ArtScroll Tanach Series®

A traditional commentary on the Books of the Bible

Rabbi Nosson Scherman/Rabbi Meir Zlotowitz
General Editors

DIVREI
hayamim I

I CHRONICLES / A NEW TRANSLATION WITH
A COMMENTARY ANTHOLOGIZED FROM TAL-
MUDIC, MIDRASHIC AND RABBINIC SOURCES.

Published by

Mesorah Publications, ltd

ספר

דברי הימים א

Translation and Commentary by
Rabbi Moshe Eisemann

Overviews by
Rabbi Moshe Eisemann
with Rabbi Nosson Scherman

Edited by
Rabbi Yehezkel Danziger

FIRST EDITION
First Impression . . . July 1987
Second Impression . . . December 1995
Third Impression . . . January 2000

Published and Distributed by
MESORAH PUBLICATIONS, Ltd.
4401 Second Avenue
Brooklyn, New York 11232

Distributed in Europe by
J. LEHMANN HEBREW BOOKSELLERS
20 Cambridge Terrace
Gateshead, Tyne and Wear
England NE8 1RP

Distributed in Israel by
SIFRIATI / A. GITLER — BOOKS
10 Hashomer Street
Bnei Brak 51361

Distributed in Australia & New Zealand by
GOLDS BOOK & GIFT CO.
36 William Street
Balaclava 3183, Vic., Australia

Distributed in South Africa by
KOLLEL BOOKSHOP
Shop 8A Norwood Hypermarket
Norwood 2196, Johannesburg, South Africa

THE ARTSCROLL TANACH SERIES
DIVREI HAYAMIM / I CHRONICLES
© *Copyright 1987 by* MESORAH PUBLICATIONS, Ltd.
4401 Second Avenue / Brooklyn, N.Y. 11232 / (718) 921-9000

ISBN
0-89906-091-9 (hard cover)
0-89906-092-7 (paperback)

Typography by CompuScribe at ArtScroll Studios, Ltd.
4401 Second Avenue / Brooklyn, N.Y. 11232 / (718) 921-9000

Printed in the United States of America by Moriah Offset
Bound by Sefercraft Quality Bookbinders, Ltd., Brooklyn, NY

ᴥৢ *Table of Contents*

◄§ Appendices

∽§ Publisher's Preface

In the infancy of the ArtScroll Series, Maran Hagaon Harav Yaakov Kamenetzky זצ״ל counseled us that of all the books in Tanach, *Divrei Hayamim / Chronicles* presented the most difficulties, and he urged us to consider an in-depth commentary on it. Within months of that conversation, the same counsel was given by להבחל״ח Maran Hagaon Harav Mordechai Gifter, *shlita.* The advice of those two great mentors remained with us and we were deeply gratified, therefore, when Rabbi Moshe Eisemann consented to devote his prodigious and profound knowledge to uncover the mysteries of *Chronicles.* As he says in his Preface, many people urged him not to attempt the "impossible," but he persevered. The results justify the effort and fulfill the hopes of the great Torah leaders.

The publication of this work is one of the high points of the history of the ArtScroll Series. We are convinced that Rabbi Eisemann's combination of new ideas and classical elucidation, his blend of philosophical thought and rigorous analysis, will become recognized as the definitive commentary on *Chronicles,* whatever the language. We are deeply grateful not only to Rabbi Eisemann, but to Rabbi Yehezkel Danziger, his editor. Both of them have devoted a major part of their lives to producing, crafting, and honing this work. We are privileged to make it available to the public.

Works of this magnitude can be produced only with the assistance of people who understand their value. Many people have helped make possible the Series in its entirety. In connection with this volume, we are especially grateful to Mr. and Mrs. Albert Reichmann of Toronto, and an admirer of Rabbi Eisemann who requests anonymity. The renaissance of Torah learning and literature in the wake of destruction is eloquent testimony to the vision and priorities of such people. May they enjoy the dividends of their largesse in the form of continued growth of the Torah community.

Rabbi Meir Zlotowitz / Rabbi Nosson Scherman

Sivan, 5747
June, 1987

◆§ Author's Preface

When, at the invitation of the editorial board of Mesorah Publications, I undertook to write a commentary to *Divrei HaYamim*, nothing could have told me how profoundly this project would shape my learning and thought over a period of many years.

Fresh from the completion of a commentary to *Yechezkel* in the same series, I had expected a difficult but not radically different task. Eager to undertake the new challenge, I paid little heed to the advice of a number of friends who felt that the book's unique characteristics would defeat any attempt to treat it within the popular format of the ArtScroll Series. The problems would prove intractable; the obstacles, too great.

As I look back now, with the commentary completed, I realize that these friends were right in many ways. There was a degree of immodesty in undertaking so vast a project. Had I known then of the years, the struggles, and the failings, I doubt that I could have summoned the courage. But now, I am happy and profoundly grateful that undertake it I did.

It proved impossible to limit the commentary to a simple anthology. For reasons discussed in the Overview, the classical commentators wrote very little on this book, and rarely addressed the many difficulties it presents. They hardly ever mentioned the wealth of aggadic material available on the genealogical tables. The historical portions are not systematically compared to, and contrasted with, the record of the same events in the earlier books. At most, the commentators might note differences with a statement that *Divrei HaYamim* is filling in details that the earlier accounts had omitted, but they do not explain why factors deemed insignificant in one account, should be considered important by another.

I felt that, to be most useful, the commentary should deal in depth with these issues. I made great efforts to enter the thought-world of the *Aggadah*, to understand how the Sages meant their teachings to guide us through the perplexing maze of the genealogies. I attempted to discover the underlying unity of the apparently disparate treatments of historical events by establishing an essential difference between the historiography of *Nevi'im* (Prophets) and *Kesuvim* (Writings), and showing this to be the reason for their different treatment of events.

All this necessitated some deviation from the normal ArtScroll format — the most striking being Section II at the end of the book. It was deemed expedient to separate these larger, more analytical pieces from the running commentary in the hope that the reader would find this arrangement both useful and helpful. When the reader seeks the simple meaning of the verse, the running commentary will supply it. The section at the end of the book provides the in-depth analysis that brings the commentary alive.

In this connection, I would like to express my deepest appreciation to R' Meir Zlotowitz and R' Nosson Scherman. All the authors who have, over the years, written for ArtScroll, have experienced their unfailing friendship and encouragement, and in this I am no different from the others. However, in connection with my work on *Divrei HaYamim*, there was something special: They had the vision and the flexibility to allow me free rein as to methodology and treatment, and by this broadmindedness, made it possible for me to approach this work as I felt I must. Had it been otherwise, my heart could not have been in what I was doing.

To these two good friends I say: The book is indeed a little different than the others in the series, but it too will, I hope, contribute to the fulfillment of the dream that has animated your efforts over the past many years — that Torah can and must reach the widest possible public.

Paradoxically, just because there is much that is new in this work, I have not sought *haskomos* (approbations) from our *Gedolim*. In principle, I subscribe strongly to the idea that published works, particularly those that purport to be original, should carry approbations. However I felt diffident about asking men who carry such awesome burdens on their shoulders, to spend precious time and energy in reading the very considerable material which makes up that part of the book which might be considered original. Instead, I have chosen to rely upon the oral encouragement which I have received from various *Roshei Yeshivah* over the years, coupled with the fact that whatever is original in this book is presented as no more than possible approaches to the solution of difficult passages. It is conjecture and nothing more. Within these limits, I carry responsibility for the material in this book.

To say that R' Yehezkel Danziger wrote this book would not be true — in fact there are passages that fall short of his exacting standards and with which he does not agree. But, short of actually writing it, he has made every word, every nuance, his own. He has been the ideal editor, goading and guiding, ruthlessly critical of all that was flabby, superficial or self-indulgent; cutting, shaping, cutting some more, until I learned to dread the mail from Lakewood. Which favorite piece would be crossed out next? Occasionally, all too rarely, the precious word of praise: "This piece is excellent;" more frequently and, to be frank, more importantly: "I am disappointed, you can do better than that!"

We worked hard and long together. The translation of a single word could, and occasionally did, take many hours, sometimes days, of thought and discussion. Passages were analyzed, solutions probed and tested. But, R' Yehezkel was always an editor. He never sought to impose his own view; choosing instead to care passionately, with an investment of time and effort beyond anything that might reasonably have been expected, that my ideas should be expressed sharply, clearly and well. Above all, because he never allowed me to lose sight of the awesome responsibility of writing Torah, he made sure that, as far as is humanly possible, they should be true. Withal, the stern editorial visage never quite managed to hide the face of a wonderful and extremely caring friend.

Because of the great bulk of the book and the many comparative charts which it contains, there were technical difficulties which, as always, were handled with grace and good taste by R' Shea Brander and primarily Eli Kroen. Rabbi Hirsh Goldwurm and Rabbi Avi Gold were always available to help; Mrs. Judi Dick and Mrs. Faigie Weinbaum proof-read exhaustively; and the typesetting was done competently and conscientiously by Mrs. Esther Feierstein, Mrs. Simie Korn and Menucha Marcus. Everyone at Mesorah Publications worked hard and conscientiously to make the publication of this beautiful book possible. To all of them — including Shimon Golding, Shmuel Klaver, Yosef Timinsky, Lea Freier, Estie Zlotowitz and Sara Adler — my sincerest thanks and appreciation.

Throughout the years during which I worked on the commentary to *Divrei Hayamim*, it has been my privilege to be associated with Yeshivas Ner Israel in Baltimore. The *Rosh HaYeshivah*, Maran HaGaon Moreinu HaRav R' Yaakov Yitzchok HaLevi Ruderman, *shlita*, has often mentioned that, in his opinion the correct teaching of Scriptures is of paramount importance. To him and to the Menahel of our Yeshiva, HaRav Naftoli Neuberger, my sincerest thanks for having given me the opportunity to be a part of this great Torah center.

Moshe Eisemann
Baltimore, Maryland
21 Nissan, 5747

ᴇ§ Editor's Note on the Transliteration

The transliteration from Hebrew to English of the numerous personal and place names found in this book has presented special problems. The standard Biblical English transliterations have in the course of time come to deviate significantly from their Hebrew pronunciations, sometimes unrecognizably so. Hardly anyone, for example, would immediately recognize Jabez as a Biblical name; more, however, might recollect Yabetz (4:9,10). By the same token, Izhar's recognition factor would be greatly enhanced by his re-transformation into Yitzhar (6:3). The need for this reversal is all the more pressing in *Divrei HaYamim* because of its strong focus on names, the greatest number of which are totally obscure to any but the most knowledgeable Biblical scholars.

At the same time, to completely alter all the spellings to conform more closely with the Hebrew would create confusion among those readers who, though not proficient in Hebrew, have gained familiarity with the great heroes and famous persons of Tanach under their accepted English names. Accordingly, a compromise system has been employed. Those names that have become widely known in English have been left unchanged, and the reader may still expect to find, for example, the names of the patriarchs given as Abraham, Isaac and Jacob. However, two exceptions have been made. First, only the names of those people who were famous by these names have remained unchanged; the transliteration of these same names when borne by lesser known people has been altered. Thus, for example, the name Samuel has been retained for the prophet of that name while that of the Yissacharite of the same name has been changed to Shemuel (7:2). Second, to assist the reader more comfortable with the traditional Hebrew pronunciation, minor changes have been introduced into even well known names where it has been deemed that these would not confuse the English reader. For example, Reuben has been changed to Reuven, Simeon to Shimeon, and Issachar to Yissachar.

All other names have been re-transliterated according to the following system:

ב ‑ v (in place of b)	פ ‑ p
ח ‑ ch (in place of h)	פ ‑ ph
י ‑ y (in place of J or I)	צ ‑ tz (in place of z)
כ ‑ ch	ש ‑ sh (in place of s)
	ת ‑ th
ע ‑ e has often been added before the vowel following the ע to indicate its presence	ִ ‑ a
	ֶ ‑ e
	ִ ‑ ia (in middle of a name)

The Sephardic pronunciation has generally been retained over the Ashkenazic because it formed the basis of the original English transliterations and is also at least familiar to most readers of today. The ח, ch and צ, tz more closely follow the Ashkenazic version because their Sephardic renditions have no precise counterpart in English, and the transliteration adopted is at least as close to the Sephardic pronunciation as is the standard English version.

It is of course inevitable that there will be some dissatisfaction with this compromise, as well as differences of opinion concerning which names should have been left unchanged. In regard to the latter problem, it should be stated that the standard considered was the level of recognition of a particular name to the average reader, not the scholar. In borderline cases, the decision was made to err in favor of the original Hebrew but to include in parenthesis the familiar English version the first time the name appears. In response to the former criticism nothing can be said except that it is the purpose of all compromises to exchange perfection for wider acceptability, a result not always achieved.

ᴥ§ Two Unknown Commentators

■ The Mefaresh

There is a commentary to *Chronicles* that has been identified by many as that of *Rashi (Shalsheles HaKabbalah, Seder HaDoros, Korei HaDoros)*, and it appears under this name in the standard editions of the Tanach. Indeed, *Rashi's* grandson *Rashbam (Deuteronomy 17:18)* testified that *Rashi* composed a commentary to *Chronicles.* It may well be that portions of the commentary found in our editions were composed by *Rashi.*

However, *Chida (Shem HaGedolim, part I, Os Shin)* and *R' Yaakov Emden* (introduction to *Eitz Avos*), among others, contend that *Rashi* is not the author of this commentary. There is convincing stylistic and textual evidence to this effect.

It is clear, however, that the author, whoever he may have been, lived in *Rashi's* time or not very long afterward. Some submit that he was *R' Saadyah* (not *R' Saadyah Gaon,* but one of the *Tosafists*) or a student of *R' Saadyah.*

Given the above doubts, we have chosen to refer to this commentary simply as the *Mefaresh,* the Commentator.

■ The Anonymous Commentator

This commentary was first published in 1874 by Rafael Kirchheim, who called it "A commentary on *Chronicles* that is attributed to a student of *R' Saadyah Gaon,*" but he found it impossible to identify the author more specifically. He established, however, that the author belonged to the tenth-century school of *R' Saadyah Gaon.* We refer to this work simply as the *Anonymous Commentator.*

The Overviews

An Overview/
The Uniqueness of Chronicles

לֹא נִתַּן דִּבְרֵי הַיָּמִים אֶלָּא לִדָּרֵשׁ

The Book of Chronicles was given only to be expounded upon homiletically (Vayikra Rabbah 1:3).

רַבִּי שִׁמְעוֹן בֶּן פַּזִּי כִּי הֲוָה פָּתַח בְּדִבְרֵי הַיָּמִים אָמַר הָכִי — כָּל דְּבָרֶיךָ אֶחָד הֵם וְאָנוּ יוֹדְעִים לְדָרְשָׁן. [פרש״י: הַרְבֵּה שֵׁמוֹת אַתָּה מַזְכִּיר ... וְכוּלָן אָדָם אֶחָד הֵם ... וְאע״פ שֶׁסָּתַמְתָּ אוֹתָן אָנוּ נוֹתְנִין אֶת לִבֵּנוּ עַד שֶׁאָנוּ יוֹדְעִים לְדָרְשָׁן.]

When R' Shimon ben Pazi began to expound upon Chronicles, he said this: "All Your words are identical and we know how to interpret them." [A single person is identified by many different names. Even though God concealed this, we apply ourselves until we are able to decipher and expound the correct meaning (Rashi).] (Megillah 13a)

בֵּין אָצֵל לְאָצֵל טָעִינוּ ד' מֵאָה גְּמַלֵּי דְּדָרְשָׁא

To expound upon the verses between [the first mention of] Atzel (I Chronicles 8:38) and [the final] Atzel (ibid. 9:44) we would need four hundred camel-loads of elucidations (Pesachim 62b).

וּמַה בְּרוּרְיָה דְּבֵיתְהוּ דְּרַבִּי מֵאִיר ... לֹא יָצְתָה יְדֵי חוֹבָתָה [(שֶׁל סֵפֶר יוֹחֲסִין — מַתְנִיתִין דְּדִבְרֵי הַיָּמִים (רש״י)] בִּתְלָת שְׁנִין וְאַתְּ אַמְרַת בִּתְלָתָא יַרְחֵי?

If even R' Meir's wife Beruriah ... could not properly complete the study [of the midrash on the Book of Chronicles (Rashi)] in three years; can you expect to do so in three months? (ibid.).

מִיּוֹם שֶׁנִּגְנַז סֵפֶר יוֹחֲסִין (פרש״י: שֶׁנִּגְנַז מֵהֶן טַעֲמֵי תוֹרָה שֶׁהָיוּ בּוֹ) תָּשַׁשׁ כֹּחָן שֶׁל חֲכָמִים וְכֵהָה מְאוֹר עֵינֵיהֶם.

From the day the Book of Genealogy [the midrash on the Book of Chronicles] was hidden [and the Sages were deprived of its principles of Torah interpretation (Rashi)] the strength of the Sages weakened and their vision was dimmed (ibid.).

The above declarations of our Sages make clear that Chronicles — especially its lengthy genealogical tables — is unique among the books of Scripture. In interpreting the other books, we hew to the principle that אֵין מִקְרָא

יֹצֵא מִידֵי פְּשׁוּטוֹ, *The verse does not depart from its simple meaning* (*Shabbos* 63a), but in *Chronicles*, the simple meaning is midrashic, not literal. Furthermore, the Sages' expound *Chronicles* in seemingly bizarre ways and elucidations of verses often seem to have no relationship to the simple meaning of the text: several names in a series may be interpreted as referring to the same person, and generations and families may be shuffled in apparent disregard of the clear meaning of the verses.

In Cronicles, the simple meaning is midrashic, not literal.

This strange phenomenon compels us to investigate the uniqueness of *Chronicles* and learn why it differs from the rest of Scripture.

I. The Difference between the Prophets and the Writings

Son and Servant

In *Ahavas Yonasan* (discourse on the Seventh of Passover) Rabbi Yonasan Eybeschuetz compares the books of the Prophets [נְבִיאִים] with those of the Writings [כְּתוּבִים]. The books of Prophets are similar to the King's "son," while the Writings are like his "servant." A personal servant glimpses more of his master than anyone else, because he is present at intimate settings where no outsider — not even a relative — may enter. And the servant may hear wishes and ideas that the King has not revealed to anyone else. On the other hand, a servant does not have the power to bring his intimate knowledge to fruition: he lacks the authority to reveal or carry out the King's will. The prince, on the other hand, hears the King's voice — his direct communication — but he does not know more than the King wants him to. In this sense, his knowledge is more meager than that of the servant. He has a great advantage, however: the power of execution. The "word" that he hears, the "voice" that is directed to him, is meant for him to act upon.

The servant may hear wishes and ideas that the King has not revealed to anyone else.

The prince does not know more than the King wants him to.

This concept is illustrated in *Daniel* 10:7, where Daniel saw a frightening vision. He reports: *I Daniel, alone saw the vision; but the people who were with me did not see the vision.* The Talmud teaches that Daniel's companions were Haggai, Zechariah, and Malachi. They were greater than Daniel, for they were prophets and he was not; but in a different sense, he was superior to them, because he saw the vision while they did not (*Megillah* 3a). *Ahavas*

Yonasan explains that Daniel who had רוּחַ הַקֹּדֶשׁ, *the spirit of holiness*, was able to see more than the three prophets, just as a servant sees more than the prince.

Two principles emerge from the above formulation of *Ahavas Yonasan:*

> 1. Embedded in the Writings are treasures of Divine wisdom, beyond those revealed to the prophets, although the King's direct voice is not heard in the Writings.
> 2. In the Prophets, God communicates openly and clearly, but makes known no more than is directly expressed or clearly implied by the text.

It is because so much is buried in the words and between the lines of the Writings that Yonasan ben Uzziel, who translated the Prophets into Aramaic [*Targum Yonasan*], was forbidden by a heavenly voice from going on to translate the Writings. Why? The Talmud answers, because the secret of the exile's deadline and the coming of Messiah [קֵץ הַיָּמִים, literally *the end of days*] is hidden in the Writings [specifically in *Daniel (Rashi)*], and Yonasan's *Targum* would have deciphered the mystery (*Megillah* 3a).

Speech and Script

On the surface it seems strange that Yonasan ben Uzziel was prohibited from translating any part of the Writings in order to avoid revelation of the secret contained in only a small part of *Daniel.* Why couldn't he have written his translation and omitted what was not to be revealed?

Maharal infers from this that the entire body of the Writings is related to the revelation of the קֵץ, [*Keitz*] the time when Messiah will come. True, the specific deadline is in Daniel, but the background that conditions the deadline is contained in all of the Writings. Therefore, the Divine Will ordained limits to how deeply we are permitted to penetrate the wisdom of the Writings. Had Yonasan's insightful, interpretive translation to the rest of the Writings been available, presumably, our perceptions would have been honed sufficiently to have deciphered the hidden message of *Daniel* as well.

The first of the above two principles can best be understood in the light of Rabbi Yitzchak Hutner's formulation in *Pachad Yitzchak (Shavuos* 2:15-16). Thought — which is by definition concealed — is unfolded on two levels: speech and script. Of the two, the greater degree of revelation is speech, because speech is a communication to someone else. By its very nature, therefore, the spoken word is the process by which one

The spoken word is the process by which one reveals his thoughts to another. reveals his thoughts to another. Script, on the other hand, is relatively private; one can write his thoughts for his personal benefit without sharing them with others. The words of the Prophets were spoken to others and set down for posterity, for the nation's edification. A prophet's message must be understood; this is the nature of a public communication. *The nature of the Writings implies a withholding of total meaning, because script is less public than speech.* The nature of the Writings, on the other hand, implies a withholding of total meaning, because script is less public than speech.

In speaking of the Messiah's coming, the Sages say לִבָּא לְפוּמָא לֹא גָלְיָא, *the heart does not reveal it* [i.e., God's innermost wish] *to the mouth* (*Koheles Rabbah* 12:10).

Accordingly, Israel's Messianic destiny cannot be revealed in the Prophets. These book are God's "mouth" — but His "heart" remains hidden from them. Only in the Writings can we get an inkling of the heart's profundities.

For the second of *Ahavas Yonasan's* two principles, we go again to *Pachad Yitzchak* (*Chanukah* 8) which explains the dictum חָכָם עָדִיף מִנָּבִיא, *a wise man is greater than a prophet* (*Bava Basra* 12a). Occasionally God's silence is more eloquent than His speech, and it takes a wise man to decipher the nuances hidden behind cryptic phrases. To the prophet, however, the message of God's silence is closed. The prophet deals in words, in revealed messages. By tradition the Hebrew for prophet, נָבִיא, is derived from נִיב שְׂפָתַיִם, *speech of the lips.*

Different Themes

In view of the above, we can understand why Ezra, the author of *Chronicles*, found it necessary to write a book of history that deals with events already related in earlier prophetic books. A history that is part of Writings will bring to bear a perspective that is radically different from the one that is presented from the viewpoint of prophecy.

We submit that *Chronicles* is the story of the Jewish people from the perspective of קֵץ, *the end*, the deadline when the Messianic era will finally arrive. This explains why Ezra reviewed many events that appear in other books *The focus of Chronicles requires it to show how history moves inexorably toward the formation of the Davidic dynasty and the rebuilding of the Temple.* (primarily *Samuel* and *Kings*), while omitting others. The focus of *Chronicles* requires it to show how history moves inexorably toward the formation of the Davidic dynasty and its return in the person of the eventual Messiah, and the rebuilding of the Temple. These twin centers of the nation — political and spiritual — embody the mission ordained by the Torah, the mission for which the universe has been created and which Israel has been chosen to bring to fruition.

If we understand the theme of a book, we can understand the criteria by which it chooses what is essential and what is tangential.

If we understand the theme of a book, we can understand the criteria by which it chooses what is essential and what is tangential. For example, the political history of a nation would assign great importance to events that would be trivial or unworthy of mention in a social history, and vice versa. A biography would not omit events that occupied its hero for many years. But if the author means only to show how his subject pursued a specific goal, then he will discard everything that is extraneous to the quest.

Our commentary will attempt to show how this thesis explains much of the content and many discrepancies between *Chronicles* and other books of Scripture.

A March Toward Eternity

It is illustrative that *Chronicles*, unlike the historical books of Prophets, begins its account of history with Adam. Furthermore, after completing the story of the First Temple era and its destruction, *Chronicles* skips two generations, makes no mention whatever of the exile, and concludes by telling us that King Cyrus authorized the return to *Eretz Yisrael* of the exiles and the construction of the Second Temple. This event is not recorded in *Kings*, which ends

If we understand Chronicles as the development of Israel's eternal mission, then the stories of Adam and Cyrus belong there.

with the Destruction. However, if we understand *Chronicles* as the development of Israel's eternal mission, then the stories of Adam and Cyrus belong there. That mission began with the creation of the first human being and is inextricably bound up with the ultimate redemption toward which Cyrus' decree pointed. Moreover, throughout *Chronicles*, the nation is called "Israel" rather than "Jacob," because Israel is the name that describes the Jewish people in its striving to gain a higher spiritual calling. "Jacob" symbolizes the nation of external events, but "Israel" symbolizes the nation that seeks purpose and fulfillment.

The first nine chapters of *Chronicles* are extremely perplexing. They seem to contain no profundities; rather, they appear to be no more than simple genealogical tables. True, the language is often complex, but the content could hardly be simpler. On the other hand, a careful analysis of these chapters shows them to be among the most profound of all the Scriptures. Let us examine both elements of the Book.

II. A Collection of Tables

A Lesser Book?

Chronicles contains the genealogy of most of Israel's tribes, with many tangential events loosely related to these family histories. In his introduction, *Radak* writes, "... because this book is a historical narrative, people are not accustomed to study it." In other words, scholars neglected the Book because they found nothing to study. For the most part, it contains nothing but dry narratives of events that have already been reported elsewhere. *Radak* adds that the Book includes material that is incomprehensible, and narratives that contradict the accounts given in the Books of *Samuel* and *Kings*.

Many others echo *Radak's* theme, in one way or another. *Ibn Caspi's* introduction cautions us not to analyze *Chronicles* as closely as we would "the book written by Moses, which was of Heavenly origin, for [this book] is but a digest and a selection [of events] made by this particular author [i.e. Ezra, who compiled *Chronicles*]. Consequently, he abridged and changed as he saw fit. As you see, he listed the order of the tribes in a confused manner ..."

This book is but a digest and a selection of events made by this particular author.

P'nei Moshe goes so far as to say that *Psalms* is holier than *Chronicles*, because it, *Psalms*, was written with רוּחַ הַקֹּדֶשׁ, *Divine Inspiration*. This implies that *Chronicles* was compiled without Divine Inspiration (*Bava Basra* 1:5).

Let us hasten to note that none of these commentators suggest that *Chronicles* is not one of the twenty-four sacred books. It clearly is (*Bava Basra* 14b), and, as such, has all the sanctity that goes with this status. Rather, as we shall show, they mean to say that much of the contents of *Chronicles* was written originally as historical narratives and genealogical tables. For many generations or centuries, these writings had no holiness whatever. Only later did Ezra select them for inclusion in *Chronicles*. The selection was undoubtedly made with prophetic inspiration and they gained sanctity once they became part of the sacred Writings, but their origin was secular, and this accounts for the relative lack of reverence with which the above commentators speak of them. Certainly, in this light, *Chronicles* is unlike *Psalms*, every word of which was composed from the start with Divine Inspiration.

Much of the contents of Chronicles was written originally as historical narratives and genealogical tables.

Collection of Material

For reasons that we shall discuss below, Ezra found it necessary to provide Israel with a detailed genealogical record of its origins and development. Of necessity, such a task required him to assemble ancient lists. By their very nature, such lists would contain errors, be incomplete, and often contradict one another. What these lists told him, he would know; what they did not contain and what had become lost or illegible with the passage of time, he could not know. To many of the leading commentators, this was not only self-evident, but presented no difficulty.

Although hardly the first to make this point, *Sha'agas Aryeh* (in *Gevuras Ari* to *Yoma*) says it very clearly in explaining how Ezra could write עַד הַיּוֹם הַזֶּה, *until this very day*, regarding conditions that had ceased to exist many generations before his time. *Sha'agas Aryeh* explains: Ezra transcribed *Chronicles* from many books that he found ...

The genealogies in Chronicles are not necessarily in chronological order; they may contradict one another. This is why the genealogies in *Chronicles* are not necessarily in chronological order, why they may contradict one another within *Chronicles* and why there are contradictions between the Books of *Ezra* and *Chronicles*, for in one of his sources he found one version and in a different source he found another. As he found them so he transcribed them. If his source used the expression "until this very day," Ezra preferred to cite it word for word rather than rephrase it.

Many of the classic commentators make the same point in their commentaries to the Book. They are:

The Mefaresh: Ezra found three books of genealogy, from which he quoted whatever he found and omitted what he did not find. This also explains why the genealogies of *Chronicles* sometimes skip about: Ezra skipped from one book to the other and combined the material in *Chronicles* (*Mefaresh*, 7:13). According to *Yerushalmi Megillah*, Ezra found three books. If two concurred against the third, he followed them. He also found many other genealogical accounts and texts, and would follow the preponderance of sources (*ibid.* 8:29).

Radak: To explain why Ezra abbreviated some of the genealogical listings, *Radak* (9:1) quotes him, as it were: *Although I have mentioned part of the genealogies, I have not mentioned them all.* "Although I have mentioned part of the genealogies, I have not mentioned them all. They are listed in the 'Books of Jewish Kings', but those books are no longer extant among us, like the Book of Rectitude and the Book of the Wars of Hashem."

On the seminal phrase וְהַדְּבָרִים עַתִּיקִים, *now these are ancient traditions* (4:22), *Radak* comments that the genealogical material is "ancient" in the sense that even facts that are not found in the Torah and Prophets were authenticated by Ezra on the basis of ancient documents or oral traditions that had been passed down from person to person.

The Anonymous Commentator: On the above expression, *now these are ancient traditions*, this commentator echoes *Radak* that Ezra's words were collected from well-established traditions that had been passed down through the ages. In his commentary to 8:3, he notes minor contradictions between *Chronicles* and *Nehemiah*, both of which were written by Ezra. He explains that according to the opinion of "people of the East," Ezra found two different written accounts and cited one in *Chronicles* and the other in *Nehemiah*.

Vilna Gaon: In his commentary to this same term, the *Vilna Gaon* writes, "these are among the things that King Chizkiah's [Hezekiah] people copied." Based on the *Gaon*'s comments to *Proverbs* 25:1, we feel that he refers to the process by which King Hezekiah restored the Torah to its traditional glory after its long period of decline under his idol-worshiping father, King Achaz. Under Hezekiah's leadership and encouragement, the scholars of his time collected a wealth of scattered information and teachings, including countless gems of King Solomon's wisdom. Had they not done so, this wealth of information would have receded gradually from the people's awareness and been lost forever. Thus, too, they collected the historical data that Ezra subsequently used in writing *Chronicles*.

Under Hezekiah's leadership and encouragement, the scholars of his time collected a wealth of scattered information and teachings.

Malbim: "This is a major principle to bear in mind throughout *Chronicles*. Ezra copied his book from the great genealogical record in which were listed the genealogy of every family, its divisions and branches from beginning to end. Ezra copied what was necessary and only what was relevant to special people ... and he omitted what was extraneous ..."(2:7).

All of the above makes clear that the text of Ezra's tables were not written originally with רוּחַ הַקֹּדֶשׁ, *Divine Inspiration*. Consequently, as *Ibn Caspi* and others have said, we should not wonder at contradictions here and there "for this text is but an abridged selection by the author." Ezra knew that there were discrepancies, but, as we shall explain below, he consciously chose to incorporate them into *Chronicles*.

Ezra knew that there were descrepancies, but, he consciously chose to incorporate them into Chronicles.

If we are correct that the tables upon which Ezra based himself were nothing more than secular jottings, how do they attain the holiness of the sacred writings?

Acquired Holiness   As *Radak* quoted above teaches, we are guided toward an answer by the precedent of Moses. In composing a song of praise for some of the miracles that God wrought as Israel crossed the Wilderness, Moses prefaced his words with a quote from the ה' מִלְחֲמוֹת סֵפֶר, *Book of the Wars of Hashem* (*Numbers* 21:14): אֶת וָהֵב בְּסוּפָה וְאֶת הַנְּחָלִים אַרְנוֹן, *The miraculous gift at the [Sea of] Reeds and at the streams of Arnon.* This poetic verse was of secular origin; but once God commanded Moses to include it in the written Torah, it attained the same sanctity as *Hear O Israel.* Whoever questions its holiness is no less a heretic than if he had denied the holiness of the Ten Commandments.

Similar is the development of Ezra's tables. Their original unknown authors intended them as nothing more than records of births or military exploits, surely not as the

Ezra came and analyzed these chronicles with an eye that would have been incomprehensible to their authors.

receptacles of Divine teachings. Then Ezra came and analyzed these chronicles with an eye that would have been incomprehensible to their authors. He sought not only the facts of history, but allusions to the underlying Divinely ordained scheme of history; not only data about people but the spiritual essence of their personalities. The outward language and appearance of these tables remained as innocuous as ever, but Ezra infused them with the holiness that flowed from their inclusion in the sacred Writings. Indeed, the Anonymous Commentator (7:18) warns us not to be misled by the surface simplicity and apparent inaccuracies of *Chronicles*, for it is part of God's Torah and He has made it a vehicle to His truth, for those who exert themselves to find its deeper meanings. For example, as our commentary will show, the seemingly bland and insignificant listing of Zerubavel's offspring (beginning 3:19) is, in the insight of the Sages, the chain of the Davidic dynasty from its outset until its climax, the King Messiah.

The question is, why did Ezra construct Chronicles in such a seemingly bizarre manner?

The question is, why did Ezra construct *Chronicles* in such a seemingly bizarre manner?

We can understand not only the Book but its construction on the basis of the dictum that "The Book of *Chronicles* was given only to be expounded upon homiletically" (*Vayikra Rabbah* 1:3). Ezra was by no means haphazard. He calculated well and his inconsistencies were inserted as clues and prods to stimulate our inquiries and lead us to the mysteries that are well concealed — but not impenetrably so — beneath the surface simplicity of *Chronicles'* welter of names and events. Countless Talmudic and Midrashic elucidations are based on these contradictions and changes, because they create the texture upon which the Sages have expounded. The Book of Genealogy, whose loss saddened the Sages (*Pesachim* 62b), was the road map to the treasures of knowledge and guidance that Ezra buried among the apparent "inconsistencies" of *Chronicles*.

Why the Genealogy

Let us begin by dealing with the most basic issue of all: What compelled Ezra to compile his amalgam of genealogical tables?

Among the primary commentators, we find the following views:

The Mefaresh: Ezra composed his book of genealogy under the guidance of the prophets Chaggai, Zechariah, and Malachi ... with the purpose of providing the family background of King David, and the family background of the Levites whom David appointed as gatekeepers,

Ezra does not relate David's shortcomings, but his victories and greatness.

watchmen, and singers of the Temple (1:1). Ezra does not relate David's shortcomings, but his victories and greatness, for this book is that of David and his dynasty (10:1). Crucial to Ezra's role was the reaffirmation of David's primacy as the progenitor of Jewish monarchy and the one who instituted the order of the Temple administration. It was Ezra who established Zerubavel as the successor to David, and Ezra who built the Second Temple, where the returning Levite families resumed the roles assigned their forebears by David.

Radak and *Abarbanel* (Introduction to *Kings*) agree that the primary purpose of *Chronicles* is to establish Zerubavel as David's successor. *Radak* also seems to hold that our *Divrei HaYamim* is the "Book of *Chronicles* of the Kings of Judah" that is mentioned frequently in the Books of *Kings*.

Meiri: (Introduction to *Psalms*:) Although Ezra was actually the prophet Malachi (*Megillah* 15a), neither the Books of *Ezra* nor *Chronicles* are part of the Prophets because their function was not to convey prophetic teachings or admonitions. Rather, their purpose was to

Their purpose was to describe the zeal with which Ezra organized the return.

describe the zeal with which Ezra organized the return to *Eretz Yisrael*. The primary prophecies of the period are in the Books of *Haggai, Zechariah,* and *Malachi*; those which appear in *Ezra* and *Chronicles* are given only incidentally.

Ramban: A different approach is that of *Ramban*. In this view — borne out by the contents of ch. 9; see our

Ezra intended to provide the family background of those who accompanied him back to Jerusalem.

commentary there — Ezra intended to provide the family background of those who accompanied him back to Jerusalem. He began with Jacob, the nation's progenitor and traced the tribes sketchily, with the exception of Judah, the leader of the nation's tribes, whose genealogy he described in detail.

Why was Ezra so concerned with the Jewish family? The reason lies in the heady hopes of that returning remnant. Small though it was in numbers, the Jewish community that came to resettle Jerusalem and build the Temple was hopeful that its handiwork would be the fulfillment of the prophecy גָּדוֹל יִהְיֶה כְּבוֹד הַבַּיִת הַזֶּה הָאַחֲרוֹן מִן הָרִאשׁוֹן, *The glory of this later House will be greater than that of the previous one (Haggai 2:9)*. In its broadest possible interpretation, Haggai's prophecy meant that the new Temple, which was being built against so much opposition and with so many difficulties, would be the herald of the final redemption, that it would be not only a second, but the final Temple, the eternal home of God's Presence.

Haggai's prophecy meant that the new Temple would be the herald of the final redemption.

The Talmud (*Kiddushin* 70b) teaches that God rests His Presence only on Jewish families whose descent is not tainted by immorality or intermarriage. Therefore, if God's Presence was indeed returning to Jerusalem in all its intensity, it could do so only to a Jewish nation that was worthy by virtue of its own purity and its direct descent from Abraham, Isaac, and Jacob, the sources of the Chosen People and its holiness. Consequently, we can well understand Ezra's concern to clarify the purity of his people's descent.

III. P'shat and D'rash

Two Worlds

A frequent cause of difficulty in Torah study is the conflict between פְּשָׁט, *the simple meaning* of Scripture, and דְּרַשׁ, *the homiletical elucidation* provided by the Sages. How can both be true if they contradict one another?

An inkling of the tension between the simple meaning and homiletical elucidation is provided by *Maharal*. He explains the Talmud's teaching (*Sotah* 12b) that the Egyptian maidservants who protested their princess' rescue of Moses went to their deaths (see *Exodus* 2:5). Their opposition, *Maharal* explains, was because their spiritual essence could not abide the survival of the Jewish child. And their "death" was not literal, but figurative: because they opposed God's will, they became "dead," that is spiritually inconsequential. Since their death was not physical, the Torah does not say explicitly that they died,

Their spiritual essence could not abide the survival of the Jewish child. And their "death" was not literal, but figurative.

because the Torah articulates only open, recognizable miracles.

From *Maharal's* elucidation we see how *p'shat* and *d'rash* can diverge without being in conflict. The Egyptian maidservants remained alive and vigorous in the world of *p'shat;* no stethoscope or electrocardiogram would have detected any diminution of life. But in the world of *d'rash,* of spiritual existence, their lives came to an end.

No stethoscope or electrocardiogram would have detected any diminution of life. But in the world of d'rash, of spiritual existence, their lives came to an end.

Genealogy can be perceived in the same way. We are accustomed in everyday discussion to speak of people as the "children" of a master or of a concept. This does not conflict with the obvious identity of their biological parents. The Sages, too, speak of teachers as the true parents of their disciples. In *Chronicles,* we will find many instances of people being ascribed to families where they do not belong — at least biologically. Since *Chronicles* is the story of the Jewish people as the bearers of God's Presence, it should be obvious that it is concerned more with spiritual ancestry than with biological parentage.

If the above assumption is correct, then we are on the road toward narrowing the chasm between the Sages' elucidations and the simple meaning of the verses. Rather than being irreconcilable, they are different facets of the same reality.

The World of Chronicles

Obviously, two worlds are before us when we study *Chronicles.* The world of *p'shat,* the simple meaning of words and phrases, flows in accordance with the rules familiar to us from the rest of Scripture, tracing the tribes from their origin until the return from Babylonia to Zion.

But there is another world in which *Chronicles* takes shape, the world of *d'rash,* the world of deeper, hidden meanings and allusions, in which chronology and physical identity are less important than the similarity of roles and common goals. Thus, *Chronicles* (4:21) can include Rachav among the children of Shelah son of Judah — despite the fact that she was a Canaanite woman who lived more than 250 years after the time of Shelah (see *Judges* ch. 2). As a purely historical statement, this is incomprehensible. But if this statement is treated in figurative or philosophical rather than literal terms — as indeed the Sages and many commentators do — it can be seen as a fact that sheds light on an entire epoch. For example, students of American history understand very well what is intended by such rhetoric as "this or that public figure is a direct descendant of Alexander Hamilton, Thomas Jefferson, or Abraham

If this statement is treated in figurative or philosophical rather than literal terms, it can be seen as a fact that sheds light on an entire epoch.

Lincoln." Such characterizations can hardly be taken literally, but they tell us more than many columns of mind-numbing statistics and curriculum vitae.

There is the physical Jerusalem, but hovering above it is the celestial Jerusalem, which is unbounded by space and time.

As an example, let us take Jerusalem. There is the physical Jerusalem, the Holy City bounded by walls and towers, and measured in feet and yards, like every city whose dimensions can be traced by map-makers and engineers. But hovering above it is the celestial Jerusalem, which is unbounded by limitations of space and time. The Heavenly Jerusalem is the glory and splendor of the earthly city below. These two cities are not separate entities; they are like body and soul to one another, שֶׁחֻבְּרָה כְּעִיר לָּהּ יַחְדָּו, *the city that is united together* (*Psalms* 122:3).

Two Nations

So, too, there are two Jewish nations. There is the nation and its tribal components that can be counted and measured; each generation and its leaders, each limited by its era and habitat. But there is also the Jewish nation that is eternal and within which all twelve tribes merge their separate identities into a single unit. This concept was symbolized when Jacob went into a personal exile, from his father's home to Laban's. On his way, he put many stones around his head to protect him as he slept, and they all fused into one. So, too, the tribes of the Jewish people, separate though they are in many respects, are part of a unified nation (*Rashi, Genesis* 28:11). In the national sense, there is a blurring of the differences between families, between cities, between tribes; in their place we find a single nation in which every segment is enriched by the talents and personality of every other segment. Just as there are not two Jerusalems, so there are not two Israels. There is one. It is a physical being that has a spiritual essence.

Just as there are not two Jerusalems, so there are not two Israels. There is one. It is a physical being that has a spiritual essence.

Only with the insights of the Sages can we see how the two are inextricably united; how the physical, chronological history of Israel is fashioned by its "meta-history" — the spiritual dimension that is above history and that molds it, the spiritual mission for which Israel was created. It is our thesis that *Chronicles* tells the story of the Jewish people from the perspective of eternity, that in *Chronicles* we are concerned not with mere dates, places, and events, but with the meta-history that is the basis of and infuses meaning into the facts.

If *p'shat* deals with physical realities and *d'rash* with inner matters, then a book whose interest lies entirely with spiritual realities will ignore the *p'shat* as irrelevant. The Book of *Chronicles* functions in the world of *d'rash*. We can now understand the above-cited teaching of the Sages that לֹא נִתַּן דִּבְרֵי הַיָּמִים אֶלָּא לִדָּרֵשׁ, *The Book of Chronicles was given only to be expounded upon homiletically* (*Vayikra Rabbah* 1:3).

In analyzing *Chronicles* the Sages recognized that it contained the secrets of the Divine Presence, the traits and achievements through which individual Jews and the entire nation can become worthy of being the chariot of the *Shechinah* [Divine Presence]. Of all the books of Scripture,

It is especially Chronicles that contains these elements of Israel's destiny, and the Sages delved into it exhaustively to uncover these mysteries.

it is especially *Chronicles* that contains these elements of Israel's destiny, and the Sages delved into it exhaustively to uncover these mysteries. These are the "four hundred camel-loads of elucidations" that were required to explain a chapter of *Chronicles* (*Pesachim* 62b); the task that consumed three years of Beruriah's life (ibid.); the Book of Genealogy whose concealment weakened the Sages and dimmed their vision (ibid.). Of the infinite wealth of Talmudic commentary on *Chronicles*, precious little remains with us. Its paucity explains why *Chronicles* is so indecipherable; its availability emboldens us to search for at least a portion of *Chronicles'* spiritual wealth.

IV. The Road to the Keitz

Chronicles and Torah

The mystery of the final Redemption is foreshadowed not only in the Book of Daniel, but in the entirety of the Writings.

The place where we can find this unifying force spelled out — if only we are capable of comprehending it — is in the Writings, for it is there that God has concealed the secret of Israel's final destiny. As we have seen above, the mystery of the final Redemption is foreshadowed not only in the Book of *Daniel*, but in the entirety of the Writings. Most of all, however, it is the Book of *Chronicles* that is the key to understanding Israel's mission and the role of that mission in fashioning history.

As a basis for this thesis, we cite the Talmud:

תָּנוּ רַבָּנָן, חֲמֵשֶׁת אֲלָפִים שְׁמֹנֶה מֵאוֹת וּשְׁמֹנִים וּשְׁמֹנֶה פְּסוּקִים הֲוֵי פְּסוּקֵי סֵפֶר תּוֹרָה. יֶתֶר עָלָיו תְּהִלִּים שְׁמֹנֶה, חָסֵר מִמֶּנָּה דִּבְרֵי הַיָּמִים שְׁמוֹנֶה.

The Rabbis taught, there are 5888 verses in the Torah. There are eight more in Psalms, and eight less in Chronicles (*Kiddushin* 30a).

Vilna Gaon emends the text to read that the Torah's verses compare to those of *Chronicles* and *Daniel* combined.[1]

---

1. This calculation is extremely difficult. According to our tradition, the Torah contains 5845 verses, *Psalms* contains 2527, *Chronicles* contains 1656, and *Daniel* contains 357. It

Why are these two in tandem compared to the Torah? Clearly, *Chronicles* and *Daniel* have something in common, and, whatever it is, it makes them parallel in a certain sense to the Torah itself. And the Book of *Psalms*, too, is likened to the Torah. Nowhere else in the Talmud do we find other portions of Scripture compared to the Torah. What is it about these books that singles them out?

The comparison between the Torah and *Psalms* is suggested in *Midrash Shochar Tov* (*Psalms* ch.1), which gives a long list of similarities between the Torah and Psalms, between the Five Books of Moses and the Five Books of David. [For elucidation of this point, see Rabbi Avrohom Chaim Feuer's Overview to the ArtScroll *Psalms*.] But what of *Chronicles*, with or without the Book of *Daniel*? On what basis do the Sages liken *Chronicles* to the Torah? In order to understand the Book, we must focus on this question.

On what basis do the Sages liken Chronicles to the Torah? In order to understand the Book, we must focus on this question.

We submit that the similarity between the books lies in their historical breadth. The Torah describes itself as זֶה סֵפֶר תּוֹלְדֹת אָדָם, *This is the account of the descendants of Adam* (*Genesis* 5:1). *Rambam* explains that the "account" is not limited to ten or twenty generations, but to the entire history of mankind. True, the events described in the Torah may be limited to the first 2488 years from Creation, but in selecting them the Torah paints the background upon which all human history is to be defined. For example, if an organization is founded on certain principles, and for the pursuit of clearly defined goals, then everything the organization does will flow from and be evaluated in the context of the original master plan. Similarly, the Torah gives us the guidelines of the universe whose creation it describes. Such principles as מַעֲשֵׂה אָבוֹת סִימָן לַבָּנִים, *the deeds of the Patriarchs are a portent for the children*; the broad strokes of Jacob's and Moses' blessings to the tribes of Israel, and the prophecies of Bilaam and *Ha'azinu*, are the bylaws of history, so to speak. If we study these portions well, we will understand — to some degree, at least — the orbits of history.

The Torah gives us the guidelines of the universe whose creation it describes.

From this perspective, *Chronicles* is indeed comparable to the Torah, for it too is the story of mankind as told through the experiences of the nation that accepted the Torah and bears God's mission on earth. And, if *Vilna Gaon* teaches that this history is to be combined with

is not within the scope of this work to solve this difficulty. The late Rabbi Chanoch Ehrentreu dealt with it rather successfully in an essay published in German. Here we concern ourselves only with the *Gaon's* comment that *Chronicles* and *Daniel* are a pair.

Daniel — the repository of the secrets of the *Keitz*, the Messianic era — then *Chronicles* is clearly designated as the book of meta-history, history on its march to redemption.

Beyond History

Thus, in the study of *Chronicles*, the main purpose of the Sages is to deal with the meta-historical aspects of the book; not with *Chronicles* as a factual, chronological record of events and personalities, but with the broad sweep and underlying purpose of history. The Canaanite woman Rachav (*Joshua* ch. 2) was not a biological descendant of Shelah son of Judah, but she is listed as one (see comm. p. 60) because her destiny, if not her genes, flowed from Shelah. The judge Boaz (*Ruth*) was not from the tribe of Benjamin, but he is included among Benjamin's offspring (see comm. p. 130) because his mission placed him there. These are the difficulties that concerned the Sages and, if we can understand their elucidations correctly, they will guide us to the solution of the contradictions, omissions, additions, and anomalies that bedevil students of *Chronicles*.

The judge Boaz was not from the tribe of Benjamin, but he is included among Benjamin's offspring because his mission placed him there.

A comment of *Maharal* (*Chiddushei Aggados, Bava Basra* 91b) helps illuminate this point. There, the Talmud notes that in the Book of *Ruth* (1:1) the sons of Elimelech were called Machlon and Kilyon, but in *I Chronicles* (4:22), they are called Yoash and Saraph. According to one Talmudic view, the names used in *Chronicles* were figurative, in order to reflect the sort of people they were: Yoash, from Hebrew יָאַשׁ, *despair*, because he despaired of redemption; and Saraph from שָׂרַף, *burning*, because he deserved to be consumed. *Maharal* explains that *Ruth* is a history of the period, and consequently it refers to its protagonists by their real names. *Chronicles*, however, is concerned with the inner dynamics — the sub-surface truths. It is not the given names of the protagonists that are significant in *Chronicles*, but the names that defined their place in history. (See following *Overview*.)

It is not the given names of the protagonists that are significant in Chronicles, but the names that defined their place in history.

The Thinking of the Sages

To understand why the Sages give us elucidations that seem totally unrelated to the simple meaning of the verse, and to explain why the Book of *Chronicles* inserts names into families where they do not belong, there are two general approaches. The first may be understood as that of *Netziv* (*Emek Ha'Netziv Bahaaloscha, Piska* 20). In commenting upon the dictum that *Chronicles* was intended for homiletical interpretation, *Netziv* notes that, unlike the rest of Scriptures where the simple meaning is paramount, *Chronicles* has no "simple meaning" in the usual sense.

The words were set down as a framework for *d'rash*, the concepts and values that are alluded to, rather than stated. How did the Sages find this unstated knowledge? Certainly not through sheer intellect, because such wisdom is above intellect. It can only be that they had רוּחַ הַקֹּדֶשׁ, *Divine Inspiration*, by means of which God permitted them to see in the words and phrases of the book ideas that could never be grasped by human intelligence. Accordingly, it is useless for us to attempt to understand the rationale behind a given *drashah*. The lessons that it teaches are significant for us; but the reason that links the *drashah* to a particular word or phrase is beyond our ken.

Maharal, however, appears to dismiss this approach. In his view, we *must* find a rationale for such things as the inclusion of strangers in families where they do not belong. And when the Sages offer an elucidation that appears to diverge from the clear meaning of a verse, we must find an underlying compelling logic for this. Obviously, the factors guiding them in these interpretations are meta-historical in nature. They are the considerations that underlie *Chronicles* — the book meant to develop the major themes of the history of the Jewish people. As an example, let us see how the *Maharal* treats the inclusion of David's family, and even Joshua, among the offspring of Shelah ben Judah:

> This verse alludes to the Davidic monarchy. It should be known that David's dynasty was intended originally to descend from Shelah, which is why Judah instructed Tamar to remain a widow until Shelah was old enough to marry her. As events developed, however, it was Judah who became the father of Tamar's children and the forerunner of the Davidic line. But because it was Shelah who was most worthy to be their ancestor, and because Joshua as the conqueror of *Eretz Yisrael* set the stage for the eventual rule of David, Shelah is listed as the head of the family (*Chiddushei Aggados, Bava Basra* 91b).

Clearly, there is no place for such calculations in literal history. In actual, physical terms, David's family descended from Peretz, not Shelah, and Joshua was from the tribe of Ephraim. But on the spiritual level of history, the area where *Maharal* excels in providing enlightenment, it is quite proper to say that the family of Peretz was inspired and nourished by Shelah in developing the traits that were necessary for kingship.

Margin notes:

How did the Sages find this unstated knowledge?

God permitted them to see in the words and phrases of the book ideas that could never be grasped by human intelligence.

David's dynasty was intended originally to descend from Shelah, which is why Judah instructed Tamar to remain a widow until Shelah was old enough to marry her.

Our Approach

We prefer to think that there must be a connection of some sort between the text and the d'rash, though it may seem subtle at times.

In our commentary, we have adopted *Maharal's* approach, because we find it difficult to accept the view that the Sages' interpretations have little or no basis in the text of *Chronicles*. We prefer to think that there must be a connection of some sort between the text and the *d'rash*, though it may seem subtle at times. Always we attempt to find a bridge between the two, and we have succeeded to a certain degree, through an analysis of the relevant teachings of the Sages and the broad range of commentaries by the masters of Aggadic literature. Granted, many of our formulations in this area are speculative and perhaps tenuous and should be segregated from a commentary that concentrates on the simple meaning. Nevertheless, no one could pretend that a commentary to *Chronicles* is adequate if it fails to deal with teachings that shed light on the approach of our Sages to the book.

Consequently, we have chosen to follow two necessary and parallel approaches:

1. To provide an acceptable commentary on the simple meaning of the text, even given the obvious fact that the "simple" meaning of *Chronicles* is hardly simple; and

2. To present the teachings of the Sages and attempt to make them comprehensible.

For the reader's convenience we have divided these tracks into two separate sections. The first appears on the page with the text, and attempts to explain its simple meaning. The second appears in the back of the book, and deals with the often esoteric teachings of the Sages.

The Book of Samuel treats David from the point of view of the here and now, while Chronicles deals with David in his capacity as the progenitor of the Messiah.

It should be clear, however, that our conjectures may well be open to dispute and that many are original to this commentary. One example is our thesis that the Book of *Samuel* treats David from the point of view of the here and now while *Chronicles* deals with David in his capacity as the progenitor of the Messiah. In our commentary, we make frequent use of this thesis to explain changes in stress and nuance in those incidents mentioned in both Books and why some aspects of David's life stressed in *Chronicles* are barely mentioned or omitted in *Samuel,* and vice versa.

It is our contention that these differences can be understood only in terms of the different tasks which the Books have set themselves. This thesis will have to stand the test of how well it manages to explain these difficult issues. [See Overview, *David the King and David the Man* (p. xlvi) where this thesis is discussed in detail.]

An Overview/
Names and their Significance
in Scripture

תָּנֵי, שְׁלֹשָׁה שֵׁמוֹת נִקְרְאוּ לָאָדָם הַזֶּה, אֶחָד שֶׁקָּרְאוּ לוֹ אָבִיו
וְאִמּוֹ וְאֶחָד שֶׁקָּרְאוּ לוֹ אֲחֵרִים וְאֶחָד שֶׁקָּרְאוּ לוֹ בְּסֵפֶר תּוֹלְדוֹת
בְּרִיָּתוֹ.

*We have learned that man is called by three
[different] names. The first is the one given him by
his father and mother; the second is the one by
which others call him. The third is the one by which
he is inscribed in the Book of Events of his
Existence (Koheles Rabbah 7:3).*

The majority of the names found in the first nine chapters of *Chronicles* are not known to us from the rest of
Scripture. Nevertheless, the Sages maintain that many of
the people listed here are identical with persons who are
mentioned in other books under different names. Although
this phenomenon is found primarily in *Chronicles*, it exists
in other books as well.[1]

The Torah views a given name as more than a simple

A person's name means of identification. A person's name — which, as we
defines his unique shall see, is never the result of happenstance — defines his
and individual unique and individual place in the Divine scheme. We may
place in the Divine say that his physical existence is no more than the tangible
scheme. form of the essence that the name expresses.

This concept enables us to understand two customs
based on names. When a person is dangerously ill, he is
given שִׁנּוּי הַשֵּׁם, *change of name,* in the prayerful hope that
this will change his destiny for the better (*Rama, Yoreh
Deah* 335:10). And *Shelah* counsels that at the conclusion
of *Shemoneh Esrei,* one should recite a verse symbolizing
his name in order to help assure that his name will "not be
forgotten" on the Day of Judgment. Since his name

1. Some examples from the Torah are:

A. The wives of Esau are given one set of names at *Genesis* 26:34, and another at
Genesis 36:2-3. See commentators for suggested solutions.

B. Moses' father-in-law is called by many different names. See *Exodus* 2:18, 3:1, 4:18,
and *Numbers* 10:29. The Sages discuss the significance of those names in a number of
places. See *Gur Aryeh* to *Exodus* 4:18 for an analysis of the various opinions expressed in
the midrashim.

C. A number of Benjamin's sons are listed by different names in *Numbers* 26:38 than
those ascribed in *Genesis* 46:21.

Since his name indicates a person's mission in life, it may sometimes be possible to change or elevate that mission through prayer. indicates a person's mission in life, it may sometimes be possible to change or elevate that mission through prayer, repentance, and personal growth. In the prayer containing the change of name for a sick person, we recite, "... even though death may have been decreed for the bearer of the previous name, it was not decreed for the bearer of the new name." In the case of a wicked person who did not fulfill his purpose in God's scheme of things, it might well be expected that his "name" will be forgotten at the time of judgment, when it becomes evident that his life failed to realize the potential that had been implicit in his name.

Definition of Names

What exactly is the relationship between a person's name and his destiny? Any analysis of this subject must begin with an attempt to define precisely, or at least generally, the Torah's concept of names.

Rashba (Responsa 4:30) associates the concept of שֵׁם, *name,* with the idea of *permanence.* The meaning of the word שֵׁם is not limited to the literal translation of the word; it also implies a lasting and meaningful status, which can best be translated as reputation or fame. The righteous will be granted יָד וָשֵׁם, *position and permanence* in God's house and His courtyards (*Isaiah* 56:5), while the שֵׁם, *name* or *reputation,* of the wicked is destined for erosion and disintegration (*Proverbs* 10:7).

Ibn Ezra, in his *Sefer HaShem,* offers an etymological analysis. He relates the word שֵׁם to שָׁם, *there,* the word that describes the location of a given object. Accordingly, a name "locates" its bearer in the sense that the combination of consonants and vowels that make a name serve as a *When we say "Reuven is wise," we mean not the letters of the name, but the person who goes by that name.* substitute for the person. When we say Reuven is wise, we mean not the letters of the name, but the person who goes by that name. We are saying that the man who carries the name Reuven is wise.

There is one other etymological suggestion. In this view, the word שֵׁם has the same meaning as שׁוּם, *assessment.* The given name is in the nature of an estimation or assessment of the object which it describes. The Torah uses the term אַנְשֵׁי הַשֵּׁם (*Genesis* 6:4, see *Rashi*) to describe people marked for destruction, because they have no intrinsic value at all. In common with a number of words in Hebrew which describe both a given state and its opposite, the word שֵׁם is viewed as describing both *value* and the *absence of value.* [A frequently cited example is the verb סקל, which is used to describe both the act of *throwing stones* and that of *removing stones.*] Interestingly, the Mishnah, sometimes uses the words שֵׁם and שׁוּם interchangeably, as in וְכָל שׁוּם שֶׁיֵּשׁ לָהּ, *any name that she has* (*Gittin* 4:2).

We have cited three interpretations of the word שֵׁם, name: permanence, location, and assessment.

We have cited three interpretations of the word שֵׁם, *name:* permanence, location, and assessment. While there are undeniable differences between the three, the thrust of them all is in the same direction. Certainly the idea of permanence attaches to that essence of a person's being that transcends the limitations of his accidental physical features and which is the substance of his value as a human being. Since it is not bound by physical limitations of space and place, it is this essence that projects the person even in his physical absence.

Names and Missions

Maharal (*Ohr Chadash*) points out that a person may corrupt himself, thereby violating the mission implied in his name. The Sages allude to this in their dictum that when Scripture introduces a righteous person, it precedes his given name with the introductory phrase 'and his name was,' as in וּשְׁמוֹ מָרְדְּכַי, *and his name was Mordechai.* In the case of an evil person, however, Scripture follows the opposite course telling us his name first, as in וְנָבָל שְׁמוֹ, *Naval was his name* (*Esther Rabbah* 6:2). Maharal explains: The name implies the person's place in the Divine plan. The righteous people who lead their lives in accordance with God's wishes fulfill their preordained destiny. Their 'name', i.e. their purpose, preceded them. However, the wicked who do not follow God's wishes deviate from their preordained destiny; they forge their own path in life. Thus, they give priority to their personal predilections over the 'name' that God ordained for them.

If indeed a name is significant, then how can its selection be left to the haphazard preferences of parents.

But, if indeed a name is such a significant part of a person's being, then how can its selection be left to the haphazard preferences of parents who are surely not privy to their child's essential nature? *Amudai HaShamayim* cites *Arizal* that the choice of a name is hardly a random matter:

> 'No name is ever given by coincidence, but [on the contrary] it all happens as a result of Divine intervention. Since it is clear [to God] what the essential nature and the activities of this person will be, the father is inspired to name him in accordance with this. For the name explicitly relates to the essence and activities of this man, whether in the direction of good or in the direction of bad …' [This quote is taken from the extensive selection, *Kuntres Krias HaShem*, in R' Moshe Bunim Pirutinsky's *Sefer HaBris* (New York, 5733).]

Arizal's assertion can be viewed as an extension of a teaching in the Talmud (*Berachos* 7b). In a homiletical reading, the Sages interpret *Psalms* 46:9 to read: 'Come, see the deeds of God who places *names* in the world!' Thus the Talmud projects the giving of names as a Divine intervention into the affairs of man. From this the Sages deduce that שְׁמָא גָרִים, *names carry influence.*

If names are Divinely inspired, then surely they must convey some message to us, and so, again and again throughout the Talmud and the Midrash, the Sages show how the names of people reflect the seeds of their destiny. 'Had the people deserved it, God would have called each individual by a name that would have indicated his nature and his destiny' (*Yalkut, Isaiah* 41:449). The *masses* of people did not live their lives in a manner that would justify this degree of personal involvement on God's part. However, because of their importance to the society around them, the names of the Kings (see *Tiferes Yisrael, Shekalim* 6:1) and the Prophets (see *Abarbanel, Introduction to Ezekiel*) are more Divinely inspired than the names of ordinary people. But even they would have enjoyed God's closer involvement had mankind lived as He wished it to.

A name, then, can be compared loosely to a computer program in the sense that it contains within itself those ingredients that determine someone's predisposition toward a certain destiny.

The above accounts for the Scriptural practice of assigning names not meant to be used in practice. Since 'names' define the potential or mission of a person, place, or thing, they can be ascribed even though they will not be put to everyday use. Rather, they may be intended simply to make a given point or define a particular nature. Thus, when Naomi returned from Moab and in her misery cried out: *Do not call me 'Naomi'* [pleasant one], *call me 'Marah'* [embittered one] *for the Almighty has dealt very bitterly with me* (*Ruth* 1:20), it seems unlikely that she actually meant to change her name; people continued to call her Naomi. Rather she meant to redefine her existence in her own and her neighbors' eyes.

Descriptive Names   Also in this category are such verses as: *And Egypt ... I have called* רַהַב הֵם שָׁבֶת, *they are conceited, idle ones* (*Isaiah* 30:7); and *Babylon ... you shall no longer be called* רַכָּה וַעֲנֻגָה, *the soft and spoiled one* (*Isaiah* 47:1). Certainly there was never any intention that the countries were ever called by those names.

Even straightforward names that seem to be meant for regular use must occasionally be seen as purely descriptive. Thus, *Maharal (Gur Aryeh, Exodus* 4:18) resolves the contradiction between various midrashim concerning the number of Yisro's names. Some maintain that he had two names. Others mention seven. *Maharal* holds that Yisro was actually called by two of his names, but the other five were descriptions that conveyed an assessment of the man and his essence.

A similar situation exists in the case of King Solomon. It is obvious that names like Agur ben Yakeh, Ithiel and Uchal (*Proverbs* 30:1), and Lemuel (*Proverbs* 31:1), which the Sages ascribe to Solomon, are purely descriptive. But his name Yedidiah (*II Samuel* 12:25) was given him by Nathan the prophet at God's command; surely it would seem that Yedidiah is a true name. Nevertheless, since it is never used in Scripture again we must conclude that even this name — which means 'Beloved of God' — is descriptive.

In this connection, we may conjecture whether names like: אִי כָבוֹד, *Ichavod* [lit. *an Absence of Honor*] (I *Samuel* 4:21); שְׁאָר יָשׁוּב, *Shear Yashuv* [lit. *The Remainder Will Return*] (*Isaiah* 7:3); מַהֵר שָׁלָל חָשׁ בַּז, *Maher Shalal Chash Baz* [lit. *Hasten Spoils, Rush Booty*] (*Isaiah* 8:3, and see *Radak* there); לֹא רֻחָמָה *Lo Ruchamah* [lit. *One Who is Shown No Mercy*] (*Hosea* 1:6); and לֹא עַמִּי *Lo Ammi* [lit. *Not My People*] (*Hoshea* 1:8), were names by which these children were actually called, or — whether for the reasons given in the context — they were descriptive names, not meant for everyday use.

The above sheds light on a related issue: the Scriptural practice of assigning a name to a place that already had that very same name.

For example, in *Genesis* 27:32-33, Isaac named a place Be'er Sheva, even though it had already been given that name a generation earlier by Abraham (ibid. 21:31). Similarly, *Genesis* 33:15 tells how Jacob gave the name Beth El to a city to which he had already given the same name some twenty-two years earlier (ibid. 28:19). *Ramban* (35:15) explains that the second naming was in the nature of a confirmation that the various truths symbolized by the respective names had once more been borne out. To reaffirm these lessons the names were given again. This can only be understood when names have the descriptive function that we have defined here. If a name were only the means of identifying a person or a thing it would be meaningless to give the same name twice.

A person can be
called by more
than one name in
Scripture provided
that both names
have the same
definition or basic
meaning.

Once we postulate that the primary function of a name is descriptive, we can readily understand a rule set forth by *Ramban* (*Numbers* 2:4), that a person can be called by more than one name in Scripture provided that both names have the same definition or basic meaning: Examples are:

— *Numbers* 1:14 gives *Deuel* as the name of Gad's leader, while *Numbers* 2:14 gives it as *Reuel*. (See fn. to 1:5-7 for a discussion of the degree to which the letters *daleth* and *reish* are interchangeable). *Ramban* suggests that both words have the same meaning. Deuel derives from יָדַע, *to know*, and means: *one who knows God*. Reuel is related to the word רַעְיוֹן, *thought* or *conjecture*, and means: *one whose thoughts are occupied by God*.

— *Genesis* 46:10 gives the name of Shimeon's son as צֹחַר, *Tzochar*. *Numbers* 26:13 gives it as זֶרַח, *Zerach* (see *Rashi*, there). *Ramban* explains that both words have the same meaning: *something that shines brightly*.

— One of the seven Canaanite nations was the חִוִּי, *Chivites* (*Genesis* 10:17 et al.). *Ramban* (*Deuteronomy* 2:23) holds that they are identical to the עַוִּים, *Avvites*, of *Deuteronomy* 2:23. Both names mean: *snake*. (חִוְיָא is the Aramaic word for snake and עַוִּים, from עוה, *to twist*, describes a snake's undulating movements.)

A person can have
two different
names based on
different
perceptions of his
nature, or one
name that lends
itself to different
interpretations.

In a radical departure from modern usage, our thesis explains how a person can have two different names based on different perceptions of his nature, or one name that lends itself to different interpretations.

As an example of the second case, *Genesis* 35:18 recounts how the dying Rachel called her second son בֶּן אוֹנִי, *Ben Oni*, but Jacob named him בִּנְיָמִין, *Benjamin*. *Rambam* comments that אוֹן can have two meanings: *sorrow* and *strength*. Rachel, who was dying in childbirth, had meant to call her son *child of sorrow*. Jacob wanted to retain at least a semblance of the name she had given but wanted it to have a pleasant connotation, so he named the baby בֶּן יָמִין, *son of the right* [*hand*], which connotes strength (the other meaning of אוֹן).

Another example is the case of Gideon's byname Yerubaal. *Judges* 6:32 tells that after Gideon had destroyed the Baal's altar, his father called him Yerubaal, to connote יָרֶב בּוֹ הַבַּעַל, *may Baal fight him* (6:32). But according to *Rosh Hashanah* 25a, when Samuel referred to Gideon as Yerubaal (*I Samuel* 12:11), he meant the name to imply: *He who fought with Baal* (see *Maharsha* there). This too is a case of differing perceptions of the same man, expressed in different interpretations of a name.

The best-known example of the first rule — that a different name will be used for the same person depending upon the context — is the Patriarch Jacob-Israel. He was called Jacob (יַעֲקֹב from עקב, *heel*) because when he was born, his hand was holding Esau's heel (*Genesis* 25:26). He was also called Israel (יִשְׂרָאֵל from שׂרה, *to rule*) because he had triumphed over an angel (*Genesis* 32:29). Thus, his original name connotes a lowly, subservient nature while the one given him later in life implies strength and victory. These two connotations determine which of the names is used in various parts of Scripture. (See *Rashi, Genesis* 32:29, *Ohr HaChayim* to *Genesis* 47:28, and *Ha'amek Davar* to *Exodus* 19:3.)

Thus, his original name connotes a lowly, subservient nature while the one given him later in life implies strength and victory.

Names, then, can reflect the perception of the person who assigns the name. The Midrash teaches that after Adam had given names to all the animals, God asked him, 'Now what should *your* name be?'

Adam answered, 'I should be called Adam for I was formed from the earth [אָדָם from אֲדָמָה, *earth*]'.

God asked, 'And what should My Name be?'

Adam answered, 'You should be called HASHEM for You are master of everything'.

Surely God did not need Adam to provide Him an objective assessment of Himself and man. Rather, God wanted Adam to spell out his own understanding of the nature of God and man.

In Summary

We may sum up as follows:

1. A name is more than a convenient way by which to address someone.

2. In a way that we cannot define precisely, there is an intimate tie between a person and the name he carries. It is analogous to a computer program in the sense that, within given parameters, it determines the range of his life experiences. This, of course, does not inhibit his free will, which he must exercise as he is faced by the choices contained within those parameters.

The name is analogous to a computer program in the sense that it determines the range of his life experiences.

3. All names are Divinely inspired. The degree to which they express absolutely the bearer's essence will vary, but in every case there is a good reason he bears a particular name. In the language of the Sages, this idea is expressed by the term שְׁמָא גָרִים, *the name carries influence*.

In every case there is a good reason he bears a particular name.

4. Many people carry more than one name. The reasons for this are as follows:

   a. Not all names of a given person were used to

address him. Some are purely descriptive and are meant only to teach a certain aspect of his character or of his historical significance.

b. Occasionally a name may point to a given aspect of the person's being and that same aspect can be expressed by a different word with a similar meaning. Scripture will then use either name.

c. There may be a number of different aspects of a person's nature, each of which is expressed by a different name.

d. Different people may view the same person from different perspectives. Each will have a different name for him. This phenomenon is the second category in the passage from *Koheles Rabbah*, with which we introduced this Overview.

e. The context within which a person is mentioned may differ from book to book, and occasionally from passage to passage. This phenomenon is the third category in the passage from *Koheles Rabbah*.

f. A name may be associated with a specific event connected with his bearer. Moses received his name because he was 'drawn from the water' [מֹשֶׁה from משה, *to draw out*]; Yissachar was given his name because Leah had 'hired' Jacob for the night [יְשָׂשׂכָר from שכר, *to hire*]. It is perfectly possible that a person may carry a number of names to commemorate given events of which we know nothing, since they are not recorded in Scripture. [This category has not been dealt with in the essay; it is discussed by *Ibn Ezra* in *Genesis* 4:19.]

In conclusion we may say that the sense of strangeness which we feel when we are confronted with a situation in which the same person appears in Scripture under different names, is rooted in a culture-gap between our generation and the thought-world of the Scriptural books and our Sages. In our society, names are fixed and rigid and, with the exception of nicknames or diminutives, they are permanent. But that is because in modern times the name has become ossified into a practically meaningless means of identification. In Scriptural times, however, a name was a sensitive, flexible tool that was responsive to and reflected meaning and situations.

An analogy to this development can best be drawn from the surname, which in its relatively short history has gone through the same metamorphosis. Such names as Schreiber, Goldsmith, Schochet were originally descriptive; they mean nothing at all to us today. If we are to enter the world of Scripture and its traditional interpretation by the Sages, we must train our minds to remember that given names developed in precisely this manner.

An Overview/
David the King and David the Man

דָּוִד מֶלֶךְ יִשְׂרָאֵל חַי וְקַיָּם

David, King of Israel, lives and endures (Rosh Hashanah 25a).

מִזְמוֹר שִׁיר־חֲנֻכַּת הַבַּיִת לְדָוִד. וְכִי דָוִד בְּנָאוֹ — וַהֲלֹא שְׁלֹמֹה בְּנָאוֹ! אֶלָּא לְפִי שֶׁנָּתַן דָּוִד נַפְשׁוֹ עָלָיו לִבְנוֹתוֹ נִקְרָא עַל שְׁמוֹ.

'A psalm — a song for the inauguration of the Temple, by David' (Psalms 30:1). But was David the one who built it; it was Solomon who built it! But because David devoted himself to building it, it was called after him (Mechilta, Beshalach).

הָיָה דָוִד אוֹמֵר לְעַצְמוֹ: וְכִי מִפְּנֵי שֶׁאָמַר לִי הַקָּדוֹשׁ בָּרוּךְ הוּא אַתָּה לֹא תִבְנֶה בַיִת, אֲנִי יוֹשֵׁב? מֶה עָשָׂה, זֵרֵז אֶת עַצְמוֹ וְהִתְקִין אֶת כָּל צְרָכָיו עַד שֶׁלֹּא מֵת.

David used to say to himself, "Will I sit idle because the Holy One Blessed is He told me, 'You will not build the Temple?' " What did he do? He motivated himself to prepare all of its needs before he died (Devarim Rabbah 2:27).

דָּוִד בָּנָה אֶת הַיְסוֹדוֹת . . . וּשְׁלֹמֹה בָּנָה אֶת הָעֶלְיוֹנוֹת . . .

David built the foundations . . . Solomon built the structures (Shir Hashirim Rabbah 1:6).

Chronicles and Samuel The first Book of *Chronicles*, from chapter 10 to the end, is more or less a review of II *Samuel*, which begins with the death of King Saul and continues to the end of King David's life. Despite all that the two books have in common, however, the differences between them outnumber their similarities. The commentary will show that *Chronicles* treats its contents from an entirely different perspective than that of *Samuel*. What is more, of the twenty-eight subjects discussed in *II Samuel*, many are not mentioned in *Chronicles* (see comparative tables below).

Ezra, the author of Chronicles, seeks to present a different perspective of David's illustrious career and monumental achievements.

Ezra, the author of *Chronicles*, portrays a "different" King David than does the Book of *Samuel*, because he seeks to present a different perspective of David's illustrious career and monumental achievements. Of course the authors do not disagree on who David was and what he did; rather each concentrates on a different aspect of the same man. Each prophet has a thesis, a perspective, which determines his presentation of David and his significance.

Obviously a great man's biography will be told differently by psychologists, political scientists, and economists. Each tells the truth, but from a different point of view. So, too, *Chronicles* presents a particular perspective of King David. How can we identify which one it is? If a narrator includes a major list of his subject's achievements, a list that a different narrator omits, we may assume that the catalogue reflects the author's entire perception of the man. Ezra's view of David is reflected in a lengthy chronicle of achievements that are not even mentioned in *Samuel*.

We will find the answer in a long and impressive description of the climax of David's service to the Jewish people.

We will find the answer in the last eight chapters of *I Chronicles*, which give us a long and impressive description of the climax of David's service to the Jewish people. Every item in the list relates to his preparations for the Temple, a building he knew he could never see: the choice and purchase of the Temple site, the great wealth he amassed for this purpose, the division of the *Kohanim* and Levites into assigned watches for the Temple service, the appointment of administrators to oversee the allocation of resources and personnel, his eloquent addresses to Solomon and the national leaders to implement their responsibility to build and maintain the Temple. That Ezra chose to give such prominence to this aspect of David's activity — laying the groundwork for the future Temple — signifies that he considered it the highlight of David's monarchy, a triumphant end to a fruitful and holy life.

He considered it the highlight of David's monarchy, a triumphant end to a fruitful and holy life.

But all these events are omitted from the Book of *Samuel*! *Samuel* ends David's life on a tragic note, telling of a three-year famine, a nearly disastrous war with the Philistines, and a census in violation of halachah, which resulted in the loss of seventy thousand lives. Its last verses tell of David's repentance and acceptance of responsibility for the calamity, upon which he was told to purchase the threshing-floor of Aravnah the Yevusite and bring an offering there — we are not even told that it was then that he realized that this was the site of the future Temple!

Are *Chronicles* and *Samuel* speaking about the same man? In a sense they are not.

The Two Davids

There is a David who was a king, a warrior, a political unifier; a flesh-and-blood human being with perhaps more than his share of opponents, suffering, and domestic heartache; the major figure in a circumscribed era of Jewish history. This is the David of *Samuel.* To treat him this way is not to diminish his greatness; it is merely to describe his years on earth without considering his impact on the broad, eternal sweep of Jewish history.

The other David is the David of *Chronicles.* Ezra depicts David's role as a prime mover in God's plan of Creation, as a pivotal figure in Israel's destiny, as the one who was instrumental in erecting the Temple — though he did not hew its stones — and in fashioning the eventful Messianic dynasty. In the life of *this* David, his activities to prepare for the Temple are essential, while a complete account of his ways and personal woes are not. In recounting David's meta-historical role, Ezra stresses what is essential to it while he minimizes what is extraneous. When we proclaim every month, "David, King of Israel, lives and endures," we mean *this* David. He is not simply a mortal human being who strode the stage of history millennia ago and now survives only in ancient books and memory. He is still alive. He transcends the era in which he was active because his ideals still move his people and because its Messianic destiny springs from him.

In recounting David's meta-historical role, Ezra stresses what is essential to it while he minimizes what is extraneous.

In the words of Henry Biberfeld's *David, King of Israel:*

> In David's life, as we shall show, ideas — and above all the idea of the omnipresence of God — acquired a singular actuality. The awareness of the Divine occupied his existence to such a degree that it completely overshadowed all other aspects of being. Where others perceived a world made and moved by concrete facts and forces, and where — if recognized at all — the forces of the spirit led a shadowy existence in the background of reality, David saw a different world. To him it was a world of the spirit, of the all-pervading and all-sustaining reality of the Divine, animating and ennobling the mechanism of the universe. This invisible reality was his true reality; the world of the idea, his world. All his thoughts and feelings, his words and actions, his wishes and impulses, were directed by

Where others perceived a world made and moved by concrete facts and forces, David saw a different world.

the influences of that unseen reality.

Painfully slow, in a development that extended over many centuries and lands, the idea of preparing the world as the Kingdom of God on earth was absorbed into the organism of the Jewish people. Relapses occurred; stagnation set in; other ideas took hold; the allure of material achievements beckoned. But beneath all this, the idea, once it had taken root, never died. It had become close, human, attainable. The impetus it received by the appearance of its human prototype carried it on through the nation's decline and exile. This idea, hope and inner certainty, aim and essence of individual and national being, is to the Jew materialized in the immortal king. Thus, as once an idea had become the very being of David, now the being of David became the idea of the Jewish people. As David was sent to prove and proclaim, in word and deed, the omnipresence of the Divine on earth, thus Israel was sent into the world as herald of the Kingdom of God. David's message was taken over by the Jewish nation. His wondrous deeds and inspired songs which expressed his inner, essential person became the vital reality, the distinctive feature of the Jewish people.

As once an idea had become the very being of David, now the being of David became the idea of the Jewish people.

The Essential David

What facet of David's personality best characterized his eternal aspect? In his last will and testament, he described himself as הַגֶּבֶר הֻקַם עָל, *the man who was established on high* (II Samuel 23:1). The Sages interpret this expression homiletically as הַגֶּבֶר שֶׁהֵקִים עוּלָהּ שֶׁל תְּשׁוּבָה, *the man who established the yoke of repentance* (Avodah Zarah 5a).

What is "repentance"? *Maharal* explains that repentance is a basic component of earthly existence. The world has no independent existence of its own. It exists by virtue of God's grace so that His will can be done. It may take years, centuries, or millennia of struggle and missteps before mankind recognizes its responsibilities to the Source of its being. *Teshuvah* comes from the root שוב, *return; teshuvah* is man's return to God with all his heart and soul. It was a pre-condition of Creation that man would eventually repent. Everything that exists must return to God, for only thereby can it exist. In particular, Israel will eventually repent. Because of its innate goodness, it is impossible for Israel not to repent (Nesiv HaTeshuvah ch. 2,4).

It was a pre-condition of Creation that man would eventually repent. Everything that exists must return to God, for only thereby can it exist.

What is the "*yoke of repentance*"? The necessity, the

inevitability of repentance, for the King Who created the world had decreed that it must eventually attain the fulfillment of His spiritual goal. King David, God's earthly surrogate, established God's authority in the kingdom of Israel, established repentance as an absolute requirement that cannot be compromised (see comm. to 17:14).

Granted — the world must fulfill its purpose, but who can guarantee that this will indeed come about? It is the Jewish soul, which is impervious to inner contamination. Because the soul always retains its essential holiness and purity, it can attain atonement through sacrificial offerings. As *Maharal* (*Gevuras Hashem*, ch. 8:62) explains, God's assurance to Abraham that nothing could destroy his offspring's claim to *Eretz Yisrael* was based on the efficacy of the offerings and the essential purity of the Jewish soul.

Because the soul's essence cannot be harmed or changed by sin, it can be cleansed by repentance and offerings. Because the soul's essence cannot be harmed or changed by sin, it can be cleansed by repentance and offerings.

But if the soul were intrinsically evil — or subject to the effects of evil — then an accumulation of sin would worm its way into the soul and eventually transform it to the point where it could no longer gain atonement by means of the sacrificial service. In the absence of the Temple, study and prayer take the place of the actual service. Thus, the echo of Temples past and future reverberates in our daily lives. If we wish to find the eternal King David who transcends the seventy years of his mortal life, we must find it in his relationship to the eternal Temple, in which there is a confluence of past, present, and future.

True, David was denied the privilege of building the Temple, but he is inextricably connected to it nonetheless, because he devoted himself to it by preparing everything that would be needed for its construction. Because of his dedication to it, it was called *his* Temple (*Mechilta Beshalach*). *In a deeper sense, David was even the builder of the Temple, because it was only in David's merit that the Ark was permitted to enter the Temple.* In a deeper sense, David was even the *builder* of the Temple, because the heart of the Temple is the Holy Ark, and it was only in David's merit that the Ark was permitted to enter the Temple. As the Talmud (*Shabbos* 30a) teaches, when Solomon inaugurated the Temple and — in the presence of the exultant nation — attempted to bring the Ark into the Holy of Holies, the Temple gates would not open to let it enter. Only when Solomon prayed and invoked his father's merit did the gates rise up to make way for the Ark. This was a public vindication of David's righteousness and proof that Solomon was his successor, not only on the throne but as the builder of the Temple.

Highlights of Chronicles

As we have shown in the Overview, *The Uniqueness of Chronicles*, the purpose of *Chronicles* is not to be a record of events, but to trace the progress of the world and Israel toward the realization of the Divine goal. Such a chronicle will be far different from a dispassionate, themeless historical narrative. Similarly, the David who is the hero of *I Chronicles* is not the David of *Samuel*. In *Chronicles*, we deal not with the king but with the king*ship*; not with the first king from the tribe of Judah but with the progenitor of Israel's Messianic dynasty, which will climax with the Messiah, offspring of David. This is our key to understanding why some events are included in *Chronicles*, while others are excluded. Let us now use this thesis as the basis to explain the contents of *Chronicles*. (Although we combine and condense some of the events, our order follows that of *Chronicles*, as listed in the table below).

1. **The Death of Saul** (ch. 10):

Chronicles recounts the downfall, but not the greatness of Saul; it recounts the greatness, but not the failures of David.

The *Mefaresh* provides a stimulating insight: *Chronicles* recounts the downfall, but not the greatness of Saul; it recounts the greatness, but not the failures of David. In doing so, Ezra did not attempt to deceive us, for we know all the relevant facts from the Book of *Samuel*. Rather his intention was to differentiate a short-lived kingship from an eternal one. Thus, the important information we need about Saul is the sin that caused him to lose his throne. David's sins, however, do not matter in this context, because they had no effect on his reign. (See comm. to 10:13-14, and footnote.) Since events 1-7 of the Book of *Samuel* (see table) are unrelated to David's kingship, they are omitted from *Chronicles*.

2. **The Coronation of David in Hebron** (11:1-3):

In our introduction to those verses, we note that the broad national consensus to accept David as king came about only as a result of a series of events centering around Avner, who took the lead in convincing the tribes to join Judah in accepting David as their king. In *Samuel,* we are led along a slow progression of events: Avner becomes disillusioned with Ish Bosheth, Saul's son and successor; he decides to switch his allegiance to David, he tries to convince the eleven tribes to do likewise, he succeeds and finally David is crowned. As always in human experience, the result was not inevitable. Avner could have reconsidered or failed. *Samuel,* which is essentially a record of events, records the suspenseful story as it occurred. But *Chronicles* omits it all. *Chronicles* deals with the inevitable. David's ascension was as necessary and as inevitable as day

Chronicles deals with the inevitable. David's ascension was as necessary and as inevitable as day and night.

and night. In the perspective of eternity, it had to be, and the details are irrelevant.

3. **The Conquest of Jerusalem** (11:4-9):

Clearly, the choice of Jerusalem and its conquest for the site of the Temple is as basic as the coronation of David, and it belongs in *Chronicles*. As *Rambam* (*Hil. Beis HaBechirah* 1:3) states, from the time the Temple was built in Jerusalem, it is forbidden to build a Tabernacle or altar anywhere else. Only Mount Moriah in Jerusalem is the proper site for the Temple.

4. **David's Warriors** (11:10-47):

David's "warriors," were primarily heroes of the spirit. That is why they are named early in his career.

In *Chronicles*, these warriors are named near the beginning of David's story; in *Samuel*, they are named at the end. The *Gra* comments that the number of these warriors is thirty-six, an allusion to the tradition that every generation includes thirty-six supremely righteous people. David's "warriors," too, were primarily heroes of the spirit (see Section Two, p. 417). That is why they are named early in his career: such people were an integral part of his rule and they characterized his mission as king.

5. **The Other Tribes Come to David's Support** (ch. 12):

This is more than a list of communities joining hands under a new national banner. The lyric tone of much of the narrative implies that their allegiance to David was motivated by a perception of the man's inner greatness (see Section Two, p. 422). These expressions of support are absent from *Samuel*, but they are listed in *Chronicles*, because they show Israel's adherence to the Messianic goal.

6. **The Nation Rejoices at His Coronation** (12:39-41):

This, too, is absent from *Samuel*, where we are told only the fact that the people crowned David and that he made a covenant with them. It is important to the theme of *Chronicles* that we know how the entire Jewish people was swept up in the enthusiasm for their national calling.

7. **The Unsuccessful Attempt to Bring the Ark to Jerusalem — The Death of Uzza** (ch. 13):

Both incidents demonstrated to the people the grave responsibility that went with their designation as God's Chosen People.

In the commentary (21:1) we note that the death of Uzza was of a piece with the plague that struck after the forbidden census. Both incidents showed that even the most righteous people are not spared when they violate God's will, and they demonstrated to the people the grave responsibility that went with their designation as God's Chosen People. And, of course, the attempt to bring the Ark to Jerusalem was part of the preparation for building the Temple.

8. **King Churam Sends Help to Build David's Palace**
(14:1-2):

Churam's desire to assist David in his construction was
symbolic of Edom's submission to Israel (see Section Two,
p. 424).

9. **David's Family in Jerusalem** (14:3-7):

Only David's children born in Jerusalem are
enumerated. Among them is Solomon, his successor and
the ancestor of Messiah.

10. **The Wars with the Philistines** (14:8-17):

In Section Two to 14:8 (p. 425), we note that these wars
were a portent of the eventual War of Gog and Magog.

11. **The Successful Ascension of the Ark to Jerusalem**
(ch. 15 and 16):

Clearly, this is all a direct preparation for the
construction of the Temple.

12. **David's Plea to Build the Temple and God's
Assurance that His Son Would Do So** (ch. 17):

In the introduction and Section Two to ch. 17, we
discuss David's status as a warrior, the factor that
prevented him from building the Temple. (Our discussion
follows the interpretation of *R' Tzadok HaKohen*; see also
Overview to ArtScroll *Shir HaShirim*.) *Chronicles'*
approach to this narrative is completely different from that
of *Samuel*. Here the subject is not David's external wars,
Our Book's but his inner lack of peace; consequently our Book's
perspective on the perspective on the Davidic dynasty, as it emerges from
Davidic dynasty, Nathan's promise and prophecy, possesses a character
possesses a unlike that which is related in *Samuel*. In fact, we may say
character unlike that this chapter holds the key to understanding the
that which is differences in approach between *Chronicles* and *Samuel*. In
related in Samuel. this regard, we will also note essential differences in
David's prayer of gratitude between the texts of *Chronicles*
and *Samuel* (see Section Two at length).

13. **David's Wars** (ch. 18):

Since David consecrated the booty of his wars for the
construction of the Temple, the wars are all preparations
for that great goal. In his battle against the allied forces of
Aram and Edom, *Samuel* stresses Aram, because it was the
Chronicles stresses larger and stronger of the allies, but *Chronicles* stresses
Edom, because in Edom, because in the perspective of eternity, Edom (the
the perspective of descendant of Esau) is the nemesis that must fall before
eternity, Edom is Israel can be triumphant (see Section Two, p. 450).
the nemesis that
must fall. 14. **David's Kindness to Ammon and the Resulting
Wars** (ch. 19):

As noted above, *Chronicles* is concerned with David's

wars only as they relate to his eternal role, and it is from this perspective that the Book reports his wars with Ammon (see comm. to ch. 19).

15. **Battles With the Three Philistine Heroes** (20:4-8): The narrative in *Chronicles* is different in many details. See Introduction to 20:4-8.

16. **The Census and Its Outcome** (ch. 21): The differences in the narratives of *Chronicles* and *Samuel* are nowhere more indicative of the dissimilar perspectives of the two books. In *Samuel* the facts are reported: the census, the epidemic, and David's offerings of repentance on the threshing-floor of Aravnah. But *Chronicles* tells us that as a result of this tragic incident David's preparations for the Temple construction were advanced considerably and he discovered the site of the Temple.

Chronicles tells us that as a result of this tragic incident David's preparations for the Trmple construction were advanced considerably.

This difference in narratives demonstrates indisputably that *Samuel's* concern is with the history of the moment, while *Chronicles* looks ahead to eternity — to the preparations for the construction of the Temple, the theme of the book.

Iyar 5747

Rabbi Moshe Eisemann
with Rabbi Nosson Scherman

Contrasts and Similarities Between Samuel and Chronicles	
The Events In Chronicles	**The Events In Samuel**
Saul's death	Saul's death; the Amalekite assassin is killed; the dirge
	David crowned by Judah in Hebron
	Ish-Bosheth is crowned by the other tribes
	Civil war — Asael is killed
	David's family
	Avner sponsors David, and is killed by Yoav
	Ish-Bosheth is assassinated
David is crowned king in Hebron	David is crowned king in Hebron
David conquers Jerusalem	David conquers Jerusalem
	Chiram helps build David's palace
David's heroes	
Many tribal units join David's banner	
The people rejoice at David's coronation	
	David's family in Jerusalem
	Two Philistine wars
Ill-fated attempt to bring Ark to Jerusalem	Ill-fated attempt to bring Ark to Jerusalem
Chiram helps build David's palace	
David's family in Jerusalem	
Two Philistine wars	
The successful transfer of the Ark	The successful transfer of the Ark
The institution of the service before the Ark	
David asks and is denied permission to build the Temple	David asks and is denied permission to build the Temple
David's prayer	David's prayer
David's wars	David's wars
	David deals kindly with Mephibosheth
Kindness to Ammon, and the resulting wars	Kindness to Ammon with the beginning of the resulting wars
	The story of Bath Sheva
	Amnon and Tamar
	Avshalom's rebellion
	The rebellion of Sheva ben Bichri
	The famine and the Giveonites
Skirmishes with three Philistine heroes	Skirmishes with four Philistine heroes
	David sings
	David prays
	David's heroes
David orders the census	David orders the census
The plague	The plague
The sacrifice	The sacrifice
Discovery of the Temple site	
Groundwork for Solomon's reign and the building of the Temple	

Divrei hayamim I

(א־ג **אָדָם** שֵׁת אֱנוֹשׁ: קֵינָן מַהֲלַלְאֵל יָרֶד: חֲנוֹךְ מְתוּשֶׁלַח
ד־ה לָמֶךְ: נֹחַ שֵׁם חָם וָיָפֶת: בְּנֵי יֶפֶת גֹּמֶר וּמָגוֹג וּמָדַי וְיָוָן

I

◄§ From Adam to Noah

1⁻4. The ten generations from Adam to Noah (Avos 5:2) listed here are identical with those listed in Genesis 5:1-32.

אָדָם — Adam. From אֲדָמָה [adamah], earth. Maharal (Tiferes Yisrael 3) teaches that he was not called אָדָם because he had been created from the earth; all the animals were made from the earth (Genesis 1:24) and such a name would not have had any meaning. Rather, by calling him אָדָם, God taught him the true nature of his being. Nothing is as valueless as a clod of earth, but again, there is nothing which does not ultimately derive from the earth. The earth is that which, while valueless in itself, nevertheless carries an infinite potential for growth and development, and that too is the nature of Man. It is Man's duty not to remain as he has been created but to achieve greatness out of the infinite resources with which he has been endowed. [See Section Two, p. 370.]

שֵׁת — Seth. The derivation of this name is given in Genesis 4:25: Because [Eve said] 'God has provided me another child in place of Abel, for Cain had killed him.' The word שֵׁת means to provide or place (see Genesis 46:4). [See further, Section Two, p. 371.]

אֱנוֹשׁ — Enosh. As Adam, so Enosh means man. However, it represents man in a deteriorated state — troubled and tainted (Hirsch) or frail and limited (Malbim) (see ArtScroll comm. to Genesis 4:24, Psalms 8:6).

[The world now entered into a long period of moral decline which eventually caused God to bring the Flood. This decline is reflected by the names given to the succeeding generations. For an analysis of this, see Section Two, p. 373.]

2. קֵינָן — Kenan. Why was his name Kenan? Because he bequeathed evil to his generation and led them astray (הִקְנָה לְדוֹרוֹ). הִקְנָה (רָעָה) is the Hiphil of קנה, to acquire, which is assumed to be the root of קֵינָן [1] (Torah Sheleimah 47).

[Sefer Yuchasin reports a different tradition according to which Kenan was a wise man who, in his time, ruled over the whole world and warned his people of the impending flood.]

מַהֲלַלְאֵל — Mahalalel. Why was his name Mahalalel? Because he repented and began praising God [Mahalalel derives from הלל, to praise] (Torah Sheleimah 49).

In this next generation the pendulum swung back. The sins of Enosh and Kenan stimulated a reaction and Mahalalel found his way back to God.

יָרֶד — Yered. Why was he called Yered? Because in his time his generation descended to the lowest depths [יָרֶד from ירד, to descend] (Torah Sheleimah 50).[2]

3. חֲנוֹךְ — Chanoch [Enoch]. There are no Midrashim to explain the derivation of this name. However, we find four people in the Book of Genesis named Chanoch. The first is the son of Cain, the second is the son of

---

1. The assumption that קֵינָן derives from קנה, to acquire, is presumably based on the derivation which the Torah (Genesis 4:1) ascribes to the similar name קַיִן: I have acquired a man with HASHEM. However, this derivation is difficult to defend grammatically since קַיִן and קֵינָן seem related to קוּן or קָן rather than to קנה. [An analogous derivation is Rashi's assertion (Exodus 7:1) that נבא, to prophesy, derives from the root ניב or נוב. See Gur Aryeh there.] Such grammatical irregularities in the derivation of proper nouns occur frequently (Ibn Ezra, Exodus 18:3) and relationship of names to their roots seems to be based more on phonetic similarity than on a strict grammatical derivation. [See Ibn Ezra, Genesis 11:1, who proves that man's original language was Hebrew from the assonance which exists between the Bible's proper nouns and the Hebrew roots from which they are derived. One of his examples is the relationship of קָן to קנה.]

The additional nun in קֵינָן can be explained as an intensification of the idea expressed in the name. See Baer, Seder Avodas Yisroel, p. 412 for such usage of the final nun in both Biblical and Rabbinic Hebrew.

2. A seemingly conflicting tradition is preserved in Midrash Aggadah, Bereishis. Why was he called Yered? Because in his days angels descended from heaven and taught mankind how to serve God (Torah Sheleimah 51).

Adam, Seth, Enosh ²Kenan, Mahalalel, Yered ³Chanoch, Methuselah, Lemech. ⁴Noah, Shem, Ham, and Japheth. ⁵The sons of Japheth — Gomer, Magog, Madai, Yavan, Tuval, Meshech,

Yered, the third is the grandson of Abraham through his concubine Keturah (25:4), and the fourth is the son of Reuven. With regard to this last one, *Sechel Tov* comments: He (Reuven) was inaugurated (חֻנַּךְ, *to inaugurate*) through him into fatherhood and named him after the righteous Chanoch (the son of Yered).

It may be that the Chanoch of this verse was also a first-born who therefore inaugurated his father into fatherhood. The precedent set here was later followed by Reuven.[1] [This would not, however, explain the grandson of Keturah being named Chanoch, since he was not a first-born.]

Haamek Davar to *Genesis* 4:17, where Cain's son is called Chanoch, remarks that the name is self-explanatory because he was the first child to be reared and educated (חֻנַּךְ, *to educate* and start a child on its life's path) by his father. [According to the teaching of the Sages, Cain and Abel had been born as grown individuals.] *Haamek Davar* does not comment on the Chanoch of our verse. Perhaps Yered, on seeing the depths to which his generation had sunk, determined to make a fresh start. His child would, as it were, make a new beginning.

For a discussion of Chanoch and his death, see ArtScroll *Genesis*, 5:22-25.

מְתוּשֶׁלַח — *Methuselah*. He was a wholly righteous man *(Yalkut)*.

According to *Seder Olam Rabbah*, he

studied under Adam for 243 years, and according to *Bava Basra* 121b, he is one of the seven[2] 'links' in the eternal chain which bridged the lifespan of mankind.

His righteousness was such that the angels eulogized him, and the Flood was postponed until the seven days of mourning for his death passed [see *Genesis* 7:10] *(Sanhedrin* 108b; *Avos d'Rabbi Nosson).*

לֶמֶךְ — *Lemech*. Concerning this Lemech the sources are silent. We do not know whether he was righteous or wicked.

נֹחַ — *Noah*. נֹחַ, from נחה, *to rest*, brought relief to a weary world ravaged by the results of the curse which had been placed on Adam *(Genesis* 5:29, *Rashi* there). [For an explanation of the etymology of נֹחַ and its relationship to נֶחָמָה, *comfort*, see ArtScroll *Genesis* to 5:29.]

As the sole righteous man of his generation it fell to him to rebuild post-diluvian mankind and set it on the path which ultimately led Israel to stand at Sinai. [See Section Two, p. 375.]

In contrast to the previous verses in which each name indicated a different generation, in our verse Noah is the father and Shem, Ham and Japheth are the sons. In addition to the fact that the separate listing of the genealogies of each of the three sons in the following verses precludes any confusion on this score, there is also the fact that Ezra was able to assume a thorough knowledge of the whole Torah on the part of the people.[3]

1. If we assume this interpretation for the name of the Chanoch in our verse — i.e., that he was called so because he was the first son of Mahalalel, then it follows that not all those listed in the genealogical lists in *Genesis* were first-born. They are named not because they were their parents' oldest children but because they were the 'soul' of their generation *(Kuzari).*

2. The Talmud notes that there were seven men whose lives spanned the entire history of man: Methuselah saw Adam; Shem [son of Noah] saw Methuselah; Jacob saw Shem; Amram [father of Moses] saw Jacob; Achiyah the Shilonite saw Amram; Elijah saw Achiyah [who did not die in the wilderness and enjoyed exceptional longevity], and Elijah is still alive *(Bava Basra* 121b).

3. According to *Sanhedrin* 69b, Japheth was the oldest of the three sons. The sequence Shem, Ham, Japheth, is in the order of their wisdom rather than their ages (see *Tosafos* and *Margolios HaYam* to *Sanhedrin* for an explanation of why, in that case, Ham is listed second; cf. ArtScroll *Genesis*, pp. 179 and 303).

The proofs which the Talmud adduces to this system come from other verses in *Genesis*, but these proofs do not exist in *Chronicles*. This verse would therefore have been misleading if a thorough knowledge of *Genesis* could not be assumed. The fact that *Chronicles* follows the order based on wisdom rather than the one based on age, as might have been expected in a genealogy, indicates that these are no simple genealogical lists. Again and again we shall find that Ezra's purpose went far beyond the mere listing of the family trees.

ו וְתֻבַל וּמֶשֶׁךְ וְתִירָס: וּבְנֵי גֹּמֶר אַשְׁכְּנַז וְדִיפַת וְתוֹגַרְמָה:

ז־ח וּבְנֵי יָוָן אֱלִישָׁה וְתַרְשִׁישָׁה כִּתִּים וְרוֹדָנִים: בְּנֵי חָם

ט כּוּשׁ וּמִצְרַיִם פּוּט וּכְנָעַן: וּבְנֵי כוּשׁ סְבָא וַחֲוִילָה וְסַבְתָּא

י וְרַעְמָא וְסַבְתְּכָא וּבְנֵי רַעְמָא שְׁבָא וּדְדָן: וְכוּשׁ יָלַד אֶת־

שֵׁם — *Shem* [lit. *a name*]. [The commentary on the three sons of Noah is based on *Maharal's* analysis of their diverse natures. See Section Two, p. 376.]

Maharal explains that of the three sons of Noah, Shem represents the true (spiritual) essence of man and thinks that this nature is implied in his name.

The name Shem literally means *name*. The Torah assigns names to things which convey their essential nature (see Overview/Names and their Significance p. xxxiv). So someone who is called *name* would be the person in whom the essence of humanity is epitomized.

An alternative explanation seems possible. *Ibn Ezra* in *Sefer HaShem* explains the etymology of the word שֵׁם, *a name*, as related to שָׁם, *there*, because we use the name to represent the person or object who is called by it. It is as though they are contained (i.e., they are 'there') in the name.

Thus the name שֵׁם, Shem, implies a presence. Something is 'there' besides the object which meets the eye. Perhaps the name שֵׁם, Shem, of Noah's son is analogous.

Adam's son שֵׁת, Seth, had been so called because מִמֶּנּוּ הוּשְׁתַת הָעוֹלָם, *from him the world received its foundation*, indicating his role in the perpetuation of mankind. So too Shem, who played a similar role among Noah's sons, in that the full destiny of man was to be realized through him, was given a name to symbolize that role. '[Shem] was righteous, born circumcised, God's name was upon him, Abraham was to be descended from him, he was a high priest before God (see *Genesis* 14:18) and the Temple was destined to be built in his portion …' (*Bereishis Rabbah* 26:3). In him

all mankind was represented.

חָם — *Ham*. The Sages do not offer any etymology for this name. But *Maharal* (*Gur Aryeh* to *Genesis* 9:23), based on the idea that Ham stands for the life-force (נֶפֶשׁ) which tends towards the craving of physical fulfillment, suggests that the name is related to חוֹם, *heat*, and describes the חוֹם טִבְעִי, *the natural heat* (desire) in a person's heart.

יֶפֶת — *Japheth*. The Sages offer no etymology for this name, but *Maharal* (*Gur Aryeh* to *Genesis* 9:23) suggests that the name is related to יוֹפִי, *beauty*. See Section Two, p. 376.

From Noah to Abraham

5-24. These verses list the descendants of Noah's sons. The seventy descendants listed here each became, according to tradition, the progenitors of a nation — the seventy nations of the ancient world. For the historical view of Israel's relationship to these nations see Section Two, p. 378.

5. בְּנֵי יֶפֶת — *The sons of Japheth*. As in the Torah, the sequence of the genealogies is: Japheth, Ham and Shem. The most important (Shem) is left to the last so that it can be given a fuller treatment (*Mefaresh*, *Radak*).[1]

With the exception of some minor differences in spelling (see below), this genealogy is identical with that of *Genesis*. [See ArtScroll *Bereishis* pp. 310-314 for a closer identification of the names mentioned here.]

Of the seven sons of Japheth, only the family tree of Gomer and Yavan is taken further. Most commentators assume that the children of the other five sons did not

---

1. The mere fact that the name mentioned last in v. 4 is treated first is not in itself noteworthy. This is a style often found in Scripture [cf. *Numbers* 33:2; *Genesis* 2:4, *I Kings* 18:10 and many more].

However, a careful analysis of our chapter shows that this is not the system which Ezra uses by choice. The genealogies of Esau's sons (vs. 36-37) follow the sequence in which they are mentioned (v. 35) as do those of the children of Seir (vs. 39-42). It is only in the case of Noah's sons (Shem, Ham and Japheth) and Abraham's sons (Isaac and Ishmael) that we find the reverse order employed. The reason is surely as the commentators assume that the less significant genealogy is first given a cursory treatment so that the important one can then be treated in detail.

and Tiras. 6 And the sons of Gomer — Ashkenaz, Diphath, and Togarmah. 7 And the sons of Yavan — Elishah, Tarshishah, Kittim, and Rodanim. 8 The sons of Ham — Cush, Mitzraim, Put, and Canaan. 9 And the sons of Cush — Seva, Chavilah, Savta, Raama, and Savtecha; and the sons of Raama — Sheva and Dedan. 10 And

develop into separate nations and are therefore subsumed under their father's nation.

Of the fourteen names in Japheth's genealogy two are spelled differently in *Chronicles* than in *Genesis*. In both cases a *daleth* (ד) and a *reish* (ר) are interchanged. Diphath of v. 6 was Riphath in *Genesis;* Rodanim (v. 7) was Dodanim in *Genesis*.[1]

6. וְדִיפַת — *And Diphath.* Here the name is written with a *daleth,* while in *Genesis* it is written with a *reish.*

At first they were soft (from רפה, *to be weak*) to Israel (hence וְרִיפַת), but in the end they became full of deceit (דוֹפִי, hence וְדִיפַת) towards them (*Mefaresh*).

Metzudos simply notes that this man must have had two names and that this constitutes an important rule in understanding the many name changes we find in Scripture. (See further in Overview/Names and their Significance.)

7. כִּתִּים וְרוֹדָנִים — *Kittim, and Rodanim.* *Gra* explains that all names occurring in

these lists without the suffix יִם-, -*im,* such as Gomer and Magog, are proper names of the children which their descendants later assumed as national names. Those names ending with the plural form יִם-, -*im,* however, are not personal names but the designation of the nations that descended from each son.

וְרוֹדָנִים — *Rodanim.* In *Genesis* they are called Dodanim.

When Israel sins they come and subjugate them (from רדה, *to rule over* or *oppress,* hence וְרוֹדָנִים); but when Israel controls them they say: You are our friends (דוֹד, *friend,* hence וְרוֹדָנִים) (*Mefaresh,* based on *Bereishis Rabbah* 37:1).

⋙ Ham's Genealogy

8⁻16. The names in Ham's genealogy are identical with those listed in *Genesis* 10:6-18 with the exception of לוּדִיים[2] (v. 11) which is written with an extra *yud.*[3]

For details, see ArtScroll *Genesis* pp. 315-325.

1. Interchanges between letters occur frequently in Hebrew. However, this is mostly the case with homorganic letters (those produced by the same organ) whereas *daleth* and *reish* belong to different groups.

Ramban points out that occasionally non-homorganic letters can also be interchanged [see *Deuteronomy* 21:14 for *aleph* (א) and *yud* (י); *Exodus* 22:15 for *reish* (ר) and *lamed* (ל)]. But, although he discusses the phenomenon of interchangeable letters at great length, he does not anywhere point out that *daleth* and *reish* are also interchangeable. On the contrary, in *Numbers* 2:4 he finds it necessary to offer an explanation for the change from דְּעוּאֵל (1:14) to רְעוּאֵל (2:14).

Nevertheless we do find *daleth* and *reish* interchanged occasionally. Cf. *Genesis* chap. 41 where *daleth* in v. 3 is replaced by *reish* in vs. 19,20 and *daleth* in v. 7 becomes *reish* in vs. 23,24 (but see commentators there); *Leviticus* 11:14 and *Deuteronomy* 14:13 (and see *Chullin* 63b); *II Samuel* 22:11 and *Psalms* 18:11.

Rashi to *Job* 15:24 does in fact claim that *daleth* and *reish* do belong to those groups of letters which are interchangeable.

2.The Massorah treats the word לוּדִיים as a *Kri-Kesiv,* an instance where the spelling is different from the pronunciation. The word is to be read as though it were written לוּדִים.

Accordingly, the form לוּדִיים is not analogous with forms like עִבְרִיִּים (Ex. 3:18) or פְּלִשְׁתִּיִּם (Amos 9:7). Those forms are the regular plural of עִבְרִי, *Hebrew,* or פְּלִשְׁתִּי, *Philistine* [עֶבֶר־עִבְרִי־עִבְרִיִּים; פְּלֶשֶׁת־פְּלִשְׁתִּי־פְּלִשְׁתִּיִּם], and instances where the words are written with a single *yud* are contractions of the regular form. Rather, the Massorah assumes the name לוּדִים to be the plural of the proper name לוּד, *Lud,* rather than of לוּדִי, *Luddite.*

3. The *Mefaresh* notes that this spelling could be the basis for the teaching of the Sages in *Bereishis Rabbah* 37:5 that: 'All of Mitzraim's coinage (the names of his descendants) are marked by the sea' [in which they were destined to drown, or, because they lived by the sea — see commentators, there]. This thought would be expressed by the double *yud* as though the word were written לוּדֵי — יָם, *Luddites of the sea.*

א יא נִמְרֹד הוּא הֵחֵל לִהְיוֹת גִּבּוֹר בָּאָרֶץ: וּמִצְרַיִם

יא־יז יָלַד אֶת־°לוּדִיִּים וְאֶת־עֲנָמִים וְאֶת־לְהָבִים וְאֶת־נַפְתֻּחִים: ק' לוּדִים

יב וְאֶת־פַּתְרֻסִים וְאֶת־כַּסְלֻחִים אֲשֶׁר יָצְאוּ מִשָּׁם פְּלִשְׁתִּים

יג וְאֶת־כַּפְתֹּרִים: וּכְנַעַן יָלַד אֶת־צִידוֹן

יד בְּכֹרוֹ וְאֶת־חֵת: וְאֶת־הַיְבוּסִי וְאֶת־הָאֱמֹרִי וְאֵת הַגִּרְגָּשִׁי:

טו־טז וְאֶת־הַחִוִּי וְאֶת־הָעַרְקִי וְאֶת־הַסִּינִי: וְאֶת־הָאַרְוָדִי וְאֶת־

יז הַצְּמָרִי וְאֶת־הַחֲמָתִי: בְּנֵי שֵׁם

עֵילָם וְאַשּׁוּר וְאַרְפַּכְשַׁד וְלוּד וַאֲרָם וְעוּץ וְחוּל וְגֶתֶר

---

10. וְכוּשׁ יָלַד אֶת־נִמְרֹד — *And Cush fathered Nimrod*. See ArtScroll *Genesis* pp. 316-317 for explanations of why Nimrod is listed separately, and page 310 there for a discussion of whether Nimrod is to be counted among the seventy nations.

If Nimrod is not to be counted among the seventy nations we may legitimately ask why he is mentioned in *Chronicles*. In *Genesis* the whole passage (vs. 8-12) can be understood as an introduction to the account of the Tower of Babel and the Dispersion (see ArtScroll *Genesis*, comm. p. 319), but in *Chronicles* that story is not told, nor are the many pertinent details from *Genesis* vs. 9-12 mentioned. We learn only that *he was the first to be a mighty person on earth*, but this information, standing by itself, seems to convey nothing.

Certain it is that Nimrod played a profoundly important part in Abraham's life and that any history of the Jewish people would be incomplete without mention being made of him.

According to the tradition of the **Sages**, Nimrod was not only the king who put Abraham's faith to the ultimate test by having him thrown into the furnace, but it was also he — as Amraphel, king of Shinar (*Genesis* 14:1) — who led the attack of the nations which was intended to wipe out the Jewish people in its

cradle.

Ezra hints at these important episodes in Israel's trek towards the קֵץ, *end*, by mentioning Nimrod. As in v. 4 (see comm. there), he relies on the people's knowledge of the Torah to flesh out the details.

הוּא הֵחֵל לִהְיוֹת גִּבּוֹר בָּאָרֶץ — *He was the first to be a mighty person on earth*. He was the first to wage war and perform feats of might (*Mefaresh*). [This accords with the tradition of the Sages (*Eruvin* 53a) identifying Nimrod with Amraphel, king of Shinar, who, in *Genesis* 14:1, is recorded as having waged the first war.]

Rashi to *Genesis* 10:9 explains: He was 'mighty' in causing the whole world to rebel against God by the plan that he devised for the generation of the Dispersion. This is based on the tradition of the Sages, 'Why was he called Nimrod? Because he stirred up the whole world to rebel (הִמְרִיד) against God's sovereignty' (*Eruvin* 53a).[1]

Radak and *Ramban* explain that in the literal sense it certainly does not mean that there was never a mighty *person* before him, or that he was the only one in his

---

1. Even in *Genesis*, where many more details are given, it is difficult to see how the text yields the many insights which the Sages teach concerning Nimrod's wickedness (see below).

The text simply says that: he was the first to be mighty (v. 8); that he was a mighty hunter (גִּבּוֹר צַיִד) before God (which expression usually has a good connotation) (v. 9); and then describes the extent of his rule (vs. 10, 11 and 12). None of this seems, in itself, to indicate that he was wicked. The various teachings of the Sages — that he was mighty in imposing idol worship on his subjects; that his hunting was a trapping of people; that 'before God' indicates that he stood in open rebellion against God, seem all to derive from an assumed basis that he was indeed wicked. [See *Ramban, Genesis* 10:9.]

But what is the basis for this assumption?

The answer may lie in the correct understanding of the term גִּבּוֹר צַיִד. The usual translation, *mighty hunter*, is only correct if each word is to be translated separately. It is, however, possible that the two words are an idiomatic expression and must be understood as a unit.

II Samuel 22:26 speaks of a גִּבּוֹר תָּמִים, *a man of perfect integrity* without any deviousness in his character. If גִּבּוֹר צַיִד is used as a contrast to גִּבּוֹר תָּמִים then it would mean *a sly man of cunning ways*.

If this is the correct translation then לִפְנֵי ה', *before HASHEM*, could only be meant in a derogatory way, and the teachings of the Sages in the rest of the passage would follow automatically.

Cush fathered Nimrod. He was the first to be a mighty person on earth. ¹¹ *And Mitzraim fathered Ludim, Anamim, Lehavim, and Naphtuchim.* ¹² *And Pathrusim and Casluchim, whence the Philistines came forth, and Caphtorim.* ¹³ *And Canaan fathered Sidon, his first-born, and Cheth.* ¹⁴ *And the Yevusite, the Emorite, and the Girgashite.* ¹⁵ *And the Chivite, the Arkite, and the Sinite.* ¹⁶ *And the Arvadite, the Tzemarite, and the Chamathite.* ¹⁷ *The sons of Shem — Elam, Ashur, Arpachshad, Lud, Aram, Utz, Chul,*

generation. Rather, the verse tells us that he was the first to subjugate others and proclaim himself a monarch over others, because until his time there was never a king; people were governed by judges and leaders.

12. אֲשֶׁר יָצְאוּ מִשָּׁם פְּלִשְׁתִּים — *Whence the Philistines came forth.* According to the Sages, our verse describes the mixed parentage of the Philistines. They were descended from both the Pathrusim and the Casluchim who exchanged wives and bore the Philistines *(Midrash* quoted by *Rashi* to *Genesis* 10:14).

However, *Ibn Ezra (Genesis* 10:13) points out that שָׁם, *whence* [lit. *there*], must refer to a geographic location. In his opinion, the names of Mitzraim's descendants derive from the places in which they lived [i.e., Pathrusim are people who lived in Pathrus *(Jeremiah* 41:1)], and the meaning of our verse is that the inhabitants of Philistia had originally emigrated from Casluah — the home of the Casluchim. *Ramban* (there) agrees that this is the simple meaning of our verse (see ArtScroll *Bereishis* p. 323).

13-16. In *Genesis* 15:19-21 Abraham was promised the land of ten Canaanite nations. *Ramban (Genesis* 10:15) explains that these were ten of the eleven descendants of

Canaan mentioned here. One of Canaan's sons never grew into a separate nation and the names of some of them had changed by the time they were promised to Abraham. [See ArtScroll *Bereishis* p. 323ff.]

◆§ Shem's Genealogy

17-23. The genealogy of Shem contained in these verses is identical with that listed in *Genesis* 10:22-30 except for two differences: (a) There, Utz, Chul, Gether and Mash [Meshech] are given as sons of Aram whereas in our verse they appear to be listed as sons of Shem; (b) the Mash of *Genesis* 10:23 is here called Meshech.

The fact that a grandson is referred to as a son is not, in itself, unusual. There are many similar cases in the Torah such as, for example, Lavan being called בֶּן נָחוֹר, *the son of Nachor (Genesis* 29:5), although he was, in fact, his grandson (cf. *Genesis* 28:5).[1]

The change from Mash to Meshech indicates that this son of Aram was known by both names *(Radak).*

The *Anonymous Commentator* offers another explanation. The letter כ, *kaf,* belongs to that group of letters which are occasionally attached to a word for no apparent reason. He cites, as an example, *Leviticus* 11:17 which mentions a bird שָׁלָךְ, *shalach.* According to *Chullin* 63a, this

---

1. When we consider terms like בֶּן חַיִל, *a brave person;* בֶּן שְׁמוֹנַת יָמִים, *eight days old;* בֶּן מָוֶת, *someone who bears death-guilt* and so on, it seems that the basic meaning of בֶּן may not be *son.* Rather, it would seem to describe someone whose nature or status reflects a given circumstance. Thus it becomes an apt expression for a son, who bears the mark of his father upon himself.

This perception of the meaning of the word בֶּן would make expressions like בְּנֵי הַנְּבִיאִים, for *students of the prophet,* or בָּנֶיךָ אֵלוּ הַתַּלְמִידִים *(the word: 'your sons,' refers to students)* readily understandable. Students are בָּנִים because in them the influence of the teacher is apparent.

Thus we should not be surprised to see grandsons called בָּנִים. Occasionally grandparents leave a sufficiently strong mark upon their granchildren that these could be referred to as their בָּנִים. Thus, *Ramban* to *Genesis* 29:5 explains that Jacob referred to Lavan as *the son of Nachor* because Nachor had exercised a much stronger influence upon Lavan than had his father Bethuel. Bethuel had been an insignificant person, while Nachor was well known.

This explanation can also hold good if, as *Ibn Janach* and *Radak* suggest, the word בֶּן derives from בנה, *to build.* The son is the means by which the father's family or house is built. This idea can surely be stretched to include the grandson.

יח וְאַרְפַּכְשַׁד יָלַד אֶת־שֶׁלַח וְשֶׁלַח
יט יָלַד אֶת־עֵבֶר: וּלְעֵבֶר יֻלַּד שְׁנֵי בָנִים שֵׁם הָאֶחָד פֶּלֶג
כ כִּי בְיָמָיו נִפְלְגָה הָאָרֶץ וְשֵׁם אָחִיו יָקְטָן: וְיָקְטָן יָלַד
כא אֶת־אַלְמוֹדָד וְאֶת־שָׁלֶף וְאֶת־חֲצַרְמָוֶת וְאֶת־יָרַח: וְאֶת־
כב הֲדוֹרָם וְאֶת־אוּזָל וְאֶת־דִּקְלָה: וְאֶת־עֵיבָל וְאֶת־אֲבִימָאֵל
כג וְאֶת־שְׁבָא: וְאֶת־אוֹפִיר וְאֶת־חֲוִילָה וְאֶת־יוֹבָב כָּל־אֵלֶּה
כד-כה בְּנֵי יָקְטָן: שֵׁם | אַרְפַּכְשַׁד שָׁלַח: עֵבֶר פֶּלֶג רְעוּ:
כו-כח שְׂרוּג נָחוֹר תֶּרַח: אַבְרָם הוּא אַבְרָהָם: בְּנֵי
כט אַבְרָהָם יִצְחָק וְיִשְׁמָעֵאל: אֵלֶּה תֹּלְדוֹתָם
ל בְּכוֹר יִשְׁמָעֵאל נְבָיוֹת וְקֵדָר וְאַדְבְּאֵל וּמִבְשָׂם: מִשְׁמָע
לא וְדוּמָה מַשָּׂא חֲדַד וְתֵימָא: יְטוּר נָפִישׁ וָקֵדְמָה אֵלֶּה הֵם
לב בְּנֵי יִשְׁמָעֵאל: וּבְנֵי קְטוּרָה פִּילֶגֶשׁ
       אַבְרָהָם יָלְדָה אֶת־זִמְרָן וְיָקְשָׁן וּמְדָן וּמִדְיָן וְיִשְׁבָּק וְשׁוּחַ
לג וּבְנֵי יָקְשָׁן שְׁבָא וּדְדָן: וּבְנֵי מִדְיָן
       עֵיפָה וָעֵפֶר וַחֲנוֹךְ וַאֲבִידָע וְאֶלְדָּעָה כָּל־אֵלֶּה בְּנֵי
לד קְטוּרָה: וַיּוֹלֶד אַבְרָהָם אֶת־יִצְחָק בְּנֵי

---

bird is so called because it *withdraws* (snatches) fish from the sea (שלה — *to withdraw*). If the name derives from the root שלה, there is no logical explanation for the ך at the end of שֶׁלַך. It must be attributed, therefore, to a linguistic quirk.

◈§ The Seed of Abraham

24-26. The previous section carried Shem's genealogy as far as it is recorded in *Genesis* 10:22-30. This completes the listing of the seventy nations which were descended from Noah.

Ezra is now ready to introduce Abraham and to do this he takes us back briefly to the family's founder, as is the practice when a great man is to be dealt with (*Ramban, Genesis* 25:19).

27. אַבְרָם הוּא אַבְרָהָם — *Abram, that is Abraham.* In *Genesis* 11:26 Terach's son is called Abram. It was he who through a Divinely ordained change of name (*Genesis* 17:5) became known as Abraham.

Since, as we have seen several times, *Chronicles* assumes a knowledge of *Genesis*, it is inconceivable that Ezra would

have found it necessary to point out such an elementary piece of information. It seems likely that this consideration caused the Sages to read deeper meanings into this verse.

According to *Berachos* 13a this verse hints at a progression. At first he was [only] father to Aram [אַבְרָם is taken as two words אַב רָם, *father of* (א)רָם,[1] then he became father to the whole world. [The additional ה hints at הֲמוֹן גּוֹיִם, *a multitude of nations*.]

Reference is to *Genesis* 17:5 where Abram's name was changed to Abraham, *... for I have made you the father of a multitude of nations.* See Section Two, p. 379.

28. יִצְחָק וְיִשְׁמָעֵאל — *Isaac and Ishmael.* As in v. 4 (see fn. there), the sons are not listed by chronological age but by importance. Isaac, not Ishmael, is considered Abraham's seed (*Genesis* 21:12; see *Ramban* to 25:19).

Gra points out that Ishmael himself had allowed his younger brother Isaac to precede him at Abraham's burial (*Genesis* 25:9). It is from this fact that *Bava Basra*

---

1. Perhaps the assumption is that אֲרָם, *Aram*, derives from רוּם, *to be great*, and that the א is prosthetic (that is, attached to aid in pronunciation) as in אֶזְרוֹעַ (*Jer.* 32:21 and *Job* 31:22) from זְרוֹעַ, *arm*. (See further *Rashi* to *Genesis* 25:3). It is unlikely that it is simply a case of the א being elided, since the same association of רָם with אֲרָם is made in *Yerushalmi Sotah* 5:6, where the word stands by itself.

Gether, and Meshech. ¹⁸ And Arpachshad fathered Shelach, and
Shelach fathered Ever. ¹⁹ And to Ever were born two sons: the name
of the first was Peleg, for in his days the land was divided; and the
name of his brother was Yoktan. ²⁰ And Yoktan fathered Almodad,
Sheleph, Chatzarmaveth, and Yerach. ²¹ And Hadoram, Uzal, and
Diklah. ²² And Eval, Avimael, and Sheva. ²³ And Ophir, Chavilah,
and Yovav; all these were the sons of Yoktan. ²⁴ Shem, Arpachshad,
Shelach. ²⁵ Ever, Peleg, Reu. ²⁶ Serug, Nachor, Terach. ²⁷ Abram,
that is Abraham. ²⁸ The sons of Abraham — Isaac and Ishmael.
²⁹ These are their descendants: Ishmael's first-born was Nevaioth;
and Kedar, Adbeel, and Mivsam. ³⁰ Mishma, Dumah, Massa,
Chadad and Tema. ³¹ Yetur, Naphish, and Kedmah. These are the
sons of Ishmael. ³² And the sons of Keturah, Abraham's concubine,
[whom] she bore — Zimran, Yokshan, Medan, Midian, Yishbak,
and Shuach. And the sons of Yokshan — Sheva and Dedan. ³³ And
the sons of Midian — Ephah, Epher, Chanoch, Avida, and Eldaah;
all these were the sons of Keturah. ³⁴ Abraham fathered Isaac. The

16b deduces that Ishmael repented his sins
during Abraham's lifetime.

It is noteworthy that in this verse only
Isaac and Ishmael are listed as sons of
Abraham, while the children of his union
with Keturah are listed as his descendants
below in vs. 32-33. Perhaps the explanation
lies in the description of Keturah as
'Abraham's concubine' in v. 32. Only the
sons of the real wives, Sarah and Hagar, are
called Abraham's children.[1]

29⁻31. The list of Ishmael's sons is identical with that in *Genesis* 25:13-15.

32. וּבְנֵי קְטוּרָה פִּילֶגֶשׁ אַבְרָהָם יָלְדָה — *And the
sons of Keturah, Abraham's concubine,
[whom] she bore.* The syntax is awkward
and must be understood as though the
word אֲשֶׁר, *whom*, was inserted before יָלְדָה,
she bore.

[The Sages teach that Keturah was
identical with Hagar, Sarah's servant,

whom Abraham had earlier taken as a
concubine and then sent away.]

The list of Keturah's descendants (בְּנֵי,
here includes grandsons — see comm. 17-
23) is identical with the list in *Genesis* 25:2-
4 with one major exception. There (v. 3) we
learn that Dedan had three sons, Ashurim,
Letushim and Leumim, but these are not
mentioned here.

There is some doubt whether these three
are proper names or whether they are
adjectives describing the prime characteristics of Dedan's descendants. [See
ArtScroll *Bereishis* pp. 967-969 for a discussion of the various opinions.] In the
latter case there would be no difficulty with
their omission here. However, *Bereishis
Rabbah* 61:5 concludes that they are
proper names *(Ramban)*. If so there seems
no persuasive reason why they should be
left out here.[2]

34. וַיּוֹלֶד אַבְרָהָם אֶת־יִצְחָק — *Abraham*

1. This explanation assumes that Keturah was, in fact, a concubine. However *Ramban* to *Genesis*
25:6 maintains that Keturah was a regular wife and that the expression 'Abraham's concubine' was
used only to underline the fact that her children were not to be considered among Abraham's heirs.

For a compendium of opinions concerning the exact status of Keturah's sons and whether they are
considered 'Abraham's seed' or not — see *Encyclopedia Talmudica* under בְּנֵי קְטוּרָה.

2. The following is offered as a possible solution. *Bereishis Rabbah* reads: Rabbi Shmuel bar
Nachman said: Although the *Targumim* render: 'merchants,' 'flaming ones' and 'heads of people'
(that is that the words are taken as descriptive), [nevertheless] they are all chiefs of nations.

It is quite possible that Rabbi Shmuel bar Nachman is not claiming that these three words are, in
fact, proper nouns. On the contrary, he postulates that the *Targumim* (which are presumably
authoritative) render them as descriptive words. Rather, he asserts that although the Torah does not
mention their actual names, but for reasons of its own describes them by the given terms, there are
nevertheless three sons of Dedan, making the descendants of Keturah sixteen rather than thirteen.

If this is the case we need not be surprised if *Chronicles* omits these three sons. Since the actual
names are not known they have no place in these genealogies.

בְּנֵי עֵשָׂו אֱלִיפַז רְעוּאֵל   לה יִצְחָק עֵשָׂו וְיִשְׂרָאֵל:

בְּנֵי אֱלִיפַז תֵּימָן וְאוֹמָר   לו וִיעוּשׁ וְיַעְלָם וְקֹרַח:

בְּנֵי רְעוּאֵל   לז צְפִי וְגַעְתָּם קְנַז וְתִמְנָע וַעֲמָלֵק:

וּבְנֵי שֵׂעִיר לוֹטָן   לח נַחַת זֶרַח שַׁמָּה וּמִזָּה:

וּבְנֵי   לט וְשׁוֹבָל וְצִבְעוֹן וַעֲנָה וְדִישֹׁן וְאֵצֶר וְדִישָׁן:

בְּנֵי   מ לוֹטָן חוֹרִי וְהוֹמָם וַאֲחוֹת לוֹטָן תִּמְנָע:

fathered Isaac. This was already said in v. 28. In *Ramban's* view (*Genesis* 25:19) an important point is made by repeating it. It is true that both Ishmael and Isaac were Abraham's sons (v. 28), but only in a physical sense. *Genesis* 21:12 had stated unequivocally that: *... through Isaac will offspring be considered yours.* Abraham's spiritual heritage passes only through Isaac.

[Another explanation of the repetition might be that this verse is analogous to v. 24. Before the introduction of an important person — in this case, Israel — the genealogy is once more traced from the beginning.]

בְּנֵי יִצְחָק עֵשָׂו וְיִשְׂרָאֵל — *The sons of Isaac — Esau and Israel.* [See Section Two, p. 381.]

וְיִשְׂרָאֵל — *And Israel.* The *Mefaresh* points out that the name Israel is used instead of Jacob out of respect to King David. As *Rashi* states (*Genesis* 32:29), Jacob is the name which implies that he received Isaac's blessings through stealth and deceit. Israel, on the other hand, teaches that he wrested them from Esau by right and in the open.

Mefaresh states in a number of places that Ezra's purpose in writing *Chronicles* was to establish King David's genealogy (cf. *Mefaresh* to 1:1 and 10:1; see Overview p. xxiv).

It is indeed noteworthy that the name Jacob does not appear in the whole *Book of Chronicles* except for ch. 16, as part of a quote from King David's prayer. When we consider that, as has been discussed in the Overviews, *Chronicles* concerns itself with the inner, essential nature of Jewish history, rather than its external features, the use of the name Israel is very apt. The guile which Jacob had to adopt in order to get the blessings was certainly only within the framework of the external exigency. Essentially, as affirmed by God's providence, the blessings were his by right. In the perspective of *Chronicles*, then, Jacob is indeed Israel.

35-37. The genealogy of Esau given in these three verses is essentially the same as that given in *Genesis* 36:10-15. There are, however, two differences which will be pointed out below.

35. The five sons of Esau given here came from three different mothers (*Genesis* there). For the purpose of the genealogy it was not necessary to point this out.

36. צְפִי — *Tzephi.* The third son of Eliphaz is given in *Genesis* as צְפוֹ, *Tzepho. Ramban* (*Job* 1:1) notes that: 'In Hebrew there are often changes in proper names provided that the meaning remains unchanged.' In his view both צְפוֹ and צְפִי derive from צפה, *to look out.* (For a more detailed discussion of *Ramban's* view, see Overview/Names and their Significance.

וְתִמְנָע — *Timna.* No Timna is mentioned among Eliphaz's children in *Genesis* 36:11. Verse 12 (there) tells that he had a concubine by that name who bore him his son, Amalek. Who is the Timna of our verse?

Rashi (from *Tanchuma*) writes that the Timna of our verse is the daughter, not the son, of Eliphaz and that she was born of an adulterous relationship with the wife of Seir (see vs. 38 and 39). Verse 39 lists her as a sister of Lotan, rather than as Seir's daughter, because, in fact, Eliphaz was her real father. For this reason, too, she is listed here among his children. Subsequently, he compounded his wickedness by incestuously taking his own daughter as a concubine.

Both *Ramban* (*Genesis*) and *Radak* (here) reject this as the simple meaning of the verse, arguing that it would be very misleading to list a daughter among the sons without some indication that she was, in fact, a daughter (cf. *Genesis* 46:15,17).

Ramban concludes that Timna must be a son. He offers several explanations for the omission in *Genesis*.

The one adopted by many of the later

sons of Isaac — Esau and Israel. [35] The sons of Esau — Eliphaz, Reuel, Yeush, Yalam, and Korach. [36] The sons of Eliphaz — Teman, Omar, Tzephi, Gatam, Kenaz, Timna, and Amalek. [37] The sons of Reuel — Nachath, Zerach, Shammah, and Mizzah. [38] And the sons of Seir — Lotan, Shoval, Tziveon, Anah, Dishon, Etzer, and Dishan. [39] And the sons of Lotan — Chori, and Homam; and the sister of

commentators (e.g., *Gra, Ksav VeHaKabbalah*) is based on a principle given in the compendium of rules for Scriptural exegesis known as the *Thirty-Two Rules of Rabbi Yose HaGlili*. The eleventh rule postulates that the first part of a new sentence may really belong to the latter part of the previous sentence. This rule has a number of different applications, among them that if the previous sentence is meant to end with the identical word with which the next one begins, then that word may be written once at the beginning of the second sentence but do service as two words. It is read as the ending of the earlier sentence and then again as the beginning of the following one.[1]

This, *Ramban* thinks, is the case with *Genesis 36:11-12*. Verse 12 begins with the word, 'And Timna' [was the concubine of Eliphaz]. This word is also to be read together with the previous sentence which lists the sons of Eliphaz by his regular wives. Thus a sixth son, Timna, is added.

The existence of this Timna makes it possible to explain another difficulty concerning the descendants of Eliphaz. *Genesis 36:16* lists a Korach among his children, yet this Korach had not appeared in the previous list. This Korach is, in fact, identical with Timna. As he grew up his father changed his name to Korach so that he should not be confused with his father's concubine who bore the same name.[2]

⋅§ Seir's Genealogy

38-42. The inclusion of Seir's genealogy in *Chronicles* is another indication that knowledge of *Genesis* is assumed. It would have no meaning here if it were not known from *Genesis 36:8ff* that Esau settled in Mt. Seir and that his descendants intermarried extensively with the local aristocracy. (For details see ArtScroll *Bereishis* p. 1541ff.)

Nevertheless, it is difficult to see what purpose the listing of this genealogy serves here. What possible purpose can there have been in repeating the involved genealogy of Seir, whose contact with Israel some fifteen hundred years earlier had only been peripheral?

Gra explains that all the names of Seir's descendants became place names, i.e., that these children of Seir settled in various locations, which subsequently took on the names of their founders. These cities were the ones which Esau and his children eventually annexed and which became known collectively as the Land of Edom. Since the Torah prohibits Israel from ever occupying any of Edom's land (*Deuteronomy 2:1-9*), it is necessary to identify the exact lands covered by this law.[3]

39. וְהוֹמָם — *And Homam.* This son of Lotan is called Hemam in *Genesis. Midrash Sechel Tov* explains that the added *vav* conveys the idea of מְהוּמָה, *confusion.*

וַאֲחוֹת לוֹטָן תִּמְנָע — *And the sister of Lotan was Timna.* This is the Timna who, according to *Genesis 36:12*, was the

1. For examples of other applications given by various commentators see: *Genesis 31:48-49 (HaKsav VeHaKaballah); Joshua 13:7-8; I Chronicles 9:41-42 (Rashbam). Gra* makes extensive use of this throughout the first nine chapters of *Chronicles.*

2. The change from Timna to Korach has an inner logic. *Midrash Sechel Tov* explains the name Timna (the concubine): Because she withheld herself (מנע, *to prevent* or *hold back*) from her family. For Korach, *Sechel Tov* offers: He slipped out (קרח, *to be bald, one from whom hair has been removed*) from under the yoke of his Creator.

Thus Timna and Korach have similar meanings and it would be natural to change the former into the latter as the need arose.

3. *Gra* assumes that the prohibition against taking any of Edom's land still had applicability in Ezra's time. This is not universally accepted. *Rambam* does not count this prohibition among the 613 *mitzvos* of the Torah and explains (*Sefer HaMitzvos, Shoresh 3*) that it applied only to Moses' generation. However, *Ramban* (*Sefer HaMitzvos, Additional Negative Commands*) cites many sources to demonstrate that this prohibition is to be counted among the 613 *mitzvos* because it has eternal validity.

שׁוֹבָל עַלְיָן וּמָנַחַת וְעֵיבָל שְׁפִי וְאוֹנָם וּבְנֵי צִבְעוֹן אַיָּה

מא וַעֲנָה: בְּנֵי עֲנָה דִּישׁוֹן   וּבְנֵי דִישׁוֹן חַמְרָן

מב וְאֶשְׁבָּן וְיִתְרָן וּכְרָן: בְּנֵי־אֵצֶר בִּלְהָן וְזַעֲוָן יַעֲקָן

מג בְּנֵי דִישׁוֹן עוּץ וַאֲרָן: וְאֵלֶּה הַמְּלָכִים אֲשֶׁר

מָלְכוּ בְּאֶרֶץ אֱדוֹם לִפְנֵי מְלָךְ־מֶלֶךְ לִבְנֵי יִשְׂרָאֵל בֶּלַע

מד בֶּן־בְּעוֹר וְשֵׁם עִירוֹ דִּנְהָבָה: וַיָּמָת בֶּלַע וַיִּמְלֹךְ תַּחְתָּיו

מה יוֹבָב בֶּן־זֶרַח מִבָּצְרָה: וַיָּמָת יוֹבָב וַיִּמְלֹךְ תַּחְתָּיו חוּשָׁם

מו מֵאֶרֶץ הַתֵּימָנִי: וַיָּמָת חוּשָׁם וַיִּמְלֹךְ תַּחְתָּיו הֲדַד בֶּן־בְּדַד

מז הַמַּכֶּה אֶת־מִדְיָן בִּשְׂדֵה מוֹאָב וְשֵׁם עִירוֹ °עִיוּת: וַיָּמָת

°עֲוִית ק'

מח הֲדַד וַיִּמְלֹךְ תַּחְתָּיו שַׂמְלָה מִמַּשְׂרֵקָה: וַיָּמָת שַׂמְלָה

מט וַיִּמְלֹךְ תַּחְתָּיו שָׁאוּל מֵרְחֹבוֹת הַנָּהָר: וַיָּמָת שָׁאוּל וַיִּמְלֹךְ

נ תַּחְתָּיו בַּעַל חָנָן בֶּן־עַכְבּוֹר: וַיָּמָת בַּעַל חָנָן וַיִּמְלֹךְ תַּחְתָּיו

הֲדַד וְשֵׁם עִירוֹ פָּעִי וְשֵׁם אִשְׁתּוֹ מְהֵיטַבְאֵל בַּת־מַטְרֵד

---

concubine of Eliphaz.

40. עַלְיָן — *Alian.* Genesis 36:23 gives this name as *Alvan.* *Rashi* (Genesis 3:20) points out that *vav* and *yud* are interchangeable as can be seen from Eve's name, חַוָּה, which was given to her because she was to be the mother of all living things (אֵם כָּל חָי).

In *Hosea* 10:9 we find the tribe of Benjamin referred to as בְּנֵי עַלְוָה. *Rashi* there explains this obscure word as denoting pride. They saw themselves as עֶלְיוֹנִים, *exalted ones.*

Thus Alian or Alvan would denote someone who is conceited.

שְׁפִי — *Shephi.* Genesis 36:23 gives this name as שְׁפוֹ, *Shepho.* [See comm., v. 36.]

Midrash Sechel Tov thinks that the name implies that its bearer was lame, as the Sages (*Sotah* 10a) interpret the same word (*Numbers* 23:3) in connection with Balaam. [*Torah Temimah* explains that this assumes that the word derives from שׁוּף, *to slip.* The bone has slipped from its socket.] *Targum* to *Numbers* interprets the word as *silent* or *alone.* *Radak* (*Sefer HaShorashim*) thinks that it implies one who is broken in spirit.

וַעֲנָה — *And Anah.* According to the Sages, this Anah is identical with the one listed in v. 38 as a son of Seir [that is, as a brother of Tziveon rather than as his son]. Tziveon committed incest with his own mother who then bore Anah. He is first listed with Seir's children because he was the child of

Seir's wife, and then again as the son of his real father, Tziveon (*Rashi, Genesis* 36:24).

Ramban and *Gra* think that there were two people of the same name. Both Seir and Tziveon had a son called Anah. (See ArtScroll *Bereishis,* p. 1549.)

41. בְּנֵי עֲנָה — *The sons of Anah.* According to *Ramban* and *Gra,* this Anah is the fourth son of Seir (v. 38), not the son of Tziveon, mentioned in v. 40. Only grandsons, not great-grandsons of Seir are listed in this genealogy.

Only one son of Anah is mentioned, so בְּנֵי must be rendered, *the son of,* rather than, *the sons of.* Such a use of the plural form בְּנֵי is irregular but not unique. See *Genesis* 46:23, *Numbers* 26:8 and below 2:8 and 3:22. *Radak* to *Genesis* 46:23 explains the usage: [as far as] *children* [are concerned there was only one] *Dishon.*

דִישׁוֹן — *Dishon.* Anah (the son of Seir) called his son by his brother's name.

Genesis 36:25 lists a daughter, Oholivamah (Esau's wife — 36:2) among Anah's children. According to *Gra* she is not mentioned here because she was the daughter of Anah, the son of Tziveon, not of Anah, the son of Seir, whose children are listed here. (See further, ArtScroll *Bereishis* p. 1533ff.)

וּבְנֵי דִישׁוֹן — *And the children of Dishon.* This Dishon is the fifth son of Seir, not the Dishon mentioned earlier in this verse as the son of Anah (*Ramban; Gra*).

Lotan was Timna. ⁴⁰ *The sons of Shoval — Alian, Manachath, Eval, Shephi, and Onam; and the sons of Tziveon — Aiah and Anah.* ⁴¹ *The sons of Anah — Dishon; and the sons of Dishon — Chamran, Eshban, Yithran, and Cheran.* ⁴² *The sons of Etzer — Bilhan, Zaavan, and Yaakan; the sons of Dishon — Utz and Aran.* ⁴³ *Now these are the kings who reigned in the land of Edom before a king reigned over the children of Israel: Bela the son of Beor, and the name of his city was Dinhavah.* ⁴⁴ *And Bela died, and Yovav the son of Zerach from Botzrah succeeded him as king.* ⁴⁵ *And Yovav died, and Chusham of the land of the Temanites succeeded him as king.* ⁴⁶ *And Chusham died, and Hadad the son of Bedad, who defeated Midian in the field of Moab, succeeded him as king; and the name of his city was Avith.* ⁴⁷ *And Hadad died, and Samlah of Masrekah succeeded him as king.* ⁴⁸ *And Samlah died, and Shaul of Rechovoth HaNahar succeeded him as king.* ⁴⁹ *And Shaul died, and Baal Chanan the son of Achbor succeeded him as king.* ⁵⁰ *And Baal Chanan died, and Hadad succeeded him as king; and the name of his city was Pai, and his wife's name was Mehetavel, daughter of*

חַמְרָן — *Chamran.* Chamran is called Chemdon in *Genesis* 36:26. [See comm. v. 6 concerning changes from *daleth* to *reish*.] *The Mefaresh* offers a midrashic explanation. Originally they were *beloved and desirable* (וְנֶחְמָדִים חֲמוּדִים, from וחמד) like righteous people, but ultimately they became ugly like *donkeys* (חֲמוֹרִים) from (חמר).

⊷§ Kings of Edom

42. This verse lists the descendants of the final two of Seir's sons. Thus, according to *Ramban* and *Gra*, the children of all of Seir's seven sons have been given.

בְּנֵי דִישׁוֹן — *The sons of Dishon.* This is the seventh of Seir's sons listed in v. 38. The fact that his name is given here as Dishon rather than Dishan, as in v. 38, is not irregular. The two endings are readily interchanged, as in חִירָם and חִירוֹם [*II Kings* 5:15, 24, 32] *(Ramban).*

43. לִפְנֵי מְלָךְ־מֶלֶךְ לִבְנֵי יִשְׂרָאֵל — *Before a king reigned over the children of Israel.* For a discussion of when these kings reigned and to which king of Israel this verse refers, see ArtScroll *Bereishis* p. 1552ff.

Concerning this latter question, *R' David Tzvi Hoffman* offers an interpretation of the verse which avoids the problem. No specific king is meant at all. But since the Torah clearly anticipates the establishment of a monarchy some time in the future (cf. *Deuteronomy* 28:36), it is perfectly legitimate for the Torah to look into the future and to say that these kings ruled in Edom long before the (anticipated) monarchy. Taken thus the intent is clear that Edom's monarchy could come about only before any monarchy arose in Israel. Once that would come about Edom's kingship would necessarily cease. See Section Two, p. 381.

46. הֲדַד — *Hadad.* In *Genesis* the name is written הֲדַר, *Hadar.* See comm. v. 6.

Hadar means *beauty. Midrash Sechel Tov* remarks that he was not able to find some midrashic source which interpreted the name of this wicked person with some kind of adverse connotation.[1]

עֲוִית — *Avith.* The name is to be read (קְרֵי) *Avith,* as it is written in *Genesis.* The spelling here (כְּתִיב) differs *(Minchas Shay).*

50. וְשֵׁם עִירוֹ פָּעִי — *And the name of his city*

---

1. It is evident from *Midrash Sechel Tov* that, had he been able to, he would have preferred an adverse interpretation for the name of a wicked person. This is in line with normal aggadic exegesis which seeks to reveal hidden layers of goodness in the names and persons of righteous people and, conversely, to uncover all kinds of evil connotations concerning wicked people. The rules governing aggadic exegesis in general, and application of this system in particular, can be found in *Maharatz Chayos, Mevo HaTalmud* chs. 19-22.

בַּת מֵי זָהָב: וַיָּמׇת הֲדַד וַיִּהְיוּ אַלּוּפֵי אֱדוֹם אַלּוּף תִּמְנָע

עֲלֺוׇה ק׳
אַלּוּף °עַלְיׇה אַלּוּף יְתֵת: אַלּוּף אׇהֳלִיבׇמׇה אַלּוּף אֵלָה

אַלּוּף פִּינֺן: אַלּוּף קְנַז אַלּוּף תֵּימׇן אַלּוּף מִבְצׇר: אַלּוּף

מַגְדִּיאֵל אַלּוּף עִירׇם אֵלֶּה אַלּוּפֵי אֱדוֹם: אֵלֶּה

בְּנֵי יִשְׂרׇאֵל רְאוּבֵן שִׁמְעוֹן לֵוִי וִיהוּדׇה יִשָּׂשׂכׇר וּזְבֻלֻן:

דׇּן יוֹסֵף וּבִנְיׇמׅן נַפְתׇּלִי גׇד וְאׇשֵׁר: בְּנֵי יְהוּדׇה

עֵר וְאוֹנׇן וְשֵׁלׇה שְׁלוֹשׇׁה נוֹלַד לוֹ מִבַּת־שׁוּעַ הַכְּנַעֲנִית

וַיְהִי עֵר | בְּכוֹר יְהוּדׇה רַע בְּעֵינֵי יהוה וַיְמִיתֵהוּ: וְתׇמׇר

כַּלָּתוֹ יָלְדׇה לּוֹ אֶת־פֶּרֶץ וְאֶת־זׇרַח כׇּל־בְּנֵי יְהוּדׇה חֲמִשָּׁה:

---

was Pai. In *Genesis* this city is called Pau. See comm. v. 36 for interchange between *vav* and *yud.*

Sechel Tov explains that this man, whose name connoted beauty (Hadar), built a beautiful city and gave it a name which implied a *shining forth* (הוֹפִיעׇה, from יפע, *to appear*).

51. וַיָּמׇת הֲדַד — *And Hadad died.* Hadad's death is not mentioned in *Genesis*. *Gra* suggests that in Moses' time he had not yet died. Ezra, however, was able to tell of his death. [*Gra* subscribes to those opinions that the *king* in the phrase, *before a king reigned over the children of Israel,* was Moses. Thus the eighth king, Hadad, was still alive when the Torah was given.]

Rashi in *Genesis* points out that the formulation of our verse ... וַיָּמׇת הֲדַד וַיִּהְיוּ, *And Hadad died and [the chiefs of Edom]*

were ..., indicates that the one followed upon the other. These chiefs ruled over Edom once the monarchy had disintegrated. (See further in ArtScroll *Bereishis* p. 1556ff.)

The list here is identical with that in *Genesis.*

אַלּוּפֵי אֱדוֹם — *The chiefs of Edom.* In *Genesis* these chiefs are called the chiefs of Esau. Perhaps the change can be explained in the same way as we understood the use of the name Israel in v. 34. *Chronicles* concerns itself with the essential rather than the external. Esau was the name given at birth, but Edom was the name by which he came to be called because of the associations concerning his nature which the name awakened. (See ArtScroll *Bereishis,* p. 1068.)

II

This chapter is a direct continuation of the previous one. 1:34 had given Isaac's children as Esau and Israel. From there till the end of the chapter the families of Esau and those of Seir were given a cursory treatment. Now Ezra turns to his main objective: an exact presentation of the families of Israel and particularly that of Judah, progenitor of the Messiah, the central figure of that קֵץ, *end,* towards which the *Book of Chronicles* is oriented (see Overview, p. xxviii).

1. The order in which the twelve sons of Jacob are listed does not follow their chronological age (see *Genesis* 29:31ff). Rather, as in *Genesis* 35:23-26 and *Exodus* 1:2-3, the sequence is: the sons of Leah, Rachel, Bilhah, and Zilpah.

In this system Dan is out of place. He is listed before Joseph without any apparent logic.

The Sages address this problem in *Bereishis Rabbah* (73:4). '*God remembered Rachel ... and opened her womb* (*Genesis* 30:22). What did God remember? Her

merit in giving her servant Bilhah to Jacob' (*Genesis* 30:3ff). Rachel's craving to share in the building of God's people was so great that she willingly gave her husband another wife in spite of the obvious disadvantage to herself. Bilhah's first son was Dan. Thus, it was in the merit of Dan that Joseph was born. Therefore Dan is mentioned here before Joseph.

◄§ Judah's descendants

3. בְּנֵי יְהוּדׇה — *The sons of Judah.* The family of Judah is listed first because the

Matred, daughter of Me Zahav. 51 *And Hadad died. And the chiefs of Edom were — the chief of Timna, the chief of Alvah, the chief of Yetheth.* 52 *The chief of Oholivamah, the chief of Elah, the chief of Pinon.* 53 *The chief of Kenaz, the chief of Teman, the chief of Mivtzar.* 54 *The chief of Magdiel, and the chief of Iram; these were the chiefs of Edom.*

These *are the sons of Israel — Reuven, Shimeon, Levi, Judah, Yissachar, and Zevulun.* 2 *Dan, Joseph, Benjamin, Naphtali, Gad and Asher.* 3 *The sons of Judah — Er, Onan and Shelah, the three born to him by Bath Shua the Canaanitess. Now Er, the first-born of Judah was evil in the eyes of HASHEM, so He killed him.* 4 *And Tamar, his daughter-in-law, bore him Peretz and Zerach. All*

main purpose of this book is to establish the genealogy of the kings of Judah *(Radak)* or, in deference to King David who was descended from Judah *(Metzudos).*

For the full account of Judah's marriage and the birth of his five sons, see *Genesis* 38.

שְׁלוֹשָׁה נוֹלַד לוֹ — *The three born to him.* The use of the singular נוֹלַד instead of the plural נוֹלְדוּ is irregular. The same irregularity recurs in 2:9, 3:1 and 3:4.

There are many instances in Scripture in which the gender or number of the predicate differs from those of the noun. This occurs quite frequently where the predicate precedes the noun, less so when it follows the noun, as in our case (e.g. *I Samuel* 2:20; *Ezekiel* 20:38).

Commentators offer explanations for some of these examples, but there is no one explanation which will explain all the instances of what may simply be a linguistic irregularity, similar to the ones found in any language.

הַכְּנַעֲנִית — *The Canaanitess.* See commentaries to *Genesis* 38:2 for a discussion of whether the term אִישׁ כְּנַעֲנִי used there to describe Judah's father-in-law is to be understood in the sense of *merchant* or that he was, in fact, of Canaanite descent. That his daughter is here described as a *Canaanitess* seems to speak for the latter interpretation.

4. וְתָמָר כַּלָּתוֹ יָלְדָה לוֹ — *And Tamar, his daughter-in-law, bore him.* The *Mefaresh* wonders why *Chronicles* would mention this embarrassing fact concerning the

ancestors of King David. [See *Mefaresh* to 10:1 for his opinion that, as a general principle, *Chronicles* (in contrast to *Samuel)* does not report those acts of King David which do not contribute to his greater glory.]

R' Yaakov Kaminetsky offers the following explanation. It is noteworthy that no mention is made of Onan and his sin *(Genesis* 38:8-10). We are simply told that Er died and that subsequently Tamar bore two sons to Judah. The matter becomes clear when we consider that the whole purpose of this section of *Chronicles* is to establish the genealogy of King David.

Now, there is no doubt that the kingship of Israel had been promised by Jacob to Judah *(Genesis* 49:10). The expectation would be that the royal line should run through Judah's first-born (see *Rashi* to *Genesis* 49:3). But from vs. 9-15 we see that David was descended from Peretz, Judah's fourth son, rather than from his first-born, Er. It is to explain this that the story of Tamar is mentioned here.

Ramban (Genesis 38:8) writes that the precept of יבום *[yibum], levirate marriage* (that a man marry the wife of his deceased brother who died childless, *Deut.* 25:5-10), was known to the ancients long before the Torah had been given. Until it was formalized by the Torah to apply only to the brother, however, any relative of the dead man, such as his father or uncle, could also perform *yibum.* The purpose of *yibum* was so that the dead man's being could be perpetuated through the first-born child of the *yibum* union. [How this comes about belongs to the secrets of the Torah which the ancients knew and we do not.]

ב ה־ז

ה־ז בְּנֵי פֶרֶץ חֶצְרוֹן וְחָמוּל: וּבְנֵי זֶרַח זִמְרִי וְאֵיתָן
ז וְהֵימָן וְכַלְכֹּל וָדָרַע כֻּלָּם חֲמִשָּׁה: וּבְנֵי כַּרְמִי עָכָר

This, then, is the explanation of our passage. Since David's lineage is traced through Peretz it was important to stress that Er had died childless; that Judah had then, through Divine Providence, performed *yibum* with Tamar; and that consequently Peretz, replacing as it were the deceased Er, was destined to become the progenitor of Judah's kings.[1]

5. חֶצְרוֹן וְחָמוּל — *Chetzron and Chamul.* *Genesis* 46:12 counts these two sons of Peretz among the seventy souls who accompanied Jacob to Egypt.

Jacob went down to Egypt just twenty-two years after Joseph was sold. [Joseph was seventeen when he was sold (*Genesis* 37:2); thirty when he stood before Pharaoh (*Genesis* 41:46); and seven years of plenty and two of famine elapsed from that time until Jacob came down (*Genesis* 45:6).] Judah married only after Joseph was sold (*Rashi, Genesis* 38:1). Thus, there were only twenty-two years during which Er was conceived and born, grew up, married Tamar and died; Onan, the second son, grew up, married Tamar and died; Shelah grew up sufficiently for Tamar to become disillusioned; Tamar conceived and bore Peretz and Zerach; and Peretz fathered Chetzron and Chamul. This calculation yields the startling conclusion that Peretz cannot have been older than 8 or 9 when he became a father.

Ramban (*Genesis* 46:15) points out that in David's ancestry there were numerous miraculous events which the Torah does not explicate (נֵס נִסְתָּר, *a hidden miracle*), but which a careful perusal of the texts will yield. *Ramban* does not explain why these miracles were necessary but feels that they are no occasion for surprise. The Torah is full of miracles which happen to God-fearing people. There is no need to point each one out particularly.

Ramban's specific reference is to the fact that David's immediate ancestors must have been unusually old when they fathered their children. In the 366 years which elapsed between the time

that Joshua entered the land and David's birth (see *Ibn Ezra,* end of *Ruth* for details and see below, comm. v. 10), there were only four generations: Salman, Boaz, Oved and Yishai. Accordingly, each one of them must have been close to ninety when he fathered; if any of them were younger the others must have been even older. Indeed, the period spanned by these generations is actually somewhat longer — see comm. to v. 10.

Radak to v. 18 here points out that, according to the tradition of the Sages that the Calev who is listed in vs. 9 and 19 as the son of Chetzron is the one whom Moses sent on the spying mission (whose father is given in *Numbers* as Yephunneh — see comm.), another such miracle must have happened. Calev was forty when he was sent on his mission in the second year after the Exodus (*Joshua* 14:7). His father, Chetzron, was already born when Jacob came to Egypt. If, as the Sages teach, Israel was in Egypt for two hundred and ten years, then Chetzron must have been approximately 172 years old when Calev was born.

On the other hand, we find other fathers at very young ages in Judah's family. Again, based on the assumption that the Calev in our chapter is identical with the one whom Moses sent on the spying mission, we must draw conclusions concerning the ages of Betzalel's forefathers. Betzalel must have been at least thirteen years old when God appointed him to build the Tabernacle in the first year after the Exodus (*Exodus* 31:2). His great-grandfather Calev, however, was then only thirty-nine years old. It follows that Calev, his son Uri and his grandson Chur must all have fathered children at the age of eight. [See further in fn. of introduction to v. 18.]

◄§ Zerach's descendants

6. זִמְרִי — *Zimri.* From *Joshua* 7:1 we know that Zerach had a son called זַבְדִּי, *Zavdi.* Since our verse makes no mention of this Zavdi, *Radak* and *Gra* identify him with Zimri.

The commentators make no attempt to

---

1. Within the framework of *Chronicles* there is an added significance to this passage. A reading of *Genesis* will show that the story of Judah and Tamar interrupts the account of Joseph's descent into slavery in Egypt. The Sages (*Bereishis Rabbah* 85:2) explain as follows: 'The tribes were busy selling Joseph, Joseph was mourning, Reuven was mourning, Jacob was mourning, Judah was busy getting married — but God was readying the light of the Messiah.'

Since the Davidic line is to descend from Judah's union with Tamar, it is from that union that the Messiah will one day be born. As R' *Yaakov Kaminetsky* puts it: The moment at which the first Jew (Joseph) descended into the first exile (Egypt) was the moment at which the groundwork for Messianic redemption had to be laid.

Thus, for *Chronicles,* the book of the קֵץ, *end,* this episode is profoundly significant.

the sons of Judah, five. ⁵ The sons of Peretz — Chetzron and Chamul. ⁶ And the sons of Zerach — Zimri, Ethan, Heman, Calcol, and Dara, five in all. ⁷ And the sons of Carmi — Achar, who brought

explain the interchanging of these two names, but two possible solutions suggest themselves.

As has been previously noted (footnote to 1:5-7), the letters *daleth* and *resh* are, at least according to *Rashi*, interchangeable. Thus we may assume that the *daleth* and *resh* in the two names have been interchanged.

Sefer HaRikmah (ch. 6) brings proofs that, since *beis* and *mem* are homorganic, they can also be substituted for the other. Therefore, in terms of spelling, זִמְרִי and זַבְדִי may well be the same.

It is also possible to trace a similarity in the meaning of the two names. זֶבֶד [*Zeved*], a gift, is used specifically for an especially exalted kind of present (*Hoffman* to *Genesis* 30:20). זֶמֶר is not only *a song* but also the produce of a land for which the land is praised or 'sung about' (commentators to *Genesis* 43:11). Thus both names connote a *good, praiseworthy portion*.

אֵיתָן וְהֵימָן וְכַלְכֹּל וָדָרַע — *Ethan, Heman, Calcol, and Dara.* In *I Kings* 5:11 we learn that Solomon's wisdom exceeded even that of: *Ethan the Ezrachite, Heman, Calcol and Darda, the children of Machol.*
The similarity in names makes it seem obvious that the reference is to Zerach's sons mentioned here. That is the opinion of *Targum* and *Rashi* there. [*Targum* there in fact renders אֵיתָן הָאֶזְרָחִי as *Ethan the son of Zerach* (rather than Ezrachite). See comm. 1:27 for an example of the occasional Scriptural style of appending an *aleph* to a name.] *Rashi* there explains that they are called בְּנֵי מָחוֹל, *the sons of Machol*, not because that was their father's name, but as a play on the word מָחוֹל, a musical instrument. They knew how to compose songs to be accompanied by musical

instruments. [Reference is to *Psalms* 88:1 and 89:1 where Heman the Ezrachite and Ethan the Ezrachite, respectively, are identified as authors of those psalms.]
It is not entirely clear what the comparison between Solomon's wisdom and that of these four men was meant to convey. Nowhere in Scripture is there any reference to particular wisdom on the part of Zerach's sons. However, *Seder Olam* 21 has preserved a tradition that Zerach's sons were prophets during the Egyptian exile. [*Targum* on our verse renders the word כֻּלָּם, *all*, as: *were leaders upon whom the spirit of prophecy rested*. See Section Two, p. 384.]
Radak thinks that the description of the four wise men as בְּנֵי מָחוֹל precludes their being the sons of Zerach mentioned here. He thinks that *Psalms* 88 and 89 were composed by Ethan ben Zerach and Heman the chorister, who are mentioned in *I Chronicles* 6:26 and 18 respectively, as descendants of Levi and that the similarity between the names of Zerach's sons and the wise men of *Kings* is merely coincidental.

כֻּלָּם חֲמִשָּׁה — *Five in all.* According to the simple meaning of the verse this phrase seems redundant.[1]

7. וּבְנֵי כַּרְמִי — *And the sons of Carmi.* In *Joshua* 7, Achan is identified as the son of Carmi, the son of Zavdi, the son of Zerach. In comm. to v. 6 we learned that Zimri is Zavdi. We therefore must read our verse as though it were written: [*The son of Zimri was Carmi*] *and the son of Carmi was Achar* (see Gra). *Radak* points out that the omission of a father's name, and the assumption that it is one of the previously mentioned people, is a common formula-

1. R' Aryeh Carmell has suggested to me that this phrase may be simply understood. It is analogous to the countless instances in which the Mishnah introduces a list with a number. E.g., *Five* [categories of people] *are unfit to give Terumah* (Mishnah, *Terumos* 1:1). Commentators (see *Meleches Shlomoh* there) suggest that this formula is used in cases where there are doubts or disagreements concerning the units which are listed. To preclude any confusion, a number is given to underline that the examples listed are correct and that no others belong in the list. Similarly this formula (which occurs often in *Chronicles*) may be used as a check against scribal error or to avoid dispute.
R' Y. Danziger has suggested that, in light of comments made several times in this commentary that Ezra copied from more extensive lists only those portions which were of significance to him for some reason (see v. 7), the numbers may be used as an indication that here the lists are complete.

ח עוֹכֵר יִשְׂרָאֵל אֲשֶׁר מָעַל בַּחֵרֶם: וּבְנֵי

ט אֵיתָן עֲזַרְיָה: וּבְנֵי חֶצְרוֹן אֲשֶׁר נוֹלַד־

י לוֹ אֶת־יְרַחְמְאֵל וְאֶת־רָם וְאֶת־כְּלוּבָי: וְרָם הוֹלִיד אֶת־

עַמִּינָדָב וְעַמִּינָדָב הוֹלִיד אֶת־נַחְשׁוֹן נְשִׂיא בְּנֵי יְהוּדָה:

יא-יב וְנַחְשׁוֹן הוֹלִיד אֶת־שַׂלְמָא וְשַׂלְמָא הוֹלִיד אֶת־בֹּעַז: וּבֹעַז

יג הוֹלִיד אֶת־עוֹבֵד וְעוֹבֵד הוֹלִיד אֶת־יִשָׁי: וְאִישַׁי הוֹלִיד

---

tion in these genealogical tables.

עָכָר עוֹכֵר יִשְׂרָאֵל — *Achar, who brought odium upon Israel.* See Joshua 7 for a description of Achan's sin. His name is given here as Achar as a play on words with the root עכר, *make odious (see Genesis 34:30).*

The *Anonymous Commentator* suggests that it is also possible that the letters *nun* and *reish* are interchangeable. He illustrated this from the name Nebuchadnezzar which often appears in Scripture as Nebuchadrezzar.

This same point is made by *Rashi to Arachin 33a* (but see *Rashi to Megillah 14b*). In his analysis of interchanging letters in *Darkei HaShinuim 2:10*, R' Shmuel Waldberg notes this example and cites various other instances in which *nun* and *reish* are substituted for one another, but is unable to find a rationale for this substitution.

The use of the plural בְּנֵי in this and the next verse, although in both cases only one son is mentioned, is irregular though not unique. See comm. 1:41 and below v. 42.

Malbim explains this usage in Chronicles in the following manner: Ezra took his information concerning the genealogies from a סֵפֶר יוּחֲסִים, *book of genealogies,* in which there was a detailed record of every single branch of every family. Ezra, for reasons to which we are not privy, made selections concerning which names to include in his *Chronicles.* Occasionally he would list only one son out of a whole goup of children. In that case, he retained the plural בְּנֵי from the book of genealogies (perhaps to indicate that there were, in fact, more children) although he listed only one of the children.

◄§ Peretz's descendants through Chetzron

9. וּבְנֵי חֶצְרוֹן — *And the sons of Chetzron.* Peretz's royal line is carried on through Chetzron. Chamul (v. 5) is not mentioned again.

Of Chetzron's three sons it is Ram who, as progenitor of David, is of greatest concern to Ezra, and for this reason his genealogy is treated first (v. 10ff). That of the first-born Yerachmeel is given in v. 28ff and that of Cheluvai (Calev — see below) in v. 18ff.

אֲשֶׁר נוֹלַד־לוֹ — *Who were born to him.* נוֹלַד is irregular for the plural בְּנֵי. See comm. to v. 3.

Targum interpolates: Who were born to him *in Timnah.* This is presumably based on an aggadic source which has been lost to us, and it presents great difficulty. Timnah is the place of Chetzron's birth (see *Genesis 38:12ff*). If Chetzron's three sons were born in Timnah they would have been alive at the time that Jacob and the seventy descendants went down to Egypt. But in that list *(Genesis 46:12)* no children are listed for Chetzron.

אֶת־יְרַחְמְאֵל ... — *Yerachmeel ...* The direct object — אֶת־יְרַחְמְאֵל — together with the passive נוֹלַד לוֹ is irregular. To balance the sentence we would have to interpolate a phrase like: 'his wife bore him' before the words: אֶת־יְרַחְמְאֵל.

כְּלוּבָי — *Cheluvai.* This is the Calev ben Chetzron mentioned in v. 18 *(Radak).*

The letter *yud* at the end of a name usually means that the name is being used to describe a family rather than an individual (cf. *Numbers 3:27*). Occasionally a name will end with an added *yud* even when an individual is meant. In that case the name describes him as progenitor of his descendants rather than as an individual (see *Sefer HaRikmah, Shaar 6,* under *yud*). The added *yud* then may imply that this son of Chetzron was significant because of the family tree he started (see *I Samuel 25:3*).

While this explanation may serve to explain the addition of the *yud*, it does not explain its being vowelized in the plural form (Cheluvai rather than Cheluvi). Cheluvai means literally *my Calevs.*

We shall see in this and the next few chapters that, according to the interpretation of the Sages, Calev is mentioned again and again under different names. We are taught many different aspects of this man's multifaceted personality. [This is

*odium upon Israel, who violated the ban. * And the sons of Ethan —
Azariah. * And the sons of Chetzron who were born to him —
Yerachmeel, Ram, and Cheluvai. * And Ram fathered Amminadav,
and Amminadav fathered Nachshon, prince of the sons of Judah.
* And Nachshon fathered Salma, and Salma fathered Boaz. * And
Boaz fathered Oved, and Oved fathered Jesse. * And Jesse fathered*

based on the assumption that Calev ben
Chetzron and Calev ben Yephunneh are the
same man. See below, comm. to v. 18 for a
lengthy discussion of the different opinions in
this matter.] Perhaps it is these many facets of
his personality which are expressed in the plural
form of his name.

10. נַחְשׁוֹן נְשִׂיא בְנֵי יְהוּדָה — *Nachshon, prince of the sons of Judah.* Nachshon is
identified as prince of the tribe of Judah in
Numbers 2:3. He was the first of the tribal
princes to offer the inaugural sacrifices for
the Tabernacle *(Numbers 7:17)*, and as
leader of the group of three tribes who
camped to the east of the Tabernacle, it was
he who led the Israelite travels through the
desert *(Numbers 10:14)*. According to the
tradition of the Sages *(Bamidbar Rabbah
13:7)*, Nachshon was the first to enter the
waters of the Red Sea and it was only after
he had entered that God divided the waters.

The fact that Nachshon was a prince
[*Sifri to Naso* 47 even calls him a king] is
stressed out of respect for King David, who
was descended from him *(Mefaresh)*. See
Section Two, p. 386.

According to *Seder Olam Rabbah* 12,
Nachshon died in the second year after the
Exodus. Since the Exodus took place in the
year 2448 after creation, it is obvious that
Nachshon's son Salma (v. 11) must at least
have been conceived by the year 2449.
Now, David was born in 2855. [Solomon
began building the Temple in the year
2928, in the beginning of the fourth year of
his reign *(I Kings 6:1)*. David had died
three years earlier at the age of seventy
(Yalkut, Genesis 42); 2928-73=2855.]
Thus, from the birth of Salma (2449) until
the birth of David there were 406 years.
These years were spanned by Salma, Boaz,
Oved, and Yishai (vs. 11 and 12). Again we
have a situation where these men must
have become fathers at an extremely
advanced age. (See comm. to v. 5.)

11. שַׂלְמָא — *Salma.* Salma is also called

שַׂלְמוֹן, *Salmon,* in *Ruth* 4:21. According to
Midrash Rabbah (Ruth 8), this second
name is a contraction of two words:
סוּלָם וְלַנְּשִׂיאִים, *a [rung] on the ladder of the
princes* (*sin* and *samech* are interchangeable). The meaning is that up to
and including Salma, Peretz's house had
produced only tribal princes but, it would
seem, some essential component of
kingship was missing from Judah's family
until Salma's son, Boaz, was joined in
mariage to the Moabite, Ruth.

בֹּעַז — *Boaz.* See *Ruth* for the events leading
up to Boaz's marriage to Ruth. According
to the tradition of the Sages, Boaz died on
the very night of his marriage. His life's
purpose had then been fulfilled — the seed
of David's kingship had been planted. (See
Overview to ArtScroll *Ruth.*) See Section
Two, p. 386.

12. עוֹבֵד — *Oved.* Oved [from עבד, *to serve*], because he served God with all his
heart *(Targum, Ruth)*.

'[He was called] Oved, *one who serves,*
because [this name hints at his] father and
mother [who acted in the service of God].
[It hints at his father Boaz] because he was
[eighty years] old and married a woman
[Ruth, not out of any physical desire but
only] with the intention of fulfilling God's
wish. Also [it hints at] his mother [Ruth]
who chose to [forsake everything in order
to] cleave to God [and follow Naomi]. She
is the *person who serves God* referred to in
Malachi 3:18' *(Midrash Lekach Tov)*.

יִשַׁי — *Jesse [Yishai].* The name of David's
father is given as אִישַׁי, *Ishai,* in the next
verse. The *Mefaresh* explains that this was
done out of respect for King David. His
father was an exalted person, worthy of
his great son. This is expressed by the
association with the word אִישׁ [*ish*], man,
which according to *Tanchuma (Shmini* 9)
is used to describe particularly important
people.[1]

1. Yishai's was a truly royal household. According to *Berachos* 58a he was constantly waited upon by
600,000 people and the same number came to hear him expound upon the Torah. [Although the

אֶת־בְּכֹרוֹ אֶת־אֱלִיאָב וַאֲבִינָדָב הַשֵּׁנִי וְשִׁמְעָא הַשְּׁלִשִׁי:
יד־יח
יד־טו נְתַנְאֵל הָרְבִיעִי רַדַּי הַחֲמִישִׁי: אֹצֶם הַשִּׁשִּׁי דָּוִיד
טז הַשְּׁבִעִי: וְאַחְיֹתֵיהֶם צְרוּיָה וַאֲבִיגָיִל וּבְנֵי צְרוּיָה אַבְשַׁי
יז וְיוֹאָב וַעֲשָׂה־אֵל שְׁלֹשָׁה: וַאֲבִיגַיִל יָלְדָה אֶת־עֲמָשָׂא
יח וַאֲבִי עֲמָשָׂא יֶתֶר הַיִּשְׁמְעֵאלִי: וְכָלֵב בֶּן־חֶצְרוֹן

Radak notes that the letters אהו"י — aleph, hey, vav, and yud — are interchangeable. The addition of the aleph is therefore simply an expansion of the yud and the essential name remains the same (see further, v. 16).

13. שִׁמְעָא — Shimea. This third son of Yishai is called שַׁמָּה, Shammah, in I Samuel 16:9. Another variant is שִׁמְעָה in II Samuel 13:3. In II Samuel 21:21 the name is written שמעי but read שִׁמְעָא.

The name שַׁמָּה occurs quite frequently in Scripture. It is the name of a grandson of Esau (Genesis 36:13); a son of one of David's warriors (II Samuel 23:11), and one of David's warriors (II Samuel 23:25). This latter is given as Shammoth in I Chronicles 11:27 and as Shamhoth in I Chronicles 27:8.

We may surmise that in all these cases the original name was שַׁמָּה. But this name has unpleasant associations because of its meaning: desolation (Jeremiah 25:38, 44:22). Perhaps, because of this, the name which was used in practice was changed to forms which did not carry this implication.

15. דָּוִיד הַשְּׁבִעִי — David the seventh. David is counted as the seventh of Yishai's sons. This seems to contradict I Samuel 16:10-11 which indicates that there were seven sons other than David and that he was, in fact, the eighth son, the small one.

The commentators assume that, as indicated here, David was really the seventh of Yishai's sons. (See Vayikra Rabbah 29:9. All 'sevens' are beloved [by God] ... [The seventh] son [is beloved] as it is written, And David was the seventh.) The eighth son, Elihu (I Chronicles 27:18), was younger than David. He is not mentioned here because once David has been 'found,' this last brother was of no concern to Ezra (Mefaresh). In I Samuel 16:11 David is called the small one, not because of his age but because of his modest bearing. He made so little of

himself that in his father's eyes he was the small one (Radak and Gra).

16. וְאַחְיֹתֵיהֶם צְרוּיָה וַאֲבִיגָיִל — And their sisters — Tzeruiah and Avigail. Since Tzeruiah and Avigail are listed as sisters of Yishai's sons rather than as daughters of Yishai, it would seem that they had a different father and were half-sisters of the seven sons of Yishai. This would agree with the simple meaning of II Samuel 17:25 where Avigail's father is given as Nachash (Malbim).

However, the Sages as well as Radak and Ralbag identify Yishai with Nachash. Radak and Ralbag (there) suggest that he may simply have had two different names. The Sages, though (Bava Basra 17a), explain that a lesson is intended. Yishai was one of four people who died without ever having sinned. Only because God had decreed that all mankind must be mortal was he also taken. God's decree had resulted from the cunning of the snake (נָחָשׁ, Nachash) who caused Eve to sin in Eden. The name נָחָשׁ, Nachash, therefore, means: The one who died because of the cunning of the snake.

אַבְשַׁי וְיוֹאָב וַעֲשָׂה־אֵל — Avshai, Yoav, and Asah-el. Nowhere in Scripture is the husband of Tzeruiah identified. In contrast to the usual practice of identifying people by their fathers, these three men are invariably referred to as sons of Tzeruiah, their mother.

Each one of these three nephews of David, but particularly Yoav, played major roles in David's life. Yoav was the loyal commander of David's armies throughout his life, and their tumultuous relationship is one of the recurring themes of II Samuel. Avshai, too, was one of the leading commanders of David's army, and it was the death of Asah-el at the hands of Saul's

number 600,000 in this context can be taken as hyperbole (see Tosafos, Bava Kama 92b and Maharal to Gittin 57a), the meaning is that his household was very large and his students unusually many. The description is of a particularly distinguished person — worthy progenitor of the royal house.]

his first-born Eliav, and Avinadav the second, and Shimea the third. [14] *Nethanel the fourth, Raddai the fifth.* [15] *Otzem the sixth, David the seventh.* [16] *And their sisters — Tzeruiah and Avigail. And the sons of Tzeruiah — Avshai, Yoav, and Asah-el, three.* [17] *And Avigail bore Amasa, and the father of Amasa was Yether the*

general, Avner, and Yoav's subsequent avenging of that death, that forever colored David's relationship with Yoav (*II Samuel* chs. 2 and 3; see further, comm. to 27:1).

שְׁלֹשָׁה — *Three.* See footnote to verse 6 for possible explanations for the use of a number at the end of a list of names. In this case *Targum* interpolates a word in order to explain the apparent redundancy. He renders: [*All*] *three were mighty* [*warriors*].

17. עֲמָשָׂא — *Amasa.* This fourth nephew of David was another one of Israel's military heroes concerning whom Scripture gives only sketchy details, but who, in the tradition of the Sages, also towered above his generation spiritually. Together with Avner, he is described (*Yerushalmi Peah* 1:1) as a *lion of Torah.*

יֶתֶר הַיִּשְׁמְעֵאלִי — *Yether the Ishmaelite.* In *II Samuel* 17:25, Amasa's father's name is given as Yithra (יִתְרָא), an *aleph* is added to the name (יֶתֶר) the *Israelite. Mefaresh* and *Radak* both explain that he was, in fact, Jewish by birth but is called the Ishmaelite here because he lived in the lands of Ishmael. *Radak* adds that *Samuel* called him an 'Israelite' specifically to avoid any misunderstanding. People called him the 'Ishmaelite' because that is where he lived; in reality he was an Israelite.

There were a number of people in David's circle whose names seem to indicate foreign descent. *II Samuel* 23:37 lists Tzelek the Ammonite among David's warriors. Verse 39 there lists Uri the Chittite, whose wife Bathsheba was later to marry David and become the mother of Solomon. *II Samuel* 15:19 mentions Ittai the Gittite (גִּתִּי), *of Gath*, a part of Philistia). *I Chronicles* 11:46 speaks of a Yithma the Moabite among David's warriors. According to *Kiddushin* 76b most of these men were Jewish by birth but were called by the names of the places in which they lived.

According to *Ruth Rabbah* (4:2), there was a disagreement among the Sages concerning Yether's origins. In one tradition, he was an Ishmaelite who strayed into the study hall of Yishai while the latter was expounding on a verse which implied that all nations could find salvation within Israel. He decided immediately to become Jewish and Yishai gave his daughter to him in marriage. According to the other tradition, he was born a Jew but 'girded a sword like an Ishmaelite,' threatening to kill anyone who disputed the halachah that Moabite and Ammonite women were not included in the Torah's ban on converts from Ammon and Moab marrying into the general community. This is the tradition of the Talmud (*Yevamos* 77a) as well [see below 8:8].[1]

◆§ **Calev — Son of Chetzron, Son of Yephunneh**

18⁻49. The next section deals with the descendants of Calev the son of Chetzron. There is another well-known Calev, however — Calev the son of Yephunneh — and the commentary to the rest of this chapter is considerably complicated by the constant need to clarify which of the many references to Calev refer to Calev ben Chetzron, and which to

---

1. Commentators suggest that if Yether was in fact a convert, this would explain the extra *aleph* in his name as it is recorded in *II Samuel* (see comm.). It is likely that on becoming Jewish he elected to change his name.

While the assumption that Yether was a convert justifies the use of 'Ishmaelite' in our verse, it leaves the appellation 'Israelite' in *Samuel* unexplained. Nowhere else in Scripture is a person described as הַיִּשְׂרְאֵלִי (except in *Leviticus* 24:10, which is an altogether different situation since no name is given there).

It may be that the appellation הַיִּשְׂרְאֵלִי, *the Israelite,* is to imply that although he was a convert, upon becoming Jewish he left every trace of his past behind. In essence and in character he was a true Israelite. [Cf. *R' Tzaddok HaKohen, Resisei Laylah* 47 for his interpretation of the teaching of the Sages (*Bereishis Rabbah, Toldos*) that Abraham was called 'Israelite'. Although Abraham was the first 'convert' (תְּחִלָּה לַגֵּרִים), he also had all the characteristics of a born Jew. No trace of his ancestry remained.]

Calev ben Yephunneh — assuming that these were two different people.

It must be stated at the outset that these complications arise only when we attempt to intertwine the Sages' traditions with the text. The written record taken by itself presents no difficulties since Calev ben Yephunneh is not mentioned at all until ch. 4. Chapter 2 in itself makes perfect sense if we assume that just one Calev, the one given in v. 9 as the third of Chetzron's sons, is being discussed. His genealogy is begun here in v. 18 and, after interrupting with Yerachmeel's family tree, the chapter once more reverts to Calev's genealogy in v. 42. Such a disrupted listing is shown by the commentators as being entirely in keeping with the system employed throughout the genealogical listings.[1] Verse 49 might be seen as a problem since Calev's daughter is given as Achsah and we know from *Joshua* that Achsah was a daughter of Calev ben Yephunneh. Even this is not an insurmountable difficulty, since it is entirely possible that Calev ben Yephunneh, who was presumably a descendant of Calev ben Chetzron, would have called his own daughter by the same name which his ancestor gave to his daughter.[2]

However, it is a firmly grounded assumption throughout aggadic literature that Moses' sister Miriam was married to Calev ben Yephunneh, that the kingly house of David was descended from that union, and that Chur was their son and Betzalel their grandson. All this is based on the tradition of the Sages that the Ephrath of v. 19 is Miriam and that the Calev whom she married is Calev ben Yephunneh, although the simple meaning of the text is that it refers to Calev ben Chetzron.

These identifications require that we make one of two assumptions: Either that the two Calevs are one and the same person; that the father was indeed Chetzron and that he is sometimes called Yephunneh [to hint at Calev's turning away (יְפֻנֶּה) from פנה, *to turn*) from the plan of the spies (*Sotah* 12a)]; or that there were two Calevs, one a son of Chetzron, and another who was descended from that first Calev, whose father was Yephunneh.

Radak to v. 18 quotes the opinion of the Sages that Calev ben Chetzron is identical with the Calev ben Yephunneh whom Moses sent to spy out the Land of Israel (see also *Yerushalmi Kiddushin* 1:2). However, he thinks this unlikely since that would force us to assume that Chetzron was some 172 years old when he fathered him. [Calev was forty when he was sent on his mission in the second year after the Exodus (*Joshua* 14:7). His father Chetzron was already born when Jacob came to Egypt (see *Genesis* 46:8,12). If, as the Sages teach, Israel was in Egypt for two hundred and ten years, then Chetzron must have been approximately 172 years old when Calev was born.]

Gra to v. 9 concurs and brings an even more persuasive proof from v. 21. There we learn that *afterwards*, at the age of sixty, Chetzron remarried. This clearly implies that the children listed earlier were born before Chetzron reached the age of sixty. Since Chetzron was among those who came to Egypt with Jacob, this would make the three sons mentioned here at least 150 years old at the time of the Exodus. However, according to *Joshua* 14:7, Calev ben Yephunneh was only forty years old in the second year after the Exodus. We must conclude, therefore, that he is not the Cheluvai or Calev ben Chetzron

---

1. The Calev, son of Chur, mentioned in v. 51 plays no role at all in the subject under discussion because, as the commentator points out, he may well be a son of Chur, who was given in v. 19 as Calev's son, and who could have been expected to name his own son after his father. Thus, whichever Calev is meant in v. 19, Calev ben Chur was his grandson and yet a third Calev.

2. Reading this entire chapter as referring to Calev ben Chetzron frees us from difficulties concerning the ages of some of the people mentioned in the Torah. Our vs. 19 and 20 give Chur, Uri, and Betzalel as descendants of Calev. Now, we know from *Joshua* 14:7 that Calev ben Yephunneh was only forty years old a year after the Exodus. Since, as *Sanhedrin* 69b points out, his great-grandson Betzalel must have been at least thirteen years old when he built the Tabernacle in the year of the Exodus, it follows that both Chur and Uri must have been extremely young when they had their respective sons. However, according to the simple meaning of our chapter, Chur, Uri, and Betzalel were descended from Calev ben Chetzron (who, as explained above, was born more than 210 years before the Exodus), not from Calev ben Yephunneh, and accordingly the ages present no difficulty at all.

Ishmaelite. ¹⁸ *And Calev the son of Chetzron fathered [children] by Azuvah, a wife, and by Yerioth; and these are her sons — Yesher,*

mentioned in vs. 9 and 18.

Thus, both *Radak* and *Gra* assume, albeit for different reasons, that there are two Calevs. One, the son of Chetzron mentioned in vs. 9 and 18, and the other, the son of Yephunneh.

In interpreting our chapter we now have a number of options:

1. We can assume that the Sages' tradition was not meant as the plain meaning of the text but as רֶמֶז, matters which are hinted at in — but not explicated by — the text. This removes the necessity of fitting the Sages' tradition into the interpretation of the text. This seems to be the position taken by *Radak* and *Malbim*.

2. We can take the apparent tradition of the Sages *(Sotah* 12a) that there was only one Calev at its face value, accept that Chetzron was 170 years old when he fathered Calev, and assume another interpretation for v. 21 which would permit us to come to some accommodation between it and the statement in *Joshua* that Calev was only forty years old a year after the Exodus.

3. We can attempt to interpret the text in such a way that the tradition of the Sages that Ephrath is Miriam and that Calev ben Yephunneh married her is reflected in the actual verses while at the same time postulating two Calevs, as logic would seem to require. This is *Gra's* approach, but it involves numerous difficulties. *Gra's* explanation will be given at each of the relevant verses, but to help the reader grasp his view a summary will appear at the end of this section.

18. וְכָלֵב בֶּן־חֶצְרוֹן הוֹלִיד — *And Calev the son of Chetzron fathered.* Chetzron had fathered three sons (v. 9). The genealogy of Ram, the middle son, was given first (vs. 10-17), because David was descended from him. We would have expected Yerachmeel as oldest to be next but Calev (Cheluvai) is listed first because he was a prince *(Metzudos).*[1]

After presenting a partial genealogy of Calev (vs. 18-24), the genealogy of Yerachmeel interrupts (vs. 25-41) before the text reverts once more to Calev (v. 42) and lists a much more complete genealogy. Commentators to v. 42 note that such a system is not uncommon in our book; the genealogy of a given person will be interrupted and then resumed once more later. The Sages, however, view our passage more as an account of Calev's marriages than as a genealogy (see below). Perhaps the existence of the other list (starting at v. 42) influenced them in their interpretation.

הוֹלִיד אֶת־עֲזוּבָה אִשָּׁה — *Fathered [children] by Azuvah, a wife* [lit. *fathered Azuvah, a woman*]. Translation follows *Radak.* Verse

19, *And Azuvah died and Calev took for himself Ephrath,* implies unambiguously that Azuvah was Calev's wife, not his daughter. On the other hand, the expression ... הוֹלִיד אֶת, *fathered,* has been used since v. 10 to describe the relationship of parent to child. What, then, is the meaning of this obscure phrase?

A number of solutions are offered:

- The Sages *(Sotah* 12a): [It says] *fathered* [which implies that Azuvah was Calev's daughter]. Did he not marry her? [The answer is that *fathered* is used instead of *married* to teach us that] whoever marries a woman with pure intentions (לְשֵׁם שָׁמַיִם) is considered as though he fathered her.

Sotah (there) assumes that Azuvah is identical with Moses' sister, Miriam, whom, in the tradition of the Sages, Calev married [see below].

— *Radak:* The word אֶת in our verse is to be translated *by* or *from.* The meaning of the verse is: *Calev fathered [children] by [his] wife Azuvah, and by [his wife] Yerioth* [see also *Targum* and *Metzudos*].

— *Gra:* Azuvah was the *daughter* of Calev ben Chetzron, and the *wife* of Calev ben Yephunneh. Our verse uses the word

---

1. *Metzudos'* assertion that Calev was a prince is based on *Numbers* 13:7 where we learn that Calev was Judah's representative among the spies. These had earlier (v. 2) been identified as 'princes.' However, this is based on the assumption that the Calev ben Chetzron in our verse is identical with the Calev ben Yephunneh of *Numbers.* In the introduction to this verse we noted that both *Radak* and *Gra* think that they were two different people.

יט וְשׁוֹבָב וְאַרְדּוֹן: וַתָּמָת עֲזוּבָה וַיִּקַּח־לוֹ כָלֵב אֶת־אֶפְרָת

כ וַתֵּלֶד לוֹ אֶת־חוּר: וְחוּר הוֹלִיד אֶת־אוּרִי וְאוּרִי הוֹלִיד

כא אֶת־בְּצַלְאֵל: וְאַחַר בָּא חֶצְרוֹן אֶל־בַּת־

מָכִיר אֲבִי גִלְעָד וְהוּא לְקָחָהּ וְהוּא בֶּן־שִׁשִּׁים שָׁנָה וַתֵּלֶד

כב לוֹ אֶת־שְׂגוּב: וּשְׂגוּב הוֹלִיד אֶת־יָאִיר וַיְהִי־לוֹ עֶשְׂרִים

אִשָּׁה, woman, in two senses. Azuvah was the first *female* descendant listed in Chetzron's genealogy and she was destined to become the *wife* of Calev ben Yephunneh.

— The *Mefaresh*: Calev had a wife called Azuvah. She died and in her memory he called a daughter by her name, Azuvah. Our verse means that he bore a daughter whom he called Azuvah after his wife. Verse 19 tells of the death of this wife.

וְאֶת־יְרִיעוֹת — *And by Yerioth.* Based on the different explanations given above, Yerioth would be either a daughter of Calev (*Mefaresh* and *Gra*), or another wife (*Radak*).

According to the Sages (*Sotah* there), Azuvah, Yerioth, and Ephrath (v. 19) are all names for Moses' sister Miriam, whom, in their tradition, Calev married. The Sages' explanation of these names will be given in the next verse.

Targum also assumes that Azuvah and Yerioth were the same woman. As do the Sages (see next verse), he interprets the name Azuvah to mean that she had been forsaken because she was sickly and barren. But for Yerioth he offers a different midrashic explanation. God saw her misery and rewarded her with great wisdom. *Shabbos* 99a (based on *Exodus* 35:26) teaches that the curtains of goat's hair which were required for the Tabernacle were made in a special way. Women of exceptional skill spun the hair straight off the goat's back. According to *Targum*, Azuvah was the particular woman who was able to do this. She was called Yerioth (יְרִיעָה, *yeriah*, curtain) to hint at that skill.

וְאֵלֶּה בָנֶיהָ — *And these are her sons.* Although in *Radak's* view Calev had two wives, Azuvah and Yerioth, the children of

only one of the two women are mentioned. *Radak* and *Metzudos* think that these are Azuvah's sons.

19. וַתָּמָת עֲזוּבָה וַיִּקַּח־לוֹ כָלֵב אֶת־אֶפְרָת — *And Azuvah died and Calev took for himself Ephrath.* According to *Radak*, this Calev is the same as the Calev of the previous verse, namely, the son of Chetzron. The verse relates that after his wife Azuvah died he married a woman called Ephrath who bore him Chur.

In the tradition of the Sages (*Sanhedrin* 69b) this verse refers to Calev ben Yephunneh. *Gra*, following this tradition,[1] explains that although verse 18 refers to Calev ben Chetzron, our verse deals with Calev ben Yephunneh (who was a descendant of the other Calev — see further in verse 24).

Malbim (comm. 2:42), however, thinks that in the view of the Sages both vs. 18 and 19 refer to Calev ben Yephunneh. He is called Calev the son of Chetzron in verse 18 only because he was descended from him [in *Malbim's* view through Ram], not because he was actually his son. Calev ben Chetzron's genealogy is dealt with in verse 42.[2]

The Sages (*Sotah* 11b) teach that Ephrath was Moses' sister, Miriam. She was called Ephrath either because it was through her that Israel was fruitful (אֶפְרָת, from פרה, *to be fruitful*) in Egypt, when she and her mother disobeyed Pharaoh's orders to kill all the first-born sons (*Tanchuma, Ki Sissa*); or, as an expression of nobility and dignity (see *Pirkei d'Rabbi Eliezer* 45).[3]

Accordingly, Calev married Miriam after Azuvah's death. But, according to the

---

1. The opinion of the Sages in *Sotah* (11b) seems to be that Calev ben Chetzron and Calev ben Yephunneh are one and the same person. The father's real name was Chetzron, but Calev was called ben Yephunneh because he turned away [יִפְנֶה from פָּנָה, *to turn away*] from the spies' plot.

2. This is *Malbim's* interpretation of the Sages' view. He himself interprets the entire passage according to its simple explanation, in essentially the same manner as *Radak*.

3. It is from the fact that Miriam is called Ephrath and that David is described as Ephrathi (*I Samuel* 17:12) that the Sages (*Sotah* 11b) deduce that David was descended from Miriam and her husband Calev. [See *Emek HaNetziv, Behaaloscha*.]

Shovav, and Ardon. ¹⁹ *And Azuvah died and Calev took for himself Ephrath, and she bore him Chur.* ²⁰ *And Chur fathered Uri, and Uri fathered Betzalel.* ²¹ *And afterwards, Chetzron came to the daughter of Machir, father of Gilead; and he took her for a wife when he was sixty years old, and she bore him Seguv.* ²² *And Seguv fathered*

teaching of the Sages, Azuvah was also Miriam. Obviously, then, the phrase *Azuvah died* in our verse is not meant literally (*Rashi, Sotah* 11b). Rather, she was stricken with *tzara'as,* a form of leprosy (*Numbers* 12:10ff), and it was considered as though she had died (see *Nedarim* 64b). When she was cured she was like a new person.

The Sages further state that this 'rebirth' was not in a figurative way, but that her youth quite literally returned to her. After she was cured, Calev performed a new marriage with her. See Section Two, p. 388, for a discussion of this idea.

חור — *Chur.* Chur was among the leaders of the people immediately after the Exodus. We find him, together with Aaron, supporting Moses' arms while he was praying to God to help the Israelites in their war with Amalek (*Exodus* 17:12). Later, Moses appointed him, again together with Aaron, to be available to judge the people while Moses ascended Mt. Sinai to receive the Torah (*Exodus* 24:14). After this, however, he disappears abruptly from history.

The Sages explain that when Moses seemed to be late in coming down from Mt. Sinai, and the people in desperation decided to make the golden calf to replace him (*Exodus* ch. 32), Chur protested and was slain (*Shemos Rabbah* 41:6). As a reward for his loyalty, God promised him that his descendants, particularly Betzalel, would be great people (*Shemos Rabbah* 48:3).

20. אוּרִי — *Uri.* The only reference to Uri in Talmudic literature is in *Sanhedrin* 69b which notes the extremely early age at which he must have become a father. See footnote to verse 5.

בְּצַלְאֵל — *Betzalel.* In *Exodus* (31:2,3) Betzalel is introduced by God to Moses as the man who is to build the Tabernacle, with the words: *See I have appointed Betzalel the son of Uri the son of Chur from the tribe of Judah. And I have filled*

him with the spirit of God in wisdom, and in understanding, and in knowledge, and in all [manner of] workmanship. [See further Section Two p. 395.]

◆§ More of Chetzron's progeny.

21. וְאַחַר בָּא חֶצְרוֹן — *And afterwards, Chetzron came.* I.e., after he had fathered the three sons mentioned in verse 9 (*Metzudos*). [It is from this that *Gra* deduces that the Calev in verse 9 cannot be identical with Calev ben Yephunneh. See introduction to v. 18.]

אֶל־בַּת־מָכִיר אֲבִי גִלְעָד — *To the daughter of Machir, father of Gilead.* Machir is the son of Menasheh, the son of Joseph (*Genesis* 50:23). His son was called Gilead (*Numbers* 26:29).

The *Mefaresh* notes that the expression, בָּא אֶל, *came to,* implies that he did not marry her but took her as a concubine. Ezra wants to record the fact that Machir was willing that his daughter should become the concubine of a sixty-year-old man because Chetzron came from Judah. This underlines the importance in which the tribe of Judah was held among the people, and it is part of *Chronicle's* aim to do honor to the Davidic line.

Radak points out that since Chetzron was among the seventy people who accompanied Jacob to Egypt (*Genesis* 46:12), his marriages must have taken place in Egypt.

וַתֵּלֶד לוֹ אֶת־שְׂגוּב — *And she bore him Seguv.* Although Seguv's son Yair seems to be mentioned in *Numbers* (see below), Seguv himself is not mentioned there.

22. וּשְׂגוּב הוֹלִיד אֶת־יָאִיר — *And Seguv fathered Yair.* In *Numbers* 32 we learn how Moses gave the eastern side of the Jordan to the tribes of Reuven, Gad and half of the tribe of Menasheh (v. 33). In that connection we learn that the land of Gilead was given to the family (see *Ramban*) of Menasheh's son, Machir (v. 40). Verse 41 goes on to say: *And Yair the son of Menasheh went and conquered its*

כג וְשָׁלוֹשׁ עָרִים בְּאֶרֶץ הַגִּלְעָד: וַיִּקַּח גְּשׁוּר־וַאֲרָם
אֶת־חַוֺּת יָאִיר מֵאִתָּם אֶת־קְנָת וְאֶת־בְּנֺתֶיהָ שִׁשִּׁים עִיר
כד כָּל־אֵלֶּה בְּנֵי מָכִיר אֲבִי־גִלְעָד: וְאַחַר מוֹת־חֶצְרוֹן בְּכָלֵב

[Gilead's] outlying cities and called them
Chavvoth Yair.

From verse 23 (here), which reports that
Geshur and Aram took Chavvoth Yair
away from them, it would seem that the
Yair mentioned in our verse is identical
with the one mentioned in Numbers as the
conqueror of Chavvoth Yair. However,
there he is called Yair the son of Menasheh
while here he is identified as the son of
Chetzron's son, Seguv, and that it was only
his grandmother who was descended from
Menasheh (v. 21).

Radak thinks that the two are, in fact,
identical. It was Ezra's purpose in
including this passage in Chronicles to
point out that although Yair is called ben
Menasheh in Numbers, his paternal
descent was in fact from Judah. His father
had married into the family of Menasheh
and had settled in the lands of his wife's
family.

However, Radak notes that the Sages
had a tradition that there were two men by
the name of Yair. The one mentioned in
Numbers was descended from Menasheh
and conquered the lands which he
subsequently named Chavvoth Yair. The
Yair of Chronicles was descended from
Judah and received his lands in Gilead
through inheriting his wife's property (see
Bava Basra 111b and 113a). See comm. to
next verse.

עֲשָׂרִים וְשָׁלוֹשׁ עָרִים — Twenty-three cities.
From verse 23 it appears that together with
Kenath and its suburbs there were
altogether sixty cities in this area, of which
twenty-three belonged to Yair himself.[1]

בְּאֶרֶץ הַגִּלְעָד — In the land of Gilead. Gilead
was also the name of Menasheh's grandson

(v. 21). Commentators do not discuss
whether there is a connection between the
two names.

23. ... וַיִּקַּח גְּשׁוּר־וַאֲרָם — Now Geshur and
Aram took ... From Deuteronomy 3:14 and
Joshua 13:13 we learn that the land
conquered by Yair ben Menasheh bordered
on Geshur and Maacha. The Aram of our
verse is probably identical with Maacha
and we do, in fact, find the expression
Aram Maacha in I Chronicles 19:6
(Anonymous Commentator and R' Dovid
Tzvi Hoffman). Or, perhaps, since Maacha
bordered on Aram, it was referred to by the
name of its neighbor (Mefaresh).

Our verse teaches that these two
neighbors of Menasheh eventually took the
whole of Chavvoth Yair away from Yair's
family. In the view of the Mefaresh, this
explains the inclusion of this passage in
Chronicles. These cities were eventually
reconquered by David and therefore their
history has a rightful place in the Book of
Chronicles which, in the Mefaresh's view,
has David as its central figure.

The history of the retaking of these cities
is nowhere explicated. From the available sources
in Scripture the following rough reconstruction
is possible.

Thirty of these cities seem to have been once
more in the possession of Israel during the reign
of the Judge, Yair (Judges 10:4). In Solomon's
time it would seem that all sixty cities were once
more Israelite property (I Kings 4:13). The
inference is that David reconquered the balance
of the cities in his campaigns which are described
in II Samuel 10:6ff (R' Dovid Tzvi Hoffman).

The Anonymous Commentator offers an
entirely novel sequence for the events
recorded in Numbers ch. 32 and here. In
his view, the conquests recorded in
Numbers did not take place at the end of

---

1. Deuteronomy 3:4 also mentions sixty cities and in verse 14 tells of Yair's conquests and the
naming of Chavvoth Yair. No mention is made in Deuteronomy of Kenath and its suburbs. These are
mentioned in Numbers 32:41-42 as having been conquered by Novach. Numbers (there) also tells of
Yair's conquests but makes no mention of any numbers.

The question arises why Deuteronomy makes no mention of Novach or Kenath. We would have
expected these to be mentioned since — as evidenced by Chronicles — they were needed to make up
the number sixty in Deuteronomy 3:14.

R' Dovid Tzvi Hoffman (Deuteronomy) concludes that Novach, and his capital, Kenath, must have
been subordinate to Yair. Consequently, his property was also known as Chavvoth Yair and
Deuteronomy had no need to mention Kenath and its suburbs separately.

2

23-24

Yair; he owned twenty-three cities in the land of Gilead. ²³ *Now Geshur and Aram took Chavvoth Yair from them, Kenath and its dependencies, sixty cities; all these [belonged to] the sons of Machir, father of Gilead.* ²⁴ *And after Chetzron died in Calev Ephrathah, the*

the fortieth year of the wandering in the desert. Rather, at the very beginning of the Egyptian exile, Machir, Yair and Novach made conquests in Gilead and built cities there. [See commentary to the Torah by *R' Yehudah HaChassid*, Jerusalem 5735, that even during the Egyptian exile there was a special dispensation for Joseph's descendants to colonize the land of Israel.] After Joseph's death, the neighboring nations, Geshur and Maachah, were emboldened to reconquer these lands. Later, when Moses led Israel to this land which had previously been owned by the Menashehites, he saw to it that this particular territory was returned to the descendants of the original owners.

אֶת־חַוֹּת יָאִיר — *Chavvoth Yair.* In verse 22 we noted that this name tends to show that the Yair of verse 22 is identical with the Yair of *Numbers* since there also the name of the area is given as Chavvoth Yair.

However, *Metzudos* points out that this is not necessarily so. It could well be that there were two people who had the same name and that this similarity prompted the later one to give his lands the same name as the earlier one had.

כָּל־אֵלֶּה בְּנֵי מָכִיר אֲבִי־גִלְעָד — *All these [belonged to] the sons of Machir, father of Gilead.* The word אֵלֶּה, *these,* refers to the cities, and the sentence must therefore be read as though בְּנֵי were written לִבְנֵי, *belonged to the sons* (*Radak* and *Metzudos*). [These commentators reject the alternative translation: *All these are the children of Machir, father of Gilead,* since the plural כָּל אֵלֶּה, *all these,* would imply that there were a number of children whereas only Seguv (v. 21) has been mentioned.]

24. וְאַחַר מוֹת־חֶצְרוֹן בְּכָלֵב אֶפְרָתָה — *And after Chetzron died in Calev Ephrathah.* The syntax of this verse is difficult. The commentators offer three possible interpretations:

1. After Chetzron died in the house of his son Calev [which was situated] in Ephrath, his [Chetzron's] wife Aviyah

[who was pregnant at the time of his death] bore him a son *(Targum).*

2. After Chetzron died in [the city of] Calev Ephrathah, his wife, Aviyah, bore him [a posthumous son] Ashchur, chieftain of Tekoa *(Mefaresh).*

3. And then, the death of Chetzron [occurred, at the time that] Calev married Ephrathah; and the wife of Chetzron was [at that time] Aviyah, and she bore him Ashchur, father of Tekoa *(Radak).*

בְּכָלֵב אֶפְרָתָה — *In Calev Ephrathah.* From the point of view of grammar and syntax, the easiest way to translate this phrase is to assume that *Calev Ephrathah* is a place name. *I Samuel* 30:14 mentions a place called Calev in the south of Israel, and in *Genesis* (35:19) Ephrathah is identified with Bethlehem. Therefore the phrase could well mean: *In Calev [which lies in the vicinity of] Ephrathah.*

The difficulty with this interpretation is contextual. For if Chetzron died in the land of Israel, he must have been at least two hundred and fifty years old at the time of his death *(Radak).* [Chetzron was among the family of Jacob who came to Egypt *(Genesis* 46:12). The 210 years which Israel stayed in Egypt, when added to the forty years in the wilderness, yield a minimum age of 250 years.]

In addition, we note the following difficulties: (1) Why should the city in which Chetzron died be mentioned? (2) The formulation ... בְּ מוֹת is unique in Scripture. (3) The fact that Calev and Ephrath occurred in v. 19 as names of people makes it likely that this is also their meaning in v. 24.

The Sages *(Tanchuma Ki Sisa* 13) take the word בְּכָלֵב [*in Calev*] as though there were two words — בָּא כָלֵב, *Calev married* [lit. *came*]. The phrase is to be rendered: *Calev married Ephrath.*

The Massorah lists nine instances in which there is an irregular dropping of the א, *aleph,* from the root בוא, *to come* (cf. *I Samuel* 25:8). But in our case there is the additional irregularity of having the two words fused into one. The *Anonymous Commentator* compares *Isaiah* 3:15, where, in the *kesiv,* the written form, the two words מַה לָּכֶם are given as one word with the *hey* deleted — מַלָּכֶם.

אֶפְרָתָה וְאֵשֶׁת חֶצְרוֹן אֲבִיָּה וַתֵּלֶד לוֹ אֶת־אַשְׁחוּר אֲבִי

כה תְקוֹעַ: וַיִּהְיוּ בְנֵי־יְרַחְמְאֵל בְּכוֹר חֶצְרוֹן הַבְּכוֹר | רָם

כו וּבוּנָה וָאֹרֶן וָאֹצֶם אֲחִיָּה: וַתְּהִי אִשָּׁה אַחֶרֶת לִירַחְמְאֵל

כז וּשְׁמָהּ עֲטָרָה הִיא אֵם אוֹנָם: וַיִּהְיוּ בְנֵי־רָם בְּכוֹר

וְאֵשֶׁת חֶצְרוֹן אֲבִיָּה — *The wife of Chetzron,
Aviyah.* Since verse 21 taught that in his
later years Chetzron married the daughter
of Machir, it was necessary to point out
that at the time of his death, he had another
wife whose name was Aviyah *(Radak).*
Targum, however, states that Aviyah was
the daughter of Machir.

אַשְׁחוּר אֲבִי תְקוֹעַ — *Ashchur, father of
Tekoa.* אֲבִי is the construct form of אָב,
father. Since the chieftain of a town can be
described as its father, the word could be
rendered *chieftain,* and this is how *Targum*
and several other commentators take it
here. However, *Radak* (vs. 42, 50, 51) is
ambivalent about the correct rendering in
this context. He mentions the possibility
that the word can be rendered *chieftain* but
feels that it is more likely that it is to be
taken in the literal sense of *father.* When
applied to a city, it means that all or
perhaps most of the inhabitants of that city
were descended from a given man. We
shall consistently translate *father* because
that word carries a dual connotation and
because *Gra,* as we shall see in 4:4,
evidently translates *father.* [*Targum's*
opinion is not clear; he sometimes
translates *chieftain* and sometimes *father.*]
Strangely, this seeming inconsistency is not
limited to *Targum* of *Chronicles. Targum
Yonason* to *Vayishlach* renders the phrase
אֲבִי אֱדוֹם as *father of Edom* in 36:9 and as
chieftain of Edom in 36:43.
Perhaps for the most accurate meaning in our
context we should go to *Genesis* 4:20, 21 where
אֲבִי is also rendered רַבְּהוֹן, *chieftain,* as it is here
but where both *Radak* and *Gra* translate: *the
first* or the *originator.* In our context it would
imply *the founder* of a particular place.
Tekoa is a city in Judah. See *II
Chronicles* 1:6.
Ashchur Avi Tekoa's descendants are
given in 4:5.
Sotah 12a takes the three words, *Ashchur Avi
Tekoa,* as descriptive of Calev ben Yephunneh.
See Section Two, p. 388.
In the prefatory remarks to v. 18 we noted
that *Gra's* opinion that there must have been two
men by the name of Calev was based on the

problem of the ages — Chetzron's son Calev
must have been at least 150 years old at the
Exodus, whereas Calev ben Yephunneh was
only forty when he was sent to spy out the land.
If Ashchur Avi Tekoa is indeed Calev ben
Yephunneh then it is quite possible that he was
born forty years before the Exodus.
But this would mean that Chetzron was the
father of both Calevs. One was born in his
earlier years and one either after or at least close
to his death.
Rather than assume this, *Gra* thinks that
Ashchur Avi Tekoa was Yephunneh, rather than
Calev ben Yephunneh. The latter was
Chetzron's grandson, not his son. The Talmud
(*Sotah* 12a quoted above) sees the father's name
as descriptive of the son. Since Yephunneh
fathered Calev some forty years before the
Exodus, we have 170 years to divide between
Chetzron and his son Yephunneh before the
latter fathered Calev.
Gra does not explain the phrase בְּכָלֵב
אֶפְרָתָה in the first part of the verse. None of the
interpretations offered are possible in his
interpretation. Chetzron must have died in the
wilderness and cannot be said to have died in the
city of Calev. Again he cannot have died when
Calev (ben Yephunneh) married Ephrath since
he died prior to Yephunneh's (Ashchur Avi
Tekoa) birth.

25. Of Chetzron's three sons (v. 9), Ram
was the first one whose genealogy was
traced, because David was to be descended
from him. Then came the genealogy of
Calev who, although the youngest, was
nevertheless a prince in Judah (comm. v.
18). [Calev's genealogy will be picked up
once more in v. 42.] Now, the genealogy of
Chetzron's first-born, Yerachmeel, is taken
up *(Gra).*

בְּנֵי־יְרַחְמְאֵל בְּכוֹר חֶצְרוֹן — *The sons of
Yerachmeel, the first-born of Chetzron.*
Because Yerachmeel's genealogy was left
for last (see v. 9), it was necessary to stress
that he was, in fact, Chetzron's first-born
(Mefaresh).

הַבְּכוֹר רָם — *Ram the first-born.* The first-
born of Yerachmeel was Ram *(Mefaresh).*
He was given the same name as his uncle,
Yerachmeel's brother (v. 9).

wife of Chetzron, Aviyah, bore him Ashchur, father of Tekoa.
²⁵ The sons of Yerachmeel, the first-born of Chetzron, were — Ram
the first-born, Bunah, Oren, Otzem, and Achiyah. ²⁶ And
Yerachmeel had another wife whose name was Atarah; she was the
mother of Onam. ²⁷ And the sons of Ram the first-born of

There are no midrashic sources extant concerning the great majority of names in the Yerachmeel line. Surely the *Sefer Yuchasin*, the Midrash on *Chronicles*, which, according to *Pesachim* 62b, was withdrawn (see Overview, p. xxix), would have taught us the significance of the names in this long list. As it is, the only one of Yerachmeel's descendants concerning whom we have some knowledge is Yishmael ben Nethaniah the murderer of Gedaliah ben Achikam. See below.

26. וַתְּהִי אַחֶרֶת לִירַחְמְאֵל — *And Yerachmeel had another wife.* The word *another* could mean simply that besides the mother of his first five sons, Yerachmeel had a second wife. Or, it is possible that the term is used to indicate that this other woman was a concubine *(Radak)*.

However, the Sages *(Yerushalmi, Sanhedrin* 2:3) have the tradition that this woman was a well-born gentile lady whom Yerachmeel married in order to pride himself (לְהִתְעַטֵּר — a play on her name: עֲטָרָה, *a crown)* with her. The son was called אוֹנָם from אוֹן, *weariness, sorrow* or *trouble,* because she brought sorrow into his house.

Yerachmeel's perfidy in marrying this gentile woman was to leave its mark on Jewish history. Many centuries later Babylon was to destroy the Temple, lay Jerusalem waste and drag the people into dark exile. But God's Providence decreed that the bond between land and people was not to be broken completely. A small, poor — and in Nebuchadnezzar's eyes — insignificant community was allowed to remain under the benign governship of Gedaliah ben Achikam.

There was every reason to hope that this small community, chastened by the holocaust which it had survived, would flourish in its ancestral home and provide the seed for Israel's regeneration. But it was not to be. Driven by jealousy (see *Abarbanel* and *Malbim* to *Jeremiah* ch. 41), Yishmael ben Nethaniah, a scion of the royal house of Judah who felt himself slighted by Gedaliah's appointment, overthrew and viciously killed the governor and numerous

innocent people. This assassination is commemorated on *Tzom Gedaliah,* the *Fast of Gedaliah* [on the 3rd of Tishrei], because its ramifications went far beyond the death of a saintly and blameless man. Terrified by the prospect of Babylonian reprisals, the small community fled to Egypt — against the advice of Jeremiah who urged them to remain — where they were ultimately destroyed. (See II *Kings* ch. 25 and *Jeremiah* ch. 41ff.)

According to the tradition of the Sages, this Yishmael ben Nethaniah was the grandson of Elishama (v. 41). Based on this they taught (*Pesikta Rabbosi* 22:5) that until the twenty-fourth generation the descendants of a proselyte are not to be trusted. [Including Yerachmeel and his wife Atarah, Yishmael ben Nethaniah is the twenty-third generation.][1]

הִיא אֵם אוֹנָם — *She was the mother of Onam.* Metzudos suggests that Onam was a well-known person and Atarah was known as his mother. However, the *Mefaresh* thinks that *mother* is not used here in the physical sense, but in the sense *of one who nurtures and educates* (as in *Judges* 5:7). We have already noted that the name Onam suggests *trouble* and *weariness.* Onam was indeed a weak and spineless person (in a spiritual sense); and his lack of personality was reflected in his descendant Sheshan (vs. 34-35), who knew no better than to marry his daughter to a slave. All this was the result of the education which Onam's gentile mother had given him. The sense of the tracing of this whole genealogy is to expose the weaknesses of the line in order to explain why the younger son Ram (brother of Yerachmeel), rather than the older son Yerachmeel, was chosen to carry the royal seed of Judah.

27. וַיִּהְיוּ בְנֵי רָם — *And the sons of Ram.* Gra to verse 28 notes that it is a firm rule that *Chronicles* only records the genealogies of heads of major families. Individuals who never attained such a status do not have their families traced. We

1. Surely the Sages do not mean to denigrate proselytes as a group. Throughout Jewish history some of the greatest personalities in Israel have been either proselytes or their descendants. Presumably, the Sages refer only to such proselytes who, like Atarah, embraced Judaism for ulterior motives.

כח יְרַחְמְאֵל מַעַץ וְיָמִין וָעֵקֶר: וַיִּהְיוּ בְנֵי־אוֹנָם שַׁמַּי וְיָדָע
כט וּבְנֵי שַׁמַּי נָדָב וַאֲבִישׁוּר: וְשֵׁם אֵשֶׁת אֲבִישׁוּר אֲבִיהָיִל
ל וַתֵּלֶד לוֹ אֶת־אַחְבָּן וְאֶת־מוֹלִיד: וּבְנֵי נָדָב סֶלֶד וְאַפָּיִם
לא וַיָּמָת סֶלֶד לֹא בָנִים: וּבְנֵי אַפַּיִם יִשְׁעִי וּבְנֵי יִשְׁעִי
לב שֵׁשָׁן וּבְנֵי שֵׁשָׁן אַחְלָי: וּבְנֵי יָדָע אֲחִי שַׁמַּי יֶתֶר
לג וְיוֹנָתָן וַיָּמָת יֶתֶר לֹא בָנִים: וּבְנֵי יוֹנָתָן פֶּלֶת וְזָזָא
לד אֵלֶּה הָיוּ בְּנֵי יְרַחְמְאֵל: וְלֹא־הָיָה לְשֵׁשָׁן בָּנִים כִּי אִם־
לה בָּנוֹת וּלְשֵׁשָׁן עֶבֶד מִצְרִי וּשְׁמוֹ יַרְחָע: וַיִּתֵּן שֵׁשָׁן אֶת־בִּתּוֹ
לו לְיַרְחָע עַבְדּוֹ לְאִשָּׁה וַתֵּלֶד לוֹ אֶת־עַתָּי: וְעַתַּי הוֹלִיד אֶת־
לז נָתָן וְנָתָן הוֹלִיד אֶת־זָבָד: וְזָבָד הוֹלִיד אֶת־אֶפְלָל וְאֶפְלָל
לח הוֹלִיד אֶת־עוֹבֵד: וְעוֹבֵד הוֹלִיד אֶת־יֵהוּא וְיֵהוּא הוֹלִיד
לט אֶת־עֲזַרְיָה: וַעֲזַרְיָה הוֹלִיד אֶת־חָלֶץ וְחָלֶץ הוֹלִיד אֶת־
מ אֶלְעָשָׂה: וְאֶלְעָשָׂה הוֹלִיד אֶת־סִסְמָי וְסִסְמַי הוֹלִיד אֶת־
מא שַׁלּוּם: וְשַׁלּוּם הוֹלִיד אֶת־יְקַמְיָה וִיקַמְיָה הוֹלִיד אֶת־
מב אֱלִישָׁמָע: וּבְנֵי כָלֵב אֲחִי יְרַחְמְאֵל מֵישַׁע בְּכֹרוֹ

---

must therefore not be surprised if of the five sons mentioned in verse 25 only Ram has his family traced.

30. לֹא בָנִים — *Without children.* The substituting of לֹא, *not*, for בְּלִי, *without*, is infrequent and occurs mostly in poetic language. Cf *II Samuel* 23:4. It is repeated in verse 34.

32. וּבְנֵי יָדָע אֲחִי שַׁמַּי — *And the sons of Yada the brother of Shammai.* See comm. 1:8 on the use of the plural *sons* where only one son is listed.

Gra thinks that it was necessary to describe Yada as *brother of Shammai* because between v. 28 and our verse Shammai's descendants have been listed and we might well have thought that Yada was also one of Shammai's grandchildren.

33. אֵלֶּה הָיוּ בְּנֵי יְרַחְמְאֵל — *These were the sons of Yerachmeel.* The descendants of Yerachmeel are traced only up to Sheshan. Although the line of Sheshan is also traced, this carries the line forward through a daughter (v. 35), and the subsequent children are not reckoned as Yerachmeel's line (*Malbim*).

34. וְלֹא־הָיָה לְשֵׁשָׁן בָּנִים — *Now Sheshan had no sons.* Verse 31 had listed Achlai as a son of Sheshan, but the commentators write

that he died during his father's lifetime. The *Mefaresh* suggests that he was called אַחְלָי from חלה, *to be ill*, because he was a weak and sickly person and died as a young man.

Alternatively, *Gra* suggests that the incident with the slave occurred before Sheshan's son was born. At that time, rather than entrust his property to a stranger, he chose to give his daughter to the slave whom he knew to have been loyal to him.

35. וַיִּתֵּן שֵׁשָׁן אֶת־בִּתּוֹ לְיַרְחָע עַבְדּוֹ לְאִשָּׁה — *So Sheshan gave his daughter as a wife to Yarcha his slave.* Sheshan's idea seems, in itself, not to have been wrong. *Pesachim* 113a teaches: 'If your daughter has reached the age of marriage — free your slave [if no other husband is available] and marry her to him.' [A freed slave is considered a proselyte.]

Surely, Sheshan did free Yarcha before he allowed him to marry his daughter. *Radak* cites a Midrash which derives this from the name יַרְחָע. The ע, *ayin*, at the end of the name stands for עֶבֶד, *slave*, and the first three letters of the name read backwards yield חָרֵי, *free*. Thus, a *freed slave. Targum* actually injects this into his translation: [And he freed him] and

Yerachmeel were Maatz, Yamin, and Eker. ²⁸ And the sons of Onam were Shammai and Yada; and the sons of Shammai — Nadav and Avishur. ²⁹ And the name of Avishur's wife was Avichail and she bore him Achban and Molid. ³⁰ And the sons of Nadav — Seled and Appaim; and Seled died without children. ³¹ And the sons of Appaim — Yishi, and the sons of Yishi — Sheshan, and the sons of Sheshan — Achlai. ³² And the sons of Yada the brother of Shammai — Yether and Yonathan; and Yether died without children. ³³ And the sons of Yonathan — Peleth and Zaza. These were the sons of Yerachmeel. ³⁴ Now Sheshan had no sons, only daughters, but Sheshan had an Egyptian slave whose name was Yarcha. ³⁵ So Sheshan gave his daughter as a wife to Yarcha his slave, and she bore him Attai. ³⁶ And Attai fathered Nathan, and Nathan fathered Zavad. ³⁷ And Zavad fathered Ephlal, and Ephlal fathered Oved. ³⁸ And Oved fathered Yehu, and Yehu fathered Azariah. ³⁹ And Azariah fathered Cheletz, and Cheletz fathered Eleasah. ⁴⁰ And Eleasah fathered Sismai, and Sismai fathered Shallum. ⁴¹ And Shallum fathered Yekamiah, and Yekamiah fathered Elishama. ⁴² The sons of Calev brother of Yerachmeel — Mesha his first-born;

Sheshan gave his daughter ...

Nevertheless, this union was forbidden since the Torah (Deuteronomy 23:8-9) forbids Egyptian proselytes to marry Jews up to the third generation. Yarcha was an Egyptian (v. 34) and thus forbidden (Radak).

Yerushalmi Horios 3:5 derives from this passage that the descendants of a freed slave must be suspect up to the sixteenth generation. [Yishmael ben Nethaniah was fifteenth in line starting from Attai the son of Yarcha and Sheshan's daughter.] (See v. 26 for a similar teaching by Pesikta Rabbosi.)

41. וַיְקַמְיָה הֹלִיד אֶת־אֱלִישָׁמָע — And Yekamiah fathered Elishama. This Elishama is the grandfather of Yishmael ben Nethaniah [see II Kings 25:25] (Gra).

◄§ Calev's genealogy continued

42. The genealogy of Calev is once more taken up (see above v. 18ff).

וּבְנֵי כָלֵב אֲחִי יְרַחְמְאֵל — The sons of Calev brother of Yerachmeel. The Mefaresh, Radak and Metzudos see no difficulty in the fact that Calev's genealogy is divided between 18ff and our passage. They say that such a treatment is common in the Book of Chronicles.

Gra offers a different explanation. Vs. 16

and 17 had introduced a number of well-known women in the line of Ram. Because of this, the genealogy of Calev was begun out of place (Yerachmeel, the first-born, should have been first) in order to list the important women of that line. After that subject, with its attendant details, was completed Yerachmeel, the first-born, is dealt with in detail. After that Calev's complete genealogy is begun.

According to Malbim's interpretation of the Sages' view (cited in comm. v. 19), the earlier passage dealt exclusively with Calev ben Yephunneh (as part of Ram's genealogy). The Calev in our passage is Calev ben Chetzron.

כָלֵב אֲחִי יְרַחְמְאֵל — Calev brother of Yerachmeel. According to those who see the earlier passage as dealing either with two different Calevs (Gra), or exclusively with Calev ben Yephunneh (Malbim), the necessity for stressing that this Calev was the brother of Yerachmeel, i.e. the son of Chetzron, is readily understood.

Furthermore, Ramban (Exodus 15:20) points out that there is a general tendency for Scripture to refer to a younger sibling as the brother (or sister) of the oldest brother.

מֵישָׁע בְּכֹרוֹ — Mesha his first-born. Assuming that the Calev of this passage is

מג הוּא אֲבִי־זִיף וּבְנֵי מָרֵשָׁה אֲבִי חֶבְרוֹן קֹרַח

מד וְתַפֻּחַ וְרֶקֶם וָשָׁמַע: וְשֶׁמַע הוֹלִיד אֶת־רַחַם אֲבִי יָרְקְעָם

מה וְרֶקֶם הוֹלִיד אֶת־שַׁמָּי: וּבֶן־שַׁמַּי מָעוֹן וּמָעוֹן אֲבִי בֵית־

מו צוּר: וְעֵיפָה פִּילֶגֶשׁ כָּלֵב יָלְדָה אֶת־חָרָן וְאֶת־מוֹצָא וְאֶת־

מז גָּזֵז וְחָרָן הֹלִיד אֶת־גָּזֵז: וּבְנֵי יָהְדָּי רֶגֶם וְיוֹתָם

מח וְגֵישָׁן וָפֶלֶט וְעֵיפָה וָשָׁעַף: פִּילֶגֶשׁ כָּלֵב מַעֲכָה יָלַד שֶׁבֶר

מט וְאֶת־תִּרְחֲנָה: וַתֵּלֶד שַׁעַף אֲבִי מַדְמַנָּה אֶת־שְׁוָא אֲבִי

נ מַכְבֵּנָה וַאֲבִי גִבְעָא וּבַת־כָּלֵב עַכְסָה: אֵלֶּה הָיוּ בְּנֵי כָלֵב

נא בֶּן־חוּר בְּכוֹר אֶפְרָתָה שׁוֹבָל אֲבִי קִרְיַת יְעָרִים: שַׂלְמָא

the same as the Calev of v. 19ff, Malbim[1] explains the splitting of the two lists as follows: The earlier list had dealt only with those of Calev's descendants who were mentioned in the Torah (Chur, Uri and Betzalel), although Chur was not really the oldest of Calev's sons. The oldest was Mesha and he is described here as the *first-born* in order to make this clear.

הוּא אֲבִי־זִיף — *He was father of Ziph.* Ziph may be the name of a person, in which case the son was more famous than the father, and the father was remembered only because of his relationship to his son. Alternatively, Ziph may be the name of a town [see *Joshua* 15:24 where it is given as one of the cities of Judah], in which case אֲבִי is to be translated chieftain as in v. 24 (*Radak*). *Targum* renders: *chieftain of Ziph* (although at the end of the verse he renders אֲבִי חֶבְרוֹן, *father of Hebron*). *Gra* explains that the residents of the city of Ziph were all descended from him. See comm. v. 24.

וּבְנֵי מָרֵשָׁה אֲבִי חֶבְרוֹן — *And his sons were Mareshah, father of Hebron.* Both *Radak* and *Gra* explain that Ziph (*Radak*) or Avi Ziph (*Gra*) are implied after the word וּבְנֵי. The phrase is to be understood: *And the sons [of Ziph or Avi Ziph] were Mareshah, the father of Hebron.* [This is another example of the plural, *the sons of* being used even though only one son is listed. See above comm. v. 7.]

Mareshah is listed in *Joshua* 15:42 among Judah's cities.

44. וְרֶקֶם הוֹלִיד ... וְשֶׁמַע הוֹלִיד — *And Shema*

fathered ... and Rekem fathered ... From v. 33 it seems that Rekem was older than Shema. However, as *Gra* notes (v. 25), the genealogy of younger sons precedes that of older sons in cases where the younger sons had children earlier than the older ones.

אֲבִי יָרְקְעָם — *Father of Yorkeam.* Yorkeam seems to have been a city in Judah. It is not mentioned elsewhere in Scripture. See above comm. v. 24 as to whether this means *father* or *chieftain*.

45. אֲבִי בֵית־צוּר — *Father of Beth Tzur.* Beth Tzur is mentioned in *Joshua* 15:58 among the Judean cities.

46. וְחָרָן הֹלִיד אֶת־גָּזֵז — *And Charan fathered Gazez.* Charan called his son by his brother's name.

47. וּבְנֵי יָהְדָּי — *And the sons of Yahdai.* No Yahdai had been mentioned among the sons of Calev's concubine Ephah. There are three different approaches among the commentators to this problem.

— *Radak* and *Metzudos:* Yahdai is a second name for one of the three sons mentioned in v. 46.

— *Gra:* The word וּבְנֵי serves the previous verse as well. It is as though the text read: [And the son of Gazez (v. 46) was Yahdai]; and the sons of Yahdai ... [See fn. to 1:36 and comm. to 8:31.]

— *Malbim:* In accordance with his view (cited in comm. 2:7) that the lists in *Chronicles* are taken from a סֵפֶר יוֹחֲסִים, *Book of Genealogies*, from which Ezra selected only those names which were important to him, he suggests that Yahdai

1. As explained in footnote to v. 19, *Malbim* himself interprets the chapter in line with *Radak*, not the Sages.

he was father of Ziph, and his sons were Mareshah, father of Hebron. ⁴³ And the sons of Hebron — Korach, and Tappuach, and Rekem, and Shema. ⁴⁴ And Shema fathered Racham, father of Yorkeam, and Rekem fathered Shammai. ⁴⁵ And the son of Shammai — Maon, and Maon was the father of Beth Tzur. ⁴⁶ And Ephah, the concubine of Calev, bore Charan, Motza, and Gazez; and Charan fathered Gazez. ⁴⁷ And the sons of Yahdai — Regem, Yotham, Geshan, Pelet, Ephah, and Shaaph. ⁴⁸ Calev's concubine was Maachah; from her he fathered Shever and Tirchanah. ⁴⁹ And she bore Shaaph, father of Madmannah, and Sheva, father of Machbenah, and the father of Givea. And Calev's daughter was Achsah. ⁵⁰ These were the sons of Calev the son of Chur, the firstborn of Ephrathah — Shoval, father of Kiriath Yearim. ⁵¹ Salma,

was a descendant of the line whose beginnings were traced in v. 46. Ezra had no need to cite the intervening names and picked up the list at Yahdai's children.

48. ... שֶׁבֶר יָלַד מַעֲכָה כָלֵב פִּילֶגֶשׁ — *Calev's concubine was Maachah; from her he fathered Shever ...*

The syntax is difficult. The translation follows most commentators who, because of the masculine form of יָלַד (instead of the feminine וַיֵּלֶד,) assume that the subject must be Calev. [See below on the feminine form וַתֵּלֶד in v. 49.]

Malbim prefers to say that the subject of יָלַד is Shever and that he and Tirchanah were the parents of Calev's concubine, Maachah. The verse is to be translated: *The concubine of Calev was Maachah [whom] Shever and Tirchanah had borne.*

49. שָׁעַף וַתֵּלֶד — *And she bore Shaaph.* According to *Malbim* (see previous verse), there is no difficulty in assuming the subject of וַתֵּלֶד, *she bore,* to be Maachah. The Maachah who was described in the verse above bore the following children.

However, if Shever and Tirchanah are children of Calev and Maachah, and their birth had been traced to Calev [יָלַד in the masculine], then it is not clear why the children mentioned in this verse are traced to Maachah [as indicated by וַתֵּלֶד, in the feminine].

Gra suggests that the subject of וַתֵּלֶד is Tirchanah (previous verse) who was a daughter of Calev. This daughter bore the children mentioned in this verse.

מַדְמַנָּה אֲבִי — *Father of Madmannah.* Madmannah is mentioned in Joshua 15:31

as a Judean city.

מַכְבֵּנָה אֲבִי — *Father of Machbenah. Gra* identifies Machbenah with Chabon which is mentioned in Joshua 15:40 as a Judean city.

עַכְסָה וּבַת־כָּלֵב — *And Calev's daughter was Achsah.* From Joshua ch. 15 and Judges ch. 1 it is clear that Achsah was the daughter of Calev ben Yephunneh. But from v. 42 (see comm. there) it is obvious that we are dealing with the genealogy of Calev ben Chetzron.

The following solutions are possible:

(1) Calev ben Chetzron and Calev ben Yephunneh are one and the same person. (See pref. notes to 18-49.)

(2) Although the list beginning in v. 42 is that of Calev ben Chetzron, this list stops at v. 45. From v. 46 onwards Calev ben Yephunneh's family is traced *(Malbim* explaining the tradition of the Sages; see comm. to v. 19).

(3) Both Calevs had a daughter named Achsah. Calev ben Yephunneh, who lived after Calev ben Chetzron, called his daughter by the same name as his forebear and namesake had called his *(Malbim).*

50. אֶפְרָתָה בְּכוֹר בֶּן־חוּר כָּלֵב בְּנֵי הָיוּ אֵלֶּה — *These were the sons of Calev the son of Chur, the first-born of Ephrathah.* Verse 19 had taught that Calev married Ephrath who bore him Chur. Thus, Chur was the son of Calev, not his father. The *Mefaresh* suggests that the verse might be read: *These are the children of Calev whose son [בֶּן, son, is read like בְּנוֹ, whose son] was Chur the first-born of Ephrath.* According to this translation the verse stresses that

נב אֲבִי בֵית־לֶחֶם חָרֵף אֲבִי בֵית־גָּדֵר: וַיִּהְיוּ בָנִים לְשׁוֹבָל
נג אֲבִי קִרְיַת יְעָרִים הָרֹאֶה חֲצִי הַמְּנֻחוֹת: וּמִשְׁפְּחוֹת
קִרְיַת יְעָרִים הַיִּתְרִי וְהַפּוּתִי וְהַשֻּׁמָתִי וְהַמִּשְׁרָעִי מֵאֵלֶּה
נד יָצְאוּ הַצָּרְעָתִי וְהָאֶשְׁתָּאֻלִי: בְּנֵי
שַׁלְמָא בֵּית לֶחֶם וּנְטוֹפָתִי עַטְרוֹת בֵּית יוֹאָב וַחֲצִי

Chur was the first-born of Ephrath only. Calev himself had other sons who were born before him.

However, the syntax is certainly difficult if this is the meaning. Most commentators assume that Chur, the son of Calev and Ephrath, called one of his sons Calev and that our verse deals with the great-grandchildren of the Calev mentioned in v. 19 (who was either Calev ben Chetzron — *Radak*; or Calev ben Yephunneh — *Gra* following the Sages). [There is no difficulty in assuming that Chur had a son Calev, although verse 20 tells only of a son Uri. As we noted in comm. to v. 42, it is possible that the earlier Calevite genealogy deals only with those names which are known to us from the Torah.] In the opinion of the *Anonymous Commentator*, this Calev is identical with Calev ben Yephunneh. [See further in Section Two p. 395*ff*.]

קִרְיַת יְעָרִים — *Kiriath Yearim.* Kiriath Yearim is mentioned in *Joshua* 15:9 and 60 among the cities of Judah.

51. אֲבִי בֵית־לָחֶם ... אֲבִי בֵית־גָּדֵר — *Father of Bethlehem ... father of Beth Gader.* In this verse *Targum* twice renders אֲבִי as *chieftain*, although in verses 44, 45 and 49 he used *father*. See further, 4:4.

52. הָרֹאֶה חֲצִי הַמְּנֻחוֹת — *Who oversaw half of Manachath.* The translation follows the *Mefaresh.* Manachath is a place name mentioned in 8:6. הָרֹאֶה, *he who sees*, can well mean: *he who oversees*, thus a ruler. Verse 54 will deal with the situation of the other half of the town of Manachath. [This phrase describes the son of Shoval and accordingly the plural בָּנִים is used as בֶּן, the singular. See above v. 7.]

Radak quotes commentators who equate מְנֻחוֹת with Jerusalem, which is elsewhere referred to as מְנוּחָה, *a place of rest* (see

Zevachim 119a).

Gra takes הָרֹאֶה as a proper name, *Haroeh,* and identifies him as the רְאָיָה, *Reaiah,* mentioned in 4:2 as a son of Shoval. [*Malbim,*[1] too, follows this explanation. He points out that the *hey* at the beginning of the word, which normally stands for the definite article but is here part of the name itself, is an irregularity which occurs fairly frequently. As examples he cites 4:3,6,8; *Ezra* 2:55; *Nehemiah* 3:21.] Accordingly, the verse should be translated as: *Now Shoval, father of Kiriath Yearim, had a son — Haroeh, ruler of half of Manachath.* [The identification of Haroeh with the Reaiah of 4:2 is also made by *Radak* and *Metzudos* there.]

חֲצִי הַמְּנֻחוֹת could also be either the names of two sons, one called חֲצִי, *Chatzi,* and one called הַמְּנֻחוֹת, *Hamenuchoth,* or the combined words could be the name of one person. [*Radak,* who also prefers to take הָרֹאֶה חֲצִי הַמְּנֻחוֹת as proper names, notes that occasionally we find names made up of words which have descriptive meanings. He cites גִּדַּלְתִּי וְרוֹמַמְתִּי, *Gidalti VeRomammi,* from 25:29. These are words which have their own meaning (*I have made great; I have exalted*) and still they serve as proper nouns.]

Targum prefers to translate this difficult phrase midrashically: הָרֹאֶה, lit. *he who sees,* becomes: *students;* and חֲצִי הַמְּנֻחוֹת becomes: *Kohanim who [have the right to] divide [חֲצִי, half, thus a portion] sacrifices* [probably from the association מְנוּחָה, *Jerusalem;* see *Radak's* opinion above].

Thus, Shoval, chieftain of Kiriath Yearim, had children who were great in Torah and who were *Kohanim.* [Since Shoval was from Judah, these *Kohanim* must have been descended from him through his daughters. Cf. v. 53.]

1. It should be noted that *Malbim's* explanation holds good according to either of the two explanations he offers at v. 49 (see comm. there). Either way the Chur of 4:1 is identical with our Chur — and his son Shoval, with our Shoval. The difference is only whether he is a son of Carmi/Calev (there) or a descendant through his daughter.

2

52-54

father of Bethlehem; Chareph, father of Beth Gader. ⁵² *Now Shoval father of Kiriath Yearim had a son who oversaw half of Manachath.* ⁵³ *And the families of Kiriath Yearim — the Yithrites, the Puthites, the Shumathites, and the Mishraites; from these the Tzorathites and Eshtaolites were descended.* ⁵⁴ *The sons of Salma — the inhabitants of Bethlehem, the Netophathites, the inhabitants of Atroth Beth*

53. וּמִשְׁפְּחוֹת קִרְיַת יְעָרִים הַיִּתְרִי וְהַפּוּתִי — *And the families of Kiriath Yearim · — the Yithrites, the Puthites.* The people of Kiriath Yearim who were descended from Shoval (v. 50) were divided into families, each family called by the name of its patriarch. This is in much the same way that the tribes of Israel were divided into families, as recorded in *Numbers* ch. 26 (*Radak*).

מֵאֵלֶּה יָצְאוּ הַצָּרְעָתִי וְהָאֶשְׁתָּאֻלִי — *From these the Tzorathites and the Eshtaolites were descended.* Judges 13:25 mentions two neighboring cities Tzorah and Eshtaol which lay in the camp of Dan. Our verse implies that these cities belonged to Judah. A number of solutions are offered.

— The *Mefaresh* suggests that the cities themselves belonged to Judah, but the territory between them was part of Dan. (See ArtScroll *Joshua* p. 294 for the relative positions of Judah and Dan in the division of the land.)

— *Radak* notes the expression *camp of Dan* which implies a temporary residence. He suggests that the cities did indeed lie in Judah's portion of the land but that Dan lived there temporarily, until its own lands had been conquered.

— *Malbim* sees no difficulty in postulating two sets of cities — one in Dan's territory referred to in *Judges* and one in Judah's territory mentioned here.

In any event, the intent of our verse is to teach that the inhabitants of these two cities were descended from the Shovalite families mentioned above. *Malbim* notes that the descent of the city of Tzorah is given in 4:2.

54. בְּנֵי שַׂלְמָא בֵּית לֶחֶם וּנְטוֹפָתִי — *The sons of Salma — the inhabitants of Bethlehem, the Netophathites.* Verse 51 had introduced Salma [the son of Chur's son Calev] as *father of Bethlehem.* His line is now taken up with the statement that the inhabitants of Bethlehem and Netophah were descended from him. From *Nehemiah* 7:26 it

appears that Netophah was a city in the vicinity of Bethlehem.

עַטְרוֹת בֵּית יוֹאָב — *The inhabitants of Atroth Beth Yoav.* *Malbim* points out that the phrase *the sons of* at the beginning of the verse is to be read together with each of the subsequent place names. The sense of the verse is that the inhabitants of each of these places were descended from Salma.

Malbim further points out that there were a number of cities which had the name Atroth. For this reason, each was identified by a further description. In our verse we deal with the Atroth which belonged to a Yoavite family. Other cities of that name, which are ascribed to other families, are mentioned in *Numbers* 32:35 and in *Joshua* 16:5 and 18:13. See further 4:3.

Targum substitutes an aggadah for the literal translation. The Mishnah in *Taanis* teaches that on a certain day of the year only members of two particular families were allowed to donate the wood to be burnt on the altar. *Yerushalmi Taanis* 4:4 explains that when Yerovoam seceded to form the Northern Kingdom, he placed sentries on the roads leading to Jerusalem to prevent people from going there for the holidays. Both these families managed to trick the sentries into letting them pass. One, who wanted to bring their *bikkurim, first fruits,* to Jerusalem hid them in baskets and covered them in such a way that they could pass through undetected. The other, who wanted to donate wood for the altar, formed the wood into ladders and pretended to be workmen going to a job. Once they came to Jerusalem they broke up the ladders and donated the wood for use on the altar. For their devotion to the Temple service these familes were rewarded by being given the exclusive right to donate wood on a given date. The name of the progenitor of the one family is given as סָלְמַי הַנְּתוֹצָתִי, *Salmai, the Nethotzathite,* which commentators interpret as a name formed from סֻלָּם, *ladder,* to commemorate the subterfuge which he had used. *Targum* must have had הַנְּטוֹפָתִי in his text of *Tannis* 28a, and assumed that reference is to the שַׂלְמָא ... נְטוֹפָתִי of our verse.

Furthermore, his tradition must have been

ב °יֹשְׁבֵי ק' נה הַמְּנֻחְתִּי הַצָּרְעִי: וּמִשְׁפְּחוֹת סוֹפְרִים °יֹשְׁבוּ יַעְבֵּץ

נה תִּרְעָתִים שִׁמְעָתִים שׂוּכָתִים הֵמָּה הַקֵּינִים הַבָּאִים וְאֵלֶּה הָיוּ בְנֵי

ג א מֵחַמַּת אֲבִי בֵית־רֵכָב:

א

---

slightly different to that of the Talmud because he combines the activities of the two families into one. He renders our verse: 'The sons of Salma ... were righteous and their name was like good spices [וּנְטוֹפָתִי, from נָטָף, *a spice*], for they annulled the sentry posts which Yerovoam set up on the road so that no one should bring up *bikkurim* to Jerusalem. So Salma's sons disguised their *bikkurim* fruits in a basket [עֲטָרוֹת from the Aramaic עטר, *to disappear*] and they would cut wood and make ladders and go up to Jerusalem to arrange wood on the altar for sacrifices. These come from the family of Yoav ben Tzeruiah (בֵּית יוֹאָב) ...'"

וַחֲצִי הַמְּנַחְתִּי — *Half of the Manachathites.* Verse 52 had recorded that half of the city of Manachath was inhabited by descendants of Shoval. Our verse now teaches that the other half was inhabited by descendants of his brother Salma (Gra).

הַצָּרְעִי — *And the Tzorathites.* According to v. 53 the town of Tzorah was inhabited by descendants of Shoval. Our verse indicates that some of the Tzorathites were also descended from Salma.

We have taken the word הַצָּרְעִי as separate from the previous phrase because that is implied by *Gra. Malbim* takes the phrase together. He translates the phrase: [Also descended from Salma:] *Half the city of Manachath in which people from Tzorah had settled.* [Those Tzorathites, however, were descended from Shoval. The verse teaches that half the residents were descended from Salma.]

55. וּמִשְׁפְּחוֹת סוֹפְרִים יֹשְׁבֵי יַעְבֵּץ — *And families of scribes, dwellers in Yabetz.* The verse continues to list families which were descended from Salma (v. 51). *Scribes* are meant here in the sense of *teachers.* These were families who taught Torah in Israel (*Radak*).

Targum, presumably based on a Midrashic source that has been lost to us, identifies וּמִשְׁפְּחוֹת סוֹפְרִים as Moses' grandson Rechaviah (see 23:17). He reads the end of the verse (הֵמָּה הַקֵּינִים) as follows: *They are the Salmaites, sons of Tziporah* [see below in *Malbim's* explanation of קֵינִים], *who are listed among the other Levites* (23:14) *who descend from Moses, leader of Israel, who was better for Israel than riders and chariots* (מֵחַמַּת אֲבִי בֵית רֵכָב).

יֹשְׁבֵי יַעְבֵּץ — *Dwellers in Yabetz.* This phrase can be understood in a number of ways. *Radak* suggests that there was a city of that name called after Yabetz (4:9ff) who had been a great and famous teacher in Israel [see below].

The *Mefaresh* in his first interpretation agrees that reference is to the Yabetz of ch. 4, but is of the opinion that our phrase does not mean that they dwelt in a city of that name but rather that they lived under his rule and tutelage. This, on the basis of 4:9 which teaches that Yabetz *was more worthy of honor than any of his brothers.*

In a second interpretation the *Mefaresh* suggests that Yabetz here may be identical with the city of Ebetz mentioned in *Joshua* 19:20, which lay in the portion of Yissachar.

תִּרְעָתִים/שִׁמְעָתִים שׂוּכָתִים — *The Tirathites, the Shimathites and the Suchathites.* These are names of the various families referred to earlier as *families of scribes* (*Mefaresh*).

הֵמָּה הַקֵּינִים הַבָּאִים מֵחַמַּת אֲבִי בֵית־רֵכָב — *They are the Kenites who are descended from Chammath, father of Beth Rechav.* There are a number of possibilities for interpreting the phrase הֵמָּה הַקֵּינִים.

The *Mefaresh* suggests that reference may be to the city קַיִן (*Joshua* 15:57). The families of scribes came from the city of Kain, for it is there that their ancestor Chammath, chieftain of Beth Rachav, lived.

This explanation is only possible according to the *Mefaresh's* first explanation of *dwellers in Yabetz.* According to his second explanation, the home city of these families is given as Ebetz and could not be Kain.

Alternatively, the *Mefaresh* as well as *Radak* suggests that קֵינִים may be the equivalent of the Aramaic קֵינָאָה (*Targum, Judges* 17:4), which is the translation of צוֹרֵף, *a smelter.* The families of scribes apparently made their living by smelting metals.

Radak also suggests that קֵינִים is the name of another of the families.

Malbim offers an entirely different interpretation. He, as do the Sages (*Sotah* 11a,

Yoav, half of the Manachathites, and the Tzorathites. ⁵⁵ And families of scribes, dwellers in Yabetz — the Tirathites, the Shimathites and the Suchathites; they are the Kenites who are descended from Chammath, father of Beth Rechav.

Sanhedrin 106a), identifies קֵינִים as the Kenites, descendants of Moses' father-in-law, Yithro (Judges 4:11). These had accompanied the Israelites into the land of Israel and had been given the area surrounding the destroyed Jericho as a homestead [see Rashi, Numbers 10:32]. Eventually these families migrated to the wilderness of Judah in order to study under Yabetz [see Section Two p. 397]. They settled among the families of Judah and, eventually, became indistinguishable from them. Ezra, therefore, found it necessary to record that these families of scholars were not, in fact, part of Judah but Kenites.

הַבָּאִים מֵחַמַּת אֲבִי בֵית־רֵכָב — Who are descended from Chammath, father of Beth Rechav. The family of Yonadav ben Rechav had been prominent in the years preceding the destruction. Jeremiah ch. 35 records how the prophet had been told by God to collect the family members and to bring them to the Temple grounds and there to offer them wine. They refused, telling Jeremiah that their father had commanded them to drink no wine, build no houses, sow no fields nor plant any vineyards, but to live a life of complete simplicity in tents. This, as Sifri to Behaaloscha teaches, was because knowing that it had already been decreed that the Temple was to be destroyed, Yonadav felt as if it' had already been destroyed. [See ArtScroll Ezekiel, pref. ch. 1 for the lesson taught by Shir HaShirim Rabbah 3:3 that all spiritual content had left the Temple long before its physical destruction.] The sensitivity of Yonadav, and the obedience which his children paid his wishes, were held up by Jeremiah as a rebuke to the people. God was their father and they had paid Him less heed than the Rechavites had paid their father.

These Rechavites were descended from a man named Chammath who was also the progenitor of the Kenites.

It should be noted that the interpretation of this last phrase of the sentence (with which all commentators concur) does not agree with the

division of the words indicated by the cantillation (trop) of the phrase. This combines הַבָּאִים (which we translated who were descended, but which translated literally means who came) with the previous phrase. That is, They are the Kenites who came. The last words, from Chammath, father of Beth Rechav, stand by themselves. This division seems to be in agreement with the interpretation of the Sages offered below.

The Sages (Sifri) teach that: Yithro, Moses' father-in-law, was called Chovav because he loved the Torah (חוֹבָב from חבב, to cherish). No proselyte ever loved the Torah as much as Yithro did. And even as he loved the Torah so did his children. (Sifri continues with a description of Jeremiah's experiences with the Rechavites cited above in the comm.)

[Now, as a reward] God appointed them scribes, as it is written [our verse] תִּרְעָתִים [from the Aramaic תַּרְעָא, gate], for they sat [as judges] at the gates of Jerusalem; שִׁמְעָתִים [from שמע, to hear], for they listened to their father's commands; שׂוּכָתִים, [from סכך, to cast shade], for they lived in huts.

[What is the meaning of] יוֹשְׁבֵי יַעְבֵּץ, dwellers in Yabetz? [It teaches that] they left Jericho and traveled to Yabetz to learn Torah from him. As it is written (4:10): And Yabetz prayed to the God of Israel ... and God brought about that for which he had asked (4:11). They lacked a teacher and he lacked students. So they who sought a teacher went to him who sought students, as it is written (Judges 1:16): And the sons of Keni, the father-in-law of Moses, went up from the city of the date trees ... (Sifri Behaaloscha). See Section Two p. 397.

⋙ Calev's genealogy/Gra

In order to help understand Gra's interpretation of Calev's genealogy, we present a list of the relevant verses according to Gra's system. We include for this purpose Gra's commentary to two relevant verses in chapter four:

2:9: The text introduces us to

דָּוִיד אֲשֶׁר נוֹלַד־לוֹ בְּחֶבְרוֹן הַבְּכוֹר | אַמְנֹן לַאֲחִינֹעַם
ב הַיִּזְרְעֵאלִית שֵׁנִי דָנִיֵּאל לַאֲבִיגַיִל הַכַּרְמְלִית: הַשְּׁלִשִׁי
לְאַבְשָׁלוֹם בֶּן־מַעֲכָה בַּת־תַּלְמַי מֶלֶךְ גְּשׁוּר הָרְבִיעִי
ג אֲדֹנִיָּה בֶן־חַגִּית: הַחֲמִישִׁי שְׁפַטְיָה לַאֲבִיטָל הַשִּׁשִּׁי

Chetzron's son Calev (*Cheluvai* — see comm.). Calev ben Yephunneh was destined to marry his daughter (see v. 18).

2:18: Calev ben Chetzron fathered a daughter — Azuvah. The text notes that this Azuvah was a woman (עֲזוּבָה אִשָּׁה) because up to this point only male descendants had been listed. In addition the word אִשָּׁה is inserted to let us know that she was also a *wife* of significance — since she eventually married Calev ben Yephunneh (who is mentioned in the next verse) and bore him the three sons mentioned in our verse.

2:19: The previous verse has taught us that Azuvah had a husband of significance but had not identified him. In this verse we learn that this husband was called Calev [who cannot have been Calev ben Chetzron since he was Azuvah's father, as in v. 18) and that after Azuvah's death this Calev married Ephrath. This Calev is the Calev ben Yephunneh whom we know from the Torah, and Ephrath is Miriam.

Chur was born from this union, and this necessitates the assumption which the Sages make in *Sanhedrin* 69b. (See above.)

2:24: Chetzron had a posthumous son called Ashchur Avi Tekoa. *Gra* identifies this Ashchur as Yephunneh, the father of the other Calev. Thus, Calev ben Yephunneh was the nephew of Calev ben Chetzron. [Ashchur Avi Takoa/Yephunneh was Chetzron's son and a brother of the first Calev.]

[*Gra's* identification is presumably based on *Sotah* 12a which interprets the names Ashchur and Avi and Takoa as refering to Calev ben Yephunneh. It cannot be that Ashchur was actually Calev because that would mean that Hebron had two sons called Calev. Rather, then, *Gra* assumes that Ashchur is the *father* of Calev ben Yephunneh and the Talmud sees qualities hinted at in the father's name reflected in the son.]

2:42: The text reverts to Calev ben Chetzron. His progeny is listed here after that of Ram and Yerachmeel because he was the youngest. He had been mentioned briefly out of turn earlier only because his female descendants were significant and some important female descendants of Ram had also been listed (v. 16). Now his line is taken up in detail.

2:48: *Gra* does not tell us which Calev is referred to here. It might be argued that since v. 42 dealt with Calev ben Chetzron, so too does this verse. On the other hand since we must assume that Calev ben Yephunneh appears in v. 50 (see below), it is possible that he is introduced already here.

2:49: See comm. for the various possibilities of identifying Calev's daughter, Achsah, and consequently Calev himself, in this verse.

2:50: Chur is introduced as the first-born of Ephrath and as among the sons of Calev. This must be Calev ben Yephunneh (see above on v. 19).

4:1: *Gra* thinks that each of the men mentioned in this verse was the son of the previous one. Thus Peretz is a son of Judah, Chetzron of Peretz, and Carmi of Chetzron. He identifies Carmi as Calev ben Chetzron. Since Chur is given next, it would seem that he was a son of Calev, son of Chetzron. Since this goes against everything which we have learned above we must assume that the implication is not so much 'son' as descendant and that Chur is descended from Calev ben Chetzron through his grandson Calev ben Yephunneh and through his daughter Azuvah. She, the Sages teach, is identical with Ephrath — both describe Moses' sister, Miriam, and she married Calev ben Yephunneh (v. 19) and bore Chur.

4:5: See above under 2:24. The Sages (*Sotah* 12a) interpret the names of the two wives Chelah and Naarah as referring to Miriam. But this would mean that they take Ashchur Avi Tekoa as being Calev ben Yephunneh. But *Gra* thinks that Ashchur is Yephunneh, not Calev. Consequently, we must understand our

3
1-4

Now these were the sons of David who were born to him in Hebron: The first-born, Amnon by Achinoam the Yezreelitess; the second, Daniel by Avigail the Carmelitess. ² The third, Avshalom the son of Maachah, the daughter of Talmai, king of Geshur; the fourth, Adoniyah son of Chaggith. ³ The fifth, Shephatiah by Avital; the sixth, Yithream by Eglah his wife. ⁴ Six

---

verse as meaning: 'He whose qualities are expressed in [his father's] name Ashchur

Avi Tekoa [that is, Calev ben Yephunneh] had two wives.'

III

⋅◆§ The Sons of David

The genealogy of Chetzron's son Ram was given in 2:10-15 up to and including David. It was then interrupted so that the story of Calev could be taken up. Our chapter picks up Ram's line once more with a listing of David's sons (Radak).

As in II Samuel 3:2-5 and 5:13-16, David's children are listed in two groups: those born to him in Hebron and those born to him in Jerusalem. [For the historical background, see the early chapters of II Samuel. See particularly 2:3-4 and 5:5 for these two periods of David's kingship.]

1. אֲשֶׁר נוֹלַד־לוֹ — Who were born to him. The use of a predicate in the singular for the plural noun בְּנֵי, sons, is irregular. See comm. 2:3.

שֵׁנִי דָּנִיֵּאל לַאֲבִיגַיִל הַכַּרְמְלִית — The second, Daniel by Avigail the Carmelitess. This Daniel is identical with the Chileav of II Samuel 3:3. Although Scripture says nothing about him, the Sages teach us that he was a man whose life was of such consummate purity that he was one of only four people who died because of the 'plot of the snake' [i.e., only because death had been decreed upon man as a result of Adam's sin] (Shabbos 55b). He was so devoted to a life of study and sanctity that he rejected any idea of inheriting his father's throne.

2. הַשְּׁלִשִׁי לְאַבְשָׁלוֹם בֶּן־מַעֲכָה בַּת־תַּלְמַי מֶלֶךְ גְּשׁוּר — The third, Avshalom the son of Maachah, the daughter of Talmai, king of Geshur. The lamed in לְאַבְשָׁלוֹם is irregular. Radak cites examples to demonstrate that occasionally a lamed is used in place of the accusative אֶת. The phrase should be understood as though it were written: הַשְּׁלִשִׁי אֶת אַבְשָׁלוֹם, Third [he fathered] Avshalom. Gra thinks that because Avshalom was so wicked that he was eventually killed for rebelling against his father (II Samuel ch. 15-19), it is not really appropriate that he should be listed among David's sons. The only reason why he is mentioned is as a bridge to his descendants.

The phrase is to be understood: The third [son is significant because of the children who would one day be born] to Avshalom. Malbim suggests that לְאַבְשָׁלוֹם should be read as though it were written לֹא אַב שָׁלוֹם. אַבְשָׁלוֹם means father of peace — the very opposite of what Avshalom turned out to be. Ezra added the lamed as a sign of scorn; this was no peaceful man.

There is another way in which Avshalom is listed differently than his two older brothers. Their relationship to their mother was stated by saying that they were born לַאֲחִינֹעַם, by Achinoam, and לַאֲבִיגַיִל, by Avigail, respectively. Avshalom is introduced as בֶּן מַעֲכָה, the son of Maachah. Malbim suggests that this is so because, as the Sages trace it, the aberrations which appeared in Avshalom's character originated in his non-Jewish mother.

הָרְבִיעִי אֲדֹנִיָּה בֶן־חַגִּית — The fourth, Adoniyah son of Chaggith. Once more we have the irregularity of בֶּן חַגִּית, son of Chaggith, instead of לְחַגִּית, by Chaggith, the formula used for the first two and last two sons. Malbim suggests that just as much of the blame for Avshalom's tragedy devolved on his mother, Maachah, so too Chaggith was responsible for much of what was wrong in Adoniyah. He did what he did because he was בֶּן חַגִּית, the son of Chaggith (cf. I Kings 1:6 and commentaries there).

3. הַחֲמִישִׁי שְׁפַטְיָה לַאֲבִיטָל — The fifth,

---

[39]   I Chronicles

ד יִתְרְעָם לְעֶגְלָה אִשְׁתּוֹ: שִׁשָּׁה נוֹלַד־לוֹ בְחֶבְרוֹן וַיִּמְלָךְ־ ג
שָׁם שֶׁבַע שָׁנִים וְשִׁשָּׁה חֳדָשִׁים וּשְׁלֹשִׁים וְשָׁלוֹשׁ שָׁנָה ד־ז
ה מָלַךְ בִּירוּשָׁלָ͏ִם: וְאֵלֶּה נוּלְּדוּ־לוֹ בִּירוּשָׁלָ͏ִם
שִׁמְעָא וְשׁוֹבָב וְנָתָן וּשְׁלֹמֹה אַרְבָּעָה לְבַת־שׁוּעַ בַּת־
ו־ז עַמִּיאֵל: וְיִבְחָר וֶאֱלִישָׁמָע וֶאֱלִיפָלֶט: וְנֹגַהּ וְנֶפֶג וְיָפִיעַ:

Shephatiah by Avital. Shephatiah does not recur in Scripture. According to *Kesubos* 62b, R' Yehudah the Prince, redactor of the Mishnah, was descended from him. [R' Yehudah the Prince (d. 190-195 c.e.) was scion of a great family descended from Hillel the Babylonian (d. 3768). The Sages teach that when Jacob blessed his son Judah (*Genesis* 49:10), promising that throughout history it would be primarily his descendants who would act as the arbiters of the law to the people, reference was to Hillel and his descendants (*Sanhedrin* 5a).]

הַשִּׁשִּׁי יִתְרְעָם לְעֶגְלָה אִשְׁתּוֹ — *The sixth, Yithream by Eglah his wife.* Throughout aggadic literature there is an undisputed tradition that Eglah is another name for Saul's daughter Michal, whom the then-king had given to David in return for his heroic feat of having killed two hundred Philistines. [See the account in *I Samuel* 18:20ff.] The Sages offer a number of explanations for the name עֶגְלָה, *Eglah,* which literally means a *calf.*

— He loved her as one would love a calf (*Sanhedrin* 21a). [A calf was a common symbol of endearment; the Talmud demonstrates this from *Judges* 14:19.]

— She refused a yoke just as a calf will not allow itself to be yoked (*Midrash*

Shocher Tov 59). [Reference is to the incident described in *I Samuel* 19:11ff, when Michal, in defiance of her father whose yoke she would not accept, helped David to escape from the soldiers whom Saul had sent to arrest him.]

— She panted like a [dying] calf and died [in childbirth] (*Yerushalmi, Succah* 5:4). [Reference is to the punishment decreed against Michal that she would not have a child עַד יוֹם מוֹתָהּ, *until the day of her death.*[1]]

The seemingly redundant expression *Eglah his wife* is noted by the commentators.

— It indicates David's special love for her (*Mefaresh*).

— She was his first wife (*Radak*).

— The expression refers not only to Eglah but to all the women mentioned in this section (*Metzudos*).

— We might have thought that Michal could not have been David's wife for one of two considerations: (a) He had previously been married to her sister, Merav (*I Samuel* 18:19), and the Torah prohibits a marriage to one's wife's sister. (b) After Michal had married David, Saul, in his hatred of David, gave her in marriage to Palti ben Laish (*I Samuel* 44). Had Palti had marital relations with her, she would have been disqualified from returning to

---

1. This refers to the incident described in *II Samuel* 6:16-23 where Michal witnessed David dancing with abandon as the Ark containing the Tablets was brought up to Jerusalem. Feeling that it demeaned the dignity of the King, Michal upbraided David for this act. Because her concern for his dignity over that of the Holy Ark, and consequently her rebuke of David, were unjustified, she was punished. *And Michal, the daughter of Saul, had no child to the day of her death* (v. 23 there).

Sanhedrin 21a points out that the punishment cannot possibly have been that Michal would be childless. Yithream had already been born in Hebron long before the incident took place. Consequently, the meaning must be that she would have no more children until she died.

But the *Yerushalmi* quoted in the commentary understood the punishment differently. She would indeed have another child but only on the day of her death. Others would bring it up — she would be denied the joy of motherhood.

This would have been an apt punishment. As *Bamidbar Rabbah* 4 tells the story, David justified his lack of reticence to Michal by comparing himself to a child in the presence of its mother. The child knows no embarrassment and will uncover himself in his mother's presence. So too did David feel no sense of shame when in the wild abandon of his dance some parts of his body were bared.

Michal apparently lacked the sensibility to understand the intimacy of such a mother-child relationship. Her punishment was that from that day onward she would never again be allowed to mother a child.

were born to him in Hebron and he reigned there for seven years and six months; and he reigned thirty-three years in Jerusalem. ⁵ And these were born to him in Jerusalem; Shimea, Shovav, Nathan, and Solomon — four to Bath Shua daughter of Ammiel. ⁶ And Yivchar, Elishama, and Eliphelet. ⁷ And Nogah, Nepheg, and Yaphia. ⁸ And

David. However, neither of these considerations were applicable. Merav had already died when David took Michal (see *Sanhedrin* 19b), and the prohibition against marrying one's wife's sister applies only during the lifetime of the wife (*Leviticus* 218:18). Furthermore, Palti, with unparalleled restraint, had refrained from touching Michal through the years in which they were ostensibly living as man and wife (*Sanhedrin* 19b). It was to stress that Michal was permitted to David, and that neither of these two considerations stood in the way, that she is described as 'his wife' (*Gra*).

4. שִׁשָּׁה נוֹלַד־לוֹ בְחֶבְרוֹן — *Six were born to him in Hebron.* See footnote to 2:6 for a discussion of the seemingly redundant numbers which are often given after a list of names.

וַיִּמְלָךְ־שָׁם שֶׁבַע שָׁנִים וְשִׁשָּׁה חֳדָשִׁים — *And he reigned there for seven years and six months.* Together with the thirty-three years which he ruled in Jerusalem, this

would give David a total of forty years and six months as king. However, *I Kings* 2:11 counts only forty years and leaves out the six months. It is, of course, possible that the total years are simply rounded off (*Yerushalmi, Rosh Hashanah* 1:1). However, *Sanhedrin* 107a proves from this discrepancy that during his six-month flight from Avshalom, David 'had leprosy, the Shechinah departed from him, and the Sanhedrin had no dealings with him,' and for this reason, they are not counted as part of his reign. According to one opinion in *Yerushalmi* (*Rosh Hashanah*, there), he had the legal status of a commoner during those six months.

5. וְאֵלֶה נוּלְדוּ־לוֹ בִּירוּשָׁלָיִם — *And these were born to him in Jerusalem.* The list of sons who were born to David in Jerusalem is given three times in Scripture. In addition to the list here, we have one in II *Samuel* 5:14ff and one later in I *Chronicles* 14:4ff. The following chart is included to facilitate comparison.

	A — **Samuel**	B — **Chronicles** (here)	C — **Chronicles** (ch. 14)
1.	שַׁמּוּעַ, Shamua	שִׁמְעָא, Shimea	שַׁמּוּעַ, Shamua
2.	שׁוֹבָב, Shovav	שׁוֹבָב, Shovav	שׁוֹבָב, Shovav
3.	נָתָן, Nathan	נָתָן, Nathan	נָתָן, Nathan
4.	שְׁלֹמֹה, Solomon	שְׁלֹמֹה, Solomon	שְׁלֹמֹה, Solomon
5.	יִבְחָר, Yivchar	יִבְחָר, Yivchar	יִבְחָר, Yivchar
6.	אֱלִישׁוּעַ, Elishua	אֱלִישָׁמָע, Elishama	אֱלִישׁוּעַ, Elishua
7.		אֱלִיפֶלֶט, Eliphelet	אֶלְפָּלֶט, Elpalet
8.		נֹגַהּ, Nogah	נֹגַהּ, Nogah
9.	נֶפֶג, Nepheg	נֶפֶג, Nepheg	נֶפֶג, Nepheg
10.	יָפִיעַ, Yaphia	יָפִיעַ, Yaphia	יָפִיעַ, Yaphia
11.	אֱלִישָׁמָע, Elishama	אֱלִישָׁמָע, Elishama	אֱלִישָׁמָע, Elishama
12.	אֶלְיָדָע, Eliada	אֱלִיָדָע, Eliada	בְּעֶלְיָדָע, Beeliada
13.	אֱלִיפֶלֶט, Eliphelet	אֱלִיפָלֶט, Eliphelet	אֱלִיפֶלֶט, Eliphelet

We note various minor spelling variations: (1) שַׁמּוּעַ (A and C) and שִׁמְעָא (B); (6) אֱלִישׁוּעַ (A and C) and אֱלִישָׁמָע (B); (7) אֱלִיפֶלֶט (B) and אֶלְפָּלֶט (C).

Of these, the first and third seem insignificant and are of a type often found in Scriptural names. The second, however, is a substantive change in meaning. אֱלִישָׁמָע

seems to mean *God hears.* אֱלִישׁוּעַ is less certain. There are three possible meanings for שׁוּעַ: *cry for help* (as in *Job* 30:24); *someone noble* or *wealthy* (as in *Job* 34:19); or it may derive from ישע, *to save* or *deliver*, hence, *salvation.* [It is unlikely that the word means *to answer a supplication*, as for example in *Genesis* 4:4,

וֶאֱלִישָׁמָע וְאֶלְיָדָע וֶאֱלִיפָלֶט תִּשְׁעָה: כָּל בְּנֵי דָוִיד מִלְּבַד

י בְּנֵי־פִילַגְשִׁים וְתָמָר אֲחוֹתָם: וּבֶן־

שְׁלֹמֹה רְחַבְעָם אֲבִיָּה בְנוֹ אָסָא בְנוֹ יְהוֹשָׁפָט בְּנוֹ:

יא־יב יוֹרָם בְּנוֹ אֲחַזְיָהוּ בְנוֹ יוֹאָשׁ בְּנוֹ: אֲמַצְיָהוּ בְנוֹ עֲזַרְיָה

יג־יד בְּנוֹ יוֹתָם בְּנוֹ: אָחָז בְּנוֹ חִזְקִיָּהוּ בְנוֹ מְנַשֶּׁה בְנוֹ: אָמוֹן

טו בְּנוֹ יֹאשִׁיָּהוּ בְנוֹ: וּבְנֵי יֹאשִׁיָּהוּ הַבְּכוֹר יוֹחָנָן הַשֵּׁנִי

---

since that word derives from the root שעה.
Cf. *Job* 14:6.]

Malbim suggests that the change to
אֱלִישׁוּעַ occured when the younger brother
was born who was also called אֱלִישָׁמָע (11).
Perhaps they tried to maintain the basic
meaning of the name — אֱלִישָׁמָע, *God hears
[and answers]*; אֱלִישׁוּעַ, *god [hears our
prayers and] sends salvation*.

In this context note should be taken of
the name of the mother of the first four
sons given in our verse: בַּת־שׁוּעַ בַּת־עַמִּיאֵל,
Bath Shua daughter of Ammiel, who is, of
course, identical with בַּת־שֶׁבַע בַּת־אֱלִיעָם,
Bathsheva daughter of Eliam (II *Samuel*
11:3). The change from בַּת־שֶׁבַע to בַּת־שׁוּעַ
can be easily explained on the basis that
beis and *vav* are interchangeable, and are in
fact often interchanged (see *Ramban*,
Genesis 30:20). *Radak* suggests that she
was known by both names and was
sometimes called by the one, sometimes by
the other. Her father's two names are not
only similar in the sense that they have
identical letters in varying order, but they
seem to be similar in meaning. Both seem to
point to an exquisite closeness between
God and nation: עַמִּיאֵל [*Ammiel*], *My
nation, God*; אֱלִיעָם, *My God, nation*.

Another discrepancy between the lists is
that the two sources in *Chronicles* list nine
sons while *Samuel* lists only seven. The
two additional ones are אֱלִיפָלֶט, *Eliphelet*,
and נֹגַה, *Nogah*. Commentators suggest
that these two died early [which would
explain why another son was also called
אֱלִיפָלֶט, *Eliphelet*] and were therefore not
listed in *Samuel*.

שִׁמְעָא ... — *Shimea* ... The sequence in
which these sons are listed is problematic.
II *Samuel* 12:24 clearly indicates that
Solomon was the first son born to David
and Bathsheba after the infant death of
their first child. We must therefore
conclude that the listing does not follow
chronology (*Metzudos*). But then we are

left with the question of why Solomon,
who was both the oldest and most
important, is listed last. Perhaps Solomon
is mentioned last because it is his genealogy
and not that of any of the others which is
taken up in v. 10. *Gra*, however, is of the
opinion that this verse proves that
Solomon was actually the youngest of
Bathsheva's four sons.

8. תִּשְׁעָה — *Nine. Gra* points out that it was
necessary to give the total number because
there are two names — אֱלִישָׁמָע, *Elishama*,
and אֱלִיפָלֶט, *Eliphelet* — which are repeated.
The stressing of the total number
emphasizes that in each case there were two
people who carried the same name.

9. כָּל בְּנֵי דָוִיד — *All these were sons of
David.* These were all the sons that he had
from his regular wives. The verse goes on
to say that there were other children born
to him from concubines (*Metzudos*).

וְתָמָר אֲחוֹתָם — *And Tamar their sister.*
Tamar is mentioned although no other
daughters are listed because she is known
to us from the episode with Amnon [II
Samuel 13:1] (*Gra*).

◄§ The Royal Line of David

10-16. These verses contain the names of
the kings of Israel [or rather the kings of
Judah, the southern kingdom, after the
kingdoms were split] from Solomon
through to the destruction of the Temple
which took place in the reign of Tzidkiahu
[Zedekiah] (v. 15). The story of each of
these kings is described later in *Chronicles*.
There are some minor spelling variations
which will be pointed out in the individual
verses. At this point it should be noted that
although all the kings are listed, they do
not cover the complete picture. Between the
reign of Achaziah (v. 11) and his son Yoash
(v. 11) there was a six-year period during
which Athaliah, Achaziah's wife, ruled the
land (see *II Chronicles* ch. 22 for details).

Elishama, Eliada, and Eliphelet — nine. ⁹ *All these were sons of David, besides the sons of the concubines, and Tamar their sister.* ¹⁰ *And the sons of Solomon — Rechovoam, his son Aviyah, his son Asa, his son Yehoshaphat.* ¹¹ *His son Yoram, his son Achaziahu, his son Yoash.* ¹² *His son Amatziahu, his son Azariah, his son Yotham.* ¹³ *His son Achaz, his son Chizkiahu, his son Menasheh.* ¹⁴ *His son Amon, his son Yoshiahu.* ¹⁵ *The sons of Yoshiahu — the first-born*

Obviously there was no need to mention her in a genealogical list.

10. אֲבִיָּה בְנוֹ — *His son Aviyah.* In *I Kings* 14:31ff this son of Rechovoam is called אֲבִיָם, *Aviyam.* From *II Chronicles* 13:20 and 21, where the name appears as אֲבִיָּהוּ, *Aviyahu,* it appears that the meaning of the name is, HASHEM *is my Father* (see below on אֲחַזְיָהוּ in v. 11).

11. יוֹרָם בְנוֹ — *His son Yoram.* This name is often given as יְהוֹרָם, *Yehoram* (cf. *II Chronicles* 21:1ff). Even within one passage we find both forms used (see *II Kings* 8:16ff). This usage is common with many of the names in Scripture which begin with the first three letters of God's ineffable Name (יְהוֹרָם means HASHEM *is exalted,* from רוּם, *to be high*). Thus, we have יְהוֹנָתָן, *Yehonathan,* and יוֹנָתָן, *Yonathan;* יְהוֹנָדָב, *Yehonadav,* and יוֹנָדָב, *Yonadav,* and many more in the same category.

אֲחַזְיָהוּ בְנוֹ — *His son Achaziahu.* In contrast to Yehoram and similar names in which three letters of God's Name begin the name, Achaziahu belongs to that category of names which end with those three letters. The name means HASHEM *holds or grasps* from אחז, *to hold.* In this category of names the final *vav* (u) is often dropped. Thus אֲחַזְיָה, *Achaziah,* and אֲחַזְיָהוּ, *Achaziahu,* are interchangeable. The same holds true for אֲמַצְיָהוּ, *Amatziahu,* and עֲזַרְיָה, *Azariah,* in v. 12; חִזְקִיָּהוּ, *Chizkiahu,* in v. 14 and יְכָנְיָה, *Yechoniah,* in v. 16. Interestingly יֹאשִׁיָהוּ, *Yoshiahu,* of v. 15 is an exception. This name appears only in that form.

12. עֲזַרְיָה בְנוֹ — *His son Azariah.* This king is also called עֻזִּיָּהוּ, *Uzziahu,* and עֻזִּיָּה, *Uzziah,* both in *Kings* and in *Chronicles.* The names have similar connotations. עֲזַרְיָה, *Azariah,* HASHEM *helps;* עֻזִּיָּה, *Uzziah,* HASHEM *is my strength.*

15. וּבְנֵי יֹאשִׁיָהוּ ... — *The sons of Yoshiahu*

... A study of *II Kings* 23:31 till the end yields the following line of succession after Yoshiahu's [Josiah] death:

Yoshiahu's son Yehoachaz [Jehoahaz] (3 months)
— Yoshiahu's son Yehoiakim [Jehoiakim] (11 years)
— Yehoiakim's son Yehoiachin/Yechoniah [Jehoiachin] (3 months)
— Yoshiahu's son Tzidkiahu [Zedekiah] (11 years)

Of the three sons of Yoshiahu mentioned there, our verse has only two: Yehoiakim and Tzidkiahu. Yehoachaz is not mentioned and instead we have two other names, Yochanan and Shallum. In *Horios* 11b, Rabbi Yochanan teaches that the Yochanan in our verse is identical with Yehoachaz. This eliminates the first problem. Yehoachaz does appear here, albeit under a different name. [The names are not far apart in meaning. יוֹחָנָן, *Yochanan,* which is a shortened form of יְהוֹחָנָן, *Yehochanan* (which also appears in Scripture; see above under יוֹרָם), means HASHEM *is merciful,* which is not a far cry from יְהוֹאָחָז, HASHEM *holds or supports.*]

R' Yochanan in *Horios* goes on to say that Shallum and Tzidkiahu are also one. The Talmud then asks: if Shallum is Tzidkiahu why is he called *the fourth* when Tzidkiahu was actually the third son of Yoshiahu. To this the answer is given that he is called fourth not because he was the fourth son but because he was the fourth king to succeed his father. [He was preceded by his two brothers and by his nephew Yehoiachin/Yechoniah.]

Gra (here) poses two questions: Why did R' Yochanan find it necessary to make this identification, and how can he say that Tzidkiahu and Shallum, whom our verse counts as two people, are really one and the same?

Gra suggests that R' Yochanan is not dealing with our verse at all. The meaning of our verse is as it seems; there were altogether four sons, one of whom, Shallum, never succeeded to the throne. The problem which R' Yochanan

טז יְהוֹיָקִים הַשְּׁלִשִׁי צִדְקִיָּהוּ הָרְבִיעִי שַׁלּוּם: וּבְנֵי יְהוֹיָקִים

יז יְכָנְיָה בְּנוֹ צִדְקִיָּה בְּנוֹ: וּבְנֵי יְכָנְיָה אַסִּר שְׁאַלְתִּיאֵל בְּנוֹ:

addresses is in *Jeremiah* 22:11 where the prophet addresses a *Shallum, son of Yoshiahu ... who rules in the place of Yoshiahu his father.* This poses a problem since, as noted, the Shallum of our verse never became king. R' Yochanan's solution is that the Shallum of *Jeremiah* (but not of *Chronicles*) is identical with Tzidkiahu. He is called Shallum not because this was his given name but because he was perfect in his deeds [שָׁלוֹם from שָׁלֵם, *perfect*] or, because the Davidic monarchy came to a close during his days [שָׁלוֹם from שָׁלֵם, *completed* — therefore, *ended*] (see *Horios*, there).

Gra interprets the Talmud's question as follows: Granted that Yoshiahu had a fourth son, Shallum, why is he listed in this section of *Chronicles* which seems concerned only with the kings in the Davidic line? Because of this problem the Talmud assumes that the word הָרְבִיעִי, *the fourth*, does not [exclusively] refer to שָׁלוֹם (who does not belong into this list at all) but refers back to Tzidkiahu. It is as though the phrase was to read: הַשְּׁלִשִׁי צִדְקִיָּה [וְהָרְבִיעִי], *the third [and the fourth] was Tzidkiahu.* To this the Talmud comments that he was called 'fourth' because he was fourth to rule.

Radak offers his own explanation that the Shallum of our verse is another name for Yechoniah/Yehoiachin, the son of Yehoiakim and therefore the grandson of Yoshiahu. He notes that in *Chronicles* it is not unusual to find a grandson listed among sons. [A different attempt to solve these complex questions is given in Appendix iv.]

הַבְּכוֹר יוֹחָנָן — *The first-born Yochanan.* As noted above, R' Yochanan in *Horios* identifies this Yochanan with the Yehoachaz of *Kings.* The Talmud there raises the question of how our verse can call this Yochanan/Yehoachaz the *first-born* when it is evident from *II Kings* 23:31 and 36 that Yehoiakim was the older of the two. The answer given is that he is called *first-born* not because he was older but because he was the first to ascend his father's throne.

הַשְּׁלִשִׁי צִדְקִיָּהוּ הָרְבִיעִי שַׁלּוּם — *The third Tzidkiahu, and the fourth Shallum.* According to *Radak's* understanding of the Talmud, Tzidkiahu is listed here under two names — his own and Shallum. According to *Gra* this Shallum is a fourth brother who never became king. Accord to *Radak's* own view, Shallum is another name of

Yechoniah son of Yehoiakim, a grandson of Yoshiahu.

As noted above, *Gra's* view is that the passage in *Horios* which identifies Tzidkiahu with Shallum does not refer to the two names in our verse. However, the simple meaning of the Talmud there implies otherwise — and is understood by *Radak* as referring to our verse.

16. יְכָנְיָה — *Yechoniah.* As we saw above, this Yechoniah [or יוֹיָכִין, יְהוֹיָכִין, יְכָנְיָהוּ, בְּנָיָהוּ (Chenaiahu, Yechoniahu, Yehoiachin, Yoiachiu) as he is variously called] succeeded his father Yehoiakim to the throne (*II Kings* 24:8). After a reign of only three months he was deposed and succeeded by his uncle Tzidkiahu (there, v. 17) who is mentioned in v. 15 above. [According to *Abarbanel* to *II Kings* ch. 24 he was succeeded by his brother Tzidkiahu (see below) rather than by his uncle.] It was during the reign of Tzidkiahu that the Temple was finally destroyed and the people exiled to Babylon.

צִדְקִיָּה בְּנוֹ — *Tzidkiah, his son.* According to the formulation used in the last six verses this would make this Tzidkiah a son of Yechoniah. However, this interpretation seems awkward for two reasons. First, בְּנֵי יְהוֹיָקִים, *the sons of Yehoiakim,* is in the plural and we would expect more than one son to be mentioned. [However, there are occasional exceptions to this in *Chronicles*; see for example, 1:41 and 2:8.] Also, since the next verse begins with the words, *And the sons of Yechoniah ...* it would seem that no sons of Yechoniah had yet been listed. [*Metzudos*, however, resolves this last difficulty by explaining the next verse to mean: The additional sons of Yechoniah (besides Tzidkiah who had already been mentioned) were ...]

Radak, Gra and *Metzudos* explain that there were two Tzidkiahu's — one the son of Yoshiahu (v. 15) who succeeded his nephew Yechoniah to the kingship, and the other (of our verse) the son of Yehoiakim (*Gra*) or Yechoniah (*Radak, Metzudos*) who was named after his uncle or great-uncle.

17-24. From v. 17 till the end of the chapter, we have a list of the progeny of Yechoniah. The list contains fifteen gener-

Yochanan, the second Yehoiakim, the third Tzidkiahu, and the fourth Shallum. ¹⁶ *And the sons of Yehoiakim — Yechoniah, his son, Tzidkiah, his son.* ¹⁷ *And the sons of Yechoniah — Assir, his*

ations according to *Gra's* interpretation of this section, and nine generations in *Malbim's* view. As follows [the disputed generations are in brackets]: Yechoniah, [Assir], Shealtiel, [Pedaiah], Zerubavel, Chananiah, [Yishaiah], [Rephaiah], [Arnan], [Ovadiah], Shechaniah, Shemaiah, Neariah, Elioanei, and Eliaonei's children (see comm. below). The extreme importance of this line lies in the fact that after Tzidkiahu's sons had been killed by Nebuchadnezzar (*II Kings* 25:7), Yechoniah was the sole survivor of the Davidic house (*Seder Olam Zuta* 7:5).[1] [*Seder Olam Zuta's* assertion must be qualified since in paragraph 7 he states explicitly that Tzidkiahu outlived his sons by thirty-seven years. Perhaps the meaning in paragraph 5 is that Yechoniah was the only one still capable of having children.]

Thus, the perpetuation of the Davidic line so inextricably bound up with Israel's Messianic destiny depended entirely on these children of Yechoniah.[2]

17. וּבְנֵי יְכָנְיָה — *And the sons of Yechoniah.* The fact that Yechoniah had children is, in itself, significant. *Jeremiah* (22:24,30) had prophesied: *For if Chenaiahu (i.e., Yechoniah), the son of Yehoiakim, king of Judah were a signet ring on My right hand — from there I would tear him off ... Thus says HASHEM: Condemn this man to childlessness, a man who will see no success in his days. For none of his seed shall ever sit on David's throne or again rule over Judah.* Such had been the fate of this wicked king. [Concerning his rule, see *II Chronicles* 36:8ff.]

And yet in Haggai's prophecy concern-

---

1. Chapter and paragraph for *Seder Olam Zuta* are from the edition published by Moshe Yair Weinstock, Jerusalem 5717.

2. When the patriarch, Jacob, gave his final blessing to his twelve sons before he died, he prophesied that: *The scepter shall not depart from Judah, nor an arbiter of law from among his descendants* (*Genesis* 49:10). *Sanhedrin* 5a interprets: *The scepter shall not depart from Judah* — this refers to the leaders of the exile (exilarchs) in Babylon who enforced their rulings over the people with a rod [שֵׁבֶט, *scepter*, is interpreted as a *rod*]; ... *nor an arbiter of law from among his descendants* — this refers to Hillel's descendants who taught the Torah in public.

Rashi to *Genesis* (there) has a different reading. For the interpretation of the *arbiter of law* he reads: These are the princes (וְשִׂיאִים) of the Land of Israel. [See *Berliner* (there) for a midrashic source for *Rashi's* reading: '... these are the princes of the family of Rabbi Yehudah the Prince who teach Torah in public in the Land of Israel.'] Thus, according to *Rashi's* reading, Jacob's prediction encompassed both branches of the leadership to which the nations looked over many centuries: The office of the *Resh Galutha, exilarch,* which was centered in Babylon and had its beginnings in the descendants of Yechoniah listed here; and that of the *Nasi,* centered in Jerusalem, of whom the first in the Davidic line was Hillel who became *Nasi* some one hundred years before the destruction of the Second Temple.

The exilarchate, which in later centuries flourished into an extremely powerful office, seems to have had its beginnings with the descendants of Yechoniah listed here.

Gra (here) writes that the first of the Exilarchs was Elioenai [the thirteenth (*Gra*) or seventh (*Malbim*) generation]. I have not been able to find a source for this. R' Moshe Isserles (*Rama*), based on *Yesod Olam* and quoted in *Sefer Yuchasin,* writes: 'With Tzidkiahu, king of Judah, the kingship of the Davidic line ended, but his descendants were in Babylon throughout the Second Temple and for a long time after the destruction. They were princes (וְשִׂיאִים) and exilarchs (רָאשֵׁי גָלִיּוֹת). The first was Shealtiel the son of Yehoiachin, king of Judah.' The implication is that the earlier generations were already considered to be in that category. Since there are no independent historical records of these early beginnings of the exilarchs we can only surmise that the institution, which later was to flourish into such a powerful force, had smaller and more modest beginnings.

The family of the Davidic princes may also be found here according to some traditions which identify Hillel with either Chizkiah [fourteenth (*Gra*) or eighth (*Malbim*) generation] (*Yesod Olam*) or with an unidentified brother (*R' Abraham ibn Daud, Sefer HaKaballah*).

However, according to *Yerushalmi, Kilaim* 9:4; *Kesubos* 13:3 and *Bereishis Rabbah* 33:3, Rabbi Yehudah the Prince, descendant of Hillel, traced his lineage to a daughter of David and not to Solomon, as would have been the case if he had been a direct descendant of Yechoniah.

יח-יט וּמַלְכִּירָם וּפְדָיָה וְשֶׁנְאַצַּר יְקַמְיָה הוֹשָׁמָע וּנְדַבְיָה: וּבְנֵי
פְדָיָה זְרֻבָּבֶל וְשִׁמְעִי וּבֶן־זְרֻבָּבֶל מְשֻׁלָּם וַחֲנַנְיָה וּשְׁלֹמִית
כ אֲחוֹתָם: וַחֲשֻׁבָה וָאֹהֶל וּבֶרֶכְיָה וַחֲסַדְיָה יוּשַׁב חֶסֶד

ing the return to Zion, it is just a grandson of this very Yechoniah who is God's chosen one and who is placed as a signet ring upon His hand: *On that day ... I will take you, Zerubavel ben Shealtiel, My servant ... and I shall place you as a signet ring, for you have I chosen; the words of HASHEM Master of Legions* (Haggai 2:23).

The bridge between these seemingly irreconcilable passages lies in the rejuvenation which repentance makes possible. As *Rambam* writes: Great is repentance, for it is the means by which a man can change his whole being. And it is Yechoniah whom *Rambam* holds up as a prime example to the efficacy of true repentance.

Vayikra Rabbah (19:6) relates that after Yechoniah had been thrown into a dungeon by Nebuchadnezzar, there to waste away until his death, the Sanhedrin worried that the Davidic line might be broken if he were to die childless. To prevent this they enlisted the help of Nebuchadnezzar's wife. When he wanted to be intimate with her she chided him: If he considered it to be his right to have conjugal relations, was Yechoniah not also entitled to live with his wife? Nebuchadnezzar allowed himself to be persuaded and gave his permission to have Yechoniah's wife lowered to him in his dungeon. Delighted to have his wife with him he wanted to approach her but she explained to him that she was a *niddah*, a menstruant woman, and that relations with her at that time were forbidden. Yechoniah immediately suppressed his desire and did not touch her. At that heroic sign of repentance, God retracted his oath and granted him children.

And so it was from Yechoniah that Zerubavel, who was to lead the Baby-

lonian exile back to Israel (see below), was descended. The man who had at one time been condemned to die childless discovered within himself the capacity to turn around God's decree and become the progenitor of the Messiah. [See *Tanchuma (Buber), Toldos* 30 and comm. to verse 24.]

See further in Section Two, p. 392.

אַסִּר — *Assir.* Yechoniah called his son Assir [from אסר, *to bind*] because he was born to him in jail *(Sanhedrin 37b).*

שְׁאַלְתִּיאֵל בְּנוֹ — *His son Shealtiel. Radak, Metzudos* and *Gra* all interpret this phrase to mean that Shealtiel was the son of Assir (in which case the introduction בְּנֵי יְכָנְיָה, *the sons of Yechoniah,* in the plural, would again be irregular since only one son is mentioned — see comm. verse 16).

Malbim suggests the possibility that the phrase means that Shealtiel was also the son of Yechoniah. The Sages in *Vayikra Rabbah* (19:6) seem to agree with this, since they interpret the name to reflect another aspect of Yechoniah's story. He called his son שְׁאַלְתִּיאֵל, *Shealtiel* [from שאל, *to ask*], because God had, so to speak, 'asked' to be freed of His oath that Yechoniah would die childless.[1] *Gra* goes so far as to say that Assir and Shealtiel were one and the same person. Both names simply imply different facets of the circumstances of his birth.

Sanhedrin 37b adds another interpretation. The name is related to שתל, *to plant,* and connotes: 'He whom God planted.' His conception was truly miraculous in that the dungeon was too narrow to allow for normal conjugal relations between Yechoniah and his wife. She conceived him in a position in which, under normal circumstances, conception would have

---

1. The idea expressed here by the Sages, that God 'asked' [evidently from the heavenly court] to have His oath [the original decree that Yechoniah should die childless] annulled, is an obvious anthropomorphism. The theory under which a court can annul a vow is based on the introduction of a new circumstance of which the taker of the oath had originally not been aware and concerning which we assume that had he known of it he would not have sworn. The concept of an oath made in ignorance of a given condition is obviously inappropriate in relation to an Omniscient God.

God's justification to, as it were, retract His oath lies in the nature of true *teshuvah* (penitence). A sinner who traverses the awesomely demanding steps of a true *teshuvah* brings about such a radical upheaval within himself, so that he can truly be described as a new person. 'Great is *teshuvah*,' writes

3

18-20

son Shealtiel. [18] *And Malchiram, Pedaiah, Shenatzar, Yekamiah, Hoshama, and Nedaviah.* [19] *And the sons of Pedaiah — Zerubavel and Shimei; and the son of Zerubavel — Meshullam and Chananiah; and Shelomith was their sister.* [20] *And Chashuvah, Ohel, Berechiah,*

been impossible.

18. ... וּמַלְכִּירָם — *And Malchiram* ... *Radak, Metzudos* and *Gra* all assume that the people mentioned here are sons of Shealtiel. *Gra,* as he often does in *Chronicles,* assumes that the word בְּנוֹ, *his son,* at the end of verse 17 refers to our verse also, so that in effect it should be read: *Shealtiel his son [and his son] Malchiram* ...

Malbim thinks that verse 18 may simply be a continuation of verse 17 and that the six men mentioned here are all sons of Yechoniah and brothers of Assir and Shealtiel.

19. זְרֻבָּבֶל — *Zerubavel.* Zerubavel is listed as a son of Pedaiah, which makes him either a grandson of Shealtiel (according to most commentators) or a nephew of Shealtiel *(Malbim;* see previous verse).

Throughout Scripture he is always called Zerubavel ben Shealtiel (cf. *Haggai* 1:1). Those commentators who assume that he was Shealtiel's grandson explain this on the basis that grandsons are often referred to in Scripture as sons (see comm. and fn. 1:17). *Malbim,* who thinks that Shealtiel and Pedaiah were brothers, explains that Shealtiel died childless and that Pedaiah then took his sister-in-law in *yibum, levirate marriage,* the law whereby a brother is required to marry the wife of his deceased brother if he died childless. The child born of this union is, of course, the biological child of the second husband, but in certain ways is considered to perpetuate the being of his mother's first husband (see comm. 2:4). In that sense Zerubavel is described as 'son' of Shealtiel.

Ibn Ezra (Haggai 1:1, *Ezra* 3:2) also

considers Zerubavel a nephew of Shealtiel and explains that Shealtiel is referred to as the father of Zerubavel because he raised him.

The name Zerubavel is, according to the Sages, a combination of two words: זֶרַע, *seed* [from זרע, *to sow*], and בְּבֶל, *Babylon.* The seed from which he grew had been sown [i.e., he had been conceived] in Babylon. This is stressed because of unusual circumstances leading up to Yechoniah's intimacy with his wife in a Babylonian dungeon (see comm. v. 17). See further in Section Two, p. 392.

From *Sanhedrin* 38a it appears that Zerubavel and Nehemiah ben Chachalaiah, the successor to Ezra, were one and the same person. It is not clear on what basis they made that identification and *Rambam,* in his *Introduction to Mishneh Torah,* considers them to be two different people. *Chida* in *Pesach Einayim* discusses this problem. See further in *Margalios HaYam* to *Sanhedrin* (there).

The life and accomplishments of Zerubavel are described in the Books of *Ezra* and *Haggai.*

וּבֶן־זְרֻבָּבֶל מְשֻׁלָּם וַחֲנַנְיָה — *And the son of Zerubavel — Meshullam and Chananiah.* The singular בֶּן, *son,* is irregular here. It must be understood as though it were written בְּנֵי, *sons.* This irregularity is repeated below in vs. 21 and 23 *(Radak).* This is the reverse of the situations pointed out several times above (v. 16, 1:41, 2:8) where the plural בְּנֵי refers to only one son.

וּשְׁלֹמִית אֲחוֹתָם — *And Shelomith was their sister.* Verse 20 continues with Zerubavel's children. They are divided into two verses, either because the ones mentioned in v. 19 were born in Babylon while those of v. 20

Rambam (Hilchos Teshuvah 7:6) ... 'it brings those that were far [from HASHEM] close [to Him]. Only yesterday this [man] was hated by God, despicable, distant and abhorrent and today he is loved and desired, close and esteemed.' *Rambam* then goes on to illustrate this very point from the experiences of Yechoniah. His *teshuvah* had wrought such a radical change within him that the very terms of abhorrence with which God had described him while he was still a sinner were subsequently turned around and used to express God's love: He had become a 'different' person.

The midrashim, in line with their general tendency to use anthropomorphic expressions in order to make their profound teachings concerning God more readily accessible, described what happened in

כא חָמֵשׁ: וּבֶן־חֲנַנְיָה פְּלַטְיָה וִישַׁעְיָה בְּנֵי רְפָיָה בְּנֵי אַרְנָן

כב בְּנֵי עֹבַדְיָה בְּנֵי שְׁכַנְיָה: וּבְנֵי שְׁכַנְיָה שְׁמַעְיָה ג

כא־כד
וּבְנֵי שְׁמַעְיָה חַטּוּשׁ וְיִגְאָל וּבָרִיחַ וּנְעַרְיָה וְשָׁפָט שִׁשָּׁה:

כג־כד וּבֶן־נְעַרְיָה אֶלְיוֹעֵינַי וְחִזְקִיָּה וְעַזְרִיקָם שְׁלֹשָׁה: וּבְנֵי

°הוֹדַוְיָהוּ ק' אֶלְיוֹעֵינַי °הֹדַיְוָהוּ וְאֶלְיָשִׁיב וּפְלָיָה וְעַקּוּב וְיוֹחָנָן וּדְלָיָה

---

were born after the return to Jerusalem (Gra); or because those of v. 19 were born from one mother, and those in v. 20 from another (Malbim).

20. חָמֵשׁ — *Five.* Gra explains that it is necessary to give the number so that it would be clear that Yushav Chesed was one name, not two. The *Anonymous Commentator* thinks that חָמֵשׁ, *Chamesh,* must be a proper name rather than a number since in that case we would have expected the masculine form — חֲמִשָּׁה.

21. וּבֶן־חֲנַנְיָה — *The sons of Chananiah.* Of Zerubavel's children, only the line of Chananiah is traced. This is another example of the singular בֶּן being used although more than one son is listed. See above v. 19 (Radak).

... בְּנֵי רְפָיָה בְּנֵי אַרְנָן — *The sons of Rephaiah, the sons of Arnan* ... The syntax of the second half of the sentence is difficult. We are not told who Rephaiah, Arnan, Ovadiah or Shechaniah are; nor, in the case of the first three, who are their children. Ignoring minor differences there are essentially two explanations offered:

Metzudos and *Gra:* The word בְּנֵי, *sons,* [which must be understood as בֶּן, *son,*] refers to the preceding rather than the following name. The sentence is to be read: *The son* [*of Yishaiah was*] *Rephaiah; the son* [*of Rephaiah was*] *Arnan* ... The shortened form is used because the meaning is obvious and the reader can be relied upon to understand.

Malbim: All the names mentioned are sons of Chananiah [in contrast to *Gra's* explanation that Rephaiah is a son of

Yishaiah, Chananiah's son, etc.]. As noted on a number of occasions, *Malbim* thinks that these lists were taken from a much more complete *Book of Genealogies.* Ezra copied out only those pieces of information which seemed pertinent. The original would have read approximately thus: The sons of Chananiah were: Pelatiah; Yishaiah; Rephaiah, whose children were ...; Arnan, whose children were ...; and so on. See Appendix II for the implications of these two explanations.

22. וּבְנֵי שְׁכַנְיָה שְׁמַעְיָה — *The sons of Shechaniah — Shemaiah.* Only one son is counted. The plural וּבְנֵי is irregular, but not uncommon to *Chronicles* (see above 1:41, 2:8).

... שִׁשָּׁה וּבְנֵי שְׁמַעְיָה — *And the sons of Shemaiah ... six.* Only five sons are counted. The following explanations are offered.

R' Shmuel ben Chofni, Gaon: The number six is meant to describe the descendants of Shechaniah, not of Shemaiah. Therefore, Shemaiah is counted together with his five sons to make a total of six descendants for Shechaniah. Or (with *Malbim*), Shemaiah died early, leaving his five sons to be brought up by his father, Shechaniah. Thus, Shemaiah is counted together with his own five sons, making a total of six sons for Shechaniah. The *Anonymous Commentator:* שִׁשָּׁה, *Shishah,* is a proper name — not a number (see v. 20).

Metzudos: When the list was composed, Shemaiah's wife was pregnant. The number of children is given as six although only five names could be listed.

Gra: The phrase *the sons of Shemaiah* is

---

terms which would have been applicable to human beings. If a man had made an oath concerning his fellow man who had wronged him, and that person had then undergone a sincere repentance, then he could certainly have gone to court and have his oath annulled because of the changed circumstance.

Chasadiah, Yushav Chesed — five. ²¹ The sons of Chananiah — Pelatiah and Yishaiah. The sons of Rephaiah, the sons of Arnan, the sons of Ovadiah, the sons of Shechaniah. ²² The sons of Shechaniah — Shemaiah; and the sons of Shemaiah — Chattush, Yigal, Bariach, Neariah, and Shaphat — six. ²³ And the sons of Neariah — Elioenai, Chizkiah, and Azrikam — three. ²⁴ And the sons of Elioenai — Hodaviahu, Eliashiv, Pelaiah, Akkuv, Yochanan, Delaiah, and Anani — seven.

to be interpreted in precisely the same way as the sons of Rephaiah etc. in the previous verse (see above). Thus it is as though it were written: The sons of Shechaniah were Shemaiah. And the sons [of Shemaiah were] Shemaiah, Chattush, etc. [i.e., Shemaiah's oldest son bore his father's name]. Thus, Shemaiah did in fact have six sons.[1]

24. וַעֲנָנִי שִׁבְעָה ... וּבְנֵי אֶלְיוֹעֵינַי — And the sons of Elioenai ... and Anani — seven. Once more the problem arises of the seemingly redundant cumulative number, seven, at the end of the verse (see fn. to v. 2:6).

However, in this case we have a midrashic interpretation which puts the whole passage in a new light, and which can indeed be seen as a key to our perception of the Book of Chronicles.

To the seventh son, Anani, Targum remarks: Anani is the Messianic king who is destined to appear.

The Mefaresh, too, had such a tradition. He writes: From Yechoniah up to Anani there are seven generations [i.e., excluding Yechoniah and Anani; including them there are at least nine, see chart]. He is the Messiah, as it is written: With the clouds of heaven, one like a man came (Daniel 7:13). Reference there is to the Messiah and a play on words is intended. Clouds of heaven are עֲנָנֵי שְׁמַיָּא, which recalls the name עֲנָנִי, Anani.

The basis for these interpretations is contained in two extant midrashic sources. The older is Tanchuma (Buber) to Toldos 30, and from that, with minor variations, it appears in Aggados Bereishis 45.

'... It is written: Who are you, O great mountain, before Zerubavel ... (Zechariah 4:7). Who is this great mountain? This is the Messianic king ... From whom is he descended? From Zerubavel who is descended from David, as it is written: [our complete passage] ... Who is Anani? He is the Messianic king, as it is written: [the quote from Daniel above]. And what is [the meaning of] seven [at the end of our verse]? It ['s significance lies in what] is written in connection with the Messiah ... seven are the eyes of HASHEM which roam around the whole earth (Zechariah 4:10).

Thus, as happens several times in this Book, both the names and the numbers contained in our passage are converted by the Sages into symbols of the unknown and unknowable mysteries surrounding the advent of the Messiah.

There is much that is strange and much that is difficult in these genealogical tables. In the Overview (p. xxix) we have surmised that the obscurity may have been intentional. Fate had decreed that the סֵפֶר הַיֻּחֲסִין, Book of Genealogies, which apparently contains the key to unlocking the secrets of these chapters, should have been lost (Pesachim 62b). The treasures of truth hidden behind the facade of these lists is to remain hidden from us until such a time when Divine Providence will once more permit them to be known. Nevertheless, here and there, a few of the teachings of the Sages have been preserved and through them we have been permitted an occasional glimpse. Several times we have surmised that these hidden truths concern the קֵץ, the end of days, the ultimate mystery of Jewish experience. In the midrash to these few verses that surmise can be confirmed.

1. I have not found other examples where a son is called by his father's name during his lifetime. Perhaps Shemaiah's oldest son took on his father's name after the latter had died and the list was completed after that time.

א וַעֲנָנִי שְׁבְעָה: בְּנֵי יְהוּדָה פֶּרֶץ חֶצְרוֹן וְכַרְמִי וְחוּר

ב וְשׁוֹבָל: וּרְאָיָה בֶן־שׁוֹבָל הוֹלִיד אֶת־יַחַת וְיַחַת הֹלִיד אֶת־

ג אֲחוּמַי וְאֶת־לָהַד אֵלֶּה מִשְׁפְּחוֹת הַצָּרְעָתִי: וְאֵלֶּה

אֲבִי עֵיטָם יִזְרְעֶאל וְיִשְׁמָא וְיִדְבָּשׁ וְשֵׁם אֲחוֹתָם

IV

◄§ Judah's genealogy continued

This chapter takes up the genealogical list of Judah from the end of chapter 2. Chapter 3, which is devoted exclusively to David's progeny, is parenthetical to these lists. According to many commentators, it is common for the *Book of Chronicles* to interrupt a given genealogical list and then to pick it up again at a later point. [See, for example, 2:42. See Overview p. xxi and Appendix II for a discussion of this and other stylistic irregularities in these lists.] The lists of Judah are concluded in v. 23; at that point Ezra moves on to Shimeon's genealogy.

1⁻4. 2:50 had begun a short list of the descendants of Chur. Our section continues with that list.

1. ... בְּנֵי יְהוּדָה — *The sons of Judah* ... The word *sons* is not meant literally in this phrase. Only Peretz was Judah's son (2:4), while the rest are descendants of Judah; see below.

... פֶּרֶץ חֶצְרוֹן — *Peretz, Chetzron.* Peretz was Judah's son (2:4), and Chetzron was the son of Peretz (2:5).

וְכַרְמִי — *Carmi.* The mention of Carmi in this verse presents great difficulties. In 2:7 he is given as a descendant of Judah's son Zerach. He seems out of place in a list which begins with Peretz (Zerach's brother) and Chetzron and ends with Chur (son of Calev, descendant of Chetzron — 2:19 and 50) and Chur's son Shoval (2:50). Clearly the passage deals with the family of Peretz, not that of Zerach.

The *Anonymous Commentator, Radak* and *Metzudos* note the facts but make no attempt to explain them. *Malbim* thinks

that our verse is not part of the following list at all but rather a check-list of names dealt with in ch. 2 against which the writer wanted to determine which family trees to develop further and which had been dealt with in sufficient detail. [See Appendix II for a discussion of the idea that the genealogical lists are written in the form of notes.]

Gra, without giving reasons, assumes that the Carmi of our verse is not the one mentioned in 2:7. The Carmi of our verse is Calev ben Chetzron under a different name. In verse 2 below, we shall see that in the tradition of the Sages, the Reaiah mentioned there is identical with Betzalel (2:20). The Sages there, also, seem to assume that this Carmi is Calev and, further, that Shoval is Uri (2:20). [See R' Zev Einhorn's comm. *Peirush Maharzav* to *Shemos Rabbah* 40:4.] Thus, the list Peretz, Chetzron, Carmi, Chur, Shoval, Reaiah — of our verse is identical with the list — Peretz, Chetzron, Calev, Chur, Uri, Betzalel.[1] For an analysis see Section Two, p. 394.

---

1. We offer the following observations on the name changes: Calev/Carmi; and Uri/Shoval.

Calev/Carmi: Maharzav suggests that Calev might be referred to as Carmi from the word כֶּרֶם [kerem], a *vineyard,* because of the grapes which the spies brought back with them from the land of Canaan (Numbers 13:23). According to the Sages (Bamidbar Rabbah 16:14), Calev had been instrumental in the decision to bring back these grapes — indeed he had drawn his sword to force the issue — and the name Carmi was therefore a fitting memorial to that occasion. In exactly the same sense, *Shemos Rabbah* 1:17 explains that the name עֲנוּב, *Anuv,* in v. 8 refers to Calev, hinting at the bunch of grapes, אֶשְׁכּוֹל עֲנָבִים [eshkol anavim], which the spies had brought back at his instigation. [See further, Section Two, p. 393.]

Uri/Shoval: We know of no sources which trace a connection between these two names but offer the following etymological observations.

The name אוּרִי, *Uri,* may well derive from the root אוֹר, light, and would then mean, *my light,* perhaps a contraction of אוּרִיאֵל [Uriel], God is my light. But from *Isaiah* 24:15 it seems that אוּר also has a different meaning. *Rashi* (there) quotes Menachem ibn Sarouk who renders אֻרִים as the caves

T*he sons of Judah — Peretz, Chetzron, Carmi, Chur, and Shoval.* *² And Reaiah son of Shoval fathered Yachath, and Yachath fathered Achumai and Lahad; these are the families of the Tzorathites. ³ And these are the fathers of Etam — Yizreel, Yishma,*

2. ... וּרְאָיָה בֶן־שׁוֹבָל הֹלִיד — *And Reaiah son of Shoval fathered* ... The *Mefaresh* notes that *Chronicles* not infrequently gives information concerning an individual of whom nothing has been said earlier. Thus we are taught that Reaiah fathered a son although it had never been said that Shoval had a son, Reaiah.

However, *Radak, Metzudos* and *Gra* all note that it is likely that the Reaiah mentioned here is identical with Haroeh who was given as Shoval's son in 2:52. [See comm. there. The *Mefaresh* is consistent with his opinion there that Haroeh is not a proper noun but means, *who oversaw.*]

אֵלֶּה מִשְׁפְּחוֹת הַצָּרְעָתִי — *These are the families of the Tzorathites.* 2:53 taught that the Tzorathites had been descended from the inhabitants of Kiriath Yearim who in turn belonged to Shoval's family. Our verse teaches that the main families of the Tzorathites were Yachath and his two sons, Achumai and Lahad *(Radak; Metzudos; Gra).*

Targum interpolates the words: *And these are the descendants of Judah who dwelt in Tzorah.* In 2:53 he had explained that the families enumerated there were Levites, descended from Moses. Thus, although Tzorah and Eshtaol are towns in Judah, no Judean inhabitants had been mentioned. Our passage lists the Judean families who lived there.

The Sages *(Shemos Rabbah* 40:4) interpret the whole verse as referring to Betzalel, builder of the Tabernacle.

God called him five [additional] names of endearment in reference to the Tabernacle:

Reaiah: For God showed him [רְאָיָה] from ראה, *to see*] to Moses and all Israel and said to them, 'From the beginning of creation I have set him aside to build the Tabernacle.'

Shoval: Because he created a dovecote for God. [שׁוֹבָל is a contraction for the words שׁוֹבָךְ לֵאלֹהִים, *a dovecote for God.*] This refers to the Tabernacle.

This is either because it was a high building, or because bird offerings were brought in it, or because Israel which is compared to a dove found shelter in it *(Commentators).* However, the term, 'a dovecote *for* God' would seem to indicate that it is for God's purposes that the dovecote was erected (see *Ramban, Exodus* 29:46). The metaphor of the dovecote seems apt when we consider passages like that in *Tikunei Zohar* 38 that, 'when God's Holy Presence (שְׁכִינְתָּא) is in exile it can be described by the verse: *And the dove was not able to find rest.*' See also *Berachos* 3a which describes a heavenly voice 'moaning like a dove.'

Yachath: Because he brought the fear [of God] upon Israel. [יַחַת from חתת, *to fear.*] Presumably reference is to the positive command to stand in awe before God's Sanctuary. See *Rambam, Beis HaBechirah*

and crevices in a rocky terrain. Other commentators there offer similar interpretations.

Now the name of Uri's father was Chur. חוּר derives from חרר, *to bore* or *pierce,* and thus becomes *a hole* and is also used for the caves and crevices in which people hide (see *I Samuel* 14:11); a meaning almost identical with the second meaning of אוּרִי.

According to 2:50, Shoval/Uri was the chieftain of Kiriath Yearim, which can be translated as *City of Forests.* The word יַעַר, which is generally translated as *forest,* is really used for any area to which access is difficult or which is unpenetrable. It derives from a root which in Arabic has the meaning of a *rugged, rough* or *difficult* place. It is, perhaps, no coincidence that this area over which Uri, son of Chur, ruled reflected the same characteristics which seem indicated in his name.

Now, the name Shoval seems to carry precisely the opposite connotation:

The root שבל implies something that is smooth and flowing easily. Hence, the train of a lady's dress *(Isaiah* 47:2), a flowing stream *(Psalms* 69:3), and a path leading through waters *(Psalms* 77:20); apparently, the precise opposite of the ideas conveyed by the other names.

Thus, we detect a relationship between the two names — if only that one is the reverse of the other.

We shall not attempt an explanation of the duality implied in these two opposite names. A number of possibilities suggest themselves but none can be considered more than conjecture. We shall only note that in Scriptural poetry the contrast between rugged, rough terrain and a smooth flowing road plays a role. Thus *Isaiah* 40:4 describes the Messianic era as a time when ... *the rough and rugged terrain shall become a straight road and the hilly ground will turn into a valley.* Perhaps some such symbolism can explain the two names given to this one person.

ד הַצְלֶלְפּוֹנִי: וּפְנוּאֵל אֲבִי גְדֹר וָעֵזֶר אֲבִי חוּשָׁה אֵלֶּה

ה בְנֵי־חוּר בְּכוֹר אֶפְרָתָה אֲבִי בֵּית לָחֶם: וּלְאַשְׁחוּר אֲבִי

ו תְקוֹעַ הָיוּ שְׁתֵּי נָשִׁים חֶלְאָה וְנַעֲרָה: וַתֵּלֶד לוֹ נַעֲרָה

אֶת־אֲחֻזָּם וְאֶת־חֵפֶר וְאֶת־תֵּימְנִי וְאֶת־הָאֲחַשְׁתָּרִי אֵלֶּה

ז־ח בְּנֵי נַעֲרָה: וּבְנֵי חֶלְאָה צֶרֶת °יִצְחָר וְאֶתְנָן: וְקוֹץ הוֹלִיד

אֶת־עָנוּב וְאֶת־הַצֹּבֵבָה וּמִשְׁפְּחֹת אֲחַרְחֵל בֶּן־הָרֻם:

°וְיִצְחָר ק'

7:1: It is a positive command to stand in awe before the Sanctuary ... [but] do not fear the Sanctuary but [fear] Him Who commanded us to stand in awe.

Achumai: Because he joined Israel to God [אֲחוּמַי from אחה, *to sew together*] and made them like brothers [אָח] to God.

Lahad: Because he brought beauty and splendor upon Israel [לָהַד from הוד, *beauty*], for the Tabernacle was their splendor. See further in Section Two, p. 394.

3. וְאֵלֶּה אֲבִי עֵיטָם — *And these are the fathers of Etam.* We follow the translation of *Targum* who translates: And these are the chieftains of Etam [fathers = chieftains; see comm. 2:24], although the syntax is problematic since אֲבִי is in the singular.

From the point of view of the syntax the simplest solution would be that of *Malbim,* that אֵלֶּה is a name and that our verse continues to list the children of Reaiah, son of Shoval. His other children were *Eleh, father of Etam, Yizreel,* etc. [The *Anonymous Commentator* notes that the conjunctive *vav* is missing from the name *Yizreel.* However, he points to *Micah* 6:4 where we have the same irregularity. This irregularity also recurs frequently in *Chronicles.* See above 1:30,31,35,37,38,40 and 3:18,20,21.]

Gra, as he did in the previous verse, interprets our passage as augmenting the passage at the end of ch. 2. In his view, עֵיטָם, *Etam,* is identical with עַטְרוֹת בֵּית יוֹאָב, *Atroth Beth Yoav,* of 2:54. After the previous verse had traced the progeny of Chur's son Shoval, our verse takes up the family of the second son, Salma (2:51). 2:54 had stated that Salma's descendants

had inhabited Atroth Beth Yoav, and our verse fills out the information that the families involved were those of Yizreel, etc. In this view, some words must be interpolated. The verse must be read roughly as follows: And these [families dwelt under the] father of Etam ...

Radak translates: And these [are also descendants of Chur and Shoval, namely]; the father of Etam; Yizreel, etc. Once more, the syntax is difficult.

וְשֵׁם אֲחוֹתָם הַצְלֶלְפּוֹנִי — *And their sister's name was Hatzlelponi. Radak* points to 3:19 where a single sister was also mentioned. He thinks that these may have been the only women in the family and that they were therefore mentioned, or that they may have been well known for some reason.

This latter explanation seems to have been accepted by the Sages who say that this Hatzlelponi[1] was the mother of the Judge, Samson *(Bava Basra* 91a).

4. וּפְנוּאֵל אֲבִי גְדֹר — *And Penuel father of Gedor. Gra* notes that Gedor is listed among Judah's cities in *Joshua* 15:58. He further equates Penuel of our verse with Chareph, father of Beth Gader of 2:51 [Beth Gader and Gedor are identical].

Thus, according to *Gra,* our passage augments the passage at the end of ch. 2. Our verse 2 expands on Shoval's progeny (vs. 50 and 52 there), and our vs. 3 and 4 expand on Shoval's brother — Salma's — progeny (vs. 51 and 54 there).

וָעֵזֶר אֲבִי חוּשָׁה — *And Ezer father of Chushah. Gra* suggests that אֲבִי, *father,* in the previous phrase וּפְנוּאֵל אֲבִי גְדֹר is to be read also with our phrase. Penuel was the father of Gedor and also of Ezer who

---

1. This is based on the Talmud's reading, which does not consider the *hey* as part of the name. *Targum* and the Midrash, however, have it as part of the name rather than as a definite article. See comm. to 2:52 for the question of personal names with the definite article.

and Yidbash, and their sister's name was Hatzlelponi. ⁴ And Penuel father of Gedor, and Ezer father of Chushah. These were the sons of Chur, the first-born of Ephrathah, the father of Bethlehem. ⁵ Now Ashchur father of Tekoa had two wives — Chelah and Naarah. ⁶ And Naarah bore him Achuzzam, Chepher, Temeni, and the Achashtarites — these were the sons of Naarah. ⁷ And the sons of Chelah — Tzereth, Tzochar, and Ethnan. ⁸ And Kotz fathered Anuv and Hatzovevah, and the families of Acharchel the son of Harum.

himself was father of Chushah — that is that most of the inhabitants of Chushah were descended from him.

חוּר בְּכוֹר אֶפְרָתָה — *Chur, the first-born of Ephrathah.* See 2:19 and 50.

חוּר ... אֲבִי בֵּית־לָחֶם — *Chur ... father of Bethlehem.* 2:51 and 54 give Salma as *father of Bethlehem. Radak* notes the apparent discrepancy but explains that the text there simply gave the information in a short form. Salma was Chur's grandson, so Chur too can be said to be father of Bethlehem.

5. וּלְאַשְׁחוּר אֲבִי תְקוֹעַ — *Now Ashchur father of Tekoa.* Ashchur father of Tekoa was listed as a son of Chetzron in 2:24. His family tree had not been given there and is picked up here *(Mefaresh; Radak).*

See comm. there for the teaching of the Sages *(Sotah* 12a) that our verse refers to Calev son of Yephunneh (or, according to *Gra,* to his father, Yephunneh).

שְׁתֵּי נָשִׁים חֶלְאָה וְנַעֲרָה — *Two wives — Chelah and Naarah.* According to the teaching of the Sages that Ashchur Avi Tekoa is Calev, these two wives really symbolize periods in the life of Calev's wife, Miriam. See Section Two to chapter 2, v. 18.

6-7. וַתֵּלֶד לוֹ נַעֲרָה ... וּבְנֵי חֶלְאָה ... — *And Naarah bore him ... And the sons of Chelah ...* The interpretation of the Sages, that Ashchur Avi Tekoa is Calev, would justify the inclusion of his genealogy at this particular point. Calev, as Carmi, had figured in the previous passage as Reaiah — Betzalel's ancestor. If we would take both passages at their face value there would be no explanation for the mention of Ashchur — a son of Chetzron — here.

In the teachings of the Sages, interpretations for Chelah's children are offered which make

these names descriptions of Miriam. See Section Two to ch. 2, v. 18. No such interpretations are given for the sons of Naarah listed in verse 6. We assume that the reason is as follows: Naarah refers to Miriam after her rejuvenation (see there), and it is natural that she should then have children. No special interpretation is called for. However, Chelah describes Miriam as she was in her sickly state. She would then not have had any children. The names in verse 7 must therefore be interpreted in a way which would not contradict this.

8. וְקוֹץ — *And Kotz.* Kotz had not been mentioned before [see comm. v. 2 on Reaiah]. *Metzudos* suggests that it may be a second name for one of the people mentioned earlier.

Gra thinks that וְקוֹץ, *and Kotz,* does double duty and should also be read together with the previous verse. *And the sons of Chelah — Tzereth, Tzohar, and Ethnan [and Kotz]. And Kotz fathered ...* [See also *Targum.*]

As they did in verse 5, the Sages interpret our verse to refer to Calev. He is called קוֹץ, *Kotz,* because he rebelled [קוֹץ from קצץ, *to cut down*] against the plot of the spies. He was called עָנוּב, *Anuv,* because he was deserving in the matter in the bunch of grapes (which the spies brought back from Israel) [עָנוּב from עֵנָב, *grape*], which were brought back only because of him. He was called צוֹבֵבָה, *Tzovevah,* because he brought about that which God desired [צוֹבֵבָה from צִבְיוֹן, *desire*] *(Shemos Rabbah* 1:17).

Perhaps the Sages offered their interpretation in order to avoid the difficulty raised above — that Kotz is introduced here without having been mentioned previously. If Kotz is indeed Calev, then his refusal to be carried along by the rest of the spies is germane to verse 5 where we learn of his willingness to marry Miriam in spite of her sickly state. See Section Two p. 388.]

וּמִשְׁפְּחוֹת אֲחַרְחֵל בֶּן־הָרֻם — *And the families of Acharchel the son of Harum.* These

ד

ט-יב

ט וַיְהִי יַעְבֵּץ נִכְבָּד מֵאֶחָיו וְאִמּוֹ קָרְאָה שְׁמוֹ יַעְבֵּץ לֵאמֹר
י כִּי יָלַדְתִּי בְּעֹצֶב: וַיִּקְרָא יַעְבֵּץ לֵאלֹהֵי יִשְׂרָאֵל לֵאמֹר
אִם־בָּרֵךְ תְּבָרֲכֵנִי וְהִרְבִּיתָ אֶת־גְּבוּלִי וְהָיְתָה יָדְךָ עִמִּי
וְעָשִׂיתָ מֵרָעָה לְבִלְתִּי עָצְבִּי וַיָּבֵא אֱלֹהִים אֵת־אֲשֶׁר
יא שָׁאָל: וּכְלוּב אֲחִי־שׁוּחָה הוֹלִיד אֶת־
יב מְחִיר הוּא אֲבִי אֶשְׁתּוֹן: וְאֶשְׁתּוֹן הוֹלִיד אֶת־בֵּית רָפָא

families were also descended from Kotz (Gra). This general statement will be further elaborated in the next verse where Yabetz, the most important member of the Acharchel family, is discussed (Gra).

Continuing with their midrashic interpretation begun in verse 5, the Sages interpret the families of Acharchel as referring to Calev's wife Miriam. She is called Acharchel because she led the women in their music and dance after the splitting of the sea (see Ex. 15:20). [אֲחַרְחֵל is taken as a contraction of two words: אַחַר, after; and חֵל, a contraction of מָחוֹל, dance.] Ben Harum also refers to Miriam. David, King of Israel, was descended from her and her husband Calev (see Section Two, p. 388ff). This kingdom was to be exalted [הָרוּם from רמם, to lift up] by God.

⇥§ Yabetz and his Prayer

9. וַיְהִי יַעְבֵּץ — *Now Yabetz was.* Yabetz was a descendant of the *family of Acharchel* [v. 9] (Gra).

Thus, according to Gra we have a family sequence: Ashchur Avi Tekoa, Kotz, Acharchel, and Yabetz.

The Sages identify Yabetz with Othniel ben Kenaz, the Judge who followed Joshua as leader of the Israelites (Temurah 16a). This will be discussed in the next verse.[1]

וַיְהִי יַעְבֵּץ נִכְבָּד מֵאֶחָיו — *Now Yabetz was the most honored of his brothers.* The Midrash remarks: *The wise shall inherit honor* (Proverbs 3:35). Honor is fitting for the Sages who exhaust themselves in the study of Torah. There are thirty-six generations (listed in Chronicles) from Adam to Yabetz. But the word honor is not written in connection with any of them except Yabetz. And why? Because he was a Torah sage who taught Torah in public, as it is

written (above 2:55): *And families of scribes, dwellers in Yabetz* (Tanchuma, Tzaveh 9). See Section Two, p. 396.

וְאִמּוֹ קָרְאָה שְׁמוֹ יַעְבֵּץ לֵאמֹר כִּי יָלַדְתִּי בְּעֹצֶב — *And his mother called him Yabetz saying, 'For I have borne in pain.'* Pain is עֹצֶב in Hebrew, and the name יַעְבֵּץ contains the same letters albeit in different order [עבץ instead of עצב]. Metzudos thinks that the change was intentional. By reversing the letters the mother wanted to imply that the sorrow of his birth should be changed into happiness.

Radak points out the phenomenon of a name being derived from a given word in a way which cannot be justified grammatically is not infrequent in Scripture. He cites three examples: נֹחַ from נחם; קַיִן from קנה; and שְׁמוּאֵל from שאל. See further in Section Two, p. 396.

10. וַיִּקְרָא יַעְבֵּץ ... לְבִלְתִּי עָצְבִּי — *And Yabetz called ... that I not be saddened.* Taken at its simplest, Yabetz's prayer was a supplication to God that the pain implicit in his name should not be realized in his own life; לְבִלְתִּי עָצְבִּי (*that I not be saddened*), is obviously a play on his name יַעְבֵּץ. [See Overview p. xxxv ff for a discussion of the idea that a person's destiny may be implied in his name.] God answered his prayers and he led a happy life (Radak).

אִם־בָּרֵךְ תְּבָרֲכֵנִי ... — *If You will surely bless me ...* The conditional if implies that some kind of a vow was made. If You will do all that I ask — then I will do such and such. However, the clause is left hanging and there is no indication what this vow may have been. Metzudos compares II Samuel 5:8 for a similar formulation.

וְהִרְבִּיתָ אֶת־גְּבוּלִי — *And enlarge my*

---

1. It should be noted that in this case the homiletic interpretation of the Sages would not be in agreement with the simple meaning of the verse as Gra understands it. The Sages teach that Ashchur Avi Tekoa is Calev. If Yabetz is Othniel ben Kenaz that would make Othniel a descendant of Calev. According to Judges 3:9, Othniel was Calev's younger brother (or half-brother — see Temurah 16a).

4

9-12

⁹ *Now Yabetz was the most honored of his brothers and his mother called him Yabetz saying, 'For I have borne in pain.'* ¹⁰ *And Yabetz called to the God of Israel saying, 'If You will surely bless me, and enlarge my boundaries, and Your hand will be with me, and You will avert evil that I not be saddened.' And God granted what he had asked.* ¹¹ *And Cheluv the brother of Shuchah fathered Mechir — he was the father of Eshton.* ¹² *And Eshton fathered Beth Rapha,*

---

boundaries. That my holdings should be large *(Malbim)*.

וְהָיְתָה יָדְךָ עִמִּי — *And Your hand will be with me.* To help me in time of need *(Metzudos)*.

וְעָשִׂיתָ מֵּרָעָה — *And You will avert evil.* You will take those evils, the intimation of which saddened my mother at my birth, and turn them into good *that I not be saddened,* as my mother had requested by calling my name Yabetz [by inverting the letters of the word עצב, *pain,* to עבץ — see above] *(Metzudos)*.

לְבִלְתִּי עָצְבִּי — *That I not be saddened.* Radak is not certain whether עָצְבִּי is to be understood as the infinitive of the intransitive verb *to be sad,* thus: *That I be not in a state of sadness;* or whether it is the passive of the transitive verb: *to sadden,* as we have translated it.

Note that in the simple translation the two words: לְבִלְתִּי עָצְבִּי, *that I not be saddened,* go together. In both interpretations of the Sages [see below] the two words are separated and each stands for a different thought.

עָצְבִּי — *Saddened.* Yabetz prayed that God should help him to fulfill His commands energetically. When a person is sad his actions tend towards lethargy *(Gra)*.

The Sages read a great deal more into this prayer *(Temurah* 16a). We have learned that Othniel [ben Kenaz, first Judge of Israel after Joshua; see *Joshua* 15-17 and *Judges* 1:3 for details] is [identical with] Yabetz ... [Why was he called] Othniel? Because God answered him. [There is a phonetic relationship between עָתְנִיאֵל and עָנָה אֹתוֹ אֵ־ל, *God answered him.*] [Why was he called] Yabetz? [Because] he counseled [יַעְבֵּץ from יעץ, *to counsel*] and spread Torah in Israel.

Now how do we know that God answered him? For it is written: *And Yabetz called to the God of Israel saying ... And God brought him all that he had asked.* [We now interpret.] *If You will*

surely bless me — with Torah [that is, that I will know much Torah]; *and enlarge my boundaries* — with students; *and Your hand will be with me* — that I will not forget my learning; *and You will avert evil* — that I will meet friends who complement my nature [a play on the word מֵרָעָה as though it derived from רֵעַ, *friend*]; *that I not* — that my evil inclination will not prevent me from learning Torah; *be saddened* — If You do all this for me — good; if not, I will go to my grave in sorrow. [This is the teaching of R' Nosson.] R' Yehudah HaNassi explained: *If You will surely bless me* — by allowing me to be fruitful; *and enlarge my boundaries* — with sons and daughters; *and Your hand will be with me* — in my business affairs; *and You will avert evil* — that neither my head, ears nor eyes will trouble me; *that I not* — that my evil inclination will not prevent me from learning Torah; *be saddened* — if You do that for me — good. If not, I will go to my grave in sorrow. See Section Two, p. 396, for a discussion of this.

11. וּכְלוּב אֲחִי־שׁוּחָה — *And Cheluv the brother of Shuchah.* Neither Shuchah nor Cheluv have been mentioned before [unless, with *Ralbag,* we identify the Shuchah of our verse with the Chushah of verse 4 and assume an inversion of letters as happens frequently with names]. They must also be part of the family of Acharchel (v. 8).

There are no extant midrashim concerning these names, and we can only assume that the lost *Sefer HaYuchasin* would have explained their significance.

הוּא אֲבִי אֶשְׁתּוֹן — *He was the father of Eshton.* In 2:24 the difficulty of knowing the exact translation of אֲבִי in this connection has been noted. Is it father or is it chieftain? From the next verse, where Eshton is reported as having fathered Beth Raphah, it would seem that Eshton is an

וְאֶת־־פָּסֵחַ וְאֶת־־תְּחִנָּה אֲבִי עִיר־־נָחָשׁ אֵלֶּה אַנְשֵׁי
רֵכָה: יג וּבְנֵי קְנַז עָתְנִיאֵל וּשְׂרָיָה וּבְנֵי עָתְנִיאֵל
חֲתַת: יד וּמְעוֹנֹתַי הוֹלִיד אֶת־עָפְרָה וּשְׂרָיָה הוֹלִיד אֶת־
יוֹאָב אֲבִי גֵּיא חֲרָשִׁים כִּי חֲרָשִׁים הָיוּ: וּבְנֵי
כָּלֵב בֶּן־יְפֻנֶּה עִירוּ אֵלָה וָנָעַם וּבְנֵי אֵלָה וּקְנַז: וּבְנֵי

individual rather than a place-name. If so, אֲבִי here would certainly be *father*.

12. וְאֶשְׁתּוֹן הוֹלִיד — *And Eshton fathered.* From this phrase it appears that Eshton is an individual rather than a place-name.

However, another explanation of our phrase is possible. *Sefer HaRikmah* points out that it is typical of Hebrew usage to shorten phrases by eliminating descriptive words in cases where the context in which the phrase appears makes a detailed description unnecessary. An example is *Genesis* 9:25. Earlier, the passage had described how Noah's son, Ham, had dealt disrespectfully with his father. Noah now punishes him by expressing a curse. But that curse reads: *May Canaan be cursed ...* Why the son rather than Ham himself who was the perpetrator of the shameful deed? *Sefer HaRikmah's* solution is that *Cursed be Canaan ...* really means *Cursed be* the father *of Canaan ...* The word אֲבִי, *the father of*, is left out because it is obvious from the context that he is meant. *Sefer HaRikmah* cites our verse as well. *Eshton* really means *father of Eshton*, as in the previous verse. The word אֲבִי is left out because it can be derived from the context. Thus, Eshton is a place-name but אֲבִי אֶשְׁתּוֹן, *The chieftain of Eshton*, fathered these children.

אֵלֶּה אַנְשֵׁי רֵכָה — *These are the men of Rechah.* The *Mefaresh* thinks that Rechah could be a place-name or it could be a name by which the family was known. He gives no reason for this, and the commentators admit ignorance of the meaning of this phrase. They assume that those people were known as *men of Rechah* for a reason which was clear at that time but which has been lost to us[1] (Radak; Metzudos; Malbim).

13. וּבְנֵי קְנַז — *And the sons of Kenaz.* Kenaz had not been mentioned earlier. *Gra* assumes that he, too, was descended from

the family of Acharchel, for which reason he is included in this sequence.

עָתְנִיאֵל — *Othniel.* Othniel ben Kenaz was the Judge who took over the mantle of leadership after Joshua's death (*Judges* 3:9). There he is described as the younger brother of Calev ben Yephunneh. The Sages (*Temurah* 16a) explain that he was actually a half-brother; they had the same mother but different fathers.

After Yephunneh died, Calev's mother married Kenaz and bore him Othniel. Calev was raised by Kenaz, for which reason he is sometimes referred to as הַקְּנִזִּי, *the Kenazite* (see comm. to v. 15). The Sages there also identify Othniel with Yabetz (vs. 9,10). It was Othniel who, by his intellect alone, rediscovered the many points of Torah law which had been forgotten in the period of mourning immediately following the death of Moses.

וּבְנֵי עָתְנִיאֵל חֲתַת — *And the sons of Othniel — Chathath.* This is another example of the plural וּבְנֵי, *the sons of*, being used for only one child (see above 1:41, 2:8).

14. וּמְעוֹנֹתַי הוֹלִיד אֶת־עָפְרָה — *And Meonothai fathered Ophrah.* Meonothai has not been mentioned before. *Gra* thinks that this is one more instance in which one word has to do double duty. Meonothai is to be read both with the previous verse and with verse 14. It is as though the text reads: *The son of Othniel was Chathath [and the son of Chathath was Meonothai]. And Meonothai fathered Ophrah.*

וּשְׂרָיָה הוֹלִיד — *And Seraiah fathered.* This Seraiah is the son of Kenaz and brother of Othniel [v. 13] (Gra).

אֲבִי גֵּיא חֲרָשִׁים — *Father of Ge Charashim.* Either Yoav's children settled Ge Charashim [lit. *the valley of the artisans*] (Radak), or he himself was chieftain of the valley (Mefaresh).

1. *Targum* renders: *These are the men of the great Sanhedrin.*

Paseach, and Techinnah, the father of Ir Nachash; these are the men of Rechah. ¹³ *And the sons of Kenaz — Othniel and Seraiah; and the sons of Othniel — Chathath.* ¹⁴ *And Meonothai fathered Ophrah, and Seraiah fathered Yoav, father of Ge Charashim, for they were artisans.* ¹⁵ *And the sons of Calev the son of Yephunneh — Iru, Elah and Naam; and the sons of Elah — Kenaz.* ¹⁶ *And the sons of*

כִּי חֲרָשִׁים הָיוּ — *For they were artisans.* The valley received its name because of the main profession of the people who lived there *(Commentators).*

◈§ Calev Son of Yephunneh

15. כָּלֵב בֶּן יְפֻנֶּה — *Calev the son of Yephunneh.* This is the first time that the name Calev ben Yephunneh occurs in *Chronicles.* The name is familiar from *Numbers* (chs. 13,14) and *Joshua* where he is mentioned as the representative of the tribe of Judah among the spies whom Moses sent to the Land of Israel. It was he, together with Joshua, who remained loyal to God and refused to join the other spies in their denigration of the Land. In *Numbers* 32:12 and *Joshua* 14:6 and 13 Calev is described as הַקְּנִזִּי, *the Kenazite,* and this is interpreted in *Temurah* 16a as indicating that Calev was the step-son of the Kenaz mentioned in verse 13. Since he is identified as belonging to the family of Kenaz, it is logical that his genealogy should be given here.

This reasoning holds good only if we assume that Calev ben Yephunneh is not identical with the Calev ben Chetzron of ch. 2 and that all references to Calev there are to Calev ben Chetzron. This has been discussed in the prefatory note to 2:18. However, as has been pointed out repeatedly, the Sages assume Calev ben Chetzron and Calev ben Yephunneh to be one and the same person. Moreover, even those commentators who, for various reasons, think they were two distinct people still interpret some passages in ch. 2 as referring to Calev ben Yephunneh. If that is so, it seems strange that another genealogical section about him should be given here. However, the *Mefaresh, Radak* and *Metzudos* all point out that it is typical of *Chronicles* to begin a genealogy, interrupt it, and then take it up again later (see e.g., 2:42).

Ralbag suggests that Yephunneh might be identical with Penuel who is listed in verse 4 as *father of Gedor.* [יְפֻנֶּה and פְּנוּאֵל both derive from the same root פנה, *to turn.*] Since verse 18 lists *Yered father of Gedor* as a descendant of Calev ben Yephunneh it could well be that verse 4 had listed Penuel/Yephunneh as 'father,' that is ancestor, of Gedor.

In order to present the opinion of the Sages that Calev ben Yephunneh and Calev ben Chetzron are the same person, clearly, we quote *Temurah* 16a:

'[*Judges* 3:9 had described Othniel ben Kenaz as Calev's younger brother. This would imply that Calev's father was Kenaz.] But was his father Kenaz? Was his father not Yephunneh? [His father was really Kenaz.] He was called Yephunneh because he turned away [יְפֻנֶּה from פנה, *to turn*] from the plans of the spies. But, still, was he the son of Kenaz? Was he not the son of Chetzron, as it is written (*Chronicles* 2:18) *And Calev ben Chetzron bore Azuvah ...?* Said Rava: [Calev's true father was indeed Chetzron. Othniel was described as Calev's younger brother because] Calev was the step-son of Kenaz.' See also *Yerushalmi, Kiddushin* 1:2.

וּבְנֵי אֵלָה וּקְנַז — *And the sons of Elah — Kenaz.* The *Mefaresh, Radak, Metzudos* and *Malbim* all explain that the *vav* in וּקְנַז is not the conjunction *and,* but is part of the name.

However, *Targum* eliminates the *vav* in his translation and renders simply: The sons of Elah — Kenaz. *Ralbag* also writes that the name is Kenaz. These commentators seem to assume that the *vav* at the beginning of the word is redundant and has no meaning at all. [See *Sefer HaRikmah* 6 under *Vav* where he writes that one of the properties of the letter *vav* is that it is occasionally added to the beginning of a word with no discernible meaning. As one example among many he quotes *Genesis* 36:24; see below 27:4.]

Gra suggests that, as we have noted so often in *Chronicles,* the word וּבְנֵי serves double duty and belongs to the earlier phrase as well: *And the sons of Calev ... and Naam,* [*and the sons of Naam were*] *Elah and Kenaz, and the son of Elah was*

יז יְהַלֶּלְאֵל זִיף וְזִיפָה תִּירְיָא וַאֲשַׂרְאֵל: וּבֶן־עֶזְרָה יֶתֶר

וּמֶרֶד וְעֵפֶר וְיָלוֹן וַתַּהַר אֶת־מִרְיָם וְאֶת־שַׁמַּי וְאֶת־יִשְׁבַּח

יח אֲבִי אֶשְׁתְּמֹעַ: וְאִשְׁתּוֹ הַיְהֻדִיָּה יָלְדָה אֶת־יֶרֶד אֲבִי גְדוֹר

וְאֶת־חֶבֶר אֲבִי שׂוֹכוֹ וְאֶת־יְקוּתִיאֵל אֲבִי זָנוֹחַ וְאֵלֶּה בְּנֵי

יט בִּתְיָה בַת־פַּרְעֹה אֲשֶׁר לָקַח מָרֶד: וּבְנֵי

אֵשֶׁת הוֹדִיָּה אֲחוֹת נַחַם אֲבִי קְעִילָה הַגַּרְמִי וְאֶשְׁתְּמֹעַ

כ הַמַּעֲכָתִי: וּבְנֵי שִׁימוֹן אַמְנוֹן וְרִנָּה בֶּן־חָנָן °וְתוֹלוֹן וּבְנֵי °וְתִילוֹן ק'

כא יִשְׁעִי זוֹחֵת וּבֶן־זוֹחֵת: בְּנֵי שֵׁלָה בֶן־יְהוּדָה עֵר אֲבִי לֵכָה

Kenaz. Thus, the *vav* is indeed the conjunction *and*, but is required only along with the implied meaning of וּבְנֵי; Naam's sons were Elah *and* Kenaz while Elah's son was also called Kenaz.

In any case, this is yet another example of the plural וּבְנֵי, *sons*, being used to describe one son. See v. 13 above.

16. וּבְנֵי יְהַלֶּלְאֵל — *And the sons of Yehallelel.* Once more *Gra* suggests that וּבְנֵי does double service, belonging also to the previous verse. It is as though the text read: ... [*and the children of Kenaz* — *Yehallelel*]. *And the children of Yehallelel* ...

Malbim thinks that Yehallelel may have been a woman's name and that she was one of Calev's wives. This would balance our verse with the next in which Ezrah seems to be a woman — presumably a wife of Calev's.

17. וּבֶן־עֶזְרָה — *And the son of Ezrah. Gra* writes that this Ezrah is a woman. Presumably his reason is that he interprets the verse in such a way that Ezrah is the subject of וַתַּהַר, *and she conceived,* at the end of the verse. See below for *Radak's* view.

וַתַּהַר — *And she conceived. Gra* assumes that the subject is Ezrah who is mentioned at the beginning of this verse. Since the expression is *she conceived,* rather than *she bore,* he deduces that the three children mentioned at the end of the verse were triplets, all conceived at the same time.

Radak disagrees on both points. Based

on his understanding of v. 18, he assumes that the subject of *she conceived* is an unnamed wife of Mered. [According to this interpretation, it is probable that he takes Ezrah at the beginning of our verse as a man's name.] Further, he feels that the translation of וַתַּהַר may well be *and she bore.* He cites an analogy from the word הוֹרִים [lit. *those who cause conception*], which means *parents,* although we would expect parents to be viewed from the point of view of birth rather than conception.

מִרְיָם — *Miriam. Radak* assumes Miriam here to be a man's name. He points out that we often find names which are used for both men and women. As an example he cites Aviyah, the name of Chetzron's wife (2:24). It is also the name of one of the Davidic kings (3:10).

18. וְאִשְׁתּוֹ הַיְהֻדִיָּה יָלְדָה ... וְאֵלֶּה בְּנֵי בִתְיָה בַת פַּרְעֹה אֲשֶׁר לָקַח מָרֶד — *And his Jewish wife bore ... and these are the sons of Bithiah the daughter of Pharaoh whom Mered had married.* There is an apparent contradiction in this verse, which begins with a list of children from a Jewish wife[1] and ends by saying that these were the children of Bithiah the daughter of Pharaoh, who seems to be a different woman. Four possible explanations are offered:

The *Mefaresh:* וְאֵלֶּה is not to be translated *and these* but is a proper name. The verse is rendered as follows: [*Calev's*] *Jewish wife bore Yered ... and Eleh was the son of Bithiah ... whom Mered had married.*

---

1. יְהֻדִיָּה has been rendered as *Jewish* following the opinion of most commentators. In the first three explanations it is used in the text in order to contrast her with Bithiah, daughter of Pharaoh, who was not of Jewish descent.

Note further that אִשְׁתּוֹ, *his wife,* could refer either to Calev or to Mered. Mered, however, may also be identical with Calev. See below.

4

17-21

Yehallel — Ziph, Ziphah, Tiria and Asarel. ¹⁷ And the son of Ezrah — Yether, Mered, Epher, and Yalon. And she conceived Miriam, and Shammai, and Yishbach, father of Eshtemoa. ¹⁸ And his Jewish wife bore Yered father of Gedor, and Chever father of Socho, and Yekuthiel father of Zanoach, and these are the sons of Bithiah the daughter of Pharaoh whom Mered had married. ¹⁹ And the sons of the wife of Hodiah, sister of Nacham — the father of Keilah the Garmite and Eshtemoa the Maachathite. ²⁰ And the sons of Shimon — Amon, Rinnah, Ben Chanan, and Tilon; and the sons of Yishi — Zocheth and Ben Zocheth. ²¹ The sons of Shelah the son of Judah — Er the father of Lechah, Ladah father of Mareshah, and the families

Radak, Ralbag, Metzudos: [Mered's] *Jewish wife bore Yered ... but these* [four sons beginning with Miriam listed at the end of the previous verse] *were the sons of Bithiah.*

Gra: יָלְדָה should not be rendered *bore* but *raised.* The word is used in accordance with the dictum of the Sages *(Megillah* 13a) that one who raises someone else's child as his own is considered as though he had given birth to that child. The verse teaches that Mered's Jewish wife raised the children but in reality these were Mered's children by Bithiah the daughter of Pharaoh.

The Sages take the view that only one woman is mentioned in this verse. They render אִשְׁתּוֹ הַיְהֻדִיָה as his *Judaic wife,* and it is a description of the daughter of Pharaoh who saved Moses from the river (see *Exodus* 2:5ff). According to the tradition of the Sages, she rejected her father's idol-worship on that day. Based on *Daniel* 3:12: אִיתַי גֻּבְרִין יְהוּדָאִין ... לֵאלָהָךְ לָא פָלְחִין, *There are Judean men ... your gods they do not worship,* they teach that anyone who rejects idol worship is called a 'Judah' person and thus Bithiah becomes אִשְׁתּוֹ הַיְהֻדִיָה, *his 'Judaic' wife.*

In this interpretation, the names of the children are all homiletically applied to Moses and, as in *Gra's* interpretation, יָלְדָה is translated *reared* or *raised* rather than bore. [For details of the Sages' interpretation see Section Two, p. 402.]

אֲבִי גְדֹר ... שׂוֹכוֹ ... וְזָנוֹחַ — *Father of Gedor ... Socho ... Zanoach.* All these are Judean cities mentioned in *Joshua;* Gedor in 15:58, Socho in 15:48, Zanoach in 15:34 and 56 *(Mefaresh).*

19. וּבְנֵי אֵשֶׁת הוֹדִיָה — *And the sons of the*

wife of Hodiah. *Radak* thinks that Hodiah is a proper name, and this verse is one more example of a given person's children being listed although he himself had not been mentioned previously.

According to *Gra,* Hodiah is an adjective, and אֵשֶׁת הוֹדִיָה is the אִשְׁתּוֹ הַיְהֻדִיָה, *his Jewish wife,* of v. 18. Our verse lists her own children while the previous verse listed the children whom she had reared but who were really children of Bithiah daughter of Pharaoh.

אֲחוֹת נַחַם — *Sister of Nacham.* Nacham is not mentioned elsewhere and we do not know who he is.

Gra again thinks that the name Nacham should be read twice. אֵשֶׁת הוֹדִיָה was a sister of Nacham and also named her son Nacham. Thus: *Nacham, father of Keilah the Garmite.*

20. וּבְנֵי שִׁימוֹן ... וּבְנֵי יִשְׁעִי — *And the sons of Shimon ... and the sons of Yishi. Gra* writes that these men were descended from the family of Acharchel (v. 8). [See *Gra* to vs. 9 and 11.] They were well known in their own right and there was no need to identify them as children of their fathers.

21. בְּנֵי שֵׁלָה בֶן־יְהוּדָה — *The sons of Shelah the son of Judah.* Shelah was Judah's third son (2:3). Although he was older than Peretz and Zerach, the children of the union between Judah and Tamar *(Genesis* ch. 38), their genealogies preceded his because it was from Peretz that David was descended. Now that the lists of the tribe of Judah come to a close there are some short notes on those of Shelah's family *(Radak).*

עֵר אֲבִי לֵכָה — *Er the father of Lechah.* Shelah called one of his sons by the name of his brother, Judah's first-born (2:3).

כב־כג

ד וְלַעְדָּה אָבִי מָרֵשָׁה וּמִשְׁפְּחוֹת בֵּית־עֲבֹדַת הַבֻּץ לְבֵית

כב אַשְׁבֵּעַ: וְיוֹקִים וְאַנְשֵׁי כֹזֵבָא וְיוֹאָשׁ וְשָׂרָף אֲשֶׁר־בָּעֲלוּ

כג לְמוֹאָב וְיָשֻׁבִי לָחֶם וְהַדְּבָרִים עַתִּיקִים: הֵמָּה הַיּוֹצְרִים

אֲבִי לֶכָה ... אֲבִי מָרֵשָׁה — *Father of Lechah ...
father of Mareshah.* Targum renders the
first אֲבִי as *father* and the second as
chieftain. See comm. 2:24.

וּמִשְׁפְּחוֹת בֵּית־עֲבֹדַת הַבֻּץ לְבֵית אַשְׁבֵּעַ — *And
the families of linen workers belonging to
the house of Ashbea.* There was, among
Shelah's descendants (*Mefaresh*), a tribal
unit called Beth Ashbea. The families belonging to this unit were linen workers
(*Metzudos*). Their products were used for
the royal garments and the priestly vestments (*Targum*) and for the hangings in
the Temple (*Mefaresh*).

The Sages have a tradition that the
descendants which are listed for Shelah
hint at a series of proselytes who joined the
Jewish people at various points in history.
In our commentary to this section (vs. 21-
23), we will follow the version of *Sifri,
Behaaloscha.*

In a long section, *Sifri* cites many
examples of how God generously rewarded
various non-Jews who had taken the
initiative to come close to God and become
proselytes. In this connection, they explain
our verse as referring to Rachav, the inn-
keeper of Jericho, who saved Joshua's spies
(*Joshua* ch. 2). After Jericho fell, she
converted to Judaism and, in the tradition
of the Sages (*Megillah* 14b), she married
Joshua. Her reward was that some of
Israel's greatest prophets descended from
her. Our verse alludes to her:

'What [is the meaning of that which] is
written: *And the families of the linen
workers from the house of Ashbea.*
[Rachav is referred to as] *linen workers*
because she hid the spies among the flax.
[She is described as] *the house of Ashbea*
[from נשבע, *to swear*] for the spies swore to
her [that she would not be harmed]' (*Sifri,
Behaaloscha*). See further in Section Two,
p. 404.

22. This verse continues with the listing of
Shelah's descendants. They are: Yokim,
the dwellers of [the city] Cozeva; Yoash;
Saraph, and Yashuvi Lechem (*Mefaresh*).

וְאַנְשֵׁי כֹזֵבָא — *And the people of Cozeva.*

Gra identifies this city with Achzivah
which is mentioned in *Joshua* 19:29.

Many commentators think that it might
be identical with the city Cheziv which,
according to *Genesis* 38:7, was the place
where Shelah was born.

וְיוֹאָשׁ וְשָׂרָף אֲשֶׁר־בָּעֲלוּ לְמוֹאָב — *And Yoash
and Saraph, who became the masters of
Moab.* The translation follows *Radak* and
others who think that בעל here is used in
the sense of owning or controlling
something [cf. *Exodus* 21:28ff]. Yoash and
Saraph had fought against Moab and had
become 'masters' of that land.

R' Shmuel Masnuth finds that the root
בעל is sometimes used in the sense *of
dwelling* (*Isaiah* 62:4). Hence, *who lived in
Moab.*

Mefaresh and a number of other
commentators take בָּעֲלוּ as indicating
marriage, thus: *who married Moabites.*
[Scripture uses בַּעַל for *husband.* Cf.
Genesis 20:3.] This follows the opinion of
the Sages who identify Yoash and Saraph
of our verse as Machlon and Kilion, the
sons of Elimelech and Naomi, who died in
Moab after they had married Ruth and
Orpah respectively (see *Book of Ruth*).

There is a controversy between Rav and
Shmuel. One says that the true names of
the brothers were Machlon and Kilion [as
given in *Ruth*]. In *Chronicles* they are
called by other names so that we may learn
something about them: Yoash [from יאש, *to
despair*] because they despaired of ever
being redeemed [from the famine which
raged in the Land of Israel (*Rashbam*); it
was only because they felt that they would
never be able to return home that they
married Moabite women (*Emek HaNetziv*)]; Saraph [from שרף, *to burn*] because
according to Divine justice they deserved
to be burned [for leaving the Land of Israel
without sufficient reason (*Rashbam*)].

The other says that their true names
were Yoash and Saraph. Their names in
Ruth teach us the following: Machlon
[from חלל, *to desecrate*] because they
lowered themselves to act in a way which
was unworthy of them; Kilion [from כלה,

דברי הימים א [60]

4

22-23

of linen workers belonging to the house of Ashbea. ²² *And Yokim and the people of Cozeva; and Yoash and Saraph, who became the masters of Moab, and Yashuvi Lechem. Now these are ancient traditions.* ²³ *They were the potters, dwellers in Netaim and*

to destroy] because they deserved to be destroyed [for leaving the Land of Israel (*Rashbam*)].

The Talmud concludes that the truth lies with that opinion which holds that their true names were Machlon and Kilion.

Maharal explains: Their given names belong in *Ruth* which deals with the outer facts of the story. *Chronicles'* interest, on the other hand, lies not with the form but the essence; it is the inner dynamics of the historical saga, the motives and drives which are part and parcel of the mystery, purpose and goal of creation, which are the core of this book. In such a context not their given names but those which point to their experience are appropriate. [This is from a difficult and profound piece of *Maharal*. For a true understanding of his views concerning the meaning of *Chronicles*, the interested reader should see *Maharal, Chidushei Aggadah* to *Bava Basra* 91b.]

וְיֹשְׁבֵי לָחֶם — *And Yashuvi Lechem. Radak* and others think that this is a proper name of one of Shelah's descendants. *Gra* writes that the words are to be understood as though they are written יוֹשְׁבֵי לֶחֶם, *dwellers of [the city] Lechem* — the Judean city of Lachmas mentioned in *Joshua* 15:40.

וְהַדְּבָרִים עַתִּיקִים — *Now these are ancient traditions.* Although the events concerning Yoash and Saraph's conquest of Moab [see *Radak's* interpretation of בְּעֲלוּ] are not generally known, that is because they happened many years ago [עֲתִיקִים from עתק, *ancient*, as in *Daniel* 7:9] (*Metzudos*). And in spite of the fact that it is not to be found in any of the Scriptural books, the story is based on a reliable tradition which was passed on from one generation to another [עֲתִיקִים from עתק, *to uproot from one place and put it down in another*, as in *Genesis* 12:8; also used when copying from one source and writing it down in another, as in *Proverbs* 25:1] (*Radak*).

In the above two interpretations this phrase refers only to the information contained in our verse. However, *Radak* points out that the phrase may well refer to all the genealogical information contained in *Chronicles*. We are not to harbor any doubts about the accuracy of those lists

which are not confirmed by any other of the Scriptural books, because all the information Ezra put down came to him through reliable traditions.

Since this last interpretation goes to the very heart of the fundamental questions concerning the origin of the genealogical lists (see Overview p. xx *ff*, Appendix II), we should carefully consider some of the other explanations of this difficult phrase. [Note that a number of interpretations are offered in the Talmud and Midrash. However, these are based on the homiletic teachings which the Sages attach to these verses.]

The *Anonymous Commentator:* These are the things which are gathered together and copied down. For they were copied down from the great history book (מִדְּבְרֵי הַיָּמִים סֵפֶר הַגָּדוֹל) from which the prophets copied them.

Gra: These are the matters which the men of Chizkiah [Hezekiah] copied down.

[*Gra's* cryptic commentary must be understood in the light of his comment to *Proverbs* 25:1 which reads: *Also these are the proverbs of Solomon which the men of Chizkiah, king of Judah, copied down.* To this *Gra* comments: For when the Men of the Great Assembly gathered all the Books of Prophets and Writings in their correct order, they found these sayings of Solomon which had been previously transcribed by the men of Chizkiah, who had re-established Torah scholarship after the death of Achaz.

Apparently *Gra* thinks that during the great revitalization of Torah study which took place when Chizkiah succeeded his wicked father Achaz, a special effort was made to collect and commit to writing as many of the old records as possible. Thus were preserved the sayings of Solomon which are recorded in *Proverbs* ch. 25 and onwards, and thus also the genealogical tables of ancient times became recorded and were still accessible to Ezra centuries later when he wrote *Chronicles* (see further in Overview p. xx *ff*).]

The Sages interpret our verse homiletically to refer to people known to us from

וְיוֹשְׁבֵי נְטָעִים וּגְדֵרָה עִם־־־־־־הַמֶּלֶךְ בִּמְלַאכְתּוֹ יָשְׁבוּ

שָׁם: כד   בְּנֵי שִׁמְעוֹן נְמוּאֵל וְיָמִין יָרִיב זֶרַח שָׁאוּל:

other parts of Scripture: *And Yokim* [from
קים, *to establish*] — this refers to Joshua
who established an oath to the Giveonites
(see *Joshua* 9:3ff); and the dwellers of
Cozeiva [from כזב, *to deceive*] — this refers
to the Giveonites who deceived Joshua;
And Yoash and Saraph — these are
Machlon and Kilion ... [see above for the
interpretation of the names]; *who married
Moabites* — because they married Moabite
women [Ruth and Orpah]; *and Yashuvi
Lechem* [from שוב, *to return*] — this refers
to the Moabite Ruth who returned and
settled in Bethlehem of Judah; *and these
are ancient traditions* — these matters were
decreed by the Ancient of Days (see *Daniel*
7:9) [God, who 'decreed' that Machlon and
Kilion should leave the Land of Israel
which resulted in Ruth marrying Boaz and
the birth of the Davidic royal dynasty]
(*Rashbam*) (*Bava Basra* 91b).

Sifri derives the same lesson from these
incidents as it does from the story of
Rachav (see v. 21). If a non-Jew makes
personal sacrifices in order to come close to
God by converting, then God will reward
that effort. The Giveonites could have
saved their lives by leaving the country,
but instead they chose to run the risk
inherent in their approach to Joshua in
order to join the Jewish people. They were
rewarded by being eternally associated
with the Temple service. Ruth gave up the
luxuries of her father's royal house to live
as an indigent in Judah. Eventually she
became the mother of Israel's kings (see
Emek HaNetziv on *Sifri*).

With these homiletic interpretations in mind,
Sifri to *Behaaloscha* has another explanation for
the phrase: *these are ancient traditions.* It
comments: 'Each of these subjects [that is the
story of Joshua and the Giveonites and the story
of Ruth] are expanded upon in their correct
place.' *Netziv* explains that in this version the
word עתיקים derives from עתק, *strong* or *fat* (as
in *I Samuel* 2:3; see also *Radak* in *Sefer
HaShorashim*). The meaning is that while here
there are only hints to various occurrences, these
matters have many important details which can
be found in other parts of Scripture.

We have seen that midrashim find references
among Shelah's descendants to Rachav, the
Giveonites and Ruth. See the Overviews (pp. xii,
xviii) for a discussion of how we are to

understand such midrashic references in light of
the fact that these people had no physical
relationship with Shelah.

23. הֵמָּה הַיּוֹצְרִים — *They were the potters.*
This refers back to the people mentioned in
the previous verse. They manufactured
earthenware utensils (*Mefaresh* and other
commentators). It is for this reason that
they lived outside the city (see below)
because there the earth was particularly
suitable for their purposes (*Radak*).

וְיוֹשְׁבֵי נְטָעִים וּגְדֵרָה — *Dwellers in Netaim and
Gederah.* The syntax is smoothest if
Netaim and Gederah are place names, and
that is how *Gra* takes them. He points
out that there were two such cities in
Judah, one called Gederah (*Joshua* 15:36),
the other, Gederoth (there, 15:41). These
names are respectively the singular and
plural form of the word גֶּדֶר, *fence.* Gederah
(sing.) was surrounded by a stone wall, for
which reason it is described in the singular.
The other was fenced in by trees and
plants, giving the impression of being
many different fences, hence the plural
form. This latter city is here called Netaim
[from נטע, *to plant*].

The *Mefaresh* and the other commentators think that our verse describes the
activities in which the people mentioned in
the previous verse were engaged. They
lived [outside the city] tending plants
(נְטָעִים) and producing fencing material
(גְדֵרָה).

עִם־הַמֶּלֶךְ בִּמְלַאכְתּוֹ יָשְׁבוּ שָׁם — *They resided
there in the service of the king. Metzudos*
thinks that this is a limiting phrase. They
dwelt in these places only as long as they
were doing the king's work. At other times
they lived in their permanent homes which
were located elsewhere. *Mefaresh* and
Radak, on the other hand, take the phrase
as explanatory. The king had arranged for
them to live there because of the work they
had to do in the royal service.

There is no indication that any particular
king is meant. We must recall that Ezra was
using ancient records [see s.v. וְהַדְּבָרִים
עַתִּיקִים] dating back to the times of the First
Temple. These families were probably in
the royal service through several gener-

4

24

Gederah; they resided there in the service of the king. ²⁴ *The sons of Shimeon — Nemuel, Yamin, Yariv, Zerach, and Shaul.* ²⁵ *His son*

ations and served many kings. *Gra*, however, writes that King Solomon is meant. [Perhaps the definite article in הַמֶּלֶךְ indicates a known king.] These people helped Solomon in the building of the Temple.

There are many aggadic interpretations of this verse. The following is from the Talmud:

... *They were the potters* — this refers to the sons of Yonadav ben Rechav [see *Jeremiah* ch. 35] who were true to the oath of their father [יוֹצְרִים from נצר, *to guard*] *(see comm. to 2:55); dwellers by the plants* — this is King Solomon, whose kingship [flourished] like a plant; *and fences* — this is the Sanhedrin who fenced in the breaches in Israel; *with the king at his work they sat there* — this is the Moabite Ruth who [was still alive during the] reign of Solomon, her grandson's grandson; as it is written: *And they placed a throne for the king's mother* (I Kings 2:19). As R' Elazar taught: This [refers to Ruth] the mother of royalty *(Bava Basra* 91b).[1]

The Rechavites were a great and holy family in Israel who were descended from Moses' father-in-law, Yithro. Yithro is, in Rabbinic literature, an example of the ideal *ger* (proselyte)

who complements the community of Israel as a gorgeous plant would be an asset to a flourishing orchard (see *Yerushalmi, Berachos* 2:8). He is the first in the long list of examples which *Sifri* to *Behaaloscha* cites (see v. 21) of non-Jews who were richly rewarded by God for their great efforts in seeking a closeness to the Divine by joining the community of Israel. It is therefore not surprising to find his descendants (the Rechavites) listed here together with Rachav, the Giveonites and Ruth (see previous verse).[2]

◆§ The Line of Shimeon

24-43. This section contains genealogical information concerning the tribe of Shimeon with a listing of the cities which they inherited. It follows directly the section on Judah because, in contrast to the other tribes whose territory in the Land of Israel was all contiguous, Shimeon had its cities scattered throughout the Judean portion of the Land [see *Joshua* 19:1] *(Mefaresh).*

24. ... בְּנֵי שִׁמְעוֹן — *The sons of Shimeon* ... Five sons are listed here for Shimeon. His children are also listed in *Genesis* (46:10) and in *Numbers* (26:12-18). The three lists are presented here in order to facilitate comparison.

	Genesis	Numbers	Chronicles
1.	יְמוּאֵל, Yemuel	נְמוּאֵל, Nemuel	נְמוּאֵל, Nemuel
2.	יָמִין, Yamin	יָמִין, Yamin	יָמִין, Yamin
3.	אֹהַד, Ohad		
4.	יָכִין, Yachin	יָכִין, Yachin	יָרִיב, Yariv
5.	צֹחַר, Tzochar	זֶרַח, Zerach	זֶרַח, Zerach
6.	שָׁאוּל, Shaul	שָׁאוּל, Shaul	שָׁאוּל, Shaul

1. The mention of Solomon and the Sanhedrin would be incongruous here if they were mentioned in their own right. We have seen that in the eyes of the Sages, our verses hint at the various proselytes who, throughout the ages, threw in their lot with the Jewish people. There seems little doubt that they are mentioned only as part of Ruth's saga. As we have seen repeatedly, *Sifri* interprets our verses to demonstrate the great rewards given to proselytes who had made the effort to come close to God. In Ruth's case the culmination of that reward came when she was privileged to sit at Solomon's right hand as he sat in judgment over Israel. [See *Pesikta deR' Kahanah* 16 which plays on the words וּתְהִי מַשְׂכֻּרְתֵּךְ שְׁלֵמָה, *and may your reward be complete (Ruth* 2:12). That reference is to Solomon (שְׁלֹמֹה = שְׁלֵמָה) who was destined to be descended from her.]

2. *Maharal* justifies the inclusion of the Rechavites in the lists contained in these verses for a different reason. The story of the Rechavites is intimately bound up with the destruction of the Temple and the loss of the land. The Giveonites are mentioned because the fact that not all Canaanite peoples were eradicated from the land contributed to the final destruction. That process, which had its roots at the very beginning of Joshua's conquest, culminated with the catastrophes which the Rechavites so clearly anticipated (see comm. to 2:55).

כה־כו שַׁלֻּם בְּנוֹ מִבְשָׂם בְּנוֹ מִשְׁמָע בְּנוֹ: וּבְנֵי מִשְׁמָע חַמּוּאֵל

כה־לב כז בְּנוֹ זַכּוּר בְּנוֹ שִׁמְעִי בְנוֹ: וּלְשִׁמְעִי בָּנִים שִׁשָּׁה עָשָׂר

וּבָנוֹת שֵׁשׁ וּלְאֶחָיו אֵין בָּנִים רַבִּים וְכֹל מִשְׁפַּחְתָּם לֹא

כח הִרְבּוּ עַד־בְּנֵי יְהוּדָה: וַיֵּשְׁבוּ בִּבְאֵר־שֶׁבַע וּמוֹלָדָה וַחֲצַר

כט־ל שׁוּעָל: וּבְבִלְהָה וּבְעֶצֶם וּבְתוֹלָד: וּבִבְתוּאֵל וּבְחָרְמָה

לא וּבְצִיקְלָג: וּבְבֵית מַרְכָּבוֹת וּבַחֲצַר סוּסִים וּבְבֵית בִּרְאִי

לב וּבְשַׁעֲרָיִם אֵלֶּה עָרֵיהֶם עַד־מְלֹךְ דָּוִיד: וְחַצְרֵיהֶם עֵיטָם

The change from יְמוּאֵל, Yemuel (1), to
נְמוּאֵל, Nemuel, is not unique to Chronicles.
This is also the form of the name in
Numbers. The irregularity is noted by R'
Shmuel ben Chofni, Gaon, who writes that
the change of single letters in a name is an
idiosyncrasy of the language (שֶׁל שִׁמּוּשָׁה
הַשָּׂפָה). See also Radak, there.

Ohad (3) is missing in Numbers and
Chronicles. Rashi there quotes a midrash
which explains that Ohad's was one of the
families wiped out in the aftermath of
Balaam's attempt to destroy Israel in the
desert (Numbers 25:1-9).

Since Ohad is already missing in
Numbers, it seems likely that יָרִיב, Yariv,
(4) is another name for יָכִין, Yachin. He is so
identified by Gra. R' Shmuel ben Chofni,
Gaon, and Radak both point out that the
same person often appears under different
names in different parts of Scripture. See
the list of giborim in ch. 11 for examples.
Rashi and Ramban in Numbers both
point out that צֹחַר, Tzohar, and זֶרַח,
Zerach, are the same person. This is an
example of the meaning of a name being
retained while the actual word is changed.
צֹחַר, related to צֹהַר, window, is something
which illuminates the interior of a building,
and זֶרַח is from זרח, to shine.

25. שַׁלֻּם בְּנוֹ — His son Shallum. Gra thinks
that בְּנוֹ, his son, refers to Shaul, the last of
Shimeon's sons listed in the previous verse.
This would mean that of the five sons of
Shimeon, only the genealogy of Shaul is
given.

Malbim thinks that the list given here
contains only the names of the princes of
the tribe. He identifies Shallum with
Shelumiel ben Tzurishaddai, who, according to Numbers 7:36, was the first
prince of Shimeon. The words his son
Shallum were taken from a book of
genealogies which contained complete

genealogical listings for Shimeon. At one
point Tzurishaddai was mentioned, and his
name was followed by the words his son,
Shallum. Ezra, who quoted only those
parts of the book which concerned him,
took only those words.

As Malbim sees it, the line of princes
then continued with Shallum's son,
Mivsam, and with Mivsam's son, Mishma.
The book then continued with the words
and the children of Mishma (v. 26), listing
their names. Since none of them were
princes, Ezra does not give these names but
instead went further down the generations
until he came to the next descendant of this
line to become a prince, Chammuel.

The verse should be read as follows:
And the descendants of Mishma his [an
unmentioned person's] son — Chammuel,
his son Zaccur … Chammuel's father's
name is not given — Mishma was his
ancestor, not father. The princely line then
continued with Chammuel's son, Zaccur,
and Zaccur's son, Shimei.

26. וּבְנֵי מִשְׁמָע — And the sons of Mishma.
According to Gra (see comm. above), this
verse continues the genealogy of Shaul
begun in the previous verse. For Malbim's
view, see above.

27. … וּלְשִׁמְעִי בָּנִים שִׁשָּׁה עָשָׂר — Now Shimei
had sixteen sons … There are no extant
Midrashic sources which tell us anything
about this Shimei or about his children.
[We assume that the lost Sefer HaYuchasin
would explain what particular significance
is attached to him.] In the context of our
verse the meaning seems to be: Although
Shimei himself had so many children, his
brothers (perhaps kinsmen rather than
actual brothers) had relatively few
children, so that all in all the Shimeonite
families were not as numerous as those of
Judah among whom they dwelled.

Shallum, his son Mivsam, his son Mishma. ²⁶ *And the sons of Mishma — his son Chammuel, his son Zaccur, his son Shimei.* ²⁷ *Now Shimei had sixteen sons and six daughters, but his brothers did not have many sons and their whole family did not multiply as much as the sons of Judah.* ²⁸ *And they dwelt in Beer Sheva, and Moladah, and Chatzar Shual.* ²⁹ *And in Bilhah, Etzem, and Tolad.* ³⁰ *And in Bethuel, Chormah, and Tziklag.* ³¹ *And in Beth Marcavoth, Chatzar Susim, Beth Biri, and Shaaraim; these were their cities until David became king.* ³² *And their towns — Etam,*

וְכָל מִשְׁפְּחֹתָם לֹא הִרְבּוּ עַד־בְּנֵי יְהוּדָה — *And their whole family did not multiply as much as the sons of Judah.* Mefaresh and Radak take this phrase as an explanation for the fact that Shimeon's cities were scattered through Judah's territory.

From the time that Jacob had decreed that Shimeon and Levi were to be *separated within Jacob and dispersed in Israel (Genesis 49:7)*, Shimeon was destined not to have one single portion of the Land as did all the other tribes, but to have his territory absorbed within the portion of another tribe *(Midrash Aggadah, Lekach Tov,* there). The tribes drew lots to determine which among them would welcome Shimeon into his portion, and the lot fell upon Judah. Consequently, when Judah set out to conquer the land which he was to inhabit, he invited Shimeon to accompany him and to share in the fruits of their joint campaign *(Judges* 1:3). God's providence brought about that Judah took in territories which were much larger than his requirements [*Joshua* 19:9] (see *R' Shmuel ben Chofni, Gaon,* to *Genesis* 49:7). These he made available to Shimeon (ibid.), happy that in this way the territories would be settled and not fall prey to wild animals *(Mefaresh).*

Our verse tells that this arrangement was mutually acceptable to the two tribes since Shimeon did not have many people and was adequately served by the cities which Judah was able to put at his disposal.

This arrangement explains why the cities ascribed to Shimeon in our section (see below) are listed in *Joshua* as belonging to Judah *(Radak).*

Metzudos interprets our verse somewhat differently. The great size of the tribe of Judah should not be ascribed to some special attribute of the land in which they

dwelled. Shimeon occupied the same area but was a comparatively small tribe.

28. בְּאֵר־שֶׁבַע וּמוֹלָדָה וַחֲצַר שׁוּעָל — *Beer Sheva, and Moladah and Chatzar Shual.* All these are listed as cities of Judah in *Joshua;* Beer Sheva and Chatzar Shual in 15:28 and Moladah in 15:26.

29. ... וּבְבִלְהָה — *And in Bilhah* ... Bilhah is not mentioned in *Joshua.* But Etzem is among Judah's cities in 15:29 and Tolad seems to be Eltolad of 15:30.

30. ... וּבְבְתוּאֵל — *And in Bethuel* ... Bethuel is not mentioned in *Joshua* (see ArtScroll comm. to 19:4), but Chormah is among Judah's cities in 15:30 and Tziklag in 15:31.

31. ... וּבְבֵית מַרְכָּבוֹת — *And in Beth Marcavoth* ... Of the cities mentioned in this verse, only Shaaraim appears among Judah's cities in *Joshua* 15:36.

The cities listed here are also given, with several changes in spelling, in *Joshua* 19:1ff. However, Beth Biri and Shaaraim of our verse do not appear there at all. Two other cities not mentioned here, Beth Levaoth and Sharuchen, are given there (v. 5). *Malbim (Joshua)* identifies them as being identical with the cities mentioned here, ascribing the differences to the normal change of names these places underwent in the centuries until *Chronicles* was written.

אֵלֶּה עָרֵיהֶם עַד־מְלֹךְ דָּוִיד — *These were their cities until David became king.* Both *Mefaresh* and *Radak* explain as follows: Shimeon had settled in various cities which Judah had put at his disposal at a time when Judah's territory far exceeded the needs of his population (see comm. to v. 27 above). However, as the size of Judah's

לג וָעַיִן רִמּוֹן וָתֹכֶן וְעָשָׁן עָרִים חָמֵשׁ: וְכָל־חַצְרֵיהֶם אֲשֶׁר
סְבִיבוֹת הֶעָרִים הָאֵלֶּה עַד־בָּעַל זֹאת מוֹשְׁבֹתָם
לד וְהִתְיַחְשָׂם לָהֶם: וּמְשׁוֹבָב וְיַמְלֵךְ וְיוֹשָׁה בֶּן־אֲמַצְיָה:
לה-לו וְיוֹאֵל וְיֵהוּא בֶּן־יוֹשִׁבְיָה בֶּן־שְׂרָיָה בֶּן־עֲשִׂיאֵל: וְאֶלְיוֹעֵינַי
לז וְיַעֲקֹבָה וִישׁוֹחָיָה וַעֲשָׂיָה וַעֲדִיאֵל וִישִׂימִאֵל וּבְנָיָה: וְזִיזָא
לח בֶן־שִׁפְעִי בֶן־אַלּוֹן בֶּן־יְדָיָה בֶן־שִׁמְרִי בֶּן־שְׁמַעְיָה: אֵלֶּה
הַבָּאִים בְּשֵׁמוֹת נְשִׂיאִים בְּמִשְׁפְּחוֹתָם וּבֵית אֲבוֹתֵיהֶם
לט פָּרְצוּ לָרוֹב: וַיֵּלְכוּ לִמְבוֹא גְדֹר עַד לְמִזְרַח הַגָּיְא לְבַקֵּשׁ
מ מִרְעֶה לְצֹאנָם: וַיִּמְצְאוּ מִרְעֶה שָׁמֵן וָטוֹב וְהָאָרֶץ רַחֲבַת
יָדַיִם וְשֹׁקֶטֶת וּשְׁלֵוָה כִּי מִן־חָם הַיֹּשְׁבִים שָׁם לְפָנִים:

---

population increased, he began to resent Shimeon's further presence in these cities. During Saul's reign, Judah made various attempts to dislodge Shimeon but Saul was too occupied with the affairs of state to be active in this matter (Mefaresh). When David became king, he aided his fellow tribesmen in regaining their cities (Radak). Subsequently, Shimeon was limited to the five cities listed below in verse 32.

Malbim (Joshua) interprets the phrase to refer to Tziklag. In I Samuel 27:6 we find Tziklag in David's possession, so by that time it was obviously not occupied by Shimeon any more.

32. וְחַצְרֵיהֶם — And their towns. From Leviticus 25:31 it appears that חָצֵר in this context is a town which has no wall around it. From Joshua 13:23 it would appear that these towns were generally associated with a larger city, and in its environs (Radak, Shorashim).

עֵיטָם ... — Etam ... With the exception of Tochen we find all these towns belonging to Judah; Etam in Judges 15:8, Ain and Rimmon in Joshua 15:32, and Ashan in Joshua 15:42.

עָרִים חָמֵשׁ — Five cities. Joshua 19:7 has עֶתֶר, Ether, instead of Etam and does not list Tochen. It also gives the total number as four. Malbim (there) suggests that Etam and Ether are one and the same, and that Tochen was built at a later date, thus appearing in Chronicles although not listed in Joshua.

Although these were not full-size cities, they were larger than most towns. Thus, the second part of this verse refers to them as five cities. As is clear from the next

verse, they were large enough to have suburbs of their own (Metzudos).

33. וְכָל־חַצְרֵיהֶם ... עַד־בָּעַל — And all their towns ... up to Baal. Joshua 19:8 has בַּעֲלַת בְּאֵר, Baalath Beer, instead of Baal.

The phrase up to Baal means that Baal or Baalath Beer was the point up to which Shimeon's territory extended. Tevuas HaAretz places it to the north, at the southernmost tip of Dan's territory. The city itself belonged to Dan (see ArtScroll Joshua, map p. 375).

וְהִתְיַחְשָׂם לָהֶם — And they have their genealogical records. The translation follows the Mefaresh. The phrase expresses the same idea as does 9:1 (see there). A cursory study of the genealogical lists shows that many tribes are dealt with in a seemingly perfunctory manner, some are omitted completely, while others like Judah and Levi are treated in great detail. This is explained in 9:1 and traced to the fact that when the northern kingdom was exiled by Sennacherib, the various tribes took their genealogical records along with them and these were consequently not available to Ezra. For the purposes of his lists he had to make use of whatever material was accessible after a lapse of some two centuries.

This could explain the fact that the Shimeon list differs from that of Judah not only in its brevity but also in its concern with geographical data seemingly inappropriate to a genealogical list. In light of Malbim's opinion (see comm. v. 25) that the names recorded in vs. 25 and 26 are the names of princes rather than of a structured family, it seems likely that we are not dealing with a genealogical list at all. Rather, Ezra seems to have drawn from a historical record dealing with Shimeon's rulers and lands rather than with

Ain, Rimmon Tochen and Ashan — five cities. ³³ *And all their towns which surrounded these cities up to Baal; these were their dwelling places; and they have their genealogical records.* ³⁴ *And Meshovav, Yamlech, and Yoshah, the son of Amatziah.* ³⁵ *And Yoel, and Yehu the son of Yoshiviah, the son of Seraiah, the son of Asiel.* ³⁶ *And Elioenai, Yaakovah, Yeshochaiah, Asaiah, Adiel, Yesimiel, and Benaiah.* ³⁷ *And Zizah the son of Shiphi, the son of Allon, the son of Yedaiah, the son of Shimri, the son of Shemaiah.* ³⁸ *These who have been mentioned by name were princes of their families and their families multiplied greatly.* ³⁹ *And they went to the approaches of Gedor, to the east side of the valley, to seek pasture for their flock.* ⁴⁰ *There they found luxurious and excellent pasture, and the land had ample room and was quiet and peaceful, because Hamites had*

---

his genealogy.

Radak and *Malbim* take our phrase together with the previous one. According to *Radak* the meaning is: *These were their dwellings and they remained identified with them.* I.e., although the Shimeonites were forced out of their cities in the time of David, these cities remained in their possession and continued to be known as Shimeonite cities. According to *Malbim,* the last phrase is rendered: *and they were identified by them.* I.e., it was the custom to call the chieftain of given units by the name of the place over which they ruled; as, for example, Ashchur, father of Tekoa (2:24). The cities of Shimeon also gave their names to the chieftains who governed them. Their enrollment in their genealogical records (הִתְיַחְשָׂם) was, so to speak, determined by the names of their cities. See below.

34⁻37. These verses contain the names of thirteen chieftains (see v. 38) who, as explained in the previous verse, were associated with the thirteen main cities (vs. 28-31) occupied by Shimeon *(Malbim).*

38. אֵלֶּה הַבָּאִים בְּשֵׁמוֹת — *These who have been mentioned by name.* This refers to the thirteen people mentioned in the previous three verses *(Metzduos; Malbim;* see below).

נְשִׂיאִים בְּמִשְׁפְּחוֹתָם — *Were princes of their families.* In contrast to the names listed in vs. 25 and 26, which described men who were princes over the whole tribe, the thirteen men mentioned here were governors only of their own cities *(Malbim).*

וּבֵית אֲבוֹתֵיהֶם פָּרְצוּ לָרוֹב — *And their families*

multiplied greatly. There was a great increase in their population so that they needed to expand their territory, as described below *(Metzudos).*

Perhaps the problem became acute from David's rule onwards when the Shimeonites suddenly lost a significant number of the cities previously available to them (see v. 31).

39. וַיֵּלְכוּ לִמְבוֹא גְדֹר — *And they went to the approaches of Gedor.* They went to find pasture for their sheep *(Mefaresh; Metzudos).*

Admas Kodesh identifies this place with a plain which lies some eighteen kilometers north of Jevel Musa [the mountain known today as Mt. Sinai] near the center of the southern part of the Sinai Peninsula. He further identifies the valley mentioned in our verse with the Wadi Agdar (or Achdas) which descends from this plain towards the Gulf of Suez. In the vicinity of this area *Admas Kodesh* found several wadis which carry names of Shimeonite princes mentioned in our passage: i.e., Yoshah (v. 34); Yeshochaiah (v. 36); and Zizah (v. 37).

40. וְהָאָרֶץ רַחֲבַת יָדַיִם — *And the land had ample room* [lit. *the land had breadth of hands*]. The metaphor of רַחֲבַת יָדַיִם, *breadth of hands,* is that of a man whose hand is large and generous; hence it denotes *plentifulness, sufficiency* (Rashi, *Genesis* 43:21).

Metzudos writes that יָד, *hand,* in this context means a place. Hence: *And the land contained extended territories.*

וְשֹׁקֶטֶת וּשְׁלֵוָה — *And was quiet and peaceful.* In *Gra's* and *Malbim's* view שָׁקֵט, *quiet,* denotes a state in which no troubles

ד

מא וַיָּבֹ֫אוּ אֵ֣לֶּה הַכְּתוּבִ֣ים בְּשֵׁמוֹת֒ בִּימֵ֣י | יְחִזְקִיָּ֣הוּ מֶֽלֶךְ־
מא-מג יְהוּדָה֒ וַיַּכּ֣וּ אֶת־אָהֳלֵיהֶ֗ם וְאֶת־הַמְּעִינִ֤ים אֲשֶׁ֣ר נִמְצְאוּ־
°הַמְּעוּנִ֖ים ק' שָׁ֔מָּה וַֽיַּחֲרִימֻם֙ עַד־הַיּ֣וֹם הַזֶּ֔ה וַיֵּשְׁב֖וּ תַחְתֵּיהֶ֑ם כִּי־
מב מִרְעֶ֥ה לְצֹאנָ֖ם שָֽׁם: וּמֵהֶ֣ם | מִן־בְּנֵ֣י שִׁמְע֗וֹן הָלְכוּ֙ לְהַ֣ר
שֵׂעִ֔יר אֲנָשִׁ֖ים חֲמֵ֣שׁ מֵא֑וֹת וּפְלַטְיָ֨ה וּנְעַרְיָ֤ה וּרְפָיָ֨ה
מג וְעֻזִּיאֵ֔ל בְּנֵ֥י יִשְׁעִ֖י בְּרֹאשָֽׁם: וַיַּכּ֕וּ אֶת־שְׁאֵרִ֥ית הַפְּלֵטָ֖ה
ה א לַעֲמָלֵ֑ק וַיֵּ֣שְׁבוּ שָׁ֔ם עַ֖ד הַיּ֥וֹם הַזֶּֽה:
א רְאוּבֵ֤ן בְּכֽוֹר־יִשְׂרָאֵל֙ כִּ֣י ה֣וּא הַבְּכ֔וֹר וּֽבְחַלְּלוֹ֙ יְצוּעֵ֣י אָבִ֔יו וּבְנֵ֖י

always lived there. ⁴¹ Then these who have been recorded by name came in the days of Yechizkiah king of Judah and they smote their tents and the Meunim that were there, and they banished them up to this day and occupied their place, because there was pasture there for their flock. ⁴² And from them, from the sons of Shimeon, five hundred men went to Mount Seir; and Pelatiah, Neariah, Rephaiah, Uzziel, the sons of Yishi, were at their head. ⁴³ And they smote the remnant of the Amalekites who had escaped and they lived there up to this day.

5

1

Ａnd the sons of Reuven, the first-born of Israel, for he was the first-born, but when he defiled his father's bed his

עַד הַיּוֹם הַזֶּה — *Up to this day.* 'This day' must mean the time at which Shimeon was exiled during the Assyrian wars. When Ezra wrote *Chronicles* Shimeon was no longer occupying Mt. Seir *(Radak).*

Alternatively, *Radak* suggests that the phrase is not to be taken literally. It means only that Amalek never came back to its former possessions, even after Shimeon had been exiled from there (see v. 41).

V

The genealogical tables began with the family of Judah since David, the central figure of *Chronicles*, was descended from him. Shimeon's genealogy then follows because his cities were scattered through Judah's territory. Having completed these two, Ezra turns to Reuven who was the actual first-born, and from whom the genealogical lists should normally have begun *(Radak).*

Together with Reuven, the records of Gad and half of Menasheh are also given since these one and a half tribes lived together with Reuven on the eastern side of the Jordan. These lists continue until v. 27, where the genealogy of Levi is taken up.

◄§ The Line of Reuven

1. וּבְנֵי רְאוּבֵן בְּכוֹר־יִשְׂרָאֵל — *And the sons of Reuven, the first-born of Israel.* This phrase is the beginning of the genealogical table which follows. This can be seen from the fact that it is repeated in v. 3 where the actual lists begin. The listing in our verse is interrupted by the insertion of an explanatory note (the second part of this verse and v. 2).

כִּי־הוּא הַבְּכוֹר — *For he was the first-born.* This phrase states the problem. Reuven was Jacob's first-born, and we would have expected his genealogy to be listed before that of any other tribe. The fact that Judah (and therefore, Shimeon) preceded him calls for an explanation. This explanation now follows.

וּבְחַלְּלוֹ יְצוּעֵי אָבִיו ... — *But when he defiled his father's bed ...* As our verse goes on to explain, the privileges which would

rightfully belong to the first-born were taken from Reuven and split between his brothers, Joseph and Judah (v. 2).

The action by which Reuven proved himself unworthy of the birthright is recounted in *Genesis* 35:22. For the purpose of our commentary, it is sufficient to quote *Rashi* there: During Rachel's lifetime, Jacob's couch [i.e. primary residence] was always in Rachel's tent; upon her death he removed it to Bilhah's [Rachel's handmaiden] tent. Reuven resented this insult to his mother [Leah] saying, 'Because my mother's sister, Rachel, was her rival, is that any reason for her [Rachel's] handmaiden to now become my mother's rival?' He therefore acted in order to right the matter.

As explained by *Rashi* there, the expression *defiled his father's bed* is not to be taken as euphemism for adultery but in a more literal sense — *he tampered with his father's couch* by removing it from Bilhah's

נִתְּנָה בִּכְרָתוֹ לִבְנֵי יוֹסֵף בֶּן־־יִשְׂרָאֵל וְלֹא לְהִתְיַחֵשׂ
ב לַבְּכֹרָה: כִּי יְהוּדָה גָּבַר בְּאֶחָיו וּלְנָגִיד מִמֶּנּוּ וְהַבְּכֹרָה
ג לְיוֹסֵף: בְּנֵי רְאוּבֵן בְּכוֹר יִשְׂרָאֵל חֲנוֹךְ וּפַלּוּא
ד חֶצְרוֹן וְכַרְמִי: בְּנֵי יוֹאֵל שְׁמַעְיָה בְנוֹ גּוֹג בְּנוֹ שִׁמְעִי בְנוֹ:

tent. Because he meddled in his father's intimate affairs, however, he is described as having *defiled his father's bed.* [This explanation is taken by *Rashi* from the Talmud *Shabbos* 55b and is the accepted opinion of the commentators. See ArtScroll comm. to *Genesis* pp. 1522-1525 for a full discussion of this matter.]

Although Reuven acted to protect his mother's position, he should not have taken it upon himself to interfere in the intimate matters which were rightfully subject to Jacob's sole discretion. Jacob deemed the impetuosity betrayed by Reuven's action sufficient reason to deny him his birthright.

The phrase וּבְחַלְּלוֹ יְצוּעֵי אָבִיו, *he defiled his father's bed,* is based on the expression which Jacob used in describing Reuven in *Genesis* 49:4. [See further ArtScroll commentary there (pp. 2135-2138).]

נִתְּנָה בִּכְרָתוֹ לִבְנֵי יוֹסֵף בֶּן־יִשְׂרָאֵל — *His primogenitureship was given to the sons of Joseph, the son of Israel.* Torah law provides that when a father's estate is divided among his sons, the first-born receives a double share; one the same as every other son and an additional one as the first-born *(Deuteronomy* 21:17).

But it was not only Jacob's estate which was at issue. As is well known, each of his sons was father of a separate tribe — the twelve tribes of Israel. Now, Jacob had been promised that one of his sons would father not one but two tribes *(Genesis* 35:11, see *Rashi* there). It was only to be expected that this privilege would devolve upon Reuven, the first-born. However, shortly before he died Jacob told Joseph

that the two sons born to him in Egypt — Ephraim and Menasheh — would henceforth have the same status as Reuven and Shimeon, i.e., each would be a separate tribe *(Genesis* 48:5). This, as our phrase in *Chronicles* explains, was the point at which the right of the first-born to two tribes shifted from Reuven to Joseph[1] (see ArtScroll *Genesis* p. 2099).

וְלֹא לְהִתְיַחֵשׂ לַבְּכֹרָה — *Although not to be enrolled as first-born.* Our translation (based on *Mefaresh* and *Radak)* follows the opinion cited in the Midrash that the subject of this phrase is Joseph. It states that although Joseph received the double share of the first-born, he was not endowed with the actual status of first-born. Had this been so, the kingship, which is also the right of the first-born (*R' Shmuel ben Chofni, Gaon,* based on *II Chronicles* 21:3), would also have belonged to Joseph. As it is, it was given to Judah, as explained in the next verse.

Another opinion in the Midrash has the phrase apply to Reuven. The birthright was given to Joseph: *So that Reuven should no longer be enrolled as the first-born.*

2. כִּי יְהוּדָה גָּבַר בְּאֶחָיו — *For Judah was mightiest among his brothers.* This verse answers the question posed by the previous verse. We would have expected the genealogical lists of Israel to begin with Reuven, the first-born. In fact they begin with Judah, who, because he was mightier than any of his brothers, was given the kingship (see end of our verse) once Reuven had forfeited that right. It is the right of royalty

---

1. *Bava Basra* 123a explains that God had originally intended that Rachel bear Jacob's first-born. This would have resulted in the primogenitureship being given to one of Rachel's sons. But because Leah had shown such spiritual greatness in her despair at the prospect of marrying Esau (see ArtScroll *Genesis* p. 1266), she was rewarded with having children before Rachel (see there p. 1281). Thus, Reuven was Jacob's first-born and would have received the double portion.

When Reuven *defiled his father's couch,* he forfeited the privilege which should have been his. At that point it was given to Joseph — a son of Rachel — as a reward for the concern he showed for her sister's dignity in preventing Leah's disgrace when Lavan had deceived Jacob into marrying Leah first (see ArtScroll *Genesis* p. 1274).

[Apparently Reuven's forfeiture was not sufficient reason for the primogenitureship to revert to Rachel automatically, although it was she who should have had it in the first place. Only the merit of Rachel's concern for her sister's dignity earned that birthright for Joseph. Without this merit it would apparently have been given to another of Leah's sons.]

primogenitureship was given to the sons of Joseph, the son of Israel, although not to be enrolled as first-born. ² *For Judah was mightiest among his brothers and royalty was to come from him — but the primogenitureship was Joseph's.* ³ *The sons of Reuven, the first-born of Israel — Chanoch, Pallu, Chetzron and Carmi.* ⁴ *The sons of Yoel — his son Shemaiah, his son Gog, his son Shimei.* ⁵ *His son*

to be counted first.

Judah's unusual strength was expressed by Jacob when he described Judah as *a young lion* [*Genesis 49:9*] *(Mefaresh)*.

וְלְנָגִיד מִמֶּנּוּ — *And royalty was to come from him*. The word נָגִיד for *prince* or *royalty* derives from the root נגד, *to be [oriented] towards*, or *opposite*. The prince is a נָגִיד because everyone turns to him for help and support *(Radak, Shorashim)*. [See fn. to 11:2 for a discussion of the exact meaning of this term.]

This verse is based on Jacob's blessing to Judah *(Genesis 49:8ff)* in which he said (v. 10): *The scepter shall never leave Judah.* This clearly implies that all future kings in Israel were to be descended from Judah *(Radak, Mefaresh)*.

Ramban (there) explains that although there were many kings who were not descended from Judah throughout the history of the monarchy, as for example Saul's dynasty and all the kings of the Northern Kingdom, this does not contradict Jacob's blessing. Saul and his line reigned before David ever became king, and Jacob's meaning was only that once Judah took up the scepter it should remain permanently with him. The kings of the Northern Kingdom were indeed illegitimate and reigned in defiance of Jacob's decree. True, Achiyah the Shilonite, a prophet, had anointed Yerovoam king in order to punish Solomon, but this did not legitimize the kings who followed Yerovoam. They should have returned the throne to its rightful rulership.

Malbim has מִמֶּנּוּ, *from him*, refer to Joseph rather than to Judah and has the word גָּבַר, *was mightiest*, of the first phrase used for the second phrase also. The whole sentence reads as follows: *For Judah was mightier than his brothers, and even with regard to the kingship* [וּלְנָגִיד], [*he was mightier*] *than Joseph* [מִמֶּנּוּ], *who was given only the primogenitureship.*

וְהַבְּכֹרָה לְיוֹסֵף — *But the primogenitureship was Joseph's*. Only the right of the double share had been given to Joseph, but Joseph did not assume all the privileges which Reuven had forfeited *(Metzudos)*.

Verses 1 and 2 have now explained why Judah's genealogy preceded that of Reuven. Now verse 3 resumes the genealogy of Reuven's family.

The purpose of these two verses was only to explain the sequence of the genealogical lists. For this reason, no mention is made here of the gift of the priesthood, which had also been intended for Reuven (see *Rashi* to *Genesis 49:3*) but was subsequently transferred to Levi.

3. ... בְּנֵי רְאוּבֵן — *The sons of Reuven* ... The four sons listed are the same as those given in *Genesis 46:9, Exodus 6:14* and *Numbers 26:5-6*.

4. ... בְּנֵי יוֹאֵל — *The sons of Yoel* ... *Mefaresh* to *9:1* notes the perfunctory way in which the genealogical records of many of the tribes are presented, explaining the reason for this as due to the fact that for many of the tribes belonging to the Northern Kingdom the records available to Ezra were very scant. When the ten tribes were exiled by the Assyrians they carried their family records with them and these were therefore lost to posterity. Ezra had to make do with whatever written fragments had by some chance survived. For this reason it is not surprising that a Yoel is introduced here of whom we have no previous information.

This approach to our verse is adopted by *Radak*. He writes that, although we know nothing of this Yoel's antecedents, it is a frequent practice of *Chronicles* to take up a name without any relationship being traced to any of the people mentioned previously.

Gra and *Malbim* approach our verse very much as they did a similar problem in 4:25 (see comm. there). *Gra* thinks that Yoel is a son of Carmi, the last of Reuven's sons. As he does frequently throughout these lists, *Gra* has the word בְּנֵי, *the sons of*, do double service. It is as though the verse were written: ... בְּנֵי [בְּנֵי כַרְמִי יוֹאֵל ו] בְּנֵי יוֹאֵל, [*The sons of Carmi was Yoel, and*] *the sons of Yoel* ...

Malbim believes that we are dealing with the princes of the tribe. As taught in verse 6, the last of the Reuvenite princes was Beerah who was taken into the Assyrian exile. This Beerah was the descendant of a

ה־ו מִיכָה בְנוֹ רְאָיָה בְנוֹ בַּעַל בְּנוֹ: בְּאֵרָה בְנוֹ אֲשֶׁר הֶגְלָה

ז תִּלְגַת פִּלְנְאֶסֶר מֶלֶךְ אַשֻּׁר הוּא נָשִׂיא לָראוּבֵנִי: וְאֶחָיו

לְמִשְׁפְּחֹתָיו בְּהִתְיַחֵשׂ לְתֹלְדוֹתָם הָראשׁ יְעִיאֵל וּזְכַרְיָהוּ:

ח וּבֶלַע בֶּן־עָזָז בֶּן־שֶׁמַע בֶּן־יוֹאֵל הוּא יוֹשֵׁב בַּעֲרֹעֵר

ט וְעַד־נְבוֹ וּבַעַל מְעוֹן: וְלַמִּזְרָח יָשַׁב עַד־לְבוֹא מִדְבָּרָה

י לְמִן־הַנָּהָר פְּרָת כִּי מִקְנֵיהֶם רָבוּ בְּאֶרֶץ גִּלְעָד: וּבִימֵי

royal line begun by the Yoel of our verse.

שְׁמַעְיָה בְנוֹ — *His son Shemaiah*. The son of Yoel, and so on through v. 6 (*Gra*).

6. בְּאֵרָה בְנוֹ — *His son Beerah*. *Gra* notes that this Beerah is identical with Beeri, the father of the prophet Hoshea (*Hosea* 1:1). *Gra's* source is *Pesikta d'Rav Kahana* which reads as follows: God said to Reuven: 'You attempted to return a beloved son to his father [when Reuven tried to save Joseph by having him put in the pit] — I swear that one who is descended from you will bring back Israel to their Heavenly Father [by calling upon them to repent].' Who is this? Hoshea! As it is written: *The word of God which came to Hoshea the son of Beeri* [who was descended from Reuven, as] it is written (our verse): *his son Beerah.*

From the structure of vs. 3-6 it seems that Ezra's interest is centered particularly on Beerah and that the previous names were brought only in order to trace his ancestry. This, too, can be understood on the basis of *Pesikta d'Rav Kahana* which continues: Why was he called Beerah? Because he was a wellspring [בְּאֵרָה from בְּאֵר, *well*] of the Torah. And why did Beerah die in exile [based on our verse that he was among the tribes exiled by Tillegath Pilneser]? So that the ten tribes would be brought back from exile in his merit.

אֲשֶׁר הֶגְלָה תִּלְגַת פִּלְנְאֶסֶר — *Whom Tillegath Pilneeser ... exiled*. This Assyrian king is called תִּגְלַת פְּלֶאֶסֶר, *Tiglath Pileser*, in *II Kings* 15:29. *Radak* points out that the sequence of letters are often interchanged in given names.

הוּא נָשִׂיא לָראוּבֵנִי — *He was prince of the Reuvenites*. Beerah was prince of the Reuvenites at the time of the Assyrian exile (*Mefaresh*).

7. וְאֶחָיו לְמִשְׁפְּחֹתָיו — *And his brothers, each according to his family*. The suffix of

מִשְׁפְּחֹתָיו is in the singular (*his* families) and does not agree with its subject, אֶחָיו (brothers), which is in the plural. [See also on בְּהִתְיַחֵשׂ in the next phrase.] Accordingly, וְאֶחָיו cannot be rendered literally as *his brothers* but must be taken as [*each of*] *his brothers* (*Metzudos*).

[Similar irregularities are not unknown in Scripture. Cf. *I Samuel* 9:13 and 16, *II Kings* 1:13, *Psalms* 46:4 and 78:15. *Targum* seems to have taken our phrase as such an irregularity since he renders לְמִשְׁפְּחֹתָיו as though it had been לְמִשְׁפְּחוֹתֵיהֶם — a plural suffix.]

The meaning of this phrase must be sought together with the next one.

בְּהִתְיַחֵשׂ לְתֹלְדוֹתָם הָראשׁ יְעִיאֵל וּזְכַרְיָהוּ — *Had in the genealogical listing of their generations the chief Yeiel and Zechariahu*. With the plural אֶחָיו, *his brothers*, we would have expected בְּהִתְיַחֲשָׂם, as for example at 7:5. See comm. above.

The meaning of the whole sentence is far from clear. Following are some interpretations:

Mefaresh: This verse should be seen as an extension of the previous list. Although only the line of Yoel is given, *his brothers* [i.e., fellow tribesmen] *are [each] listed by their families*. In the [formal] genealogies [lit. *in the reckoning of their generations*] *Yeiel and Zechariahu* are heads of lists. [It is not clear whether *Mefaresh* takes *his brothers* as referring to Yoel's brothers or Beerah's brothers.]

Metzudos: And [when] his [Beerah's] brother's families were listed by their genealogies [it was discovered that] *Yeiel and Zechariahu* were the most prominent [i.e., had the most distinguished family tree].

Gra: Reference is not to Beerah but to Carmi's descendants. Our verse tells us that his three brothers also had genealogical tables devoted to their families. These tables listed *Yeiel and Zechariahu* — as well as the people mentioned in the following verses — as chiefs. [Our translation has

Michah, his son Reaiah, his son Baal. 6 His son Beerah, whom Tillegath Pilneeser the king of Assyria exiled; he was prince of the Reuvenites. 7 And his brothers, each according to his family, had in the genealogical listing of their generations the chief Yeiel and Zechariahu. 8 And Bela the son of Azaz, the son of Shema, the son of Yoel dwelled from Aroer as far as Nevo and Baal Meon. 9 And to the east he dwelled until the approach to the desert from the river Euphrates, for their flocks increased in the land of Gilead. 10 Now in

adopted this explanation because of its simplicity.]

Malbim: And his brothers, at the time they established their genealogical lines [in the days of Yotham and Yerovoam — see below, v. 17], *had as their heads Yeiel and Zechariahu.*

The significance of who headed the family at the time of the last formal arrangement of genealogies may be understood on the basis of *Malbim's* remarks to *Ezra* 8:1. He explains there that the system used to record the genealogy of each individual was for each person to record how he was related (paternally) to the head of the family to which he belonged. The head of the family, in turn, held a record of how he was descended from the father of the tribe of which his family was a member. Thus, when the genealogies of these families were established, they were traced through the records of Yeiel and Zechariahu — the heads of the family.

8. ... וּבֶלַע בֶּן־עָזָז — *And Bela the son of Azaz.* Shema and Yoel, respectively grandfather and great-grandfather of Bela, are identified by *Radak* as being the Yoel and Shemaiah mentioned in verse 4. This, however, is only possible if the term *his brothers* in the previous verse refers to the brother of Beerah, as most commentators assume (see above). In that case we are still dealing with the lineage of Carmi. If, with *Gra*, we take וְאֶחָיו as referring to Carmi, then we are now dealing with descendants of Reuven's other sons.

הוּא יוֹשֵׁב בַּעֲרֹעֵר — *Dwelled from* [lit. *in*] *Aroer.*[1] The Reuvenites mentioned in this

verse lived in Aroer. But while the two other cities, Nevo and Baal Meon, were indeed part of Reuven's territory (see *Numbers* 32:38), Aroer seems to have belonged to Gad (v. 34, there). *Radak* suggests two possibilities. The word בַּעֲרֹעֵר could be translated *from Aroer* rather than *in Aroer.* [*Radak* demonstrates that the prefix ב, *beis,* is occasionally used with such a meaning.] Our verse would then mean that the Reuvenites lived in territory which bordered on Aroer. The city itself did not belong to them. The second possibility is that *in Aroer* means in the outskirts of the city, which lay in Reuven's land. The city proper belonged to Gad.

וְעַד־נְבוֹ וּבַעַל מְעוֹן — *As far as Nevo and Baal Meon.* See *Numbers* 32:38 for these cities. *Metzudos* points out that our verse describes the dimension of the territory from the south to the north while the next verse deals with the expansion eastwards.

9. ... וְלַמִּזְרָח יָשַׁב — *And to the east he dwelled* ... The vast holdings of this family extended eastwards.

לְמִן־הַנָּהָר פְּרָת — *From the river Euphrates.* According to *Radak,* the territory went up to the western bank of the Euphrates but did not go beyond it. *Metzudos* thinks that לְמִן הַנָּהָר implies that it crossed the river.

When God promised Abraham that the Land of Israel would be his, He gave the Euphrates as one of the boundaries of the Land (*Genesis* 15:18). The eastern boundary described in *Numbers* ch. 34 lies considerably west of the Euphrates. *Tevuas HaAretz* explains that the two passages are not contradictory. The passage in *Numbers* gives those boundaries which were

---

1. The use of the present tense, יוֹשֵׁב, instead of the past tense, יָשַׁב, as in the next verse, is unexpected. Without offering an explanation for why this irregularity should appear here, we note that the present tense can be found in Scripture to denote the past and the future as well. One example of the former is *Joshua* 5:4. The text reads: *All the people who are going out of Egypt* ... which *Targum* renders: ... *who went out of Egypt.* An example of the latter is *I Kings* 8:19 which reads: ... *but the son who is born from you,* which *Targum* renders: ... *the son who will be born from you.*

שָׁאוּל עָשׂוּ מִלְחָמָה עִם־הַהַגְרִאִים וַיִּפְּלוּ בְּיָדָם וַיֵּשְׁבוּ
יא בְּאָהֳלֵיהֶם עַל־כָּל־פְּנֵי מִזְרָח לַגִּלְעָד: וּבְנֵי־
יב גָד לְנֶגְדָּם יָשְׁבוּ בְּאֶרֶץ הַבָּשָׁן עַד־סַלְכָה: יוֹאֵל הָרֹאשׁ
יג וְשָׁפָם הַמִּשְׁנֶה וְיַעְנַי וְשָׁפָט בַּבָּשָׁן: וַאֲחֵיהֶם לְבֵית

realistic for the small nation which Israel was at that time. The Land described in *Genesis* is an ideal which would be realized as the people multiplied. During the reigns of David and Solomon, these boundaries were, in fact, reached.

Thus, according to *Radak*, Reuven's expansion eastwards took place within the boundaries which had been provided to Abraham. According to *Metzudos* it went beyond them.

The statement that Reuven's territory extended eastwards to the Euphrates requires some explanation. A glance at the map will show that after a great bulge towards the west opposite southern Turkey and northern Syria, the Euphrates flows steadily eastwards until it empties into the Persian Gulf. As R' Y.M. Tucazinsky's *HaAretz LeGevuloseha* makes clear, it is the western bulge which constitutes the north-eastern boundary of Israel. At that point it extends slightly west of the 38° longitudinal mark. Opposite Reuven's territory at the very south of Israel, the Euphrates is many hundreds of miles away running along the eastern border of Iraq. If our verse is to be taken literally, Reuven's lands would have extended almost to Iran.

It seems likely that *from the river Euphrates* means from the point to which a straight line could be drawn from the western extremity of the Euphrates [which lies hundreds of miles to the north of that point]. According to *HaAretz LeGevuloseha* (under *The Boundaries of the Patriarchs*) it was such a straight line which defined the boundaries of the Land in patriarchal times.

כִּי מִקְנֵיהֶם רָבוּ — *For their flocks increased.* The expansion eastwards was necessary because of their many sheep (*Radak*).

בְּאֶרֶץ גִּלְעָד — *In the land of Gilead.* Gra notes that Gilead was originally occupied by Gad (*Joshua* 13:25). At some point in history Reuven must have absorbed some of Gad's lands.

10. ... וּבִימֵי שָׁאוּל עָשׂוּ מִלְחָמָה — *Now in the days of Saul they waged war* ... This verse describes the historical events which made the expansion eastwards possible (*Malbim*). Verses 18-22 describe a war which the tribes on the eastern bank of the Jordan waged against the Hagrites. From *Bereishis Rabbah* 98:15 it appears that this

is the same war described in our verse. The two passages must therefore be studied together. [However, see comm. below for *Malbim's* opinion that they were two separate wars.]

עִם־הַהַגְרִאִים — *Against the Hagrites.* Verse 19 identifies the Hagrites more closely. Their names are Yetur, Naphish, and Nodav. The similarity of the first two names to two sons of Ishmael (*Genesis* 25:15) makes it obvious that the general name Hagrites derives from their matriarch, Hagar (*commentators*). Nodav is presumably another name for Kedmah (*Maharzav to Bereishis Rabbah*).

Psalms 83:7 speaks of *the tents of Edom, Ishmael, Moab, and Hagrim.* Many commentators interpret that name as they do ours — Hagrim are descendants of Hagar (see *Rashi, Ibn Ezra, Radak,* there). However, the *Anonymous Commentator* thinks that Hagrim in *Psalms* is a different nation, unrelated to the descendants of Hagar (perhaps because Ishmael is mentioned separately there). He stresses that the Hagrites of our passage are not descendants of Hagar but are to be identified with the nation mentioned in *Psalms.*

וַיִּפְּלוּ בְּיָדָם — *And they fell into their hands.* The Hagrites fell into the hands of the armies of Reuven and Gad. See verse 20.

וַיֵּשְׁבוּ בְּאָהֳלֵיהֶם — *And they settled in their tents.* The Reuvenites settled in the Hagrite dwellings (*Metzudos*). It was the custom of Arabs to dwell in tents (*Mefaresh*).

עַל־כָּל־פְּנֵי מִזְרָח לַגִּלְעָד — *Throughout all the land east of Gilead.* The translation follows *Targum*, who eliminates the prefix *lamed* from his rendering of לַגִּלְעָד. *Metzudos* translates: *towards Gilead.*

Our translation has followed the simple meaning of this sentence which, as we have seen above, is meant to give the background to Reuven's push to the east. There is also a midrashic interpretation to this sentence:

While Israel was conquering and dividing the land, the tribes of Reuven and Gad were with them, having left their small children behind [in the fortified cities of the

the days of Saul they waged war against the Hagrites, and they fell
into their hands; and they settled in their tents throughout all the
land east of Gilead. ¹¹ And near them, the sons of Gad dwelled in the
land of Bashan up to Salchah. ¹² Yoel, the chief, and Shapham the
second, and Yanai and Shaphat in the Bashan. ¹³ And their brothers

Transjordan — see *Numbers* ch. 32, *Joshua*
ch. 22]. They returned home after seven
years of war and seven years of dividing
the land. One who had left his son aged ten
found him now at twenty-four ... [while
they were gone] three evil tribes attacked
[their families] — Yetur, Naphish, and
Kedmah. This is what is meant by the
verse: *Now in the days of Saul* — this refers
to Joshua. Why is he called Saul? Because
his kingship was a 'borrowed' one [שָׁאוּל
from שאל, *to borrow*].

[The meaning of the next few lines in the
Midrash is unclear. According to *Yepheh
Toar* based on *Os Emmes* the correct
reading yields a description of the warring
factions.] Both the attacking Arabs and the
Jewish fighters wore their hair long. As a
result, the returning armies of Reuven and
Gad did not, at first, realize that their
own children were involved in the
fighting. So God inspired the children to
call out: 'Answer us, O God of Abraham,
Isaac and Jacob,' as it is written (v. 20):
*they were helped ... and the Hagrites ...
were given into their hands ... (Bereishis
Rabbah* 98:15). See Section Two, p. 408.

◄§ The Line of Gad

11⁻17. Reuven's genealogy followed
Judah's and Shimeon's because he was the
first-born (see comm. to vs. 1 and 2). Now,
Gad follows Reuven because they were
neighbors on the eastern side of the Jordan.

11. וּבְנֵי־גָד לְנֶגְדָּם — *And near them, the sons
of Gad.* See *Genesis* 33:12 for another
example of נֶגֶד meaning *near* rather than
the more usual, *opposite* (Mefaresh).

יָשְׁבוּ בְּאֶרֶץ הַבָּשָׁן עַד־סַלְכָה — *Dwelled in the
land of Bashan up to Salchah.* From
Deuteronomy 3:13 it would appear that the
area known as the Bashan was given to the
half-tribe of Menasheh which received its
portion on the eastern bank, rather than to
Gad, as indicated here.

Radak thinks that our passage refers to
sections of the Bashan which were never
given to Menasheh. The words: *all of the
Bashan* in *Deuteronomy* mean only the

whole of the Bashan ruled over by Og the
king of Bashan, mentioned there. There
were, however, enclaves over which he
never ruled and these fell to Gad's portion.

Gra and *Malbim* both think that
we are dealing with later shifts in the
population. Initially, the whole Bashan was
given to Menasheh, as *Deuteronomy*
implies. Between that time and the Assyrian exile, events occurred which caused
the population to shift and in the end the
land was in the possession of Gad.
Chronicles deals with these later circumstances.

12. We have already noted a number of
times that Ezra did not have the complete
genealogies of the ten tribes available to
him. These lists had been taken along into
the Assyrian exile and were thus lost to
those who remained. Ezra therefore had to
make use of such records as had survived
for one reason or another. In the case of
Gad, there seems to have been no records
which traced any of the family back to
Gad's own children. [For Gad's children,
see *Numbers* 26:15-17.] We cannot know
to which period the people listed here
belong [but see below on Shaphat].

יוֹאֵל הָרֹאשׁ וְשָׁפָם הַמִּשְׁנֶה — *Yoel, the chief,
and Shapham the second. Radak* writes
that the four people mentioned in this verse
were well-known heads of families who at
one time ruled in the Bashan.

The word מִשְׁנֶה, *the second,* in our
context seems to indicate someone *second
in rank* (see e.g. *II Chronicles* 28:7).
Targum renders: *Yoel, head of the Sanhedrin; Shapham, head of the house of
learning.*

וְיַעֲנַי וְשָׁפָט בַּבָּשָׁן — *And Yanai and Shaphat
in the Bashan. Targum* renders: *And Yanai
and Shaphat were judges in the Bashan.*

In the tradition of the Sages (*Pesachim*
68a), the Shaphat mentioned in our verse is
the father of the prophet Elisha (*I Kings*
19:16). This would date our list as belonging approximately to the reigns of Omri or
Achav in Israel. See further in verse 17.

אֲבוֹתֵיהֶם מִיכָאֵל וּמְשֻׁלָּם וְשֶׁבַע וְיוֹרַי וְיַעְכָּן וְזִיעַ וָעֵבֶר
יד שִׁבְעָה: אֵלֶּה ׀ בְּנֵי אֲבִיחַיִל בֶּן־חוּרִי בֶּן־
טו יָרוֹחַ בֶּן־גִּלְעָד בֶּן־מִיכָאֵל בֶּן־יְשִׁישַׁי בֶּן־יַחְדּוֹ בֶּן־בּוּז: אֲחִי
טז בֶן־עַבְדִּיאֵל בֶּן־גּוּנִי רֹאשׁ לְבֵית אֲבוֹתָם: וַיֵּשְׁבוּ בַּגִּלְעָד
יז בַּבָּשָׁן וּבִבְנֹתֶיהָ וּבְכָל־מִגְרְשֵׁי שָׁרוֹן עַל־תּוֹצְאוֹתָם: כֻּלָּם
הִתְיַחְשׂוּ בִּימֵי יוֹתָם מֶלֶךְ־יְהוּדָה וּבִימֵי יָרָבְעָם מֶלֶךְ־

13. וַאֲחֵיהֶם — *And their brothers.* In our context, this must be understood as their fellow tribesmen *(Metzudos).*

שִׁבְעָה — *Seven.* See footnote to 2:6 for an explanation of this apparent redundancy.

Targum renders: *All seven of them were leaders.*

The *Anonymous Commentator* and *Malbim* both point out that according to *Genesis* 46:16 Gad had seven sons and that consequently it seems likely that the seven family heads mentioned here corresponded to the seven families who made up the tribe of Gad. [See, however, *Gra's* comm. to next verse.]

14. ... אֵלֶּה בְּנֵי אֲבִיחַיִל — *These are the sons of Avichail ...* The seven leaders mentioned in the previous verse were all the sons of one man *(Gra).* Once more, any Midrashim on these names have been lost to us.

15. אֲחִי בֶן־עַבְדִּיאֵל — *Achi the son of Avdiel.* אֲחִי is a proper noun and is not to be translated 'the brother of' *(Malbim; Gra).*

רֹאשׁ לְבֵית אֲבוֹתָם — *Was the head of their families* [lit. *the house of their fathers*]. He was the leader of the people mentioned above *(Gra).*

16. וַיֵּשְׁבוּ בַּגִּלְעָד בַּבָּשָׁן — *And they dwelled in Gilead, in Bashan.* Radak notes that בַּגִּלְעָד בַּבָּשָׁן should be read as though it were written בַּגִּלְעָד וּבַבָּשָׁן, *In Gilead [and] in Bashan.* According to 3:12, Gad did indeed occupy parts of Gilead. See verse 11 for a discussion of the statement that he lived in the Bashan.

וּבִבְנֹתֶיהָ — *And its dependencies* [lit. *its daughters*]. This usage occurs in *Numbers* 32:42.

וּבְכָל־מִגְרְשֵׁי שָׁרוֹן — *And in all the open spaces of Sharon.* According to *Rashi* to *Numbers* 35:2, a מִגְרָשׁ is a *clearing* surrounding the city for its beautification.

Metzudos thinks that the word describes the houses outside the city walls. They appear as though they have been expelled [מִגְרָשׁ from גרש, *to drive away*] from the city.

עַל־תּוֹצְאוֹתָם — *Up to their limits. Metzudos* notes that the עַל in this phrase must be translated *up to* [as thought it were written, עַד] rather than the more usual *on* or *besides.*

תּוֹצָאָה, *limit,* derives from the root יצא, *to go out.* It is that which 'goes out' as far as possible from the center.

In comm. to vs. 9 and 10 we noted *Malbim's* opinion that during the Hagrite wars there was a huge expansion eastwards, far beyond the boundaries which had originally been assigned to the tribes on the eastern bank. *Malbim* bases his interpretation of our verse on that same assumption. Gad lived in Gilead and Bashan, locations which fell into the boundaries which Moses had laid down. In addition, they expanded beyond those boundaries [תּוֹצָאָה describes a *spreading-out beyond*] to the area of Sharon.

17. כֻּלָּם הִתְיַחְשׂוּ — *The genealogical lines of all of them were established.* It is not clear from the text whether this verse is to be read with the preceding or the following section [although the fact that immediately following upon our verse there is a פָּרָשָׁה סְתוּמָה,*semi-paragraph* in the Massorah, seems to argue for the former option].

According to the first possibility, our verse teaches that the genealogical information given about Gad was gleaned from records which were established in the reigns of the kings mentioned in our verse. This seems to be the opinion of *Metzudos.*

According to the second possibility it is an introduction to the war described in the following verses. From *Numbers* 1:2-3 it is evident that censi taken for military purposes included the establishment of

according to their families — Michael, Meshullam, Sheva, Yorai, Yacan, Zia, and Ever — seven. 14 *These are the sons of Avichail the son of Churi, the son of Yaroach, the son of Gilead, the son of Michael, the son of Yeshishai, the son of Yachdo, the son of Buz.* 15 *Achi the son of Avdiel, the son of Guni was the head of their families.* 16 *And they dwelled in Gilead, in Bashan and its dependencies, and in all the open spaces of Sharon up to their limits.* 17 *The genealogical lines of all of them were established in the days of Yotham the king of Judah, and in the days of Yerovoam the king*

---

genealogical lines. Thus, the Hagrite wars described here were the occasion of an extensive genealogical survey of the tribes on the eastern bank (*Radak*).

בִּימֵי יוֹתָם מֶלֶךְ־יְהוּדָה וּבִימֵי יָרָבְעָם מֶלֶךְ־יִשְׂרָאֵל — *In the days of Yotham the king of Judah, and in the days of Yerovoam the king of Israel.* The Yerovoam of our verse refers to Yerovoam the son of Yoash, not to Yerovoam the son of Nevat (founder of the Northern Kingdom).

Commentators point out that the reigns of these two kings did not coincide. According to the dates given in *Kings*, the reign of Uzziah, the father of Yotham, extended many years beyond the death of Yerovoam the king of Israel. Uzziah became king in the twenty-seventh year of Yerovoam's reign (*II Kings* 15:1) which, according to 14:23, lasted forty-one years. According to 15:2, Uzziah reigned for fifty-two years, which places the end of his reign some thirty-eight years after Yerovoam's death. Thus, Yotham the son of Uzziah did not become king until long after Yerovoam's death.

Radak offers two possibilities. According to *II Kings* 15:5, Uzziah became a leper at some point during his reign at which time his son, Yotham, became the effective ruler of the people. Thus, although Yotham did not formally become king until much later, it is quite possible that for all practical purposes his leadership of the people could have coincided with Yerovoam's reign. Alternatively, *Radak* suggests that our verse may refer to two separate countings, one which took place while Yerovoam was king and the other several decades later.

That Yotham king of Judah is mentioned at all in this connection is worthy of note. The tribes on the eastern bank were a part of the Northern Kingdom, and we would not expect a king of Judah to be involved in

their census. *Gra* suggests that Yotham was only mentioned in order to date the occurrence by the reign of a righteous king. Yerovoam, who was wicked (*II Kings* 14:24), is mentioned only with reluctance. [It is obvious from this that *Gra* agrees with *Radak's* first explanation. If two different censi took place, *Gra's* explanation would not be possible.]

Malbim, who agrees with *Radak's* second explanation that there were two separate censi, suggests that the necessity for a census during Yerovoam's reign was due to the fact that he reconquered vast tracts of land which had been taken by Aram in earlier years (ibid:25). Apparently, then, much of the eastern bank had not been under Jewish control for some time before his reign and was only restored to the two and a half tribes as a result of his campaigns. As the rightful owners resettled in their lands, it became necessary to re-establish correct family records.

✌ The Hagrite War

18. This verse begins the account of the war between the tribes on the eastern bank and the Hagrites. In comm. to v. 10 we noted that in the view of the Sages the war described here is the same as that mentioned in v. 10. *Malbim*, however, thinks that we are dealing with a different war. In the first campaign, waged during Saul's reign, the Hagrites had been driven eastwards and their territory was annexed by Reuven, as described in v. 10. However, during the reign of Yehoachaz, king of Israel, the tribes of the eastern bank lost their hold on many of their possessions because of the ascendancy of Aram, as described in *II Kings* 13:3ff. The Hagrites seized this opportunity to return to their former lands. When Yerovoam came to power and led Israel to the huge victories described there in 14:25, the eastern tribes

יח בְּנֵי־רְאוּבֵ֣ן וְגָדִ֗י וַחֲצִ֣י שֵֽׁבֶט־מְנַשֶּׁה֮ מִן־ יִשְׂרָאֵל֒:
בְּנֵי־חַ֣יִל אֲ֠נָשִׁים נֹשְׂאֵ֨י מָגֵ֤ן וְחֶ֙רֶב֙ וְדֹ֣רְכֵי קֶ֔שֶׁת וּלְמוּדֵ֖י
מִלְחָמָ֑ה אַרְבָּעִ֨ים וְאַרְבָּעָ֥ה אֶ֛לֶף וּשְׁבַע־מֵא֥וֹת וְשִׁשִּׁ֖ים

יט יֹצְאֵ֥י צָבָֽא: וַיַּעֲשׂ֥וּ מִלְחָמָ֖ה עִם־הַהַגְרִיאִ֑ים וִיט֖וּר וְנָפִ֥ישׁ

כ וְנוֹדָֽב: וַיֵּעָזְר֣וּ עֲלֵיהֶ֔ם וַיִּנָּתְנ֤וּ בְיָדָם֙ הַהַגְרִיאִ֔ים וְכֹ֖ל
שֶֽׁעִמָּהֶ֑ם כִּ֠י לֵאלֹהִ֤ים זָעֲקוּ֙ בַּמִּלְחָמָ֔ה וְנַעְתּ֥וֹר לָהֶ֖ם כִּי־

כא בָ֥טְחוּ בֽוֹ: וַיִּשְׁבּ֣וּ מִקְנֵיהֶ֗ם גְּמַלֵּיהֶ֞ם חֲמִשִּׁ֥ים אֶ֙לֶף֙ וְצֹ֗אן
מָאתַ֙יִם֙ וַחֲמִשִּׁ֣ים אֶ֔לֶף וַחֲמוֹרִ֖ים אַלְפָּ֑יִם וְנֶ֥פֶשׁ אָדָ֖ם מֵאָ֥ה

כב אָֽלֶף: כִּֽי־חֲלָלִ֤ים רַבִּים֙ נָפָ֔לוּ כִּ֥י מֵהָאֱלֹהִ֖ים הַמִּלְחָמָ֑ה

כג וַיֵּשְׁב֥וּ תַחְתֵּיהֶ֖ם עַד־הַגֹּלָֽה: וּבְנֵ֗י חֲצִ֤י שֵׁ֙בֶט֙ מְנַשֶּׁ֔ה

---

became emboldened to wage a new campaign against the Hagrites and they then regained their lost territories, as described here.

בְּנֵי־רְאוּבֵן ... מִן־בְּנֵי־חַיִל — *From the sons of Reuven ... warriors* [gathered]. The syntax is extremely difficult. *Metzudos* inserts the word *gathered* in his rendering and it appears that the word מִן, *from* [among], is interpreted as though it came at the beginning of the sentence.

וַחֲצִי שֵׁבֶט־מְנַשֶּׁה — *And the half-tribe of Menasheh*. Although the initial request for territory on the eastern bank had only come from Reuven and Gad (*Numbers* 32:1ff), the Torah tells that half the tribe of Menasheh also took their inheritance (v. 33). For this reason, they too were involved in the Hagrite war.

The genealogy of Menasheh begins in verse 23.

וְדֹרְכֵי קֶשֶׁת — *Proficient with bow* [lit. *treaders upon the bow*]. In order to achieve maximum force, it was necessary to plant one's foot on the bottom of the longbow. Therefore, bowmen were called דֹּרְכֵי קֶשֶׁת, *those who tread* [דֹּרְכֵי from דרך, *to tread upon*] *upon the bow* (*Metzudos*).

וּלְמוּדֵי מִלְחָמָה — *And trained for war*. למד, *to learn*, can also have the meaning *to gain experience* (*Metzudos*).

יֹצְאֵי צָבָא — *Fit for combat* [lit. *who go out to war*]. *Metzudos* explains this to mean those fit to go out to war.

19. וַיַּעֲשׂוּ מִלְחָמָה עִם־הַהַגְרִיאִים — *And they made war on the Hagrites* ... See

comm. to verse 10 for identification of the Hagrites and the others mentioned here.

20. וַיֵּעָזְרוּ עֲלֵיהֶם — *And they were helped against them*. עזר, *to help*, together with the preposition עַל, means to help someone overpower an enemy. Cf. *II Chronicles* 26:7.

The implication of the *nifal*, passive voice, is that they were helped by someone other than themselves, but the verse does not identify this helper. *Targum* renders: *They were helped by their brother Israelites*. The comm. to v. 10 quoted *Bereishis Rabbah* 98:15 that the armies of these two and a half tribes, which had crossed the Jordan in order to fulfill their obligation to help in the conquest of the land, returned during the heat of the battle. Because they had been gone so long they did not recognize their own children and did not realize that their own families were involved in the fighting. God inspired the children to pray out loud. When the fathers heard these prayers, they jumped into the fray and turned the tide of battle. Accordingly, the unnamed helper may refer to God Who inspired the children to pray, or it may refer to the returning armies who made the victory possible.

וְכֹל שֶׁעִמָּהֶם — *And all that were with them*. *Radak* and *Metzudos* interpret this to mean the other nations or mercenaries who were assisting the Hagrite armies.

According to the Midrash, it refers to those children of the two and one half tribes who had been captured by the Hagrites.

of Israel. ¹⁸ From the sons of Reuven and Gad and the half-tribe of Menasheh warriors [gathered], men bearing shield and sword, proficient with bow and trained for war, forty-four thousand seven hundred and sixty fit for combat. ¹⁹ And they made war on the Hagrites, Yetur, Naphish, and Nodav. ²⁰ And they were helped against them, and the Hagrites and all that were with them were given into their hands; for they cried out to God in the war, and He answered them because they trusted in Him. ²¹ So they captured their possessions: fifty thousand of their camels, two hundred and fifty thousand sheep; two thousand asses; and one hundred thousand people. ²² For many were slain, because the war was from God. And they settled in their lands until the exile. ²³ And the sons

כִּי לֵאלֹהִים זָעֲקוּ — *For they cried out to God.* According to the simple meaning of the verse this phrase explains why the Jewish armies were victorious. They had prayed to God and He answered their prayers.

According to the Midrash, the phrase explains how the returning armies realized that their own children were involved in the fighting. The children had grown long hair just like that of their attackers. The only way to tell that they were Israelites was by their children's cry to God. [See further in Section Two, p. 408.]

וַנֶעְתּוֹר לָהֶם — *And He answered them.* עתר means *to pour out an abundance of prayer* (see *Genesis* 25:21). The form used here could be rendered either: *He made Himself accessible to their entreaties;* or, *He allowed Himself to be persuaded by their entreaties.*

21. וְנֶפֶשׁ אָדָם מֵאָה אָלֶף — *And one hundred thousand people.* Given the relatively small size of the Jewish army (v. 18), the number of captives seems excessive. The next verse will explain (*Malbim*).

נֶפֶשׁ אָדָם — *People* [lit. *souls of men*]. When Scripture gives the number of persons in a given group, the preferred term is נֶפֶשׁ (cf. *Exodus* 1:5; *Numbers* 31:28; *Deuteronomy* 10:22). The word אָדָם is added to נֶפֶשׁ when groups of animals are counted in the same context. Besides our verse, *Numbers* 31:35 and 46 can serve as examples.

22. כִּי־חֲלָלִים רַבִּים נָפָלוּ — *For many were slain* [lit. *for many corpses fell*]. This verse explains the unexpectedly high number of captives taken. Many of the Hagrites surrendered when they saw how many of

their number were killed (*Metzudos*).

כִּי מֵהָאֱלֹהִים הַמִּלְחָמָה — *Because the war was from God.* Verse 20 described how the army of the two and a half tribes cried to God in their distress. God answered their entreaties and many more enemy soldiers fell than could have been expected under normal circumstances.

וַיֵּשְׁבוּ תַחְתֵּיהֶם עַד־הַגֹּלָה — *And they settled in their lands* [lit. *they dwelled in their stead*] *until the exile.* The two and a half tribes spread eastward into the lands which they conquered from the Hagrites (*Metzudos*). They remained in these lands until the Assyrian exile described in verse 26.

◆§ Menasheh on the East Bank

23. After the genealogical information concerning Gad has been completed, Ezra turns to the half-tribe of Menasheh who was the neighbor of Reuven and Gad on the eastern bank. *Ramban* notes that the initial request to Moses came only from Reuven and Gad. However, when the time came to divide the land it became obvious that there was too much territory for just two tribes. Moses asked for volunteers and part of Menasheh, perhaps because they were also rich in flocks, agreed to stay on the eastern bank.

וּבְנֵי חֲצִי שֵׁבֶט מְנַשֶּׁה — *And the sons of the half-tribe of Menasheh.* Ramban (*Numbers* 32:33) points out that the word חֲצִי, *half*, in this context should really be taken as *part*. Menasheh comprised eight families (*Numbers* 26:29-32), and only two of those took their portion east of the Jordan (see *Joshua* 17:2).

יָשְׁבוּ בָּאָרֶץ מִבָּשָׁן עַד־בַּעַל חֶרְמוֹן וּשְׂנִיר וְהַר־חֶרְמוֹן הֵמָּה
כד רָבוּ: וְאֵלֶּה רָאשֵׁי בֵית־אֲבוֹתָם וָעֵפֶר וְיִשְׁעִי וֶאֱלִיאֵל
וְעַזְרִיאֵל וְיִרְמְיָה וְהוֹדַוְיָה וְיַחְדִּיאֵל אֲנָשִׁים גִּבּוֹרֵי חַיִל
כה אַנְשֵׁי שֵׁמוֹת רָאשִׁים לְבֵית אֲבוֹתָם: וַיִּמְעֲלוּ

יָשְׁבוּ בָּאָרֶץ — *Settled in the land.* After the war with the Hagrites they returned to dwell in their own land (*Metzudos*).

מִבָּשָׁן ... — *From Bashan ...* But, because their population increased greatly [הֵמָּה רָבוּ] (*Gra; Metzudos*), they expanded beyond their original boundaries into areas which had previously been occupied by the other two tribes who had now moved over to the newly conquered Hagrite territories.

מִבָּשָׁן — *From Bashan.* Bashan had been the original territory which Moses had assigned to the half-tribe of Menasheh (see *Deuteronomy* 3:13 and comm. to v. 11 above).

עַד־בַּעַל חֶרְמוֹן — *To Baal Hermon. Ramban* (*Deuteronomy* 3:9) suggests that Baal Hermon could be the name of a city or fortress, or that the name Baal derived from the fact that an idol of that name was located there.

וּשְׂנִיר וְהַר־חֶרְמוֹן — *And Senir and Mount Hermon.* From *Deuteronomy* 3:9 it appears that Hermon and Senir are two names for the same mountain. *Gra* explains that each of the mountain's four slopes had its own name. The west slope was called Senir and the south slope was called Hermon. The meaning of our verse is that the Menashites settled west and south of the mountain.

הֵמָּה רָבוּ — *[For] they became numerous.* The expansion of their territory became necessary because of their increase in numbers (*Gra; Metzudos*).

24. וְאֵלֶּה רָאשֵׁי בֵית־אֲבוֹתָם — *Now these are the heads of their families.* This verse does not contain all the genealogical data that was available to Ezra concerning the tribe of Menasheh; a much more thorough treatment is given in 7:14ff.

With the exception of *Malbim*, the commentators do not explain the significance of this list, and he confines himself to writing that the seven names mentioned here could correspond to the seven families ascribed to Menasheh's son, Machir, in *Numbers* 26:29ff (see comm. to v. 13).

[This explanation is difficult to understand, since of the seven families of Machir six received their shares on the western side of the Jordan (see *Joshua* 17:2). The context of these verses though would seem to indicate that these men were all heads of families residing on the eastern bank.]

It is possible that the seven family heads mentioned here lived at the time of the Hagrite war and were involved in it. This would explain why they are mentioned here, although the main genealogical treatment is left to ch. 7 where the whole tribe is dealt with as one unit.

וָעֵפֶר — *Epher. Radak* thinks that the *vav* is not part of the name. He notes that occasionally a proper name is introduced by a redundant *vav*, as in *Genesis* 36:24.

Malbim prefers to assume that the *vav* is part of the name (see above 4:15).

אֲנָשִׁים גִּבּוֹרֵי חַיִל — *Men of outstanding quality.* The word חַיִל is a term of extreme plasticity and versatility, and it is used throughout Scripture to describe many different qualities. These have in common only that they are inspired by a sense of zeal and devotion which makes them exceptional. Thus, in the case of a judge, it would describe a man of unusual intelligence, earnestness and rectitude; in a warrior, a soldier of bravery and dedication, knowledgeable and trained in the intricacies of warfare; and in the case of a housewife, one who runs her home with energy and devotion (*Ramban, Exodus* 18:21; see also *Rashi* to *Exodus* 47:6).

Accordingly, a אִישׁ חַיִל or an בֶּן חַיִל would be a man with outstanding qualities who stands out from the crowd. The particular quality meant depends on the context.

גִּבּוֹר from גבר, *to be strong* or *mighty*, is used in Scripture to denote physical prowess (cf. *Proverbs* 16:32). However, when used in advance in conjunction with another word, it is likely that it serves only to accentuate the other word in the phrase. Thus, גִּבּוֹר תָּמִים (*II Samuel* 22:26) would mean a *paragon of integrity*, and גִּבּוֹר צַיִד (*Genesis* 10:9) would be an *expert hunter.*

of the half-tribe of Menasheh settled in the land from Bashan to Baal Hermon and Senir and Mount Hermon, [for] they became numerous. 24 *Now these are the heads of their families — Epher, Yishi, Eliel, Azriel, Yirmiah, Hodaviah, Yachdiel, men of outstanding quality, men of names, heads of their families.* 25 *But*

Accordingly, גִּבּוֹר חַיִל would denote a paragon of the particular quality expressed in חַיִל. [See *Mefaresh* to 26:8.]

Given the wide range of meanings this phrase can have, the translation of this book will specify a quality only when the context makes it obvious that a particular quality is meant. Where there is ambiguity, חַיִל will be rendered simply as *quality* [e.g., *men of quality*], and גִּבּוֹר חַיִל will be rendered as a *person of outstanding quality*.

אַנְשֵׁי שֵׁמוֹת — *Men of names.* These men were known by their names because of their great importance *(Metzudos).*

The word שֵׁם is used throughout Scripture to denote renown (cf. among countless examples: *Genesis* 11:4 and 12:2). Thus, to the expression אַנְשֵׁי הַשֵּׁם in *Genesis* 6:4, *Gra* remarks: Those known in the world for either their own eminence, their actions or their family are called אַנְשֵׁי שֵׁם. However, the use of the plural, שֵׁמוֹת, in our verse seems to indicate that *names* rather than *renown* is intended.

The form אַנְשֵׁי שֵׁמוֹת, which is unique to *Chronicles*, is repeated at 12:30.

⋖§ Exile of the Eastern Tribes

25⁻26. This treatment of the sins and exile of the two and a half east-bank tribes is unique to *Chronicles*. *Kings* does not distinguish their fate from that of the rest of the tribes of the Northern Kingdom.

The description of the sins contained in verse 25 is a very much shortened version of the much more detailed review of *II Kings* 17:7ff. The listing of the place names to which they were exiled (v. 26) is an almost exact repetition of v. 6 there. Our passage is special only in the sense that what was said there in connection with the whole of the Northern Kingdom is said here in connection with the tribes of the eastern bank only. *Chronicles* does not mention the exile of the other tribes of the Northern Kingdom.[1]

The exile of the Northern Kingdom occurred in three waves. *II Kings* 15:29 tells how during the reign of Pekach ben Remaliahu (the penultimate king of the Northern Kingdom) the Assyrian king Tiglath Pileser[2] took many of Israel's cities and exiled the tribe of Naphtali and, as appears from *Isaiah* 8:23, Zevulun.

---

1. Even the account of the exile of the three tribes of the eastern bank is not given in the historical part of the book, which begins with ch. 10, but as part of the genealogical listings here — possibly as a quote from the source from which Ezra drew the lists given here. This, because in contrast to *Kings* which details the histories of both the northern and southern kingdoms, *Chronicles'* narrative deals only with Judah.

Why does *Kings* not mention this exiling of the eastern bank, which may even have been the earliest of the three waves — see commentary — separately? The following may be a possible explanation:

The entire institution of the monarchy, beginning with the reigns of David and Solomon and ending with the tragedy of the Babylonian exile, did not live up to the kingship which God had wanted for Israel and which, throughout the prophetic books, is envisioned for the Messianic era. [For a detailed exposition, see ArtScroll *Ezekiel* p. 531.]

From the moment of its inception — against God's will — the monarchy went into a decline (see *Shemos Rabbah* 15:26 which compares it to a waning moon, ending in darkness as Tzidkiahu was blinded), and it may well be that it is the purpose of the *Book of Kings* to chronicle that decline.

Such a chronicle would concern itself primarily with the area in which, had God's will been done, the monarchy should have flourished. Now, in *Ezekiel*, where the Israel of the Messianic future is described and the boundaries of that ideal state are delineated, the eastern branch of the Jordan is not included. It seems clear that although in a political sense, and to some extent a halachic one, the boundaries of Israel will surely extend to the east and indeed encompass many areas never before conquered, the focus of the sanctity of Israel, the dwelling place of the Divine Presence, is specifically in *Eretz Yisrael* proper. [See ArtScroll *Ezekiel* p. 740ff.] That is where the monarchy should have fulfilled its role, and it is there that its disintegration engages the attention of *Kings*. The exile of the three tribes on the eastern bank has no place in that account.

2. In *Chronicles* the name of the Assyrian king is always given as Tillegath Pilneser or Pilneeser (see above, v. 6), while in *Kings* it is Tiglath Pileser.

בֵּאלֹהֵי אֲבֹתֵיהֶם וַיִּזְנוּ אַחֲרֵי אֱלֹהֵי עַמֵּי־הָאָרֶץ אֲשֶׁר־
כו הִשְׁמִיד אֱלֹהִים מִפְּנֵיהֶם: וַיָּעַר אֱלֹהֵי יִשְׂרָאֵל אֶת־רוּחַ |
פּוּל מֶלֶךְ־אַשּׁוּר וְאֶת־רוּחַ תִּלְּגַת פִּלְנֶסֶר מֶלֶךְ אַשּׁוּר
וַיַּגְלֵם לָראוּבֵנִי וְלַגָּדִי וְלַחֲצִי שֵׁבֶט מְנַשֶּׁה וַיְבִיאֵם לַחְלַח
כז וְחָבוֹר וְהָרָא וּנְהַר גּוֹזָן עַד הַיּוֹם הַזֶּה: בְּנֵי לֵוִי

Then, 17:6ff describes the final and total destruction of Shomron (Samaria). In addition to these two stages, there is the exile of the eastern bank described in our verse.

There is a disagreement among the Sages concerning the sequence of the exiles. *Pesichta* to *Eichah Rabbosi* (5) records two opinions: According to one, Naphtali was taken first; according to the other, the tribes on the eastern bank.

The Talmud's tradition seems to have been that Reuven and Gad went first, since *Arachin* 32b teaches that from the time of the exile of the eastern bank, the *Yovel* [Jubilee] year was no longer observed. [The laws of the *Yovel* apply only when the land is occupied by all twelve tribes (*Gra*).] In addition, there are many Midrashim which teach that the impetuousness which Reuven and Gad displayed in demanding that they receive their inheritance on the eastern bank was punished by having them be the very first of Israel's tribes to lose their land (cf. *Rashi* to *Proverbs* 21:1).

Gra thinks that our passage argues in favor of this opinion. Verse 26 tells that the exile of the eastern bank was brought about by two Assyrian kings: Pul and Tillegath Pilneser. From a comparison of *II Kings* 15:19 and 15:29, it is clear that Pul reigned before Tillegath Pilneser. Since our verse indicates that the exile of the eastern bank took place during the reigns of both Pul and Tillegath Pilneser, this would seem to mean that it took place during the end of Pul's reign and the very beginning of Tillegath Pilneser's reign. It would therefore seem to predate the exile of Naphtali which, in *II Kings* 15:29, is ascribed solely to Tillegath Pilneser and presumably took place in a later part of his reign. *Rashi* (*II Kings* 17:1), however, accepts the opinion that the exile of Naphtali preceded that of the tribes of the eastern bank.

Malbim interprets the fact that both Pul and Tillegath Pilneser are mentioned, differently. He believes that this indicates

that the tribes of the eastern bank were themselves exiled in two waves, one during Pul's reign, and the remainder during Tillegath Pilneser's reign when he conquered Naphtali and Zevulun. [In *Malbim's* view, this explains the phrase in verse 23: *And the sons of the half-tribe of Menasheh settled in the land.* It means that they remained in the land even after the exile mentioned in verse 22. It also explains the verse in *Isaiah* 8:23 which mentions Gilead among the areas taken by Tillegath Pilneser, implying that at the time of his campaign Gilead, that is the eastern bank, was still in Jewish hands.

25. וַיִּמְעֲלוּ בֵּאלֹהֵי אֲבֹתֵיהֶם וַיִּזְנוּ — *But they dealt faithlessly with the God of their fathers and strayed …* [lit. *and committed harlotry*]. The translation follows the *Targumim* which consistently render מעל as שקר, *to be false* or *deceptive*.

Toras Kohanim to *Leviticus* 5:15 uses our verse to demonstrate that מעל can be extended to mean *change.* In our case, it means exchanging the God of their fathers for the idols of the local population. This fits very well with the use of the term מעל in conjunction with זנה.

זנה, which usually means *to to commit fornication* or *be a harlot*, has been translated as *strayed*, in the sense that it is used in *Numbers* 15:39. However, *Toras Kohanim* takes it in the sense of misappropriating a given object — in this case loyalty to one's God. See *Rashi* to *Leviticus* 19:29.

אֲשֶׁר־הִשְׁמִיד אֱלֹהִים מִפְּנֵיהֶם — *Whom God had exterminated before them.* It should have been expected that the impotence of these idols would have been demonstrated by their inability to help the nations who had worshiped them. Nevertheless, Israel succumbed to the worship of these idols (*Mefaresh* and *Metzudos*).

26. וַיָּעַר אֱלֹהֵי יִשְׂרָאֵל — *And the God of Israel incited.* The translation follows

they dealt faithlessly with the God of their fathers and strayed after the gods of the peoples of the land whom God had exterminated before them. ²⁶ *And the God of Israel incited the spirit of Pul the king of Assyria, and the spirit of Tillegath Pilneser the king of Assyria, and he exiled them — the Reuvenites, the Gadites, and the half-tribe of Menasheh — and brought them to Chalach, Chavor, Hara and the river of Gozan until this day.* ²⁷ *The sons of Levi —*

Targum, who renders וְגֵרִי.

However, *Metzudos* translates *aroused* in the sense of rousing to activity. This seems to be the opinion of *Targum* to the books of the prophets who, when עוּר is used in conjunction with רוּחַ as it is in our verse (cf. *Jeremiah* 51:11; *Haggai* 1:14), renders it as *awakening* (cf. *Zechariah* 4:1).

אֱלֹהֵי יִשְׂרָאֵל — *The God of Israel.* The parallel verses in *Kings* use HASHEM rather than *God of Israel* (cf. *II Kings* 17:18ff). In fact the use of *God of Israel* as the subject in a narrative passage such as this is unique to our verse. Perhaps it is used to add poignancy to what is being described.

A period, unique in Jewish history, was about to come to a close. With Solomon's reign, the ideal state of Israel's nationhood had been attained. Every institution envisioned by the Torah was in place — the monarchy stood at its peak; the Temple functioned flawlessly; the *Kohen Gadol* (High Priest) wearing the *Urim VeTumim* was available for Divine guidance; prophecy — the most direct form of communication between God and man — was freely bestowed on those who had risen to the requisite heights of personal sanctity. Every condition for a national and individual life guided solely by Torah was fulfilled. Even the *Yovel* (Jubilee) year, that highest expression of sanctity of which Israel as a nation is capable, could be celebrated because the stringent condition for its application — that the majority of all Jews should be living in their land — was fulfilled.

If God had a purpose in creation, and that purpose could come to fruition by means of His chosen people living an exemplary Torah life within the boundaries of His Holy Land, then beginning with Solomon's reign it could be said that the fulfillment of God's purpose had become possible.

The exile of the tribes of the eastern bank constituted the first overt break in this ideal. Once they were taken into captivity the *Yovel* laws ceased to apply and the ideal state of Israel's nationhood ceased to be a practical reality. Thenceforth, and until the advent of the Messiah, it would be a dream of the future. The long trek of *galus* (exile) had begun.

God's love for His people, expressed most clearly in the name *God of Israel,* was not enough to avert the tragedy. Israel's sins had, as it were, forced the hand of the *God of Israel,* who had previously delighted in the perfection of their state, to incite Assyria against them.

פּוּל מֶלֶךְ־אַשּׁוּר ... תִּלְגַת פִּלְנֶסֶר ... — *Pul the king of Assyria ... Tillegath Pilneser ...* According to *Gra* the exile took place during the end of Pul's reign and the beginning of his successor Tillegath Pilneser's reign. According to *Malbim* two different exiles are referred to here (see above, comm. to 25-26).

וַיַּגְלֵם לָראוּבֵנִי ... — *And he exiled them — the Reuvenites ...* The information given here for the destination of the tribes of the eastern bank is almost identical with that given in *II Kings* 17:6. The difference is only that the *Hara* mentioned here is not given there while *Kings* lists *cities of Media* which are not mentioned here.

עַד הַיּוֹם הַזֶּה — *Until this day.* The tribes of the eastern bank did not return from their exile when Judah returned from Babylon to build the Second Commonwealth *(Radak).*

⋈§ The Tribe of Levi

27-41. Ezra now turns his attention to the tribe of Levi. Verses 27-41 trace the lineage of Aaron's son Eleazar through Tzadok, from whom all the *Kohanim Gedolim* (High Priests) of the First Temple were descended. Chapter 6 will treat the genealogical lists of the tribe in a more general way.

27. ... בְּנֵי לֵוִי — *The sons of Levi ...* This verse is repeated in 6:1. In our verse it serves as an introduction to the Tzadokite

כח גֵּרְשׁוֹן קְהָת וּמְרָרִי: וּבְנֵי קְהָת עַמְרָם יִצְהָר וְחֶבְרוֹן
כט וְעֻזִּיאֵל: וּבְנֵי עַמְרָם אַהֲרֹן
וּמֹשֶׁה וּמִרְיָם וּבְנֵי אַהֲרֹן נָדָב וַאֲבִיהוּא אֶלְעָזָר וְאִיתָמָר:

---

line which is traced up to the destruction of the First Temple. In ch. 6 it introduces the genealogy of the whole tribe.

גֵּרְשׁוֹן קְהָת וּמְרָרִי — *Gershon, Kehath and Merari. Genesis* 46:11 lists these names in identical form. V. 6:1 has גֵּרְשׁוֹם, *Gershom,* instead of גֵּרְשׁוֹן, *Gershon.*

28. ... וּבְנֵי קְהָת — *And the sons of Kehath ...* Chapter 6 will list the families of Gershon and Merari in addition to that of Kehath. In our passage, which is the record of the Tzadokite line, only Kehath is mentioned. The same four sons listed here are given in *Exodus* 6:18.

29. וּבְנֵי עַמְרָם ... מִרְיָם — *And the children of Amram ... Miriam.* The best translation of בְּנֵי in our phrase is probably *children* since Miriam is mentioned. Hebrew generally uses the masculine plural to describe mixed groups. Although when the genealogical lists give daughters they usually identify them as women (cf. 4:3), in the case of Miriam that was unnecessary since she is well known from the Torah.

... וּבְנֵי אַהֲרֹן — *And the sons of Aaron ...* The same four sons listed here are given in *Exodus* 6:23 and many other places.

The two oldest, Nadav and Avihu, were killed by a heavenly fire when they sinned at the inauguration of the Tabernacle (*Leviticus* 10:1*ff*). At Aaron's death the third son, Eleazar, succeeded him as *Kohen Gadol* (High Priest) (*Numbers* 20:23*ff*).

◄§ The Kohanim Gedolim?

30‾41. We have already noted that the main genealogy of the tribe of Levi begins with 6:1. The list in our chapter must therefore have a special function.

Many commentators (*Tosafos, Yoma* 9a; *Mefaresh; Gra*) assume that this passage is not simply a genealogical record but a list of the *Kohanim Gedolim* (High Priests) who served from the time of Aaron till the destruction of the First Temple. The position of the *Kohen Gadol* is passed from father to son where the son is sufficiently wise and God-fearing to fill that post (*Rambam, Klei Mikdash* 4:20). According to these opinions, throughout the years of

the First Temple there were always sons worthy of succeeding their fathers. [Cf. *Vayikra Rabbah* 21:8: In the First Temple, since they served faithfully ... they were succeeded by their sons and grandsons ...]

Such an interpretation of our passage would indeed explain why it exists separately from the general genealogical tables of ch. 6. There are, however, great difficulties in assuming that our list is a record of the *Kehunah Gedolah* (High-Priesthood). To facilitate discussion a numbered list of the names is given here:

1. Aaron
2. Eleazar
3. Pinechas
4. Avishua
5. Bukki
6. Uzzi
7. Zerachiah
8. Meraioth
9. Amariah (a)
10. Achituv (a)
11. Tzadok (a)
12. Achimaatz
13. Azariah (a)
14. Yochanan
15. Azariah (b)
16. Amariah (b)
17. Achituv (b)
18. Tzadok (b)
19. Shallum
20. Chilkiah
21. Azariah (c)
22. Seraiah
23. Yehotzadak

A number of *Kohanim* whom we know to have been *Kohanim Gedolim* are missing from the list.

In the period before the Temple was built by Solomon, we have Scriptural reference to the *Kehunah Gedolah* of Eli (*I Samuel* 1); his great-grandson Achiyah [the son of Achituv, the son of Pinechas, the son of Eli] (*I Samuel* 14:3); Achiyah's brother, Achimelech [who was killed by Saul in the priesly city of Nov] (*I Samuel* 22:9); and Achimelech's son, Eviathar, who served as *Kohen Gadol* for David (*I Samuel* 30:7) and continued in this post until Solomon replaced him with Tzadok [11 on the list] (*I Kings* 2:35). [According to

5

28-29

Gershon, Kehath and Merari. [28] *And the sons of Kehath — Amram, Yitzhar, Chevron, and Uzziel.* [29] *And the children of Amram — Aaron, and Moses, and Miriam; and the sons of Aaron — Nadav*

Josephus, Antiquities 6:6:5, Achituv, the son of Eli's son Pinechas, was also a *Kohen Gadol*.]

According to *Eliyahu Rabbah* 11, Eli, and therefore of course his dynasty, were descended from Aaron's son Ithamar. The *Kehunah Gedolah* had originally been promised to Eleazar's son, Pinechas, and should have remained his eternally. However, as the Sages teach, Pinechas did not provide the leadership which his times required and as a result the *Kehunah Gedolah* was given to Eli and his descendants who came from Ithamar. It was not returned to the descendants of Pinechas (son of Eleazar) until Solomon's reign when he installed Tzadok (11) as *Kohen Gadol*. From that time on, the *Kehunah Gedolah* remained with the descendants of Tzadok (see *Rashi* to *I Samuel* 2:30).

This entire episode in the history of the *Kehunah Gedolah* is not reflected in our list and, indeed, from this analysis it would follow that Avishua (4), Bukki (5), Uzzi (6), Zerachiah (7), Meraioth (8), Amariah (9), and Achituv (10) were never *Kohanim Gedolim*, since between Pinechas and Tzadok the *Kehunah Gedolah* was vested in the descendants of Ithamar.

[Following *Rambam* [Introduction to Mishneh Torah] we assume that the *Kehunah Gedolah* passed directly from Pinechas to Eli and have eliminated seven names. *Josephus, Antiquities* 5:11:5, claims that Pinechas was followed by Avishua (4); Bukki (5) and Uzzi (6). Accordingly, the *Eliyahu Rabbah* does not mean that the *Kehunah Gedolah* passed directly from Pinechas to Eli but that it passed to him from Pinechas' descendants. This eliminates the problem of how Pinechas, who appears during the wanderings in the desert, remained alive until Eli's ascension to the *Kehunah Gedolah*. See *Kiryas Melech* of R' Chaim Kanievski *shlita.*

In addition, our list does not record Yehoiada (*II Kings* 11:4ff), who was *Kohen Gadol* during the reigns of Athaliah and Yehoash, nor Uriah who seems to have been *Kohen Gadol* during the reign of Achaz (*II Kings* ch. 16) [see *Metzudos, II Kings* 11:4 and 16:10].

Malbim also doubts that our passage is a list of the *Kohanim Gedolim* of the First Temple. He cites *Seder Olam Zuta* which offers a list of the *Kohanim Gedolim* who officiated in the reign of each king, and only

a few of these names coincide with the ones listed here.

The following is *Seder Olam Zuta's* list: [*Kohanim Gedolim* not mentioned in our verse are given in brackets.]

1. Solomon — Tzadok
2. Rechovoam — Achimaatz
3. Aviyah — Azariah
4. Asa — [Yehoram]
5. Yehoshaphat — [Yehoachaz]
6. Yehoram — [Yehoshaphat]
7. Achaziah — [Yehoshaphat]
8. Yehoash — [Yehoiada, Pedaiah]
9. Amatziah — [Tzidkiah]
10. Uzziahu — [Yoel]
11. Yotham — [Yotham]
12. Achaz — [Uriah]
13. Chizkiah — [Neraiah]
14. Menasheh — [Hoshaiah]
15. Amon — Shallum
16. Yoshiahu — Chilkiah
17. Yehoachaz — Chilkiah
18. Yehoiakim — Azariah
19. Yehoiachin — Seraiah
20. Tzidkiah — Yehotzadak

Based on this list, *Malbim* concludes that we are dealing with a genealogical list and not a list of the *Kohanim Gedolim*. This seems to be the opinion of *Radak* as well. The reason this list is given separately from the genealogical tables of ch. 6 may be because it is the direct line of descent of Yehoshua the son of Yehotzadak (23), the first *Kohen Gadol* of the Second Temple who, together with Zerubavel, headed the return of the exiles from Babylon. Ezra may have wanted to stress his descent from the illustrious Tzadokite line.

Those commentators who interpret our list as a record of the *Kohanim Gedolim* view this passage as the source from which the Sages drew their information concerning the number of *Kohanim Gedolim* who served in the First Temple.

Yoma 9a reads: 'The First Temple stood for four hundred and ten years and throughout this period there were only eighteen *Kohanim Gedolim.*' No source is given for this statement, but many commentators assume that it is based on our text. *Riva* in *Tosafos*, there, suggests that the text should be emended to read *eight* instead of *eighteen*. This he bases on our verse 36 which states that *he* Azariah (b) (15) *served as Kohen in*

ל אֶלְעָזָר הוֹלִיד אֶת־פִּינְחָס פִּינְחָס הֹלִיד אֶת־אֲבִישׁוּעַ:

לא-לב וַאֲבִישׁוּעַ הוֹלִיד אֶת־בֻּקִּי וּבֻקִּי הוֹלִיד אֶת־עֻזִּי: וְעֻזִּי

לג הוֹלִיד אֶת־זְרַחְיָה וּזְרַחְיָה הוֹלִיד אֶת־מְרָיוֹת: מְרָיוֹת

הוֹלִיד אֶת־אֲמַרְיָה וַאֲמַרְיָה הוֹלִיד אֶת־אֲחִיטוּב:

לד וַאֲחִיטוּב הוֹלִיד אֶת־צָדוֹק וְצָדוֹק הוֹלִיד אֶת־אֲחִימָעַץ:

the House that Solomon built in Jerusalem — presumably during Solomon's reign. If we assume that Yehotzadak (23) who was exiled is not counted then we have eight *Kohanim Gedolim* spanning the period under discussion. *Tosafos* goes on to suggest that if it is postulated that the count begins with Azariah (b) (15) as *Riva* thinks, then it would not be necessary to emend the text. We could count Yehotzadak (23), making nine *Kohanim Gedolim* and then these together with their auxiliary *Kohanim Gedolim* [known in Scripture as *Kohen Mishneh*] would be eighteen.

Based on a a reading of *Sifrei* (beginning of *Pinchas*) which seems to count the eighteen *Kohanim Gedolim* from Pinechas himself, *Tosafos* suggests that the Talmud does not mean that the eighteen served only during the period of the First Temple. Rather, it means that those of the listed *Kohanim Gedolim* who served during the period of the Temple made the number of Pinechas' descendants who served as *Kohanim Gedolim* eighteen. According to this system the count begins with Pinechas' son Avishua (4) and does not count Seraiah (22) or Yehotzadak (23) who, even if they served as *Kohanim Gedolim*, did not complete their terms since Seraiah was taken captive during the first wave of exiles in Yehoiakim's reign and Yehotzadak met the same fate eleven years later when Nebuchadnezzar finally destroyed the Temple.

Both explanations assume that verse 36 is to be taken literally and that Azariah (b) (15) was, in fact, *Kohen Gadol* during Solomon's reign. This assumption is, however, far from simple. It is clear from Scripture (*I Kings* 2:35) that Tzadok (a) (11) was *Kohen Gadol* during Solomon's reign and it is quite unthinkable that the office changed hands four times during his lifetime. For this reason, *Yalkut (Korach* 654) maintains that this verse refers to Azariah the *Kohen Gadol* who served during the reign of King Uzziahu, some one hundred and seventy years after Solomon's rule. He 'served' in Solomon's Temple by protecting its sanctity. Uzziahu, not satisfied with his royal mantle, coveted the prerogatives of the *Kohen Gadol* and wanted to offer incense in the Temple. Azariah, at great risk to himself, protested and thus preserved the integrity of the *Kehunah* (see *II Chronicles* 28:16ff).

Tosafos cites this opinion without explaining how the eighteen *Kohanim Gedolim* are to be

counted according to this system.

Gra reads *twelve* instead of *eighteen* and takes the count from Tzadok (a) (11) who, as we saw above, was *Kohen Gadol* in Solomon's reign. Yehotzadak (23) is not counted. In *Gra's* opinion, he was not a *Kohen Gadol* himself but his son, Yeshua, was to be the first *Kohen Gadol* of the rebuilt Temple.

Gra hesitates to accept *Yalkut's* solution that Azariah (b) (15) is the *Kohen Gadol* who officiated during Uzziahu's reign. He points out that the *Kohen Gadol* during Yehoshaphat's reign was called Amariah (*II Chronicles* 19:11) and that this is probably the Amariah (b) (16), the son of Azariah (b) (15). Since Yehoshaphat reigned long before Uzziahu it is impossible to place Azariah in Uzziahu's reign [see below for a possible answer to this problem which *Gra* poses]. Rather, he suggests that Azariah (b) (15) be identified with the *Kohen Gadol* Yehoiada who was instrumental in preserving the Davidic line of succession when he saved the infant Yehoash from his grandmother Athaliah's murderous intentions (*II Kings* ch. 11). Since Athaliah dismantled the Temple service and it was only restored as a result of Yehoiada and Azariah's efforts, he is described as serving in Solomon's Temple.

Malbim thinks that *Seder Olam Zuta's* listing can help explain v. 36. According to the *Seder Olam* list the *Kohen Gadol* during Aviyah's reign (3) was Azariah. Which Azariah was this — (a) or (b)? Verse 36 points out that it was the second Azariah, that is Azariah (b) (15) *who served in the House that Solomon built*, i.e., who served as *Kohen Gadol* (during the reign of Aviyah), rather than his grandfather, Azariah (a) (13). The first Azariah, however, never served as *Kohen Gadol* at all. [In this, *Malbim* follows his view that our list here is not a list of the *Kohanim Gedolim* but a genealogical list; see comm.]

This would mean, though, that *Yalkut (Korah* 654) disagrees with *Seder Olam Zuta* because it identifies Azariah (b) (15) as the man who protested so forcefully when King Uzziahu tried to bring incense in the Temple. However, *Yalkut* is in any case in disagreement with the *Seder Olam* since *Seder Olam* lists Yoel (10) and not Azariah as *Kohen Gadol* during Uzziahu's reign. Although the verse itself states that the *Kohen Gadol* who barred Uzziahu's way was Azariah, *Malbim* suggests that the term כֹּהֵן הָרֹאשׁ, *head Kohen*, used to describe Azariah in that episode

and Avihu, Eleazar and Ithamar. ³⁰ *Eleazar fathered Pinechas, Pinechas fathered Avishua.* ³¹ *And Avishua fathered Bukki, and Bukki fathered Uzzi.* ³² *And Uzzi fathered Zerachiah and Zerachiah fathered Meraioth.* ³³ *Meraioth fathered Amariah, and Amariah fathered Achituv.* ³⁴ *And Achituv fathered Tzadok, and Tzadok*

(II Chronicles 26:20) does not mean *Kohen Gadol* but *head Kohen,* the priest who dealt with the administrative details of the priesthood in the Temple. This is the meaning of the phrase, ... *who served in the Temple which Solomon built* (v. 36). He served there in the capacity of administrator — not as *Kohen Gadol.* The actual *Kohen Gadol* of that time, though, was Yoel, according to *Seder Olam Zuta.*

Malbim further notes that *Seder Olam Zuta* gives the *Kohen Gadol* in the reign of Yehoshaphat as Yehoachaz. Thus, the Amariah given in *II Chronicles* 19:11 as the *head Kohen* was also not *Kohen Gadol,* but the priestly administrator. If the Sages interpret the term *head Kohen* as does *Malbim,* this would answer the problem raised by *Gra* against their interpretation of verse 36. We have noted above that in the view of many commentators the Sages view our passage as a list of *Kohanim Gedolim.* But they also say that Azariah (b) (15) was *Kohen Gadol* during Uzziahu's reign. *Gra* asked how this is possible since Amariah (16) was *Kohen Gadol* during the reign of Yehoshaphat which antedated that of Uzziahu. According to *Malbim's* understanding of the term *head Kohen* the difficulty disappears. The Amariah of Yehoshaphat's reign is not the Amariah (16) of our list. Our list deals with *Kohanim Gedolim* and the Amariah of Yehoshaphat's reign was only a *head Kohen.*

30. אֶלְעָזָר הוֹלִיד אֶת־פִּינְחָס — *Eleazar fathered Pinechas.* As explained above, many commentators assume this section to be a list of *Kohanim Gedolim.* Pinechas succeeded his father as *Kohen Gadol,* as may be seen from *Judges* 20:28.

אֲבִישׁוּעַ — *Avishua.* There is no record in Scripture that this son of Pinechas ever became *Kohen Gadol.* But *Josephus* (*Antiquities* 5:11:5) reports that Pinechas' son, Aviezer, followed his father in the office. It is possible that Aviezer and Avishua are the same person.

31. בֻּקִּי ... עֻזִּי — *Bukki ... Uzzi.* According to *Josephus* (ibid.), Bukki became *Kohen Gadol* after his father, Avishua (Aviezer — see above), and was succeeded by his son, Uzzi.

32. זְרַחְיָה — *Zerachiah.* As *Josephus* (ibid.) records it, the *Kehunah Gedolah* passed to Eli and his dynasty — descendants of

Aaron's son Ithamar — after Uzzi's death (see discussion, above). If this is so, then this Zerachiah is the first in the line who was not a *Kohen Gadol.* We have noted above that *Gra's* opinion is that all the people in our list were *Kohanim Gedolim.*

מְרָיוֹת — *Meraioth.* The *Anonymous Commentator* identifies Meraioth with Eli. He is called Meraioth [from מַר, *bitter*] because of the double tragedy [Meraioth in the plural] of his life. Both his sons were destined to die on one day (see *I Samuel* 2:24).

According to this tradition, Eli would belong to Eleazar's dynasty, while according to the Sages, quoted above, he was descended from Ithamar.

In *Ezra* ch. 7, Ezra's own genealogy is traced. He is introduced as the son of Seraiah (22), and the line is taken back to Azariah (b) (15). This Azariah is given as the son of Meraioth (8), and the line then continues back till Aaron. Six generations are left out. *Radak* thinks that this was done for the sake of brevity, and *Malbim* adds that since Ezra wrote *Chronicles* before he wrote *Ezra,* the complete genealogy was available in *Chronicles* and it was possible to be less detailed in *Ezra.*

34. צָדוֹק — *Tzadok.* If we can rely on *Josephus,* Tzadok was already an important *Kohen* during Saul's reign (*Antiquities* 7:2:2).

In Scripture he appears first as ... *a young man of exceptional quality and his family — twenty-two chieftains* (*I Chronicles* 12:29) who was among those who came to Hebron to declare David king over all Israel.

He remained loyal to David during Absalom's uprising and Adoniyahu's pretension. Eventually, Solomon took the *Kehunah Gedolah* away from Eviathar, a descendant of Eli belonging to the family of Ithamar, and gave it to Tzadok. At that point the *Kehunah Gedolah* returned to Eleazar's line never to be lost again.

Tzadok's descendants remained loyal to the Torah throughout the tragic years of the decline of the First Temple. None of

לה וַאֲחִימַעַץׂ הוֹלִיד אֶת־עֲזַרְיָה וַעֲזַרְיָה הוֹלִיד אֶת־יוֹחָנָן:
לו וְיוֹחָנָן הוֹלִיד אֶת־עֲזַרְיָה הוּא אֲשֶׁר כִּהֵן בַּבַּיִת אֲשֶׁר־
לז בָּנָה שְׁלֹמֹה בִּירוּשָׁלָ͏ִם: וַיּוֹלֶד עֲזַרְיָה אֶת־אֲמַרְיָה וַאֲמַרְיָה
לח הוֹלִיד אֶת־אֲחִיטוּב: וַאֲחִיטוּב הוֹלִיד אֶת־צָדוֹק וְצָדוֹק
לט הוֹלִיד אֶת־שַׁלּוּם: וְשַׁלּוּם הוֹלִיד אֶת־חִלְקִיָּה וְחִלְקִיָּה
מ הוֹלִיד אֶת־עֲזַרְיָה: וַעֲזַרְיָה הוֹלִיד אֶת־שְׂרָיָה וּשְׂרָיָה
מא הוֹלִיד אֶת־יְהוֹצָדָק: וִיהוֹצָדָק הָלַךְ בְּהַגְלוֹת יהוה אֶת־
א יְהוּדָה וִירוּשָׁלָ͏ִם בְּיַד נְבֻכַדְנֶאצַּר: בְּנֵי
ב לֵוִי גֵּרְשֹׁם קְהָת וּמְרָרִי: וְאֵלֶּה שְׁמוֹת בְּנֵי־גֵרְשׁוֹם

them ever succumbed to the lure of idol worship which attracted members of the other priestly families. For this reason the Messianic visions of Ezekiel assume a *Kehunah* made up, in the first place, from Tzadok's descendants (*Ezekiel* 44:15; see ArtScroll comm. there).

Nehemiah's list of the *Kohanim Gedolim* of the Second Temple shows that throughout the period of the Scriptures the *Kehunah Gedolah* continued in Tzadokite hands (*Nehemiah* ch. 12).

אֲחִימַעַץ — *Achimaatz.* Achimaatz is mentioned as Tzadok's son in *II Samuel* and various other places. According to *Seder Olam Zuta*, he was *Kohen Gadol* during the reign of Solomon's son, Rechovoam.

35. עֲזַרְיָה — *Azariah.* According to *Seder Olam Zuta*, Azariah was *Kohen Gadol* during the reign of Rechovoam's son Aviyah.

The *Kohanim Gedolim* listed in *Seder Olam Zuta* after Azariah do not correspond to the names in our list until Shallum (19). This has been discussed above in comm. 30-41.

36. הוּא אֲשֶׁר כִּהֵן בַּבַּיִת אֲשֶׁר־בָּנָה שְׁלֹמֹה בִּירוּשָׁלַ͏ִם — *He is the one who served as Kohen in the House that Solomon built in Jerusalem.* There are many interpretations of this verse and its significance. *Tosafos* (*Yoma* 9a) assume that this means that this second Azariah served as *Kohen Gadol* (High Priest) in the times of Solomon. This, however, poses several difficulties, one of which is that from *I Kings* 2:35 we know that Azariah's great-great-grandfather, Tzadok, was appointed *Kohen Gadol* at the beginning of Solomon's reign. *Yalkut* (*Korah* 654) states that the Azariah of our verse is identical with the

Azariah who prevented King Uzziahu from offering incense in the Temple (see *II Chronicles* 28:16ff). Since he risked his life to preserve the integrity of the *Kehunah* (priesthood) and the Temple, he is credited as having been *the Kohen* of Solomon's Temple.

Gra identifies the Azariah of our verse with the famous *Kohen Gadol* Yehoiada of *II Kings* ch. 11 (and *II Chronicles* ch. 23,24) who saved the Davidic line by overthrowing the wicked Queen Athaliah and placing on the throne the last-surviving child of the Davidic line, Yoash. It was Yehoiada who taught Yoash to go in the ways of God (*II Kings* 12:3). Since it was through this influence that Yoash restored the Temple service which had been dismantled by Athaliah, Azariah-Yehoiada is singled out as having served as *Kohen* in Solomon's Temple.

Malbim suggests that Azariah of our verse is the Azariah who, according to *Seder Olam Zuta* (see list above, p. 85), served as *Kohen Gadol* in the reign of Aviyah. Our verse emphasizes that it was only the Azariah of our verse, and not his grandfather of the same name (v. 35), who ever served as *Kohen Gadol* in Solomon's Temple.

Each of his explanations is beset by various difficulties. These have been discussed at length above in the introductory notes to vs. 30-41.

37. אֲמַרְיָה — *Amariah.* See comm. 30-41 for a discussion of whether this is the Amariah mentioned in Scripture during the reign of Yehoshaphat.

38. שַׁלּוּם — *Shallum. Seder Olam Zuta* lists Shallum as *Kohen Gadol* during the reign of Amon.

39. חִלְקִיָּה — *Chilkiah.* Chilkiah was *Kohen*

fathered Achimaatz. 35 Achimataz fathered Azariah, and Azariah fathered Yochanan. 36 And Yochanan fathered Azariah; he is the one who served as Kohen in the House that Solomon built in Jerusalem. 37 And Azariah fathered Amariah, and Amariah fathered Achituv. 38 And Achituv fathered Tzadok, and Tzadok fathered Shallum. 39 And Shallum fathered Chilkiyah, and Chilkiyah fathered Azariah. 40 And Azariah fathered Seraiah, and Seraiah fathered Yehotzadak. 41 And Yehotzadak went when HASHEM exiled Judah and Jerusalem at the hands of Nebuchadnezzar.

The sons of Levi — Gershom, Kehath and Merari. 2 And these are

Gadol during the reign of Yoshiahu (Josiah). It was his discovery of a surviving Torah scroll which triggered the major repentance movement inaugurated by Yoshiahu and described in detail in *II Kings* ch. 22.

עֲזַרְיָה — *Azariah*. *Seder Olam Zuta* has this Azariah as *Kohen Gadol* during the reign of Yehoiakim — the first king exiled by the Babylonians.

40. שְׂרָיָה — *Seraiah*. Seraiah, described as כֹּהֵן הָרֹאשׁ, the head *Kohen*, in *II Kings* 25:18, was murdered by Nebuchadnezzar at Rivlah, at the destruction of the Temple (ibid. vs. 20-21). From the Scriptural account it would therefore seem that he was the very last of the *Kohanim Gedolim* who served in the First Temple. This would mean that his son Yehotzadak was never a *Kohen Gadol.*

However, *Seder Olam Zuta* (see list given above; see also *Josephus, Antiquities* 10:8:5,6) mentions Yehotzadak as a *Kohen Gadol.* This could mean that for some reason lost to us he was made *Kohen Gadol*

during his father's lifetime.

Shir HaShirim Rabbah 5:4 seems to bear this out. The Midrash explains that Yehoshua ben Yehotzadak, rather than Ezra, became *Kohen Gadol* when the Second Temple was built (see *Haggai* 1:1) because Yehoshua's father — Yehotzadak — had previously held that office.

Although from the description of Ezra's own lineage (*Ezra* 7:1ff) it is clear that Ezra was also the son of Seraiah and a brother of Yehotzadak (*Mefaresh* below, 24:2, *Radak* and *Ibn Ezra* to *Haggai* 1:1), the line of the *Kehunah Gedolah* had already passed to Yehotzadak during the first Temple. Thus, it was Yehotzadak's son — Yehoshua — who had first claim to the office of *Kohen Gadol* rather than Ezra (*Ibn Ezra* there).[1] This would seem to be the Midrash's intent as well.

41. ... וִיהוֹצָדָק הָלַךְ — *And Yehotzadak went* ... The Tzadokite line was to continue in the Second Temple. The first *Kohen Gadol* after the return to Zion was Yehoshua, the son of Yehotzadak (see *Haggai* 1:1).

VI

◄§ Gershon, Kehath, Merari

1. This verse is a repetition of 5:27. There, Levi's sons were brought as an introduction to the genealogy of the *Kohanim Gedolim* (see comm. there). Our chapter deals with the genealogy of the tribe as a whole and leads to David's organization of the choristers for the Temple service which

begins with v. 16.

גֵּרְשֹׁם — *Gershom*. 5:27 had Gershon with a *nun* rather than the *mem* used here. *Radak* points out that *nun* and *mem* are readily interchangeable.

2-4. The names of the third generation of Levi's family are identical with those listed in *Exodus* 6:17-19.

1. There is no Scriptural or Talmudic source that Ezra was ever a *Kohen Gadol*. Nevertheless, both *Rambam* in his introduction to *Mishneh Torah* and *Meiri* in his introduction to *Avos* state that he did hold the post. This is possibly based on *Koheles Rabbah* 1:4. See *Kiryas Melech* on *Rambam* ad loc.

Sefer HaYuchasin writes: 'After Yehoshua the *Kohen Gadol* died it appears that Ezra became *Kohen Gadol* since we find that Ezra dealt with a *parah adumah* (see *Rambam, Parah* 3:4). However, it appears from the *Book of Ezra* [Nehemiah] that his (Yehoshua's) son Yehoiakim and grandson

ג לִבְנֵי וְשִׁמְעִי: וּבְנֵי קְהָת עַמְרָם וְיִצְהָר וְחֶבְרוֹן וְעֻזִּיאֵל:
ד בְּנֵי מְרָרִי מַחְלִי וּמֻשִׁי וְאֵלֶּה מִשְׁפְּחוֹת הַלֵּוִי לַאֲבֹתֵיהֶם:
ה-ו לְגֵרְשׁוֹם לִבְנִי בְנוֹ יַחַת בְּנוֹ זִמָּה בְנוֹ: יוֹאָח בְּנוֹ עִדּוֹ

וְאֵלֶּה מִשְׁפְּחוֹת הַלֵּוִי לַאֲבֹתֵיהֶם — *And these are the Levitical families according to their fathers.* The genealogies of the sons are traced to their fathers (*Metzudos*).

The similarity between our list and that of *Exodus* is great enough to make a change in expression particularly noteworthy. The list in *Exodus* ends with the words: אֵלֶּה מִשְׁפְּחֹת הַלֵּוִי לְתֹלְדֹתָם, *these are the Levitical families according to their generations.* Why, then, does our phrase substitute: *according to their fathers?*

Perhaps, the fact that our phrase begins with the prefatory וְאֵלֶּה, *and these,* instead of אֵלֶּה, *these,* as in *Exodus,* points to a solution. This wording seems to indicate that the phrase refers to that which is to follow, rather than to the names which preceded it.

Now, the following lists seem to be an introduction to David's organization of the choristers (v. 16ff). That organization was arranged along the lines of the three Levite families, Gershom, Kehath and Merari (see vs. 18-23; 24-27; and 29-32). For this reason the three sons of Levi are introduced as family heads. [לַאֲבֹתֵיהֶם may be a contracted form of לְבֵית אֲבוֹתָם rather than as individuals.]

5. לְגֵרְשׁוֹם — *To Gershom.* The genealogical lists follow the order of birth. Gershom was the first-born and his family is treated first. Later when the choristers are traced back to their forefathers, Heman from Kehath is listed first because he was the most important among them.

לִבְנִי בְנוֹ — *His son Livni.* Shimei's genealogy is not given. Similarly, from the line of Kehath, only Yitzhar's is traced and from Merari only that of Mushi (see below on v. 14). *Radak* explains that in this section Ezra traces only those families who were to be involved with David's organization of the choristers.

לִבְנִי ... יַחַת ... זִמָּה — *Livni ... Yachath ... Zimmah.* There are some differences between the line of descent as given here and as it appears in vs. 24-28 where the genealogy of Gershom's descendant, Asaph the chorister, is traced.

To facilitate comparison we offer the following lists.

List A — Gershom	
I. (vs. 2-6)	**II. (vs. 24-28)**
1. גֵּרְשׁוֹם, Gershom	1. גֵּרְשֹׁם, Gershom
2. לִבְנִי, Livni	
3. יַחַת, Yachath	3. יַחַת, Yachath
	4. שִׁמְעִי, Shimei
5. זִמָּה, Zimmah	5. זִמָּה, Zimmah
6. יוֹאָח, Yoach	
	6. אֵיתָן, Ethan
7. עִדּוֹ, Iddo	7. עֲדָיָה, Adaiah
8. זֶרַח, Zerach	8. זֶרַח, Zerach
9. יְאָתְרַי, Yeathrai	9. אֶתְנִי, Ethni
	10. מַלְכִּיָּה, Malchiyah
	11. בַּעֲשֵׂיָה, Baaseiah
	12. מִיכָאֵל, Michael
	13. שִׁמְעָא, Shimea
	14. בֶּרֶכְיָהוּ, Berechiahu
	15. אָסָף, Asaph

Eliashiv, and Yodaiah ben Eliashiv, and Yonathan ben Yodaiah were *Kohanim Gedolim* — and not Ezra. Although it appears from the beginning of the *Book of Knowledge* (*Rambam*) that Ezra was *Kohen Gadol* before Shimon HaTzaddik — there is no source for this in any historical record.

From *Shir HaShirim Rabbah* 5:4 it seems that Ezra was not *Kohen Gadol*. The *Midrash* explains that although he was a righteous man the office was given to Yehoshua who was the son of the previous *Kohen Gadol* and was denied to Ezra (see comm. to v. 40).

The *Mefaresh* to verse 40 also indicates that Ezra was never *Kohen Gadol*.

the names of Gershom's sons — Livni and Shimei. ³ And the sons of Kehath — Amram, Yitzhar, Chevron and Uzziel. ⁴ The sons of Merari — Machli and Mushi; and these are the Levitical families according to their fathers. ⁵ To Gershom — his son Livni, his son Yachath, his son Zimmah. ⁶ His son Yoach, his son Iddo, his son

List B — Kehath	
I. (vs. 7-13)	**II. (vs. 18-23)**
1. קְהָת, Kehath	1. קְהָת, Kehath
2. עַמִּינָדָב, Amminadav	
	2. יִצְהָר, Yitzhar
3. קֹרַח, Korach	3. קֹרַח, Korach
4. אַסִּיר, אֶלְקָנָה, אֲבִיָסָף Eviasaph, Elkanah, Assir,	4. אֲבִיָסָף, Eviasaph
5. אַסִּיר, Assir	5. אַסִּיר, Assir
6. תַּחַת, Tachath	6. תַּחַת, Tachath
7. אוּרִיאֵל, Uriel	
	7. צְפַנְיָה, Tzephaniah
8. עֻזִּיָה, Uzziah	8. עֲזַרְיָה, Azariah
9. שָׁאוּל, Shaul	
	9. יוֹאֵל, Yoel
10. אֶלְקָנָה, Elkanah	10. אֶלְקָנָה, Elkanah
11. עֲמָשַׂי, Amasai	11. עֲמָשַׂי, Amasai
12. אֲחִימוֹת, Achimoth	12. מַחַת, Machath
13. אֶלְקָנָה, Elkanah	13. אֶלְקָנָה, Elkanah
14. צוֹפַי, Tzophai	14. צוּף, Tzuph
15. נַחַת, Nachath	15. תּוֹחַ, Toach
16. אֱלִיאָב, Eliav	16. אֱלִיאֵל, Eliel
17. יְרֹחָם, Yerocham	17. יְרֹחָם, Yerocham
18. אֶלְקָנָה, Elkanah	18. אֶלְקָנָה, Elkanah
19. שְׁמוּאֵל, Samuel	19. שְׁמוּאֵל, Samuel
20. וַשְׁנִי, אֲבִיָּה, Vashni, Aviyah	20. יוֹאֵל, Yoel
	21. הֵימָן, Heman

List C — Merari	
I. (vs. 14-15)	**II. (vs. 29-32)**
1. מְרָרִי, Merari	1. מְרָרִי, Merari
	2. מוּשִׁי, Mushi
2. מַחְלִי, Machli	3. מַחְלִי, Machli
3. לִבְנִי, Livni	
4. שִׁמְעִי, Shimei	
5. עֻזָּה, Uzzah	
6. שִׁמְעָא, Shimea	
7. חַגִּיָה, Chaggiah	
8. עֲשָׂיָה, Asaiah	
	4. שֶׁמֶר, Shemer
	5. בָּנִי, Bani
	6. אַמְצִי, Amtzi
	7. חִלְקִיָּה, Chilkiah
	8. אֲמַצְיָה, Amatziah
	9. חֲשַׁבְיָה, Chashaviah
	10. מַלּוּךְ, Malluch
	11. עַבְדִּי, Avdi
	12. קִישִׁי, Kishi
	13. אֵיתָן, Ethan

ז בְּנוֹ זֶרַח בְּנוֹ יְאָתְרַי בְּנוֹ: בְּנֵי קְהָת עַמִּינָדָב בְּנוֹ קֹרַח בְּנוֹ

ח-ט אַסִּיר בְּנוֹ: אֶלְקָנָה בְנוֹ וְאֶבְיָסָף בְּנוֹ וְאַסִּיר בְּנוֹ: תַּחַת בְּנוֹ

י אוּרִיאֵל בְּנוֹ עֻזִּיָּה בְנוֹ וְשָׁאוּל בְּנוֹ: וּבְנֵי אֶלְקָנָה עֲמָשַׂי

יא וַאֲחִימוֹת: אֶלְקָנָה °בְּנוֹ אֶלְקָנָה צוֹפַי בְּנוֹ וְנַחַת בְּנוֹ:

יב-יג אֱלִיאָב בְּנוֹ יְרֹחָם בְּנוֹ אֶלְקָנָה בְּנוֹ: וּבְנֵי שְׁמוּאֵל הַבְּכֹר

ז-יג

°בְּנֵי ק'

There are three general observations to be made concerning these lists before we submit them to more detailed study.

(1) As has been noted several times, the word בֵּן, *son*, in lists such as these can mean *descendant* and need not mean a direct son.

In our lists this becomes obvious when we consider that lists II of A, B and C all go down to David's time since they trace the families of the three choristers, Heman, Asaph, and Ethan, whom David appointed. List B has twenty-one names while lists A and C have fourteen and thirteen respectively spanning the same period. It seems likely that lists A and C leave out a number of generations who were, perhaps, less significant than the others. [In David's own family only ten generations spanned this same period (see 2:4-15). However, this is a special situation and belongs to the category of the other miraculous circumstances which attended the development of Israel's royal family. See above 2:5.]

(2) As we have seen many times, the same people often appear in Scripture under different names. [For a detailed discussion see Overview/Names and their Significance.] In the lists with which we are dealing here this is particularly obvious in list B where list II gives Korach's father as Yitzhar, as it is given in the Torah, while list I gives the name Amminadav.

Thus, in analyzing the lists two options are available to explain the discrepancies. Either one or both lists may have skipped one or more generations as explained in (1). Or the same person may be listed under two different names.

(3) We have established that Ezra made use of many different sources in compiling his lists. [For a detailed discussion see Overview p. xxff.] It seems clear that list I of A, B and C is a regular genealogical record with no involvement with David's choristers, while list II is manifestly a record of the choristers. This can best be seen in A where list I goes only up to יְאָתְרָי, Yeathrai (9), [probably the same as אֶתְנִי,

Ethni (9) in list II] although the chorister from Gershom's family was Asaph (15), six generation later. [Malbim surmises that Yeathrai must have been an important personage whose lineage was, for some reason, available to Ezra.] Thus, we should not be surprised to find various apparent discrepancies between the two records in much the same way that these occur in all cases in which material is drawn from different sources.

A glance at A shows that Livni [I(2)] is omitted in list II while Shimei [II(4)] is omitted in list I.

6. יוֹאָח — *Yoach*. It is possible that in list A Yoach [I(6)] is omitted in II and that Ethan [II(6)] is omitted in I (*Malbim*). But it is also possible that Yoach and Ethan are different names for the same person (*Gra*).

יְאָתְרָי — *Yeathrai*. The Gershonite list stops here although Ezra knew of at least six other generations as can be seen in A:II. Yeathrai must have been an important person whose genealogy had been preserved (*Malbim*).

7. The genealogy of Levi's second son, Kehath, is now taken up.

עַמִּינָדָב — *Amminadav*. Amminadav is not mentioned among the four sons of Kehath listed in v. 3. Moreover, he is given here as father of Korach whom the Torah identifies as a son of Yitzhar (*Numbers* 16:1). Commentators are unanimous in identifying Amminadav as Yitzhar but offer no explanation for a connection between the two names.

The correct translation of עַמִּינָדָב, Amminadav, is probably *my kinsman is noble* [from עַם, a *people*, and נָדָב as in נָדִיב, *to be noble, princely, in rank* (cf. *I Samuel* 2:8)].

יִצְהָר, Yitzhar, is also used in the sense of nobility. The word literally means *oil* (cf. *Deuteronomy* 7:13), which was used to anoint nobility. *Zechariah* 4:14 describes king and *Kohen Gadol* as בְּנֵי יִצְהָר, lit. *sons of oil*, because they attain their rank

Zerach, his son Yeathrai. ⁷ The sons of Kehath — his son
Amminadav, his son Korach, his son Assir. ⁸ His son Elkanah, and
his son Eviasaph, and his son Assir. ⁹ His son Tachath, his son Uriel,
his son Uzziah, and his son Shaul. ¹⁰ And the sons of Elkanah —
Amasai and Achimoth. ¹¹ [His son] Elkanah; and the sons of
Elkanah — his son Tzophai, his son Nachath. ¹² His son Eliav, his
son Yerocham, his son Elkanah. ¹³ And the sons of Samuel — the
first-born Vashni and Aviyah. ¹⁴ The sons of Merari — Machli, his

through anointing (see commentators there). *Targum* there renders בְּנֵי יִצְהָר as בְּנֵי רַבְרְבַיָּא, *sons of princes*, which is the term he uses to translate נְדִיבִים in *Psalms* 146:3.

אַסִּיר — *Assir*. This Assir is the son of Korach, as seen from *Exodus* 6:24. See further, next verse.

8. אֶלְקָנָה בְנוֹ וְאֶבְיָסָף בְּנוֹ — *His son Elkanah, and his son Eviasaph.* According to *Exodus* 6:24 both Elkanah and Eviasaph [spelled Aviasaph there] were also sons of Korach. Consequently, in both instances the word בְּנוֹ, *his son*, means Korach's son. This is in contrast to the rest of the list where בְּנוֹ, *his son*, is always used in the sense of the son of the person immediately preceding him.

וְאַסִּיר בְּנוֹ — *And his son Assir.* From v. 22 it is obvious that this Assir was the son of Eviasaph *(Gra)*.

9. אוּרִיאֵל — *Uriel.* Uriel [B:I(7)] is missing in list II. There we have Tzephaniah [II(7)] who, in turn, is missing in list I. Either each list omits one name *(Malbim)*, or we must assume that the same person was known by both names *(Ralbag; Gra)*.

עֻזִּיָּה — *Uzziah.* Uzziah [B:I(8)] is the same as Azariah in list II(8).[1]

שָׁאוּל — *Shaul.* Shaul [I(9)] is omitted in list

II and Yoel [II(4)] is missing in list I. Again, either one is missing from each list or it is the same person under two names.

10⁻11. The syntax of these two verses is difficult. *Gra* suggests that they should be understood as though they were written as follows: [His son Elkanah] and the sons of Elkanah were Amasai [and the son of Amasai was] Achimoth. [The son of Achimoth was] Elkanah and the sons of Elkanah ...

We have noted many times that בְּנֵי, *sons* (in the plural), is occasionally used when only one son is listed. *Malbim* explains that the original list may have contained more names but that Ezra selected only those people who were important to him.

13. הַבְּכֹר וַשְׁנִי וַאֲבִיָּה — *The first-born Vashni and Aviyah.* According to *I Samuel* 8:2, Samuel's first-born was called Yoel and that name is given below in v. 18. The commentators therefore assume that Vashni is another name for Yoel.

The *Mefaresh* suggests that a *hey* may have been elided from וַשְׁנִי which should read וְהַשֵּׁנִי, *the second one.* The verse would then read as follows: *And the sons of Samuel [were] the first-born* [whose name is not given here but who is later identified as Yoel] *and 'the second one' was Aviyah.*[2]

1. Interestingly, the same name change occurs in the case of a king of Judah. In *II Kings* ch. 15 he is called Azariah, but in vs. 32 and 34 there, as well as in *II Chronicles* (ch. 26) and several other places in Scripture, he is called Uzziah.

2. The suggestion of the *Mefaresh* has the merit of bringing our passage structurally in line with *I Samuel* 8:2 which reads: וַיְהִי שֶׁם בְּנוֹ הַבְּכוֹר יוֹאֵל וְשֵׁם מִשְׁנֵהוּ אֲבִיָּה, *And the name of his first-born son was Yoel and the name of his second one was Aviyah.* The fact that the name Yoel is left out here can perhaps be explained by the fact that, as *I Samuel* (there) states, *he did not walk in the path of his father*, Samuel. The Sages *(Midrash Samuel* 1:6) take this further and describe him as a רָשָׁע, *a wicked person.* [This explanation is less than satisfying since the Sages (there) also describe Aviyah as 'wicked.' Perhaps Yoel, the first-born, was more to blame and was therefore eliminated from this list.]

The first opinion is that Vashni is another name for Yoel. This would fit with the Sages' tradition that Samuel's son Yoel became the prophet Yoel (Joel) [the second in the Book of Twelve Prophets]. Although *Samuel* describes him as not walking in the path of his father, and indeed some Sages (as quoted above) considered him wicked, there is a tradition that he eventually repented and changed his

יד וַשְׁנִי וַאֲבִיָּה: בְּנֵי מְרָרִי מַחְלִי לִבְנִי בְנוֹ שִׁמְעִי בְנוֹ עֻזָּה

טו-טז בְנוֹ: שִׁמְעָא בְנוֹ חַגִּיָּה בְנוֹ עֲשָׂיָה בְנוֹ: וְאֵלֶּה אֲשֶׁר הֶעֱמִיד

14. בְּנֵי מְרָרִי מַחְלִי — *The sons of Merari — Machli.* Verse 4 had taught that Merari had two sons, Machli and Mushi. It would seem at first glance that here we are tracing the genealogy of Machli. Two considerations speak against this: (1) Ethan, the chorister from the family of Merari (vs. 29-32), is a descendant of Mushi (v. 32); (2) according to 23:21 Machli had two sons, Eleazar and Kish, but had no son Livni (the name given here for Machli's son). From v. 31 and 23:23 we see that Mushi, Merari's other son, also had a son Machli (carrying the same name as his uncle). It therefore seems likely that we are dealing with Mushi's line here. The Machli [C:I(2)] mentioned here is identical with Machli [II(3)] and is the son of Mushi [who is omitted from our list] *(Malbim).*

לִבְנִי בְנוֹ — *His son Livni.* List II gives Shemer [II(4)] as Machli's son. There seem to be a number of possibilities. Either list I traces Machli's line through his son Livni while list II traces it through another son, Shemer *(Malbim)*; numbers 4-9 of list II are identical with 3-8 of list I and all those people went under two names; or list II skips some generations and Shemer [II(4)] may be the son of Asaiah [I(8)].

15. עֲשָׂיָה — *Asaiah.* Malbim thinks that this Asaiah may be identical with the prince of Merari's family mentioned in 15:6. The importance of this man would explain why his family records were preserved. (See comm. to Yeathrai in v. 6.)

◄§ Lineage of the Choristers

16-17. These verses introduce the listing

of the families of the choristers. David appointed three choristers, one each from the families of Gershom, Kehath and Merari, to *serve through song* (v. 17). Some historical and halachic background is necessary to understand the significance of these appointments.

David's forty-year rule is divided by Scripture into two periods. During the first seven years he was only accepted as king by his own tribe, Judah, and the royal seat was in Hebron. When the rest of Israel decided to accept his kingship they came to Hebron to crown him king and from then on he made his capital in Jerusalem. There he reigned for thirty-three years. (See *II Samuel* 5:1-10 and *I Chronicles* ch. 11ff.) One of his first acts as king in Jerusalem was to bring the אָרוֹן, *the Holy Ark*, which was at that time in Kiriath Yearim (see I *Samuel* 6:1 and 7:2), and lodge it in a tent which he had erected in Jerusalem for that purpose.[1] It remained there forty-three years (thirty-three years of David's reign and the first ten years of Solomon's reign, while the Temple was being completed).

During these forty-three years the Tabernacle was at Giveon, where it had been moved after Saul had destroyed its previous location, the priestly city of Nov (see *Zevachim* 112b and 118b). Thus, during this forty-three-year period there were two locations for public worship, the tent in Jerusalem where the Holy Ark rested, and the Tabernacle at Giveon where the daily sacrifices were brought. Now שִׁיר [*shir*], *song,* was an integral part of the daily sacrifices, as derived from the Torah *(Arachin* 11a). As the wine libation (נֶסֶך)

ways, becoming one of Israel's great prophets. The name Vashni [from שנה, *to change*] hints at that change in character. See the comm. of *Mahari HaKohen* to *Midrash Shocher Tov* to *Psalm* 80.

1. When the Holy Ark is mentioned in this connection, it is not absolutely clear which Ark is meant. There are some opinions that the Ark in the Tabernacle was the only one in existence and that whenever an Ark is mentioned reference is to that one. There are, however, other opinions that there were two Arks: One which held the tablets of stone which Moses brought down from Sinai, and which stood in the Tabernacle; and another which contained the fragments of the original tablets which Moses broke when he came down from Sinai the first time. In this opinion, the Ark which contained the tablets was never moved out of the Tabernacle. The one which was taken out to war, captured by the Philistines and subsequently taken to Kiriath Yearim and from there, by David, to Jerusalem, was the one which contained the fragments of the first tablets. [The interested reader can find an exhaustive analysis of this question in *Rabbi Eliezer Silver's Anfei Errez* under the heading אֲרוֹן בְּרִית ה׳.] For the purpose of our comm. it is simplest to assume that only one Ark existed and that reference throughout is to that same one.

6

14-16

son Livni, his son Shimei, his son Uzzah. [15] His son Shimea, his son Chaggiah, his son Asaiah. [16] Now these are the ones whom David

was performed at the morning and evening sacrifices (תְּמִידִים), a minimum of twelve Levites would stand on a special platform (דּוּכָן) and sing a psalm assigned to that particular day. This song was accompanied by musical instruments, although this accompaniment was not mandatory (see *Rambam, Klei HaMikdash* ch. 3). Since *shir* is an integral part of the sacrificial service, we must assume that this was performed even before David initiated the organization described here and in greater detail in ch. 16. What was it then that David initiated?

It is of course possible that David simply introduced a system into the recitation of the *shir*. Whereas until his time it could have been performed by any twelve Levites, he now ordained that one each of the three great Levitic families must be involved. Again, it is possible that David introduced the specific texts which were to be said on a given day. The Mishnah in *Tamid* (7:4) specifies a particular psalm to be said on each day of the week. [Those psalms have become part of our daily morning prayers.] It is conceivable that up to David's time the Levites were not bound to any particular text and that it was David who ordained the specific psalms to be used. The alternative to this is to assume that the text of the seven psalms which were used predated David and that he merely incorporated them into his book of *Psalms*.[1]

However it seems from the tradition of the Sages, as recorded in *Seder Olam* ch. 14, that David's innovation was much more radical. As noted above, during the forty-three years between David's ascension to the throne and the completion of

Solomon's Temple there were two places of public worship. Apart from the Tabernacle at Giveon, where presumably the *shir* had been and continued to be said together with the daily sacrifice, there was also the tent in Jerusalem where the Holy Ark rested. From *Seder Olam* [and, as we shall see, according to *Malbim* from the text of our section] it appears that David innovated an entirely new form of *shir* that was to be performed daily in front of the Holy Ark — independent of any sacrificial service.[2]

Seder Olam reports that the psalm quoted in 16:8-36 was divided into two parts. The first part was sung by the Levites at morning service and the second in the evening. This entirely new kind of *shir* had no source other than David's decree (see 16:4).

It is not absolutely clear from the sources whether this *shir* in front of the Ark was ordained only for the forty-three-year interim period or whether it was continued in the service in Solomon's Temple when this became the location of both the altar and the Ark. The text of *Seder Olam* seems to suggest that it was only a temporary measure (וכך היו כל הארבעים תשלש שנה לפני הארון). However, as is well known, the recitation of the psalm from 16:8-36 has found its way into the morning prayers according to most rituals, and this is justified by *Tur, Orach Chaim* 51: '... because David ordained that it should be said daily before the Ark.' *Tur's* words seem to suggest that it was a permanent ordinance.

16. ... וְאֵלֶּה אֲשֶׁר הֶעֱמִיד דָּוִיד — *Now these are the ones whom David apppointed* ... David appointed these Levites when the Ark was brought from the house of Oved-Edom where it had been since the tragedy of Uzzah's death [see *II Samuel* 6:10ff] (Mefaresh).

1. A similar uncertainty exists concerning the text of *Hallel*. If we assume that the obligation to recite *Hallel* is of Torah origin it is possible that the recitation of *Hallel* preceded David but that different texts were used. Or it may be that *Hallel* always consisted of the psalms which we know today and that David incorporated them into his book. See *Rambam* and *Ramban* in *Sefer HaMitzvos, Shoresh* 1, for a discussion.

2. However, *Radak* to 15:37 believes that there was also a form of sacrificial service in the tent in Jerusalem. While the בָּמָה גְדוֹלָה, *great communal altar*, stood in Giveon, a בָּמָה קְטַנָּה, a private or small altar, was put up in the tent in which the Ark was placed. Private altars were at this time still permissible (see Mishnah *Zevachim* 14:7 and Gem. 119a; cf. *Radak* to *I Kings* 3:3). Thus, that *shir* was also said in conjunction with the bringing of a daily sacrifice.

In support of *Radak's* opinion it should be noted that in *I Kings* ch. 3 it is clear that Solomon

ו

יז-כג

יז דָּוִיד עַל־יְדֵי־־שִׁיר בֵּית יְהֹוָה מִמְּנוֹחַ הָאָרוֹן וַיִּהְיוּ
מְשָׁרְתִים לִפְנֵי מִשְׁכַּן אֹהֶל־מוֹעֵד בַּשִּׁיר עַד־בְּנוֹת שְׁלֹמֹה
אֶת־בֵּית יְהֹוָה בִּירוּשָׁלָ͏ִם וַיַּעַמְדוּ כְמִשְׁפָּטָם עַל־עֲבוֹדָתָם:
יח וְאֵלֶּה הָעֹמְדִים וּבְנֵיהֶם מִבְּנֵי הַקְּהָתִי הֵימָן הַמְשׁוֹרֵר
יט בֶּן־יוֹאֵל בֶּן־שְׁמוּאֵל: בֶּן־אֶלְקָנָה בֶּן־יְרֹחָם בֶּן־אֱלִיאֵל
כ-כא בֶּן־תּוֹחַ: בֶּן־°צִיף בֶּן־אֶלְקָנָה בֶּן־מַחַת בֶּן־עֲמָשָׂי: בֶּן־
כב אֶלְקָנָה בֶּן־יוֹאֵל בֶּן־עֲזַרְיָה בֶּן־צְפַנְיָה: בֶּן־תַּחַת בֶּן־אַסִּיר
כג בֶּן־אֶבְיָסָף בֶּן־קֹרַח: בֶּן־יִצְהָר בֶּן־קְהָת בֶּן־לֵוִי בֶּן־יִשְׂרָאֵל:

°צוּף ק'

עַל־יְדֵי־שִׁיר — *Over the song.* Gra writes that עַל יְדֵי is to be understood as עַל, *over.* Since עַל יַד often means *next to,* the idea expressed would probably be that these main choristers were to be 'next to' the song that is close by the other choristers so that they would be able to control the music.

Ibn Ezra to *Ezra* 3:10 takes the phrase עַל יְדֵי in a similar context as an idiom referring to instrumental music, since music is drawn from the instrument by the hands (לְהַלֵּל אֶת ה' עַל יְדֵי דָּוִיד מֶלֶךְ יִשְׂרָאֵל, *to praise HASHEM with the music of David king of Israel*). Accordingly, our verse here would mean *over the music of the song of the House of HASHEM.*

עַל־יְדֵי־שִׁיר בֵּית ה' — *Over the song of the House of HASHEM.* Malbim thinks that *House of HASHEM* in our verse is in contrast to *Tabernacle of the Tent of Meeting* in the next verse. Our verse refers to the tent in Jerusalem in which the Ark rested, while the next verse refers to the Tabernacle in Giveon. Thus, the song in our verse is the recitation of the psalm quoted in 16:8-36, and the verse refers to the events described in 16:37.

מִמְּנוֹחַ הָאָרוֹן — *When the Ark came to rest.* Up to the time that David brought the Ark to Jerusalem it had moved several times. When it came to Jerusalem it had reached its final resting place *(Metzudos).*

When we consider that at 28:2 David describes the Temple as a בֵּית מְנוּחָה, *resting place,* for the Ark — the location of its

ultimate *resting,* then it seems likely that מִמְּנוֹחַ הָאָרוֹן would mean *from the time that the Ark will have entered its final resting place,* that is, from the time that it will have been brought into the Temple.

This would mean that בֵּית ה' in our verse would refer to the Temple precisely as the phrase is used in the next verse. This would eliminate the necessity of assuming that in our verse the word בַּיִת is used to describe a temporary structure which everywhere else is described as an אֹהֶל.

The sense of our verse and the next would then be as follows: Chapters 23-26 tell how David, even though he was denied the right to build the Temple, nevertheless made many of the dispositions regarding its future administration. Chapter 25 tells how he organized twenty-four groups of Levites for the *shir.* These groups were based on the three Levite families, Gershom, Kehath and Merari as represented by Asaph, Heman and Yeduthun. [For a discussion of the relationship of Ethan-Yeduthun, see 16:4.] Thus, our verse would be referring to those dispositions: These are the Levite families whom David appointed to undertake the *shir* once the Temple will have been built [and in the meantime] they were to serve ...

Given this interpretation, it follows that verse 17 would refer to the Tabernacle at Giveon [as מִשְׁכַּן אֹהֶל מוֹעֵד would imply] since it is that Tabernacle, and not the temporary shelter which David erected for the Ark, which stood in the stead of the Temple which was yet to be built.

sacrificed at both the great altar in Giveon (v. 3 there) and at a private altar upon his return to Jerusalem (v. 15 there). It is therefore not unreasonable to postulate that such an altar would have been present before the Ark and that it had already been there at the time of David. [For a wide-ranging discussion of this see R' Yitzchak Isaac HaLevi's *Tekufas HaMikrah,* particularly ch. 33.]

It must, however, be noted that the obligation of *shir* did not pertain to a private altar. Since whatever altar existed in Jerusalem only had the status of a בָּמָה קְטַנָּה, *private altar,* David's institution of *shir* there was still an innovation.

appointed over the song of the House of HASHEM when the Ark came to rest. ¹⁷ They served through song before the Tabernacle of the Tent of Meeting until Solomon built the House of HASHEM in Jerusalem, and they carried on with their service according to their custom. ¹⁸ And these are the ones who carried on, and their sons: From the sons of Kehath — Heman the chorister, the son of Yoel, the son of Samuel. ¹⁹ The son of Elkanah, the son of Yerocham, the son of Eliel, the son of Toach. ²⁰ The son of Tzuph, the son of Elkanah, the son of Machath, the son of Amasai. ²¹ The son of Elkanah, the son of Yoel, the son of Azariah, the son of Tzephaniah. ²² The son of Tachath, the son of Assir, the son of Eviasaph, the son of Korach. ²³ The son of Yitzhar, the son of Kehath, the son of Levi, the son of

---

17. לִפְנֵי מִשְׁכַּן אֹהֶל־מוֹעֵד — *Before the Tabernacle of the Tent of Meeting. Malbim* explains this to mean the Tabernacle in Giveon. Thus, the song mentioned in our verse would seem to be the regular recitation of given psalms which, as we have seen above, were an integral part of the sacrificial service (see 16:41).

Although the previous verse stated that David appointed the Levites to sing in front of the Ark in Jerusalem, this does not mean that all stayed there. In 16:37ff we learn that only Asaph remained in Jerusalem and was responsible for the service there. Heman was stationed in Giveon (*Malbim*).

Metzudos interprets the phrase to refer to the tent in Jerusalem.

עַד־בְּנוֹת שְׁלֹמֹה ... — *Until Solomon built* ... Our phrase could be interpreted to mean that the special arrangement instituted by David lasted only *until* the Temple was built (see above, comm. 16-17). But whether this is true or not would depend on the correct understanding of the next phrase.

וַיַּעַמְדוּ כְמִשְׁפָּטָם עַל־עֲבוֹדָתָם — *And they carried on with their service.* The idiom עמד על עבודה [lit. *to stand on the service*] is unusual and we cannot know its meaning with any certainty. עמד (*stand*) could carry the connotation of *persistence* (as in *Koheles/Eccl.* 8:3), in which case the phrase would mean *and they performed their service conscientiously.* On the other hand, עמד is often used to describe a sense of permanence and continuity (see e.g. *Psalms* 111:3), in which case a more correct translation would be *and they continued with their service.* If the latter is the case, the implication would be that their service

continued after Solomon built his Temple, and this is *Metzudos'* opinion.

כְמִשְׁפָּטָם — *According to their custom.* For the use of מִשְׁפָּט as *custom* see *I Samuel* 2:13.

18. וְאֵלֶּה הָעֹמְדִים וּבְנֵיהֶם — *And these are the ones who carried on, and their sons. Targum* adds: *They and their sons.* The text does not make clear whether the meaning is that the choristers were joined in song by their sons [this seems to be *Malbim's* opinion who renders: *with their sons*], or whether the meaning is that the sons of these choristers were to carry on their father's service after the fathers had died.

Gra in contrast to *Malbim* seems to render: *And their sons,* but either of the two meanings seems possible.

הֵימָן הַמְשׁוֹרֵר — *Heman the chorister.* In contrast to the genealogies at the beginning of the chapter, where Gershom's descendants are listed first, here the Kehathite line is given precedence. This is because Heman was the most important among the three choristers. This can be seen from the fact that Heman was to stand in the middle with Asaph (from Gershom) and Ethan (from Merari) ranged on his right and left respectively (see vs. 24 and 29). It is also evidenced by the fact that whereas the genealogy of Asaph and Ethan are only traced up to Levi, that of Heman is taken up to Jacob [Israel] (*Radak*).

For a comparison between these names and those given at the beginning of the chapter see chart. The differences are minor and have been noted above.

23. בֶּן־לֵוִי בֶּן־יִשְׂרָאֵל — *The son of Levi, the son of Israel. Radak's* opinion is that

כד וְאֶחָיו אָסָף הָעֹמֵד עַל־יְמִינֶו אָסָף בֶּן־בֶּרֶכְיָהוּ בֶּן־שִׁמְעָא:

כה-כו בֶּן־מִיכָאֵל בֶּן־בַּעֲשֵׂיָה בֶּן־מַלְכִּיָּה: בֶּן־אַתְנִי בֶן־זֶרַח בֶּן־

כז-כח עֲדָיָה: בֶּן־אֵיתָן בֶּן־זִמָּה בֶּן־שִׁמְעִי: בֶּן־יַחַת בֶּן־גֵּרְשֹׁם בֶּן־

כט לֵוִי: וּבְנֵי מְרָרִי אֲחֵיהֶם עַל־הַשְּׂמֹאול אֵיתָן בֶּן־

ל קִישִׁי בֶּן־עַבְדִּי בֶּן־מַלּוּךְ: בֶּן־חֲשַׁבְיָה בֶן־אֲמַצְיָה בֶּן־

לא-לב חִלְקִיָּה: בֶּן־אַמְצִי בֶן־בָּנִי בֶּן־שָׁמֶר: בֶּן־מַחְלִי בֶּן־מוּשִׁי בֶּן־

לג מְרָרִי בֶּן־לֵוִי: וַאֲחֵיהֶם הַלְוִיִּם נְתוּנִים לְכָל־עֲבוֹדַת

לד מִשְׁכַּן בֵּית הָאֱלֹהִים: וְאַהֲרֹן וּבָנָיו מַקְטִירִים עַל־מִזְבַּח

הָעוֹלָה וְעַל־מִזְבַּח הַקְּטֹרֶת לְכֹל מְלֶאכֶת קֹדֶשׁ הַקֳּדָשִׁים

Heman's ancestry is traced to Israel, in contrast to that of Asaph and Ethan which is only traced to Levi, because of his importance as the main chorister.

The Sages (Bamidbar Rabbah 18:4) offer a different explanation. When the Torah describes Korach's rebellion against Moses he is introduced as Korach the son of Yitzhar, the son of Kehath, the son of Levi (Numbers 16:1). Jacob's name is not mentioned because he prayed that his name not be associated with any discord that would arise among his descendants (see ArtScroll[1] comm. to Genesis 49:6). But wicked as Korach was, his progeny was to play a major role in the choral music of the sacred Temple service. Heman, the main

chorister, came from Korach's line (v. 22). In order to make up for the omission of Jacob's name in Korach's genealogy as it is given in Numbers, Chronicles traces Heman to Israel.[1]

24-32. These verses give the genealogies of Asaph, the chorister from the family of Gershom, and of Ethan, the chorister from the family of Merari. Asaph, being the next most exalted, stood to the right of Heman while Ethan, who ranked third, stood to the left.[2]

For a comparison between the names in this list and those given at the beginning of the chapter see charts A and C. The differences are noted in the comm. there.

1. From the Sages' assumption that Jacob's name should have been mentioned in the context of the story of Korach's rebellion and was left out only because of his prayer, it seems likely that by the detailed listing of Korach's progenitors, the Torah means to lay some of the blame of his sin at their door. Korach was the son of Yitzhar, of Kehath and Levi, and yet he sinned! There must have been some imperfection in these great fathers if such a son sprang from them. But not in Jacob who knew himself to be free from the slightest taint of disharmony.

But Korach's sons were also the masters of *shir*, songs of jubilation to God. Although they had originally plotted with their father against Moses, they parted ways with him when they realized the enormity of the schism they were generating. When the earth swallowed up Korach and his followers they were miraculously given a refuge within the chasm, and from there, at the very edge of the abyss, they sang songs of exquisite yearning to God (see *Rashi* to *Psalms* 42:1). Their song speaks of a closeness born of distance, of a craving for God which only one upon the very edge of a bottomless abyss can know.

Here was a reflection of Jacob's own essence. He too had known the terror of alienation from the Divine source of his inspiration. As the patriarch who was to teach Israel to cope with the bitter experience of exile, he was forced to leave the Holy Land and to make his life in the household of Lavan. As he set out on the journey which was to keep him away for twenty long years from the house of his father and the Divine Presence which dwelt there, he turned to God and instituted the *Maariv* prayer — the prayer of the night when man feels most alone and from his very loneliness turns to find that God is near after all. For this reason, when the choristers descended from Korach are listed, their genealogy is traced to Israel. It was the song of his soul that burst from their lips.

2. The relative importance of the choristers is a reflection of the relative standing of these families. In the arrangement of the camp in the wilderness, Kehath was placed to the south near the camp of Reuven, Shimeon and Dan, which, in the Torah's listing takes precedence over the camp of Ephraim, Menasheh, and Benjamin which lay to the west together with the family of Gershom. Merari lay to

Israel. ²⁴ *And his brother Asaph who stood at his right — Asaph the son of Berechiahu, the son of Shimea.* ²⁵ *The son of Michael, the son of Baaseiah, the son of Malchiyah.* ²⁶ *The son of Ethni, the son of Zerach, the son of Adaiah.* ²⁷ *The son of Ethan, the son of Zimmah, the son of Shimei.* ²⁸ *The son of Yachath, the son of Gershom, the son of Levi.* ²⁹ *And the sons of Merari their brother, on the left — Ethan the son of Kishi, the son of Avdi, the son of Malluch.* ³⁰ *The son of Chashaviah, the son of Amatziah, the son of Chilkiyah.* ³¹ *The son of Amtzi, the son of Bani, the son of Shemer.* ³² *The son of Machli, the son of Mushi, the son of Merari, the son of Levi.* ³³ *And their brother Levites were appointed for all the service of the Tabernacle of the House of God.* ³⁴ *And Aaron and his sons offered sacrifices upon the altar of the burnt offering and upon the incense*

33. וַאֲחֵיהֶם הַלְוִיִם — *And their brother Levites.* The three mentioned above were heads of families (רָאשֵׁי אָבוֹת) and were choristers in the Tabernacle and had no other duties besides the *shir*. Their brother Levites were to perform the other necessary tasks *(Radak)*.

נְתוּנִים לְכָל־עֲבוֹדַת מִשְׁכַּן ... — *Were appointed for all the service of the Tabernacle ...* They served as gatekeepers and also skinned the sacrifices, as can be seen from *II Chronicles* 35:11 *(Mefaresh)*. They were also charged with the upkeep of the Tabernacle *(Radak)*.

◄§ **The Line of Aaron**

34⁻38. Having completed the description of the Levite families and their functions, Ezra now turns to the priestly line within the tribe of Levi. Since the list carries Aaron's children only up to Tzadok's son Achimaatz, rather than to the destruction of the first Temple as in 5:30-41, *Malbim* surmises that the list used here was written during the reigns of David and Solomon. See comm. v. 34.

We have bracketed v. 34 together with vs. 35-38, although it is not clear that they belong together. It may well be that v. 34 stands on its own, or together with v. 33, and that its purpose is simply to contrast the function of the *Kohanim* with that of the Levites *(Radak)*. The list in vs. 35-38 then follows independently. This may be indicated by the *Massorah* which brackets

vs. 33 and 34 in one *parashah* (self-contained paragraph) and has vs. 35-38 in another *parashah*. The consideration which speaks for seeing v. 34 as part of the section 35-38 is the conjunction *vav, and,* which begins v. 35. This could indicate that the words, *And these are the sons of Aaron ... refer* back to the phrase, *And Aaron and his sons ...* in v. 34.

34. וְאַהֲרֹן וּבָנָיו ... לְכָל מְלֶאכֶת קֹדֶשׁ הַקֳּדָשִׁים — *And Aaron and his sons ... for all the service of the Holy of Holies.* Although in the time of David it was his descendant Tzadok who was *Kohen Gadol,* Aaron is mentioned here as leading the Temple service since the *Kehunah Gedolah* was descended from him *(Radak).* Or, as *Malbim* puts it, any *Kohen Gadol* can be called 'Aaron' since he fills the position originally occupied by Aaron.

If Aaron describes the *Kehunah Gedolah* (High Priesthood), וּבָנָיו, *and his sons,* could mean those *Kohanim Gedolim* who followed him, or it could mean the ordinary *Kohanim* who served with him. The correct understanding of the phrase would depend on the meaning of the later phrase, ... *for all the service of the Holy of Holies.* If, as *Malbim* thinks, this refers to the Yom Kippur service (which took place in the Holy of Holies), then our whole verse would seem to be dealing with the *Kehunah Gedolah,* because only the *Kohen Gadol* was allowed to perform the Yom Kippur service. On the other hand, *Metzudos* interprets the phrase to mean simpy that whereas the upkeep of the rest of the Tabernacle was the responsibility of the Levites

the north near Gad, Naphtali, and Asher, the sons of the handmaidens (see *Numbers 3:27ff*).

Similarly, when the Tabernacle was transported through the wilderness, Kehath carried the Ark and the other sacred vessels — the most holy components of the Tabernacle; Gershom carried the cloth components of the Tabernacle — the next level of sanctity; while Merari carried the beams, bolts and sockets.

וּלְכַפֵּר עַל־יִשְׂרָאֵל כְּכֹל אֲשֶׁר־צִוָּה מֹשֶׁה עֶבֶד

לה הָאֱלֹהִים: וְאֵלֶּה בְּנֵי אַהֲרֹן אֶלְעָזָר בְּנוֹ

לו פִּינְחָס בְּנוֹ אֲבִישׁוּעַ בְּנוֹ: בֻּקִּי בְנוֹ עֻזִּי בְנוֹ זְרַחְיָה בְנוֹ:

לז־לח מְרָיוֹת בְּנוֹ אֲמַרְיָה בְנוֹ אֲחִיטוּב בְּנוֹ: צָדוֹק בְּנוֹ אֲחִימַעַץ

לט בְּנוֹ: וְאֵלֶּה מוֹשְׁבוֹתָם לְטִירוֹתָם

בִּגְבוּלָם לִבְנֵי אַהֲרֹן לְמִשְׁפַּחַת הַקְּהָתִי כִּי לָהֶם הָיָה

(v. 33), these were not allowed to enter the Holy of Holies and this therefore had to be serviced by the *Kohanim*. If so, the term *and his sons* could well be referring to regular *Kohanim*.

If our verse does describe the *Kehunah Gedolah*, this would argue against bracketing our verse with vs. 35-38, since as discussed at 5:30-41, not all the people mentioned in this list were, in fact, *Kohanim Gedolim*.

This problem is also dealt with by the Sages, who derive an important rule from it. 'Rabbi Simai taught: It is written, *And Aaron and his sons offered sacrifices on the altar*. But were Aaron and his sons still alive at that time? Were the current priests not Tzadok and his sons? [The unexpected formulation] teaches us that [even if] Aaron and his sons had been alive at that time, Tzadok and his sons would have taken precedence over them [because they were the current office-holders] at that time' (*Koheles Rabbah* 1:4).

The example from our verse is one of several which the Midrash there brings to show that if a person holds an office at a particular time then he takes precedence over people who, although greater than he, are not official office-holders.

מַקְטִירִים — *Offered sacrifices*. The verb קטר occurs only in the *hiphil, causative*. It refers to the smoke which rises up from the burning of a sacrifice, hence מַקְטִיר, *to cause smoke to rise*, that is, to bring the offering up on to the altar so that it may burn. [See

Rashbam to Leviticus 9:10.]

מִזְבַּח הָעוֹלָה ... מִזְבַּח הַקְּטֹרֶת — *The altar of the burnt offering ... the incense altar*. The altar of the burnt-offering is the altar which stood in the courtyard of the Tabernacle and Temple. The incense altar is the golden altar that stood inside the Sanctuary.

וּלְכַפֵּר עַל־יִשְׂרָאֵל — *And to atone for Israel*. This refers to the various sin offerings (חַטָּאוֹת וַאֲשָׁמוֹת) brought by the *Kohanim*.

כְּכֹל אֲשֶׁר־צִוָּה מֹשֶׁה עֶבֶד הָאֱלֹהִים — *In accordance with all that Moses the servant of God had commanded*. In the context of our passage this phrase could have the purpose of contrasting the service of the *Kohanim* with the singing of the choristers mentioned above. Whereas that had been an arrangement made by David (v. 16), the *Kohanim* served entirely according to the laws laid down in the Torah.[1]

עֶבֶד הָאֱלֹהִים — *The servant of God*. The commentators do not explain why Moses is given this title in the context of our verse. The description of Moses as *servant of God* occurs a number of times throughout the book. Occasionally he is also called *servant of* HASHEM (see II:24:6,9).

35-38. For a discussion of the names in

1. It is possible, however, that an explanation for this phrase must be sought in the broader context of the book rather than in the narrow requirements of our particular passage. Throughout the book we find a tendency to state that the sacrificial service and attendant ceremonies were performed in accordance with the Torah's directions. I have not been able to find an explanation for this phenomenon either in midrashic literature or in any of the classical commentators. Nevertheless, this system is used so consistently that it seems likely that it reflects some general theme rather than specific ideas within the context of each verse. Some other examples of this are: 'To bring the burnt offering to HASHEM on the altar of the burnt offering in the morning and evening, *according to all that is written in* HASHEM's *Torah which He commanded Israel*' (16:40); 'And day by day to offer up *according to the command of Moses* for Sabbaths and new moons ...' (II:8:13); '... for the burnt offerings of morning and evening and the burnt offerings for Sabbaths and new moons and festivals *as it is written in* HASHEM's *Torah*' (II:31:3). There are many more examples of similar usages in related areas. [In Appendix I a hypothesis was offered that while the genealogical lists of the first nine chapters were written by Ezra, the rest of the book may have been written by Nehemiah. In this context, it is noteworthy that our verse, which comes among the genealogical lists, has the same stylistic peculiarities which we have detected in the later parts of the book.]

6

35-39

altar for all the service of the Holy of Holies and to atone for Israel,
in accordance with all that Moses the servant of God had
commanded. 35 Now these were the sons of Aaron — his son Eleazar,
his son Pinechas, his son Avishua. 36 His son Bukki, his son Uzzi,
his son Zerachiah. 37 His son Meraioth, his son Amariah, his son
Achituv. 38 His son Tzadok, his son Achimaatz. 39 Now these are
their dwelling places, their townships within their borders — to the
sons of Aaron of the family of the Kehathites, for the lot came out

this list see 5:30-41. See also comm. above
34-38.

◄§ The Levitical Cities

39⁻66. This section lists the cities assigned
to the *Kohanim* and Levites from each of
the tribes of Israel. The tribe of Levi had
been excluded from a share in the land
(Numbers 26:62) because their lives were
to be totally dedicated to the service of
God; He was their 'portion' and the
territorial base appropriate to the other
twelve tribes [twelve, because Joseph was
divided into two tribes — Ephraim and
Menasheh] would have distracted them
from their exalted purpose *(Numbers*
18:20; cf. *Rambam, Shemittah VeYovel*
13:10ff).* Instead, each of the tribes was
expected to give some of its cities to Levi,
forty-two in all, so that together with the
six cities of refuge which were also
assigned to them, the *Kohanim* and Levites
would own forty-eight cities throughout
the land of Israel *(Numbers* ch. 35 and see
v. 6 there).

Radak notes that the listing of these
cities is appropriate here. We have just
learned that the Levites were to be the
choristers and general factotums of the
Temple and that the *Kohanim* were to
devote their lives to the sacred service. It
was because sanctity was to be the mission,
focus, and aspiration of their lives that
these cities were given to them.

Our section is largely a repetition of
Joshua ch. 21. The four charts offered
below will demonstrate both the major and
minor differences between the two
passages.

39. וְאֵלֶּה מוֹשְׁבוֹתָם לְטִירוֹתָם בִּגְבוּלָם — *Now
these are their dwelling places, their
townships within their borders.* It is
difficult to know the exact meaning of the

prefix *lamed* in לְטִירוֹתָם, *their townships.*
According to *Sefer HaRikmah* (6) a *lamed*
can occasionally have the same connotation
as a *beis* which normally means *in.*
Therefore our phrase might be correctly
translated: *Their dwelling places within
their townships.* Again according to
Rikmah, a *lamed* may have the same
meaning as a *vav, and.* Thus: *Their
dwelling places and their townships.*
Rikmah also notes that the *lamed* may have
no translation at all, and this is how we
have translated the phrase.

The meaning of טיר is obscure.
Metzudos renders *palace.* [*These are their
dwelling places (locations) for their palaces
within their borders.*] The idea that טיר may
be a building is confirmed by *Targum* to
Numbers 31:10 who renders טירתָם as
houses of worship. However, it is not clear
why the houses in the Levite cities would
be sufficiently ornate to be described as
palaces. *Targum* to *Genesis* 25:16, the only
other place in the Torah which uses the
word, renders כְּרַךְ, which usually denotes a
fortified city (cf. *Targum* to *Numbers*
13:28). This is, however, inappropriate for
the Levite cities which also served as refuge
cities *(Rambam, Rotzeach Ushmiras Nefesh*
8:9) since the Talmud states expressly
(Makkos 10a) that fortified cities (כְּרַבִּין)
cannot be used as refuge cities. *Targum*
here renders כפר which is used in the
Targumim to denote the small outlying
townships which are part of a larger-city
complex (see e.g. *Numbers* 21:25 and
32:41), therefore, *a small town. Aruch*
(under טר) is of the same opinion and
renders, *small, strong city.* This is the
translation which we have used.[1]

לִבְנֵי אַהֲרֹן לְמִשְׁפַּחַת הַקְּהָתִי — *To the sons of
Aaron of the family of the Kehathites.*
Kehath, the middle son of Levi, was the
grandfather of Aaron (54:27-9). Aaron and

1. The usage of the word seems to have changed between Scriptural and Talmudic times. Whereas
our verse uses the word טיר to describe the Levitic cities which were also cities of refuge, *Makkos* 10a
quotes a teaching of the Sages that the cities of refuge were not to be טירין קְטַנִּים, *small villages.*

מ הַגּוֹרָל: וַיִּתְּנוּ לָהֶם אֶת־חֶבְרוֹן בְּאֶרֶץ יְהוּדָה וְאֶת־
מא מִגְרָשֶׁיהָ סְבִיבֹתֶיהָ: וְאֶת־שְׂדֵה הָעִיר וְאֶת־חֲצֵרֶיהָ נָתְנוּ
מב לְכָלֵב בֶּן־יְפֻנֶּה: וְלִבְנֵי אַהֲרֹן נָתְנוּ אֶת־

מ–מב

his descendants were chosen from among all the Levitic families to serve as *Kohanim*. As a result, the family of Kehath was treated as two entities — Aaron's family, the *Kohanim*, and the other Kehathites who remained Levites.

כִּי לָהֶם הָיָה הַגּוֹרָל — *For the lot came out for them.* I.e., first. The Levites were divided into four groups: the *Kohanim*, Kehathites, Gershonites and Merarites. Lots were drawn among them and the first lot pointed to the *Kohanim*. They were to receive their cities from the three tribes, Judah, Shimeon and Benjamin (*Joshua* 21 and see comm. below). This was determined in a miraculous fashion. As the lot for Aaron and his sons was drawn, the names of the three tribes who were to be the ones to give the cities lit up on the *choshen*, the breastplate of the *Kohen Gadol* (*Malbim* to *Joshua*).

40–41. The actual listing of the cities begins in v. 42. Our two verses interrupt the flow of the narrative in order to explain the status of Hebron, the first of the cities to be given to Aaron and his sons. *Joshua* 14:6ff tells how Calev ben Yephunneh, the spy who together with Joshua had remained loyal to God (see *Numbers* ch. 13ff), came to Joshua to demand a portion of the land and that in fulfillment of his request he was given Hebron. (See v. 13, there.) However, in *Joshua* 20:7 Hebron is listed as one of the cities of refuge which indicates that it did not belong to Calev. *Makkos* 10a raises this question and answers that Calev did not receive the actual city. This was one of the cities of refuge and it and the open land surrounding it were never given to any individual. Calev received only the outlying fields and villages which lay beyond the city and its open land but which were called Hebron after the name of their mother city. This information is, in effect, contained in our two verses. Verse 40 and 42 tell that Hebron along with its clearings was one of the cities given to the *Kohanim*. Verse 41 explains that this does not contradict that which we know from *Joshua* that Hebron belonged to Calev because it was only the outlying areas which were given to him.

40. וְאֶת־מִגְרָשֶׁיהָ — *With its clearings.* All the cities given to the Levites had a מִגְרָשׁ, a cleared space, around them (*Numbers* 35:1). *Rashi* (there) writes that its purpose was to beautify the city. It was forbidden to build or plant in that area.

41. ... וְאֶת־שְׂדֵה הָעִיר — *But the outlying areas of the city ...* When Moses sent the twelve spies to report on conditions in the land of Israel it is told that their travels brought them to Hebron. But instead of the expected phrase וַיָּבֹאוּ עַד חֶבְרוֹן, *and they came to Hebron*, the Torah uses the singular form, וַיָּבֹא, *and he came*. The Sages deduce from this that only Calev actually went to Hebron. He wanted to pray at the grave of the Patriarchs — the cave of Machpelah — to entreat God to help him to distance himself from the perfidy of the other spies. As a reward, God promised to give him and his descendants the land *upon which he had trodden* (*Deuteronomy* 1:36). Therefore, when Calev came to claim his portion, Joshua gave him Hebron (*Joshua* 14:16). Our verse explains that he was not given the city itself but only its outlying area.

חֲצֵרֶיהָ — *Its towns.* The word is used to describe unwalled towns or villages in contrast to the bigger, walled-in cities. See above 4:32.

42–66. [To facilitate the comm. of the next section we offer a comparative listing of *Joshua* ch. 21 and our verses on pp. 104, 105.]

Before going to the individual lists we should note the general structure of this section as it compares to the parallel passage in *Joshua*. Our section seems to miss the inner logic of the structure there. There are four Levite units: *Kohanim*, the Kehathites, Gershonites, and the Merarites. Since twelve tribes contributed cities, each unit would be supplied by three tribes. In *Joshua* 21:4-7 we have such a breakdown, stating which of the four Levite units received how many cities from which group of three tribes. Then from v. 13 onwards, the names of the individual cities and the tribes from which they came are given. Here the same information is given,

for them. ⁴⁰ They gave them Hebron in the land of Judah with its surrounding clearings. ⁴¹ But the outlying areas of the city and its towns they gave to Calev the son of Yephunneh. ⁴² To the sons of

but the structuring is different. Verses 42-45 give the names of the cities which were given to the Kohanim but without the introductory statement (found in Joshua) that the Kohanim were to receive thirteen cities from the tribes Judah, Shimeon, and Benjamin. This omission would not in itself be noteworthy if Chronicles would have dispensed with this information completely. But immediately following the listing of the cities which the Kohanim received, vs. 46-49 do give the general information concerning the later three of the four Levite units and only then does v. 50 give the information concerning the cities of the Kohanim which had already been listed earlier. After this, vs. 51-66 give the individual listings for the later three Levitical families. Thus, if we number the individual passages in Joshua from 1-8 [the general statements concerning which Levitical unit received how many cities from which three tribes are 1-4; the individual listings are 5-8], then the sequence in Chronicles would have to be numbered: 5, 2, 3, 4, 1, 6, 7, 8. Numbers 1 and 5 are interchanged.

One other irregularity should be noted. When the individual cities of the Kohanim are listed in vs. 42-45, no mention is made of the fact that the first nine of the thirteen cities came from Judah and Shimeon [a fact that is stressed in Joshua 21:16]. Only the four last cities are identified as coming from Benjamin (v. 45).

The answer to these difficulties may lie in the historical realities which existed at the time that Chronicles was written. Sotah 48b teaches that with the destruction of the First Temple the institution of Levitical cities came to an end. Why they were not revived during the period of the Second Temple is unclear (see Meshech Chochmah to Massei), but the fact remains that when Ezra wrote Chronicles the Levitical cities were, in a formal sense, a thing of the past. Nevertheless, as we see in 9:22, the Levites at the time of the return did settle in some of the cities which had been theirs in the past, or at least in the outskirts of those cities. In view of the fact that so few Levites returned, it can certainly be assumed that the cities which they chose to resettle would be those closest to Jerusalem — that

is, those from Judah and Shimeon.

Thus it may well be that vs. 42-44 do not reflect the original division made by lot in Joshua's time. Rather, the nine cities listed are the actual cities — in light of the above the only cities — which were Levitical cities at the time Chronicles was written. As a reproduction of a list compiled at a later date, there was no reason to be bound to the formula used by Joshua, which was to preface with a general statement (1) the enumeration of the specific cities (5). Again, since during the period of the return these were the only cities extant, there was no reason to describe them as coming from Judah and Shimeon. This description belonged only to a time when all tribes supplied a given number of cities and it was necessary to have an accounting of how this was done. Certainly by the time of the return, all tribal distinction with regard to these cities had become meaningless. It was only the last four cities which are described as coming from Benjamin because that section, in fact, derived from earlier times when all Levitical cities were described by the tribe from which they came. After the cities of the Kohanim were listed (5), the only source for the other cities was from the earlier era — that is from the records in Joshua. Consequently, the formula from Joshua is used and numbers 2, 3, 4 follow naturally to be followed in turn by numbers 6, 7, 8. Number 1 (v. 50) was interpolated after number 4 to preserve the integrity of the general listings.

42-44. These are the cities which, according to Joshua 21:4 and our v. 50, were given by the two tribes, Judah and Shimeon. The verses do not however indicate which were from which tribe. A careful check of the city names yields that all of them, with the possible exception of Ayin [I(7)], are identified as belonging to Judah. Verse 40 states clearly that Hebron was in the land of Judah. As for the others in list I, see: 2 — Joshua 15:42; 3 — 15:45; 4 — 15:50; 5 — 15:51; 6 — 15:15; 8 — 15:55; 9 — II Kings 14:11, II Chronicles 28:21. Ayin (7) is mentioned in Shimeon's territory in Joshua 19:7 but also among Judah's cities in 15:32. To solve this problem Margalios HaYam (Sanhedrin

עָרֵי הַמִּקְלָט אֶת־חֶבְרוֹן וְאֶת־לִבְנָה וְאֶת־מִגְרָשֶׁיהָ וְאֶת־ מג־מה

יַתִּר וְאֶת־אֶשְׁתְּמֹעַ וְאֶת־מִגְרָשֶׁיהָ וְאֶת־חִילֵז וְאֶת־ מג

מִגְרָשֶׁיהָ אֶת־דְּבִיר וְאֶת־מִגְרָשֶׁיהָ וְאֶת־עָשָׁן וְאֶת־ מד

מִגְרָשֶׁיהָ וְאֶת־בֵּית שֶׁמֶשׁ וְאֶת־מִגְרָשֶׁיהָ וּמִמַּטֵּה בִנְיָמִן מה

אֶת־גֶּבַע וְאֶת־מִגְרָשֶׁיהָ וְאֶת־עָלֶמֶת וְאֶת־מִגְרָשֶׁיהָ וְאֶת־

עֲנָתוֹת וְאֶת־מִגְרָשֶׁיהָ כָּל־עָרֵיהֶם שְׁלֹשׁ־עֶשְׂרֵה עִיר

111b) quotes *Radak* to *Joshua* 15:32. *Radak* demonstrates that many of the cities given as Judean actually belonged to Shimeon. They were listed among Judah's cities because they were scattered throughout Judah's land. Therefore, it is possible that a number of the cities mentioned here,

though traced to lists of Judean cities in *Joshua* ch. 15, may in fact have come from Shimeon.

45. שְׁלֹשׁ־עֶשְׂרֵה עִיר — *Thirteen cities.* Only eleven cities are listed here. A glance at list A shows that two cities, *Yuttah* [I(8)] and

A. The thirteen cities of the *Kohanim* taken from the tribes of Judah, Shimeon and Benjamin.	
I: Joshua	**II: Chronicles**
JUDAH AND SHIMEON	
1. חֶבְרוֹן [מִקְלָט], *Hebron* [refuge]	1. חֶבְרוֹן [מִקְלָט], *Hebron* [refuge]
2. לִבְנָה, *Livnah*	2. לִבְנָה, *Livnah*
3. יַתִּר, *Yattir*	3. יַתִּר, *Yattir*
4. אֶשְׁתְּמֹעַ, *Eshtemoa*	4. אֶשְׁתְּמֹעַ, *Eshtemoa*
5. חֹלֹן, *Cholon*	5. חִילֵז, *Chilez*
6. דְּבִר, *Devir*	6. דְּבִיר, *Devir*
7. עַיִן, *Ayin*	7. עָשָׁן, *Ashan*
8. יֻטָּה, *Yuttah*	9. בֵּית שֶׁמֶשׁ, *Beth Shemesh*
9. בֵּית שֶׁמֶשׁ, *Beth Shemesh*	
BENJAMIN	
10. גִּבְעוֹן, *Giveon*	
11. גֶּבַע, *Geva*	11. גֶּבַע, *Geva*
12. עֲנָתוֹת, *Anathoth*	13. עֲנָתוֹת, *Anathoth*
13. עַלְמוֹן, *Almon*	12. עָלֶמֶת, *Alemeth*
B. The ten cities of the Kehathites taken from the tribes of Ephraim, Dan and Menasheh [the half-tribe of Menasheh who dwelt west of the Jordan].	
I: Joshua	**II: Chronicles**
EPHRAIM	
1. שְׁכֶם [מִקְלָט], *Shechem* [refuge]	1. שְׁכֶם [מִקְלָט], *Shechem* [refuge]
2. גֶּזֶר, *Gezer*	2. גֶּזֶר, *Gezer*
3. קִבְצַיִם, *Kivtzaim*	3. יָקְמְעָם, *Yokmeam*
4. בֵּית חֹרוֹן, *Beth Choron*	4. בֵּית חוֹרוֹן, *Beth Choron*
DAN	
5. אֶלְתְּקֵא, *Eltekei*	
6. גִּבְּתוֹן, *Gibethon*	
7. אַיָּלוֹן, *Aiyalon*	7. אַיָּלוֹן, *Aiyalon*
8. גַּת רִמּוֹן, *Gath Rimmon*	8. גַּת רִמּוֹן, *Gath Rimmon*
[HALF] MENASHEH	
9. תַּעְנָךְ, *Taenach*	9. עָנֵר, *Aner*
10. גַּת רִמּוֹן, *Gath Rimmon*	10. בִּלְעָם, *Bileam*

6

43-45

Aaron they gave the cities of refuge — Hebron and Livnah and its clearings, and Yattir and Eshtemoa and its clearings. 43 And Chilez and its clearings, and Devir and its clearings. 44 And Ashan and its clearings, and Beth Shemesh and its clearings. 45 And from the tribe of Benjamin — Geva and its clearings, Alemeth and its clearings, and Anathoth and its clearings. All their cities, thirteen cities among

Giveon (10), are missing from our list. *Malbim* suggests that the cities which are not listed here may not have existed any more by the time that *Chronicles* was written. [The other cities are listed because, although as stated above they had long since ceased to be specifically Levitical cities, they were nevertheless occupied and

C. The thirteen cities of the Gershonites taken from the tribes of Yissachar, Asher, Naphtali and Menasheh [the half-tribe of Menasheh who dwelt east of the Jordan].	
I: Joshua	**II: Chronicles**
[HALF] MENASHEH	
1. גּוֹלָן [מקלט], Golan [refuge]	1. גּוֹלָן [מקלט], Golan [refuge]
2. בְּעֶשְׁתְּרָה, Beeshterah	2. עַשְׁתָּרוֹת, Ashtaroth
YISSACHAR	
3. קִשְׁיוֹן, Kishion	3. קֶדֶשׁ, Kedesh
4. דָּבְרַת, Davrath	4. דָּבְרַת, Dovrath
5. יַרְמוּת, Yarmuth	5. רָאמוֹת, Ramoth
6. עֵין גַּנִּים, En Gannim	6. עָנֵם, Anem
ASHER	
7. מִשְׁאָל, Mishal	7. מָשָׁל, Mashal
8. עַבְדּוֹן, Avdon	8. עַבְדּוֹן, Avdon
9. חֶלְקַת, Chelkath	9. חוּקֹק, Chukok
10. רְחֹב, Rechov	10. רְחֹב, Rechov
NAPHTALI	
11. קֶדֶשׁ [מקלט], Kedesh [refuge]	11. קֶדֶשׁ [מקלט], Kedesh [refuge]
12. חַמֹּת דֹּאר, Chammoth Dor	12. חַמּוֹן, Chammon
13. קַרְטָן, Kartan	13. קִרְיָתַיִם, Kiriathaim

D. The twelve cities of the Merarites taken from the tribes of Reuven, Gad and Zevulun.	
I: Joshua	**II: Chronicles**
ZEVULUN	
1. יָקְנְעָם, Yokneam	1. רִמּוֹנוֹ, Rimmono
2. קַרְתָּה, Kartah	2. תָּבוֹר, Tavor
3. דִּמְנָה, Dimminah	
4. נַהֲלָל, Nahalal	
REUVEN	
	5. בֶּצֶר [מקלט], Betzer [refuge]
	6. יַהְצָה, Yahtzah
	7. קְדֵמוֹת, Kedemoth
	8. מֵיפָעַת, Mephaath
GAD	
9. רָמֹת [מקלט], Rammoth [refuge]	9. רָאמוֹת [מקלט], Ramoth [refuge]
10. מַחֲנַיִם, Machanaim	10. מַחֲנַיִם, Machanaim
11. חֶשְׁבּוֹן, Cheshbon	11. חֶשְׁבּוֹן, Cheshbon
12. יַעְזֵר, Yaezer	12. יַעְזֵיר, Yaazer

מו וּלְבְנֵי קְהָת הַנּוֹתָרִים   בְּמִשְׁפְּחוֹתֵיהֶם:
מִמִּשְׁפַּחַת הַמַּטֶּה מִמַּחֲצִית מַטֵּה מְנַשֶּׁה בַּגּוֹרָל
מז עָרִים עָשֶׂר: וְלִבְנֵי גֵרְשׁוֹם לְמִשְׁפְּחוֹתָם
מִמַּטֵּה יִשָּׂשכָר וּמִמַּטֵּה אָשֵׁר וּמִמַּטֵּה נַפְתָּלִי וּמִמַּטֵּה
מח מְנַשֶּׁה בַּבָּשָׁן עָרִים שְׁלֹשׁ עֶשְׂרֵה: לִבְנֵי
מְרָרִי לְמִשְׁפְּחוֹתָם מִמַּטֵּה רְאוּבֵן וּמִמַּטֵּה־גָד וּמִמַּטֵּה
מט זְבֻלוּן בַּגּוֹרָל עָרִים שְׁתֵּים עֶשְׂרֵה: וַיִּתְּנוּ בְנֵי־יִשְׂרָאֵל
נ לַלְוִיִּם אֶת־הֶעָרִים וְאֶת־מִגְרְשֵׁיהֶם: וַיִּתְּנוּ
בַגּוֹרָל מִמַּטֵּה בְנֵי־יְהוּדָה וּמִמַּטֵּה בְנֵי־שִׁמְעוֹן וּמִמַּטֵּה
בְּנֵי בִנְיָמִן אֵת הֶעָרִים הָאֵלֶּה אֲשֶׁר־יִקְרְאוּ אֶתְהֶם
נא בְּשֵׁמוֹת: וּמִמִּשְׁפְּחוֹת בְּנֵי קְהָת וַיְהִי
נב עָרֵי גְבוּלָם מִמַּטֵּה אֶפְרָיִם: וַיִּתְּנוּ לָהֶם אֶת־עָרֵי הַמִּקְלָט
אֶת־שְׁכֶם וְאֶת־מִגְרָשֶׁיהָ בְּהַר אֶפְרָיִם וְאֶת־גֶּזֶר וְאֶת־
נג מִגְרָשֶׁיהָ: וְאֶת־יָקְמְעָם וְאֶת־מִגְרָשֶׁיהָ וְאֶת־בֵּית חוֹרוֹן
נד וְאֶת־מִגְרָשֶׁיהָ: וְאֶת־אַיָּלוֹן וְאֶת־מִגְרָשֶׁיהָ וְאֶת־גַּת־רִמּוֹן
נה וְאֶת־מִגְרָשֶׁיהָ: וּמִמַּחֲצִית מַטֵּה מְנַשֶּׁה אֶת־עָנֵר וְאֶת־
מִגְרָשֶׁיהָ וְאֶת־בִּלְעָם וְאֶת־מִגְרָשֶׁיהָ לְמִשְׁפַּחַת לִבְנֵי־קְהָת
נו הַנּוֹתָרִים: לִבְנֵי גֵרְשׁוֹם מִמִּשְׁפַּחַת

---

known by name.]

In addition, there are some minor changes in the spelling of some of the names. Such changes occur very frequently throughout *Chronicles*. There are some changes, however, which cannot be taken as variations in spelling and must be seen as different names. *Radak* suggests two possibilities. It is possible that the same town was known by two different names, just as we find that Scripture occasionally refers to the same person by different names (see 11:10-47); or, the city which was indicated by the lot at Joshua's division may have remained in Canaanite hands so that another city had to be substituted.

בְּמִשְׁפְּחוֹתֵיהֶם — *Among their families.* The word refers to the *Kohanim* mentioned in v. 42. The thirteen cities were divided among the families of the *Kohanim*. *Malbim* to *Joshua* notes that Divine Providence, through the drawing of the lot, decreed that just the *Kohanim* — the most exalted among the Levites — received their portion in the holiest part of the land — in the vicinity of Jerusalem and the holy Temple.

46. וּלְבְנֵי קְהָת הַנּוֹתָרִים — *And to the remaining sons of Kehath.* I.e., besides the *Kohanim* who were also the sons of Kehath [see v. 39 above] (*Mefaresh*).

מִמִּשְׁפַּחַת הַמַּטֶּה מִמַּחֲצִית חֲצִי מְנַשֶּׁה — *From the family of the tribe and from the half-tribe, half of Menasheh.* Our verse must be studied together with vs. 51-55 which give the details of the cities received by the remaining Kehathites. We find an apparent contradiction. Our verse seems to ascribe all ten cities to the half-tribe of Menasheh while vs. 51-54 ascribe the cities numbered II(1-8) on list B to Ephraim. Both our verse and v. 54 seem to be in contradiction with *Joshua* 21:23 which ascribes the four cities numbered I(5-8) to Dan. The *Chronicles* list omits the cities I(5-6) completely and ascribes the cities numbered 7 and 8 to Ephraim rather than to Dan. Our verse, of course, makes no mention of Dan either, in apparent contradiction to *Joshua* 21:5 which lists Dan in the general statement.

Malbim offers the following solution. From *Judges* 1:34 it appears that Dan was never able to conquer the territory which

their families. ⁴⁶ *And to the remaining sons of Kehath, from the family of the tribe and from the half-tribe, half of Menasheh, ten cities.* ⁴⁷ *To the sons of Gershom according to their families — from the tribe of Yissachar, from the tribe of Asher, from the tribe of Naphtali, and from the tribe of Menasheh in Bashan — thirteen cities.* ⁴⁸ *To the sons of Merari according to their families — from the tribe of Reuven, and from the tribe of Gad, and from the tribe of Zevulun by lot — twelve cities.* ⁴⁹ *The children of Israel gave the cities and their clearings to the Levites.* ⁵⁰ *And they gave by lot — from the tribe of the sons of Judah, from the tribe of the sons of Shimeon, and from the tribe of the sons of Benjamin — the cities which have been named.* ⁵¹ *For some of the families of the sons of Kehath, the cities of their possession were from the tribe of Ephraim.* ⁵² *They gave them the refuge cities — Shechem and its clearings in Mount Ephraim, and Gezer and its clearings.* ⁵³ *And Yokmeam and its clearings, and Beth Choron and its clearings.* ⁵⁴ *And Aiyalon and its clearings, and Gath Rimmon and its clearings.* ⁵⁵ *And from the half-tribe of Menasheh — Aner and its clearings, and Bileam and its clearings — to the family of the remaining sons of Kehath.* ⁵⁶ *To the sons of Gershom, from the*

---

had been assigned to him. Therefore, although the lot which was cast by Joshua determined that Dan was to supply a number of cities to the Levites, this never came about. The cities numbered I(5 and 6) were never conquered and are therefore missing from the *Chronicles* list. Cities 7 and 8, which should have fallen to Dan, were instead conquered by Ephraim (see *Judges* 1:35) and are therefore ascribed to him in the *Chronicles* list. Thus, the second Levite unit received all its cities from Ephraim and Menasheh rather than from Dan as had been assumed in *Joshua*. *Malbim* thinks that this is reflected in our verse and that Ephraim is, in fact, mentioned albeit not by name. The sentence is to be translated as follows: *From [the complete] family* [i.e., Ephraim] *of the tribe* [of Joseph who was divided into two families, and] *from a half-tribe — the half-tribe of Menasheh* [who was only a partial family from the tribe of Joseph]. *Malbim's* rendering eliminates the apparent contradiction between our verse and v. 51ff.

However, *Malbim's* assertion that Dan never conquered its territory is somewhat problematical. His proof is based on a very early period in the settlement of the land, when much of the territory which made up *Eretz Yisrael* had not yet been conquered. It seems unlikely that

David, in his wars of conquest, would have allowed the territory of one of the tribes to remain in alien hands. It may be, though, that the territory of Dan was not conquered for many centuries after the entry into the land, by which time the Levites had already been given other cities to settle. Thus, by the time Dan finally conquered its territory, the full complement of Levitical cities had already been distributed.

חֲצִי מְנַשֶּׁה — *Half of Menasheh.* Verse 47 tells that Gershom's portion came in part from *the tribe of Menasheh in Bashan.* That is the half of Menasheh from the eastern shore of the Jordan. Consequently, the half-tribe Menasheh mentioned in our verse is the one in the land of Israel proper.

48. בְּגוֹרָל — *By lot.* They drew lots to determine which cities each tribe was to give *(Metzudos).*

55. לִבְנֵי־קְהָת הַנּוֹתָרִים — *Of the remaining sons of Kehath.* The Kehathites are described as *remaining* because the *Kohanim,* who were also descendants of Kehath, had already taken their portion *(Metzudos).* These remaining Kehathites are the same as those mentioned in v. 46.

56⁻66. See lists C and D for a comparison of our list and the one in *Joshua.* See also remarks in comm. 42-45.

חֲצִי מַטֵּה מְנַשֶּׁה אֶת־גּוֹלָן בַּבָּשָׁן וְאֶת־מִגְרָשֶׁיהָ וְאֶת־
נז עַשְׁתָּרוֹת וְאֶת־מִגְרָשֶׁיהָ: וּמִמַּטֵּה
יִשָּׂשכָר אֶת־קֶדֶשׁ וְאֶת־מִגְרָשֶׁיהָ אֶת־דָּבְרַת וְאֶת־
נח מִגְרָשֶׁיהָ: וְאֶת־רָאמוֹת וְאֶת־מִגְרָשֶׁיהָ וְאֶת־עָנֵם וְאֶת־
נט מִגְרָשֶׁיהָ: וּמִמַּטֵּה אָשֵׁר אֶת־מָשָׁל וְאֶת־מִגְרָשֶׁיהָ
ס וְאֶת־עַבְדּוֹן וְאֶת־מִגְרָשֶׁיהָ: וְאֶת־חוּקֹק וְאֶת־מִגְרָשֶׁיהָ
סא וְאֶת־רְחֹב וְאֶת־מִגְרָשֶׁיהָ: וּמִמַּטֵּה נַפְתָּלִי אֶת־
קֶדֶשׁ בַּגָּלִיל וְאֶת־מִגְרָשֶׁיהָ וְאֶת־חַמּוֹן וְאֶת־מִגְרָשֶׁיהָ
סב וְאֶת־קִרְיָתַיִם וְאֶת־מִגְרָשֶׁיהָ: לִבְנֵי מְרָרִי
הַנּוֹתָרִים מִמַּטֵּה זְבוּלֻן אֶת־רִמּוֹנוֹ וְאֶת־מִגְרָשֶׁיהָ אֶת־
סג תָּבוֹר וְאֶת־מִגְרָשֶׁיהָ: וּמֵעֵבֶר לְיַרְדֵּן יְרֵחוֹ לְמִזְרַח הַיַּרְדֵּן
מִמַּטֵּה רְאוּבֵן אֶת־בֶּצֶר בַּמִּדְבָּר וְאֶת־מִגְרָשֶׁיהָ וְאֶת־יַהְצָה
סד וְאֶת־מִגְרָשֶׁיהָ: וְאֶת־קְדֵמוֹת וְאֶת־מִגְרָשֶׁיהָ וְאֶת־מֵיפָעַת
סה וְאֶת־מִגְרָשֶׁיהָ: וּמִמַּטֵּה־גָד אֶת־רָאמוֹת בַּגִּלְעָד
סו וְאֶת־מִגְרָשֶׁיהָ וְאֶת־מַחֲנַיִם וְאֶת־מִגְרָשֶׁיהָ: וְאֶת־חֶשְׁבּוֹן
א וְאֶת־מִגְרָשֶׁיהָ וְאֶת־יַעְזֵיר וְאֶת־מִגְרָשֶׁיהָ: וְלִבְנֵי

א־ב ק׳ יָשׁוּב° ב יִשָּׂשכָר תּוֹלָע וּפוּאָה °יָשִׁיב וְשִׁמְרוֹן אַרְבָּעָה: וּבְנֵי תוֹלָע

---

62. לִבְנֵי מְרָרִי הַנּוֹתָרִים — *To the remaining sons of Merari.* I.e., those who remained from the Levite families. The others had already taken their portions (*Metzudos*). Perhaps the expression *remaining* is used to explain a notable omission in *Joshua*. The general statements concerning the first three Levite units (vs. 4-6) all stress that the decision of which tribes were to supply cities to which particular unit was taken by lot. This is not mentioned in v. 7 in con-

nection with Merari. *Malbim* (there) explains that since Merari was the last Levite unit left it was obvious that his portion was to come from the three tribes which remained. This may be implied by the word *remaining* in our verse.

63-64. List D shows that *Joshua* does not give the cities which Reuven set aside for the Merarites. See ArtScroll *Joshua* there for a discussion.

VII

⧫ The Line of Yissachar

After having completed the description of the Levite families and their cities, Ezra goes back to the genealogies of the other tribes. In general, the genealogies seem to be listed according to a geographical pattern with Jerusalem as its focal point (see map in ArtScroll comm. to *Joshua*, p. 294). Given this orientation, we have three groups of tribes — those to the south of Jerusalem; those to the east across the Jordan; and those to the north. These three groups are dealt with in a counter-clockwise sequence — from south to east to north. The treatment of the first two of these three units is entirely logical. We begin with Judah and Shimeon in the south. [Shimeon, who did not have a clearly defined area of the Land, and whose cities were primarily in Judah's territory (4:24-43), is considered to be one with Judah.] We then move to the eastern shore of the Jordan where Reuven, Gad and half

family of the half-tribe of Menasheh — Golan in Bashan and its clearings, and Ashtaroth and its clearings. [57] *And from the tribe of Yissachar — Kedesh and its clearings, Dovrath and its clearings.* [58] *And Ramoth and its clearings, and Anem and its clearings.* [59] *From the tribe of Asher — Mashal and its clearings, and Avdon and its clearings.* [60] *And Chukok and its clearings, and Rechov and its clearings.* [61] *And from the tribe of Naphtali — Kedesh in Galilee and its clearings, and Chammon and its clearings, and Kiriathaim and its clearings.* [62] *To the remaining sons of Merari from the tribe of Zevulun — Rimmono and its clearings, and Tavor and its clearings.* [63] *From Transjordan at Jericho to the east of the Jordan, from the tribe of Reuven — Betzer in the desert and its clearings, and Yahtzah and its clearings.* [64] *And Kedemoth and its clearings, and Mephaath and its clearings.* [65] *And from the tribe of Gad — Ramoth in Gilead and its clearings, and Machanaim and its clearings.* [66] *And Cheshbon and its clearings, and Yazer and its clearings.*

A*nd for the sons of Yissachar — Tola, Puah, Yashuv, and*

Menasheh are dealt with, from south to north.

Although the northern group is taken next, within this section we do not have the same consistency. The last of the tribes listed is Benjamin (in ch. 8) which, by returning to the area of Jerusalem, seems to bear out the general thesis. But we would have expected the remaining northern tribes to be listed from north to south. This, however, is not done and the sequence — Yissachar [Benjamin — see comm. v. 6], [Dan — see comm. v. 13], Naphtali, Menasheh, Ephraim, Asher, Benjamin — shows no discernible pattern.

If we are unable to discern a logical sequence for the five [or six, see below] tribes listed in our chapter, it may still be in place to examine possible causes for the juxtaposition of any two of the tribes.

Thus *Daas Soferim* suggests that it may indeed have been natural for Ezra to have treated Yissachar after Levi. Because of the special position Levi occupied as teacher and guardian of the Torah (see *Deuteronomy* 33:10), we may surmise that its cities were centers of Torah learning and spiritual elevation for the whole land. In the tradition of the Sages — based on *I Chronicles* 12:33 — Yissachar, too, was devoted to intensive Torah study, more so than any other tribe (see *Yoma* 26a). Thus, its position in Israel closely resembled that of Levi and this may well account for Ezra's turning to him after completing Levi. *Daas Soferim* thinks that this affinity between the two tribes may explain the use of the conjunction *and* to open verse 1.

1. תּוֹלָע וּפוּאָה יָשׁוּב וְשִׁמְרוֹן — *Tola, Puah, Yashuv, and Shimron.* These four names are essentially the same as those listed for Yissachar's sons in *Genesis* 46:13 and *Numbers* 26:23-24. Differences are that the name of the second son is spelled פֻּוָה, *Puvah,* there and the third son, who is called יָשׁוּב, *Yashuv,* here and in *Numbers,* is called יוֹב, *Yov,* in *Genesis.*[1]

אַרְבָּעָה — *Four.* See 2:6 for a discussion of why the cumulative number is occasionally given after a listing of the names. Here, no midrashic interpretations are extant and the explanations suggested in the footnote there do not seem apt in a situation such as ours where the names, being already listed in the Torah, seem to preclude any ambiguities.

1. *Sifri Zuta (Nasso 7:18)* explains the change to יָשׁוּב, *Yashuv. Numbers* 7:2 tells how the princes of Israel donated six wagons and twelve oxen on their own initiative, to be used in transporting the Tabernacle from place to place. Tradition has it that it was Yissachar's son יוֹב, *Yov,* who gave the princes this idea. As a result the ש was added to his name so that it would now connote מֵשִׁיב עֵצָה, *one who gives advice.* [For use of the verb שׁוּב in this sense cf. *Proverbs* 26:16.]

עֻזִּי וּרְפָיָה ְוִירִיאֵל ֖וְיַחְמַי וְיִבְשָׂם וּשְׁמוּאֵל רָאשִׁים לְבֵית־
אֲבוֹתָם לְתוֹלָע גִּבּוֹרֵי חַיִל לְתֹלְדוֹתָם מִסְפָּרָם בִּימֵי דָוִיד
ג עֶשְׂרִים-וּשְׁנַיִם אֶלֶף וְשֵׁשׁ מֵאוֹת: וּבְנֵי עֻזִּי
יִזְרַחְיָה וּבְנֵי יִזְרַחְיָה מִיכָאֵל ֙וְעֹבַדְיָה וְיוֹאֵל יִשִּׁיָּה חֲמִשָּׁה
ד רָאשִׁים כֻּלָּם: וַעֲלֵיהֶם לְתֹלְדוֹתָם לְבֵית אֲבוֹתָם גְּדוּדֵי
צְבָא מִלְחָמָה שְׁלֹשִׁים וְשִׁשָּׁה אֶלֶף כִּי-הִרְבּוּ נָשִׁים וּבָנִים:
ה וַאֲחֵיהֶם לְכֹל מִשְׁפְּחוֹת יִשָׂשכָר גִּבּוֹרֵי חֲיָלִים שְׁמוֹנִים
ו וְשִׁבְעָה אֶלֶף הִתְיַחְשָׂם לַכֹּל: בִּנְיָמִן בֶּלַע וָבֶכֶר
ז וִידִיעֲאֵל שְׁלֹשָׁה: וּבְנֵי בֶּלַע אֶצְבּוֹן וְעֻזִּי ֙וְעֻזִּיאֵל וִירִימוֹת

2. ... עֻזִּי — *Uzzi* ... All six sons mentioned here were heads of separate family units which descended from them. The family unit of Uzzi was formed by all his sons (none of whose names are mentioned) except for Yizrachiah (v. 3), whose progeny was numerous enough to be considered a family unit in its own right (*Malbim*; see further to v. 3).

לְתוֹלָע — *of Tola.* All six family groups were sub-groups of the larger family group of Tola.

גִּבּוֹרֵי חַיִל לְתֹלְדוֹתָם — *Mighty warriors throughout their generations.* All the generations of these chieftains produced mighty warriors. The number of their descendants during David's reign was twenty-two thousand and six hundred (*Metzudos*). Above in 5:24 the term גִּבּוֹרֵי חַיִל was defined as *men of outstanding quality.* In the context of this chapter, it is evident that whatever general qualities they may have possessed, they are being cited here specifically for their military prowess. This may explain the plural חֲיָלִים in גִּבּוֹרֵי חֲיָלִים verses 5, 7, and 11. Accordingly, throughout this chapter this term will be translated as *mighty warriors.*

Above, Yissachar's special place among the ten tribes of Israel as student and teacher of the Torah was discussed. If here their fame seems to be predicated upon their valor as warriors this need not surprise us. In Scripture and in midrashic literature the two activities go together. See Section Two p. 417ff.

3. וּבְנֵי עֻזִּי יִזְרַחְיָה — *And the sons of Uzzi — Yizrachiah.* The plural וּבְנֵי seems to indicate that Uzzi had more sons than the Yizrachiah mentioned here (see comm. 2:8). The families of these sons were not large enough to make them family heads in their own right. Since Yizrachiah formed

his own family unit, it is through the unmentioned sons that Uzzi is considered the head of a separate family unit in the previous verse.

וּבְנֵי יִזְרַחְיָה ... חֲמִשָּׁה רָאשִׁים — *And the sons of Yizrachiah ... five heads ...* Four sons are listed but the number of heads of families is given as five. Yizrachiah had other sons besides the four mentioned here, but their families were not large enough to be separately constituted. Yizrachiah himself, therefore, was chieftain over them. He, and the four sons whose families were large enough to be considered separately, formed five family units (*Malbim*).

4. וַעֲלֵיהֶם לְתֹלְדוֹתָם — *And under them* [lit. *on them*] *by their generations.* Their numerous descendants were organized under the five chieftains mentioned in the previous verse (*Malbim*). They reached the number of thirty-six thousand. Thus, the one son of Uzzi, Yizrachiah, had a family which was much larger than the combined descendants of all of Uzzi's other sons — *for they had many wives and children.*

Since we must assume that the numbers given here describe these families at the time of David, as do those in verse 2, the word עֲלֵיהֶם, *under them,* which refers to the five chieftains mentioned in the previous verse, presents a problem. The great-grandson of Yissachar would not likely have been alive in David's time. One of two solutions is possible: Either the וּבְנֵי in verse 3 does not mean *son* but *descendant,* as we have seen before, in which case the names given may well have belonged to officers who lived during David's reign; or, the leadership of the family units continued to bear the names of the original chieftains long after these had died.

5. וַאֲחֵיהֶם לְכֹל מִשְׁפְּחוֹת יִשָׂשכָר — *And their brothers in all the families of Yissachar.* This refers to the descendants of Tola's

Shimron — four. ² And the sons of Tola — Uzzi, Rephaiah, Yeriel, Yachmai, Yivsam, and Shemuel, heads of their families of Tola, mighty warriors throughout their generations; their number in the days of David was twenty-two thousand six hundred. ³ And the sons of Uzzi — Yizrachiah; and the sons of Yizrachiah — Michael, Ovadiah, Yoel, Yishiah — five heads in all. ⁴ And under them by their generations according to their families, formed into military units — thirty-six thousand men, for they had many wives and children. ⁵ And their brothers in all the families of Yissachar, mighty warriors — eighty-seven thousand; all had their genealogical records. ⁶ Benjamin — Bela, Becher, and Yediael — three. ⁷ And the

brothers, the other three sons of Yissachar (Radak; Malbim).

התיחשם לכל — All had their genealogical records. The translation follows Metzudos. All eighty-seven thousand Yissacharite warriors possessed records of their family trees. Targum seems to agree with this translation since he renders לכל as all of them rather than the more usual everything. Examples of כל used in this manner where Targumim also render all of them, are II Kings 24:16 and Jeremiah 44:12.

◄§ Benjamin's Sons

6-12. Commentators are of two minds concerning this passage. It is possible that the Benjamin mentioned in verse 6 is another of Yissachar's descendants and that the description of Yissachar's family continues until Naphtali's genealogy is taken up in verse 13. The other possibility is that the Benjamin in verse 6 is Jacob's youngest son and that a genealogy of the Benjaminite tribe is inserted here between the lists of Yissachar and Naphtali.

List A — Benjamin's Sons			
I: Genesis 46:21	**II:** Numbers 26:38-40	**III:** I Chron. 7:6-7	**IV:** I Chron. 8:1-5
1. בֶּלַע, Bela	בֶּלַע, Bela	בֶּלַע, Bela	בֶּלַע, Bela
2. בֶּכֶר, Becher		בֶּכֶר, Becher	
3. אַשְׁבֵּל, Ashbel	אַשְׁבֵּל, Ashbel	יְדִיעֵאל], Yediael]	אַשְׁבֵּל, Ashbel
4. גֵּרָא, Gera			
5. נַעֲמָן, Naaman			
6. אֵחִי, Echi	אֲחִירָם, Achiram		אַחְרַח, Achrach
7. ראש, Rosh			
8. מֻפִּים, Muppim	שְׁפוּפָם, Shephupham		נוֹחָה], Nochah]
9. חֻפִּים, Chuppim	חוּפָם, Chupham		רָפָה], Raphah]
10. אָרְדְּ, Ard			
List B — Bela's Sons			
	II	**III**	**IV**
	אַרְדְּ, Ard		אַדָּר, Addar
	נַעֲמָן, Naaman		נַעֲמָן, Naaman
		אֶצְבּוֹן, Etzbon	גֵּרָא, Gera
		עֻזִּי, Uzzi	אֲבִיהוּד, Avihud
		עֻזִּיאֵל, Uzziel	אֲבִישׁוּעַ, Avishua
		יְרִימוֹת, Yerimoth	אֲחוֹחַ, Achoach
		עִירִי, Iri	גֵּרָא, Gera
			שְׁפוּפָן, Shephuphan
			חוּרָם, Churam

ז

וְעֵירִי חֲמִשָּׁה רָאשֵׁי בֵית אָבוֹת גִּבּוֹרֵי חֲיָלִים וְהִתְיַחְשָׂם
ח עֶשְׂרִים וּשְׁנַיִם אֶלֶף וּשְׁלֹשִׁים וְאַרְבָּעָה: וּבְנֵי
בֶּכֶר זְמִירָה וְיוֹעָשׁ וֶאֱלִיעֶזֶר וֶאֶלְיוֹעֵינַי וְעָמְרִי וִירֵמוֹת
ט וַאֲבִיָּה וַעֲנָתוֹת וְעָלֶמֶת כָּל־אֵלֶּה בְּנֵי־בָכֶר: וְהִתְיַחְשָׂם
לְתֹלְדוֹתָם רָאשֵׁי בֵית אֲבוֹתָם גִּבּוֹרֵי חָיִל עֶשְׂרִים אֶלֶף
וּמָאתָיִם: י וּבְנֵי יְדִיעֲאֵל בִּלְהָן וּבְנֵי בִלְהָן °יעיש °יעוש ק'
יא וּבְנְיָמִן וְאֵהוּד וּכְנַעֲנָה וְזֵיתָן וְתַרְשִׁישׁ וַאֲחִישָׁחַר: כָּל־
אֵלֶּה בְּנֵי יְדִיעֲאֵל לְרָאשֵׁי הָאָבוֹת גִּבּוֹרֵי חֲיָלִים שִׁבְעָה־
יב עָשָׂר אֶלֶף וּמָאתַיִם יֹצְאֵי צָבָא לַמִּלְחָמָה: וְשֻׁפִּם וְחֻפִּם

There are potent arguments for both sides of this question. The names of the first two sons of this Benjamin, Bela and Becher, are the same as those given in *Genesis 46:21*, indicating that the two Benjamins are identical. The fact that Yediael, the third son mentioned here, is not given in *Genesis* need not be seen as contradicting the thesis since, as we have seen countless times in *Chronicles*, the same people are often known by different names and Yediael may be another name for Ashbel or one of the other sons.

There are, however, serious considerations which speak against the assumption that we are dealing here with the Benjaminite tribe. In the first place, the whole of ch. 8 is devoted to Benjamin and there seems no obvious reason why his genealogy should be split into two with one part inserted between Yissachar and Naphtali. Again, as noted in the prefatory remarks to this chapter, the listing of the tribes seems to follow a general geographical pattern. In this system, Benjamin belongs at the very end of the tribes [which is, in fact, his position in ch. 8] but has no place between Yissachar and Naphtali. Furthermore, none of the names

of the five children listed here for Benjamin's son Bela (v. 7) bears any resemblance to Bela's children given in *Numbers 26:40* or those listed below in 8:3-4. Also, the cumulative number שְׁלֹשָׁה, *three*, in verse 6 is apt only if these were the only three sons of Benjamin (see comm. 2:6). If, however, for whatever reason [see below] verse 6 lists only three of Benjamin's ten sons there seems little logic to the *three* being added.

Radak considers both possibilities and does not decide between them.[1] Most commentators, including *Gra*, assume that we are dealing with the Benjaminite line, while *Malbim* takes for granted that the Benjamin listed here belongs to Yissachar's family.

6. ... בִּנְיָמִן בֶּלַע וָבֶכֶר — *Benjamin — Bela, Becher* ... If a Yissacharite is meant it is possible that all three names belong to one generation, although *Malbim* assumes that even in that case Benjamin was the father and Bela and Becher the sons. If Jacob's son Benjamin is meant then, of course, Bela and Becher are his sons, as seen from *Genesis 46:21* (see comm. 1:4).

וִידִיעֲאֵל — *And Yediael.* If Jacob's son

1. Although *Radak* makes no attempt to decide between the two options, a question which he raises in ch. 8 may shed some light upon the view of the Sages in this matter.

A glance at the chart will show that although *Genesis* lists ten sons for Benjamin, *Numbers* has only five. *Rashi* to *Numbers* quotes the explanation which the Sages offer: five Benjaminite families were wiped out on a certain occasion during the journey through the wilderness. *Radak* questions this explanation. One of the families which is missing in *Deuteronomy* is that of Becher. Nevertheless, Becher appears in our list [A:III(2)]. If the family of Becher was wiped out in the wilderness we would not expect it to be listed in *Chronicles*. If, however, the Sages assumed our list to deal with a Yissacharite rather than a Benjaminite family, there is, of course, no problem.

However, as a possible answer to *Radak's* question, R' Y. Danziger has suggested that the five families may not have been wiped out completely but merely that their number was so greatly reduced that they ceased to qualify as 'families.' If so, it is possible that in the course of time the family of Becher multiplied to the point that it again qualified for the distinction of being considered as a 'family' and was so reconstituted.

sons of Bela — Etzbon, Uzzi, Uzziel, Yerimoth, and Iri, five heads of families, mighty warriors; and their genealogical records listed twenty-two thousand and thirty-four. ⁸ And the sons of Becher — Zemirah, Yoash, Eliezer, Elioenai, Omri, Yeremoth, Aviyah, Anathoth, and Alemeth — all these were the sons of Becher. ⁹ And their genealogies by their generations — [for they were] heads of their families — mighty warriors, twenty-two thousand and two hundred. ¹⁰ And the sons of Yediael — Bilhan; and the sons of Bilhan — Yeush, Benjamin, Ehud, Chenaanah, Zethan, Tarshish, and Achishachar. ¹¹ All these were the sons of Yediael, family heads, mighty warriors — seventeen thousand and two hundred who go out

Benjamin is meant, this Yediael would be another name for the third son, Ashbel (*Mefaresh; Gra*).

If the three names given here are indeed the first three of Benjamin's ten sons, we would need to know why just these three are listed here. *Gra* suggests that since the families mentioned here are all described as *mighty warriors* (vs. 7,9 and 11) the list of Benjaminites here forms an appendix to the lists of the Yissacharite mighty warriors in David's army (v. 2).

שְׁלֹשָׁה — *Three.* See above, prefatory comment to 6-12.

7. וּבְנֵי בֶלַע ... — *And the sons of Bela* ... A glance at list B on the chart will show that none of Bela's sons listed here seem to be given either in *Numbers* or in ch. 8 where the children of Benjamin's son, Bela, are listed. *Malbim* feels that this proves that we are dealing here with a Yissacharite family. The other commentators must assume either that some sons of Bela are listed here and others in ch. 8, or that five of Bela's sons went under two names.

וְהִתְיַחְשָׂם ... — *And their genealogical records listed* ... *Targum* seems to understand the phrase as we have translated it. Their family lists contained twenty-two thousand and thirty-four.

8. וּבְנֵי בֶכֶר ... — *And the sons of Becher* ... No children of Becher are listed either in *Numbers* or in ch. 8. *Malbim* takes this as another proof that we are dealing with a Yissacharite Benjamin here. *Gra*, however, surmises that in Moses' time Becher's children had not yet had large enough families to be counted as separate units. By the time that Ezra wrote *Chronicles*, however, their progeny was large enough to

warrant a separate listing.

Radak notes that two of Becher's sons, Anathoth and Alemeth, seem to have given their names to Benjaminite cities (see above 6:45). This, of course, tends to bear out the opinion which sees our section as a Benjaminite listing.

9. וְהִתְיַחְשָׂם לְתֹלְדוֹתָם — *And their genealogies by their generations.* Commentators do not explain the meaning of this phrase, which occurs in only one other place (5:7). It is not clear whether it is an idiomatic expression or whether the words are to be translated literally. In the context of our verse the meaning may be that the genealogical status of the sons of Becher was not as sons of their father but as fathers of their own families. Each had a large enough family to be known as an independent family head. According to this interpretation, the next phrase, [*for they were*] *heads of their families*, is to be understood as an explanation of our phrase.

10. וּבְנֵי יְדִיעֲאֵל בִּלְהָן — *And the sons of Yediael — Bilhan.* There have been a number of instances in *Chronicles* in which the phrase בְּנֵי, *sons*, is used although only one son is listed. See comm. to 2:7.

11. לְרָאשֵׁי הָאָבוֹת — *Family heads.* אָבוֹת, literally *fathers*, would seem to be an abbreviated form of בָּתֵּי אָבוֹת, *fathers' houses*, thus *families*. See comm. to 24:31.

יֹצְאֵי צָבָא לַמִּלְחָמָה — *Who go out in the army to war.* Ramban (*Numbers* 1:3) points out that the word צָבָא does not necessarily mean *army*, but can be used to describe any large group of people. When an army is meant the word לַמִּלְחָמָה, *to war*, is added.

We find many different ways in which the term is used to describe men who

יג בְּנֵי עִיר חֻשִׁם בְּנֵי אַחֵר:
יד וְגוּנִי וְיֵצֶר וְשַׁלּוּם בְּנֵי בִלְהָה:

בְּנֵי נַפְתָּלִי יַחֲצִיאֵל
בְּנֵי מְנַשֶּׁה

---

belong to the army: יוֹצֵא צָבָא *(Numbers* 1:3
et al.); אַנְשֵׁי יוֹצְאֵי צָבָא לַמִּלְחָמָה (here);
יוֹצְאֵי צָבָא עֹרְכֵי (12:8 et al); צָבָא לַמִּלְחָמָה
מִלְחָמָה (12:33), and others. It seems likely
that these are technical terms describing
army groupings which were well known at
the time these expressions were used but
are lost to us.

From *I Samuel* 30:24 it is clear that there
were units in the army which did the actual
fighting and others whose duty it was to
guard the stores. The fighters there are
described as הַיֹּרֵד לַמִּלְחָמָה, *those who go
down to war.* This implies that even within
the army not all were involved in מִלְחָמָה.
We may therefore surmise that terms
which combine צָבָא, *army,* and מִלְחָמָה, *war,*
such as our phrase, describe the fighting
arm of the army.

12. In the Overview (p. xx ff) and in the
commentary to הַדְּבָרִים עַתִּיקִים (4:22) the
point has been made that the genealogical
tables of *Chronicles* were drawn from older
sources from which Ezra compiled his lists
according to various criteria. Our verse
more than any other seems to bear out this
thesis. The verse stands by itself and does
not in any way follow from the previous
section. It has all the indications of being
simply a fragment from an earlier source
which Ezra inscribed here for reasons
which we cannot follow. We know nothing
about the brothers Shuppim and Chuppim
nor about their father, Ir [unless, with
Radak and *Gra,* we assume that Ir is
identical with Bela's son, Iri, from verse 7],
nor are Chushim or Acher mentioned
before. Obviously, the verse must have
been a part of a larger, more complete,
genealogical source within which the
information contained in it had meaning.

Both the *Mefaresh* and *Radak* note the
unusual nature of this verse.

Mefaresh writes: Ezra, who wrote
this genealogy, was in doubt whether the
people mentioned in this verse were
Benjaminites, and therefore mentioned
them separately. Moreover, he was
perplexed by verse 15 [in which it would
appear that Shuppim and Chuppim were
descended from Menasheh (see comm.
there)].

[Note that the *Massorah* places our verse in

one *parashah* together with verses 10 and 11.]

Radak writes: [The reason why] the
genealogies are written in a truncated form
is that Ezra was able to write down only
what he found in genealogical sources or
what was handed down to him by tradition.

Only the *Anonymous Commentator*
attempts an explanation. In his view our
verse serves as background for verse 15 by
teaching the genealogy of the woman
whom Machir took. For the *Anonymous
Commentator's* understanding of Chushim
ben Acher, see verse 13.

וְשֻׁפִּם וְחֻפִּם — *And Shuppim and Chuppim.*
Shuppim and Chuppim are mentioned
again in verse 15. See there.

חֻשִׁם בְּנֵי אַחֵר — *Chushim the sons of Acher.*
Again, this information seems to convey
nothing to us.

Malbim thinks that Acher must have
had a number of sons of whom only
Chushim was of interest to Ezra. Hence the
plural form בְּנֵי.

Gra surmises that אַחֵר, *Acher,* may be
identical either with אֲחִישָׁחַר, *Achishachar,*
of verse 10 or with אַחְרַח, *Achrach,* of 8:1.

For the *Anonymous Commentator's* and
Malbim's suggestion concerning Chushim
ben Acher, see next verse.

◆§ Naphtali

13. בְּנֵי נַפְתָּלִי — *The sons of Naphtali ...*
The four sons of Naphtali mentioned here
are, with minor changes in spelling, the
same as those mentioned in *Genesis* 47:24
and *Numbers* 26:48ff.

Ezra's treatment of Naphtali does not
go beyond these names. The *Mefaresh* explains that the sources available to him
simply did not yield any additional
information. [See Overview p. xxi for a
detailed discussion of the theory which the
Mefaresh develops here concerning the
methodology which Ezra used in compiling
his lists.]

If, in spite of this, Ezra found it
worthwhile to list the sons of Naphtali,
whom we already know from the Torah,
this makes the omission of any mention of
Dan from these lists extremely problematic. Even if no detailed family history was
available it would, at the very least, have

in the army to war. ¹² And Shuppim and Chuppim the sons of Ir; Chushim the sons of Acher. ¹³ The sons of Naphtali — Yachatziel, Guni, Yetzer, and Shallum, the sons of Bilhah. ¹⁴ The sons of

been possible to record his family as it is given in the Torah.[1]

The *Anonymous Commentator* and *Malbim* both think that Dan is, in fact, mentioned. In their view, the unexplained *Chushim ben Acher* in the previous verse is Chushim the son of Dan who is mentioned in *Genesis* 46:23. Dan is called Acher

because of the idea of אָחוֹר, *backwards*, expressed in Jacob's blessing to Dan *(Genesis* 49:17), *... and his rider will fall backwards (Anonymous Commentator);* or, because Dan, as the last of all the camps *(Numbers* 10:25), traveled *behind* [אָחַר from אחר, *to be behind]* all the other tribes *(Malbim).*[2]

1. It has been noted several times that differences in spellings may well be the source for homiletical interpretation. Thus, the minor differences in spelling which we saw in the Naphtali list might explain the inclusion of this list in *Chronicles.*

Again, there is the ending *the sons of Bilhah* in our verse. *Radak* notes that there is an aggadic explanation for the mention of Bilhah here. When Leah decided to give her maidservant Zilpah to Jacob, the Torah uses the phrase, *... and she 'took' her maidservant Zilpah and gave her to Jacob (Genesis* 30:9). Earlier, when Rachel had made the same decision concerning Bilhah, the phrase is *... and she 'gave' him Bilhah, her maidservant, as a wife* (v. 4, there). Bilhah was more than willing to marry Jacob and there was no need for her mistress to 'take' her. Her willingness to marry Jacob is here rewarded by mentioning her specifically as the mother of his progeny *(Bereishis Rabbasi).* Thus, if Ezra found a genealogical record of Naphtali's family with the ending בְּנֵי בִלְהָה, this may have been sufficient reason for him to include the record in *Chronicles* even though it does not take the family further than those names already given in the Torah.

2. There are a number of considerations which speak for the interpretation offered by the *Anonymous Commentator* and *Malbim:* (1) The ending, *the sons of Bilhah,* is much more meaningful if both Dan and Naphtali are mentioned. (2) The name Chushim at this point would be a great coincidence if Dan's son was not meant. This, together with the fact that both in *Numbers* ch. 1 and in ch. 26 Dan follows Benjamin in the census, speaks strongly for this identification. (3) In this way Dan is not omitted from Ezra's listing.

There are, however, two counter-indications: (1) Why would Dan be called Acher here? The solutions offered are justifications, not explanations. It is possible to describe Dan as Acher, but why should it be done? (2) Why should Dan be listed in the same verse as Benjamin?

It is possible to answer these two objections if we accept a different explanation for the name אַחֵר, *Acher,* than those offered in the commentary.

Of all the twelve tribes, Dan is the one most closely associated with idol worship. When *Deuteronomy* 27:17 considers the possibility of a tribe in Israel harboring a propensity towards idol worship, the Midrash *(Shocher Tov* 101) says that this refers to Dan. The Midrash there tells how God had asked Moses to propose a tribe from which the priesthood might come. His suggestion that Dan might be chosen was rejected. God said, 'They are idol worshipers!' [Reference is to the infamous idol of Michah in *Judges* ch. 17.] *Sifri* to *Deuteronomy* 34:1 which tells how God showed Moses ... the whole land of Gilead *up to Dan* comments: 'This teaches us that He showed him the tribe of Dan serving idols.' And *Shemos Rabbah* 40:4 talks of Dan as being '... the most fallen [וְאֵין לְךָ יָרוּד מְשֵׁבֶט דָן] of the tribes.'

These negative qualities determined Dan's position in the wilderness encampment according to the Midrash quoted by *Ramban* in *Numbers* 2:2. 'The north is the direction from which darkness descends upon the world. It is there that the tribe of Dan is located for it was he who darkened the world with the idols which Yerovoam erected, as it is written, *... and the one he put in Dan* ... They shall travel last (v. 27), for all who serve idols go backwards, not forwards.'

Thus, we see clearly that the concept אָחוֹר, *backwards,* or its derivative אַחֵר, *Acher,* was associated with Dan. We may speculate that the source from which Ezra drew his listing came from a period in which Dan's propensity to idol worship expressed itself in some overt act (such as the time in which they formally erected Michah's statue), and that at that time there was a reluctance to use Dan's name. He was therefore called אַחֵר, *Acher,* in the records to underline his deviation from the expected norm. [A parallel to this is the appellation אַחֵר, *Acher,* attached to the one-time *Tanna,* Elisha ben Avuya, when he renounced the practice of Torah *(Chagigah* 15a). That name change may well have had its origin in the usage here.]

It is clear that all the references quoted here present only one aspect of Dan's nature. There are many other Midrashim which describe the heights of sanctity to which Dan rose. A full discussion of the implication of this apparent duality is beyond the scope of this footnote. We may, however,

אַשְׂרִיאֵל אֲשֶׁר יָלְדָה פִּילַגְשׁוֹ הָאֲרַמִּיָּה יָלְדָה אֶת־מָכִיר
טו אֲבִי גִלְעָד: וּמָכִיר לָקַח אִשָּׁה לְחֻפִּים וּלְשֻׁפִּים וְשֵׁם
אֲחֹתוֹ מַעֲכָה וְשֵׁם הַשֵּׁנִי צְלָפְחָד וַתִּהְיֶינָה לִצְלָפְחָד בָּנוֹת:

It should further be noted that Zevulun is also missing completely from the genealogical lists of the first nine chapters. If Dan is in fact listed, the fact that Zevulun is missing becomes even more striking.

◄§ Menasheh's Sons

14-19. The difficulties in understanding the next five verses are typical of the structural idiosyncrasies of the genealogical lists in general. A glance at the charts accompanying this passage will show the widely diverging opinions of five commentators and, in the commentary, we shall see how difficult it is to reconcile any of these interpretations with the simple meaning of the text. [See chart here and pp. 120, 121.]

Our passage is a prime example of the problems discussed in Appendix II, and it must be understood in light of the solution offered there. We must certainly assume that the lost *Sefer HaYuchasin* contained the key to understanding the obscurity of the passage. We have no extant midrashim to help unravel its mysteries.

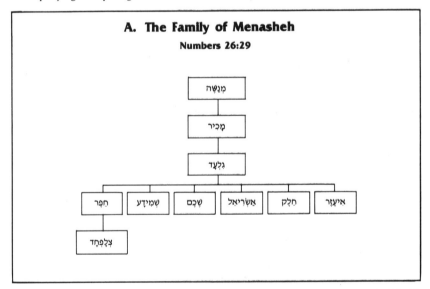

A. The Family of Menasheh

Numbers 26:29

14. בְּנֵי מְנַשֶּׁה אַשְׂרִיאֵל — *The sons of Menasheh — Asriel.* A glance at list A will show that Asriel was not a son of Menasheh but a grandson of Menasheh's son, Machir, through Gilead. Commentators point out that throughout the book grandsons are occasionally listed as sons.

Radak wonders why of Gilead's six sons only Asriel is mentioned here. He suggests that his family may have been a particularly important one. He notes that

there is an aggadic explanation which holds that Asriel is mentioned because his name is similar to Israel, the forefather of the tribes.

Radak further notes the seeming incongruity of mentioning Asriel, Machir's grandson, before Machir himself. He suggests that this may be explained because Asriel was born from a regular wife while Machir's mother was an Aramean concubine [see below].

surmise that the power which enabled him to rise above the baser aspects of his nature derived from his association with Benjamin, that tribe whose essence is the ability to spread sanctity to areas where none had been before. See Section Two p. 414.

Menasheh — Asriel whom she bore. His Aramean concubine bore
Machir the father of Gilead. 15 And Machir took a wife [who was a
sister] to Chuppim and Shuppim, and his sister's name was
Maachah, and the name of the second was Tzelophchad, and

אֲשֶׁר יָלְדָה — Whom she bore. According to
the Massorah there is a break here. The
next phrase, His Aramean concubine bore
Machir the father of Gilead, stands by
itself. If this is so, the subject of our
predicate is missing. The reference is to an
unnamed wife of Gilead who bore him
Asriel.[1]

Metzudos indicates that the reason for
leaving out the name of the mother was
that in contrast to the next phrase which
describes Machir's mother as an Aramean
concubine, there was nothing remarkable
about Asriel's mother.

Gra assumes that the subject of our
phrase is also the Aramean concubine
mentioned in the next phrase. יָלְדָה here is
not meant in the literal sense, she bore, but,
as it sometimes occurs (see comm. 4:18),
she raised. The Aramean concubine raised
[her great-grandson] Asriel [presumably
after his mother died], but she bore [next
phrase] Machir the father of Gilead.

פִּילַגְשׁוֹ הָאֲרַמִּיָּה יָלְדָה אֶת־מָכִיר — His
Aramean concubine bore Machir. Most
commentators take this phrase to mean that
Menasheh himself married the Aramean
concubine. Only the Anonymous Commentator is of the opinion that it was
Machir, and not his father Menasheh, who
married her. [The Anonymous Commentator takes אֶת as meaning together with
rather than indicating the accusative.]

We need not be surprised at how
Menasheh, or his son Machir, who lived and
died in Egypt came to marry an Aramean
woman. The travels of the Ishmaelite or
Midianite merchants mentioned in the story
of Joseph (Genesis ch. 37) clearly indicate
the existence of active trade routes between
Egypt and its neighbors to the north and
east.

15. וּמָכִיר לָקַח אִשָּׁה לְחֻפִּים וּלְשֻׁפִּים — And
Machir took a wife [who was a sister] to
Chuppim and Shuppim. Verse 12 spoke of
Shuppim and Chuppim as descendants of
either Yissachar or Benjamin (see comm. to
v. 6). Therefore, the simple translation that

Machir took a wife for Chuppim and
Shuppim [who in such a context would
presumably be his children] is untenable.
Consequently, Radak, Gra and Metzudos
think that a sister of Chuppim and
Shuppim is meant, i.e., Machir took a wife
[related to] Chuppim and Shuppim.

In this context, the next phrase, And his
sister's name was Maachah, gives the name
of Machir's wife as Maachah who was the
sister of Chuppim (Radak; Gra). [She was
also the sister of Shuppim. The singular is
used because it was Chuppim who was the
more important of the two and the sister is
therefore identified as his (Chuppim's)
sister (Radak).] Our translation follows
this explanation.

The Anonymous Commentator assumes
that the reference is to Machir marrying a
daughter of Chuppim [the daughter of
Shuppim will be mentioned later (v. 18)]
who is identified in the following phrase as
Maachah. The next phrase states that
Machir took his sister (i.e., kinswoman),
Maachah, as his wife. Although she was
actually the daughter of Chuppim, she is
described as Machir's sister because she
was related to him. [Her ancestor Benjamin
was Machir's great-uncle.] Scripture often
uses the terms 'brother' or 'sister' to
describe such relationships (see, e.g.
Genesis 20:12).

וְשֵׁם הַשֵּׁנִי צְלָפְחָד — And the name of the
second was Tzelophchad. The extreme
obscurity of this phrase is reflected in the
widely divergent opinions of the commentators concerning its meaning. From list A
we see that Tzelophchad was the son of
Gilead's sixth son, Chepher. In what way
can he be described as the second?

Radak thinks that second means the
second of Gilead's descendants to be
mentioned. In all, only Asriel (v. 14),
Shemida (v. 19), and Chepher, in the
person of his son Tzelophchad, will be
dealt with. Therefore, Tzelophchad is the
second. He is mentioned instead of his
father, Chepher, because the other sons of
Chepher were unremarkable. The only one

1. Radak points out that such usage occurs in Scripture in Numbers 26:59 and I Kings 1:6 where
יָלְדָה is used without any indication of who the mother was.

טז וַתֵּלֶד מַעֲכָה אֵשֶׁת־מָכִיר בֵּן וַתִּקְרָא שְׁמוֹ פֶּרֶשׁ וְשֵׁם אָחִיו

יז שֶׁרֶשׁ וּבָנָיו אוּלָם וָרָקֶם: וּבְנֵי אוּלָם בְּדָן ֶאֵלֶּה בְּנֵי גִלְעָד

יח בֶּן־מָכִיר בֶּן־מְנַשֶּׁה: וַאֲחֹתוֹ הַמֹּלֶכֶת יָלְדָה אֶת־אִישׁ הוֹד

יט וְאֶת־אֲבִיעֶזֶר וְאֶת־מַחְלָה: וַיִּהְיוּ בְּנֵי שְׁמִידָע אַחְיָן וָשֶׁכֶם

כ וְלִקְחִי וַאֲנִיעָם: וּבְנֵי אֶפְרַיִם

of Chepher's sons to achieve distinction was Tzelophchad, and he is therefore mentioned in place of his father.

Metzudos takes *second* to mean the next generation. Asriel was Gilead's son, Tzelophchad his grandson. In that sense Tzelophchad can be described as the *second*.

Gra postulates the existence of yet another sister of Shuppim and Chuppim who was also called Maachah. The first Maachah married Machir, while the second became Tzelophchad's wife. The verse is to be understood as follows: And his sister's name was Maachah and [this also] was the name of the second [the wife of] Tzelophchad (see list D, below p. 120).

According to the *Anonymous Commentator*, Tzelophchad is the *second* relative to Asriel (v. 14). He is second in line to Asriel because he was descended from him. Evidently the *Anonymous Commentator* assumes that when *Numbers* talks of the sons of Gilead (26:30) and then lists six names, this does not mean that all the six were sons of Gilead. Rather, he assumes that only the first two, Iezer and Chelek were, in fact, Gilead's sons. Thus he is free to explain that Chepher was a son of Asriel and that, relative to him, Chepher's son, Tzelophchad, can be called *the second* (see list B, p. 121).

וַתֵּהְיֶינָה לִצְלָפְחָד בָּנוֹת — *And Tzelophchad had daughters.* As recorded in the Torah (*Numbers* 26:33 and 27:1ff), Tzelophchad had only daughters.

16. וַתֵּלֶד מַעֲכָה אֵשֶׁת־מָכִיר בֵּן — *And Maachah the wife of Machir bore a son.* The necessity of describing Maachah as *the wife of Machir* is used by *Gra* to support his opinion that there were two sisters called Maachah, one of whom married Machir while the other married Tzelophchad. Our verse deals with the one who married Machir.

וַתִּקְרָא שְׁמוֹ פֶּרֶשׁ ... וּבָנָיו ... — *And she called his name Peresh ... and his sons ...* For the

sake of continuity we continue with *Gra's* interpretation. Peresh and Sheresh were born to Maachah from an earlier husband. She, not Machir, gave them their names. But *his sons*, meaning the sons descended from Machir, were Ulam and Rekem. *Gra* points out that since Ulam and Rekem are described as *sons of Gilead* in v. 17 we must take the word *sons* in our phrase in a broader sense. They were not his direct sons but were descended from him through his son, Gilead (see list D, p. 120).

The *Anonymous Commentator* believes that Peresh and Sheresh are sons of Machir. But since the Torah gives Machir's son as Gilead, he proposes that Peresh and Sheresh are not two people at all but are two names by which Gilead was known. Peresh [from פרש, *to separate*] and Sheresh [from שרש, *to take root*] together form the idea of growth and height [i.e., that which separates itself from its root in order to grow]. This recalls גִּלְעָד, the high mountainous region from which the name derives.

Thus the sons of Gilead, who was also known as Peresh and Sheresh, are Ulam and Rekem. The *Anonymous Commentator* believes Ulam and Rekem to be other names for Iezer [אלם, *to be strong*, recalls אִיעֶזֶר from עזר, *to help*] and Chelek [רֶקֶם from רקם, *to empty out*, recalls חֵלֶק, from חלק, *to divide*]. These are given here as sons of Gilead, as indeed they are given in the Torah (see list A, p. 116). As has been noted above (in connection with Asriel and Chepher), in the opinion of the *Anonymous Commentator* the other four names are not sons of Gilead.

In the opinion of *Radak* and *Metzudos*, Peresh and Sheresh and their progeny are simply children born to Machir and Maachah. *Chronicles* fills in details which were not given in the Torah, which lists only Gilead as a son of Machir (see list C, p. 120).

17. וּבְנֵי אוּלָם בְּדָן — *And the sons of Ulam — Bedan.* This is another instance in which

Tzelophchad had daughters. ¹⁶ *And Maachah the wife of Machir bore a son and she called his name Peresh and the name of his brother Sheresh; and his sons — Ulam and Rekem.* ¹⁷ *And the sons of Ulam — Bedan. These are the sons of Gilead the son of Machir the son of Menasheh.* ¹⁸ *And his sister who ruled bore Ish Hod, Aviezer, and Machlah.* ¹⁹ *And the sons of Shemida were Achyan, Shechem, Likchi, and Aniam.* ²⁰ *And the sons of Ephraim — Shuthelach, and*

the plural בְּנֵי is used even though only one son is listed (see comm. 2:7).

אֵלֶּה בְּנֵי גִלְעָד — *These are the sons of Gilead.* The *Anonymous Commentator*, who identified Peresh and Sheresh (v. 16) with Gilead, has no problems with this phrase. All the people mentioned in the last two verses are, indeed, children of Gilead.

Radak and *Metzudos* are forced to explain the phrase as referring to Asriel (v. 14) and Tzelophchad (v. 15). These two are the son and grandson of Gilead respectively (list A). The purpose of our phrase is to make clear that although they were descended from Menasheh they were not his actual sons, as a casual reading of the text might imply.

Gra has the phrase refer to Ulam and Rekem. In his view (see above), v. 16 had given these two people as sons of Machir. Our verse makes clear that they were not his actual sons but were descended from him through Gilead.

18. וַאֲחֹתוֹ הַמֹּלֶכֶת — *And his sister who ruled.* Our translation follows *Radak* and *Metzudos.* The sister of Gilead [presumably through his father Machir] was a powerful woman who ruled over some areas of land. She was significant enough to have the names of her children recorded.

The *Anonymous Commentator* thinks that מֹלֶכֶת is a proper name, *Molecheth.* Verse 15 had recorded that Machir has taken a wife לְחֻפִּים וּלְשֻׁפִּים, *of Chuppim and Shuppim.* According to the *Anonymous Commentator* this meant that he had taken a wife (Maachah) who was a daughter of Chuppim. That verse implied, however, that he had also taken a daughter of Shuppim but no name was given for her. Our verse deals with that woman. Molecheth is the daughter of Shuppim whom Machir married. She is described as his [Machir's] *sister* just as Maachah was in v. 15 because both these women were related to Machir.

The *Anonymous Commentator* believes that אִישׁ הוֹד, *Ish Hod,* is identical with שְׁמִידָע, *Shemida* (v. 19). [אִישׁ הוֹד, *a man of imposing appearance,* recalls שְׁמִידָע, *one whose name is well known* (because of his striking looks).] This would make the Shemida mentioned in *Numbers* (list A) a son of Machir rather than of Gilead. The Shechem mentioned in v. 19 as a son of Shemida is the same Shechem as the one mentioned in *Numbers.*

Thus, a careful reading of the *Anonymous Commentator's* interpretation of our passage yields the following reading of the list in *Numbers:* Iezer and Chelek [here called Ulam and Rekem] are sons of Gilead; Asriel is a son of Machir; Shechem is a son of Shemida [Ish Hod] the son of Machir; Chepher is a son of Asriel. (See list B.)

Gra also thinks that Molecheth is a proper name. She is the sister of Chuppim. *Gra* identifies her three sons with names given in the Torah as having belonged to Gilead's sons. *Gra* therefore writes that this Molecheth married Gilead.

In his view, Ish Hod is identical with Shemida and Machlah with Chelek. Although he does not say so explicitly, we assume that he identifies Aviezer with Iezer. Thus, according to his interpretation (see list D), we have five of the six sons ascribed by *Numbers* to Gilead mentioned here. The exception is Shechem. We assume that *Chronicles* had no reason to mention him, or that Shechem the son of Shemida (v. 18) is the Shechem of the Torah, and the list in the Torah includes a grandson.

19. For שֶׁכֶם, see comm. above.

We have seen how very obscure the phrasing of this section on Menasheh is. In concluding it is worth quoting the *Anonymous Commentator* who, apparently struck by the difficulty of this passage, ends his commentary with the following remarks (slightly paraphrased):

שׁוּתָלַח וּבֶרֶד בְּנוֹ וְתַחַת בְּנוֹ וְאֶלְעָדָה בְנוֹ וְתַחַת בְּנוֹ:

'Consider these matters carefully and do not allow your pride to cause you to read them as one would a letter or other Scriptural passages. For these sections, which are closely tied to passages in the Torah in *Numbers* and in *Deuteronomy*, are woven with delicate threads — they are the words and riddles of the wise. It is not right to read them superficially without particular care because they are Divine words. Are not these words like fire and like a mallet shattering rocks and cliffs? If you think deeply into them you will find satisfaction. But it is only given to those who can suffer to obtain the truth to understand them. God himself will grant visions to him who struggles by night and by day and will light up his eyes by allowing His holy truth to reach his mouth and his heart so that he may see the things as they truly are.'

20⁻27. These verses deal with the tribe of

Ephraim and trace the family down to Joshua the son of Nun, successor to Moses.

⋙ Ephraim's Sons

20. וּבְנֵי אֶפְרַיִם שׁוּתָלַח וּבֶרֶד בְּנוֹ וְתַחַת בְּנוֹ — *And the sons of Ephraim — Shuthelach, and his son Bered, and his son Tachath.* *Numbers* 26:35 gives the sons of Ephraim as: Shuthelach, Becher and Tachan. *Radak* surmises that our Bered and Tachath might be the same as Becher and Tachan. In that case both words, בְּנוֹ, *his son*, refer to Ephraim.

This opinion is shared by the *Anonymous Commentator* who notes that the conjunction *vav* in וּבֶרֶד and וְתַחַת indicates that they were indeed sons of Ephraim. In lists which use similar formulations for different generations the *vav* is not used. Had separate generations been meant our verse would have read: בֶּרֶד בְּנוֹ תַחַת בְּנוֹ.

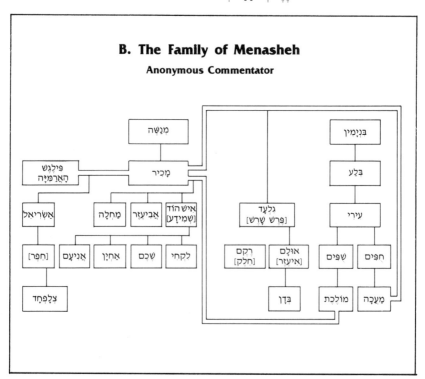

B. The Family of Menasheh
Anonymous Commentator

מְנַשֶּׁה · בִּנְיָמִין · פִּילֶגֶשׁ הָאֲרַמִּיָּה · מָכִיר · בֶּלַע · אַשְׂרִיאֵל · אִישׁ הוֹד [שְׁמִידָע] · אֲבִיעֶזֶר · מַחְלָה · גִּלְעָד [פֶּרֶשׁ שֶׁרֶשׁ] · עֵירִי · [חֵפֶר] · אֲנִיעָם · אָחְיָן · שֶׁכֶם · לִקְחִי · רֶקֶם [חֵלֶק] · אוּלָם [אִיעֶזֶר] · שָׁפִים · חֻפִּים · צְלָפְחָד · בְּדָן · מוֹלֶכֶת · מַעֲכָה

דברי הימים א   **[120]**

his son Bered, and his son Tachath, his son Eleadah, and his son

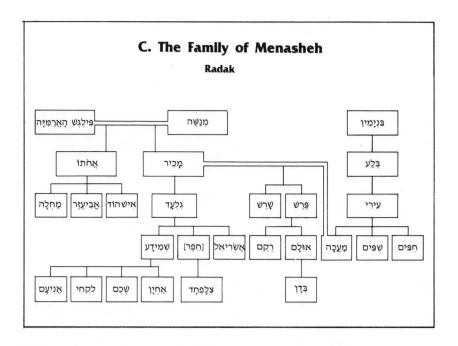

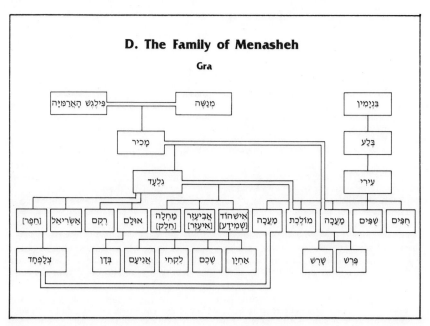

כא וְזָבָד בְּנוֹ וְשׁוּתֶלַח בְּנוֹ וְעֵזֶר וְאֶלְעָד וַהֲרָגוּם אַנְשֵׁי־גַת
כב הַנּוֹלָדִים בָּאָרֶץ כִּי יָרְדוּ לָקַחַת אֶת־מִקְנֵיהֶם: וַיִּתְאַבֵּל
כג אֶפְרַיִם אֲבִיהֶם יָמִים רַבִּים וַיָּבֹאוּ אֶחָיו לְנַחֲמוֹ: וַיָּבֹא
אֶל־אִשְׁתּוֹ וַתַּהַר וַתֵּלֶד בֵּן וַיִּקְרָא אֶת־שְׁמוֹ בְּרִיעָה כִּי

Radak also considers the other possibility, that only Shuthelach is an actual son of Ephraim. The others each form a new generation.

21. וַהֲרָגוּם אַנְשֵׁי־גַת — *But the men of Gath ... killed them.* There are essentially four different ways in which the commentators deal with this obscure reference.

The problem is with the timing of this incident. Verse 22 makes it clear that it happened during Ephraim's lifetime. But Ephraim was certainly not among those who entered the Land of Israel. Quite apart from the problem of age — he had already been born when Jacob and his sons came to Egypt — we know that of all the people who were above twenty when they left Egypt only Joshua and Calev entered the land *(Radak).*[1] How then could this incident, which apparently took place in Israel [*The men of Gath (Philistia), natives of the land*], have taken place during his lifetime?

Ralbag offers the simplest explanation. בָּאָרֶץ, *of the land*, refers to Egypt. There was a colony of Philistines who had been born in Egypt, and some of Ephraim's sons raided this colony for cattle and were killed in the process. [This explains why *Numbers* 26:35 lists only three out of the nine sons mentioned here. The other six were killed on that occasion.]

The other commentators seem to reject the possibility of a Philistine colony in Egypt, feeling that the term *men of Gath* would only be used for those who lived in the Land of Israel.

To solve this problem *R' Yehudah HaChassid* suggests that even during the Egyptian exile the Pharaohs allowed Joseph's descendants to move freely between Egypt and Israel. Joseph had, after all, been a ruler of Egypt and out of respect

for his position his children were allowed freedoms denied the other tribes. Thus, while the incident certainly took place in Israel, it could well have happened during the early years of the exile. *R' Yehudah HaChassid* feels that this could serve to explain another difficulty in our passage. Verse 24 implies that Ephraim's daughter, Sheerah, built certain cities in Israel *after* this incident took place. Then, verses 25-27 proceed to list the five generations leading to Joshua, the conquerer of the Land. It is only possible that there were five generations between this incident and the conquest if indeed we pre-date the massacre to the early years of the exile.

Radak assumes that the incident must have taken place at the end of the forty years in the wilderness when the conquest of the eastern side of the Jordan took place. Ephraim must still have been alive at that time but died before the entry into the land. *Radak* suggests two possible explanations for the description, *who were born in the land.* It could refer to the Philistines and have the purpose of explaining the debacle. The Philistines who had been born there knew the land intimately and were able to defend it effectively against the invading Ephraimites who were unfamiliar with the terrain. Alternatively, he suggests that the phrase is a description of the Ephraimites. The Torah tells that Joseph was still alive in Egypt when Ephraim's grandchildren were born *(Genesis* 50:23). These descendants of Ephraim are described here as being *born in the land;* that is, the land of Egypt.

The Sages have a different tradition. [See *Targum* and *Yalkut Shimoni* here, and *Targum Yonason* to *Exodus* 13:17. All these are based on *Pirkei d'Rabbi Eliezer* 48.] At some point during the Egyptian exile, Genon, an Ephraimite, claimed that he had been sent by God to take the Jews

---

1. According to *Bava Basra* 121b, those who were already over sixty at the time that the spies were sent were not included in God's decree that the generation of the spies would not enter the land. Thus, it would have been possible for Ephraim to have entered if he had still been alive.

Tachath. 21 *And his son Zavad, his son Shuthelach, and Ezer and Elead. But the men of Gath, who were born in the land, killed them as they came down to carry off their cattle.* 22 *And their father Ephraim mourned over them many days, and his brothers came to comfort him.* 23 *And he came to his wife and she conceived and bore a son and he called his name Beriah, for she had come into his house*

out of Egypt. His tribesmen, who because they knew themselves to be of royal blood [they were destined to rule over the Northern Kingdom *(Radal,* comm. to *Pirkei d'Rabbi Eliezer)*] particularly chafed under Egyptian domination, followed him. Two hundred thousand of their number, relying on their military might (see *Psalms* 78:9), managed to escape from mighty Egypt, from which previously no slave had ever escaped. They thus anticipated the redemption by thirty years (see *Rashi, Sanhedrin* 92b and *Ramban, Exodus* 12:42). In doing so, they contravened the oath which Joseph's brothers had sworn to him (see *Mechilta* to *Beshalach)* that they would not attempt to leave Egypt before God would redeem them. When they did battle with the Philistines on their way into Israel they were defeated and a terrible slaughter took place. [See Section Two, p. 411.]

There is one opinion among the Sages that it was this debacle which caused God not to take Israel up to the Promised Land by the shortest and most direct route when He brought them out of Egypt. This route would have taken them through Philistia *(Exodus* 13:17), where the sight of the bones of their defeated brothers would have weakened their resolve and might have caused them to want to return to Egypt *(Shemos Rabbah* 20:10).

22. וַיִּתְאַבֵּל אֶפְרַיִם אֲבִיהֶם — *And their father Ephraim mourned.* This phrase places the incident described in the last verse during Ephraim's lifetime (see comm. to v. above).

וַיָּבֹאוּ אֶחָיו לְנַחֲמוֹ — *And his brothers came to comfort him. Metzudos* feels that the conjunction *vav* should, in this phrase, be translated as *in spite of* rather than as *and.* The sentence must be read as one thought. In spite of the fact that his brothers came to comfort him, Ephraim could not bring himself to stop mourning for many days.

Who were the brothers who came to comfort Ephraim?

Radak and *Metzudos* translate the word broadly, in the sense of kin rather than actual brothers. This, because we know of only one brother, Menasheh, for Ephraim. *Ralbag* thinks that Joseph may, in fact, have had additional sons. He bases this on *Genesis* 45:6 which seems to hint at other children whom Joseph was destined to bear. *Ramban* in his commentary there also expresses this opinion.

Malbim believes that *his brothers* refers to Ephraim's son, Shuthelach, mentioned in verse 20. According to *Malbim,* all the names mentioned in v. 20 after Shuthelach are his sons and descendants. All these were killed by the Philistines. Since that entire line was wiped out there was no one left to comfort the bereaved Ephraim except Shuthelach's brothers. The names of these brothers are not given.

23. וַיָּבֹא אֶל־אִשְׁתּוֹ — *And he came to his wife.* Most commentators assume this to refer to Ephraim. *Malbim,* though, believes that Shuthelach is meant. The Torah *(Numbers* 26:36), after listing Ephraim's sons and their families, goes on to say, *Now these are the sons of Shuthelach — Eran ...* No children of Ephraim's other sons are given. *Malbim* explains that עֵרָן, *Eran,* is the בְּרִיעָה, *Beriah,* of our verse. The root רַע, *evil* or *misfortune,* is changed around to עַר to avoid the negative connotation. When the Torah writes, *Now these are the sons of Shuthelach ...* the meaning is, *only* these. The others had been killed by the Philistines.

... — וַיִּקְרָא אֶת־שְׁמוֹ בְּרִיעָה כִּי בְרָעָה הָיְתָה בְּבֵיתוֹ *And he called his name Beriah, for she had come into his house in misfortune.* Ephraim gave his son the name Beriah because from the time he had taken Beriah's mother misfortune had dogged his house. His other children were killed after he had taken that wife *(Radak).*

כד בְרִיעָה הָיְתָה בְּבִיתוֹ: וּבִתּוֹ שֶׁאֱרָה וַתִּבֶן אֶת־בֵּית־חוֹרוֹן
כה הַתַּחְתּוֹן וְאֶת־הָעֶלְיוֹן וְאֵת אֻזֵּן שֶׁאֱרָה: וְרֶפַח בְּנוֹ וְרֶשֶׁף
כו וְתֶלַח בְּנוֹ וְתַחַן בְּנוֹ: לַעְדָּן בְּנוֹ עַמִּיהוּד בְּנוֹ אֱלִישָׁמָע
כז-כח בְּנוֹ: נוֹן בְּנוֹ יְהוֹשֻׁעַ בְּנוֹ: וַאֲחֻזָּתָם וּמשְׁבוֹתָם
בֵּית־אֵל וּבְנֹתֶיהָ וְלַמִּזְרָח נַעֲרָן וְלַמַּעֲרָב גֶּזֶר וּבְנֹתֶיהָ
כט וּשְׁכֶם וּבְנֹתֶיהָ עַד־עַיָּה וּבְנֹתֶיהָ: וְעַל־יְדֵי בְנֵי־מְנַשֶּׁה בֵּית־
שְׁאָן וּבְנֹתֶיהָ תַּעְנַךְ וּבְנֹתֶיהָ מְגִדּוֹ וּבְנוֹתֶיהָ דּוֹר וּבְנוֹתֶיהָ
ל בְּאֵלֶּה יָשְׁבוּ בְּנֵי יוֹסֵף בֶּן־יִשְׂרָאֵל: בְּנֵי אָשֵׁר
לא יִמְנָה וְיִשְׁוָה וְיִשְׁוִי וּבְרִיעָה וְשֶׂרַח אֲחוֹתָם: וּבְנֵי בְרִיעָה
לב חֶבֶר וּמַלְכִּיאֵל הוּא אֲבִי °בִרְזָוֶת: וְחֶבֶר הוֹלִיד אֶת־יַפְלֵט

°בִּרְזָיֶת ק'

24. בֵּית־חוֹרוֹן הַתַּחְתּוֹן וְאֶת־הָעֶלְיוֹן — *The lower and upper Beth Choron.* These cities are mentioned in *Joshua* ch. 16 as lying in Ephraim's territory. If *Numbers* 32:40, *And Moses gave Gilead to Machir the son of Menasheh …* is to be taken literally, then this would indicate that Machir was alive at the time of the conquest. Similarly, a daughter of Ephraim may also have been living then and she could well have built these cities. However, this would assume an inordinately old age for them, and both *Ibn Ezra* and *Ramban* to *Numbers* take *Machir* as an eponym — the name of the man standing for his family. If so, we assume that these cities were built long before the conquest of the land by Moses and Joshua. See comm. to v. 21.

אֻזֵּן שֶׁאֱרָה — *Uzzen Sheerah.* She gave her own name to the city which she built (*Mefaresh*). *Metzudos* thinks that there may have existed another city with the name Uzzen. She gave her own name to the city which she built to distinguish it from the other.

25. וְרֶפַח בְּנוֹ — *And his son Rephach.* 'His son' refers to Beriah [v. 23] (*Mefaresh; Metzudos; Gra; Malbim*). See below for *Radak's* view.

וְרֶשֶׁף וְתֶלַח בְּנוֹ — *And Resheph and his son Telach. Malbim* suggests that since all the names in our verse are joined by a *vav*, all may be assumed to be sons of Beriah. (See comm. to v. 20.) Laedan of v. 26 would then be a son of Tachan and the rest of the names till Joshua (v. 27) would each represent a new generation. In this view,

Joshua's genealogy would read: Joshua, Non, Elishama, Ammihud, Laedan, Tachan, Beriah, Ephraim. Other commentators (*Mefaresh; Metzudos; Gra*) think that each of the names in our verse also represents a different generation. If so, two generations — those of Telach and Rephach — must be added between Laedan and Beriah. *Malbim* notes that the interpretations given for the last few verses would be incompatible with the view of the Sages in *Sanhedrin* 92b that the Ephraimites left Egypt only thirty years before the Exodus. Since v. 23 implies that Beriah was born after that debacle there would not be time for all the generations between Beriah and Joshua to be born. According to that tradition, we would have to assume that Rephach and his descendants were not the children of Beriah, but that *And his son Rephach* refers to Shuthelach of v. 20. A careful reading of *Radak* could also yield that interpretation.

26. עַמִּיהוּד … אֱלִישָׁמָע — *Ammihud … Elishama. Numbers* 7:48 gives the prince of Ephraim as Elishama the son of Ammihud.

27. נוֹן בְּנוֹ יְהוֹשֻׁעַ בְּנוֹ — *His son Non, his son Joshua.* In the Torah, Joshua's father is known as Nun rather than Non. *Ibn Ezra* in his *Safah Berurah* proves from this that the *u* and *o* sounds are interchangeable in Hebrew.

In view of the truncated form of many of the genealogical tables we would not normally attach any significance to the fact that Ephraim's family is only traced to Joshua. Rather, we would assume that

in misfortune. ²⁴ And his daughter, Sheerah, built the lower and upper Beth Choron and Uzzen Sheerah. ²⁵ And his son Rephach, and Resheph and his son Telach, and his son Tachan. ²⁶ His son Laedan, his son Ammihud, his son Elishama. ²⁷ His son Non, his son Joshua. ²⁸ And their holdings and their dwelling places — Beth El and its dependencies, and to the east — Naaran, and to the west Gezer and its dependencies, and Shechem and its dependencies, up to Ayah and its dependencies. ²⁹ And close by to the sons of Menasheh — Beth Shean and its dependencies, Taenach and its dependencies, Megiddo and its dependencies, Dor and its dependencies. In these dwelled the sons of Joseph the son of Israel. ³⁰ The sons of Asher — Yimnah, Yishvah, Yishvi, Beriah, and their sister Serach. ³¹ And the sons of Beriah — Chever and Malkiel; he was the father of Birzaith. ³² And Chever fathered Yaphlet, Shomer,

because of Joshua's great importance his ancestry had to be traced but his children were of no particular significance. However, the Sages (Eruvin 63a, Pesachim 119b, and Megillah 14b) derive from the fact that the list stops here that Joshua died without any sons.

28. וַאֲחֻזָּתָם וּמֹשְׁבוֹתָם — And their holdings and their dwelling places. Metzudos thinks that these two words have essentially the same meaning. They are used here to describe Ephraim's towns.

בֵּית־אֵל וּבְנֹתֶיהָ ... — Beth El and its dependencies. ... Beth El is described as belonging to Joseph's descendants in Joshua 16:1. Naaran appears in Joshua 16:7 as Naarathah (Gra). Gezer is mentioned in 16:3 and Shechem in 20:7. According to Gra the four cities mentioned here describe the boundaries of the Ephraimite territories: Beth El to the south; Naaran to the east [וְלַמִּזְרָח נַעֲרָן] is to be translated, And to the east (of Ephraim) lay Naaran]; Gezer to the west and Shechem to the north.

Metzudos takes 'east' and 'west' as relating to Beth El. Naaran lay east of Beth El and Gezer lay to the west of Beth El.

עַד־עַיָּה וּבְנֹתֶיהָ — Up to Ayah and its dependencies. Minchas Shay points out that although some editions have עַזָּה [and some commentators seem to have had that reading — see Gra], the correct reading according to all sources is עַיָּה.

29. וְעַל־יְדֵי בְנֵי־מְנַשֶּׁה — And close by to the sons of Menasheh. Ephraim's territory described in the verse above was close to

that of his brother, Menasheh. Rashi to Numbers 2:17 explains that the expression עַל יַד [lit. near the hand] means close by in the sense that it describes the area to a person's side which he can reach with his hand.

בֵּית שְׁאָן ... — Beth Shean ... The four places mentioned here are all listed in Joshua 17:11. The name spelled דוֹר here is called דְּאר there.

בְּאֵלֶּה יָשְׁבוּ בְּנֵי יוֹסֵף — In these dwelled the sons of Joseph. The Ephraimites dwelled in the cities counted in the previous verse, the sons of Menasheh in the cities mentioned here (Mefaresh).

◄§ The Line of Asher

30⁻40. Ezra now turns to the genealogy of Asher. The sequence in which the tribes are dealt with has been discussed at the beginning of this chapter.

30. בְּנֵי אָשֵׁר ... — The sons of Asher ... Asher's children listed here, as well as Beriah's, are identical with those listed in Genesis 46:17.

31. הוּא אֲבִי בִרְזָיִת — He was the father of Birzaith. Mefaresh and Gra take Birzaith to be the name of a city. Gra adds that it would be an oil-producing region (זַיִת, an olive). The Anonymous Commentator thinks that it is the name of a person — בַּר זַיִת, one who has affinity to the olive — a fitting name for a man of the tribe of Asher which had been blessed by Moses that he would dip his foot in oil (Deuteronomy 33:24). This opinion is reflected in Bereishis Rabbah quoted by the Mefaresh.

לג וְאֶת־שׁוֹמֵר וְאֶת־חוֹתָם וְאֵת שׁוּעָא אֲחוֹתָם: וּבְנֵי יַפְלֵט

לד פָּסַךְ וּבִמְהָל וְעַשְׁוָת אֵלֶּה בְּנֵי יַפְלֵט: וּבְנֵי שֶׁמֶר אֲחִי

לה °וְרָהְגָּה ק' לה °וְרָהְגָּה יַחְבָּה וַאֲרָם: וּבֶן־הֶלֶם אָחִיו צוֹפַח וְיִמְנָע וְשֵׁלֶשׁ

לו-לז וְעָמָל: בְּנֵי צוֹפָח סוּחַ וְחַרְנֶפֶר וְשׁוּעָל וּבֵרִי וְיִמְרָה: בֶּצֶר

לח וָהוֹד וְשַׁמָּא וְשִׁלְשָׁה וְיִתְרָן וּבְאֵרָא: וּבְנֵי יֶתֶר יְפֻנֶּה

לט-מ וּפִסְפָּה וַאֲרָא: וּבְנֵי עֻלָּא אָרַח וְחַנִּיאֵל וְרִצְיָא: כָּל־אֵלֶּה

בְנֵי־אָשֵׁר רָאשֵׁי בֵית־הָאָבוֹת בְּרוּרִים גִּבּוֹרֵי חֲיָלִים רָאשֵׁי

הַנְּשִׂיאִים וְהִתְיַחְשָׂם בַּצָּבָא בַּמִּלְחָמָה מִסְפָּרָם אֲנָשִׁים

עֶשְׂרִים וְשִׁשָּׁה אָלֶף:

א וּבִנְיָמִן הוֹלִיד אֶת־בֶּלַע בְּכֹרוֹ אַשְׁבֵּל הַשֵּׁנִי וְאַחְרַח

ב-ג הַשְּׁלִישִׁי: נוֹחָה הָרְבִיעִי וְרָפָא הַחֲמִישִׁי: וַיִּהְיוּ בָנִים

ד לְבֶלַע אַדָּר וְגֵרָא וַאֲבִיהוּד: וַאֲבִישׁוּעַ וְנַעֲמָן וַאֲחוֹחַ:

There Birzaith is taken as a generic name rather than as the name of an individual. The daughters of Malkiel would marry either *Kohanim Gedolim* or kings, both of whom were anointed with oil upon their appointment to office. Asher's daughters were particularly beautiful because the abundance of oil in their territory made it possible to treat their skin in the most becoming manner.

34. Four sons are given for Shemer. אֲחִי in this verse is a proper noun.

35. וּבֶן־הֶלֶם אָחִיו — *And the son of his brother Helem. Metzudos* notes that וּבֶן, *the son of*, should be understood as though it were written וּבְנֵי, *the sons of*, since more than one son is listed. He further thinks that אָחִיו, *his brother*, means that Helem was the brother of each of the men listed in the previous verse. Thus, he assumes him to be a son of Shemer. However, the *Anonymous Commentator* and *Gra* both think that Helem is identical with Chotham in v. 32. *His brother* identifies him as a brother of Shemer in the previous verse. The *Anonymous Commentator* traces the association between the names. חוֹתָם, *Chotham*, derives from חתם, *to seal*, while הֶלֶם, *Helem*, derives from הלם, *to strike* (see e.g. *Judges* 5:26). Since a seal is used by bringing it down heavily on the paper the two names may well be interchanged. Four sons are given for Helem.

36-37. Eleven sons are given for Helem's son Tzophah.

38. וּבְנֵי יֶתֶר — *And the sons of Yether.* Yether is the Yithran of v. 37 (*Metzudos*).

39. וּבְנֵי עֻלָּא — *And the sons of Ulla.* Ulla has not been listed before. *Metzudos* suggests that he may be one of the people mentioned previously under a different name. *Gra*, as he has done frequently in these genealogical lists, suggests that the word וּבְנֵי, *the sons of*, does double duty. It is as though the text read as follows: And the son of Ara was Ulla, and the son of Ulla ...

40. בְּרוּרִים גִּבּוֹרֵי חֲיָלִים — *Select mighty warriors.* The genealogical records for Asher were apparently taken from army records (see below). The names mentioned here were all of people who were mighty warriors chosen for their valor.

We have bracketed בְּרוּרִים, *select*, together with the following phrase in accordance with *Targum* and *Radak*. It can also be treated as an adjective describing *heads of families*, that is, *select heads of families*, and this may be indicated by the *trop* (cantillation).

ברר, *to separate* or *select*, is used in the later Scriptural books where בחר might have been used in earlier books. *Targum* renders בְּחִירַיָּא.

וְהִתְיַחְשָׂם בַּצָּבָא בַּמִּלְחָמָה — *Their genealogies were traced in the army during the war. Kiddushin* 76b derives from our phrase that only such soldiers who could trace their genealogies were permitted to fight in

Chotham, and their sister Shua. ³³ And the sons of Yaphlet —
Pasach, and Bimhal, and Ashvath; these are the sons of Yaphlet.
³⁴ And the sons of Shemer — Achi, Rahgah, Chubbah, and Aram.
³⁵ And the son of his brother Helem — Tzophach, Yimna, Shelesh,
and Amal. ³⁶ The sons of Tzophach — Suach, Charnepher, Shual,
Beri, and Yimrah. ³⁷ Betzer, Hod, Shamma, Shilshah, Yithran, and
Beera. ³⁸ And the sons of Yether — Yephunneh, Pispa, and Ara.
³⁹ And the sons of Ulla — Arach, Channiel, and Ritzia. ⁴⁰ All these
were the sons of Asher, heads of families, select mighty warriors,
chiefs of the princes. Their genealogies were traced in the army
during the war; they numbered twenty-six thousand men.

And Benjamin fathered Bela his first-born, Ashbel the second and
Achrach the third. ² Nochah the fourth and Rapha the fifth.
³ Now Bela had sons — Addar, Gera, and Avihud. ⁴ And Avishua,

---

David's armies. When faced with dangers of battle, it was important that the soldiers should be able to rely upon the merit of their fathers. *Ramban (Deuteronomy 33:24)* points out that this description of Asher's descendants shows them to have been mightier and more valiant than any of the other tribes. He suggests that this qualitative advantage may have been contained in Moses' blessing there: *May Asher be blessed [more] than [the other] sons.*

VIII

◄§ The Tribe of Benjamin

This chapter is devoted to the genealogy of the tribe of Benjamin. [See pref. remarks to ch. 7 for a discussion of the sequence in which the tribes are treated.] In 7:6 we examined the question of whether the Benjamin mentioned there is an unknown Yissacharite, as some commentators assume, or, as is the opinion of most commentators, that there also the tribe of Benjamin is meant. This chapter must be studied in conjunction with the passage in ch. 7, together with the chart offered there. Some of the problems of our chapter have been discussed in the comm. there. Many commentators note that the detailed family lists given here for the tribe of Benjamin have as their purpose to establish a correct genealogy for King Saul, who is mentioned in verse 33.

1⁻2. Five sons are given for Benjamin. A glance at the chart in ch. 7 will show that Bela appears as the first-born on all four lists. Ashbel appears in (I), II and IV and commentators assume that Yediael [III(3)] is identical with Ashbel. He is called *the second* here, although according to (I) he was the third son. Since Becher [I(2)] is omitted here, in the context of our list Ashbel is, indeed, the second *(Radak)*.

Achrach appears to be the Echi of I(6) and the Achiram of II(6) *(Gra)*.

Gra writes that Nochah and Rapha are the Muppim [I(8)] and Chuppim [I(9)] of *Genesis* (or the Shephupham [II(8)]and Chupham [II(9)] of *Numbers*). He does not, however, indicate his source. It is possible that he assumes this identification

because that would make the five sons mentioned in our chapter identical with the five sons mentioned in *Numbers*.

Rashi (Numbers 26:13) quotes the Sages' answer to the problem of the five missing families in *Numbers*. According to that tradition, five Benjaminite families were wiped out in an internecine battle which took place in the wilderness. (See there for details.) This would also explain why only five families are mentioned here.

R' Shmuel ben Chofni, Gaon, explains the absence of five of the families mentioned in *Genesis* by stating that in *Chronicles* Ezra was interested only in such families as were large enough in number to have attained an independent standing. The other Benjaminite sons had families

ה־יז וְגֵרָא וּשְׁפוּפָן וְחוּרָם: וְאֵלֶּה בְּנֵי אֵחוּד אֵלֶּה הֵם רָאשֵׁי
ז אָבוֹת לְיוֹשְׁבֵי גֶבַע וַיַּגְלוּם אֶל־מָנָחַת: וְנַעֲמָן וַאֲחִיָּה
ח וְגֵרָא הוּא הֶגְלָם וְהוֹלִיד אֶת־עֻזָּא וְאֶת־אֲחִיחֻד: וְשַׁחֲרַיִם
הוֹלִיד בִּשְׂדֵה מוֹאָב מִן־שִׁלְחוֹ אֹתָם חוּשִׁים וְאֶת־בַּעֲרָא

which were too small to be considered in *Chronicles.*

3-5. Nine sons are given for Benjamin's oldest son, Bela. See 7:7 for a discussion of the problem that none of the names of Bela's sons given there seem to agree with the names given here. [See list B on the Benjaminite chart.]

Two names among these nine, Addar [list B:IV(1)] and Naaman [IV(2)], seem to be the same as those given for Bela's sons in *Numbers.* These names themselves seem to parallel the names which appear in the *Genesis* list under Benjamin's sons [list A:I(5) and (10)]. *Radak* suggests the possibility that the *Genesis* list contains the names of both sons and grandsons. The other possibility which *Radak* considers is that Bela may have given his children the names of their uncles. *R' Shmuel ben Chofni, Gaon,* agrees with this latter opinion. He rejects the other possibility because if, indeed, the *Genesis* list had contained both sons and grandsons, we would have expected the grandsons to be listed together. As it is, Naaman is number 5, and Ard is number 10 on that list.

The solution offered for the appearance of the names Addar (Ard) and Naaman among Bela's sons are also required to explain the name Gera [list B:IV(8)], who was also listed as the fourth son of Benjamin in the *Genesis* list. Similarly, if Shephuphan and Churam [13 and 14 on list B:IV] are identical with Shephupham and Chupham [A:II(8) and (9)], and Muppim and Chuppim [A:I(8) and (9)], one of the above solutions must be adopted.

6-7. These two verses are obscure, and a number of interpretations are possible. The only thing that can be said with certainty is that the inhabitants of Geva [apparently a Benjaminite city — see *Joshua* 18:24] were at one time exiled [or moved away — *Radak* below] from their city. Beyond this one point, the verses lend themselves to various interpretations.

6. וְאֵלֶּה בְּנֵי אֵחוּד — *And these are the sons*

of *Echud.* Who is Echud? *Radak* and *Metzudos* seem to assume that he is Bela under a different name. This, since the *heads of families* who were his sons seem to be identified as Naaman, Achiyah and Gera in verse 7 and these are given as Bela's sons in vs. 3-5. [אֲחִיָּה, Achiyah (v. 7), is assumed to be identical with אֲחוֹחַ, Achoach, of verse 4.]

The import of the verses, then, is that three of Bela's sons became chieftains in the Benjaminite city of Geva after moving the inhabitants of that city to Manachath. Manachath, to judge from 2:52 and 54 above, seems to have been a city in Judah. [It is not clear how the Benjaminite inhabitants of Geva could have been moved to a Judean city.]

In any event, reference is to an event of which there are no other extant records and its significance is lost to us.

Gra thinks that Echud is Bela's son Avihud from v. 3. He believes that the six names in vs. 4 and 5 are not sons of Bela but rather sons of Avihud, the last name mentioned in verse 3. Accordingly, וְאֵלֶּה, *and these are,* of our verse refers back to these just-mentioned six sons of Avihud-Echud and is a concluding description of that list. [This type of summation occurs frequently both in *Genesis* (10:20 and 32; 22:23; 25:4; to cite just a few) and throughout this book (see last verse of this chap.).] The next phrase is taken by *Gra* to mean that they served as family heads only in Geva. Later, however, they were exiled to the Judean city of Manachath by the three of these brothers mentioned in verse 7. Once more, the significance of this event is lost to us.

The *Anonymous Commentator* suggests an entirely original interpretation in the name of *R' Saadiah Gaon.* אֵחוּד, Echud, is not the name of a man but of a place. It refers to יְהֻד, Yehud, a city which, according to *Joshua* 19:45, belonged to the tribe of Dan. This city of Yehud lay far distant from the bulk of Danite cities and was situated at the border which Dan shared with Benjamin. The Benjaminite city of Geva (*Joshua* 18:24) was in the

Naaman, and Achoach. ⁵ And Gera, Shephuphan, and Churam.
⁶ And these are the sons of Echud — they were heads of families of
the inhabitants of Geva, and they made them move to Manachath.
⁷ And Naaman, Achiyah, and Gera, he made them move; and he
fathered Uzza and Achichud. ⁸ And Shacharaim fathered [children]
in the field of Moab from Shilcho Otham [and] Chushim and from

vicinity and, in time, the Danites from Yehud, cut off as they were from the main population center of their tribe, gravitated towards Geva and eventually became chieftains in that city.

The Benjaminite Geva also lay close to Ephraimite territory. [This can be seen from *Joshua* ch. 18, where Geva is listed together with Tzemaraim (v. 22). *II Chronicles* 13:4 identifies this city as belonging to Ephraim.] When the Assyrian king [referred to in verse 7 by the names Naaman, Achiyah and Gera] swept away the tribe of Ephraim together with the other tribes of the the Northern Kingdom, he took the inhabitants of Geva with him. Consequently, the Danites who had become chieftains in that city were taken into captivity together with its Benjaminite population.

The fact that the Danites and the Benjaminites were exiled together is expressed by the word מְנָחַת, which is a contraction of the two words מָנָה אַחַת, *one portion*. The implication is that the Danites and the Benjaminites shared one fate, i.e., they were taken to one place in the Assyrian exile and there remained neighbors with one another.[1]

וַיַּגְלוּם — *And they made them move.* Our translation follows *Radak* who points out that although גלה generally means *to go into exile*, it can also be used to describe simple movement from one place to another. [In his *Michlol* he compares this to *II Samuel* 15:19.]

אֶל־מָנָחַת — *To Manachath.* As explained above, the commentators offer two possible explanations of מְנָחַת. Most commentators (*Radak; Metzudos; Gra*) identify it as a city

in Judah, as may be seen from above 2:52,54. *R' Saadiah Gaon*, however, interprets it as a contraction of the words מָנָה אַחַת, *one portion*, i.e., they were exiled together to one place.

7. וְנַעֲמָן וַאֲחִיָּה וְגֵרָא — *And Naaman, Achiyah, and Gera.* All three names have been mentioned among Bela's sons [אֲחִיָּה, *Achiyah*, as אֲחוֹחַ, *Achoach*]. Either these three brothers made the inhabitants of Geva move (*Metzudos*), or they made the rest of their brothers move (*Gra*).

According to *R' Saadiah Gaon* these are names of an Assyrian king. [See above.]

הוּא הֶגְלָם — *He made them move.* The use of this phrase indicates that one of the three was the initiator. According to *Metzudos* it refers to Gera, the one mentioned last; *Gra* appears to have it refer to Naaman, the first in the list.

וְהוֹלִיד אֶת־עֻזָּא וְאֶת־אֲחִיחֻד — *And he fathered Uzza and Achichud.* The brother who initiated the move (see above) fathered these two children.

8. וְשַׁחֲרַיִם הוֹלִיד בִּשְׂדֵה מוֹאָב — *And Shacharaim fathered [children] in the field of Moab.* This Shacharaim is one of the descendants of Benjamin. As on numerous other occasions in *Chronicles*, his progeny is given although his ancestry is not. He went to dwell in Moab either because of a famine or for some other unknown cause (*Radak*).

הוֹלִיד ... מִן־שִׁלְחוֹ אֹתָם — *Fathered ... from Shilcho Otham.* The relationship in this verse and the next are obscure, and there are a number of different interpretations.

Radak and *Metzudos:* שִׁלְחוֹ אֹתָם, *Shilcho Otham*, is the name of one of Shacharaim's

---

1. This is one of the few extant interpretations explicitly ascribed to *R' Saadiah Gaon*. Besides its interest as an illuminating interpretation to an otherwise obscure passage, it sheds light on how this giant of the Geonic period viewed the text of the book of *Chronicles*.

Certainly, this explanation cannot be said to be conveyed by a simple reading of the text. There are too many assumptions of historical data which would be unknown even to readers of Ezra's own generation and the identification of those names in verse 7 as referring to Sennacherib would not be understood from the text. Nevertheless, *R' Saadiah Gaon* offers his explanation, not as a homiletical

ט נָשָׁיו: וַיּוֹלֶד מִן־חֹדֶשׁ אִשְׁתּוֹ אֶת־יוֹבָב וְאֶת־צִבְיָא וְאֶת־
י מֵישָׁא וְאֶת־מַלְכָּם: וְאֶת־יְעוּץ וְאֶת־שָׂכְיָה וְאֶת־מִרְמָה
יא אֵלֶּה בָנָיו רָאשֵׁי אָבוֹת: וּמֵחֻשִׁים הוֹלִיד אֶת־אֲבִיטוּב
יב וְאֶת־אֶלְפָּעַל: וּבְנֵי אֶלְפַּעַל עֵבֶר וּמִשְׁעָם וָשָׁמֶד הוּא בָּנָה
יג אֶת־אוֹנוֹ וְאֶת־לֹד וּבְנֹתֶיהָ: וּבְרִעָה וָשֶׁמַע הֵמָּה רָאשֵׁי
הָאָבוֹת לְיוֹשְׁבֵי אַיָּלוֹן הֵמָּה הִבְרִיחוּ אֶת־יוֹשְׁבֵי גַת:
יד־טז וְאַחְיוֹ שָׁשָׁק וִירֵמוֹת: וּזְבַדְיָה וַעֲרָד וָעָדֶר: וּמִיכָאֵל
יז וְיִשְׁפָּה וְיוֹחָא בְּנֵי בְרִיעָה: וּזְבַדְיָה וּמְשֻׁלָּם וְחִזְקִי וָחָבֶר:
יח־יט וְיִשְׁמְרַי וְיִזְלִיאָה וְיוֹבָב בְּנֵי אֶלְפָּעַל: וְיָקִים וְזִכְרִי וְזַבְדִּי:
כ־כא וֶאֱלִיעֵנַי וְצִלְּתַי וֶאֱלִיאֵל: וַעֲדָיָה וּבְרָאיָה וְשִׁמְרָת בְּנֵי
כב־כד שִׁמְעִי: וְיִשְׁפָּן וָעֵבֶר וֶאֱלִיאֵל: וְעַבְדּוֹן וְזִכְרִי וְחָנָן: וַחֲנַנְיָה
כה־כו וְעֵילָם וְעַנְתֹתִיָּה: °וּפְנִיאֵל וְיִפְדְיָה °וּפְנוּאֵל ק' בְּנֵי שָׁשָׁק: וְשַׁמְשְׁרַי

---

wives. The others were Chushim and Baara. The children are listed in verse 9 and onwards.

Mefaresh: Shacharaim is one of the men who moved away from Geva, as described in the previous two verses. At some point he was *sent away* from his place of exile *after which* (מִן שִׁלְחוֹ אֹתָם) he fathered children by his wives, named, respectively, Chushim, Baara, and Chodesh (v. 9).

Gra: Shacharaim is another son of Naaman (v. 7); that is, our verse is to be read as a direct continuation of the previous one. This Shacharaim had two wives, Chushim and Baara, whom he had divorced (שִׁלְחוֹ אֹתָם, *sent them away*) and subsequently remarried. In verse 9 we learn that he had children by his wife Chodesh. She is the Baara of our verse (since Chushim is mentioned in v. 11) who was called חֹדֶשׁ, *Chodesh* [from חָדָשׁ, *new*], because she was the first of the two to become his new wife when he remarried her.

The Sages (*Yerushalmi, Yevamos* 8:3) offer a homiletical interpretation to our verse which has it refer to Boaz and his efforts to establish the laws that Moabite women converts are permitted to marry Jewish men:

'Shacharaim is Boaz, who was unburdened [שַׁחֲרַיִם from חרר, *to be free*] by sin.

Fathered in the field of Moab means that he married Ruth the Moabite. *From Shilcho Otham,* he was descended from the tribe of Judah concerning whom it is written, *And he sent* (שָׁלַח), from שלח, *to send*] *Judah ahead of him ... to Goshen* (Genesis 46:28). *Chushim, Baara his wives* ... means that he hastened [חוּשִׁים from חש, *to hasten*] like a leopard and clarified [בַּעֲרָא related to באר, *to explain*] the halachah. And he fathered from his wife Chodesh ... for through her the law was renewed [חֹדֶשׁ from חדש, *to renew*] that [the Torah's prohibition against a Moabite convert marrying a Jew applies only to a] male Moabite but not to a female Moabite. See Section Two, p. 414.

חוּשִׁים — *Chushim.* One of the wives of Shacharaim. Her progeny is taken up in verse 11.

9. ... וַיּוֹלֶד מִן־חֹדֶשׁ אִשְׁתּוֹ — *And he fathered from his wife Chodesh* ... According to *Radak* and *Metzudos,* Chushim is another name for Shilcho Otham; according to *Gra,* she is Baara; according to *Mefaresh* she is yet another wife, previously unmentioned. See v. 8.

... אֶת־יוֹבָב — *Yovav* ... Seven sons are listed in this verse and the next. They were born to Shacharaim from his wife Chodesh.

10. אֵלֶּה בָנָיו רָאשֵׁי אָבוֹת — *These were his*

---

interpretation, but as the plain meaning the text wishes to convey.

The conclusion seems inevitable that R' *Saadiah Gaon* looked upon the text of *Chronicles,* or at least on the genealogical lists contained in the first nine chapters, as having a character of its own in which the meaning of the writer is not yielded as expressly and clearly as it is in other parts of Scripture. This concept has been discussed in detail in Appendix II and Overview.

Baara, his wives. 9 And he fathered from his wife Chodesh — Yovav, Tzivia, Mesha, and Malcam. 10 And Yeutz, Sachiah, and Mirmah — these were his sons, heads of families. 11 And from Chushim he fathered Avituv and Elpaal. 12 And the sons of Elpaal — Iver, Misheam, and Shemed; he built Ono and Lod and its dependencies. 13 And Beriah and Shema, they were the heads of the families of those who lived in Aiyalon. They put to flight the inhabitants of Gath. 14 And Achio, Shashak, and Yeremoth. 15 Zevadiah, Arad, and Eder. 16 And Michael, Yishpah, and Yocha, the sons of Beriah. 17 And Zevadiah, Meshullam, Chizki, and Chever. 18 And Yishmerai, Yizliah, and Yovav, the sons of Elpaal. 19 And Yakim, Zichri, and Zavdi. 20 And Elienai, Tzillethai, and Eliel. 21 And Adaiah, Beraiah, and Shimrath, the sons of Shimei. 22 And Yishpan, Ever, and Eliel. 23 And Avdon, Zichri, and Chanan. 24 And Chananiah, Elam, and Anthothiyah. 25 And Yiphdeiah and Penuel, the sons of Shashak. 26 And Shamsherai, Shechariah, and Athaliah.

sons, heads of families. All the sons of Shacharaim were significant enough to be considered heads of families.

11. ... וּמֵחֻשִׁים הוֹלִיד — And from Chushim he fathered ... Chushim was one of the wives mentioned in verse 8.

12. הוּא בָּנָה אֶת־אוֹנוֹ וְאֶת־לֹד — He built Ono and Lod. These two cities are mentioned in Nehemiah 11:35 as belonging to Benjamin.[1] Ezra 2:33 and Nehemiah 7:37 also speak of a man Ono who had a son Lod, but there is nothing in those texts to tie those people to Benjamin.

13. אַיָּלוֹן — Aiyalon. There were a number of different cities with the name Aiyalon in Israel. Joshua 21:24 speaks of one in the territory of Dan, while Judges 12:12 has one in Zevulun. Nowhere is an Aiyalon specifically identified as belonging to Benjamin, although II Chronicles 11:10 mentions Aiyalon among a group of cities identified as belonging to Judah and Benjamin.

הֵמָּה הִבְרִיחוּ אֶת־יוֹשְׁבֵי גַת — They put to flight the inhabitants of Gath. This refers to a historical event which has been lost to us.

14. ... וְאַחְיוֹ — And Achio ... From the ending of verse 16 it would seem that the names contained in vs. 14-16 are not of sons of Elpaal but of his son Beriah (v. 13) (Mefaresh). Although vs. 17 and 18 seem once again to be sons of Elpaal (see end of verse 18), Gra sees no difficulty. It could well be that certain grandsons of Elpaal were listed before his own sons because they were older. Or, sons of Elpaal may mean descendants (Metzudos).

16. בְּנֵי בְרִיעָה — Sons of Beriah. Beriah is given as a son of Elpaal in verse 13. See previous verse 14.

19⁻21. Verse 21 identifies the people mentioned in these verses as the sons of Shimei. Metzudos and Gra identify this Shimei with the Shema of verse 13. Thus we have here a listing of grandsons of Elpaal.

22⁻25. Verse 25 identifies the people mentioned in these verses as the sons of Shashak. Shashak is mentioned in verse 14 and, according to verse 16, he was a son of Beriah (v. 13). We have therefore in these verses great-grandsons of Elpaal.

26⁻27. Verse 27 identifies the people mentioned in these verses as the sons of Yerocham. Yerocham has not been mentioned before and Metzudos thinks that he may be one of the people who have already been listed under a different name.

1. Megillah 4a traces the history of these two cities. They were already flourishing in Joshua's days but were destroyed during the terrible internecine wars which raged between Benjamin and the other tribes in connection with the incident of the concubine in Giveah (Judges chs. 19-21). Thus, the sons of Elpaal did not originally build these cities but rebuilt them after their destruction. For halachic purposes they are deemed as having been walled cities from the time of Joshua.

כז וּשְׁחַרְיָה וַעֲתַלְיָה: וְיַעֲרֶשְׁיָה וְאֵלִיָּה וְזִכְרִי בְּנֵי יְרֹחָם:
כח אֵלֶּה רָאשֵׁי אָבוֹת לְתֹלְדוֹתָם רָאשִׁים אֵלֶּה יָשְׁבוּ
כט בִירוּשָׁלָם: וּבְגִבְעוֹן יָשְׁבוּ אֲבִי גִבְעוֹן וְשֵׁם אִשְׁתּוֹ
ל-לא מַעֲכָה: וּבְנוֹ הַבְּכוֹר עַבְדּוֹן וְצוּר וְקִישׁ וּבַעַל וְנָדָב: וּגְדוֹר
לב וְאַחְיוֹ וָזָכֶר: וּמִקְלוֹת הוֹלִיד אֶת־שִׁמְאָה וְאַף־הֵמָּה נֶגֶד
לג אֲחֵיהֶם יָשְׁבוּ בִירוּשָׁלַם עִם־אֲחֵיהֶם: וְנֵר הוֹלִיד אֶת־
קִישׁ וְקִישׁ הוֹלִיד אֶת־שָׁאוּל וְשָׁאוּל הוֹלִיד אֶת־יְהוֹנָתָן

Gra identifies him with Yevemoth (v. 14), the brother of Shashak.

וְאֵלִיָּה — *And Eliyah.* Radak quotes a Midrash which equates this Eliyah with Elijah the prophet. According to *Bereishis Rabbah* 71:9, there is a disagreement among the Sages whether Elijah was descended from Benjamin or from Gad [*Eliyahu Zuta* 15 has them arguing whether he was descended from Jacob's wife Rachel or from his wife Leah]. Those who claim that he was descended from Benjamin [Rachel] cite our verse, which deals with the progeny of Benjamin. See Section Two.

28. אֵלֶּה רָאשֵׁי אָבוֹת לְתֹלְדוֹתָם רָאשִׁים — *These are the heads of families, heads of their descendants.* Our translation follows the cantillation which makes a minor break after אָבוֹת and connects רָאשִׁים to לְתֹלְדוֹתָם. *Malbim* suggests that the meaning of our verse is to differentiate between the Benjaminites listed here and those listed at 9:7-9. Those are described as רָאשֵׁי אָבוֹת לְבֵית אֲבֹתֵיהֶם, *heads of families for their family units*, which makes them more important chieftains than those listed here who were heads only of their immediate descendants.

אֵלֶּה יָשְׁבוּ בִירוּשָׁלָם — *These lived in Jerusalem.* Jerusalem was partly within the borders of Judah and partly in Benjamin. Thus the Benjaminites mentioned here could well have lived in Jerusalem (*Radak*).

29-38. This section with minor changes is repeated in 9:35-44. The *Mefaresh* sees this as a prime example of his theory that Ezra used whatever sources were available to him to produce as complete a record as possible. When various sources were in contradiction with one another he would choose on the basis of the majority of manuscripts. However, in cases where the

sources varied by only minor differences, he would include both in his book. According to *Mefaresh*, our passage falls into this category (see Overview p. vii).

While in theory it is quite possible that the commentators agree with the basic premises of the *Mefaresh*, they have a different explanation for the repetition of our passage in ch. 9. As part of the Benjaminite genealogy it belongs in our chapter. It is repeated in ch. 9, however, because it describes the ancestry of King Saul, whose story is taken up in ch. 10.

29. וּבְגִבְעוֹן יָשְׁבוּ אֲבִי גִבְעוֹן — *And in Giveon lived the father of Giveon.* In 9:35 this chieftain is identified as Yeiel (*Gra*).

30. In 9:36 another name, נֵר, *Ner*, is given between Baal and Nadav. The family of this Ner is given in verse 33.

30. Chapter 9:37 has Zechariah for Zecher. In addition, it mentions a fourth son, Mikloth. He is not mentioned in our verse although his genealogy is taken up in verse 32.

Malbim points out that this can serve as a proof for the system which we have seen countless times in this book [particularly in the view of *Gra*], that the word at the beginning of a sentence may be meant to do double service in that it should be understood to refer also to the end of the previous verse. Thus in our case, *and Mikloth* at the beginning of verse 32 should also be read at the end of verse 31. Wherever this system has been used till now by the commentators, it was done on the basis of conjectures, without actual proof that was indeed the meaning of the verse. However, in our list, the comparison to the list in ch. 9 yields this explanation without any doubt.

32. The Shimah of our verse is called Shimam at 9:38.

וְאַף־הֵמָּה נֶגֶד אֲחֵיהֶם יָשְׁבוּ בִירוּשָׁלַם — *And they too lived with their brothers in Jerusalem.*

²⁷ *And Yaareshiah, Eliyah, and Zichri, the sons of Yerocham.*
²⁸ *These are the heads of families, heads of their descendants; these
lived in Jerusalem.* ²⁹ *And in Giveon lived the father of Giveon, and
the name of his wife was Maachah.* ³⁰ *And his first-born son was
Avdon; and Tzur, Kish, Baal, and Nadav.* ³¹ *And Gedor, Achio, and
Zecher.* ³² *And Mikloth fathered Shimah; and they too lived with
their brothers in Jerusalem, together with their brothers.* ³³ *And Ner
fathered Kish; and Kish fathered Saul; and Saul fathered Jonathan,*

Metzudos thinks that the נֶגֶד of our phrase
is equivalent to the עִם, *with*, of the next
phrase, which is merely a repetition for the
sake of emphasis. The meaning of the
whole verse is that although the main
dwellings of the people listed here were
located in Giveon (v. 29), they occasionally
came to Jerusalem to live there with their
brothers who were located permanently in
Jerusalem (v. 28).

Gra has a different interpretation for נֶגֶד.
In his view the people who lived in
Jerusalem — the most holy city in the land
— did so as representatives of all the people
who were not able to live there (see
ArtScroll comm. to *Ezekiel* 48:19). This is
the meaning of the first part of the phrase.
They lived in Jerusalem נֶגֶד, *in place of* their
brothers who were not able to do so. The
verse then goes on to say that in Jerusalem
they lived together with those other
Benjaminites mentioned previously. See
Pref. Remarks to ch. 9.

Malbim also prefers to assign different
meanings to the two phrases. He translates
נֶגֶד as *against*. The last two Benjaminites,
Mikloth and his son Shimah, lived in

Jerusalem together with the other Benjaminites who lived there, against the wish
of the rest of their family whose home was
in Giveon (v. 29).

33. וְנֵר הוֹלִיד אֶת־קִישׁ — *And Ner fathered
Kish.* See comm. to verse 30 that Ner was a
son of Yeiel who is mentioned in ch. 9 but
is omitted in our list. According to our
verse, Ner was the father of Kish who was
the father of Saul. But *I Samuel* 9:1 gives
Kish's father as Aviel. *Yerushalmi (Sheviis*
3:7) explains that while the real name of
Kish's father was indeed Aviel he was
given the name Ner [נֵר, *lamp*] because it
was his practice to light lamps in dark
streets so that people might be helped by
their light. In the merit of this good deed he
was rewarded that his grandson became
king.

וְשָׁאוּל הוֹלִיד ... — *And Saul fathered ...*
Scripture gives two other lists of Saul's
sons, one at *I Samuel* 14:49 (when Saul
became king), and another at 31:2 (there),
which gives the sons of Saul who died with
him on Mt. Gilboa.

I Samuel 14:49	I Samuel 31:2	Chronicles
יוֹנָתָן, Jonathan	יְהוֹנָתָן, Jonathan	יְהוֹנָתָן, Jonathan
יִשְׁוִי, Yishvi	אֲבִינָדָב, Avinadav	מַלְכִּי שׁוּעַ, Malki Shua
מַלְכִּי שׁוּעַ, Malki Shua	מַלְכִּי שׁוּעַ, Malki Shua	אֲבִינָדָב, Avinadav
		אֶשְׁבָּעַל, Eshbaal

Jonathan and Malki Shua are common to
all three lists. Of the four sons listed in
Chronicles, list 1 misses Avinadav and
Eshbaal but substitutes Yishvi, while list 2
misses only Eshbaal.

Radak assumes that the Yishvi of list 1 is

Avinadav. This would make lists 1 and 2
the same. Eshbaal is certainly the same as
Ish Bosheth,[1] the son who succeeded Saul
as king (*II Samuel* 2:8-9). List 2 mentions
only those sons of Saul who were killed
with him in battle. Eshbaal-Ish Bosheth,

---

1. Commentators point out that throughout Scripture names ending in בַּעַל, *baal*, such as אֶשְׁבָּעַל,
Eshbaal, are often changed to בּוֹשֶׁת, *bosheth*. Thus אֶשְׁבָּעַל, *Eshbaal* = אִישׁ בּוֹשֶׁת, *Ish Bosheth*. This,
because Baal was the name of an idol. In order to avoid mention of this idol, it was the practice to
change the name to בּוֹשֶׁת, *shame*. An example is the name יְרֻבַּעַל, *Yerubaal*, which was given to
Gideon (*Judges* 6:32). In *II Samuel* 11:21 it appears as יְרֻבֶּשֶׁת, *Yerubesheth*. *Radak* notes that we do
not know the reason why such a name would have been given to Saul's son in the first place.

לד וְאֶת־מַלְכִּי־שׁוּעַ וְאֶת־אֲבִינָדָב וְאֶת־אֶשְׁבָּעַל: וּבֶן־יְהוֹנָתָן
לה מְרִיב בָּעַל וּמְרִיב בַּעַל הוֹלִיד אֶת־מִיכָה: וּבְנֵי מִיכָה
לו פִּיתוֹן וָמֶלֶךְ וְתַאְרֵעַ וְאָחָז: וְאָחָז הוֹלִיד אֶת־יְהוֹעַדָּה
וִיהוֹעַדָּה הוֹלִיד אֶת־עָלֶמֶת וְאֶת־עַזְמָוֶת וְאֶת־זִמְרִי וְזִמְרִי
לז הוֹלִיד אֶת־מוֹצָא: וּמוֹצָא הוֹלִיד אֶת־בִּנְעָא רָפָה בְנוֹ
לח אֶלְעָשָׂה בְנוֹ אָצֵל בְּנוֹ: וּלְאָצֵל שִׁשָּׁה בָנִים וְאֵלֶּה
שְׁמוֹתָם עַזְרִיקָם ׀ בֹּכְרוּ וְיִשְׁמָעֵאל וּשְׁעַרְיָה וְעֹבַדְיָה וְחָנָן
לט כָּל־אֵלֶּה בְּנֵי אָצַל: וּבְנֵי עֵשֶׁק אָחִיו אוּלָם בְּכֹרוֹ יְעוּשׁ
מ הַשֵּׁנִי וֶאֱלִיפֶלֶט הַשְּׁלִשִׁי: וַיִּהְיוּ בְנֵי־אוּלָם אֲנָשִׁים
גִּבּוֹרֵי־חַיִל דֹּרְכֵי קֶשֶׁת וּמַרְבִּים בָּנִים וּבְנֵי בָנִים מֵאָה
א וַחֲמִשִּׁים כָּל־אֵלֶּה מִבְּנֵי בִנְיָמִן: וְכָל־

---

who succeeded his father to the throne, has no place in that list, since he did not at that time go out to war (see Gra).

Metzudos thinks that the Yishvi of list 1 is Eshbaal-Ish Bosheth. This would explain why he is not listed in list 2. Avinadav who appears in lists 2 and 3 may not have been born when Saul became king.

34. וּבֶן־יְהוֹנָתָן מְרִיב בָּעַל — And the son of Jonathan was Meriv Baal. From II Samuel 9:6 we know Jonathan's son as מְפִיבֹשֶׁת, Mephibosheth. Radak and Metzudos explain that Meriv Baal is another name for Mephibosheth, since Baal changes to Bosheth (see footnote to the previous verse). Radak thinks that Meriv [from ריב, quarrel, argument] and Mephi [from פֶּה, mouth] would also be related since speech is the prime source of argument. He was given this name because of some unrecorded incident.

35. Chapter 9 verse 41 has תַּחְרֵעַ, Tachrea, instead of תַּאְרֵעַ, Tarea, in our verse. Our verse lists אָחָז, Achaz, whose progeny is given in the next verse, while 9:41 does not list him, although verse 42 there lists his children. See there.

36. Chapter 9 verse 42 substitutes יַעְרָה, Yaerah, for יְהוֹעַדָּה, Yehoadah.

37. רָפָה בְנוֹ — His son Raphah. Raphah is the son of Bineah, Eleasah is the son of Raphah and Atzel is the son of Eleasah (Metzudos).

38. וּלְאָצֵל שִׁשָּׁה בָנִים — And Atzel had six sons. Pesachim 62b teaches: From the time

that the Sefer HaYuchasin [the midrash to Chronicles — Rashi] was hidden, the strength of the wise became weakened and their eyes darkened. Mar Zutra taught: Between Atzel [of our verse] and Atzel [of verse 9:44], there are sufficient homiletical interpretations to load up four hundred camels.

Even granting that four hundred camel-loads is גוּזְמָא, exaggeration, which forms an integral part of aggadic exposition [see Maharitz Chayos, Mevo HaTalmud ch. 30], it is nevertheless clear that the Sages had the tradition that there was a vast body of homiletical interpretation attached to the text of the genealogical lists. This Sefer HaYuchasin is not extant and, as we can see from the quotation from Pesachim 62b, the Sages bemoaned the wealth of insights which were thus denied them. [Some of the homiletical interpretations of the Sages have, of course, been preserved in various Talmudic and Midrashic sources, and these have been quoted in the course of the commentary.]

39. וּבְנֵי עֵשֶׁק אָחִיו — And the sons of his brother Eshek. The brother of Atzel (Metzudos; Gra). He was not counted among the sons of Motza (v. 37) because he was not as important as the others (Malbim).

40. ... בְנֵי־אוּלָם — And the sons of Ulam ... We know of no reason why the family list in our chapter is taken down to Ulam's sons and their descendants while the similar list in ch. 9 stops at Atzel's sons (Malbim).

Malki Shua, Avinadav, and Eshbaal. [34] *And the son of Jonathan was Meriv Baal; and Meriv Baal fathered Michah.* [35] *And the sons of Michah — Pithon, Melech, Tarea and Achaz.* [36] *And Achaz fathered Yehoadah; and Yehoadah fathered Alemeth, Azmaveth, and Zimri; and Zimri fathered Motza.* [37] *And Motza fathered Bineah; his son Raphah; his son Eleasah; his son Atzel.* [38] *And Atzel had six sons, and these are their names: Azrikam, Bocheru, Yishmael, Sheariah, Ovadiah, and Chanan; all these were the sons of Atzel.* [39] *And the sons of his brother Eshek — Ulam his first-born, Yeush the second, and Eliphelet the third.* [40] *And the sons of Ulam were men who were mighty warriors, bow-men, who had many sons and grandsons — one hundred and fifty. All these are from the sons of Benjamin.*

IX

◦§ The Returning Exiles

The genealogical lists which begin the book of *Chronicles* have been completed in the first eight chapters. The narrative section which will recount the history of the Jewish people from David's accession to the throne up to the destruction of the First Temple begins with ch. 10. Chapter 9, which contains a brief record of the settlement of Jerusalem in Ezra's time, seems to fit with neither section. Its historical setting postdates the end of *Chronicles'* historical record by many decades, and the people with whom it deals seem to have no connection with the families traced in the earlier genealogical lists. What, then, is the function of ch. 9 in the structure of the book of *Chronicles?*

Furthermore, the entire structure of *Chronicles* requires explanation. There seems to be little that connects the genealogical lists with which the book begins with the narrative section.

Ramban, in his *Sefer HaGeulah*, addresses these issues and provides not only the setting for ch. 9, but gives coherence to the structure of the entire book. The key to *Chronicles'* purpose, *Ramban* believes, is to be found in its final two verses: Cyrus' proclamation that whoever wished to might go up and begin the slow and painful reclamation of wasted and desolate Israel. The last two verses of *Chronicles* are the same two verses with which *Ezra* begins. This, as *Ramban* sees it, indicates that Ezra meant to make *Chronicles* a preface to his own book. The book of *Ezra*, the account of the שִׁיבַת צִיּוֹן, *the return to Zion*, is to be read against the background supplied by *Chronicles.*

This concept places chapter 9 — the brief account of the settlement of Jerusalem in Ezra's time — at the very center of the book. The genealogical lists, *Ramban* thinks, are given in order to supply the family background of the returnees who settled in Jerusalem and thus, they are as it were an introduction to this chapter. The historical survey contained in the rest of the book is there in order to tell their story up to the point at which the book of *Ezra* will pick it up.

Taken superficially, *Ramban's* suggestions leave two major questions unanswered:

Firstly, if indeed the genealogical lists are meant to provide background for the families which settled in Jerusalem, we would have expected that the names given in ch. 9 should be traceable to the earlier lists. This is not generally the case. Most of the names of the returnees given in ch. 9 (vs. 2-17) are not traceable to the families described in the earlier chapters.

Secondly the listings in ch. 9 require analysis. As the commentators point out, vs. 2-17 of our chapter are, with minor changes, the record of the inhabitants of Jerusalem given in *Nehemiah* ch. 11. But it is clear from the chronology of *Ezra* and *Nehemiah* that this list describes a state of affairs that obtained relatively late in the history of the period; that is, after the building and inauguration of the city wall by Nehemiah. At that time it was recognized that the sparsely occupied city was still too difficult to defend and consequently efforts were made tò encourage people who had settled in the outlying areas to move into the city. The list contained in our chapter describes the state of affairs at that time. Why would such a list have a place in *Chronicles* which, as we have seen from *Ramban*, is an *introduction* to the book of *Ezra*? Would the list of families who came up with Ezra such as the one given in *Ezra* ch. 2 not have been more appropriate? Moreover, why limit the list to the people who for one reason or another settled in Jerusalem when the listing in *Nehemiah* goes on to describe the settlement of the people throughout the Land?

Accepting *Ramban's* general delineation of the structure of the book[1] as our starting point, we must probe beyond it to find an answer to our questions. We must begin by asking why the particular historiography of *Chronicles* is a more appropriate background to the Book of *Ezra* than that of *Samuel* and *Kings*. As we have seen in the Overview *Chronicles* brings a perspective of its own to bear on the events which it describes — specifically, that it views events not from the context of the time in which they occurred but from the perspective of נֵצַח יִשְׂרָאֵל, *Israel's eternity*, as expressed in its Messianic destiny.

Why did *Ezra* require the one rather than the other? The answer would seem to lie in the high hopes which Ezra and his generation entertained that the modest beginnings of the return to Zion could be made to grow into the Messianic era *(Rashi to Ezekiel 43:11; see discussion at 11:17-20 in ArtScroll ed. p. 198)*. In the Overview, we suggested that his preoccupation with the genealogies was grounded in the teaching that the *Shechinah* rests only among such families in Israel as have a pure lineage (מִשְׁפָּחוֹת הַמְיוּחָסוֹת בְּיִשְׂרָאֵל) *(Kiddushin 70b)*. [Although the Sages teach that one of the five things lacking in the Temple was the *Shechinah*, had Israel risen to the challenge of the hour it might well have been different — and it was Ezra's hope that indeed it might be so.]

The era was pregnant with Messianic potential. The people were led by Zerubavel — scion of the Davidic line (see *Ezra* ch. 2 and above 3:19). Together with him was Yeshua the *Kohen Gadol*, scion of the Tzadokite line of *Kohanim Gedolim* in whom the prophet Ezekiel had seen the *Kehunah* of the Messianic era vested (see *Ezekiel* 44,15). Thus, there existed the triad which in Zechariah's visions *(Zechariah 4:1-8)* would combine to bring the Messianic light to the world — people, king and *Kohen*. It was towards this destiny that Ezra wished to educate his generation.

But there is yet a fourth element on which the Messianic vision focuses — the city of Jerusalem. The triumphant ending of Ezekiel's vision of the future concerns the sacred city from which the light of the Messiah will go out to the world (see ArtScroll *Ezekiel* 48:30ff).

This is the special place which Jerusalem occupies in Ezra's vision of the return to Zion. In 8:32 we saw that *Gra* renders the difficult phrase: וְאַף־הֵמָּה נֶגֶד אֲחֵיהֶם יָשְׁבוּ בִירוּשָׁלַיִם, *and they, too, dwelled in Jerusalem as representatives of their brothers*. This is reminiscent of the events described in *Nehemiah* 11:1ff, where lots were cast to determine which of the returnees would settle in Jerusalem, and of *Ezekiel* which tells of *the workers in the [sacred] city* who are to draw their sustenance from the rest of the people of Israel because they will act as representatives of the entire people in dwelling in the holy city. Life there will be a life of absolute sanctity in the one place on earth pervaded completely by the presence of God.

This is how the ninth chapter of *Chronicles* is to be understood. *Nehemiah*, in the parallel lists [see comm.], deals with the facts as they occurred — who settled in Jerusalem, under what circumstances, and who settled elsewhere. In *Chronicles*, however, Ezra takes the same historical events and blows the soul of eternity into them — the full settlement of Jerusalem is for him the focus of his story. It is to embody Israel's future and therefore, as we shall see below, he describes it specifically in terms of Israel's glorious past — sparing

---

1. *Ramban* himself notes in *Sefer HaGeulah* that he gives his explanation only in passing — the structure of the book of *Chronicles* is of only peripheral interest to the thesis which he develops there — and thus it is not surprising that his ideas focus only on the general outline rather than on the particulars which we have considered.

And all Israel had their genealogies registered — and they are recorded in the book of the kings of Israel; but Judah was exiled

no effort to cast the rather prosaic realities of the present in the mold of a majestic past which hid within itself the seeds of a splendid and resplendent future.

It may very well be that *Ramban's* meaning is not so much that the technical knowledge of which of these people belonged to which of the families in the previous chapters which is significant, as much as it is to know that those taking up residence in Jerusalem did so as representatives of a people whose lineage was impeccable. Their function was to reestablish the *Shechinah* in Israel, and for this purpose it was necessary to establish the genealogies of this reborn nation. It was only against such a background that the story which Ezra had to tell in his book was significant.

1. וְכָל־יִשְׂרָאֵל הִתְיַחְשׂוּ — *And all Israel had their genealogies registered.* Most commentators take this as a general remark, made in closing, concerning the genealogical tables contained in the first eight chapters. In contrast to Judah, who has been dealt with at great length, many tribes have been given only a cursory treatment; and some, like Zevulun and perhaps Dan (see comm. 7:12), have not been mentioned at all. Nevertheless, all the tribes kept meticulous genealogical records and their absence from this book is because they were lost when the Assyrian conquest swept away the Northern Kingdom. Most likely the exiles took their family records along with them, but these remained unavailable to Ezra. Whereas *Judah was exiled to Babylon* because of their sins, and therefore their records were available to Ezra in Babylon.

As noted in the prefatory remarks to this chapter, *Ramban* differs. He explains the genealogical tables as a means of establishing the lineage of the families which settled in Jerusalem when Ezra returned from Babylon. While, in the tradition of the Sages (see *Tosafos, Arachin* 32a, and see further below on verse 3), representatives from a number of tribes returned with the exiles, it is nevertheless true that only Judah and Benjamin returned in sufficient numbers to warrant their being treated as tribal units. Accordingly, our verse explains that the genealogies of the other tribes had been treated in a more superficial manner because only the two tribes (Benjamin and Judah) which were part of the kingdom of Judah (... הָגְלוּ וִיהוּדָה) were really significant to Ezra. They had been exiled to Babylon by Nebuchadnezzar and the second commonwealth was theirs. For this reason their genealogies are given in detail while those of the other tribes are of no significance to Ezra. He assumes that their family records accompanied them into exile.

There are many similarities — but also many differences — between our passage and *Nehemiah* 11:1-23 (see prefatory remarks). We shall note, and to some extent analyze, the similarities and differences in the commentary to the individual verses. As a general introduction it may be said that most commentators assume the two lists to be essentially the same, attributing the differences in names and numbers to the kind of discrepancies which we have noted throughout the book.

It must, however, be noted that in our case the differences are much more pronounced than in any of the other lists which we have analyzed. Perhaps it is because of this that *Malbim* strongly rejects this approach and claims that the two lists must be viewed as separate lists augmenting one another — not as different versions of the same list. As *Malbim* sees it the list in *Nehemiah* has the sole purpose of filling in details which for one reason or another are missing from the *Chronicles* list.

Since the other commentators make no real attempt to resolve the apparent discrepancies between the two lists, our commentary will be based, for the most part, on *Malbim's* approach.

2. For a proper understanding of this verse and the next, some background information is required. Many problems beset the original settlers in the Holy Land. Among them was the need to make Jerusalem a viable capital city for the fledgling nation. It was a large city with very few inhabitants and not many houses had been built since it had been laid waste (*Nehemiah* 7:4).

It was natural for the leaders of the people to make their houses in Jerusalem, but efforts were also made to have as many

ב וִיהוּדָה הָגְלוּ לְבָבֶל בְּמַעֲלָם: וְהַיּֽוֹשְׁבִים הָרִאשֹׁנִים אֲשֶׁר
בַּאֲחֻזָּתָם בְּעָרֵיהֶם יִשְׂרָאֵל הַכֹּהֲנִים הַלְוִיִּם וְהַנְּתִינִים:
ג וּבִירוּשָׁלַ͏ִם יָשְׁבוּ מִן־בְּנֵי יְהוּדָה וּמִן־בְּנֵי בִנְיָמִן וּמִן־בְּנֵי
ד אֶפְרַיִם וּמְנַשֶּׁה: עוּתַי בֶּן־עַמִּיהוּד בֶּן־עָמְרִי בֶּן־אִמְרִי בֶן־

as possible of the ordinary citizens move there. Accordingly, it was decided that one tenth of the population should take up residence there and lots were cast to determine who would be the ones to go (*Nehemiah* 11:1). In addition to those who had to go because they were selected by the lot, there were also those who voluntarily left the comfort of the countryside for the more congested condition of city life (see *Kesubos* 110b). The nation showed much gratitude to these volunteers (v. 2, there).

Nehemiah 11:3 goes on to say: *Now these are the heads of the community who settled in Jerusalem.* [Those that are listed there from verse 4 (equivalent to our verse 3) and onward (*Metzudos*).] *But in the cities of Judah people lived in their ancestral houses in their cities, Israelites, Kohanim ...* Dr. Raphael Breuer in his comm. to *Nehemiah* suggests that this interaction is meant to stress once more the heroism of the people who volunteered to shoulder the hardships of life in Jerusalem. In the other cities in Judah there were flourishing communities where all manner of people [Israelites, *Kohanim*, Nethinites ... (see below)] lived together in harmony. Nevertheless, there were people willing to give up those amenities for the hard life of pioneering a viable community in Jerusalem. Our verse is the parallel of that verse in *Nehemiah* and should be interpreted in the same vein.

וְהַיֹּשְׁבִים הָרִאשֹׁנִים ... — *Now the first settlers* ... This refers to the people who came up in the original wave of returnees with Zerubavel before Ezra's return (*Metzudos*). [The first wave of returnees was led by Zerubavel ben Shealtiel (*Ezra* 2:2). Ezra came to Israel at the head of the second wave some twenty-three years later (*Ezra* 7:1ff).]

בַּאֲחֻזָּתָם — *In their holdings.* אחז is *to grasp* or *take possession.* It is used often to describe land owned by virtue of inheritance and thus might mean here that the settlers had returned to the land which had belonged to their respective families before

the exile (*Metzudos* to *Nehemiah* and *Malbim*). *Metzudos* here seems to interpret otherwise: Each one settled in the land which he [now] *grasped* or *took possession of.*

בְּעָרֵיהֶם — *In their cities.* That is, in cities other than Jerusalem.

יִשְׂרָאֵל — *Israelites.* Israelites from all the ten tribes. These were individuals from among the exiled tribes who, for reasons of their own, had settled among Judah and Benjamin and were therefore taken to Babylon. Their numbers were never large enough to form tribal units of their own (*Metzudos*). *Ramban* (*Sefer HaGeulah*) makes clear that although there is a tradition among the Sages that many of the Assyrian exiles were brought back by Jeremiah during Yoshiah's (Josiah's) reign (*Yalkut Shimoni, Melachim* 248), these did not remain permanently. Eventually they drifted back to join their tribes. Consequently they were not among the returnees from Babylon. See, however, *Tosafos* to *Gittin* 36a who believes that Jeremiah brought back actual tribal units and that these did share the Babylonian exile and later returned with these exiles. Still, *Tosafos* stresses that not all the Assyrian exiles returned, and we may assume that those who did were relatively few in number. Thus no detailed accounting of them was warranted.

הַכֹּהֲנִים הַלְוִיִּם — *The Kohanim, the Levites.* As it stands this phrase would be understood as Levites being a description of *Kohanim.* This form occurs many times in Scripture. [For a list, see *R' David Cohen's Ohel David*, part I.] However, the text in the parallel passage in *Nehemiah* reads הַכֹּהֲנִים וְהַלְוִיִּם, *the Kohanim and the Levites,* and that is how *Targum* here renders it. It therefore seems likely that our phrase is a shortened form and should in fact be translated: *The Kohanim and the Levites.*

וְהַנְּתִינִים — *And the Nethinites.* These were descendants of the Giveonites, a group

to Babylon because of their faithlessness. ² Now the first settlers, who were in their holdings in their cities, were Israelites, the Kohanim, the Levites, and the Nethinites. ³ Now in Jerusalem there settled from the sons of Judah and from the sons of Benjamin and from the sons of Ephraim and Menasheh. ⁴ Uthai, the son of Ammihud, the son of Omri, the son of Imri, the son of Bani, from

belonging to the seven Canaanite nations whom Joshua had been commanded to destroy. They deceived Joshua into thinking that they were a foreign people, thereby convincing him to allow them to convert and join the nation of Israel. Joshua swore to them that they would come to no harm, but later, upon learning of the deception, he condemned them to eternal servitude as wood-choppers and drawers of water in the Temple (see *Joshua* chapter 9).[1]

These Nethinites, although Jewish, were forbidden to intermarry with the regular Jewish population. [There are differences among the authorities whether this prohibition is a Biblical one or whether it stems from a Rabbinic decree.] In general they lived a segregated existence because leaders from David to Ezra felt that their ethical and moral standards were such that it would be best if they did not mingle more than necessary with the regular population.[2]

In addition to the groups mentioned in our verse, *Nehemiah* lists also בְּנֵי עַבְדֵי שְׁלֹמָה, *sons of Solomon's servants*. These, according to *Yevamos* 16b, were a group of powerful nobles of gentile origin who had served as servants to Solomon and who had in the course of time married Jewish women. They had apparently become an identifiable group since they occur frequently in *Ezra* and *Nehemiah*. The thesis propounded in the prefatory remarks may explain why they are not mentioned in *Chronicles*. The thrust of *Chronicles* is to describe the community of settlers in Jerusalem who could form the nucleus around which the Messianic future could build. Our verse tells that many of the people who could have been involved in this Jerusalemite community instead

settled in the outlying cities. In this context the Nethinites, who were to function as Temple servants, have a place but not the *sons of Solomon's servants*. They are, however, mentioned in *Nehemiah* since that book is concerned with the historical realities rather than with the essential dynamics of the times.

3. וּבִירוּשָׁלַם ... וּמִן־בְּנֵי אֶפְרַיִם וּמְנַשֶּׁה — *Now in Jerusalem ... from the sons of Ephraim and Menasheh.* The parallel list in *Nehemiah* 11:4 leaves out Ephraim and Menasheh. Their numbers were too insignificant to warrant special mention, as can be seen from the fact that even *Chronicles*, which does record their presence, does not give any individual names as it does for Judah, Benjamin and the *Kohanim* and Levites.

The mention of people from Ephraim and Menasheh confirms that although only Judah and Benjamin went into the Babylonian exile as tribal units, there were nevertheless members of other tribes who had chosen to live among them before the exile (see *II Chronicles* 15:9 and 34:9), and who therefore went into exile with them (see *Rambam, Sefer HaGeulah*).

Nevertheless, we should ask why *Chronicles* thought it important to mention the presence of those people. It may well be that this too can be explained by the thesis suggested in the prefatory remarks. The community which Ezra wished to build up in Jerusalem required representatives of the entire nation. Judah, Benjamin, *Kohanim* and Levites were all to some degree involved in the Temple. Ephraim and Menasheh provided at least a minimal representation of the tribes of the Northern Kingdom.

4. עוּתַי בֶּן־עַמִּיהוּד ... — *Uthai, the son of*

1. The expression used there is וַיִּתְּנֵם יְהוֹשֻׁעַ בַּיּוֹם הַהוּא חֹטְבֵי עֵצִים ..., *and on that day Joshua condemned them to be wood-choppers ...* וַיִּתְּנֵם derives from the root נתן, *to give* or *place*, and, as a result, these Giveonites and their descendants were known as נְתִינִים, *Nethinites.*

2. For background material concerning the events which led to the Nethinites' somewhat degraded standing among the Jewish people, see *Yevamos* 78b and *Yerushalmi Kiddushin* 4:1.

° פְּנֵי מִן ק'

ה ק° בְּנֵימִן־בְּנֵי פֶרֶץ בֶּן־יְהוּדָה: וּמִן־הַשִּׁילוֹנִי עֲשָׂיָה הַבְּכוֹר
ו וּבָנָיו: וּמִן־בְּנֵי זֶרַח יְעוּאֵל וַאֲחֵיהֶם שֵׁשׁ־מֵאוֹת וְתִשְׁעִים:
ז וּמִן־בְּנֵי בִּנְיָמִן סַלּוּא בֶּן־מְשֻׁלָּם בֶּן־הוֹדַוְיָה בֶּן־הַסְּנֻאָה:
ח וְיִבְנְיָה בֶּן־יְרֹחָם וְאֵלָה בֶן־עֻזִּי בֶּן־מִכְרִי וּמְשֻׁלָּם בֶּן־
ט שְׁפַטְיָה בֶּן־רְעוּאֵל בֶּן־יִבְנִיָּה: וַאֲחֵיהֶם לְתוֹלְדֹתָם תְּשַׁע
מֵאוֹת וַחֲמִשִּׁים וְשִׁשָּׁה כָּל־אֵלֶּה אֲנָשִׁים רָאשֵׁי אָבוֹת

Ammihud. The first name listed in *Nehemiah* 11:4 is עֲתָיָה בֶן עֻזִּיָה. The name עֲתָיָה is sufficiently close to עוּתַי, *Uthai*, and the name of one of his progenitors, אֲמַרְיָה, is sufficiently close to the אִמְרִי, *Imri*, of our verse, that we must assume עֲתָיָה and עוּתַי to be the same man. *Malbim* explains the discrepancies between the lineage of two lists by assuming that Ezra in *Chronicles* and Nehemiah in *Nehemiah* were working from different records. Ezra's list was incomplete and Nehemiah, from sources available to him, filled in names which Ezra had not known, but did not find it necessary to repeat those names which Ezra had already recorded. Accordingly the word בֶן is not to be taken as son but as descendent (as has been noted many times in this book).

The following list makes *Malbim's* opinion clear.

Chronicles	Nehemiah
עוּתַי, Uthai	עֲתָיָה, Athaiah
עֲמִיהוּד, Ammihud	
עָמְרִי, Omri	
	עֻזִּיָה, Uzziah
	זְכַרְיָה, Zechariah
אִמְרִי, Imri	אֲמַרְיָה, Amariah
בָּנִי, Bani	
	שְׁפַטְיָה, Shephatiah
	מַהֲלַלְאֵל, Mahalalel
פֶרֶץ, Peretz	פֶרֶץ, Peretz

5. ... וּמִן־הַשִּׁילוֹנִי — *And from the Shilonite ...* I.e., a descendent of Judah's son Shelah *(Metzudos)*. Of this Shilonite family, the one who settled in Jerusalem was the first-born of this family, Asaiah, and his sons. *Nehemiah* 11:5 tells of a

מַעֲשֵׂיָה, *Maaseiah,* whom it traces back six generations to Shiloni. *Malbim* explains that עֲשָׂיָה and מַעֲשֵׂיָה are the same person. Whereas Ezra in *Chronicles* was satisfied simply to state that he was descended from Shiloni, Nehemiah supplied some of the names of the intervening generations.

6. וּמִן־בְּנֵי זֶרַח יְעוּאֵל — *And from the sons of Zerach — Yeuel.* We have now had descendants from all three of Judah's sons who did not die childless (see 2:2): Peretz (v. 4), Shelah (v. 5), and Zerach.

Nehemiah makes no mention of any descendants of Zerach. This may be because there were probably too few Zerachites to be numerically significant (see *Malbim* below). Symbolically, however, their presence was important. Each of Judah's three sons had a specific role to play in the historical process. [Peretz, of course, was progenitor of the royal line. The roles of Zerach and Shelah have been discussed in Section Two to ch. 2.] Thus, if Judah is to play an important part in being host to the *Shechinah,* it must be in his totality as represented by all facets of his progeny. Thus, the paucity of Zerachites which could keep their mention out of the factual listings in *Nehemiah* could not stand in the way of their being mentioned in *Chronicles.*

שֵׁשׁ־מֵאוֹת וְתִשְׁעִים — *Six hundred and ninety.* Verse 6 in *Nehemiah* reads: *All the sons of Peretz who dwelled in Jerusalem [numbered] four hundred and sixty-eight men of quality.* *Metzudos* thinks that the number 690 in our verse refers to the families of Yeuel (from Shelah's son) and Asaiah (from Zerach's son), while the number given in *Nehemiah* refers only to the sons of Peretz. *Malbim's* opinion is that our number of 690 includes all of Judah's descendants. *Nehemiah* adds only the clarification that of these 690, 468 came from Peretz.

7. ... וּמִן־בְּנֵי בִּנְיָמִין סַלּוּא בֶּן־מְשֻׁלָּם — *And from the sons of Benjamin — Sallu, the son*

the sons of Peretz the son of Judah. ⁵ And from the Shilonite —
Asaiah the first-born and his sons. ⁶ And from the sons of Zerach —
Yeuel; and their brothers — six hundred and ninety. ⁷ And from the
sons of Benjamin — Sallu, the son of Meshullam, the son of
Hodaviah, the son of Hassenuah. ⁸ And Yivneyah the son of
Yerocham; Elah, the son of Uzzi, the son of Michri; and Meshullam,
the son of Shephatiah, the son of Reuel the son of Yivneyah. ⁹ And
their brothers according to their generations nine hundred and fifty-

---

of Meshullam ... Our verse gives
Meshullam as a 'son' of Hodaviah.
Nehemiah 11:7 also mentions a Sallu the
son of Meshullam but then mentions six
generations of ancestors not mentioned
here. As before, *Malbim* explains that
Nehemiah found records which filled in
those generations between Meshullam and
Hodaviah.

8. This verse lists three men of whom
there is no mention in *Nehemiah*. See next
verse.

9. וַאֲחֵיהֶם לְתוֹלְדֹתָם — *And their brothers
according to their generations.* The
brothers of Sallu, Yivneyah, Elah, and
Meshullam who were the descendants of
the same ancestors as these four men. [The
two pronouns *their* stand for two different
groups of people: The first, to the four
Benjaminites who had been listed as
dwellers in Jerusalem; the second to the
fathers (i.e., ancestors) of these four men
who had also been mentioned in vs. 7-8
(*Metzudos*).][1] Thus, the meaning of the
verse is — their *kinsmen*, i.e., their relatives
from among their (extended family).

תְּשַׁע מֵאוֹת וַחֲמִשִּׁים וְשִׁשָּׁה — *Nine hundred
and fifty-six.* Verse 8 in *Nehemiah* reads:
*And after him [Sallu] Gabbai Sallai — nine
hundred and twenty-eight.* We thus have a
discrepancy of twenty-eight. If we were to
assume that this is the number contributed
by the three men mentioned in our v. 8 who
do not appear in *Nehemiah* (*Malbim*), this

would leave a very small number for each
of those three families.

Radak (Nehemiah) suggests that the
number given in *Nehemiah* refers only to
the family of Gabbai Sallai who is not
mentioned at all in *Chronicles*, while the
number here refers to the families of the
four Benjaminites mentioned here. Thus,
there is no need to correlate the two
numbers.

But why would a family that was
significant to Nehemiah not be mentioned
in *Chronicles* and, conversely, why were
the three men mentioned in our v. 8 not
important to Nehemiah?

This might tend to confirm the thesis
suggested in the prefatory remarks — that
the two books may have different foci of
interest. It is eminently possible that from
the political standpoint (*Nehemiah*),
Gabbai Sallai occupied a more significant
role, while from the point of view of
populating Jerusalem so that it might once
more become a resting place for the
Shechinah (Chronicles), the other Benjaminite families were important.

That the relative importance of various
people could vary with the perspectives of
the two books may be illustrated from the
following: *Nehemiah* (v. 9) speaks of a
יְהוּדָה בֶּן הַסְּנוּאָה, *Yehudah the son of
Hassenuah*, who was second in command
over the city — evidently an important
functionary. Now it seems evident that he
is the same as הוֹדַוְיָה בֶּן הַסְּנָאָה, *Hodaviah the
son of Hassenuah*,[2] who is mentioned in
our v. 7, not in his own right but only as an

---

1. אָח, *brother*, is a noun formed from the root אחה, *to bind* or *tie together*. It can therefore be used to
describe many different types and degrees of relationship.

A careful reading of a number of listings in the *Chronicles* and *Nehemiah* chapters with which we
are dealing show a tendency to give a group of names and then to follow that with, ... וַאֲחֵיהֶם. [For
Chronicles see vs. 6, 9, 13, 17 and 25; for *Nehemiah*, vs. 12, 14 and 19.] In a number of these cases it
seems possible that the meaning is *colleagues* [cf. *Nehemiah* vs. 12 and 19]. If so, it would be
reasonable to expect that where actual family is meant, this would be underlined.

2. The name הוֹדַוְיָה, *Hodaviah*, is the same as יְהוּדָה, *Yehudah*, with the *yud* shifted from the
beginning of the name to the middle and a *vav* added. This name change occurs elsewhere. Cf. *Ezra*
2:40 and 3:9.

י לְבֵית אֲבֹתֵיהֶם: וּמִן־הַכֹּהֲנִים יְדַעְיָה וִיהוֹיָרִיב

יא וְיָכִין: וַעֲזַרְיָה בֶן־חִלְקִיָּה בֶּן־מְשֻׁלָּם בֶּן־צָדוֹק בֶּן־מְרָיוֹת

יב בֶּן־אֲחִיטוּב נְגִיד בֵּית הָאֱלֹהִים: וַעֲדָיָה

ancestor of Sallu. Evidently his important role was of no significance to *Chronicles*.

כָּל־אֵלֶּה ... — *All these ...* The simplest interpretation of the phrase would be to say that *all men* refers to the four Benjaminites identified by name and that the sense is that these four were the family heads of the various family units into which the nine hundred and fifty-six people were divided.

אֲנָשִׁים — *Men.* Men of importance (*Metzudos*).

רָאשֵׁי אָבוֹת — *Family heads. Targum* equates this with רָאשֵׁי בֵית אָבוֹת.

לְבֵית אֲבֹתֵיהֶם — *Of their families.* I.e., the family units of the nine hundred and fifty-six men — see above.

⏤§ **The Returning Kohanim**

10. וּמִן־הַכֹּהֲנִים — *And from the Kohanim.* Verse 2 had taught that *Kohanim* were

among the settlers in the outlying cities. We now learn that some of these also settled in Jerusalem.

יְדַעְיָה וִיהוֹיָרִיב וְיָכִין — *Yedaiah, Yehoiariv and Yachin.* Nehemiah (v. 10) gives: יְדַעְיָה בֶן־יוֹיָרִיב יָכִין, *Yedaiah the son of Yoiariv, Yachin,* telling us that Yedaiah was a son of Yoiariv but also leaving out Yehoiariv in his own right. There were only two *Kohanim* of significance: Yedaiah [son of Yoiariv] and Yachin.

Chronicles lists Yehoiariv in his own right. Once more we see the phenomenon discussed in the previous verse. From the political perspective (*Nehemiah*), Yoiariv the father of Yedaiah was unimportant. In the context of the settlers who readied Jerusalem to be focus for the *Shechinah* (*Chronicles*) he was significant.[1]

11. The list contained in this verse occurs, with minor changes, four times in Scripture.

(1) Chronicles 5:38-41	(2) Ezra 7:1-2	(3) Chronicles 9:11	(4) Nehemiah 11:11
אֲחִיטוּב, *Achituv*	אֲחִיטוּב, *Achituv*	אֲחִיטוּב, *Achituv*	אֲחִיטוּב, *Achituv*
		מְרָיוֹת, *Meraioth*	מְרָיוֹת, *Meraioth*
צָדוֹק, *Tzadok*	צָדוֹק, *Tzadok*	צָדוֹק, *Tzadok*	צָדוֹק, *Tzadok*
שַׁלּוּם, *Shallum*	שַׁלּוּם, *Shallum*	מְשֻׁלָּם, *Meshullam*	מְשֻׁלָּם, *Meshullam*
חִלְקִיָּה, *Chilkiyah*	חִלְקִיָה, *Chilkiyah*	חִלְקִיָּה, *Chilkiyah*	חִלְקִיָּה, *Chilkiyah*
עֲזַרְיָה, *Azariah*	עֲזַרְיָה, *Azariah*	עֲזַרְיָה, *Azariah*	שְׂרָיָה, *Seraiah*
שְׂרָיָה, *Seraiah*	שְׂרָיָה, *Seraiah*		
יְהוֹצָדָק, *Yehotzadak*			

1. All three names of our verse appear among the *mishmares* (watches) of *Kohanim* listed in ch. 24. [Yedaiah is number 2, Yehoiariv is number 1, and Yachin is number 21.] We might therefore be inclined to see our verse as a listing not of individuals but of families — representatives of the respective *mishmaros* of Yedaiah, Yehoiariv and Yachin.

However, a close reading of the books of *Ezra* and *Nehemiah* yields that many of the individual *Kohanim* of that era carried names identical with those of the original *mishmares* [cf. חָרִם (3); מַלְכִּיָּה (5); מִיָּמִן (6); אֲבִיָּה (8); שְׁבַנְיָה (10); בִּלְגַּי (15); אִמֵּר (16); מַעַזְיָה (24) among the signers of the אֲמָנָה, covenant organized by Nehemiah (*Nehemiah* ch. 10)]. We therefore have no real reason to assume that the listing here does not refer to individuals.

In this connection, though, the following points are noteworthy:

(1) The three *Kohanim* listed in our verse, if indeed they are individuals, were obviously among the most important *Kohanim*. Nevertheless, not one of these three is listed among the signatories.

(2) Nehemiah (12:1ff) lists the *Kohanim* who came back to the land together with Zerubavel and Yehoshua the *Kohen Gadol* — that is, those who comprised the first wave of the returnees: Among them we find: אֲמַרְיָה [= אִמֵּר (16)] (v. 2); מַלּוּךְ [= מַלְכִּיָּה (5)] (v. 2); רְחֻם [possibly a conversion of חָרִם (3)] (v. 3); שְׁבַנְיָה (10) (v. 3); מַלְכִּיָּה (5) (v. 2); בִּלְגָּה (15) (v. 5); מִיָּמִן (6) (v. 5); אֲבִיָּה (8) (v. 4); מִיָּמִין (6) (v. 5); יְדַעְיָה (2) (v. 6); יוֹיָרִיב (1) (v. 6). יָכִין, who is listed here among the important *Kohanim*, does not appear on that list; nor does עֲזַרְיָה [our v. 11, although his father חִלְקִיָּה may be the one mentioned in *Nehemiah* v. 7 and מְרָיוֹת, his ancestor, may be the אֲמַרְיָה of v. 2 there], or עֲזָיָה [our v. 12, although his father יְרוֹחָם may be the רְחֻם of v. 3 there and his great-grandfather מַלְכִּיָּה is probably the מַלּוּךְ of v. 2 there],

six. All these were men who were family heads of their families. [10] *And from the Kohanim — Yedaiah, Yehoiariv and Yachin.* [11] *And Azariah, the son of Chilkiyah, the son of Meshullam, the son of Tzadok, the son of Meraioth,. the son of Achituv, governor of the*

In spite of the similarity between lists (1) and (2) on the one hand and lists (3) and (4) on the other they cannot be the same. The שְׂרָיָה, Seraiah, of lists (1) and (2) is, according to the tradition of the Sages, the Kohen Gadol who functioned at the end of the First Temple (see 5:40) who was murdered by Nebuchadnezzar at Rivlah (II Kings 25:18-21). Thus he cannot be the man who was a Temple functionary in Ezra's time at the beginning of the Second Temple. By the same token, Azariah of our verse [list (3)] cannot be the Azariah of lists (1) and (2) since that Azariah was a Kohen Gadol during Yehoiakim's reign during the period of the First Temple (see comm. to 5:39) and could also not be meant here. Thus, despite the similarities in the names of their ancestors we must conclude that while the Azariah and Seraiah of lists (1) and (2) are Kohanim Gedolim at the end of the First Temple, the Azariah of list (3) and the Seraiah of list (4) are different people who served in the early years of the Second Temple.

As can be seen from list (4), Nehemiah substitutes Seraiah for Azariah. Both Gra and Malbim assume these to be two different names for the same man. If the thesis which we have suggested a number of times is true — that Nehemiah deals with the politically important personalities while Chronicles is interested in those who contributed towards the establishment of Jerusalem as focus for the Shechinah — then the following seems possible:

Nehemiah 10:3 lists both a Seraiah and an Azariah among the signatories of Nehemiah's covenant who were Kohanim. They may well have been brothers — both sons of Chilkiyah — see below — who both held the position of נְגִיד בֵּית הָאֱלֹהִים, Governor of the House of God, at different times. The one may have been an important political figure, the other more

significant as a religious head. For this reason, Nehemiah lists one while Chronicles lists the other.

Malbim (to Nehemiah) suggests that Azariah/Seraiah of lists (3) and (4) are indeed descendants of Chilkiyah (all lists), not through the line of Azariah and Seraiah of lists (1) and (2), but through a different son. If so, the genealogical lists from Chilkiyah and up are indeed identical in all four lists, and the assumptions made in fn. to v. 10 concerning the ancestry of Azariah and the generation spread among the Jerusalem settlers would be incorrect. In fact, they would all belong essentially to the same generation.

However, it must be said that from the textual viewpoint that if this is indeed the case, Chronicles is very misleading by giving Azariah as a son of Chilkiyah in both its lists (1 and 3) while having two different people in mind.

From this point of view it might be better to explain as follows: Among the returnees we find a Kohen by the name of Chilkiyah (Nehemiah 12:7); a Kohen by the name of Meshullam (Nehemiah 10:8); a scribe Tzadok who from the context also appears to have been a Kohen (Nehemiah 13:13 — based on the cantillation there); and a Kohen called Meremoth (Nehemiah 12:3) who is later referred to as Meraioth (v. 15) there. It is evident that these names were popular in the Kohanic families. It is even conceivable that the names in our verse refer to these returnees and that a series of names which had occurred much earlier within this same family was repeated either by coincidence or by design in later generations. As a glance at the list of Kohanim Gedolim at 5:30-41 will show, not only were the same names constantly repeated but also the repetition of a block of three names — see there where 9, 10 and 11 are repeated in the same order in 15, 16 and 17.

נְגִיד בֵּית הָאֱלֹהִים — Governor of the House of God. This cannot mean the position of Kohen Gadol, since that was held by Yehoshua the son of Yehotzadok in Ezra's time (Malbim).

or מַעֲשַׂי [our v. 12, although his ancestor אִמֵּר is probably the אֲמַרְיָה of v. 2 there].

(3) If indeed the יְהוֹיָרִיב and יְדַעְיָה of our verse are the same as the men of that name mentioned in Nehemiah ch. 12 as suggested above, and moreover, the מַלְכִּיָּה and מְרָיוֹת and אִמֵּר given in the next two verses are also identical with the names in that Nehemiah list, then we have a remarkable spread of generations among the Jerusalem settlers. The men mentioned in vs. 11 and 12 would be several generations removed from the ones mentioned in our verse. See comm. to v. 11.

בֶּן־יְרֹחָם בֶּן־פַּשְׁחוּר בֶּן־מַלְכִּיָּה וּמַעְשַׂי בֶּן־עֲדִיאֵל בֶּן־

יג יַחְזֵרָה בֶּן־מְשֻׁלָּם בֶּן־מְשִׁלֵּמִית בֶּן־אִמֵּר: וַאֲחֵיהֶם רָאשִׁים

לְבֵית אֲבוֹתָם אֶלֶף וּשְׁבַע מֵאוֹת וְשִׁשִּׁים גִּבּוֹרֵי חֵיל

יד מְלֶאכֶת עֲבוֹדַת בֵּית־הָאֱלֹהִים: וּמִן־הַלְוִיִּם שְׁמַעְיָה

טו בֶן־חַשּׁוּב בֶּן־עַזְרִיקָם בֶּן־חֲשַׁבְיָה מִן־בְּנֵי מְרָרִי: וּבַקְבַּקַּר

There must certainly have been many other positions in the hierarchy of the Temple. In *Jeremiah* 20:1 we find one Pashchur described as פְּקִיד נָגִיד בְּבֵית ה'. Apparently, as part of his position of authority, we find him jailing Jeremiah for a perceived crime, and so too we find the function of פְּקִידִים described as entailing the physical restraining of people prophesying in a crazed ecstasy (*Jeremiah* 29:26).

12. ... וּמַעְשַׂי ... וַעֲדָיָה — *And Adaiah ... and Masai ...* See comm. to v. 13.

13. וַאֲחֵיהֶם ... אֶלֶף וּשְׁבַע מֵאוֹת וְשִׁשִּׁים — *And their brothers ... one thousand seven hundred and sixty.* Nehemiah, instead of giving a total at the end of the listing of all the *Kohanim*, gives separate numbers for each of the three mentioned: For Seraiah [Azariah], 822; for Adaiah, 242; and for Amashsai, 128. If we add these numbers we get 1192, which is 568 short of the number given here.

Malbim's solution is that despite the similarity of their names, Masai of our verse and Amashsai of *Nehemiah* are two different people and that the larger number is the sum for four, not three, families. However, for this to be true we would have to assume that *Chronicles* adds into its totals a family which it did not even mention. Furthermore, the great similarity between the names of their respective ancestors points strongly to Masai and Amashsai being the same person.

Perhaps the thesis we have suggested throughout this chapter may serve to explain the discrepancy in numbers. *Nehemiah* may only have been concerned with politically significant functionaries while *Chronicles* takes into account even less public figures who could have played an important role in the religious life of the people.

רָאשִׁים לְבֵית אֲבוֹתָם — *Heads of their families.* It seems unlikely that all seventeen

hundred and sixty men were family heads. The text in *Nehemiah* may throw light upon the true meaning of this verse. We have already noted that in *Nehemiah* the totals for each of the three families of *Kohanim* are given separately. In addition, a different category seems to be assigned to each:

For Seraiah/Azariah v. 12 there adds: וַאֲחֵיהֶם עֹשֵׂה הַמְּלָאכָה לַבַּיִת, *And their brothers performed the service of the House;* for Adaiah: וְאֶחָיו רָאשִׁים לְאָבוֹת, *And his brothers, heads of families;* for Amashsai/Masai: וַאֲחֵיהֶם גִּבּוֹרֵי חָיִל, *And their brothers, accomplished experts.* Similarly, there are three categories mentioned in our verse: רָאשִׁים לְבֵית אֲבוֹתָם, *heads of their families;* גִּבּוֹרֵי חַיִל, *accomplished experts;* מְלֶאכֶת עֲבוֹדַת בֵּית־הָאֱלֹהִים, *in the performance of the service of the House of God.* Though from our text they would all seem to apply to the total number of people mentioned, the text in *Nehemiah* strongly indicates that they are, in fact, to be broken down into various groups. Only 242 (v. 13) are heads of family units.

The fact that *Nehemiah* breaks the information down into the units described above, assigning a particular number and function to each name, while *Chronicles* just gives the totals and a general description of the functions filled, may serve to bear out the thesis which we have suggested. In the *Nehemiah* perspective the focus is the position and by whom and in what way it was filled. The description of the settlement is made up of just such details. In *Chronicles* it is the people rather than the positions who are important. It is they who welcome the *Shechinah* into their midst.

We find a similar difference in approach in the Levite listings in the next few verses — see below.

גִּבּוֹרֵי חַיִל — *Accomplished experts.* This term, which is more frequently used to

House of God. ¹² *And Adaiah, the son of Yerocham, the son of Pashchur, the son of Malkiyah; and Masai, the son of Adiel, the son of Yachzerah, the son of Meshullam, the son of Meshillemith, the son of Immer.* ¹³ *And their brothers, heads of their families, one thousand seven hundred and sixty — accomplished experts in the performance of the service of the House of God.* ¹⁴ *And from the Levites — Shemaiah, the son of Chashuv, the son of Azrikam, the son of Chashaviah, from the sons of Merari.* ¹⁵ *And Bakbakkar,*

describe military heroes, is used here for the *Kohanim* and their activities in the Temple. גבור, from גבר, *to be strong*, is usually translated *hero*. This does not fit in our context, where it seems to mean someone who commands whatever skills and attributes are necessary in a given context, in this case the Temple service. See comm. 5:24.

As explained above, only some of the *Kohanim* are described in *Nehemiah* as גבורי חיל, *accomplished experts*, and this seems to point to some particular quality or expertise for this general term. Its precise connotation in this context is lost to us.

מְלֶאכֶת עֲבוֹדַת בֵּית־הָאֱלֹהִים — *In the performance of the service of the House of God.* Both מְלָאכָה and עֲבוֹדָה can be used to describe physical work. We have translated according to the meaning apparent from the context. מְלָאכָה, which most often means *work*, can also describe any kind of activity (*Psalms* 107:23) or *sphere of concern* (*Exodus* 22:6). עֲבוֹדָה is often used to describe the sacred Temple service.

⋖§ The Levites and their Stations

14. שְׁמַעְיָה ... — *Shemaiah ... Nehemiah* (v. 15) has the identical listing except that it takes the lineage up one more stage — to Buni. *Malbim* (*Nehemiah*) notes that both Chashaviah and Buni appear among Merari's descendants in 6:30, 31 respectively. He suggests that *Nehemiah* adds Buni because he was the better known.

But this would mean that the Chashav-

iah of our verse is the one mentioned in 6:30, an ancestor of Ethan, the chorister of David's time — that is, a man who lived many centuries earlier. Yet *Ezra* 8:19 speaks of a Merarite Chashaviah contemporary with himself, and there is a Levite Buni signed on Nehemiah's covenant (*Nehemiah* 9:4), which makes it likely that Shemaiah's grandfathers mentioned in our verse and in *Nehemiah* are Levites from the early period of the return.[1]

Since in v. 15 a descendant of Asaph the chorister is mentioned who is himself described as a chorister in *Nehemiah* 11:17, and in v. 16 we have descendants from the chorister Yeduthun and also a man whose home was in Netophathi which, as it appears from *Nehemiah* 12:28 was settled by Levite choristers, it seems likely that all the Levite's mentioned here, including Shemaiah of our verse, were מְשׁוֹרְרִים, *choristers*. The listing of the Levite gatekeepers begins in v. 17.

מִן־בְּנֵי מְרָרִי — *From the sons of Merari.* Although we have deduced that Shemaiah was a chorister, his lineage is not traced to any of the original choristers but simply to the founder of this Levite family — Merari. This, in contrast to Mattaniah in the next verse who is traced to Asaph [the Gershonite chorister — see 6:24ff] and Ovadiah of v. 16 who is traced to Yeduthun — the Merarite contemporary of Asaph. *Nehemiah* does not even make the point that Shemaiah was a Merarite.[2]

15. וּבַקְבַּקַּר ... וּמַתַּנְיָה ... — *And Bakbakkar*

---

1. This would be another instance of names being repeated within the same dynasty (see comm. to v. 11).

We have yet much to learn concerning the confluence of names among the Levite dynasties. We meet up with associations which seem to go beyond the likelihood of coincidence:

Thus, Chashaviah is not only the name of an ancestor of the Merarite chorister Ethan but also a son of the chorister Yeduthun (25:3) [who apparently replaced Ethan at some later date; see 16:41]. In the list of Yeduthun's sons Chashaviah follows Yishaiah. Again in *Ezra* 8:19 we have Ezra being joined by several Merarite Levites — the two mentioned by name are Chashaviah and Yishaiah.

2. In this section all three major Levite families are represented among the dwellers of Jerusalem. Descendants of Asaph of Gershom, and Yeduthun of Merari, are mentioned in vs. 15 and 16.

טז חֶרֶשׁ וְגָלָל וּמַתַּנְיָה בֶּן־מִיכָא בֶּן־זִכְרִי בֶּן־אָסָף: וְעֹבַדְיָה
בֶּן־שְׁמַעְיָה בֶּן־גָּלָל בֶּן־יְדוּתוּן וּבֶרֶכְיָה בֶן־אָסָא בֶּן־
יז אֶלְקָנָה הַיּוֹשֵׁב בְּחַצְרֵי נְטוֹפָתִי: וְהַשֹּׁעֲרִים שַׁלּוּם וְעַקּוּב

... and Mattaniah ... These would seem to be identical with the Mattaniah and Bakbukiah of Nehemiah (v. 17).[1]

חֶרֶשׁ וְגָלָל — Cheresh and Galal. The name Cheresh does not recur in Scripture and Galal only in the next verse as an ancestor of Ovadiah. If indeed they were important people it is surprising that they do not appear in one of the many Levite listings contained in Chronicles, Ezra and Nehemiah. Perhaps they appear under other names in these lists — possibly Shabbathai and Yozavad of Nehemiah 11:16.

... וּמַתַּנְיָה — And Mattaniah ... See Nehemiah 11:17 for a description of Mattaniah's function in the Temple service.[2]

בֶּן־זִכְרִי בֶּן־אָסָף — The son of Zichri, the son of Asaph. Nehemiah has זַבְדִּי, Zavdi, instead of Zichri. At 25:2 Asaph's son is given as זַכּוּר, Zaccur, and this could be the Zichri of our verse. However, we also find a Zaccur among the signatories of the covenant (Nehemiah 10:13), and it is possible that he is the ancestor referred to here.

16. ... וְעֹבַדְיָה — And Ovadiah ... Ovadiah is עַבְדָּא, Avda, in the Nehemiah account.

וּבֶרֶכְיָה ... הַיּוֹשֵׁב בְּחַצְרֵי נְטוֹפָתִי — And Berechiah ... who lived in the towns of the Netophathites. Berechiah is not mentioned in Nehemiah and we must assume that within that context he was not significant. The fact that he lived in the towns of the Netophathites indicates that he was one of

the Levite musicians (see Nehemiah 12:28). [Metzudos thinks that the descriptions ... who lived ... must refer to Elkanah, the grandfather, rather than to Berechiah himself since he is listed here among the dwellers in Jerusalem.]

17-27. The following verses list the Levite gatekeepers and their positions. In these lists we notice an unusual phenomenon: Verse 17 lists the four heads of the gatekeepers in Ezra's time. Verse 18 then tells us that this was a continuation of the system that had already obtained in the First Temple from David's time onwards. Verses 19 and 20 there made reference to the guarding of the sacred precincts during Moses' time in the desert. [See Gra in comm. to v. 18.] Verse 22 once more ties the arrangements of various Levite cadres to antiquity by associating them with David's and Samuel's ordinances. And verse 24 can really only be understood as a reference to the desert encampment (see comm. there).

What could be the meaning of the constant interplay between these three periods?

We can best understand this on the basis of Ramban's comments (Numbers 1:53 and glosses to Seder HaMitzvos, Positive Command 36) that the gatekeepers of the Temple era were, so to speak, the direct halachic descendants of the Levite encampments around the Tabernacle in the wilderness. That which in the wilderness took the form of the camping of the three Levite families around the Tabernacle with Moses, Aaron and his sons filling the

---

Shallum of v. 17 is likely either identical with or a representative of the Shallum of v. 19 (see comm. to v. 17) — a Kahathite through his descent from Korach.

It should also be noted that, against our expectations, Chronicles occasionally traces different people within the same grouping to various stages of antiquity. Thus in II Chronicles ch. 29 we have Elitzaphan, Asaph (v. 13), and Heman and Yeduthun (v. 14) given as ancestors together with Gershom, Kehath and Merari (v. 12).

1. Nehemiah assigns particular functions to the various Levites [Mattaniah is described there as the one to lead off the prayers, with Bakbukiah second to him] while Chronicles does not. This may be explained by the suggestion made in the commentary to v. 13. Nehemiah, in line with his perspective, is concerned with the formal role which people played within the community. Chronicles is concerned with the person himself.

2. Mattaniah is another name which appears again and again within the same clan. Thus we have an Asaphite Levite of that name in the ancestry of Yachaziel — a contemporary of King Yehoshaphat (II Chronicles 20:14) and again in Chizkiah's days (29:13, there). See comm. to v. 11 and fn. to v. 14.

Cheresh and Galal; and Mattaniah, the son of Michah, the son of Zichri, the son of Asaph. ¹⁶ And Ovadiah, the son of Shemaiah, the son of Galal, the son of Yeduthun; and Berechiah, the son of Asa, the son of Elkanah, who lived in the towns of the Netophathites. ¹⁷ And the gatekeepers — Shallum, Akkuv, Talmon, and Achiman;

eastern position *(Numbers* 3:38) was later represented by the שֹׁעֲרִים, *gatekeepers.*

Ramban's opinion may be borne out by the form in which the Torah tells of the Levite positions around the Tabernacle. These were assigned in the context of their responsibilities for the various components of the Tabernacle. Thus, for example, the Gershonites were to camp to the west — and were to carry the various cloth components *(Numbers* 3:23-26); the Kehathites were to camp in the south — and their responsibilities were the utensils, and so on. Thus, the position in which they camped seems also to have been a function of their serving capacity.

Thus we have a single continuum, a thread running from the antiquity of the desert encampment, through the glories of Solomon's Temple to the muted and modest realities of the return to Zion. And it was important to Ezra to stress this continuum.

The theme which so clearly Ezra sought to perpetuate may be understood as follows: The nationhood of Israel has focus and direction. At its center lies its most precious spiritual possession — embodied in the Holy Ark ensconced in the inner sanctum of the Temple — or, even as it was in the second commonwealth, in the empty Holy of Holies which, in its very devastation, reminded Israel of a more glorious past and thereby beckoned it towards a more resplendent future.

It was the function of the Levites to stand guard over this focal point of Israel's

nationhood. Through the reestablishment of the Levite *mishmaros* (watches) with their intimations of the past, Ezra sought to confirm the new settlement in Jerusalem as the seed containing Israel's Messianic future.

17. וְהַשֹּׁעֲרִים — *And the gatekeepers.* Rambam in *Klei Mikdash* (3:12) states: The entire progeny of Levi is set aside for Temple service ... It is a positive command that the Levites be unencumbered and prepared for the service of the Temple whether they wish to be or not ... Their duty is to guard the Temple. Some of them are to be gatekeepers to open the gates of the Temple and to close its doors. And some of them are to be choristers, to accompany the daily sacrifices with song ...[1]

Our v. 17 lists four gatekeepers: Shallum, Akkuv, Talmon, and Achiman who, together with their *brothers*, guarded the Temple. Shallum is the leader. In v. 26 these four men are described as גִּבֹּרֵי הַשֹּׁעֲרִים, *the outstanding gatekeepers*, an exceedingly unusual expression which appears to place their position in a very special category.

Ezra 2:42 lists six families of gatekeepers who came with him to the land of Israel: The sons of: Shallum, Ater, Talmon, Akkuv, Chatita and Shovai. Thus, three of our four are mentioned there with Achiman missing. Shallum is listed first there which seems appropriate since, as we learn in our verse, he was a leader.[2]

Against this background we are struck by the

1. The pattern of listing שֹׁעֲרִים, *gatekeepers*, apart from the general grouping of Levites is a recurring one in the books of *Ezra* and *Nehemiah*. Thus, for example, *Ezra* 2:40ff, which parallels *Nehemiah* 7:43ff and gives the list of returnees who came with Ezra, lists *Levites* in v. 40; מְשֹׁרְרִים, *choristers* in v. 41 and שֹׁעֲרִים, *gatekeepers* in v. 42.

This could be explained on the basis of *Taanis* 17a and *Tosefta* to *Taanis* 2:2 from which it transpires that not every *Kohen* was allotted to a *mishmar* but that some were left free to augment whichever one was in need of their help (see Rambam, glosses to *Sefer HaMitzvos*, Positive Command 36). In the same way it may be that Levites, too, were left unmentioned.

This could perhaps help to explain the cryptic verse at *Nehemiah* 12:25 where, according to the simple meaning, Mattaniah, Bakbukiah and Ovadiah seem to be listed as gatekeepers although in the commentary above we recognized them as musicians. Since they are given as *Levites* it is possible that they functioned in different capacities at different points of their lives. They may have been musicians at one time and gatekeepers at another.

2. Since the *Ezra* listing talks of *sons of* ..., we must assume that the names given there are names of families or clans. Thus, Shallum, Akkuv, and Talmon are family names. In our verse they appear as individuals. Perhaps when *Ezra* talks of *sons of* ..., he means that these descendants came with their

ט יח וְטַלְמֹן וַאֲחִימֶן וַאֲחִיהֶם שַׁלּוּם הָרֹאשׁ: וְעַד־הֵנָּה בְּשַׁעַר

יכ־יט יט הַמֶּלֶךְ מִזְרָחָה הֵמָּה הַשֹּׁעֲרִים לְמַחֲנוֹת בְּנֵי לֵוִי: וְשַׁלּוּם

Nehemiah parallel to our verse. Nehemiah 11:19 has: The gatekeepers Akkuv and Talmon and their brothers who guard the gates … That only two out of the four are given is not problematic. We have seen throughout this section that the two books do not always list the same people and various explanations have been put forth for this. But it is difficult to understand why Shallum is not mentioned though he was the leader.

שֹׁעֲרִים from שַׁעַר, gate, means gatekeepers. The gatekeepers, however, were also assigned other functions. Thus we have שֹׁעֲרִים (gatekeepers) at 15:23 and 24 preceding and following the Ark to make sure that no unauthorized person approach.

Moreover, from our vs. 26-32 it is clear that the gatekeepers [in contrast to the choristers who were relieved of any other duties — see v. 33] had many other areas of jurisdiction assigned to them. Apparently, the שַׁעַר is less specifically a gatekeeper than a general Temple functionary. They assumed all the varied roles assigned to the Levites in the wilderness.

18⁻26. Nehemiah does not have this entire section. Its account of the Jerusalem settlers ends with the verse parallel to our v. 17. The very fact that Chronicles attaches this section to the list of the settlers puts the entire list into an entirely different perspective. Because the thrust of this passage is continuity — the identification of different generations of Temple function-aries into one body of Levitic guardianship of all that is holy to Israel — the indication is that the Jerusalem lists, too, have continuity as their hallmark. The returnees to Jerusalem are the link between Israel's historic past and Messianic future.

Radak seems to underline this theme of continuity by tying together the הֵמָּה הַשֹּׁעֲרִים, they are the gatekeepers, of v. 18 with the הֵמָּה יִסַּד דָּוִיד וּשְׁמוּאֵל הָרֹאֶה בֶּאֱמוּנָתָם, it is they whom David and Samuel the Seer established for all time of v. 22. We shall examine the meaning of these phrases within the context of the verses in which they occur, but in the broad view of the passage as a whole the meaning seems to

be: These [four guards of Ezra's time] are the [very embodiment of] gatekeepers of earlier times, they are the ones whom David and Samuel the Seer established as a permanent fixture. The people have changed but they are like the skin cells of a human body which continuously renew themselves while the person of whom they are a part remains the same. Shallum of Ezra's time is the Shallum of David's time.

18. … וְעַד־הֵנָּה — And up to now … Translation follows Radak. Radak seems to take this verse together with v. 22. The just-mentioned gatekeepers are the em-bodiment of those who from the earliest days of the Temple until now faithfully stood guard at its portals. The role they fill today is the same one they performed throughout the years of the First Temple.

בְּשַׁעַר הַמֶּלֶךְ — At the king's gate. Ralbag writes that it was called שַׁעַר הַמֶּלֶךְ because it was through that gate that the king used to enter the Temple from his palace. However, this name seems inappropriate for Ezra's time when there was no king in Israel. It is also unlikely that the name is a holdover from the period of the First Temple, since nowhere do we find this name used for the eastern gate. From II Chronicles 23:5 it appears that the eastern gate was commonly called שַׁעַר הַיְסוֹד (or שַׁעַר סוּר— see comm. there), and in Ezekiel it is commonly referred to as the entry gate (Ezekiel 40:14), or the outer gate (cf. Ezekiel 44:1).

In order to understand this we postulate the following:

We have previously shown that the description of the gatekeepers reaches back into hoariest antiquity. It would also seem that it looks ahead to the Messianic future as well, and that its perceptions and de-scriptions are anchored not in the present but in that mystic anticipation which animated Ezra's activities in Jerusalem.

In the Third Temple, as described in the final chapters of Ezekiel, the eastern entrance to the Temple courtyard is to be kept closed at all times, except only on Shabbos and Rosh Chodesh at which times

progenitor and these patriarchs subsequently became their leaders. Other possibilities would be that our verse, in contrast to the previous verses, means families instead of individuals, or that children of the respective families carried the names of the family founders.

their brother Shallum was the chief. [18] *And up to now at the king's gate in the east — they are the gatekeepers for the Levite camps.* [19] *And Shallum, the son of Kore, the son of Eviasaph, the son of*

it is to be opened so that the *Nasi* — the Messianic king — might make his entrance from there (*Ezekiel* 46:1, and see ArtScroll comm. there). Thus, with a view to that situation the name שַׁעַר הַמֶּלֶךְ, *king's gate,* seems entirely apt.

By the same token, the fact that this was now to be the Messianic entrance would surely make the eastern approach the most significant one and the location at which the most important of the gatekeepers would stand watch.

This may perhaps explain the extremely difficult wording of v. 26: כִּי בֶאֱמוּנָה הֵמָּה אַרְבַּעַת הַשֹּׁעֲרִים הֵם הַלְוִיִּם, *For they, the four outstanding gatekeepers, are permanently established; they are the Levites.* None of the commentators offers a clear explanation for the seemingly redundant phrase הֵם הַלְוִיִּם, *they are the Levites.* As we understand the verse the meaning is clear. The four outstanding gatekeepers were בֶאֱמוּנָה, *permanently established,* that is, part of a constant and eternal system stretching from the most distant past all the way to the furthest future — הֵם הַלְוִיִּם, *they are the Levites.* They, in their persons, represented the Levite presence which is an integral part of the Divine Presence in Israel.

מִזְרָחָה — *In the east.* The meaning cannot be that the four men mentioned in the previous verse all stood guard at the eastern gate, since v. 24 makes clear that the guarding described in this passage took care of all the four sides of the Temple.

The explanation may be as follows: As will be explained at 26:17, *Rosh* to *Tamid* states that the guards at all the Temple gates faced eastwards because, inasmuch as the main entrance was in the east, they were all, in a sense, guarding that gate. Perhaps our phrase has the same sense: The eastern — main — entrance of the Temple was still being guarded by all the Levites whose efforts ultimately tended towards that gate.

הֵמָּה הַשֹּׁעֲרִים — *They are the gatekeepers.* This phrase is to be read together with the הֵמָּה ... of v. 22. The earlier part of that verse states, *They are registered in their towns.* Its meaning is: look up their genealogies and you will find that indeed

these men can trace their family lines back to the gatekeepers of yesteryear. This, too, is the meaning of our verse: These are the descendants of the original gatekeepers; the families who occupied these positions in the past are still (וְעַד הֵנָּה) the ones who now are the Temple guardians.

לְמַחֲנוֹת בְּנֵי לֵוִי — *For the Levite camps.* In the encampment in the wilderness there was a hierarchy of three distinct areas, each with its own level of sanctity. The most holy was the מַחֲנֵה שְׁכִינָה, *the camp of the Divine Presence,* which included the Tabernacle and its courtyard. The second level was the מַחֲנֵה לְוִיָּה, *the Levite camp,* which was the inner circle of the encampment around the Tabernacle. After that came the מַחֲנֵה יִשְׂרָאֵל, *the Israelite camp,* the outer circle around the Tabernacle.

This hierarchy of sanctity was duplicated in the Temple. The city of Jerusalem had the character of מַחֲנֵה יִשְׂרָאֵל, the Temple Mount was the מַחֲנֵה לְוִיָּה, and the Temple proper had the character of the מַחֲנֵה שְׁכִינָה (see *Rambam, Bias Mikdash* ch. 3).

Thus, the guardians of the eastern gate leading onto the Temple Mount could be said to be the gatekeepers of the Levite camp. This is how *Metzudos* takes the phrase. [According to *Middos* 1:1, the five gates of the Temple Mount were among the twenty-four places at which a guard was required in the Temple.]

It should be noted that *Chronicles* seems to use the word מַחֲנוֹת ה' as a synonym for the Temple. See *II Chronicles* 31:2 and *Metzudos* there.

Ralbag thinks that מַחֲנוֹת in our context refers to the מִשְׁמָרוֹת, *the divisions* or *cadres* of the Levites who stood guard at the gates. The word מַחֲנֶה occurs frequently in Scripture to denote a *company of people* (cf. *Genesis* 34:8-11), and thus this usage would be entirely apt.

19. ... וְשַׁלּוּם — *And Shallum* ... This Shallum is clearly the Shallum of David's time whose genealogy is given at 26:1 and who, according to 26:14, was assigned the watch at the eastern gate. Following upon the previous verse our verse seems to be saying: Indeed, the gatekeepers of Ezra's time are the family descendants of those

בֶּן־קוֹרֵא בֶּן־אֶבְיָסָף בֶּן־קֹרַח וְאֶחָיו לְבֵית־אָבִיו הַקָּרְחִים
עַל מְלֶאכֶת הָעֲבֹדָה שֹׁמְרֵי הַסִּפִּים לָאֹהֶל וַאֲבֹתֵיהֶם עַל־
כ מַחֲנֵה יהוה שֹׁמְרֵי הַמָּבוֹא: וּפִינְחָס בֶּן־אֶלְעָזָר נָגִיד הָיָה
כא עֲלֵיהֶם לְפָנִים יהוה ׀ עִמּוֹ: זְכַרְיָה בֶּן מְשֶׁלֶמְיָה שֹׁעֵר

who functioned under David: The Shallum
of Ezra (v. 17) is the successor to the
Shallum of David's time. The verse then
continues:

וְאֶחָיו לְבֵית־אָבִיו הַקָּרְחִים — And his brothers
from his family, the Korachites. This
phrase places the function assigned within
a family context. Shallum functioned not
only as an individual but also as a scion of
the family who merited this great task.
They in turn were the continuations of
their father's activities (וַאֲבֹתֵיהֶם) — and
therefore we can expect that privilege to
continue to be vested in the future
generations of that family.

עַל מְלֶאכֶת הָעֲבֹדָה ... — In charge of the work
of the service ... In connection with the
Temple service these two words are
frequently used but never as a separate
term — מְלֶאכֶת עֲבוֹדָה. It is invariably either
in the construct, as for example in v. 13,
מְלֶאכֶת עֲבוֹדַת בֵּית הָאֱלֹהִים (cf. also Exodus
36:1 and 3 and many other places) or, as in
our case, together with the definite article
— מְלֶאכֶת הָעֲבֹדָה. In such a usage it seems
likely that the definite article replaces the
information supplied by the construct form
— thus מְלֶאכֶת הָעֲבֹדָה, the work of the
[sacred] service [of the Temple].
Which work is meant here? Metzudos
thinks that שֹׁמְרֵי הַסִּפִּים לָאֹהֶל is in
apposition to our phrase. Thus the work
referred to here is the act of guarding the
Temple.

שֹׁמְרֵי הַסִּפִּים לָאֹהֶל — Guardians of the
doorposts to the Tent. סַף according to
Radak in Shorashim is either a doorpost or
a threshold.
Radak renders אֹהֶל as the Holy of Holies.
In the wilderness this section was housed in
the Tabernacle (tent), and during the time
of David's reign (when the Shallum of our
verse served), the Sanctuary was again in a
tent in the city of Giveon (see comm. to
17:5). Thus, the term tent is quite fitting.
According to Radak, the phrases, שֹׁמְרֵי
הַסִּפִּים לָאֹהֶל ... שֹׁמְרֵי הַמָּבוֹא are to be read
together with the middle phrase: וַאֲבֹתֵיהֶם
עַל־מַחֲנֵה ה' taken parenthetically. The
meaning is as follows: The Korachites
guarded the doorposts of the Holy of
Holies (שֹׁמְרֵי הַסִּפִּים לָאֹהֶל), even as their
forefathers (the Korachites were descended
from the Kehathites) had had charge of the
holy vessels (מַחֲנֵה ה') in the Tabernacle (see
Numbers 3:27-31).
Evidently Radak does not equate the
שֹׁמְרֵי הַסִּפִּים with the regular gatekeepers.
Gra seems to agree with Radak that the
שֹׁמְרֵי הַסִּפִּים are not identical with the
gatekeepers. But whereas Radak has אֹהֶל
refer to the Holy of Holies, Gra renders it
הֵיכָל, the Sanctuary.[1]
Metzudos renders אֹהֶל as עֲזָרָה, the
Temple courtyard. Evidently he equates
שֹׁמְרֵי הַסִּפִּים with the regular gatekeepers.
He does not, however, explain why the
courtyard should, in this connection, be
called an אֹהֶל. Perhaps they would be called

1. The term שֹׁמְרֵי הַסַּף occurs in Scripture with reference to the Temple administration — particularly
with regard to the treasury. Thus at II Kings 12:10 we have the כֹּהֲנִים שֹׁמְרֵי הַסַּף administering the
money that had been collected for Temple repairs and much later, in Yoshiahu's reign, we have
לְיַם שֹׁמְרֵי הַסַּף going about the land in order to collect money for that same purpose.
Rashi to the Kings passage writes that the שֹׁמְרֵי הַסַּף had charge of the keys to the various Temple
gates. This on the basis of Targum who renders the term אֲמַרְכָּלִים, and with reference to Shekalim 5:2
where we find seven Temple officials with that title who, according to Tosefta there, were charged
with the keys. As the ArtScroll commentary to the Mishnah there suggests, these keys may well have
been ones which provided access to the treasury chambers.
Rashi's opinion, then, seems to be that the שֹׁמְרֵי הַסַּף are not identical with the שֹׁעֲרִים, gatekeepers,
and we must assume that in our verse too he would interpret as he does in Kings.
Given Rashi's interpretation that we are dealing with the officials known as אֲמַרְכָּלִים we can readily
understand how these are described as Kohanim in Kings and as Levites in Chronicles. Tosefta
Shekalim makes clear that since these functionaries were not involved in the actual sacrificial service
they could be drawn from either Kohanim, Levites, or Israelites. It is completely possible that, during
the reign of one king, Kohanim were charged with these duties and during the reign of a different
king, Levites.

Korach, and his brothers from his family, the Korachites, were in charge of the work of the service, guardians of the doorposts to the Tent; as their forefathers had been in charge of the camp of HASHEM, guardians of the entry. ²⁰ And Pinechas the son of Eleazar was prince over them in the past, [for] HASHEM was with him.

guardians of the Tent because the watchmen at the courtyard entrance were guarding the approaches to the Sanctuary. [Since this verse describes the dispositions in David's time, when the Temple had not yet been built, the term אֹהֶל is appropriate.] An analogy would be *I Samuel* 1:9 when we have ... *and Eli the Kohen sat at the doorposts of the Sanctuary of HASHEM.* R' Yaakov Emden (see *Mor Uktziah* to *Orach Chaim* 102) points out that the courtyard doorposts must be meant since sitting in the actual courtyard is forbidden *(Nachalas Shimon).*

וַאֲבֹתֵיהֶם עַל מַחֲנֵה ה' — *As their forefathers had been in charge of the camp of HASHEM.* Shallum and his brethren were descendants of Korach who was, in turn, a Kehathite. In the wilderness (see *Numbers* 3:27-31), Shallum's forefathers — the Kehathites — had the duty of transporting and guarding the sacred vessels of the Tabernacle — the Ark, the inner altar, the menorah and the table [מַחֲנֵה ה', *the camp of HASHEM*]. They were themselves warned *(Numbers* 4:17-20) to take precautions against any unauthorized approach to these vessels. Thus, the descendants of those Kehathites — Shallum and his brethren — were the logical choice to fulfill this similar duty [שֹׁמְרֵי הַסִּפִּים לָאֹהֶל, *guardians of the doorposts to the Tent*] in David's time *(Radak,* see also *Gra* and *Metzudos).*

20. ... וּפִינְחָס בֶּן־אֶלְעָזָר — *And Pinechas the son of Eleazar* ... This appears to be another glance backwards at the glorious past of the Korachite שֹׁעֲרִים, *gatekeepers.* They were part of a tradition which was associated with no less a personality than the great Pinechas — a man concerning whom it might be said — ה' עִמּוֹ, *HASHEM is with him!* All his endeavors seemed to enjoy the blessed success of one constantly in the presence of God.

Pinechas must have been the leader of

the gatekeepers at about the time of the entry into the Land *(Malbim),* because up to that point the general supervisory position over the Kehathites (and therefore the Korachites) was exercised by his father Eleazar (see *Ramban* to *Numbers* 4:7). Indeed, *Radak* makes the point that Pinechas inherited his positions from Eleazar.

But why then is Pinechas, rather than Eleazar, mentioned and what is the significance of an association with him that this should be underlined here? [*Radak,* indeed, quotes opinions that the Pinechas son of Eleazar mentioned in our verse is not the one known to us from the Torah at all, but he rejects this position.]

Radak quotes a tradition of the Sages that Pinechas lived a phenomenally long life — several hundred years — and this may be the explanation of his significance. Over centuries it was he with whom the exercise of the guardianship of the Temple was associated and the mere mention of his name could well have awakened a sense of pride and commitment on the part of the Korachites who were to function as gate-keepers for the returning exiles. They were a part of a glorious past.

We may perhaps suggest another possibility. Ezra himself, as well as Yeshua the *Kohen Gadol,* were descendants of Eleazar and Pinechas (see *Ezra* 7:1-5). It seems reasonable to assume that just as in antiquity the gatekeepers had been under the leadership of a *Kohen,* so too now the *Kohen Gadol* or Ezra himself may well have occupied that post. If so, then, in context of the thrust of our entire chapter which is to establish the continuity which bound together the generations, it would be germane to point out that the supervisory role, too, was hereditary and vested in Ezra's family. This could be established by showing that the position had indeed passed from Eleazar to Pinechas.[1]

לְפָנִים ... ... *in the past.* Pinechas goes back to earliest times since he was already born at the time of the Exodus *(Ralbag).*

1. The suggested thesis may help to explain a textual oddity: Wherever Pinechas son of Eleazar is mentioned in Scripture he is almost always described either as a *Kohen* or a descendant of Aaron, which makes his *Kehunah* clear. Our reference is an exception. Perhaps the explanation is that here Ezra's *Kehunah* is known and assumed. At issue is that fact that Pinechas the son took over from Eleazar the father. It is the relationship, not the identity, which is important.

ה' עמו — *HASHEM was with him.* Pinechas attained a high position because *Hashem was with him (Radak; Metzudos).*

The term seems out of place in this context. Throughout Scripture when this or similar forms are used it is invariably in a situation fraught with difficulties in which the person, due to God's help, was able to overcome problems and achieve his objectives. Usually it appears to explain a king's ability to consolidate his rule in spite of obstacles. This explanation does not seem to fit here.

It is perhaps for this reason that the Sages read our sentence differently. Rather than reading לְפָנִים, *in the past*, together with the first phrase: 'Pinechas had been the prince of the Levites *in the past*' as we have translated it, the Sages *(Yerushalmi, Yoma* 1:1) read it with the latter part of the sentence: לְפָנִים ה' עמו, *in the past HASHEM had been with him.* According to this reading, there came a time in the life of Pinechas when HASHEM's special assistance to him ceased — because he failed to maintain the high standards which had originally earned him God's approbation. [Sources vary concerning the events which led to this decline. See discussion in 5:30.]

Perhaps this idea is significant within the context in which it is taught. Certainly when confronted with the glorious past of their families, the functionaries of Ezra's time would have been acutely sensitive to the reduced status of their present situation. *Ezra* 3:12 tells how the elders of the people — those to whom the memories of the First Temple were still alive — wept when they realized how greatly reduced the grandeur of the Second Temple was. How much more so the Levites whose entire activity was supposed to be performed as the continuation of a great tradition! Ezra may therefore have felt it appropriate to point out to them that even the great Pinechas had had to cope with a diminution of his relationship with God — and had nonetheless managed to leave his positive mark upon the duties which he controlled.

21. ... זְכַרְיָה בֶּן מְשֶׁלֶמְיָה — *Zechariah the son of Meshelemiah* ... At 26:2 and 14 we find that the first-born of the Meshelemiah of David's line was called Zechariah, and this would seem to indicate that this verse also refers back to that time, just as vs. 19 and 20 have done.

However, there are a number of considerations which speak against this assumption: (1) There seems little purpose in telling about Zechariah's post at this point more than that of any of the other gatekeepers described in ch. 26. (2) If indeed the Zechariah of earlier times is meant, he should have been listed before Pinechas. The statement that Pinechas had been in charge of the gatekeepers seems to be meant to sum up that section, and there seems little logic in describing Zechariah's position after that verse. (3) At 26:14 Zechariah is assigned by lot to the northern side of the Temple while the פֶּתַח לְאֹהֶל מוֹעֵד, *the entrance to the Tent of Meeting*, of our verse seems to indicate the eastern entrance.

It therefore seems more likely that the Meshelemiah of our verse is the same as the Shallum of v. 17 — the official from Ezra's time. As we have seen so many times in this chapter, names repeated themselves in the later generations of a family. The Shallum/Meshelemiah of Ezra's time gave his son the same name that the earlier Shallum/Meshelemiah had given his.

As transpires from vs. 17 and 18, the guardianship of the eastern gate would have fallen to Shallum who, as leader, would have been given this most important of all the positions. However, since he was one of the גִּבּוֹרֵי הַשֹּׁעֲרִים, *the officers of the gatekeepers* (v. 26), who were in general charge of all the arrangements, it is unlikely that he himself would have taken the actual guard duty. Rather, our sense tells us, this duty was assigned to his son Zechariah.

Thus, as we read our verse, it is a direct continuation of v. 17, with the intervening verses in a parenthetical relationship to the main narrative: Shallum was the leader ... and was represented by his son.

פֶּתַח לְאֹהֶל מוֹעֵד — *Of the entrance to the Tent of Meeting.* The term אֹהֶל מוֹעֵד, *Tent of Meeting*, would seem inappropriate as a description of the Temple. However, in the context of this whole section the term is fitting. The meaning is to define Ezra's Temple as the אֹהֶל מוֹעֵד, *Tent of Meeting*, of his generation. What the Tabernacle had

9

21-22

²¹ *Zechariah the son of Meshelemiah was the gatekeeper of the entrance to the Tent of Meeting.* ²² *All those selected to be keepers of the doorposts were two hundred and twelve; they are registered*

been in the wilderness the Temple now replaced.

22. כֻּלָּם ... מָאתַיִם וּשְׁנֵים עָשָׂר — *All those ... were two hundred and twelve.* Metzudos renders the phrase: *All those that were chosen as keepers of the doorposts numbered two hundred and twelve.*

Nehemiah 11:19 gives the number of gatekeepers as one hundred and seventy-two. *Metzudos'* solution is that *Nehemiah's* number refers only to the Levites who stood guard at the Temple Mount. Our number, however, includes those whose duty it was to stand guard at the entrances of the courtyard.

Malbim explains differently. The Mishnah in *Middos* 1:1 enumerates twenty-four locations in the Temple at which guards stood watch.[1] He demonstrates that a group of thirty Levites would be required daily in the Temple; twenty-four for guard duty and another six for the six areas of responsibility assigned to the Levites in vs. 26-32. [If responsibility for the *chavittim* sacrifices in verse 31 is to be counted, then *holy vessels* and *flour, wine, oil* etc. in verse 29 are counted as one. If the *chavittim* of verse 31 are not to be counted, then verse 29 is to be divided into two areas of responsibility.] With a separate group serving each day, we arrive at a total of 210 (7 x 30) for each מִשְׁמָר, *division.*

Additionally, both the gatekeepers and the Levites who controlled the six areas of responsibility would have an executive officer who would organize and assign the various duties. These two leaders would raise the total to two hundred and twelve, which is the number given in our verse.

Nehemiah speaks of 172 Levites because he counts only the gatekeepers, who numbered 168 (7 x 24), and the four Levites mentioned by name in verse 17 who, since they are identified specifically, must have been leaders and organizers [this is also *Radak's* view] and would not have been included in the twenty-four.

הַבְּרוּרִים — *Selected.* This term is elsewhere used only in the sense of groups of people chosen from within a larger group (see 7:40, 16:41). Since the number given here describes *all* the gatekeepers serving at that time, its usage here seems unusual.

However, v. 25 indicates that these were not all the gatekeepers there were but that there were others who lived in their villages who came periodically to serve *with these.* This would mean that the actual pool of gatekeepers was larger than the 212 given here, and it may be that in this sense, the 212 who lived in Jerusalem the year round were *selected.*

In the context of our understanding of the whole passage the meaning of this may be that the 212 were the actual descendants of the gatekeepers of the First Temple — the actual direct carriers of the proud tradition described in the passage. The ones not counted in that number would be new gatekeepers co-opted into the group during the period of the Second Temple.

Having established this we can take it a step further. Our verse talks of שַׁעֲרִים בַּסִּפִּים, an obvious reference to the שֹׁמְרֵי הַסִּפִּים of v. 19. Now, with the apparent exception of *Metzudos*, the commentators do not equate these with the regular gatekeepers. We saw that *Rashi* thinks that they are Temple functionaries in charge of the keys while *Radak* and *Gra* see them as guards charged with making sure that no one unauthorized approached the Holy of Holies or the Sanctuary, respectively. Since these duties are nowhere, except here, associated with the gatekeepers in general, we must assume that only particular gatekeepers were charged with these additional duties; specifically these would be the family members described in our section.

הֵמָּה בְּחַצְרֵיהֶם הִתְיַחְשָׂם — *They are registered in their towns.* Our translation follows *Metzudos* who interprets the verse to mean that the genealogical records of these Levites are to be found in their towns — the

---

1. The Mishnah states that three of these locations were manned by *Kohanim* and the others by Levites. However, some commentators understand this to mean that at three of the locations there were *Kohanim* in addition to Levites. For the purpose of his comm., *Malbim* assumes this opinion.

כג דָּוִיד וּשְׁמוּאֵל הָרֹאֶה בֶּאֱמוּנָתָם: וְהֵם וּבְנֵיהֶם עַל־
כד הַשְּׁעָרִים לְבֵית־יְהוָה לְבֵית הָאֹהֶל לְמִשְׁמָרוֹת: לְאַרְבַּע
כה רוּחוֹת יִהְיוּ הַשֹּׁעֲרִים מִזְרָח יָמָּה צָפוֹנָה וָנֶגְבָּה: וַאֲחֵיהֶם
בְּחַצְרֵיהֶם לָבוֹא לְשִׁבְעַת הַיָּמִים מֵעֵת אֶל־עֵת עִם־אֵלֶּה:

small townships clustered around Jerusalem where the Levites lived in order to be close to the Temple.

Metzudos does not explain why the genealogical lists are mentioned here, nor does he make clear why the Levites were living in these towns instead of in the Levite cities assigned in ch. 6. Now, it would be possible to assume that the returnees did not return to their original holdings but took possession of whatever land seemed most suitable for them. In that case the Levites may well have chosen land near Jerusalem. But this would seem to contradict *Metzudos* to *Nehemiah* (quoted in comm. to v. 2) that the returnees did indeed settle in their original holdings.

Radak translates: *They lived in the towns [which were determined] by their lineage.* Contrary to *Metzudos*, *Radak* assumes that the חֲצֵרוֹת are the ancestral towns of these Levites — those assigned to their families of Joshua's time. Each of these Levites lived in the particular town to which his genealogy entitled him. The point of mentioning this here is to underline that although these Levites were gatekeepers in the Temple, they were not there constantly. As v. 25 teaches, they came to the Temple periodically for seven days — the rest of the time living in their ancestral towns.

In *Radak's* interpretation, too, it is not clear why this information should be given here. Moreover, the parallel section in *Nehemiah* seems to be saying that these Levites lived in Jerusalem.

Perhaps the purpose of our phrase is to point out that although this entire section is describing those who settled in Jerusalem, the Levites mentioned here did not actually live there. They were reckoned a part of Jerusalem because of their Temple duties, but their actual homes were in their ancestral townships.

In comm. to v. 18 we have presented our understanding of this phrase. The genealogies of these Levites are significant because they identify them as scions — and therefore carriers of the tradition — of the original Levite gatekeepers.

But why stress חַצְרֵיהֶם?

First, an analysis of the term: חֲצֵרוֹת are open cities (*Rashi*, *Genesis* 25:16 and *Leviticus* 25:31) as opposed to טִירוֹת, *fortified* cities (*Genesis*, there and see

comm. to 6:39). Now the Levite cities in the First Commonwealth were described as טִירוֹת (6:39). Why did they now live in חֲצֵרוֹת? [This point speaks in favor of *Metzudos'* explanation (above) that the returnees did not settle in their ancestral cities but chose smaller towns (חֲצֵרוֹת) in the vicinity of Jerusalem.]

It is possible that *Radak's* opinion is as follows: From *Joshua* 13:28 and above 6:41 it is clear that חֲצֵרוֹת can be towns which belong together with a larger city. They are the outlying townships of that city. If so, it is possible that the returnees, while returning to their ancestral holdings, chose to occupy only the חֲצֵרוֹת, *outlying townships*, of those cities rather than the larger cities themselves. This, because their small numbers made it unnecessary to activate the complex living structures of a large city.

Perhaps, then, the meaning of the phrase is: Even in their חֲצֵרוֹת, symbol of the reduced state in which these Levites now functioned, you will still find the proud records of their exalted lineage.

Another possibility is suggested by 4:33 where a similar statement — that the genealogies are to be found in the חֲצֵרוֹת — is made in connection with the tribe of Shimeon. Perhaps the explanation is that in contrast to the other tribes whose territory was contiguous and whose genealogical records would be maintained in one central city, Shimeon and Levi who were scattered in different cities had smaller archives in each of their separate locations (R' Y. Danziger).

הֵמָּה יִסַּד דָּוִיד וּשְׁמוּאֵל הָרֹאֶה בֶּאֱמוּנָתָם — *It is they whom David and Samuel the Seer established for all time.* The translation follows *Radak.* הֵמָּה, *they,* refers to the 212 gatekeepers. David and Samuel ordained that there should always be a minimum of this number of gatekeepers and that they should be divided into מִשְׁמָרוֹת [*mishmaros*], *divisions.*

The use of the singular יִסַּד, *he established,* may be explained by the fact that in a formal sense it was David alone who established the *mishmaros.* This appears from the text of ch. 23 and particularly vs. 1-6 which make clear that

in their towns; it is they whom David and Samuel the Seer established for all time. 23 *They and their sons were in charge of the gates to the House of HASHEM, to the House of the Tent, in divisions.* 24 *The gatekeepers are to be in the four directions — to the east, the west, the north and the south.* 25 *And their brothers in their*

the division into *mishmaros* took place late in David's life at a time when Samuel had long since died. The role that Samuel played is nowhere explicated in Scripture, but the Sages *(Taanis* 27a) explain that it was Samuel who taught David that it was permissible and proper to expand the number of Levitical divisions from those originally established by Moses (when the population was much smaller).

בְּאֱמוּנָתָם — *For all time.* Both *Radak* and *Metzudos* associate the word with permanence. David and Samuel gave permanence to the *mishmar* arrangement.

The word אֱמוּנָה occurs a number of times in *Chronicles* (I: 9:22, 26, 31; II: 19:9; 31:12, 15, 18; 34:12), and it is noteworthy that it always is used in connection with some Levite involvement in the Temple or general administration. In most of these cases it is clear that the word is meant to describe the earnest dedication and reliability with which given tasks are performed. Thus at v. 31 it tells us how faithfully and conscientiously a given Levite dealt with the difficult task of preparing the *chavittim* — see comm. there.

In view of this usage throughout the book it seems logical to assign this meaning here also — while at the same time incorporating the connotation of permanence. David and Samuel were dedicated servants to the concept of establishing the Divine Presence in Israel. They had labored long and hard to find the correct spot for the Temple long before there was any real chance of its actually being built *(Zevachim* 54b based on *I Samuel* 19:18). Their אֱמוּנָה to God's service and to the perpetuation of His Presence in Israel inspired them to go further than the identification of a suitable location for the Temple, and to lay plans for the *ideal* fulfillment of the Divine service within it. Hence the inspiration for the establishment of the permanent *mishmaros.*

23. וְהֵם וּבְנֵיהֶם עַל־הַשְּׁעָרִים — *They and their sons were in charge of the gates.* This is a continuation of the *permanency* expressed in the previous verse. The children of the men whom David appointed continued to perform the same tasks as their fathers *(Malbim).* But see comm. to v. 26 for an alternative interpretation.

לְבֵית־ה׳ לְבֵית הָאֹהֶל — *To the House of*

HASHEM, to the House of the Tent. Metzudos thinks that these terms are synonymous; both denote the Temple. *Malbim* explains that *House of HASHEM* is Solomon's Temple whereas *House of the Tent* denotes the Tabernacle which served as the sanctuary during David's days.

But in that case the sequence seems difficult. We would have expected the Tabernacle to be mentioned before the Temple.

In the sense in which we have understood the thrust of our chapter we can readily understand the two terms to be in apposition. The meaning is that the בֵּית ה׳, the Temple of Solomon, is the successor to the Tabernacle. The Tabernacle which Moses had erected in the wilderness is, so to speak, the soul of Solomon's Temple. In that sense the Levite gatekeepers of David's time can readily be seen as the embodiment of the Levite encampment in the wilderness.

לְמִשְׁמָרוֹת — *In divisions.* Not all the Levite gatekeepers served at the same time. They were divided into divisions serving on a rotating basis. In the tradition of the Sages there were twenty-four מִשְׁמָרוֹת [*mishmaros*] or *divisions,* each of which served one complete week every twenty-four weeks (see *Rambam, Klei HaMikdash* 3:9).

24. לְאַרְבַּע רוּחוֹת — *In the four directions.* The Levites guarded the Temple on all four sides. For details see 26:17-18.

25. ... וַאֲחֵיהֶם — *And their brothers* ... As explained in the comm. to v. 22, the simple meaning of this verse is that the *brothers* are those *shoarim* who are not included in the count of 212. *Radak,* however, seems to understand our verse to mean that the 212 mentioned there did not all serve at the same time but were divided into *mishmaros* who lived in their townships and came to the Temple for only seven-day stretches when their turn arrived.

לָבוֹא לְשִׁבְעַת הַיָּמִים — *To come for seven days.* Each מִשְׁמָר, *division,* of Levites was

כו כִּי בֶאֱמוּנָה הֵמָּה אַרְבַּעַת גִּבֹּרֵי הַשֹּׁעֲרִים הֵם הַלְוִיִּם
כז וְהָיוּ עַל־הַלְּשָׁכוֹת וְעַל־הָאֹצָרוֹת בֵּית הָאֱלֹהִים: וּסְבִיבוֹת
בֵּית־הָאֱלֹהִים יָלִינוּ כִּי־עֲלֵיהֶם מִשְׁמֶרֶת וְהֵם עַל־הַמַּפְתֵּחַ
כח וְלַבֹּקֶר לַבֹּקֶר: וּמֵהֶם עַל־כְּלֵי הָעֲבֹדָה כִּי בְמִסְפָּר יְבִיאוּם
כט וּבְמִסְפָּר יוֹצִיאוּם: וּמֵהֶם מְמֻנִּים עַל־הַכֵּלִים וְעַל כָּל־כְּלֵי

to come to Jerusalem to serve for seven days.

מֵעֵת אֶל־עֵת — *At fixed periods* [lit. *from time to time*]. In *Ezekiel* 4:10 and 11 the expression מֵעֵת עַד עֵת denotes a twenty-four-hour period. In our context it means a full week. In both instances the phrase conveys the same idea — from one point in time until the return of that point.

עִם־אֵלֶּה — *With these*. See above that these are the 212 referred to in v. 22. *Metzudos* thinks that it refers to those Levites who had earlier been identified by name.

26. כִּי בֶאֱמוּנָה הֵמָּה ... — *For they ... are permanently established*. *Metzudos* again understands אֱמוּנָה here to mean *permanently*, as above in verse 22. Our verse is a continuation of the previous one, explaining that the rotation worked smoothly and continuously because it had initially been designed to be permanent. [See comm. to v. 18, s.v. בְּשַׁעַר הַמֶּלֶךְ.]

Malbim translates אֱמוּנָה in our verse in its more usual meaning of *faithful*. The Levites discharged their duties faithfully and were therefore given charge of other Temple functions as described in this and subsequent verses.

אַרְבַּעַת גִּבֹּרֵי הַשֹּׁעֲרִים — *The four outstanding gatekeepers*. The four Levites mentioned above in verse 17 (*Metzudos*) were permanently stationed in the Temple and as officers did not serve on a rotating basis. [For the translation of גִּבֹּרֵי as *outstanding*, see comm. to 5:24.]

They, the four permanent officers of the gatekeepers, were the very embodiment of the ancient Levites, *shoarim*. They were not only heirs to the glorious Levite heritage (vs. 18-20; see comm. there), but also worthy successors to those illustrious ancestors. Under the leadership of their four officers, the Levites of the Second Temple re-established the Levite traditions of the First Temple and the Tabernacle.

Thus, this section (vs. 17-32) begins by listing the four officers of the gatekeepers (v. 17), proceeds to trace their work against the historical background of the Levites (vs. 18-20), and then describes the duties and manner of their service (vs. 21-27). Verses 28-32 then describe the additional duties assigned to the gatekeepers.

Metzudos renders this verse: *For they* [the Levitical organization] *are permanently established* — *both the four officers of the gatekeepers and the* [rest of the] *Levite* [gatekeepers].

וְהָיוּ עַל־הַלְּשָׁכוֹת ... — *They shall* [also] *be in charge of the chambers* ... The translation follows *Metzudos*, according to whom this is a new thought. In addition to their duties at the gates, the Levites were also given these other responsibilities.

Malbim, based on his interpretation of בֶאֱמוּנָה as *faithful*, explains this as following from the previous phrase. Because they — the officers and Levites — were faithful in discharging their guard duty, they were *also* appointed over the chambers and storage rooms in the Temple.

The subject of *they* are the *brothers* of v. 25 rather than the four leaders mentioned in v. 26. This is obvious from the following verses which retain the pronoun and are manifestly talking of more than four Levites.

עַל־הַלְּשָׁכוֹת ... — ... *In charge of the chambers*. *Gra* writes that chambers refers to areas like the לִשְׁכַּת הַטְּלָאִים, the *chamber* in which animals were checked for blemishes which might disqualify them as sacrifices (see *Middos* 1:6). The *storage rooms* are areas in which the voluntary gifts made to the Temple were stored.

But why should the stewardship which the Levites practiced over the chambers and storage rooms be mentioned before the guard duty described in v. 27? Surely, in a section dealing with gatekeepers we would have expected that their obligation to spend the night around the Temple (v. 27) should be mentioned first, and only then, that the Levites who were *shoarim* had additional

towns are to come for seven days at fixed periods with these. ²⁶ For they, the four outstanding gatekeepers, are permanently established; they are the Levites. They shall [also] be in charge of the chambers and the storage rooms of the House of God. ²⁷ They are to spend the night round about the House of God, because they are responsible for the guard and they are in charge of the key, [to open the gates] each morning. ²⁸ And some of them [were charged] with the vessels of the service, for they would bring them and remove them by number. ²⁹ And some of them were appointed over the vessels and over all the vessels of the Sanctuary, and over the flour,

duties imposed upon them.

The answer lies in the fact that as we have noted in the prefatory remarks to this section, the Levites were assigned their guard duties within the context of their other responsibilities. Their original responsibility in the wilderness was for the care and transportation of the various utensils and components of the Tabernacle. The chambers and storage rooms of our verse would thus be the equivalent of the various Tabernacle components which the Levites were called upon to carry. Having just summed up the entire section with the statement that *they are* [the embodiment of] *the* [original] *Levites*, the verse adds a description of these additional duties of theirs which are so reminiscent of their original tasks.

27. יָלִינוּ — *They are to spend the night.* לון has the primary meaning *to spend the night,* although it is occasionally used for *sleeping.* In our case the watchmen, of course, did not sleep.

The guarding of the Temple entrances took place only during the night (*Rambam, Beis HaBechirah* 8:2).

וְהֵם עַל־הַמַּפְתֵּחַ — *And they are in charge of the key.* It was the duty of the Levites to lock the gates at night (*Anonymous Commentator*) and to reopen them in the morning.

וְלַבֹּקֶר לַבֹּקֶר — [*To open the gates*] *each morning.* The *vav* in the first וְלַבֹּקֶר is redundant but not unusual in Scripture. See, for example, *II Samuel* 15:34. For a more complete list see *Sefer HaRikmah* 6 under *vav.*

Our verse teaches that the key of the Temple courtyard (*Mefaresh*) or gates (*Metzudos*) were in the charge of the Levite *shoarim.* But according to *Tamid* 1:1 and *Middos* 1:8 the courtyard keys were in the

charge of the elders of the Kohanite family unit serving on that particular day. How does this agree with our verse?

Perhaps, if we can rely on the authenticity of Josephus' tradition, the solution can be found in *Against Apion* 8 where we hear that at midday every day the keys were issued to the *Kohanim.* Perhaps, then, our verse talks of the overall responsibility for the keys — this was vested in the Levites. The keys, however, were issued each day to the *Kohanim* serving on that day.

28. וּמֵהֶם עַל־כְּלֵי הָעֲבֹדָה — *And some of them* [*were charged*] *with the vessels of the service.* According to *Tamid* 3:4 a total of ninety-three vessels and implements were needed for the daily service in the Temple. These were kept in a special chamber, and it was the duty of the Levites to take them out in the morning and replace them in the evening.

בְּמִסְפָּר יְבִיאוּם וּבְמִסְפָּר יוֹצִיאוּם — *They would bring them and remove them by number.* In the morning they would *bring* them to the altar. They would count them as they brought them out, and they would count them again when they removed them from the altar area to return them to the chambers in which they were kept (*Metzudos*). This was done to make sure that none of them were mislaid or lost (*Ralbag*).

29. עַל־הַכֵּלִים וְעַל כָּל־כְּלֵי הַקֹּדֶשׁ — *Over the vessels and over all the vessels of the Sanctuary.* The first *vessels* refers to those implements not directly involved in the sacrificial service, such as cooking utensils for preparing the meat of the sacrifices which was to be eaten. *Vessels of the Sanctuary* are the candelabrum, the table of the show-bread and similar vessels

הַקֹּדֶשׁ וְעַל־הַסֹּלֶת וְהַיַּיִן וְהַשֶּׁמֶן וְהַלְּבוֹנָה וְהַבְּשָׂמִים:

ל-לא וּמִן־בְּנֵי הַכֹּהֲנִים רֹקְחֵי הַמִּרְקַחַת לַבְּשָׂמִים: וּמַתִּתְיָה מִן־הַלְוִיִּם הוּא הַבְּכוֹר לְשַׁלֻּם הַקָּרְחִי בֶּאֱמוּנָה עַל

לב מַעֲשֵׂה הַחֲבִתִּים: וּמִן־בְּנֵי הַקְּהָתִי מִן־אֲחֵיהֶם עַל־לֶחֶם

לג הַמַּעֲרָכֶת לְהָכִין שַׁבַּת שַׁבָּת: וְאֵלֶּה הַמְשֹׁרְרִים °פְּטוּרֵים ק' רָאשֵׁי אָבוֹת לַלְוִיִּם בַּלְּשָׁכֹת °פְּטִירִים כִּי־יוֹמָם וָלַיְלָה

לד עֲלֵיהֶם בַּמְּלָאכָה: אֵלֶּה רָאשֵׁי הָאָבוֹת לַלְוִיִּם לְתֹלְדוֹתָם רָאשִׁים אֵלֶּה יָשְׁבוּ בִירוּשָׁלִָם:

°יְעִיאֵל ק' לה וּבְגִבְעוֹן יָשְׁבוּ אֲבִי־גִבְעוֹן °יעואל וְשֵׁם אִשְׁתּוֹ מַעֲכָה:

לו-לז וּבְנוֹ הַבְּכוֹר עַבְדּוֹן וְצוּר וְקִישׁ וּבַעַל וְנֵר וְנָדָב: וּגְדוֹר

לח וְאַחְיוֹ וּזְכַרְיָה וּמִקְלוֹת: וּמִקְלוֹת הוֹלִיד אֶת־שִׁמְאָם וְאַף־

לט הֵם נֶגֶד אֲחֵיהֶם יָשְׁבוּ בִירוּשָׁלִַם עִם־אֲחֵיהֶם: וְנֵר

(Metzudos). They were presumably charged with keeping these clean and in good repair.

... וְעַל־הַסֹּלֶת — And over the flour ... The flour and oil were used for the מְנָחוֹת, meal offerings; the נְסָכִים, wine for the libations; the frankincense was placed on top of the לֶחֶם הַפָּנִים, show-bread, and the spices were used for the קְטֹרֶת, incense (Metzudos).

30. ... וּמִן־בְּנֵי הַכֹּהֲנִים — But [those who blended the mixture of spices] were from among the Kohanim. Although the Levites were charged with taking care of the spices for the incense (v. 29), the actual blending was done by Kohanim.

31. בֶּאֱמוּנָה — Served faithfully. The translation follows Gra. Apparently the preparation of the chavittim was a difficult task and, in addition, it had to be done very early in the morning (see Rambam, Temidim U'Musafim 6:1). Only a faithful and conscientious person could be entrusted with its preparation.

Metzudos translates אֱמוּנָה as he did earlier in verses 22 and 26. The appointment was a lasting one.

... חֲבִתִּים — Chavittim. The Kohen Gadol was required to bring a daily meal offering (Leviticus 6:12ff). It was made out of one tenth of an ephah of flour and brought in two parts — one in the morning and one in the afternoon. This daily offering was known as the chavittim of the Kohen Gadol. The name derives from the word מַחֲבַת, a kind of frying pan, which was used in its preparation (see Rambam, Temidim

U'Musafim 3:18ff).

Our verse teaches that it was part of the Levites' duty to see that this offering was prepared and brought at its correct time (Metzudos).

32. וּמִן־בְּנֵי הַקְּהָתִי מִן־אֲחֵיהֶם — And from [among] the Kehathites, from [among] their brothers. The Levite duties detailed up to now had been performed by Korachites (v. 19) who were part of the Kehathite family (see Numbers 16:1). The duty described in our verse was to be performed by other Kehathites, not Korachites. Thus it would be done by their brothers (Metzudos).

עַל־לֶחֶם הַמַּעֲרָכֶת — Over the bread of the rows. Every Sabbath, twelve fresh loaves of bread were arranged upon the table which stood in the Sanctuary. [For details, see Rambam, Temidim U'Musafim 5:1ff.] The loaves were arranged in two stacks of six each — hence the expression מַעֲרֶכֶת, which connotes some kind of arrangement [from עֲרֹךְ, to arrange or to set in a row].

לְהָכִין — To prepare. כּן usually means to set up, prepare or organize something. Thus we may suppose that it was the duty of these Levites to see to it that the arrangement of the bread should be done punctually and in the correct manner. However, the term sometimes also means to prepare food in the sense of cooking or baking (cf. Exodus 16:5). Thus our phrase may mean that they were in charge of baking the bread.

33. וְאֵלֶּה הַמְשֹׁרְרִים — But these choristers.

wine, oil, incense, and the spices. ³⁰ *But those who blended the mixture of the spices were from among the Kohanim.* ³¹ *And Mattithiah from among the Levites, he was the first-born of Shallum the Korachite, served faithfully over the preparation of the chavittim.* ³² *And from [among] the Kehathites, from [among] their brothers, [were given responsibility] over the bread of the rows to prepare [it] each Sabbath.* ³³ *But these choristers [who were] the family chiefs of the Levites [had their place] in the Chambers of the Released because their duties were day and night.* ³⁴ *These are the heads of the families of the Levites, heads of their descendants. These dwelled in Jerusalem.* ³⁵ *And in Giveon dwelled the father of Giveon — Yeiel, and his wife's name was Maachah.* ³⁶ *And his first-born son — Avdon and Tzur and Kish and Baal and Ner and Nadav.* ³⁷ *And Gedor and Achio and Zechariah and Mikloth.* ³⁸ *And Mikloth fathered Shimam. They too lived with their brothers in Jerusalem, in conjunction with their brothers.* ³⁹ *And Ner fathered*

Metzudos thinks that this refers to Shemaiah and the other Levites mentioned in vs. 14-16.

Metzudos' assumption is that those Levites were choristers. But if so, there does not seem to be any persuasive reason why the information contained in our verse was not given in vs. 14-16 instead of being kept till after the list of gatekeepers.

Furthermore, as we noted above, it seems customary for the books of *Ezra* and *Nehemiah* to list three categories: Levites, choristers and gatekeepers, and if, as can be expected, *Chronicles* follows that system, then the men listed in vs. 14-16 would be the Levites, other than choristers and gatekeepers.

Thus, we cannot ignore the possibility that our v. 33 is a fragment from a list of choristers which for some reason is not given in whole. [This would be analogous to the apparently meaningless listing of the Naphtalites at 7:13 (see comm. there) and would be part of the pattern traced in detail in Appendix II.] Verse 34 might then be the ending of that list or the rounding off of the entire Levite section of our chapter, as suggested in comm. to that verse.

בְּלִשְׁכַת פְּטוּרִים — [*had their place] in the Chambers of the Released. Gra* writes that פְּטוּרִים [lit. *free* or *released from work*] is a proper noun. The chambers were called Chambers of the Released because they were assigned to the choristers who were free from any other duties. Other commentators, however, render: *These choristers ... [who sat] in the chambers, were released [from all other activities]* (*Radak; Mefaresh; Metzudos*).

כִּי־יוֹמָם וָלַיְלָה עֲלֵיהֶם בַּמְּלָאכָה — *Because their*

duties were [lit. *upon them] day and night.* The music of the Levites accompanied certain of the sacrifices in the Temple. Certainly no sacrifices were brought during the night. The meaning of the phrase is that they were busy day and night rehearsing their music and acquiring skill with their instruments *(Metzudos)*. [For details of the Levitic music see *Rambam, Klei HaMikdash* ch. 3.]

34. ... אֵלֶּה — *These are* ... Verse 3 began a list of the returnees from Babylon who settled in Jerusalem. Our verse puts the Levites in the same category.

◆§ The Line of Saul

35-44. This section is, with only minor differences, a repetition of 8:29-38. See comm. there for a discussion of why this repetition was necessary. We have noted the various minor differences between the two lists in the parallel verses in ch. 8.

Gra's states that this section is repeated here because it contains Saul's genealogy. As such it is an apt introduction to the next chapter which deals with Saul's death.

35. יְעִיאֵל — *Yeiel.* This name is not given in ch. 8.

36. This *Ner* is not given in ch. 8.

37. See comm. 8:31 for some changes in spelling. Mikloth is not mentioned there.

38. See 8:32 for a change in the spelling of Shimam. The rest of the sentence is explained there.

הוֹלִיד אֶת־קִישׁ וְקִישׁ הוֹלִיד אֶת־שָׁאוּל וְשָׁאוּל הוֹלִיד
אֶת־יְהוֹנָתָן וְאֶת־מַלְכִּי־שׁוּעַ וְאֶת־אֲבִינָדָב וְאֶת־אֶשְׁבָּעַל:
מ וּבֶן־יְהוֹנָתָן מְרִיב בָּעַל וּמְרִי־בַעַל הוֹלִיד אֶת־מִיכָה:
מא־מב וּבְנֵי מִיכָה פִּיתֹן וָמֶלֶךְ וְתַחְרֵעַ: וְאָחָז הוֹלִיד אֶת־יַעְרָה
וְיַעְרָה הוֹלִיד אֶת־עָלֶמֶת וְאֶת־עַזְמָוֶת וְאֶת־זִמְרִי וְזִמְרִי
מג הוֹלִיד אֶת־מוֹצָא: וּמוֹצָא הוֹלִיד אֶת־בִּנְעָא וּרְפָיָה בְנוֹ
מד אֶלְעָשָׂה בְנוֹ אָצֵל בְּנוֹ: וּלְאָצֵל שִׁשָּׁה בָנִים וְאֵלֶּה
שְׁמוֹתָם עַזְרִיקָם ׀ בֹּכְרוּ וְיִשְׁמָעֵאל וּשְׁעַרְיָה וְעֹבַדְיָה וְחָנָן
אֵלֶּה בְּנֵי אָצַל:
א וּפְלִשְׁתִּים נִלְחֲמוּ בְיִשְׂרָאֵל וַיָּנָס אִישׁ־יִשְׂרָאֵל מִפְּנֵי
ב פְלִשְׁתִּים וַיִּפְּלוּ חֲלָלִים בְּהַר גִּלְבֹּעַ: וַיַּדְבְּקוּ פְלִשְׁתִּים
אַחֲרֵי שָׁאוּל וְאַחֲרֵי בָנָיו וַיַּכּוּ פְלִשְׁתִּים אֶת־יוֹנָתָן וְאֶת־

---

39. See 8:33.

40. This verse is discussed in 8:34. The change from מְרִיב בָּעַל to מְרִי בַעַל in our verse is no different than the minor spelling variations which are common throughout Scripture.

41. See 8:41 for spelling variations.

The verse there has an additional son, Achaz. Our verse does not mention him but takes up his genealogy in the next verse. *Rashbam* cites this as an example of

the Scriptural usage which we have traced a number of times (see 1:36). Occasionally a word or phrase at the beginning of a sentence does double duty and must be read also together with the foregoing sentence. In our case it is as though Achaz were written twice — at the end of our sentence and at the beginning of the next.

42. See 8:36.

43. See 8:37.

44. See 8:38.

X

The genealogical lists have been completed and *Chronicles* now turns its attention to the saga of the royal house of David — the central theme of the book of *Chronicles*.

When we think of kingship in Israel we think of David, the chosen servant of God (*Psalms* 78:70), scion of the royal house of Judah, embodiment of every regal quality, loyal shepherd of God's people (*Bereishis Rabbah* 59:5).

But before David there had been another king. Saul, from the tribe of Benjamin, had been chosen by God to rule over Israel and to save them from their Philistine oppressors (*I Samuel* 9:16). The tragedy of Saul's inability to live up to his great calling is the subject of the first book of *Samuel*. It was Saul's failure which made David king; it was Saul's rulership which was passed on to David (v. 14, see *Malbim* there).

It would have been possible to simply depose Saul and appoint David king while Saul was still alive. But, 'the rule of one king may in no way encroach upon the rule of another' (*Taanis* 5a), and furthermore, as *Zohar* (*Vayelech*) teaches, it would have been no kindness to keep Saul alive only to see his erstwhile servant rule over him.

Consequently, if David was to rule, Saul must first die. Thus, the Davidic saga properly begins with Saul's death; and it is there that *Chronicles* begins its account.

Although our chapter is an almost exact parallel of I *Samuel* 31:1-13, there are some small changes in language and emphasis. These can mostly be explained by an awareness of the purpose of the two books in reporting the incident. In *Samuel* the story belongs within the framework of the general history with which that book deals, while *Chronicles'* interest in the event is only inasmuch as Saul's death was a prelude to David's succession. The significant variations will be pointed out in the commentary.

Kish; and Kish fathered Saul; and Saul fathered Jonathan, and Malki Shua, and Avinadav, and Eshbaal. ⁴⁰ *And the sons of Jonathan — Meriv Baal, and Meri Baal fathered Michah.* ⁴¹ *And the sons of Michah — Pithon and Melech and Tachrea.* ⁴² *And Achaz fathered Yarah; and Yarah fathered Alemeth, Azmaveth, and Zimri, and Zimri fathered Motza.* ⁴³ *And Motza fathered Binea, and his son Rephaiah, his son Eleasah, his son Atzel.* ⁴⁴ *And Atzel had six sons and these were their names — Azrikam, Bocheru, Yishmael, Sheariah, Ovadiah, and Chanan — these were the sons of Atzel.*

N*ow the Philistines fought against Israel, and the men of Israel fled before the Philistines and they fell slain on Mount Gilboa.* ² *The Philistines pursued closely after Saul and after his sons, and*

◈§ The Death of King Saul

1. וּפְלִשְׁתִּים נִלְחֲמוּ בְיִשְׂרָאֵל — *Now the Philistines fought against Israel.* There is a particular poignancy in the fact that Saul meets his end at the hands of the Philistines. He had been made king so that he might save Israel from the Philistines (*I Samuel* 9:16). He failed, and it was just the Philistines who became God's tools when this great man had to die (*R' Yehudah Bachrach, Mah Bein Shaul Le'David*).

In Saul's case we are told only of his downfall whereas when the story of David is taken up we are told only of his greatness. David's weak points are never mentioned in *Chronicles*, for this book is for his sake and the sake of the kings of Judah (*Mefaresh*).[1]

וַיָּנָס אִישׁ־יִשְׂרָאֵל — *And the men* [lit. *man*] *of Israel fled.* In the account in *Samuel* the

plural form is used — וַיָּנֻסוּ אַנְשֵׁי יִשְׂרָאֵל. Normally the use of the plural form in such a case indicates the significance of each individual [of which their are many], while the singular is used when the whole community is viewed as one unit (see *Rashi* to *Exodus* 19:2). Perhaps in *Chronicles*, where the whole thrust of the narrative is to describe Saul's death, the rest of the people recede in importance and are all seen as one anonymous unit.

וַיָּנָס ... וַיִּפְּלוּ חֲלָלִים — *And* [they] *fled ... and they fell slain. Malbim* detects a cause and effect relationship. They fell *because* they fled. As *Sotah* 44b teaches: falling [in battle] begins with flight.

2. וַיַּדְבְּקוּ פְלִשְׁתִּים — *The Philistines pursued closely.* As they pursued them they caught up with them, coming very close [to their quarry] (*Metzudos*). [See ArtScroll *Genesis*

---

1. Taken at face value the *Mefaresh's* comment seems to betray a chauvinism unsuited to Scripture. In reality however this treatment of Saul's shortcomings and David's merits reflects their true standing as taught by the Sages: 'R' Huna taught: How safe from worry is a man whom God helps! [For, see] Saul sinned [only] once and it proved a catastrophe for him, but David sinned twice and it did not prove a catastrophe for him' (*Yoma* 22b).

Saul spared Agag's life when Samuel had told him that it was God's wish that Amalek should be totally wiped out. Because of this one transgression, his kingship was taken from him. [See comm. to v. 13.] David sinned twice: he had Uriah, the husband of Bath-Sheba killed (*II Samuel* chs. 11,12), and later, he counted Israel in a manner and under circumstances which were not appropriate (see ch. 2). Yet, he remained king.

Maharal (*Gevuros HaShem* 9) explains: David came from the royal tribe of Judah; he was always destined to be king and was inherently suited to the mantle of royalty. In the broader picture, his sins were aberrations which did not affect his essential being and suitability for the kingship. Saul, however, was a Benjaminite; it was only his personal greatness of character which caused God's choice to fall on him. He had no inherent qualities of kingship and, as a result, even one sin was enough to shake his tenuous hold on the throne. [*Ramban* to *Genesis* 49:10 states that if Saul had not sinned David would still have become king. But in that case Saul would have retained a vice-regal status, second only to David, and perhaps his rule over his own tribe of Benjamin.]

Thus, in *Chronicles'* perspective, the sins of David were aberrations which have no place in the

ג אֲבִינָדָב וְאֶת־מַלְכִּי־שׁוּעַ בְּנֵי שָׁאוּל: וַתִּכְבַּד הַמִּלְחָמָה
עַל־שָׁאוּל וַיִּמְצָאֻהוּ הַמּוֹרִים בַּקָּשֶׁת וַיָּחֶל מִן־הַיּוֹרִים:
ד וַיֹּאמֶר שָׁאוּל אֶל־נֹשֵׂא כֵלָיו שְׁלֹף חַרְבְּךָ | וְדָקְרֵנִי בָהּ
פֶּן־יָבֹאוּ הָעֲרֵלִים הָאֵלֶּה וְהִתְעַלְּלוּ־בִי וְלֹא אָבָה נֹשֵׂא
כֵלָיו כִּי יָרֵא מְאֹד וַיִּקַּח שָׁאוּל אֶת־הַחֶרֶב וַיִּפֹּל עָלֶיהָ:
ה וַיַּרְא נֹשֵׂא־כֵלָיו כִּי מֵת שָׁאוּל וַיִּפֹּל גַּם־הוּא עַל־הַחֶרֶב
ו וַיָּמֹת: וַיָּמָת שָׁאוּל וּשְׁלֹשֶׁת בָּנָיו וְכָל־בֵּיתוֹ יַחְדָּו מֵתוּ:
ז וַיִּרְאוּ כָּל־אִישׁ יִשְׂרָאֵל אֲשֶׁר־בָּעֵמֶק כִּי נָסוּ וְכִי־מֵתוּ
שָׁאוּל וּבָנָיו וַיַּעַזְבוּ עָרֵיהֶם וַיָּנֻסוּ וַיָּבֹאוּ פְלִשְׁתִּים וַיֵּשְׁבוּ
ח בָּהֶם: וַיְהִי מִמָּחֳרָת וַיָּבֹאוּ פְלִשְׁתִּים לְפַשֵּׁט
אֶת־הַחֲלָלִים וַיִּמְצְאוּ אֶת־שָׁאוּל וְאֶת־בָּנָיו נֹפְלִים בְּהַר
ט גִּלְבֹּעַ: וַיַּפְשִׁיטֻהוּ וַיִּשְׂאוּ אֶת־רֹאשׁוֹ וְאֶת־כֵּלָיו וַיְשַׁלְּחוּ

וַיִּדְבְּקוּ] derives from דבק, to p. 1352 on
cleave to or to join.

3. וַתִּכְבַּד הַמִּלְחָמָה עַל־שָׁאוּל — *The battle
bore down heavily on Saul.* Only Saul is
mentioned, his sons having already been
killed. Since he was now alone, the battle
became particularly heavy for him
(*Metzudos*).

וַיִּמְצָאֻהוּ הַמּוֹרִים בַּקָּשֶׁת — *And the bowmen
located him.* The tribe of Benjamin had
always been particularly skillful marksmen
with bow and sling (cf. 12:2). Now that
Saul had incurred God's displeasure, there
was a particular irony to the tragedy that it
was just the enemy archers who brought
about his downfall (*Mefaresh*).

[The *Mefaresh* seems to understand the
word וַיִּמְצָאֻהוּ [from מצא, to find] in the
sense: ... their [arrows] found him, that is,
that he was hit by the bowmen. Perhaps he
would then translate the last phrase וַיָּחֶל
מִן הַיּוֹרִים as, and he was wounded [וָחֵל from
חלה to be sick] by the archers, as in II Kings
1:2. We have taken וַיָּחֶל as deriving from
חול, to fear, in accordance with Targum. In
that case, we should take our phrase in the
sense to discover or locate. He was located
by the archers. This is how *Metzudos*
renders it.]

וַיָּחֶל מִן־הַיּוֹרִים — *And he became frightened
of the bowmen.* He was afraid that the
archers would capture him and seek to
amuse themselves with his suffering (see v.

4). יָחֶל is the *hiphil*, causative, of חול, to
fear or tremble (*Metzudos*).

4. It is outside the scope of this commentary to analyze in detail the rights and
wrongs of Saul's attempted suicide. [For a
wide-ranging discussion of this important
and complex problem, see *Nachalas
Shimon* to I Samuel 58.] The issue revolves
around the question of whether, when
faced with the prospect of unbearable
torture, a person is allowed to take his own
life. Basic source material can be found in:
Bereishis Rabbah to Genesis 9:5; *Daas
Zekeinim MiBaalei Tosafos*, there; and *Beis
Yosef* to Yoreh Deah 15b.

וְהִתְעַלְּלוּ־בִי — *And torture me.* The root עלל
combines the idea of causing someone pain
and amusing oneself at his expense
(*Metzudos*).

כִּי יָרֵא מְאֹד — *For he was very much afraid.*
He was afraid of how God would punish
him for killing His anointed one
(*Metzudos*).

5. כִּי מֵת שָׁאוּל — *That Saul was dead.* Saul
had not really died at that point. As is
evident from the account of the Amalekite
(II Samuel 1:10), it was he who actually
killed Saul. However Saul was so gravely
wounded that he appeared dead to his
weapon-bearer (*Radak to Samuel*).

6. וַיָּמָת שָׁאוּל וּשְׁלֹשֶׁת בָּנָיו וְכָל־בֵּיתוֹ — *And
Saul, his three sons and all his household*

---

total picture. Saul's shortcomings, on the other hand, are an essential part of the Davidic saga because
they were the immediate cause of David's ascension to the throne.

10

3-9

the Philistines slew Jonathan, Avinadav and Malki Shua the sons of Saul. ³ The battle bore down heavily on Saul and the bowmen located him; and he became frightened of the bowmen. ⁴ So Saul said to his armor-bearer, 'Draw your sword and pierce me with it lest these uncircumcised men come and torture me.' But the armor-bearer was unwilling, for he was very much afraid. So Saul took the sword and fell upon it. ⁵ And the armor-bearer saw that Saul was dead, and he too fell upon the sword and died. ⁶ And Saul, his three sons and all his household died; they died together. ⁷ And all the men of Israel who were in the valley saw that they had fled and that Saul and his sons were dead, and they forsook their cities and fled; and the Philistines came and occupied them. ⁸ On the next day, the Philistines came to strip the corpses; and they found Saul and his sons fallen on Mount Gilboa. ⁹ And they stripped him and took his head and armor, and they sent around the land of the Philistines to

died. I Samuel 31:6 reads: And Saul, his three sons, his weapon-bearer and all his men died. Thus it adds the information that the weapon-bearer died and talks of all his men which has wider implications than all his household. As explained in the preface to this chapter, the interest of Chronicles is directly centered on Saul's death rather than on the broader historical context.

We have taken the phrase וְכָל בֵּיתוֹ, and all his household, together with the first part of the verse rather than together with the last two words, in accordance with the cantillation. However, in this sense, the יַחְדָּו מֵתוּ, they died together, at the end of the verse seems redundant. If we could take the entire second half of the phrase together the sentence would read: So Saul and his three sons died; and thus his whole household [that is, those who were with him on the battlefield (Targum)] died in one stroke.

7. וַיִּרְאוּ כָּל־אִישׁ יִשְׂרָאֵל אֲשֶׁר־בָּעֵמֶק — And all the men of Israel who were in the valley saw. The valley referred to is the valley of Yizreel, as is clear from I Samuel 29:1 (Malbim). I Samuel 31:7 adds: ... and which were on the other side of the Jordan. Again we notice the narrower concern of Chronicles. Mention of the wider involvement is appropriate to the text concerned with the history of Israel. The thrust of our narrative, however, concerns only Saul and his family and it therefore omits some of the broader details.

כִּי נָסוּ — That they had fled. This must refer to the men of Israel mentioned in v. 1, since in the previous verse there is no mention of anyone fleeing. I Samuel 31:7 has clearly:

That the men of Israel had fled. Again, our verse concentrates only on the death of Saul and his sons.

8. לְפַשֵּׁט אֶת־הַחֲלָלִים — To strip the corpses. In the קַל the root פשט is used with clothes as the object (cf. Leviticus 6:4). In the פִּעֵל the object is the body. Hence, to strip a corpse.

נֹפְלִים — Fallen. The root נפל, to fall, is used not only to describe the act of falling but also the state of having fallen (see e.g. I Samuel 19:24). Therefore, the use of the present tense is appropriate.

9⁻10. In the account of the Philistines' gruesome actions, the accounts in Samuel and Chronicles complement one another. Samuel explicates the decapitation of Saul, which is assumed here. Samuel tells of the disposition which the Philistines made of Saul's belongings and of his body but does not mention what was done with his head. Chronicles tells what was done with the belongings and the head but makes no direct mention of the body. Verse 12, which tells of the kindness which the people of Yavesh Gilead did to Saul's body, assumes a knowledge of its disposition from Samuel. See further in commentary.

9. וַיִּשְׁלְחוּ ... סָבִיב — And they sent around. No direct object is given and we can only surmise what it is they sent. Perhaps it was the head and weapons mentioned earlier in the verse or it may mean that they sent messengers to apprise the people of what had occurred.

בְּאֶרֶץ־פְּלִשְׁתִּים סָבִיב לְבַשֵּׂר אֶת־עֲצַבֵּיהֶם וְאֶת־הָעָם:
י וַיָּשִׂימוּ אֶת־כֵּלָיו בֵּית אֱלֹהֵיהֶם וְאֶת־גֻּלְגָּלְתּוֹ תָקְעוּ בֵּית
יא דָּגוֹן: וַיִּשְׁמְעוּ כֹּל יָבֵישׁ גִּלְעָד אֵת כָּל־אֲשֶׁר־
יב עָשׂוּ פְלִשְׁתִּים לְשָׁאוּל: וַיָּקוּמוּ כָּל־אִישׁ חַיִל וַיִּשְׂאוּ אֶת־
גּוּפַת שָׁאוּל וְאֵת גּוּפֹת בָּנָיו וַיְבִיאוּם יָבֵישָׁה וַיִּקְבְּרוּ אֶת־
עַצְמוֹתֵיהֶם תַּחַת הָאֵלָה בְּיָבֵישׁ וַיָּצוּמוּ שִׁבְעַת יָמִים:

לְבַשֵּׂר אֶת־עֲצַבֵּיהֶם וְאֶת־הָעָם — *To carry the news to their idols and the people.* Metzudos explains this to mean to the priests of the idols. In his commentary to *Samuel*, Malbim suggests that the announcement to the idols was made by putting the belongings in *the house of Ashtaroth* (there v. 10), which is here called *the house of their gods*; and the announcement to the people was made by nailing the body onto the wall of Beth Shan (v. 10 there). [As noted in prefatory remarks to 9-10, no mention is made here of the disposition of the body although it is assumed in v. 12.]

10. בֵּית אֱלֹהֵיהֶם — *The house of their gods.* This expression is substituted for *house of Ashtaroth* in *Samuel*, and it indicates that Ashtaroth was an idol. The commentators write that this idol was made in the form of a sheep. This is based on the fact that עַשְׁתְּרֹת is used in Scripture (*Deuteronomy* 7:13) to denote a flock of sheep.

וְאֶת־גֻּלְגָּלְתּוֹ תָקְעוּ בֵּית דָּגוֹן — *And his skull they fastened in the house of Dagon.* Isaiah 22:33 uses תקע to describe the act of

driving in a nail. In *Genesis* 31:25 תקע is used for pitching a tent, presumably because the tent pegs have to be driven into the ground. *Judges* 3:21 uses תקע to describe a sword being thrust into a body. Thus, it would seem that Saul's skull was fastened to the temple of Dagon by means of nails or pegs.

Malbim to *Samuel* suggests that the Philistines may have had a very specific reason for choosing the temple of Dagon for displaying the vanquished king's head. Many years earlier when they had captured the holy ark from the Jewish army (*I Samuel* 55ff), they had brought it to Dagon's temple. In the presence of the Holy Ark, Dagon had tumbled down and his head, arms and legs had broken off (v. 4 there). It must have seemed sweet vengeance to the Philistines to display the severed head of Saul at that particular location.

See pref. to these verses that the account in *Samuel* makes no mention of the fate of Saul's head.[1]

11. Yavesh Gilead [i.e., the city of Yavesh

1. While we know of no teaching of the Sages to guide us in this matter it may be possible to explain this difference between the narratives in *Samuel* and *Chronicles* as follows: It would seem that it was no coincidence that the great and righteous Saul had to suffer the terrible indignity of decapitation after his death. Saul is described as having stood 'from his shoulder and up' above everyone else (*I Samuel* 9:2). The pure and selfless nature which singled him out as an ideal king for Israel was reflected in an imposing, regal stature, which, in spite of his modest and retiring nature, drew everyone's glance towards him.

Sotah 10a teaches that there were five people, part of whose being was akin to the divine. Each of them met his downfall from that very aspect of his being which was so particularly exalted. [See *Maharal*, there, for an explanation of this phenomenon.] In the case of Saul it was his neck which was god-like [since he stood higher than everyone else from his shoulders up — *Rashi*]. He met his downfall by his neck because when he fell upon his sword (v. 4) it pierced him in the place where the sword normally cuts — the neck (Talmud, there).

Surely, then, the particularly gruesome act of decapitating Saul is to be seen as underlining his failure as king in that very part of his being where the greatness of his potential had been most striking. No more graphic indication of the catastrophe of his life could be imagined than that his head should be fastened to Dagon's temple.

It is, perhaps, for this reason that *Samuel* keeps silent concerning this detail but that *Chronicles*, concerned as it is with presenting the rationale for David's rise to the kingship (see pref. to this chapter), cannot gloss over this final great indignity perpetrated against Israel's first king.

carry the news to their idols and the people. ¹⁰ *And they placed his armor in the house of their gods and his skull they fastened in the house of Dagon.* ¹¹ *Now all of Yavesh Gilead heard all that the Philistines had done to Saul.* ¹² *And every man of noble spirit arose, and they carried off the body of Saul and the bodies of his sons, and brought them to Yavesh; and they buried their bones under the oak in Yavesh and fasted for seven days.* ¹³ *Saul died for the*

---

in the land of Gilead] lay on the eastern side of the Jordan in the portion of Menasheh. [For Gilead, see *Numbers* 32:39ff.] At one time they had been under attack by Nachash, king of Ammon, who threatened them with the vilest torture. Saul heard of their plight, collected an army from the whole of Israel and came to their rescue. [For details see *I Samuel* ch. 11.] From that time onwards, the inhabitants of Yavesh Gilead viewed Saul with special veneration. Now that his terrible fate had overtaken him, it was they who took the initiative to end the shameful display of his body (*Pirkei d'R' Eliezer* 17; *Radak*).

12. בָּל־אִישׁ חַיִל — *Every man of noble spirit.* See comm. to 5:24 that the meaning of the word חַיִל changes according to the context. Only truly noble men would have been moved to risk their lives to retrieve Saul's body.

וַיִּשְׂאוּ אֶת־גּוּפַת שָׁאוּל — *And they carried off the body of Saul.* The bodies of Saul and his sons, which were hanging on the walls of a city, were accessible to them. Saul's head — in Dagon's temple — was probably well guarded and they were unable to get to it (*Malbim*).

... בְּיָבֵשׁ וַיִּקְבְּרוּ אֶת־עַצְמוֹתֵיהֶם — *And they buried their bones ... in Yavesh.* This grave was not to be Saul's final resting place. *II Samuel* 21:12ff tells how David eventually brought his bones and those of his sons [none of which had in any way disintegrated (*Pirkei d'R' Eliezer* 17)] and buried them in the grave of Saul's father, Kish, in the land of Benjamin.

וַיָּצוּמוּ שִׁבְעַת יָמִים — *And fasted for seven days. Pirkei d'R' Eliezer* 17 teaches that during these seven days of fasting they

mourned and eulogized Saul. For this they are to be rewarded when the Messianic redemption arrives. At that time, the half-tribe of Menasheh which dwelled in Gilead will be the very first to be gathered in.

The *Mefaresh* suggests that these seven days were in repayment for what Saul had done for Yavesh Gilead in the days of its danger (see comm. v. 11). When Ammon had threatened, the people of the town had asked for a seven-day grace period within which they might find someone to help them. They had found their salvation through Saul and now mourned him for these seven days.

In addition, the *Mefaresh* points out that these seven days might be the customary seven days of mourning for the death of a relative. It could well be that the people of Yavesh Gilead were related to Saul's family since, from the time of the incident of the 'concubine in Giveah' (see *Judges* ch. 19ff), there was much intermarriage between the tribe of Benjamin and the inhabitants of Yavesh Gilead (see ch. 21, there).

13-14. These two verses have no parallel in *Samuel*, where for the purposes of the historical narrative there is no need to spell out the sins for which Saul died so tragically. Within the framework of *Chronicles*, however, where this incident is related as background to David's succession (see pref. remarks to this chapter), this explanation is appropriate.[1]

David's greatness is to be understood against the background of Saul's weakness. If Saul, in spite of his personal, impeccable goodness (see below), lost the kingship because he could not live up to the uncompromising standards which the Torah expects from Israel's king, then all

---

1. Although the description of Saul's death in *Samuel* is not accompanied by any explanation as it is in *Chronicles*, the reason is given in an earlier passage. In *I Samuel* ch. 28 we have the account of how Saul communicated with Samuel after the latter's death through the agency of the witch of Ein Dor. On that occasion Samuel prophesied Saul's death at the hands of the Philistines and ascribed it to Saul's disobedience in failing to wipe out Amalek, as he had been commanded to do.

יג וַיָּמָת שָׁאוּל בְּמַעֲלוֹ אֲשֶׁר־מָעַל בַּיהוֹה עַל־דְּבַר יהוה
יד אֲשֶׁר לֹא־שָׁמָר וְגַם־לִשְׁאוֹל בָּאוֹב לִדְרֹוֹשׁ: וְלֹא־דָרַשׁ
בַּיהוֹה וַיְמִיתֵהוּ וַיַּסֵּב אֶת־הַמְּלוּכָה לְדָוִיד בֶּן־יִשָׁי:

the more does David's towering personality appear in all its grandeur.

13. וַיָּמָת שָׁאוּל — *Saul died.* If we take these words literally then the sins enumerated here are the causes of Saul's death, not the reasons why he lost his kingship. *Maharitz Chayos* suggests that this could be the answer to the apparent discrepancy between our verses and *Yoma* 22b which teaches that Saul lost his kingship because of only one fault, while here, as we shall see, five or six sins are enumerated. If our verses deal only with the causes of Saul's death, then there is no contradiction.

בְּמַעֲלוֹ אֲשֶׁר־מָעַל בַּה׳ עַל־דְּבַר ה׳ אֲשֶׁר לֹא־שָׁמַר — *For the faithlessness with which he acted towards HASHEM* [lit. *which he was unfaithful against HASHEM*] *in that he did not obey the words of HASHEM.* No particular sin is specified at this point. Since *Chronicles* obviously assumes a familiarity with Saul's story from *Samuel,* the simple meaning of our phrase appears to be a reference to the sin which is described in *Samuel* as having cost Saul his crown: his ill-considered mercy on Amalek in the face of Samuel's expressed command to eradicate them completely (*Metzudos*). The Sages, however, saw hints of a number of different transgressions in this and the following phrases. See below.

וְגַם־לִשְׁאוֹל בָּאוֹב לִדְרֹוֹשׁ — *And for consulting the necromancer for guidance.* The story of Saul's desperate attempt to learn the truth about Israel's fate from the necromancer (בַּעֲלַת אוֹב) of Ein Dor, after he had failed to elicit any response from God, is told in *I Samuel* 28:7ff. It seems remarkable that whereas in *Samuel* there is no indication of any kind that Saul's means of communicating with Samuel was considered sinful, *Chronicles* puts it at the very center of the causes of Saul's downfall. The Torah certainly forbids necromancy (*Leviticus* 20:27 and *Deuteronomy* 18:11) and, moreover, the Sages indicate that Saul's actions at Ein Dor fell within this prohibition. In *Midrash Samuel* 24 and *Vayikra Rabbah* 26 they teach that the 'man' and 'woman' mentioned in *Leviticus*

there in regard to the prohibition of necromancy hint at Saul and the woman of Ein Dor.

Nevertheless, it is equally certain that Saul did not violate the Torah's wishes in a formal sense. The Torah makes provision for a king, when necessity arises, to act in ways normally prohibited by the Torah, provided he does so on a purely temporary and emergency basis (הוֹרָאַת שָׁעָה). Saul was desperate and needed help. The *Urim VeTumim* had not answered his queries, the prophets whom he had consulted had found no vision to guide him, and his dreams had not yielded any hints of what the future might hold. As a final resort he turned to the magic of the necromancers. All other avenues had been closed to him (*Teshuvos Radvaz* 485).

But if it was not a formal transgression it was nevertheless a travesty of the kingly role. Israel's pride had always been its holy and direct communion with God for which reason it had no need for the dark magic rites to which the others nations had descended. *For these nations whom you inherit, they listen to soothsayers and magicians. But you, not so has HASHEM your God made you (Deuteronomy* 18:14). In abjectly disguising himself and creeping to the sorceress in the dark of night, Saul betrayed the very essence of his people. Israel must look to God, not to the filthy wiles of the necromancer. David was later to sing that *the king trusts in HASHEM and in the kindness of the Most High, that will not falter (Psalms* 21:8). By contrast Saul turned to magic — and showed himself unworthy to be king. *And Saul disguised himself (I Samuel* 28:8) — he became released from his kingship (*Midrash Samuel* 23 — a play on the word וַיִּתְחַפֵּשׂ (with a שׂ, *and he disguised himself,* which can also be read with a שׁ — וַיֵּחָפֵשׁ, *he became free*).

And thus, this final act of Saul was in a sense the worst. It was not the formal cause for the loss of the kingship — that, as explicated in various places in *Samuel,* came because of the debacle at the Amalekite war. But it goes to the essence of that failure; it revealed that which without

faithlessness with which he acted towards HASHEM in that he did not obey the words of HASHEM and for consulting the necromancer for guidance. 14 *And he did not seek out HASHEM, so He killed him; and He transferred the kingship to David the son of Jesse.*

it might have remained hidden. Saul had to lose his kingship not because of what he did but because of what he was. In the final analysis Saul's rule was doomed not because of misjudgments or disobedience but because those very acts which were the direct cause of his rejection derived from an erosion of the inner nobility upon which the outer trappings of royalty must be based.

And so, for *Samuel* which deals with the outer contours of the story, the implications of the visit to Ein Dor are of no particular significance — there was no formal violation of the halachah there. But for *Chronicles* it goes to the very heart of Saul's rejection and the choice of David. If it alone among all the transgressions is explicated while the others are only alluded to, it is because in a sense all those are only the outer manifestations of this essential failing.

The Sages (*Vayikra Rabbah* 26) find that Saul deserved to die for five reasons and see all five alluded to in our verse and in the first phrase of v. 14:

'Because of five sins was this righteous man killed.

— *For the faithlessness:* This refers to the wiping out of Nov, city of the *Kohanim* (*I Samuel* chs. 21 and 22);

— *with which he acted:* This refers to his having mercy on Agag (*I Samuel* 15:9);

— *in that he did not obey:* Because he did not wait for Samuel who had said to expect him in seven days (*I Samuel* 10:8);

— *and for consulting ...:* This is the sin of seeking guidance from the necromancer;

— *and he did not seek out HASHEM* (v. 14): This refers to the time Saul ordered the *Kohen* to refrain from consulting the *Urim VeTumim* (*I Samuel* 4:9).'

14. וְלֹא־דָרַשׁ בַּה' — *And he did not seek out*

HASHEM. *Radak* points out that Saul did indeed seek out *Hashem* to learn his fate through the *Urim VeTumim* and the prophets. Why then does it say that he did not search out *Hashem*? *Radak* answers that the statement is figurative. Once Saul resorted to necromancy it was as though he had never sought out God. If the dark wiles of a sorceress are considered a legitimate alternative to the prophets then they too are stripped of any sacred content.

Metzudos' solution is that Saul did not try enough. If he had really seen God as the only possible source of salvation then the initial rejection would not have deterred him from praying and seeking again and again.

וַיְמִיתֵהוּ — *So He killed him.* *Chronicles* takes us beneath the surface appearance. The narratives of the battle both in *Samuel* and here make no mention of God's role in Saul's death; Saul's death could have been ascribed to the normal consequences of battle. *Chronicles* now teaches that the Philistine archers were no more than tools in God's hands.

וַיַּסֵּב אֶת־הַמְּלוּכָה ... — *And He transferred the kingship ...* The use of the root סבב[1] to describe the transfer of the kingship from Saul to David is significant. Elsewhere we find the kingship being *given* to David (*I Samuel* 15:28, 28:17), and the kingship being *removed* from Saul and David's throne being *established* (*II Samuel* 3:10). But the use of סבב is unique to *Chronicles* where it is repeated in even more striking form at 12:23. There we learn that the officers came to Hebron לְהָסֵב מַלְכוּת שָׁאוּל אֵלָיו כְּפִי ה', *to transfer Saul's kingship to him* [David] *in accordance with God's words.*

In our context two possibilities suggest

---

1. The root סבב (when it does not mean *to surround*) has many complex nuances. These range from a simple change of direction (e.g. *Exodus* 13:18) to a significant change of status which may be either undesired, as when Adoniyah complained to Bath-Sheva that Solomon had, so to speak, 'usurped' his kingship — וַתִּסֹּב הַמְּלוּכָה וַתְּהִי לְאָחִי, *and the kingship was transferred and became my brother's* (*I Kings* 2:15); or desirable, as in *Jeremiah* 31:21 which predicts a change of heart for Israel in which [the nation] *who had been weak as a female will become strong like a male,* נְקֵבָה תְּסוֹבֵב גָּבֶר (Ibn Janach and *Metzudos*).

א וַיִּקָּבְצ֧וּ כָל־יִשְׂרָאֵ֛ל אֶל־דָּוִ֖יד חֶבְר֣וֹנָה לֵאמֹ֑ר הִנֵּ֛ה עַצְמְךָ֥
ב וּבְשָׂרְךָ֖ אֲנָֽחְנוּ: גַּם־תְּמ֣וֹל גַּם־שִׁלְשׁ֗וֹם גַּ֚ם בִּהְי֣וֹת שָׁא֣וּל
מֶ֔לֶךְ אַתָּ֗ה הַמּוֹצִ֥יא וְהַמֵּבִ֖יא אֶת־יִשְׂרָאֵ֑ל וַיֹּ֨אמֶר יְהוָ֤ה
אֱלֹהֶ֙יךָ֙ לְךָ֔ אַתָּ֞ה תִרְעֶ֣ה אֶת־עַמִּ֣י אֶת־יִשְׂרָאֵ֔ל וְאַתָּה֙

themselves. סבב may connote a simple transfer of the kingship which, as an institution, remained inviolate despite Saul's failures. From having been vested in Saul, it now came to David for whom it had always been destined.

On the other hand, the word may connote a profound change. In this sense the kingship undergoes a basic and therefore highly significant change as it moves from Saul to David.

Saul's kingship had never been that kingship which the Torah had intended. That had been promised to Judah (see *Genesis* 49:10 and comm. to 5:1-2) and could never be vested in any other tribe. The nature of Saul's kingship must be understood as only a *temporary mandate* (מַלְכוּת שָׁעָה) to rule over Israel. When the people asked for a king during Samuel's lifetime they angered God. His providence over them was, through Samuel's presence,

still so direct that they should not have felt the need of any other kind of leadership. In His anger God gave them a kingship which from its start was doomed to failure. Even if Saul had not sinned, David would eventually have become king. In that case Saul would either have continued ruling over a small segment of the nation — perhaps Rachel's descendants — Benjamin, Ephraim, and Menasheh — or he would have served in some subsidiary position to David. Because of his shortcomings he forfeited even these posts (*Ramban* to *Genesis* 49:10).

The true Jewish kingship, which carries within itself the seeds of Messianic redemption, came into being only with David's ascension to the throne. A very narrow and limited kingship now became a historic institution, central to the very concepts of Jewish nationhood and universal redemption.

XI

◄§ The Tribes ask David to be King

Verses 1-3 of our chapter parallel *II Samuel* 5:1-3 while verses 4-9 parallel verses 6-10 there.

At the time of Saul's death David was in Tziklag, a town in Philistia which had been placed at his disposal by Achish, king of the Philistines. Subsequently, God indicated to him that he should move to Hebron where his own tribe, Judah, crowned him king over them. He remained there ruling over his own tribe for seven years until, upon the initiative of Avner ben Ner, Saul's general, the rest of the tribes of Israel came to Hebron and crowned him king over all Israel. This is the point at which *Chronicles* picks up David's story. Since it assumes knowledge of the book of *Samuel* [without which the last chapter, starting as it does with Saul's death, would have been meaningless], there is no need to point out that the coronation in Hebron did not immediately follow the death of Saul. Moreover, from 3:4 we already know that David ruled seven years in Hebron before moving to Jerusalem, and this is repeated in 29:27.

1. וַיִּקָּבְצוּ כָל־יִשְׂרָאֵל — *And all Israel gathered. Samuel* has: *And all the tribes of Israel came (II Samuel 5:1). Radak* there explains that the stress on the fact that *all* the tribes came is to underline that even the tribe of Benjamin (Saul's tribe), which might have been expected to absent itself from David's moment of triumph, also joined in the coronation. Our text, then, omits this nuance. There are two possible

explanations for this. Firstly, the list of officers who participated in the coronation (12:23ff) makes clear that all the tribes, including Benjamin (12:29), attended and there was consequently no need to stress it here. Secondly, the nature of the narrative in *Chronicles* is different from that in *Samuel*. There, the whole historical background of the incident is provided, including the efforts of Avner to persuade

11

1-2

And all Israel gathered to David at Hebron and said, 'Behold we are your bone and your flesh. ² Even in times past, even while Saul was king, it was you who led Israel out and in; and HASHEM your God said to you, "You shall shepherd My people Israel and

the rest of Israel to accept David as king. To that end, Avner spoke first to the elders of Israel (II *Samuel* 3:17) and then, separately, to the tribe of Benjamin (v. 19). Within that context, it was significant that all the tribes of Israel, including Benjamin, came to proclaim David king. In *Chronicles*, however, where this background is omitted, the narrative beginning with the assembly in Hebron, underlining the fact that *all* the tribes came, would have had no special meaning.

This difference in approach can also explain the choice of the verb. Where *Samuel* used וַיָּבֹאוּ, *and they came*, *Chronicles* uses וַיִּקָּבְצוּ, *and they gathered*. The former is apt in the context of a complete narrative. The people whom we had met before discussing the desirability of accepting David as king now *came to* Hebron. בּוֹא, *to come*, bridges between a point of departure and the given destination. *Chronicles*, on the other hand, knows nothing of the people before they arrived in Hebron and describes them only as they arrive there. In Hebron, they *gathered*.

הִנֵּה — *Behold. Samuel* has הִנְנוּ, *here we are!* This has an entirely different connotation. It is more apt in *Samuel* where the thrust of the narrative is to underline the surprising submission of the Benjaminites (see above).

עַצְמְךָ וּבְשָׂרְךָ אֲנָחְנוּ — *We are your bone and your flesh. Gra* thinks that when this term is used to denote relationship, then *your bone* refers to a paternal relationsip while *your flesh* refers to a maternal relationship. The people meant to convey that whatever doubt had existed concerning David's descent from Ruth the Moabite had now been laid to rest — his father's status was considered as impeccable as his mother's.

Metzudos explains that this argument was made to dissuade David from limiting his kingship to his own tribe of Judah. Since all the tribes were descended from one man — Jacob — he was related to all of them.

2. *Metzudos* explains that this verse continues the argument of the previous one. Just as David should not consider himself bound to Judah alone by ties of kinship, so too, he should not consider Judah as having been the only tribe loyal to him over the years. All of Israel had, in effect, been led by him even during Saul's reign.

גַּם־תְּמוֹל גַּם־שִׁלְשׁוֹם — *Even in times past* [lit. *even yesterday even two days ago*]. As is obvious from the context, the events referred to happened years, not days, before. The phrase is a common Biblical idiom for the more recent past.

גַּם בִּהְיוֹת שָׁאוּל מֶלֶךְ — *Even while Saul was king*. This גַּם, *even*, is omitted in *Samuel* and thus, the two passages have different points of emphasis. In *Samuel* the translation reads: *Even in times past while Saul was king*. The phrase *while Saul was king* explains the times past but makes no particular issue out of the fact that David was in effect a ruler even while Saul was still alive — a fact which reflects badly on Saul. The word גַּם, *even*, in our verse does seem to bring out that point and is in line with the point made in the preface to ch. 10 that *Chronicles* focuses on the rule of David.

אַתָּה הַמּוֹצִיא וְהַמֵּבִיא אֶת־יִשְׂרָאֵל — *It was you who led Israel out and in*. The expression could well be idiomatic and should, perhaps, not be translated literally. The people are simply saying that David had controlled their lives even during Saul's reign. However, the *Targumim* tend to translate even idiomatic expressions literally.[1]

Thus, *Targum* to *Samuel* translates as we have done. *Targum* here renders: You lead us out — to war; and brought us in — to the study hall, and taught us [Torah].

אַתָּה תִרְעֶה אֶת־עַמִּי אֶת־יִשְׂרָאֵל — *You shall shepherd My people Israel*. You were

---

1. E.g., *Onkelos* to *Genesis* 41:44. Pharaoh told Joseph that without him no man was to *raise his hand or foot. Targum* renders: To raise his hand — to hold a weapon; to raise his foot — to ride upon a horse.

ג תִּהְיֶה נָגִיד עַל עַמִּי יִשְׂרָאֵל: וַיָּבֹאוּ כָל־זִקְנֵי יִשְׂרָאֵל
אֶל־הַמֶּלֶךְ חֶבְרוֹנָה וַיִּכְרֹת לָהֶם דָּוִיד בְּרִית בְּחֶבְרוֹן לִפְנֵי
יהוה וַיִּמְשְׁחוּ אֶת־דָּוִיד לְמֶלֶךְ עַל־יִשְׂרָאֵל כִּדְבַר יהוה
ד בְּיַד־שְׁמוּאֵל: וַיֵּלֶךְ דָּוִיד וְכָל־יִשְׂרָאֵל יְרוּשָׁלַ͏ִם

appointed shepherd over *all* Israel, not just over one tribe *(Metzudos)*. The description of the king as shepherd places the monarchy in its correct perspective. Far from being a self-fulfilling source of power for the king, it is an institution in which even the smallest, weakest and apparently least significant segment of the populace can find help and protection. '... the Torah called [the king] *shepherd* ... (see *Psalms 78:70-72*), and the way of a shepherd is taught in Scripture *(Isaiah 40:11)*: *As a shepherd looks after his flock, gathering the lambs in his arm, carrying them in his lap, and guiding the little ones'* (Rambam, *Hilchos Melachim 2:6*).

When God told David, 'You shall shepherd My people,' David said, 'The Lord is my shepherd, I shall not want' *(Psalms 23:1)*. David said, 'You tell me to tend [Your flock]. How can I tend them — I am powerless! You [God] be my shepherd so that I shall not want and then I too will be able to fulfill their needs' *(Mefaresh)*.

נָגִיד — *Prince.* This word for prince derives from the root נגד, *to be [oriented] towards*, or *opposite*. The prince is a נָגִיד because everyone turns towards him for help and

support *(Radak, Sefer HaShorashim)*.[1] See further at 29:22.

3. וַיָּבֹאוּ כָל־זִקְנֵי יִשְׂרָאֵל — *And all the elders of Israel came.* These elders of Israel are not identical with *all Israel* of v. 1. The sequence of events was as follows: First all Israel came to Hebron to beg David to extend his kingship over them. After they had done this, the elders who were to be involved in the actual coronation remained behind, made the covenant (see below), and anointed David king *(Abarbanel* to *Samuel)*.

Radak (to *Samuel*) traces a reverse sequence. וַיָּבֹאוּ in our verse is to be rendered: *And* [the elders of Israel] *had already come* [*previously*]; i.e., we are now being informed of events which form the background of those described in vs. 1 and 2. Before any steps could be taken to crown David king over all Israel the elders needed to know whether David would hold their earlier allegiance to Saul's son, Ish Bosheth (see *II Samuel 2:8ff*), against them. Moreover, there had been a five-year period during which the monarchy had been allowed to lapse completely. [See *Sanhedrin 20a* and *Rashi* and *Tosafos*

1. Perhaps this etymology can help us to understand a difference in wording between *Samuel* and *Chronicles*. The phrase in *Samuel* reads: וְאַתָּה תִּהְיֶה לְנָגִיד עַל יִשְׂרָאֵל, while *Chronicles* reads: וְאַתָּה תִּהְיֶה נָגִיד עַל עַמִּי יִשְׂרָאֵל. Where *Samuel* has לְנָגִיד, *Chronicles* has נָגִיד and adds עַמִּי.

The word נָגִיד as *prince* does not appear in Scripture before *Samuel* and it seems likely that it was not in use before then. New words are formed based on given perceptions of the thing which they describe. It is a truism that in the early periods of their use they continue to convey the idea which is the basis for their development and are so understood by the people who use them. As time goes on, however, these words cease to be strictly associated in the minds of people with the ideas which originally animated them and become neutral nouns bereft of their original meaning. We may surmise that when the word נָגִיד was used in *Samuel's* time, it conveyed the idea of *turning towards* or *orientation*, but that in later centuries it came to mean *prince* and no more.

Now in Scripture the root היה with the prefix ל — הָיָה ל ... — usually means: *to become.* Thus, the phrase in *Samuel* may mean: God said to you, *You shall shepherd My people Israel, and* [through that] *you will become* [...] the one to whom all Israel turns. The phrase וְאַתָּה תִּהְיֶה לְנָגִיד ... does not parallel the first phrase but describes a result of it. Hence, it does not have to balance the first phrase and עַמִּי has no place in it. By the time *Chronicles* was written, however, the word נָגִיד had lost its original connotation and simply meant *prince.* The form הָיָה ל ... would have meant nothing. In these circumstances the second phrase is parallel to the first and the word עַמִּי is inserted for balance. [It is also possible that the dropping of the prefix ל has no particular significance and is part of the development of language between the time *Samuel* was written and the time *Chronicles* was written. Other examples of the dropped ל in this construction are *Chronicles 18:2* compared to *II Samuel 8:2* and *Chronicles 17:21* compared to *II Samuel 7:23*. (But cf. *II Chronicles 23:16* where the הָיָה ל... is retained.)]

you shall be a prince over My people Israel." ³ And all the elders of Israel came to the king at Hebron and David made a covenant with them in Hebron before HASHEM; and they anointed David king over Israel in accordance with the word of HASHEM at the hand of Samuel.⁴ Then David and all Israel went to Jerusalem — that is

there.] All this worried the elders and they sought reassurance from David on these points. The covenant which they made with David concerned these matters and through it David promised them that these lapses would not affect his attitude towards them. Subsequently, all Israel came to promise their allegiance (vs. 1-2) and the coronation took place.

וַיִּכְרֹת לָהֶם דָּוִיד בְּרִית בְּחֶבְרוֹן — *And David made a covenant with them in Hebron.* A covenant implies that the participants — in this case apparently David and the people — shoulder certain obligations. The people swore allegiance to him and he swore that he would judge them and lead them righteously *(R' Yeshaya di Trani to Samuel)* and fight their wars for them *(Mefaresh).* For *Radak's* view of the covenant, see above.

לִפְנֵי ה' — *Before HASHEM.* When something is described as taking place *before HASHEM* this usually means that it happened in the Temple or the Tabernacle. Since the Tabernacle did not stand in Hebron, an explanation is necessary. The following solutions are offered:

— From *II Samuel* 15:7 we see that there was a public altar (בָּמָה) in Hebron. This would be sufficient for Hebron to be described as *before HASHEM (Ralbag to Samuel).*

— Wherever all of Israel, or a majority of Israel, is assembled, the Divine Presence (שְׁכִינָה) rests upon them. What they do is done *before HASHEM (Radak to Samuel).*

— Any covenant is always made *before HASHEM (Mefaresh),* because God is invoked as a witness to their commitments *(Radak to Samuel).*

— The Holy Ark was brought to Hebron temporarily for the purpose of the coronation *(Metzudos).*

וַיִּמְשְׁחוּ אֶת־דָּוִיד לְמֶלֶךְ עַל־יִשְׂרָאֵל — *And they anointed David king over Israel.* David had already been anointed by Samuel *(I Samuel* 16:13) and by the tribe of Judah *(II Samuel* 2:4). Nevertheless, he was anointed once more to stress that henceforth his kingship was to be over all Israel *(Radak to Samuel).*

כִּדְבַר ה' בְּיַד־שְׁמוּאֵל — *In accordance with the word of HASHEM at the hands of Samuel.* Samuel had anointed David king over all of Israel. Only now was Samuel's appointment realized *(Radak to Samuel).*

◄§ The Establishment of Jerusalem

4. ... וַיֵּלֶךְ דָּוִיד וְכָל־יִשְׂרָאֵל — *Then David and all Israel went* ... There was a tradition that Zion was to be the seat of Israel's monarchy and that it would not be captured by anyone who was not king over all Israel. Now was the first time these conditions were fulfilled, since Saul's kingship was not destined to last *(Radak to Samuel).* Therefore David's first act as king over all Israel was to wage the campaign against the Yevusites in Jerusalem.

The *Mefaresh* offers a different explanation for the campaign at this time. David was afraid that people might think that his military successes during Saul's lifetime were to be attributed to Saul's merit, and that he would prove impotent now that Saul was dead. He promptly set out to conquer Jerusalem in order to dispel this notion.

Samuel has, 'And David and *his men* went ...' in place of *all Israel. Radak* there notes this discrepancy but says that once David was king, all Israel were considered *his men.*

Radak must be understood as follows: It is obvious that the term אֲנָשָׁיו, *his men,* has a limiting connotation. Its meaning is to point to *his men* in contrast to some other group. However, there is no one specific way in which his men are to be differentiated from the others. It may be, as it surely meant in the many instances in which the term is used in *Samuel* up to this point, that *his men* are the ones loyal to him as opposed to those whose loyalty lay elsewhere. On the other hand, it may also mean his soldiers or army, in contrast to the rest of the people who were not fighting men. That is surely its meaning in *II Samuel* 5:21 where we learn that David and *his men* took the Philistine idols forsaken on the battlefield; the context there allows for no other interpretation. *Chronicles,* by the use of *all Israel* instead of *his men,* points out the correct meaning of the term. This was necessary because up to that point the term had been used in the former sense.

ה הִיא יְבוּס וְשָׁם הַיְבוּסִי יֹשְׁבֵי הָאָרֶץ: וַיֹּאמְרוּ יֹשְׁבֵי יְבוּס
לְדָוִיד לֹא תָבוֹא הֵנָּה וַיִּלְכֹּד דָּוִיד אֶת־מְצֻדַת צִיּוֹן הִיא
ו עִיר דָּוִיד: וַיֹּאמֶר דָּוִיד כָּל־מַכֵּה יְבוּסִי בָּרִאשׁוֹנָה יִהְיֶה
לְרֹאשׁ וּלְשָׂר וַיַּעַל בָּרִאשׁוֹנָה יוֹאָב בֶּן־צְרוּיָה וַיְהִי
ז לְרֹאשׁ: וַיֵּשֶׁב דָּוִיד בַּמְּצָד עַל־כֵּן קָרְאוּ־לוֹ עִיר דָּוִיד:
ח וַיִּבֶן הָעִיר מִסָּבִיב מִן־הַמִּלּוֹא וְעַד־הַסָּבִיב וְיוֹאָב יְחַיֶּה

יְרוּשָׁלַם הִיא יְבוּס — *Jerusalem — that is
Yevus.* Yevus is the name of the city;
Yevusites (later in this verse) is the name of
its inhabitants *(Gra).* The Jerusalem which
was later to become David's capital city
was at the time of Joshua's conquest in the
hands of the Yevusites *(Joshua 15:8, 15:63,
18:28. Judges 1:21, 19:10).* They were the
family of one Yevus, himself descended
from Avimelech, the Philistine king with
whom Abraham had made a covenant (see
Genesis 21:22ff). [That is, the name Yevus
does not in this instance refer to the
Canaanite nation of that name; see below.]
He had built a mighty fortress there some
twenty-five years after the exodus in order
to protect himself from the anticipated
Israelite invasion (see *Seder HaDoros,* year
2473).

וְשָׁם הַיְבוּסִי יֹשְׁבֵי הָאָרֶץ — *And there were the
Yevusites, dwellers in the land.* As the
Sages teach it *(Sifri,* see *Rashi* to *Joshua
15:63),* the following story emerges. Al-
though from a military standpoint
Jerusalem could well have been taken

earlier, Joshua and subsequent generations
were unable to do so because they were
bound by Abraham's vow to Avimelech
that he would not deal falsely with
Avimelech's grandchildren *(Genesis
21:23).* As a result, the tribes of Judah and
Benjamin did take some parts of the city
which had not been covered by the pact,
but had to accept the presence of enclaves
of Yevusites in their midst.

This apparently redundant phrase may
be explained by this teaching of the Sages.
It was only the fact of the Yevusites living
there, and the consequent constraints of
Abraham's pact with Avimelech, which
had prevented the area from being conquered long before *(R' Y.M.
Tucazinsky).* [1]

5-9. These five verses which describe the
conquest of Jerusalem parallel *II Samuel*
5:6-10. Our passage differs from the
passage in *Samuel* in two ways. It fills in
some details left unexplained there (see v.
6), and it reports some of the dialogue in
simpler and shorter form:

Chronicles	Samuel
5. לֹא תָבוֹא הֵנָּה, *You shall not come here.*	**6.** לֹא־תָבוֹא הֵנָּה, *You shall not come here*
	כִּי אִם־הֱסִירְךָ הָעִוְרִים וְהַפִּסְחִים לֵאמֹר לֹא־יָבוֹא דָוִד הֵנָּה *You shall not come here unless you remove the blind and the lame, saying David shall not come here.*
6. ... כָּל־מַכֵּה יְבוּסִי בָּרִאשׁוֹנָה, *Whoever kills a Yevusite first ...*	**8.** כָּל־מַכֵּה יְבֻסִי וְיִגַּע בַּצִּנּוֹר, *Whoever kills a Yevusite and will reach the tower*
	וְאֶת־הַפִּסְחִים וְאֶת הָעִוְרִים שְׂנֻאֵי נֶפֶשׁ דָּוִד, *and the lame and the blind, those reviled by David's soul.*
	עַל־כֵּן יֹאמְרוּ עִוֵּר וּפִסֵּחַ לֹא יָבוֹא אֶל־הַבָּיִת, *Therefore they say the blind and lame shall not enter the house.*

Thus the account in *Chronicles* omits
all reference to the *blind and lame* (עִוֵּר

and פִּסֵּחַ) and furthermore, it substitutes
בָּרִאשׁוֹנָה, *first,* for the very obscure וְיִגַּע

1. For a thorough discussion and analysis of the geographical and military details of David's
campaign see *R' Y.M. Tucazinsky's* monumental *Ir HaKodesh VeHaMikdash* vol. 1, part 2, ch. 1.

Yevus — and there were the Yevusites, dwellers in the land. ⁵ *The inhabitants of Yevus said to David, 'You shall not come here'; and David captured the Fortress of Zion, which is in the City of David.* ⁶ *And David said, 'Whoever kills a Yevusite first shall be a chief and an officer'; Yoav the son of Tzeruiah went up first and so he became a chief.* ⁷ *David took up residence in the fortress; therefore they called it the City of David.* ⁸ *And he built the city round about, from the plaza to the surrounding area, while Yoav restored the rest of the*

בְּצָנוֹר, *will reach the tower.* Abarbanel (to *Samuel*) feels that nothing omitted in *Chronicles* can have been an integral part of the message. Rather, the additional phrases found in *Samuel* were added for emphasis and the essential meaning of the message is in no way distorted by their omission. We may further surmise that the phrases may have been idiomatic and conveyed a vivid image at the time when they were in general use but which in subsequent centuries fell into disuse. *Chronicles* either omits them entirely [as in the case of *the blind and the lame*] or substitutes a more familiar phrase [as in וַיִּגַע בַּצִּנּוֹר, *will reach the tower*].

5. ... וַיִּלְכֹּד דָּוִיד — *And David captured* ... Abarbanel (*Samuel*) postulates the existence of two Yevusite enclaves in the area. One was the fortress discussed in our verse. This David captured by himself without the help of Yoav and it was therefore called the City of David, in his honor. The next verses deal with the capture of a second enclave which was in the city and this was captured by the efforts of Yoav — see below. According to *Radak* (to *Samuel*), however, there was only one enclave. Our verse makes the general statement that David captured it. The next verses describe how it was done.

6. כָּל־מַכֵּה יְבוּסִי ... יִהְיֶה לְרֹאשׁ — *Whoever kills a Yevusite ... shall be a chief.* Samuel (v. 18) does not spell out the reward to be gained for killing the Yevusite. This is analogous to *Genesis* 4:15 where a threat is implied to whomever kills Cain but no mention is made of what the punishment would be. *Chronicles* spells out *shall be a chief* because it turned out that this was how Yoav was rewarded. [Yoav ben Tzeruiah was David's nephew (above 2:16), and served as his general throughout his reign (see *II Samuel*).]

יִהְיֶה לְרֹאשׁ וּלְשָׂר — *Shall be a chief and an officer.* Malbim suggests that the terms are

not synonymous. A שָׂר would be an army officer while a רֹאשׁ would be a leader of the people. David mentioned both positions in case the conqueror turned out to be an army officer who was already a שָׂר. His reward would have to come to him as a *chief*. In the event, this proved to be the case. Yoav was already an officer so his reward was that he become *a chief*. For this reason it fell to Yoav's lot to supervise the non-military restoration of Jerusalem (v. 8, see there).

7. וַיֵּשֶׁב דָּוִד בַּמְצָד — *David took up residence in the fortress.* He settled there permanently (*Abarbanel* to *Samuel*). We have translated בַּמְצָד, *in the fortress,* and assumed that reference is to the מְצוּדָה, *fortress,* mentioned in v. 5, since this is the opinion of most commentators. The parallel verse in *Samuel* expressly has בַּמְצֻדָה. If this is the correct translation then the phrase, *therefore they called it the City of David,* relates to v. 5 which stated that the Fortress of Zion and the City of David are one. Our verse explains how the fortress came to be called the City of David.

Malbim, however, offers an entirely original interpretation. He believes that מְצוּדָה describes a man-made fortress but that מְצָד is a natural fortress — a mountain. Our passage is not a repetition of what was said in *Samuel* but an addition to it. The Fortress of Zion was built on top of a mountain. Initially, David overran the fortress, made it his home and called it City of David (v. 5). Subsequently, the fortress became too small and David's household overflowed onto the mountain (v. 7). Eventually people קָרְאוּ לוֹ, *'they called it,'* in the plural] began calling this expanded home of David by the name that he had originally given to the fortress — City of David.

8. וַיִּבֶן הָעִיר מִסָּבִיב מִן־הַמִּלּוֹא וְעַד־הַסָּבִיב — *And he built the city round about, from the*

יא   ט אֶת־שְׁאָר הָעִיר: וַיֵּלֶךְ דָּוִיד הָלוֹךְ וְגָדוֹל וַיהוָה צְבָאוֹת
ט-יא   עִמּוֹ:
י וְאֵלֶּה רָאשֵׁי הַגִּבֹּרִים אֲשֶׁר לְדָוִיד הַמִּתְחַזְּקִים עִמּוֹ
בְמַלְכוּתוֹ עִם־כָּל־יִשְׂרָאֵל לְהַמְלִיכוֹ כִּדְבַר יהוה עַל־
יא יִשְׂרָאֵל: וְאֵלֶּה מִסְפַּר הַגִּבֹּרִים אֲשֶׁר לְדָוִיד
°הַשְּׁלִישִׁים ק' יָשָׁבְעָם בֶּן־חַכְמוֹנִי רֹאשׁ °הַשְּׁלוֹשִׁים הוּא־עוֹרֵר אֶת

plaza to the surrounding area. מִלּוֹא is a plaza inside the city walls (Radak, Shorashim) in which the people used to gather. David made sure not to build in that area in order not to inconvenience the public. He developed only that ground which lay between the plaza and the walls of the fortress in which he had taken up residence (Radak).

Much later, David's son Solomon was not to show the same sensitivity to the people's wishes. He built up the plaza (see I Kings 11:27), and this precipitated the quarrel with Yeravoam the son of Nevat which eventually resulted in the establishment of the Northern Kingdom.

The word סָבִיב is used first as an adverb (as in Genesis 23:17) meaning around, then as a noun (as in Numbers 22:4) meaning surrounding area. In our verse it refers to the area surrounding the fortress in which David now lived. He built the city between the plaza and the area around his fortress (Radak; Ralbag).

Other interpretations of מִלּוֹא are: moat, that which is filled (מלא, to fill) with water (Abarbanel to Samuel); and abutment or rampart, a small protective wall around the actual city wall. It is called מִלּוֹא because it was a double wall filled with earth (Rashi and Gra). Abarbanel also suggests that סָבִיב as a noun may mean the city wall [that which surrounds].

Since it seems unlikely that David would build up the area between the moat or abutment (which were beyond the city wall) and the city wall, since this would deprive those living there of the protection of the wall, we suggest an alternative way of rendering our verse. [I am indebted to R' Y. Danziger for this suggestion.] The word סָבִיב may take on both a general and specific meaning; i.e., the general area surrounding the city — the perimeter — and specifically the structure which was built around the city — the abutment or moat. The thrust of this verse is to describe the division of responsibility for building the city between David and Yoav. To that end the verse states that David built the perimeter of the city (וַיִּבֶן הָעִיר מִסָּבִיב), while Yoav restored the interior (שְׁאָר הָעִיר). The verse then interjects an elaboration of what David did — namely, that he

built all of the perimeter, both the abutment (or moat) and the wall of the city. The prepositions מִן and עַד are not to be taken literally as connoting direction but should be understood idiomatically as meaning the entirety of, a common Biblical idiom as in מֵחוּט וְעַד שְׂרוֹךְ נַעַל (Genesis 14:23), or מִנַּעַר וְעַד זָקֵן (Esther 3:13).

The verse would thus be translated: And he built the perimeter of the city — both the abutment (or moat) and the wall — while Yoav restored the rest of the city.

Malbim, continuing with his assumption in the previous verse, explains as follows: He assumes מִלּוֹא to be an open place or plaza, as does Radak. Samuel, which told only of David's occupation of the fortress, reported that David's building had been limited to inwards of the plaza, that is, within the fortress. Chronicles, however, tells of David's household spilling over onto the mountain (previous verse) and now tells that after that David expanded his building activities onto the mountain, that is round about the fortress. But this building activity was limited to From the open space to the places round about. The open space itself was not built up, but was left available for the people to congregate there (as according to Radak).

וְיוֹאָב יְחַיֶּה אֶת־שְׁאָר הָעִיר — While Yoav restored the rest of the city. Yoav was given this privilege as a reward for having conquered the city (Malbim, see comm. to v. 6). יְחַיֶּה derives from חיה, to live; that is, he brought the city back to life. Metzudos explains that he made sure that all the buildings were in good repair. Gra explains that he rebuilt the parts which had been burned down during the conquest (Judges 1:8). Malbim thinks that the expression denotes a breathing of life into the city, either by making sure to increase its population or by generating a feeling of joy and bustling activity. It would also mean guaranteeing a sufficient supply of food and drink to assure everyone's comfort. Targum takes it in this latter sense, translating Yoav supported the rest of the city.

דברי הימים א   [174]

city. ⁹ David grew steadily greater and HASHEM, Master of Legions, was with him. ¹⁰ These are the chief mighty men of David who supported him forcefully in his kingship, with all Israel, to crown him; in accordance with the word of HASHEM concerning Israel. ¹¹ Now this is the tally of David's mighty men: Yashoveam the son of Chachmoni, the chief of the captains. He brandished his spear

9. הָלוֹךְ וְגָדוֹל — *Grew steadily greater.* The form indicates a constant progression (*Metzudos*).

וַה' צְבָאוֹת עִמּוֹ — *And HASHEM, Master of Legions, was with him. Targum* substitutes *was a help for him* in accordance with *Targum's* aim, manifest throughout Scripture, to avoid even the appearance of anthropomorphisms. *Samuel* has: וַה' אֱלֹהֵי צְבָאוֹת, *Hashem the Lord of Hosts.*

⋄§ The Giborim

10⁻47. This section contains a list of גִּבֹּרִים [*giborim*], *mighty men,* who were involved in David's coronation and were part of his retinue. In the course of this commentary the transliterated term *gibor (giborim)* will be used instead of *mighty man (men)* because, as the Sages make clear, the term must be understood in a very special way for which the customary terms such as mighty man, hero, or warrior, neither suffice nor reflect.

The names and exploits recounted up to Uriah the Hittite in v. 41 are either identical with or very similar to those given in *II Samuel* 23:8ff. From Zavad the son of Achlai (v. 41) until the end of the chapter, the names of the *giborim* are unique to *Chronicles.* The very similarity between the lists makes the numerous apparent discrepancies between them all the more striking, and the comm. will examine the different explanations offered by the commentators. These explanations tend to address each individual difference as a separate issue and the solutions offered are particular rather than general in nature. In light of a number of extant midrashim, it would seem that the Sages took a more general approach to the problem, seeing in these discrepancies great troves of aggadic material. Furthermore, throughout this section, they see the tales of heroic exploits as referring to great Torah accomplishments. It seems only fitting that the great King David, who was at the same time the mighty general and monarch as well as the great psalmist of history, should have been surrounded by a circle of men noted for their heroism in both of life's battlefields — that of the military conflict and that of the soul. This theme will be more fully developed in Section Two, p. 417.

Quite apart from discrepancies between our list and the one in *Samuel,* the comm. to this section is complicated by some internal difficulties. There are references to groups of three and groups of thirty, and the commentators find difficulty in determining the precise functions and standings of these various groups. The thirty [concerning whose identity there are disagreements among the commentators (see below)] would seem not to have been quite as close to the king as the three but to have nevertheless occupied a special place in his retinue.[1]

In order to simplify the comm., we offer on the following page a comparative list of the *giborim* as they appear here and as they

1. Since *Shir HaShirim* 3:7 talks of sixty *giborim* surrounding Solomon's bed it can surely be no coincidence that David had thirty *giborim* to serve him. According to *Maharal* (*Aggados* to *Sotah* 10a) the number sixty connotes a number that is full and complete. Thus, if a given unit is described in measurements of sixty the implication is that this unit comprised every possible aspect of the quality under discussion. Thus, for example, the width of Samson's shoulders is given by the Talmud there as sixty cubits because he was endowed with every conceivable quality of strength. *Maharal* there cites the sixty *giborim* of Solomon as another example; Solomon's guard comprised every possible expression of might. [Cf. also: Sleep is one sixtieth of death (*Berachos* 57b); a dream is one sixtieth of prophecy (there).]

Thus, the thirty *giborim* of David indicate a fraction of the possible. This would be significant in determining the relationship of David to Solomon. In general, aggadic literature views David's life as being a state of development which found its fulfillment in the life of his son, Solomon. (See *R'*

Chronicles	Samuel
1. יָשָׁבְעָם בֶּן חַכְמוֹנִי, *Yashoveam the son of Chachmoni*	1. יֹשֵׁב בַּשֶּׁבֶת תַּחְכְּמֹנִי ... הוּא עֲדִינוֹ הָעֶצְנִי, *Yoshev Basheveth Tachkemoni ... he is Adino the Etznite*
2. אֶלְעָזָר בֶּן דּוֹדוֹ הָאֲחוֹחִי, *Eleazar the son of Dodo the Achochite*	2. אֶלְעָזָר בֶּן דֹּדוֹ בֶּן אֲחוֹחִי, *Eleazar the son of Dodo the son of Achochi*
3. —	3. שַׁמָּה בֶן אָגֵא הָרָרִי, *Shammah the son of Agei [the] Hararite*
4. אַבְשַׁי אֲחִי יוֹאָב, *Avshai the brother of Yoav*	4. אֲבִישַׁי אֲחִי יוֹאָב, *Avishai the brother of Yoav*
5. בְּנָיָה בֶּן יְהוֹיָדָע, *Benaiah the son of Yehoiada*	5. בְּנָיָהוּ בֶּן יְהוֹיָדָע, *Benaiahu the son of Yehoiada*
6. עֲשָׂהאֵל אֲחִי יוֹאָב, *Asahel the brother of Yoav*	6. עֲשָׂהאֵל אֲחִי יוֹאָב, *Asahel the brother of Yoav*
7. אֶלְחָנָן בֶּן דּוֹדוֹ מִבֵּית לָחֶם, *Elchanan the son of Dodo from Bethlehem*	7. אֶלְחָנָן בֶּן דֹּדוֹ בֵּית לָחֶם, *Elchanan the son of Dodo [from] Bethlehem*
8. שַׁמּוֹת הַהֲרוֹרִי, *Shammoth the Harorite*	8. שַׁמָּה הַחֲרֹדִי, *Shammah the Charodite*
9. —	9. אֱלִיקָא הַחֲרֹדִי, *Elika the Charodite*
10. חֶלֶץ הַפְּלוֹנִי, *Cheletz the Pelonite*	10. חֶלֶץ הַפַּלְטִי, *Cheletz the Paltite*
11. עִירָא בֶן עִקֵּשׁ הַתְּקוֹעִי, *Ira the son of Ikkesh the Tekoite*	11. עִירָא בֶן עִקֵּשׁ הַתְּקוֹעִי, *Ira the son of Ikkesh the Tekoite*
12. אֲבִיעֶזֶר הָעֲנְּתוֹתִי, *Aviezer the Anethothite*	12. אֲבִיעֶזֶר הָעֲנְּתֹתִי, *Aviezer the Anethothite*
13. סִבְּכַי הַחֻשָׁתִי, *Sibbechai the Chushathite*	13. מְבֻנַּי הַחֻשָׁתִי, *Mevunai the Chushathite*
14. עִילַי הָאֲחוֹחִי, *Ilai the Achochite*	14. צַלְמוֹן הָאֲחֹחִי, *Tzalmon the Achochite*
15. מַהְרַי הַנְּטוֹפָתִי, *Mahrai the Netophathite*	15. מַהְרַי הַנְּטֹפָתִי, *Mahrai the Netophathite*
16. חֵלֶד בֶּן בַּעֲנָה הַנְּטוֹפָתִי, *Cheled the son of Baanah the Netophathite*	16. חֵלֶב בֶּן בַּעֲנָה הַנְּטֹפָתִי, *Chelev the son of Baanah the Netophathite*
17. אִיתַי בֶּן רִיבַי מִגִּבְעַת בְּנֵי בִנְיָמִן, *Ithai the son of Rivai from Giveah of the Benjaminites*	17. אִתַּי בֶּן רִיבַי מִגִּבְעַת בְּנֵי בִנְיָמִן, *Ittai the son of Rivai from Giveah of the Benjaminites*
18. בְּנָיָה הַפִּרְעָתוֹנִי, *Benaiah the Pirathonite*	18. בְּנָיָהוּ פִּרְעָתֹנִי, *Benaiahu the Pirathonite*
19. חוּרַי מִנַּחֲלֵי גָעַשׁ, *Churai from Nachalei Gaash*	19. הִדַּי מִנַּחֲלֵי גָעַשׁ, *Hiddai from Nachalei Gaash*
20. אֲבִיאֵל הָעַרְבָתִי, *Aviel the Arvathite*	20. אֲבִי עַלְבוֹן הָעַרְבָתִי, *the father of Alvon the Arvathite*
21. עַזְמָוֶת הַבַּחֲרוּמִי, *Azmaveth the Bacharumite*	21. עַזְמָוֶת הַבַּרְחֻמִי, *Azmaveth the Barchumite*
22. אֱלְיַחְבָּא הַשַּׁעַלְבֹנִי, *Eliachba the Shaalvonite*	22. אֶלְיַחְבָּא הַשַּׁעַלְבֹנִי, *Eliachba the Shaalvonite*
23. בְּנֵי הָשֵׁם הַגִּזוֹנִי, *The sons of Hashem the Gizonite*	23. בְּנֵי יָשֵׁן יְהוֹנָתָן, *the sons of Yashen, Yehonathan*
24. יוֹנָתָן בֶּן שָׁגֵה הַהֲרָרִי, *Yonathan the son of Shageh the Hararite*	24. שַׁמָּה הַהֲרָרִי, *Shammah the Hararite*
25. אֲחִיאָם בֶּן שָׂכָר הַהֲרָרִי, *Achiam the son of Sachar the Hararite*	25. אֲחִיאָם בֶּן שָׂרָר הָאֲרָרִי, *Achiam the son of Sharar the Ararite*
26. אֱלִיפַל בֶּן אוּר, *Eliphal the son of Ur*	26. אֱלִיפֶלֶט בֶּן אֲחַסְבַּי בֶּן הַמַּעֲכָתִי, *Eliphelet the son of Achasbai the son of the Maachathite*
27. חֵפֶר הַמְּכֵרָתִי, *Chepher the Mecherathite*	27. אֱלִיעָם בֶּן אֲחִיתֹפֶל הַגִּלֹנִי, *Eliam the son of Achithophel the Gilonite*
28. אֲחִיָּה הַפְּלֹנִי, *Achiyah the Pelonite*	
29. חֶצְרוֹ הַכַּרְמְלִי, *Chetzro the Carmelite*	28. חֶצְרַי הַכַּרְמְלִי, *Chetzrai the Carmelite*
30. נַעֲרַי בֶּן אֶזְבָּי, *Naarai the son of Ezbai*	29. פַּעֲרַי הָאַרְבִּי, *Paarai the Arbite*
31. יוֹאֵל אֲחִי נָתָן, *Yoel the brother of Nathan*	30. יִגְאָל בֶּן נָתָן מִצֹּבָה, *Yigal the son of Nathan from Tzovah*
32. מִבְחָר בֶּן הַגְרִי, *Mivchar the son of Hagri*	31. בָּנִי הַגָּדִי, *Bani the Gadite*
33. צֶלֶק הָעַמּוֹנִי, *Tzelek the Ammonite*	32. צֶלֶק הָעַמֹּנִי, *Tzelek the Ammonite*
34. נַחְרַי הַבֵּרֹתִי, *Nachrai the Berothite*	33. נַחֲרַי הַבְּאֵרֹתִי, *Nachrai the Beerothite*
35. עִירָא הַיִּתְרִי, *Ira the Yithrite*	34. עִירָא הַיִּתְרִי, *Ira the Yithrite*
36. גָּרֵב הַיִּתְרִי, *Garev the Yithrite*	35. גָּרֵב הַיִּתְרִי, *Garev the Yithrite*
37. אוּרִיָּה הַחִתִּי, *Uriah the Hittite*	36. אוּרִיָּה הַחִתִּי, *Uriah the Hittite*

are given in *Samuel*.

The other sixteen names in our chapter have no parallel in *Samuel*. [Although *Chronicles* 3 and 9 are blank, we have counted them on the assumption that the names were left out for some reason. This seems likely since C2 and 4 and C8 and 10 parallel S2 and 4 and S8 and 10. On the other hand, since C28 has no parallel in the S list the numbering of the two lists has to diverge at that point. Note further that *Malbim* thinks that S26 is really two names in which case the S list would also end up with thirty-seven names.[1]]

10-11. The two verses seem to speak of two different groups of people. Verse 10 deals with the *chief giborim of David who supported him forcefully in his kingship ... to crown him ...*, that is, *giborim* who were involved in his coronation. Verse 11, however, is the list of *David's giborim* with no reference to the coronation, and as we have seen, it is a list [up to C37] which is almost identical with the list in *Samuel* which makes no mention of the coronation. *Malbim's* solution is that this explains the additional sixteen *giborim* who are listed from the middle of v. 41 [from C37] onwards which are not listed in *Samuel*. These sixteen were involved in the coronation but were not part of the regular roster of *giborim*. Thus, v. 10 gives a general introduction to the complete list: All these *giborim* were involved in the crowning. Then v. 11 begins a list of *giborim* whose involvement with David did not end with the coronation but who remained with him constantly, with the ones present at the coronation only appended to the end of it (v. 41ff).

10. הַמִּתְחַזְּקִים עִמּוֹ — *Who supported him forcefully.* חזק, *to be strong*, in the הִתְפָּעֵל, *reflexive*, usually means: *to strengthen oneself, to take strength* or *courage*. It is rarely used with עִם, *with*. See *Daniel* 10:21.

כִּדְבַר ה' עַל־יִשְׂרָאֵל — *In accordance with the word of* HASHEM *concerning Israel.* When

Samuel speaks of David's coronation it does not stress that it accorded with *Hashem's* promise. It may well have been the perspective of history which justified this assessment. At the time, many obstacles had still to be hurdled before it bcame clear that the Davidic line was indeed to be a permanent one.

⚜ The Group of Three

11. יָשָׁבְעָם בֶּן־חַכְמוֹנִי — *Yashoveam the son of Chachmoni.* This is C1 in our list. S1 has: יֹשֵׁב בַּשֶּׁבֶת תַּחְכְּמֹנִי רֹאשׁ הַשָּׁלִשִׁי הוּא עֲדִינוֹ הָעֶצְנִי, *Yoshev Basheveth Tachkemoni, chief of the three, he is Adino the Etznite.* Additionally, our verse states that he slew three hundred men in one battle, whereas *Samuel* has it as eight hundred. Following are some of the solutions offered:

— *Mefaresh:* חַכְמוֹנִי, *Chachmoni* = תַּחְכְּמוֹנִי, *Tachkemoni. Samuel* talks of the father, *Chronicles* of the son. The former killed eight hundred in battle (see there), the latter only three hundred.

The translation of the verse in *Samuel* would then be as follows: The phrase יֹשֵׁב בַּשֶּׁבֶת [*Yoshev Basheveth*] is taken separately. It is not a name but means: *he who sat in the seat* [of judgment] (שֶׁבֶת is a *seat*, cf. *Amos* 6:3). The Sages explain it as the Sanhedrin. Thus: *These are the names of David's giborim. The [first] one who sat in the Sanhedrin [was called] Tachkemoni. He was the leader of the [group of] three and he was [also known as] Adino the Etznite. He was able to brandish his spear over eight hundred slain at one time.* [Note that the cantillation marks there do indeed separate יֹשֵׁב from בַּשֶּׁבֶת תַּחְכְּמֹנִי.]

— *Radak* (to *Samuel*): תַּחְכְּמֹנִי, *Tachkemoni,* and בֶּן חַכְמוֹנִי, *the son of Chachmoni,* are not names but descriptive words relating to this *gibor's* wisdom. בֶּן is not being used in the sense of *son* but in the sense of one possessed of a certain quality [as in בֶּן חַיִל]. Here the meaning would be *one* [who has the quality] *of wisdom.* The name of the *gibor* was actually *Adino the Etznite.* The name יָשָׁבְעָם, *Yashoveam,* here is a contraction of the two words יוֹשֵׁב

Tzadok HaKohen, *Tzidkas HaTzadik* 244 and R' *Yitzchak Hutner, Pachad Yitzchak to Pesach* 68. See further in Section Two to ch. 17, p. 437.) The fact that David had only a half of the possible number of *giborim,* while Solomon had the full complement, would tend to confirm this. It is worthy of note that R' *Shmuel ben Chofni, Gaon,* in a comm. to *Deuteronomy* 1:15 which talks of *officers of the thousand, hundred, fifty, and ten,* expresses surprise that no mention is made of officers commanding groups of thirty. Our passage clearly indicates that such groups existed. In light of the above, it is possible that the groups of thirty were unique to David's army, for the reasons discussed here.

1. *II Samuel* 23:39 states clearly that there were thirty-seven *giborim.* See *Radak* and *Metzudos* there for their explanations of the reckoning.

יב חֲנִיתוֹ עַל־שְׁלֹשׁ־מֵאוֹת חָלָל בְּפַעַם אֶחָת: וְאַחֲרָיו אֶלְעָזָר
יג בֶּן־דּוֹדוֹ הָאֲחוֹחִי הוּא בִּשְׁלוֹשָׁה הַגִּבֹּרִים: הוּא־הָיָה עִם־
דָּוִיד בַּפַּס דַּמִּים וְהַפְּלִשְׁתִּים נֶאֶסְפוּ־שָׁם לַמִּלְחָמָה וַתְּהִי
חֶלְקַת הַשָּׂדֶה מְלֵאָה שְׂעוֹרִים וְהָעָם נָסוּ מִפְּנֵי פְלִשְׁתִּים:
יד וַיִּתְיַצְּבוּ בְתוֹךְ־הַחֶלְקָה וַיַּצִּילוּהָ וַיַּכּוּ אֶת־פְּלִשְׁתִּים

הָעָם [בְּרֹאשׁ], *one who sits at the head of the people,* and he was called this because, due to his wisdom (תַּחְכְּמֹנִי), he sat among the advisors of the king (יָשֵׁב בַּשֶּׁבֶת). The problem of the number of slain attributed to him can be solved by assuming that the two numbers refer to two different occasions. At one time he killed eight hundred and at another three hundred.

— *Malbim:* This first of the *giborim* excelled in two areas — in his love of wisdom and in his valor in battle. *Samuel* deals with his love of wisdom which was so great that it made him chief [in that area] of *the three* (רֹאשׁ הַשְּׁלֹשִׁי). *Chronicles* deals with his military prowess. This was less remarkable and did not make him chief of the three but of the thirty (רֹאשׁ הַשָּׁלִישִׁים), who constituted a lower echelon. [*Malbim* takes the word שָׁלִישִׁים as *thirty* rather than as *captains.*] His name was Adino the Etznite but he was also called יָשָׁבְעָם בֶּן חַכְמוֹנִי, *Yashoveam the son of Chachmoni,* which are contractions meaning: יָשֵׁב־עָם, *he who sits at the head of the people,* and בֶּן חָכָם, *son of a wise man.* There is no contradiction between the numbers eight hundred and three hundred because the two accounts describe different aspects of his might. *Samuel* is to be read as follows: *Adino the Etznite, the chief of the three, loved wisdom* [so much that] *he would sit in the council of the wise even after a battle in which he killed eight hundred people* [and he would not use his exhaustion as an excuse to absent himself from the study hall]. *Chronicles* tells us of his physical strength. *He was able to brandish his spear* [without any effort] *even after* [he had exerted himself by] *slaying three hundred men.*

רֹאשׁ הַשָּׁלִישִׁים — *The chief of the captains.* The word is used in this sense in *Exodus* 14:7. *Samuel* has: *chief of the three.* See above for *Malbim's* explanation. *Radak* (to *Samuel*) thinks that שָׁלִשִׁי in *Samuel* is to be understood as though it were written שָׁלִשִׁים [that is, identical with the text in

Chronicles] and cites examples where the final ם of the plural form is dropped.

Although the word here is to be read שָׁלִשִׁים, *captains,* it is written שְׁלֹשִׁים, *thirty.* It may be that the captains were organized into groups of thirty. (See pref. to these verses.)

הוּא־עוֹרֵר אֶת־חֲנִיתוֹ — *He brandished his spear.* עוֹר, commonly translated *to awaken,* is often used in the sense of *arousing* or *inciting to action* (cf. *Judges* 5:12 and many more). Thus, עוֹרֵר אֶת־חֲנִיתוֹ might be rendered literally, *he activated his spear.* It refers either to the movements made with the spear as it is used in battle, or the triumphant waving of the spear over the vanquished foe.

12. וְאַחֲרָיו — *After him.* While this *gibor,* too, belonged to the three who were apparently closest to David (see below), he was lower in rank then Yashoveam (*Metzudos*).

אֶלְעָזָר בֶּן־דּוֹדוֹ הָאֲחוֹחִי — *Eleazar the son of Dodo the Achochite.* In *Samuel* he is listed as, *Eleazar, the son of Dodo, the son of Achochi.* The name Achochite here refers to a family, not a place — i.e., of the family of Achochi (*Radak* to *Samuel*).

הוּא בִּשְׁלוֹשָׁה הַגִּבֹּרִים — *He was among the three mighty men.* *Rashi* to *Samuel* remarks: The greatest among the *giborim.* Apparently there were three *giborim* who were a higher echelon than all the others. They were Yashoveam, Eleazar and Shammah the son of Agei (S3), who is mentioned in *Samuel* but not in *Chronicles.*

Metzudos thinks that this phrase is just a shortened form of the phrase in *Samuel: Among the three giborim who were with David when they shamed the Philistines ...* According to this there is no indication that these three *giborim* were particularly important; they just happened to be with David on that occasion. *Samuel* tells of a major military exploit performed by this Eleazar. In one of the battles with the

over three hundred slain men at one time. ¹² *After him was Eleazar the son of Dodo the Achochite. He was among the three mighty men.* ¹³ *He was with David at Pas Damim, where the Philistines had gathered for battle, and there was a tract of land full of barley; and the people had fled from before the Philistines.* ¹⁴ *But they made a stand in the tract and saved it, and they smote the Philistines. And*

Philistines, he smote the enemy until *his hand cleaved to the sword*, and on that occasion God granted a great deliverance to Israel. *Chronicles* does not tell of this adventure — we know it from *Samuel*, and *Chronicles* had nothing to add *(Malbim).* [See next verse for the exploit which *Chronicles* does ascribe to Eleazar.]

13⁻14. The exploit ascribed in these verses to Eleazar is almost identical with one which *Samuel* ascribes to the third *gibor*, Shammah the son of Agei, who is not mentioned here at all. In spite of the similarity between the two narratives, there are some differences: Our passage talks of a field full of barley while *Samuel* has a field full of lentils; v. 14 describes the stand of this *gibor* through which he saved the crop in the plural while *Samuel* has the singular form. In the comm. to v. 19 we shall discuss the solution which the Sages offer for the discrepancy in the crops — they do not address the other two dissimilarities. Here we shall list the approach of some of the commentators.

— *Radak:* The words הוּא הָיָה, *he was*, in v. 13 do not refer to Eleazar (C2 and S2) but to Shammah (S3). Although he is not mentioned here by name, he is hinted at in v. 12 which talks of the *three* of which, according to *Samuel*, he was a a part. Thus it is understood that reference is to him. It may be that Eleazar helped him in this exploit and that is why the plural form is used in v. 14. The main hero, however, was Shammah and for that reason *Samuel* talks only of him and uses the singular. The different crops present no problem. The field had already been harvested and now was used as a drying area for sheaves from other fields. There were sheaves of barley and of lentils. One narrative mentions one so the second talks of the other.

— *Gra, Metzudos:* The differences between the two narratives indicate that they describe two different exploits which were only superficially alike. The one from *Samuel* was performed by Shammah and the one described here by Eleazar. The

plural form is explained because he was helped by David *(Gra).*

Malbim: The exploit described here is an expansion of the exploit which *Samuel* ascribes to Eleazar (v. 10 there). *Samuel* only tells of the great slaughter which he perpetrated until *his hand cleaved to his sword. Chronicles* fills in the details by telling that this battle revolved around a barley field. [It is not the same exploit ascribed by *Samuel* (v. 11) to Shammah.] *Samuel* does not elaborate as *Chronicles* does because, as is evident from the plural form in v. 14, Eleazar had the help of his company in accomplishing his victory. *Samuel* records only those exploits which were done by the *gibor* alone.

13. בַּפַּס דַמִּים — *At Pas Damim.* Commentators suggest that this may be identical with אֶפֶס דַמִּים of *I Samuel* 17:1 which had earlier been the site of another Philistine attack.

וְהַפְּלִשְׁתִּים נֶאֱספוּ־שָׁם לַמִּלְחָמָה — *Where the Philistines had gathered for battle.* They had gathered there to avenge the slaughter which Eleazar had wreaked upon them in the episode recorded in *Samuel* (v. 10) but not here. [See comm. to previous verse.]

וַתְּהִי חֶלְקַת הַשָּׂדֶה מְלֵאָה שְׂעוֹרִים — *And there was a tract of land full of barley.* The Philistines had apparently come to steal the produce of the land *(Ralbag* and *Abarbanel* to *Samuel).*

וְהָעָם נָסוּ מִפְּנֵי פְלִשְׁתִּים — *And the people had fled from before the Philistines.* Terrified by the marauders, the people had abandoned the field.

14. ... וַיִּתְיַצְּבוּ — *But they made a stand ...* As explained in the preface to 13-14, the use of the plural here indicates that the stand was made by more than one person. Those involved were either Shammah and Eleazar *(Radak)*, the entire company of three, including Yashoveam *(Malbim)*, or Eleazar and David *(Gra).*

15⁻19. The exploit described in these ver-

טו וַיּוֹשַׁע יהוה תְּשׁוּעָה גְדוֹלָֽה: וַיֵּרְדוּ שְׁלוֹשָׁה֩ מִן־
הַשְּׁלוֹשִׁים רֹאשׁ עַל־הַצֻּר אֶל־דָּוִיד אֶל־מְעָרַת עֲדֻלָּם
טז וּמַחֲנֵה פְלִשְׁתִּים חֹנָה בְּעֵמֶק רְפָאִֽים: וְדָוִיד אָז בַּמְּצוּדָֽה
יז וּנְצִיב פְּלִשְׁתִּים אָז בְּבֵית לָֽחֶם: וַיִּתְאָו דָּוִיד וַיֹּאמַר מִי
יח יַשְׁקֵנִי מַיִם מִבּוֹר בֵּֽית־לֶחֶם אֲשֶׁר בַּשָּֽׁעַר: וַיִּבְקְעוּ
הַשְּׁלֹשָׁה בְּמַחֲנֵה פְלִשְׁתִּים וַיִּֽשְׁאֲבוּ־מַיִם מִבּוֹר בֵּֽית־לֶחֶם
אֲשֶׁר בַּשַּׁעַר וַיִּשְׂאוּ וַיָּבִאוּ אֶל־דָּוִיד וְלֹֽא־אָבָה דָוִיד
יט לִשְׁתּוֹתָם וַיְנַסֵּךְ אֹתָם לַֽיהוָֽה: וַיֹּאמֶר חָלִילָה לִּי מֵֽאֱלֹהַי

ses was performed by three *giborim* whose names are not given. [But see below to v. 20.] The story is also told in *Samuel*.

15. וַיֵּרְדוּ שְׁלוֹשָׁה מִן־הַשְּׁלוֹשִׁים רֹאשׁ — *And three who were leaders among the thirty went down.* The syntax is difficult but the translation follows *Radak* and *Metzudos*. Each one of the three was a leader (ראש) among the thirty. Verse 20 tells that Avshai, brother of Yoav (C4 and S4), was the *leader of the three.* The implication is that there were at least two groups of three. The first and most prestigious was the one consisting of Yashoveam-Adino (C1, S1), Eleazar (C2, S2) and Shammah (S3). The second group (presumably our three anonymous *giborim*) consisted of Avshai, Benaiah and Asahel (C,S, 4-6). Avshai, then, was the leader of this second group of three (v. 20) which ranked lower than the first group (v. 21). There is a clear implication in our verse that at least this second group of three were part of a group of thirty.[1]

Malbim (Samuel) suggests that the thirty are to be counted as follows: The first two groups of three are to be included in the count, which would make twenty-nine to Paarai the Arbite (S29). In *Malbim's* view, however, Eliphelet the son of Achasbai the son of the Maachathite (S26) is to be counted as two [Eliphelet the son of Achasbai; the son of the Maachathite], thus making Paarai the Arbite the thirtieth in the list. From Paarai onward there are another seven names of *giborim* who were not significant enough to be counted among the thirty. The last verse in the *Samuel* list ends with the words: ... *all [together] thirty-seven.* That is, according to *Malbim*, thirty and seven. All this is true for the *Samuel* list. In the *Chronicles* list Eliphal the son of Ur (C26) replaces Eliphelet the son of

Achasbai (S26) and there is no son of the Maachathite. Naarai the son of Ezbai (C30) is the parallel of Paarai the Arbite and is therefore the thirtieth on the list. [Achiyah the Pelonite (C28), who is not counted in the *Samuel* list, makes up for the son of the Maachathite.]

Malbim's computation agrees with the implication of our verse, that the second three are included in the thirty and there is no reason to suppose that the first three were not also included. However, most commentators do not count the first two groups of three among the thirty, as will be explained below (v. 25).

וַיֵּרְדוּ ... עַל־הַצֻּר אֶל־דָּוִיד — *Went down upon the crag to David.* Since the *giborim* went down upon the crag, they must have been higher up the mountain, with David's cave somewhat lower (*Radak*).

אֶל־מְעָרַת עֲדֻלָּם — *To the cave of Adullam.* Adullam is a city in the portion of Judah (see *Joshua* 15:35). *Radak* thinks that this incident took place before David was crowned king, since we also find him hiding in the cave of Adullam while he was a fugitive from Saul (*I Samuel* 22:1). *Abarbanel* thinks it more likely that this incident happened after the coronation. *II Samuel* 5:17 reports that when the Philistines heard that David had been crowned king they gathered to make war against him, and upon hearing this, David went to the *fortress.* This could well be the fortress described here (v. 16). Furthermore, it says there (v. 18) that in that campaign the Philistine army was in the valley of Rephaim, as it says here.

16. וְדָוִיד אָז בַּמְּצוּדָה — *David was then in the fortress.* The cave of Adullam is described as a fortress (*Metzudos*).

1. Both the *Targum* here and *Targum Yonasan* to *Samuel* know nothing of any groups of thirty because they render every שְׁלִשִׁים that occurs in the text as גִּבְרַיָּא, *giborim.* That is, they read the word as though it were written שָׁלִישִׁים, *captains.* As noted in v. 11, the word there is spelled שְׁלוֹשִׁים but read as שָׁלִשִׁים. However, the שְׁלוֹשִׁים of our verse is read as it is written and there seems no reason to render it *giborim. Rashi* and *Radak* to *Samuel* note *Targum's* rendering.

HASHEM *brought about a great salvation.* 15 *And three who were leaders among the thirty went down upon the crag to David, to the cave of Adullam, while a camp of Philistines was encamped in the Valley of Rephaim.* 16 *David was then in the fortress and a Philistine garrison was then in Bethlehem.* 17 *And David craved and said, 'Who will give me water to drink from the cistern in Bethlehem which is by the gate?'* 18 *So the three breached the Philistine camp, and drew water from the cistern of Bethlehem which was by the gate; and they carried it off and brought it to David. But David did not want to drink it and he poured it as a libation to HASHEM.* 19 *And*

וּנְצִיב פְּלִשְׁתִּים אָז בְּבֵית לָחֶם — *And a Philistine garrison was then in Bethlehem. Rashi* (to *Samuel*) assumes נְצִיב to have been a unit of the army. He writes that although the main army was in the valley of Rephaim, their מַצָּב [that is the term used in *Samuel* instead of נְצִיב] was in Bethlehem. Seemingly he takes the word to mean a garrison.

Radak and *Metzudos* take the word to mean *officer.* The officers with a small group of soldiers camped in Bethlehem away from the main body of the army. Until early in David's reign much of the land was in Philistine hands.

Mefaresh understands the verse to mean a Philistine governor or prefect who was stationed in Bethlehem.

17. וַיִּתְאָו דָוִיד — *And David craved. Samuel* has וַיִּתְאַוֶּה, a more usual form of אוה, *to desire.* However, it is not unusual for the final *hey* to be dropped; cf. *Psalms* 45:12.

מִי יַשְׁקֵנִי מַיִם מִבּוֹר בֵּית־לָחֶם — *Who will give me water to drink from the cistern in Bethlehem.* David had come from Bethlehem (*I Samuel* 17:12 and 58) and therefore craved the water whose taste he had known as a child (*Mefaresh*). Since from v. 19 it is obvious that he had not actually intended that the water be brought to him, we understand the phrase as a wistful thought: 'If only I had some of the refreshing water of my youth!' (*Metzudos*).

אֲשֶׁר בַּשָּׁעַר — *Which is by the gate.* According to the simple meaning of the verse, this was the location of the particular well David had in mind. The apparent pedantry of identifying the well so precisely and repeating it in the next verse was surely one of the indications which caused the Sages to give the passage the interpretation that שַׁעַר, *gate,* refers to the seat of the Sanhedrin and that David was

not longing for water but for instruction on a point in halachah (see below).

18. וַיִּבְקְעוּ הַשְּׁלשָׁה בְּמַחֲנֵה פְלִשְׁתִּים — *So the three breached the Philistine camp.* When they heard that David craved the water they went on their own initiative in order to give him pleasure (*Metzudos*).

This too may well have induced the Sages to interpret the incident as discussed below. It is inconceivable that David's men would have held life so cheap that they would risk almost certain death in order to satisfy David's thirst.

The root בקע has the basic meaning of: *cleave, break open* or *through* (see *Ecclesiastes* 10:9; *Judges* 15:19; and *Amos* 1:18). The *Mefaresh* explains that the Philistines had gathered around the cistern in order to prevent access and the three *giborim* drove a wedge through them to get to the water.

וַיִּשְׁאֲבוּ ... וַיִּשְׂאוּ — *And drew [water] ... and they carried it off ...* The commentators point to the heroism and skill of the *giborim.* While they were engaged in drawing the water they would have been unable to defend themselves, and in fighting their way back to their own lines we might have expected the water to spill. Nevertheless they managed to accomplish all that they had set out to do.

וְלֹא־אָבָה דָוִיד לִשְׁתּוֹתָם — *But David did not want to drink it.* David's refusal to drink the water is explained in the next verse. He could not bear to put the water which had been obtained by such heroism to such a trivial use. It had become too precious to be used for anything but a libation before *Hashem.*

וַיְנַסֵּךְ אֹתָם לַה׳ — *And he poured it as a libation to HASHEM.* The use to which an object is put should reflect the cost at which it was obtained (*Abarbanel*).

מֵעֲשׂוֹת זֹאת הֲדַם הָאֲנָשִׁים הָאֵלֶּה אֶשְׁתֶּה בְנַפְשׁוֹתָם
כִּי בְנַפְשׁוֹתָם הֱבִיאוּם וְלֹא אָבָה לִשְׁתּוֹתָם אֵלֶּה עָשׂוּ
כ שְׁלֹשֶׁת הַגִּבֹּרִים: וַאֲבִשַׁי אֲחִי־יוֹאָב הוּא הָיָה
רֹאשׁ הַשְּׁלוֹשָׁה וְהוּא עוֹרֵר אֶת־חֲנִיתוֹ עַל־שְׁלֹשׁ מֵאוֹת
כא חָלָל °וְלֹא־שֵׁם בַּשְּׁלוֹשָׁה: מִן־הַשְּׁלוֹשָׁה בַשְּׁנַיִם נִכְבָּד
כב וַיְהִי לָהֶם לְשָׂר וְעַד־הַשְּׁלוֹשָׁה לֹא־בָא:

°וְלוֹ ק'

בְּנָיָה

It is not simple to determine the exact nature of this libation:

The *Mefaresh*, quoting Bar Kaparah (from *Yerushalmi Sanhedrin* 2:5), states that it was the festival of Succos, at which time a libation of water had to be made on the altar. *Yerushalmi* adds that in Bar Kaparah's opinion there was a *bamah*, a private altar, in the place where David was encamped.[1]

Many commentators (*Radak, Metzudos, R' Yeshaya diTrani*) think that the libation was not made on an altar at all, since the halachah knows of no water libation except the communal one on Succos, which could not have been meant here. They explain that David poured the water out upon the ground in honor of *Hashem*.

Abarbanel, however, explains that David did not make the libation at that moment. He set aside the water and made the libation later when he came to the central altar.

19. חָלִילָה לִי — *Far be it from me.* From the root חלל, *to pollute, defile, profane,* is derived the word חֹל, *profaneness, commonness* (e.g. *I Samuel* 21:5). Hence the mishnaic term, חוּלִין, *that which is not holy,* and the biblical term חָלִילָה which commentators render: *It is* חוּלִין *for me,* an act which is not worthy of me.

הֲדַם הָאֲנָשִׁים הָאֵלֶּה אֶשְׁתֶּה — *Shall I drink the blood of these men?* Since they risked their lives in bringing me this water it is as though they had brought me their very life's blood (*Metzudos*).

כִּי בְנַפְשׁוֹתָם הֱבִיאוּם — *For they brought it with their lives.* Because they risked their lives in bringing it (*Mefaresh*).

We have on this passage the interpreta-tion of the Sages which serves to illustrate how the Sages viewed the entire matter of David's *giborim*. As the Sages teach it, David's thirst was not for the sweet waters of Bethlehem but for instruction in Torah. [Water is frequently used as a metaphor for Torah.] The Sanhedrin [hinted at in the word שַׁעַר, *gate,* in v. 17 — the courts sat at the city gates; see *Deuteronomy* 25:7] was located in Bethlehem, and David needed guidance concerning certain halachic problems. The three *giborim* crashed through the Philistine lines in order to reach the Sanhedrin, posed the problems which needed resolution and brought the rulings back to David. David, horrified that they had risked their lives for a Torah ruling under circumstances in which there was no justification for such disregard for human life, punished them in a manner appropriate to their failing. See below.

For the purpose of their interpretation the Sages take the two episodes — the one with the barley field (vs. 13-14) and the one with the water — as one. This, although according to the simple meaning of the passages they seem to be two different incidents.

According to the Sages, the two armies were deployed opposite one another. David's forces were in Jewishly held land where a barley field was located, while the Philistines were in their own territory where there was a field of lentils owned by Philistine farmers. David's soldiers wanted to commandeer the barley of the Jewish farmers to feed their animals on the anticipation that they would repay the owners with the lentils which they were about to capture from the Philistines. The question arose whether this was permissible. David did not know the halachah and

---

1. *Rashash* to *Ruth Rabbah* notes that this opinion of the *Yerushalmi* is not without problems. The libation made on Succos was a communal sacrifice and such sacrifices can never be brought on a private altar even when such altars were permissible.

he said, 'Far be it from me before my God to do this! Shall I drink the blood of these men [when they jeopardized] their lives [for it]? For they brought it with their lives.' And so he would not drink it. These deeds were performed by the three mighty men.[20] *And Avshai the brother of Yaov was the leader of the three; he brandished his spear over three hundred slain men; he was illustrious among the three.*[21] *He was the most respected among the second three and he became their officer, but he did not come to*

---

bemoaned the fact that the Sanhedrin was not available to guide him.

The answer which the *giborim* brought back from the Sanhedrin was that under normal circumstances it would be forbidden to take an object unlawfully [in this case the barley for fodder] even with the intention of repaying. Nevertheless, what is forbidden to a commoner may be allowed a king, whose royal prerogative extends to confiscation of property where that is appropriate. Verse 18 tells that David refused to avail himself of this special dispensation.

In the Sages' interpretation, the phrase, *and he poured it as a libation to HASHEM*, is to be taken metaphorically. Since he desisted from availing himself of the royal privilege which entitled him to commandeer the barley as fodder for his soldiers' animals, and since this was a religiously appropriate stance, it was considered as though he had made a libation to God with the 'water' [ruling] which he had obtained.

Bava Kama 60b (which suggests two other possibilities for the problem for which David sought guidance) considers the answer which David received one which he could have used in good conscience. Therefore, his refusal to drink must be given a different interpretation from the one given above. The Talmud there interprets as follows: Normally a person who teaches a given halachic ruling is entitled to have his name attached to that ruling; it is to be taught in his name. The three *giborim* who would, under different circumstances, have merited this honor, lost their right to it in this case because they risked their lives in a situation in which they should not have done so. Therefore, David refused to say it in their name [*David did not want to drink it*] but reported the halachic ruling which they had obtained anonymously (מִשְׁמָא דְּגְמָרָא), as part of the huge body of law which is, so to speak, the property of the whole community rather than being attached to

any individual. Thus, *he poured it out as a libation for HASHEM.*

20. וְאַבְשַׁי אֲחִי־יוֹאָב — *And Avshai the brother of Yoav.* Avshai was David's nephew (2:16) and a general in his army. He is mentioned several times in *Samuel.* We would have expected Yoav, the greatest of David's warriors, to be listed among the *giborim*, but his very stature precluded this. Since he was the general over all of them he could not be listed among them (*Mefaresh*).

הוּא הָיָה רֹאשׁ הַשְּׁלוֹשָׁה — *Was the leader of the three.* He was the leader of the three *giborim* whose exploit in bringing David water was described in 15-19 (*Mefaresh, Radak*).

וְלוֹ־שֵׁם בַּשְּׁלֹשָׁה — *He was illustrious* [lit. *had a name*] *among the three.* Since he, too, was able to brandish his spear over three hundred victims as Yashoveam had done, he was highly esteemed by the people. That esteem did not put him completely into the category of the first three who were, after all, more exalted than he (v. 21), but he was not altogether of a different caliber (*Malbim*).

21. מִן־הַשְּׁלוֹשָׁה בַשְּׁנַיִם נִכְבָּד — *He was the most respected among the second three.* The syntax is difficult and the translation follows *Malbim.* There were two groups of three *giborim.* Avshai, although he was respected even among the first three (v. 20), nevertheless belonged to the second three and was the most illustrious of them.

Radak has שְׁנַיִם, *two*, referring to the other two *giborim* in the second three. He was more respected than the other two *giborim* in his group.

וְעַד־הַשְּׁלוֹשָׁה לֹא־בָא — *But he did not come to the [first] three.* In the hierarchy of the *giborim*, he was not counted among the first three. While his exploits in the matter of the three hundred slain was the same as that of Yashoveam, he nevertheless did not have his standing (*Malbim*).

בֶּן־יְהוֹיָדָע בֶּן־אִישׁ־חַיִל רַב־פְּעָלִים מִן־קַבְצְאֵל הוּא הִכָּה
אֵת שְׁנֵי אֲרִיאֵל מוֹאָב וְהוּא יָרַד וְהִכָּה אֶת־הָאֲרִי בְּתוֹךְ
כג הַבּוֹר בְּיוֹם הַשָּׁלֶג: וְהוּא הִכָּה אֶת־הָאִישׁ הַמִּצְרִי אִישׁ
מִדָּה | חָמֵשׁ בָּאַמָּה וּבְיַד הַמִּצְרִי חֲנִית כִּמְנוֹר אֹרְגִים
וַיֵּרֶד אֵלָיו בַּשָּׁבֶט וַיִּגְזֹל אֶת־הַחֲנִית מִיַּד הַמִּצְרִי וַיַּהַרְגֵהוּ
כד בַּחֲנִיתוֹ: אֵלֶּה עָשָׂה בְּנָיָהוּ בֶּן־יְהוֹיָדָע וְלוֹ־שֵׁם בִּשְׁלוֹשָׁה

22. בְּנָיָה בֶּן־יְהוֹיָדָע — *Benaiah the son of Yehoiada.* See below, v. 24, whether Benaiah belonged to the three *giborim* who brought the water. In *Samuel* (see S5) this *gibor* is called בְּנָיָהוּ *Benaiahu.* This spelling is also used in v. 24.

With the exception of Avshai, Benaiah is better known to us from Scripture than any of the other *giborim.* Particularly in the time of Solomon, we find him as an important member of the king's household who was entrusted with the execution of Solomon's judgment against Adoniah (*I Kings* 2:25); Yoav (there 29-34) and Shimei ben Gera (there 41-46). After Yoav's death he was appointed general in his place (there, 2:35 and 4:4).

In *II Samuel* 8:18 and 20:23 we find Benaiah appointed over the *Cherethi* and *Pelethi.* There is much uncertainty concerning the meaning of this term. *Targum* renders: *bowmen and slingers,* assuming Benaiahu to have been in charge of certain segments of the army. In the tradition of the Sages, Benaiahu was אַב בֵּית דִּין, *head of the Sanhedrin (Berachos* 4a). According to *Tosafos* there this is implied by the words: The Sanhedrin renders definite and precise decisions כְּרֵתִי from כרת, *to cut*], and as a group they are distinguished in the quality of their judgments פְּלֵתִי is similar to מוּפְלָא, one who is special or distinguished]. (See also *Midrash Tehillim* to *Psalms* 3.)

Once more we have the link between greatness in Torah and greatness on the battlefield. Benaiah is commander of the marksmen and at the same time president of the court. See Section Two.

בֶּן־אִישׁ־חַיִל — *A valiant man. Targum* renders: *One who shuns evil* [lit. *fears sin*].

The *Mefaresh* writes that בֶּן here is not to be translated as *son* but as denoting possession of quality, as in the expression בֶּן בְּלִיַּעַל, *a worthless person* (*I Samuel* 25:17). *Malbim* to *Exodus* 18:21 comments that the adjective חַיִל always denotes that

the person has all the skills and attributes required for the task at hand. Thus a בֶּן אִישׁ חַיִל would be one eminently suited for the role he is to play — in the simple context of our passage it would be that of a valiant soldier.

Radak takes בֶּן literally and assumes that Benaiah's father, Yehoiada, was also a mighty warrior. *Abarbanel* also translates בֶּן as *son* but treats the expression as a metaphor. It tells us that Benaiah's military skill was so great that it seemed that he had inherited it; it flowed in his veins, so to speak.

In *Samuel* the phrase is written בֶּן אִישׁ חַי, *a living man,* although, there too, it is read בֶּן אִישׁ חַיִל as it is here. The *Mefaresh* explains that the כְּתִיב, *written form,* defines the essence of the קְרִי, *pronounced form.* Valor (חַיִל) is the most graphic form of life (חַי). When seeing a hero in action one is wont to say that he is full of life.

Berachos (18a,b) wonders what the meaning of בֶּן אִישׁ חַי, *son of a living man,* can be. Are people ever born from dead men? The phrase must mean that life was the very essence of Benaiah's being. He typified the great *tzaddik,* who even in death is described as alive (צַדִּיקִים בְּמִיתָתָן נִקְרְאוּ חַיִּים). See Section Two, p. 417, for a discussion of this.

רַב־פְּעָלִים — *Of many deeds.* He performed many heroic acts (*Mefaresh*). This description is unique to Benaiah.

מִן־קַבְצְאֵל — *From Kavtzeel.* This is a city in Judah's territory mentioned in *Joshua* 15:21 (*Gra*).

Berachos 18b takes this phrase together with the earlier one רַב־פְּעָלִים מִן־קַבְצְאֵל, *he increased and gathered Torah deeds* (קַבְצְאֵל from קבץ, *to gather*).

הוּא הִכָּה אֵת שְׁנֵי אֲרִיאֵל מוֹאָב — *He smote the two Moabite heroes. Targum* here expands on *Targum* of *Samuel. Targum* there simply renders: *Two great ones of Moab. Targum* here adds: Who were like [as

the [first] three. ²² Benaiah the son of Yehoiada, a valiant man of
many deeds from Kavtzeel. He smote the two Moabite heroes, and
he went down and smote the lion in the pit on a snowy day. ²³ And
he slew an Egyptian — a man of great size, five cubits — and in the
Egyptian's hand was a spear like a weaver's beam, and he went
down to [face] him with a staff. He tore the spear away from the
hand of the Egyptian and slew him with his own spear. ²⁴ These
deeds did Benaiahu the son of Yehoiada perform. He was illustrious

---

fearsome as] lions [אֲרִיאֵל from אֲרִי, lion].
Mefaresh explains that the word אֲרִיאֵל is
used to describe a mighty warrior because
both אֲרִי, lion, and אֵל, mighty one (see
Ezekiel 17:13), carry associations of
strength. Thus, mighty as lions.

Ralbag agrees to the etymological
derivation but thinks that אֲרִיאֵל refers to a
fortress. Thus he [Benaiah] conquered two
Moabite fortresses.

Berachos 18b, continuing its interpretation of the passage as dealing with Benaiah
the Torah leader rather than Benaiah the
warrior, offers: He put to shame [הִכָּה,
smote, denigrate] the periods שָׁנֵי from
שָׁנִים, years rather than שְׁנֵי, two] of the two
Temples [אֲרִיאֵל is used in Scripture to
describe the Temple (Isaiah 29:1) which
could be described as a Temple of Moabites
because it was built by Solomon who was
descended from the Moabite Ruth].
Throughout those two periods there was
no one who could be compared to him.

וְהִכָּה אֶת־הָאֲרִי בְּתוֹךְ הַבּוֹר בְּיוֹם הַשָּׁלֶג — And
smote the lion in the pit on a snowy day. A
lion is even more difficult to fight in a
narrow place (such as a pit) where the
attacker has little room to maneuver
(Metzudos). A freezing day also tends to
impair the agility of the hunter more than
the lion (Metzudos), and moreover affords
the lion the opportunity to blind his
attacker by kicking snow in his eyes
(Mefaresh). Nevertheless Benaiah managed
to kill the lion.

Once more Berachos 18b reads this
phrase as a description of Benaiah's
righteousness. Either the phrase tells us
that he smashed the ice of a river (according to Targum, the Shiloach stream) in
order to immerse himself in the water to
obtain ritual cleanliness [perhaps the 'lion'
in this case is the extreme and fearful cold
of the water], or, that he studied the whole
of Toras Kohanim (an extremely complicated set of halachos) on a short winter's

day [according to Targum, on the tenth of
Teves]. אֲרִי, in this version, is apparently
related to the Aramaic אוֹרְיָן, study or
Torah. Thus בַּר אוֹרְיָן, one who is a learned
person.

We have noted the midrashic interpretations from Berachos although it is clear that
there is much in them which requires
further elucidation. For example, the fact
that just here the Moabite descent of
Solomon should be stressed in connection
with the Temple which he built certainly
calls for further study. The purpose in
bringing these interpretations is to stress
once more the duality which the Sages see
in David's giborim, how the valiant warrior
and the righteous Torah scholar fuse into
one.

23. אִישׁ מִדָּה חָמֵשׁ בָּאַמָּה — A man of great
size, five cubits. Samuel has instead: אִישׁ
מַרְאֶה, a man of [fearful] appearance. Radak
points out that the meaning is the same.
The expression אִישׁ מִדָּה is similar to אַנְשֵׁי
מִדּוֹת (Numbers 13:22). There Rashi
comments that it denotes a person who is
so tall that one would have to specify his
size to get a real grasp of his appearance.

חֲנִית כִּמְנוֹר אֹרְגִים — A spear like a weaver's
beam. The spear was as thick as a weaver's
beam (Targum), a size proportionate to the
giant. Samuel leaves out this description of
the spear. This expression is also found
below in 20:5 and II Samuel 21:19.

וַיֵּרֶד אֵלָיו בַּשָּׁבֶט — And he went down to
[face] him with a staff. Against this
awesomely armed and mighty warrior,
Benaiah went down armed only with a
stick. He managed to disarm the Egyptian
and to kill him with his own weapon.

24. וְלוֹ־שֵׁם בִּשְׁלוֹשָׁה הַגִּבֹּרִים — He was illustrious among the three mighty men.
There is disagreement among the commentators whether Benaiah belonged to the
second group of three [who had brought

כה הַגִּבֹּרִים: מִן־הַשְּׁלוֹשִׁים הִנּוֹ נִכְבָּד הוּא וְאֶל־הַשְּׁלֹשָׁה
וְגִבּוֹרֵי

כו לֹא־בָא וַיְשִׂימֵהוּ דָוִיד עַל־מִשְׁמַעְתּוֹ:

הַחֲיָלִים עֲשָׂהאֵל אֲחִי יוֹאָב אֶלְחָנָן בֶּן־דּוֹדוֹ מִבֵּית

כז־כח לָחֶם: שַׁמּוֹת הַהֲרוֹרִי חֵלֶץ הַפְּלוֹנִי: עִירָא

כט בֶּן־עִקֵּשׁ הַתְּקוֹעִי אֲבִיעֶזֶר הָעַנְּתוֹתִי: סִבְּכַי

ל הַחֻשָׁתִי עִילַי הָאֲחוֹחִי: מַהְרַי הַנְּטֹפָתִי חֵלֶד

לא בֶּן־בַּעֲנָה הַנְּטֹפָתִי: אִיתַי בֶּן־רִיבַי מִגִּבְעַת

לב בְּנֵי בִנְיָמִן בְּנָיָה הַפִּרְעָתֹנִי: חוּרַי מִנַּחֲלֵי גָעַשׁ

לג אֲבִיאֵל הָעַרְבָתִי: עַזְמָוֶת הַבַּחֲרוּמִי אֶלְיַחְבָּא

לד הַשַּׁעַלְבֹנִי: בְּנֵי הָשֵׁם הַגִּזוֹנִי יוֹנָתָן בֶּן־שָׁגֵה

לה הַהֲרָרִי: אֲחִיאָם בֶּן־שָׂכָר הַהֲרָרִי אֱלִיפַל בֶּן־

לו־לז אוּר: חֵפֶר הַמְּכֵרָתִי אֲחִיָּה הַפְּלוֹנִי: חֶצְרוֹ

---

the water (vs. 15-19)]. Most commentators agree that he did indeed belong to those three and that is the meaning of our phrase (*Mahari Kara; Abarbanel; Malbim*). According to this view the phrase in the next verse, ... *but he did not come up to the three*, means that he did not attain the stature of the first group of three.

Metzudos, however, thinks that he was not even among the second three and that that is the meaning of the phrase in the next verse. Our verse simply relates that the second group of three respected him for his prowess although he was not one of them.

25. מִן־הַשְּׁלוֹשִׁים הִנּוֹ נִכְבָּד הוּא — *He was more respected than the thirty*. In comm. to v. 15 we noted *Malbim's* opinion, that the first six *giborim* are part of the count of the thirty. The meaning of our phrase must then be that although Benaiah belonged to the thirty he was nevertheless more important than the others. *Malbim* explains that this was because he was the head of the Sanhedrin (see v. 22). However, most commentators assume that the count of the thirty begins after the first six (see below). In that case our verse means that since he was more illustrious than these thirty he was not counted among them.

וְאֶל־הַשְּׁלֹשָׁה לֹא־בָא — *But he did not come up to the three*. See comm. to v. 24. The logic of our verse is clear according to *Metzudos*. Benaiah was more illustrious than the thirty, and was therefore not counted among them, but he was also not quite as

illustrious as the second three and was therefore not counted among them either. According to the commentators who are of the opinion that he did indeed belong to the second group of three, and that our phrase refers to the first 'three,' we must see our sentence as an explanation of the previous one. Verse 24 counted Benaiah among the second 'three.' Verse 25 tells us the reason: He was more illustrious than the thirty but not up to the first three.

וַיְשִׂימֵהוּ דָוִיד עַל־מִשְׁמַעְתּוֹ — *And David placed him in command of* [lit. *over*] *his loyal followers*. מִשְׁמַעַת [from שמע, *to hear*] is taken as a group of people who are obedient to some central commander by *Targum* to *I Samuel* 22:14. Our translation is based on that *Targum* and is followed by several commentators. In Benaiah's case, these loyal followers of David would be the *Cherethi* and *Pelethi* (*Malbim*) which are identified by *Targum* (see *II Samuel* 8:18 and 20:23) as *bowmen and slingers*.

Metzudos defines the word as meaning a person who listens to another and does his bidding. Our phrase would thus be rendered: *And David appointed Benaiahu as his adjutant.*

It has been noted (comm. to v. 22) that Benaiahu is often mentioned in *Samuel* and *Kings* as being a prominent part of David and Solomon's retinue, and in many instances it was he who executed their wishes. Our verse may explain why Benaiahu, who stood only fifth in the hierachy of *giborim*, is mentioned so often while the others occur only as a group. The special role to which David appointed him may

among the three mighty men. ²⁵ He was more respected than the thirty but he did not come up to the three, and David placed him in command of his loyal followers. ²⁶ Now, the mighty men of the armies were Asahel the brother of Yoav, Elchanan the son of Dodo from Bethlehem. ²⁷ Shammoth the Harorite, Cheletz the Pelonite. ²⁸ Ira the son of Ikkesh the Tekoite, Aviezer the Anethothite. ²⁹ Sibbechai the Hushathite, Ilai the Achochite. ³⁰ Mahrai the Netophathite, Cheled the son of Baanah the Netophathite. ³¹ Ithai the son of Rivai from Giveah of the Benjaminites, Benaiah the Pirathonite. ³² Churai from Nachalei Gaash, Aviel the Arvathite. ³³ Azmaveth the Bacharumite, Eliachba the Shaalvonite. ³⁴ The sons of Hashem the Gizonite, Yonathan the son of Shageh the Hararite. ³⁵ Achiam the son of Sachar the Hararite, Eliphal the son of Ur. ³⁶ Chepher the Mecherathite, Achiyah the Pelonite. ³⁷ Chetzro the

have thrust him into the position which he held. *Targum* here renders: *And David appointed him as Rosh HaYeshivah over the students.*

26. וְגִבּוֹרֵי הַחֲיָלִים — *Now, the mighty men of the armies.* This phrase introduces a list of *giborim* who, while valiant soldiers, were not at the level of the earlier five *(Mefaresh)*.

עֲשָׂהאֵל אֲחִי יוֹאָב — *Asahel the brother of Yoav.* *Samuel* has: *And Asahel the brother of Yoav with the thirty,* which would imply that Asahel is to be counted among the group of thirty. This, however, cannot be the case. Firstly, a glance at the list will show that if we count Asahel there would be thirty-one *giborim* with Uriah the Hittite. Secondly, most commentators assume that Asahel was among the three who brought the water [Avshai, Benaiahu, Asahel] and these stood higher in the hierachy than the thirty. *Malbim* suggests that he did indeed belong to the second three of the more exalted six. Nevertheless he was not as close to David as the other five, and he took his place with the group of thirty although he was not in fact part of them. [Asahel died before David's coronation *(II Samuel* 2:23). His association with David, therefore, must have been from earlier times.]

אֶלְחָנָן בֶּן־דּוֹדוֹ — *Elchanan the son of Dodo.* From here through Uriah the Hittite (v. 41) is the list of the thirty *giborim.* It parallels the list in *Samuel* in most details. A glance at the list will show that there are two types of discrepancies between the lists. The first is relatively minor differences in spelling [see e.g. שָׁמּוֹת (C8) for שָׁמָּה (S8)], a type of

deviation which, as can be seen from numerous instances in the genealogical lists of the first nine chapters, is extremely common. The second is the case where a completely different name is used [see, e.g., Sibbechai (C13) for Mevunai (S 13)], but where there is nevertheless a strong indication that the same person is meant [both are described as Hushathites]. In such cases the commentators *(R' Shmuel ben Chofni, Gaon, Metzudos, Malbim)* assume that the person may have had two names, one of which is given in *Samuel,* the other in *Chronicles.* Alternatively, *Malbim* suggests that the original *gibor* may have died and he was later replaced by another. [See Section Two for what seems to have been the opinion of the Sages.]

In one instance a *gibor* from *Samuel* [אֱלִיקָא הַחֲרֹדִי (S9)] has been left out altogether, and the number is made up by inserting אֲחִיָּה הַפְּלֹנִי (C28), who has no parallel in the *Samuel* list.

31. מִגִּבְעַת בְּנֵי בִנְיָמִין — *From Giveah of the Benjaminites.* By leaving גִּבְעַת untranslated rather than rendering רָמָא as they do at other places, the *Targumim* indicate that the word is a proper noun and is not to be taken as *hill.*

34. בְּנֵי הָשֵׁם הַגִּזוֹנִי יוֹנָתָן בֶּן־שָׁגֵה הַהֲרָרִי — *The sons of Hashem the Gizonite, Yonathan the son of Shageh the Hararite.* Here we have a substantive difference between the lists. *Samuel* has בְּנֵי יָשֵׁן יוֹנָתָן, linking Yehonathan to *the sons of Yashen,* which seems parallel to our *the sons of Hashem.* For our *Yonathan the son of Shageh the Hararite,* Samuel has *Shammah the Hararite.*

לח הַכַּרְמְלִי נַעֲרַי בֶּן־אֶזְבָּי: יוֹאֵל אֲחִי נָתָן מִבְחָר

לט בֶּן־הַגְרִי: צֶלֶק הָעַמּוֹנִי נַחְרַי הַבֵּרֹתִי נֹשֵׂא כְּלֵי

מ־מא יוֹאָב בֶּן־צְרוּיָה: עִירָא הַיִּתְרִי גָּרֵב הַיִּתְרִי אוּרִיָּה

מב הַחִתִּי זָבָד בֶּן־אַחְלָי: עֲדִינָא בֶן־שִׁיזָא הָראוּבֵנִי

מג רֹאשׁ לָראוּבֵנִי וְעָלָיו שְׁלֹשִׁים: חָנָן בֶּן־מַעֲכָה

מד וְיוֹשָׁפָט הַמִּתְנִי: עֻזִּיָּא הָעֲשְׁתְּרָתִי שָׁמָע °וִיעוּאֵל

°וִיעִיאֵל ק'

מה בְּנֵי חוֹתָם הָעֲרֹעֵרִי: יְדִיעֲאֵל בֶּן־שִׁמְרִי וְיֹחָא

מו אָחִיו הַתִּיצִי: אֱלִיאֵל הַמַּחֲוִים וִירִיבַי וְיוֹשַׁוְיָה

מז בְּנֵי אֶלְנָעַם וְיִתְמָה הַמּוֹאָבִי: אֱלִיאֵל וְעוֹבֵד וְיַעֲשִׂיאֵל

הַמְּצֹבָיָה:

א וְאֵלֶּה הַבָּאִים אֶל־דָּוִיד לְצִיקְלַג עוֹד עָצוּר מִפְּנֵי שָׁאוּל

ב בֶּן־קִישׁ וְהֵמָּה בַּגִּבּוֹרִים עֹזְרֵי הַמִּלְחָמָה: נֹשְׁקֵי קֶשֶׁת

מַיְמִינִים וּמַשְׂמִאלִים בָּאֲבָנִים וּבַחִצִּים בַּקָּשֶׁת מֵאֲחֵי

ג שָׁאוּל מִבִּנְיָמִן: הָרֹאשׁ אֲחִיעֶזֶר וְיוֹאָשׁ בְּנֵי הַשְּׁמָעָה

---

41. אוּרִיָּה הַחִתִּי — *Uriah the Hittite.* Uriah is the last of the names listed in *Samuel* and ends the list of the thirty. Names like Uriah the Hittite at first glance seem to indicate that David had non-Jewish men among his followers. According to the Talmud (*Kiddushin* 7b), however, these descriptions refer to the places in which they lived rather than to their nationality. In fact, they were all Jewish.

זָבָד בֶּן־אַחְלָי — *Zavad the son of Achlai.* This *gibor* begins a list of sixteen names which have no parallel in *Samuel.* In comm. to vs.

10-11 the point has been made that this group of *giborim* were specifically involved with David's coronation but were not part of his regular retinue.

42. רֹאשׁ לָראוּבֵנִי — *Head of the Reuvenites.* *Targum* inserts: head of the tribe of Reuven.

וְעָלָיו שְׁלֹשִׁים — *And there were thirty attached to him. Targum* adds: thirty *giborim.* These thirty *giborim* are not all listed since only another fourteen names follow *(Ralbag).*

XII

Our chapter deals with the different groups of followers who attached themselves to David at various stages of his career prior to his becoming king. In this, it backtracks from the previous chapter to the time when Saul was still king and David was fleeing from him. The rest of the chapter lists the military heroes who came to Hebron to participate in the transfer of power from Saul's descendants to David.

These lists do not appear in *Samuel.* We can only surmise why *Chronicles* included them in its account of these events. Perhaps it is in line with the emphasis which *Chronicles* places on legitimizing David's kingship as against that of Saul (see above, comm. to 10:13,14; 11:2). If even during Saul's lifetime substantial numbers of the other tribes defected to David, this would tend to show the high esteem in which David was held even then by the people of Israel.

Our chapter uses many terms describing aspects of the military, the exact meaning of which is not clear to us. We cannot really grasp the varying nuances in expressions such as: יוֹצְאֵי צָבָא לַעֲרֹךְ מִלְחָמָה (v. 36), or יוֹצְאֵי צָבָא עֹרְכֵי מִלְחָמָה (v. 33); (v. 25); גִּבּוֹרֵי חַיִל לַצָּבָא without a precise knowledge of how the armies in David's time were organized. We have therefore translated as closely to the meaning of the Hebrew words as possible,

Carmelite, Naarai the son of Ezbai. ³⁸ Yoel the brother of Nathan, Mivchar the son of Hagri. ³⁹ Tzelek the Ammonite, Nachrai the Berothite, the armor-bearer of Yoav the son of Tzeruiah. ⁴⁰ Ira the Yithrite, Garev the Yithrite. ⁴¹ Uriah the Hittite, Zavad the son of Achlai. ⁴² Adina the son of Shiza the Reuvenite, head of the Reuvenites; and there were thirty attached to him. ⁴³ Chanan the son of Maachah, Yoshaphat the Mithnite. ⁴⁴ Uzzia the Ashterathite, Shama and Yeiel the sons of Chotham the Aroerite. ⁴⁵ Yediael the son of Shimri, Yocha his brother, the Titzite. ⁴⁶ Eliel the Machavimite, Yerivai and Yoshaviah the sons of Elnaam, Yithmah the Moabite. ⁴⁷ Eliel, Oved and Yaasiel the Metzovaites.

These are the ones who joined David at Tziklag, while he was still constrained by Saul the son of Kish; they were among the mighty men who assisted in the war. ² Armed with bow, and ambidextrous with [both] stones and arrows and bow, they were from among Saul's brothers, from Benjamin. ³ The chief was Achiezer and Yoash the sons of Hashemaah the Giveathite, Yeziel

---

recognizing the likelihood that there is an occasional idiom for which a literal translation may well be inappropriate.

⋖ The Forces coming over to David

1⁻7. In the face of constant harassment by Saul, David had finally decided to leave the Holy Land. He knew well the spiritual void which would be his lot if he left that land in which the proximity of God was most felt, and he was keenly aware of the magnitude of that loss. As he movingly described his plight when he called out to Saul from the mountain after having spared his life ... *for they have driven me out this day, [preventing me] from being contained within HASHEM's land, as if to say, 'Go and serve other gods' (I Samuel* 26:19). [From this the Sages deduce that whoever lives outside the Holy Land is like one who has no God.] But the risk of falling into Saul's hands was too great. So, accompanied by a loyal band of six hundred men, he made his way to the Philistine Achish, king of Gath. He was kindly received and, upon his request, he was allowed to settle with his followers in an outlying town — Tziklag. From there David went marauding against Israel's enemies, such as the Amalekites, while allowing Achish to think that he was, in fact, fighting against the Israelites. When the climactic battle in which Saul was killed by the Philistines took place, David and his men were forced by the Philistine officers, who did not trust them,

to remain in Tziklag (see *I Samuel* chs. 27 and 29 for details).

1. עוֹד עֲצוּר — *While he was still constrained.* The translation follows *Malbim.* Other commentators render *hidden.* This seems to be the opinion of *Targum* as well. He renders בָּבוּשׁ, a term which is also used to translate words which connote hiding — see e.g., *Exodus* 3:6. The basic meaning of the root עצר is *to restrain.*

עֹזְרֵי הַמִּלְחָמָה — *Who assisted in the war.* They were to assist him in the war which he would wage *(Malbim).*

2. מַיְמִינִים וּמַשְׂמְאֵלִים — *Ambidextrous* [lit. *able to use both right and left hand*]. From *Judges* 20:16 it appears that many Benjaminites were left-handed *(Malbim).*

בָּאֲבָנִים — *With [both] stones.* Stones hurled from slings could be deadly projectiles. It was in this manner that David slew Goliath *(I Samuel* 17:49). Both *Mefaresh* and *Metzudos* seem to think that the stones in this context were projectiles propelled by a bow.

מֵאֲחֵי שָׁאוּל מִבִּנְיָמִן — *They were from among Saul's brothers, from Benjamin.* אָח in our context is to be understood as *relative*

הַגִּבְעָתִי °וַיּוֹאֵל וָפֶלֶט בְּנֵי עַזְמָוֶת וּבְרָכָה וְיֵהוּא ק׳ °וְיִזְאֵל
הָעֲנָתֹתִי: ד וְיִשְׁמַעְיָה הַגִּבְעוֹנִי גִּבּוֹר בַּשְּׁלֹשִׁים וְעַל־
הַשְּׁלֹשִׁים: ה וְיִרְמְיָה וְיַחֲזִיאֵל וְיוֹחָנָן וְיוֹזָבָד הַגְּדֵרָתִי:
ו אֶלְעוּזַי וִירִימוֹת וּבְעַלְיָה וּשְׁמַרְיָהוּ וּשְׁפַטְיָהוּ °הַחֲרוּפִי ק׳ °הַחֲרִיפִי:
ז אֶלְקָנָה וְיִשִּׁיָּהוּ וַעֲזַרְאֵל וְיוֹעֶזֶר וְיָשָׁבְעָם הַקָּרְחִים:
ח-ט וְיוֹעֵאלָה וּזְבַדְיָה בְּנֵי יְרֹחָם מִן־הַגְּדוֹר: וּמִן־הַגָּדִי נִבְדְּלוּ
אֶל־דָּוִיד לַמְצַד מִדְבָּרָה גִּבֹּרֵי הַחַיִל אַנְשֵׁי צָבָא
לַמִּלְחָמָה עֹרְכֵי צִנָּה וָרֹמַח וּפְנֵי אַרְיֵה פְּנֵיהֶם וְכִצְבָאִים
עַל־הֶהָרִים לְמַהֵר: עֵזֶר הָרֹאשׁ עֹבַדְיָה הַשֵּׁנִי
יא-יב אֱלִיאָב הַשְּׁלִשִׁי: מִשְׁמַנָּה הָרְבִיעִי יִרְמְיָה הַחֲמִשִׁי: עַתַּי
יג הַשִּׁשִּׁי אֱלִיאֵל הַשְּׁבִעִי: יוֹחָנָן הַשְּׁמִינִי אֶלְזָבָד הַתְּשִׁיעִי:
יד-טו יִרְמְיָהוּ הָעֲשִׂירִי מַכְבַּנַּי עַשְׁתֵּי עָשָׂר: אֵלֶּה
מִבְּנֵי־גָד רָאשֵׁי הַצָּבָא אֶחָד לְמֵאָה הַקָּטָן וְהַגָּדוֹל לְאָלֶף:
טז אֵלֶּה הֵם אֲשֶׁר עָבְרוּ אֶת־הַיַּרְדֵּן בַּחֹדֶשׁ הָרִאשׁוֹן וְהוּא
מְמַלֵּא עַל־כָּל־°גְּדִיתָיו ק׳ °גְּדוֹתָיו וַיַּבְרִיחוּ אֶת־כָּל־הָעֲמָקִים לַמִּזְרָח

rather than the more frequent use of *brother* (*Metzudos*). [The word probably derives from the root אחה, *to tie together*, and can therefore be used to describe any close relationship or, indeed, friendship.] See Section Two, p. 421.

3. הָרֹאשׁ אֲחִיעֶזֶר וְיוֹאָשׁ בְּנֵי הַשְּׁמָעָה — *The chief was Achiezer and Yoash the sons of Hashemaah.* As indicated by the singular ראש, *chief*, this description refers only to Achiezer. He was the chief of the Benjaminites who came and he was accompanied by his brother Yoash (*Metzudos*).

Malbim, with an eye to verse 4 which describes the Yishmaiah mentioned there as being in charge of *thirty*, notes that altogether twenty-three Benjaminites are listed here between our verse and verse 6. Then verses 9 through 13 count eleven Gadites who also came to join David, a total, therefore, of thirty-four.

If we postulate that each company of ten had its own officer this would account for thirty-three out of the thirty-four men. The thirty-fourth, Yishmaiah, could then be described as chief of *thirty*, i.e., he was the overall commander of this group of thirty men. According to this scheme, *Malbim* explains the description *chief* of our verse as referring to both Achiezer and Yoash.

They were each chief of one company of ten.

4. גִּבּוֹר בַּשְּׁלֹשִׁים — *Mighty among the thirty.* The translation follows *Malbim's* interpretation of verse 3. However, *Metzudos* renders שלשים in our verse as *captains*, as in Exodus 14:7 (see also above 11:11).

Some texts have verses 4 and 5 combined into one (see *Mikraos Gedolos*). We have followed *Minchas Shai* in separating them.

8. מִן־הַגְּדוֹר — *From Gedor.* Some texts have מִן־הַגְּדוּד, *from the troop* (see *Mikraos Gedolos*, Lublin ed.). Our text follows *Mikraos Gedolos*, Warsaw ed. and *Koren*. This version is also found in *Mordechai Breuer's* text which is taken from the *Kether Aram Zova*, the remnants of the *Ben Asher* manuscript considered by *Rambam* to be the most reliable text. [Both versions are cited by *Minchas Shai*.]

9. The Gadites enumerated here joined David while he was in *the stronghold in the wilderness*. The commentators assume that this refers to the period recorded in *I Samuel* ch. 23 where David is described as being in *strongholds in the wilderness* (v. 14 there). Accordingly, this took place before the Benjaminites of the previous verses joined forces with him — since they

and Pelet the sons of Azmaveth, Berachah, and Yehu the Anathothite. ⁴ And Yishmaiah the Giveonite, mighty among the thirty and over the thirty. ⁵ And Yirmiyah, Yachaziel, Yochanan, Yozavad the Gederaite. ⁶ Eluzai, Yerimoth, Bealiah, Shemariahu, and Shephatiahu the Charuphite. ⁷ Elkanah, Yishiahu, Azarel, Yoezer, and Yashoveam, the Korachites. ⁸ And Yoelah and Zevadiah the sons of Yerocham from Gedor. ⁹ From the Gadites there defected to David at the stronghold in the wilderness the mighty among the soldiery, fighting men of the army, able to wield shield and spear; their faces like the face of a lion, and as fleet as roedeer upon the mountains. ¹⁰ Ezer, the chief, Ovadiah the second, Eliav the third. ¹¹ Mishmannah the fourth, Yirmiyah the fifth. ¹² Attai the sixth, Eliel the seventh. ¹³ Yochanan the eighth, Elzavad the ninth. ¹⁴ Yirmiyahu the tenth, Machbannai the eleventh. ¹⁵ These of the Gadites were chiefs of the army; the least was equal to a hundred, the greatest to a thousand. ¹⁶ These are the ones who crossed the Jordan in the first month when it was overflowing all its banks, and they put to flight all the [dwellers of the] low-lying areas

came to him in Tziklag to which he went after abandoning his wilderness strong-holds (see ch. 27 there).

This would make the Gadites the very first tribal unit to throw in their lot with David. See Section Two, p. 423.

וּמִן־הַגָּדִי נִבְדְּלוּ — *From the Gadites there defected.* Malbim points out that verse 14 identifies these Gadites as chiefs of companies. They defected from their companies in order to join up with David.

וּפְנֵי אַרְיֵה פְּנֵיהֶם — *Their faces like the face of a lion.* According to *Gra* the valor implied in this description expressed itself when they routed the *dwellers of the low-lying areas,* as described in verse 16.

15. רָאשֵׁי הַצָּבָא — *Chiefs of the army.* They had all been chiefs in their army before their defection (*Malbim*).

צָבָא is a term which connotes a multitude and can be used for many different types of groupings (see above 7:11). The context here suggests that an army is meant.

אֶחָד לְמֵאָה הַקָּטָן וְהַגָּדוֹל לְאָלֶף — *The least was equal to a hundred, the greatest to a thousand.* The Torah (*Leviticus* 26:8) had promised that if Israel would walk in the statutes of God, one hundred of their number would put ten thousand of their enemies to flight. This would pit one soldier against one hundred. The Torah's

promise was fulfilled with the weakest of the Gadites (*Mefaresh*).

16. בַּחֹדֶשׁ הָרִאשׁוֹן — *In the first month.* Nissan is counted as the first month. In the early spring all the snows have melted and the waters of the Jordan would be particularly swollen (*Mefaresh*).

וְהוּא מְמַלֵּא עַל־כָּל־גְּדוֹתָיו — *When it was overflowing all its banks* [lit. *and it was full above all its banks*]. The translation follows *Metzudos.* The Jordan was full to overflowing because of the melting snows. To be able to ford it at such a time required particular strength and courage (*Metzudos*).

וַיַּבְרִיחוּ אֶת־כָּל־הָעֲמָקִים — *And they put to flight all the [dwellers of the] low-lying areas.* Most commentators think that עֲמָקִים, *low-lying areas,* refers to the residents of those areas. As the Gadites crossed the Jordan, the people who lived on both sides of the river fled from before them, assuming that they were coming to make war (*Radak*).

Metzudos interprets this as another indication of the strength and determination of the Gadites. Even though they must have been exhausted from their efforts in fording the Jordan, they were still able to route those of Saul's supporters who came to meet them.

יז וְלַמַּעֲרָב: וַיָּבֹאוּ מִן־בְּנֵי בִנְיָמִן וִיהוּדָה
יח עַד־לַמְצָד לְדָוִיד: וַיֵּצֵא דָוִיד לִפְנֵיהֶם וַיַּעַן וַיֹּאמֶר לָהֶם
אִם־לְשָׁלוֹם בָּאתֶם אֵלַי לְעָזְרֵנִי יִהְיֶה־לִּי עֲלֵיכֶם לֵבָב
לְיָחַד וְאִם־לְרַמּוֹתַנִי לְצָרַי בְּלֹא חָמָס בְּכַפַּי יֵרֶא אֱלֹהֵי
יט אֲבוֹתֵינוּ וְיוֹכַח: וְרוּחַ לָבְשָׁה אֶת־עֲמָשַׂי
הַשְּׁלִישִׁים ק' רֹאשׁ °הַשְּׁלוֹשִׁים לְךָ דָוִיד וְעִמְּךָ בֶן־יִשַׁי שָׁלוֹם שָׁלוֹם
לְךָ וְשָׁלוֹם לְעֹזְרֶךָ כִּי עֲזָרְךָ אֱלֹהֶיךָ וַיְקַבְּלֵם דָּוִיד וַיִּתְּנֵם
כ בְּרָאשֵׁי הַגְּדוּד: וּמִמְּנַשֶּׁה נָפְלוּ עַל־דָּוִיד
בְּבֹאוֹ עִם־פְּלִשְׁתִּים עַל־שָׁאוּל לַמִּלְחָמָה וְלֹא עֲזָרֻם כִּי
בְעֵצָה שִׁלְּחֻהוּ סַרְנֵי פְלִשְׁתִּים לֵאמֹר בְּרָאשֵׁינוּ יִפּוֹל

17. לַמְצָד — *Stronghold.* At the beginning of our chapter we learned of Benjaminites who joined David at Tziklag. Here we have a record that even before them, when David was still in his stronghold in the wilderness (see v. 8), some people from Benjamin and Judah joined him.

The *Mefaresh* thinks that the Benjaminites, who were, after all, members of Saul's tribe, made sure that some members of David's tribe, Judah, accompany them to David so that he not suspect them of duplicity. For this reason they also made sure to be accompanied by David's nephew, Amasai.

18. וַיֵּצֵא דָוִיד ... — *And David went out ...* David was still suspicious of their intentions, so he went out from his stronghold (*Mefaresh* and *Metzudos*) to question them.

יִהְיֶה־לִּי עֲלֵיכֶם לֵבָב — *It will be my desire* [lit. *I will have a heart upon you*]. The heart (לֵב or לֵבָב) is perceived in Scripture as the seat of the understanding and of many emotions. The idiom, 'to have one's heart upon someone,' means to have a strong emotional interest in him. It is used to denote good will (as in our verse) as well as anger (e.g., *II Samuel* 14:1).

לְיָחַד — *That we unite* [lit. *to unite*]. The verb יחד, in one of its meanings, denotes *joining two things together* (see *Genesis* 49:6 and *Isaiah* 14:20).

The *Mefaresh* reads לֵבָב לְיָחַד together. Thus he renders: *Our hearts will be joined together.*

Metzudos translates the whole phrase slightly differently. He renders: *God will inspire me to recognize your goodwill*

towards me so that we will love one another. [Perhaps *Metzudos* understood the phrase in this way because it then parallels the next phrase in which the word וְיוֹכַח indicates to him that God would *demonstrate* their duplicity to him.]

בְּלֹא חָמָס בְּכַפַּי — *Though there is no wrongdoing in my hands.* Though I am innocent of any wrongdoing.

יֵרֶא ... — ... *Witness.* Roots ending in ה [as for example ראה, *to see*] drop their third root-letter in certain forms of the future tense. To compensate for the dropped letters, the vowel sound of the first letter is sometimes lengthened. Thus יֵרֶא for יִרְאֶה.

יֵרֶא ... וְיוֹכַח — *Witness ... and judge.* The combination of the two words recalls *Genesis* 31:42, רָאָה ... וַיּוֹכַח. This suggests that the phrase might be idiomatic, in which case the precise meaning does not exactly follow the translation of the individual words.

Targum renders וְיוֹכַח as וְיִתְפְּרַע, which suggests *punishment* or *vengeance.* The root יכח also appears with the meaning *judge* (cf. *Isaiah* 11:3) and this, too, would be apt in our context. *Rashi* in *Genesis* renders *admonish. Metzudos* has *demonstrate.* God will reveal your perfidy to all.

19. וְרוּחַ לָבְשָׁה אֶת־עֲמָשַׂי — *And a spirit took hold of Amasai* [lit. *And a spirit clothed Amasai*]. *Mefarash, Radak,* and *Metzudos* all stress that the spirit referred to here is not the רוּחַ הַקֹּדֶשׁ, *Divine inspiration,* which occasionally grips a person, but is used simply to describe the enthusiasm which prompted Amasai to assume the role of spokesman for his companions. The Sages of the Talmud (*Megillah* 14b),

to the east and west. ¹⁷ Benjaminites and Judeans came to David at the stronghold. ¹⁸ And David went out to meet them and responded to them saying, 'If you have come to me in peace to help me, it will be my desire that we unite; but if to betray me to my enemies though there is no wrongdoing in my hands, let the God of our fathers witness and judge.' ¹⁹ And a spirit took hold of Amasai, chief of the officers: 'We are yours, David, and with you, son of Jesse. Peace, peace to you and peace to your helper, for your God has helped you.' So David accepted them and put them at the head of the troop. ²⁰ And from Menasheh there fell in with David when he came with the Philistines to do battle against Saul, but he did not help them, because the lords of the Philistines sent him away by design, saying,

however, assume that Amasai did speak here with Divine inspiration.

לְךָ דָוִיד וְעִמְּךָ בֶּן־יִשַׁי — [We are] yours, David, and with you, son of Jesse. We come to you in peace and want to be part of your company so that we can help you (Mefaresh).

Metzudos renders לְךָ דָוִיד as, for your benefit, David (see Rashi to Genesis 12:1).

Gra notes the double appellation: David and son of Jesse. We come to you both because of your personal worthiness and because of the prominence that is yours from your father.

שָׁלוֹם שָׁלוֹם לְךָ — Peace, peace to you. In the previous verse David had wondered whether they were coming in peace. Amasai answers that they certainly have nothing but peace in mind.

The double expression Peace, peace requires some explanation. Metzudos sees the repetition merely as a means of emphasis. Targum renders: Peace by day and peace by night. Ralbag thinks that it means: Peace to those of your supporters who are far away and also to those who are close by.

The Sages in Gittin 62a derive from our verse that: 'It is fitting that in greeting a king the word שָׁלוֹם, peace, should be said twice.' Maharal explains that the greeting to a king addresses him on two levels, as a person and in his capacity as monarch, on whose well-being the welfare of the whole country depends. Thus, peace to you as an individual and peace to you as a public figure.

כִּי עֲזָרְךָ אֱלֹהֶיךָ — For your God has helped you. You owe us no thanks for joining us. It was God's decree that we should come to you (Mefaresh).

Metzudos takes this statement with the previous one: Since both you and your helpers are at peace despite all of Saul's efforts, it is obvious that God is helping you. Why then should we wish to deceive you?

20-23. These verses refer to events that transpired during the Philistine campaign against Saul which climaxed with the death of Saul and his three sons on Mt. Gilboa. David, as bodyguard of Achish, had joined the Philistine army [of course without any intention of actually helping them (Mefarsh)] and was ready to travel with them. Over Achish's objections, his officers prevailed upon him to send David back home to Tziklag. They were afraid that David would betray them to Saul in order to curry favor with the king who had pursued him so relentlessly. As he was returning to Tziklag, he was joined by the Menashehites who are identified here.

20. וּמִמְּנַשֶׁה נָפְלוּ עַל־דָוִיד — And from Menasheh there fell in with David. Targum renders שְׁרוֹ עִם דָוִד, from שׁרה, which the Targumim use to describe an army or a company of soldiers. Thus it was a military group that joined with David. The idiom ... נָפַל עַל to describe the joining of forces with someone is not unusual in Scripture. See, for example, II Kings 25:11.

בְּבֹאוֹ עִם־פְּלִשְׁתִּים — When he came with the Philistines. For details see I Samuel chs. 28 and 29.

וְלֹא עֲזָרָם כִּי בְעֵצָה שִׁלְחֻהוּ — But he did not help them, because [the lords of the Philistines] sent him away by design. The implication of this is that had the officers not interfered, David would indeed have aided the Philistines against Saul's army. In the light of what we know from Samuel

כא אֶל־אֲדֹנָיו שָׁאוּל: בְּלֶכְתּוֹ אֶל־צִיקְלַג נָפְלוּ עָלָיו ׀ מִמְּנַשֶּׁה עַדְנַח וְיוֹזָבָד וִידִיעֲאֵאל וּמִיכָאֵל וְיוֹזָבָד וֶאֱלִיהוּא וְצִלְּתַי כב רָאשֵׁי הָאֲלָפִים אֲשֶׁר לִמְנַשֶּׁה: וְהֵמָּה עָזְרוּ עִם־דָּוִיד עַל־ כג הַגְּדוּד כִּי־גִבּוֹרֵי חַיִל כֻּלָּם וַיִּהְיוּ שָׂרִים בַּצָּבָא: כִּי לְעֶת־ יוֹם בְּיוֹם יָבֹאוּ עַל־דָּוִיד לְעָזְרוֹ עַד־לְמַחֲנֶה גָדוֹל כְּמַחֲנֵה כד אֱלֹהִים: וְאֵלֶּה מִסְפְּרֵי רָאשֵׁי הֶחָלוּץ לַצָּבָא

---

about how David repeatedly spared Saul's life even when he had the opportunity of killing him, and how, even while he was living in Tziklag under the protection of the Philistine king, he directed all his military activities against Israel's enemies while pretending to Achish that he was fighting the Jews, this is inconceivable.

The answer seems to be that David certainly never intended to fight against his own brothers. But being in a position where he was forced to show loyalty to Achish, he pretended to be interested in doing battle with Saul, all the while relying on some form of Divine intervention to save him from catastrophe. In the event, it turned out that the mistrust of the Philistine lords was the means by which David escaped.

Perhaps this itself explains the inclusion of this seemingly irrelevant phrase in our sentence. After all, since the purpose of *Chronicles* here is to tell us about the Menashehites who joined David on his return to Tziklag, why mention within that context that David never helped the Philistines?

The answer may be that since none of the episodes which so graphically show David's concern for Saul are mentioned in *Chronicles*, it was necessary to stress that David never actually fought Saul but only pretended to do so.

כִּי בְעֵצָה — *Because ... by design.* Again the word עֵצָה, *design*, seems superfluous here. There is no mention in the passage in *Samuel* of any particular plan, and the fears of the officers seem perfectly natural — as they themselves explained.

In line with remarks made concerning the previous phrase, it is possible that a Divine design is meant here. [Compare *Sotah* 10b — עֵצָה עֲמוּקָה שֶׁל מַלְכוּ שֶׁל עוֹלָם, *the deep designs of God, the King of the world.*] The fears of the officers were implanted in them by Divine Providence so

that David should not be placed in the position of fighting his own brothers.

בְרֹאשֵׁינוּ — *With our heads.* This paraphrases the sentence in *I Samuel 29:4*: *With what would he curry favor with his [former] master if not with the heads of these men!*

יִפּוֹל אֶל־אֲדֹנָיו שָׁאוּל — *Will he fall in with his master Saul.* יִפּוֹל in this phrase is identical in meaning to the נָפְלוּ earlier in our verse. In the present context it means to return to Saul's favor.

22. וְהֵמָּה עָזְרוּ עִם־דָּוִיד עַל־הַגְּדוּד — *They aided David against the troop.* After Achish sent David home on the advice of his officers, David made his way back to Tziklag. When he arrived there he found that a band of Amalekites had sacked the city and had taken all the women and children captive. David pursued the Amalekites and eventually recovered all that they had taken (*I Samuel* ch. 30). The Menashehites who joined David on his way back to Tziklag aided him in his campaign against the Amalekite band (*Mefaresh* and *Metzudos*).

וַיִּהְיוּ שָׂרִים בַּצָּבָא — *So they became officers in the army.* As a result of the help which the Menashehites gave David in his campaign against the Amalekites, David made them officers over his men (*Metzudos*).

23. כִּי לְעֶת־יוֹם בְּיוֹם — *For with each new day.* The expression יוֹם בְּיוֹם is normally translated *daily.* People came constantly, daily, to join David. The addition of the word עֵת adds another dimension. Each new day would bring new excitement as an additional group came to swell the ranks of David's men. The term לְעֵת יוֹם, which does not recur in Scripture, seems to have the same meaning as, for example, לְעֵת עֶרֶב (*Genesis* 8:11), *as the evening came.*

The verse is, in effect, saying that there is no necessity of detailing the various

'With our heads will he fall in with his master Saul.' ²¹ *When he went to Tziklag there fell in with him from Menasheh — Adnach, Yozavad, Yediael, Michael, Yozavad, Elihu and Tzillethai, chiefs of the thousands of Menasheh.* ²² *They aided David against the troop, for all of them were mighty among the soldiery, so they became officers in the army.* ²³ *For with each new day men would come to David to aid him, until they grew to be a camp of awesome size.* ²⁴ *Now this is the count of the leaders of those armed for battle,*

groups who came; sufficient to say that each day brought its own contingent until the small band of men originally supporting David grew into a vast army (*Mefaresh; Metzudos*).

עַד־לְמַחֲנֶה גָדוֹל כְּמַחֲנֵה אֱלֹהִים — *Until they grew to be a camp of awesome size* [lit. *a great camp, like a camp of God*]. Most commentators explain that the expression, *a camp of God*, simply means an extremely large camp. Scripture often describes something especially large as being God-like. For example, עִיר גְדוֹלָה לֵאלֹהִים, *an enormously large city* [lit. a city great to God], depicts the Assyrian capital Nineveh in *Jonah* 3:3 (see ArtScroll comm. there).

The *Mefaresh* suggests that here the expression may be meant more literally. Only Divine Providence could explain the rapid growth of David's following.

⏤§ **David's Coronation**

24⁻41. This section gives an accounting of the cadres from the various tribes who came to Hebron in order to transfer the kingship from Saul's descendants to David. *Chronicles* makes no mention of the seven years during which David was accepted as king by only his own tribe, Judah (see *II Samuel* 2:4 and 5:5). Apparently, in the long-range view of *Chronicles*, this episode was not significant. The facts would be known to readers from *Samuel* and, moreover, ch. 3, in dividing David's sons into those born in Hebron and those born in Jerusalem, hints quite clearly at that period of David's life.

The section lists the representatives from each tribe in Israel who came to attend David's coronation [Levites and *Kohanim* are listed separately, as are the two halves of the tribe of Menasheh]. It will be seen from this list that some tribes sent measurably fewer than others. In most cases the commentators offer some explanation.

Judah — 6,800
Shimeon — 7,100
Levi — 4,600
Kohanim — 3,700
Tzadok — 22
Benjamin — 3,000
Ephraim — 20,800
half of Menasheh — 18,000
Yissachar — 200
Zevulun — 50,000
Naphtali — 38,000
Dan — 28,000
Asher — 40,000
Reuven, Gad, half of Menasheh — 100,000

It will be seen from the list that the sequence of the tribes follows a geographic pattern. It begins with Judah and Shimeon (whose portion was interspersed in Judah's) in the south. It then runs north along the eastern segment of the land all the way to Naphtali in the north. It then returns south and lists Dan and Asher whose portion lay in the western half of the land. From there it moves to the eastern bank of the Jordan.

24. וְאֵלֶה מִסְפְּרֵי רָאשֵׁי הֶחָלוּץ לַצָּבָא — *Now this is the count of the leaders of those armed for battle.* In 11:1 and 3 we noted two groups which were involved in David's coronation. One was described as כָּל יִשְׂרָאֵל, *all of Israel*, the other as כָּל זִקְנֵי יִשְׂרָאֵל, *all the elders of Israel*. It is not clear from the text whether the people mentioned in our section are a third group or whether they are the ones who were described as *all of Israel*.

Malbim understands the phrase מִסְפְּרֵי רָאשֵׁי הֶחָלוּץ to mean that the head of each cadre counted the people in his group and informed David of the totals. *These were the [individual] counts of the leaders of the troops.*

חָלוּץ denotes an armed man (*Metzudos*).

בָּאוּ עַל־דָוִיד — *[Who] came to David.* The word *who* is understood. It is as though the

יב

בָּאוּ עַל־דָּוִיד חֶבְרוֹנָה לְהָסֵב מַלְכוּת שָׁאוּל אֵלָיו כְּפִי

כה יְהוָה: בְּנֵי יְהוּדָה נֹשְׂאֵי צִנָּה וָרֹמַח שֵׁשֶׁת אֲלָפִים

כו וּשְׁמוֹנֶה מֵאוֹת חֲלוּצֵי צָבָא: מִן־בְּנֵי שִׁמְעוֹן

כז גִּבּוֹרֵי חַיִל לַצָּבָא שִׁבְעַת אֲלָפִים וּמֵאָה: מִן־בְּנֵי

כח הַלֵּוִי אַרְבַּעַת אֲלָפִים וְשֵׁשׁ מֵאוֹת: וִיהוֹיָדָע הַנָּגִיד

כט לְאַהֲרֹן וְעִמּוֹ שְׁלֹשֶׁת אֲלָפִים וּשְׁבַע מֵאוֹת: וְצָדוֹק נַעַר

ל גִּבּוֹר חָיִל וּבֵית־אָבִיו שָׂרִים עֶשְׂרִים וּשְׁנָיִם: וּמִן־

בְּנֵי בִנְיָמִן אֲחֵי שָׁאוּל שְׁלֹשֶׁת אֲלָפִים וְעַד־הֵנָּה מַרְבִּיתָם

לא שֹׁמְרִים מִשְׁמֶרֶת בֵּית שָׁאוּל: וּמִן־בְּנֵי אֶפְרַיִם

עֶשְׂרִים אֶלֶף וּשְׁמוֹנֶה מֵאוֹת גִּבּוֹרֵי חַיִל אַנְשֵׁי שֵׁמוֹת

לב לְבֵית אֲבוֹתָם: וּמֵחֲצִי מַטֵּה מְנַשֶּׁה שְׁמוֹנָה

לג עָשָׂר אֶלֶף אֲשֶׁר נִקְּבוּ בְּשֵׁמוֹת לָבוֹא לְהַמְלִיךְ אֶת־

דָּוִיד: וּמִבְּנֵי יִשָּׂשכָר יוֹדְעֵי בִינָה לַעִתִּים לָדַעַת

---

phrase were written: אֲשֶׁר בָּאוּ עַל־דָּוִיד. The use of עַל rather than אֶל to denote direction can occasionally be found in Scripture. As an example, see *II Samuel* 15:20.

לְהָסֵב מַלְכוּת שָׁאוּל אֵלָיו — *To transfer the kingship of Saul to him.* The use of the root סבב in this context is unique to *Chronicles* (see comm. to 10:14).

25. בְּנֵי יְהוּדָה ... שֵׁשֶׁת אֲלָפִים ... — *Sons of Judah ... six thousand ...* It is not surprising that relative to the other tribes so few people came from Judah. It was really unnecessary for anybody from Judah to come since David had been ruling over them for the past seven years. His coronation now served only to spread his kingship over the other tribes who up till now had been loyal to Saul and his children (*Mefaresh*).

26. The commentators do not note the comparatively small numbers who came from Shimeon. We can assume that since Shimeon's cities were interspersed among Judah's territory, David was effectively ruling over them, as well. Few Shimeonites came just as few Judeans came.

28. וִיהוֹיָדָע הַנָּגִיד לְאַהֲרֹן — *And Yehoiada the prince of Aaron.* Commentators assume that this Yehoiada is the father of the Benaiah who is mentioned in 11:22 among David's *giborim*. He is described as a prince of the *Kohanim*. [See 11:2 for a discussion of the meaning of the term נָגִיד.] In our

context, *Radak* thinks that it means that he was the *Kohen Gadol* (High Priest). *Mefaresh* and *Metzudos* take it simply as a position of leadership.

Note that Yehoiada does not appear in the list of *Kohanim* given at 5:30-41. As discussed in commentary there, many commentators consider that to be the list of the *Kohanim Gedolim*. If so, the absence of Yehoiada indicates that he was never a *Kohen Gadol*.

29. וְצָדוֹק נַעַר — *And Tzadok, a young man.* This is the Tzadok who appears throughout the story of David and Solomon. *Mefaresh* sees our verse as an explanation of verse 27, which made Yehoiada the leader of the *Kohanim*. Would we not have expected Tzadok to have been the main *Kohen*? Our verse gives the answer. At that time he was still a young man, not yet ready for the mantle of leadership.

נַעַר גִּבּוֹר חָיִל — *A young man of exceptional quality.* See comm. to 5:24.

וּבֵית־אָבִיו שָׂרִים עֶשְׂרִים וּשְׁנָיִם — *And his family — twenty-two chieftains.* Metzudos interprets the second part of the verse to say that Tzadok, together with twenty-two kinsmen who were princes, came to join David in Hebron.

Mefaresh sees this as a continuation of the point made in the first part of the verse. Tzadok was not yet *Kohen Gadol* because he was still a young man. He was eventually given the office because, in

[who] came to David at Hebron to transfer the kingship of Saul to him, in accordance with the word of HASHEM. ²⁵ Sons of Judah, bearers of shield and spear — six thousand eight hundred, armed for battle. ²⁶ From the sons of Shimeon, men of military prowess attached to the army — seven thousand one hundred. ²⁷ From the sons of Levi, four thousand six hundred. ²⁸ And Yehoiada the prince of Aaron; and with him — three thousand and seven hundred. ²⁹ And Tzadok, a young man of exceptional quality, and his family — twenty-two chieftains. ³⁰ And from the Benjaminites, the brothers of Saul — three thousand, the majority of whom had until now supported the House of Saul. ³¹ From the sons of Ephraim — twenty thousand eight hundred, men of military prowess, men of distinction in their families. ³² From the half-tribe of Menasheh there were eighteen thousand who had been designated by name to come and crown David king. ³³ From the sons of Yissachar, those with a profound understanding of the times so that they knew what

addition to being an exceptional individual, he was from an extremely prominent family, as witness the twenty-two chieftains in his family. [The verse, however, makes no statement as to whether they did indeed attend the coronation.]

30. וְעַד־הֵנָּה מַרְבִּיתָם — *The majority of whom had until now.* The possessive תָם, *their,* could refer to the sons of Benjamin or to the three thousand.

Radak and *Metzudos* think that this phrase contrasts the Benjaminites mentioned here with those mentioned at the beginning of the chapter, who joined David while he was still in Tziklag. Of the three thousand who came for David's coronation, a majority of their number had until now been serving Saul. *Ralbag* adds that the verse is emphasizing that though most of these people had been loyal followers of Saul up to this time they now came willingly to join David.

The *Mefaresh* seems to assume that the subject of *whom* is the tribe of Benjamin as a whole and that it explains why only three thousand came from Benjamin. The answer is that the majority of Benjaminites had, until now, been loyal to the House of Saul. [Compare, for example, the attitude of Shimei ben Gera the Benjaminite to David, as described in *II Samuel* 16:7-8.]

שֹׁמְרִים מִשְׁמֶרֶת — *Had ... supported.* They made efforts to maintain his rule over Israel (*Metzudos*).

31. אַנְשֵׁי שֵׁמוֹת — *Men of distinction* [lit. *men of names*]. See comm. to 5:24 for

remarks concerning this expression. According to *Metzudos*, this phrase means men who were renowned enough to be known individually by name.

Ibn Ezra (noted in Overview/*Names and their Significance in Scripture*) associates the ideas of שֵׁם, *name,* and שְׁמָמָה, *desolation. Rashi's* remarks to *Genesis* 6:4 on the phrase אַנְשֵׁי הַשֵּׁם — *Men of desolation who laid the world waste* — is based on the same notion. Perhaps a similar meaning could be ascribed in our verse. The Ephraimites were mighty warriors in front of whom enemy territory would be laid waste.

32. אֲשֶׁר נִקְּבוּ בְּשֵׁמוֹת — *Who had been designated by name. Metzudos* adduces *Leviticus* 24:16 to demonstrate that the meaning of the root נקב is *to state something clearly.*

33. יוֹדְעֵי בִינָה לָעִתִּים — *Those with a profound understanding of the times.* In a phrase such as ours, where common words are combined to form an uncommon expression [it does not recur in Scripture], the meaning must be derived from an analysis of the usage of the words, both singly and in combination, elsewhere in Scripture — always bearing in mind the possibility that the phrase may be an idiom which cannot be translated literally.

The root ידע, *to know,* is found combined with both בִּינָה, *understanding,* and עֵת, *time.* Thus, *Isaiah* 29:24 looks forward to the time that וְיָדְעוּ תֹעֵי־רוּחַ בִּינָה, those of erring spirit shall *know un-*

מַה־יַּעֲשֶׂה יִשְׂרָאֵל רָאשֵׁיהֶם מָאתַיִם וְכָל־אֲחֵיהֶם עַל־ **יב**
פִּיהֶם: לד מִזְּבֻלוּן יוֹצְאֵי צָבָא עֹרְכֵי **לד**
מִלְחָמָה בְּכָל־כְּלֵי מִלְחָמָה חֲמִשִּׁים אָלֶף וְלַעֲדֹר בְּלֹא־לֵב

derstanding, and *Proverbs* 4:1 exhorts us
וְהַקְשִׁיבוּ לָדַעַת בִּינָה, to listen carefully so that
you shall *know understanding*. Similarly,
in *Esther* 1:13 we find Ahasuerus
consulting לַחֲכָמִים יֹדְעֵי הָעִתִּים, the experts
who *knew the times*.

What are עִתִּים, *times*? As used in
Chronicles it seems to refer not to specific
points in time but rather to an era. Thus,
the history of David's reign is described (*I
Chronicles* 29:30) as הָעִתִּים אֲשֶׁר עָבְרוּ עָלָיו,
the times that passed over him, and *II
Chronicles* 15:5 describes turbulent periods
of history as ... וּבָעִתִּים הָהֵם אֵין שָׁלוֹם, *in
those times there was no peace*.

On the other hand, *Isaiah* 33:6 seems to use
עִתִּים as *fixed seasons* [*of the years*] (see *Rashi*
there), and in *Ezra* 10:14 and *Nehemiah* 10:35
the word certainly has the meaning of a point in
time.

It seems likely that there is a qualitative
difference between לֵידַע בִּינָה, *to know
understanding*, and the simpler לְהָבִין, *to
understand*. The former expression
describes one who not only understands a
given point but is able to apply it in a
practical way. Accordingly, the phrase
יוֹדְעֵי בִינָה לָעִתִּים would be people who have
a thorough and practical grasp of the needs
and problems of a given era, or those who
are able to analyze a situation so well that
they can grasp opportunity as it arises and
act at exactly the right moment.

The *Mefaresh* seems to take the phrase
in the first way. The Yissacharites were to
be David's political advisors in his attempts
to consolidate his kingship in the face of
continued opposition by Saul's heirs.

Metzudos seems to favor the second
interpretation. The Yissacharites were to
determine which times were most suitable
for military action.

In both of these two interpretations the
phrase לָדַעַת מַה יַּעֲשֶׂה יִשְׂרָאֵל fits smoothly.
Israel would take its guidance from the
Yissacharites.

In the context of the section as a whole
these explanations seem to fit the simple
meaning of the phrase. As did the cadres
from the other tribes who came as soldiers,
the Yissacharites also had a role to play in
David's political or military affairs.

Both *Radak* and *Metzudos*, however,
cite the interpretation of the Sages that our
phrase refers to Yissachar's special
expertise in the field of astronomy. They
understood the theories of time and season
and were therefore able to advise in the
halachic question of when the תְּקוּפוֹת,
seasons, began, which years should have
an extra month in order to balance the
lunar with the solar calendar, and other
related issues.

Furthermore, this verse is brought
throughout the Talmud and in many
midrashim to demonstrate that the tribe of
Yissachar was especially great in the
knowledge of Torah. This is understood to
be the thrust of Jacob's blessing to
Yissachar in *Genesis* 49:14ff, and this is
the basis of the midrashic interpretation of
the sacrifices which Yissachar's prince
brought in the wilderness (see *Bamidbar
Rabbah* to *Numbers* 7:18ff). Throughout
Rabbinic literature it is well established
that Yissachar as a unit was steeped in
Torah learning. In fact, based on Moses'
blessing to Yissachar and Zevulun
(*Deuteronomy* 33:18), these two became
the prototype of the fruitful partnership
between the man who is immersed in the
study of Torah and the one who, perhaps
unable to learn by himself, gives of his
wealth in order to support the Torah
scholar, thus sharing in his Torah.

From the fact that so many sources point
to our verse as proof of Yissachar's Torah
greatness, despite the clear implication of
the context that the verse refers to worldly
knowledge, it would seem that we are being
offered an unambiguous glimpse into the
thought world of the Sages. It was clear to
them that only someone wholly steeped in
Torah was able to have a truly objective
and accurate grasp of an era or a given
situation. Our verse, as the Sages read it,
seems clearly to postulate the idea that true
wordly wisdom goes hand in hand with
Torah wisdom and that only the
Yissacharites of a given generation can be
its true leaders.

רָאשֵׁיהֶם מָאתַיִם — *Two hundred chiefs.*
Were there only two hundred Yissacharites

Israel should do — two hundred chiefs together with all their brothers by their orders. 34 *From Zevulun, those who go forth with the army — fifty thousand; fighters with all manner of weapons of war, able to form formations with an undivided heart.* 35 *From*

who joined David? If so, the difference in number between this and the other tribes would be striking. The question depends on the understanding of the next phrase: וְכָל־אֲחֵיהֶם עַל־פִּיהֶם, *with all their brothers by their orders.* Gra interprets this to mean that their *kinsmen* actually came with them. Two hundred chiefs came together with all the many people who regarded them as their leaders.

In a somewhat different vein, *Metzudos* explains that since everything which the brothers or adherents of these two hundred men did was only upon their direction, it was equivalent to their having come. Once the two hundred leaders accepted the rule of David, the people who followed them in everything they did would certainly prove loyal to him. It was therefore unnecessary for them to personally come and declare their allegiance.

The Sages teach that the two hundred chiefs were רָאשֵׁי סַנְהֶדְרָאוֹת, *heads of Sanhedrins,* the halachic courts in whose hands the religious leadership of the people resided [in accordance with the Torah law that every town should have its own judges *(Deuteronomy* 16:18)].

Having been taught by the Sages that it was Yissachar's function to be the teachers of Torah and the administrators of Torah law in Israel, the disparity in the numbers which they supplied to David's camp and those which the other tribes sent need no longer trouble us. In David's army it was taken for granted that the study of Torah and the administration of justice was as important to victory in battle as a well-equipped and valiant army. Thus, *Sanhedrin* 49a remarks on the juxtaposition of two thoughts in *II Samuel* 8:16: *And David administered justice and charity to all his people; and Yoav the son of Tzeruiah was [general] over the army.* Why was David able to administer justice and charity? Because Yoav was in control of the army. And why was Yoav's army successful? Because David was administering justice and charity.

וְכָל־אֲחֵיהֶם עַל־פִּיהֶם — *Together with all their brothers by their orders.* See above for Gra's and *Metzudos'* interpretation of this phrase.

The Sages *(Bereishis Rabbah* 72:5), in line with their tradition that the Yissacharites were the main repository of halachah in Israel *(Yoma* 26a), interpret: *And all their brothers* [when they needed halachic guidance did everything solely] by their [Yissachar's] *mouth.* [They required no explanation for the rulings which Yissachar offered but accepted them as though they had been handed to Moses at Sinai *(Tifereth Zion,* there).]

34. עֹרְכֵי מִלְחָמָה — *Fighters.* ערך means *to arrange in a given order.* In the case of an army it would describe the deployment into suitable formations. The Hebrew idiom uses the term in a wider sense to describe the fighting in general, not only the specific drawing of the battle lines (see *Genesis* 14:8).

בְּכָל־כְּלֵי מִלְחָמָה — *With all manner of weapons of war.* The phrase lends itself to two possible interpretations. It may be part of the earlier phrase: *Fighters with all manner of weapons,* or it may stand on its own and describe the Zevulunites who joined David for his coronation — they came in full battle-gear. This latter is perhaps the more likely since it puts our verse in line with vs. 24 and 37 where this is surely the meaning.

וְלַעֲדֹר — *To form formations.* עדר in this context is unique. The commentators, based on v. 38, assume it to have a similar meaning to ערך, *to arrange.* They surmise that a flock of sheep is called עֵדֶר because they are an organized group.

בְּלֹא־לֵב וָלֵב — *With an undivided heart.* See *Psalms* 12:3 where dishonest people are described as speaking בְּלֵב וָלֵב, *a double heart.* In our context the meaning is probably that they were wholeheartedly behind David. There was no residual loyalty to Saul *(Radak).* He does not make clear, however, why the individual loyalty of the Zevulunites should be mentioned in connection with the ordering of formations.[1]

1. R' Y. Danziger suggests that לֵב וָלֵב [lit. *heart and heart*] might be equivalent to the English phrase, 'of two minds,' which connotes uncertainty or hesitation. The phrase would thus mean: capable of forming all [the diverse] formations without hesitation.

לה וָלֵב: וּמִנַּפְתָּלִי שָׂרִים אֶלֶף וְעִמָּהֶם בְּצִנָּה וַחֲנִית

לו שְׁלֹשִׁים וְשִׁבְעָה אָלֶף: וּמִן־הַדָּנִי עֹרְכֵי מִלְחָמָה

לז עֶשְׂרִים־וּשְׁמוֹנָה אֶלֶף וְשֵׁשׁ מֵאוֹת: וּמֵאָשֵׁר

לח יוֹצְאֵי צָבָא לַעֲרֹךְ מִלְחָמָה אַרְבָּעִים אָלֶף: וּמֵעֵבֶר

לַיַּרְדֵּן מִן־הָראוּבֵנִי וְהַגָּדִי וַחֲצִי ׀ שֵׁבֶט מְנַשֶּׁה בְּכֹל כְּלֵי

לט צְבָא מִלְחָמָה מֵאָה וְעֶשְׂרִים אָלֶף: כָּל־אֵלֶּה אַנְשֵׁי

מִלְחָמָה עֹדְרֵי מַעֲרָכָה בְּלֵבָב שָׁלֵם בָּאוּ חֶבְרוֹנָה

לְהַמְלִיךְ אֶת־דָּוִיד עַל־כָּל־יִשְׂרָאֵל וְגַם כָּל־שֵׁרִית יִשְׂרָאֵל

מ לֵב אֶחָד לְהַמְלִיךְ אֶת־דָּוִיד: וַיִּהְיוּ־שָׁם עִם־דָּוִיד יָמִים

מא שְׁלוֹשָׁה אֹכְלִים וְשׁוֹתִים כִּי־הֵכִינוּ לָהֶם אֲחֵיהֶם: וְגַם

הַקְּרוֹבִים־אֲלֵיהֶם עַד־יִשָּׂשכָר וּזְבֻלוּן וְנַפְתָּלִי מְבִיאִים

לֶחֶם בַּחֲמוֹרִים וּבַגְּמַלִּים וּבַפְּרָדִים וּבַבָּקָר מַאֲכָל קֶמַח

דְּבֵלִים וְצִמּוּקִים וְיַיִן וְשֶׁמֶן וּבָקָר וְצֹאן לָרֹב כִּי שִׂמְחָה

38. The Reuvenites, Gadites and half of the tribe of Menasheh had settled on the east bank of the Jordan River.

39. וְגַם כָּל־שֵׁרִית יִשְׂרָאֵל לֵב אֶחָד — *And all the rest of Israel were also of one heart.* Even those people who did not come to Hebron to take part in the coronation were also totally loyal to David. The *Mefaresh* suggests that שֵׁרִית, *remainder*, is spelled here without the usual *aleph* in order to underline the fact that the number of people who did not come to Hebron was insignificant. Most made the effort to be present. [It is unlikely that the people who came formed an actual majority of the total population. We assume that *Mefaresh* means that a majority of the people for whom it was appropriate to come, that is, the people's leaders, came to take an active part.]

In concluding the commentary to this list we point to the lyric tone of some of the passages — in particular Amasai's address to David (v. 19) and phrases like: לְךָ וָלֵב, עֹדְרֵי מַעֲרָכָה בְּלֵבָב שָׁלֵם (v. 33) and וְלֹא־עֵדֶר בְּלֹא in our verse. The tenor of the whole section points to the profound significance of the moment.

40-41. The description of the joyous celebration which accompanied David's coronation does not appear in *Samuel*. Where *Chronicles* stresses the enthusiastic unity of the whole people — *And all the rest of Israel were also of one heart* (v. 38)

... *for there was joy in Israel* (v. 40) — *Samuel* is satisfied with a factual presentation of the coronation itself and the making of the covenant that accompanied it.

On many occasions this commentary will note the tendency of *Chronicles* to stress the involvement of the people in a given event even in cases in which the original account in *Samuel* and *Kings* makes no issue of it (see particularly comm. 1-4 to ch. 13). Moreover, there is a marked propensity on the part of *Chronicles* to underline the joy of participation which frequently animated the people. [Besides our passage, see e.g. I:29:9 and 17; II:15:15; and II:24:10.] All this can be readily understood when we consider the point that whereas the books of *Samuel* and *Kings* tend to view the events of the day from the perspective of the monarchy, *Chronicles* deals with the totality of Israel's odyssey within which the period of the monarchy is no more than a fleeting moment. This can be seen from the fact that *Chronicles* sets the stage for its account by beginning with Adam and which concludes its story with a glance towards the future redemption by mentioning the return to Zion under Cyrus. Thus, from *Chronicles'* perspective it is necessary to stress that the crowning of David was not a matter of the aristocracy which left the lives of the people untouched. The whole of Israel was involved, and joyously

*Naphtali — a thousand officers; and with them — thirty-seven thou-
sand with shield and spear.³⁶ From the Danites — twenty-eight thousand six hundred fighters.³⁷ From Asher, those who go forth with the
army to fight — forty thousand.³⁸ And from the other side of the
Jordan, from the Reuvenites and the Gadites and the half-tribe of
Menasheh, with all the implements of a fighting army — one hundred
and twenty thousand.³⁹ And these, warriors able to form for battle,
came wholeheartedly to Hebron to crown David king over all Israel;
and all the rest of Israel were also of one heart to make David king.⁴⁰
They remained there with David for three days, eating and drinking,
for their brothers had prepared for them.⁴¹ And also those that were
close by to them, including even Yissachar, Zevulun and Naphtali,
brought for them — on asses, camels, mules and oxen — flour products, cakes of pressed figs, raisins, wine, oil, cattle, and sheep in
quantity — for there was joy in Israel.*

involved, in proclaiming David — the repository of its Messianic destiny — king.[1]

40. כִּי־הֵכִינוּ לָהֶם אֲחֵיהֶם — *For their brothers
had prepared for them.* Only because the
Hebronites had made it their business to
prepare for the great influx of people from
the other tribes did these find enough
provisions for the festivities *(Metzudos).*

41. וְגַם הַקְּרוֹבִים־אֲלֵיהֶם עַד־יִשָּׂשׂכָר וּזְבֻלוּן
וְנַפְתָּלִי — *And also those that were close by
to them, including even Yissachar,
Zevulun and Naphtali.* Yissachar,
Zevulun, and Naphtali, the most northerly
tribes, were certainly not close by to

Hebron. *Metzudos* thinks that they can
nevertheless be described as close because
they were not as far away as those who
dwelt on the eastern shore of the Jordan.

Our translation assumes that close by
does not refer to these three tribes but
should be understood as though it were
said that not only those that were close by
but even the three most distant tribes
contributed to the joyful celebration. In
this sense the use of the word עַד would be
analogous to its use in *Leviticus* 11:42.

כִּי שִׂמְחָה בְיִשְׂרָאֵל — *For there was joy in
Israel.* Israel rejoiced in having a strong and
wise king *(Mefaresh).*

XIII

◄§ Tragic attempt to bring the Holy Ark to Jerusalem

This chapter parallels *II Samuel,* ch. 6 in its account of David's ill-fated attempt to
convey the Holy Ark from Kiriath Yearim to Jerusalem. The differences between the two
accounts will be addressed at the appropriate place in the commentary.

Initially the Ark[2] had been together with the rest of the Tabernacle at Shiloh where Eli
was *Kohen Gadol.* The center of communal worship had been there and, just as was the
case in the wilderness, the Ark was an integral part of the Tabernacle.

During a major battle with the Philistines the tide of war turned against the Israelites
and, in desperation, they decided to bring the Ark from Shiloh, hoping that its presence in
their midst would save them. In fact, it spurred the Philistines to even greater efforts and
they not only defeated the Israelites but also captured the Ark *(I Samuel* ch. 4).

After God inflicted plagues upon the Philistines, they decided to return the Ark to the

---

1. We have several times quoted *Mefaresh's* assertion that it is the purpose of *Chronicles* is to exalt
the Davidic dynasty and that this affects the selection of the topics treated [see preface to ch. 10]. This
is entirely true within the treatment which *Chronicles* devotes to the monarchy. There is a clear
difference between the treatment of Saul and that of David and his descendants. This, however, does
not alter the fact that the monarchy, as such, is not the sole or even the main focus of the book.

2. As at 6:16, the commentary will assume that there was only one Ark, rather than two.

א וַיִּוָּעֵץ דָּוִיד עִם־שָׂרֵי הָאֲלָפִים וְהַמֵּאוֹת   בְּיִשְׂרָאֵל: ב לְכָל־נָגִיד: וַיֹּאמֶר דָּוִיד לְכֹל | קְהַל יִשְׂרָאֵל אִם־עֲלֵיכֶם טוֹב וּמִן־יהוה אֱלֹהֵינוּ נִפְרְצָה נִשְׁלְחָה עַל־אַחֵינוּ הַנִּשְׁאָרִים בְּכֹל אַרְצוֹת יִשְׂרָאֵל וְעִמָּהֶם הַכֹּהֲנִים וְהַלְוִיִּם ג בְּעָרֵי מִגְרְשֵׁיהֶם וְיִקָּבְצוּ אֵלֵינוּ: וְנָסֵבָּה אֶת־אֲרוֹן אֱלֹהֵינוּ

Jews. Chapter 6 of *I Samuel* describes how it was brought to Kiriath Yearim, to the house of Avinadav, there to remain until the events described in our chapter.

In the meanwhile, the Tabernacle at Shiloh had been dissolved and it was then moved from place to place until it finally reached Giveon, where it was at the time that the events recounted in our chapter took place.

The question must be raised why no attempt was made in all those years to reunite the Ark with the rest of the Tabernacle. Surely we would have expected that as soon as the Ark was sent back by the Philistines it would have been returned to its rightful place in the Holy of Holies. *R' Yitzchak Isaac Halevi* raises this question in his *Doros HaRishonim, Tekufas HaMikra*, and suggests that there was a Scriptural basis for not doing so. *Deuteronomy* 12:9, as interpreted by the Sages, speaks of two distinct epochs concerning the Tabernacle. One is called מְנוּחָה, *resting place*, and refers to Shiloh. The other is called נַחֲלָה, *inheritance*, and refers to Jerusalem (see *Zevachim* 119a). From this it was deduced that the Torah envisioned only these two locations for the Tabernacle complete with all of its components. Consequently, once Shiloh was destroyed and before a permanent Temple was built there was no sanction to return the Ark to the Tabernacle.

Thus the anomalous situation of two distinct foci for public worship (discussed at length in 6:16) came about.

1-4. This passage is missing entirely from the account in *Samuel*. Chapter 6:1 there simply states that David gathered thirty thousand young men of Israel, and v. 2 tells how he took them with him in order to bring the Ark from Kiriath Yearim. No mention is made there of any prior consultation with the people.

Perhaps the answer lies in the difference noted at 12:4-41 between the books of *Samuel* and *Kings* on the one hand and *Chronicles* on the other. The point was made there that where *Samuel* and *Kings* can be described as histories of the monarchy, it is *Chronicles* which views the events more through the perspective of the people. A detail which was irrelevant from

the perspective of the impact of this tragic event upon David becomes highly significant in a context in which the people of Israel are the focus. It was they who, once David took the initiative, recognized the centrality of Jerusalem to the religious life of the nation. They also understood that it would have been an aberration to have kept the Ark in Kiriath Yearim once Jerusalem had been taken. It seems likely that for the returning exiles, to whom *Chronicles* must have been primarily addressed, this populist insight would have been highly significant.[1]

וַיִּוָּעֵץ דָּוִיד — *David consulted.* See pref. remarks to vs. 1-4, and see comm. v. 3 for

1. *Ramban* (to *Numbers* 16:2) states that when David was disqualified from building the Temple because he was a *man of blood*, this was only because the initiative to build it came from him. It would therefore have been considered his Temple which, in view of the many wars he had been compelled to fight, was deemed inappropriate. Had the initiative to build the Temple come from the people, then even though the actual building would still have gone through David's hands, there would have been no disqualification, since in that situation he would only have been acting as executor of the people's will.

It is clear that a given result is ascribed not necessarily to the person who physically brings it about but rather to the person whose initiative inspired the project and spurred it to completion. Even according to the account in *Chronicles*, the idea of transporting the Ark clearly came from David. He initiated it and in that sense it was he, and only he, who brought it about. Hence, the account in *Samuel* lays it entirely at his door.

Nonetheless, by seeking the advice of the people and eliciting their agreement he allowed them to

David consulted with the officers of the thousands and the hundreds, every leader. ² And David said to the entire congregation of Israel, 'If it appears right to you and HASHEM our God is agreed, let us send out far and wide for our brothers who remain in all the lands of Israel, and with them the Kohanim and the Levites in their cities surrounded by clearings, to assemble to us. ³ And let us

the remarks of the *Mefaresh* to our verse.

לְכָל־נָגִיד — *Every leader*. He did not bring all the chiefs into the discussion; only the leaders among them *(Radak; Metzudos)*.

2. לְכֹל קְהַל יִשְׂרָאֵל — *To the entire congregation of Israel*. Verse 1 had David consulting with the leaders among the chiefs. Here he addresses the whole congregation of Israel. *Malbim's* solution is that by speaking to their representatives it was as though he was speaking to all the people.

וּמִן־ה' אֱלֹהֵינוּ — *And HASHEM our God is agreed*. The translation follows *Metzudos*.

נִפְרְצָה נִשְׁלְחָה — *Let us send out far and wide*. The translation follows *Radak* (Shorashim). *Metzudos* and *Malbim* render: Let us show *strength* or *enthusiasm* (see v. 11). It would be a mark of respect for the Ark if more people were present for the transfer *(Mefaresh)*.

אַחֵינוּ הַנִּשְׁאָרִים בְּכֹל אַרְצוֹת יִשְׂרָאֵל — *Our brothers who remain in all the lands of Israel*. Those that remained in their lands and did not come with you *(Metzudos)*.

Metzudos does not make clear which people were with David and which had remained at home. 11:1ff describes David's investiture at Hebron, then the conquest of Jerusalem, a list of David's *giborim* and, in the beginning of ch. 12, a list of those who had joined David at Tziklag. The text then apparently reverts to the investiture at 12:23. The incident recorded in our chapter follows that passage.

We have two alternatives. If only one investiture took place — and there is no textual indication that it was otherwise — then that was followed by the conquest of Jerusalem [together with *all Israel* (11:4)], and the events described here followed that. In that case, the remaining people mentioned in our verse would be the ones who had not taken part in the conquest of

Jerusalem.

There is also the possibility that there were two separate ceremonies involved in David's becoming king. First there was the formal investiture described at 11:1ff. This was followed by the conquest of Jerusalem and only then was the coronation celebrated as described in 12:23ff. [This sequence would have the advantage of explaining why the story of the conquest of Jerusalem interrupted the accounts in 11:1ff and 12:23ff.] In that case David would have meant those of Israel who had not attended the coronation celebrations.

In either case, David seems to be faulting the laggards who had not seen fit to take part in the important events of the past, busying themselves instead with their private concerns in their cities. In order to urge them to at least take part in the transfer of the Ark, it would be necessary to go into all the scattered areas, *all the lands of Israel*, not forgetting the Levite cities [which because of their special nature might not have been visited by someone making the rounds of Israel's cities], to pry these people away from their concerns and to urge them to participate in the significant event which was about to occur.

בְּעָרֵי מִגְרְשֵׁיהֶם — *In their cities surrounded by clearings*. The Levite cities were called עָרֵי מִגְרָשׁ because the Torah ordained that they must have a מִגְרָשׁ, *clearing*, around them *(Numbers 35:2) (Metzudos)*.

3. וְנָסֵבָּה — *And let us transfer ... back*. This term is not used in connection with the transfer of the Ark in *Samuel*. It is possible that it is used here in order to parallel the expression וַיִּסֹב, *and He transferred*, in 10:14 and לְהָסֵב, *to transfer*, in 12:23. Just as these terms implied the beginnings of a completely new stage of the monarchy (see comm. to 10:14), so David argues that a changed attitude is required towards the Ark. When verse 1 taught of

share in the great undertaking. As a good king who had not only the physical but also spiritual elevation of his people at heart, he made sure that they too would be able to express their love and respect for the Ark.

ד אֵלֵינוּ כִּי־לֹא דְרַשְׁנֻהוּ בִּימֵי שָׁאוּל: וַיֹּאמְרוּ כָל־הַקָּהָל
ה לַעֲשׂוֹת כֵּן כִּי־יָשַׁר הַדָּבָר בְּעֵינֵי כָל־הָעָם: וַיַּקְהֵל דָּוִיד
אֶת־כָּל־יִשְׂרָאֵל מִן־שִׁיחוֹר מִצְרַיִם וְעַד־לְבוֹא חֲמָת
ו לְהָבִיא אֶת־אֲרוֹן הָאֱלֹהִים מִקִּרְיַת יְעָרִים: וַיַּעַל דָּוִיד
וְכָל־יִשְׂרָאֵל בַּעֲלָתָה אֶל־קִרְיַת יְעָרִים אֲשֶׁר לִיהוּדָה
לְהַעֲלוֹת מִשָּׁם אֵת אֲרוֹן הָאֱלֹהִים | יהוה יוֹשֵׁב הַכְּרוּבִים

David seeking counsel with the chiefs, *Mefaresh* (there) remarks: He told them: You have now looked after yourselves by providing for yourselves a king to look after your welfare; it is now time to worry about the respect due to God. This thought is eloquently expressed by the use of the term וְנָסֵבָּה.

אֲרוֹן אֱלֹהֵינוּ — *The Ark of our God.* The Ark is often referred to as the Ark of HASHEM, or the Ark of God, or the Ark of the covenant of God, and so on, but never as the Ark of our God. It is possible that David used the term here to evoke the people's feelings. The Ark is the Ark of *our* God Who is always good to us. It is our responsibility therefore to treat His Ark with the proper respect.

כִּי־לֹא דְרַשְׁנֻהוּ בִּימֵי שָׁאוּל — *For we did not seek it out in the days of Saul.* דרש means *to seek* or *inquire after* as in *Leviticus* 10:16. In the present context it is used in the sense of: We did not show proper concern and respect for it (see below 15:13).

When Saul destroyed Nov, the city of *Kohanim* (*I Samuel* ch. 21), he decimated the ranks of the *Kohanim* whose duties revolved around the Ark. Thereby, he diminished the standing of the Ark (*Radak* and *Metzudos*). [Although when the slaughter of Nov took place the Ark was in Kiriath Yearim, not Nov (see prefatory remarks to this chapter), the *Kohanim* of Nov were involved with the Ark in Kiriath Yearim. Consequently, the killing at Nov affected the standing of the Ark, too.]

It is noteworthy that instead of blaming Saul for his lack of attention to the Ark, David includes himself in his strictures. *We* were not concerned enough about the Ark during Saul's reign.

5. מִן־שִׁיחוֹר מִצְרַיִם וְעַד־לְבוֹא חֲמָת — *From the Shichor of Egypt to the approaches of Chamath.* The Shichor river is the southern

boundary of the land and Chamath is the northern boundary (*Gra*). All the inhabitants of the land were involved in the transfer of the Ark.

6. ... וַיַּעַל דָּוִיד — *And David ... went up.* Samuel has וַיֵּלֶךְ דָּוִד, *and David went.* Chronicles intends a simple play on words with the city name בַּעֲלָתָה, which *Samuel* does not have — see below.

There may also be a more profound purpose. As our verse stands, we are struck by a seeming contradiction in terms. David *went up* (from Jerusalem) to Kiriath Yearim, and his purpose was *to bring up* (לְהַעֲלוֹת) the Ark to Jerusalem. To go up to a place implies that the point of departure lies lower down, while to bring up from a place implies that one is moving to a higher place. It would seem, therefore, that the terms are not meant in a geographic sense. David *went up* to Kiriath Yearim because as long as the Ark was lodged there going there implied a spiritual ascension. He wanted to bring the Ark up to Jerusalem because as the place most eminently suited for the Ark, it is a place to which the Ark rises.

The stress on the sanctity of the Ark implied in the expression וַיַּעַל is most apt in the context of this passage, where David blames himself and all Israel (v. 3) for not having paid sufficient respect to the Ark.

בַּעֲלָתָה — *To Baalah.* In *Joshua* (15:9) Baalah is given as another name for Kiriath Yearim. Our verse then means that David went up to Baalah, which is Kiriath Yearim.

The text in *Samuel* is less simple ... וַיֵּלֶךְ דָּוִד מִבַּעֲלֵי יְהוּדָה לְהַעֲלוֹת מִשָּׁם, *And David went from Baalei Judah to bring up from there the Ark ...* The text does not tell us his destination [he went *from* Baalei Judah] and says that they took up the Ark *from there* — although no place had been given for the location of the Ark. *Rashi* (there) equates Baalei Judah with Baalah

transfer the Ark of our God back to us, for we did not seek it out in the days of Saul.' ⁴ *And the whole congregation said to do so because the matter appeared right in the eyes of all the people.* ⁵ *So David assembled all Israel, from the Shichor of Egypt to the approaches of Chamath, to bring the Ark of God from Kiriath Yearim.* ⁶ *And David and all Israel went up to Baalah, to Kiriath Yearim of Judah, to bring up from there the Ark of God, HASHEM,*

(and thus Kiriath Yearim) but does not explain why the verse says that they went from there rather than to there.

The solution may lie in *I Samuel* 7:1. The house of Avinadav is described there as being בַּגִּבְעָה, *on the hill.* Now *Rashi* to *II Samuel* 6:2 asserts that בַּעַל [*baal*] means *a plain.* Thus בַּעֲלֵי יְהוּדָה, *Baalei Judah*, would seem to mean *the plain of Judah.* The town lay on a plain but Avinadav's house lay on a hill overlooking it. In *Samuel*, where the location of the Ark was known from previous passages, there was no need to say that it was in Kiriath Yearim. We are told, only, how the transfer was made. The multitudes gathered on the plain — Baalei Judah (Kiriath Yearim) — from where they went up to Avinadav's house on the hill to take the Ark. *Chronicles*, having made no previous mention of where the Ark was, was forced to say that David and all Israel went to Baalah, which was Kiriath Yearim.

אֲרוֹן הָאֱלֹהִים ה' יוֹשֵׁב הַכְּרוּבִים — *The Ark of God, HASHEM, Who is enthroned upon the Cheruvim.* According to *Targum* the phrase ה' יוֹשֵׁב הַכְּרוּבִים, *HASHEM, Who is enthroned upon the Cheruvim,* stands in apposition to הָאֱלֹהִים, *God.*

To understand the significance of the phrase in our context it is best to set our verse next to that in *Samuel* (*II*: 6:2) so that the differences between the two may be more readily apparent.

Chronicles	Samuel
1. ... לְהַעֲלוֹת מִשָּׁם אֶת אֲרוֹן הָאֱלֹהִים ה' יוֹשֵׁב הַכְּרוּבִים, *to bring up from there the Ark of God, HASHEM, Who is enthroned upon the Cheruvim*	1. לְהַעֲלוֹת מִשָּׁם אֶת אֲרוֹן הָאֱלֹהִים ..., *to bring up from there the Ark of God*
2. אֲשֶׁר נִקְרָא שֵׁם, *which was called a name*	2. אֲשֶׁר נִקְרָא שֵׁם, *which was called a name*
	3. שֵׁם ה' צְבָאוֹת יוֹשֵׁב הַכְּרוּבִים עָלָיו, *the name of HASHEM, Master of Legions, Who is enthroned upon the Cheruvim, is upon it.*

It will be seen that the appositional phrase is missing in *Samuel*, which, however, gives the same information in its section (3). This, in turn, is entirely missing from our sentence.

It is possible that our text uses the appositional phrase to explain the events which follow. Why was Uzza killed for the seemingly innocent act of trying to support the Ark? Our verse gives the answer: HASHEM is the One Who is enthroned atop the *Cheruvim* [which are, of course, part of the cover of the Ark]. In stretching out his hand to support the Ark, Uzza approached too close to the manifestation of the Divine Presence. This explanation needed to be emphasized only in *Chronicles*, where the story is told to people to whom the Holy Ark was not a tangible reality. [The latest date given by the Sages for its removal from the Temple is the reign of Yehoiachin (*Yoma* 53b), many decades before *Chronicles* was written.] When *Samuel* was written, however, the Ark was in the midst of the people, an object of daily veneration, and no explanation would be necessary to explain Uzza's fault.

ה' יוֹשֵׁב הַכְּרוּבִים — *HASHEM, Who is enthroned upon the Cheruvim.* The parallel passage in *Samuel* has ה' צְבָאוֹת, *HASHEM Master of Legions.* This is one of several places in *Chronicles* where the name צְבָאוֹת is omitted from an identical phrase in the earlier books. Compare, for example, *I:15:2* with *II Samuel* 6:18; and *I:17:25* with *II Samuel* 7:21 (cf. comm. v. 8).

ז אֲשֶׁר־נִקְרָא שֵׁם: וַיַּרְכִּבוּ אֶת־אֲרוֹן הָאֱלֹהִים עַל־עֲגָלָה
ח חֲדָשָׁה מִבֵּית אֲבִינָדָב וְעֻזָּא וְאַחְיוֹ נֹהֲגִים בָּעֲגָלָה: וְדָוִיד
וְכָל־יִשְׂרָאֵל מְשַׂחֲקִים לִפְנֵי הָאֱלֹהִים בְּכָל־עֹז וּבְשִׁירִים
וּבְכִנֹּרוֹת וּבִנְבָלִים וּבְתֻפִּים וּבִמְצִלְתַּיִם וּבַחֲצֹצְרוֹת:
ט וַיָּבֹאוּ עַד־גֹּרֶן כִּידֹן וַיִּשְׁלַח עֻזָּא אֶת־יָדוֹ לֶאֱחֹז אֶת־

אֲשֶׁר־נִקְרָא שֵׁם — *Which was called a name.*
The Ark of God was called by a name. The
name is not given here but refers to the one
given in *Samuel* [phrase (3)] which says
that *the name of HASHEM, Master of
Legions, Who is enthroned upon the
Cheruvim, is upon it.* The name is not
repeated here, possibly because the basic
information was already given in phrase (1)
here (*Rashi to Samuel*).[1]

Radak notes that this high praise of the
Ark was stressed here rather than at any
other reference to the Ark in Scripture
because it had gained its most widespread
fame by the havoc which it had wreaked
among the Philistines, as described in *I
Samuel* chs. 5 and 6.

In contrast to the previous assumption
that שֵׁם is to be taken as a common noun,
Ibn Ezra (*Sefer HaShem*) and *Radak* (in
Samuel) seem to interpret the שֵׁם in our
phrase as a proper noun. The Ark is called
שֵׁם, *Name. Ibn Ezra* explains this on the
basis of his etymology of the word שֵׁם. As
seen in Overview/Names and their
Significance, he thinks that it is related to
שָׁם, *there*, the word describing the location
of a given object. The thinking is that a
name locates its bearer. When we use a
person's name we treat it as though its
bearer were in our presence [see there for a
more detailed presentation].

Thus אֲשֶׁר נִקְרָא שֵׁם might be rendered:
Which is called 'Presence.' The verse in

Samuel then goes on to explain that the
name Presence is appropriate for the Ark
because through it the presence of God in
this world is manifest.

7. וַיַּרְכִּבוּ אֶת־אֲרוֹן הָאֱלֹהִים — *And they
loaded the Ark of God.* As the Sages
explain it, this loading of the Ark upon a
wagon was a terrible mistake on David's
part, and it set the stage for Uzza's tragic
death. According to *Numbers 7:9*, the
articles which the Kehathites were supposed to transport in the wilderness were to
be carried upon the shoulders and — in
contrast to the burdens of Gershon and
Merari — not to be placed upon a carriage.
By having the Ark placed upon the wagon,
David was ignoring one of the Torah's
commandments.

Radak suggests that David's reasoning
may have been that the Torah's insistence
that the holy vessels be carried on the
shoulders was only applicable during the
desert wanderings. When the transportation of the Tabernacle was an everyday
occurrence, it was necessary to stress the
special sanctity of the holy vessels by
assigning a special mode for carrying them.
Treating them in precisely the same way as
the rest of the Tabernacle would have
tended to obscure their special standing.
But once the Tabernacle was permanently
or almost permanently established in one
place, David thought it no longer necessary

---

1. What is the significance of something being called by the name of God? There are two passages
which throw light on this.

In *Genesis 33:20* we find Jacob building an altar, and calling it אֵל אֱלֹהֵי יִשְׂרָאֵל, which translates as
Almighty God, God of Israel. Rashi points out that Jacob did not call the altar God. Rather he wanted
that the altar should awaken for him the association of the miraculous salvation which God had granted
him. *Ramban* there points out that the concept is much the same as when names like Tzuriel, which
translates as *God is my rock*, are given to people. By means of the name the person will serve as a reminder
of a particular aspect of God's goodness.

In other passages we find the people of Israel and even individuals among them being called by the
name of God. Thus, for example, *Jeremiah* (15:16) speaks of the great joy which God's
communication caused him: *For Your name is called upon me, O HASHEM, God of Legions.* The
meaning is apparently that he is identified entirely with God's wishes and that he has no existence
besides his function as God's messenger — his whole being becomes merely a tool of God's will. Thus,
the name given in *Samuel* and alluded to here implies an existence which is entirely a projection of
God's presence on earth.

13

7-9

Who is enthroned upon the Cheruvim, which was called a name.
⁷ And they loaded the Ark of God upon a new wagon from the
house of Avinadav, and Uzza and Achio drove the wagon. ⁸ And
David and all Israel rejoiced before God with all their might and
with songs, harps, nevalim, tupim, cymbals and trumpets. ⁹ They
came to the threshing floor of Kidon, and Uzza stretched out his

to stress that special standing by carrying them. In this reasoning he erred and the relocation of the Ark was marred by Uzza's death.

Gra (and *Tiferes Zion* to *Bamidbar Rabbah* 4:20) thinks that David's reasoning was that in the wilderness the people were on a high level of sanctity and were therefore worthy to be direct bearers of the Divine Presence which rested, so to speak, upon the Ark. In David's own time, after the centuries of the period of the Judges had passed during which idol worship had several times occurred, David thought that humans could no longer be worthy bearers of the Ark, and he decided to transport it by wagon.

The *Mefaresh* explains that David decided on the use of a wagon because that is how the Philistines had brought it to Kiriath Yearim. Perhaps *Mefaresh* agrees with *Radak* that David thought that the Torah law had changed. This was indicated to him by the fact that nothing untoward happened when the Philistines used a wagon to return the Ark.

מִבֵּית אֲבִינָדָב — *From the house of Avinadav.* See *I Samuel* 7:1.

8. מְשַׂחֲקִים — *Rejoiced.* שחק, which often means *to laugh*, is also used in the sense of expressing joy. See for example *Genesis* 21:6 where at Isaac's birth Sarah calls out צְחֹק עָשָׂה לִי אֱלֹהִים, *God has provided me with* צְחֹק. In that context *laughter* would certainly not be an apt translation and, indeed, *Targum* renders *joy*.

לִפְנֵי הָאֱלֹהִים — *Before God. Samuel* has HASHEM instead of our ELOHIM [God]. In this connection we note the following: Throughout *Chronicles* the name of God is often given differently than in *Samuel* and *Kings*. This is occasionally even true in direct quotes (e.g. *I*:17:17 as compared to II *Samuel* 7:19). In our own section the change from HASHEM to ELOHIM here occurs several more times. These changes will be noted without any attempt at

explanation. The various uses of God's names touches upon levels of truth beyond our understanding and therefore beyond conjecture.

בְּכָל־עֹז וּבְשִׁירִים ... — *With all their might and with songs ... Samuel* (v. 8) has בְּכָל עֲצֵי בְרֹשִׁים, *with all kinds of cypress wood.*

וּבִנְבָלִים — *Nevalim.* From *Arachin* 13b and *Rashi* there it seems that a *nevel* is a wind instrument. Since its precise nature is unknown to us, the word is left untranslated. The same is done for *tupim.*

וּבִמְצִלְתַּיִם — *Cymbals.* The *Mefaresh* notes on the basis of v. 15:16 below that this instrument's purpose was to make a loud noise [presumably for rhythm], rather than melody. He describes it as an instrument upon which one beats with a stick to produce sound — perhaps a drum. The double ending מְצִלְתַּיִם, however, suggests an instrument consisting of two equal parts similar to cymbals. This is the view of *Metzudos.*

9. גֹּרֶן כִּידֹן — *The threshing floor of Kidon.* Our text has *Kidon* where *Samuel* has *Nachon. Radak* suggests two possible solutions: The owner of the threshing floor may have had two names; or, Kidon which is related to כִּידוֹ, *calamity* (*Job* 21:20), may be a name given to the place because of the tragedy which happened there.

Sotah 35b has a different solution. Originally it was called כִּידוֹן [*Kidon*], *spear,* because Uzza was killed there (as if struck down by a spear — *Rashi*). In the end it was called נָכוֹן [*Nachon*], *established,* because the house of Oved Edom was blessed for taking in the Ark.

וַיִּשְׁלַח עֻזָּא אֶת־יָדוֹ לֶאֱחֹז אֶת־הָאָרוֹן — *And Uzza stretched out his hand to take hold of the Ark.* The difference between our text and *Samuel,* which has וַיֹּאחֶז בּוֹ, *and he took hold of it,* is striking enough to require examination. Did Uzza only attempt to take hold of the Ark (the implication of our text) or did he actually take hold of it (as stated in *Samuel*)?

[207]   *I Chronicles*

י הָאָרוֹן כִּי שָׁמְטוּ הַבָּקָר: וַיִּחַר־אַף יהוה בְּעֻזָּא וַיַּכֵּהוּ עַל
אֲשֶׁר־שָׁלַח יָדוֹ עַל־הָאָרוֹן וַיָּמָת שָׁם לִפְנֵי הָאֱלֹהִים:
יא וַיִּחַר לְדָוִיד כִּי־פָרַץ יהוה פֶּרֶץ בְּעֻזָּא וַיִּקְרָא לַמָּקוֹם
יב הַהוּא פֶּרֶץ עֻזָּא עַד הַיּוֹם הַזֶּה: וַיִּירָא דָוִיד אֶת־הָאֱלֹהִים

	Chronicles		Samuel
1.	וַיִּשְׁלַח עֻזָּא אֶת־יָדוֹ לֶאֱחֹז אֶת־הָאָרוֹן, *And Uzza stretched out his hand to take hold of the Ark*	1.	וַיִּשְׁלַח עֻזָּה אֶל־אֲרוֹן הָאֱלֹהִים וַיֹּאחֶז בּוֹ ..., *And Uzzah stretched out for the Ark of God and took hold of it ... (v. 6).*
2.	וַיִּחַר־אַף ה' בְּעֻזָּא, *And the anger of HASHEM flared against Uzza (v. 10)*	2.	וַיִּחַר־אַף ה' בְּעֻזָּה, *And the anger of HASHEM flared against Uzzah*
3.	וַיַּכֵּהוּ עַל אֲשֶׁר־שָׁלַח יָדוֹ עַל־הָאָרוֹן, *and He struck him down because he stretched out his hand upon the Ark;*	3.	וַיַּכֵּהוּ שָׁם הָאֱלֹהִים עַל־הַשַּׁל, *and God struck him down there because of the error*
4.	וַיָּמָת שָׁם לִפְנֵי הָאֱלֹהִים, *and he died there before God.*	4.	וַיָּמָת שָׁם עִם אֲרוֹן הָאֱלֹהִים, *and he died there by the Ark of God.*

It would seem that we have here a classic example of *Chronicles* serving as a midrash, an in-depth explanation of the text in *Samuel*.

The first question which must be asked is: What sins were committed in this matter? *Abarbanel* (in *Samuel*) finds four.

(a) The Ark should have been carried on the shoulders of the Levites rather than on a wagon.

(b) The Ark itself should never have been touched. It was to be borne by means of its poles only. Uzza touched the Ark itself.

(c) Only *Kohanim* and Levites were allowed to handle the Ark. Uzza was an ordinary Israelite.

(d) Uzza should have realized that the Ark was not in danger of falling. Even when borne in the proper manner, the Ark really 'carried those that bore it' (*Sotah* 35a). How obvious, then, that it could never require human interference to prevent it from falling! (*Sotah* there.)

When we examine Uzza's guilt and try to determine for which of these shortcomings he was punished, we can eliminate (a) since this was not Uzza's fault but David's. Of the rest we may say that (b) and (c) were sins of action [an unqualified man touching the Ark] while (d) was clearly a fault of the mind — an inadequate awareness of the sanctity of the Ark.

Was it the action or the attitude which condemned Uzza to die? The answer is apparently given in (3) of *Samuel*. God

smote Uzza there — עַל הַשַּׁל. *Targum* and the commentators there render: *because of the error* (from the Aramaic שְׁלָא, to err). The fault lay not in what he did but in what he thought; his mistake made him liable to death (see *Rashi* there). Accordingly, in the composite action consisting of *stretching out the hand* and then *taking hold*, the weight of the fault is with stretching out the hand. The mistaken attitude would be reflected in the attempt whether or not it succeeded.

But *Samuel* seems to underline the fact that he actually took hold of the Ark. The explanation would seem to be that *Samuel* states the historical truth as it happened. Uzza did, in fact, take hold of the Ark, thus transgressing sins (b) and (c) in addition to (d). In phrase (3), however, it is made clear that the severity of the punishment came because of only one of the three sins. This truth *Chronicles* makes clear by stating in phrase (1) that Uzza *stretched out his hand* in order to support the Ark. The fact that in addition to this he also touched it is not especially relevant to the story. God was angered at his intention (phrase 3), not at his holding the Ark. Thus, what *Samuel* makes clear with the expression עַל הַשַּׁל, a word borrowed from Aramaic which never recurs in Scripture, *Chronicles* teaches by presenting only the aspect of the attempt.

What of the differences in phrases (4)? It seems evident that the אֱלֹהִים, *God*, of *Chronicles* is synonymous with the אֲרוֹן הָאֱלֹהִים, *Ark of God*, of *Samuel* (Me-

13
10-12

hand to take hold of the Ark because the cattle shook [it]. ¹⁰ *And the anger of HASHEM flared against Uzza and He struck him down because he stretched out his hand upon the Ark; and he died there before God.* ¹¹ *David was greatly disturbed because HASHEM had made a breach in Uzza, and he called that place Peretz-Uzza until this day.* ¹² *And David feared God on that day and said, 'How can I*

tzudos). By referring to the Ark as אֱלֹהִים, that is, by stressing the proximity to the Divine which is experienced by one who is in the presence of the Ark, *Chronicles* answers the problem of how Uzza could have been punished for an oversight.[1] It places Uzza's forgetfulness into the category of a חִלּוּל הַשֵּׁם, *desecration of God's Name* — a sin which is punishable even when committed inadvertently (see *Avos* 4:4 and *Kiddushin* 40a).

Samuel opted for a different lesson. It used אֲרוֹן הָאֱלֹהִים, *Ark of God,* rather than אֱלֹהִים, *God,* in order to make possible the Talmud's teaching that Uzza did not forfeit his portion in the World to Come. Just as the Ark lives eternally, so, too, does Uzza *(Sotah* 35a).

כִּי שָׁמְטוּ הַבָּקָר — *Because the cattle shook [it].* This phrase is irregular because it would seem to require a direct object such as כִּי שָׁמְטוּ ... [אֶת הָאָרוֹן], *shook ... [the Ark],* which is lacking in our verse *(Rashi* to *Samuel).* It is possible that the direct object was omitted to avoid any implication that the Ark was actually in danger of slipping. According to *Sotah* 35a, Uzza's sin had been just that — that he had thought the Ark to be in danger of falling when he

should have realized that it was not (see above). For this reason, the transitive verb is left, as it were, hanging. Although the animals acted in a way which could, and indeed should, have resulted in the teetering of the Ark, in actual fact, the Ark remained steady.

Radak to *Samuel* thinks that here the verb may have been used intransitively. The oxen were literally shaken apart. Their very limbs were dislocated because of the enormity of having the holy Ark on the carriage which they were pulling.

11. וַיִּחַר לְדָוִיד — *David was greatly disturbed.* The translation follows *Metzudos.*

כִּי־פָרַץ ה' פֶּרֶץ בְּעֻזָּא — *Because HASHEM had made a breach in Uzza.* In 15:13, where David recounts the events described in our chapter, he uses the expression: פָּרַץ ה' אֱלֹהֵינוּ בָּנוּ, *HASHEM our God made a breach in us.* This seems to indicate that a better translation for our phrase might be: *Because HASHEM made a breach [in Israel] through Uzza* (see comm. to 15:13).

The expression פֶּרֶץ, which connotes *to break open,* does not recur in Scripture in connection with a punishment. From the fact that the use of the word was immortalized by naming the place

1. We can further explain the harsh punishment meted out to Uzza for an inadvertent transgression in the following manner: *Yerushalmi, Makkos* 2:6 reads: 'Wisdom was asked: What punishment shall be meted out to an [unwitting] sinner? Wisdom answered: May evil pursue the evildoer. Prophecy was asked the same question. Prophecy answered: The soul that sins [unwittingly] shall die. Then God was asked what shall become of the unwitting sinner? He answered: Let him repent and he shall be forgiven.' Wisdom and Prophecy, it would seem, deal in a truth which is absolute, and in an absolute sense a soul which was sent by God into the world for a given purpose has its *raison d'être* defined by that purpose. If it deviates from that purpose then the life it has been given has no justification — the evil pursues the evildoer and the sinning soul must die.

God Himself recognizes that man does not live in an absolute world. He Himself placed man in surroundings which obscure the truth. The soul is a stranger in an environment which is unrelievedly hostile to the values which alone have meaning for it. And so God says: Let the soul consider, let it rally its forces and come to its senses. Even in the physical world the truth can be found. Let it find the way back to its essence — it will repent and be forgiven.

But all this is true only when one is not in the presence of the Ark. The Ark is the one point in a physical world at which the curtains part and the truth — incontrovertible and undeniable — shines through. As *Ibn Ezra* explained above (v. 6), the Ark is Presence! אֲשֶׁר נִקְרָא שֵׁם, the Name of God is upon it. It carries its bearers, it is bereft of physical dimensions (see *Yoma* 21a and *Bava Basra* 99a); it is, in short, an other-worldly intruder into the realm of the physical. For one who is blind even to that shining light there is indeed no hope. Thus, for Uzza the absolute judgments of Wisdom and Prophecy held sway.

יג בַּיּוֹם הַהוּא לֵאמֹר הֵיךְ אָבִיא אֵלַי אֵת אֲרוֹן הָאֱלֹהִים:

יג־יד יג וְלֹא־הֵסִיר דָּוִיד אֶת־הָאָרוֹן אֵלָיו אֶל־עִיר דָּוִיד וַיַּטֵּהוּ

אֶל־בֵּית עֹבֵד־אֱדֹם הַגִּתִּי: וַיֵּשֶׁב אֲרוֹן הָאֱלֹהִים עִם־בֵּית

עֹבֵד אֱדֹם בְּבֵיתוֹ שְׁלֹשָׁה חֳדָשִׁים וַיְבָרֶךְ יהוה אֶת־בֵּית

עֹבֵד־אֱדֹם וְאֶת־כָּל־אֲשֶׁר־לוֹ:

יד °חוּרָם ק' א וַיִּשְׁלַח °חִירָם מֶלֶךְ־צֹר מַלְאָכִים אֶל־דָּוִיד וַעֲצֵי אֲרָזִים

א־ד ב וְחָרָשֵׁי קִיר וְחָרָשֵׁי עֵצִים לִבְנוֹת לוֹ בָּיִת: וַיֵּדַע דָּוִיד

כִּי־הֱכִינוֹ יהוה לְמֶלֶךְ עַל־יִשְׂרָאֵל כִּי־נִשֵּׂאת לְמַעְלָה

ג מַלְכוּתוֹ בַּעֲבוּר עַמּוֹ יִשְׂרָאֵל: וַיִּקַּח דָּוִיד

ד עוֹד נָשִׁים בִּירוּשָׁלָם וַיּוֹלֶד דָּוִיד עוֹד בָּנִים וּבָנוֹת: וְאֵלֶּה

Peretz-Uzza it can be seen that it carried a particular significance. Perhaps one of the following solutions explains its use:

As will be seen in the commentary to ch. 14, there is a good possibility that the Philistine wars described there took place before the events described in our chapter. As told there (v. 11), David, deeply impressed by the miraculous victory granted him by God, declared: פָּרַץ הָאֱלֹהִים אֶת אוֹיְבַי בְּיָדִי כְּפֶרֶץ מָיִם, God has broken open my enemies by my hand like the bursting forth of water, and to commemorate the event he called the place בַּעַל פְּרָצִים, Baal Peratzim. When subsequently the tragic death of Uzza occurred — because as David realized, he himself had been at fault — he was struck by the uncompromising consistency of God's justice. When he deserved it God smashed open his enemies before him; when he fell short of his obligations God created the same kind of breach in Israel.

Another possible explanation is based on the points raised in the commentary to v. 9. As explained there, Uzza was punished for an *unwitting* transgression. Thus, in this case, the defense of ignorance and error did not hold good. God *broke open* this usually protective position and punished him for the reasons explained above.

The possibility must also be considered that David intended a play on words. The unbounded enthusiasm with which he had laid the plans for the transportation of the Ark had been expressed by the use of the term נִפְרְצָה [lit. *let us spread forth*] (v. 2, see comm. there). This 'spreading out' through the ranks of Israel had now become a breach. [Such a play on words is not infrequent in Scripture. Compare, for example, Haman's פּוּר, *lot*, which when salvation came was turned into the joyous Purim.]

12. וַיִּירָא דָוִיד אֶת־הָאֱלֹהִים — *And David feared God.* In this verse *Chronicles* has אֱלֹהִים, *God*, where *Samuel* has HASHEM. See remarks to v. 8.

However, in v. 10 it was noted that *Chronicles* uses אֱלֹהִים as a synonym for אֲרוֹן הָאֱלֹהִים (see comm., v. 9). It is therefore possible that this verse means that David feared the God Who was manifest in the Ark (cf. comm. to v. 6).

13. עֹבֵד־אֱדֹם הַגִּתִּי — *Oved Edom the Gittite.* Since Oved Edom is mentioned among the Levites at 15:18, *Mefaresh* thinks that he is called the Gittite because he used to live in Gath — not because he was a Philistine (see comm. to 2:17).

14. שְׁלֹשָׁה חֳדָשִׁים — *Three months.* The story of the Ark will be taken up once more in ch. 15.

XIV

◄§ David Establishes Himself in Jerusalem

Our chapter covers the same topics as those described in II Samuel 5:11-25. They are: (1) Churam sends workers and materials to help David build a palace. (2) David marries more wives in Jerusalem and fathers additional children. (3) David fights two battles against the Philistines.

There is, however, one striking difference between the account in *Samuel* and that in *Chronicles*. Whereas in *Chronicles* all these events follow the transport of the Ark from Kiriath Yearim (previous chapter), in *Samuel* they precede it. To contrast the two accounts, the following comparison is offered. The coronation of David was followed by:

13

13-14

bring the Ark of God to me?' ¹³ So David did not move the Ark near himself to the city of David, but he directed it to the house of Oved Edom the Gittite. ¹⁴ And the Ark of God stayed with the household of Oved Edom, in his house, for three months; and HASHEM blessed the house of Oved Edom and all that he had.

14

1-4

And Churam, King of Tyre, sent messengers to David with cedar wood, and masons and carpenters to build a house for him. ² Thus David realized that HASHEM had firmly established him as king over Israel, that his kingdom had been raised high for the sake of His people Israel. ³ David took more wives in Jerusalem, and David fathered more sons and daughters. ⁴ These are the names of

Chronicles	Samuel
1. The conquest of Jerusalem	1. The conquest of Jerusalem
2. The abortive transfer of the Ark	2. Churam's ambassadors
3. Churam's ambassadors	3. David's marriages
4. David's marriages	4. Two Philistine attacks
5. Two Philistine attacks	5. The abortive transfer of the Ark
6. The successful transfer of the Ark	6. The successful transfer of the Ark

Abarbanel to Samuel notes the discrepancy. He demonstrates that the actual historical sequence is probably the one presented in Samuel and concludes that the sequence in Chronicles is not determined by the chronology of the events. He does not, however, offer an explanation for the particular order chosen by Chronicles. See Section Two, p. 424 for a possible explanation.

1. ... וַיִּשְׁלַח חוּרָם מֶלֶךְ־צֹר — And Churam, King of Tyre, sent ... For a discussion of the place which Churam, King of Tyre, played in Jewish history, see ArtScroll Ezekiel pp. 460-465.

וַעֲצֵי אֲרָזִים — With [lit. and] cedar wood. The vav here (וַעֲצֵי) serves in place of a beis (בְּעֲצֵי) (R' Yonah ibn Janach in HaRikmah).

As Metzudos explains, the function of the people whom Churam sent was to bring the wood.

וְחָרָשֵׁי קִיר — And masons [lit. wall builders]. Samuel has וְחָרָשֵׁי אֶבֶן קִיר, stonemasons, making clear that these were artisans who worked in stone rather than wood.

2. וַיֵּדַע דָּוִד — Thus David realized. The commentators explain that David realized that his kingship had been firmly established when he saw foreign kings willingly subjugate themselves to him (Radak; Mefaresh; Metzudos). Gra adds that it was especially significant that Tyre, an Edomite nation, recognized David's supremacy. See Section Two for a fuller discussion of this.

כִּי־הֱכִינוֹ ה' — That HASHEM had firmly established him. הֱכִינוֹ is from כּוּן, to set firmly or to establish. It is occasionally used to describe a strong unopposed rulership, as in I Kings 2:46.

בַּעֲבוּר עַמּוֹ יִשְׂרָאֵל — For the sake of His people Israel. David also realized that the heights to which his kingship had been elevated had not been for him personally but for the sake of God's people, Israel (Metzudos).

3. עוֹד נָשִׁים — More wives. This expression is not really appropriate for Chronicles, since it makes no mention in its narrative of the wives and children whom David had previously had in Hebron (see II Samuel 3:2ff). [The wives and children from Hebron are, however, mentioned in ch. 3 above.] This is one example among many (see 1:4) that Chronicles was written on the assumption that the reader was familiar with the earlier books.

Samuel has פִּלַגְשִׁים וְנָשִׁים, concubines and wives. It may be that Chronicles omits mention of the concubines because by the

שְׁמוֹת הַיְלוּדִים אֲשֶׁר הָיוּ־לוֹ בִּירוּשָׁלָ͏ִם שַׁמּוּעַ וְשׁוֹבָב נָתָן

ו־ז וּשְׁלֹמֹה: וְיִבְחָר וֶאֱלִישׁוּעַ וְאֶלְפָּלֶט: וְנֹגַהּ וְנֶפֶג וְיָפִיעַ:

ח וֶאֱלִישָׁמָע וּבְעֶלְיָדָע וֶאֱלִיפָלֶט: וַיִּשְׁמְעוּ פְלִשְׁתִּים כִּי־

נִמְשַׁח דָּוִיד לְמֶלֶךְ עַל־כָּל־יִשְׂרָאֵל וַיַּעֲלוּ כָל־פְּלִשְׁתִּים

ט לְבַקֵּשׁ אֶת־דָּוִיד וַיִּשְׁמַע דָּוִיד וַיֵּצֵא לִפְנֵיהֶם: וּפְלִשְׁתִּים

י בָּאוּ וַיִּפְשְׁטוּ בְּעֵמֶק רְפָאִים: וַיִּשְׁאַל דָּוִיד בֵּאלֹהִים לֵאמֹר

time this was written it was apparent that David's concubines had no significant impact on history, and thus there was no reason to record their existence.

4-7. For an examination of these names and a discussion of the differences between this list and other lists of David's sons, see comm. to 3:5ff.

8-12. With minor differences this account parallels the one in *Samuel*. One major change between the two passages is that the אֱלֹהִים, *God*, of v. 10 is HASHEM in the account in *Samuel*. See remarks to 13:8.

❧ The Philistine Wars

8. וַיִּשְׁמְעוּ פְלִשְׁתִּים כִּי־נִמְשַׁח דָּוִיד לְמֶלֶךְ עַל־כָּל־יִשְׂרָאֵל — *And the Philistines heard that David had been anointed king over all Israel.* Israel had long been subservient to the Philistines. As long as David ruled only over Judah in Hebron they did not feel themselves challenged. Now that David had been crowned king over all Israel, they felt the need to reassert their supremacy (*Mefaresh*).

וַיַּעֲלוּ כָל־פְּלִשְׁתִּים — *So all the Philistines went up.* They mustered all their forces because David's military prowess was well known to them (*Metzudos*).

It was on the occasion of this battle that David composed the second psalm, which sings of the futility of the nations of the world gathering their forces to fight against God and His anointed one (*Radak*). See Section Two, p. 425.

לְבַקֵּשׁ אֶת־דָּוִיד — *To seek out David.* Targum renders לְמִתְבַּע, which is the term favored by the *Targumim* to translate the root דרש, *to seek out.* Thus, *Targum* indicates that בקש, which usually means to ask, is here used in the same sense as דרש, *to seek out.* See *Judges* 6:29 where the two terms are used synonymously.

וַיֵּצֵא לִפְנֵיהֶם — *And went out against them.* This expression is very unusual in the sense in which it is used here. יָצָא לִפְנֵי always means *to go out at the head of an army,* as it is used in v. 15 of our chapter. The idea of going out *against* is normally expressed with the form יָצָא לִקְרַאת (see, e.g., *I Samuel* 4:1). We do find לִפְנֵי with the meaning *against* but that normally occurs only with the prefix ב, *beis* (as e.g. *Deuteronomy* 7:24 and 11:25), rather than with ל, *lamed.* The meaning *against* used in conjunction with the prefix *lamed* can be found in *Job* 41:2 but not with the root יצא. It is not clear why *Chronicles* substitutes this unusual expression for the phrase וַיֵּרֶד אֶל הַמְּצוּדָה, *And he went down to the fortress,* which *Samuel* has.

9. בְּעֵמֶק רְפָאִים — *Through the Valley of Rephaim.* Joshua (15:8) mentions this valley as being in the vicinity of Jerusalem.

10. וַיִּשְׁאַל דָּוִיד בֵּאלֹהִים — *And David inquired of God.* David consulted the *Urim VeTumim,* the oracular breastplate worn by the *Kohen Gadol* (High Priest) (see *Exodus* 28:30), before committing himself to the fight. The midrashim praise David for not taking any step in war without first asking God. See further comm. to v. 14.

הַאֶעֱלֶה עַל־פְּלִשְׁתִּים — *Shall I go up against the Philistines.* The term עלה is an idiom for waging war. Thus David was actually asking, 'Shall I wage war against the Philistines?' For this reason, the expression is used even though the Philistines were in the Valley of Rephaim and thus presumably at a lower elevation than David.

11. וַיַּעֲלוּ בְּבַעַל־פְּרָצִים — *So they went up to Baal Peratzim.* The end of our verse makes it obvious that this name was given to the area after the Philistine defeat. *Chronicles,* however, refers to it even initially by its subsequently well-known name.

פָּרַץ הָאֱלֹהִים אֶת־אוֹיְבַי בְּיָדִי — *God has broken open my enemies by my hand.* The use of פרץ in the sense of breaking open a people

those born, whom he had in Jerusalem: Shammua, Shovav, Nathan, and Solomon. ⁵ Yivchar, Elishua, and Elpelet. ⁶ Nogah, Nepheg, and Yaphia. ⁷ Elishama, Beeliada, and Eliphelet. ⁸ And the Philistines heard that David had been anointed king over all Israel, so all the Philistines went up to seek out David; and David heard and went out against them. ⁹ And the Philistines had come and fanned out through the Valley of Rephaim. ¹⁰ And David inquired of God

[in our case, smashing an army] is found elsewhere in Scripture (see, e.g., *Psalms* 60:3). However, its use with בְּיָדִי [lit. *into my hand*] is unique. *Samuel* has לְפָנַי, *before me.* It seems that the phrase should be translated *by my hand* rather than *into my hand.* David now recognizes himself as a tool in the hands of God.

כְּפֶרֶץ מָיִם — *Like the breaking of water.* The simile suggests the breaking waves of the ocean *(Mefaresh).* *Metzudos* understands the phrase as conveying a sense of suddenness. *God has broken open my enemies as* [swiftly as] *a flood of water* [breaks through a barrier].

12. וַיַּעַזְבוּ־שָׁם אֶת־אֱלֹהֵיהֶם — *And they abandoned their gods there.* It seems the Philistines had taken out their idols with them to battle. When fleeing their crushing defeat, they abandoned their idols on the battlefield.

וַיִּשָּׂרְפוּ בָּאֵשׁ — *And they were burnt in a fire.* They burnt the idols which the Philistines had left behind in accordance with the Torah's law which forbids any benefit to be derived from anything that had been used for idol worship (see *Avodah Zara* 44a).

Our verse serves as another example of *Chronicles* elucidating an obscure passage in the earlier books by its choice of words. In place of our וַיִּשָּׂרְפוּ בָּאֵשׁ, *and they were burnt in a fire, Samuel* has וַיִּשָּׂאֵם which would normally be translated, *and they*

carried *them away* — apparently to put them to some use. However, *Targum* and the commentators there render וַיִּשָּׂאֵם, *and they burnt them* (see *Rosh Hashanah* 22b). Our verse makes this meaning clear.

13. In spite of the defeat which they suffered, the Philistines regrouped for another attack. They were to suffer another ignominious defeat (v. 16), but even this would not eliminate them as enemies of the Jews. In 18:1 we see that at a later date David had to wage yet another war against them.

14. וַיִּשְׁאַל עוֹד דָּוִד בֵּאלֹהִים — *And David inquired once more of God.* We are not told precisely what question David asked. Perhaps the fact that the question is not quoted in itself indicates that it was precisely the same question asked in v. 10. Consequently, there was no necessity to repeat it. [Whenever the *Urim VeTumim* was consulted the answer seems to have been precisely matched to the question asked. See v. 10; see also I *Samuel* 23:2; 30:8 and II *Samuel* 2:1. On that basis, since the answer, at least in part, is לֹא תַעֲלֶה, *do not go up,* the assumption is that the question was הַאֶעֱלֶה, *shall I go up,* as in v. 10. But see below.]

לֹא תַעֲלֶה אַחֲרֵיהֶם — *Do not go up after them.* God's answer here seems different in important aspects from the one given in the parallel verse in *Samuel.* The two answers:

Chronicles	Samuel
1. וַיֹּאמֶר ... לֹא תַעֲלֶה אַחֲרֵיהֶם, And [God] said ... 'Do not go up after them,	1. וַיֹּאמֶר ... לֹא תַעֲלֶה, And [God] said ... 'Do not go up,
2. הָסֵב מֵעֲלֵיהֶם, turn away from them	2. הָסֵב אֶל אַחֲרֵיהֶם, circle behind them,
3. ... וּבָאתָ לָהֶם, and come at them ...'	3. ... וּבָאתָ לָהֶם, and come at them ...'

The most striking difference is that in phrase (1) of *Chronicles* he is told not to go up אַחֲרֵיהֶם [which usually means *behind*

them], whereas in phrase (2) of *Samuel* it seems that is just what he is supposed to do. It would seem that although the words

יד פְּלִשְׁתִּים ק' הַאֶעֱלֶה עַל־°פְּלִשְׁתִּיים וּנְתַתָּם בְּיָדִי וַיֹּאמֶר לוֹ יְהוָה יא-טז
יא עֲלֵה וּנְתַתִּים בְּיָדֶךָ: וַיַּעֲלוּ בְּבַעַל־פְּרָצִים וַיַּכֵּם שָׁם דָּוִיד
וַיֹּאמֶר דָּוִיד פָּרַץ הָאֱלֹהִים אֶת־אוֹיְבַי בְּיָדִי כְּפֶרֶץ מָיִם
יב עַל־כֵּן קָרְאוּ שֵׁם־הַמָּקוֹם הַהוּא בַּעַל פְּרָצִים: וַיַּעַזְבוּ־שָׁם
יג אֶת־אֱלֹהֵיהֶם וַיֹּאמֶר דָּוִיד וַיִּשָּׂרְפוּ בָּאֵשׁ: וַיֹּסִיפוּ
יד עוֹד פְּלִשְׁתִּים וַיִּפְשְׁטוּ בָּעֵמֶק: וַיִּשְׁאַל עוֹד דָּוִיד בֵּאלֹהִים
וַיֹּאמֶר לוֹ הָאֱלֹהִים לֹא תַעֲלֶה אַחֲרֵיהֶם הָסֵב מֵעֲלֵיהֶם
טו וּבָאתָ לָהֶם מִמּוּל הַבְּכָאִים: וִיהִי כְּשָׁמְעֲךָ אֶת־קוֹל
הַצְּעָדָה בְּרָאשֵׁי הַבְּכָאִים אָז תֵּצֵא בַמִּלְחָמָה כִּי־יָצָא
טז הָאֱלֹהִים לְפָנֶיךָ לְהַכּוֹת אֶת־מַחֲנֵה פְלִשְׁתִּים: וַיַּעַשׂ דָּוִיד

in *Samuel* and *Chronicles* are similar, they are used in different senses. Both the word תַעֲלֶה and the word אַחֲרֵיהֶם can have more than one meaning. When the root עלה is used in connection with war [as, for example, in David's question: הַאֶעֱלֶה], an idiomatic translation would be: *Shall I wage war* rather than: *Shall I go up to war*. That is, although the basic meaning of עלה is *to go up*, its use in connection with war is not influenced by the geographical location of the enemy. [Compare usage like מִי יַעֲלֶה לָנוּ אֶל הַכְּנַעֲנִי ... לְהִלָּחֶם בּוֹ, lit. *who will go up for us to the Canaanite ... to fight him*, in *Judges* 1:1.]

Thus, God's answer to David's first question עֲלֵה, *go up* (v. 10), really means — *go wage war*, not ascend a height. However, with עלה used in that sense it cannot be correct to say, as *Chronicles* does in our verse, לֹא תַעֲלֶה אַחֲרֵיהֶם, *do not wage war* [lit. *go up*] *after them*. One does not wage war *after* or *behind* them. If any word should be used it would be לִקְרָאתָם, *against them*, or a similar expression. It seems therefore clear that the two phrases must be translated in two different ways.

Now אַחֲרֵיהֶם can also have two meanings. It can describe a location, as (*Genesis* 18:10) *behind them*, but it can also mean *following someone* as, for example, in *Deuteronomy* 13:5, תֵּלֵכוּ אַחֲרֵי ה' אֱלֹהֵיכֶם, *You shall follow after HASHEM your God*. Thus, *Samuel* has God saying: (1) *Do not wage war* [yet, i.e., do not meet them head on]. (2) *Move around behind them*. In *Chronicles* the message is: (1) *Do not follow them up* [to the elevated ground which they occupy]. (2) *Turn away from them*.

We can best understand the difference between the two messages when we consider *Radak's* remarks in *Samuel*. He comments: Do not go up against them yet for the moment of salvation has not yet come. In the meantime move to the rear and come up to them from the *becha* trees. Then, when you hear the sound — move in to attack.

Later on, *Radak* explains the sound that they are to hear. The text (v. 15) calls it קוֹל הַצְּעָדָה, *the sound of footsteps*, and *Radak* explains: I shall allow you to hear a sound which will strengthen the hearts of your men. They will hear a sound as though there were footsteps atop the trees — as though angels were coming to smite the Philistines.

The intent of *Radak* is clear. The verse in *Samuel* does not mean that this battle could not be won by a frontal assault and that a stratagem was therefore necessary. Rather, God was prescribing a means of delaying the moment of confrontation. In contrast to the earlier battle which was David's, this fight was to be God's. His angels were to go out to smite the Philistines; David's men were to see clearly that they were but the tools of Divine intervention. But this interpretation is not reflected in the words of the text. Read simply they convey directions for setting a trap for the Philistines. It is the text in *Chronicles* which gives the words their correct shading. As rendered here they in no way connote military strategy. They are simply an exhortation to avoid contact with the Philistines. [See below, comm. to v. 15, on other changes in the text which convey the same idea.]

saying, 'Shall I go up against the Philistines and will You deliver them into my hand?' And HASHEM said to him, 'Go up and I shall deliver them into your hand.' [11] *So they went up to Baal Peratzim and David smote them there. And David said, 'God has broken open my enemies by my hand like the breaking of water.' They therefore called the name of that place Baal Peratzim.* [12] *And they abandoned their gods there, and David commanded and they were burnt in a fire.* [13] *And the Philistines once more fanned out through the valley.* [14] *And David inquired once more of God. And God said to him, 'Do not go up after them, turn away from them and come at them from in front of the becha trees.* [15] *And it shall be when you hear the sound of footsteps in the tops of the becha trees then proceed to battle, for God has gone out before you to smite the Philistine camp.'*

For David to relinquish the battle into God's hands must not have been easy, particularly after the victory which his forces had won in the earlier battle. The normal tendency would have been to take matters into his own hands. But, as the *Mefaresh*, followed by *Metzudos*, quotes from the Sages, David was being deliberately challenged to submerge his own interest to God's will. When God rejected Saul in favor of David the heavenly court objected until God told them: 'Come, I will show you the difference between David and Saul.' That difference lay in David's ability to submit. Where Saul had sometimes substituted his own thinking for God's directions, David followed each detail of God's plan meticulously.

The ideal king of Israel is no more than the conduit through whom God exercises His stewardship of His people. To the extent that the king asserts himself he blocks out God's rulership. The man who cannot obey God in every detail is not the man who can be Israel's king. David's bearing in this battle was to vindicate his choice as king.

15. וַיְהִי כְּשָׁמְעֲךָ אֶת־קוֹל הַצְּעָדָה בְּרָאשֵׁי הַבְּכָאִים — *And it shall be when you hear the sound of footsteps in the tops of the becha trees. Radak's* explanation of this phrase

has been quoted in the commentary to the previous verse. The footsteps are those of God's angels who are coming to wage war against the Philistines.

Ralbag sees this as part of a stratagem to take the Philistines by surprise. David was told not to advance from the grove of trees until a wind blew and the rustling of the branches would resemble the sound of marching feet. At that moment his advance would go unnoticed since the Philistines would think that the noise they heard was caused by the wind in the trees.

אָז תֵּצֵא בַמִּלְחָמָה — *Then proceed to battle.* That this phrase was substituted for the אָז תֶּחֱרָץ, *then you shall act decisively*, of *Samuel*, is entirely consistent with the other changes which have been noted. The maneuver which brings the army into position is itself part of the battle. The moment of attack is merely that point in time when decisive action is taken. For this reason, *Samuel*, which describes the maneuver, uses the phrase *then you shall act decisively*. By contrast, *Chronicles*, which pays scant attention to the maneuver, but more clearly emphasizes the supernatural aspect of this battle, marks the beginning of the battle from the sound of the footsteps.[1]

16. וַיַּעַשׂ דָּוִיד כַּאֲשֶׁר צִוָּהוּ הָאֱלֹהִים — *And*

---

1. It was not easy for David and his men to refrain from attacking until the appointed hour. *Midrash Shocher Tov* 27 describes that as they came up behind the Philistines they were less than eight cubits away from them. When the Philistines saw them, Israel said to David: 'Why are we standing still?' He answered them: 'God has commanded us not to attack until we see the shaking of the treetops. If we attack we will be killed. Better that we die innocently (by adhering to God's command) than die guiltily. Let us all raise our eyes to our Father in Heaven.' When they showed their trust in God the trees began to shake and they went to the attack … Then God said to the angels: 'See the difference between Saul and David!'

כַּאֲשֶׁר צִוָּהוּ הָאֱלֹהִים וַיַּכּוּ אֶת־מַחֲנֵה פְלִשְׁתִּים מִגִּבְעוֹן

יז וְעַד־גָּזְרָה: וַיֵּצֵא שֵׁם־דָּוִיד בְּכָל־הָאֲרָצוֹת וַיהוָה נָתַן אֶת־

א פַּחְדּוֹ עַל־כָּל־הַגּוֹיִם: וַיַּעַשׂ־לוֹ בָתִּים

ב בְּעִיר דָּוִיד וַיָּכֶן מָקוֹם לַאֲרוֹן הָאֱלֹהִים וַיֶּט־לוֹ אֹהֶל: אָז אָמַר דָּוִיד לֹא לָשֵׂאת אֶת־אֲרוֹן הָאֱלֹהִים כִּי אִם־הַלְוִיִּם כִּי־בָם ׀ בָּחַר יהוה לָשֵׂאת אֶת־אֲרוֹן יְהוָה וּלְשָׁרְתוֹ עַד־

ג עוֹלָם: וַיַּקְהֵל דָּוִיד אֶת־כָּל־יִשְׂרָאֵל אֶל־יְרוּשָׁלִָם לְהַעֲלוֹת אֶת־אֲרוֹן יהוה אֶל־מְקוֹמוֹ אֲשֶׁר־הֵכִין לוֹ:

ד־ה וַיֶּאֱסֹף דָּוִיד אֶת־בְּנֵי אַהֲרֹן וְאֶת־הַלְוִיִּם: לִבְנֵי

ו קְהָת אוּרִיאֵל הַשָּׂר וְאֶחָיו מֵאָה וְעֶשְׂרִים: לִבְנֵי

ז מְרָרִי עֲשָׂיָה הַשָּׂר וְאֶחָיו מָאתַיִם וְעֶשְׂרִים: לִבְנֵי

ח גֵּרְשׁוֹם יוֹאֵל הַשָּׂר וְאֶחָיו מֵאָה וּשְׁלֹשִׁים: לִבְנֵי

David did as God had commanded him. The Midrash points out that this phrase takes on special significance in view of what has previously been explained. David obeyed God's commands in spite of the fact that this required unusual heroism and a highly disciplined sense of submission to the Divine. This obedience vindicated God's choice of David as king.

17. This verse has no parallel in *Samuel.* Perhaps it needed the perspective of history to appreciate the significant effects of these victories over the surrounding nations.

XV

⋘ The Ark Comes to Jerusalem

Chapter 13 ended with the diversion of the Ark to the house of Oved Edom the Gittite. During the three months that it remained there it brought abundant blessings to his house (v. 14). Our chapter resumes that story and tells how it finally was brought to Jerusalem. Many more details are given than in the parallel section in II *Samuel* 6:12-23.

1. וַיַּעַשׂ־לוֹ בָתִּים — *And he built for himself houses.* The verb עשה is used here idiomatically in place of the more common בנה. However, see Section Two, p. 426 for other possible explanations.

וַיָּכֶן מָקוֹם ... וַיֶּט־לוֹ אֹהֶל — *And he prepared a place ... and spread out a covering for it.* David prepared a building for the Ark which had walls of stone but a ceiling made out of curtains. מָקוֹם, *place*, refers to the stone walls; אֹהֶל, *covering*, describes the curtains of the ceiling (*Gra*). [Although אֹהֶל in Scripture generally describes the entire tent and not just the ceiling, its use as roof, ceiling, or cover is very widespread in Rabbinic literature. Apparently this usage had already achieved currency at the time *Chronicles* was written.]

2. ... אָז — *Then* ... When Uzza died (*Metzudos*). When Uzza died David

realized that he was at least indirectly responsible for his death. Had David followed the Torah's requirement that the Ark be carried on the shoulders of the Levites, perhaps God would have shielded Uzza from making the miscalculation which cost him his life (see comm. 13:9). Or perhaps, even though Uzza erred, his punishment might not have been as immediate and as severe.

כִּי אִם־הַלְוִיִּם — *But the Levites.* Rambam's opinion (*Sefer HaMitzvos, Positive Command* 34) is that the halachah requires that the Ark be borne by the *Kohanim* Although the Torah seems to qualify any of the descendants of Kehath to carry the Ark (*Numbers* 7:8), including the Levites, this applied only in the wilderness when there were very few *Kohanim.* Once the Israelites entered the Land of Israel,

16 *And David did as God had commanded him and they smote the Philistine camp from Giveon up to Gezer.* 17 *And David's fame spread through all the countries, and* HASHEM *cast a fear of him over all the nations.*

A nd he built for himself houses in the City of David; and he prepared a place for the Ark of God and spread out a covering for it. 2 *Then David said that no one but the Levites was to carry the Ark of God, for it was they whom* HASHEM *chose to carry the Ark of God and to serve before Him forever.* 3 *And David assembled all Israel at Jerusalem to bring up the Ark of* HASHEM *to its place which he had prepared for it.* 4 *And David gathered the sons of Aaron and the Levites.* 5 *Of the sons of Kehath* — *Uriel, the officer, and one hundred and twenty of his brothers.* 6 *Of the sons of Merari* — *Asaiah, the officer, and two hundred and twenty of his brothers.* 7 *Of the sons of Gershom* — *Yoel, the officer, and one hundred and*

---

however, the duty of carrying the Ark devolved exclusively on the *Kohanim.* Many other authorities disagree and are of the opinion that both *Kohanim* and Levites were always equally qualified.[1]

According to *Rambam,* the word *Levites* in our text must mean *Kohanim.* They are called Levites because they were descended from Levi. [Cf. R' Yehoshua ben Levi's assertion *(Yevamos* 86b) that there are twenty-four places in Scripture where *Kohanim* are referred to as Levites. For an exhaustive analysis of this, see *Kuntros HaKohanim HaLeviim* in *R' David Cohen's Ohel Dovid.*]

בִּי־בָם בָּחַר ה' לָשֵׂאת אֶת־אֲרוֹן ה' — *For it was they whom* HASHEM *chose to carry the Ark of God.* See *Numbers* 7:9.

Although that verse deals with all the vessels of the Tabernacle, and does not in any way single out the Ark, the commentators note that as far as the other vessels were concerned, the requirement that they be carried only on the shoulder was temporary and did not extend beyond their entry into the Land. (See *Encyclopedia Talmudis* under אָרוֹן, vol. 2 p. 178.)

3. ... וַיַּקְהֵל דָּוִיד אֶת־כָּל־יִשְׂרָאֵל — *And David assembled all Israel* ... Once more the

difference in emphasis between *Samuel* and *Chronicles* is notable. In *Samuel* it states simply, ... *and David went and brought up the Ark* ... and no mention is made of *all Israel.* See prefatory remarks to 13:1-4.

4. ... וַיֶּאֱסֹף דָּוִיד — *And David gathered* ... The purpose for which David gathered the *Kohanim* and the Levites is made clear in v. 11ff.

5. אוּרִיאֵל הַשָּׂר — *Uriel, the officer.* An Uriel is listed under the sons of Kehath at 6:9. There seems little doubt that this is not the Uriel mentioned here since the one in ch. 6 is number 7 on list I (found in v. 5 there), while the Heman who was appointed chorister at this time (v. 17 here) is number 21 on List II there — a difference of fourteen generations. On the other hand, there is also the identity of names between Asaiah, the officer of the Merarites (v. 6), and an Asaiah who is listed at I(8) in the Merari list of ch. 6. It is, of course, possible that the similarity in the names is a coincidence. Moreover, the same names do frequently recur within the same family line.

וְאֶחָיו מֵאָה וְעֶשְׂרִים — *And one hundred and twenty of his brothers.* I.e., fellow members

---

1. The controversy is far reaching and is beyond the scope of this commentary. The basis for the controversy is the interpretation of various verses in Scripture, some of which occur in *Chronicles.* The commentary will note those verses which *Rambam* feels support his position, although the commentary will generally adhere to the other opinion since it fits more smoothly into the simple meaning of the text.

ט אֱלִיצָפָן שְׁמַעְיָה הַשָּׂר וְאֶחָיו מָאתָיִם: לִבְנֵי

י חֶבְרוֹן אֱלִיאֵל הַשָּׂר וְאֶחָיו שְׁמוֹנִים: לִבְנֵי עֻזִּיאֵל

יא עַמִּינָדָב הַשָּׂר וְאֶחָיו מֵאָה וּשְׁנֵים עָשָׂר: וַיִּקְרָא

דָוִיד לְצָדוֹק וּלְאֶבְיָתָר הַכֹּהֲנִים וְלַלְוִיִּם לְאוּרִיאֵל עֲשָׂיָה

יב וְיוֹאֵל שְׁמַעְיָה וֶאֱלִיאֵל וְעַמִּינָדָב: וַיֹּאמֶר לָהֶם אַתֶּם

רָאשֵׁי הָאָבוֹת לַלְוִיִּם הִתְקַדְּשׁוּ אַתֶּם וַאֲחֵיכֶם וְהַעֲלִיתֶם

יג אֵת אֲרוֹן יהוה אֱלֹהֵי יִשְׂרָאֵל אֶל־הֲכִינוֹתִי לוֹ: כִּי

לְמַבָּרִאשׁוֹנָה לֹא אַתֶּם פָּרַץ יהוה אֱלֹהֵינוּ בָּנוּ כִּי־לֹא

יד דְרַשְׁנֻהוּ כַּמִּשְׁפָּט: וַיִּתְקַדְּשׁוּ הַכֹּהֲנִים וְהַלְוִיִּם לְהַעֲלוֹת

טו אֶת־אֲרוֹן יהוה אֱלֹהֵי יִשְׂרָאֵל: וַיִּשְׂאוּ בְנֵי־הַלְוִיִּם אֵת

אֲרוֹן הָאֱלֹהִים כַּאֲשֶׁר צִוָּה מֹשֶׁה כִּדְבַר יהוה בִּכְתֵפָם

טז בַּמֹּטוֹת עֲלֵיהֶם: וַיֹּאמֶר דָּוִיד לְשָׂרֵי

of his family (Metzudos).

8. לִבְנֵי אֱלִיצָפָן — Of the sons of Elitzaphan. It is only here and in II Chronicles 29:13, during the reign of Chizkiah, that we find Elitzaphan as a family head. In the Torah he is given as the son of Uzziel (v. 10 here), who in turn was a son of Kehath. Moses appointed Elitzaphan as chief of the Kehathites at Numbers 3:30. We must assume that the reason why his family is listed here before that of his father (by his other sons) in v. 10 is that in David's time his was the more important family.

9-10. Chevron and Uzziel are both sons of Kehath (6:3). It is only in Chronicles that they appears as families.

11. לְצָדוֹק וּלְאֶבְיָתָר — Tzadok and Eviathar. In the commentary to 12:28 it was noted that when Tzadok joined David at Hebron, he must still have been very young and not yet ready for the mantle of leadership. In spite of his youth, David turned to him here to organize the transfer of the Ark.

Eviathar, a descendant of Eli the Kohen Gadol (High Priest), seems to have been Kohen Gadol early in David's career (I Samuel 30:7). He continued in this post until Solomon replaced him with Tzadok (I Kings 2:35). It seems significant that Tzadok is mentioned here before Eviathar, who was Kohen Gadol and must have been considerably older than Tzadok. It may be that even then Tzadok's great spiritual grandeur shone through, or perhaps it is Chronicles with the hindsight of history

which places Tzadok before Eviathar. (With Solomon's appointment of Tzadok, the Tzadokite line replaced that of Eli, of which Eviathar was the last, as Kohanim Gedolim.)

וְלַלְוִיִּם לְאוּרִיאֵל ... — And the Levites, Uriel ... The names are in apposition to the Levites. To which Levites did he call? To Uriel, etc. The names are the ones given in vs. 5-10 as the officers of the various Levitical families. According to Rambam, that the Ark was to be carried by Kohanim (see comm. v. 2), it must be that David called the two Kohanim to attend to the carrying and the Levites to act as choristers, as described below. According to the other opinions, the function of the Kohanim must have been to cover the Ark with the various covers prescribed by the Torah (see Numbers 5:4) so that the Levites would then be able to carry it (Malbim).

12. אַתֶּם רָאשֵׁי הָאָבוֹת לַלְוִיִּם — You are the heads of the Levitical families. Because of this it is your responsibility to see that everything is in order (Metzudos).

הִתְקַדְּשׁוּ — Prepare yourselves. The translation follows Targum. Rashi attaches this same meaning to the word in Exodus 19:22. Metzudos has purify yourselves.

אֶל־הֲכִינוֹתִי לוֹ — To the place which I have prepared for it. The phrase must be understood as though it were written, אֶל [הַמָּקוֹם אֲשֶׁר] הֲכִינוֹתִי לוֹ (Radak and Metzudos).

thirty of his brothers. ⁸ Of the sons of Elitzaphan — Shemaiah, the officer, and two hundred of his brothers. ⁹ Of the sons of Chevron — Eliel, the officer, and eighty of his brothers. ¹⁰ Of the sons of Uzziel — Amminadav, the officer, and one hundred and twelve of his brothers. ¹¹ And David called Tzadok and Eviathar the Kohanim, and the Levites, Uriel, Asaiah, Yoel, Shemaiah, Eliel, and Amminadav. ¹² And he said to them, 'You are the heads of the Levitical families; prepare yourselves, you and your brothers, that you may transfer the Ark of HASHEM, the God of Israel, to the place which I have prepared for it. ¹³ Because from the first it was not you, HASHEM our God made a breach in us; for we did not seek it out as the law requires.' ¹⁴ So the Kohanim and the Levites prepared themselves in order to bring up the Ark of HASHEM, the God of Israel. ¹⁵ And the Levites carried the Ark of God, as Moses had commanded in accordance with the word of HASHEM, on their shoulders, by the poles on them. ¹⁶ And David told the officers of the

---

13. כִּי לְמַבָּרִאשׁוֹנָה לֹא אַתֶּם — *Because from the first it was not you.* Because you, the Kohanim and Levites, were not involved in the original attempt to transport the Ark, the breach which God made in us through which Uzza's death came about *(Radak and Metzudos).*

כִּי־לֹא דְרַשְׁנֻהוּ בַּמִּשְׁפָּט — *For we did not seek it out as the law requires.* We did not show proper care for it as the law requires in that we transported it on a wagon instead of having it carried on the shoulders of the Levites *(Radak).* [For דרש in this context see comm. to 13:3.]

פָּרַץ ה' אֱלֹהֵינוּ בָּנוּ — *HASHEM our God made a breach in us.* Even though it was Uzza who erred, David still identifies with him. By striking Uzza (13:11), He made a breach in us *(Metzudos).* If Uzza is hurt it touches all of us.

The meaning of the phrase could also be that by Uzza's death the community as a whole was breached by the loss of one of its valued members. If this indeed is meant, it suggests an alternative meaning for the phrase at 13:11: ... *for HASHEM has made a breach* [in Israel] *through* [the death of] *Uzza.*

The following speaks for the latter explanation. פרץ means *to break open.* This implies that something is left standing. This meaning is not preserved when the word is used as a synonym for *killing.*

15. כַּאֲשֶׁר צִוָּה מֹשֶׁה כִּדְבַר ה' — *As Moses had commanded in accordance with the word of HASHEM.* Where did Moses command? [In

Numbers 7:9 when he disposed of the wagons which were available for the transport of the Tabernacle and the Torah it says:] *But to the sons of Kehath he did not give* [any wagons] *for the service of the sanctified* [objects] *was their duty — they shall carry on the shoulder (Sifrei, Nasso).* *Ramban (Sefer Hamitzvos Shoresh 3)* explains that *as Moses had commanded* refers to the requirement that the Levites who carried the Ark should be between thirty and fifty years of age.

בַּמֹטוֹת עֲלֵיהֶם — *By the poles on them.* The use of מֹט for *pole* is noteworthy. *Exodus* 25:13 specifies בַּדִּים for carrying the Ark. From *Numbers* 4:6, 8 and 10 it appears that the two terms are not synonymous since in connection with the Ark and the table, בַּדִּים are used (as specified in *Exodus*), but in the case of the candelabrum (where *Exodus* does not specify בַּדִּים), מֹט is used. *Ibn Ezra* to *Numbers* points out that the text seems to differentiate between בַּד and מֹט. If this is the case, our verse is problematic since the Torah specifies בַּדִּים not מֹט for the Ark. However, *Rashi* to *Exodus* 12:13 seems to equate בַּד with מֹט. If the two were indeed originally different from one another we would have to conclude that the difference between them became lost over the centuries and that by the time *Chronicles* was written the terms were interchangeable. [See further in *Wertheimer's* study of *Synonyms in Scripture.*]

16. לְשָׂרֵי הַלְוִיִם — *The officers of the Levites.* These are the men mentioned in vs.

הַלְוִיִּם֙ לְהַעֲמִ֣יד אֶת־אֲחֵיהֶ֣ם הַמְשֹׁרְרִ֔ים בִּכְלֵי־שִׁ֖יר
נְבָלִ֤ים וְכִנֹּרוֹת֙ וּמְצִלְתָּ֔יִם מַשְׁמִעִ֖ים לְהָרִ֣ים־בְּק֑וֹל
לְשִׂמְחָֽה: יז וַיַּעֲמִ֣ידוּ הַלְוִיִּ֗ם אֵ֚ת הֵימָ֣ן בֶּן־יוֹאֵ֔ל
וּמִן־אֶחָ֖יו אָסָ֣ף בֶּן־בֶּרֶכְיָ֑הוּ וּמִן־בְּנֵ֤י מְרָרִי֙ אֲחֵיהֶ֔ם אֵיתָ֖ן
בֶּן־קֽוּשָׁיָֽהוּ: יח וְעִמָּהֶ֖ם אֲחֵיהֶ֣ם הַמִּשְׁנִ֑ים זְכַרְיָ֡הוּ בֵּ֣ן וְיַעֲזִיאֵ֡ל
וּשְׁמִֽירָמ֣וֹת וִֽיחִיאֵ֡ל ׀ וְעֻנִּ֡י אֱלִ֠יאָב וּבְנָיָ֤הוּ וּמַעֲשֵׂיָ֙הוּ֙
וּמַתִּתְיָ֔הוּ וֶאֱלִֽיפְלֵ֙הוּ֙ וּמִקְנֵיָ֔הוּ וְעֹבֵ֥ד אֱדֹ֖ם וִֽיעִיאֵ֑ל
הַשֹּׁעֲרִֽים: יט וְהַֽמְשֹׁרְרִ֑ים הֵימָ֣ן אָסָ֣ף וְאֵיתָ֔ן בִּמְצִלְתַּ֥יִם נְחֹ֖שֶׁת
לְהַשְׁמִֽיעַ: כ וּזְכַרְיָ֨ה וַעֲזִיאֵ֜ל וּשְׁמִֽירָמ֤וֹת וִֽיחִיאֵל֙ וְעֻנִּ֣י
וֶאֱלִיאָ֣ב וּמַעֲשֵׂיָ֔הוּ וּבְנָיָ֖הוּ בִּנְבָלִ֣ים עַל־עֲלָמֽוֹת: כא וּמַתִּתְיָ֣הוּ
וֶאֱלִֽיפְלֵ֗הוּ וּמִקְנֵיָ֙הוּ֙ וְעֹבֵ֤ד אֱדֹם֙ וִֽיעִיאֵ֣ל וַֽעֲזַזְיָ֔הוּ בְּכִנֹּר֖וֹת
כב עַל־הַשְּׁמִינִ֣ית לְנַצֵּֽחַ: וּכְנַנְיָ֥הוּ שַֽׂר־הַלְוִיִּ֖ם בְּמַשָּׂ֑א יָסֹ֖ר

5-10 above.

אֶת־אֲחֵיהֶם הַמְשֹׁרְרִים — *Their brothers, the choristers.* The nature of the שִׁיר, *song*, as part of the Temple service has been discussed in the prefatory remarks to 6:16-17. There it was noted that according to *Arachin* 11a שִׁיר is *choral music.* It could be accompanied by instrumental music, but this was not mandatory. Hence, the מְשֹׁרְרִים, *choristers*, were really singers and their skill as instrumental musicians was of only secondary importance. However, for the great joy that was to accompany the bringing up of the Ark, David insisted on instrumental music. The text does not make clear whether the choristers also sang on this occasion. The expression לְהָרִים קוֹל cannot indicate anything since קוֹל is also used to describe the sound of instruments. [See, e.g., *Exodus* 19:16. But see further at v. 22.]

וּמְצִלְתָּיִם — *And cymbals.* See comm. to 13:8. In contrast to the cantillation, which separates מְצִלְתַּיִם from מַשְׁמִעִים, *Metzudos* reads the two words together, thus indicating that the function of the מְצִלְתַּיִם is to make sounds rather than a tune — hence a percussion instrument. According to the cantillation, מַשְׁמִעִים goes with the next phrase which refers back to all the instruments mentioned before. They were all there to be heard and thereby to generate the joy which David wanted for this great occasion. See further at 16:42.

לְשִׂמְחָה — *In joy.* To inspire joy at the transport of the Ark (*Metzudos*).

17. וַיַּעֲמִידוּ הַלְוִיִּם — *So the Levites set up.* Perhaps the sense of the phrase is as though the word שָׂרֵי, *officers*, is injected. From v. 16 we see that it was the officers of the Levites who were to make the appointments.

הֵימָן ... אָסָף ... אֵיתָן — *Heman ... Asaph ... Ethan.* The three main choristers who were to function in connection with the transport of the Ark are the same three who were appointed by David to be the choristers when the Ark was established in Jerusalem. See 6:18-32 and the lists offered there. [The only change in our verse is that the father of Ethan is given here as Kushaiahu while he appears in ch. 6 as Kishi.] Verse 19 will describe what these three choristers did in the procession.

18. וְעִמָּהֶם אֲחֵיהֶם הַמִּשְׁנִים — *And with them their brothers who were second in rank.* The three choristers mentioned in v. 17 were the main ones. The Levites mentioned in this verse played a secondary role. They were really gatekeepers [הַשֹּׁעֲרִים, at the end of the verse], but on this occasion they helped out with the musical accompaniment. *Malbim* points out that although the Levites were not normally allowed to exchange their duties and a chorister could not help out in the gatekeeper's job nor the gatekeeper in the chorister's (see *Rambam*, *Klei HaMikdash* 3:10), this interdiction did not apply here. The music which was played here did not have the character of the ritual שִׁיר [*shir*], *song*, that was performed during the bringing of the

Levites to set up their brothers, the choristers, with instruments, nevalim, harps, and cymbals, playing loudly so as to resound in joy. ¹⁷ *So the Levites set up Heman the son of Yoel, and from his brothers, Asaph, the son of Berechiah, and from the sons of Merari their brother, Ethan the son of Kushaiahu.* ¹⁸ *And with them their brothers who were second in rank — Zechariahu Ben, Yaaziel, Shemiramoth, Yechiel, Unni, Eliav, Benaiahu, Maaseiahu, Mattithiahu, Eliphelehu, Mikneiahu, and Oved Edom, and Yeiel, the gatekeepers.* ¹⁹ *The choristers were Heman, Asaph, and Ethan with brass cymbals to play loudly.* ²⁰ *And Zechariah, Aziel, Shemiramoth, Yechiel, Unni, Eliav, Maaseiahu, and Benaiahu with nevalim on alamoth.* ²¹ *Mattithiahu, Eliphelehu, Mikneiahu, Oved Edom, Yeiel and Azaziahu had harps to perform according to sheminith.* ²² *And Chenaniahu was the musical director of the Levites; he directed the music because he was an expert.* ²³ *Berechiah*

---

sacrifices. It was just a means of generating joy among the people and had no halachic standing.

זְכַרְיָהוּ בֵּן — *Zechariahu Ben.* Mefaresh, Radak and Metzudos all point out that בֵּן here is a proper noun. It cannot, however, be a separate person since in vs. 20 and 21 the name does not recur. The assumption is that the first of the Levites listed in this verse had two names.

וְעֹבֵד אֱדֹם — *And Oved Edom.* The Oved Edom mentioned here is a Levite who was usually a gatekeeper but functioned here as a musician. The Oved Edom of v. 24 was a Kohen — see below.

הַשֹּׁעֲרִים — *The gatekeepers.* The men listed here were either assigned to be gatekeepers once the Ark was established in Jerusalem [but see 16:5 where it is evident that some of them functioned as musicians even after the Ark was in Jerusalem], or they had previously been gatekeepers of the Tabernacle at Shiloh, Nov and Giveon (Radak). Their function in the procession is described in vs. 20-21.

19. The three main choristers listed in v. 17 were to play on copper cymbals.

20-21. These two verses describe the functions of the secondary musicians listed in v. 18. There were to be two groups, each to play a different instrument. The instruments mentioned are: עֲלֶמֶת נֵבֶל and כִּנּוֹר עַל הַשְּׁמִינִית. These instruments are discussed in ArtScroll *Psalms* 33:2, and we follow the usage of that work not to offer any translation since we cannot really

know the exact nature of any given instrument. We offer the following general remarks: נֵבֶל, *nevel*, really means *a bag* — usually a leather wine bag. Thus the נֵבֶל seems to be an instrument which produces sound by having the air in a bag expelled (Rashi). עֲלֶמֶת, *alemeth*, is related to עֶלֶם, *a youth.* Meiri supposes that it is an instrument which plays a vigorous, happy sound particularly suited to young people. In this context it is difficult to know the precise meaning of עַל. It may mean *on* or *with.*

כִּנּוֹר is obviously a string instrument since עַל הַשְּׁמִינִית denotes that it had eight strings (Metzudos). It is generally supposed to be a harp-like instrument.

21. וַעֲזַזְיָהוּ — *And Azaziahu.* Azaziahu was not mentioned in v. 18 because he was not one of the gatekeepers (Malbim).

לְנַצֵּחַ — *To perform.* Metzudos explains that the root נצח, *to conquer,* is an apt way to describe musical performers because in a harmony different voices rise to predominate over the others. The term לַמְנַצֵּחַ is familiar as a heading for many psalms and is discussed in ArtScroll *Psalms* 4:1.

22. וּכְנַנְיָהוּ שַׂר־הַלְוִים בְּמַשָּׂא — *And Chenaniahu was the musical director of the Levites.* We know of three main choristers (v. 17) and of the secondary musicians (v. 18). Now we have one person who was in general control of all the music. His job was to conduct [יָסֹר from יסר, *to discipline* or *admonish*] the musicians, telling them when to play loudly and when to play quietly (Mefaresh).

כג בַּמַּשָּׂא כִּי מֵבִין הוּא: וּבֶרֶכְיָה וְאֶלְקָנָה שֹׁעֲרִים לָאָרוֹן:

כד וּשְׁבַנְיָהוּ וְיוֹשָׁפָט וּנְתַנְאֵל וַעֲמָשַׂי וּזְכַרְיָהוּ וּבְנָיָהוּ

וֶאֱלִיעֶזֶר ק' מַחְצְרִים° הַכֹּהֲנִים בַּחֲצֹצְרוֹת לִפְנֵי אֲרוֹן

כה הָאֱלֹהִים וְעֹבֵד אֱדֹם וִיחִיָּה שֹׁעֲרִים לָאָרוֹן: וַיְהִי דָוִיד

וְזִקְנֵי יִשְׂרָאֵל וְשָׂרֵי הָאֲלָפִים הַהֹלְכִים לְהַעֲלוֹת אֶת־אֲרוֹן

כו בְּרִית־יהוה מִן־בֵּית עֹבֵד־אֱדֹם בְּשִׂמְחָה: וַיְהִי

בֶּעֱזֹר הָאֱלֹהִים אֶת־הַלְוִיִּם נֹשְׂאֵי אֲרוֹן בְּרִית־יהוה וַיִּזְבְּחוּ

כז שִׁבְעָה־פָרִים וְשִׁבְעָה אֵילִים: וְדָוִיד מְכֻרְבָּל | בִּמְעִיל בּוּץ

מַשָּׂא is taken as music. The root is נשא, *to lift up* or *to raise*, and is used for music because in it the voice or sound is raised (*Radak* and *Metzudos*). [See further in *Arachin* 11a where an association between the root נשא and music is made.] *Ralbag* and *Malbim* think that מַשָּׂא as music refers specifically to choral music. Since the songs of the Levites talked of the praises of God, they were spiritually uplifting and the expression מַשָּׂא is apt for them (*Malbim*). *Ralbag* also points out that this would explain the use of the phrase כִּי מֵבִין הוּא, *for he was understanding*. The singer of God's praises must be an understanding person.

יָסַר בַּמַּשָּׂא — *He directed the music. Radak* and *Metzudos* think that the ס, *samech*, is substituted here for a שׂ, *sin*, making it the verb form of the noun שַׂר, *officer. Radak* also suggests that this second מַשָּׂא may mean prophecy [see *Nachum* 1:1 as one of several places where this word is used in this sense]. *Chenaniahu taught the music because he was chief among the* [*Levitical*] *prophets* (see 25:1). The *Mefaresh's* understanding of יָסַר in our context is that *he conducted the music.*

כִּי מֵבִין הוּא — *Because he was an expert* [lit. *because he was understanding*]. He was chosen musical director because of his great understanding and mastery of music (*Mefaresh; Metzudos*). See below, 25:7.

23. שֹׁעֲרִים לָאָרוֹן ... — ... *were warders* [lit. *gatekeepers*] *for the Ark.* The Levites mentioned in v. 18 were really gatekeepers, but for the purpose of the procession they had been pressed into service as musicians. The two mentioned here were warders for the Ark during the procession. *Malbim* explains this as follows. The Ark was preceded in the procession by the *Kohanim* who blew trumpets in front of it (v. 24),

and it was followed by the Levite orchestra described above. To prevent the Levitical musicians from approaching too close to the Ark there were two Levite warders, the two mentioned in our verse, who walked between the Ark and the Levites who followed it. Similarly, there were two *Kohanim* who acted as warders (end of v. 24), and these walked between the Ark and the *Kohanim* who walked in front of it.

Kohanim — trumpeters
Two *Kohanim* — warders
Ark
Two *Levites* — warders
Levites — musicians

24. Seven *Kohanim* were to precede the Ark blowing trumpets.

וְעֹבֵד אֱדֹם וִיחִיָּה שֹׁעֲרִים לָאָרוֹן — *And Oved Edom and Yechiah were warders for the Ark.* The two warders whose duty it was to go behind the Ark and act as a buffer between it and the Levite orchestra (v. 23) were Levites. The two mentioned here, who were to walk before the Ark to make sure that the *Kohanim* who preceded it did not come too close, were *Kohanim* (*Malbim*). Thus, the *Oved Edom* of our verse who was a *Kohen* cannot be the same as the one mentioned in v. 18 who was a Levite.

25. וַיְהִי ... בְּשִׂמְחָה — *And ... were joyous.* The translation follows *Metzudos* who takes the whole sentence together. Although the singular וַיְהִי, *and he was,* is irregular, Scripture often uses that form to describe the activities of a group when the initiative for that action came mainly from one member of the group. Thus, *Genesis* 9:23 says וַיִּקַּח שֵׁם וָיֶפֶת אֶת־הַשִּׂמְלָה, *Shem and Yapheth took the garment,* using the singular וַיִּקַּח instead of the plural וַיִּקְחוּ, because, as the Sages teach, the initiative

and Elkanah were warders for the Ark. ²⁴ Shevaniahu, Yoshaphat, Nethanel, Amasai, Zechariahu, Benaiahu, and Eliezer, the Kohanim, blew the trumpets before the Ark of God; and Oved Edom and Yechiah were warders for the Ark. ²⁵ And David, and the elders of Israel, and the officers of the thousands who went to bring up the Ark of the Covenant of HASHEM from the house of Oved Edom were joyous. ²⁶ And it was when God helped the Levites who carried the Ark of the Covenant of HASHEM that they sacrificed seven bulls and seven rams. ²⁷ And David was hooded in a linen robe, as were all the

came from Shem. In our case, David — who as described in v. 29 and in more graphic detail in *II Samuel* 6:16 was jubilant at the ceremony, dancing with absolute abandon at the sheer joy of the occasion — may well be considered the true celebrant of the joy which all the people felt. The others were caught up in the spell of David's jubilation.

There are a number of considerations, however, pointing to a different interpretation of the verse. (1) The combination בְּשִׂמְחָה and הָיָה does not recur in Scripture. We do rarely find a similar combination

such as *Ecclesiastes* 7:14, הֱיֵה בְּטוֹב, but it is by no means a common usage. On the other hand, if בְּשִׂמְחָה qualifies לְהַעֲלוֹת *(to bring up in joy)*, then this is entirely normal usage and moreover it parallels the passage in *Samuel* (see below). (2) The cantillation marks make a stop at הָאֲלָפִים, which would not be expected if הַהֹלְכִים, *who went,* is a description of David and the elders ... (3) A parallel between the second half of our verse and the passage in *Samuel* is readily discernible from the following chart:

Chronicles	Samuel
1. וַיְהִי דָוִיד ... [הַהֹלְכִים] לְהַעֲלוֹת אֶת אֲרוֹן ... בְּשִׂמְחָה, *And David ... [who went] to bring up the Ark ... joyous*	1. וַיֵּלֶךְ דָוִד וַיַּעַל אֶת אֲרוֹן ... בְּשִׂמְחָה, *And David went and he brought up the Ark ... in joy*
2. וַיְהִי בֶּעְזֹר ... וַיִּזְבְּחוּ ..., *And it was when [God] helped ... that they sacrificed*	2. וַיְהִי כִּי צָעֲדוּ ... וַיִּזְבַּח ..., *And it was when they had gone ... that he sacrificed*

This would tend to indicate that the first part of our verse should be seen as being parallel to its counterpart in *Samuel*. Thus the translation of our verse might best be given as: *And it was David, the elders of Israel and the officers of the thousands, who went to bring up the Ark ... in joy.* This would then be an elaboration of the description of the episode in *Samuel*. In line with the rest of the account in *Chronicles* which, as we have seen, is at pains to demonstrate that the bringing up of the Ark was done with the involvement of the whole of Israel, our verse stresses that involvement.

26. וַיְהִי בֶּעְזֹר הָאֱלֹהִים ... וַיִּזְבְּחוּ שִׁבְעָה פָרִים וְשִׁבְעָה אֵילִים — *And it was when God helped ... that they sacrificed seven bulls and seven rams.* Samuel has: *And it was when those who carried the Ark had gone six steps that they sacrificed an ox and a fatling.* Metzudos suggests that our passage tells of a sacrifice brought by the

Levites in gratitude to God for their not having come to any harm carrying the Ark. This was in addition to the ox and fatling brought by David as part of the ceremony. [Note the singular וַיִּזְבַּח in *Samuel,* in contrast to the plural וַיִּזְבְּחוּ here.]

The Sages (*Sotah* 35b and *Bamidbar Rabbah* 4:20) offer various other solutions. The one closest to the simple meaning of the texts is that שׁוֹר וּמְרִיא in *Samuel* does not refer to a single ox and a single fatling but is a generic term meaning oxen and fatlings (cf. *Genesis* 32:5). *Chronicles* gives the exact number. [מְרִיא, *fatling*, would then refer to *rams*. See *Radak's Shorashim* that it can refer to any animal that has been fattened.]

27. וְדָוִיד מְכֻרְבָּל בִּמְעִיל בּוּץ — *And David was hooded in a linen robe.* The commentators render כרבל as עטף, *to wrap oneself*. *Mefaresh* refers to the Talmudic כַּרְבַּלְתָּא דְתַרְנְגוֹלָא, *the crest of a cock,* and this implies a head covering. *Ralbag* states

וְכָל־הַלְוִיִּם֩ הַנֹּשְׂאִ֨ים אֶת־הָאָר֜וֹן וְהַמְשֹׁרְרִ֗ים וּכְנַנְיָ֛ה הַשַּׂ֥ר

כח הַמַּשָּׂא֙ הַמְשֹׁרְרִ֔ים וְעַל־דָּוִ֖יד אֵפ֣וֹד בָּ֑ד וְכָל־יִשְׂרָאֵ֗ל

מַעֲלִים֙ אֶת־אֲר֣וֹן בְּרִית־יְהֹוָ֔ה בִּתְרוּעָ֖ה וּבְק֣וֹל שׁוֹפָ֑ר

כט וּבַחֲצֹֽצְר֗וֹת וּבִמְצִלְתַּ֙יִם֙ מַשְׁמִעִ֔ים בִּנְבָלִ֖ים וְכִנֹּר֑וֹת וַיְהִ֣י

אֲר֣וֹן בְּרִ֣ית יְהֹוָ֗ה בָּ֚א עַד־עִ֣יר דָּוִ֔יד וּמִיכַ֣ל בַּת־שָׁא֗וּל

נִשְׁקְפָ֣ה ׀ בְּעַ֣ד הַֽחַלּ֗וֹן וַתֵּ֨רֶא אֶת־הַמֶּ֤לֶךְ דָּוִיד֙ מְרַקֵּ֣ד

א וּמְשַׂחֵ֔ק וַתִּ֥בֶז ל֖וֹ בְּלִבָּֽהּ׃ וַיָּבִ֙יאוּ֙ אֶת־אֲר֣וֹן הָאֱלֹהִ֔ים

וַיַּצִּ֣יגוּ אֹת֔וֹ בְּת֣וֹךְ הָאֹ֔הֶל אֲשֶׁ֥ר נָֽטָה־ל֖וֹ דָּוִ֑יד וַיַּקְרִ֙יבוּ֙

ב עֹל֣וֹת וּשְׁלָמִ֔ים לִפְנֵ֖י הָאֱלֹהִֽים׃ וַיְכַ֣ל דָּוִ֔יד מֵהַעֲל֥וֹת

ג הָעֹלָ֖ה וְהַשְּׁלָמִ֑ים וַיְבָ֥רֶךְ אֶת־הָעָ֖ם בְּשֵׁ֥ם יְהֹוָֽה׃ וַיְחַלֵּ֗ק

---

clearly that it refers to a hood attached to the linen shirt.

Samuel makes no mention of this מְעִיל בּוּץ, *linen robe*, but only of an אֵפוֹד בָּד, *linen ephod*. However, *Rashi* and *Radak*, based on *Targum* there, say that the *linen ephod* is actually the same as the *linen robe* [in contrast to the אֵפוֹד, *ephod*, and מְעִיל, *robe*, mentioned in the Torah in connection with the vestments of the *Kohen Gadol* which were two different kinds of garments]. This interpretation makes our verse, which mentions the מְעִיל בּוּץ and the אֵפוֹד בָּד separately, a little difficult, unless we assume that, although both refer to the same garment, the first phrase tells us about its hood while the end of the verse deals with the actual garment. Simpler, as far as our verse is concerned, would be to take it as does *Metzudos* that we are dealing with two separate kinds of garments. The first, the מְעִיל, *robe*, was worn not only by David but also by all the musicians, while the אֵפוֹד בָּד, *linen ephod*, was worn only by David. This, however, leaves the question of why *Chronicles* makes a point of mentioning the מְעִיל while *Samuel* omits any mention of it. See Section Two, p. 428.

וְכָל־הַלְוִיִּם הַנֹּשְׂאִים אֶת־הָאָרוֹן — *As were* [lit. *and*] *all the Levites who carried the Ark*. These Levites, too, were dressed in the hooded linen robe.

הַשַּׂר הַמַּשָּׂא הַמְשֹׁרְרִים — *The musical director of the choristers*. The grammar of this verse is somewhat awkward. *Radak* writes that the phrase must be understood as though another word, שַׂר, were inserted —

וּכְנַנְיָה הַשַּׂר, [שַׂר] הַמַּשָּׂא הַמְשֹׁרְרִים, *and Chenaniah, the officer, the musical director of the choristers*.

28. וְכָל־יִשְׂרָאֵל — *And all Israel*. It seems highly significant that the parallel verse in *Samuel* has, *And David and all the house of Israel*. In prefatory remarks to 13:1-4, the relationship of David and the people in this matter was traced. David was the initiator to whose merit the accomplishment of the transfer of the Ark would always be ascribed, but the people of Israel were willing and enthusiastic collaborators who, once they were inspired by their king, became equal participants. It is entirely appropriate that *Chronicles*, which deals with the eternal history of the people of Israel, should emphasize this aspect.

בִּתְרוּעָה וּבְקוֹל שׁוֹפָר — *With the soundings and blasts of the shofar*. תְּרוּעָה, *soundings*, refers to the short staccato sounds of the *shofar*, while קוֹל, *blasts*, refers to the longer blasts (*Metzudos*).

29. ... וּמִיכַל בַּת־שָׁאוּל — *Michal, the daughter of Saul* ... In contrast to *Samuel*, which elaborates and gives the entire dialogue between Michal and David on this matter, *Chronicles* restricts itself to this one terse remark. *Mefaresh* explains that this accords with *Chronicles'* intent to report only those events which reflect honor on David and his royal line (see comm. to 10:1). It could also be that *Chronicles'* interest centered less on the incident itself than on the light which it shed on the difference between Saul and David. [As noted several times from ch. 10 onward,

Levites who carried the Ark, the choristers, and Chenaniah, the musical director of the choristers; and David wore a linen ephod. ²⁸ And all Israel transported the Ark of the Covenant of HASHEM with the soundings and blasts of the shofar, and with trumpets and cymbals, playing with nevalim and harps. ²⁹ And when the Ark of the Covenant of HASHEM arrived at the city of David, Michal, the daughter of Saul, looked out through the window, and when she saw King David dancing and frolicking she felt contempt for him in her heart.

16

1-3

S̲o they brought the Ark of God and set it up under the cover which David had spread out for it; and they offered burnt-offerings and peace-offerings before God. ² And David finished offering the burnt-offerings and the peace-offerings, and he blessed the people with the Name of HASHEM. ³ And he gave out to every

---

this is the thrust of much that *Chronicles* has taught in these chapters.] For this, a

report of the entire dialogue was not necessary. See Section Two.

XVI

◁§ At the Tent of the Ark

This chapter continues with the story of the transfer of the Ark, covering much the same ground as does *Samuel,* but also adding much that is not given there.

1. וַיָּבִיאוּ אֶת־אֲרוֹן הָאֱלֹהִים — *So they brought the Ark of God.* They must refer to *all Israel* in 15:28, just as the *they* of *Samuel* in the parallel verse refers to *David and the whole house of Israel* in the earlier verse there. *Chronicles,* as we saw above, is consistent in recording the matter from the point of view of the people (see 13:1-4). In that context, the end of our verse is particularly significant.

וַיַּקְרִיבוּ עֹלוֹת וּשְׁלָמִים — *And they offered burnt-offerings and peace-offerings.* In *Samuel* it is David who brings the offerings to God. As we have seen before, the initiative came from David, and in that sense it can be rightfully ascribed to him. But the people allowed themselves to be drawn into full and enthusiastic participation, and in that sense it is entirely appropriate for *Chronicles* to speak of their bringing the sacrifices.

2. וַיְכַל דָּוִיד — *And David finished.* The previous verse had talked of all of Israel offering the sacrifices. Our verse, precisely as does the verse in *Samuel,* talks of David finishing the sacrificial service. This con-

firms the point suggested in the previous verse. The entire sacrificial service was initiated and supervised by David, hence our verse can talk of his finishing the service. Nevertheless, v. 1 speaks of *all* Israel bringing the sacrifices because of their enthusiastic agreement and participation.

וַיְבָרֶךְ אֶת־הָעָם בְּשֵׁם ה' — *And he blessed the people with the Name of HASHEM.* David blessed the people after their efforts at transporting the Ark had been crowned with success. In the same way we find that Moses and Aaron blessed the people after the dedication of the Tabernacle was completed (*Leviticus* 9:23, and see *Ramban* there to v. 22), and that Solomon bestowed a blessing on the people at the dedication ceremonies which celebrated the completion of the Temple (*I Kings* 8:22).

בְּשֵׁם ה' — *With the Name of HASHEM.* *Samuel* has בְּשֵׁם ה' צְבָאוֹת, *with the Name of HASHEM, Master of Legions.* The commentary has noted at 13:5 that *Chronicles* has a tendency to leave out the name צְבָאוֹת, *Master of Legions,* even where it was used in the earlier books. See also our remarks at 13:8.

Metzudos appears to explain our phrase to mean that he used the Ineffable Name of

לְכָל־אִישׁ יִשְׂרָאֵל מֵאִישׁ וְעַד־אִשָּׁה לְאִישׁ כִּכַּר־לֶחֶם
ד וְאֶשְׁפָּר וַאֲשִׁישָׁה: וַיִּתֵּן לִפְנֵי אֲרוֹן יהוה מִן־הַלְוִיִּם
מְשָׁרְתִים וּלְהַזְכִּיר וּלְהוֹדוֹת וּלְהַלֵּל לַיהוה אֱלֹהֵי
ה יִשְׂרָאֵל: אָסָף הָרֹאשׁ וּמִשְׁנֵהוּ זְכַרְיָה יְעִיאֵל
וּשְׁמִירָמוֹת וִיחִיאֵל וּמַתִּתְיָה וֶאֱלִיאָב וּבְנָיָהוּ וְעֹבֵד אֱדֹם
וִיעִיאֵל בִּכְלֵי נְבָלִים וּבְכִנֹּרוֹת וְאָסָף בַּמְצִלְתַּיִם מַשְׁמִיעַ:
ו וּבְנָיָהוּ וְיַחֲזִיאֵל הַכֹּהֲנִים בַּחֲצֹצְרוֹת תָּמִיד לִפְנֵי אֲרוֹן

God in his blessing. As the Sages interpret *Numbers 6:27* (see *Rashi* there), this name of God was to be used only in the Kohanic blessing which was part of the Temple service. Outside the Temple, even *Kohanim* giving their public blessings had to use another of God's Names. David, of course, was not a *Kohen* and his blessing on this occasion had no legal standing. His use of the Ineffable Name must have been in the nature of a הוֹרָאַת שָׁעָה, *a temporary ruling,* born out of the exalted spiritual context of the moment that God's Presence, associated with the Ark (see 13:6), came to rest in Jerusalem.

3. וְאֶשְׁפָּר — *A serving of meat.* Targum translates simply as *a serving.* Metzudos to *Samuel,* however, adds *a serving of meat.* *Rashi* to *Samuel* explains that the word is a contraction of [אֶחָד] מִשִּׁשָּׁה בְּפָר, one-sixth of an ox. Each portion was this size.

וַאֲשִׁישָׁה — *And a flagon.* A flagon of wine (*Rashi* and commentators).

At this point *Samuel* concludes with the statement that after this all the people went back to their homes and that David then also went home to greet his own family. It then picks up the story of how Michal taunted David for his performance. Here, this information is delayed till v. 43. [The encounter with Michal is not given at all — see comm. 15:27.] *Chronicles* instead interrupts the narrative with a detailed account of the dispositions which David made for the service at the location of the Ark.

The contrast between the relatively terse narrative in *Samuel* and the expansive detail that is lavished on the story here is striking. This difference is not limited to our chapter, which deals specifically with the Ark in Jerusalem, but was equally apparent in the previous chapter, which dealt with the Ark while it was still en route.

Perhaps the difference lies in the circumstances in which the two books were written. When Nathan and Gad wrote this part of the book of *Samuel* (see *Bava Basra* 15a), the Ark was a tangible presence in Israel. The immediate generation to whom the book was addressed needed only to go to Jerusalem to bask in the aura of holiness which surrounded it and to acquaint itself with the form and structure of the Kohanic and Levitic functions attendant upon it. The forms of the service described in our two chapters were practiced daily in their midst.

When the chapters in *Chronicles* were written, however, the Ark was only a memory. It had either been buried or carried into exile (see *Yoma* 53b). In the vivid and graphic descriptions contained in our chapters, the writer may well have intended to bring the past glory of Zion alive for the people who needed to live with the knowledge that the Temple in their midst was only a pale shadow of the one which had originally stood in its place.

In addition there is the dictum of the Sages (*Menachos* 110a) that whoever studies the laws of the sacrifices is considered as though he had offered them. By immersing themselves in the details of the service that had once surrounded the Ark, the generations who would live through the dark ages of its absence would, in a sense, be able to share in the blessings which it showered upon the people in the days of their glory.

4. וַיִּתֵּן לִפְנֵי אֲרוֹן ה' מִן־הַלְוִיִּם מְשָׁרְתִים — *And he assigned some of the Levites to serve before the Ark of HASHEM as ministrants.* Only some of the Levites, because the bulk of them serviced at the Tabernacle in Giveon (see comm. to 6:16-17). The ministering of these Levites consisted of maintaining the physical upkeep of the tent of the Ark, besides the functions

person in Israel, both men and women, to each a loaf of bread, a serving of meat and a flagon. ⁴ And he assigned some of the Levites to serve before the Ark of HASHEM as ministrants, to proclaim, to give thanks and to praise HASHEM, God of Israel. ⁵ Asaph was the chief and Zechariah second to him; and Yeiel, Shemiramoth, Yechiel, Mattithiah, Eliav, Benaiahu, Oved Edom and Yeiel played nevalim and harps; and Asaph, the sounding cymbals. ⁶ And Benaiahu and Yachaziel the Kohanim blew the trumpets daily before

mentioned in the second part of the verse.

וּלְהַזְכִּיר וּלְהוֹדוֹת וּלְהַלֵּל — *To proclaim, to give thanks and to praise.* To proclaim God's deeds in the distant past; to thank God for His favors; and to praise Him by relating His greatness *(Malbim).* The *Mefaresh* offers: לְהַזְכִּיר, *to proclaim* — to say those psalms which have לְהַזְכִּיר in their title *(Psalms* 38 and 70), וּלְהוֹדוֹת, *to give thanks* — to say *Psalm* 105 which begins with the word הוֹדוּ; and וּלְהַלֵּל, *to praise* — to say those psalms which begin with the word הַלְלוּיָהּ.

A third possibility is suggested by the fact that לְהַזְכִּיר is bracketed together with words connoting thanks and praise. Perhaps this indicates that the root זכר in the *hiphil* also connotes a form of praise.

Indeed, verses like *Isaiah* 12:4 and 63:7 and *Psalms* 20:8 and 45:18 might well have such a meaning. This could also be the meaning of לְהַזְכִּיר in the headings of *Psalms* 38 and 70.

5. אָסָף הָרֹאשׁ — *Asaph was the chief.* From the dispositions which David made concerning the choristers (recorded in ch. 6) it is clear that Heman, not Asaph, was to be the chief one. He was to stand in the middle with Asaph and Ethan to be ranged on his right and left respectively (see 6:18-23 and 24). We must assume that Asaph was chief only of the group of Levites who functioned in the presence of the Ark in Jerusalem. In the Tabernacle at Giveon, Asaph was indeed second to Heman *(Ralbag).* [See further at vs. 39-42.]

וּמִשְׁנֵהוּ זְכַרְיָה — *And Zechariah second to him.* The cantillation indicates a stop after Zechariah. Thus from among the Levites listed here only Zechariah is designated as second to Asaph. This is further indicated by the fact that after Zechariah, Yeiel is given without the conjunctive *vav* [*and*], indicating that he stands at the beginning of a separate list of those who served, not as a continuation of the list of officers.

זְכַרְיָה ... יְעִיאֵל ... — *... Zechariah ... Yeiel*

... All the Levites given here were listed in 15:68 among the gatekeepers who had been pressed into service to act as musicians while the Ark was being transported. However, not all who participated there are listed here.

יְעִיאֵל — *Yeiel.* At the end of our list another Yeiel is given. Perhaps the first Yeiel is the Yaaziel given at 15:18 and not listed here.

6. וּבְנָיָהוּ וַחֲזִיאֵל הַכֹּהֲנִים — *And Benaiahu and Yachaziel the Kohanim.* Throughout David's reign and up to the time that Solomon built the Temple in Jerusalem, the Tabernacle stood at Giveon — which was therefore the site of all communal service (see 6:16-17). Whatever form of service David established in front of the Ark after he had taken it to Jerusalem was therefore only a temporary innovation and was in no way based on the specifications found in the Torah. The Torah does talk of the *Kohanim* blowing trumpets as part of the Temple service *(Numbers* 10:1-10), but only on the holy days and *Rosh Chodesh* (the new moon) *(Rambam, Klei Hamikdash* 3:5). Our verse seems to describe a daily function for these *Kohanim,* and this must be seen as one of the temporary innovations which David established for the special service before the Ark.

The fact that this service was essentially one of שִׁיר [*shir*], *song,* rather than sacrifice, may explain why here the Levites are mentioned before the *Kohanim* while below (vs. 39-42), in regard to the service at Giveon, the verse speaks first of Tzadok the *Kohen* (v. 39) and only then of Heman and Yeduthun the Levites (v. 41). Since the focus of the service at Giveon was the sacrifice, the *Kohanim* were central and the *shir* of the Levites only an accompaniment to that central activity. In Jerusalem there was only *shir,* and in that the Levites were pre-eminent.

תָּמִיד — *Daily.* Although literally translated, the word תָּמִיד should be rendered

ז בְּרִית־הָאֱלֹהִים: בַּיּוֹם הַהוּא אָז נָתַן דָּוִיד בְּרֹאשׁ לְהֹדוֹת
לַיהוָה בְּיַד־אָסָף וְאֶחָיו:
ח-ט הוֹדוּ לַיהוָה קִרְאוּ בִשְׁמוֹ הוֹדִיעוּ בָעַמִּים עֲלִילֹתָיו: שִׁירוּ
י לוֹ זַמְּרוּ־לוֹ שִׂיחוּ בְּכָל־נִפְלְאֹתָיו: הִתְהַלְלוּ בְּשֵׁם קָדְשׁוֹ
יא יִשְׂמַח לֵב מְבַקְשֵׁי יְהוָה: דִּרְשׁוּ יְהוָה וְעֻזּוֹ בַּקְּשׁוּ פָנָיו

---

constantly; its connotation is *daily* — see
Rashi to *Leviticus* 23:3.

7. בַּיּוֹם הַהוּא — *On that day.* On the day
that the Ark was brought to Jerusalem.

אָז נָתַן דָּוִיד בְּרֹאשׁ לְהֹדוֹת לַה' — *David
established* [*this*] *as pre-eminent in the
praise of HASHEM.* The translation follows
Malbim. The psalm which follows was to
be the first among all the psalms which the
Levites would sing to praise God. [This
appears to be also the opinion of *R' Yaakov
Emden* in his comm. to the siddur.]

Mefaresh takes רֹאשׁ as *leader.* The
reading of this psalm was to be responsive.
There was to be a leader who said each
verse, and he would be followed by the rest
of the Levites repeating it (see *Mefaresh*
11:17 and *Rashi* and *Ibn Ezra* there).

The interpretation of the *Mefaresh*
influenced liturgical form some thousand years ago. The
siddur of *R' Shlomo ben Shimshon of Worms*
reports that it was the custom in Mainz (based
on our verse) that when the הודו was said (see
below), the leader would say the first verse and
the congregation would then respond.

הודו/Song of Praise

8-36. According to *Seder Olam* 14, the
songs of praise contained in this section
were divided into two. The section
consisting of vs. 8-22 was sung in the
morning, and the section consisting of vs.
23-36 in the evening. *Seder Olam* cites no
source for this assertion so we must assume
that it is relaying an oral tradition. The
tradition may be based on the fact that the
two sections seem to derive from two
separate psalms. It would seem that the
first section corresponds to *Psalm* 105:1-
15, while the greater part of the second
section corresponds to *Psalm* 96:1-13. The
final three verses are vs. 1 and 47-48 of
Psalm 106.

However, though the resemblance to
these *Psalms* is striking, most of the verses
being exact repetitions of those found in
Psalms, it is quite possible that the sections
used here take on a slightly different

meaning in their new form. By choosing
only certain parts of larger *Psalms* and by
dedicating them to the daily service before
the Ark, David subtly altered their focus.
This may account for the differences which
exist between the two texts. Since this
necessitates analyzing the chapter as a
whole, this hypothesis will be examined in
detail in Section Two (p. 430). For the verse
to verse commentary it is only necessary to
know that there are two basic approaches
among the commentators: There are those
who interpret the psalm in general terms —
as it was surely meant in its form in *Psalms*
— and there are those who, in its present
form, see direct reference to the Ark and
the story surrounding it.

8. הוֹדוּ לַה' — *Give thanks to HASHEM.*
David is addressing the choristers and the
congregation *(Mefaresh).* *Ibn Ezra* thinks
that this psalm was said while they were
carrying the Ark.

הוֹדוּ has been rendered *give thanks*
following *Gra.* However, *Targum (Psalms)*
renders: *praise.* The root ידה carries both
connotations and in addition also is used
for the verb, *to admit.* The basic meaning
of the root is *to throw,* thus, to throw
oneself, that is to subjugate oneself to
someone either by admitting fault [to
admit], acknowledging superiority [to
praise] or dependence [to thank].

קִרְאוּ בִשְׁמוֹ — *Proclaim His Name. Ibn Ezra*
thinks that the phrase connotes the
spreading of the teaching of God. He also
ascribes this meaning to *Genesis* 21:33.

Mefaresh renders: *Pray to HASHEM —
that He may extend His help to His Ark.* He
compares this verse to *I Kings* 18:24
where the phrase is used with the
connotation of praying.

Gra interprets the phrase as an
exhortation of the people to ascribe all their
successes to God (compare *Genesis* 21:33).

הוֹדִיעוּ בָעַמִּים עֲלִילֹתָיו — *Make His acts
known among the nations.* The root עלל

the Ark of the Covenant of God. ⁷ On that day, on that occasion, David established [this] as pre-eminent in the praise of HASHEM, under the direction of Asaph and his brothers — ⁸ Give thanks to HASHEM, proclaim His Name, make His acts known among the nations. ⁹ Sing to Him, make music to Him, speak of all His wondrous acts. ¹⁰ Glory in His Holy Name; be glad of heart, you who seek HASHEM. ¹¹ Search out HASHEM and His might, seek out

---

has a number of different nuances. It can be used simply to describe God's works, in a rough parallel to פֶּלֶא, wonder (Psalms 77:12), or to פָּעַל, deed (v. 13, there), but it can also express the idea of making sport of something. Thus, in Exodus 10:2, God tells that through the plagues He made sport out of Egypt.

Those commentators who read the message of this psalm to refer specifically to the Ark (e.g., Mefaresh) take the word in the latter sense. They explain that the phrase refers to the manner in which God treated the Philistines while the Ark was in their possession, having been captured in a war against Israel (see I Samuel ch. 5). God plagued them with severe intestinal diseases to demonstrate their impotence in the face of God, forcing them to return the Ark to Israel.

Others (e.g., Metzudos) see the phrase simply as an exhortation to make God's wondrous acts known among the nations of the world.

Tiferes Zion (to Bereishis Rabbah 54:6) points out that the miracles which occurred while the Ark was held by the Philistines were unique in that they happened solely to a gentile people. In that sense, they spread the knowledge of God's deeds among the nations of the world more than other miracles which were performed in the presence of Jews and therefore presumably for their benefit.

9. שִׁירוּ לוֹ זַמְּרוּ־לוֹ — Sing to Him, make music to Him. We have translated according to most commentators (Mefaresh; Ibn Ezra; Metzudos) who explain that שִׁיר means choral music while זְמֵר is instrumental music. Targum renders שִׁירוּ as praise. This, because frequently the word שִׁיר carries the specific connotation of a song of praise — see for example Psalms 28:7 and 69:31. R' Shlomo ben Shimshon

of Worms adds: Sing to Him ... in thanks for the miracles that He performed in connection with the Ark.

שִׂיחוּ בְּכָל־נִפְלְאוֹתָיו — Speak of all His wondrous acts. The wondrous acts which he performed in connection with the Ark (R' Shlomo ben Shimshon of Worms). According to one of the Sages in Avodah Zarah 24b, the song which the cows 'sang' as they pulled the carriage bringing back the Ark from Philistia to Israel (see I Samuel 6:12)[1] was Psalms 98:1, which underlines the wondrous acts performed by Hashem.

10. הִתְהַלְלוּ בְּשֵׁם קָדְשׁוֹ — Glory in His Holy Name. In the הִתְפַּעֵל, reflexive, הלל, to praise, becomes to praise oneself; to boast; to take pride (see for example Psalms 34:3).

In our context, it is not HASHEM but His Holy Name in which David's listeners are to pride themselves. Israel is to pride itself that it alone among the nations was given God's Ineffable Name to use and relate to. Other nations know God and describe Him only as He reveals Himself to them through His deeds. Only Israel has the name which relates to God's essence (see Ibn Ezra, Gra).

יִשְׂמַח לֵב מְבַקְשֵׁי ה׳ — Be glad of heart, you who seek HASHEM. Those who wish to seek HASHEM by going to visit the Ark will henceforth find it in its rightful place in Jerusalem (R' Shlomo ben Shimshon of Worms).

Radak suggests that the seekers of Hashem may even belong to the gentile nations. They, too, will rejoice as they strive for the truth.

The connection between the first and second halves of the verse is best understood if we take the latter phrase as does R' Yosef Albo (see ArtScroll, Tehillim p. 1270): In the pursuit of material gain, happiness depends upon the attainment of

---

1. This is the aggadic interpretation of I Samuel 6:12: וַיִּשַּׁרְנָה הַפָּרוֹת בַּדֶּרֶךְ, which the Sages interpret to mean: And the cows sang on the way [to Beth Shemesh]. See Section Two, p. 436.

יב תָּמִיד: זִכְרוּ נִפְלְאֹתָיו אֲשֶׁר עָשָׂה מֹפְתָיו וּמִשְׁפְּטֵי־פִיהוּ:
יג־יד זֶרַע יִשְׂרָאֵל עַבְדּוֹ בְּנֵי יַעֲקֹב בְּחִירָיו: הוּא יהוה אֱלֹהֵינוּ
טו בְּכָל־הָאָרֶץ מִשְׁפָּטָיו: זִכְרוּ לְעוֹלָם בְּרִיתוֹ דָּבָר צִוָּה
טז לְאֶלֶף דּוֹר: אֲשֶׁר כָּרַת אֶת־אַבְרָהָם וּשְׁבוּעָתוֹ לְיִצְחָק:

one's aim; thus the seeker is dissatisfied because, as yet, he lacks the object of his desire. Such, however, is not the case in the search for God. In this case, the seeking and finding occur simultaneously. A person who dedicates himself to seeking God demonstrates that he recognizes God as the ultimate good fortune; therefore he rejoices while he seeks.

Thus, the second half of the verse connects with the first. We are to glory in our possession of God's Name because it lends meaning and content to our striving.

11. דִּרְשׁוּ ה' וְעֻזּוֹ — *Search out* HASHEM *and His might.* Attempt to discover the extent of God's might (*Metzudos*). Many commentators think that עֹז, *might,* refers here specifically to the Ark,[1] since in *Psalms* 78:61 the phrase וַיִּתֵּן לַשְּׁבִי עֻזּוֹ, *And He placed His might in captivity,* is interpreted by the Sages to refer to the capture of the Ark by the Philistines.

The *Mefaresh* goes so far as to suggest that the Uzza who was killed while transporting the Ark, and who is identified in *II Samuel* 6:3 as a son of Avinadav, is really Avinadav's son Elazar who, according to *I Samuel* 7:1, had been appointed to watch over the Ark. He was called עֻזָּא, *Uzza,* because of his contact with the Ark which is the עֹז, *the manifestation of the strength of God.*[1]

בַּקְשׁוּ פָנָיו תָּמִיד — *Seek out His Presence always.* Through prayer and song (*R' Shlomo ben Shimshon of Worms*).

12. זִכְרוּ — *Remember.* Remember in your hearts (*Ibn Ezra*). [*Ibn Ezra's* intention is to stress that although the root זכר occasionally means *to mention* (even when the קל, *simple form,* is used), here it means *to remember.*]

נִפְלְאֹתָיו — *His wonders.* The *Mefaresh* thinks it refers to the wonders connected with the return of the Ark: The plague of the mice;[2] the straight and consistent path taken by the nursing cows although their calves had been locked up behind them (*I Samuel* 6:10 and 12); and the tragic death of Uzza. *Ibn Ezra* sees it as a reference to the creation of heaven and earth.

מֹפְתָיו — *His marvels.* According to *Ibn Ezra* this refers to the miracles in Egypt. *Gra* differentiates between פֶּלֶא [the root of נִפְלְאֹתָיו, *wonders*] and מֹפֵת, *a sign.* In the case of a *sign* nothing new is created; rather, God's providence is manifested upon an already existing object. A *wonder* is the creation of a new form. [Examples would be: The plague of the wild beasts which created nothing new but utilized existing animals for God's purpose would be a מֹפֵת; the manna which fell miraculously from heaven would be a פֶּלֶא.]

וּמִשְׁפְּטֵי־פִיהוּ — *And the decrees of His mouth.* According to *Ibn Ezra* this refers to the laws God gave at Sinai, while *R' Shlomo ben Shimshon of Worms* sees it as a reference to the judgment of the mice which God made against the Philistines (see above).

13. זֶרַע יִשְׂרָאֵל עַבְדּוֹ — *O seed of Israel, His servant.* This verse identifies the people addressed in the previous verses. Who is to praise and to remember? The seed of Israel... (*Mefaresh*). *Radak* notes that *Psalms* has: *The seed of Abraham, His servant.* He explains that our text is an elucidation of that text. *Seed of Abraham* could include the other descendants of Abraham. Our text makes clear that only

1. Two roots which describe strength in Hebrew are עֹז and עֹצֶם. In his study of synonyms, *Beur Shemos HaNirdaphim,* *R' Shlomo Wertheimer* demonstrates that whereas עֹצֶם describes physical strength, עֹז is invariably used for the force of the spirit. This agrees with *Maharal's* definition of the word (see, e.g., *Derech Chaim* to *Avos* 5:20). *Maharal* sees עֹז as the aggressive, overpowering vehemence by which a person exerts his will over another. Thus the Ark, the conduit through which God seeks with the irresistible force of spirit to overpower a mankind made sluggish by a physical world, is aptly called God's עֹז, *might.*

2. The Sages interpret the obscure טְחֹרִים of *I Samuel* 5:6 as a swarm of mice who came and entered the body orifices of the Philistines and came out again dragging their intestines with them.

16

12-16

His Presence always. ¹² Remember His wonders that He has wrought, His marvels and the decrees of His mouth. ¹³ O seed of Israel, His servant; the children of Jacob, His chosen ones. ¹⁴ He is HASHEM our God, over all the earth are His judgments. ¹⁵ Remember forever His covenant, the word He ordained for a thousand generations. ¹⁶ That He made with Abraham, and His vow for Isaac.

Israel is meant. [See Section Two for a different perception of the change from Abraham to Israel.]

בְּנֵי יַעֲקֹב בְּחִירָיו — The children of Jacob, His chosen ones. Who were chosen by God from among the idolatrous nations (Metzudos).

14. הוּא ה' אֱלֹהֵינוּ — He is HASHEM our God. Both Radak and Gra see this verse as dealing with the problem of Israel's having been singled out in the face of the universality of God's kingship. Radak offers: Although His judgment extends over the whole world, He is still our God and we are His people. Gra renders: Although we speak of Him as our God, nevertheless, His judgment extends over the whole world.

Metzudos renders: He is still the same God Whose judgment — as it did in the past — extends over the whole earth.

R' Shlomo ben Shimshon of Worms again sees the verse from the perspective of the Ark: Just as He punished the Philistines for having taken the Ark, He will punish the other nations for their transgressions.

15. זִכְרוּ לְעוֹלָם בְּרִיתוֹ — Remember forever His covenant. The covenant mentioned here was made with Abraham (v. 16) and concerned the land of Canaan (v. 18). It was to be given to him and to specified descendants — see below.

Thus, our passage is an exhortation to the people to remember constantly their special relationship to the Land of Israel. An exhortation which was particularly apt now that the Ark, and with it the Divine Presence, had come to rest in Jerusalem, thereby imbuing the land with its spiritual essence.

Rashi and the Mefaresh interpret בְּרִית as referring to the Torah, which was given to Israel as part of a covenant. The thousand generations in the second part of the sentence hints at an aggadic tradition that God had originally intended to give the Torah after one thousand generations but, seeing that the world could not

long exist without the Torah, He decided to wait only twenty-six generations. Metzudos also interprets בְּרִית as referring to the Torah. His explanation of the thousand generations is based on a different aggadic tradition. God by-passed nine hundred and seventy-four generations during which He could have created the world. Thus, when He gave the Torah twenty-six generations later, it resulted in the Torah being given in the thousandth generation. Apart from the difficult aggadic concepts involved in these explanations, it would seem that the equation of בְּרִית with תּוֹרָה in this context belongs to the realm of דְּרוּשׁ, homiletical interpretation, rather than to the simple meaning. As we have seen, vs. 16 and 18 clearly indicate that the subject is the covenant concerning the land.

דָּבָר צִוָּה לְאֶלֶף דּוֹר — The word He ordained for a thousand generations. The root צוה, which generally means to command, can also have the meaning to ordain, to decree (Radak). The promise of the land which God made to Abraham at the Covenant Between the Pieces (Genesis ch. 15) was to be an everlasting one. The expression for a thousand generations is used as a synonym for always (Ibn Ezra), as in Exodus 20:6: He does kindness to thousands, to those that love Him and guard His commands — for a thousand generations (Rashi).

16. אֲשֶׁר כָּרַת אֶת־אַבְרָהָם — That He made with Abraham. As it is written: On that day HASHEM made a covenant with Abram, saying: 'To your descendants have I given this land ...' [Genesis 15:18] (Radak).

וּשְׁבוּעָתוֹ לְיִצְחָק — And His vow for Isaac. The translation for Isaac rather than to Isaac follows Radak. In all of Torah there is no mention that God ever made a direct oath to Isaac concerning the land. The most that is found in Genesis 26:3 where God promises Isaac to give him and his descendants the land because of the oath which He had made to Abraham. The intent of our verse must therefore be that the oath which promised the land to Abraham's descendants was limited to Isaac and his children, and excluded Ishmael and his descendants (Radak).

יז־יח וַיַּעֲמִידֶהָ לְיַעֲקֹב לְחֹק לְיִשְׂרָאֵל בְּרִית עוֹלָם: לֵאמֹר לְךָ

יז־כד יט אֶתֵּן אֶרֶץ־כְּנָעַן חֶבֶל נַחֲלַתְכֶם: בִּהְיוֹתְכֶם מְתֵי מִסְפָּר

כ כִּמְעַט וְגָרִים בָּהּ: וַיִּתְהַלְּכוּ מִגּוֹי אֶל־גּוֹי וּמִמַּמְלָכָה

כא אֶל־עַם אַחֵר: לֹא־הִנִּיחַ לְאִישׁ לְעָשְׁקָם וַיּוֹכַח עֲלֵיהֶם

כב־כג מְלָכִים: אַל־תִּגְּעוּ בִּמְשִׁיחָי וּבִנְבִיאַי אַל־תָּרֵעוּ: שִׁירוּ

כד לַיהוה כָּל־הָאָרֶץ בַּשְּׂרוּ מִיּוֹם־אֶל־יוֹם יְשׁוּעָתוֹ: סַפְּרוּ

---

17. וַיַּעֲמִידֶהָ לְיַעֲקֹב לְחֹק — *And He es-tablished it for Jacob as a statute.* Radak continues with the theme of Israel's selection. Just as Isaac, and not Ishmael, was to be the heir to God's commitment to Abraham, so it was Jacob, and not Esau, who would inherit the land. This was Isaac's meaning when, in bidding farewell to Jacob, he said: *May He grant you the blessing of Abraham, to you and to your offspring with you, that you may possess the land of your sojournings which God gave to Abraham (Genesis 28:4).*

The term חֹק signifies a decree or enactment with a connotation of certainty or permanence. Cf. *Psalms 2:7; Job 28:26.* In our verse it seems to serve as a synonym for בְּרִית עוֹלָם, *an everlasting covenant.*

18. לְךָ אֶתֵּן אֶרֶץ־כְּנָעַן — *'To you I shall give the Land of Canaan.* To you and not to Ishmael and Esau, although they too are descendants of Abraham *(Metzudos).* Radak, noting the singular לְךָ, *to you* [in contrast to the plural נַחֲלַתְכֶם, *your heritage,* at the end of the verse], suggests that the singular signifies that a separate promise was made to each of the Patriarchs.

חֶבֶל נַחֲלַתְכֶם — *The lot of your heritage.'* The word חֶבֶל, *portion,* is often used in conjunction with נַחֲלָה, *heritage.* Cf. *Deuteronomy 32:9.*

19. בִּהְיוֹתְכֶם מְתֵי מִסְפָּר — *When you were but few men.* During the days of the Patriarchs the Jewish people were very few in number *(Radak and Metzudos),* and even so God promised them the land. This demonstrates that their claim to the land is not based on the strength of their numbers *(Mefaresh).* [In context, this point is extremely apt. The psalm is a celebration of the settlement of the Ark in Jerusalem. This draws attention to the fact that the Land is important as the land of the Divine Presence — not for its physical properties. It stands to reason, then, that mere numbers can in no way influence the bond

between Israel and the Land of Israel.]

כִּמְעַט וְגָרִים בָּהּ — *Few and sojourning in it.* From most commentators it seems that the כ, *kaf,* of כִּמְעַט is treated as a pleonasm, that is, that the word is to be understood exactly as if it had been written without the *kaf* and that for purposes of translation the letter is redundant. The meaning of the whole verse would be: *When you were but few men,* [and not only] *few* [but also merely] *sojourning in the land.* An analogy would be the כִּמְעַט of *Isaiah 1:9,* which many commentators (but not *Rashi)* treat as though the *kaf* were not there. However, *Radak* to *Isaiah* there thinks of that *kaf* as an emphasizing tool [he calls it כ"ף הָאֲמִתּוּת], thus: as few as can be. Here also he would render the verse: *When you were but few men, indeed very few, and sojourning in it.*

The *Mefaresh* notes the logical dynamic of the verse which we indicated in the comm. above. The mere fact that you were few would itself have made God's promise remarkable. But even a few people who are firmly established in a place can be said to have some legitimate claim to it. You, however, were only sojourners in the land. [The next verse carries this thinking one step further. The truth is that you were not even bona fide sojourners but were really only travelers.] In spite of this lack of permanent status, God gave you the land.

20. וַיִּתְהַלְּכוּ מִגּוֹי אֶל־גּוֹי — *And they wan-dered from people to people.* The *Mefaresh* points to the use of וַיִּתְהַלְּכוּ, *wandered,* rather than וַיֵּלְכוּ, *went.* The connotation is towards an aimless wandering rather than to a firm, purposeful journey (see *I Samuel* 13:13). The term is used to underscore the impermanence of their status in the lands in which they journeyed. This lack of standing could have exposed them to much petty cruelty on the part of the permanent residents.

Mefaresh identifies the wanderings of

16

17-24

¹⁷ *And He established it for Jacob as a statute, for Israel as an everlasting covenant.* ¹⁸ *Saying: 'To you I shall give the Land of Canaan, the lot of your heritage.'* ¹⁹ *When you were but few men, few and sojourning in it.* ²⁰ *And they wandered from people to people, and from one kingdom to another nation.* ²¹ *He allowed no man to oppress them, and He rebuked kings for their sake:* ²² *'Dare not touch My anointed ones, and to My prophets do no harm.'* ²³ *Sing to HASHEM, all the earth, announce His salvation daily.*

---

the Patriarchs: Abraham visited Egypt and Gerar in Philistia; Isaac also spent time among the Philistines; and Jacob spent twenty-two years in Lavan's house, and later went down to Egypt.

21. לֹא־הִנִּיחַ לְאִישׁ לְעָשְׁקָם — *He allowed no man to oppress them.* These unprotected wanderers must have seemed easy prey to the general populace, yet God did not allow this to happen (*Mefaresh; Metzudos*).

וַיּוֹכַח עֲלֵיהֶם מְלָכִים — *And He rebuked kings for their sake.* Even more than to the general populace, ordinary strangers would surely have been at the mercy of the despots who ruled those lands. Nevertheless, both Pharaoh (*Genesis* 12:17) and Avimelech (20:3) were severely chastised when they attempted to take Sarah away from Abraham (*Radak*).

22. אַל־תִּגְּעוּ בִמְשִׁיחָי — *'Dare not touch My anointed ones.* The plagues which descended upon Pharaoh and Avimelech warned them as eloquently as words could have done (*Metzudos*).

My anointed ones does not mean that the Patriarchs were actually anointed with oil. The term is used to describe any especially important or princely person — see, for example, *Isaiah* 45:1 (*Metzudos*), the Patriarchs were looked upon as royalty, as can be seen in the case of Abraham who was called *Prince of God* by the Chittites (*Genesis* 23:6); and in the case of Isaac, for whose friendship the Philistine king was willing to bend his dignity and come to him instead of demanding his attendance [*Genesis* 26:26] (*Radak*).

וּבִנְבִיאַי אַל־תָּרֵעוּ — *And to My prophets do no harm.'* The Patriarchs were prophets (see *Rashi, Megillah* 14a), and in the case of Abraham this is attested to by *Genesis* 20:7 (*Radak*).

At this point that part of the psalm which comes from *Psalms* 105 ends. With the next verse the section taken from *Psalm*

96 begins. As noted above from *Seder Olam*, the first part of the psalm — up to our verse — was said in the morning, the second part in the evening.

23. This verse is really a contraction of vs. 1 and 2 of *Psalm* 96. The second halves of each verse are combined, the first halves are omitted. This change in the wording of the psalm, which was apparently made by David when he established it as the song to be recited in front of the Ark, is of course striking and may indeed establish the tone of the whole service in front of the Ark. This is discussed in the analysis of this chapter in Section Two (p. 430*ff*).

שִׁירוּ לַה׳ כָּל־הָאָרֶץ — *Sing to HASHEM, all the earth.* כָּל הָאָרֶץ is short for כָּל [יוֹשְׁבֵי] הָאָרֶץ, *all the [inhabitants of] earth* (*Ibn Ezra*). Since v. 24 turns specifically to the nations of the world [סַפְּרוּ בַגּוֹיִם], *Ibn Ezra* thinks that our verse refers to all the inhabitants of the Land of Israel. For this reason he also thinks that בַּשְּׂרוּ, *announce,* in our verse is an exhortation to the people of Israel to talk of God's wonders among themselves. In *Ibn Ezra's* view, then, this section of our psalm begins with exhortations to Israel and then goes on to talk to the nations of the world.

Since none of the other commentators make this point, it seems likely that they take the whole passage as addressing the gentile nations. Accordingly, כָּל הָאָרֶץ should well be translated, *all the earth,* and the intention would be to call all the nations of the world to God's service.

מִיּוֹם־אֶל־יוֹם — *Daily* [lit. *from day to day*]. Every single day God shows His wonders, and these should be appreciated and discussed.

יְשׁוּעָתוֹ — *His salvation.* HASHEM is constantly saving His people. The specific salvation in our context refers to the miracles by which God forced the Philistines to give up the Ark which they

כה בַּגּוֹיִם אֶת־כְּבוֹדוֹ בְּכָל־הָעַמִּים נִפְלְאֹתָיו: כִּי גָדוֹל יהוה
כו וּמְהֻלָּל מְאֹד וְנוֹרָא הוּא עַל־כָּל־אֱלֹהִים: כִּי כָּל־אֱלֹהֵי
כז הָעַמִּים אֱלִילִים וַיהוה שָׁמַיִם עָשָׂה: הוֹד וְהָדָר לְפָנָיו
כח עֹז וְחֶדְוָה בִּמְקֹמוֹ: הָבוּ לַיהוה מִשְׁפְּחוֹת עַמִּים הָבוּ
כט לַיהוה כָּבוֹד וָעֹז: הָבוּ לַיהוה כְּבוֹד שְׁמוֹ שְׂאוּ מִנְחָה
ל וּבֹאוּ לְפָנָיו הִשְׁתַּחֲווּ לַיהוה בְּהַדְרַת־קֹדֶשׁ: חִילוּ מִלְּפָנָיו

had captured in battle [*I Samuel* ch. 5,6] (*Radak*).

24. סַפְּרוּ בַגּוֹיִם אֶת־כְּבוֹדוֹ — *Relate His glory among the peoples.* The matter of the Ark served as a great glorification of God. With all their military might, the Philistines were still forced to give it up (*Radak*).

25. וְנוֹרָא הוּא עַל־כָּל־אֱלֹהִים — *Awesome is He above any lord.* In the context it would be simplest to take אֱלֹהִים as *idol*, and see this phrase as a reference to the Philistine idol Dagon which repeatedly fell and was eventually smashed because of the presence of the Ark in the idolatrous temple (*I Samuel* 5:1-5). *Radak* and *Malbim* both suggest this interpretation. However, certainly no reference to Dagon was intended in the original form of the psalm when it had not yet been chosen as part of the ritual to be performed in front of the Ark. What then did the psalmist mean when he described God as more awesome than any אֱלֹהִים?

Metzudos explains that the *heavenly princes* (שָׂרֵי מַעְלָה), who have charge of the gentile nations, are meant. As *Metzudos* understands our verse, the nations are exhorted to recognize that God is more awesome than any of the heavenly creatures who stand between them and God.

Deuteronomy 4:19 declares a prohibition against serving a heavenly host (צְבָא הַשָּׁמַיִם) *whom God had apportioned to all the nations ...* (אֲשֶׁר חָלַק לְכֹל הָעַמִּים ...). *Ramban* there explains that all the nations, with the exception of Israel, have a heavenly angel through whom their destiny is controlled and who represents them in the heavenly court. Israel is special in that it has no intermediary but relates directly to God Himself. The verse in *Deuteronomy* teaches that these heavenly hosts have no independent power and function entirely as agents of God; they must, therefore, not be regarded as deities. The meaning of our verse, then, would be precisely the same as *Deuteronomy* 10:17, where God is described as אֱלֹהֵי אֱלֹהִים, *Lord of all lords*, which *Ramban* there interprets as referring to those

heavenly agents through whom God controls the destiny of the nations of the world.

26. כִּי כָּל־אֱלֹהֵי הָעַמִּים אֱלִילִים — *For all the lords of the nations are nothingness.* אֱלִיל is often, though not exclusively, used to describe the deities of the nations. In other contexts we find the word meaning *falsehood* (*Jeremiah* 14:14); and *worthless* (*Zechariah* 11:17; *Job* 13:4). Thus, when it is used in connection with the foreign deities it intends to stress their absolute impotence. According to *Metzudos'* explanation of the previous verse, this description is particularly apt. The nations are called upon to apprehend the supremacy of God. They are not to be led astray by the existence of intermediaries, however holy and exalted they might be. In relation to God they are *nothingness* [אֱלִיל from אַל, *nothing*]. Our verse may well be suggesting a play on words. The powers whom the nations revere are not אֱלֹהִים [from אֵל, *strong*], but אֱלִילִים [from אַל, *nothing*] (*R' Dovid Hoffman* to *Leviticus* 19:4).

27. הוֹד וְהָדָר לְפָנָיו — *Glory and majesty are before Him.* *Malbim* defines הוֹד as the intrinsic *glory* which is the true essence of God, whereas הָדָר is the external majesty which is visible to the observer (cf. ArtScroll *Tehillim* p. 1188).

עֹז וְחֶדְוָה בִּמְקֹמוֹ — *Might and delight are in His place.* *Psalms* has עֹז וְתִפְאֶרֶת בְּמִקְדָּשׁוֹ, *strength and majesty are in His Sanctuary.* The change is explained in the analysis of the chapter in Section Two.

28-29. These two verses are particularly significant in that they exhort the nations of the world to worship God in precisely the same terms as *Psalm* 29 addresses Israel. There we have הָבוּ לַה' בְּנֵי אֵלִים, *Render to HASHEM, you sons of the powerful* [which the Sages in *Megillah* 17b interpret as referring to the descendants of

²⁴ *Relate His glory among the peoples, among all the nations His wonders.* ²⁵ *For HASHEM is great and exceedingly lauded, awesome is He above any lord.* ²⁶ *For all the lords of the nations are nothingness, but HASHEM made heaven!* ²⁷ *Glory and majesty are before Him, might and delight are in His place.* ²⁸ *Render to HASHEM, O families of nations, render to HASHEM honor and might.* ²⁹ *Render to HASHEM honor worthy of His Name; take an offering and come before Him, prostrate yourselves before HASHEM in majestic holiness.* ³⁰ *Tremble before Him, all the earth, indeed, the world is fixed so that it cannot*

the Patriarchs], instead of our הָבוּ לַה׳ מִשְׁפְּחוֹת עַמִּים, *Render to HASHEM, O families of nations.* Otherwise the verses are identical except that our verse 29 has the exhortation to *take an offering and come before Him*, which *Psalm* 29 does not have.[1]

It would appear that this verse is meant to speak to the nations of the world and to assure them of God's concern for them, even though He allows His presence to rest in Israel. There can be no greater assurance to the nations than to invite them to serve God in precisely the same form in which the children of God's beloved Patriarchs are exhorted. The appropriateness of this idea just here will become apparent in the analysis in Section Two.

28. הָבוּ ... הָבוּ — *Render ... render.* The second phrase is an explanation of the first. The families of the nations are exhorted: *Render to HASHEM!* What they are to render is told in the second phrase.

הָבוּ לַה׳ כָּבוֹד וָעֹז — *Render to HASHEM honor and might.* Say that honor and strength are His and in His control *(Metzudos).*

29. הָבוּ לַה׳ כְּבוֹד שְׁמוֹ — *Render to HASHEM honor worthy of His Name.* The honor that is due to His Name *(Metzudos).* *Mefaresh* sees specific reference to the name HASHEM which denotes mastery of the universe. Accordingly, *Ascribe to HASHEM the glory befitting the Master of the universe.* Ibn Ezra associates the *honor of His Name* with the Ark which, as seen in 13:6, was called שֵׁם, *name.* Thus, *Render to HASHEM the*

honor surrounding the Ark.

שְׂאוּ מִנְחָה וּבֹאוּ לְפָנָיו — *Take an offering and come before Him. Psalms* has וּבֹאוּ לְחַצְרוֹתָיו, *and come to His courtyards.* This change is much the same as the one noted in v. 27, where *Chronicles* substitutes *His place* for *in His Sanctuary* (see Section Two). *Ibn Ezra,* who considers the first part of the verse an allusion to the Ark, explains that the second phrase is based on the first. Because of the glory surrounding the Ark, it is fitting that one come to God's courtyards or place.

הִשְׁתַּחֲווּ לַה׳ בְּהַדְרַת־קֹדֶשׁ — *Prostrate yourselves before HASHEM in majestic holiness. Mefaresh* points to v. 27 which taught of God's הָדָר, *majesty.* Evidently he understands our verse to mean: *Bow down to HASHEM in* [the awareness of His] *majestic holiness.*

Metzudos takes הַדְרַת קֹדֶשׁ as a description of the tent in which the Ark was kept [in *Psalms,* as a description of God's Temple]. The meaning is: *Worship God in* [the tent of the Ark] *which is splendorous in its sanctity.*

From *Berachos* 30b it appears that the Sages took the phrase as describing the person who is worshiping God. R' Yehudah used to dress himself up before he prayed, based on our verse which enjoins one to bow down before God in majestic holiness.

30. חִילוּ מִלְּפָנָיו כָּל־הָאָרֶץ — *Tremble before Him, all the earth.* As in v. 21, the phrase is presumably to be taken as *all the*

---

1. As a possible explanation for this omission in *Psalm* 29 we offer the following: It seems clear that the Sages had a tradition that *Psalm* 29 comprises the elements which constitute the ideal form of Israel's prayer. *Megillah* 17b derives the first three blessings of the *Shemoneh Esrei* from the first two verses of that psalm. The last blessing — a prayer for peace — is an obvious reflection of the final verse of *Psalm* 29. In addition, the Talmud teaches that the *Shemoneh Esrei* consists of eighteen blessings, reflecting the eighteen times that God's Name is mentioned in this psalm. In this psalm then, descriptive as it is of the basic form of prayer, reference to an offering to be brought before God would not be appropriate since prayer by its very nature is not confined to a specific place but can be

לא כָּל־הָאָרֶץ אַף־תִּכּוֹן תֵּבֵל בַּל־תִּמּוֹט יִשְׂמְחוּ הַשָּׁמַיִם
לב וְתָגֵל הָאָרֶץ וְיֹאמְרוּ בַגּוֹיִם יהוה מָלָךְ: יִרְעַם הַיָּם
לג וּמְלוֹאוֹ יַעֲלֹץ הַשָּׂדֶה וְכָל־אֲשֶׁר־בּוֹ: אָז יְרַנְּנוּ עֲצֵי הַיָּעַר
לד מִלִּפְנֵי יהוה כִּי־בָא לִשְׁפּוֹט אֶת־הָאָרֶץ: הוֹדוּ לַיהוה
לה כִּי טוֹב כִּי לְעוֹלָם חַסְדּוֹ: וְאִמְרוּ הוֹשִׁיעֵנוּ אֱלֹהֵי יִשְׁעֵנוּ
וְקַבְּצֵנוּ וְהַצִּילֵנוּ מִן־הַגּוֹיִם לְהֹדוֹת לְשֵׁם קָדְשֶׁךָ
לו לְהִשְׁתַּבֵּחַ בִּתְהִלָּתֶךָ: בָּרוּךְ יהוה אֱלֹהֵי יִשְׂרָאֵל
מִן־הָעוֹלָם וְעַד הָעֹלָם וַיֹּאמְרוּ כָל־הָעָם אָמֵן וְהַלֵּל
לז לַיהוה: וַיַּעֲזָב־שָׁם לִפְנֵי אֲרוֹן בְּרִית־יהוה לְאָסָף
וּלְאֶחָיו לְשָׁרֵת לִפְנֵי הָאָרוֹן תָּמִיד לִדְבַר־יוֹם בְּיוֹמוֹ:

[inhabitants of] *earth.*

אַף־תִּכּוֹן תֵּבֵל בַּל־תִּמּוֹט — *Indeed, the world is fixed so that it cannot falter.* Both in *Psalm* 96 and in 93:1 the picture of the world being *fixed so that it cannot falter* is mentioned in connection with God's kingship. In the thought-world of Scripture, the earth or the world is metaphorically imagined to be resting upon foundations (cf. *II Samuel* 22:16), and the placing of the world upon these foundations is a function of God's might (cf. *Psalms* 89:11). Thus the idea is expressed that God's rulership is absolute. His control is complete, and so the world which He originally placed upon its foundations remains firmly ensconced there.

Mefaresh explains the verse as follows: A mortal king exploits his power. When he sees that his subjects fear him, he seeks to increase their fear so that he becomes ever more their master. But when God observes that His creatures fear and serve Him, He lets them be. Indeed, God then brings additional stability to the earth so that man will feel a sense of security. When the whole earth trembles before Him, He makes sure that the world is fixed so that it cannot falter.

31. יִשְׂמְחוּ הַשָּׁמַיִם וְתָגֵל הָאָרֶץ — *Let the heavens rejoice and the earth be glad.* Not only the nations of the world rejoice at their recognition of God's omnipresence; nature itself jubilates at the prospect of the coming of God to judge the world. In this context the next phrase וְיֹאמְרוּ בַגּוֹיִם ה' מָלָךְ, *let them declare among the peoples, 'HASHEM reigns,'* which deals with the recognition of

the nations rather than with the jubilation of nature, seems inappropriate. Its insertion is discussed in the analysis of the chapter in Section Two.

32. יִרְעַם הַיָּם וּמְלֹאוֹ — *Let the sea and its fullness roar.* רַעַם is *thunder* and is used here in a borrowed sense. Its fullness refers to the creatures which populate the sea (*Metzudos*).

33. כִּי־בָא לִשְׁפּוֹט אֶת־הָאָרֶץ — *For He comes to judge the earth.* The concept of God coming to judge the earth belongs in the framework of the Messianic era. Indeed, this is how *Rashi* to *Psalms* explains it. However, as will be shown in the analysis of the chapter in Section Two, David, by designating this song for the service of the Ark, was relating the song to the present. How then do we understand our phrase?

It would appear that the key to the correct understanding of the phrase lies in the elimination in *Chronicles* of the appositional phrase, יִשְׁפֹּט תֵּבֵל בְּצֶדֶק וְעַמִּים בֶּאֱמוּנָתוֹ, *He will judge the world with righteousness and the nations with His faithful truth,* which appears in v. 13 of *Psalms.* With this appositional phrase in place it is clear that לִשְׁפּוֹט does indeed mean *to judge,* a concept which *Rashi* applies to Messianic times. Without this phrase, the לִשְׁפּוֹט of our verse may well have a different meaning. The root שפט is sometimes used in the sense of *to vindicate* or *to defend* (cf. *Isaiah* 1:17, 23). Our verse may intend this meaning. The sea, the fields and the trees in the forest all exult in the knowledge that God defends them, vindicates their existence and guarantees

offered wherever man's heart turns towards God. In our psalm, however, which deals specifically with the idea of coming to *God's place,* the reference to bringing a gift is entirely appropriate.

falter. ³¹ *Let the heavens rejoice and the earth be glad, let them declare among the peoples, 'HASHEM reigns.'* ³² *Let the sea and its fullness roar, let the field and everything in it exult.* ³³ *Then the trees of the forest will sing joyously before HASHEM, for He comes to judge the earth.* ³⁴ *Give thanks to HASHEM, for He is good, for His kindness endures forever.* ³⁵ *And say, 'Save us, O God of our salvation, gather us and deliver us from among the peoples, to give thanks to Your Holy Name, to glory in Your praise.'* ³⁶ *Blessed is HASHEM, God of Israel, from the most distant past to the remotest future. Then all the people said: 'Amen, and praise to HASHEM.'* ³⁷ *And he left there, before the Ark of the Covenant of HASHEM, Asaph and his brothers — to serve before the Ark continually,*

their sustenance.

34⁻36. These last three verses are taken from *Psalm 106* and are respectively the first and the last two verses of that psalm.

34. הודוּ לַה' כִּי טוֹב — *Give thanks to HASHEM, for He is good.* Radak thinks that this verse is the subject of the jubilation of nature described in the previous two verses. Nature sings of God's goodness and His eternal kindness.

35. לְהִשְׁתַּבֵּחַ בִּתְהִלָּתֶךְ — *To glory in Your praise.* שבח means *to laud* or *praise.* In the reflexive it means *to praise oneself;* that is, *to boast* of an accomplishment or *to glory* in a circumstance. Save us, so that we may glory in the fact that we can come close to You (*Metzudos*).

36. אֱלֹהֵי יִשְׂרָאֵל מִן־הָעוֹלָם וְעַד־הָעֹלָם — *God of Israel, from the most distant past to the remotest future.* Translation follows *Hirsch.* See further at 29:10.

וַיֹּאמְרוּ כָל־הָעָם אָמֵן וְהַלֵּל לַה' — *Then all the people said: 'Amen, and praise to HASHEM.'* David ordained that after the conclusion of the psalm, all the people present should affirm its contents by saying *Amen,* meaning *it is true;* and then each of those present should offer praises to God in accordance with his ability (*Metzudos*).

These are the last words of the psalm. The next phrase does not belong to the text of the psalm (*Radak*).

⊷§ Levites at Jerusalem and Giveon

37. וַיַּעֲזָב־שָׁם ... לְאָסָף וּלְאֶחָיו — *And he left there ... Asaph and his brothers.* See comm. to v. 5. *Gra* identifies *his brothers* as Zechariah and Yeiel and the others mentioned there.

The use of *lamed* (לְאָסָף) in place of the

אֶת, which in Hebrew appears before the direct object, is unusual but not unique. *Ibn Janach* cites numerous examples in *Sefer HaRikmah.* See, for example, *I Samuel 22:7.*

לְשָׁרֵת לִפְנֵי הָאָרוֹן — *To serve before the Ark.* The service meant here is to sing the appropriate psalms daily in front of the Ark (*Mefaresh*). *Radak* also mentions a daily sacrifice. Apparently, he assumes that the daily *shir* was sung in conjunction with a sacrifice on a *bamah* (private altar) set up by the Ark (see prefatory remarks to 6:16-17). Although being on a *bamah* this sacrifice would not have had the halachic status requiring *shir* (only communal sacrifices had this status, and those were brought on the communal altar in Giveon), David nevertheless introduced such a *shir.* *Radak* himself notes that this daily sacrifice in front of the Ark could be brought by Levites [only Asaph and his brothers are mentioned here; nothing is said of the *Kohanim* who were listed in v. 6] since the altar was a private one. Only in vs. 39-40, which deal with the communal altar in Giveon (בָּמָה הַגְּדוֹלָה), is there an insistence on *Kohanim.*

תָּמִיד לִדְבַר־יוֹם בְּיוֹמוֹ — *Continually, according to the daily requirements.* According to the requirement for a twice-daily service; in the morning and in the evening (*Mefaresh*). *Metzudos* interprets this to mean that there was to be a different *shir* for every day. Each day they were to recite the psalm appropriate for that particular day.

It would seem that he refers to the different psalms enumerated in the mishnah in *Tamid* which are incorporated in our daily morning prayers. Apparently, *Metzudos* thinks that these

לח וְעֹבֵד אֱדֹם וַאֲחֵיהֶם שִׁשִּׁים וּשְׁמוֹנָה וְעֹבֵד אֱדֹם בֶּן־
לט יְדִיתוּן וְחֹסָה לְשֹׁעֲרִים: וְאֵת ׀ צָדוֹק הַכֹּהֵן וְאֶחָיו הַכֹּהֲנִים
מ לִפְנֵי מִשְׁכַּן יהוה בַּבָּמָה אֲשֶׁר בְּגִבְעוֹן: לְהַעֲלוֹת עֹלוֹת
לַיהוה עַל־מִזְבַּח הָעֹלָה תָּמִיד לַבֹּקֶר וְלָעָרֶב וּלְכָל־
מא הַכָּתוּב בְּתוֹרַת יהוה אֲשֶׁר צִוָּה עַל־יִשְׂרָאֵל: וְעִמָּהֶם הֵימָן

were recited in addition to the psalm in our chapter.

At 6:16-31 all three main choristers, Heman, Asaph and Ethan (Yeduthun — see below to v. 41), are apparently assigned to the *shir* at Giveon: Heman is to stand in the center, Asaph at his right and Ethan (Yeduthun) at his left. How, then, are we to understand our verse and v. 41 which teaches that the choristers were separated: Asaph to the Ark and the other two to the Tabernacle at Giveon?

Two solutions seem possible: The dispositions described in ch. 6 may have applied only before the Ark was brought to Jerusalem. Once this occurred, Asaph was separated from the others. This, however, is not possible if מִמְּנוֹחַ הָאָרוֹן in v. 16 there is interpreted as meaning: *From the time that the Ark came to rest* in its temporary tent in Jerusalem — see comm. there.

Another possibility is that when ch. 6 teaches that Asaph is to stand at Heman's right this does not mean necessarily Asaph the man, but whoever of his clan is assigned to the *shir* (see ch. 25 for the divisions of the choristers). Thus, our verse may mean that Asaph himself, together with [some of] his brothers, was assigned to the Ark but that members of his clan were still part of the service at Giveon and filled his place there.

38. ... וְעֹבֵד אֱדֹם וַאֲחֵיהֶם — *And Oved Edom and their brothers.* The meaning of the verse is that these men were also left by David to perform the services in front of the Ark. The irregular plural form is explained by *Radak* as a Scriptural shortening which should be understood as though it were written: וְעֹבֵד אֱדֹם [וּבָנָיו] וַאֲחֵיהֶם, *And Oved Edom [and his sons] and their brothers.* He compares this to 26:8 where we have precisely this formulation. *Malbim* points out that if we accept *Radak's* explanation we are faced with an apparent discrepancy since the family of Oved Edom is then numbered here as sixty-eight while at 26:8 it is given as sixty-two.

He suggests that between the two countings some family members may have died. *Malbim* himself suggests that there is no need to insert *his sons*. Their brothers may refer to the colleagues of Oved Edom and Chosah, who were sixty-eight in number.

וְעֹבֵד אֱדֹם בֶּן־יְדִיתוּן וְחֹסָה — *And Oved Edom the son of Yedithun and Chosah.* According to *Gra*, Chosah, too, was a son of Yedithun.

This Oved Edom would seem to be the same as the one mentioned at the beginning of the verse. However, it is not clear why just in this context Oved Edom is identified as a son of Yedithun. Oved Edom is mentioned almost twenty times in Scripture and nowhere else is any mention made of his father.

Moreover, who is Yedithun? An almost identical name occurs frequently as one of the Levite choristers (Yeduthun — cf. v. 41), and that would be the most obvious identification. However, in a number of lists of choristers (cf. 25:1), that Yeduthun seems to take the place of Ethan who was listed together with Heman and Asaph in ch. 6. We must assume either that Yeduthun is another name for Ethan or that at some point he took Ethan's place (see footnote to v. 41). In either case, that would make Yeduthun a Merarite [since Ethan was a descendant of Levi's son Merari]. But Oved Edom is apparently identified in 26:4 as a Korachite (see v. 1 there), and therefore a descendant of Kehath. We must conclude, then, that either the Yeduthun of our verse is a different man, or that the Oved Edom of the second part of the verse is not identical with the Oved Edom of the first part of the verse but a Merarite of the same name, and the son of the head of the Merarite choristers.

Both the awkwardness of the syntax and the vexing question of why Oved Edom's father, Yedithun, is mentioned here make it likely that this Oved Edom is indeed not

according to the daily requirements. ³⁸ *And Oved Edom and their brothers — sixty-eight; and Oved Edom the son of Yedithun and Chosah to be gatekeepers.* ³⁹ *And Tzadok the Kohen and his brother Kohanim served before the Tabernacle of HASHEM at the bamah in Giveon.* ⁴⁰ *To offer burnt-offerings regularly, morning and evening, to HASHEM upon the Altar of the Burnt-Offering, and all that is written in the Torah of HASHEM which He decreed for Israel.* ⁴¹ *With*

the one mentioned in the first part of the verse, and that his father is mentioned here in order to differentiate him from the other Oved Edom mentioned in the verse.

Moreover, *Gra's* assertion that Chosah is also a son of Yedithun makes it clear that this second Oved Edom is certainly a Merarite, since 26:10 clearly identifies Chosah as a Merarite. This buttresses the possibility that Yedithun is indeed identical with the famous Merarite chorister, Yeduthun.

There is also the possibility that this Oved Edom is the *Kohen* of that name mentioned in 15:24. However, in ch. 26 the Levite Oved Edom is mentioned as a gatekeeper together with Chosah who is also mentioned here (see vs. 4ff and 10ff). This makes it likely that here, too, the Levite Oved Edom is meant. We must then conclude that there were three Oved Edoms — the Kehathite of the first part of our verse, who is also mentioned in ch. 26; a Merarite brother of Chosah and son of Yedithun; and the *Kohen* mentioned in 15:24.

39. וְאֵת צָדוֹק הַכֹּהֵן — *And Tzadok the Kohen* ... After the dispositions which David made for the service in front of the Ark in Jerusalem have been described, *Chronicles* turns for a moment to the other center of public worship at Giveon.

מִשְׁכַּן ... בָּמָה — *Tabernacle ... bamah.* The word בָּמָה for *altar* is generally used for those altars which were situated outside the Tabernacle or Temple. The altar in the Tabernacle or Temple is called מִזְבֵּחַ. Its usage here therefore is unusual.

The solution lies in the duality which existed from the time that the Ark was captured by the Philistines in Eli's days to the time that Solomon finally restored it to its rightful place when he built the Temple. [See 6:16-17 and prefatory remarks to ch. 13.] Throughout that time, the remnants of the Tabernacle which Moses had built stood at various locations, and these were

the sites of all communal service. However, in the absence of the Ark, the altar there had the halachic character of a בָּמָה, *bamah,* rather than of a מִזְבֵּחַ. [See *Zevachim* 112b, 117a,b; see also *R' Yitzchak Isaac HaLevi's Tekufas HaMikrah* ch. 45 for a detailed discussion.] In spite of the fact that in halachic terms it fell short of a true Tabernacle, it was nevertheless called מִשְׁכָּן because that had been its name from the earliest times.

40. עֹלוֹת ... תָּמִיד לַבֹּקֶר וְלָעָרֶב — *Burnt-offerings regularly, morning and evening.* Reference is to the twice-daily *tamid* sacrifice ordained in *Numbers* ch. 28.

מִזְבַּח הָעֹלָה — *Altar of the Burnt-Offering.* This was the altar upon which all sacrifices were brought. It is in contrast to the מִזְבַּח הַקְטֹרֶת, *incense altar.*

וּלְכָל־הַכָּתוּב בְּתוֹרַת ה' — *And all that is written in the Torah of HASHEM.* This refers to all the other sacrifices mandated by the Torah, such as the additional sacrifices for special days [מוּסָפִים] *(Metzudos).*[1]

However, although the בָּמָה גְדוֹלָה, *communal bamah,* served in place of the מִזְבֵּחַ, *altar,* during the periods of *bamos,* not all sacrifices could be offered on it. See *Zevachim* 117a,b.

41. וְעִמָּהֶם ... — *With them* ... Together with the *Kohanim* mentioned in v. 39, the following Levites also served.

הֵימָן וִידוּתוּן — *Heman and Yeduthun.* See comm. to v. 5 above. In our verse Yeduthun is mentioned where we would have expected Ethan on the basis of what we learned in ch. 6 (see also 15:17). It would seem that either Yeduthun is another name for Ethan or that at some point he replaced him as chief of the Merarite musicians.[2]

---

1. See footnote to 6:34.

2. There are considerations which make it likely that Ethan and Yeduthun are the same man:
    (1) Verse 5:17 has Ethan among those who accompanied the Ark to Jerusalem; our verse says that

טז וִידוּתוּן וּשְׁאָר הַבְּרוּרִים אֲשֶׁר נִקְּבוּ בְּשֵׁמוֹת לְהֹדוֹת

מב-מג מב לַיהֹוָה כִּי לְעוֹלָם חַסְדּוֹ: וְעִמָּהֶם הֵימָן וִידוּתוּן חֲצֹצְרוֹת וּמְצִלְתַּיִם לְמַשְׁמִיעִים וּכְלֵי שִׁיר הָאֱלֹהִים וּבְנֵי יְדוּתוּן מג לַשָּׁעַר: וַיֵּלְכוּ כָל־הָעָם אִישׁ לְבֵיתוֹ וַיִּסֹּב דָּוִיד לְבָרֵךְ

יז א אֶת־בֵּיתוֹ:   וַיְהִי כַּאֲשֶׁר יָשַׁב דָּוִיד בְּבֵיתוֹ וַיֹּאמֶר

א

וּשְׁאָר הַבְּרוּרִים אֲשֶׁר נִקְּבוּ בְּשֵׁמוֹת — *And the rest of those selected who were designated by name.* The commentators do not say who these men were. Perhaps some or all of those mentioned in 15:18ff are meant.

42. וְעִמָּהֶם הֵימָן וִידוּתוּן — *With them, with Heman and Yeduthun.* The two names stand in apposition to עִמָּהֶם, *with them.* Thus the phrase must be understood as *with them,* [that is, with] *Heman and Yeduthun (Radak).* Ralbag thinks that the implication of our verse is that Heman and Yeduthun were choral musicians and that those with them accompanied them with musical instruments.

חֲצֹצְרוֹת וּמְצִלְתַּיִם לְמַשְׁמִיעִים — *Trumpets and cymbals to play loudly.* We have followed the *trop* (cantillation) division which indicates that לְמַשְׁמִיעִים, *to play loudly* [lit. *to make themselves heard*], describes both the trumpets and the cymbals. From *Metzudos* here together with his comment to 15:16, it would seem that he takes מַשְׁמִיעִים to describe the cymbals only. The entire purpose of a percussion instrument is to add loudness. See comm. to 15:16.

וּכְלֵי שִׁיר הָאֱלֹהִים — *As well as the instruments of God.* I.e., the other instruments which were used to make music in the Tabernacle of God (*Metzudos*).

Throughout Scripture, when there is a need to emphasize the size or importance of an object, it is idiomatically attached to God's name. See for example *Psalms* 6:7; 80:11; *Shir HaShirim* 8:6;

Jeremiah 2:31 (*Radak* to *Jonah* 3:3). Perhaps here too the meaning is particularly beautiful sounding instruments.

וּבְנֵי יְדוּתוּן לַשָּׁעַר — *And the sons of Yeduthun were to be at the gate.* According to *Gra,* the Yeduthun of this verse is identical with the Yedithun of v. 38. The sons of Yeduthun are Oved Edom and Chosah of that verse, who, in *Gra's* view, were both sons of Yeduthun. They were placed in charge of the gate. See comm. to v. 38 above.

43. וַיֵּלְכוּ כָל־הָעָם אִישׁ לְבֵיתוֹ — *Then all the people departed, each to his house.* In II *Samuel* 6:19 this phrase follows immediately upon the information that David gave each person bread, meat and wine to celebrate the bringing of the Ark, which in our chapter is mentioned in v. 3. *Chronicles,* which records the dispositions which David made for the service before the Ark, waits up to this point to record the return of the people to their houses.

וַיִּסֹּב דָּוִיד לְבָרֵךְ אֶת־בֵּיתוֹ — *And David turned away to greet his household.* David turned aside from the tent of the Ark (*Metzudos*). *Samuel* has ... וַיָּשָׁב דָּוִד לְבָרֵךְ, *and David returned to greet* ... The change can be readily explained. It is only here in *Chronicles* where David's detailed dispositions are recorded, where his concentration was so to speak riveted on the tent of the Ark, that his return home is described as a *turning away.* In *Samuel* the implication is

---

immediately upon its arrival in Jerusalem Yeduthun was assigned to Giveon. If Ethan would have died or in some way been disqualified during this brief interlude, it seems likely that some explanation would have been given, or at least some mention made of the circumstance surrounding his replacement — particularly in the light of the importance attached to Ethan in ch. 6, where his genealogy is traced together with that of Heman.

(2) In ch. 6 Heman, Asaph, and Ethan are assigned to duties at Giveon. [See comm. there for how vs. 16 and 17 are to be understood. Our assertion that these Levite families are assigned to Giveon does not accord with *Metzudos.*] At least superficially, our verse, which has Yeduthun and not Ethan assigned to Giveon, would contradict that passage if they were not the same person.

(3) *Bava Basra* 14b teaches that Asaph, Heman and Yeduthun all contributed to the book of *Psalms.* No mention is made of Ethan. While it is possible that Ethan was an exception among the major choristers and did not in fact contribute, it seems more likely that Yeduthun is Ethan.

them were Heman, Yeduthun, and the rest of those selected who were designated by name, to praise HASHEM, for His kindness is everlasting. ⁴² With them, with Heman and Yeduthun, were trumpets and cymbals to play loudly, as well as the instruments of God. And the sons of Yeduthun were to be at the gate. ⁴³ Then all the people departed, each to his house, and David turned away to greet his household.

17

1

It was when David lived in his house that David said to Nathan,

simply that he returned home after bringing the Ark from the house of Oved Edom.

לְבָרֵךְ אֶת-בֵּיתוֹ — *To greet his household.* We follow *Radak* in *Samuel* who takes the root ברך as meaning *to greet* [as in II *Kings* 4:29]. David had been away on a journey

and now that he had returned he went to greet his wife. *Metzudos* takes ברך to mean *bless,* as it was used in v. 2. Having blessed the people he now wanted to bless his family. In *Samuel* an account of Michal's confrontation with David follows. *Chronicles'* different perspective on the event has been discussed in 15:27.

XVII

◄§ David Asks to Build the Temple

This chapter parallels *II Samuel*, ch. 7. In it we learn how David felt inspired to seek a more permanent home for the Holy Ark than the tent which he had erected for it in anticipation of its return from the house of Oved Edom. God sends Nathan, the Prophet, to tell David that not he, but a son of his, heir to his royal line, has been chosen for the task of building a Temple to God. In a prayer suffused with gratitude for all the favors which God has showered upon him, David accepts God's decision.

The reason for David's present desire to build the Temple is given in *II Samuel* (7:1): *It was when the king lived in his house and HASHEM had given him rest from all his enemies round about ...* The Torah teaches (*Deuteronomy* 12:10,11) that the obligation to build a Temple begins only after all of Israel's enemies have been defeated — *When God shall have given you rest from all your enemies round about and you dwell in tranquillity, and it shall be the place which HASHEM your God shall choose to install His Name there ...* The implication that the investiture of God's name in a chosen place is dependent on peace reigning in Israel is clear. This halachic principle is formulated in *Sanhedrin* 20b, and the parallel verse in *Samuel* is cited as one of the proofs (see also *Rambam, Melachim* 1:2).

David now thought that this state had been reached and that therefore it was his duty as king to build the Temple. As Nathan was to inform him, however, and as is evident from the next chapter, true lasting peace was not yet at hand and the time was not yet ripe for the erection of the Temple. The origins of David's mistaken assessment will be further discussed in the preface to chapter 18.

As elsewhere in this book, there are differences between the presentation of the incident in *Chronicles* and *Samuel* — some striking, some subtle. From the number of times they occur, it seems likely that they represent not so much specific shifts of focus as a general difference in perspective between the two books. The broad treatment required for such an analysis necessitates dealing with the chapter as a whole. This will be done in Section Two (p. 437*ff*), with the commentary restricting itself to just noting the discrepancies.

1. וַיְהִי כַּאֲשֶׁר יָשַׁב דָּוִיד בְּבֵיתוֹ — *It was when David lived in his house.* David was dwelling in a house (14:1) befitting his rank (*Metzudos*). How inappropriate, therefore, that the Ark should still be

consigned to a tent! So David turns to Nathan.

There are two differences between this verse and its parallel in *II Samuel* 7:1 which are particularly noticeable.

דָּוִיד אֶל־נָתָן הַנָּבִיא הִנֵּה אָנֹכִי יוֹשֵׁב בְּבֵית הָאֲרָזִים

ב וַאֲרוֹן בְּרִית־יהוה תַּחַת יְרִיעוֹת: וַיֹּאמֶר נָתָן אֶל־דָּוִיד

ג כֹּל אֲשֶׁר בִּלְבָבְךָ עֲשֵׂה כִּי הָאֱלֹהִים עִמָּךְ:   וַיְהִי

ד בַּלַּיְלָה הַהוּא וַיְהִי דְּבַר־אֱלֹהִים אֶל־נָתָן לֵאמֹר: לֵךְ

וְאָמַרְתָּ אֶל־דָּוִיד עַבְדִּי כֹּה אָמַר יהוה לֹא אַתָּה תִּבְנֶה־לִּי

ה הַבַּיִת לָשָׁבֶת: כִּי לֹא יָשַׁבְתִּי בְּבַיִת מִן־הַיּוֹם אֲשֶׁר

הֶעֱלֵיתִי אֶת־יִשְׂרָאֵל עַד הַיּוֹם הַזֶּה וָאֶהְיֶה מֵאֹהֶל אֶל־

ו אֹהֶל וּמִמִּשְׁכָּן: בְּכֹל אֲשֶׁר־הִתְהַלַּכְתִּי בְּכָל־יִשְׂרָאֵל הֲדָבָר

דִּבַּרְתִּי אֶת־אַחַד שֹׁפְטֵי יִשְׂרָאֵל אֲשֶׁר צִוִּיתִי לִרְעוֹת אֶת־

Chronicles	Samuel
1(a) וַיְהִי כַּאֲשֶׁר יָשַׁב דָּוִיד בְּבֵיתוֹ, *It was when David lived in his house*	1(a) וַיְהִי כִּי־יָשַׁב הַמֶּלֶךְ בְּבֵיתוֹ, *It was when the king lived in his house,*
	(b) וַיהוה הֵנִיחַ לוֹ מִסָּבִיב מִכָּל־אֹיְבָיו, *and HASHEM gave him rest from all his enemies round about,*
(b) וַיֹּאמֶר דָּוִיד אֶל־נָתָן הַנָּבִיא ..., *that David said to Nathan the prophet*	2. ... וַיֹּאמֶר הַמֶּלֶךְ אֶל־נָתָן הַנָּבִיא, *that the king said to Nathan the prophet...*

Whereas *Samuel* speaks of *the king*, *Chronicles* has *David*. Furthermore, phrase (b) from *Samuel*, *And HASHEM gave him rest from all his enemies round about*, is missing here entirely. See Section Two.

הִנֵּה אָנֹכִי יוֹשֵׁב בְּבֵית הָאֲרָזִים וַאֲרוֹן בְּרִית־ה' תַּחַת יְרִיעוֹת — *Behold, I am living in the house of cedars while the Ark of the Covenant of HASHEM is under curtains.* The statement implies a rhetorical question. Can it be right that while I am living in a palace which befits my rank, the Ark of *Hashem* should be in a tent which is manifestly not appropriate for it (*Metzudos*)? See Section Two.

בְּבֵית הָאֲרָזִים — *In the house of cedars.* The use of the definite article indicates that David's palace was known as the *house of cedars*. Cedars shipped from Tyre were obviously rare and their use in the building gave it its unique character.

2. כֹּל אֲשֶׁר בִּלְבָבְךָ עֲשֵׂה — *Do all that is in your heart.* Nathan was not talking as a prophet. Even a prophet can know the absolute truth only when God chooses to reveal it to him. His approval here was based on his personal judgment that David was justified in his aspirations (*Radak*).

Because righteous people dedicate their hearts to the service of God, their instincts

are generally reliable. [As recounted in *Shocher Tov*: ... Nathan said ... 'If it would not have been God's wish that you should built the Temple, it would not have occurred to you to build it ...'.] In the event, however, Nathan's judgment proved to be wrong.

◆§ God's Reply

3. וַיְהִי בַּלַּיְלָה הַהוּא — *And it was that very night.* The Sages explain that God hastened to send Nathan that very night because He knew David to be a man of action. Unless he was stopped right away, he might well go out the very next day to hire workers, or perhaps make a vow that he would not eat or drink until he had accomplished his purpose. In either case, he would be embarrassed (*Mefaresh*).

4. ... לֹא אַתָּה תִּבְנֶה־לִּי — *You shall not build for Me ...* Samuel gives the reply as a rhetorical question: הַאַתָּה תִּבְנֶה־לִּי בַיִת לְשַׁבְתִּי, *Will you build a house for me for My dwelling?*

The Sages (*Pesikta Rabbasi* quoted in *Yalkut*) offer the following assessment of the change. When a message is couched in the form of a rhetorical question, it is not as absolute as when it is given as a categorical statement. Therefore, the form in *Samuel*

17

2-6

the prophet, 'Behold, I am living in the house of cedars while the Ark of the Covenant of HASHEM is under curtains.' ² And Nathan said to David, 'Do all that is in your heart, for God is with you.' ³ And it was that very night that the word of God came to Nathan saying: ⁴ 'Go tell David My servant: Thus has HASHEM said, you shall not build for Me the house to dwell in. ⁵ For I have not dwelled in a house from the day that I brought Israel up until this very day, but I have moved from tent to tent and from tabernacle [to tabernacle]. ⁶ Wherever I have traveled in all of Israel, did I ever

modifies the implications of *Chronicles*. As they see it, there are three possible modifications:

(1) You personally are excluded but your son will build the Temple. [The implication is that Solomon will function as an extension of his father David.]

(2) You will not complete the building but you will lay its foundations. [David's involvement in the planning of the Temple and in the laying of its foundations are discussed from ch. 22 onwards.]

(3) You will not build the Temple but, after it is built, the heavenly fire will descend upon the altar in your merit.

See further in Section Two.

5. ... בִּי לֹא יָשַׁבְתִּי בְּבַיִת — *For I have not dwelled in a house* ... The בִּי, *because*, of this phrase cannot be taken as expressing a direct relation between our phrase and the previous one. David was not denied permission to build the Temple *because* God had not had a permanent Temple from the time of the Exodus. Rather, it is meant to answer an implied question: Why was David denied permission when there was seemingly an urgent need for a permanent home for the Ark? To which the reply was that the need was not urgent, as evidenced by history. [For the use of בִּי as an introduction to an answer to an implied question, see *Isaiah* 28:27 and *Job* 22:1.]

The thrust of the explanation contained in this and the next verse may be as follows: The model of God's rulership over the world is His kingship over Israel. Towards this end, He seeks to *dwell* among Israel. David's thinking may well have been that just as he, a mortal king, craved to be firmly established among his people, as epitomized by a splendid and permanent palace, so too it was only fitting that God's Presence be firmly manifested in a permanent home.

To this God answered that it is the presence but not the permanence which is imperative. God wishes His Presence among the people to reflect their spiritual state. As long as the state of Israel is one of flux and movement, God, too, does not wish to be ensconced in a permanent home. Indeed, as Ezekiel was to teach many centuries later in his visions of the *Merkavah*, God would willingly leave this Temple in order to accompany His children into exile. Permanence is thus not an absolute end but merely one of many possible postures. From the time of the Exodus, God had not sought a permanent home, even during the days of the Judges when the halachic requirements may have been fulfilled (see below), because Israel's spiritual state had not yet ripened into the maturity which could have been appropriately reflected in a permanent Temple.

וָאֶהְיֶה מֵאֹהֶל אֶל-אֹהֶל וּמִמִּשְׁכָּן — *But I have moved from tent to tent and from tabernacle [to tabernacle]*. The Tabernacle wandered from the wilderness to Gilgal, from Gilgal to Shiloh and from there to Nov and Giveon. In none of these places was there a really permanent building *(Radak)*. Even in Shiloh, where the Tabernacle stood for a number of centuries, only the walls were of stone. They were covered with a ceiling made of curtains (see *Zevachim* 112a,b).

The term וּמִמִּשְׁכָּן, *from tabernacle*, should be understood as though it were written וּמִמִּשְׁכָּן לְמִשְׁכָּן, *from tabernacle to tabernacle*, and is the parallel of the earlier phrase, *from tent to tent*. The intent is obvious and therefore the text relies on the reader's understanding *(Radak; Metzudos)*. See analysis in Section Two for another understanding of this omission.

6. אֶת-אַחַד שֹׁפְטֵי יִשְׂרָאֵל — *To one of Israel's Judges. Samuel* has אֶת אַחַד שִׁבְטֵי יִשְׂרָאֵל. The word שֵׁבֶט, which also means *tribe*, is obviously used there in the sense of a *rod*

ז עַמִּי לֵאמֹר לָמָּה לֹא־בְנִיתֶם לִי בֵּית אֲרָזִים: וְעַתָּה כֹּה־
תֹאמַר לְעַבְדִּי לְדָוִד כֹּה אָמַר יהוה צְבָאוֹת אֲנִי לְקַחְתִּיךָ
מִן־הַנָּוֶה מִן־אַחֲרֵי הַצֹּאן לִהְיוֹת נָגִיד עַל עַמִּי יִשְׂרָאֵל:
ח וָאֶהְיֶה עִמְּךָ בְּכֹל אֲשֶׁר הָלַכְתָּ וָאַכְרִית אֶת־כָּל־אוֹיְבֶיךָ
מִפָּנֶיךָ וְעָשִׂיתִי לְךָ שֵׁם כְּשֵׁם הַגְּדוֹלִים אֲשֶׁר בָּאָרֶץ:
ט וְשַׂמְתִּי מָקוֹם לְעַמִּי יִשְׂרָאֵל וּנְטַעְתִּיהוּ וְשָׁכַן תַּחְתָּיו וְלֹא
יִרְגַּז עוֹד וְלֹא־יוֹסִיפוּ בְנֵי־עַוְלָה לְבַלֹּתוֹ כַּאֲשֶׁר בָּרִאשׁוֹנָה:
י וּלְמִיָּמִים אֲשֶׁר צִוִּיתִי שֹׁפְטִים עַל־עַמִּי יִשְׂרָאֵל וְהִכְנַעְתִּי

or *scepter*. Thus: He who wields the scepter — the judge (*Radak*, comp. *Genesis* 49:10).[1]

From our verse it seems that God could have asked one of the Judges to build the Temple. This is difficult in light of the Talmud's statement (*Sanhedrin* 20b) that a pre-condition for the Temple's erection is the appointment of a king. *R' Reuven Margolies* in *Margalios HaYam* infers that, for the purpose of this halachah, a Judge would qualify as a king.

7-15. In both *Samuel* and *Chronicles* this section is introduced by the words: *Now, so shall you say to My servant, to David*, indicating that what is to follow is a new thought and not a continuation of what was said before.

The first part of Nathan's message denied David the right to build the Temple. What would have been the crowning glory of his life was now beyond his reach. David had now to redefine his life in terms other than those which he had once anticipated. Nathan is to reveal to him his true destiny.

7. וְעַתָּה כֹּה־תֹאמַר לְעַבְדִּי לְדָוִד — *Now so shall you say to My servant, to David.* R' Tzvi Binyamin Wolf in his *Sefer Shmuel Al Pi HaMesorah* suggests that the term *My servant* is used in order to stress that no fault is attached to David for wanting to build the Temple. The *Mefaresh* goes so far as to say that all that follows in Nathan's prophecy is meant to be a reward for that initiative.

לְקַחְתִּיךָ מִן־הַנָּוֶה — *I took you from the shepherd's hut.* Mefaresh and Metzudos take נָוֶה as we have translated it. *Radak*

translates *sheep-pens*.

God reminds David of the favors He has done for him in the past (*Metzudos*).

לִהְיוֹת נָגִיד — *To be a prince.* See comm. 11:2.

8. וָאַכְרִית אֶת־כָּל־אוֹיְבֶיךָ מִפָּנֶיךָ — *And I have destroyed all your enemies from before you.* And it is for this reason that it occurred to you to build the Temple, in accordance with the Torah's directions (*Rashi* to *Samuel*).

וְעָשִׂיתִי לְךָ שֵׁם — *And I made a name for you.* I spread your fame among the nations. See 14:17 (*Mefaresh* and *Radak*).

Up to this point the conversive *vav* (ו' ההפוך) has been used together with the future form to convey the past tense (וָאֶהְיֶה ... וָאַכְרִית). As *Mefaresh* and *Radak* render וְעָשִׂיתִי, *and I made* (past tense), a change in style is assumed. At this point the past tense is conveyed by using the past form and the *vav* is no longer conversive.

If we were to assume that the *vav* in וְעָשִׂיתִי is also a conversive, this would convert the word into the future tense, *I will make ...* and make the phrase the first of the promises contained in the next verse (וְשַׂמְתִּי ... וּנְטַעְתִּיהוּ). This seems to be the opinion of the Sages quoted by *Metzudos*. He notes that the Sages (*Pesachim* 117b) have a homiletical interpretation for our verse. David was promised that God would make him a name like the name of the *great ones in the land,* meaning the Patriarchs. The 'name' which is to be given to David is that just as God is described as the *shield of*

---

1. R' Aryeh Carmel has pointed out to me that we have here an instance in which the linguistic usage of *Chronicles* can throw light on a difficult passage in the Torah.

If a שֹׁפֵט, *judge*, can indeed be referred to as a שֵׁבֶט, *staff*, then we have a simple translation for *Deuteronomy* 29:9. The verse lists: רָאשֵׁיכֶם, *your leaders*; שִׁבְטֵיכֶם זִקְנֵיכֶם, *your elders*; and שֹׁטְרֵיכֶם, *your officers.* In this context the translation of שִׁבְטֵיכֶם as *your tribes* would have little meaning. Rendered as *your judges*, the verse is self-explanatory.

speak to one of Israel's Judges whom I commanded to shepherd My people, saying: Why have you not built for Me a house of cedar? [7] Now so shall you say to My servant, to David: Thus has HASHEM, Master of Legions, said: I took you from the shepherd's hut, from behind the sheep, to be a prince for My people Israel. [8] And I have been with you wherever you have gone and I have destroyed all your enemies from before you; and I made a name for you like that of the great men in the land. [9] And I will make a place for My people Israel, and establish him so that he will live in his place and be disturbed no more, nor shall evil people continue to wear him away as formerly, [10] and as from the days that I appointed Judges over My people Israel. I will subdue all your enemies; and I have told you

Abraham in the first blessing of the *Shemoneh Esrei*, so too, He is described as the *shield of David* in one of the blessings which is recited after the *Haftorah*.

9. וְשַׂמְתִּי מָקוֹם לְעַמִּי יִשְׂרָאֵל — *And I will make a place for My people Israel.* Rashi to *Samuel* writes: I will bring tranquillity to My people — they will be at peace in your son's reign. Thus, *Rashi* interprets this verse as a refutation of David's thinking. David had thought that peace had already been attained; God now tells him that much is still to be done before that condition is achieved but assures him that it will yet come.

Radak, in accordance with *Targum*, explains that it refers not to peace but to the harmonious interaction between the people and the land. The heavens will give their water, and the earth will produce its harvests.

The Sages (*Berachos* 7b) take *place* to refer to the Temple (see below for their explanation).

וּנְטַעְתִּיהוּ — *And establish* [lit. *plant*] *him.* The object must be עַמִּי יִשְׂרָאֵל. The singular *him* is used because the people are viewed as a single cohesive unit.

וְלֹא יִרְגְּזוּ עוֹד — *And be disturbed no more.* Their tranquillity will not be disturbed anymore, to be forced to move out of the land (*Metzudos*).

לְבַלֹּתוֹ — *To wear him away. Samuel* has לְעַנּוֹתוֹ, *to afflict him,* which, *Mefaresh* explains, has essentially the same meaning.

See Section Two.

The Talmud's interpretation (*Berachos* 7b)[1] is that in the early years of the Temple the nations of the world were in no way able to inflict any suffering at all upon Israel (לְעַנּוֹתוֹ, *to afflict him*). However, the promise of such complete freedom from suffering at the hands of the nations was conditional upon Israel living up to the demands which the Torah placed upon them (*Ralbag*). When Israel's level of observance became ever less, they were indeed subjected to suffering at the hands of the nations. At that time all that was left of God's promise was that the nations would not be allowed to destroy them completely.

כַּאֲשֶׁר בָּרִאשׁוֹנָה — *As formerly.* As it was before God sent the Judges to protect His people (*Metzudos*). See further below.

10. וּלְמִימִים אֲשֶׁר צִוִּיתִי שֹׁפְטִים עַל־עַמִּי יִשְׂרָאֵל — *And as from the days that I appointed Judges over My people Israel.* Rashi to *Samuel* maintains that this is to be read as a continuation of the thought expressed in the previous verse. The enemies will not wear you away as they did in the early days before the advent of the Judges (previous verse) and as they continued to do during the period of the Judges (this verse). Although the Judges consistently saved them from their enemies, they were, nevertheless, intermittently exposed to danger in the periods between the Judges (*Radak*).

1. The Talmud homiletically reads לְבַלֹּתוֹ as לְכַלֹּתוֹ, *to destroy him.* The substitution of a כ, *caf,* for a ב, *beis,* or indeed any two letters which are similar in appearance, in a homiletical interpretation is a common form employed by the Sages which does not imply any textual emendation. See R' Shmuel Woldenberg's exhaustive analysis of the methods of the Sages in the realm of *aggadah* — *Darkei HaShinuyim* 2:5.

יא אֶת־כָּל־אוֹיְבֶיךָ וָאַגִּד לָךְ וּבַיִת יִבְנֶה־לְּךָ יהוה: וְהָיָה
כִּי־מָלְאוּ יָמֶיךָ לָלֶכֶת עִם־אֲבֹתֶיךָ וַהֲקִימוֹתִי אֶת־זַרְעֲךָ
יב אַחֲרֶיךָ אֲשֶׁר יִהְיֶה מִבָּנֶיךָ וַהֲכִינוֹתִי אֶת־מַלְכוּתוֹ: הוּא
יג יִבְנֶה־לִּי בָיִת וְכֹנַנְתִּי אֶת־כִּסְאוֹ עַד־עוֹלָם: אֲנִי אֶהְיֶה־
לּוֹ לְאָב וְהוּא יִהְיֶה־לִּי לְבֵן וְחַסְדִּי לֹא־אָסִיר מֵעִמּוֹ
יד כַּאֲשֶׁר הֲסִירוֹתִי מֵאֲשֶׁר הָיָה לְפָנֶיךָ: וְהַעֲמַדְתִּיהוּ בְּבֵיתִי
טו וּבְמַלְכוּתִי עַד־הָעוֹלָם וְכִסְאוֹ יִהְיֶה נָכוֹן עַד־עוֹלָם: כְּכֹל
הַדְּבָרִים הָאֵלֶּה וּכְכֹל הֶחָזוֹן הַזֶּה כֵּן דִּבֶּר נָתָן אֶל־

וְהִכְנַעְתִּי אֶת־כָּל־אוֹיְבֶיךָ — *I will subdue all your enemies.* Samuel has וַהֲנִיחֹתִי, *I will grant you peace.* Malbim explains the change in the same vein as the Sages in the previous verse. When Israel lives up to its high calling they will be completely at peace from all their enemies (*Samuel*). When they are not as they should be, they will not be granted perfect peace, although God will subdue their enemies before them (*Chronicles*). [See Section Two for another explanation.]

וָאַגִּד לָךְ וּבַיִת יִבְנֶה־לְּךָ ה' — *And I have told you that HASHEM will build a house for you.* The translation follows *Targum* who inserts אֲרוּם, *that,* and reads וּבַיִת ... as though it was written כִּי בַיִת as, indeed, the verse reads in the *Samuel* account. See Section Two.

וּבַיִת יִבְנֶה־לְּךָ ה' — *That HASHEM will build a house for you.* You intended to build a house for My name — in that measure will be your reward. God announces to you that He will give you a son who will rule after you and occupy Israel's throne in your place, thus establishing a royal house (*Mefaresh*). In this phrase God announces to David the continuity of the Davidic line. It is this promise which prompts David's outpouring of gratitude in the prayer which is recorded in vs. 16-27.

Metzudos sees this promise as designed to comfort David for the hurt of having been denied permission to build the Temple. God's promises to David are so great that the fact that He does not let him build the Temple should not matter.

Samuel has בַּיִת יַעֲשֶׂה לָּךְ, *will make a house for You,* instead of יִבְנֶה לָּךְ, *will build a house for You.* Commentators offer no explanation. It is possible that the word יִבְנֶה, *build,* is substituted here because *Chronicles* made use of the idiom וַיַּעַשׂ לוֹ בָתִּים with a different connotation at 15:1 (see there and Section Two p. 426).

11. וְהָיָה כִּי־מָלְאוּ יָמֶיךָ — *And it shall be when your time will have come* [lit. *when your days have been filled*]. This will not happen soon. I shall wait until your days are full and complete before passing your throne on to your son (*Mefaresh*).

לָלֶכֶת עִם־אֲבֹתֶיךָ — *To go the way of your fathers* [lit. *to walk with your fathers*]. *Samuel* has וְשָׁכַבְתָּ אֶת אֲבֹתֶיךָ, *and you shall lie with your fathers.* See Section Two.

אֲשֶׁר יִהְיֶה מִבָּנֶיךָ — *Who shall be from among your sons. Samuel* has אֲשֶׁר יֵצֵא מִמֵּעֶיךָ, *who will come forth from your insides.*

13. This verse telescopes two verses in *Samuel* into one.

Chronicles		Samuel	
13(a) אֲנִי אֶהְיֶה־לּוֹ לְאָב וְהוּא יִהְיֶה־לִּי לְבֵן, *I will be a father to him and he shall be a son to Me.*		14(a) אֲנִי אֶהְיֶה־לּוֹ לְאָב וְהוּא יִהְיֶה־לִּי לְבֵן, *I will be a father to him and he shall be a son to Me*	
		(b) אֲשֶׁר בְּהַעֲוֹתוֹ וְהֹכַחְתִּיו בְּשֵׁבֶט אֲנָשִׁים וּבְנִגְעֵי בְּנֵי אָדָם, *that if he sins, I will chasten him with the rod of men and with the afflictions of mankind.*	
(b) וְחַסְדִּי לֹא־אָסִיר מֵעִמּוֹ, *I will not*		15(a) וְחַסְדִּי לֹא־יָסוּר מִמֶּנּוּ, *But My*	

that HASHEM will build a house for you. [11] *And it shall be when your time will have come to go the way of your fathers, I will raise up your offspring who shall be from among your sons to succeed you and I will establish his kingdom.* [12] *He shall build a house for Me and I will maintain his throne forever.* [13] *I will be a father to him and he shall be a son to Me: I will not remove My benevolence from him as I removed it from him who preceded you.* [14] *And I will install him in My house and in My kingdom forever, and his throne shall be established forever.'* [15] *In accordance with all these words and in*

Chronicles	Samuel
remove My benevolence from him	*benevolence shall not depart from him*
	(b) בַּאֲשֶׁר הֲסִרֹתִי מֵעִם שָׁאוּל, *as I removed it from Saul,*
(c) בַּאֲשֶׁר הֲסִירוֹתִי מֵאֲשֶׁר הָיָה לְפָנֶיךָ, *as I removed it from him who preceded you.*	(c) אֲשֶׁר הֲסִרֹתִי מִלְּפָנֶיךָ, *whom I removed from before you.*

The *Mefaresh*, following a previously stated thesis, writes that *Samuel* 14(b) is omitted in *Chronicles* because *Chronicles* wishes to avoid any reference which reflects badly upon David's dynasty (see comm. to 10:1).

However, a careful reading of the two passages will show that in spite of the similarity between the two, the differences may give the verse in *Chronicles* an entirely different thrust than that of the two verses in *Samuel*.

The issue can best be clarified by defining the precise meaning of חֶסֶד, *benevolence*, in 15(a) of *Samuel* and 13(b) of *Chronicles*. This is never to be taken away from David as it was once taken away from Saul. But how was it taken away from Saul? *Samuel* answers in 15(c): his kingship was terminated. This answer is missing entirely in *Chronicles*.

We can paraphrase v. 15 in *Samuel* thus: I will never take away Solomon's kingship as I once took away Saul's kingship. Given this we read vs. 14 and 15 together as follows: I will be a father to Solomon; he will be My son. Even if he is ever exposed to the punishing rod and afflictions of his antagonists in punishment for his sins, it will never result in a permanent break in his rule. His throne will never be taken from him as it was once taken from Saul.

By contrast, *Chronicles* says nothing about Saul losing his kingship. The חֶסֶד, *benevolence*, which Saul lost but which will never be taken from Solomon may thus well refer to the state of being possessed by the spirit of God. *I Samuel*

16:14 teaches that: ... *the spirit of HASHEM departed from Saul* (סָרָה מֵעִם שָׁאוּל, as in our ... בַּאֲשֶׁר הֲסִירוֹתִי), *and an evil spirit from before HASHEM possessed him.* Here, God promises that His spirit shall never depart from Solomon. In this context, reference to the fact that he might well be exposed to *rods and afflictions* at the hand of his enemies has no place.

מֵאֲשֶׁר הָיָה לְפָנֶיךָ — *From him who preceded you.* Saul is not mentioned by name as he is in *Samuel*. As a king he had failed, and in *Samuel*, where his rule is detailed and contrasted to that of David, there is no reason to cover up this failure.

As a man, however, his greatness in many ways rivaled that of David (*Moed Kattan* 16b), and so David could not have wished to hear his spiritual downfall explicated. It is with exquisite sensitivity that *Chronicles* blocks out from Nathan's message the mention of Saul's name, which David would not have wanted to hear. See further in Section Two.

14. בְּבֵיתִי וּבְמַלְכוּתִי — *In My house and in My kingdom. Samuel* has: וְנֶאְמַן בֵּיתְךָ וּמַמְלַכְתְּךָ, *Your [David's] house and your kingship will be secured.* See Section Two.

עַד־עוֹלָם — *Forever.* For his children after him (*Metzudos*).

15. כְּכֹל הַדְּבָרִים הָאֵלֶּה — *In accordance with all these words.* Although originally Nathan had agreed with David's suggestion (v. 2), he was not ashamed to retract his words and to convey God's message of refusal (*Metzudos*).

טז דָּוִיד: וַיָּבֹא הַמֶּלֶךְ דָּוִיד וַיֵּשֶׁב לִפְנֵי יהוה

וַיֹּאמֶר מִי----אֲנִי יהוה אֱלֹהִים וּמִי בֵיתִי כִּי הֲבִיאֹתַנִי

יז עַד-הֲלֹם: וַתִּקְטַן זֹאת בְּעֵינֶיךָ אֱלֹהִים וַתְּדַבֵּר עַל-בֵּית-

עַבְדְּךָ לְמֵרָחוֹק וּרְאִיתַנִי כְּתוֹר הָאָדָם הַמַּעֲלָה יהוה

◄§ David's Prayer of Gratitude

16-27. This section contains the prayers of thanksgiving which David offered to God in gratitude for the promise which Nathan had made that the kingship of Israel would be eternally vested in his family. It parallels the passage in *II Samuel* 7:18-29 but, once more, there are changes in the text which are sufficiently significant to reflect the particular perspective which *Chronicles* has shown throughout in its approach to the whole incident.

Whether here or in *Samuel*, however, this prayer is somewhat puzzling. Why does David make no mention of the Temple? Why no word of his submission to God's decree of denial? Why no word to express his joy that his own frustrated aspirations would yet come to fruition through his son Solomon? It seems as though the outpouring of gratitude for the perpetuation of the kingship has submerged the idea of the Temple — which had previously been central to David's thinking — completely.

Perhaps we may surmise as follows: When God assured David of Israel's kingship in perpetuity, the implication of this promise went far beyond whatever individual satisfaction David may have derived from this. Jeremiah speaks of David's kingship as a cosmic necessity: *Thus says HASHEM: If I were to break My covenant with day and night, that day and night would no more come in their appointed time; then also would My covenant with David break — that he should have a son reigning upon his throne (Jeremiah 33:20, 21).* That cosmic necessity can be nothing other than the Messianic era, the focus of world history, the purpose and justification of creation. That Messianic era coalesces around the Messianic king, scion of Israel's royal house and, from the moment that David was identified as progenitor of that kingly line, identified absolutely with David himself. In the moment that David was

promised the kingship he was plucked from the temporal limitations of his physical existence and transformed into a figure of eternity. The man who had functioned as king of Israel became the kingship of Israel incarnate, in whose bosom burned the spark which God's providence, through the agency of the movement of history, would one day fan into the Messianic flame.

The building of a Temple may well be the fulfillment of any man's life. No individual can possibly look upon a more exalted *raison d'être* than to have been instrumental in bringing the manifestation of the Divine Presence to a permanent place in Israel. But in the long-range perspective of eternity, even the Temple itself becomes but a milestone along the road to the fulfillment of God's purpose. More than God wishes to dwell in a house, He wishes to dwell in Israel's hearts. It is the function of the Messiah to make the hearts of Israel the true *House of HASHEM*, the true focus of Godliness on earth, to which the Temple will be only secondary in significance (see ArtScroll *Ezekiel*, prefatory remarks to ch. 48, pps. 747-751, for a fuller discussion).

It was a different David who poured out his heart in gratitude before God than the man who had wanted so much to be the builder of God's Temple. Before Nathan's prophecy he had been an individual whose life would have reached its pinnacle with the construction of the Temple. After Nathan had spoken David became fused with the eternal Israel; the 'Temple' he would build was even greater than the one he had once envisioned.

16. וַיָּבֹא הַמֶּלֶךְ דָּוִיד וַיֵּשֶׁב לִפְנֵי ה' — *And King David came and sat down before HASHEM.* He sat down before the Ark *(Rashi).* [To sit down before the Ark is considered as sitting down *before HASHEM* since the Ark is the focus of God's presence on earth.][1]

Our verse serves as the basis for the ruling that no one but kings from the

---

1. Commentators to *Samuel* and *Chronicles* all seem to agree with *Rashi* that *before HASHEM* here is to be taken as *before the Ark.* A difficulty, however, arises in light of the Sages citing our verse as the

accordance with all this vision did Nathan speak to David. ¹⁶ *And King David came and sat down before HASHEM and said: 'Who am I, O HASHEM God, and who is my house that You have brought me to this point?* ¹⁷ *And this was still too little in Your eyes, O God, so that You spoke concerning the house of Your servant into the distant future, and You have seen me as a man of noble nature, O HASHEM,*

Davidic line is permitted to sit in the Temple courtyard *(Yoma* 25a). Apparently, the Sages assume that the text would not have made an issue of the fact that David sat before *Hashem* if this would not have had some halachic significance.

כִּי הֲבִיאֹתַנִי עַד־הֲלֹם — *That You have brought me to this point.* הֲלֹם is an adverb of place. Thus, for example, *Exodus* 3:5: אַל־תִּקְרַב הֲלֹם, *do not approach hither.* Here it is used figuratively in the sense of *to this point of dignity and greatness.* David is thanking God for having granted him the gift of kingship. [Based on this, *Zevachim* 102a derives from our verse that whenever הֲלֹם is used in Scripture it carries a connotation of kingship (אֵין הֲלֹם אֶלָּא מַלְכוּת).]

At this point he is talking about his personal kingship. The gift of the kingship being granted to his family in perpetuity is mentioned in the next verse.

17. וַתִּקְטַן זֹאת בְּעֵינֶיךָ אֱלֹהִים — *And this was still too little in Your eyes, O God.* As if making me king was not a sufficient kindness, you went even further —

וַתְּדַבֵּר עַל־בֵּית־עַבְדְּךָ לְמֵרָחוֹק — *So that You spoke concerning the house of Your servant into the distant future.*

The promise was not limited to me but

extended into the future. My kingship is to be passed on to my descendants forever *(Mefaresh; Metzudos).*

וּרְאִיתַנִי כְּתוֹר הָאָדָם הַמַּעֲלָה — *And You have seen me as a man of noble nature.* תּוֹר is obscure. We find it used as a necklace in *Shir HaShirim* 1:10, and *Radak* suggests there that it describes the beautiful way in which the various ornaments on the necklace are arranged. Thus it suggests the smooth interaction of the qualities or properties of a given object or series of objects. Used in connection with a man, it would describe the harmony with which his various characteristics interact with one another — hence, his *nature.*

Radak's interpretation of the phrase is: You have looked upon me as having the nature of an exalted person, when, in fact, I am lowly and undeserving.

Samuel has וְזֹאת תּוֹרַת הָאָדָם. There, too, *Radak* takes תּוֹרָה to mean *nature* [תּוֹר in the feminine form, תּוֹרָה] and interprets the phrase as a rhetorical exclamation: The kindness You have shown me *befits a noble man!* [The definite article הָ makes הָאָדָם equal אָדָם הַמַּעֲלָה of our phrase.] The exclamation is meant to imply: but not one as undeserving as I am. Thus, the two phrases have essentially the same meaning. See Section Two for further explanation.

source for the halachah that kings from the Davidic line were specially privileged in that they were allowed to sit while everyone else was required to stand in the Temple courtyard. Sitting before the Ark, which was at that time in Jerusalem (16:1), was not the same as sitting in the Temple courtyard, which was then located in Giveon.

Ritva to *Yoma* 25a derives from the use of our verse as the source for the permission that even while the Tabernacle was in its temporary locations of Shiloh, Nov, or Giveon, its courtyard had the legal status of עֲזָרָה, *Temple courtyard.* He evidently thinks that the words *before HASHEM* of our verse mean that David went to Giveon to offer up his prayer and not before the Ark in Jerusalem.

Perhaps *Rashi* and those commentators who think that David sat before the Ark assume that the prohibition to sit in the Temple courtyard derives from the presence of the Ark in the Holy of Holies. Therefore, although there was no formal courtyard in the tent which David erected before the Ark, the analogy may still be made. If David was allowed to sit before the Ark, he would also be allowed to sit in the courtyard. The difficulty with this theory is that although there was no Ark in the Second Temple, the Talmud (cf. *Yoma* 25a) applies this ban to sitting in that Temple's courtyard as well.

According to both explanations, this dispensation is based on the permanence of the Davidic monarchy, for which reason it was not accorded to any of the other Jewish kings [e.g., Saul or the kings of the Northern Kingdom; see *Rashi* and *Radak* to *I Kings* 12:27, from *Sanhedrin* 101b]. In this context, then, it is entirely appropriate that our verse should use הַמֶּלֶךְ דָּוִיד, *King David,* where up to now the title had not been used. This act of sitting down before HASHEM was an expression of the just-granted permanent status of this kingship and this is reflected in the text.

יח אֱלֹהִים: מַה־יּוֹסִיף עוֹד דָּוִיד אֵלֶיךָ לְכָבוֹד אֶת־עַבְדֶּךָ
יט וְאַתָּה אֶת־עַבְדְּךָ יָדָעְתָּ: יהוה בַּעֲבוּר עַבְדְּךָ וּכְלִבְּךָ
עָשִׂיתָ אֵת כָּל־הַגְּדוּלָּה הַזֹּאת לְהֹדִיעַ אֶת־כָּל־הַגְּדֻלּוֹת:
כ יהוה אֵין כָּמוֹךָ וְאֵין אֱלֹהִים זוּלָתֶךָ בְּכֹל אֲשֶׁר־שָׁמַעְנוּ
כא בְּאָזְנֵינוּ: וּמִי כְּעַמְּךָ יִשְׂרָאֵל גּוֹי אֶחָד בָּאָרֶץ אֲשֶׁר הָלַךְ
הָאֱלֹהִים לִפְדּוֹת לוֹ עָם לָשׂוּם לְךָ שֵׁם גְּדֻלּוֹת וְנֹרָאוֹת
כב לְגָרֵשׁ מִפְּנֵי עַמְּךָ אֲשֶׁר־פָּדִיתָ מִמִּצְרַיִם גּוֹיִם: וַתִּתֵּן
אֶת־עַמְּךָ יִשְׂרָאֵל לְךָ לְעָם עַד־עוֹלָם וְאַתָּה יהוה הָיִיתָ
כג לָהֶם לֵאלֹהִים: וְעַתָּה יהוה הַדָּבָר אֲשֶׁר דִּבַּרְתָּ עַל־עַבְדְּךָ
כד וְעַל־בֵּיתוֹ יֵאָמֵן עַד־עוֹלָם וַעֲשֵׂה כַּאֲשֶׁר דִּבַּרְתָּ: וְיֵאָמֵן
וְיִגְדַּל שִׁמְךָ עַד־עוֹלָם לֵאמֹר יהוה צְבָאוֹת אֱלֹהֵי יִשְׂרָאֵל
כה אֱלֹהִים לְיִשְׂרָאֵל וּבֵית־דָּוִיד עַבְדְּךָ נָכוֹן לְפָנֶיךָ: כִּי אַתָּה
אֱלֹהַי גָּלִיתָ אֶת־אֹזֶן עַבְדְּךָ לִבְנוֹת לוֹ בָּיִת עַל־כֵּן מָצָא

18. ... מַה־יּוֹסִיף עוֹד דָּוִיד אֵלֶיךָ — *What more can David proceed to ask of You* ... What other requests does David need to make (*Mefaresh*)?

לְכָבוֹד אֶת־עַבְדֶּךָ — *To honor Your servant.* This phrase continues the previous one: What more should David ask to increase his honor (*Mefaresh; Metzudos*)?

וְאַתָּה אֶת עַבְדְּךָ יָדָעְתָּ — *When You know Your servant.* When You know me so well that You grant me my wishes without my ever having to ask for them (*Mefaresh; Metzudos*).

Rashi (*Samuel*) takes ידע in the sense of *evince an interest.* Thus: *What more could David ask of You ... when You have given me all my needs.*

19. בַּעֲבוּר עַבְדְּךָ — *For Your servant's sake.* There are several changes in the next two verses from the corresponding section in *Samuel.* See Section Two.

וּכְלִבְּךָ — *And in accordance with Your heart.* You did what You did because it was Your wish, not because I deserved it (*Rashi; Metzudos*).

The expression may derive from *I Samuel* 13:14 where, when Saul was disqualified from the kingship, he was told that God would ... *search out a man in accordance with His heart* (אִישׁ כִּלְבָבוֹ). David recognizes now that he is that man whom God had described in those terms (*H. Biberfeld* in *David, King of Israel*).

לְהֹדִיעַ אֶת־כָּל־הַגְּדֻלּוֹת — *To make known all the greatness. Rashi* to *Samuel*, which has לְהוֹדִיעַ אֶת עַבְדֶּךָ, *to make known to Your servant*, remarks: To let me know the great promise of my future.

20. ה' אֵין כָּמוֹךָ — *HASHEM, there is none like You.* If there were anyone at all like You we would be able to form some idea of the extent of Your wisdom by contrasting it to him. As it is, there is no one like You (*Metzudos*).

Samuel has: עַל כֵּן גָּדַלְתָּ ה' אֱלֹהִים כִּי אֵין כָּמוֹךָ. See Section Two.

וְאֵין אֱלֹהִים זוּלָתֶךָ — *And there is no God besides You.* Even among the nations there is no other deity at all (*Mefaresh*).

בְּכֹל אֲשֶׁר־שָׁמַעְנוּ בְּאָזְנֵינוּ — *In all that we have heard with our ears.* All the wondrous things that we have heard concerning You confirm that there is none like You (*Metzudos*).

21. וּמִי כְּעַמְּךָ יִשְׂרָאֵל גּוֹי אֶחָד בָּאָרֶץ — *And who is like Your people, Israel, a unique nation in the land.* In what are they unique? The answer comes in the next part of the verse (*Mefaresh*). Israel's uniqueness expresses itself in their history — God moved heaven and earth to redeem them from slavery — and it is through them that His Presence is manifest on earth.

Metzudos interprets the phrase as continuing from the previous verse. Since God is unique, so too must be His people.

God. ¹⁸ *What more can David proceed to ask of You to honor Your servant when You know Your servant?* ¹⁹ HASHEM, *for Your servant's sake, and in accordance with Your heart, You have done this great thing, to make known all the greatness.* ²⁰ HASHEM, *there is none like You and there is no God besides You, in all that we have heard with our ears.* ²¹ *And who is like Your people, Israel, a unique nation in the land, whom God went to redeem for Himself as a nation; to provide a name for Yourself for greatness and awesomeness; to drive out nations from before Your people whom You redeemed from Egypt?* ²² *And You have set Your people Israel for Yourself as an eternal nation, and You,* HASHEM, *have been a God for them.* ²³ *Now,* HASHEM, *let the promise You made concerning Your servant and his house become true forever, and do as You have promised.* ²⁴ *And let it come true, and thus Your Name will become great forever, with people saying,* HASHEM, *Master of Legions, the God of Israel is God to Israel; and the house of Your servant David endures before You.* ²⁵ *For You, my God, have disclosed to Your servant that You will build a house for him;*

לָשׂוּם לְךָ שֵׁם גְּדֻלּוֹת וְנוֹרָאוֹת — *To provide a name for Yourself for greatness and awesomeness.* See Section Two concerning the change from *Samuel's* wording.

לְגָרֵשׁ ... גּוֹיִם — *To drive out nations.* The word גּוֹיִם, *nations,* at the end of the verse is to be read together with לְגָרֵשׁ, *to drive out.* It refers to the Canaanite nations who were driven out of the land so that Israel might settle there.

22. וַתִּתֵּן אֶת־עַמְּךָ יִשְׂרָאֵל לְךָ לְעָם עַד־עוֹלָם — *And You have set Your people Israel for Yourself as an eternal nation. Samuel* has וַתִּכוֹנֵן from כּוּן, *to establish.* There is a difference in connotation. וַתִּתֵּן seems to describe the original act of taking Israel as God's special people. וַתִּכוֹנֵן describes their continuing existence. They were not only *taken* but *established* as a people. This term is particularly appropriate for *Samuel,* where a special point is made of God's purpose to make a name for Himself (see Section Two), a purpose best fulfilled through Israel's permanent existence.

לְעָם עַד־עוֹלָם — *As an eternal nation.* At the Covenant Between the Pieces, Abraham was told that the land would not be his until the fourth generation, at which time the iniquity of the Emorites would be full (*Genesis* 15:16). The implication is that while God does not punish the Gentile nations without sufficient cause, He does not prevent their guilt from building up to

the point where they must be destroyed.

By contrast, Abraham was promised the land *for an everlasting possession* (17:8 there) which, according to *Ramban* (15:18 there), implies that even if they should ever be driven out of the land because of their sins, this would only be temporary; eventually they would return.

As explained in *Kuzari* (2:36-44), this contrast lies at the very essence of the difference between Israel and the nations. The destiny of God's will on earth is, as it were, so intimately tied to Israel that He will never permit Israel's sins to become so heavy as to require their destruction.

24. וְיֵאָמֵן וְיִגְדַּל שִׁמְךָ עַד־עוֹלָם לֵאמֹר ... — *And let it come true, and thus Your Name will become great forever, with people saying* ... By making Your promise concerning my house come true, Your Name will be made great forever, as people point to its fulfillment as proof that You are our God forever and that Your word may be relied upon to be unchanging (*Metzudos*).

Mefaresh sees וְיֵאָמֵן as being joined to וְיִגְדַּל, May Your name be [accepted as] *true and become great forever* ...

אֱלֹהִים לְיִשְׂרָאֵל — *Is God to Israel.* He directs their destiny in every detail. Compare *I Samuel* 17:46.

25. גָּלִיתָ אֶת־אֹזֶן עַבְדְּךָ — *You* ... *have disclosed to* [lit. *uncovered the ear of*] *Your servant.* This expression signifies

כו עַבְדְּךָ לְהִתְפַּלֵּל לְפָנֶיךָ: וְעַתָּה יהוה אַתָּה־הוּא הָאֱלֹהִים

כז וַתְּדַבֵּר עַל־עַבְדְּךָ הַטּוֹבָה הַזֹּאת: וְעַתָּה הוֹאַלְתָּ לְבָרֵךְ

אֶת־בֵּית עַבְדְּךָ לִהְיוֹת לְעוֹלָם לְפָנֶיךָ כִּי־אַתָּה יהוה

א בֵּרַכְתָּ וּמְבֹרָךְ לְעוֹלָם: וַיְהִי

---

broaching a subject [comp. *Ruth* 4:4]. David justifies his audacity in asking for the eternity of his monarchy by emphasizing that it was not he who first suggested the idea (*Metzudos*).

עַל־כֵּן — *Therefore* ... It is only for this reason that I presume to make my prayer (*Metzudos*).

26. אַתָּה־הוּא הָאֱלֹהִים — *You are the Almighty.* We have used *Almighty* instead of the usual *God* because of the context. David means that God is all powerful and therefore in a position to bring His promise to fulfillment (*Metzudos*).

וַתְּדַבֵּר עַל־עַבְדְּךָ — *And You have spoken ... for Your servant.* Although the prophecy had not been to David directly but had come to him through Nathan, David

realizes that Nathan, as God's true prophet, could be relied upon to convey God's intention. It is therefore as though God Himself had spoken to him (*Metzudos*).

27. This final verse, which *Chronicles* makes as a statement, is given in *Samuel* in the form of a prayer. See Section Two.

וְעַתָּה הוֹאַלְתָּ ... — *Now, You have desired ...* The root יאל is used in Scripture in two different senses. It can mean *to begin* and *to desire*. *Rashi* and other commentators render *desire*, and we have used this in our translation. *Targum*, however, renders *begin*.

וּמְבֹרָךְ לְעוֹלָם — *It is blessed forever.* Translation follows *Mefaresh*. *Targum* and *Metzudos* see the phrase as a prayer: *May it be blessed forever.*

XVIII

◄§ David Subdues his Neighbors

Our chapter parallels *II Samuel* ch. 8. The chapter contains the account of a number of successful campaigns which David waged against Israel's neighbors. The introduction in v. 1 — וַיְהִי אַחֲרֵי כֵן, *and it was after this* — indicates some connection with the events described in the previous chapters. This connection requires further exploration.

Malbim explains as follows: From *II Samuel* 7:1 it appears that David's initiative in suggesting that he should build the Temple derived from his thinking that the degree of tranquillity required by the Torah had already been attained (see Section Two to ch. 17). God's message through Nathan had revealed to him that there was much still to be done and many battles still to be fought. Therefore, David now took up arms, and where till now he had satisfied himself with repulsing the incursions which Israel's enemies made into the land, he now undertook a series of aggressive wars designed to carry the fight into enemy territory, so that those belligerent neighbors could be subdued and subjugated to Jewish control. In this way, by the time Solomon became king there would be perfect peace and the long-awaited building of the Temple could begin. Moreover, the spoils taken in these wars could be set aside for use in the building of the Temple, thereby affording David the opportunity of at least assisting in the building in a positive way.

In order to obtain a better understanding of these wars, we should analyze the basis for David's original misconception. What had made him think that, in fact, the state described in the Torah's words, *when God shall have given you rest from all your enemies from round about and you dwell in tranquillity* (*Deuteronomy* 12:10), had come about, and what was it that God had shown him to be fallacious in his thinking?

The Torah speaks only of God having given rest from all enemies — not of having conquered them. It is entirely conceivable that if all Israel's enemies had come to recognize Israel's unique destiny and special relationship with God, and had desired to win her friendship instead of hating and fighting her, that too would have brought about the required state of peace. That being so, we can readily understand David's thinking. He had every reason to suppose that, in fact, the time had come when Israel's enemies were

therefore Your servant has ventured to pray before You. ²⁶ *Now,*
HASHEM, You are the Almighty, and You have spoken of this
goodness for Your servant. ²⁷ *Now, You have desired to bless the*
house of Your servant that it may remain before You forever; and
because You, HASHEM, have blessed it, it is blessed forever.'

willing to recognize her role in history and to seek out her friendship. This, from the fact that even her traditional archenemy, Edom, as represented by Churam, king of Tyre, had extended such a gesture of amity as sending material and workmen to build the new king's palace (see Section Two to ch. 14). Surely, this subjugation of Edom seemed to presage an era in which no one would anymore feel the need to lift a sword against Israel. Even the Philistine wars which followed immediately upon this event could be viewed as affirming this interpretation of events, for those wars were viewed by the Sages as harbingers of the Gogian wars against the Messiah (see Section Two to ch. 14) — the final, futile attempt to deny reality, the last flickering of the flame before its extinction. David would have been justified in thinking that after those conquests there would be no more wars.

Thus David's thinking. During a time when, in fact, no one was attacking Israel he thought that, following Churam's example, all Israel's neighbors were now at peace with her — a foretaste of the Messianic era. God revealed to him that this was not so. Israel's neighbors were still her enemies and they would have to be subdued by military might. The era of peace and understanding had not yet come.

But if that is so, then this must have been a shattering revelation to David. As Solomon was later to teach *(Proverbs 16:7): When God looks with favor upon a man's ways — even his enemies make peace with him.* If, indeed, he would still have to fight so many wars, did this not mean that God did not yet look with favor upon his life? Indeed, it showed that David's personal, inner battles were, in fact, far from over (see Section Two to ch. 17). It would not be until just before his death that he would achieve the inner tranquillity of 'God's beloved' which was to be the hallmark of his son Solomon's life. [See *II Samuel* 12:25 where Nathan, in God's behalf, called Solomon יְדִידְיָה, *beloved of God.*][1]

Against this background it is possible to view these campaigns from two perspectives. On the one hand David, by subjugating his potential enemies, was consolidating his rule and creating the peace and tranquillity which were required if Solomon was to build the Temple. On the other hand, these battles were outer manifestations of David's inner conflicts, and his victories were milestones on his path to the inner harmony which would find expression in the life of his son Solomon. From this perspective, their significance must be determined entirely by the degree to which they can be viewed as preparations for that ultimate point at which David would find vindication through Solomon. It is possible

1. In light of this it is possible to explain the difficult *Psalm* 60 which David sang ... *when he made war against Aram Naharaim and Aram Tzovah and Yoav returned and smote Edom ...,* that is, on the occasion of the events described in our chapter.

We would have expected a psalm composed on the occasion of such major triumphs to be a song of jubilation, extolling God for the victory He granted over Israel's enemies. Instead, we are surprised by the introductory verses which would be more in place in a dirge bemoaning a defeat. *O God, You forsook us, You breached us, You were angry with us, O restore us* ... Even when the psalm eventually sings of the victories (v. 8ff), it intersperses a verse of utter depression: *Did not You, O God, forsake us and not go forth, O God, with our legions?*

Commentators offer a variety of explanations (see ArtScroll *Psalms* there), but all these assume calamities which are nowhere hinted at in the text. An interpretation which takes the psalm as it is offered would be forced to see the wars, in and of themselves, to be the source of David's ambivalent feelings. As we have understood the implications of the past few chapters in *Chronicles* (see Section Two), this is indeed the case. 'If God had indeed been present in our camp, not a single soldier would have fallen' (see *Ramban* to *Numbers* 21:1). The wars of Israel should in no way be normal ones in which both victor and vanquished suffer casualties. That David won the campaigns described here was small comfort for the fact that he realized that because of his own failings they fell far short of the unmitigated קִדּוּשׁ הַשֵּׁם, *sanctification of God's Name,* which Israel's wars would ideally be. And so the psalm reflects an ambivalence. David's joy at his mighty victories is tempered by his sorrows at the imperfect state in which he felt himself and his armies to be.

אַחֲרֵי־כֵן וַיַּ֤ךְ דָּוִיד֙ אֶת־פְּלִשְׁתִּ֔ים וַיַּכְנִיעֵ֑ם וַיִּקַּ֥ח אֶת־גַּ֛ת

ב וּבְנֹתֶ֖יהָ מִיַּ֣ד פְּלִשְׁתִּֽים: וַיַּ֣ךְ אֶת־מוֹאָ֑ב וַיִּהְי֤וּ מוֹאָב֙ עֲבָדִ֔ים

ג לְדָוִ֖יד נֹשְׂאֵ֥י מִנְחָֽה: וַיַּ֥ךְ דָּוִ֛יד אֶת־הֲדַדְעֶ֥זֶר מֶֽלֶךְ־צוֹבָ֖ה

ד חֲמָ֑תָה בְּלֶכְתּ֕וֹ לְהַצִּ֥יב יָד֖וֹ בִּנְהַר־פְּרָֽת: וַיִּלְכֹּ֨ד דָּוִ֜יד מִמֶּ֗נּוּ

אֶ֣לֶף רֶ֗כֶב וְשִׁבְעַ֤ת אֲלָפִים֙ פָּרָשִׁ֔ים וְעֶשְׂרִ֥ים אֶ֖לֶף אִ֑ישׁ

---

that these two perspectives form the respective views which *Samuel* and *Chronicles* take of the events recorded here.

1. וַיְהִי אַחֲרֵי־כֵן — *It was after this.* After David had intended to build the Temple and God had told him not to, David decided that he would at least organize and prepare everything so that when the time came for his son to build it everything would be ready. The text now concentrates on showing how David prepared everything — fighting his enemies and setting aside the spoils for the building of the Temple (*Mefaresh*).

וַיַּךְ דָּוִיד אֶת־פְּלִשְׁתִּים — *That David smote the Philistines.* David had already repulsed two Philistine attacks, as recounted in ch. 14. This time he invaded their territory and took one of their main cities.

2. וַיַּךְ אֶת־מוֹאָב — *And he smote Moab.* David was allowed to attack Moab although Moses had been forbidden to do so (*Deuteronomy* 2:9) because Moab had forfeited their right to the Torah's protection by hiring Balaam to curse the Jews (*Bereishis Rabbah* 74:15).

In the case of the Moabite campaign, *Chronicles* omits a significant passage from the parallel section in *Samuel*:

Chronicles	Samuel
2(a) וַיַּךְ אֶת־מוֹאָב, *And he smote Moab*	2(a) וַיַּךְ אֶת־מוֹאָב, *And he smote Moab*
(b)	(b) וַיְמַדְּדֵם בַּחֶבֶל הַשְׁכֵּב אוֹתָם אַרְצָה, *and he measured them with rope laid down on the ground*
(c)	(c) וַיְמַדֵּד שְׁנֵי־חֲבָלִים לְהָמִית וּמְלֹא הַחֶבֶל לְהַחֲיוֹת, *and he measured two ropes to put to death and the length of one to keep alive*
(d) וַיִּהְיוּ מוֹאָב עֲבָדִים לְדָוִיד נֹשְׂאֵי מִנְחָה, *and Moab became tribute-paying servants to David*	(d) וַתְּהִי מוֹאָב לְדָוִד לַעֲבָדִים נֹשְׂאֵי מִנְחָה, *and Moab became tribute-paying servants to David*

Samuel tells that after David had conquered Moab he *measured them with a rope,* laying them down on the ground and condemning two thirds of them to death and allowing one third to live. Why does *Chronicles* omit this passage?

Furthermore, why did David undertake this seemingly cruel and arbitrary action? According to *Pirkei d'R' Eliezer*, David wanted to punish the Moabites for a singularly vicious and vindictive crime which they had committed. When David was fleeing from Saul, he had asked the

Moabite king to allow David's parents and brothers to remain with him and be protected by him. Mindful of his own descent from Moab through his ancestress Ruth, David had thought that his family would be in safe hands. The Moabite king agreed to extend his protection to David's family (*I Samuel* 22:4) but subsequently murdered them all with the exception of one of David's brothers. David, then, was avenging the murder of his family.

The selection was also not as arbitrary as would at first appear. As *Zohar* to *Balak*

It was after this that David smote the Philistines and subdued them; and he took Gath and its dependencies from the Philistines. ² And he smote Moab, and Moab became tribute-paying servants to David. ³ And David smote Hadadezer, king of Tzovah, towards Chamath as he was going to establish his presence at the River Euphrates. ⁴ David captured from him one thousand chariots, seven thousand riders and twenty thousand infantry. David hamstrung all

(190a) teaches, Divine Providence assured that only the completely wicked Moabites were condemned to death by this system.

In spite of all this, it is clear that David's action in this matter was prompted by a strict adherence to דִּין, justice, untempered by רַחֲמִים, mercy. Now, as Ramban (Numbers 16:22) teaches, it was this very quality of David's, that he was an אִישׁ מִשְׁפָּט וּמַחֲזִיק בְּמִדַּת הַדִּין, a man of law, adhering to strict justice, which disqualified David from building the Temple, the very purpose of which was to elicit God's mercy upon His people.

We may therefore conclude that however justified David's actions were in this matter, his dealings with the Moabites could in no way be interpreted as being a positive step in the preparation for the building of the Temple. Consequently, Chronicles, which looks upon the campaigns described in our chapters from the perspective of their being steps in the preparation for the building of the Temple (see prefatory remarks), omits this part.

⤳ The War against Aram

3. חֲמָתָה — Towards Chamath. Chamath was a country whose king, To'u, had been a longstanding enemy of Hadadezer (v. 10). As David headed northward in order to

establish a presence near the Euphrates (see below), he met the Tzovian forces.

בְּלֶכְתּוֹ לְהַצִּיב יָדוֹ בִּנְהַר פְּרָת — As he was going to establish his presence at the River Euphrates. The phrase lends itself to two interpretations. Rashi (to Samuel), Radak and Metzudos see the subject of בְּלֶכְתּוֹ, as he was going, as Hadadezer; Gra sees it as David.

If, indeed, it refers to David we understand well why the point is made. As in all the other campaigns described in this chapter, David was attempting to consolidate his hegemony over the entire area, and he was moving north when Hadadezer met him.

If the subject is Hadadezer, it is less easy to see why this is of interest to us. Radak suggests that in his move towards the Euphrates, Hadadezer was encroaching upon Israelite territory, and this caused David to attack him. But it is difficult to reconcile this with the geographical position of Aram Tzovah (Aleppo), which lies well to the north of any Israelite territory of which we are aware.

4. אֶלֶף רֶכֶב וְשִׁבְעַת אֲלָפִים פָּרָשִׁים — One thousand chariots, seven thousand riders. There is a significant discrepancy between our verse and the one in Samuel.

Chronicles	Samuel
4(a) וַיִּלְכֹּד דָּוִיד מִמֶּנּוּ, David captured from him	4(a) וַיִּלְכֹּד דָּוִד מִמֶּנּוּ, David captured from him
(b) אֶלֶף רֶכֶב, one thousand chariots,	(b)
(c) וְשִׁבְעַת אֲלָפִים פָּרָשִׁים, seven thousand riders,	(c) אֶלֶף וּשְׁבַע־מֵאוֹת פָּרָשִׁים, one thousand and seven hundred riders,
(d) וְעֶשְׂרִים אֶלֶף אִישׁ רַגְלִי, and twenty thousand infantry.	(d) וְעֶשְׂרִים אֶלֶף אִישׁ רַגְלִי, and twenty thousand infantry

Samuel makes no mention of the רֶכֶב, chariots, which Chronicles has in (b). Additionally, under (c) Samuel lists 1700

riders while Chronicles has 7000.

Radak suggests that the two accounts complement one another and that

רַגְלִי וַיְעַקֵּר דָּוִד אֶת־כָּל־הָרֶכֶב וַיּוֹתֵר מִמֶּנּוּ מֵאָה רָכֶב:
ה וַיָּבֹא אֲרַם דַּרְמֶשֶׂק לַעְזוֹר לַהֲדַדְעֶזֶר מֶלֶךְ צוֹבָה וַיַּךְ
ו דָוִד בַּאֲרָם עֶשְׂרִים־וּשְׁנַיִם אֶלֶף אִישׁ: וַיָּשֶׂם דָּוִד בַּאֲרַם
דַּרְמֶשֶׂק וַיְהִי אֲרָם לְדָוִיד עֲבָדִים נֹשְׂאֵי מִנְחָה וַיּוֹשַׁע
ז יהוה לְדָוִיד בְּכֹל אֲשֶׁר הָלָךְ: וַיִּקַּח דָּוִיד אֵת שִׁלְטֵי הַזָּהָב
ח אֲשֶׁר הָיוּ עַל עַבְדֵי הֲדַדְעֶזֶר וַיְבִיאֵם יְרוּשָׁלָ͏ִם: וּמִטִּבְחַת
וּמִכּוּן עָרֵי הֲדַדְעֶזֶר לָקַח דָּוִיד נְחֹשֶׁת רַבָּה מְאֹד בָּה ׀
עָשָׂה שְׁלֹמֹה אֶת־יָם הַנְּחֹשֶׁת וְאֶת־הָעַמּוּדִים וְאֵת כְּלֵי
ט הַנְּחֹשֶׁת: וַיִּשְׁמַע תֹּעוּ מֶלֶךְ חֲמָת כִּי הִכָּה דָוִיד

Chronicles simply fills in information not given in *Samuel*. Thus, it mentions the chariots which *Samuel* omits. Furthermore, *Samuel* lists only the important officers among the horsemen, of which there were 1700, while *Chronicles* lists all the riders, of which there were 7000.

Ralbag explains that the 1700 of *Samuel* were captured on the battlefield. Later, when David entered Hadadezer's cities, he captured many more.

Malbim believes that the number 1700 [written as אֶלֶף וּשְׁבַע מֵאוֹת, *one thousand and seven hundred*] is made up of the 1000 chariots mentioned in *Chronicles* (b) and seven hundred horsemen who were in command of each team of horses. Each of these comprised ten horses and therefore ten riders, which makes the 7000 in *Chronicles*. Since *Samuel* deals with the commanding officers who controlled the whole chariot, it makes sense to give the chariots and officers in one number of 1700. *Chronicles*, which lists the individual riders, each of whom was involved with only one horse, lists horses (רֶכֶב) and riders separately.

וַיְעַקֵּר דָּוִיד אֶת־כָּל־הָרָכֶב — *David hamstrung all the chariot horses.* The term רֶכֶב is used in this verse to refer both to the chariots and the teams needed to operate them. Thus, David hamstrung all the horses but kept one hundred *chariots of them*, i.e., their teams.

The Torah forbids a king to own more horses than he needs to pull his chariots. To be accompanied by horses who are not pulling chariots is a sign of pride and arrogance which the Torah prohibits (see *Rambam, Hilchos Melachim* 3:3). For this reason David hamstrung all the horses

which he did not need and retained only the hundred teams which he was able to use (*Commentators*).

The process of hamstringing the horse must have caused them a great deal of pain, and most codifiers agree that it is forbidden by the Torah to cause an animal needless suffering.

In *Joshua* 11:6 we find God commanding Joshua to hamstring the horses which he was to capture in a battle with the Canaanites. *Tosafos* to *Avodah Zarah* 13a suggests that Joshua was allowed to do this only because it was a special decree from God. In David's case no such decree was given.

Perhaps David assumed that God's decree was not limited to the particular war for which it was made but was meant to apply to all wars which were to be fought in the long process of bringing peace to the country.

An alternative approach would be to say that the prohibition against inflicting pain on animals applies only to needless pain. If some useful purpose is served, as for example here where David's motive is to avoid transgressing the Torah law against having too many horses, it is permitted. This seems to be *Rashi's* opinion in *Avodah Zarah*. (See R' *Shimon Krasner's Nachalas Shimon* on *Joshua* ch. 37.)

5. אֲרַם דַּרְמֶשֶׂק — *Aram Darmesek.* Aram was a huge area with many districts, each of which had its own name. Thus, besides Aram Darmesek [Damascus], we have Aram Naharaim and Aram Maachah (19:6). Collectively all these places are simply known as Aram [see v. 12 and others, there] (*Radak* to *Samuel*).

6. וַיָּשֶׂם דָּוִיד בַּאֲרַם דַּרְמֶשֶׂק — *David then placed [governors] in Aram Darmesek.* The verse actually omits the word נְצִבִים, *governors*, between the words דָּוִיד and בַּאֲרָם, which the parallel passage in *Samuel* has. *Metzudos* implies that the word is left

18

5-9

the chariot horses except for one hundred chariots of them. 5 And Aram Darmesek came to help Hadadezer the king of Tzovah; and David slew twenty-two thousand men of Aram. 6 David then placed [governors] in Aram Darmesek, and Aram became tribute-paying servants to David; and HASHEM gave victory to David wherever he went. 7 And David took the gold shields borne by the servants of Hadadezer and brought them to Jerusalem. 8 And from Tivchath and Cun, the cities of Hadadezer, David captured huge quantities of copper; from these Solomon made the copper sea, the pillars and the copper vessels. 9 To'u, king of Chamath, heard that David had

out here because it is self-understood.[1] *Targum* inserts the word in order to make the meaning clear.

וַיְהִי אֲרָם לְדָוִיד עֲבָדִים — *And Aram became ... servants to David.* This statement seems to refer to Aram only. We find the forces of Hadadezer again ranged against David in ch. 19 and it is only at the end of that chapter that Hadadezer is finally subjugated.

וַיּוֹשַׁע ה׳ לְדָוִיד בְּכֹל אֲשֶׁר הָלָךְ — *And HASHEM gave victory to David wherever he went.* God was not pleased with David's conquest of Aram. He should have first cleared out the Canaanite pockets which remained in the land before he set his sights on territory outside the land. In the words of *Sifrei* (to *Deuteronomy* 11:24), his actions were שֶׁלֹּא כַּתּוֹרָה, *not in accordance with the Torah.* As a result of this, the territory which he conquered [which was later known as סוּרְיָא, *Suria*] never became part of Israel proper for halachic purposes, but was given the status of כִּבּוּשׁ יָחִיד, *an individual* [as opposed to a communal] *conquest.*

In the light of this tradition our verse must be understood that although David did not act in accordance with God's wishes

in this matter, God nevertheless helped him in his enterprise *(Malbim).*

◆§ David Consecrates the Spoils

7. וַיִּקַּח דָּוִיד ... וַיְבִיאֵם יְרוּשָׁלָיִם — *And David took ... and brought them to Jerusalem.* David brought the captured shields to Jerusalem and placed them in the vaults which contained the sacred property set aside for Temple use *(Radak, Samuel).*

8. וּמִטִּבְחַת וּמִכּוּן — *And from Tivchath and Cun. Samuel* has בֶּטַח, *Betach,* and בֵּרֹתַי, *Berothai. Radak* suggests that the cities may each have had two names and, moreover, he points out that טִבְחַת and בֶּטַח seem to be identical but with the letters inverted. *Malbim* thinks that the names of the cities may well have changed from the time that *Samuel* was written until the time that the *Chronicles* account was written.

... בָּהּ עָשָׂה שְׁלֹמֹה — *From these Solomon made ...* This phrase is understandably missing from *Samuel.* At the time *Samuel* was written this had not yet taken place.

9. וַיִּשְׁמַע תֹּעוּ ... — *To'u ... heard ...* It seems likely that this incident is recorded because of the valuables which To'u sent to David, which David subsequently set aside

1. *Samuel* tells how David established governors in Aram Darmesek (v. 6) and in Edom (v. 14). A careful reading reveals a subtle difference in the nuances of the two verses:
(6) וַיָּשֶׂם דָּוִד נְצִבִים בַּאֲרַם דַּמֶּשֶׂק, *And David placed governors in Aram Darmesek.*
(14) וַיָּשֶׂם בֶּאֱדוֹם נְצִבִים, *And he placed in Edom governors.*
In the case of Aram, the governors are mentioned before the location; in the case of Edom the location is mentioned first.
It is possible that the emphasis of the phrase lies on the earlier word. Verse 6 tells that David established governors in the territory which he had conquered. There is no particular significance in the fact that the territory was Aram. In the case of Edom, however, the emphasis is specifically that David was able to establish governors in Edom — Israel's archenemy with whose destiny Israel's own is so intimately bound.
As we shall see below, Israel's role vis-à-vis Edom is stressed much more in *Chronicles* than in *Samuel.* In the perspective of *Chronicles,* the governors which David established in Aram sink into absolute insignificance when contrasted with those which he established in Edom (v. 13).
The deemphasis of the governors of Aram, which *Samuel* accomplishes by varying the syntax, is brought out more sharply in *Chronicles* by omitting the word נְצִבִים, *governors,* entirely.

יח ' אֶת־כָּל־חֵיל הֲדַדְעֶזֶר מֶלֶךְ־צוֹבָה: וַיִּשְׁלַח אֶת־הֲדוֹרָם־

י־יב ק' לִשְׁאָל־ בְּנוֹ אֶל־הַמֶּלֶךְ־דָּוִיד °לִשְׁאָול־לוֹ לְשָׁלוֹם וּלְבָרֲכוֹ עַל

אֲשֶׁר נִלְחַם בַּהֲדַדְעֶזֶר וַיַּכֵּהוּ כִּי־אִישׁ מִלְחֲמוֹת תֹּעוּ הָיָה

יא הֲדַדְעֶזֶר וְכֹל כְּלֵי זָהָב וָכֶסֶף וּנְחֹשֶׁת: גַּם־אֹתָם הִקְדִּישׁ

הַמֶּלֶךְ דָּוִיד לַיהֹוָה עִם־הַכֶּסֶף וְהַזָּהָב אֲשֶׁר נָשָׂא מִכָּל־

הַגּוֹיִם מֵאֱדוֹם וּמִמּוֹאָב וּמִבְּנֵי עַמּוֹן וּמִפְּלִשְׁתִּים

יב וּמֵעֲמָלֵק: וְאַבְשַׁי בֶּן־צְרוּיָה הִכָּה אֶת־אֱדוֹם בְּגֵיא הַמֶּלַח

---

for the building of the Temple.

10. כִּי־אִישׁ מִלְחֲמוֹת תֹּעוּ הָיָה הֲדַדְעֶזֶר — *For Hadadezer had been To'u's enemy in war.* Mefaresh points out that this explains the mention of Chamath in v. 3. Hadadezer was on his way to wage war against To'u when David attacked him.

וְכֹל כְּלֵי זָהָב ... — *With all sorts of gold ... vessels.* The phrase implies that Hadoram brought all these precious vessels to David. *Samuel* makes this clearer by saying: וּבְיָדוֹ הָיוּ ..., *and with him were ...*

11. גַּם־אֹתָם הִקְדִּישׁ הַמֶּלֶךְ דָּוִיד לַה' — *Those, too, King David consecrated to HASHEM.* David not only consecrated the spoils of war; he also gave the gifts which Hadoram had brought in friendship to the sacred treasury.

מֵאֱדוֹם — *From Edom.* Samuel has *from Aram* and does not have *from Edom.* See comm. to next verse.
The war against Edom is taken up in the next verse.

וּמִמּוֹאָב — [And from] Moab. See v. 2.

וּמִבְּנֵי עַמּוֹן — [And from] Ammon. The wars against Ammon are taken up in ch. 19.
Radak (II Chronicles 20:1) points out that the nation of Ammon is invariably called בְּנֵי עַמּוֹן [lit. *the children of Ammon*]. [An exception is *Psalms* 83:8. In his view, when the plural עַמּוֹנִים is used to describe a nation — and this always occurs without the בְּנֵי — this refers to a different people who settled in Ammonite territory.] The individuals from Ammon, though, are known as עַמּוֹנִי, without בֶּן. R' Y. Danziger suggests that the reason goes back to the origins of the nation. When Lot's daughters conceived by their father (*Genesis* 19:30ff), the older called

her son מוֹאָב, *Moab,* but the younger used the name בֶּן עַמִּי, *ben Ammi.* The word בֶּן, *ben,* became a part of the name of the nation [and does not mean *the children of*], and is so used throughout Scripture.

וּמִפְּלִשְׁתִּים — [*And from*] *the Philistines.* See v. 1.

וּמֵעֲמָלֵק — *And* [*from*] *Amalek.* We do not find any wars which David waged against Amalek after he became king. However, in *I Samuel* ch. 30 there is an account of a campaign against Amalek while Saul was still king. In v. 20 there, there is mention of spoils which David took, and we must assume that it is to those spoils that our verse refers.

◈§ The Edomite War

12. וְאַבְשַׁי בֶּן־צְרוּיָה הִכָּה אֶת־אֱדוֹם בְּגֵיא הַמֶּלַח — *And Avshai the son of Tzeruiah smote Edom in the Valley of Salt.* This verse must be seen in contrast to its parallels in *Samuel* and *Psalms* 60(opposite page).

All three sources refer to a battle in the Valley of Salt (d), but where *Samuel* has it as a battle against Aram (c), the other two sources have it against Edom (c). It is unlikely that two different campaigns are meant and that these took place in the same location by coincidence, since both *Samuel* and *Chronicles* talk of smiting 18,000 men (e). But this number is also problematic since *Psalms,* apparently referring to the same battle, talks of 12,000 killed (e).

All three sources diverge from one another in the identity of the person who waged the battle (b). *Samuel* ascribes it to David, *Psalms* to Yoav, and *Chronicles* to Avshai.

Rashi to *Samuel* (and *Metzudos* here) quotes the opinion of the Sages that *Samuel* (and *Chronicles*) refers to one

smitten the entire army of Hadadezer, king of Tzovah. ¹⁰ And he sent his son Hadoram to King David to greet him and bless him for having fought Hadadezer and smitten him — for Hadadezer had been To'u's enemy in war — with all sorts of gold, silver and bronze vessels. ¹¹ Those, too, King David consecrated to HASHEM, together with the silver and gold which he carried off from all the nations; from Edom, Moab, Ammon, the Philistines and Amalek. ¹² And Avshai the son of Tzeruiah smote Edom in the Valley of Salt —

Chronicles	Psalms	Samuel
12(a)	2(a)	13(a) וַיַּעַשׂ דָּוִד שֵׁם, And David made a name [for himself],
(b) וְאַבְשַׁי בֶּן־צְרוּיָה, And Avshai the son of Tzeruiah	(b) וַיָּשָׁב יוֹאָב, and Yoav returned	(b) בְּשֻׁבוֹ, on his return
(c) הִכָּה אֶת־אֱדוֹם, smote Edom	(c) וַיַּךְ אֶת־אֱדוֹם, and smote Edom	(c) מֵהַכּוֹתוֹ אֶת־אֲרָם, from smiting Aram,
(d) בְּגֵיא הַמֶּלַח, in the Valley of Salt —	(d) בְּגֵיא־מֶלַח, in the Valley of Salt —	(d) בְּגִיא־מֶלַח, in the Valley of Salt —
(e) שְׁמוֹנָה עָשָׂר אָלֶף, eighteen thousand men.	(e) שְׁנֵים עָשָׂר אָלֶף, twelve thousand men.	(e) שְׁמוֹנָה עָשָׂר אָלֶף, eighteen thousand men.

battle in which 18,000 of the enemy were slain, while *Psalms* refers to another battle where 12,000 were killed. This latter battle was led by Yoav, while the former was directed by Avshai. Although *Samuel* ascribes this victory to David, this is because as king the battle was fought on his behalf and the victory was thus considered his. [It is common for Scripture to attribute a victory to a king although he did not necessarily lead the army.] The discrepancy between the two books as to the identity of the opponent may be simply solved. The enemy was Edom. *Samuel* does not identify the enemy as Aram but says only that he was engaged when David was *returning* from Aram. The fact that in the very next verse (14) *Samuel* states that David established governors in Edom makes this abundantly clear.

Radak, however, assumes that all three battles were one and the same. He suggests the following solution:

The war against Edom was waged at the same time as the one against Aram. [See *Psalms* 60: *When he made war against*

Aram Naharaim and Aram Tzovah, and Yoav returned and smote Edom in the Valley of Salt.] The total of 18,000 victims came from both nations together. The initial campaign was waged by Avshai, who killed six thousand. Subsequently Yoav took over [see *Psalms: And Yoav returned ...*] and killed another 12,000, making a total of 18,000. *Chronicles* ascribes the full total to Avshai because he was the first general to engage in that battle and it was really his war. *Samuel* credits the whole war to David because it was fought on his behalf.

Furthermore, *Samuel* describes the campaign as having taken place against Aram because the Edomites fought at the side of the Arameans in the Valley of Salt. It was thus part of the general Aramean campaign, although separate from the battles described in vs. 3-5. [For this reason the casualty count for this battle is also given separately and is not included in the earlier count.] *Psalms* and *Chronicles*, however, describe it as a separate battle against Edom, since it was really removed

יג שְׁמוֹנָה עָשָׂר אָלֶף: וַיָּשֶׂם בֶּאֱדוֹם נְצִיבִים וַיִּהְיוּ כָל־אֱדוֹם
עֲבָדִים לְדָוִיד וַיּוֹשַׁע יהוה אֶת־דָּוִיד בְּכֹל אֲשֶׁר הָלָךְ:
יד וַיִּמְלֹךְ דָּוִיד עַל־כָּל־יִשְׂרָאֵל וַיְהִי עֹשֶׂה מִשְׁפָּט וּצְדָקָה
טו לְכָל־עַמּוֹ: וְיוֹאָב בֶּן־צְרוּיָה עַל־הַצָּבָא וִיהוֹשָׁפָט בֶּן־
טז אֲחִילוּד מַזְכִּיר: וְצָדוֹק בֶּן־אֲחִיטוּב וַאֲבִימֶלֶךְ בֶּן־אֶבְיָתָר
יז כֹּהֲנִים וְשַׁוְשָׁא סוֹפֵר: וּבְנָיָהוּ בֶּן־יְהוֹיָדָע עַל־הַכְּרֵתִי
וְהַפְּלֵתִי וּבְנֵי־דָוִיד הָרִאשֹׁנִים לְיַד הַמֶּלֶךְ:

from the main theater of operations and the
Edomites were the primary opponents in
this battle.[1]

According to Radak's explanation we
have an explanation for our verse 11
which, as we see above, substitutes Edom
for the Aram in Samuel. The two books are
thus entirely consistent. Samuel, which
ascribes the whole war to Aram, talks of
the spoils of Aram; Chronicles, which sees
it as a war against Edom, uses that
description in v. 11.

For a further analysis of this, see Section
Two p. 450.

13. וַיּוֹשַׁע ה' אֶת־דָּוִיד בְּכֹל אֲשֶׁר הָלָךְ — And
HASHEM gave victory to David wherever he
went. This phrase is repeated here (see v. 6)
because of the special significance which
Edom had in Israel's history (see Section
Two). God granted David a victory which
was a harbinger of the Messianic era
(Malbim).

14. וַיִּמְלֹךְ דָּוִיד עַל־כָּל־יִשְׂרָאֵל — David ruled
over all Israel. After all the outstanding
victories which David won on the
battlefield no one in Israel had any doubts
concerning the legitimacy of his rule
(Radak).

וַיְהִי עֹשֶׂה מִשְׁפָּט וּצְדָקָה לְכָל־עַמּוֹ — And
practiced justice and charity towards all his
people. As king, David was responsible for
the administration of justice in the land (see
Proverbs 29:4). Our verse teaches that he
saw to it that all litigants would have their
disagreements adjudicated. But David did
not stop at doing what he had to do. As the

occasion demanded, he would help out
needy people, drawing on his own
resources to practice ... charity (Metzudos).

The Sages interpret our verse to mean
that he was able to combine charity with
justice. When two litigants came in front of
him for judgment, he would lay down the
law for them but then pay the required
amount out of his own pocket (Avos d'R'
Nosson 33).

The Mefaresh interprets our verse to
mean that David withdrew from the
waging of war and gave over his life
completely to the exercise of justice and
charity. For this reason the generalship of
the armies was given over to Yoav (next
verse). However, this explanation is
difficult in light of II Samuel 21:17 which
states that it was only much later that,
upon the insistence of his men, David
withdrew from any actual involvement in
combat (R' Tzvi Binyomin Wolf).

15. וְיוֹאָב בֶּן־צְרוּיָה עַל־הַצָּבָא — And Yoav the
son of Tzeruiah commanded the army. As
the Sages (Sanhedrin 49a) read our phrase,
it serves as an important source for the
understanding of the relationship between
those people who are able to devote their
whole lives to the study of the Torah and
those who are active in other areas. They
read our phrase together with the end of
the last verse and see in this combination
the mutual dependence of David and Yoav.
It is true that David was able to study the
Torah [as can be seen from the fact that he
administered justice — something that

1. Another possibility may be to combine Rashi's assumption that the victims came only from Edom
with Radak's suggestion that the disparity between the numbers need not indicate three separate
wars.

While David and Yoav went north to fight Aram, Avshai was charged with attacking Edom in the
Valley of Salt. He did so — killing six thousand men. After the northern campaign had been brought
to a successful conclusion, David and Yoav joined Avshai, killing another twelve thousand, thus
bringing the total to eighteen thousand.

eighteeen thousand men. ¹³ And he then placed governors in Edom, and all Edom became servants to David; and HASHEM gave victory to David wherever he went. ¹⁴ David ruled over all Israel and practiced justice and charity towards all his people. ¹⁵ And Yoav the son of Tzeruiah commanded the army; and Yehoshaphat the son of Achilud was the chronicler. ¹⁶ And Tzadok the son of Achituv, and Avimelech the son of Eviathar were Kohanim; and Shavsha was the scribe. ¹⁷ And Benaiah the son of Yehoiada was in charge of the Cherethi and the Pelethi; and the sons of David were first at the king's side.

would have been impossible without the study of Torah] — but only because Yoav was a conscientious general in whose charge David was able to leave the army without having to worry about it. On the other hand, Yoav needed David, because if not for the merit of studying the Torah, Yoav could never have been so successful on the battlefield.

מַזְכִּיר ... וִיהוֹשָׁפָט — And Yehoshaphat ... was the chronicler. He kept a record of the cases which came before David for judgment. His scribe was Shavsha, mentioned in the next verse (Mefaresh).

Metzudos thinks that he recorded historical events for posterity. He wrote the סֵפֶר הַזִּכְרוֹנוֹת, the book of records.

16. כֹּהֲנִים ... וַאֲבִימֶלֶךְ ... וְצָדוֹק — And Tzadok ... and Avimelech ... were Kohanim.

They were the Kohanim who filled official posts. Tzadok was the מְשׁוּחַ מִלְחָמָה, the Kohen whose duty it was to officiate at the mustering of the army preparing for war (see Deuteronomy 20:1-9). Avimelech was סְגָן, assistant to the Kohen Gadol. The Kohen Gadol, Eviathar (see 6:30-41), is not mentioned here because he had been appointed at the very beginning of David's reign and our passage lists only those functionaries who were appointed now. It is also possible that since Eviathar was eventually relieved of the Kehunah Gedolah (see above at 5:30-41), Chronicles did not list him (Metzudos).

וְשַׁוְשָׁא סוֹפֵר — And Shavsha was the scribe. He assisted Yehoshaphat, the chronicler (Mefaresh).

17. עַל־הַכְּרֵתִי וְהַפְּלֵתִי — In charge of the Cherethi and the Pelethi. There are many opinions concerning the meaning of these obscure terms.

Targum (to Samuel) renders: bowmen and slingers (see also Gra), which would make Benaiahu an officer of the army. Rashi (there) quotes the Sages who equate כְּרֵתִי וּפְלֵתִי with the Urim VeTumim, the hidden name of God which the Kohen Gadol carried in his breastplate which would miraculously provide answers to the questions asked of God by the king through the Kohen Gadol. It was Benaiahu's duty to help decide what questions should be asked of the Urim VeTumim and to work out the details of how the question should be posed (Wolf).

Tosafos (Berachos 4a) thinks that this term identifies Benaiahu as head of the Sanhedrin, the High Court. [The Sanhedrin renders definite and precise decision (כְּרֵתִי from כרת, to cut) and, as a group, are distinguished in the rendering of judgments פְּלֵתִי similar to מוּפְלָה, one who is special or distinguished).] Other commentators think that כְּרֵתִי and פְּלֵתִי are the names of two distinguished families who were close to David.

הָרִאשֹׁנִים — Were first. The sons of David were the ones who were closest to the king, always ready to do his bidding (Mefaresh).

XIX

◄§ David's Kindness Rebuffed

This chapter and the next deal with the wars which David waged against the Ammonites. They parallel chs. 10 and 11 in II Samuel. Chapter 18 here paralleled ch. 8 in Samuel. Chapter 9 in Samuel, which describes David's kindness in seeking out Jonathan's son, Miphibosheth, and establishing him as a member of the royal household, is not

א וַיְהִי אַחֲרֵי־כֵן וַיָּמׇת נָחָשׁ מֶלֶךְ בְּנֵי־עַמּוֹן וַיִּמְלֹךְ בְּנוֹ
ב תַּחְתָּיו: וַיֹּאמֶר דָּוִיד אֶעֱשֶׂה־חֶסֶד ׀ עִם־חָנוּן בֶּן־נָחָשׁ
כִּי־עָשָׂה אָבִיו עִמִּי חֶסֶד וַיִּשְׁלַח דָּוִיד מַלְאָכִים לְנַחֲמוֹ
עַל־אָבִיו וַיָּבֹאוּ עַבְדֵי דָוִיד אֶל־אֶרֶץ בְּנֵי־עַמּוֹן
ג אֶל־חָנוּן לְנַחֲמוֹ: וַיֹּאמְרוּ שָׂרֵי בְנֵי־עַמּוֹן לְחָנוּן הַמְכַבֵּד
דָּוִיד אֶת־אָבִיךָ בְּעֵינֶיךָ כִּי־שָׁלַח לְךָ מְנַחֲמִים הֲלֹא
בַּעֲבוּר לַחְקֹר וְלַהֲפֹךְ וּלְרַגֵּל הָאָרֶץ בָּאוּ עֲבָדָיו אֵלֶיךָ:
ד וַיִּקַּח חָנוּן אֶת־עַבְדֵי דָוִיד וַיְגַלְּחֵם וַיִּכְרֹת אֶת־מַדְוֵיהֶם
ה בַּחֵצִי עַד־הַמִּפְשָׂעָה וַיְשַׁלְּחֵם: וַיֵּלְכוּ וַיַּגִּידוּ לְדָוִיד

reviewed in *Chronicles*. This is consistent with *Chronicles'* approach of omitting the personal episodes of David's life. See further in Section Two p. 452.

2. וַיֹּאמֶר דָּוִיד אֶעֱשֶׂה־חֶסֶד עִם־חָנוּן בֶּן־נָחָשׁ —. *And David said, 'I will show kindness to Chanun the son of Nachash.* As is evident from below, this attempt was a terrible mistake. His intentions were misread and this resulted in much bloodshed and suffering. The reason for this is provided by the Sages.

Although it is written in the Torah *(Deuteronomy 20:10): When you approach a city to make war against it, invite it first to make peace,* to these [Ammon and Moab] do not do so: *Do not seek their peace or their benefit! (Deuteronomy 23:7).*

It can be shown that whoever deals mercifully with them will eventually be embarrassed and be involved in suffering. Who is [an example of] this? David — David said, 'Let me deal kindly with Chanun the son of Nachash.' God said to him, 'You intend to transgress My commands, for I have written, *Do not seek their peace or their benefit* — and you wish to deal kindly with them!' *Do not be excessively righteous! (Eccl. 7:16).* No one has the right to ignore the words of the Torah — and this one sends messengers to comfort the Ammonites and to do kindness to them.

Eventually he became embarrassed ... and became involved in wars ... Who brought all this about? David, who ignored God's command and attempted to do kindness to them *(Bamidbar Rabbah 21:5).*

The question, however, remains what David's motivation was. Surely he would not have

willingly transgressed the Torah's command that we are not to seek the peace and benefit of Ammon and Moab.

The commentators suggest that the Torah only forbids a kindness shown to them gratis. In David's case, where it was a matter of repaying a kindness done to him by Nachash, the Torah's prohibition would not be operative *(Kesef Mishneh* to Rambam, *Melachim* 6:6, quoting *Mizrachi).* Indeed had David shown appreciation to Nachash himself, there would have been no problem. David erred in thinking that the same dispensation would also apply to Nachash's son. For this the Sages castigated him *(Ohr Sameach* to Rambam *ibid.).*

Perhaps a different solution is possible. *Rambam (Melachim* 6:6) applies the prohibition: *Do not seek their peace or their benefit* only to certain clearly defined categories — that Ammon and Moab are excluded from the obligation to offer peace when preparing to wage war against a city, and that they are excluded from attaining the status of a *ger toshav,* the privileged position granted to non-Jews who elect to subscribe to the seven Noahide laws (see *R' Yitzchok Zev Soloveitchik).* He makes no mention at all of any prohibition against showing private kindnesses to individuals of these nations, indicating that no such prohibition exists. Thus, David did not transgress any actual prohibition.

Nevertheless, David erred. Even though the *halachah* may be limited to the instances given above, the language of the Torah — *Do not seek their peace or their benefit* — implies that any friendly approach, even when not expressly forbidden by the *halachah,* is frowned upon by the Torah.[1]

כִּי־עָשָׂה אָבִיו עִמִּי חֶסֶד — *For his father*

1. The Torah frequently uses certain modes of expression to indicate the thrust of its thinking even when not every aspect of that particular direction may be reflected in *halachah.* The Torah may use this method to indicate displeasure at a given action even when that action is not actually forbidden. This concept is discussed and many examples are adduced in *R' Y. Copperman's* לפשוטו של מקרא.

*I*t was after that, that Nachash the king of Ammon died, and his
son became king in his place. ² And David said, 'I will show
kindness to Chanun the son of Nachash, for his father showed
kindness to me.' So David sent messengers to console him
concerning his father; and David's servants came to the land of
Ammon to Chanun, to console him. ³ And the princes of Ammon
said to Chanun, 'Do you perceive David as honoring your father by
sending you consolers? Surely his servants have come to you to
investigate, scrutinize and reconnoiter the land. ⁴ So Chanun took
David's servants, and shaved them and cut their garments off at the
midpoint, the buttocks, and sent them away. ⁵ They went and

---

showed kindness to me.' The Sages had a
tradition that when the Moabite king
slaughtered all of David's family (see
comm. to 18:2), one brother managed to
escape and to find refuge with Nachash
king of Ammon. Nachash resisted pressure
from the Moabites to surrender him. See
further at 20:3 concerning this tradition.

Why did David wait till Nachash's death
to express his gratitude? *Malbim* thinks
that he specially waited for an innocuous
occasion, such as a visit of consolation, so
that it would not imply any wish to
establish a treaty between the two nations
and would not even give the appearance of
going against the Torah's wishes. Had he
sent a delegation during Nachash's lifetime
it would have had to take the form of an
offer to establish a treaty. This David did
not want to do. *Malbim* suggests that this is
borne out by the text. Where *Samuel*
simply says: *And David's servants came to
the land of Ammon, Chronicles* adds: *to
Chanun, to console him.* This, in order to
stress the private nature of the visit.

3. ... וַיֹּאמְרוּ שָׂרֵי בְנֵי־עַמּוֹן — *And the princes
of Ammon said ...* As the Sages (quoted by
Mefaresh) explain it, the princes were
convinced that David would not have
transgressed the Torah's prohibition
against making peace with Ammon. Surely
then, his motivation in sending the delegation must have been to spy out the land.

וְלַהֲפֹךְ — *To scrutinize* [lit. *to turn over*].
This is the translation of *Targum* to
Samuel. As *Metzudos* explains, in order to
examine something closely it must be
turned and viewed from all sides.

4. וַיְגַלְּחֵם — *And shaved them. Samuel* has,
... and he shaved half of their beards. By

stressing that he shaved only half of their
beards, *Samuel* puts the next phrase ... *and
he cut their clothes in half up to their
buttocks,* into a particular perspective. The
stress is on the concept of *halves:* half a
beard, half a garment. *Chronicles,* which
omits the fact that he shaved half of the
beard, loses the stress on *half* in the second
phrase. The emphasis is on the shameful
treatment of revealing the buttocks and the
statement that Chanun cut the clothes in
half is only to say how this was effected.

Malbim, quoting *Abarbanel,* explains
the symbolism of the halves. Chanun was
saying: Your intentions were only half
good. You wanted to deal kindly in order to
repay the favor my father had done to you
but you also wanted to spy out the land.

But why should *Chronicles* not include this in
its account? R' Y. Danziger has suggested that
cutting off half a man's beard and making him
look ridiculous could well be a bigger insult than
cutting off the whole beard. *Samuel* faithfully
reports the details of this insult because it was
well known at the time and heightened the sense
of outrage of both the king and the people.
Chronicles, however, does not wish or consider
it proper to report any more of their indignity
than is absolutely necessary because it is an
affront to the Davidic kingship. The basic story
had to be told to explain the outbreak of the war
but there was no need to explicate non-essential
details which were best forgotten. In the case of
the cutting of their clothes, however, it was
necessary to tell that only half are cut away since
otherwise it would have left an impression that
the men had been left completely naked.

הַמִּפְשָׂעָה — *The buttocks.* פֶּשַׂע [equivalent
to the word פסע] is a *step* (see *I Samuel*
20:3). Thus מִפְשָׂעָה is the organ of the body
which enables it to move — the hips or
buttocks (*Metzudos*).

---

1. In the light of an analysis of the different perspectives which *Chronicles* and *Samuel* seem to take
of the incident (see Section Two p. 455), another explanation is possible. See there.

עַל־הָאֲנָשִׁים וַיִּשְׁלַח לִקְרָאתָם כִּי־הָיוּ הָאֲנָשִׁים נִכְלָמִים **יט**

מְאֹד וַיֹּאמֶר הַמֶּלֶךְ שְׁבוּ בִירֵחוֹ עַד אֲשֶׁר־יְצַמַּח זְקַנְכֶם **ו־י**

וּשַׁבְתֶּם: ו וַיִּרְאוּ בְּנֵי עַמּוֹן כִּי הִתְבָּאֲשׁוּ עִם־דָּוִיד

וַיִּשְׁלַח חָנוּן וּבְנֵי עַמּוֹן אֶלֶף כִּכַּר־כֶּסֶף לִשְׂכֹּר לָהֶם מִן־

אֲרָם נַהֲרַיִם וּמִן־אֲרָם מַעֲכָה וּמִצּוֹבָה רֶכֶב וּפָרָשִׁים:

ז וַיִּשְׂכְּרוּ לָהֶם שְׁנַיִם וּשְׁלֹשִׁים אֶלֶף רֶכֶב וְאֶת־מֶלֶךְ מַעֲכָה

וְאֶת־עַמּוֹ וַיָּבֹאוּ וַיַּחֲנוּ לִפְנֵי מֵידְבָא וּבְנֵי עַמּוֹן נֶאֶסְפוּ

מֵעָרֵיהֶם וַיָּבֹאוּ לַמִּלְחָמָה: ח וַיִּשְׁמַע דָּוִיד וַיִּשְׁלַח

אֶת־יוֹאָב וְאֵת כָּל־צָבָא הַגִּבֹּרִים: ט וַיֵּצְאוּ בְּנֵי עַמּוֹן

וַיַּעַרְכוּ מִלְחָמָה פֶּתַח הָעִיר וְהַמְּלָכִים אֲשֶׁר־בָּאוּ לְבַדָּם

בַּשָּׂדֶה: י וַיַּרְא יוֹאָב כִּי־הָיְתָה פְנֵי־הַמִּלְחָמָה אֵלָיו פָּנִים

5. וַיֵּלְכוּ וַיַּגִּידוּ לְדָוִיד — *They went and reported to David.* The delegates, too embarrassed to appear in Jerusalem in person, sent messengers to David to apprise him of their plight (*Metzudos*). David, in turn, feeling their plight, told them to remain in Jericho until their beards grew back sufficiently for them to return to the capital without shame.

⮜§ The War of Ammon

6. הִתְבָּאֲשׁוּ — *They had made themselves odious.* באש means *to have a bad smell, to stink.* Thus, figuratively, to give oneself a bad smell, that is to make oneself odious (*Metzudos*).

וַיִּשְׁלַח חָנוּן וּבְנֵי עַמּוֹן ... — *Chanun and the Ammonites sent ...* Having realized how greatly they had antagonized David, they feared an outbreak of war. Feeling themselves no match for David's armies, they sought to protect themselves by hiring mercenary armies to fight at their side.

7. There are substantive differences between *Samuel* and *Chronicles* concerning the numbers, components and nationalities of the mercenary armies hired by Ammon, as may be seen at a glance from the chart on the opposite page.

The following are some of the suggested solutions:

Samuel mentions Aram Beth Rechov but not Aram Naharaim; *Malbim* suggests they

may be the same. If we assume that the king of Maachah and his people in *Chronicles* refers to the thousand men mentioned of the king of Maachah in *Samuel*, then we are left with *Samuel* talking of thirty-two thousand men while *Chronicles* talks of the same numbers of chariots and horsemen. It is, of course, possible that the *infantry* of *Samuel* are identical to the *horsemen* of *Chronicles* and then we would simply be faced with the fact that *Chronicles* mentions chariots while *Samuel* does not.[1]

Malbim thinks that *Chronicles* describes a different stage of the negotiations than does *Samuel*. He notes that *Samuel* makes no mention of the thousand talents of silver which *Chronicles* records. He suggests that after the initial contract the additional money was paid in order to hire the chariots and horsemen.

8. כָּל־צָבָא הַגִּבּוֹרִים — *The whole army and the mighty men.* The translation follows *Radak* that צָבָא stands by itself (otherwise the construct would have been צְבָא).

10. כִּי־הָיְתָה פְנֵי־הַמִּלְחָמָה אֵלָיו פָּנִים וְאָחוֹר — *That mighty warriors pressed him* [lit. *that the face of the war was to him*] *both front and rear.* The effect of the division of the enemy forces into two armies was that Yoav had to contend with attacks from both front and rear (*Mefaresh*). He was thus forced to divide his army as well to

1. If this solution is correct we must assume that רַגְלִי means *men* (as in *Exodus* 12:37) rather than infantry as it means at 18:4. This would seem borne out at v. 18 of our chapter where *Chronicles* uses

reported to David about the men and he sent to meet them, for the men were very humiliated; and the king said, 'Remain in Jericho until your beards grow back, then return.' ⁶ And the Ammonites saw that they had made themselves odious with David, so Chanun and the Ammonites sent a thousand talents of silver to hire for themselves chariots and horsemen from Aram Naharaim, Aram Maachah, and from Tzovah. ⁷ They hired for themselves thirty-two thousand chariots and the king of Maachah and his people, and they came and camped before Medeva; and the Ammonites too assembled from their cities and came out to battle. ⁸ And David heard; and he sent out Yoav and the whole army and the mighty men. ⁹ The Ammonites went out and deployed for battle at the city gates, while the kings who had come stayed alone in the field. ¹⁰ Now Yoav saw that mighty warriors pressed him both front and

Chronicles	Samuel
6(a) וַיִּרְאוּ בְּנֵי עַמּוֹן כִּי הִתְבָּאֲשׁוּ עִם־דָּוִיד, And the Ammonites saw that they had made themselves odious with David,	6(a) וַיִּרְאוּ בְּנֵי עַמּוֹן כִּי נִבְאֲשׁוּ בְּדָוִד, And the Ammonites saw that they had become odious with David
(b) וַיִּשְׁלַח חָנוּן וּבְנֵי עַמּוֹן אֶלֶף כִּכַּר־כֶּסֶף, so Chanun and the Ammonites sent a thousand talents of silver	(b) וַיִּשְׁלְחוּ בְּנֵי־עַמּוֹן, so the Ammonites sent
(c) לִשְׂכֹּר לָהֶם, to hire for themselves	(c) וַיִּשְׂכְּרוּ, and hired
(d) מִן־אֲרַם נַהֲרַיִם, from Aram Naharaim	(d) אֶת־אֲרַם בֵּית־רְחוֹב, Aram Beth Rechov
(e) וּמִן־אֲרַם מַעֲכָה, and from Aram Maachah	(e) •
(f) וּמִצּוֹבָה, and from Tzovah	(f) וְאֶת־אֲרַם צוֹבָא, and Aram Tzovah —
(g) רֶכֶב וּפָרָשִׁים, chariots and horsemen.	(g)
7(a) וַיִּשְׂכְּרוּ לָהֶם שְׁנַיִם וּשְׁלֹשִׁים אֶלֶף רֶכֶב, They hired for themselves thirty-two thousand chariots	(h) עֶשְׂרִים אֶלֶף רַגְלִי, twenty thousand infantry,
(b) וְאֶת־מֶלֶךְ מַעֲכָה וְאֶת־עַמּוֹ, and the king of Maachah and his people	(i) וְאֶת־מֶלֶךְ מַעֲכָה אֶלֶף אִישׁ, and the king of Maachah — one thousand men,
	(j) וְאִישׁ טוֹב שְׁנֵים־עָשָׂר אֶלֶף אִישׁ, and Ish Tov — twelve thousand men.

defend against the two-pronged attack.

Because the face is to the front of the body, the word פָּנִים, *face*, is used to denote the foreward part of any given unit [cf. פְּנֵי אֹהֶל מוֹעֵד, *the front of the Tabernacle* (*Leviticus* 9:5 and many other places)]. Since the forward ranks of an army is composed of its mightiest warriors, they

are referred to as the face of the battle (*Targum* and *Radak* to *Samuel*).

Radak there notes that the feminine verb הָיְתָה is used because of the feminine noun מִלְחָמָה although we would have expected the masculine plural since it seemingly describes the word פְּנֵי. Similar constructions occur elsewhere in Scripture.

אִישׁ רַגְלִי to describe the same people who in the *Samuel* account (*II Samuel* 16:18) are described as פָּרָשִׁים. We should, however, note the oddity that the two books seem to change expressions: when the one uses רַגְלִי the other uses פָּרָשִׁים and vice versa.

וְאָחוֹר וַיִּבְחַר מִכָּל־בָּחוּר בְּיִשְׂרָאֵל וַיַּעֲרֹךְ לִקְרַאת אֲרָם:

יא וְאֵת יֶתֶר הָעָם נָתַן בְּיַד אַבְשַׁי אָחִיו וַיַּעַרְכוּ לִקְרַאת

יב בְּנֵי עַמּוֹן: וַיֹּאמֶר אִם־תֶּחֱזַק מִמֶּנִּי אֲרָם וְהָיִיתָ לִּי

יג לִתְשׁוּעָה וְאִם־בְּנֵי עַמּוֹן יֶחֱזְקוּ מִמְּךָ וְהוֹשַׁעְתִּיךָ: חֲזַק

וְנִתְחַזְּקָה בְּעַד־עַמֵּנוּ וּבְעַד עָרֵי אֱלֹהֵינוּ וַיהוה הַטּוֹב

יד בְּעֵינָיו יַעֲשֶׂה: וַיִּגַּשׁ יוֹאָב וְהָעָם אֲשֶׁר־עִמּוֹ לִפְנֵי אֲרָם

טו לַמִּלְחָמָה וַיָּנוּסוּ מִפָּנָיו: וּבְנֵי עַמּוֹן רָאוּ כִּי־נָס אֲרָם וַיָּנוּסוּ

גַם־הֵם מִפְּנֵי אַבְשַׁי אָחִיו וַיָּבֹאוּ הָעִירָה וַיָּבֹא יוֹאָב

טז יְרוּשָׁלָ͏ִם: וַיַּרְא אֲרָם כִּי נִגְּפוּ

לִפְנֵי יִשְׂרָאֵל וַיִּשְׁלְחוּ מַלְאָכִים וַיּוֹצִיאוּ אֶת־אֲרָם אֲשֶׁר

יז מֵעֵבֶר הַנָּהָר וְשׁוֹפַךְ שַׂר־צְבָא הֲדַדְעֶזֶר לִפְנֵיהֶם: וַיֻּגַּד

לְדָוִיד וַיֶּאֱסֹף אֶת־כָּל־יִשְׂרָאֵל וַיַּעֲבֹר הַיַּרְדֵּן וַיָּבֹא אֲלֵהֶם

וַיַּעֲרֹךְ אֲלֵהֶם וַיַּעֲרֹךְ דָּוִיד לִקְרַאת אֲרָם מִלְחָמָה וַיִּלָּחֲמוּ

יח עִמּוֹ: וַיָּנָס אֲרָם מִלִּפְנֵי יִשְׂרָאֵל וַיַּהֲרֹג דָּוִיד מֵאֲרָם שִׁבְעַת

אֲלָפִים רֶכֶב וְאַרְבָּעִים אֶלֶף אִישׁ רַגְלִי וְאֵת שׁוֹפַךְ

וַיִּבְחַר מִכָּל־בָּחוּר בְּיִשְׂרָאֵל — *So he chose from among all the young men of Israel.* בָּחוּר, *a young man*, is formed from the root בחר, *to choose*, because there is a tendency to choose young men over older ones for any work that must be done or war that must be waged (*Radak, Shorashim*).

וַיַּעֲרֹךְ לִקְרַאת אֲרָם — *And he deployed to meet Aram.* From the whole narrative it seems clear that Aram was the stronger of the two adversaries.

12. וְהָיִיתָ לִּי לִתְשׁוּעָה ... וְהוֹשַׁעְתִּיךָ — *You will be my rescue ... I shall rescue you.* The wording makes clear that Yoav was the stronger and more confident of the two. Avshai would be a help to Yoav, but Yoav would rescue Avshai.

The form וְהוֹשַׁעְתִּיךָ is considerably more emphatic than the wording in *Samuel*: וְהָלַכְתִּי לְהוֹשִׁיעַ לָךְ, *I shall go to rescue you.* Perhaps the wording in *Samuel* is a verbatim quote while that in *Chronicles* was written with the hindsight of history, which saw Yoav in the full strength of his military prowess. In the event, neither had to help the other.

13. חֲזַק וְנִתְחַזְּקָה — *Be strong and we will be strong.* Yoav is exhorting Avshai to show valor in battle [חֲזַק] and promising him that Yoav and his forces will be equally courageous [נִתְחַזְּקָה] (*Metzudos*).

בְּעַד־עַמֵּנוּ וּבְעַד עָרֵי אֱלֹהֵינוּ — *For the sake of our people and the cities of our God. For our people* — that they not be taken captive. *For the cities of our God* — that they not be captured (*Metzudos*).

וַה' הַטּוֹב בְּעֵינָיו יַעֲשֶׂה — *And may HASHEM do as He sees fit.* Although we will make every effort (חֲזַק וְנִתְחַזְּקָה), nevertheless we realize that ultimately our salvation is in the hand of God (*Radak*). However, even if God will not help us we will accept His decision with love (*Metzudos*).

15. וַיָּבֹא יוֹאָב יְרוּשָׁלָ͏ִם — *And Yoav came to Jerusalem.* Samuel expands this phrase: וַיָּשָׁב יוֹאָב מֵעַל בְּנֵי עַמּוֹן וַיָּבֹא יְרוּשָׁלַיִם, *and Yoav turned away from the Ammonites and came to Jerusalem.* The implication is that after the Ammonites had retreated into their city, Yoav joined forces with Avshai and could have besieged the city. He chose not to and instead returned to Jerusalem, leaving the destruction of Ammon to a later date, as described in the next chapter.

16. וַיַּרְא אֲרָם כִּי נִגְּפוּ — *Aram saw that they had been smitten.* The change from the singular (וַיַּרְא) to the plural (נִגְּפוּ) is noteworthy, particularly since Samuel retains the singular form: וַיַּרְא אֲרָם כִּי נִגַּף. Our verse then goes on: וַיִּשְׁלְחוּ לִפְנֵי יִשְׂרָאֵל, מַלְאָכִים, *and they sent messengers* in contrast to *Samuel* which has: וַיִּשְׁלַח

rear, so he chose from among all the young men of Israel and he deployed to meet Aram. ¹¹ And the rest of the people he put under Avshai his brother and they deployed to meet Ammon. ¹² And he said, 'If Aram will be too powerful for me you will be my rescue, and if the Ammonites will be too powerful for you, I shall rescue you. ¹³ Be strong and we will be strong for the sake of our people and the cities of our God, and may HASHEM do as He sees fit.' ¹⁴ Then Yoav and the people with him approached Aram to battle, and they fled before him. ¹⁵ And the Ammonites saw that Aram had fled so they too fled before his brother Avshai and entered the city; and Yoav came to Jerusalem. ¹⁶ Aram saw that they had been smitten by Israel, so they sent messengers and brought out the Arameans who were on the other side of the river, and at their head was Shophach, the general of Hadadezer's army. ¹⁷ It was reported to David, and he mobilized all Israel, and crossed the Jordan, and he came and maneuvered towards them. David deployed for battle against Aram and they fought with him. ¹⁸ And Aram fled before Israel and David slew seven thousand charioteers and forty

הַדַּדְעֶזֶר, and Hadadezer sent.

The singular form is used for describing a group of people when they act as a unit, as one man. When the discipline of the unit disintegrates and they act as individuals, then the plural form is apt.

It is obvious from the course of the narrative that in the wake of the terrible defeat which Aram suffered, Hadadezer lost control of his people. This can be shown from v. 19 there where we read: *And the kings, the servants of Hadadezer saw that they had been smitten before Israel, and they made peace with Israel and served them.* The kings are described as 'servants of Hadadezer' and nevertheless they, not he, are the ones who assess the situation and decide to make peace with Israel. It may well be then that, though the actions appeared outwardly to be the result of concerted action, beneath the surface there had already been a disintegration of unity.

Thus, the account in *Samuel* saw Aram as a united people even in defeat (נִגַּף), and when Hadadezer sent for reinforcements this was interpreted as his own initiative, taken as the leader of his people.

In the eyes of *Chronicles*, the basic unity was already shattered with the initial defeat (כִּי נִגְּפוּ); and while it may have been Hadadezer who actually sent for the reinforcements his action was only the expression of the will of the people (וַיִּשְׁלְחוּ).

וְשׁוֹפַךְ שַׂר־צְבָא הֲדַדְעֶזֶר — *And ... Shophach, the general of Hadadezer's army.* Samuel has שׁוֹבַךְ instead of שׁוֹפַךְ. *Radak* and *Ramban* (*Exodus* 15:10) point out that the letters פ and ב are often interchanged. The Sages have a homiletical explanation for the change. He was called שׁוֹבַךְ [as שׁוֹבָךְ, a *dove-cote*] because of his great height; and he was called שׁוֹפַךְ [from שׁפַךְ, *to pour out*] because of the great amount of blood which he shed (*Sotah* 42b).

17. וַיַּעֲרֹךְ אֲלֵהֶם — *And he ... maneuvered towards them.* The next phrase reads: וַיַּעֲרֹךְ דָּוִיד לִקְרַאת אֲרָם מִלְחָמָה, *and David deployed [his forces] for battle against Aram.* Metzudos explains the first וַיַּעֲרֹךְ as describing the preparations for deployment and the second one to describe the actual deployment.

18. שִׁבְעַת אֲלָפִים רֶכֶב וְאַרְבָּעִים אִישׁ רַגְלִי — *Seven thousand charioteers and forty thousand infantrymen.* Samuel has: *seven hundred charioteers and forty thousand cavalry.* Radak explains the discrepancy as follows. Among the seven thousand, there were seven hundred of exceptional quality. These are the seven hundred mentioned in *Samuel*, which ignores the ones of lesser quality. It is by coincidence that the number of cavalry and infantrymen killed in each case was forty thousand. *Samuel* mentions only the cavalry, *Chronicles* only the infantry.

יט שַׂר־הַצָּבָא הֵמִית: וַיִּרְאוּ עַבְדֵי הֲדַדְעֶזֶר כִּי נִגְּפוּ לִפְנֵי

יִשְׂרָאֵל וַיַּשְׁלִימוּ עִם־דָּוִיד וַיַּעַבְדֻהוּ וְלֹא־אָבָה אֲרָם

א לְהוֹשִׁיעַ אֶת־בְּנֵי־עַמּוֹן עוֹד: וַיְהִי לְעֵת תְּשׁוּבַת

הַשָּׁנָה לְעֵת ׀ צֵאת הַמְּלָכִים וַיִּנְהַג יוֹאָב אֶת־חֵיל הַצָּבָא

וַיַּשְׁחֵת ׀ אֶת־אֶרֶץ בְּנֵי־עַמּוֹן וַיָּבֹא וַיָּצַר אֶת־רַבָּה וְדָוִיד

ב יֹשֵׁב בִּירוּשָׁלָ͏ִם וַיַּךְ יוֹאָב אֶת־רַבָּה וַיֶּהֶרְסֶהָ: וַיִּקַּח דָּוִיד

---

19. וַיִּרְאוּ עַבְדֵי הֲדַדְעֶזֶר ... וַיַּשְׁלִימוּ — *And the servants of Hadedezer saw ... and they made peace.* As is clear from *Samuel*, these servants were the kings who were vassals to Hadadezer. See comm. to v. 16.

וְלֹא־אָבָה אֲרָם לְהוֹשִׁיעַ אֶת־בְּנֵי־עַמּוֹן עוֹד — *Henceforth, Aram was no longer willing to come to the rescue of Ammon.* This information is given as an introduction to the war against Ammon described in the next chapter. When Yoav later attacked Ammon, Aram no longer extended any kind of help to the Ammonites.

XX

◄§ The Conquest of Ammon

The first three verses of this chapter describe David's final and victorious campaign against Ammon. It was during this war that David's tragic encounter with Bathsheba and Uriah took place (II *Samuel* ch. 11). *Chronicles* makes no mention of this episode, perhaps, because its significance was only for David, the man. The mark which his kingship left upon Israel was not affected by it — as the Sages (*Sanhedrin* 106a) teach he was destined to marry Bathsheba anyway — and it therefore has no place in *Chronicles'* broad perspective of the period of the monarchy.

1. וַיְהִי לְעֵת תְּשׁוּבַת הַשָּׁנָה — *And it was at the time of year's end* [lit. *at the time of the turn of the year*]. This is *Targum's* rendering. The root of תְּשׁוּבָה is שׁוּב, *to return.* In this connection it means at the time when the year returns to the point from which it set out, the end of the year. The next phrase, *at the time when the kings go out* [to war], explains why the campaign was put off till then. At that time of year the fields are full of grain and there is an abundance of fodder for the horses (*Rashi; II Samuel* 11:1). *Radak* and *Metzudos* think that the *kings* refer to the Aramean kings mentioned in the previous chapter as the allies of Ammon. The first and second phrases taken together mean: *One year after the kings had originally come out to aid the Ammonites.*

וְדָוִיד יֹשֵׁב בִּירוּשָׁלַ͏ִם — *While David stayed in Jerusalem.* This phrase, which parallels the phrase in *Samuel* 11:1, is problematic in *Chronicles.* In *Samuel* the phrase serves as an introduction to the story of Bathsheba: *... and David stayed in Jerusalem. Now it was towards the evening* ... Here, the incident of Bathsheba is not recorded and the fact that David stayed in Jerusalem seems irrelevant. Moreover, adding the statement that David stayed in Jerusalem makes v. 2, which states that David took the crown off the head of the Ammonite king (implying David's presence in Ammon), and v. 4, which reports David's return to Jerusalem, seem awkward. The background to these two verses lies in a section of the account of the battle recounted in *Samuel* but omitted here. According to that account Yoav had captured a part of the Ammonite capital, and had sent messengers to David that he should come to the front and complete the taking of the city and thus gain the glory of the conquest for himself. Thus *Samuel* makes clear David's exit from Jerusalem to Ammon. *Chronicles*, however, says nothing of Yoav's message to David and it is never stated that David came to the front. Accordingly, the phrase assuming David's presence in Ammon is jarring, since it seems to contradict the opening statement that David stayed in Jerusalem.

The reason why *Chronicles* states that David stayed in Jerusalem may perhaps be better understood if we recognize some other changes in emphasis between the two accounts:

thousand infantrymen from Aram; and he put Shophach, the
general, to death. ¹⁹ And the servants of Hadadezer saw that they
had been smitten by Israel and they made peace with David and
served him. Henceforth, Aram was no longer willing to come to the
rescue of Ammon.

And it was at the time of year's end, the time when the kings go
out, that Yoav led out the army and devastated the land of
Ammon; and he came and besieged Rabbah, while David stayed in
Jerusalem. And Yoav smote Rabbah and laid it waste. ² David took

Chronicles 20:1	Samuel 11:1
1(a) ... וַיְהִי לְעֵת תְּשׁוּבַת הַשָּׁנָה, And it was at the time of year's end ...	1(a) ... וַיְהִי לִתְשׁוּבַת הַשָּׁנָה, And it was at year's end ...
(b) וַיִּנְהַג יוֹאָב אֶת־חֵיל הַצָּבָא, that Yoav led out the army	(b) וַיִּשְׁלַח דָּוִד אֶת־יוֹאָב וְאֶת־עֲבָדָיו עִמּוֹ וְאֶת־כָּל־יִשְׂרָאֵל, that David sent Yoav, and his servants with him, and all Israel
(c) וַיַּשְׁחֵת אֶת־אֶרֶץ בְּנֵי־עַמּוֹן, and devastated the land of Ammon;	(c) וַיַּשְׁחִתוּ אֶת־בְּנֵי עַמּוֹן, and they devastated Ammon;
(d) וַיָּבֹא וַיָּצַר אֶת־רַבָּה, and he came and besieged Rabbah	(d) וַיָּצֻרוּ עַל־רַבָּה, and they besieged Rabbah
(e) וְדָוִיד יֹשֵׁב בִּירוּשָׁלָם, while David stayed in Jerusalem,	(e) וְדָוִד יֹשֵׁב בִּירוּשָׁלָם, while David stayed in Jerusalem.
	12:29
(f) וַיַּךְ יוֹאָב אֶת־רַבָּה וַיֶּהֶרְסֶהָ, and Yoav smote Rabbah and laid it waste.	29. וַיֶּאֱסֹף דָּוִד אֶת־כָּל־הָעָם וַיֵּלֶךְ רַבָּתָה וַיִּלָּחֶם בָּהּ וַיִּלְכְּדָהּ, And David gathered all the people and went to Rabbah; and he attacked it and conquered it.
2. ... וַיִּקַּח דָּוִיד אֶת־עֲטֶרֶת־מַלְכָּם, David took the crown of their king ...	30. ... וַיִּקַּח אֶת־עֲטֶרֶת־מַלְכָּם, And he took the crown of their king ...

It is notable that *Chronicles* ascribes every aspect of the battle to Yoav while *Samuel* stresses David's involvement:

1. In *Samuel* (1b) David sends Yoav in the company of his servants and all Israel. In *Chronicles* (1b) it is Yoav leading the army, apparently on his own initiative.

2. In *Samuel* (1c) the destruction of the Ammonite land is credited to all the people [David's agents] who were sent to fight [וַיַּשְׁחִתוּ, *they devastated*]. In *Chronicles* (1c) it is credited to Yoav himself.

3. In *Samuel* it is David who finally destroys Ammon's capital, Rabbah (12:29), while in *Chronicles* (1f) the destruction is credited to Yoav.

The last of these points seems particularly noteworthy. As seen above, *Samuel* tells how, after it appeared that Rabbah would surely fall, Yoav had loyally sent for David. He told his messengers to

say (12:28): *I have fought against Rabbah and I have captured the water-city. Now gather the rest of the people, camp against the city and conquer it, lest I capture the city and my name will be called upon it.* In *Chronicles'* account, the very thing that Yoav had sought to avoid seems to have happened — the credit for taking the city was given to him rather than to David.

The explanation for *Chronicles'* approach may be as follows: *Rambam* (*Melachim* 4:10), in discussing the role of the monarchy in the view of the Torah, states: '... the purpose of establishing a king is only in order that he may execute justice and wage war, as it is written: *Let our king judge us and go out before us and wage our battles (I Samuel* 8:20). Although *Rambam* does not say so explicitly, it is implied, and borne out by countless stories throughout Scripture, that the duty of

אֶת־עֲטֶרֶת־מַלְכָּם מֵעַל רֹאשׁוֹ וַיִּמְצָאָהּ l מִשְׁקַל כִּכַּר־זָהָב
וּבָהּ אֶבֶן יְקָרָה וַתְּהִי עַל־רֹאשׁ דָּוִיד וּשְׁלַל הָעִיר הוֹצִיא
ג הַרְבֵּה מְאֹד: וְאֶת־הָעָם אֲשֶׁר־בָּהּ הוֹצִיא וַיָּשַׂר בַּמְּגֵרָה
וּבַחֲרִיצֵי הַבַּרְזֶל וּבַמְּגֵרוֹת וְכֵן יַעֲשֶׂה דָוִיד לְכֹל עָרֵי בְנֵי־
ד עַמּוֹן וַיָּשָׁב דָּוִיד וְכָל־הָעָם יְרוּשָׁלָ͏ִם: וַיְהִי אַחֲרֵי־
כֵן וַתַּעֲמֹד מִלְחָמָה בְּגֶזֶר עִם־פְּלִשְׁתִּים אָז הִכָּה סִבְּכַי
ה הַחֻשָׁתִי אֶת־סִפַּי מִילִדֵי הָרְפָאִים וַיִּכָּנֵעוּ: וַתְּהִי־

---

conducting wars is a personal one. It seems to require that the king himself go out to battle (see *Rashi* to *Joshua* 7:10). Indeed this was David's own custom until in his old age his men became afraid for his safety (*II Samuel* 21:17). Why then did David elect to stay in Jerusalem and send Yoav to take Ammon on this occasion?

In the absence of any express teaching by the Sages we can only surmise. But perhaps David felt himself to blame for the horror and bloodshed of this war. As seen in ch. 19, it was his unwarranted impetuousness in attempting to befriend Chanun, the Ammonite king, which precipitated the war between the two people. Perhaps in these circumstances he felt it improper to assume a formal role in the battle and decided to delegate the task to Yoav.

But, was this a correct decision? The events which followed seem to indicate that it was not: ... *while David stayed in Jerusalem. And it was towards evening that David got up from his bed and strolled upon the palace roof, and from the roof he saw a woman washing and the woman was very beautiful* (*II Samuel* 11:1-2). The text surely indicates that the debacle with Bathsheva flowed *directly* from David's decision to stay in Jerusalem and not merely chronologically upon it.

This insight may yield the following conclusion: The matter of Bathsheva would not have happened if David had not erred in electing to stay in Jerusalem. If so, his conduct of this war was not as it should have been. Consequently, although in fact

it was David who sent Yoav to do battle, the initiative should be credited to the brave and loyal Yoav who throughout the affair acted in an entirely exemplary fashion. This would explain *Chronicles'* approach to the story and his reason for stating that David remained in Jerusalem, in spite of the textual difficulties which this causes. It is in our context an implied criticism of David and is inserted to explain the perspective which *Chronicles* takes of the events of this war.[1]

2. וַיִּקַּח דָּוִיד אֶת־עֲטֶרֶת־מַלְכָּם מֵעַל רֹאשׁוֹ — *David took the crown of their king from upon his head.* The translation follows the simple meaning of the verse (*Targum* to *II Samuel* 12:30; *Radak*; *Metzudos*). The Sages (*Avodah Zarah* 44a), however, note that the national idol of Ammon was called מַלְכֹּם, *Milcom* (*I Kings* 11:5), or מֹלֶךְ, *Molech* (v. 7 there). It is possible, then, that מַלְכָּם, *their king* [*Malcam*], in our verse is to be taken as a proper noun — the idol's name — and that the verse means that David took the crown which had rested on the head of the idol of Ammon and placed it on his own head. The Sages assume this meaning and discuss the question of how David could have used this crown for his own purpose, inasmuch as the Torah forbids us to derive any benefit from an object that had been used for idol worship. See there.

וַתְּהִי עַל־רֹאשׁ דָּוִיד — *And it became David's crown* [lit. *and it was on David's head*]. A crown weighing a talent of gold would be

---

1. If this analysis is correct, then our passage in *Chronicles* is a sort of Midrash on *Samuel*. It takes a section of Scripture and explicates teachings which are implicit in the text, in much the same way that the Sages of the Talmud did in later centuries.

We could imagine the same Midrash in Talmudic language as reading approximately: God said to David: 'Do you sit in comfort in Jerusalem while My children are in the field of battle? By your life, their victory will not be ascribed to you.'

the crown of their king from upon his head — he found it to weigh a talent of gold, and in it was a precious stone — and it became David's crown; and he brought out of the city a great quantity of booty. ³ And he brought out the people who were in it and cut them with saws and with iron files and with axes. So did David treat all the Ammonite cities. Then David and all the people returned to Jerusalem. ⁴ After this a war arose at Gaza with the Philistines. On that occasion Sibbechai the Chushathite killed Sippai, a descendant of the Rephaim, and they were subdued. ⁵ And there was another

much too heavy for the human head to bear. The Sages (*Avodah Zarah* 44a) offer a number of explanations:

— David did not really wear the crown; our verse means only that it fit his head (see below), not that he actually put it on.

— There was a magnetic contraption fixed into the ceiling above David's throne which lifted the weight of the crown off David's head;

— The crown did not really weigh a talent of gold. Reference is to the precious stone in it, which had the value of a talent of gold.

This crown which David captured from the Ammonites was to play an important role in the saga of the Davidic royal line. David himself saw the fact that it fitted him perfectly as a sign that he was indeed suited to the kingship (*Avodah Zarah* there), and subsequent claimants to the throne were tested by whether or not the crown could sit comfortably on their heads. Thus, Adoniyah was shown to be a pretender without rights to the throne when the crown did not fit him (see *Sanhedrin* 21b), and it was used as proof to establish Yehoash's legitimacy as king when the boy-king was crowned (see *II Kings* 11:12 and *Rashi*). See Section Two p. 456.

3. מְגֵרוֹת ... חֲרִיצֵי הַבַּרְזֶל ... מְגֵרָה — *Saws ... iron files ... axes.* *Rashi* and most other commentators assume these instruments to be implements of torture. [וַיָּשַׂר from נשר, is lit. *to saw.*] We rendered מְגֵרוֹת as *axes* although the word is simply the plural form of מְגֵרָה at the beginning of the verse which is taken as *saw.* This is because the parallel passage in *Samuel* (12:31) has מְגֵרֹת, from גזר, *to split* [wood] (*Metzudos* to *Samuel*). *Metzudos* here, however, explains that מְגֵרוֹת are also *saws* but smaller ones than those described as מְגֵרָה. For David's reasons for acting as he did, see Section Two p. 457.

◆§ Defeat of the Philistine Heroes

4⁻8. We have an account of three wars

against the Philistines, in each of which one great Philistine warrior was killed. The passage parallels *II Samuel* 21:18-22. Note, however, that in *Samuel* (vs. 15-17) there is an account of yet another war against the Philistines in which yet another of their heroes was killed. Why does *Chronicles* omit the account of that battle? The *Mefaresh* suggests that *Chronicles* left out the description of that battle because it does not reflect well on David. As told in *Samuel*, David suddenly tired during that fight and was about to be killed by Yishvi Benov of the Philistine army. He was saved only by the intervention of Avshai. On that occasion it was decided that it was too risky to allow David to go out to war any more and that henceforth he would stay off the battlefield and allow his soldiers to do the fighting. All this adds no particular honor to David and it is therefore omitted. See further, Section Two p. 458.

4. מִילִידֵי הָרְפָאִים — *A descendant of the Rephaim.* The reading רְפָאִים here follows *Minchas Shai.* There are some texts which have הָרָפָא and offer הָרְפָאִים as an alternative reading. [See the *Pardes* edition of *Mikraos Gedolos.*] In *Samuel*, three of the four Philistine heroes are identified as children of הָרָפָה, and the final verse in that passage rounds off the account: אֶת־אַרְבַּעַת אֵלֶּה יֻלְּדוּ לְהָרָפָה בְּגַת, *these four were born to 'Haraphah' in Gath.* In the tradition of the Sages (*Sotah* 42b), *Haraphah* is the name of a woman and refers to עָרְפָּה, *Orpah,* the sister-in-law of Ruth, who elected to return to her people rather than accompany Naomi on her way home. In *Chronicles*, however, the word is spelled הָרָפָא (with an aleph א not with a ה *hey*). Verses 5 and 8 identify the three warriors as being born to הָרָפָא (again with an *aleph*). The mere change of a *hey* to an *aleph* would not, on its own, be significant; it could be viewed

ר־ח

כ ק׳ יָעִיר ° עוֹד מִלְחָמָה אֶת־פְּלִשְׁתִּים וַיַּ֤ךְ אֶלְחָנָן בֶּן־°יָעוֹר אֶת־לַחְמִי

ו אֲחִי גָּלְיָת הַגִּתִּי וְעֵץ חֲנִיתוֹ כִּמְנוֹר אֹרְגִים: וַתְּהִי־

עוֹד מִלְחָמָה בְּגַת וַיְהִי ׀ אִישׁ מִדָּה וְאֶצְבְּעֹתָיו שֵׁשׁ־וָשֵׁשׁ

ז עֶשְׂרִים וְאַרְבַּע וְגַם־הוּא נוֹלַד לְהָרָפָא: וַיְחָרֵף אֶת־

ח יִשְׂרָאֵל וַיַּכֵּהוּ יְהוֹנָתָן בֶּן־שִׁמְעָא אֲחִי דָוִיד: אֵל נוּלְדוּ

as an Aramaism which would not be surprising in *Chronicles* whose Hebrew reflects the propensity towards Aramaic forms which were common when Ezra wrote the book. But v. 4 identifies Sippai as being from the descendants of הָרְפָאִים, *the Rephaim*, a nation often mentioned in Scripture and manifestly not the name of an individual woman. This makes it likely that הָרָפָא of vs. 6 and 8 means *the Rapha* and is simply a shortening of הָרְפָאִים, *the Rephaim*, that is, a people not an individual. It is thus that *R' Shmuel ben*

Chofni (p. 506) takes it. He traces the connection of the Rephaim to the Philistines from 14:9 which talk of a Philistine campaign which brought them into the territory of the *Rephaim*. He surmises that they intermarried so that it is no surprise that there were descendants of the Rephaim in the Philistine army.

5. ... וַיַּךְ אֶלְחָנָן בֶּן־יָעִיר — *And Elchanan the son of Yair killed* ... The parallel verse in *Samuel* reads differently, yet is tantalizingly similar:

Chronicles	II Samuel 21:19
5(a) וַיַּךְ אֶלְחָנָן בֶּן־יָעִיר, *And Elchanan the son of Yair killed*	19(a) וַיַּךְ אֶלְחָנָן בֶּן־יַעְרֵי אֹרְגִים, *And Elchanan the son of Yaarei Orgim*
(b) אֶת־לַחְמִי, *Lachmi*	(b) בֵּית הַלַּחְמִי, *the Bethlehemite killed*
(c) אֲחִי גָּלְיָת הַגִּתִּי, *the brother of Goliath the Gittite;*	(c) אֵת גָּלְיָת הַגִּתִּי, *Goliath the Gittite;*
(d) וְעֵץ חֲנִיתוֹ כִּמְנוֹר אֹרְגִים, *the shaft of his spear was like a weaver's beam.*	(d) וְעֵץ חֲנִיתוֹ כִּמְנוֹר אֹרְגִים, *the shaft of his spear was like a weaver's beam.*

Are the two passages describing the same incident? On the one hand there is the fact that in *Samuel* the victim is Goliath, while in *Chronicles* it is Goliath's brother, Lachmi. On the other hand it seems certain that the Elchanan mentioned in (a) on both passages is one and the same person [the difference between יַעְרֵי, *Yaarei*, in *Samuel* and יָעִיר, *Yair*, in *Chronicles* is surely the kind of minor change that occurs in given names throughout Scripture]. It would surely be stretching coincidence to say that the same man killed both Goliath and his brother, or that the two Elchanans are different people, but that the killer of both Goliath and his brother bore the same name. Again who is the Goliath mentioned in *Samuel*? If he is the Goliath whom we know from *I Samuel* ch. 17, then surely he

was slain by David, not by Elchanan the son of Yair. Is he then a different Goliath? It is true that the Goliath in our passage is called *the Gittite* [from Gath], while the one whom David killed is described as *the Philistine*. [On this basis the *Mefaresh* does indeed think that they were two different people, see further.] But it is also true that from *I Samuel* 17:4 and 23 it is clear that Goliath the Philistine came from Gath. Were there then two Gittite Goliaths, who were both mighty warriors and both slain in battle with Israel?

A simple solution is suggested by *Ibn Janach* in ch. 25 of *Sefer HaRikmah*. In that chapter he demonstrates an idiosyncrasy of Scriptural writing which he calls חֶסְרוֹן, *missing* [*words*]. This theory postulates that many verses in Scripture

*war with the Philistines, and Elchanan the son of Yair killed Lachmi
the brother of Goliath the Gittite; the shaft of his spear was like a
weaver's beam.* **6** *There was another war at Gath; and there was a
man of extraordinary stature with six digits on each of his limbs,
twenty-four digits; he too was born to the Rapha.* **7** *He taunted
Israel, and Yehonathan the son of Shimea, David's brother killed
him.* **8** *These were born to the Rapha in Gath; and they fell by the*

cannot be understood unless we assume
that a word or two was intentionally
omitted and left to the reader to supply.
[This idea is not unique to *Ibn Janach;*
many earlier commentators, notably *R'
Saadiah Gaon,* make use of this principle.]
Among the many examples which he
adduces is the verse in *Samuel.* Based on
Chronicles, he takes it for granted that
Elchanan killed not Goliath but his brother,
and he consequently sees a word 'missing'
from the verse. The word אֲחִי, *brother of,* is
to be understood before גָּלְיָת, *Goliath.* By
this simple assumption the two verses
agree with one another and have no bearing
on the confrontation between David and
Goliath.

Ibn Janach does not, however, address the
strange coincidence of the names: that the
Israelite warrior should be called בֵּית הַלַּחְמִי, *the
Bethlehemite* in *Samuel,* where the name of the
Philistine is not given, and should be called לַחְמִי,
Lachmi in *Chronicles* where the warrior is not
called the Bethlehemite.

Metzudos (Samuel) offers the following
solution: בֵּית הַלַּחְמִי, in *Samuel,* is not part
of the warrior's name but is a direct object
of the verb וַיַּךְ, *and he killed Beth Halachmi.* This *Beth Halachmi* is the same as
the Lachmi mentioned in *Chronicles.* [We
would thus have expected אֶת בֵּית הַלַּחְמִי,
but this accusative particle is occasionally
omitted; see for example *II Samuel*
15:14.] The אֶת in the phrase אֶת גָּלְיָת הַגִּתִּי is
not an accusative particle but is to be
translated *with.* The meaning is that
Elchanan managed to kill Beth Halachmi,
the Philistine, although the mighty Goliath
himself was engaged in that battle and
might have been expected to help him —
the more so since from *Chronicles* we see
that he was his own brother.

Malbim makes an entirely novel
suggestion. The story as it actually
happened is described in *Chronicles.*
Elchanan the son of Yair killed Lachmi who
was the brother of Goliath. The *Samuel*
version is the form in which the storytellers

preserved the record of the event. The
coincidence — that Lachmi's brother
Goliath had been killed by David the
Bethlehemite who could thus be described
as בֵּית הַלַּחְמִי and that, moreover, this
Lachmi was as mighty a warrior as his
brother Goliath, and that therefore his
defeat had the same miraculous overtones
— prompted them to immortalize the story
of that combat in terms which would have
been appropriate in describing David's
victory over Goliath — Beth Halachmi
killed Goliath. In this way people knew
that reference was to the defeat of Lachmi
at the hands of Elchanan but at the same
time they were made aware of just how
miraculous an event this was.

Targum and *Rashi* interpret the verse in
Samuel as describing David's victory over
Goliath. Elchanan ben Yaarei Orgim is
really David, as shown by the description
the Bethlehemite. He is called Elchanan
because God showed him favor [אֶלְחָנָן from
חָנַן, *to show favor*], and he is given as a son
of יַעְרֵי אֹרְגִים, *Yaarei Orgim,* because his
family used to weave [אֹרְגִים from ארג, *to
weave*] the curtain which separated the
Holy from the Holy of Holies in the
Tabernacle. [יַעַר, *forest,* is used as a
metaphor for the Temple which is called
יַעַר הַלְּבָנוֹן, *the forest of Lebanon.*] The idea
of the verse is that God's justice was meted
out *measure for measure.* Goliath, who
wielded a spear whose handle was as thick
as a weaver's beam, was defeated by David
whose family used the weaver's beam for
the glory of God. [In line with *Targum's*
interpretation *Rashi* notes that although
David's battle with Goliath took place at
the beginning of Saul's reign, that is, long
before the other skirmishes with the
Philistines mentioned here, it is repeated
together with them, outside the
chronological sequence, in order to bring
the death of all the four sons of Orpah
(*Haraphah* — see comm. to v. 4) together.]

Targum to *Chronicles* bases his interpretation
on *Targum* to *Samuel* and has Elchanan the son

of Yair refer to David. He is called the son of Yair [from נער, *to wake up*] because it was his custom to arise in the middle of the night in order to sing God's praises. Our verse teaches that on the same day that David killed Goliath he also killed Goliath's brother. [See further in Section Two.]

8. בְיַד־דָּוִיד וּבְיַד־עֲבָדָיו — *By the hand of David and by the hands of his servants.* In his comm. to *Samuel*, *Wolf* notes that this verse seems a clear proof to the interpreta-

tion of the Sages that the Elchanan mentioned there is David (see above). If not, there would be no justification to say that these warriors fell to David, since they were all killed by different people. However, since all the commentators do not see David mentioned in *Chronicles'* account of these events, it seems more likely that David is mentioned because as king he was in general command of the battle, not because he actually killed the men.

XXI

◄§ The Ill-fated Census

The story of the census which David initiated, together with its tragic aftermath, is the subject of our chapter. In the parallel section in *Samuel*, it forms the final chapter of that book and brings the account of David's reign to an end. By contrast, our chapter, which tells essentially the same story, concludes with the identification of the site upon which David sacrificed to end the plague as the site for the future Temple (22:1). It is then followed by detailed descriptions of the preparations and dispositions which David made for the Temple which Solomon was to build (chs. 22-29). Indeed, in the *Chronicles* arrangement, the entire account of the census and subsequent plague may be seen as a prelude to the discovery of the Temple site and the preparations for its construction.

This difference in thrust between the *Chronicles* and *Samuel* accounts helps to explain the numerous and significant textual differences that mark these parallel chapters. By and large, the commentators do not address these points. Since a full explanation requires a comprehensive analysis of the chapter as a whole, the commentary will basically restrict itself to an explanation of the verses as they appear here, only occasionally comparing the two versions, while the resolution of the differences between our book and *Samuel* will be treated in Section Two, p. 460ff.

1. וַיַּעֲמֹד שָׂטָן עַל־יִשְׂרָאֵל — *An adversary rose up against Israel.* Samuel begins the account of this incident with the phrase: וַיֹּסֶף אַף־ה' לַחֲרוֹת בְּיִשְׂרָאֵל, *The wrath of HASHEM was once more kindled against Israel.*

This introduction immediately suggests that what follows comes as retribution for a sin.[1] By omitting the introductory sentence, *Chronicles* sets a different tone and proceeds to tell a different aspect of the story.

When שָׂטָן is to be taken as a proper

noun, *Satan*, Scripture invariably uses הַשָּׂטָן, *the Satan.* For this reason, *Radak* and *Metzudos* think that here it is not a name but a word describing the יֵצֶר הָרָע, *evil inclination*, which lies within every person. There was something in David which allowed him no rest and urged him to count the people. This proved to be a tragedy for Israel.

וַיָּסֶת אֶת־דָּוִיד ... — *And provoked David ...* The contrast between this verse and its parallel in *Samuel* is noteworthy.

Chronicles	Samuel
(a) וַיָּסֶת אֶת־דָּוִיד, *and provoked David*	(a) וַיָּסֶת אֶת־דָּוִד בָּהֶם לֵאמֹר, *and incited David against them, saying,*
(b) לִמְנוֹת אֶת־יִשְׂרָאֵל, *to count Israel*	(b) לֵךְ מְנֵה אֶת־יִשְׂרָאֵל וְאֶת־יְהוּדָה, *go count Israel and Judah*

1. Israel's sin is not explicated. *Rashi (Samuel)* admits ignorance. *Ramban (Numbers 1:3)* suggests that they failed, of their own accord, to suggest that the time had come to build the Temple, leaving it to David to take the initiative.

1

An adversary rose up against Israel and provoked David to count

The root סוּת from which וַיָּסֶת is formed is used in Scripture with a number of different nuances. Together with the prefix ב (... סוּת ב) it invariably means *to instigate someone against someone else* (see, e.g., I Samuel 26:19). Without the prefix it has the meaning of provoking someone to take a given course or perform a given action (see Joshua 15:18). Thus, while the *Samuel* verse tells us that David was incited against Israel, our verse states only that David was provoked into counting them.

לִמְנוֹת אֶת־יִשְׂרָאֵל — *To count Israel*. Why did David want to count the people and in what way did this counting offend against the Torah?

Motives:

(a) *Bamidbar Rabbah* 2:17 calls David's census a needless one (שֶׁלֹּא לְצוֹרֶךְ). Based on this, *Ramban (Numbers* 1:3) thinks that David simply wanted to take pleasure in contemplating the size of the nation over which he ruled.

(b) *Ralbag* sees David as putting his trust in his military might. Evidently, he thinks that David wanted the census so that he could be sure of the number of soldiers available to him.

(c) *Malbim* suggests a political motive. In the early years of David's reign the people had been absolutely loyal to him. If he needed soldiers he let the fact be known and had no trouble filling the ranks of his army. Things changed after Absalom's rebellion, as can be seen from the thousands who joined the insurrection of Sheva ben Bichri *(II Samuel* ch. 20). David thought that if, in the future, he would have to draft an army, he would not be able to rely on volunteers. He ordered the census, and included the whole nation — even the infants — so that if ever the need arose he would be able to organize a draft and would know who had attained military age.

Transgression:

(a) The counting took place without the shekalim prescribed by the Torah. *Exodus* 30:11ff prescribes that when Israel is to be counted, each person must give half a shekel and the total is to be arrived at by counting the money rather than the people. According to *Berachos* 62b, David forgot

this rule and wanted the people themselves counted.

Ramban (Numbers 1:3) believes this to be unlikely. Why would David ignore such a clear ruling in the Torah, and moreover, what prevented Yoav from ordering the use of shekalim on his own initiative?

(b) For this reason *Ramban* suggests a different transgression: David counted *all* Israel — including those under twenty — thus contravening the Torah which limits all censi to people over twenty.

The Torah's reason would be as follows: The Torah teaches that the people of Israel are never to be defined in terms of their number; God wants to increase them ... *as the stars of heaven*. If counting is ever found necessary, then it must be limited to a given segment of the people — as, for example, the ones to be drafted into the army. The nation itself is to remain beyond number. *Ramban* bases his explanation on 27:23-24, which imply that Yoav counted the whole people — see comm. there.

(c) The counting was unnecessary, as taught in *Bamidbar Rabbah* quoted above. From the careful provisions which the Torah makes for a census, and the stipulations that if done incorrectly it could cause Israel to be smitten by the plague *(Exodus* 30:11), it is clear that the Torah does not favor a census except for the most pressing needs (see *Yoma* 22b). No such need existed when David ordered the counting. *Ramban* suggests this as a possibility, and this is also *Radak's* view.

(d) David trusted his army too much: Ralbag suggests that David wanted the census in order to assure himself of having sufficient soldiers for his army. This indicated a lack of trust in God. There are those among the commentators who support this view on the basis of the fact that in *Samuel*, the story of the census follows immediately upon the listing of David's *giborim*, mighty warriors [see above ch. 11] *(Wolf)*.

אֶת־יִשְׂרָאֵל ... — *Israel ... Samuel* has *Israel and Judah*. It must be assumed that David, in his order, did in fact separate Israel from Judah since Yoav gave separate numbers for the two entities (v. 5). *Malbim*, following his explanation of David's motive, explains that *Chronicles* does not

ב וַיֹּאמֶר דָּוִיד אֶל־יוֹאָב וְאֶל־שָׂרֵי הָעָם לְכוּ סִפְרוּ אֶת־
יִשְׂרָאֵל מִבְּאֵר שֶׁבַע וְעַד־דָּן וְהָבִיאוּ אֵלַי וְאֵדְעָה אֶת־
ג מִסְפָּרָם: וַיֹּאמֶר יוֹאָב יוֹסֵף יְהֹוָה עַל־עַמּוֹ ׀ כָּהֵם מֵאָה
פְעָמִים הֲלֹא אֲדֹנִי הַמֶּלֶךְ כֻּלָּם לַאדֹנִי לַעֲבָדִים לָמָּה
ד יְבַקֵּשׁ זֹאת אֲדֹנִי לָמָּה יִהְיֶה לְאַשְׁמָה לְיִשְׂרָאֵל: וּדְבַר־
הַמֶּלֶךְ חָזַק עַל־יוֹאָב וַיֵּצֵא יוֹאָב וַיִּתְהַלֵּךְ בְּכָל־יִשְׂרָאֵל
ה וַיָּבֹא יְרוּשָׁלָ‍ִם: וַיִּתֵּן יוֹאָב אֶת־מִסְפַּר מִפְקַד־הָעָם אֶל־
דָּוִיד וַיְהִי כָל־יִשְׂרָאֵל אֶלֶף אֲלָפִים וּמֵאָה אֶלֶף אִישׁ שֹׁלֵף
חֶרֶב וִיהוּדָה אַרְבַּע מֵאוֹת וְשִׁבְעִים אֶלֶף אִישׁ שֹׁלֵף חָרֶב:

mention Judah because David's main interest was in the rest of Israel. David knew that his own tribe, Judah, would be loyal to him under all circumstances.

2. וַיֹּאמֶר דָּוִיד אֶל־יוֹאָב וְאֶל־שָׂרֵי הָעָם — *And David said to Yoav and the officers of the people.* Samuel does not mention the officers. On the other hand, where in v. 4 we have ... *and Yoav went out,* Samuel has ... *and Yoav and the officers of the army went out.*

Perhaps the explanation is as follows: David's original order was given to Yoav alone. When, contrary to David's expectations, Yoav balked at the task and had to be forced to undertake the project, his own authority waned and his officers were given a share of the responsibility. This explains the passage in *Samuel. Chronicles* — which sees the matter in retrospect, and is really only giving the general outlines of the story while omitting many of the details given in *Samuel* — tells the story as it turned out in the end and mentions the officers immediately. Having done so, there was no need to mention them once more in v. 4.

מִבְּאֵר שֶׁבַע וְעַד־דָּן — *From Beersheva to Dan.* Samuel has ... *from Dan to Beersheva,* that is, from north to south rather than from south to north. The form which *Samuel* uses is familiar from other places in Scripture (*Judges* 20:1; *I Samuel* 3:20; *II Samuel* 3:10, 24:15, 17:11, 24:2,15; *I Kings* 5:5), but the sequence used here occurs only one more time, in *II Chronicles* 30:5.

It may be that by the time *Chronicles* was written the idiom had changed, or that we are dealing with the type of chiasm which is frequently found in Scripture.

וְהָבִיאוּ אֵלַי — *And bring it to me.* The object of the verb *bring* is not stated by the verse but is understood: *Count Israel and bring [the count] to me.*

3. ... וַיֹּאמֶר יוֹאָב — *But Yoav said ...* Yoav now warns David that he is making a terrible mistake by counting the people and pleads with him that it is both unnecessary and dangerous to Israel. As *Exodus* 30:12 teaches, improper counting of Israel can result in a plague.

Malbim, based on his explanation above, sees Yoav as assuring David that the people are all loyal to David — *are they not ... all servants to my lord?*

4. וַיֵּצֵא יוֹאָב וַיִּתְהַלֵּךְ בְּכָל־יִשְׂרָאֵל וַיָּבֹא יְרוּשָׁלָ‍ִם — *And Yoav went out and traveled through all Israel and came back to Jerusalem.* This verse is a contraction of four verses in *Samuel.* The words וַיֵּצֵא יוֹאָב, *and Yoav went out,* are expanded there by the addition ... *to count the people — Israel.* Our word וַיִּתְהַלֵּךְ, *and traveled,* does duty for a detailed description of the places which he visited. וַיָּבֹא יְרוּשָׁלַיִם, *and he came back to Jerusalem,* is expanded there to read, *And he came back at the end of nine months and twenty days to Jerusalem.*

5. אֶת־מִסְפַּר מִפְקַד־הָעָם — *The number of the tally of the people.* The terms מִסְפָּר [from ספר, *to count*] and מִפְקָד [from פקד, which is also used in the sense, *to count*] seem synonymous. Indeed, *Radak* and *Metzudos* take them as having identical meanings and adduce examples from other parts of Scripture where two words with essentially similar meanings are used together for emphasis.

Ramban (Numbers 1:1) finds that the root פקד has a different nuance than ספר even when it is used with the meaning *to count.* פקד carries a connotation of attending to something, concentrating

Israel. ² And David said to Yoav and the officers of the people, 'Go count Israel from Beersheva to Dan; and bring it to me so that I may know their number.' ³ But Yoav said, 'May HASHEM add upon His people a hundred times as many as they are now; are they not, my lord king, all servants to my lord? Why does my lord seek this thing? Why should it occasion guilt upon Israel?' ⁴ But the king's words prevailed over Yoav, and Yoav went out and traveled through all Israel and came back to Jerusalem. ⁵ And Yoav reported the number of the tally of the people to David; and all Israel came to one million, one hundred thousand men capable of drawing a sword, and Judah came to four hundred and seventy thousand men

upon it or recalling it. When it is used in the sense *to count* it implies a counting made by collecting objects from the people — presumably the half-shekel mandated by the Torah — and counting those in order to arrive at a correct total of the people. Accordingly, the term מִסְפַּר מִפְקָד is to be understood as the number (מִסְפָּר) of the people arrived at by tallying the shekalim collected from them (מִפְקָד). [As explained in v. 1, *Ramban* believes that Yoav did use the shekalim to count the people.]

Rashi quotes *Pesikta, Bamidbar Rabbah* and *Midrash Shmuel* which maintain that the two terms refer to two separate accountings which Yoav was prepared to deliver — a large one and a small one. He hoped that David would be satisfied with the small one but would submit the large one if the king demanded it.

Malbim adds that the small one was a simple statement of the total number of people, while the large one accounted for each individual and broke the census down into its component parts. A simple statement of the numerical strength of the nation would have been less offensive to the Torah's values than a detailed breakdown of the populace.

Wolf, based on *Ramban's* opinion that David's sin was to count the whole nation and not only those above the age of twenty, suggests that the small one was limited to those over twenty who were counted legitimately, while the large one contained the names of all the people.

אֶלֶף אֲלָפִים וּמֵאָה אֶלֶף ... — *One million, one hundred thousand* ... While *Chronicles* gives the number from Israel as 1,100,000 and from Judah as 470,000, *Samuel* has the number from Israel as 800,000 and from Judah as 500,000.

The Sages *(Thirty-two Midos of R' Eliezer ben R' Yose HaGlili)* address the question of the discrepancy in the numbers from Israel but do not comment on the 30,000 discrepancy in the number from Judah.

For the extra 300,000 in *Chronicles*, two solutions are offered. According to 27:1 there were 24,000 functionaries employed at the king's court every month. Multiplied by twelve for the months of the year this yields 288,000. For each tribe in Israel there were also 1000 officials, which makes 12,000, yielding a total of 300,000 for all those in service. These men were already listed in the registers that were available to David and therefore there was no need for Yoav to count them, for which reason *Samuel* gives 800,000 as the total which Yoav counted. *Chronicles* gives 1,100,000, adding in the 300,000 officials.

The other solution is based on the fact that, as v. 6 in *Chronicles* reports, Yoav did not count Levi or Benjamin. The census without these two tribes yielded 800,000. *Chronicles*, noting that Yoav did not count these two tribes, adds as a historical footnote that the two tribes which were not counted had 300,000 men, thus yielding a total of 1,100,000 *(Rashi to Samuel).*

Malbim points out that this second explanation will also explain the discrepancy in the Judah census. As is well known, many Levites and Benjaminites lived in Judah's territory in Jerusalem. *Samuel*, which has no figure for the tribes of Levi and Benjamin, incorporated those of them who lived in Jerusalem in the Judah count, thus yielding an extra 30,000 men for Judah. Since *Chronicles* gives the total including the two tribes, the 30,000 appear in the total figure and are therefore subtracted from the Judah count.

ו וְלֵוִי וּבִנְיָמִן לֹא פָקַד בְּתוֹכָם כִּי־נִתְעַב דְּבַר־הַמֶּלֶךְ אֶת־

ז יוֹאָב: וַיֵּרַע בְּעֵינֵי הָאֱלֹהִים עַל־הַדָּבָר הַזֶּה וַיַּךְ אֶת־

ח יִשְׂרָאֵל: וַיֹּאמֶר דָּוִיד אֶל־הָאֱלֹהִים חָטָאתִי מְאֹד אֲשֶׁר עָשִׂיתִי אֶת־הַדָּבָר הַזֶּה וְעַתָּה הַעֲבֶר־נָא

ט אֶת־עֲווֹן עַבְדְּךָ כִּי נִסְכַּלְתִּי מְאֹד: וַיְדַבֵּר יהוה

י אֶל־גָּד חֹזֵה דָוִיד לֵאמֹר: לֵךְ וְדִבַּרְתָּ אֶל־דָּוִיד לֵאמֹר כֹּה אָמַר יהוה שָׁלוֹשׁ אֲנִי נֹטֶה עָלֶיךָ בְּחַר־לְךָ אַחַת

יא מֵהֵנָּה וְאֶעֱשֶׂה־לָּךְ: וַיָּבֹא גָד אֶל־דָּוִיד וַיֹּאמֶר לוֹ כֹּה־

יב אָמַר יהוה קַבֶּל־לָךְ: אִם־שָׁלוֹשׁ שָׁנִים רָעָב וְאִם־שְׁלֹשָׁה חֳדָשִׁים נִסְפֶּה מִפְּנֵי־צָרֶיךָ וְחֶרֶב אוֹיְבֶיךָ ׀ לְמַשֶּׂגֶת וְאִם־שְׁלֹשֶׁת יָמִים חֶרֶב יהוה וְדֶבֶר בָּאָרֶץ וּמַלְאַךְ יהוה מַשְׁחִית בְּכָל־גְּבוּל יִשְׂרָאֵל וְעַתָּה רְאֵה מָה־אָשִׁיב אֶת־

יג שֹׁלְחִי דָּבָר: וַיֹּאמֶר דָּוִיד אֶל־גָּד צַר־לִי מְאֹד אֶפְּלָה־נָּא בְיַד־יהוה כִּי־רַבִּים רַחֲמָיו מְאֹד וּבְיַד־

---

6. וְלֵוִי וּבִנְיָמִן לֹא פָקַד בְּתוֹכָם — *But he did not tally Levi and Benjamin among them.* The Sages (*Yalkut, Samuel*) explain that Yoav felt he could reasonably avoid the king's orders with these two tribes. In the case of Levi he could argue that the tribe had also been excluded from the general census in Moses' days (*Numbers* 1:48 ff.). As for Benjamin, that tribe had suffered catastrophic losses during the tragic affair of the concubine in Giveah (*Judges* chs. 19-21). David would surely understand that this tribe should not now be exposed to the dangers of a census which, as *Exodus* teaches, might well result in a plague.

As *Malbim* explains the discrepancy in the previous verse, our verse is a comment on the previous one. The verse explains that the reason why the numbers are different here than in *Samuel* is because Levi and Benjamin had not been a part of the general census given there.

7. וַיַּךְ אֶת־יִשְׂרָאֵל — *And He smote Israel.* Verses 11-14 indicate that the plague started later, when David chose that punishment over the other two alternatives which God offered him. *Malbim* thinks that our verse makes it obvious that, in a small way, the plague already began earlier. However, he does not explain why this information was not given in *Samuel*. This is particularly problematic if, as seems from our text, it was that plague which made David realize his folly and pray to God for forgiveness (v. 8). In *Samuel* no cause is ascribed to David's conscience pangs, and if they were stimulated by the beginnings of a plague it would surely have been in place to mention that.

Metzudos does not agree that there was any plague before the one mentioned in v. 14. He thinks that our verse is looking ahead and reporting what happened later. See Section Two.

8. הַעֲבֶר־נָא אֶת־עֲווֹן עַבְדְּךָ — *Forgive now, I pray, the transgression of Your servant.* The *Mefaresh* notes that this is one of only four places in Scripture in which עֲווֹן, *transgression*, appears with the extra *vav*. He suggests that the extra *vav* is there to hint at the fullness or seriousness of the transgression.

It should, however, be noted that the word עֲוֹן does not recur in *Chronicles*, and that taken by itself, the insertion of the *vav* does not seem significant since all spelling in *Chronicles* tends towards the writing out of the quiescent letters. The most blatant example of this is the spelling of David as דָּוִיד throughout *Chronicles*, inserting the *yud* which, throughout the rest of Scripture, is left out.

9. חֹזֵה דָוִיד — *David's seer.* Gad is called David's seer because all his recorded prophecies were communications to David (*Radak* to *II Samuel* 24:11).

capable of drawing a sword. ⁶ But he did not tally Levi and Benjamin among them, for the word of the king was repugnant to Yoav. ⁷ This matter was bad in the eyes of God, and He smote Israel. ⁸ And David said to God, 'I have sinned greatly that I have done this thing; forgive now, I pray, the transgression of Your servant, for I have acted very foolishly.' ⁹ And HASHEM spoke to Gad, David's seer, saying: ¹⁰ 'Go and speak to David, saying, "Thus has HASHEM said: I offer you three; choose one of these and I will do it to you."' ¹¹ And Gad came to David and said to him, 'Thus says HASHEM, accept upon yourself: ¹² Whether three years of famine; or three months to be swept away before your oppressors, with the sword of your enemies overtaking you; or three days with the sword of HASHEM, a plague in the land, and the angel of HASHEM destroying throughout the borders of Israel. Now see what answer I shall reply to Him Who sent me.' ¹³ David said to Gad, 'I am greatly distressed; let me fall, I pray, into the hand of HASHEM, for His mercies are very

⊷§ The Plague

10. שָׁלוֹשׁ אֲנִי נֹטֶה עָלֶיךָ — *I offer you three.* The meaning is one of three. David was to have a choice concerning which of three punishments was to be given.

The root נטה usually means *to incline.* Its use in the sense *to offer* is unique to this passage. See Section Two p. 466.

What is the significance of the choice which David was given? *Wolf* points to the case of Solomon who, in *I Kings* 3:5, was given a choice in the nature of a test; that is, that there was a right and a wrong choice to make. Here, too, Gad really wanted David to choose the correct punishment. The expressions which Gad used to urge David to make the choice [*Samuel* has דַּע וּרְאֵה, *consider and analyze* (v. 13); *Chronicles* has only רְאֵה, *analyze* (v. 12), see Section Two] indicate how crucial the choice was. Moreover, *Midrash Shocher Tov* 17, quoted by *Radak (Samuel* v. 13), states that the seemingly redundant word דָּבָר in the phrase, מָה־אָשִׁיב שֹׁלְחִי דָּבָר, *what 'answer' shall I reply to Him Who has sent me,* was meant to hint to David that the desired choice was the plague, since דֶּבֶר, *plague,* and דָּבָר, *matter,* have the same letters. *Wolf* suggests that the plague was the expected choice, since according to *Exodus* 30:12, a census not sanctioned by the Torah would be punished by a plague.

11. קַבֶּל־לָךְ — *Accept upon yourself. Malbim* suggests that the phrase implies: Accept God's justice with love.

12. אִם־שָׁלוֹשׁ שָׁנִים רָעָב — *Whether three years of famine. Samuel* has seven years. *Radak* explains that in fact Gad said only three years, as stated in *Chronicles.* However, immediately prior to the incident of the census there had been a three-year famine because of the matter of the Giveonites (see *II Samuel* ch. 21). Since three years of famine would inevitably be followed by another year of hunger during which the new crop would first have to grow, there would, in fact, have been a famine of seven years.

נִסְפֶּה — *To be swept away.* For a similar usage see *Genesis* 18:23,24.

13. צַר־לִי מְאֹד — *I am greatly distressed.* You tell me to choose the least among them! The choice is hard for me and distresses me. It is comparable to telling a man: You are going to die. Do you wish to be buried near your father or near your mother? He answered them: Woe to the ears that must hear such words! *(Midrash Shocher Tov* 17, quoted by *Mefaresh).*

אֶפְּלָה־נָּא בְיַד־ה' ... — *Let me fall, I pray, into the hand of HASHEM.* David chose the plague, which is a punishment which comes exclusively from God's hands. Both defeat at the hands of his enemies and a famine in which the populace would have to depend on the largess of the wealthy among them involve people who cannot be counted upon to have the degree of mercy which *Hashem* would surely show.

יד אָדָם אַל־אֶפֹּל: וַיִּתֵּן יהוה דֶּבֶר בְּיִשְׂרָאֵל וַיִּפֹּל מִיִּשְׂרָאֵל
טו שִׁבְעִים אֶלֶף אִישׁ: וַיִּשְׁלַח הָאֱלֹהִים ׀ מַלְאָךְ ׀ לִירוּשָׁלִַם
לְהַשְׁחִיתָהּ וּכְהַשְׁחִית רָאָה יהוה וַיִּנָּחֶם עַל־הָרָעָה
וַיֹּאמֶר לַמַּלְאָךְ הַמַּשְׁחִית רַב עַתָּה הֶרֶף יָדֶךָ וּמַלְאַךְ
טז יהוה עֹמֵד עִם־גֹּרֶן אָרְנָן הַיְבֻסִי: וַיִּשָּׂא
דָוִיד אֶת־עֵינָיו וַיַּרְא אֶת־מַלְאַךְ יהוה עֹמֵד בֵּין הָאָרֶץ
וּבֵין הַשָּׁמַיִם וְחַרְבּוֹ שְׁלוּפָה בְּיָדוֹ נְטוּיָה עַל־יְרוּשָׁלָ͏ִם
יז וַיִּפֹּל דָּוִיד וְהַזְּקֵנִים מְכֻסִּים בַּשַּׂקִּים עַל־פְּנֵיהֶם: וַיֹּאמֶר
דָּוִיד אֶל־הָאֱלֹהִים הֲלֹא אֲנִי אָמַרְתִּי לִמְנוֹת בָּעָם
וַאֲנִי־הוּא אֲשֶׁר־חָטָאתִי וְהָרֵעַ הֲרֵעוֹתִי וְאֵלֶּה הַצֹּאן מֶה
עָשׂוּ יהוה אֱלֹהַי תְּהִי נָא יָדְךָ בִּי וּבְבֵית אָבִי וּבְעַמְּךָ
יח לֹא לְמַגֵּפָה: וּמַלְאַךְ יהוה אָמַר אֶל־גָּד
לֵאמֹר לְדָוִיד כִּי ׀ יַעֲלֶה דָוִיד לְהָקִים מִזְבֵּחַ לַיהוה בְּגֹרֶן
יט אָרְנָן הַיְבֻסִי: וַיַּעַל דָּוִיד בִּדְבַר־גָּד אֲשֶׁר דִּבֶּר בְּשֵׁם יהוה:

Again, if David would have chosen either of the other two alternatives, the people might have thought that he had specially chosen a punishment which would not touch him personally. In a war he would be defended by his personal guard and in a famine his wealth would protect him from real hunger. He chose the plague to which he was as vulnerable as any man (*Targum* and commentators).

14. שִׁבְעִים אֶלֶף אִישׁ — *Seventy thousand men*. The Sages (*Pirkei d'R' Eliezer* 43 and other midrashic sources) argue whether this number is to be taken literally or whether it refers to only one man — Avshai the son of Tzeruiah, David's nephew and general, who was so great that his death hurt Israel as much as if seventy thousand men had died. [*Berachos* 62b also has the tradition that Avshai the son of Tzeruiah died in this plague. However, this is derived from the word רַב, *Enough!* (in v. 15) which the Talmud interprets: God said to the angel: 'Take the greatest among them (רַב), for with his death many debts can be repaid (i.e., I can punish Israel for many sins).' At that moment Avshai the son of Tzeruiah died.]

15. וּכְהַשְׁחִית רָאָה ה' — *But as he destroyed,*

HASHEM saw. What did *Hashem* see that persuaded Him to tell the angel to desist from further slaughter?

Berachos 62b has a number of different opinions, all of which are hinted at in the wording of our phrase: He saw [or recalled] the merit of the patriarch, Jacob; the 'ashes' of Isaac from the *Akeidah*[1]; the half-shekalim which the Jews had given when they had originally been counted in the wilderness and concerning which God had promised that they would atone for future sins; the Temple which was to be built in Jerusalem.

According to *Aggados Bereishis* the angel whom God had sent to spread the plague was really an angel of mercy. As soon as he came to Jerusalem, he went straight to Mount Moriah — the future Temple mountain — and stood there reminding God of the superhuman sacrifice which Abraham had brought there when he was willing to offer up his son Isaac to God. God 'saw' Abraham's merit and called a halt to the plague.

Pirkei d'R' Eliezer states that God saw David's penitence, which is described in the next verse.

All the explanations besides this last one present a problem. All the various merits

---

1. That is, the ashes of the ram which Abraham offered in place of Isaac when the angel told him not to sacrifice his son (*Maharsha* there).

great, and let me not fall into the hand of man.' ¹⁴ So HASHEM sent a plague against Israel, and seventy thousand men of Israel fell. ¹⁵ And God sent an angel to Jerusalem to destroy it; but as he destroyed, HASHEM saw and reconsidered the evil, and He said to the destroying angel, 'Enough! Now withhold your hand'; and the angel of HASHEM was standing by the threshing floor of Ornan the Yevusite. ¹⁶ David lifted up his eyes and saw the angel of HASHEM standing between earth and heaven, with his sword drawn in his hand, stretched out over Jerusalem; and David and the elders, covered in sackcloth, fell upon their faces. ¹⁷ And David said to God, 'Is it not I who ordered the people to be counted, and I who have sinned and committed evil? But what have these sheep done? O HASHEM God, may Your hand be upon me and upon my father's house, but let Your people not be plagued.' ¹⁸ And the angel of HASHEM told Gad to tell David, that David should erect an altar to HASHEM on the threshing floor of Ornan the Yevusite. ¹⁹ So David went up in accordance with the word of God which he had spoken

suggested were known to God before he sent the angel to Jerusalem. Why did He send the angel and then, upon contemplating those merits, tell him to desist from further killing?

Perhaps all the various opinions listed above agree with that of *Pirkei d'R' Eliezer.* God saw David's penitence in the first place. When David demonstrated his true contrition God 'remembered' the many merits of Israel and told the angel to stop.

This would explain why the verse states simply that 'God saw' but does not specify what He saw. There were, in fact, a number of different factors, and giving any single one of them would have presented a one-dimensional and therefore distorted picture. As it is, the phrase is left open to be filled in by the sensitive insight of Israel's sages.

וַיִּנָּחֶם עַל־הָרָעָה — *And reconsidered the evil.* Ramban to *Genesis* 6:6 notes the difficulty of depicting God as reconsidering or regretting, and explains that the expression is anthropomorphic because, 'the Torah speaks in the language of man.' Man perceives this Divine manifestation as if it were regret.

For a wide-ranging discussion, see ArtScroll *Genesis*, vol. I, p. 190.

רַב — *Enough!* The translation follows *Metzudos. Berachos* 62b renders: Take the greatest one (רַב) from among them. This refers to Avshai the son of Tzeruiah who was as great as a majority of the Sanhedrin.

וּמַלְאַךְ ה' עֹמֵד עִם־גֹּרֶן אָרְנָן הַיְבוּסִי — *And the angel of HASHEM was standing by the*

threshing floor of Ornan the Yevusite. God made sure that the angel should be next to the threshing floor of Ornan so that David should see him there, and pray and be answered by God in that place. Having the plague cease at that place would be a sign to him that this place was particularly suited for prayer and that this should be the site of the Temple *(Radak).*

16. ... וַיִּשָּׂא דָוִיד אֶת־עֵינָיו — *David lifted up his eyes* ... This verse and the next record David's prayer of repentance. According to *Pirkei d'R' Eliezer* quoted above, that God had seen David's repentance, what is told here must have happened earlier. Our verse must be read as though it were written, *And David* [had previously] *lifted up his eyes* ...

17. הֲלֹא אֲנִי אָמַרְתִּי לִמְנוֹת בָּעָם — *Is it not I who ordered the people to be counted.* David attempts to deflect the punishment from the community and have the burden shifted upon himself and his family.

Whenever God's wrath is unleashed against a larger group, it is always best to focus it on one individual, who would in any case be included, thereby saving everyone else *(Ramban to Numbers* 16:21).

As noted in comm. to v. 15, this prayer was apparently offered before the events described in v. 15. Thus, God accepted David's entreaty and immediately terminated the plague, but in His mercy He did not turn His anger against David's family.

כ וַיָּשָׁב אָרְנָן וַיַּרְא אֶת־----הַמַּלְאָךְ וְאַרְבַּעַת בָּנָיו עִמּוֹ

כא מִתְחַבְּאִים וְאָרְנָן דָּשׁ חִטִּים: וַיָּבֹא דָוִיד עַד־אָרְנָן וַיַּבֵּט

אָרְנָן וַיַּרְא אֶת־דָּוִיד וַיֵּצֵא מִן־הַגֹּרֶן וַיִּשְׁתַּחוּ לְדָוִיד אַפַּיִם

כב אָרְצָה: וַיֹּאמֶר דָּוִיד אֶל־אָרְנָן תְּנָה־לִּי מְקוֹם הַגֹּרֶן

וְאֶבְנֶה־בּוֹ מִזְבֵּחַ לַיהוָה בְּכֶסֶף מָלֵא תְּנֵהוּ לִי וְתֵעָצַר

כג הַמַּגֵּפָה מֵעַל הָעָם: וַיֹּאמֶר אָרְנָן אֶל־דָּוִיד קַח־לָךְ וְיַעַשׂ

אֲדֹנִי הַמֶּלֶךְ הַטּוֹב בְּעֵינָיו רְאֵה נָתַתִּי הַבָּקָר לָעֹלוֹת

כד וְהַמּוֹרִגִים לָעֵצִים וְהַחִטִּים לַמִּנְחָה הַכֹּל נָתָתִּי: וַיֹּאמֶר

הַמֶּלֶךְ דָּוִיד לְאָרְנָן לֹא כִּי־קָנֹה אֶקְנֶה בְּכֶסֶף מָלֵא כִּי לֹא־

כה אֶשָּׂא אֲשֶׁר־לְךָ לַיהוָה וְהַעֲלוֹת עוֹלָה חִנָּם: וַיִּתֵּן דָּוִיד

כו לְאָרְנָן בַּמָּקוֹם שִׁקְלֵי זָהָב מִשְׁקָל שֵׁשׁ מֵאוֹת: וַיִּבֶן שָׁם

דָּוִיד מִזְבֵּחַ לַיהוָה וַיַּעַל עֹלוֹת וּשְׁלָמִים וַיִּקְרָא אֶל־יְהוָה

כז וַיַּעֲנֵהוּ בָאֵשׁ מִן־הַשָּׁמַיִם עַל מִזְבַּח הָעֹלָה: וַיֹּאמֶר

כח יְהוָה לַמַּלְאָךְ וַיָּשֶׁב חַרְבּוֹ אֶל־נְדָנָהּ: בָּעֵת הַהִיא בִּרְאוֹת

דָּוִיד כִּי----עָנָהוּ יְהוָה בְּגֹרֶן אָרְנָן הַיְבוּסִי וַיִּזְבַּח שָׁם:

---

20. וַיָּשָׁב אָרְנָן — *Ornan turned.* He turned his face (*Metzudos*).

וַיַּרְא אֶת־הַמַּלְאָךְ — *And saw the angel.* *Ralbag* points out that although it is rare for an angel to be actually seen by humans, this may occasionally happen when there is a particular need. He cites Belshazzar's vision of the handwriting on the wall as an example.

•§ Purchase of the Future Temple Site

21. וַיָּבֹא דָוִיד עַד־אָרְנָן — *David came up to Ornan.* This seeming repetition of what was said in v. 18 becomes necessary because of the interjection here of v. 20.

22. בְּכֶסֶף מָלֵא — *At full price.* As David explains in v. 24, he did not want the place as a gift but wanted to pay its full price so that each of Israel's tribes would be able to contribute towards the purchase of the Temple site. See below.

23. וְהַמּוֹרִגִים — *The threshing instruments.* According to *Zevachim* 116b, the מוֹרַג is an implement used in threshing which has sharp teeth set into it with which to break up the chaff.

25. שִׁקְלֵי זָהָב מִשְׁקָל שֵׁשׁ מֵאוֹת — *Gold shekels, six hundred by weight.* The verse in *Samuel* is substantially different.

Chronicles	Samuel
(a) וַיִּתֵּן דָּוִיד לְאָרְנָן בַּמָּקוֹם, *So David gave Ornan for the place*	(a) וַיִּקֶן דָוִד אֶת־הַגֹּרֶן וְאֶת־הַבָּקָר, *And David purchased the threshing floor and the cattle*
(b) שִׁקְלֵי זָהָב מִשְׁקָל שֵׁשׁ מֵאוֹת, *gold shekels, six hundred by weight.*	(b) בְּכֶסֶף שְׁקָלִים חֲמִשִּׁים, *for silver — fifty shekels.*

There are two apparent discrepancies. In *Samuel* we have silver and 50 shekels; in *Chronicles*, gold and 600.

The Sages (*Zevachim* 116b and *Sifri* to *Nasso*) suggest a number of solutions, among them that David collected one twelfth of the selling price [600 gold shekalim] from each tribe in silver. I.e., each tribe donated an amount of silver equivalent to 50 gold shekels. Thus each of the tribes donated an equal portion for the purchase of the Temple site.

Both the syntax and the *trop* in *Samuel* bear out this interpretation. It does not say *fifty silver*

in the name of HASHEM. ²⁰ Ornan turned and saw the angel, but his four sons who were with him were hiding — now Ornan was threshing wheat. ²¹ David came to Ornan; and Ornan looked and saw David, and he came off the threshing floor and prostrated himself before David. ²² David said to Ornan, 'Give me the place of this threshing floor so that I may build on it an altar to HASHEM; give it to me at full price, so that the plague may be held back from this people.' ²³ And Ornan said to David, 'Take it, and let my lord the king do what seems good in his eyes. See, I am giving the oxen for burnt-offerings, the threshing instruments for wood, and the wheat for a meal-offering; I give it all.' ²⁴ But King David said to Ornan, 'No, for I will buy it at full price. I will not offer to HASHEM what belongs to you nor sacrifice a burnt-offering that costs nothing.' ²⁵ So David gave Ornan for the place gold shekels, six hundred by weight. ²⁶ And David built an altar there for HASHEM and brought up burnt-offerings and peace-offerings; and he called to HASHEM, Who answered him with fire from heaven upon the altar of the burnt-offering. ²⁷ And HASHEM spoke to the angel, and he returned his sword to its sheath. ²⁸ At that time, when David saw that HASHEM answered him at the threshing-floor of Ornan the Yevusite,

---

shekalim but, as we translated above: silver — fifty shekels.

Another solution suggested by the Sages is that the fifty shekels of Samuel paid for the cattle and the threshing-floor [the small piece of ground upon which the altar actually stood]. The six hundred shekels of gold mentioned in Chronicles were for the entire place (בַּמָּקוֹם) — the surrounding area upon which the Temple was later built (Radak).[1]

26. וַיַּעֲנֵהוּ בָאֵשׁ מִן־הַשָּׁמַיִם — Who answered him with fire from heaven. God showed His acceptance of David's prayer by sending a fire down from heaven to consume the offerings (Ralbag).

Samuel simply states that God allowed Himself to be entreated (וַיֵּעָתֵר) by David and caused the plague to stop. This, in fact, is the end of the narrative in Samuel and with it the book comes to a close. The fire

descending from heaven — which must have been the signal to David that here, indeed, was the Temple site — is not mentioned. Samuel, in contrast to Chronicles, presents the story only as it affected Israel through the plague. The incident as the means by which God revealed the Temple site to David is confined to Chronicles. See prefatory remarks to this chapter.

28. בָּעֵת הַהִיא ... וַיִּזְבַּח שָׁם — At that time ... he offered sacrifices there. Metzudos and Gra understand the phrase to mean that from that time on David made it a practice to offer his sacrifices on the altar which he had built on Ornan's threshing floor. The first part of the sentence explains that David began doing this because on the first occasion that he offered sacrifices there — the occasion described in our chapter — God answered him (v. 26). This indicated

---

1. The place as a whole would seem to refer to the entire area which later became the Temple — i.e., the entire Temple Mount. The Mishnah (Middos 2:1) states that this area was 500 x 500 cubits. The area of the altar in the First Temple was 28 x 28 cubits (Middos 3:1). Thus the ratio of the area of the Temple Mount to that of the altar was approximately 319 to 1.

Now a gold shekel was worth 25 silver shekels (Bava Metzia 45b). Accordingly, the 600 gold shekels given in our verse equalled 15,000 silver shekels — 300 times the amount reported in Samuel. If we further consider that the Samuel sum included payment for the cattle and farm implements and allow three silver shekels for that, then the actual purchase price for the altar site was only forty-seven shekels — again for a ratio of just about 1 to 319. Thus the difference in the two prices accurately reflects the difference in the sizes of the two pieces of land (R' Y. Danziger).

כט וּמִשְׁכַּן ˒יְהוָה אֲשֶׁר־עָשָׂה מֹשֶׁה בַמִּדְבָּר וּמִזְבַּח הָעוֹלָה בָּעֵת הַהִיא בַּבָּמָה בְּגִבְעוֹן: ל וְלֹא־יָכֹל דָּוִיד לָלֶכֶת לְפָנָיו א לִדְרֹשׁ אֱלֹהִים כִּי נִבְעַת מִפְּנֵי חֶרֶב מַלְאַךְ יְהוָה: וַיֹּאמֶר דָּוִיד זֶה הוּא בֵּית יְהוָה הָאֱלֹהִים וְזֶה־מִזְבֵּחַ לְעֹלָה לְיִשְׂרָאֵל: ב וַיֹּאמֶר דָּוִיד לִכְנוֹס אֶת־הַגֵּרִים אֲשֶׁר בְּאֶרֶץ יִשְׂרָאֵל וַיַּעֲמֵד חֹצְבִים לַחְצוֹב אַבְנֵי גָזִית לִבְנוֹת בֵּית הָאֱלֹהִים: ג וּבַרְזֶל ׀ לָרֹב לַמִּסְמְרִים לְדַלְתוֹת הַשְּׁעָרִים וְלַמְחַבְּרוֹת הֵכִין דָּוִיד וּנְחֹשֶׁת לָרֹב אֵין מִשְׁקָל:

to David that this was to be the site of the future Temple. See below to vs. 29 and 30.

29. ... וּמִשְׁכַּן ה' — *Now the Tabernacle of HASHEM* ... The *Mefaresh* points out that the last three verses of our chapter are like one long sentence. He seems to mean that the previous verse flows directly into this one and relates to it as does an explanation to a problem. The two verses might be paraphrased as follows: In spite of the fact that the Tabernacle which Moses had built was at Giveon (v. 29) [and we might have expected that David would go there to bring the sacrifices which he wished to offer] still, since on the first occasion that he offered here he was answered (v. 28), he made it a habit to continue to sacrifice here. See below to v. 30.

בַּבָּמָה בְּגִבְעוֹן — *At the bamah at Giveon.* See comm. 6:16-17 for a wide-ranging discussion of the status of the Tabernacle at Giveon. As explained there, the Holy Ark had been separated from the Tabernacle since the catastrophic Philistine wars which are recounted at the beginning of *I Samuel*, and was now in the tent which David had erected for it in Jerusalem. For this reason Giveon did not have the status of a regular מִשְׁכָּן, *Tabernacle*, and is described as a בָּמָה, *bamah*, lit. *a high place.*

Although the term *bamah* generally refers to the altar, it is used here to refer to the Sanctuary at Giveon as a whole (*Radak*).

30. ... וְלֹא־יָכֹל דָּוִיד — *But David was not able* ... *Gra* explains as follows: The previous verse taught that although the Tabernacle was at Giveon and we would have expected David to sacrifice there, he nevertheless made it his habit to sacrifice at the altar which he had erected on Ornan's threshing floor. This was due to the success of his first sacrifice there, when God had answered him with heavenly fire, which convinced him that this was indeed the Temple site.

But why did he bring the first sacrifice there? Why did he not bring that one at Giveon? Our verse gives the answer. At that time he had been so afraid of the celestial sword which the angel had wielded over Jerusalem (v. 16) that he was physically unable to make the trip to Giveon.[1]

1. *Gra's* interpretation requires some explanation. Surely David brought the first sacrifice on Ornan's threshing floor because he was commanded to do so by Gad who had been told by the angel to bring this message to David (v. 18).

However, a careful reading of that verse shows that David was not commanded to bring sacrifices; only to build the altar. *HaLevi* (Doros HaRishonim, Tekufos HaMikra ch. 37) argues persuasively that from the time of the Patriarchs it had been customary to build altars, the purpose of which was not to offer sacrifices but to serve as a place suitable for prayer and to 'proclaim the name of HASHEM.' He demonstrates this from numerous places in Scripture, although he does not cite our passage.

It is clear that this was also *Gra's* view. The angel had Gad command David to build an altar. To fulfill this command it would have been sufficient to build the altar and to pray there as, indeed, David did (v. 26). The idea of bringing sacrifices came to David because Ornan offered his cattle and threshing instruments for that purpose (v. 23). David could have refused the offer and explained that he would rather bring sacrifices at the great *bamah* at Giveon. Our verse explains why he did not do so.

he offered sacrifices there. ²⁹ Now the Tabernacle of HASHEM which Moses had made in the wilderness and the altars of the burnt-offerings were at the bamah at Giveon at that time. ³⁰ But David was not able to go before it to consult God, because he was terrified by the angel's sword.

D avid said, 'This is the House of HASHEM, God, and this is the altar for burnt-offerings of Israel.' ² David commanded to gather the alien residents in the Land of Israel, and he assigned masons to hew dressed stones to build the House of God. ³ And David prepared large quantities of iron for the nails of the doors of the gates and for the couplings, and vast quantities of copper

XXII

1. זֶה הוּא בֵית ה' הָאֱלֹהִים — *This is the House of HASHEM, God. Targum* renders: *This* [is the place upon which] *the House of HASHEM, God* [is to be built]. So also in the next phrase: *This is the altar which is* [destined to be] *for Israel's burnt-offerings.*

The commentators in general agree with *Targum's* rendering since the building of the Temple and the establishment of a permanent altar still lay in the future. However, the *Mefaresh* takes the second phrase as meaning that henceforth anyone wanting to bring a burnt-offering should use the altar which David had erected.

לְעֹלָה — *For burnt-offerings.* The great majority of required sacrifices offered on the Temple altar were עֹלוֹת, *burnt-offerings,* and that is why the altar was called by this name. In fact, of course, many other types of offerings were also brought upon this altar (*Metzudos*).[1]

◄§ David's Preparations for the Temple

2. This verse begins the detailed account of the preparations which David made for the building of the Temple which his son, Solomon, was to undertake. The interest which *Chronicles* has in these preparations — which are entirely absent from the books of *Samuel* and *Kings* — have been discussed in the footnote to p. 441.

לִכְנוֹס אֶת־הַגֵּרִים — *To gather the alien residents.* From *II Chronicles* 8:7-9 it is evident that the laborers for Solomon's building projects were drawn from the descendants of the Canaanite nations who were dwelling among the Jews in the Land of Israel. The Israelites themselves were occupied with military obligations. These Canaanite sojourners had not become Jewish but had forsaken the idol worship of their ancestors (*Radak* to *Chronicles* 2:16). David, too, made use of such alien residents. *Mefaresh* thinks that he did not want to impose the heavy labor involved upon the Israelites.

Ralbag and *Metzudos* think that reference is to the Giveonites (known in the Talmud as נְתִינִים, *Nethinim*), who, since the time of Joshua (see *Joshua* ch. 9), had been Temple servants for the menial labors which had to be done.

וַיַּעֲמֵד חֹצְבִים לַחְצוֹב ... — *And he assigned masons to hew ... Malbim* suggests that our phrase also refers to the beginning of the next sentence. The masons had to hew stone (v. 2) and also to mine iron (v. 3) for the nails and other metal implements which were required for the building.

3. וְלַמְחַבְּרוֹת — *And for the couplings.* Most commentators assume that these couplings (מְחַבְּרוֹת from חבר, *to join*], which

---

1. Our verse, and indeed the thrust of the narrative in the previous chapter, implies that this was the first inkling which David had concerning the location of the future Temple.

This seems to contradict a tradition of the Sages (*Zevachim* 54b) that David, together with the prophet Samuel, had discovered the Temple location many years earlier. Moreover, *Succah* 53a,b has a tradition that David had dug the foundation of the altar years earlier, while Achitophel was still alive. For attempted solutions to these difficulties see *Rashi* to *Makkos* 11a, *Maharsha* to *Succah* 53b, and *Wolf, Sefer Shmuel al pi HaMesorah.* See further, fn. to 28:2.

ד וַעֲצֵי אֲרָזִים לְאֵין מִסְפָּר כִּי־הֵבִיאוּ הַצִּידֹנִים וְהַצֹּרִים
ה עֲצֵי אֲרָזִים לָרֹב לְדָוִיד: וַיֹּאמֶר דָּוִיד שְׁלֹמֹה
בְנִי נַעַר וָרָךְ וְהַבַּיִת לִבְנוֹת לַיהֹוָה לְהַגְדִּיל ׀ לְמַעְלָה
לְשֵׁם וּלְתִפְאֶרֶת לְכָל־הָאֲרָצוֹת אָכִינָה נָּא לוֹ וַיָּכֶן דָּוִיד
ו לָרֹב לִפְנֵי מוֹתוֹ: וַיִּקְרָא לִשְׁלֹמֹה בְנוֹ וַיְצַוֵּהוּ לִבְנוֹת בַּיִת
ז לַיהֹוָה אֱלֹהֵי יִשְׂרָאֵל: וַיֹּאמֶר דָּוִיד לִשְׁלֹמֹה
בְּנִי ק׳ °בְנוֹ אֲנִי הָיָה עִם־לְבָבִי לִבְנוֹת בַּיִת לְשֵׁם יהֹוָה אֱלֹהָי:
ח וַיְהִי עָלַי דְּבַר־יהֹוָה לֵאמֹר דָּם לָרֹב שָׁפַכְתָּ וּמִלְחָמוֹת

were used to join wooden panels to one another, were made out of iron. *Malbim*, however, points out that in *II Chronicles* 34:11 we learn of מְחַבְּרוֹת made out of wood. Consequently, he renders: ... *nails for the doors of the gates and for the [wooden] brackets* ... i.e., the nails were to be used in the doors and in the brackets.

4. הַצִּידֹנִים וְהַצֹּרִים — *The Sidonians and the Tyrians.* I Kings 5:16ff tells how Solomon requested the help of Chiram, king of Tyre, in cutting trees from Lebanon for use in building the Temple. Now Chiram, throughout Scripture, is always identified as king of Tyre. However, in *I Kings* 5:20, Solomon explains why he asks Chiram's help: ... *for there is none among us who knows how to cut down trees as the Sidonians do.* Rashi there points out that the Sidonians lived in close proximity to the forest and that they were also subjects of Chiram.

5. נַעַר וָרָךְ — *Young and tender.* נַעַר refers to his age, רָךְ to his physical state *(Gra).*

According to *Seder Olam Rabbah* 14, Solomon was only twelve years old when he ascended the throne. If the events recorded here took place in the last year of David's reign, Solomon would have been eleven.

לְהַגְדִּיל לְמַעְלָה לְשֵׁם וּלְתִפְאֶרֶת לְכָל־הָאֲרָצוֹת — *Must be exceedingly great so that it should be famous and glorious in all the lands.* In *II Chronicles* 2:4 we learn how Solomon sent a message to Chiram, king of Tyre, requesting his help because, ... *the house which I am building is great, for our God is greater than all [other] gods.* The implication is that God's greatness makes it necessary that the Temple be a particularly large and imposing building.

But, besides the fact that it is patently ridiculous to think that God's greatness is somehow enhanced by a large building, this idea is contradicted by the teaching of the Sages:

When God said to Moses, *They shall make a Sanctuary for Me,* Moses said to Him, 'Master of the world! Is it not written, *The heavens and the high heavens cannot contain You,* and You tell me to build a Sanctuary for You?' God answered him, 'Moses, it is not as you think. [Make] twenty beams to the north, twenty to the south and eight in the west and I will come and contain My Presence there ...' (*Yalkut Shimoni, Terumah* 364).

It seems probable, therefore, that Solomon was only using imagery which was suited to the perception of the gentile king, Chiram. He would indeed be inclined to think that a grandiose building would do particular honor to God. [See ArtScroll *Ezekiel,* vol. 2, pp. 463-4 for a description and discussion of an edifice which Chiram later raised to his own glory because he ascribed a degree of divinity to himself.]

In the same sense we can understand David's statement here. It would be necessary to make the Temple very great indeed — but not because God would demand a magnificent building for this glory. Rather, it would be needed to impress the gentile nations (לְכָל־הָאֲרָצוֹת, *all the lands*) with its fame and splendor (see *Gra*).

6. וַיִּקְרָא לִשְׁלֹמֹה בְנוֹ ... — *And he called his son Solomon* ... See footnote to 23:1 for a discussion of when this conversation took place.

וַיְצַוֵּהוּ ... — *And charged him* ... This phrase introduces vs. 7-16 which give the details of this charge. David's charge to

beyond weighing. ⁴ *And innumerable cedar logs; for the Sidonians and the Tyrians brought large quantities of cedar logs to David.* ⁵ *And David said, 'My son Solomon is young and tender and the house to be built for HASHEM must be exceedingly great so that it should be famous and glorious in all the lands, therefore I will make preparations for him'; so David made abundant preparations before his death.* ⁶ *And he called his son Solomon and charged him to build a house for HASHEM, God of Israel.* ⁷ *David said to Solomon, 'My son, I had intended to build a house for the name of HASHEM, my God.* ⁸ *But the word of HASHEM came to me, saying, ''You have shed*

Solomon runs from v. 7 through v. 16. It is mainly concerned with Solomon's destiny as the builder of the Temple, but from vs. 12-13 it appears to deal also with Solomon's kingship. In fact, this may have been the occasion on which David informed Solomon that he was to be the successor to the throne (see further in fn. to 23:1). If so, our phrase, ... *to build a house for HASHEM, God of Israel,* is significant. It puts the kingship of Israel into perspective. The central purpose of the Davidic king is to bring the Divine Presence to dwell among the people (see *Rambam, Melachim* 1:1).

7. ... אֲנִי הָיָה עִם־לְבָבִי — *I had intended* [lit. *I had in my heart*] ... See ch. 17.

8. עָלַי דְּבַר־ה' לֵאמֹר — *But the word of HASHEM came to me, saying.* It is not recorded where God said the things mentioned in this verse to David, but this message may have come to him at the same time that Nathan told him that he was not to build the Temple. *Radak* also suggests that God never said these things in so many words but that David understood this to have been God's meaning when He denied him permission to build the Temple. This would not be the only instance where Scripture makes reference to a conversation not previously recorded. See, for example, *Deuteronomy* 1:22 (*Radak*).

Malbim, however, thinks that the two prophecies came at two separate times. When David initially wanted to build the Temple, as recorded in ch. 17, God's reason for refusing permission was that the state of being at rest from all enemies, which is the Torah's precondition for building the Temple, had not yet been attained (see there). It was for this reason that David then set out to wage the wars which are recounted in ch. 18. When he had success-

fully executed those battles, he thought that now, at last, God would allow him to start building. But, at that time God once more refused him permission, this time because of the abundance of blood which David had shed in all these wars, as recorded in our verse.

דָּם לָרֹב שָׁפַכְתָּ — *You have shed much blood.* David is disqualified from building the Temple because he has shed much blood in his lifetime.

Radak feels that *innocent* blood must be meant. Many people who had done no wrong were killed, either by David himself, or on his orders, or indirectly because of him. Uriah, the husband of Bathsheva, was among these (*II Samuel* ch. 11), and the *Kohanim* of the city of Nov whom Saul had slaughtered because they had extended hospitality to David (*I Samuel* chs. 21-2) also belong to this category. Again, among all the many enemies who had fallen in the battles which David had waged there must have been people who were innocent of any wrongdoing. It is not that David was being punished for the death of these people, since his reasons for waging war were always legitimate. But all the killing of innocents made him unsuitable to build the Temple, which is a place of peace, forgiveness of sin, and acceptance of prayer. In this sense David's rejection is comparable to the Torah's prohibition against any iron instrument being used in the manufacture of the stones for the altar (*Exodus* 20:22); the altar cannot derive from the sword.

Ramban, however, assumes that it was not the innocent blood but the wars themselves which disqualified David. He writes that by his martial exploits David showed himself to be, '... a man of Law, adhering to strict justice, and therefore not suitable for [building] a house [which was

גְּדֹלוֹת עָשִׂיתִי לֹא־תִבְנֶה בַיִת לִשְׁמִי כִּי דָמִים רַבִּים
ט שָׁפַכְתָּ אַרְצָה לְפָנָי: הִנֵּה־בֵן נוֹלָד לָךְ הוּא יִהְיֶה אִישׁ
מְנוּחָה וַהֲנִיחוֹתִי לוֹ מִכָּל־אוֹיְבָיו מִסָּבִיב כִּי שְׁלֹמֹה יִהְיֶה
י שְׁמוֹ וְשָׁלוֹם וָשֶׁקֶט אֶתֵּן עַל־יִשְׂרָאֵל בְּיָמָיו: הוּא־יִבְנֶה
בַיִת לִשְׁמִי וְהוּא יִהְיֶה־לִּי לְבֵן וַאֲנִי־לוֹ לְאָב וַהֲכִינוֹתִי
יא כִּסֵּא מַלְכוּתוֹ עַל־יִשְׂרָאֵל עַד־עוֹלָם: עַתָּה בְנִי יְהִי יהוה
עִמָּךְ וְהִצְלַחְתָּ וּבָנִיתָ בֵּית יהוה אֱלֹהֶיךָ כַּאֲשֶׁר דִּבֶּר
יב עָלֶיךָ: אַךְ יִתֶּן־לְךָ יהוה שֵׂכֶל וּבִינָה וִיצַוְּךָ עַל־יִשְׂרָאֵל
יג וְלִשְׁמוֹר אֶת־תּוֹרַת יהוה אֱלֹהֶיךָ: אָז תַּצְלִיחַ אִם־תִּשְׁמוֹר
לַעֲשׂוֹת אֶת־הַחֻקִּים וְאֶת־הַמִּשְׁפָּטִים אֲשֶׁר צִוָּה יהוה
אֶת־מֹשֶׁה עַל־יִשְׂרָאֵל חֲזַק וֶאֱמָץ אַל־תִּירָא וְאַל־תֵּחָת:

to serve as a focus for God's] mercy.'

Gra writes that the Temple was to be called מְנוּחָה, *rest*, and required a man whose nature would be one of tranquillity (see v. 9). [It would seem that *Gra* refers to *Deuteronomy* 12:9, where it seems that מְנוּחָה is used to describe the Temple. But see *Rashi* there.]

Although *Gra* says no more than this, it seems that his perception of the matter agrees with that of R' Tzadok HaKohen whose interpretation of the matter was quoted and discussed in Section Two, p. 438.

From the Midrash (*Yalkut Shimoni* to *Samuel* 145), it would also appear that it was not the innocent blood which David had shed, but the wars which he waged which made him unsuitable to be the Temple builder:

When David heard [that he was told not to build the Temple because of the large amount of blood which he had shed] he was afraid. He said: 'Am I then [personally] disqualified from building the Temple?' ... So God answered him, 'Do not be afraid, David. I swear that I regard [the people whom you have killed] as ... [so many] sacrifices that you brought before Me.' So David asked, 'If so, why may I not be allowed to build the Temple?' God answered, 'If you were to build it, it would

stand eternally, and never be destroyed.' And David said to Him, 'Would this not be all to the good?' But God answered him, 'I know that [Israel] will one day sin before Me. I intend to pour out My anger upon the [physical] building [rather than on the people themselves; for this reason I do not want a Temple which can never be destroyed].'[1]

לְפָנָי — *Before Me*. It is from this expression that the midrash quoted above derives that all the soldiers killed by David's armies in battle were considered by God to be so many sacrifices.

9. הוּא יִהְיֶה אִישׁ מְנוּחָה — *He shall be a man of rest*. God had not used these exact words. However, the idea is implied in the language which Nathan used in his message to David at 17:13. See comm. there.

וַהֲנִיחוֹתִי לוֹ מִכָּל־אוֹיְבָיו מִסָּבִיב — *And I will give him rest from all his enemies round about*. This is a reference to *Deuteronomy* 12:10, where a precondition for the building of the Temple is that Israel should be at peace with all the surrounding nations. See Section Two p. 437.

שְׁלֹמֹה ... שָׁלוֹם — *Solomon ... peace*. The name שְׁלֹמֹה, *Solomon*, is from the root שלם,

1. For a discussion of this cryptic midrash, see R' E.E. Dessler's *Michtav M'Eliyahu*, vol. 2, p. 275. He explains: For an action to be described as taking place *before HASHEM*, it must be performed with completely pure and disinterested motives. Any personal interest would disqualify it from being seen as an act of service before God. When David had been told that he could not build the Temple because he had shed much blood, he had been afraid that his motives in waging war were being impinged. Could it be that he had, indeed, the nature of a killer? God reassured him. David's wars were fought *before HASHEM*. No personal interest of David's was involved, no blot upon his soul.

much blood and waged great wars; you shall not build a house for My name for you have shed much blood upon the ground before Me. ⁹ Behold, a son will be born to you, he shall be a man of rest, and I will give him rest from all his enemies round about; for his name shall be Solomon, and I will bestow peace and quiet upon Israel in his time. ¹⁰ He shall build a house for My name, he shall be a son to Me and I will be a father to him, and I will establish the throne of his kingdom over Israel forever." ¹¹ Now, my son, may HASHEM be with you, and you shall be successful in building a house for HASHEM your God, as He has said concerning you. ¹² Let only HASHEM give you intelligence and understanding and appoint you over Israel, and to observe the law of HASHEM your God. ¹³ Then you will be successful, if you keep the statutes and judgments which HASHEM commanded Moses concerning Israel; be strong and

meaning *peace.*

10. וְהוּא יִהְיֶה־לִּי לְבֵן וַאֲנִי־לוֹ לְאָב — *He shall be a son to Me and I will be a father to him.* In 17:13 the sequence is the other way around: *I will be a Father to him and he will be a son to Me.*

Perhaps the explanation is as follows: God, in His overflowing goodness, shoulders the responsibility for the relationship. He promises to be a Father to Solomon and, as a reaction, Solomon will want to be a son to Him. This is the message which, on God's command, Nathan delivered to David. David, as a father exhorting his son, however, placed the onus for the establishment of the relationship on Solomon. You, my son, should be a son to God; He will then be a Father to you.

וַהֲכִינוֹתִי כִּסֵּא מַלְכוּתוֹ ... עַד־עוֹלָם — *And I will establish the throne of his kingdom ... forever.* The implications of this promise are discussed in Section Two, ch. 17.

12. שֵׂכֶל וּבִינָה — *Intelligence and understanding.* שֵׂכֶל describes the kind of wisdom which can cope with difficult situations and bring them to a successful resolution *(Gra to Proverbs 3:4;* at 1:3 there, he compares *I Samuel* 18:14 where מַשְׂכִּיל is used to describe *success).* בִּינָה is the ability to analyze knowledge and, by a closer understanding, to produce new insights *(Sifri to Deuteronomy 13).*

וִיצַוְּךָ עַל־יִשְׂרָאֵל — *And appoint you over Israel.* The combination צוה עַל usually means *to appoint over* (see 17:10). This is how *Targum* renders our phrase: *appoint*

you king over Israel.

Metzudos understands the phrase differently: *Let God give you the intelligence and understanding to guide Israel.* Since it is God Who will imbue Solomon with the wisdom to guide Israel, it is as though He Himself is commanding what should be done for Israel.

וְלִשְׁמוֹר אֶת־תּוֹרַת ה' אֱלֹהֶיךָ — *And to observe the law of HASHEM your God.* I.e., to rule Israel and to lead them in the path of God's laws *(Ralbag). Metzudos,* following his explanation of the previous phrase, has: Let God give you the intelligence to observe the law of *HASHEM your God.*

13. חֲזַק וֶאֱמָץ — *Be strong and persevere. Malbim (Joshua* 1:6) explains that the root חזק describes the initial determination to overcome an obstacle and אמץ is the perseverance in that determination.

Beur Shemos HaNirdofim SheBiTanach (Wertheimer) demonstrates from many proofs that אמץ always implies a greater degree of effort than does חזק. According to him, the phrase means — *be exceedingly strong* — be strong, but do not be satisfied with just ordinary strength. You are called upon to make superhuman efforts.

אַל־תִּירָא וְאַל־תֵּחָת — *Do not fear and do not falter.* ירא and חתת are the opposite of חזק and אמץ. One who fears does not have the courage to make the initial commitment, and one who falters does not persevere *(Malbim).*

Wertheimer demonstrates that חתת always describes the faint-heartedness that is somewhat less than actual fear. The phrase implies: Do not be afraid and do not even be faint hearted.

יד וְהִנֵּה בְעָנְיִי הֲכִינוֹתִי לְבֵית־יהוה זָהָב כִּכָּרִים מֵאָה־אֶלֶף וְכֶסֶף אֶלֶף אֲלָפִים כִּכָּרִים וְלַנְּחֹשֶׁת וְלַבַּרְזֶל אֵין מִשְׁקָל כִּי לָרֹב הָיָה וְעֵצִים וַאֲבָנִים הֲכִינוֹתִי וַעֲלֵיהֶם תּוֹסִיף:
טו וְעִמְּךָ לָרֹב עֹשֵׂי מְלָאכָה חֹצְבִים וְחָרָשֵׁי אֶבֶן וָעֵץ וְכָל־
טז חָכָם בְּכָל־מְלָאכָה: לַזָּהָב לַכֶּסֶף וְלַנְּחֹשֶׁת וְלַבַּרְזֶל אֵין
יז מִסְפָּר קוּם וַעֲשֵׂה וִיהִי יהוה עִמָּךְ: וַיְצַו דָּוִיד לְכָל־שָׂרֵי
יח יִשְׂרָאֵל לַעְזֹר לִשְׁלֹמֹה בְנוֹ: הֲלֹא יהוה אֱלֹהֵיכֶם עִמָּכֶם וְהֵנִיחַ לָכֶם מִסָּבִיב כִּי | נָתַן בְּיָדִי אֵת יֹשְׁבֵי הָאָרֶץ
יט וְנִכְבְּשָׁה הָאָרֶץ לִפְנֵי יהוה וְלִפְנֵי עַמּוֹ: עַתָּה תְּנוּ לְבַבְכֶם וְנַפְשְׁכֶם לִדְרוֹשׁ לַיהוה אֱלֹהֵיכֶם וְקוּמוּ וּבְנוּ אֶת־מִקְדַּשׁ יהוה הָאֱלֹהִים לְהָבִיא אֶת־אֲרוֹן בְּרִית־יהוה וּכְלֵי קֹדֶשׁ הָאֱלֹהִים לַבַּיִת הַנִּבְנֶה לְשֵׁם־יהוה:
א וְדָוִיד זָקֵן וְשָׂבַע יָמִים וַיַּמְלֵךְ אֶת----שְׁלֹמֹה בְנוֹ עַל----

The *Targumim* render the word as *to be broken* (see *Targum* to *Deuteronomy* 1:21 and *Radak, Sefer HaShorashim*). In that sense it can be seen as a result of fear. Thus: Do not fear in order that you should not be broken by it.

14. ... וְהִנֵּה בְעָנְיִי — *And now, in my poverty* ... Relative to the infinite power of God, even the richest man would be considered poor. אֵין עֲשִׁירוּת בִּפְנֵי מִי שֶׁאָמַר וְהָיָה הָעוֹלָם, *there is no wealth in the presence of the Creator of the world* (*Yalkut*). *Midrash Shocher Tov*, however, derives עָנְיִי from ענה, *to be afflicted;* thus, *and now, by my painful efforts.* David was referring to the extreme efforts which he expended in his extensive preparations for the building of the Temple. [The Sages explain that the Temple was called David's (cf. *Psalms* 30:1) because מָסַר נַפְשׁוֹ עָלָיו, *he sacrificed greatly for it.*]

Targum preserves the tradition of the Sages (see *Yalkut Shimoni*) that David set aside the very food from his mouth to add to the Temple treasury. This עָנְיִי describes the hunger which David suffered as he fasted in order to contribute the food which

he was denying himself.

15. וְכָל־חָכָם בְּכָל־מְלָאכָה — *And every craftsman for every manner of work.* The phrase is obviously shortened. The meaning is: *all sorts of craftsmen for all kinds of work* (*Metzudos*).

17. ... וַיְצַו דָּוִיד — *David commanded* ... In our opening remarks to ch. 23 it will be shown that this charge to the officers probably took place at a later date than the charge to Solomon contained in vs. 7-16.

19. לִדְרוֹשׁ לַה' אֱלֹהֵיכֶם — *To seeking HASHEM, your God.* The root דרש means to *search out* or to *turn to* God. It usually appears with the accusative אֶת. Its use with the prefix ל, *lamed,* is unique to *Chronicles.* From *II Chronicles* 15:12-13 it seems obvious that the meaning is precisely the same whether אֶת or ל is used.

וּכְלֵי קֹדֶשׁ הָאֱלֹהִים — *And the sacred vessels of God.* This presumably refers to the remains of Moses' Tabernacle, which was then standing at Giveon. See *II Chronicles* 5:5.

XXIII

◆§ The Levitical Mishmaros

This chapter begins the description of the dispositions which David made for the building, administration, and service of the Temple which Solomon was destined to build.

The *Kohanim* and Levites were each to be divided into twenty-four מִשְׁמָרוֹת, *mishmaros* [lit. *watches*], each *mishmar* to serve on a rotating basis for one week in the Temple service. The details of this arrangement can be found in *Rambam, Klei HaMikdash* chs. 3

persevere, do not fear and do not falter. ¹⁴ *And now, in my poverty, I have prepared for the House of* HASHEM *a hundred thousand talents of gold, a million talents of silver, and copper and iron beyond counting, because there was so much; I have prepared wood and stone but you should add to these.* ¹⁵ *And with you will be numerous workers, quarrymen, stone and wood masons and every craftsman for every manner of work — for gold, silver, bronze and iron, beyond count. Go and do, and may* HASHEM *be with you.'* ¹⁷ *David commanded all the officers of Israel to assist his son Solomon.* ¹⁸ *'Surely* HASHEM *your God is with you and He will give you peace from all around you; for He has given the inhabitants of the land into my hand, and the land has been subdued before* HASHEM *and before His people.* ¹⁹ *Now set your hearts and souls to seeking* HASHEM *your God; rise and build the sanctuary of* HASHEM *God so that the Ark of the covenant of* HASHEM *and the sacred vessels of God may be brought into the house which is to be built for the name of* HASHEM.'

David was old and full of days and he made his son Solomon king

and 4. The commentators assume that our chapter traces the development of the twenty-four Levite *mishmaros*, while ch. 24 deals with those of the *Kohanim*. Some additional details concerning the Levite lists are given at the end of ch. 24 vs. 20-31, while the special sub-groups of the Levites — the choristers and gatekeepers — are given in chs. 25 and 26 respectively. Due to the great complexity of these chapters and the questions that they raise, it is necessary to subject them to a broader analysis than is appropriate to the commentary on any one verse. This will be done in Appendix V.

1. The dispositions which David made concerning the service and administration of the Temple are described in conjunction with Solomon's elevation to the throne. Our verse, which talks of David being *old and full of days*, recalls I Kings 1:1 which begins with almost the identical words. It is thus reasonable to assume that the sec-

ond part of v. 1, ... *and he made his son Solomon king over Israel*, is a brief summation of the events described in that chapter. These are: Adoniyah's pretension; Bathsheva and Nathan's intercession on Solomon's behalf; and David's immediate action to assure Solomon's succession.[1]

1. Some clarification concerning the sequence of events is necessary. The narrative there does not make clear how Nathan and Bathsheva knew that Solomon was supposed to be king. In her speech to the king, Bathsheva talks of an oath which David had made to her, but this is never explicated in Scripture. The Sages find only a hint of it in II Samuel 12:24-25. Nevertheless, it seems clear that it was generally assumed that Solomon was to be king, since Adoniyah invited neither him nor anyone else of the king's inner circle to the coronation which he organized for himself (I Kings 1:10).

At 28:5, David talks of God's choosing Solomon from among all his sons to be king over Israel. In our commentary there we surmise that this was indicated when, at Solomon's birth, God sent the prophet Nathan to call the child Yedidiah — *beloved of God* — after David had called him Solomon, indicating that he saw him as the fulfillment of the prediction made at 22:9.

Thus, in David's mind it must have been clear that Solomon was to succeed him and this is indicated in 22:5ff. Since the events in ch. 22 would seem to have preceded those in ch. 23, then from v. 6 there it is obvious that Solomon, too, had already been informed of his destiny before Adoniyah's pretensions. This raises the question of why Bathsheva makes no mention of this in her argument to David.

We must conclude one of two possibilities: Either this charge to Solomon was generally known and Bathsheva, too, was privy to it but she nevertheless preferred to press her claim for Solomon by referring to an oath which had been made to her privately, rather than to David's earlier decision

ב וַיֶּאֱסֹף֙ אֶת־כָּל־שָׂרֵ֣י יִשְׂרָאֵ֔ל וְהַכֹּהֲנִ֖ים יִשְׂרָאֵֽל׃ ב

ג וְהַלְוִיִּֽם׃ וַיִּסָּֽפְרוּ֙ הַלְוִיִּ֔ם מִבֶּ֛ן שְׁלֹשִׁ֥ים שָׁנָ֖ה וָמָ֑עְלָה וַיְהִ֣י ב־ז
מִסְפָּרָ֧ם לְגֻלְגְּלֹתָ֛ם לִגְבָרִ֖ים שְׁלֹשִׁ֥ים וּשְׁמוֹנָ֖ה אָֽלֶף׃

ד מֵאֵ֗לֶּה לְנַצֵּ֙חַ֙ עַל־מְלֶ֣אכֶת בֵּית־יְהֹוָ֔ה עֶשְׂרִ֥ים וְאַרְבָּעָ֖ה

ה אָ֑לֶף וְשֹׁטְרִ֥ים וְשֹׁפְטִ֖ים שֵׁ֣שֶׁת אֲלָפִ֑ים וְאַרְבַּ֙עַת֙ אֲלָפִ֔ים
שֹֽׁעֲרִ֔ים וְאַרְבַּ֤עַת אֲלָפִים֙ מְהַֽלְלִ֣ים לַֽיהֹוָ֔ה בַּכֵּלִ֖ים אֲשֶׁ֥ר

ו עָשִׂ֖יתִי לְהַלֵּֽל׃ וַיֶּחָלְקֵ֥ם דָּוִ֖יד מַחְלְק֑וֹת לִבְנֵ֣י

ז לֵוִ֔י לְגֵרְשׁ֖וֹן קְהָ֥ת וּמְרָרִֽי׃ לַגֵּרְשֻׁנִּ֖י לַעְדָּ֑ן

2. וַיֶּאֱסֹף אֶת־כָּל־שָׂרֵי יִשְׂרָאֵל — *He gathered all the officers of Israel.* The actual division of the Levites into their groups was made by David himself (v. 6). Nevertheless, it seems to have been a sufficiently significant innovation to require the presence of the officers of Israel. Perhaps, too, the leaders were required because the Levite activities were not limited to the Temple service but included educational and administrative duties throughout the land (see v. 24).

3. מִבֶּן שְׁלֹשִׁים שָׁנָה וָמָעְלָה — *From the age of thirty and up.* In *Numbers* 4:35 the age at which a Levite is responsible for the Temple service is given as thirty years. In 8:24 it is given as twenty-five years. The Sages explain that at twenty-five years the Levites began learning the many intricate details of their service but that they only began serving at age thirty. It therefore seems logical that David would take his census from among those Levites who were already thirty.

Both passages in *Numbers* specify that the Levites must retire from their service at age fifty. No mention is made here that David counted only those under fifty.

Ramban (Sefer HaMitzvos, Shoresh 3) suggests that since the verse states that only those Levites of thirty and over were counted, as specified by the Torah, it is understood that those over fifty were also excluded.

R' Yeshayah Reicher, in his work *Mikra U'Massores,* thinks that since this count of the Levites was made not only for the purpose of service in the Temple but also in order to appoint שֹׁטְרִים, *sheriffs,* and שֹׁפְטִים, *judges* (v. 4), there was no reason to exclude those over fifty since, with greater age, they would make better leaders.[1]

לְגֻלְגְּלֹתָם ... — *Taken individually* ... See v. 24, below.

4. ... מֵאֵלֶּה — *Of these* ... These are David's actual words. This can be seen from the use of עָשִׂיתִי, *I made,* in the next verse *(Gra; Malbim).*

which was, after all, revocable. Or, that the charge in ch. 22 was made privately to Solomon — was, in fact, not generally known, and Adoniyah's perception of Solomon as a rival was based not on any solid knowledge but on his observations of David's special bearing towards his chosen son.

It seems clear, however, that the charge to the officers recounted at 22:17 must have taken place at a later date — that is, some time after the events recounted at the beginning of ch. 22, and indeed after the events described in the first verse of our chapter. It is inconceivable that Bathsheva and Nathan should not have referred to such a public pronouncement if it had taken place before Adoniyah's pretension. Moreover, if David had already publicized Solomon's succession, then Adoniyah would not have been engaged in a superficially justified pretension [by virtue of the fact that he was the oldest remaining son of David] but in an insurrection against David's wishes. Under such circumstances, it would have been inconceivable for a man of Yoav's stature to join him in rebelling against the king's official designation.

It need not surprise us that the charge to the officers should have been included in ch. 22 even though it took place some time later. It is well-established Scriptural usage to tell a complete story even at the cost of a strictly organized chronology. [As an example, see *Exodus* 16:33ff where, as part of the story of the manna, we have Moses telling Aaron to deposit some of the heavenly food at the side of the Holy Ark, although the Torah had not yet been given and certainly no Ark existed. The later passage was included in order to complete the story which was being told there.]

1. *Ramban* seems to reject this. In a controversy with *Rashi (Numbers* 8:25) whether the age limitation of the Levites applied also to the Levite service of שִׁיר, *song,* he cites our v. 5 as proof that

over Israel. ² He gathered all the officers of Israel and the Kohanim and the Levites. ³ The Levites were counted from the age of thirty and up; their numbers, taken individually, came to thirty-eight thousand. ⁴ Of these twenty-four thousand to oversee the administration of the House of HASHEM, and six thousand sheriffs and judges. ⁵ And four thousand gatekeepers and four thousand to praise HASHEM with the instruments which I made for praise. ⁶ David divided them into divisions according to the sons of Levi — for Gershon, Kehath and Merari. ⁷ For the Gershonites — Ladan and

---

לְנַצֵּחַ — *To oversee.* The translation follows *Targum.* See also *Radak (Shorashim)* and *Ibn Ezra* (to *Ezra* 3:8). *Ralbag* suggests that these 24,000 Levites were appointed over the tasks described below in verse 28, see there. See further in Appendix V.

At 15:21, however, this term was used to describe performing music, and *Gra*[1] and *Metzudos* offer this same explanation here.

Presumably, *Targum* did not take the term in this sense since it describes all the 24,000 Levites, and from the next verse we see that only 4,000 were musicians. However, *Gra* and *Metzudos* anticipate this problem and explain that these 24,000 were choristers who did not play an instrument, while the 4,000 mentioned in the next verse were musicians.

וְשֹׁטְרִים וְשֹׁפְטִים ... — *Sheriffs and judges.* *Metzudos* takes שֹׁטְרִים in its usual sense — officials of the court who enforce the rulings of the judges. Apparently, he takes שֹׁפְטִים as does *Ralbag*, that the Levites served as *judges* in disproportionate numbers. This was due to the fact that they were the primary teachers of the Torah (*Deuteronomy* 33:10) and therefore had greater Torah knowledge.

Thus, we assume that in David's plans, the judiciary throughout the land was to be under Levite control, and they were to supply a large share of the judges and court officials.

However, a careful analysis of our verse together with 26:29 would indicate that their function was broader than that of sheriffs. See comm. there.

5. שֹׁעֲרִים — *Gatekeepers.* See 9:17ff and below 26:1ff.

מְהַלְלִים לַה׳ בַּכֵּלִים — *To praise HASHEM with the instruments.* See 6:16-17 for a wide-ranging discussion of the obligation of the Levites to function as choristers and musicians during the Temple service.

6. וַיֶּחָלְקֵם דָּוִיד מַחְלְקוֹת — *David divided them into divisions.* The commentary will follow *Gra* and *Malbim*, who find the Levite *mishmaros* actually listed in this section. See, however, Appendix V for another possible explanation.

This verse begins to describe the twenty-four *mishmaros* which David established for the Levites. As will become clear from the commentary below, *mishmaros* in Ezra's time were not quite the same as those in David's time. The passage should be studied together with 24:20ff.

In studying these lists it must be remembered that the word בֶּן, *son,* may mean *descendant* rather than son. The names given are the heads of *mishmaros* in David's time by which time many more generations had elapsed from the sons of Levi than those recorded in our text (*Malbim*). This can be readily seen by checking against the lists given at 6:5 for the choristers, where between 13 and 21 generations are listed between Levi's sons and the functionaries of David's time.

7. לַגֵּרְשֻׁנִּי — *For the Gershonites.* To facilitate discussion the following chart is offered. Each name is followed by a number in order to show how the twenty-four *mishmaros* are counted according to *Gra.* In some instances *Malbim* differs with *Gra* and this will be discussed in the commentary.

---

indeed for this purpose also the age limitation applied. It is evident that *Ramban* feels that the age limitation applied to all the activities listed in vs. 4-5, including therefore also the officials and judges. [See also *Rambam, Klei HaMikdash* 3:8, who agrees with *Rashi* in this respect.]

1. *Gra* here offers a novel explanation for the root נצח being used to describe music. It derives from the fact that with the power of music it is possible for a person to conquer (נצח) the evil inclination within himself.

ח וְשִׁמְעִי: בְּנֵי לַעְדָּן הָרֹאשׁ יְחִיאֵל וְזֵתָם וְיוֹאֵל

ט שְׁלֹשָׁה: בְּנֵי שִׁמְעִי °שְׁלֹמוֹת וַחֲזִיאֵל וְהָרָן שְׁלֹשָׁה

י אֵלֶּה רָאשֵׁי הָאָבוֹת לְלַעְדָּן: וּבְנֵי שִׁמְעִי יַחַת

יא זִינָא וִיעוּשׁ וּבְרִיעָה אֵלֶּה בְנֵי־שִׁמְעִי אַרְבָּעָה: וַיְהִי־יַחַת

הָרֹאשׁ וְזִיזָה הַשֵּׁנִי וִיעוּשׁ וּבְרִיעָה לֹא־הִרְבּוּ בָנִים וַיִּהְיוּ

יב לְבֵית אָב לִפְקֻדָּה אֶחָת: בְּנֵי קְהָת עַמְרָם

יג יִצְהָר חֶבְרוֹן וְעֻזִּיאֵל אַרְבָּעָה: בְּנֵי עַמְרָם

אַהֲרֹן וּמֹשֶׁה וַיִּבָּדֵל אַהֲרֹן לְהַקְדִּישׁוֹ קֹדֶשׁ קָדָשִׁים הוּא־

וּבָנָיו עַד־עוֹלָם לְהַקְטִיר לִפְנֵי יהוה לְשָׁרְתוֹ וּלְבָרֵךְ בִּשְׁמוֹ

יד עַד־עוֹלָם: וּמֹשֶׁה אִישׁ הָאֱלֹהִים בָּנָיו יִקָּרְאוּ עַל־שֵׁבֶט

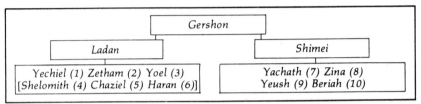

At 6:2, as in the Torah, the sons of Gershon are given as Livni and Shimei. Who, then, is the Ladan mentioned here? *Radak* suggests that Ladan is another name for Livni. *Malbim* feels that it is possible that Ladan is a descendant of Livni, perhaps many generations removed from him.

8. ... בְּנֵי לַעְדָּן — *The sons of Ladan* ... The three sons of Ladan mentioned in this verse are the heads of the first three of the twenty-four *mishmaros*.

שְׁלֹשָׁה — *Three.* In the genealogical lists in chs. 1-8 we have frequently observed that a list of names may be followed by a number which seems to be redundant. This has been discussed at 2:6.

9. ... בְּנֵי שִׁמְעִי — *The sons of Shimei* ... The three names listed in this verse seem problematic since they are given as *sons of Shimei* but are then listed at the end of the verse as *heads of families of Ladan.*

Gra identifies this *Shimei* as Gershon's other son. Nevertheless, some of his children became leaders in Ladan's family, which was so large that more leaders were required than it was able to produce from within its own ranks.

Malbim's solution is that the Shimei of our verse is not the same one mentioned in verse 7. A glance at the Gershonite list given at 6:5 shows another Shimei [II(3)]

who can be seen, by combining lists I and II there, to be a grandson of Livni. It is his descendants who are given in our verse and all the descendants of Livni — those of our verse and the previous one — are then subsumed under Ladan. The Shimei in the next verse is the one mentioned in verse 7 as Gershon's son.

The three sons mentioned in our verse take the count from (4) to (6).

10. ... וּבְנֵי שִׁמְעִי — *The sons of Shimei* ... According to *Gra*, the four names mentioned in this verse take us from (7) through (10).

11. ... וִיעוּשׁ וּבְרִיעָה לֹא־הִרְבּוּ בָנִים — *But Yeush and Beriah did not have many sons* ... The verse goes on to say that because they were only few in number they were joined into one *mishmar* (*Metzudos*). *Gra*, however, counts both of these towards the count of twenty-four. He therefore explains that this remark is parenthetical and describes the situation in Ezra's time. Many centuries after David's dispositions were made, the two families had indeed shrunk and were merged into one *mishmar.* However, in David's time there were sufficient numbers to form two *mishmaros.* See 24:27.

לְבֵית אָב לִפְקֻדָּה אֶחָת — *One family, one order.* פְּקֻדָּה [lit. *tally*] seems to be used here

Shimei. 8 *The sons of Ladan — the chief was Yechiel and Zetham and Yoel, three.* 9 *The sons of Shimei — Shelomith, Chaziel and Haran, three; these were the heads of the families of Ladan.* 10 *The sons of Shimei — Yachath, Zina, Yeush and Beriah; these were the sons of Shimei, four.* 11 *Yachath was the chief, and Zizah the second. But Yeush and Beriah did not have many sons, so they became one family, one order.* 12 *The sons of Kehath — Amram, Yitzhar, Chevron and Uzziel, four.* 13 *The sons of Amram — Aaron and Moses; and Aaron was set apart to sanctify him as holy of holies, he and his descendants forever, to burn [offerings] before HASHEM, to serve before Him and to bless in His name forever.* 14 *But as for Moses, the man of God, his sons are reckoned among the tribe*

---

to correspond to family; that is, an organized group assigned to a specific task — an *order*. Since they were so few in number, they were counted for the tasks of the Levites as one unit. See further, at 24:3.

12. ... בְּנֵי קְהָת — *The sons of Kehath* ... The following chart illustrates *Gra's* count of the *mishmaros* descended from Kehath.

13. ... וַיִּבָּדֵל אַהֲרֹן — *And Aaron was set apart* ... Aaron's descendants are not to be counted among the Levite groups. Although he was descended from Levi, he and his children were set aside from the Levites and imbued with the sanctity of the *Kehunah*, priesthood. They had their own twenty-four *mishmaros*, as recounted in the next chapter.

לְהַקְדִּישׁוֹ קֹדֶשׁ קָדָשִׁים — *To sanctify him as holy of holies.* The rest of the Levite tribe was holy; Aaron's descendants — the *Kohanim* — were holy of holies (*Ralbag*).

לְהַקְטִיר לִפְנֵי ה' — *To burn [offerings] before* HASHEM. The verb קטר, which is generally transitive, is used here without an object. It is used most frequently throughout Scripture in connection with the קְטֹרֶת, incense.

However, *II Kings* 16:15 uses it to describe the bringing of the daily burnt-offering and it also is occasionally used to describe the burning of the fats of various sacrifices.

וּלְבָרֵךְ בִּשְׁמוֹ עַד־עוֹלָם — *And to bless in His name forever.* One of the duties of the *Kohanim* was to bless the people in God's name (*Numbers* 6:22-27). However, the Sages may have understood the prefix ב in the sense of *with*, that is that God's Ineffable Name is to be used in the priestly blessing (see e.g., *Arachin* 11a).

14. וּמֹשֶׁה ... בָּנָיו יִקָּרְאוּ עַל־שֵׁבֶט הַלֵּוִי — *But as for Moses ... his sons are reckoned among the tribe of Levi.* Although Aaron's descendants are not counted among the Levites, Moses' children are.

It would seem that it was necessary to stress this because Moses also functioned in the priesthood. The Sages teach that during the seven inaugural days leading to Aaron's induction into the priesthood, Moses functioned as *Kohen Gadol*.

This was also reflected in the encampment around the Tabernacle in the wilderness. The three Levite families were ranged on the southern, western, and northern sides respectively, but Aaron, Moses and his sons camped in the east side (*Numbers* 3:38). This, because of

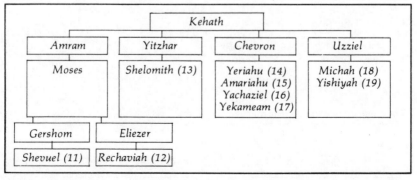

בְּנֵי מֹשֶׁה גֵּרְשׁוֹם וֶאֱלִיעֶזֶר: בְּנֵי גֵרְשׁוֹם

יז שְׁבוּאֵל הָרֹאשׁ: וַיִּהְיוּ בְנֵי־אֱלִיעֶזֶר רְחַבְיָה הָרֹאשׁ

וְלֹא־הָיָה לֶאֱלִיעֶזֶר בָּנִים אֲחֵרִים וּבְנֵי רְחַבְיָה רָבוּ

יח־יט לְמָעְלָה: בְּנֵי יִצְהָר שְׁלֹמִית הָרֹאשׁ:   בְּנֵי

חֶבְרוֹן יְרִיָּהוּ הָרֹאשׁ אֲמַרְיָה הַשֵּׁנִי יַחֲזִיאֵל הַשְּׁלִישִׁי

כ וְיָקַמְעָם הָרְבִיעִי: בְּנֵי עֻזִּיאֵל מִיכָה הָרֹאשׁ

כא וְיִשִּׁיָּה הַשֵּׁנִי: בְּנֵי מְרָרִי מַחְלִי וּמוּשִׁי בְּנֵי

כב מַחְלִי אֶלְעָזָר וְקִישׁ: וַיָּמָת אֶלְעָזָר וְלֹא־הָיוּ לוֹ בָּנִים כִּי

כג אִם־בָּנוֹת וַיִּשָּׂאוּם בְּנֵי־קִישׁ אֲחֵיהֶם: בְּנֵי מוּשִׁי מַחְלִי

כד וְעֵדֶר וִירֵמוֹת שְׁלֹשָׁה: אֵלֶּה בְנֵי־לֵוִי לְבֵית אֲבֹתֵיהֶם

רָאשֵׁי הָאָבוֹת לִפְקוּדֵיהֶם בְּמִסְפַּר שֵׁמוֹת לְגֻלְגְּלֹתָם עֹשֵׂה

הַמְּלָאכָה לַעֲבֹדַת בֵּית יהוה מִבֶּן עֶשְׂרִים שָׁנָה וָמָעְלָה:

Moses' status as a *Kohen*.

Our verse teaches that this status notwithstanding, his sons were to be counted among the Levites and became part of the twenty-four *mishmaros*.

15. גֵרְשׁוֹם וֶאֱלִיעֶזֶר — *Gershom and Eliezer.* These are the names of Moses' sons as given in *Exodus* 18:3-4. They themselves are not part of the count of twenty-four but are mentioned here because of their descendants.

16-18. ... שְׁבוּאֵל ... רְחַבְיָה ... שְׁלֹמִית — *Shevuel ... Rechaviah ... Shelomith ...* These are heads of *mishmaros* 11-13 in *Gra's* count.

19. ... בְּנֵי חֶבְרוֹן — *The sons of Chevron ...* The descendants of Chevron are numbers 14 through 17 in *Gra's* count.

Based on 24:23, *Malbim* concludes that the last three mentioned in our verse were actually sons of Yeriahu. *Gra* and *Metzudos*, though, consider all of them to be the sons of Chevron and explain that verse differently. See there.

20. ... בְּנֵי עֻזִּיאֵל — *The sons of Uzziel ...* The two descendants of Uzziel are numbers 18 and 19 in *Gra's* count.

21. ... בְּנֵי מְרָרִי — *The sons of Merari ...* The following chart covers Merari's descendants.

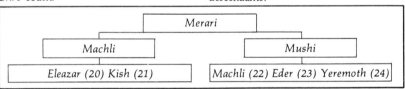

אֶלְעָזָר — *Eleazar.* As indicated in the chart, Eleazar is the twentieth in *Gra's* count. However, since v. 22 teaches that he had no sons, he can only have headed a *mishmar* in his own lifetime. After his death the *mishmar* named after him must have received a different leader. See 24:27.

23. ... בְּנֵי מוּשִׁי — *The sons of Mushi ...* The three descendants of Mushi complete the count of twenty-four.

24. אֵלֶּה בְנֵי־לֵוִי לְבֵית אֲבוֹתֵיהֶם — *These are the sons of Levi according to their families.* Reference is to the lists beginning at v. 7. Verse 6 had introduced these lists by saying that David had created divisions for: לִבְנֵי לֵוִי לְגֵרְשׁוֹן קְהָת וּמְרָרִי, and our phrase must be understood as referring back to that verse:

24. אֵלֶּה בְנֵי־לֵוִי, *These are the sons of Levi*	**6.** לִבְנֵי לֵוִי, *For the sons of Levi,*
לְבֵית אֲבוֹתֵיהֶם, *according to their families.*	לְגֵרְשׁוֹן קְהָת מְרָרִי, *for Gershon, Kehath and Merari.*

of Levi. ¹⁵ *The sons of Moses — Gershom and Eliezer.* ¹⁶ *The sons of Gershom — Shevuel, the chief.* ¹⁷ *The sons of Eliezer — Rechaviah, the chief; Eliezer had no other sons but the sons of Rechaviah were exceedingly numerous.* ¹⁸ *The sons of Yitzhar — Shelomith, the chief.* ¹⁹ *The sons of Chevron — Yeriahu, the chief, Amariah, the second, Yachaziel the third, and Yekameam the fourth.* ²⁰ *The sons of Uzziel — Michah the chief, and Yishiyah the second.* ²¹ *The sons of Merari — Machli and Mushi; the sons of Machli — Eleazar and Kish.* ²² *And Eleazar died, and he had no sons, only daughters; and their kinsmen, the sons of Kish, married them.* ²³ *The sons of Mushi — Machli, Eder and Yeremoth — three.* ²⁴ *These are the sons of Levi according to their families, the heads of the families for their countings, by name-tally, taken individually — those who did the work for the service of the House of* HASHEM *— from the age of*

 רָאשֵׁי הָאָבוֹת לִפְקוּדֵיהֶם — *The heads of the families for their countings.* רָאשֵׁי הָאָבוֹת is short for רָאשֵׁי בָּתֵּי הָאָבוֹת. Although the introduction had been אֵלֶּה בְנֵי-לֵוִי, not all the Levites are listed — only their family heads.

The word פְּקוּדָה in this context generally means *tally* or *muster* (see *Numbers* ch. 1). The people listed above were the heads of the families of all those counted in the tribe of Levi (*Metzudos*).

בְּמִסְפַּר שֵׁמוֹת לְגֻלְגְּלֹתָם — *By name-tally, taken individually.* This phrase is familiar from the census taken at the beginning of *Numbers. Numbers* 1:20-21 reads: תּוֹלְדֹתָם לְמִשְׁפְּחֹתָם לְבֵית אֲבֹתָם בְּמִסְפַּר שֵׁמוֹת ... לְגֻלְגְּלֹתָם ... פְּקֻדֵיהֶם — ... *their generations, according to their families, according to their father's houses, by name-tally, taken individually ... their count ... Gra* there (*Aderes Eliyahu*) explains that the census which Moses took consisted of two distinct parts: actual counting and the establishment of genealogical lines. *Gra* interprets the first verse as being concerned with the genealogical issues and only with the next verse, beginning with פְּקֻדֵיהֶם, *their count,* does the numbering begin.

The meaning of בְּמִסְפַּר שֵׁמוֹת, in this context, is that the genealogical tables were concerned not only with the בָּתֵּי אָבוֹת, *family units,* but with each individual who was listed by name. Moreover, he had to appear in person — לְגֻלְגְּלֹתָם, *individually.* HaKesav VeHakabbalah explains that in *Gra's* view מִסְפַּר does not derive from ספר, *to count,* but from סַפֵּר, *to tell.* מִסְפַּר is that

which is told (as in *Judges* 7:15 — אֶת-מִסְפַּר הַחֲלוֹם, *the telling of the dream*) and the phrase בְּמִסְפַּר שֵׁמוֹת לְגֻלְגְּלֹתָם would mean: ... *with names explicated by each person as he appeared individually.*

This could well be the meaning here also. David did not satisfy himself with simply assigning so and so many groupings to each of the three major Levitical divisions. He identified each of the leaders of the sub-groupings by name and, moreover, had them appear before him in person to ascertain their suitability for the tasks assigned to them.

There may be yet another explanation for מִסְפַּר שֵׁמוֹת, based upon *Rashi's* interpretation of *Numbers* 14:29. There, the decree of wandering for forty years in the wilderness is expressed in regard to כָּל-פְּקֻדֵיכֶם לְכָל-מִסְפַּרְכֶם. *Rashi* renders this difficult phrase by taking פְּקֻדָה as referring to the actual counting and מִסְפַּר as the tally. He renders the phrase: All of you who were counted in the various tallies which had been previously held [whether for the army, the shekels or anything else].

Then, מִסְפַּר שֵׁמוֹת may mean: a tally held for the purpose of ascertaining the names in a given group [and not necessarily for the purpose of knowing the number of people involved]. This verse has been interpreted as referring back to the earlier lists. As shall be seen below, another explanation is possible.

מִבֶּן עֶשְׂרִים שָׁנָה וָמָעְלָה — *From the age of twenty and up.* Verse 3 had said that census applied to Levites from age *thirty* and up — this in accordance with the

כה כֵּי אָמַר דָּוִיד הֵנִיחַ יהוה אֱלֹהֵי־יִשְׂרָאֵל לְעַמּוֹ וַיִּשְׁכֹּן
כו בִּירוּשָׁלַ͏ִם עַד־לְעוֹלָם: וְגַם לַלְוִיִּם אֵין־לָשֵׂאת אֶת־הַמִּשְׁכָּן
כז וְאֶת־כָּל־כֵּלָיו לַעֲבֹדָתוֹ: כִּי בְדִבְרֵי דָוִיד הָאַחֲרֹנִים הֵמָּה
כח מִסְפַּר בְּנֵי־לֵוִי מִבֶּן עֶשְׂרִים שָׁנָה וּלְמָעְלָה: כִּי מַעֲמָדָם
לְיַד־בְּנֵי אַהֲרֹן לַעֲבֹדַת בֵּית יהוה עַל־הַחֲצֵרוֹת וְעַל־
הַלְּשָׁכוֹת וְעַל־טָהֳרַת לְכָל־קֹדֶשׁ וּמַעֲשֵׂה עֲבֹדַת בֵּית

Torah's specification at *Numbers 4:35*.

The solution seems to be contained in verse 27. There were two countings. The earlier one included only those Levites who were above thirty [and below fifty — see comm. to v. 3], while the later one included also those who were twenty and over [and, presumably, even those over fifty].

Why did David change the age in his second counting?

Malbim and *Metzudos* assume that David did not initially realize that the Torah law restricting Levitical service to those between thirty and fifty applied only in the desert years when a prime function of the Levites was to carry the Ark (see *Chullin* 24a). [For this, strength was needed, and the peak of strength is in this age bracket *(Malbim).*] When he saw that this would no longer be necessary, he realized that the law no longer applied and he therefore recounted the Levites from twenty and up. *Ramban,* in his commentary to *Numbers 8:25* and in his glosses to *Sefer HaMitzvos, Shoresh 3,* has a different view. The Talmud *(Chullin 24a)* teaches that the age limitations set for the Levites do not apply to Shiloh and the Temple. In contrast to *Rambam* [that 'Shiloh and the Temple' is an expression describing the entire period after Israel entered the Promised Land], *Ramban* is of the opinion that the phrase is to be taken literally. Even after Israel entered the Promised Land, the age limitations still applied during the times when the Tabernacle did not stand at Shiloh and when the Temple had not yet been built.

Ramban believes that the two censi described in this chapter bear out his opinion. When David made the earlier one, he had in mind the period of time which

would elapse before the Temple would be built by Solomon. The Torah's limitations were still applicable then and consequently only those Levites above thirty were counted.[1]

The second counting was for the purpose of organizing the Levites for the Temple period. Then, as *Chullin* teaches, the limitations were to be lifted and, like the Israelites, the Levites would also be counted from age twenty.

Given *Ramban's* interpretation, it would seem that the interpretation of the earlier part of the verse may also change. אֵלֶּה ... בְּנֵי־לֵוִי is not a summation of the earlier lists but an introduction to what is to follow. The meaning would be: *These Levites* [who were mentioned above, were also the ones which were counted in a second census which David took] ... *from age twenty and up.*

From David's time onward it apparently became customary to count the Levites from age twenty and up; cf. *II Chronicles 31:17* and *Ezra 3:8.*

In this context it may also be that the word לִפְקוּדֵיהֶם is not to be taken in its usual sense of *countings,* but as *orders* with specific assignments or charges. These Levites, according to their families [now became] the heads of their families for their [new] orders. See below, 24:3.

עֹשֵׂה הַמְּלָאכָה — *Those who did the work.* Whether it be gatekeeping, singing, or any of the other functions *(Metzudos).*

25. הֵנִיחַ ה' אֱלֹהֵי־יִשְׂרָאֵל לְעַמּוֹ — *HASHEM, God of Israel, has given rest to His people.* This verse and the next explain why David now counted the Levites from age twenty. This was because David understood that no one would ever again have to carry the sacred vessels. God had given them rest,

---

1. The reasoning would seem to be that since between Shiloh and the Temple the Ark was not in a permanent resting place, it stood to be transported at any time. For that reason, transporting the Ark was still considered a prime function of the Levites and only those Levites eligible for that service were allowed to serve in any capacity.

twenty and up. ²⁵ For David said, 'HASHEM, God of Israel, has given rest to His people, and He will dwell in Jerusalem forever. ²⁶ So, too, the Levites will no longer have to carry the Tabernacle and all its vessels for its service. ²⁷ For according to David's later words they are the tally of the sons of Levi — from twenty years and up. ²⁸ Because their place is beside the sons of Aaron for the service of the House of HASHEM — to care for the courtyards, the chambers, and the purity of all the holy things; and the matters concerning the

and the Temple in Jerusalem would be their permanent location *(Metzudos)*.

וַיִּשְׁכֹּן — *And He will dwell.* When David spoke, the dwelling of God still lay in the future. It would come about only once the Temple was built. Nevertheless, the past tense (future plus the conversive *vav*) is used in accordance with Scriptural custom that even an event which has not yet taken place is described by the past tense if it is absolutely certain that it will occur. Cf. *Genesis* 23:11, *Judges* 1:2.

26. וְגַם לַלְוִיִּם — *So, too, the Levites.* The phrase is to be understood as follows: Verse 25 had spoken of a sustained peace. The implication is that the holy Ark would never more have to be carried to battle. Now, the Ark could be carried by the *Kohanim* or Levites.[1]

Thus v. 25 is not dealing with specifically Levite concerns. However, the other parts of the Tabernacle were carried exclusively by Levites. Therefore, our verse introduces its subject with the phrase: *So, too, the Levites.* The meaning is that not only would the state of peace preclude the carrying of the Ark [by either *Kohanim* or Levites] into battle (v. 25) but, also, the purely Levite concern of carrying the rest of the appurtenances would not occur any more because the Temple site would never more be changed *(Mikra U'Massores)*.

אֵין־לָשֵׂאת אֶת־הַמִּשְׁכָּן — *Will no longer have to carry the Tabernacle.* Ramban (see comm. to v. 24) explains as follows: As long as the Ark had to be transported, the Torah disqualified over- and under-age Levites even from unrelated services, such as the *shir*, the musical accompaniment to the sacrificial service. This, so that Levites of an inappropriate age might not come, inadvertently, to carry the Ark. Once no

more transporting had to be done, the age disqualifications were removed for all kinds of service.

27. ... כִּי בְדִבְרֵי דָוִיד הָאַחֲרוֹנִים — *For according to David's later words ...* See comm. to v. 24.

הֵמָּה מִסְפַּר בְּנֵי־לֵוִי — *They are the tally of the sons of Levi.* See comm. to v. 24, s.v. *they are the sons of Levi.* Our verse belongs to this pattern. This, the larger number of Levites, including those from age twenty and up, is the true Levite tally for the time when the Temple will be standing.

28. כִּי מַעֲמָדָם לְיַד־בְּנֵי אַהֲרֹן — *Because their place is beside the sons of Aaron.* Since the Levites are not to serve independently but under the control of the *Kohanim*, there is no need that they should be older than twenty *(Metzudos)*. Or, because they had so many responsibilities, there were not enough Levites over thirty. Therefore, the twenty-year-olds were also counted and given the less important tasks *(Malbim)*.

עַל־הַחֲצֵרוֹת ... — *To care for the courtyards* ... The various tasks enumerated now are in apposition to the previous phrase. The Levites are to function in *the service of HASHEM's House* by taking care of the courtyards, etc.

וְעַל־טָהֳרַת לְכָל־קֹדֶשׁ — *And the purity of all the holy things.* Radak compares *II Chronicles* 29:16, where we find the Levites helping the *Kohanim* to remove unclean objects which were found in the Temple and to carry them out to the valley of Kidron.

וּמַעֲשֵׂה עֲבֹדַת בֵּית הָאֱלֹהִים — *And the matters concerning the service of the House of God.* The many other needs of the Temple

1.. For the controversy between *Rambam* and *Ramban* whether after the entry into the land only *Kohanim* were qualified to carry the Ark *(Rambam)* or whether either could serve *(Ramban)*, see

כט הָאֱלֹהִים: וּלְלֶחֶם הַמַּעֲרֶכֶת וּלְסֹלֶת לְמִנְחָה וְלִרְקִיקֵי
ל הַמַּצּוֹת וְלַמַּחֲבַת וְלָמֻרְבָּכֶת וּלְכָל־מְשׂוּרָה וּמִדָּה: וְלַעֲמֹד
לא בַּבֹּקֶר בַּבֹּקֶר לְהֹדוֹת וּלְהַלֵּל לַיהוָה וְכֵן לָעָרֶב: וּלְכֹל
הַעֲלוֹת עֹלוֹת לַיהוָה לַשַּׁבָּתוֹת לֶחֳדָשִׁים וְלַמֹּעֲדִים
לב בְּמִסְפָּר כְּמִשְׁפָּט עֲלֵיהֶם תָּמִיד לִפְנֵי יְהוָה: וְשָׁמְרוּ אֶת־
מִשְׁמֶרֶת אֹהֶל־מוֹעֵד וְאֵת מִשְׁמֶרֶת הַקֹּדֶשׁ וּמִשְׁמֶרֶת בְּנֵי
א אַהֲרֹן אֲחֵיהֶם לַעֲבֹדַת בֵּית יְהוָה: וְלִבְנֵי אַהֲרֹן
מַחְלְקוֹתָם בְּנֵי אַהֲרֹן נָדָב וַאֲבִיהוּא אֶלְעָזָר וְאִיתָמָר:
ב וַיָּמָת נָדָב וַאֲבִיהוּא לִפְנֵי אֲבִיהֶם וּבָנִים לֹא־הָיוּ לָהֶם
ג וַיְכַהֲנוּ אֶלְעָזָר וְאִיתָמָר: וַיֶּחָלְקֵם דָּוִיד וְצָדוֹק מִן־בְּנֵי

not explicated above (Ralbag).

29. ... וּלְלֶחֶם הַמַּעֲרֶכֶת — *And for the arranged bread ...* The verse lists the other areas of Levite responsibilities. They were to prepare the לֶחֶם הַפָּנִים, *Panim bread*, which was arranged in rows upon the table in the Sanctuary every week. They were also responsible for the fine flour that was required for the meal-offering (*Metzudos*).

וְלִרְקִיקֵי הַמַּצּוֹת וְלַמַּחֲבַת וְלָמֻרְבָּכֶת — *The unleavened wafers, that which is pan-baked and that which is boiled.* All these are forms of meal-offerings (מִנְחָה) — see *Leviticus* 2:4,5; 7:12. The Levites, however, were responsible only for their preparation; the actual offering was performed by the *Kohanim*.

וּלְכָל־מְשׂוּרָה וּמִדָּה — *And for every liquid and dry measure.* It was the Levites' responsibility to see that all liquid and dry measures were accurate (*Metzudos; Rashi, Leviticus* 19:35). Radak (*Shorashim*) takes מְשׂוּרָה as a small measure, מִדָּה as a large one.

30. ... וְלַעֲמֹד בַּבֹּקֶר — *And to stand each morning ...* The sacrificial service in the Temple began every morning with a burnt-offering (תָּמִיד שֶׁל שַׁחַר), and concluded with a burnt-offering in the evening תָּמִיד שֶׁל בֵּין הָעַרְבַּיִם. These offerings were accompanied by choral music — the *shir* — sung by the Levites, as were all communal burnt offerings.

31. ... וּלְכֹל הַעֲלוֹת עֹלוֹת לַה׳ — *And whenever burnt-offerings were to be brought to HASHEM.* Radak and *Metzudos* interpret our verse as a continuation of the previous one. The Levites were responsible not only for the *shir* which was sung every day at the morning and evening sacrifice, but also for the *shir* accompanying the sacrifices of the special days mentioned in our verse. *Mefaresh*, however, sees this sentence as a new thought. The Levites were in charge of the paddocks in which the animals for the sacrifices were kept. Our verse tells that it was their duty to deliver to the *Kohanim* as many animals as would be needed for that day's sacrifices.

32. וְשָׁמְרוּ אֶת־מִשְׁמֶרֶת אֹהֶל־מוֹעֵד — *And they shall stand watch over the Tent of Meeting.* The word מִשְׁמֶרֶת is used in several different ways in this verse. In this first phrase *Metzudos* believes that it is to be taken at its most basic meaning — *to stand watch* or *to guard.* The verse refers to the function of the Levites as gatekeepers of the Temple (see above 9:23ff).

The term אֹהֶל מוֹעֵד, *Tent of Meeting,* for the Temple is unusual. See above 9:17-23 and particularly comm. to vs. 21, 23.

וְאֵת מִשְׁמֶרֶת הַקֹּדֶשׁ — *Have charge of the holy.* Here מִשְׁמֶרֶת is not used in the sense of *guarding* but of having *charge* or responsibility over something. The Levites were charged with the responsibility of

Sefer HaMitzvos, Shoresh 3. *Ramban,* there, notes that even though normally there are no age limitations on *Kohanim* (*Chullin* 24a), these would nevertheless apply for *Kohanim* who carry the Ark.

House of God. 29 *And for the arranged bread, the fine flour of the meal-offering, the unleavened wafers, that which is pan-baked and that which is boiled; and for every liquid and dry measure.* 30 *And to stand each morning to give thanks and praise to* HASHEM, *and in the evening too,* 31 *and whenever burnt-offerings were to be brought to* HASHEM *on the Sabbaths, the New Moon and festivals, in accordance with the numbers required of them — regularly before* HASHEM. 32 *And they shall stand watch over the Tent of Meeting, have charge of the holy, and serve their brothers, the sons of Aaron, in the service of the House of* HASHEM.

F*or the sons of Aaron, their divisions — the sons of Aaron were Nadav, Avihu, Eleazar, and Ithamar.* 2 *Nadav and Avihu died before their father and they had no sons; and Eleazar and Ithamar filled the office of Kohen.* 3 *David, with Tzadok from the sons of*

---

preserving the sanctity of the holy vessels and other objects *(Metzudos),* to see that they were not defiled.

וּמִשְׁמֶרֶת בְּנֵי אַהֲרֹן אֲחֵיהֶם — *And serve their brothers, the sons of Aaron.* Here מִשְׁמֶרֶת is

used in the sense of a *duty* or *function.* They were to help the *Kohanim* in those parts of the sacrificial service — such as skinning the animals — for which a *Kohen* was not required *(Mefaresh* and *Metzudos).*

XXIV

◄§ The Kohanic Mishmaros

Having concluded the listing of the twenty-four Levite *mishmaros,* the book now turns to those of the *Kohanim.*

1. וְלִבְנֵי אַהֲרֹן מַחְלְקוֹתָם — *For the sons of Aaron, their divisions.* The translation follows *Metzudos.* The *Mefaresh* renders as though it were written: *Now these are the sons of Aaron according to their divisions.*

2. וַיָּמָת נָדָב וַאֲבִיהוּ לִפְנֵי אֲבִיהֶם — *Nadav and Avihu died before their father.* See *Leviticus* 10:1ff.

וּבָנִים לֹא־הָיוּ לָהֶם — *And they had no sons.* Because they left no sons, the *Kehunah Gedolah* (High Priesthood) was given to Eleazar (see end of verse). However, if Nadav and Avihu had left sons, one of them would have become *Kohen Gadol* rather than Eleazar *(Mefaresh).* [1]

וַיְכַהֵן אֶלְעָזָר וְאִיתָמָר — *And Eleazar and Ithamar filled the office of Kohen.* *Metzudos* translates the verse to mean: [*they*] *remained Kohanim.* However, according to *Mefaresh,* quoted above, the reference here seems to be the *Kehunah Gedolah* and the correct translation is *became.* For a list of the *Kohanim Gedolim* descended from Eleazar and Ithamar, see comm. to 5:30.

3. The divisions into the twenty-four *mishmaros* were made by David, aided by Tzadok — a descendant of Eleazar — and Achimelech — a descendant of Ithamar — so that both priestly families were represented.

וְצָדוֹק מִן־בְּנֵי אֶלְעָזָר — *With Tzadok from the sons of Eleazar.* For genealogy and details concerning Tzadok, see 5:34 and also Section Two to 5:32.

---

1. The *Mefaresh* proves this point from the succession to the *Kehunah Gedolah* at the return to Zion after the Babylonian exile. The *Kohen Gadol* at that time was Yehoshua, who was the son of Yehotzadak, who was the son of Seraiah, the last *Kohen Gadol* of the First Temple. Ezra was also a son of Seraiah and the younger brother of Yehotzadak, yet he was not made *Kohen Gadol.* [See pref. remarks 5:30-41, and also footnote to 5:41 for a discussion of whether Ezra was ever *Kohen Gadol.* See also ArtScroll *Ezra* 3:2.]

אֶלְעָזָ֤ר וַאֲחִימֶ֙לֶךְ֙ מִן־־־בְּנֵ֣י אִֽיתָמָ֔ר לִפְקֻדָּתָ֖ם בַּעֲבֹדָתָֽם:

ד וַיִּמָּצְא֣וּ בְנֵֽי־־־אֶלְעָזָ֗ר רַבִּ֛ים לְרָאשֵׁ֥י הַגְּבָרִ֖ים מִן־־־בְּנֵ֣י
אִֽיתָמָ֑ר וַיַּחְלְק֑וּם לִבְנֵ֣י אֶלְעָזָ֣ר רָאשִׁ֤ים לְבֵֽית־אָבוֹת֙ שִׁשָּׁ֣ה

ה עָשָׂ֔ר וְלִבְנֵ֥י אִֽיתָמָ֖ר לְבֵ֣ית אֲבוֹתָ֑ם שְׁמוֹנָֽה: וַֽיַּחְלְק֞וּם
בְּגֽוֹרָל֤וֹת אֵ֙לֶּה֙ עִם־־־אֵ֔לֶּה כִּֽי־־־הָ֤יוּ שָֽׂרֵי־־־קֹ֙דֶשׁ֙ וְשָׂרֵ֣י

ו הָֽאֱלֹהִ֔ים מִבְּנֵ֥י אֶלְעָזָ֖ר וּבִבְנֵ֥י אִֽיתָמָֽר: וַיִּכְתְּבֵ֡ם
שְׁמַֽעְיָה֩ בֶן־נְתַנְאֵ֨ל הַסּוֹפֵ֜ר מִן־הַלֵּוִ֗י לִפְנֵ֨י הַמֶּ֤לֶךְ וְהַשָּׂרִים֙
וְצָד֣וֹק הַכֹּהֵ֗ן וַאֲחִימֶ֙לֶךְ֙ בֶּן־־־אֶבְיָתָ֔ר וְרָאשֵׁ֥י הָֽאָב֖וֹת
לַכֹּֽהֲנִ֣ים וְלַלְוִיִּ֑ם בֵּֽית־אָ֣ב אֶחָ֗ד אָחֻז֙ לְאֶלְעָזָ֔ר וְאָחֻ֥ז ׀ אָחֻ֖ז

ז לְאִֽיתָמָֽר: וַיֵּצֵ֞א הַגּוֹרָ֧ל הָֽרִאשׁ֛וֹן לִיהֽוֹיָרִ֖יב

וַאֲחִימֶלֶךְ מִן־בְּנֵי אִיתָמָר — *And Achimelech from the sons of Ithamar.* Ralbag points out that our verse must be the source of the tradition that the *Kohen Gadol*, Eli, and his family were descended from Ithamar (see pref. remarks 5:30-41 for a detailed discussion). The Achimelech of our verse is identified in v. 6 as a son of Eviathar. Eviathar, in turn, was a son of Achituv (*I Samuel* 22:20) who was a son of Eli's son, Pinechas (*I Samuel* 14:3).

לִפְקֻדָּתָם בַּעֲבֹדָתָם — *Into their orders for their service.* פְּקֻדָּה is that for which a person is responsible (*Rashi* to *Numbers* 4:16 — וּפְקֻדַּת אֶלְעָזָר). From this basic meaning it would seem from 23:11 that the word came to be [almost] synonymous with בֵּית אָב, *family*, in much the same way that מִשְׁמָר, *mishmar* [from מִשְׁמֶרֶת], is used for such groupings (25:8). Thus וַיַּחְלְקֵם ... לִפְקֻדָּתָם may well have the essential meaning: He divided them into their *mishmaros*. See above, 23:11.

Metzudos, though, takes the word as *numbers* (see also *Targum*). The divisions were based on the census figures.

4. וַיִּמָּצְאוּ בְנֵי־אֶלְעָזָר רַבִּים לְרָאשֵׁי הַגְּבָרִים — *And the sons of Eleazar were found to be more numerous by the count of men.* The Talmud (*Taanis* 27a) discusses the development of the institution of the *mishmaros*. Already in the time of Moses there were eight *mishmaros* — four from Eleazar and four from Ithamar; or according to a different opinion there were sixteen, eight from each of the two families. All agree that by Samuel's time there were

sixteen *mishmaros* functioning at Shiloh.

Our verse teaches that David's innovation was to double the number of *mishmaros* from Eleazar. His count showed that the family of Eleazar had increased much more than that of Ithamar and he therefore doubled Eleazar's eight *mishmaros* to sixteen, while leaving Ithamar's at eight. Thus, there were a total of twenty-four (see further in v. 6).

רָאשִׁים לְבֵית־אָבוֹת — *Heads of families.* Throughout this section this term is used as a synonym of *mishmar*.

5. וַיַּחְלְקוּם בְּגוֹרָלוֹת אֵלֶּה עִם־אֵלֶּה — *So they divided them by lots, these against those.* In determining the order in which the *mishmaros* were to serve, David used a lottery. As the next part of the verse teaches, the descendants of both Eleazar and Ithamar were of an extremely high level of sanctity and it would have been impossible to decide on the basis of personal merit (*Commentators*).

כִּי־הָיוּ שָׂרֵי־קֹדֶשׁ וְשָׂרֵי הָאֱלֹהִים ... — *For there were saintly and godly men ...* The commentators are silent concerning the precise meaning of these terms which are unique to our verse.

For parallels we would have to go to expressions such as שַׂר שָׁלוֹם in *Isaiah* 9:5, or perhaps נְשִׂיא אֱלֹהִים in *Genesis* 23:6.

Perhaps these terms are not to be translated literally but are to be taken as composite terms denoting particular greatness in a given quality. The translation has treated them in this way.[1] This is close to

---

1. See also discussion of the terms גִּבּוֹר חַיִל in comm. 5:24 and גִּבּוֹר תָּמִים in fn. to 1:10.

Eleazar and by Achimelech from the sons of Ithamar, divided them into their orders for their service. ⁴ And the sons of Eleazar were found to be more numerous by the count of men than the sons of Ithamar, so they divided them; to the sons of Eleazar sixteen heads of families, to the sons of Ithamar eight heads of families. ⁵ So they divided them by lots, these against those, for there were saintly and godly men from the sons of Eleazar and among the sons of Ithamar. ⁶ And Shemaiah the son of Nethanel the scribe, of the Levites, wrote them down in the presence of the king; the officers, Tzadok the Kohen, and Achimelech the son of Eviathar, the family heads of the Kohanim and the Levites — one [extra] unit for Eleazar, but for Ithamar the unit as the unit had been. ⁷ The first lot came out for

---

Targum's rendition: Great men who were holy and great men serving in front of God.

The *midrashim* translate the words literally and take the word שׂר in its basic meaning from the root שׂרר, to rule; thus, someone who gives orders and can expect them to be followed. They deduce from our verse that the צַדִּיקִים, *righteous people*, rule over the upper spheres שָׂרֵי הָאֱלֹהִים is taken as 'lords over the angels') and over the lower spheres (שָׂרֵי קֹדֶשׁ, 'lords over the holy ones [Israel]'). The truly righteous people can decide the destiny of the world *(Pesikta d'R' Kahanah and Aggados Bereishis)*.

6. וַיִּכְתְּבֵם שְׁמַעְיָה בֶן־נְתַנְאֵל הַסּוֹפֵר מִן־הַלֵּוִי — *And Shemaiah the son of Nethanel the scribe, of the Levites, wrote them down.* He recorded the order of the *mishmaros* which was yielded by the drawing of the lots *(Mefaresh).* Or, he wrote down the names of the twenty-four *mishmaros* on the twenty-four lots that were to be drawn *(Radak* and *Metzudos).*

The Sages interpret the verse homiletically in such a way that it refers to Moses and Aaron: *Shemaiah* [is Moses] for God heard (שמע, *to hear*) his prayers; *ben Nethanel*, who was given (נתן, *to give*) the Torah from God's hand into his; *the scribe*, for he was Israel's scribe; *the Levite*, who came from the tribe of Levi; *before the king*, in front of the King of kings and His court; and *Tzadok*, that is Aaron the Kohen; *and Achimelech*, who was brother (אָח, *brother*) of the king [Moses]; *ben Eviathar*, for whom God overlooked (ותר, *to overlook*) the sin of the golden calf *(Vayikra Rabbah 1:3).*

Commentators to the midrash explain that the Sages were moved to this interpretation because while our text seems to yield that David was the innovator of the system of the *mishmaros*, v. 19 states that it was *by the hand of their father*

Aaron. That is, the concept of the *mishmaros* dated back to the days of Moses and Aaron (see *Taanis* 27a and comm. to v. 4). The Sages thought that this should be indicated in the text. In our verse they were struck by the identification of the scribe who wrote the names on the chips for the drawing of the lots. Why was it important to know who performed this apparently insignificant task? They took this as the justification to interpret the verse in accordance with v. 19 and their tradition concerning the great antiquity of the institution of the *mishmaros*.

בֵּית־אָב אֶחָד אָחֻז לְאֶלְעָזָר וְאָחֻז אָחֻז לְאִיתָמָר — *One [extra] unit for Eleazar, but for Ithamar the unit as the unit had been.*

We have rendered this difficult phrase as *Taanis* 27a seems to take it and in a way that it accords with what we learned in v. 4. The number of *mishmaros* from Eleazar was doubled, so that for every unit which existed before there were now two. For Ithamar the units remained the same.

The term אָחֻז (derived from אחז, *to hold*, thus, *to take out from a group*) is best translated as *unit* in our context. Compare *Numbers* 31:30.

Malbim takes the meaning of the verse as follows: Up to the sixteenth *mishmar* lots were drawn alternately — one from Eleazar and one from Ithamar. The ones from seventeen through twenty-four came from Eleazar only. Now the *mishmaros* from Eleazar — even those among the first eight — could have been new *mishmaros*, while those from Ithamar were all original ones. For this reason the text uses אֶחָד אָחֻז when dealing with Eleazar. It is a neutral term which can apply equally to a *mishmar* which was now added and to one which had previously existed. But when talking of Ithamar it uses אָחֻז אָחֻז, meaning, *a unit from among the original units.*

7ᐨ18. These verses list the twenty-four

ח לִידַעְיָה הַשֵּׁנִי לְחָרִם הַשְּׁלִשִׁי לִשְׂעֹרִים הָרְבִעִי:
ט-י לְמַלְכִּיָּה הַחֲמִישִׁי לְמִיָּמִן הַשִּׁשִּׁי לְהַקּוֹץ הַשְּׁבִעִי לַאֲבִיָּה
יא-יב הַשְּׁמִינִי: לְיֵשׁוּעַ הַתְּשִׁעִי לִשְׁכַנְיָהוּ הָעֲשִׂרִי: לְאֶלְיָשִׁיב
יג עַשְׁתֵּי עָשָׂר לְיָקִים שְׁנֵים עָשָׂר: לְחֻפָּה שְׁלֹשָׁה עָשָׂר
יד לְיֶשֶׁבְאָב אַרְבָּעָה עָשָׂר: לְבִלְגָּה חֲמִשָּׁה עָשָׂר לְאִמֵּר
טו שִׁשָּׁה עָשָׂר: לְחֵזִיר שִׁבְעָה עָשָׂר לְהַפִּצֵּץ שְׁמוֹנָה עָשָׂר:
טז-יז לִפְתַחְיָה תִּשְׁעָה עָשָׂר לִיחֶזְקֵאל הָעֶשְׂרִים: לְיָכִין אֶחָד
יח וְעֶשְׂרִים לְגָמוּל שְׁנַיִם וְעֶשְׂרִים: לִדְלָיָהוּ שְׁלֹשָׁה וְעֶשְׂרִים
יט לְמַעַזְיָהוּ אַרְבָּעָה וְעֶשְׂרִים: אֵלֶּה פְקֻדָּתָם לַעֲבֹדָתָם
לָבוֹא לְבֵית־יְהוָה כְּמִשְׁפָּטָם בְּיַד אַהֲרֹן אֲבִיהֶם כַּאֲשֶׁר
כ צִוָּהוּ יְהוָה אֱלֹהֵי יִשְׂרָאֵל: וְלִבְנֵי לֵוִי הַנּוֹתָרִים לִבְנֵי
כא עַמְרָם שׁוּבָאֵל לִבְנֵי שׁוּבָאֵל יֶחְדְּיָהוּ: לִרְחַבְיָהוּ לִבְנֵי
כב רְחַבְיָהוּ הָרֹאשׁ יִשִּׁיָּה: לַיִּצְהָרִי שְׁלֹמוֹת לִבְנֵי שְׁלֹמוֹת
כג יָחַת: וּבְנֵי יְרִיָּהוּ אֲמַרְיָהוּ הַשֵּׁנִי יַחֲזִיאֵל הַשְּׁלִישִׁי יְקַמְעָם
כד-כה הָרְבִיעִי: בְּנֵי עֻזִּיאֵל מִיכָה לִבְנֵי מִיכָה °שָׁמִיר שׁמוּר: אֲחִי מִיכָה

°שָׁמִיר ק'

---

mishmaros of the Kohanim in the order in which they served. After the twenty-fourth mishmar had served, the order rotated once more to the first.

15. לְחֵזִיר שִׁבְעָה עָשָׂר — *The seventeenth for Chezir.* *Gra* believes that this name is no coincidence. Before David's innovation there were just sixteen *mishmaros.* After the sixteenth the order would 'return,' i.e., start once more from the beginning. As a reminder of this, the seventeenth *mishmar* was named חֵזִיר from חזר, *to return.*

19. פְקֻדָּתָם לַעֲבֹדָתָם — *These are their orders for their service.* See comm. to v. 3. *Metzudos,* though, takes פקד in its usual sense, *to count.* The phrase means: This is the number of the *mishmaros* who were to serve in the Temple. *Targum* renders מִנְיָנֵיהוֹן which agrees with *Metzudos.*

לָבוֹא לְבֵית־ה' כְּמִשְׁפָּטָם — *To come to the House of HASHEM according to the rule fixed for them.* David made no innovation. The institution of the *mishmaros* dated back to Moses and Aaron. David's dispositions were limited to increasing the number of *mishmaros* (see comm. to v. 4).

כַּאֲשֶׁר צִוָּהוּ ה' אֱלֹהֵי יִשְׂרָאֵל — *As HASHEM the God of Israel had commanded him.* See comm. to 15:2 where we discussed the controversy between *Rambam* and

Ramban whether subsequent to their entry into the Land of Israel the Ark was to be borne specifically by the *Kohanim (Rambam)* or whether the Levites were still qualified *(Ramban).*

Our verse plays a significant role in this controversy. It is quoted and interpreted by *Sifri* to *Nasso* 46, and *Rambam* and *Ramban* disagree in the meaning of *Sifri's* interpretation. As *Rambam* reads *Sifri,* our phrase, which refers back to the earlier phrase, *at the hands of their father Aaron,* hints at the Torah's command to carry the Ark upon the shoulder. Since Aaron is mentioned, the implication is clear that it is the *Kohanim* (sons of Aaron) who are to be the bearers. *Ramban* interprets the passage in such a way that the entire passage refers only to the *mishmaros* and that nothing is taught concerning the carrying of the Ark. For details see *Ramban's* glosses to *Sefer HaMitzvos* to *Shoresh* 3.

◄§ The Remaining Levites

20-31. This passage augments the Levite lists given in ch. 23. As indicated in the comm. there, certain changes came about after the first generation of these *mishmaros.* These changes are given here.

20. וְלִבְנֵי לֵוִי הַנּוֹתָרִים — *And for the remaining Levites.* The Levite *mishmaros* which

Yehoiariv, the second for Yedaiah. ⁸ The third for Charim, the fourth for Seorim. ⁹ The fifth for Malciyah, the sixth for Miyamin. ¹⁰ The seventh for Hakkotz, the eighth for Aviyah. ¹¹ The ninth for Yeshua, the tenth for Shechaniahu. ¹² The eleventh for Eliashiv, the twelfth for Yakim. ¹³ The thirteenth for Chuppah, the fourteenth for Yeshevav. ¹⁴ The fifteenth for Bilgah, the sixteenth for Immer. ¹⁵ The seventeenth for Chezir, the eighteenth for Happitzetz. ¹⁶ The nineteenth for Pethathiah, the twentieth for Yechezkel. ¹⁷ The twenty-first for Yachin, the twenty-second for Gamul. ¹⁸ The twenty-third for Delaiahu, the twenty-fourth for Maaziahu. ¹⁹ These are their orders for their service, to come to the House of HASHEM according to the rule fixed for them at the hands of their father Aaron, as HASHEM the God of Israel had commanded him. ²⁰ And for the remaining Levites: for the sons of Amram — Shuvael; for the sons of Shuvael — Yechdeiahu. ²¹ For Rechaviahu: for the sons of Rechaviahu — Yishiyah, the chief. ²² For the Yitzharites — Shelomoth; for the sons of Shelomoth — Yachath. ²³ And the sons — Yeriahu, Amariahu the second, Yachaziel the third, and Yekameam the fourth. ²⁴ And the sons of Uzziel — Michah; for the sons of Michah — Shamir. ²⁵ The brother of Michah was Yishiyah; for the

---

are dealt with in this passage are called the *remaining* ones because the *mishmaros* of *Kohanim*, which were also descended from Levi, have already been completed. Moreover, the changes recorded here applied only to the descendants of Kehath and Merari, while the Gershonite *mishmaros* recorded in ch. 23 remained unchanged (*Metzudos*). See further in Appendix V.

לִבְנֵי עַמְרָם שׁוּבָאֵל לִבְנֵי שׁוּבָאֵל יֶחְדְּיָהוּ — *For the sons of Amram — Shuvael; for the sons of Shuvael — Yechdeiahu.* In the chart given at 23:12, Shuvael [Shevuel] was listed as number 11 of the *mishmaros*. After his death the *mishmar* came to be known by his son's name — Yechdeiahu (*Metzudos*).

21. לִרְחַבְיָהוּ ... — *For Rechaviahu* ... At 23:12 Rechaviahu is listed as number 12. After his death his *mishmar* came to be known by the name of his descendant Yishiyah (*Metzudos*).

22. שְׁלֵמוֹת — *Shelomoth.* Shelomoth [Shalomith] is listed as number 13 at 23:12. After his death, the *mishmar* came to be known by the name of his descendant Yachath (*Metzudos*).

23. וּבְנֵי יְרִיָּהוּ — *And the sons — Yeriahu.* The four names mentioned in our verse are 14,15,16, and 17 in the chart at 23:12. All

are sons of Chevron. *Gra* does not believe that any changes took place in this group. They are listed here only because from Shuvael and on all the *mishmaros* are listed, whether there were changes or not. The verse is to be understood as though it were written: *And the sons [of Chevron were] Yeriahu, Amariahu, the second* ...

Metzudos, however, differs. He thinks that after Yeriahu's (14) death, his *mishmar* became too small and was merged into that of Amariahu (15). [See below at v. 27 how the count of twenty-four was then made up.] The phrase is to be rendered: *And for the sons of Yeriahu [they became one with] Amariahu, the second one.*

Malbim (23:19) concludes from this verse that the last three are actually the sons of Yeriahu; see there. According to him, the verse reads: *For the sons of Yeriahu: Amariahu, the second* ...

24. לִבְנֵי מִיכָה שָׁמִיר — *For the sons of Michah — Shamir.* The *mishmar* of Michah (18) became known after his death by the name of his descendant Shamir (*Metzudos*).

25. אֲחִי מִיכָה יִשִּׁיָּה — *The brother of Michah was Yishiyah.* The *mishmar* of Yishiyah (19), who was the brother of Michah (19), became known after his death

כו יְשִׁיָּה לִבְנֵי יִשִׁיָּה זְכַרְיָהוּ: בְּנֵי מְרָרִי מַחְלִי וּמוּשִׁי בְּנֵי
כז יַעֲזִיָּהוּ בְּנוֹ: בְּנֵי מְרָרִי לְיַעֲזִיָּהוּ בְנוֹ וְשֹׁהַם וְזַכּוּר וְעִבְרִי:
כח-כט לְמַחְלִי אֶלְעָזָר וְלֹא־הָיָה לוֹ בָּנִים: לְקִישׁ בְּנֵי־קִישׁ
ל יְרַחְמְאֵל: וּבְנֵי מוּשִׁי מַחְלִי וְעֵדֶר וִירִימוֹת אֵלֶּה בְּנֵי
לא הַלְוִיִּם לְבֵית אֲבֹתֵיהֶם: וַיַּפִּילוּ גַם־הֵם גּוֹרָלוֹת לְעֻמַּת |
אֲחֵיהֶם בְּנֵי־אַהֲרֹן לִפְנֵי דָוִיד הַמֶּלֶךְ וְצָדוֹק וַאֲחִימֶלֶךְ
וְרָאשֵׁי הָאָבוֹת לַכֹּהֲנִים וְלַלְוִיִּם אָבוֹת הָרֹאשׁ לְעֻמַּת

by the name of his descendant, Zechariahu (*Metzudos*).

26. ... בְּנֵי מְרָרִי — *The sons of Merari* ... *Metzudos* renders this verse as follows. From the chart at 23:21 we see that the *mishmaros* from the Merari line came only from Machli and Mushi. Subsequently, additional *mishmaros* from Merari's son Yaaziyahu were added to make up the number twenty-four.

27. ... לְיַעֲזִיָּהוּ בְנוֹ — *By his son Yaaziyahu* ... Yaaziyahu had three sons: Shoham, Zaccur and Ivri. These are used to make up the count of twenty-four.

According to *Metzudos* they make up for: Yeush (9) and Beriah (10) who, according to 23:10, were made into one *mishmar*, thus eliminating one *mishmar* from Gershon; Yeriahu (14) and Amariahu (15) who, according to *Metzudos'* interpretation of v. 23 above, were merged into one *mishmar*, thus eliminating one *mishmar* from Kehath; and Eleazar (20) who died without sons, which eliminates one *mishmar* from Merari. By adding three new *mishmaros* to Merari, the total of twenty-four is preserved.

Gra (who disagrees with *Metzudos'* in his interpretation of v. 23 — see above) has only two *mishmaros* missing: one from Gershon, because of the merging of Yeush (9) and Beriah (10); and one from Merari, because of the elimination of Eleazar (20), who died without sons (v. 28).

Gra does not explain why three *mishmaros* were required to replace them, but the solution may be given by *Malbim*, whose count is the same as that of *Gra*. *Malbim* takes us back to the Merari list at 6:14. He identifies Yaaziyahu with Uzzah [CI(5)] and Shoham with Shimea [CI(6)]. He thinks that Zaccur and Ivri were sons (not brothers) of Shoham and that in

reality only those two (not three) *mishmaros* were added. Thus the total of twenty-four is preserved.

28. לְמַחְלִי אֶלְעָזָר — *For Machli — Eleazar*. Our verse repeats what we know from 23:17 — that Eleazar died childless.

29. בְּנֵי־קִישׁ יְרַחְמְאֵל — *The sons of Kish, Yerachmeel*. After Kish (21) died, his *mishmar* came to be called by the name of his descendant Yerachmeel.

30. ... וּבְנֵי מוּשִׁי — *And the sons of Mushi* ... The sons of Mushi remained unchanged, thus bringing the count of the Levite *mishmaros* to twenty-four — see comm. to v. 27.

31. וַיַּפִּילוּ גַם־הֵם גּוֹרָלוֹת — *They also cast lots*. Verse 5 taught that the order in which the twenty-four *mishmaros* of the *Kohanim* served was determined by lots. Our verse teaches that this method was also used for the Levites.

לְעֻמַּת אֲחֵיהֶם בְּנֵי־אַהֲרֹן — *Corresponding to their brothers, the sons of Aaron*. *Metzudos* translates: *just as ... the sons of Aaron*. However, לְעֻמַּת usually means *opposite* or *parallel to*, and for this reason *Malbim* explains that the lots which were cast for the Levites were to determine which *mishmaros* of the Levites would serve together with which *mishmar* of *Kohanim*. Thus the lots were meant to put the Levites 'opposite' [corresponding to] the *Kohanim*.

אָבוֹת הָרֹאשׁ לְעֻמַּת אָחִיו הַקָּטָן — *Avoth, the chief, against his younger brother*. The phrase is obscure. The translation follows *Radak* and *Metzudos*. They take Avoth as a proper noun and understand the intent of the phrase as being the same as that expressed in v. 5 in connection with the lots

sons of Yishiyah — Zechariahu. ²⁶ The sons of Merari — Machli and Mushi; [and] the sons of Yaaziyahu his son. ²⁷ The sons of Merari by his son Yaaziyahu — Shoham, Zaccur and Ivri. ²⁸ For Machli — Eleazar, and he had no sons. ²⁹ For Kish — the sons of Kish, Yerachmeel. ³⁰ And the sons of Mushi were Machli, Eder and Yerimoth. These were the Levites according to their families. ³¹ They also cast lots, corresponding to their brothers, the sons of Aaron, in the presence of King David, Tzadok, Achimelech, and the family heads of the Kohanim and the Levites. Avoth, the chief, against his younger brother.

of the *Kohanim*. No distinction was to be made on the basis of personal greatness; all were to be equal participants in the lottery. And thus, Avoth, the most important among the Levites, was put into the lottery in the same way as was his most insignificant brother. *Radak* compares 25:8. See there.

Perhaps because the name Avoth is found nowhere else among the Levites, and also because in this interpretation the word לְעֻמַּת has an entirely different meaning than it has in the beginning of the verse, *Ralbag* has a different interpretation. אֲבוֹת הָרֹאשׁ are the heads of the seven individual family units within each *mishmar*, each of whom did service on one of the seven days of the week which was assigned to the whole *mishmar* (see *Rambam, Klei HaMikdash* 4:11). Our phrase teaches that just as the *mishmar* of the Levites was placed opposite a given *mishmar* of the *Kohanim*, so too each family unit within the Levite *mishmar* was assigned a particular day, always to be the same as a given family unit among the *Kohanim*. Thus the phrase is saying that the head of every family unit was placed *opposite his brother*, that is the head of a particular family unit among the *Kohanim*. He is called הַקָּטָן, *the small one*, in contrast to the leader of the entire *mishmar*.

We may suggest another possibility for the interpretation of this very obscure phrase:

It would seem that the frequently used term בֵּית אָב, family [lit. *father's house*], or, in the plural בָּתֵּי אֲבוֹת is often shortened to אֲבוֹת [lit. *fathers*]. This is probably the correct explanation of terms like רָאשֵׁי אֲבוֹת, *heads of families*, which if translated literally *(heads of fathers)* would make little sense. This can be readily illustrated from *Exodus* ch. 6 where we have a genealogical section introduced by ... *these are the*

heads of their בֵּית אֲבוֹת [lit. *father's house* (v. 14)] and concluded with ... *these are the heads of the* אֲבוֹת [lit. *fathers*] *of the Levites* (v. 25). This is surely also the explanation of a term such as נְשִׂיאֵי הָאָבוֹת לִבְנֵי יִשְׂרָאֵל, *princes of the families* [lit. *fathers*] *of the children of Israel (I Kings* 8:1). See comm. to v. 31.

If we now study 25:8, a verse with obvious similarities to ours, we note the following phrasing: ... *one mishmar corresponding to* ... *the small with the great, the expert with the student*. That is, a correspondence is established between the *mishmaros* and also between the individual members of a given *mishmar*.

Note further that correspondence of the *mishmaros* is given there in truncated form: ... מִשְׁמֶרֶת לְעֻמַּת. [The comm. there will discuss the possible rationale for this.] Now, just as the verse there truncated the phrase: מִשְׁמֶרֶת לְעֻמַּת [מִשְׁמֶרֶת], *a mishmar corresponding to* [*a mishmar*], here too this may have been done. If so, אֲבוֹת may be taken as an independently standing phrase — a truncated form of [לְעֻמַּת אֲבוֹת] אֲבוֹת. The remaining phrase: הָרֹאשׁ לְעֻמַּת אָחִיו הַקָּטָן, is then a perfectly balanced phrase, and this verse would be the parallel of that one. It would mean: *The families* [one opposite the other], *the chief opposite his younger brother*.

Another possibility is that אֲבוֹת may be a contraction of רָאשֵׁי הָאָבוֹת, *the family heads*, which occurs frequently [and is itself a contraction of וְרָאשֵׁי בָּתֵּי הָאָבוֹת]. The phrase would then be understood as follows: *The leaders* [of the various *mishmaros*] *the chief opposite his younger brother*. [That is, the *mishmaros* which were headed by a leader — who was designated רֹאשׁ (see 23:11 et al., and 26:10) — did not serve before those headed by less exalted leaders. Each had to take its turn as determined by lots.] (R' Y. Danziger).

כה א אֲחָיו הַקָּטָן׃ וַיַּבְדֵּל דָּוִיד וְשָׂרֵי הַצָּבָא לַעֲבֹדָה
א־ב °הַנִּבְּאִים ק׳ לִבְנֵי אָסָף וְהֵימָן וִידוּתוּן °הַנְּבִיאִים בְּכִנֹּרוֹת בִּנְבָלִים
ב וּבִמְצִלְתָּיִם וַיְהִי מִסְפָּרָם אַנְשֵׁי מְלָאכָה לַעֲבֹדָתָם׃ לִבְנֵי
אָסָף זַכּוּר וְיוֹסֵף וּנְתַנְיָה וַאֲשַׂרְאֵלָה בְּנֵי אָסָף עַל יַד־אָסָף

XXV

◄§ The Choristers

In ch. 23 vs. 4 and 5 the tasks of the Levites were divided into four general categories: Temple administration; court officers and judges; gatekeepers; and musicians to praise God. Our chapter and the next take up these general categories and treat them in greater detail. Here we learn that within the group of 4000 musicians mentioned in 23:5 there was another division into twenty-four groups [corresponding with the twenty-four *mishmaros*] of twelve each.

1. ... וַיַּבְדֵּל דָּוִיד — *David ... separated ...* This verse does not deal with the division of the Levites into twenty-four groups but their separation from the other Levites. David separated the sons of Asaph, Heman and Yeduthun to be the musicians and the other Levites to be the gatekeepers and officials over the Temple treasures (*Radak*).

When we consider that the number of musicians dealt with in our chapter was 288 (v. 7 = 24 x 12) while 23:5 talks of 4000 Levites assigned to 'praise God with instruments,' it seems likely that the meaning of the phrase is that the 288 mentioned in our chapter were separated out of the much larger pool of Levite musicians (cf. *Malbim*).

The meaning would be as follows. The Mishnah in *Arachin* 13b rules that there had to be at least twelve choristers for the *shir*. Instrumental accompaniment was optional (see *Rambam, Klei Hamikdash* 3:3), but if instruments were used, they too had to be a minimum of twelve.

Thus, it seems likely that while there was a general pool of 4000 musicians who could be used to augment either the choir or orchestra, our chapter deals with a group of Levites who were separated to take responsibility over the obligatory aspects of the *shir* (see Talmud, *Arachin* there).

From *Metzudos* to v. 7 it appears that the twelve selected for each *mishmar* were the most accomplished musicians.

וְשָׂרֵי הַצָּבָא לַעֲבֹדָה — *And the officials of the service corps.* The translation follows *Malbim*, who compares this to *Numbers* 4:30. The word צָבָא [lit. *host*] is used in Scripture to describe any group or company of people gathered together, whether for waging war or any other

purpose (*Ramban, Numbers* 1:3).

Metzudos separates לַעֲבֹדָה from וְשָׂרֵי הַצָּבָא [although *trop* seems to favor their combination]. Thus the sentence is to be rendered: *David and the officials separated* [the various groups] *each to its* [individual] *service.*

אָסָף וְהֵימָן וִידוּתוּן — *Asaph, Heman and Yeduthun.* See comm. to 6:16. For Yeduthun, see fn. to 16:41.

Up to this point these choristers have been mentioned in connection with the *shir* in the temporary locations which existed before Solomon built the Temple — that is at Giveon and in front of the Ark at Jerusalem. Here David is making dispositions which are to be valid for the Temple.

It is noteworthy that here the Gershonite Asaph is mentioned first, followed by the Kehathite Heman and the Merarite Yeduthun — that is, the order of birth is followed. In ch. 6, though, Heman is given the honored central place and Asaph and Ethan are assigned to his right and left. We may surmise that when the three are to serve together, then indeed, Kehath stands at the place of honor, just as in the wilderness it was he who dealt with the most holy vessels of the Tabernacle. However, when the issue is the division into *mishmaros*, each independent of the other, the essential sanctity of a particular family is not relevant and the logical way to mention the three brothers is by their ages.

הַנִּבְּאִים בְּכִנֹּרוֹת בִּנְבָלִים וּבִמְצִלְתָּיִם — *Who prophesied to the accompaniment of the harps, nevalim and cymbals.* A number of psalms in the book of *Psalms* are ascribed to one or another of the choristers mentioned in our verse. Since the psalms were written with Divine inspiration (רוּחַ הַקֹּדֶשׁ), and moreover, often contain

David and the officials of the service corps separated the sons of Asaph, Heman and Yeduthun, who prophesied to the accompaniment of the harps, nevalim and cymbals, and their number was in accordance with the number of people required for their service. ² For the sons of Asaph — Zaccur, Yoseph, Nethaniah and Asarelah, the sons of Asaph; under the tutelage of Asaph, who

prophetic visions of the future, the compositions of these psalms can be described as prophecy. The choristers attained the sublime level necessary for the spirit of prophecy to rest upon them from the music made by the musicians playing under them (*Radak*), in much the same way that the spirit of God descended upon Elisha the prophet to the accompaniment of music [*II Kings* 3:15] (*Mefaresh*).

Malbim believes that the verb נבא is not limited to prophetic utterances. Any speech which uses exalted idioms and talks of Godly matters can be described by that word, especially when said under the influence of Divine inspiration (see *Targum* and *Radak* to *I Samuel* 10:5). Hence, נבא is used to describe the *shir*.

Metzudos sees the word הַנִּבְּאִים as separate from the rest of the phrase. הַנִּבְּאִים is a description of Asaph, Heman and Yeduthun — *they who prophesied* — while the rest of the verse is a description of the service they were to perform. *David ... separated the sons of Asaph, Heman, and Yeduthun, who prophesied, to play with harps, nevalim, and cymbals.*

Note that the *kesiv* is הַנְּבִיאִים, *the prophets*, as opposed to the *keri* הַנִּבְּאִים, *who prophesy*. This would tend to confirm *Metzudos'* rendering, since Asaph, Heman and Yeduthun are described below as seers of David (see v. 5; also II:29:30 and II:35:15).

וַיְהִי מִסְפָּרָם אַנְשֵׁי מְלָאכָה לַעֲבדָתָם — *And their number was in accordance with the number of people required for their service.* The translation follows *Malbim*. The 288 Levites numbered below constituted the minimum number required for each of the twenty-four *mishmaros* (see above).

Metzudos' takes אַנְשֵׁי מְלָאכָה as an idiom denoting *expert: Experts in the service* [required of them]. This, in accordance with his interpretation of v. 7.

2. עַל יַד־אָסָף — *Under the tutelage* [lit. *by the hand*] *of Asaph.* The sons of Asaph were taught their musical skills by their father (*Metzudos*).

In the context in which this phrase occurs another explanation seems possible.

Asaph's children are described here as performing their service עַל יַד [lit. *by the hand of*] their father, who in turn is described as הַנִּבָּא עַל יְדֵי הַמֶּלֶךְ [lit. *who prophesied by the hands of the king*]. Again, Yeduthun's sons are also described as serving עַל יְדֵי [lit. *by the hands of*] their father, whose function is: הַנִּבָּא עַל־הוֹדוֹת ... וְהַלֵּל, *who prophesied thanks and praise to HASHEM* (v. 3). However, the sons of Heman, whose function is given in v. 5 as חֹזֵה הַמֶּלֶךְ בְּדִבְרֵי הָאֱלֹהִים לְהָרִים קָרֶן, *the king's seer who prophesied God's promise to exalt*, are not given as being עַל יַד, *by the hand*, their father.

However, in v. 6 where the function of all three choristers is given as: ... בְּשִׁיר ... לַעֲבדַת בֵּית הָאֱלֹהִים ... *in the song ... for the service of the House of God*, all the sons — including Heman's — are described as being עַל יְדֵי, *by the hand of*, their respective fathers.

Again, we note the oddity in sequence. At v. 1 we noted that when all the choristers are together, Heman from Kehath is central, but that otherwise the order of birth would logically be used. But the sequence in which the descendants are listed in vs. 2-5 is Asaph (Gershon), Yeduthun (Merari), and Heman (Kehath), and this seems illogical.

Perhaps, the various functions ascribed to the three choristers in vs. 2-5 are not part of the Temple service but positions which they held in the king's household. The sense of the three verses might then be that each of these main choristers had a certain important position — in relation to the king — the sequence of their description being determined by their relative significance, and it was these important functionaries whom David chose to be the Temple choristers. In these functions Asaph and Yeduthun were joined by their sons (עַל יַד) but Heman was not. However, during the *shir* in the Temple (v. 6) all were together with their sons.

In this context עַל יַד (*by the hand*) would mean *next to* or *together with*, as in *Exodus* 2:5 and many other places.

ג הַנִּבָּא עַל־יְדֵי הַמֶּלֶךְ: לִידוּתוּן בְּנֵי יְדוּתוּן גְּדַלְיָהוּ וּצְרִי
וִישַׁעְיָהוּ חֲשַׁבְיָהוּ וּמַתִּתְיָהוּ שִׁשָּׁה עַל יְדֵי אֲבִיהֶם יְדוּתוּן
ד בַּכִּנּוֹר הַנִּבָּא עַל־הוֹדוֹת וְהַלֵּל לַיהוה: לְהֵימָן בְּנֵי
הֵימָן בֻּקִּיָּהוּ מַתַּנְיָהוּ עֻזִּיאֵל שְׁבוּאֵל וִירִימוֹת חֲנַנְיָה חֲנָנִי
אֱלִיאָתָה גִּדַּלְתִּי וְרֹמַמְתִּי עֶזֶר יָשְׁבְּקָשָׁה מַלּוֹתִי הוֹתִיר
ה מַחֲזִיאוֹת: כָּל־אֵלֶּה בָנִים לְהֵימָן חֹזֵה הַמֶּלֶךְ בְּדִבְרֵי
הָאֱלֹהִים לְהָרִים קָרֶן וַיִּתֵּן הָאֱלֹהִים לְהֵימָן בָּנִים אַרְבָּעָה
ו עָשָׂר וּבָנוֹת שָׁלוֹשׁ: כָּל־אֵלֶּה עַל־יְדֵי אֲבִיהֶם בַּשִּׁיר בֵּית

הַנִּבָּא עַל־יְדֵי הַמֶּלֶךְ — *Who prophesied under
the tutelage of the king.* David himself had
gradually guided Asaph to the high
spiritual level at which he was enabled to
prophesy (*Metzudos*).

If our suggestion above is correct, then
this phrase would describe a function
which Asaph filled in the king's household.
Thus, ... *who prophesied near,* or, *in the
presence of the king.* Much as Gad the
prophet is called *David's seer* (*II Samuel*
24:1), that is, apparently, a seer who stood
constantly at the disposal of the king; so
too was Asaph available to David to fill the
function of נִבָּא [lit. *prophesy*].

The precise nature of this act is difficult
to ascertain. Certainly it is not limited to
predicting the future (cf. *I Samuel* 10:10
and many other places). The Sages see a
much more general meaning. They deduce
from this phrase that Asaph was a בֶּן תּוֹרָה
(*Koheleth Rabbah* 7:39), *a person imbued
with the spirit of the Torah.* Thus, we may
suppose that Asaph was the man who bore
the general responsibility for the spiritual
matters of David's household.[1] In this he
was helped by his sons.

Of the three functions assigned to the
three choristers this was the most important and is therefore mentioned first.

3. בְּנֵי יְדוּתוּן ... שִׁשָּׁה — *The sons of
Yeduthun ... six.* Only five names are
given; the sixth son would be Shimei (v.
17), whose name does not occur among the
names listed in vs. 2-4.

The Sages have a tradition that at the
time that this count was made, Yeduthun,
in fact, had only five sons. However, his
wife was pregnant and David saw in
prophetic vision that this sixth child, too,
would grow up worthy to head a group of

Levites.

Commentators suggest that Shimei may
already have been born but did not yet
prophesy (*Radak*) or was under the age of
thirty (*Malbim*) and was therefore not
mentioned. However, he showed his
potential for exceptional greatness and was
therefore included in the count. *Malbim*
suggests that pending Shimei's coming of
age, his father Yeduthun headed a group in
his place.

עַל יְדֵי אֲבִיהֶם יְדוּתוּן בְּכִנּוֹר — *Under the
tutelage of their father, Yeduthun, on the
harp.* Yeduthun taught his sons the skills
of the harp (*Metzudos*).

According to the thesis expressed in the
previous verse בְּכִנּוֹר would imply that
Yeduthun's was a musical function in the king's
household — perhaps akin to that filled by David
in Saul's tine.

It is significant that Yeduthun appears in the
heading of three psalms — 39, 62 and 77. As
Rashi takes it there, it is clear that the word
functions not only as a man's name but also as
the name of a musical instrument. It seems
possible that if, indeed, Yeduthun was the
musician *par excellence,* that he lent his name to
an instrument — perhaps a form of the harp —
which he played with particular virtuosity.

הַנִּבָּא עַל־הוֹדוֹת וְהַלֵּל לַה׳ — *Who prophesied
thanks and praise to HASHEM.* Yeduthun's
prophecy expressed itself in thanking and
praising God (*Metzudos*).

Mefaresh renders: *Who prophesied as
thanks and praise were given to HASHEM.*
Yeduthun prophesied while his sons
played psalms beginning with the word
הוֹדוּ, *Thank!* (עַל הוֹדוֹת), and הַלְלוּיָהּ, *Praise
God!* (וְהַלֵּל).

Literally, our phrase would be rendered: *Who
prophesied over 'to thank' and 'to praise'
HASHEM.* The syntax is unusual, although a
careful analysis of the relevant Scriptural

---

1. We may even surmise that Asaph's position in David's household may have been the reason why
while the Ark was still separated from the Tabernacle, it was he who was assigned to the Ark in
Jerusalem while the other two functioned in Giveon (16:37ff). It may be that David required Asaph's
presence in Jerusalem.

prophesied under the tutelage of the king. ³ For Yeduthun — the sons of Yeduthun: Gedaliahu, Tzeri, Yeshaiahu, Chashaviahu and Mattithiahu, six; under the tutelage of their father, Yeduthun, on the harp, who prophesied thanks and praise to HASHEM. ⁴ For Heman — the sons of Heman: Bukkiahu, Mattaniahu, Uzziel, Shevuel, Yerimoth, Chananiah, Chanani, Eliathah, Giddalti, Romamti Ezer, Yoshbekashah, Mallothi, Hothir and Machazioth. ⁵ All these were sons to Heman, the king's seer who prophesied God's promise to exalt; God gave Heman fourteen sons and three daughters. ⁶ All these under the tutelage of their fathers — to

passages yields that in connection with singing praises to God there is frequent use of the infinitive. Thus we have Ezra 3:11: וַיַּעֲנוּ בְּהַלֵּל וּבְהוֹדֹת לַה׳ כִּי טוֹב ..., and Nehemiah 12:46: ... וְשִׁיר תְּהִלָּה וְהוֹדוֹת ...

Perhaps the reason for this is that the use of the infinitive is particularly appropriate for describing the act of praising or thanking God. The infinitive expresses the idea of the verb in the abstract, that is, it speaks of an action without expressing who does the action and without regard to circumstances of time or mood under which it takes place. It is an ideal form to use when the agent of the action recedes completely into the background and is assigned no significance whatever.

While the chazzan repeats the blessing of מוֹדִים in the Shemoneh Esrei prayer it is customary for the congregation to say a silent מוֹדִים prayer of their own. This is known as מוֹדִים דְּרַבָּנָן, because it is a combination of various prayers composed by different Rabbis. However, the basic form of that prayer is the one said by Rav (Sotah 40a): מוֹדִים אֲנַחְנוּ לָךְ ... עַל שֶׁאָנוּ מוֹדִים לָךְ, We thank You ... for having inspired us to thank You (Rashi). Thus we see that the act of praising or thanking God consists of such total self-abnegation that not only that for which we thank is ascribed to God, but we do not take credit even for the idea of expressing thanks — that too is seen as deriving entirely from God.

It lies in the very nature of singing God's praises that the agent seeks total anonymity. This is best achieved by the use of the infinitive.

4. ... לְהֵימָן — For Heman ... Fourteen sons are mentioned (Romamti Ezer is one name — see v. 31). Thus we have four sons from Asaph, six from Yeduthun, and fourteen from Heman, for a total of twenty-four. These led groups of twelve each (see v. 7), which paralleled the twenty-four mishmaros of the Kohanim. Yoseph from Asaph (v. 9) would serve together with Yehoiariv, the first of the mishmaros of the Kohanim (24:7) (Radak).

5. חֹזֵה הַמֶּלֶךְ בְּדִבְרֵי הָאֱלֹהִים לְהָרִים קָרֶן — The king's seer who prophesied God's promise to exalt. The translation follows Radak and Metzudos who have לְהָרִים קָרֶן as part of the prophecy which Heman saw for the king. He prophesied that the horn [glory]

of Israel would be restored and raised high [even after it went into exile] (Radak) or that David's kingship would be exalted (Ralbag; Metzudos) . [This is the sense of this expression in I Samuel 2:10.]

Mefaresh takes לְהָרִים קָרֶן as a description of Heman's role as a seer. He was a mighty seer of God's words for the king. I.e., the level of his prophecy concerning God's words (בְּדִבְרֵי הָאֱלֹהִים) was exalted.

Targum does not take לְהָרִים קָרֶן as an idiom but renders it literally: to blow the horn. Just as Yeduthun was associated with the harp (v. 3), so Heman was associated with the horn or shofar.

The difficulty with this explanation is that the shofar is not mentioned among the instruments which the Levites were supposed to play.

We have noted above that, in contrast to the families of Asaph and Yeduthun, the sons of Heman are not described as being עַל יַד, by the side, of their father. On the other hand we find a phenomenon in Heman's family which is not duplicated in the case of the others: There are among his sons highly unusual names — גְּדַלְתִּי; רוֹמַמְתִּי עֶזֶר — which require explanation.

The explanation of both points may lie in a further understanding of Heman's function.

When we consider the frequent Scriptural use of אֵל and אֱלֹהִים to denote unusual strength, might or beauty — cf. comm. to 12:23; Jonah 3:3; Ezekiel 31:8 and 9, Psalms 36:7 and many more — we may read דִּבְרֵי הָאֱלֹהִים as weighty or important matters.

לְהָרִים קָרֶן denotes a feeling of pride and success (cf. Psalms 75:5ff and many others) and is often used to describe the help that God extends to His people (cf. Psalms 148:14).

Perhaps, then, Heman's task was to interpret significant events in such a way that they would imply an uplifting or successful conclusion. He was the interpreter of current events and was called upon to do this in the most positive form. This, quite possibly, was something that required maturity and wisdom of which only he, not his sons, was capable. They could not be at their father's side in this matter.

On the other hand, it would be entirely appropriate for him to name his children in such a way that they would reflect the ideals to which he dedicated his life. This would be in much the same way that Isaiah called his children שְׁאָר

יְהֹוָה בְּמִצְלְתַּ֫יִם נְבָלִים וְכִנֹּרוֹת לַעֲבֹדַת בֵּית הָאֱלֹהִים
עַל יְדֵי הַמֶּלֶךְ

ז אָסָף וִידוּתוּן וְהֵימָן: וַיְהִי מִסְפָּרָם עִם־אֲחֵיהֶם מְלֻמְּדֵי־שִׁיר

ח לַיהֹוָה כָּל־הַמֵּבִין מָאתַיִם שְׁמוֹנִים וּשְׁמוֹנָה: וַיַּפִּילוּ גּוֹרָלוֹת

ט מִשְׁמֶרֶת לְעֻמַּת כַּקָּטֹן כַּגָּדוֹל מֵבִין עִם־תַּלְמִיד: וַיֵּצֵא

הַגּוֹרָל הָרִאשׁוֹן לְאָסָף לְיוֹסֵף גְּדַלְיָהוּ הַשֵּׁנִי הוּא־וְאֶחָיו

י וּבָנָיו שְׁנַיִם עָשָׂר: הַשְּׁלִשִׁי זַכּוּר

יא בָּנָיו וְאֶחָיו שְׁנַיִם עָשָׂר: הָרְבִיעִי לַיִּצְרִי

יב בָּנָיו וְאֶחָיו שְׁנַיִם עָשָׂר: הַחֲמִישִׁי נְתַנְיָהוּ

יג בָּנָיו וְאֶחָיו שְׁנַיִם עָשָׂר: הַשִּׁשִּׁי בֻּקִּיָּהוּ

יד בָּנָיו וְאֶחָיו שְׁנַיִם עָשָׂר: הַשְּׁבִיעִי יְשַׂרְאֵלָה

טו בָּנָיו וְאֶחָיו שְׁנַיִם עָשָׂר: הַשְּׁמִינִי יְשַׁעְיָהוּ

טז בָּנָיו וְאֶחָיו שְׁנַיִם עָשָׂר: הַתְּשִׁיעִי מַתַּנְיָהוּ

יז בָּנָיו וְאֶחָיו שְׁנַיִם עָשָׂר: הָעֲשִׂירִי שִׁמְעִי

יח בָּנָיו וְאֶחָיו שְׁנַיִם עָשָׂר: עַשְׁתֵּי־עָשָׂר עֲזַרְאֵל

יט בָּנָיו וְאֶחָיו שְׁנַיִם עָשָׂר: הַשְּׁנֵים עָשָׂר לַחֲשַׁבְיָה

כ בָּנָיו וְאֶחָיו שְׁנַיִם עָשָׂר: לִשְׁלֹשָׁה עָשָׂר שׁוּבָאֵל

שׁוּב, She'ar Yashuv [lit. the remainder shall return], and מַהֵר שָׁלָל חָשׁ בַּז, Maher Shalal Chash Boz [lit. hasten booty, bring on plunder speedily], to reflect aspects of his prophecy.

6. כָּל־אֵלֶּה עַל־יְדֵי אֲבִיהֶם ... אָסָף וִידוּתוּן וְהֵימָן — All these under the tutelage of their fathers ... Asaph, Yeduthun and Heman. The translation follows Ralbag, who takes Asaph, Yeduthun and Heman at the end of the sentence in apposition to their fathers. The sentence thus means : All these [were trained] by their fathers — and the king — Asaph, Yeduthun, and Heman, [to perform] in the song of the House of HASHEM.

Metzudos does not take the names in apposition to their fathers. He translates: All these learned to perform the song of the House of HASHEM ... as composed by the king, Asaph, Yeduthun and Heman. The songs played in the service were psalms of David and Asaph, Yeduthun and Heman.

In line with the suggested translation of עַל יַד as together with in vs. 2 and 3, the first part of this verse would mean that all the sons [including Heman's] served with their respective fathers when it came to the Divine service.

For the second part of the verse: עַל יְדֵי הַמֶּלֶךְ אָסָף וִידוּתוּן וְהֵימָן, the following should be considered: Once more, the sequence is unexpected. Why is the Kehathite, Heman, mentioned after the Merarite, Yeduthun? It

seems possible that reference here is to the psalms which these choristers composed. In the book of Psalms, twelve compositions are ascribed to Asaph, three to Yeduthun, and only one to Heman. It is perhaps reasonable to conclude that Yeduthun reached a higher standing in this matter than Heman and he is therefore mentioned first.

Given this we may understand עַל יְדֵי הַמֶּלֶךְ as follows: In a widely appearing midrash (see, for example, Koheleth Rabbah 7:39), the Sages teach that although many people created liturgical compositions, these became a part of the Divinely inspired psalms of all Israel only when David incorporated them into his book (Tifereth Zion). Only David, whose heart was the heart of all Israel, could imbue these compositions with the universality needed to touch the heart of every Jew in every generation and elicit the responding music of his soul.

It was by the hand of the king [not David, the individual, but the king — the all-encompassing soul of Israel] that Asaph, Yeduthun and Heman achieved their ultimate standing in relation to the shir of the House of HASHEM.

7. וַיְהִי מִסְפָּרָם עִם־אֲחֵיהֶם ... — Their number — together with their brothers ... was ... The twenty-four heads, together with the rest of their group of twelve each (see below), came to 288 (Metzudos).

מָאתַיִם שְׁמוֹנִים וּשְׁמוֹנָה — Two hundred and eighty-eight. See comm. to v. 1. There were

perform in the song of the House of HASHEM to the accompaniment of cymbals, nevalim and harps, for the service of the House of God — under the tutelage of the king, Asaph, Yeduthun and Heman. 7 Their number — together with their brothers who were trained in songs to HASHEM, all masters — was two hundred and eighty-eight. 8 They cast lots, one watch against [another], small and great, the master with the student. 9 The first lot came out to Asaph, to Yoseph; Gedaliahu, the second, he, his brothers and his sons — twelve. 10 The third, Zaccur, his sons and his brothers — twelve. 11 The fourth to Yitzri, his sons and brothers — twelve. 12 The fifth, Nethaniahu, his sons and his brothers — twelve. 13 The sixth, Bukkiahu, his sons and his brothers — twelve. 14 The seventh, Yesarelah, his sons and his brothers — twelve. 15 The eighth, Yeshaiah, his sons and his brothers — twelve. 16 The ninth, Mattaniahu, his sons and his brothers — twelve. 17 The tenth, Shimei, his sons and his brothers — twelve. 18 The eleventh, Azarel, his sons and his brothers — twelve. 19 The twelfth to Chashaviah, his sons and his brothers — twelve. 20 For the thirteenth, Shuvael,

---

288 experts (כָּל הַמֵּבִין) out of the pool of 4,000. These were composed of the twenty-four leaders recorded above and their groups of eleven each, which made up twenty-four groups of twelve.

8. וַיַּפִּילוּ גּוֹרָלוֹת מִשְׁמֶרֶת לְעֻמַּת — They cast lots, one watch against [another]. The complete phrase should certainly read מִשְׁמֶרֶת לְעֻמַּת מִשְׁמֶרֶת, one watch against another watch (see Targum). As Mefaresh, Radak and Metzudos point out, the omission of the second מִשְׁמֶרֶת recalls 17:5 where, in a similar formulation, the phrase-ending לְמִשְׁכָּן was left out. Since the ending is self-understood there is no need for the text to include it (Metzudos).

See the analysis in Section Two there of that chapter where a possible explanation for that omission was offered. In a similar vein, we have seen that our section has stressed that the determination of the order in which the various mishmaros were to serve was left to absolute chance (see 24:5, 31 and the end of our verse). Perhaps our phrase, too, is deftly worded to convey this idea. There was to be no planning of any kind to determine which group of Levites was to serve with which mishmar of the Kohanim. Each mishmar of Levites would fall against ... whichever mishmar of Kohanim would be determined by the lots. Nothing else was to interfere with the element of chance.

בְּקָטֹן כַּגָּדוֹל מֵבִין עִם-תַּלְמִיד — Small and great, the master with the student. The least significant group was to have the same chance as the greatest to be first. The most expert group (מֵבִין) from בּוּן, to understand) was to have no preference over another group which had yet to attain that level of mastery (Commentators).

This interpretation assumes that even among the 288 experts (כָּל הַמֵּבִין) there were still some who could be described as תַּלְמִיד, student, relative to the more accomplished musicians.

Perhaps the phrase can be taken as relating to the Kohanic mishmaros to which these twenty-four groups of musicians were to correspond. Even the greatest in the Levite groups might have to serve with a mishmar of Kohanim who could be described relatively as students.

9-31. This section lists the sequence in which the twenty-four Levite groups of twelve were to serve — as yielded by the lottery. Thus Yoseph, the second son of Asaph (v. 2), whose lot came out first (v. 9), served with Yehoiariv, the first of the Kohanic mishmaros. Gedaliahu, the oldest son of Yeduthun (v. 3), served with Yedaiah, the second Kohanic mishmar (24:7), and so on. All the names given here were listed above (vs. 2-4) under their respective fathers, with the exception of Shimei (v. 17), the sixth of Yeduthun's sons — see comm. to v. 3.

9. לְאָסָף לְיוֹסֵף — To Asaph, to Yoseph. Among Asaph's sons, the first lot fell to Yoseph (Metzudos).

הוּא-וְאֶחָיו וּבָנָיו שְׁנֵים עָשָׂר — He, his brothers and his sons — twelve. This formula is used throughout this section. In our verse it does service for both Yoseph, the first of the groups, and Gedaliahu, the second. Since both are mentioned in the same verse it sufficed to write it just once (Mefaresh).

‫לְאַרְבָּעָה עָשָׂר מַתִּתְיָהוּ‬ ‫עָשָׂר שְׁנַיִם וְאֶחָיו בָּנָיו כא‬

‫לַחֲמִשָּׁה עָשָׂר לִירֵמוֹת‬ ‫עָשָׂר שְׁנַיִם וְאֶחָיו בָּנָיו כב‬

‫לְשִׁשָּׁה עָשָׂר לַחֲנַנְיָהוּ‬ ‫עָשָׂר שְׁנַיִם וְאֶחָיו בָּנָיו כג‬

‫לְשִׁבְעָה עָשָׂר לְיִשְׁבְּקָשָׁה‬ ‫עָשָׂר שְׁנַיִם וְאֶחָיו בָּנָיו כד‬

‫לִשְׁמוֹנָה עָשָׂר לַחֲנָנִי‬ ‫עָשָׂר שְׁנַיִם וְאֶחָיו בָּנָיו כה‬

‫לְתִשְׁעָה עָשָׂר לְמַלּוֹתִי‬ ‫עָשָׂר שְׁנַיִם וְאֶחָיו בָּנָיו כו‬

‫לְעֶשְׂרִים לֶאֱלִיָּתָה‬ ‫עָשָׂר שְׁנַיִם וְאֶחָיו בָּנָיו כז‬

‫לְאֶחָד וְעֶשְׂרִים לְהוֹתִיר‬ ‫עָשָׂר שְׁנַיִם וְאֶחָיו בָּנָיו כח‬

‫לִשְׁנַיִם וְעֶשְׂרִים לְגִדַּלְתִּי‬ ‫עָשָׂר שְׁנַיִם וְאֶחָיו בָּנָיו כט‬

‫לִשְׁלֹשָׁה וְעֶשְׂרִים לְמַחֲזִיאוֹת‬ ‫עָשָׂר שְׁנַיִם וְאֶחָיו בָּנָיו ל‬

‫לְאַרְבָּעָה וְעֶשְׂרִים לְרוֹמַמְתִּי עָזֶר‬ ‫עָשָׂר שְׁנַיִם וְאֶחָיו בָּנָיו לא‬

‫לְמַחְלְקוֹת לְשֹׁעֲרִים לַקָּרְחִים‬ ‫עָשָׂר שְׁנַיִם וְאֶחָיו בָּנָיו א‬

‫וְלִמְשֶׁלֶמְיָהוּ בָּנִים‬ ‫מְשֶׁלֶמְיָהוּ בֶּן־קֹרֵא מִן־בְּנֵי אָסָף: ב‬

‫זְכַרְיָהוּ הַבְּכוֹר יְדִיעֲאֵל הַשֵּׁנִי זְבַדְיָהוּ הַשְּׁלִישִׁי יַתְנִיאֵל‬

‫הָרְבִיעִי: עֵילָם הַחֲמִישִׁי יְהוֹחָנָן הַשִּׁשִּׁי אֶלְיְהוֹעֵינַי ג‬

‫הַשְּׁבִיעִי: וּלְעֹבֵד אֱדֹם בָּנִים שְׁמַעְיָה הַבְּכוֹר יְהוֹזָבָד ד‬

‫הַשֵּׁנִי יוֹאָח הַשְּׁלִשִׁי וְשָׂכָר הָרְבִיעִי וּנְתַנְאֵל הַחֲמִישִׁי:‬

‫עַמִּיאֵל הַשִּׁשִּׁי יִשָּׂשכָר הַשְּׁבִיעִי פְּעֻלְּתַי הַשְּׁמִינִי כִּי בֵרְכוֹ ה‬

As throughout *Chronicles*, the word אֶחָיו, *his brothers*, means colleagues subsumed under his name, not necessarily sons of his father *(Mefaresh).*

XXVI

⋅§ The gatekeepers and their stations

Having dealt with the divisions of the musicians in the previous chapter, the account now turns to the gatekeepers, who were also mentioned at 23:32 among the Levite functionaries.

The listings in this chapter are extremely complex, particularly when taken together with what was learned about the gatekeepers in Ezra's time in ch. 9. The commentary will follow *Malbim's* understanding of these groupings.

Malbim bases his commentary on the assumption that the Levites stood guard at twenty-four locations in the Temple (see comm. to 9:22). Based on 9:22, he postulates a different Levite at each of these twenty-four locations for every day of the week [7 x 24 = 168]. *Malbim* also assumes twenty-four weekly rotations for the gatekeepers, just as there were for the musicians.[1] This would yield a total of 7 x 24 x 24 = 4,032 Levites. Now 23:5 gave the number of gatekeepers as 4,000. *Malbim* explains that number by saying that it does not include the twenty-four heads of the various divisions which are listed in our chapter (as *Malbim* explains it) and that it also does not include the four overall leaders of the Levites who are given in our chapter — Meshelemiahu, Oved Edom, Shemaiah and Chosah. [*Malbim* points to his commentary at 9:22 where he demonstrates that four overall leaders were indeed required for the Levites. See our comm. there.] These division heads and leaders bring the number up to 4,028. Rather than detail the extra four Levites, *Chronicles* preferred to round off the number at 4,000.

1. The *Mefaresh*, however, writes that the gatekeepers did not serve in weekly relays as did the musicians but were divided only according to the locations at which they performed their duties. But see at 9:23.

his sons and his brothers — twelve. ²¹ For the fourteenth, Mattitiahu, his sons and his brothers — twelve. ²² For the fifteenth, to Yeremoth, his sons and his brothers — twelve. ²³ For the sixteenth, to Chananiahu, his sons and his brothers — twelve. ²⁴ For the seventeenth, to Yoshbekashah, his sons and his brothers — twelve. ²⁵ For the eighteenth, to Chanani, his sons and his brothers — twelve. ²⁶ For the nineteenth, to Mallothi, his sons and his brothers — twelve. ²⁷ For the twentieth, to Eliyathah, his sons and his brothers — twelve. ²⁸ For the twenty-first, to Hothir, his sons and his brothers — twelve. ²⁹ For the twenty-second, to Giddalti, his sons and his brothers — twelve. ³⁰ For the twenty-third, to Machazioth, his sons and his brothers — twelve. ³¹ For the twenty-fourth, to Romamti Ezer, his sons and his brothers — twelve.

For the divisions of the gatekeepers: from the Korachites — Meshelemiahu, the son of Kore, from the sons of Asaph. ² And Meshelemiahu had sons: Zechariahu his firstborn, Yedaial the second, Zevadiahu the third, Yethniel the fourth. ³ Elam the fifth, Yehochanan the sixth, and Eliehoenai the seventh. ⁴ And Oved Edom had sons: Shemaiah his firstborn, Yehozavad the second, Yoach the third, Sachar the fourth, Nethanel the fifth. ⁵ Ammiel the sixth, Yissachar the seventh, and Peullethai the eighth — for God

---

1. לַקְרָחִים מְשֶׁלֶמְיָהוּ בֶן־קֹרֵא מִן־בְּנֵי אָסָף — From the Korachites — Meshelemiahu, the son of Kore, from the sons of Asaph. Malbim notes that this Meshelemiahu seems to be identical with the Shallum of 9:19. That Shallum is also identified as a Korachite and his genealogy is given as *the son of Kore*. At v. 18 there we learn that this Shallum guarded the eastern gate, the position assigned to Meshelemiahu in our v. 14. Accordingly, we must assume that the name Asaph in the phrase, מִן־בְּנֵי אָסָף, *from the sons of Asaph*, at the end of the description of Meshelemiahu's parentage, is a shortening of Eviasaph, Korach's son (see 6:22 and 9:19), and not Asaph the Levite singer who has been mentioned so frequently in the past chapters. That Asaph was not descended from Korach [i.e., from the family of Kehath], but from the family of Gershon (see 6:24-28). [See comm. to 9:18,19.]

In *Malbim's* count the sons of this Meshelemiahu (vs. 2, 3) are counted among the division heads, but Meshelemiahu himself is not in the count of twenty-four. He belongs among the four overall leaders.

2⁻3. Seven sons are given for Meshelemiahu and, in *Malbim's* count, these are seven of the twenty-four division heads mentioned in the commentary above.

The oldest son, Zechariahu, is also mentioned at 9:21; see there.

4⁻5. Eight sons are listed for Oved Edom. Of these only seven are included in the count of twenty-four since the oldest son, Shemaiah, belongs not to the twenty-four but to the four main leaders. His own sons are included in the count of twenty-four and are listed in v. 7.

5. כִּי בֵרְכוֹ אֱלֹהִים — For God blessed him. This Oved Edom is the same one who welcomed the Holy Ark into his house after Uzza's untimely death (13:14). There we learn that, as a reward, God blessed the house of Oved Edom and all that was his. Our phrase is a reference to that blessing.

Since eight sons do not seem to be an excessively large number of children, the Sages interpret the phrase as follows: In v. 8 we learn that Oved Edom had sixty-two descendants. After Oved Edom's wife gave birth to the eight sons enumerated here, she herself bore sextuplets. [*For God blessed him* describes not the first eight children, but that which happened after this birth.] In addition, each of the daughter-in-law's by his first eight sons also bore sextuplets. Thus, 9 x 6 = 54 which together with the original eight yields sixty-two [see below to v. 8] (*Berachos* 63b and 64a).

ו אֱלֹהִים: וְלִשְׁמַעְיָה בְנוֹ נוֹלַד בָּנִים הַמִּמְשָׁלִים לְבֵית
ז אֲבִיהֶם כִּי־גִבּוֹרֵי חַיִל הֵמָּה: בְּנֵי שְׁמַעְיָה עָתְנִי
וּרְפָאֵל וְעוֹבֵד אֶלְזָבָד אֶחָיו בְּנֵי־חָיִל אֱלִיהוּ וּסְמַכְיָהוּ:
ח כָּל־אֵלֶּה מִבְּנֵי־עֹבֵד אֱדֹם הֵמָּה וּבְנֵיהֶם וַאֲחֵיהֶם אִישׁ־חַיִל
ט בַּכֹּחַ לַעֲבֹדָה שִׁשִּׁים וּשְׁנַיִם לְעֹבֵד אֱדֹם: וְלִמְשֶׁלֶמְיָהוּ
י בָּנִים וְאַחִים בְּנֵי־חַיִל שְׁמוֹנָה עָשָׂר: וּלְחֹסָה מִן־
בְּנֵי־מְרָרִי בָּנִים שֹׁמְרֵי הָרֹאשׁ כִּי לֹא־הָיָה בְכוֹר וַיְשִׂימֵהוּ
יא אָבִיהוּ לְרֹאשׁ: חִלְקִיָּהוּ הַשֵּׁנִי טְבַלְיָהוּ הַשְּׁלִשִׁי זְכַרְיָהוּ
יב הָרְבִעִי כָּל־בָּנִים וְאַחִים לְחֹסָה שִׁשָּׁה עָשָׂר: לְאֵלֶּה
מַחְלְקוֹת הַשֹּׁעֲרִים לְרָאשֵׁי הַגְּבָרִים מִשְׁמָרוֹת לְעֻמַּת

6. וְלִשְׁמַעְיָה בְנוֹ נוֹלַד בָּנִים — *And sons were born to Shemaiah his son.* As explained in comm. 4-5 above, Shemaiah, the oldest son of Oved Edom, is among the four overall leaders. His six sons, listed in v. 7, are among the twenty-four.

הַמִּמְשָׁלִים לְבֵית אֲבִיהֶם — *Who exercised leadership in their family.* The translation follows *Metzudos*, who treats מִמְשָׁלִים as a verb — albeit in an irregular form. *Targum*, *Mefaresh* and *Malbim* take it as a noun and render: *leaders.* Thus, *who were leaders in their family.* *Radak* is alone in deriving the word not from משל, *to rule,* but from the alternative meaning, *to be similar to.* He takes our phrase together with the next and renders: *Who were similar to their father's family* [in that] *they were men of outstanding quality* [just as their father's family had been].

כִּי־גִבּוֹרֵי חַיִל הֵמָּה — *For they were men of outstanding quality.* Expressions such as אִישׁ חַיִל or גִבּוֹר חַיִל always denote men of exceptional ability. See above, 5:24.

7. ... בְּנֵי שְׁמַעְיָה — *The sons of Shemaiah ...* Six sons are listed for Shemaiah, all of whom are to be counted among the twenty-four division leaders according to *Malbim.* [However, *Metzudos* takes the phrase אֶחָיו בְּנֵי־חַיִל (see below) as proper nouns, that is, one son was called אֶחָיו, another בְּנֵי חָיִל. This would add two additional sons to the list.]

... אֶחָיו בְּנֵי־חָיִל — *Whose brothers were men of quality.* See above, that *Metzudos* takes this phrase as proper nouns. However, *Targum* renders as we have done (and so too must *Malbim,* who counts only six sons for Shemaiah).

The phrase is obscure. Whose brothers

were men of outstanding quality? And who were these brothers? The commentators offer no explanations. Taken simply it seems to imply that the two younger brothers of Elzavad — Elihu and Semachiahu — were men of outstanding quality. However, there is no obvious reason why these two men should be described as *brothers of Elzavad.*

8. הֵמָּה וּבְנֵיהֶם וַאֲחֵיהֶם ... — *They, their sons and their brothers. They* are the sons of Oved Edom who are mentioned here by name; *their sons* are the twenty-four descendants enumerated here; and *their brothers* are other relatives who were not mentioned here at all *(Radak).*

אִישׁ־חַיִל בַּכֹּחַ לַעֲבֹדָה — *Men of special strength for the service.* As explained in 5:24 the term אִישׁ חַיִל denotes a person of special quality. In this context, the quality is given as strength for [Temple] service.

שִׁשִּׁים וּשְׁנַיִם לְעֹבֵד אֱדֹם — *Sixty-two for Oved Edom.* See comm. to v. 5. At 16:38 we have a record of sixty-eight members of Oved Edom's family, an apparent discrepancy. See comm. there for *Malbim's* solutions.

Metzudos' here suggests that between the time when David brought the Ark to Jerusalem [which is the event described in ch. 16] and David's old age [which is the period dealt with in our chapter], it could well be that some of Oved Edom's family died.

9. ... וְלִמְשֶׁלֶמְיָהוּ — *And Meshelemiahu ...* The immediate descendants of Meshelemiahu were listed in vs. 2 and 3 and numbered seven. It seems possible that a more encompassing number is given here because this was also done for Oved Edom's descendants in v. 8. *Malbim* thinks

blessed him. ⁶ And sons were born to Shemaiah his son, who exercised leadership in their family, for they were men of outstanding quality.⁷ The sons of Shemaiah were Othni, and Rephael, and Oved, Elzavad, whose brothers were men of quality, Elihu and Semachiahu. ⁸ All these were from the sons of Oved Edom; they, their sons and their brothers, men of special strength for the service — sixty-two for Oved Edom. ⁹ Meshelemiahu had sons and brothers of quality — eighteen. ¹⁰ Chosah, from the sons of Merari, had sons: Shimri was the chief, though he was not a firstborn, but his father appointed him chief. ¹¹ Chilkiahu the second, Tevaliahu the third, Zechariahu the fourth; all Chosah's sons and brothers came to thirteen. ¹² To these were [given over] the divisions of the gatekeepers — to these, the leaders of the men —

that this verse is added here so that by contrast we can see the degree to which God blessed Oved Edom. From his eight sons came a family of sixty-two, while Meshelemiahu's seven sons yielded only eighteen.

10⁻11. The fourth of the overall leaders is Chosah [who was also mentioned at 16:38]. The four sons mentioned here by name complete the count of twenty-four — seven from Meshelemiahu, seven from Oved Edom, six from Shemaiah and four from Chosah.

10. כִּי לֹא־הָיָה בְכוֹר — Though he was not a firstborn. The context seems to demand the translation of כִּי as though instead of the more usual because. Examples of this usage are Leviticus 11:4 and Psalms 25:11 (see Metzudos there).

Metzudos here renders the word because. The phrase explains why Shimri was called chief rather than firstborn, as had been the main brothers in vs. 2 and 4. Our phrase answers that he was, in fact, not the firstborn.

11. כָּל־בָּנִים וְאַחִים לְחֹסָה שְׁלֹשָׁה עָשָׂר — All Chosah's sons and brothers came to thirteen. Besides the four sons mentioned by name there were other relatives; together the whole group came to thirteen. This information given concerning Chosah's group parallels that given about Oved Edom in v. 8 and Meshelemiahu in v. 9.

To sum up the count as Malbim has it, we now have twenty-eight Levites to add to the count of 4,000 given at 23:5 as the number of gatekeepers. They are the twenty-four division heads and the four overall leaders mentioned in our chapter. This number falls just four short of the

4,032 Levites which were needed to discharge the duties of the gatekeepers as Malbim computes them. See comm. to v. 1.

12. לְאֵלֶּה מַחְלְקוֹת הַשֹּׁעֲרִים — To these were [given over] the divisions of the gate-keepers. The twenty-four (Malbim) or more (Metzudos) people counted up in the section above were placed in charge of the division of the mishmaros of the gate-keepers (Metzudos; Malbim).

As we have seen in the comm. up to this point, Malbim counts exactly twenty-four division heads while Metzudos has more. This disagreement brings about a difference in the treatment of the next phrase in the sentence. Metzudos divides the sentence as follows: לְרָאשֵׁי הַגְּבָרִים מִשְׁמָרוֹת / לְעֻמַּת אֲחֵיהֶם, while Malbim has: / לְרָאשֵׁי הַגְּבָרִים מִשְׁמָרוֹת לְעֻמַּת אֲחֵיהֶם.

According to Malbim, לְרָאשֵׁי הַגְּבָרִים, to the leaders of the men, is in apposition to לְאֵלֶּה, these [men]. The meaning of the sentence in its entirety is: These men [each of the twenty-four mentioned above] were given the leadership of the [twenty-four] mishmaros of gatekeepers which were established corresponding (לְעֻמַּת) to their brothers [the other mishmaros, such as those of the musicians. Their purpose was] to serve [as gatekeepers] in the House of HASHEM.

Metzudos cannot agree with Malbim. There were only twenty-four mishmaros, but according to Metzudos, more than twenty-four men were mentioned. Consequently, the men counted here cannot have been the actual division heads but were rather in general charge of the group of 4,000 and were responsible for dividing them into twenty-four mishmaros [unequal — since 4,000 is not divisible by twenty-

יג אֲחֵיהֶם לְשָׁרֵת בְּבֵית יהוה: וַיַּפִּילוּ גוֹרָלוֹת כַּקָּטֹן כַּגָּדוֹל
יד לְבֵית אֲבוֹתָם לְשַׁעַר וָשָׁעַר: וַיִּפֹּל הַגּוֹרָל מִזְרָחָה
לְשֶׁלֶמְיָהוּ וּזְכַרְיָהוּ בְנוֹ יוֹעֵץ | בְּשֶׂכֶל הִפִּילוּ גוֹרָלוֹת וַיֵּצֵא
טו גוֹרָלוֹ צָפוֹנָה: לְעֹבֵד אֱדֹם נֶגְבָּה וּלְבָנָיו בֵּית הָאֲסֻפִּים:

four]. The meaning of the sentence
according to *Metzudos* is: *To these [men
fell the responsibility of creating] divisions,
mishmaros made up of specific numbers of
men, corresponding to those of their
brothers, to serve in the House of HASHEM*.

13. וַיַּפִּילוּ גוֹרָלוֹת ... לְבֵית אֲבוֹתָם — *They cast
lots ... according to their families*. From the
comm. to the next few verses it will become
clear that *families* in our verse refers to the
four major families of Meshelemiahu,
Oved Edom, Shemaiah, and Chosah. Lots
were cast among these few families to
determine which of them would stand
watch at which location [in contrast to the
lots which were cast by the *Kohanim* and
the musicians which were to determine the
order in which they were to serve
(*Metzudos*)]. The decisions were determined by Providence, and the relative
greatness or insignificance of a given
family group played no role.

לְשַׁעַר וָשָׁעַר — *For the various gates*.
According to *Middos* 1:1, watchmen stood
at twenty-four locations in the Temple, as
follows: Five at the entrances to the Temple
Mount [one gate each at the east, north,
and west, and two on the south]; five at the
entrances to the courtyard [two each on the
north and south sides, and one on the east];
eight for the corners of the Temple Mount
and courtyard walls [one at each of the four
exterior corners of the Temple Mount wall
and one at each of the four exterior corners
of the courtyard wall]; five in various
chambers; and one behind the back wall of
the Holy of Holies. Three of the chambers
were manned by *Kohanim*.
Evidently the watches stood not only at
gates but also at other locations within the
Temple areas and in various chambers.
Thus, *for the various gates* requires some
explanation.
From vs. 14-16 it appears that the lots
were cast for the four leaders identified
above. Each of these may have been
assigned to a particularly significant gate
on one of the four sides of the Temple and
the rest of each group, as enumerated in vs.

17 and 18, were subsidiary to them. Thus
the lots cast for these four leaders were *for
the various gates*.

14. וַיִּפֹּל הַגּוֹרָל מִזְרָחָה לְשֶׁלֶמְיָהוּ — *The lot for
the east fell to Shelemiahu*. See comm. to v.
1 where we assumed with *Malbim* that the
Shallum mentioned above in 9:19 as
watchman of the eastern gate is identical
with our Shelemiahu.
We noted in comm. to v. 13 that the lots
were cast for the allocation of the *gate*
positions. Therefore Shelemiahu was the
gatekeeper to the east. Since both the
Temple Mount and the Temple courtyard
had only one gate in the east (*Middos* 1:3
and 4), our verse could mean either than he
stood guard at the gate of the Temple
Mount or at the gate of the courtyard.
We postulated above that as leader, he
would have been assigned to the most
significant gate. It could be argued that the
one leading into the courtyard was the
more important because of the greater
sanctity of the courtyard. On the other
hand, the gate leading onto the Temple
Mount was the first one encountered by
someone entering from that direction, and
this may have given it special significance.
According to the dispositions described
in *Middos* for the northern side, at which
there was one gate leading onto the Temple
Mount and three leading into the courtyard, there were guardᵈ aᵗ only two of the
three inner gates — thosᵉ .urthest to east
and west; the center gate had no one
assigned to it. Since of the courtyard gates
the center gate, which might have been
seen as the most important, had no guard at
all, the only one which stood out as unique
would be the single one leading onto the
Temple Mount.
If we further postulate that the three
sides — east, north and south — had similar
arrangements, then it follows that to the
east, the gate leading onto the Temple
Mount was meant as Shelemiahu's special
preserve.

וּזְכַרְיָהוּ בְנוֹ יוֹעֵץ בְּשֶׂכֶל ... וַיֵּצֵא גוֹרָלוֹ צָפוֹנָה — *As*

watches corresponding to their brothers; to serve in the House of
HASHEM. ¹³ They cast lots — small and great alike, according to their
families — for the various gates. ¹⁴ The lot for the east fell to
Shelemiahu; as for Zechariahu his son, a wise counsellor, they cast
lots and his lot came out to the north. ¹⁵ To Oved Edom, the south;
and to his sons, the additional chambers. ¹⁶ to Shuppim and Chosah,

---

for Zechariahu his son, a wise counsellor ...
and his lot came out to the north. Of the
four main leaders of the Levites isolated by
Malbim in the earlier part of this chapter,
only Shemaiah is from the second
generation; he was himself counted among
Oved Edom's sons. We would have
expected that one of the main gates would
be assigned to him. Nonetheless, the
northern gate is allotted to Zechariahu the
son of Shelemiahu, whose progeny is not
given earlier, and Shemaiah is not
mentioned in our section by name (see
below v. 15). The reason must be
Zechariahu's great personal standing
which is expressed in the assessment that
he was a יוֹעֵץ בְּשֵׂכֶל, a wise counsellor.

צָפוֹנָה — To the north. Since the courtyard
had three northern gates (Middos 1:4) and
the Temple Mount had only one, we
assume that it is to that one gate that
Zechariahu was assigned — see above and
comm. to v. 15.

15. לְעֹבֵד אֱדֹם נֶגְבָּה — To Oved Edom, the
south. Middos 1:3 has two gates on the
southern side of the Temple Mount and 1:4
has three gates for the courtyard on that
side. Thus, in contrast to the eastern and
northern sides, there is no ready reason to
conclude that his post was a Temple Mount
gate rather than a courtyard gate.
This leads us to consider the possibility
that, in contrast to the Second Temple, the
First Temple had only one gate leading into
the Temple Mount from the south. In the
introductory remarks to vs. 17 and 18
below, we will explore the consideration
that there may have been several more or
less structural changes between the two
buildings. Rashi to II Kings 22:14 does,
indeed, talk of only one gate named after
the prophetess Chuldah, where Middos
1:3, which describes the Second Temple,
talks of two gates of Chuldah.

וּלְבָנָיו ... — And to his sons ... Since
Shemaiah is among the four main Levites
and had his progeny listed in v. 7, we

suspect that his sons here may mean
Shemaiah in particular. It was he to whom
the northern gate should logically have
gone, as noted in comm. to v. 14. In the
event Zechariahu received that honor and
Shemaiah was therefore given charge of the
בֵּית הָאֲסֻפִּים, additional chambers.

בֵּית הָאֲסֻפִּים — The additional chambers.
From our verse and from v. 17 it is clear
that this structure was part of the southern
watch. But what precisely was it? Radak
(Shorashim) and Metzudos confess
ignorance. It is simply the name of a
structure on the south side of the Temple
which was known to the people of Ezra's
time but whose meaning has become lost to
us.
Rosh to Tamid 27a, on the basis of the
Gemara there as he understands it,
attempts to reconcile as much as possible
the arrangements in the First Temple with
the description given in Middos of the
Second Temple. In his explanation, he sees
this phrase as the source of those watches
which were stationed in various chambers.
These chambers were not part of the
original scheme of the building but were
added later by prophetic fiat (אֲסֻפִּים from
יסף, to add), hence, additional chambers [of
which there were two separate double
chambers; thus four in all — see v. 17]. Our
translation follows Rosh.
Targum renders בֵּית שִׁקְפַּיָא, the term which
Targumim favor for סִיף [see, for example,
Targum to 9:19]. These are parts of the structure
of a door-frame, as for example in Exodus 12:7
where it is used for the beam above the door.
This opinion of Targum is also held by Rabbeinu
Tam quoted by Rosh to Tamid 27a. [See also Ibn
Ezra to Nehemiah 12:25.] But what is a house of
door-frames?
It has been suggested that house of door-
frames may simply be the בֵּית שַׁעַר, the
gatekeeper's lodge, or vestibule which occurs
frequently in Mishnah and Talmud. Witness
אסיפא דביתא of Bava Kamma 104b, which some
commentators render as בֵּית שַׁעַר; and a geniza
fragment of Geonic interpretations where בֵּית
שַׁעַר (Mishnah, Bava Basra 1:5) is rendered
אסופא ארמית.

If so, the בֵּית הָאֲסֻפִּים would be a gatekeeper's lodge attached to the southern gate. This lodge, it has been suggested, may well have had two sections (see *Radak*) — one on either side of the gate. Those would be the two posts, each of which required two watchmen.

16. ... לְשֻׁפִּים — *To Shuppim* ... This name has not been mentioned in the previous lists. *Metzudos* surmises that it may be someone previously listed under a different name. But, inasmuch as our section deals only with the four leaders of the gate-keepers [unless specifically explained, as in the case of Zechariahu — see comm. to v. 14 above], why should one of the subsidiary Levites be mentioned in this context — and why under a name which we cannot even recognize?

The answer may be that the western side required six watchmen, as we shall see in v. 18. But Chosah, to whose lot it fell, had only four sons identified in the earlier list. He together with them would be only five. Because of this, a son from a different family had to be co-opted into Chosah's group. The name may have been intentionally changed into one which perhaps was not given at birth but which — as is often the case with names in *Chronicles* — was attached later because of some deed or quality displayed. This would stress that his presence in this watch was based not on his family but on his own qualities.

But why, in this case, should he be mentioned first?

Perhaps the explanation lies in the responsibility to which he was assigned. We shall see below that the guard detail on the west had two tasks: The guarding of the *parbar* (outlying area — v. 18, see there) and the *path* mentioned in our verse. It may be that Shuppim was in charge of the detail assigned to the *path* while Chosah guarded the *parbar*. Since v. 18 mentions the *path* before the *parbar* (see comm. below) — perhaps it was the more important — Shuppim is mentioned before Chosah.

עִם שַׁעַר שַׁלֶּכֶת בַּמְסִלָּה הָעוֹלָה — *By the Shallecheth gate, on the path that led upwards.* The reference is obscure. No Shallecheth gate or path is mentioned in *Middos* and therefore we have nothing but the text of our verse and of v. 18 to guide us.

Middos has four guards on the west assigned to the corners of the courtyard and the Temple Mount and, as we shall see in the prefatory remarks to vs. 17 and 18, *Rosh* believes that these positions are reflected in v. 18. However, *Rosh* offers no explanation for our verse and furthermore, his interpretation of v. 18 is based on an unusual rendering of מְסִלָּה in that verse which is not shared by other commentators, as we shall see below. We shall therefore attempt to understand our verse on its own merits based on the rendering of the word מְסִלָּה in v. 18 as *path*.

In the prefatory remarks to 17-18 we shall see that, as *Rosh* interprets *Tamid* 27a, it appears that, in contrast to the Second Temple, the First Temple did not have a western gate. But, if so, what is the שַׁעַר שַׁלֶּכֶת, and what is the *path*?

Malbim suggests that the שַׁעַר שַׁלֶּכֶת was the gate through which the Temple wastes were taken out [שַׁלֶּכֶת from שלך, *to throw*, *fling* or *cast*]. If we combine this with *Metzudos* who renders מְסִלָּה הָעוֹלָה, *the path that leads up the mountain*, we can surmise as follows:

Somewhere to the west of the Temple complex [whether within or without the Temple grounds] there was a path along which the wastes were removed to the place set aside for this purpose. There was a gate in the western wall — the שַׁעַר שַׁלֶּכֶת — which led onto this path. This gate did not have a watchman, as did the other gates of the Temple, since it was a service gate rather than one which warranted a ceremonial watch. However, four watchmen were required for the path — they may have been stationed along it or patrolled it in some way — and these had their main station near the Shallecheth gate which led onto the path (עִם שַׁעַר שַׁלֶּכֶת).

In the Second Temple there were other arrangements for the waste disposal [today we know of a שַׁעַר הָאַשְׁפָּה (lit. *dung gate)* to the south] and thus there was no path and no Shallecheth gate. The four watchmen who had been assigned to the path were now freed and were henceforth stationed at the four corners of the courtyard and the Temple Mount precisely as was the case on the eastern side.

26

16-17

the west, by the Shallecheth gate, on the path that led upwards; one watch corresponding to the other watch. ¹⁷ To the east, six Levites; to the north, four, facing the sun; to the south, four, facing the sun,

מִשְׁמָר לְעֻמַּת מִשְׁמָר — *One watch corresponding to the other watch.* The two groups within Chosah's watch divided the two responsibilities equitably. After one group had watched the path and the other the *parbar*, they would exchange positions *(Metzudos).*

When we consider that both guard details were stationed within the *parbar* (outlying) area (see v. 18), there may be a more simple meaning: The two details (the one on the path and the one in the outlying area) stood opposite one another within the same area.

17⁻18. *Middos* 1:1 teaches that the Second Temple was guarded at twenty-four locations. Of these, twenty-one were manned by *Levites* and three by *Kohanim*.

Tamid 27a teaches that the numbers of positions given in the mishnah is derived from vs. 17-18 here. According to one opinion, these verses deal only with the twenty-one Levite positions; according to another, they include all twenty-four.

As *Rosh* explains the first opinion, our verses are to be understood as follows:

Of the six watchmen assigned to the eastern side in v. 17, one was stationed at the gate leading on to the Temple Mount, one at the gate of the courtyard, one at each of the eastern corners of the Temple Mount, and one at each of the eastern corners of the courtyard.

Of the four assigned to the north, one guarded the gate leading onto the Temple Mount, two guarded two of the three gates leading onto the courtyard, and one guarded one of the Temple chambers located on that side.

Of the four to the south, two guarded the two gates of Chuldah which led onto the Temple Mount from the south, and another two guarded two of the three gates which led into the courtyard on that side.

The *assupim* of v. 17 [which *Rosh* renders as *additional chambers*] have two watchmen, one for each set of two chambers — see comm.

Of the six watchmen assigned to the west in v. 18, four guarded the corners of the courtyard and Temple Mount [מְסִלָּה is taken to mean *end* — the rear of the Temple complex], and two stand guard together

behind the Holy of Holies. [The position behind the Holy of Holies was isolated and the guard needed a companion *(Gemara).*]

According to these dispositions we have a total of twenty-two Levites standing watch at twenty-one positions. However, no arrangement is made for a western gate to the Temple Mount and we must assume that, in contrast to the Second Temple, the First Temple did not have such a gate.

Rosh does not explain the second opinion of the *Gemara*, that the text yields all twenty-four positions, but we assume as follows: East, north and south remain same. *Assupim* had four watchmen [2+2], and of the six of v. 18, four stood guard at the corners, one behind the Holy of Holies and one at a western gate (if one existed in the First Temple), or in the Temple Mount area (if, as is obvious according to the first opinion, there was no formal gate to the Temple Mount on the western side).

Rosh is able to maintain his opinion that our text yields that even in the First Temple four on the western side stood guard at the corners of the courtyard and Temple Mount, only by rendering מְסִלָּה as *end* — the extremity of the Temple. But other commentators, including *Targum*, take the word in its more usual meaning — *path* — and our commentary follows that meaning.

17. לַמִּזְרָח הַלְוִיִּם שִׁשָּׁה — *To the east, six Levites.* These six positions are precisely those delineated by *Middos*: One each at each eastern corner of the Temple Mount and the courtyard, and one each at the gates leading to each area.

In the commentary to v. 18 we shall see that in the First Temple the western corners of the courtyard and Temple Mount did not have guards. These positions were filled when the four watchmen assigned to the *path* in v. 16 became unnecessary. This being so we can define the function of the watchmen at the corners as being an extension of the watches of the eastern gates — witness that in the west where there was no gate there were no watches at the corners.

לַצָּפוֹנָה ... אַרְבָּעָה לַנֶּגְבָּה ... אַרְבָּעָה — *To the north, four ... to the south, four.* We saw above how these four are apportioned in

יח שְׁנָיִם: לַפַּרְבָּר לַמַּעֲרָב אַרְבָּעָה לַמְסִלָּה שְׁנַיִם לַפַּרְבָּר:
יט אֵלֶּה מַחְלְקוֹת הַשֹּׁעֲרִים לִבְנֵי הַקָּרְחִי וְלִבְנֵי מְרָרִי:
כ וְהַלְוִיִּם אֲחִיָּה עַל־אוֹצְרוֹת בֵּית הָאֱלֹהִים וּלְאֹצְרוֹת הַקֳּדָשִׁים:
כא בְּנֵי לַעְדָּן בְּנֵי הַגֵּרְשֻׁנִּי לְלַעְדָּן רָאשֵׁי הָאָבוֹת לְלַעְדָּן לְלַעְדָּן

Rosh's view that the arrangements in the First Temple were the same as those in the Second. However, in themselves the verses could yield a different interpretation, particularly as we have surmised that according to many commentators it is possible that the arrangement in the First Temple was significantly different than in the Second. In v. 15 we suggested that the First Temple had only one gate leading onto the Temple Mount on the southern side. In that case, the four on each side could well have been assigned — one to the gate leading onto the Temple Mount and three to the three gates leading into the courtyard.

לַיּוֹם ... — *Facing the sun.* The translation follows *Rosh (Tamid)* who suggests that the guards had to face east, either because this is a Torah requirement whose meaning is too deep for us to fathom (גְּזֵירַת הַכָּתוּב), or because the focus of all the guarding was mainly the eastern gate. See *Chullin* 60a for the use of יוֹם as *sun.*

Rosh's interpretation has the advantage of explaining why לַיּוֹם is only said in relation to north and south. The eastern watchmen presumably faced east anyway.

Malbim, who as we saw in ch. 9 and above thinks that the twenty-four watchmen were changed every day, interprets our phrase as meaning *per day.*

וְלָאֲסֻפִּים שְׁנַיִם שְׁנָיִם — *And for the two pairs of additional chambers.* See comm. to v. 15. We followed *Rosh* there and continue with his interpretation here. The chambers were added to the Temple plan in pairs at two different times (which is why they are listed separately). They either had two watchmen, one for each pair (according to the first explanation of the *Gemara),* or four watchmen, one for each chamber (according to the second explanation there). See above.

If אֲסֻפִּים is a gatehouse it may well be that there were sections on either side of the gate, each requiring two watchmen.

18. לַפַּרְבָּר לַמַּעֲרָב — *For the outlying areas to the west.* *Ramban (Genesis* 30:20) makes the point that the letters *beis* (ב) and *vav* (ו) are often interchangeable. One example he cites is פַּרְבָּר, which he believes to be the same word as פַּרְוָר *(II Kings* 23:11), which means an area lying outside the city walls.[1]

Thus פַּרְבָּר would be an outlying area of the Temple — presumably the entire section west of the Holy of Holies incorporating both the part lying within the courtyard (eleven cubits in the Second Temple) and the western areas of the Temple Mount.

The verse can best be rendered as follows: [As] *for the outlying areas to the west* [there were two separate details stationed there;] *four* [men] were assigned] *to* [guard] *the path; two* [men were assigned] *to* [guard] *the outlying area* [proper].

19. לִבְנֵי הַקָּרְחִי וְלִבְנֵי מְרָרִי — *For the sons of the Korachites and the sons of Merari.* Meshelemiahu is introduced in 26:1 as a Korachite and Chosah in v. 10 as being descended from Merari. A simple reading of the text seems to imply that Oved Edom, and therefore his son Shemaiah also, were Korachites. See discussion at 16:38 and 42.

⁓§ **Temple Functionaries**

20. וְהַלְוִיִּם — *And the Levites:* The following duties also belonged to the Levites *(Metzudos).* From 23:4 it is clear that the administration of Temple affairs also fell within the duties of the Levites.

Alternatively, we might render the phrase: *The Levites* [who filled the following positions] *were:*

אֲחִיָּה — *Achiah.* This Levite has not been previously mentioned.

---

1. See *Numbers* 35:2 and *Ezekiel* 27:28 where the *Targumim* use the word פַּרְוָר to render מִגְרַשׁ which *Metzudos* to *Ezekiel* explains as denoting an area which was, so to speak, expelled (גרש, *to send away)* from the walled-in area.

and for the two pairs of additional chambers. [18] *For the outlying areas to the west, four for the path, two for the outlying area.* [19] *These are the divisions of the gatekeepers for the sons of the Korachites and the sons of Merari.* [20] *And the Levites: Achiah was in charge of the treasuries of the House of God and the treasuries of the consecrated [animals].* [21] *The sons of Ladan of the sons of the Gershonites: Now Ladan had heads of families; for Ladan the*

R' David Cohen, in his *Ohel David* vol. II, suggests that this may be the prophet Achiah the Shilonite (see *I Kings* chs. 11-15). According to *Rambam (Introduction to Mishneh Torah)*, Achiah the Shilonite was a Levite. There is no known source for this and *R' Cohen* surmises that *Rambam* may have derived it from our verse.

Certainly, if we are dealing here with the mysterious Shilonite whose life spanned many centuries [*Rambam*, based on *Bava Basra* 121b, states that he was alive at the time of the Exodus and he was still a prophet in the times of Solomon and his son Rechavoam], this would help us grasp the import of this verse. Verses 21-32 are obviously connected to the earlier lists given in chs. 23 and 24, and they detail the responsibilities of the Gershonites and the Kehathites. In this context our verse, which talks of an unidentified Achiah whose parentage we do not know and cannot derive from this verse, seems out of place. But if it is the towering personality of the Shilonite who, in his own person, provided a link to Sinai, then no further explanation or identification is necessary.

עַל־אוֹצְרוֹת בֵּית הָאֱלֹהִים — *Was in charge of the treasuries of the House of God.* These were the funds set aside for the needs of the building *(Metzudos)*.

וּלְאֹצְרוֹת הַקֳּדָשִׁים — *And the treasuries of the consecrated [animals].* This was the money from which the communal sacrifices were bought *(Mefaresh* and *Metzudos)*.

21. בְּנֵי לַעְדָּן בְּנֵי הַגֵּרְשֻׁנִּי — *The sons of Ladan of the sons of the Gershonites.* See 23:7. The Yechiel mentioned here as Ladan's son is also mentioned at 23:8. The meaning of our verse is that the sons of Ladan were also among those Levites who had administrative duties in the Temple.

The wording of our verse, however, is obscure. *Metzudos* renders as follows: *The sons of Ladan [who were among] the sons of the Gershonites — now Ladan [was*

blessed with a great number of] *heads of families* — [the most prominent son] *of Ladan the Gershonite was Yechieli.*

R' Y. Danziger has suggested the following rendering for this obscure verse. At 23:9 we noted *Gra's* opinion that some of the heads of families in the Ladan clan, came from Shimei. Our verse may mean that for the position of treasurer which was assigned to the clan, only such chiefs were chosen who were actually descended from Ladan himself. The verse should be rendered: *The sons of Ladan [who are to represent] the Gershonite descendants, for [the family of] Ladan, heads of families who were [actual] descendants of Ladan the Gershonite — Yechieli.*

The verse is sufficiently complex for us to attempt yet another solution.

In addition to the inherent difficulty of this verse, two other points require elucidation. First, there is the problem of how functionaries in David's time could be removed no more than two or three generations from Levi's son Gershon. Second, Zetham and Yoel are given in the next verse as sons of Yechieli where earlier (23:5) they were given as brothers. These points taken together lead us to surmise that we are dealing with two Ladans, the first the son of Gershon and the second his descendant and namesake of many years later. This may be further bolstered by noting the appellation *Ladan the Gershonite* in our verse. It seems unlikely that the actual son of Gershon should have been so called and this again leads to the premise that we are dealing with a second Ladan. This second Ladan had a son and he may well have called his son by the same name which his illustrious forefather had chosen for his son — Yechieli. This [second] Yechieli, in turn, may have wanted to perpetuate other names which had been honored in the clan. Alternatively, these names may not have been given names at all but official ones which had become attached to the offices which they held (see

כב הַגֵּרְשֻׁנִּי יְחִיאֵלִי: בְּנֵי יְחִיאֵלִי זֵתָם וְיוֹאֵל אָחִיו עַל־
כג אֹצְרוֹת בֵּית יהוה: לַעַמְרָמִי לַיִּצְהָרִי לַחֶבְרוֹנִי לָעֻזִּיאֵלִי:
כד־כה וּשְׁבָאֵל בֶּן־גֵּרְשׁוֹם בֶּן־מֹשֶׁה נָגִיד עַל־הָאֹצָרוֹת: וְאֶחָיו
לֶאֱלִיעֶזֶר רְחַבְיָהוּ בְנוֹ וִישַׁעְיָהוּ בְנוֹ וְיֹרָם בְּנוֹ וְזִכְרִי בְנוֹ
כו וּשְׁלֹמוֹת בְּנוֹ: הוּא שְׁלֹמוֹת וְאֶחָיו עַל כָּל־אֹצְרוֹת
כז הַקֳּדָשִׁים אֲשֶׁר הִקְדִּישׁ דָּוִיד הַמֶּלֶךְ וְרָאשֵׁי הָאָבוֹת לְשָׂרֵי־
הָאֲלָפִים וְהַמֵּאוֹת וְשָׂרֵי הַצָּבָא: מִן־הַמִּלְחָמוֹת וּמִן־
כח הַשָּׁלָל הִקְדִּישׁוּ לְחַזֵּק לְבֵית יהוה: וְכֹל הַהִקְדִּישׁ שְׁמוּאֵל
הָרֹאֶה וְשָׁאוּל בֶּן־קִישׁ וְאַבְנֵר בֶּן־נֵר וְיוֹאָב בֶּן־צְרוּיָה כֹּל
כט הַמַּקְדִּישׁ עַל יַד־שְׁלֹמִית וְאֶחָיו: לַיִּצְהָרִי
כְּנַנְיָהוּ וּבָנָיו לַמְּלָאכָה הַחִיצוֹנָה עַל־יִשְׂרָאֵל לְשֹׁטְרִים

°וּשְׁלֹמִית ק'

Appendix V). Thus, it was the son and grandson of the latter Ladan who were the Yechieli, Zetham, and Yoel of David's times.

Our verse could now be rendered as follows: *The children of* [the second] *Ladan,* [the ones who were to represent] *the Gershonite descendants* [of the clan of the first] *Ladan, these* [children] *of the Gershonite Ladan* [who were to be] *family heads — Yechieli.*

22. בְּנֵי יְחִיאֵלִי זֵתָם וְיוֹאֵל אָחִיו — *The sons of Yechieli — Zetham and Yoel his brother.* At 23:8 these two seem to be Yechieli's brothers. *Radak* suggests that either they were actually the children of Yechieli but were counted there among Ladan's children in accordance with the rule that grandchildren can be considered children; or, that in fact they are not the same people but that Yechieli called his children by his brothers' names [as in the case of Mushi, the son of Merari, who called his son by his brother's name — Machli; see above 23:21,23].

עַל־אֹצְרוֹת בֵּית ה' — *The treasuries of the House of HASHEM.* These are the silver and gold objects that lay in the Temple treasury (*Metzudos*). See 29:8.

23. לַעַמְרָמִי ... — *For the Amramites ...* The four names mentioned here are the four sons of Kehath. The meaning of the verse is that descendants of each one of these four people were also involved in the adminstration of the Temple. The rest of our chapter gives the names of these

descendants but does not list any for the last son, Uzziel. *Metzudos* suggests that perhaps Uzziel's descendants are given together with those of Chevron, but he does not say why that should be done.

Malbim indicates that the descendants of Uzziel are indeed omitted. Perhaps no list which detailed the appointments of the children of Uzziel was available when *Chronicles* was written.

24. וּשְׁבָאֵל ... נָגִיד עַל־הָאֹצָרוֹת — *Shevuel ... the official in charge of the treasuries.* This means either that one of the treasuries not yet mentioned was in his charge, or that he was the official in overall charge of all the treasuries (*Mefaresh*).

Since it is highly improbable that a grandson of Moses would still have been alive in David's time, it seems likely that our verse refers to a Shevuel who was a functionary in an earlier time, or that, as has been suggested previously, the name of an early holder of the office had become attached to the office and was adopted by all later holders.

25. וְאֶחָיו לֶאֱלִיעֶזֶר — *His brothers through Eliezer.* That is, Shevuel's cousins, the sons of Moses' other son, Eliezer (see above 23:15ff).

רְחַבְיָהוּ בְנוֹ ... — *His son Rechaviahu ...* Rechaviahu was Eliezer's only son (23:17), but he himself had many sons (there). The rest of those mentioned in this verse are all Rechaviahu's sons.

וִישַׁעְיָהוּ בְנוֹ — *His son Yeshaiahu.* Although a number of sons are counted, the most

Gershonite — Yechieli. [22] *The sons of Yechieli — Zetham and Yoel his brother, were in charge of the treasuries of the House of* HASHEM. [23] *For the Amramites, the Yitzharites, the Chevronites and the Uzzielites:* [24] *Shevuel, the son of Gershom, the son of Moses, the official in charge of the treasuries.* [25] *His brothers through Eliezer — his son Rechaviahu, his son Yeshaiahu, his son Yoram, his son Zichri, and his son Shelomith.* [26] *This Shelomoth and his brothers were in charge of all the treasuries of consecrated things which King David and the family heads who were officers over the thousands and the hundreds and the officers of the army had consecrated.* [27] *They consecrated from the wars and from the spoils in order to strengthen the House of* HASHEM. [28] *And all that Samuel the seer, Saul the son of Kish, Avner the son of Ner, and Yoav the son of Tzeruiah had consecrated; all who consecrated — by the hand of Shelomith and his brothers.* [29] *For the Yitzharites — Chenaniahu and his sons for the outside work over Israel, as sheriffs and judges.*

significant among them was the youngest, Shelomith, as can be seen from the next verse which talks of *Shelomoth and his brothers (Radak).*

It is not clear why *Radak* explains the verse as he does. Verse 26 makes it clear that the Shelomith mentioned at the end of the verse actually functioned in David's time. This would obviously be more likely if each of the names mentioned represented a new generation. Compare 3:10 and countless other examples.

26. עַל כָּל־אֹצְרוֹת הַקֳּדָשִׁים אֲשֶׁר הִקְדִּישׁ דָּוִיד הַמֶּלֶךְ ... — *Of all the treasuries of consecrated things which King David ... had consecrated.* *Radak* suggests that the Levites mentioned earlier were in charge of various treasuries which had been consecrated since the time of Moses. Shelomoth and his relatives were in charge of those treasuries which had come to the Temple from David's reign onwards.

וְרָאשֵׁי הָאָבוֹת לְשָׂרֵי־הָאֲלָפִים וְהַמֵּאוֹת — *And the family heads who were officers over the thousands and the hundreds.* The translation follows *Metzudos* who reads the phrase as though the words *who were* appeared in the text.

R' Y. Danziger has suggested an alternative translation. Perhaps the preposition ל in לְשָׂרֵי־ הָאֲלָפִים can be rendered, *together with* [for ל as interchangeable with עִם, *with*, compare: אִינֶנּוּ עִמּוֹ ... (*Genesis* 31:2 and 5), or ... מֵעַזֹב לוֹ, אִינֶנּוּ אֵלַי (*Exodus* 23:5), or usages such as: כִּי־ תֶּעֱזֹב עִמּוֹ, יַעֲמֹד לִימִין אֶבְיוֹן (*Psalms* 109:31) — see *Michlol* of *Radak*].

Given this translation we have two donors besides the king — the family heads and the army

officers. This would reflect precisely the arrangement ordained in the Torah (*Numbers* 31:25ff) that spoils of war are to be shared between the soldiers and the people and that each group must donate a part of its portion for sacred purposes.

27. מִן־הַמִּלְחָמוֹת וּמִן־הַשָּׁלָל הִקְדִּישׁוּ — *They consecrated from the wars and from the spoils.* They consecrated that which they took in their wars and which they took as spoils from the territories which they conquered (*Metzudos*).

28. ... וְכֹל הַהִקְדִּישׁ שְׁמוּאֵל הָרֹאֶה — *And all that Samuel the seer ... had consecrated.* *Ramban* (*Deuteronomy* 3:13) demonstrates that the prefix ה can be used in place of אֲשֶׁר, *that which.* Thus הַהִקְדִּישׁ, *that which he consecrated.*

עַל יַד־שְׁלֹמִית וְאֶחָיו — *By the hand of Shelomith and his brothers.* See v. 26. Shelomith was in charge of all the treasures which came into the Temple treasury from the time of Samuel, Saul and David and onwards.

29. לַמְּלָאכָה הַחִיצוֹנָה עַל־יִשְׂרָאֵל לְשֹׁטְרִים וּלְשֹׁפְטִים — *For the outside work over Israel, as sheriffs and judges.* Most commentators take outside to mean outside the city — to cut down cedars and quarry stones and to plough the fields belonging to the Temple treasury (*Mefaresh*). *Radak* adds that the words *over Israel* refers to the supervision and responsibility over the harvest and collection of produce consecrated by people for the Temple. All these activities were to

ל וּלְשֹׁפְטִים: לַחֶבְרוֹנִי חֲשַׁבְיָהוּ וְאֶחָיו

בְּנֵי־חַיִל אֶלֶף וּשְׁבַע־מֵאוֹת עַל פְּקֻדַּת יִשְׂרָאֵל מֵעֵבֶר

לַיַּרְדֵּן מַעְרָבָה לְכֹל מְלֶאכֶת יהוה וְלַעֲבֹדַת הַמֶּלֶךְ:

לא לַחֶבְרוֹנִי יְרִיָּה הָרֹאשׁ לַחֶבְרוֹנִי לְתֹלְדֹתָיו לְאָבוֹת בִּשְׁנַת

הָאַרְבָּעִים לְמַלְכוּת דָּוִיד נִדְרָשׁוּ וַיִּמָּצֵא בָהֶם גִּבּוֹרֵי חַיִל

לב בְּיַעְזֵיר גִּלְעָד: וְאֶחָיו בְּנֵי־חַיִל אַלְפַּיִם וּשְׁבַע מֵאוֹת רָאשֵׁי

---

be overseen by Chenaniahu and his sons. They were to be officers and judges over the many workers who were occupied by these activities (*Radak* and *Metzudos*).

According to this interpretation, there is no indication in our verse that the Levites functioned as judges or court officers in a more general sense (see comm. to 23:4). *Malbim*, however, takes *sheriffs and judges* in its broader sense. In addition to being in charge of the Temple's outside interests, Chenaniahu and his sons also served as general law-enforcers and judges in Israel.

Ralbag has an altogether different view. He understands *outside work* as referring to any Temple related activities which took place outside the Temple confines (rather than outside the city). These Levites' duties were to encourage the people to pay the annual levy of half a shekel and to fulfill their sacrificial pledges. They were also judges and law-enforcers charged with the duty of guiding the people on a path of righteousness and goodness, since the Levites in particular were the Torah sages. [In this capacity they functioned for the king whose duty it is to see that there should be justice in the land. This is the meaning of the words ... *and for the service of the king*, in the next verse.] See above at 23:4 for *Ralbag's* interpretation there.

A careful analysis of the Scriptural usages of the word שֹׁטֵר may yield another explanation. It is true that we find Levites שֹׁטְרִים in the sense of court-officials at II:19:11 where Yehoshaphat establishes his judicial reforms. After making sure that the courts would function in all the areas of concern, he says ... *and the Levites are available to you as* שֹׁטְרִים, which in the context surely means officials of the court. Moreover, in that same context (v. 8 there), Yehoshaphat appoints Levites as judges in the Jerusalem court which was to be composed of ... *Levites, Kohanim, and family heads of Israel* [in accordance with the halachah (*Rambam, Sanhedrin* 2:2) that an ideal Sanhedrin should contain both *Kohanim* and Levites among its members].

Nevertheless, the שֹׁטֵר function of the Levites

is not limited to that of court-functionary. Thus, during the building projects of the king Yoshiah, where the verse in *II Chronicles* (34:12-13) states that the Levites supervised the projects, they are also described as שֹׁטְרִים. This, in much the same way that שֹׁטְרִים oversaw the Israelite labor in Egypt (*Exodus* ch. 5).

The Mishnah considers the position of שֹׁטֵר a position of dignity. In *Kiddushin* 4:5 the Mishnah rules: ... 'Those whose fathers were established as שֹׁטְרֵי הָרַבִּים and as administrators of charities [in Jerusalem] may be married by *Kohanim* without any further checking [of their lineage] required.' The assumption is clearly that such שֹׁטְרִים could come only from the most impeccable family backgrounds. Levites would, then, be particularly suitable for these functions.

This passage in *Kiddushin* gives us further insight into the term שֹׁטְרִים. The discussion there makes it clear, and *Rashi* states so explicitly, that the functionaries referred to in the mishnah are not sheriffs but judges who sit on the minor, three-man courts and who are not co-opted into the standing courts of twenty-three judges.

Thus we see that the term שֹׁטֵר is flexible [we have now met them as court-enforcers, work-supervisors and judges — see also *Deuteronomy* 20:9 where they appear as army officers]. The term connotes a community functionary with a standing higher than that of the ordinary person. The meaning of שֹׁפְטִים, too, does not seem to be limited to a judge in a court of law. The שֹׁפְטִים, *Judges*, who ruled Israel in the period before the kings were rulers rather than judges and many verses in Scripture (e.g., *Isaiah* 40:23) equate the שֹׁפֵט with a ruler.

Now when we consider that v. 29 here seems clearly to be part of a section continuing with vs. 30-32, which describe appointees over various sections of the country, we may surmise that the Levites of our verse were appointed as governors and administrators over the various territories described in those verses for the מְלֶאכֶת ה', *work of HASHEM*, described in v. 30.

What sort of work was this? This expression seems to parallel the one from v. 32 where we have it used in conjunction with דְּבַר הָאֱלֹהִים, *matters of God*. Indeed, we find מְלָאכָה used in the description of purely religious concerns as, for example, in *Ezra* 10:13, where the term relates to the expulsion of the gentile wives.

We may thus conclude that the Levites were

³⁰ *For the Chevronites — Chashaviahu and his brothers, seventeen hundred men of quality, in charge of the administration of Israel in the western part of the Transjordan, for all the work of HASHEM and the service of the king.* ³¹ *For the Chevronites, Yeriah was the chief of the Chevronites, according to his descendants, for each of the families. In the fortieth year of David's reign they were searched out and men of extraordinary ability were found among them in Yaezer in Gilead.* ³² *And his brothers, men of quality, two thousand seven*

governors and administrators of the religious concerns in the territories described and that, in conjunction with these religious activities, they also managed the king's concerns.

This analysis may help explain the unusual sequence — שטרים before שפטים [in contrast to *Deuteronomy* 16:18]. When court officials are meant, it is logical to mention judges before sheriffs since the latter's function begins only after judgment has been rendered. As religious functionaries, though, it is likely that the שטרים, who were presumably a lower echelon than the שפטים, were more numerous and in closer contact with the people. For this reason, they are mentioned first.

30. ... לַחֶבְרוֹנִי — *For the Chevronites.* See v. 23.

בְּנֵי־חַיִל — *Men of quality.* See comm. to 5:24.

עַל פְּקֻדַּת יִשְׂרָאֵל מֵעֵבֶר לַיַּרְדֵּן מַעֲרָבָה — *In charge of the administration of Israel in the western part of the Transjordan.* Since the territory beyond the Jordan lies to the east of the Land of Israel, the meaning of the phrase must be that we are dealing with the western part of Transjordan, that is, the part that lies closest to the land of Israel (*Radak; Metzudos*).

לְכֹל מְלֶאכֶת ה' וְלַעֲבֹדַת הַמֶּלֶךְ — *For all the work of HASHEM and for the service of the king.* Chashaviahu and his group were responsible for all the people who worked for the Temple (*Metzudos*) and the property of the king and his storage houses in that area (*Mefaresh*).

Ralbag identifies the two categories with the areas of responsibility which he had defined under *outside work* in the previous verse. *Work of HASHEM* is the responsibility for the half-shekels and the sacrifices which had been promised; *service of the king* is the administration of Torah law.

31. לַחֶבְרוֹנִי יְרִיָּה הָרֹאשׁ — *For the Chevronites, Yeriah was the chief.* See 23:19.

לַחֶבְרוֹנִי לְתֹלְדֹתָיו לְאָבוֹת — *Of the Chevronites, according to his descendants, for each of the families.* We assume that the possessive in לְתֹלְדֹתָיו, *his descendants,* refers back to Chevron and that the word stands in apposition to לַחֶבְרוֹנִי. Thus: For Chevron — that is, for Chevron's descendants.

לְאָבוֹת is short for בָּתֵי אָבוֹת, *family units* (*Metzudos*).

בִּשְׁנַת הָאַרְבָּעִים לְמַלְכוּת דָּוִיד נִדְרָשׁוּ — *In the fortieth year of David's reign they were searched out.* The dispositions which David made for all the *mishmaros* took place in the last years of his life, as can be seen from 23:1: *And David was old and full of days.* This is in contrast to the arrangements of which we learn in the next chapter, which were made early on in David's reign (*Radak*).

R' Y. Danziger has suggested another meaning for this verse. Yeriah was the son of Chevron (23:19), and he was of course no longer alive in David's days. Now above, in 24:23, *Metzudos* suggested that upon his death, his family ceased to exist as a separate entity and its members were incorporated into one of the other families. However, when it came time to appoint the various Levitical functionaries, David wished to accord a distinction to the line of Yeriah — the original head of the Chevronite clan — by appointing a descendant of his to one of the posts. Accordingly, he searched through the genealogical tables to find Yeriahites who were fit for the position. He had to institute a search because there was no longer any family group known as Yeriahites in his time.

Thus, the verse may be understood as follows: *Of the Chevronites, Yeriah was the chief of the Chevronites in the genealogy of the families.* [I.e., although his line no longer served as the head family of the Chevronites, the genealogical records of the clan reveal that it had once been so. Consequently,] *in the fortieth year of David's reign they were searched out and there were found to be of them men of outstanding quality in Yaezer in Gilead.*

בְּיַעְזֵיר גִּלְעָד — *In Yaezer in Gilead.* The town

הָאָבוֹת וַיַּפְקִידֵ֗ם דָּוִ֣יד הַמֶּ֑לֶךְ עַל־הָראוּבֵנִ֥י וְהַגָּדִ֖י וַחֲצִי֙
שֵׁ֣בֶט הַֽמְנַשִּׁ֔י לְכָל־דְּבַ֥ר הָאֱלֹהִ֖ים וּדְבַ֥ר הַמֶּֽלֶךְ׃ וּבְנֵ֣י א
יִשְׂרָאֵ֣ל ׀ לְֽמִסְפָּרָ֡ם רָאשֵׁ֣י הָאָב֣וֹת וְשָׂרֵ֣י הָאֲלָפִ֣ים ׀ וְהַמֵּא֗וֹת
וְשֹׁטְרֵיהֶם֮ הַמְשָׁרְתִ֣ים אֶת־הַמֶּ֒לֶךְ֒ לְכֹ֣ל ׀ דְּבַ֣ר הַֽמַּחְלְק֗וֹת
הַבָּאָ֤ה וְהַיֹּצֵאת֙ חֹ֣דֶשׁ בְּחֹ֔דֶשׁ לְכֹ֖ל חָדְשֵׁ֣י הַשָּׁנָ֑ה הַֽמַּחֲלֹ֙קֶת֙
הָֽאַחַ֔ת עֶשְׂרִ֥ים וְאַרְבָּעָ֖ה אָֽלֶף׃ עַ֞ל הַמַּחֲלֹ֣קֶת ב
הָרִֽאשׁוֹנָה֙ לַחֹ֣דֶשׁ הָֽרִאשׁ֔וֹן יָֽשָׁבְעָ֖ם בֶּן־זַבְדִּיאֵ֑ל וְעַ֨ל
מַ֣חֲלֻקְתּ֔וֹ עֶשְׂרִ֥ים וְאַרְבָּעָ֖ה אָֽלֶף׃ מִן־בְּנֵי־פֶ֙רֶץ֙ הָרֹ֔אשׁ ג
לְכָל־שָׂרֵ֥י הַצְּבָא֖וֹת לַחֹ֥דֶשׁ הָרִאשֽׁוֹן׃ וְעַ֞ל ד
מַֽחֲלֹ֣קֶת ׀ הַחֹ֣דֶשׁ הַשֵּׁנִ֗י דּוֹדַ֤י הָאֲחוֹחִי֙ וּמַ֣חֲלֻקְתּ֔וֹ וּמִקְל֖וֹת
הַנָּגִ֑יד וְעַל֙ מַֽחֲלֻקְתּ֔וֹ עֶשְׂרִ֥ים וְאַרְבָּעָ֖ה אָֽלֶף׃ שַׂ֣ר ה

---

of Yaezer which stood in the land of Gilead
(Metzudos).

Gilead lies on the east bank of the Jordan
and, as can be seen from the next verse, the
Levitical family mentioned in our verse
discharged their duties among the two-
and-a-half tribes who lived on the east
bank.

Since according to 6:62,66 Yaezer was a
Levite city assigned to the Merarites, we
must assume that in the course of the years
some Chevronites [of the Kehathite clan]

came to settle there.

32. עַל הָראוּבֵנִי וְהַגָּדִי וַחֲצִי שֵׁבֶט הַמְנַשִּׁי — Over
the Reuvenites, the Gadites and the half-
tribe of the Menashehites. This must refer
to the eastern segment of the east bank.
The western segment which was closest to
the land of Israel was under the charge of
Chashaviahu (v. 30).

לְכָל־דְּבַר הָאֱלֹהִים וּדְבַר הַמֶּלֶךְ — For all matters
pertaining to God and matters pertaining to
the king. See comm. to vs. 29 and 30.

XXVII

◆§ The Officers of the Realm

The first section of this chapter describes the institution of monthly relays, twenty-four
thousand men each, who were to be at the king's disposal to help in the execution of his
royal duties. These relays functioned throughout David's reign (see v. 7) and, strictly
speaking, have no place in this part of the book, which deals with dispositions which
David made in his old age (23:1) in preparation for the building of the Temple. They are
mentioned here only because of the similarity between the monthly relays and the weekly
mishmaros of Kohanim and Levites described in the last few chapters (Mefaresh).

1. ... וּבְנֵי יִשְׂרָאֵל לְמִסְפָּרָם — The children of
Israel according to their numbers ... The
numbers are the twelve divisions of 24,000
each at the end of the verse. Mefaresh
points out there that there were vastly more
people in Israel than the 288,000 yielded by
those divisions but that only the strongest
and wealthiest people were drafted for this
purpose since only they could afford to
ignore their own concerns for the period of
a month. Accordingly, בְּנֵי יִשְׂרָאֵל here
means, [The elite of] the children of Israel.

See below for Metzudos' rendering of
מִסְפָּר which seems to accord with the Sages
as quoted by Malbim.

רָאשֵׁי הָאָבוֹת ... — The family heads ... The
phrase is appositional. The divisions of
twenty-four thousand included the officials listed here (Ralbag).

But in the view of the Sages (cited by
Malbim at 21:5 — see there for their
solution to the problem of the discrepancies
between the census figures of Samuel and
Chronicles) the officials listed in this
phrase were not included in the number
twenty-four thousand but were a separate
group of twelve thousand people — one
thousand to a tribe. Thus the phrase is not
appositional. It would seem that the Sages
take מִסְפָּר as does Metzudos — a numbered

hundred heads of families; King David appointed them over the Reuvenites, the Gadites and the half-tribe of Menashehites, for all matters pertaining to God and matters pertaining to the king.

The children of Israel according to their numbers — the family heads, officers of the thousands and hundreds and their sheriffs, who served the king in the matter of the divisions which rotated monthly through all the months of the year, each division consisting of twenty-four thousand men: ² In charge of the first division, for the first month — Yashoveam the son of Zavdiel; in his division were twenty-four thousand men. ³ Of the sons of Peretz, the head of all the corps commanders, for the first month. ⁴ In charge of the division of the second month — Dodai the Achochite, and his divisional aide, Mikloth the prince; in his division were twenty-four

unit — and render the verse as follows: *As for Israel's numbered units* [they were in the charge of] *family heads* ... [who governed] *in all matters concerning the divisions* ... *each division consisting of twenty-four thousand men*.

הַמַּחֲלֹקֶת הָאַחַת עֶשְׂרִים וְאַרְבָּעָה אָלֶף — *Each division consisting of twenty-four thousand men*. Each month a corps of twenty-four thousand men stood at the king's disposal.

2. עַל הַמַּחֲלֹקֶת הָרִאשׁוֹנָה ... יָשְׁבְעָם בֶּן־זַבְדִּיאֵל — *In charge of the first division ... Yashoveam the son of Zavdiel*. *Ralbag* and *Gra* suggest that this is the Yashoveam who is the first of David's *giborim* at 11:11. Although there his father's name is given as Chachmoni, it may well be that he went under two names. As will be seen below, almost all the division heads are among David's *giborim*.

3. מִן־בְּנֵי־פֶרֶץ — *Of the sons of Peretz*. Yashoveam was descended from Judah's son Peretz, the same lineage from which David himself came. It is for this reason that David appointed him chief of all the division heads (*Mefaresh*).

לְכָל־שָׂרֵי הַצְּבָאוֹת — *Of all the corps commanders*. The term צָבָא applies to any large group of people gathered together for a specific purpose. See comm. to 25:1.

לַחֹדֶשׁ הָרִאשׁוֹן — *For the first month*. The previous verse had already stated that he was assigned to the first month. Perhaps this phrase follows on what was said

before. Because he was the leader of all the division heads, he served in the first month.

4. דּוֹדַי הָאֲחוֹחִי — *Dodai the Achochite*. This seems to be the father of the second of David's *giborim* in ch. 11 (*Ralbag*). But *Gra* identifies him with Elchanan ben Dodo, who is seventh in that list.

וּמַחֲלֻקְתּוֹ וּמִקְלוֹת הַנָּגִיד — *And his divisional aide, Mikloth the prince*. If this phrase were omitted, the description of Dodai's stewardship would have been precisely parallel to that of all the other twelve divisions. This phrase, inserted as it were in the middle of the general formula, is difficult to translate. From v. 6 it is clear that the term מַחֲלֹקֶת, *division*, is used in a secondary sense to refer to the person who is in charge of it as well (*Radak*). Thus, in our context it would refer to the assistant head (since Dodai was the chief).

Both *Metzudos* and *Malbim* suggest that the *vav* before Mikloth is to be read as part of the name, *Umikloth*, rather than *and Mikloth*. However, both *Ralbag* and *Targum* see the *vav* as extra, a Scriptural irregularity which occasionally occurs but which does not alter the meaning. See above, 4:15. However, the *trop* combines וּמַחֲלֻקְתּוֹ with the previous phrase and separates it from וּמִקְלוֹת הַנָּגִיד, *Mikloth the prince*, and it would thus seem to indicate a different meaning than the similar phrase in v. 6.

While we cannot know for certain the precise responsibilities of the monthly relays described in our chapter, it seems that they

הַצָּבָא הַשְּׁלִישִׁי לַחֹדֶשׁ הַשְּׁלִישִׁי בְּנָיָהוּ בֶן־־־־־יְהוֹיָדָע
ו הַכֹּהֵן רֹאשׁ וְעַל מַחֲלֻקְתּוֹ עֶשְׂרִים וְאַרְבָּעָה אָלֶף: הוּא
בְנָיָהוּ גִּבּוֹר הַשְּׁלֹשִׁים וְעַל־הַשְּׁלֹשִׁים וּמַחֲלֻקְתּוֹ עַמִּיזָבָד
ז בְּנוֹ: הָרְבִיעִי לַחֹדֶשׁ הָרְבִיעִי עֲשָׂהאֵל אֲחִי
יוֹאָב וּזְבַדְיָה בְנוֹ אַחֲרָיו וְעַל מַחֲלֻקְתּוֹ עֶשְׂרִים וְאַרְבָּעָה
ח אָלֶף: הַחֲמִישִׁי לַחֹדֶשׁ הַחֲמִישִׁי הַשַּׂר שַׁמְהוּת
ט הַיִּזְרָח וְעַל מַחֲלֻקְתּוֹ עֶשְׂרִים וְאַרְבָּעָה אָלֶף: הַשִּׁשִּׁי
לַחֹדֶשׁ הַשִּׁשִּׁי עִירָא בֶן־עִקֵּשׁ הַתְּקוֹעִי וְעַל מַחֲלֻקְתּוֹ
י עֶשְׂרִים וְאַרְבָּעָה אָלֶף: הַשְּׁבִיעִי לַחֹדֶשׁ הַשְּׁבִיעִי
חֶלֶץ הַפְּלוֹנִי מִן־בְּנֵי אֶפְרָיִם וְעַל מַחֲלֻקְתּוֹ עֶשְׂרִים

were available to the king for the full range of royal responsibilities. Among these was certainly some military activity — particularly when we recall that these relays began early in David's reign, long before he even came to Jerusalem (see comm. to v. 7), at a time when his kingship had in no sense yet been consolidated. Hence the title שַׂר צָבָא [the head of all the corps], usually a military title, for the division head (vs. 3,5 and 8). [In this regard, it is certainly significant that the divisional heads were drawn from the ranks of David's giborim, military heroes.]

Now, an active general would presumably have his own staff of adjutants and these could well be considered his personal מַחֲלֶקֶת, division, within the larger division which he commanded. Thus, following the trop we could render our verse: In charge of the division of the second month was Dodai the Achochite, his [personal] staff, and Mikloth the prince.

5. שַׂר הַצָּבָא הַשְּׁלִישִׁי — The commander of the third corps. All division heads were שָׂרֵי צָבָא (v. 3), but this is stressed only in the case of Benaiahu (see also at v. 8). This is so either in order to do special honor to Benaiahu (Mefaresh; Metzudos) who, although a lesser gibor than the Yashoveam of v. 2 (see list of giborim in ch. 11), was nevertheless much more active in governing Israel; or, because he is introduced in v. 6 as the gibor of the thirty (Radak), probably a military position.

בְּנָיָהוּ בֶן־יְהוֹיָדָע הַכֹּהֵן רֹאשׁ — Benaiahu the son of Yehoiada, the Kohen, [who was] the

head. The Mefaresh points out that כהן and ראש are not to be taken together as כהן ראש (the head Kohen or Kohen Gadol) since the Kohanim Gedolim of David's reign were Eviathar and Tzadok.

But what is the meaning of the statement that he was the head? He has already been introduced as commander.

The answer may depend on the correct understanding of the next verse. If מַחֲלֻקְתּוֹ there can be understood as we have suggested in v. 4 — his staff of adjutants — then the verse may mean as follows: Benaiahu was the gibor of the thirty and their leader (וְעַל הַשְּׁלֹשִׁים). These thirty, under the leadership of his son Ammizavad, were his personal מַחֲלֶקֶת, division, within the larger group.

Given the presence of such a large and distinguished staff within the division, the designation ראש for Benaiahu could have one of two meanings: Either that he was only the nominal head but, because of his many other activities (see comm. v. 7), was not involved in daily administrative details; or, on the contrary, that he was the head or actual leader notwithstanding the fact that there were many others who could have handled the burdens of leadership.

6. הוּא בְנָיָהוּ גִּבּוֹר הַשְּׁלֹשִׁים — This was Benaiahu the mighty man of the thirty. The translation follows the Mefaresh. Reference is to the group of thirty, an elite among the giborim, who occupied a special place in David's retinue. [For a discussion of these thirty see prefatory remarks to 11:10-47, see also comm. to 11:15.] This interpretation assumes that Benaiahu belonged to the group of thirty and was moreover their leader (וְעַל הַשְּׁלֹשִׁים). This is

thousand men. ⁵ The commander of the third corps, for the third month, was Benaiahu the son of Yehoiada, the Kohen, the head; in his division were twenty-four thousand men. ⁶ This was Benaiahu the mighty man of the thirty and over the thirty; his divisional aide was Ammizavad, his son. ⁷ The fourth, for the fourth month, Asahel, the brother of Yoav, and Zevadiah, his son, after him; in his division were twenty-four thousand men. ⁸ The fifth, for the fifth month, the commander, Shamhuth the Zerachite; in his division were twenty-four thousand men. ⁹ The sixth, for the sixth month, Ira the son of Ikkesh the Tekoite; in his division were twenty-four thousand men. ¹⁰ The seventh, for the seventh month; Cheletz the Pelonite of the Ephraimites; in his division were twenty-four

in agreement with the opinion of some commentators to 11:25 (see there).

Other commentators, however, read the passage in ch. 11 in such a way that Benaiahu was not part of the thirty but was part of an even higher echelon (see comm. to 11:15). These commentators would have to follow *Metzudos* in his rendering of our passage. He takes שְׁלִשִׁים as שָׁלִישִׁים, that is *captains*. Benaiahu was mighty among the king's officers and chief among them.

We should note *Targum's* opinion. As we saw in ch. 11, *Targum* there and also in *Samuel* renders every שְׁלִשִׁים as גִבָּרַיָא, *captains*, just as *Metzudos* does here. Nevertheless, in our passage he renders the word שְׁלִשִׁים as *thirty*.

וּמַחֲלֻקְתּוֹ עֲמִיזָבָד בְּנוֹ — *His divisional aide was Ammizavad, his son.* Benaiahu's son, Ammizavad, assisted him in the administration of his division *(Radak)*, or succeeded him after his death *(Ralbag)*. See comm. to v. 7.

7. עֲשָׂהאֵל אֲחִי יוֹאָב — *Asahel, the brother of Yoav.* Since Asahel is one of the division heads, it is clear that the institution of the monthly divisions stems from the earliest days of David's reign — in contrast to the *mishmaros* of the *Kohanim* and the Levites which were organized when David was already in his old age (23:1). Asahel was killed by Avner long before David even came to Jerusalem (see *II Samuel* 2:12ff) *(Radak).*

וּזְבַדְיָה בְּנוֹ אַחֲרָיו — *And Zevadiah, his son, after him.* After Asahel's death, his son Zevadiah became the division head.

In the second, third and fourth months we have had mention of someone assisting or taking

over from the original division head. This is not the case with any of the others.

In each of these three cases there may have been a special circumstance. As noted above, most of the division heads were drawn from among David's *giborim*. However, Dodai the Achochite of the second month was the father of a *gibor* (see comm. v. 4). He may well have been considerably older than any of the division heads and therefore required an assistant.

Benaiahu ben Yehoiada is introduced as שַׂר הַצָּבָא, *the commander of the corps*, and may well have carried responsibilities besides administering his division (see 11:22 that in the tradition of the Sages he was אַב בֵּית דִּין, *head of the court*). Under such circumstances it is natural that he too would require an assistant. In the case of Asahel, his early death necessitated a successor.

8. שְׁמָהוּת הַיִּזְרָח — *Shamhuth the Zerachite.* The *Mefaresh* renders יִזְרָח as descended from Zerach. In vs. 11 and 13 the division heads of the eighth and tenth months are also traced to Zerach. In v. 3, we learned how David appointed Yashoveam as leader of all the division heads because he was descended from David's own ancestor Peretz. It is therefore not surprising that descendants of Peretz's brother Zerach should also figure prominently among the important administrators.

Gra identifies Shamhuth with Shammoth the Harorite, number eight on the list of David's *giborim* (ch. 11).

9. עִירָא בֶן־עִקֵּשׁ — *Ira the son of Ikkesh.* He is number eleven on the list of David's *giborim*.

10. חֶלֶץ הַפְּלוֹנִי — *Cheletz the Pelonite.* He is number ten on the list of David's *giborim*.

<table>
<tr><td>יא וְאַרְבָּעָה אָלֶף׃</td><td>הַשְּׁמִינִי לַחֹדֶשׁ הַשְּׁמִינִי</td></tr>
</table>

יא וְאַרְבָּעָה אָלֶף׃ הַשְּׁמִינִי לַחֹדֶשׁ הַשְּׁמִינִי
סִבְּכַי הַחֻשָׁתִי לַזַּרְחִי וְעַל מַחֲלֻקְתּוֹ עֶשְׂרִים וְאַרְבָּעָה
יב אָלֶף׃ הַתְּשִׁיעִי לַחֹדֶשׁ הַתְּשִׁיעִי
אֲבִיעֶזֶר הָעֲנְּתוֹתִי °לַבֵּן | יְמִינִי ק לבנימיני וְעַל מַחֲלֻקְתּוֹ עֶשְׂרִים
יג וְאַרְבָּעָה אָלֶף׃ הָעֲשִׂירִי לַחֹדֶשׁ הָעֲשִׂירִי
מַהְרַי הַנְּטוֹפָתִי לַזַּרְחִי וְעַל מַחֲלֻקְתּוֹ עֶשְׂרִים וְאַרְבָּעָה
יד אָלֶף׃ עַשְׁתֵּי־עָשָׂר לְעַשְׁתֵּי עָשָׂר הַחֹדֶשׁ
בְּנָיָה הַפִּרְעָתוֹנִי מִן־בְּנֵי אֶפְרַיִם וְעַל מַחֲלֻקְתּוֹ עֶשְׂרִים
טו וְאַרְבָּעָה אָלֶף׃ הַשְּׁנֵים עָשָׂר לִשְׁנֵים עָשָׂר
הַחֹדֶשׁ חֶלְדַּי הַנְּטוֹפָתִי לְעָתְנִיאֵל וְעַל מַחֲלֻקְתּוֹ עֶשְׂרִים
טז וְאַרְבָּעָה אָלֶף׃ וְעַל שִׁבְטֵי יִשְׂרָאֵל
לָרְאוּבֵנִי נָגִיד אֱלִיעֶזֶר בֶּן־זִכְרִי לַשִּׁמְעוֹנִי שְׁפַטְיָהוּ בֶּן־
יז מַעֲכָה׃ לְלֵוִי חֲשַׁבְיָה בֶן־קְמוּאֵל לְאַהֲרֹן
יח צָדוֹק׃ לִיהוּדָה אֱלִיהוּ מֵאֲחֵי דָוִיד לְיִשָּׂשכָר
יט עָמְרִי בֶּן־מִיכָאֵל׃ לִזְבוּלֻן יִשְׁמַעְיָהוּ בֶּן־
כ עֹבַדְיָהוּ לְנַפְתָּלִי יְרִימוֹת בֶּן־עַזְרִיאֵל׃ לִבְנֵי
אֶפְרַיִם הוֹשֵׁעַ בֶּן־עֲזַזְיָהוּ לַחֲצִי שֵׁבֶט מְנַשֶּׁה יוֹאֵל בֶּן־
כא פְּדָיָהוּ׃ לַחֲצִי הַמְנַשֶּׁה גִּלְעָדָה יִדּוֹ בֶּן־זְכַרְיָהוּ
כב לְבִנְיָמִן יַעֲשִׂיאֵל בֶּן־אַבְנֵר׃ לְדָן עֲזַרְאֵל בֶּן־יְרֹחָם
כג אֵלֶּה שָׂרֵי שִׁבְטֵי יִשְׂרָאֵל׃ וְלֹא־נָשָׂא דָוִיד מִסְפָּרָם לְמִבֶּן

---

11. סִבְּכַי הַחֻשָׁתִי — *Sibbechai the Chushathite.* He is number thirteen on the list of *giborim*.

12. אֲבִיעֶזֶר הָעֲנְּתוֹתִי — *Aviezer the Anathothite.* He is number twelve on the list of *giborim*.

13. מַהְרַי הַנְּטוֹפָתִי — *Maharai the Netophathite.* He is number fifteen on the list of *giborim*.

14. בְּנָיָה הַפִּרְעָתוֹנִי — *Benaiah the Pireathonite.* He is number eighteen on the list of *giborim*.

15. חֶלְדַּי הַנְּטוֹפָתִי — *Cheldai the Netophathite.* He is number sixteen on the list of *giborim*.

16-22. This section gives a list of leaders of the various tribes. Their precise function is not stated. Furthermore, the list is incomplete — Gad and Asher are missing.

Nevertheless, there are thirteen names, since the *Kohanim* are listed separately from the other Levites (v. 17), and the two halves of Menasheh — those in the main part of the land and those east of the Jordan — each have their own leader.

It is possible that the sources available to the author of *Chronicles* did not have any information on these tribes. This would also explain why Dan (v. 22) is out of place. The sequence of the tribes is given according to their mothers: first Leah's sons up to Zevulun (v. 19), then Naphtali (v. 19) from Bilhah, then Rachel's sons through Benjamin (v. 21). In this order Dan belongs before Naphtali, but it appears only at the end of the list. The main source from which the author drew may well have been missing Dan also, and he therefore does not appear in the list. However, the name of Dan's leader was available through a different source and was appended to the end. Such an explanation would be entirely compatible with the approach of the commentators to the genealogical lists in the first eight chapters of this book.

16. לָרְאוּבֵנִי נָגִיד — *The prince for the Reuvenites.* None of the other leaders are given the title נָגִיד, *prince. Daas Soferim* thinks it possible that the Reuvenite leader was particularly powerful and that because

thousand men. [11] The eighth, for the eighth month, Sibbechai the Chushathite of the Zerachites; in his division were twenty-four thousand men. [12] The ninth, for the ninth month, Aviezer the Anathothite of the Benjaminites; in his division were twenty-four thousand men. [13] The tenth, for the tenth month, Maharai the Netophathite of the Zerachites; in his division were twenty-four thousand men. [14] The eleventh, for the eleventh month, Benaiah the Pireathonite of the Ephraimites; in his division were twenty-four thousand men. [15] The twelfth, for the twelfth month, Cheldai the Netophathite of Othniel; in his division were twenty-four thousand men. [16] In charge of the tribes of Israel: The prince for the Reuvenites — Eliezer the son of Zichri; for the Shimeonites — Shephatiah the son of Maachah. [17] For Levi — Chashaviah the son of Kemuel; for Aaron — Tzadok. [18] For Judah — Elihu from among David's brothers; for Yissachar — Omri the son of Michael. [19] For Zevulun — Yishmaiahu the son of Ovadiahu, for Naphtali — Yerimoth the son of Azriel. [20] For the Ephraimites — Hoshea the son of Azaziahu; for the half-tribe of Menasheh — Yoel the son of Pedaiahu. [21] For the half-tribe of Menasheh in Gilead — Yiddo the son of Zechariahu; for Benjamin — Yaasiel the son of Avner. [22] For Dan — Azarel the son of Yerocham. These were the chiefs of the tribes of Israel. [23] But David did not count those twenty years and

of this his leadership extended beyond his own tribe to that of Reuven's neighbor, Gad. This would explain why our list contains no leader for Gad. [See above for another possible explanation.]

R' Y. Danziger has suggested that the term נָגִיד applies to all the leaders listed; it is used here, and then left inexplicit in the rest of the cases. Certainly this would seem true for Shimeon in the second half of the verse and thus can be applied to all the tribes listed.

17. לְאַהֲרֹן צָדוֹק — *For Aaron — Tzadok.* Within the Levite tribe, the *Kohanim* had their own leader — Tzadok.

As in the case of the other tribes we must assume that some sort of secular leadership is meant. Certainly, Tzadok did not become *Kohen Gadol* until Solomon's reign (see comm. to 5:30 and 34).

18. לִיהוּדָה אֱלִיהוּ מֵאֲחֵי דָוִיד — *For Judah — Elihu from among David's brothers.* No Elihu in mentioned among Jesse's sons at 2:13-15. Nevertheless, since *Chronicles* lists only seven sons for Jesse, while *I Samuel* 16:10-11 indicates that there were

eight sons, the Sages conclude that there must have been another son who is not mentioned in *Chronicles* for reasons discussed in comm. to 2:13-15. They identify this son as Elihu *(Radak).*

21. לַחֲצִי הַמְנַשֶּׁה גִלְעָדָה — *For the half-tribe of Menasheh in Gilead.* This is the half-tribe of Menasheh which settled on the eastern bank of the Jordan.

23-24. In the last few chapters, we have had detailed accounts of the various *mishmaros* and divisions which David established. In each of these cases it was necessary to count the people in order to be able to divide them into groups of appropriate size.

In these two verses we learn of the care which David took to make sure that the various censi conform to the Torah's wishes. Sobered by the catastrophic results of the count which had been taken by Yoav some years earlier (ch. 21), David made sure that the mistakes of the past would not be repeated.

23. וְלֹא־נָשָׂא דָוִיד מִסְפָּרָם ... — *But David did*

עֶשְׂרִים שָׁנָה וּלְמַטָּה כִּי אָמַר יהוה לְהַרְבּוֹת אֶת־יִשְׂרָאֵל
כד כְּכוֹכְבֵי הַשָּׁמָיִם: יוֹאָב בֶּן־צְרוּיָה הֵחֵל לִמְנוֹת וְלֹא כִלָּה
וַיְהִי בָזֹאת קֶצֶף עַל־יִשְׂרָאֵל וְלֹא עָלָה הַמִּסְפָּר בְּמִסְפַּר
כה דִּבְרֵי הַיָּמִים לַמֶּלֶךְ דָּוִיד: וְעַל אֹצְרוֹת
הַמֶּלֶךְ עַזְמָוֶת בֶּן־עֲדִיאֵל וְעַל הָאֹצָרוֹת בַּשָּׂדֶה בֶּעָרִים
כו וּבַכְּפָרִים וּבַמִּגְדָּלוֹת יְהוֹנָתָן בֶּן־עֻזִּיָּהוּ: וְעַל
עֹשֵׂי מְלֶאכֶת הַשָּׂדֶה לַעֲבֹדַת הָאֲדָמָה עֶזְרִי בֶּן־----
כז כָּלוּב: וְעַל־הַכְּרָמִים שִׁמְעִי הָרָמָתִי וְעַל שֶׁבַּכְּרָמִים
כח לְאֹצְרוֹת הַיַּיִן זַבְדִּי הַשִּׁפְמִי: וְעַל־הַזֵּיתִים

not count those ... On all occasions which David had to count the people in order to divide them into *mishmaros* or other divisions, David took care to count only those who were over twenty *(Commentators).*

שָׁנָה וּלְמָטָּה עֶשְׂרִים לְמִבֶּן — *Twenty years and under.* The prohibition against counting the whole populace — including those below twenty — is not explicated in the Torah *(Ramban, Numbers 1:1).* Nevertheless, since at Exodus 30:14 the Torah limited that particular census to men above the age of twenty, it can be deduced that God's will is that all censi be conducted within only that group.

Our verse explains why those under twenty are to be excluded. God wishes to make Israel as numerous as the stars of the heavens. Their numbers are to be so overwhelming as to defy any attempt to express them in any exact number. At any given moment in history the reality may not reflect this blessing of God, but this shortfall should not be spelled out. As long as only a segment is counted, they may be regarded — if only in theory — as limitless. As soon as the entire nation is defined in terms of an exact number, the reality which does not reflect God's wish will have been expressed.

24. ... בֶּן־צְרוּיָה יוֹאָב — *Yoav the son of Tzeruiah ...* There are two main opinions among the commentators concerning the relationship of this verse to the previous one. Most commentators take it to show the reason for the care which David took. Yoav, too, had counted only those over twenty and, even so, his census had ended in tragedy.

Ramban, however, sees Yoav's experience as the source from which David learned his lesson. Yoav had counted everybody, including those under twenty, and this brought on the plague. David made sure not to repeat this error. See below.

וְלֹא כִלָּה לִמְנוֹת הֵחֵל — *Began to count but did not finish.* He began to count those that were older than twenty but did not complete the census since he did not count the tribes of Levi and Benjamin (see 21:6). Nevertheless, God's anger was kindled against Israel — see ch. 21 *(Metzudos).*

The meaning according to *Metzudos* would be as follows: Yoav took care to count only those people who were older than twenty, conforming to the Torah's wishes. In addition, knowing that it was not the wish of God that the census should be performed at all, he omitted two tribes from the count. In spite of these precautions God sent the plague against Israel for the reasons discussed at 21:1. From this David concluded that even under the best circumstances a census could spell danger for the people. He took care that nothing should go wrong this time.

Ramban's opinion (discussed at 21:1) is that Yoav counted the whole people — including those under twenty — and that this was the sin which caused God to bring the plague upon Israel. In his view this is what our verse tells us. David was careful to count only those people who were above twenty so that he would not repeat Yoav's mistake. *Ramban* does not explain what the expression, *began ... but did not finish,* refers to, nor what place it has in the argument as he understands it. A careful reading of *Ramban* there yields that Yoav

under, because HASHEM had promised to make Israel as numerous as
the stars of the heavens. ²⁴ Yoav the son of Tzeruiah began to count
but did not finish, because through this wrath came upon Israel; and
the number was not recorded in the census records of King David's
chronicles. ²⁵ In charge of the king's treasuries — Azmaveth the son
of Adiel; in charge of the stores in the fields, cities, villages and
towers — Yehonathan the son of Uzziahu. ²⁶ In charge of those who
worked the fields in farming — Ezri the son of Cheluv. ²⁷ In charge
of the vineyards — Shimei the Ramathite; in charge of the output of
the vineyards for the stores of wine — Zavdi the Shiphmite. ²⁸ In

counted only the strong and able bodied,
leaving out the sick, the weak and the old.
This may be how he understands our verse.
Even though Yoav only began to count but
did not finish — since he left out sizeable
segments of the community — his census
ended in tragedy because he included
people under twenty. Because of this David
made sure that his count would be limited
to those over twenty.

ולֹא עָלָה הַמִּסְפָּר ... — And the number was
not recorded ... Metzudos who, as we saw,
thinks that Yoav counted only those who
were over twenty, finds in this the solution
to the discrepancy in the census results
reported in Samuel and Chronicles which
were discussed at 21:5. The additional
300,000 given in Chronicles are the ones
under twenty which had not been included
in the total in Samuel, which gave only the
numbers which Yoav actually counted.
This is the meaning of our verse. Because
Yoav had not counted the people under
twenty, his total did not reach the total
which is given in Chronicles. He therefore
translates: So the number did not reach the
number in King David's chronicles.[1]

Ramban, however, cannot agree with
this interpretation, since in his opinion
Yoav also counted the people under
twenty. Perhaps he would interpret this
phrase as seems to be Malbim's understanding: [Because Yoav's census elicited
God's anger,] therefore, the census results
were not recorded in the official chronicles
of King David's reign. The translation
follows this interpretation.

25-34. This section gives a list of other
functionaries in the royal court. Though it
has no bearing upon David's preparations
for the Temple, it follows in connection
with the monthly divisions which served
the king. The record of the functionaries of
David's court was retained to give us an
idea of just how great and mighty a king he
was (Mefaresh).

25. וְעַל אֹצְרוֹת הַמֶּלֶךְ — In charge of the
king's treasuries. The king's personal
treasury (Mefaresh).

וְעַל הָאֹצָרוֹת בַּשָּׂדֶה — In charge of the stores
in the fields. Storehouses of produce,
foodstuffs, and beverages (Mefaresh).

בֶּעָרִים וּבַכְּפָרִים וּבַמִּגְדָּלוֹת — In the ... cities,
villages and towers. I.e., the stores of arms
kept in the cities, villages and towers
(Metzudos).

26. וְעַל עֹשֵׂי מְלֶאכֶת הַשָּׂדֶה — In charge of
those who worked the fields. Ezri
scheduled the people who ploughed the
fields and procured their equipment for
them (Mefaresh).

27. וְעַל-הַכְּרָמִים ... וְעַל שֶׁבַּכְּרָמִים לְאֹצְרוֹת הַיַּיִן
— In charge of the vineyards ... in charge
of the output of the vineyards for the stores
of wine. Shimei was in charge of caring for
the vines and harvesting the crop; Zavdi
was in charge of processing the grapes into
wine (Radak; Metzudos).

28. וְעַל-הַזֵּיתִים — In charge of the olive
trees. To plant olive trees and to pick them
(Mefaresh).

1. It is noteworthy that in this interpretation we have the name of our book given as דִּבְרֵי הַיָּמִים לַמֶּלֶךְ
דָּוִיד, King David's Chronicles. This would tend to confirm the opinion of those commentators who
think that Chronicles' interest centers specifically upon David and the glory of his royal dynasty.
This point has been made repeatedly by the Mefaresh; cf. comm. to 10:1.

וְהַשִּׁקְמִים אֲשֶׁר בַּשְּׁפֵלָה בַּעַל חָנָן הַגְּדֵרִי וְעַל־אֹצְרוֹת

כט הַשֶּׁמֶן יוֹעָשׁ: וְעַל־הַבָּקָר הָרֹעִים בַּשָּׁרוֹן °שִׁטְרַי

ל הַשָּׁרוֹנִי וְעַל־הַבָּקָר בָּעֲמָקִים שָׁפָט בֶּן־עַדְלָי: וְעַל־

הַגְּמַלִּים אוֹבִיל הַיִּשְׁמְעֵלִי וְעַל־----הָאֲתֹנוֹת יֶחְדְּיָהוּ

לא הַמֵּרֹנֹתִי: וְעַל־הַצֹּאן יָזִיז הַהַגְרִי כָּל־אֵלֶּה שָׂרֵי

לב הָרְכוּשׁ אֲשֶׁר לַמֶּלֶךְ דָּוִיד: וִיהוֹנָתָן דּוֹד־דָּוִיד

יוֹעֵץ אִישׁ־מֵבִין וְסוֹפֵר הוּא וִיחִיאֵל בֶּן־חַכְמוֹנִי עִם־בְּנֵי

לג הַמֶּלֶךְ: וַאֲחִיתֹפֶל יוֹעֵץ לַמֶּלֶךְ וְחוּשַׁי הָאַרְכִּי רֵעַ הַמֶּלֶךְ:

לד וְאַחֲרֵי אֲחִיתֹפֶל יְהוֹיָדָע בֶּן־בְּנָיָהוּ וְאֶבְיָתָר וְשַׂר־צָבָא

וְהַשִּׁקְמִים אֲשֶׁר בַּשְּׁפֵלָה — *And sycamores in the valley.* The sycamore trees growing in the lowlands. These were a variety of fig tree (*Metzudos*) (ficus sycomorus) which were grown primarily for their wood (*Sheviis* 4:5, *Bava Basra* 5:6) [see *HaTzomeach VeHaChai BaMishnah* by Dr. Y. Feliks].

29. וְעַל־הַבָּקָר הָרֹעִים בַּשָּׁרוֹן — *In charge of the cattle grazing in the plains.* *Targum* and *Metzudos* take שָׁרוֹן in the lower case (plain) rather than identifying it with the geographic area of that name.

30. אוֹבִיל הַיִּשְׁמְעֵלִי — *Ovil the Ishmaelite.* Ovil was Jewish but was called the Ishmaelite because he had lived among them for a time (*Radak*). *Mefaresh* thinks that the description Ishmaelite refers to his expertise in the care of camels.

31. יָזִיז הַהַגְרִי — *Yaziz the Hagrite.* These were a pastoral people adept at raising sheep (*Mefaresh*).

Malbim thinks that the functionaries identified in this section by their countries were non-Jews who offered their services to David. He sees in this an echo of Isaiah's prophecy (61:5) that there would be times when ... *strangers shall come to shepherd your sheep.*

Radak's interpretation to v. 30 would mean that in this verse, too, he thinks that the people mentioned are Jews who happened to have lived in gentile lands — perhaps to study the skills which they were later to employ in the service of their own people. See also at 11:41.

32-34. In these three verses the members of the more immediate royal household are given. It recalls a similar listing at 18:15-17. The two lists are quite different from

one another. Perhaps the one from ch. 18 is of people who held official positions in the realm, while the ones given here were David's personal advisors (R' Y. Danziger). In this case Yoav's title of שַׂר צָבָא (v. 34) would be meant as military aide or advisor rather than as general.

32. וִיהוֹנָתָן דּוֹד־דָּוִיד יוֹעֵץ — *Yehonathan, David's uncle, was a counselor.* The same title is also given to Achitophel in v. 32. *Metzudos* suggests that Achitophel was the official permanent counselor, while Yehonathan only advised occasionally.

Perhaps, too, they served at different times during the reign. Yehonathan was David's uncle and presumably older than he. He could well have functioned during the early years of David's reign, while Achitophel, who was active during Absalom's revolt and was relatively young at the time (*Sanhedrin* 106b), would be the advisor of the later period (R' Y. Danziger).

אִישׁ־מֵבִין וְסוֹפֵר הוּא — *A wise and learned man.* The translation follows *Metzudos*. For the use of סוֹפֵר as *a learned man* or *scholar* [rather than *scribe*], see *Doros HaRishonim* vol. 5, ch. 4, p. 174. [See also ArtScroll *Ezra* 7:6 (p. 254).] It is used in this sense in the Talmud (*Chullin* 108).

עִם־בְּנֵי הַמֶּלֶךְ — *With the king's sons.* His duty was to teach and raise the king's sons and to be their mentor (*Commentators*).

At 18:17 we have David's sons described as ... *first at the hand of the king,* that is, in some kind of official capacity. This would have made it possible to interpret that Yechiel was somehow involved in that function. However, according to the thesis advanced above that here we are dealing with David's personal staff, the interpretation of the commentators seems the more likely.

33. וַאֲחִיתֹפֶל יוֹעֵץ לַמֶּלֶךְ — *Achitophel was*

charge of the olive trees and sycamores in the valley — Baal Chanan
the Gederite; and in charge of the oil stores — Yoash. ²⁹ In charge of
the cattle grazing in the plains — Shitrai the Sharonite; and in charge
of the cattle in the valley — Shaphat the son of Adlai. ³⁰ In charge of
the camels — Ovil the Ishmaelite; and in charge of the she-asses —
Yehdaiahu the Meronothite. ³¹ In charge of the sheep — Yaziz the
Hagrite. All these were the officials in charge of the property
belonging to King David. ³² Yehonathan, David's uncle, was a
counselor, a wise and learned man, and Yechiel the son of
Chachmoni was with the king's sons. ³³ Achithophel was the king's
counselor, and Chushai the Archite was the king's friend.
³⁴ Achithophel was succeeded by Yehoiada the son of Benaiahu and

the king's counselor. See comm. to v. 32
that *Metzudos* thinks that Achitophel was
the king's main counselor, in contrast to
the Yehonathan mentioned there who only
advised the king occasionally.

The quality of Achitophel's counsel is
described at *II Samuel* 16:23 as creating a
feeling of standing in the very presence of
God. Indeed, as the Sages read that verse,
Achitophel himself was more like an angel
than a human being with human limitations. His whole being was suffused with
wisdom *(Shocher Tov* 3:4).

With such gifts, Achitophel should have
been one of the great luminaries of Jewish
history. Instead, he came to an ignominious
end. During Absalom's rebellion he
deserted David and became Absalom's
advisor, and it was he who gave the
shameful counsel that Absalom should
violate David's concubines *(II Samuel*
16:21). Later, he urged a plan upon
Absalom which, if it would have been
carried out, would have guaranteed victory
for the rebel forces. Its implementation was
thwarted by Chushai the Archite (see
below), and Achitophel returned to his
home and committed suicide *(II Samuel*
17:23).

As the Sages teach it, Achitophel's
tragedy derived from an unbounded
personal ambition which persuaded him
that he himself might one day be king (see
Sanhedrin 101a and *Yalkut Shimoni* 151).

וְחוּשַׁי הָאַרְכִּי רֵעַ הַמֶּלֶךְ — *And Chushai the
Archite was the king's friend.* He was
constantly together with the king so that
David could divert himself with him
(Metzudos).

During Absalom's rebellion, Chushai
proved to be Achitophel's nemesis. It was
he who gained Absalom's confidence in
order to subvert any realistic plan that the
rebels might make *(II Samuel* 16:16ff), and
he who persuaded Absalom that
Achitophel's strategy was not viable *(II
Samuel* 17:5ff).

It may perhaps be that Achitophel and
Chushai are mentioned together here because of
that fateful association. In contrast to
Achitophel, Chushai was a true *friend* of the
king.

34. ... וְאַחֲרֵי אֲחִיתֹפֶל — *Achitophel was
succeeded by* [lit. *And after Achitophel* ...]
Most commentators understand this phrase
to mean that after Achitophel's early death
(according to *Sanhedrin* 106b, he was only
thirty-three when he died) his position was
filled by two new advisors. Yehoiada the
son of Benaiahu is presumably the son of
Benaiahu the son of Yehoiada and was
named after his grandfather (see *Tosafos* to
Berachos 4a).

In this interpretation the last phrase in
the sentence ... *and the king's general was
Yoav*, is not connected to the earlier phrase
but simply lists Yoav as another
functionary of the king.

However, *Berachos* 3b connects the last
phrase to the previous ones and takes the
sentence as one unit. When a war was
contemplated, the first man to be consulted
would be Achitophel. With his brilliant
mind he would suggest the most promising
strategy for gaining victory. The people
would then go to Yehoiada in his capacity
as head of the Sanhedrin (the assumption is
that he succeeded his father to that post —
see *Tosafos* there) so that the elders of the

א לַמֶּ֫לֶךְ יוֹאָ֑ב: וַיַּקְהֵ֣ל דָּוִיד֘ אֶת־כָּל־שָׂרֵי

יִשְׂרָאֵל֒ שָׂרֵ֣י הַשְּׁבָטִ֡ים וְשָׂרֵ֣י הַמַּחְלְקוֹת֩ הַֽמְשָׁרְתִ֨ים

אֶת־הַמֶּ֜לֶךְ וְשָׂרֵ֣י הָאֲלָפִ֣ים וְשָׂרֵ֣י הַמֵּא֗וֹת וְשָׂרֵ֨י כָל־רְכוּשׁ־

וּמִקְנֶ֣ה ׀ לַמֶּ֣לֶךְ וּלְבָנָ֗יו עִם־הַסָּרִיסִ֛ים וְהַגִּבּוֹרִ֖ים וּֽלְכָל־

ב גִּבּ֣וֹר חָ֑יִל אֶל־יְרוּשָׁלָֽ͏ִם: וַיָּ֛קָם דָּוִ֥יד הַמֶּ֖לֶךְ עַל־רַגְלָ֑יו

Sanhedrin might pray for their success (*Radak*). They would then go to Eviathar, who was *Kohen Gadol*, so that he would consult the *Urim VeTumim* to predict whether they would be victorious. Only after that would Yoav feel ready to serve as *the king's general* and lead the people into battle.

XXVIII

◄§ David Passes the Crown to Solomon

David's preparations are now complete. The time has come to charge Solomon in the presence of all Israel with the execution of his father's carefully laid plans. [David had already talked to him in private, as recorded in 22:6ff.] He is to build the Temple and institute the *mishmaros* in accordance with the dispositions made by David. God will be with him and support all his endeavors, provided only that he remain loyal to the Torah. The people gladly accept David's exhortations, donate generously towards the building of the Temple, and amid popular rejoicing, crown Solomon king.

1. אֶת־כָּל־שָׂרֵי יִשְׂרָאֵל — *All the leaders of Israel.* These leaders are broken down into several different categories in the next part of the verse.

שָׂרֵי הַשְּׁבָטִים — *The leaders of the tribes.* Those listed from 27:16ff (*Mefaresh*).

וְשָׂרֵי הַמַּחְלְקוֹת הַמְשָׁרְתִים אֶת־הַמֶּלֶךְ — *The leaders of the divisions which served the king.* These are listed from 27:1ff (*Mefaresh*).

וְשָׂרֵי הָאֲלָפִים וְשָׂרֵי הַמֵּאוֹת — *The officers of the thousands and the officers of the hundreds.* These are also mentioned at 27:1.

וְשָׂרֵי כָל־רְכוּשׁ־וּמִקְנֶה לַמֶּלֶךְ וּלְבָנָיו — *And the officials in charge of all the property and livestock belonging to the king and his sons.* These are the functionaries listed from 27:25ff. It is possible that these functionaries oversaw the property of the king's sons, as well, although this was not mentioned before. Or, perhaps, reference is to the tutor of the king's children mentioned at 27:32.

עִם־הַסָּרִיסִים — *Together with the officers of the court.* סָרִיס often means a eunuch (*Jeremiah* 38:7 among many), but it is also used to describe any official (*Radak, Shorashim; Metzudos*). Here officials of the royal court are meant although their function is not explicated.

וְהַגִּבּוֹרִים — *The mighty men.* The *giborim* of David are listed at 11:11ff.

וּלְכָל־גִּבּוֹר חָיִל — *And every man of outstanding quality.* No one of any important standing was missing (*Metzudos*).

2. וַיָּקָם דָּוִיד הַמֶּלֶךְ עַל־רַגְלָיו — *Then King David rose to his feet.* Although David was weak from old age, he forced himself to rise out of respect for the high officials who had come to Jerusalem (*Metzudos*).

Aggados Bereishis 38 has a similar thought. David had been gravely ill for thirteen years as a result of the penance to which he had subjected himself in atonement for what he had done in the matter of Bathsheva. When the time came to hand over the Temple plans (מְגִילַת בִּנְיַן בֵּית הַמִּקְדָּשׁ) to Solomon, he prayed to God that he be given the strength to rise so that he would be able to pass them on from a standing position.[1]

As noted at 23:1, our passage must surely

---

1. The reference to a מְגִילַת בִּנְיַן בֵּית הַמִּקְדָּשׁ, *scroll containing the building plans for the Temple,* is based on *Midrash Shemuel* 15:3, which traces the history of the scroll. In this account, it was originally handed from God to Moses, then from Moses to Joshua, from him to the elders, from them

Eviathar; and Yoav was the commander of the king's army.

David assembled all the leaders of Israel — the leaders of the tribes, the leaders of the divisions which served the king, the officers of the thousands and the officers of the hundreds and the officials in charge of all the property and livestock belonging to the king and his sons, together with the officers of the court, the mighty men and every man of outstanding quality, to Jerusalem. ² Then King David rose to his feet and said, 'Listen to me, my brothers and

have taken place after Adoniyah's attempted usurpation, described in *I Kings* ch. 1.

Accordingly, David's rising to his feet was really a superhuman effort. At that time David was bedridden — not merely old. It was not really to be expected anymore that David should stand up. He had not gotten out of bed even when Bathsheva and Nathan came to speak to him (*I Kings* 1:15), or when the servants had come to tell him that Solomon had been crowned (1:47). Thus, his standing for this charge was a remarkable event.

This would also go far to explain his reason for wanting to stand. This was David's last official act as king; he was giving his farewell address to the people and his coronation speech for Solomon. The speech begun here ends in 29:22 with the formal anointment of Solomon for the second time (so that it be in the presence of all Israel, not just the residents of Jerusalem — as the commentators explain there). It is no wonder then that David struggled to his feet for this momentous address (*R' Y. Danziger*).

Shir HaShirim Rabbah 1:6 sees an

entirely new thought in our phrase — it hints at the fact that David built the foundation of the Temple. He, so to speak, set the Temple upon its feet. In addition to all the preparations which are described in the previous chapters, he even took part in the actual building.[1]

Commentators grapple with the question of why the phrase should not be simply understood as telling us that David got to his feet.

Gra thinks that the problem lies with the combination of the verb וַיָּקָם, *he rose*, with עַל רַגְלָיו, *on his feet*. He demonstrates from many examples that the root קום does not mean *to rise* or *to get up upon one's feet*. For this the root עמד is the correct word. Rather, קום is used to describe a change of position or of attitude or of relationship. Its use with עַל רַגְלָיו is irregular and therefore points to other connotations not explicated in the text. *Gra* adduces other examples where the combination of קום with עַל רַגְלָיו is interpreted midrashically.

In our case the Sages understand the phrase to

to the prophets and from them to David. David then gave it to Solomon, as recounted in our passage. The Midrash makes the point that in each case the transfer took place in a standing position. Why was this necessary?

Our Sages teach that אֵין יְשִׁיבָה לְמַעְלָה, *there is no sitting on high* — God's angels never sit. They are מַלְאֲכֵי הַשָּׁרֵת, *ministering angels* who must be constantly poised for action. Their legs are רֶגֶל יְשָׁרָה, *a straight leg* (*Ezekiel* 1:7), because no joints are required to facilitate sitting (*Rashi* and *Metzudos* there). Their very being makes the indolence and languor, implicit in being seated in the presence of the Divine, an impossibility.

Perhaps the same idea underlies the insistence that the transfer of the scroll containing the building plans for the Temple be done standing. Those in possession of the plans had to impress upon themselves the urgency of implementing them. If centuries had to pass before the time would be ripe, that was part of God's inscrutable plan. But for their part, the people entrusted with the means had to be in a constant state of readiness to do their part. When the time would come that God would be willing to have His Presence come to rest in a permanent abode among His people, no moment was to be lost because of indolence or unpreparedness.

1. There is some question concerning the time when David built the foundations. From *Succah* 53b it appears that he dug them when Achitophel was still alive, which appears to contradict ch. 21 which implies that David only discovered the Temple site on Ornan's threshing-floor towards the end of his life.

Rashi to *Makkos* 11a offers the following solution: *Zevachim* 54b implies that David had discovered the Temple site many years earlier together with Samuel. That is when he dug the foundations with the permission of the owner. At the time of the plague, his original choice of location was confirmed and he bought the area from Ornan.

See also *Maharsha* to *Succah* 53b and see fn. below.

כח

ג-ו

וַיֹּאמֶר שְׁמָעוּנִי אַחַי וְעַמִּי אֲנִי עִם־לְבָבִי לִבְנוֹת בֵּית
מְנוּחָה לַאֲרוֹן בְּרִית־יהוה וְלַהֲדֹם רַגְלֵי אֱלֹהֵינוּ וַהֲכִינוֹתִי
לִבְנוֹת: ג וְהָאֱלֹהִים אָמַר לִי לֹא־תִבְנֶה בַיִת לִשְׁמִי כִּי אִישׁ
מִלְחָמוֹת אַתָּה וְדָמִים שָׁפָכְתָּ: ד וַיִּבְחַר יהוה אֱלֹהֵי יִשְׂרָאֵל
בִּי מִכֹּל בֵּית־אָבִי לִהְיוֹת לְמֶלֶךְ עַל־יִשְׂרָאֵל לְעוֹלָם כִּי
בִיהוּדָה בָּחַר לְנָגִיד וּבְבֵית יְהוּדָה בֵּית אָבִי וּבִבְנֵי אָבִי
בִּי רָצָה לְהַמְלִיךְ עַל־כָּל־יִשְׂרָאֵל: ה וּמִכָּל־בָּנַי כִּי רַבִּים
בָּנִים נָתַן לִי יהוה וַיִּבְחַר בִּשְׁלֹמֹה בְנִי לָשֶׁבֶת עַל־כִּסֵּא
מַלְכוּת יהוה עַל־יִשְׂרָאֵל: ו וַיֹּאמֶר לִי שְׁלֹמֹה בִנְךָ הוּא־
יִבְנֶה בֵיתִי וַחֲצֵרוֹתָי כִּי־בָחַרְתִּי בוֹ לִי לְבֵן וַאֲנִי אֶהְיֶה־לּוֹ

convey a change in relationship to the building of the Temple. From having been engaged in preparing for the building David now moved to active participation.[1]

אַחַי וְעַמִּי — My brothers and my people. I can treat you in one of two ways. If you listen to me you shall be my brothers; if you don't I shall treat you as my people and impose my rule upon you (Sotah 40a).

Rambam (Melachim 2:6) deduces from our verse the degree of care and sensitivity with which a king should address his people: 'Let him consider the dignity of even the smallest among them; and when he addresses a group, let him use the plural and speak considerately to them, as it is written: Listen to me, my brothers and my people.'

בֵּית מְנוּחָה — A resting place [lit. a house of rest]. It is called a place where God's presence is going to rest because this would be the permanent location for the Temple. It would never be moved to another place (Ralbag). [See Rambam, Beis HaBechirah 1:3.]

וְלַהֲדֹם רַגְלֵי אֱלֹהֵינוּ — And as a footstool for our God. Once the Divine Presence is ensconced in the Sanctuary, the Temple court-yards become its footstool (Gra).

וַהֲכִינוֹתִי לִבְנוֹת — And I have made preparations to build. I have prepared everything that might possibly be needed (Metzudos); i.e., all the preparations described from ch. 22ff.

3. וְהָאֱלֹהִים אָמַר לִי — But God said to me.

1. But why would such an important fact be only hinted at in the text? If David did, indeed, begin the building of the Temple, surely Scripture could have mentioned this explicitly among the detailed accounts in chs. 22-29 of the preparations which David made.

Perhaps the midrash does not really mean that David actually dug the foundations. Maharal in Gevuros Hashem 17 teaches that physical events which take place in a physical context are explicated in the text. Where the text is not explicate but only hints that a given event took place, then we can assume that a metaphysical, rather than physical, event is meant (see Maharal there, under וַתֵּרֶד).

If this principle holds good not only in the Torah but also in the rest of Scripture, then we would be forced to conclude that the midrash's statement that David built the foundations of the Temple, which is only hinted at in our verse, describes a metaphysical truth. It is meant to reflect the ideas which have been discussed in Section Two to ch. 17, that David's and Solomon's reigns are to be viewed as one long continuum, and that although Solomon was the actual builder of the Temple, it was David's house that he was building.

If that interpretation is correct, we would be relieved from attempting to solve the question of the historical sequence (see fn. above), since we are not dealing with events which actually happened but with metaphysical realities which the Sages are expressing in the aggadic idiom.

At the same time, we could suggest a reasonable way in which the Sages saw this in the words of our verse without resorting to Gra's solution. We surmised in the fn. above that the plans of the Temple were handed over from a standing position to indicate the zealous preparedness of the people who were entrusted with these plans. Now David had already been disqualified from any part of the building; why then was it necessary for him to stand? From this the Sages deduced a partnership in Solomon's activities. David, too, was 'building' the Temple — with Solomon's hands. He stood in eager anticipation of his involvement in the realization of his dreams.

*my people. I had in my heart to build a resting place for the Ark of
the Covenant of HASHEM and as a footstool for our God, and I have
made preparations to build. ³ But God said to me, "You shall not
build a house for My Name for you are a man of war and have shed
blood." ⁴ Now, HASHEM, the God of Israel, chose me from among all
my father's family to be king over Israel forever; for He chose Judah
to be prince, and within the house of Judah, my father's family, and
from among my father's sons, it was me that He desired to make
king over all Israel. ⁵ And from all my sons, for HASHEM has given
me many sons, He chose my son Solomon to occupy the throne of
HASHEM's kingship over Israel. ⁶ And He said to me, "Your son
Solomon, he shall build My house and My courtyards, for I have
chosen him to be a son to Me, and I will be a father to him. ⁷ I will*

See chapter 17 and 22:8.

4. וַיִּבְחַר ה' אֱלֹהֵי יִשְׂרָאֵל בִּי — *Now, HASHEM,
the God of Israel, chose me.* Do not think
that because I was disqualified from
building the Temple that this means that I
am not suited to be king. On the contrary,
God chose me specifically to be king
(*Metzudos*).

כִּי בִיהוּדָה בָּחַר לְנָגִיד — *For He chose Judah to
be prince.* This can be seen from the
blessing which Jacob gave his sons before
he died [see *Genesis* 49:8ff] (*Ralbag*).

וּבִבְנֵי אָבִי בִּי רָצָה לְהַמְלִיךְ — *And from among
my father's sons, it was me that He desired
to make king.* My father had many sons.
God could easily have denied me the
kingship if I would not have been deemed
worthy.

5. וַיִּבְחַר בִּשְׁלֹמֹה בְנִי — *He chose my son
Solomon.* The circumstances of Solomon's
birth from Bathsheba in no way disqualified him from being king. David had
many sons and God could easily have made
any of them king. He chose Solomon
because he was indeed the one who was
worthy (*Metzudos*).

כִּסֵּא מַלְכוּת ה' עַל־יִשְׂרָאֵל — *The throne of
HASHEM's kingship over Israel.* See Section
Two p. 437ff for a discussion of the idea
that the Davidic line represents God's
kingship over Israel.

6. וַיֹּאמֶר לִי שְׁלֹמֹה בִנְךָ הוּא־יִבְנֶה בֵיתִי וַחֲצֵרוֹתָי
— *And He said to me, "Your son Solomon,
he shall build My house and My
courtyards.*" There is no express prophecy
recorded identifying Solomon as David's
heir. Nathan's message at 17:11 speaks

only of one of David's sons. However, at
22:9 David tells Solomon of having
received a prophecy in which he was told
of a son to be born to him who would be a
man of peace and that this will be reflected
in his name — שְׁלֹמֹה, Solomon, from שָׁלוֹם,
peace.

When his son by Bathsheba was born,
David *called his name Solomon — and God
loved him* (*II Samuel* 12:24). Subsequently
God sent Nathan the prophet to announce
that God wished the child to be called יְדִידְיָה
[*Yedidiah*], *beloved of God* (v. 25). It seems
that David, on his own initiative, decided
that this child was to be the Solomon
whose birth had been predicted by God. By
sending the message that He wished the
child to be known as Yedidiah, God seems
to have confirmed that choice. This could
well be what David means when he says
here that God told him that Solomon was to
build the Temple. This was implicit in
God's confirmation of David's decision to
call this son Solomon.

כִּי־בָחַרְתִּי בוֹ לִי לְבֵן וַאֲנִי אֶהְיֶה־לּוֹ לְאָב — *For I
have chosen him to be a son to Me, and I
will be a father to him.* At 22:10 the
commentary suggested that the sequence,
*he shall be a son to Me and I will be a father
to him,* implies that the onus of creating the
relationship would fall upon Solomon. If
he would be to God as a son, then God
would act towards him as a father.

In our verse the point is made that the
status of being a son is also to be conferred
upon Solomon. God chooses him as a son,
and he is, accordingly, a Divinely ordained
king. It will nevertheless be up to Solomon
to determine the intensity and direction of

ז לְאָב: וַהֲכִינוֹתִי אֶת־מַלְכוּתוֹ עַד־לְעוֹלָם אִם־יֶחֱזַק
ח לַעֲשׂוֹת מִצְוֹתַי וּמִשְׁפָּטַי כַּיּוֹם הַזֶּה: וְעַתָּה לְעֵינֵי כָל־
יִשְׂרָאֵל קְהַל־יהוה וּבְאָזְנֵי אֱלֹהֵינוּ שִׁמְרוּ וְדִרְשׁוּ כָּל־
מִצְוֺת יהוה אֱלֹהֵיכֶם לְמַעַן תִּירְשׁוּ אֶת־הָאָרֶץ הַטּוֹבָה
ט וְהִנְחַלְתֶּם לִבְנֵיכֶם אַחֲרֵיכֶם עַד־עוֹלָם: וְאַתָּה שְׁלֹמֹה־בְנִי
דַּע אֶת־אֱלֹהֵי אָבִיךָ וְעָבְדֵהוּ בְּלֵב שָׁלֵם וּבְנֶפֶשׁ חֲפֵצָה
כִּי כָל־לְבָבוֹת דּוֹרֵשׁ יהוה וְכָל־יֵצֶר מַחֲשָׁבוֹת מֵבִין

that relationship, to fashion, so to speak, the kind of father that God will be to him. This is the meaning of 22:10.

7. אם־יֶחֱזַק לַעֲשׂוֹת מִצְוֹתַי וּמִשְׁפָּטַי — *If he will be strong in performing My commandments and My laws.* The implication is clear. The establishment of Solomon's kingship eternally is to be conditional on his adherence to God's commandments and laws. The same idea is expressed in *I Kings* 8:25, where Solomon prays to God that He keep the promise made to David that ... *no descendant of yours will ever be denied Israel's throne if only your children watch their ways, to walk before Me as you have walked before Me.*

In both places the implication is that God's gift of kingship to David was conditional upon his descendants remaining loyal to the Torah. But the only prophecy about the kingship recorded — that of Nathan at *II Samuel* 7:14-15 — seems to imply the opposite. *And I shall be a father to him and he shall be to Me a son, so when he sins I shall chastise him with rods of men and with affliction of the sons of men. But My kindness shall not depart from him as I removed it from Saul, whom I removed from before you.* In this prophecy God appears to be saying that although Solomon may be severely punished for any sins he may commit, the kingship will remain with him eternally and unconditionally. *Abarbanel* raises this question and suggests that there may be a difference between idol worship — which would relieve God of this promise because it would no longer be true that the relationship could be described as that of a father to a son — and other transgressions.

A more encompassing answer may lie in *Malbim's* interpretation of the passage in *Samuel.* As he renders the phrase, God's promise is not that He will punish Solomon

with physical punishments instead of taking the kingship away from him, but rather that at the smallest transgressions God will immediately expose him to a *warning* — not a punishing *rod* — so that his negligence will never escalate into the kind of wickedness necessitating his loss of the throne. Thus, the phrase וְחַסְדִּי לֹא יָסוּר מִמֶּנּוּ is not to be translated '... *but* My kindness shall not depart from him,' but '... *so that* My kindness shall not depart from him.'

Rendered thus, the implication is clear that if Solomon does indeed ignore God's cautionary chastisements and continues to sin, then he will indeed lose his kingship.

This may be the meaning of *Rambam, Melachim* 1:7 who writes: 'Once David was anointed, he acquired the crown of kingship and thus the kingship belongs to him and his male descendants forever ... But he acquired it only for [those of his sons who are] righteous, as it is written, ... *if your sons keep My covenant.* Even though he acquired it only for the righteous ones, kingship will never be torn away from David's seed. God promised him this, as it is written: *If his sons forsake My Torah and walk not in My judgments ... Then I will punish with the rod their transgression, and with afflictions their iniquity. But My kindness I shall not remove from him ... (Psalms 89:31-34).'*

Perhaps, too, *Rambam* means that even in the event that one or another of David's descendants would lose the kingship because of his wickedness, it would eventually revert to the Davidic line through another descendant.

For a detailed discussion, see R' Z. Hoberman's *Lechem Chuki* I:47.

8. וְעַתָּה לְעֵינֵי כָל־יִשְׂרָאֵל — *Now, in the presence of all Israel* [lit. *in the sight of all Israel*]. David wishes to exhort his people while all of them are present (*Metzudos*). No one should have the excuse of saying they were not there and could not have known.

וּבְאָזְנֵי אֱלֹהֵינוּ — *And in the presence of our*

establish his kingdom forever, if he will be strong in performing My commandments and My laws as he does now." ⁸ Now, in the presence of all Israel, the congregation of HASHEM, and in the presence of our God, observe and seek out all the commandments of HASHEM your God, so that you may possess the good land and bequeath it to your children after you forever. ⁹ And you, my son Solomon, know the God of your father and serve Him with a whole heart and a willing soul, for HASHEM examines all hearts and understands the formations of all thoughts; if you seek Him out, He

---

God [lit. *in the hearing of our God*]. As in the first phrase of this verse, this expression is idiomatic (see *Targum*). In order to see, a person must be more immediately present than in order to hear. For this reason the eyes are used to describe the presence of the people but the ears are more aptly used to describe the presence of God, Whose being is intangible.

וְדִרְשׁוּ ... — ... *and seek out.* A similar use of the root דרש can be found in *Psalms* 119:45, 94 and 155. In this context the word is to be understood as — seek with a determination to find.

לְמַעַן תִּירְשׁוּ אֶת־הָאָרֶץ הַטּוֹבָה — *So that you may possess the good land.* Although the root ירש is mostly used in the sense of taking possession of new territory, *Metzudos* here renders it as meaning to keep possession of what one already has. He apparently assumes that towards the end of David's reign the whole land had already been conquered and that it was only a question of retaining it.

But see ArtScroll *Joshua*, fn. to 13:1, that it was only in Solomon's time that the entire territory was taken. At the time of Yoav's census the Jews had apparently not yet settled the northernmost areas of the promised land. If so, it might be that David meant that the rest of the conquest was dependent on the conscientious guarding of the Torah's laws.

9. וְאַתָּה שְׁלֹמֹה־בְנִי — *And you, my son Solomon.* Our obligations to serve God increases in proportion to the favors which He showers upon us. The rest of Israel must guard and seek out the commandments of the Torah in gratitude for the gift of the land (v. 8); but you, Solomon, whom God has chosen as His son, must go much further (*Malbim*).

דַּע אֶת־אֱלֹהֵי אָבִיךָ — *Know the God of your father.* A person *knows* that which has

been proved to him, not that which he accepts on faith. The exhortation דַּע, *know*, would seem to indicate that David charged Solomon with proving to himself — through philosophical and scientific investigation — that God created the world and rules it. This is the way the verse is understood by *Rambam, Guide* 3:51, and *Malbim* here. However, *Kuzari* is of the opinion that historical truths handed down from fathers to sons and accepted could also be described as knowledge, and that it is to these truths that our verse refers.

Radak and *Metzudos* take the exhortation as combining both approaches. The command דַּע, *know*, does indeed demand that Solomon use his critical faculties for the philosophical quest of achieving an understanding of God. The words אֱלֹהֵי אָבִיךָ, *the God of your father*, imply that pending that proof, he should accept God on the basis of the received tradition.

וְעָבְדֵהוּ בְּלֵב שָׁלֵם ... כִּי כָל־לְבָבוֹת דּוֹרֵשׁ ה׳ — *And serve Him with a whole heart ... for Hashem examines all hearts.* Scripture uses both לֵב and לְבָב to mean *heart.* The change within the same verse is noteworthy and *Mefaresh* offers the following explanation. The two letters ב in לְבָב imply a degree of duality and are used to denote the multiple urges — towards good and towards evil — within man's heart. By contrast the single ב in לֵב connotes a heart not torn by these conflicting drives but wholly in the service of God.

Thus David exhorts Solomon to have only a single — *whole* — heart entirely devoted to God and with no other loyalty within it. This, because God examines all the divided hearts, knowing full well their inclination towards evil.

וְכָל־יֵצֶר מַחֲשָׁבוֹת מֵבִין — *And understands the formations of all thoughts.* The root יצר means *to form;* thus יֵצֶר מַחֲשָׁבוֹת are the

אִם־תִּדְרְשֶׁנּוּ יִמָּצֵא לָךְ וְאִם־־תַּעַזְבֶנּוּ יַזְנִיחֲךָ לָעַד׃

י רְאֵה ׀ עַתָּה כִּי־יְהוָה בָּחַר בְּךָ לִבְנוֹת־בַּיִת לַמִּקְדָּשׁ חֲזַק
יא וַעֲשֵׂה׃ וַיִּתֵּן דָּוִיד לִשְׁלֹמֹה בְנוֹ אֶת־תַּבְנִית
הָאוּלָם וְאֶת־בָּתָּיו וְגַנְזַכָּיו וַעֲלִיֹּתָיו וַחֲדָרָיו הַפְּנִימִים
יב וּבֵית הַכַּפֹּרֶת׃ וְתַבְנִית כֹּל אֲשֶׁר הָיָה בָרוּחַ עִמּוֹ לְחַצְרוֹת

images formed in the person's thoughts, the aspirations and hopes of his desires whether good or bad (Radak). [For a detailed discussion of the terms, see ArtScroll Bereishis vol. 1, p. 188.]

וְאִם־תַּעַזְבֶנּוּ יַזְנִיחֲךָ לָעַד — *But if you forsake Him, He will spurn you forever.* זָנַח, *spurn,* is stronger than עזב, *forsake* (Mefaresh).

10. בַּיִת לַמִּקְדָּשׁ — *A house for the sacred [Ark].* I.e., to house the Ark. The translation follows *Mefaresh,* who takes the word in the sense in which it is used in *Numbers* 10:21. There the Kehathites, whose task was to carry the Ark, are described as carrying the מִקְדָּשׁ.[1] *Metzudos,* however, renders, *to serve as a Sanctuary.*

◄§ The Temple Plans

11־19. David now hands over the Temple plans to Solomon. The midrash (quoted above in v. 2) traces these plans all the way back to the time of Moses. Indeed, as we shall see below, all the details of the plan are ascribed either to a prophetic tradition or to Divinely inspired study of Torah texts which yielded certain parts. Thus, long before the Temple was built, the plans, down to the smallest detail, had already been meticulously laid down. Because they were Divinely inspired, they remained binding not only for Solomon's Temple but for the Second Temple and for the Messianic Temple which is to rise in the future, as well (*Rambam, Introduction to Zeraim;* see *Eruvin* 104a as one of many passages in the Talmud which insist that, based on our v. 19, even the smallest changes in the Temple structure were prohibited).

11. אֶת־תַּבְנִית הָאוּלָם — *The plan of the Hall.* תַּבְנִית from בנה, *to build.* The plan according to which the Hall is to be built, i.e., its dimensions (*Mefaresh*).

הָאוּלָם ... וַחֲדָרָיו הַפְּנִימִים — *The Hall ... inner rooms.* The אוּלָם, *Hall,* is the entrance hall which led into the Sanctuary. The Sanctuary, in turn, lay in front of the Holy of Holies, which is mentioned below (בֵּית הַכַּפֹּרֶת).

Why is the הֵיכָל, *Sanctuary,* not mentioned? Surely David would have included it in the plans which he handed over to Solomon?

Malbim, apparently to deal with this problem, explains that *the inner chambers* mentioned here refer to the Sanctuary. But why should the Sanctuary be described as an inner room of the Hall? We would suppose that the Sanctuary, with its greater degree of sanctity, would be considered the more significant of the two and would rate mention in its own right.

In light of the *Mefaresh's* explanation of the previous verse, it appears that the entire Temple takes its significance specifically from the Holy of Holies — the place in which the Ark rested — and that all its other components are considered ancillary to it. In such a context it might well be that all that lay in front of the Holy of Holies is termed אוּלָם, *an entrance hall,* and that אוּלָם here indeed includes the Sanctuary.

See *I Kings* ch. 7 in the description of Solomon's palace. A careful study of the plans yields that there were a number of chambers which lay in front of the main palace and each of them is called אוּלָם. Thus we see that this name is not limited to the outermost chamber but can be used to describe any halls which are ancillary to the main ones.

1. *Ibn Ezra* there agrees with the *Mefaresh* in his interpretation of that verse, but *Rashi* there seems to disagree, interpreting מִקְדָּשׁ as *sacred objects* — not specifically the Ark.
    The interpretation of the *Mefaresh* is significant in that it defines the function of the Temple as primarily that of housing the Holy Ark. This is also the implication of 17:1, where David's desire to build the Temple is focused on building a proper house for the Ark. The particular stress on the function of housing the Ark would seem to derive from the identification between the Ark and the Divine Presence on earth — see comm. to 13:6.

will make Himself available to you, but if you forsake Him, He will spurn you forever. [10] *Take heed now, HASHEM has chosen you to build a house for the sacred [Ark] be strong and do it.'* [11] *Then David handed over to Solomon his son the plan of the Hall, its chambers, storage places, attics, inner rooms, and the chamber of the Ark-cover.* [12] *And the plan of everything which came to him through the Divine spirit, for all the courtyards of the House of HASHEM and all the chambers round about, which were for the*

וְאֶת־בָּתָּיו — *Its chambers. Metzudos* explains that this refers to the בֵּית הַחֲלִיפוֹת, the *knife depository,* a long, narrow building which was attached to the hall.

Malbim renders בָּתָּיו as יְצִיעִים, *cells,* and apparently means the cells referred to in *I Kings* 6:5, see there. But that verse indicates that those cells were built only into the walls of the Holy of Holies and the Sanctuary, and not of the entrance hall. *Malbim* in his comm. to *Kings* stresses this point. It is therefore difficult to see why these יְצִיעִים should be described as belonging to the entrance hall.

וְגַנְזַכָּיו — *Storage spaces.* The translation follows *Mefaresh* and *Radak.* The word does not recur in Scripture. It is evidently derived from the root גנז, *to hide* or *store (Metzudos).*

וַעֲלִיֹּתָיו — *Attics. Ralbag* points out that the walls of the hall towered to a height of 120 cubits. Contained within this huge structure there must have been numerous chambers.

וַחֲדָרָיו הַפְּנִימִים — *Inner rooms.* As seen above, *Malbim's* opinion is that this refers to the הֵיכָל, *Sanctuary. Ralbag* has it refer to chambers which may have been arranged over the Sanctuary.

וּבֵית הַכַּפֹּרֶת — *And the chamber of the Ark-cover.* This is the Holy of Holies *(Metzudos).* [See *Aruch* under בֵּית כַּפֹּרֶת and כפר (10), Mishnah, *Middos* 1:1, and other references adduced in *Aruch HaShalem.* See also *Targum* to *Leviticus* 16:2.] The golden lid which covered the Ark was called the כַּפֹּרֶת (see *Exodus* 25:17ff). [כפר is taken in the sense *to cover* (see *Rashi* to *Exodus* 25:17 and *Rashbam* and *Ibn Ezra* there, based on *Ibn Ezra* to *Genesis* 32:21], thus, a lid. Accordingly,

בֵּית הַכַּפֹּרֶת would be the chamber in which the כַּפֹּרֶת, *Ark-cover,* was kept, that is the Holy of Holies *(Aruch* under בֵּית כַּפֹּרֶת).

But why would the Holy of Holies be described as the place of the Ark-cover? *Tosefos Yom Tov* to *Middos* 1:1 explains because the Ark-cover together with the two cherubim which were fashioned from it formed the throne (מֶרְכָּבָה, *Merkavah)* for the Divine Presence. Hence it is specifically the Ark-cover which is the focal point of the Holy of Holies.[1] This is also the opinion of *Ralbag.*

Tiferes Yisrael (there) has a similar explanation. The main significance of the Holy of Holies is that God communicated there with Moses from atop the Ark-Cover (see *Exodus* 25:22). For this reason the Holy of Holies is described as housing the Ark-cover.

R' Dovid Tzvi Hoffman in his commentary to *Leviticus* dissents. He shows that the root כפר in the פָּעַל never means *to cover.* For this reason he argues (and is borne out by *Tanchuma* to *VaYakhel)* that the בֵּית הַכַּפֹּרֶת was so called because the *atonement* service on Yom Kippur, the most significant atonement procedure of the year, took place in it (כַּפֵּר, *to atone).* Thus, the translation would be the *Atonement Chamber.* [See also *HaKesav VeHakabbalah, Exodus* 25:17:2.]

12. כֹּל אֲשֶׁר הָיָה בָרוּחַ עִמּוֹ — *And the plan of everything which came to him through the Divine spirit.* All the plans handed to Solomon had been Divinely revealed either to David or to Samuel, who passed them on to David *(Radak).*

The commentators are unanimous that our verse refers to a spirit of prophecy — and indeed this seems borne out by v. 19, see there. However, the word רוּחַ often means the human mind as, e.g., in *Ezekiel* 10:32, and this is also

---

1. This interpretation is difficult in the context of our passage. While the cherubim on the Ark may have served this function in the Tabernacle, in Solomon's Temple it was the standing cherubim which served in this capacity — see below, on v. 18.

בֵּית־יהוה וּלְכָל־הַלְּשָׁכוֹת סָבִיב לְאֹצְרוֹת בֵּית הָאֱלֹהִים
יג וּלְאֹצְרוֹת הַקֳּדָשִׁים: וּלְמַחְלְקוֹת הַכֹּהֲנִים וְהַלְוִיִּם וּלְכָל־
מְלֶאכֶת עֲבוֹדַת בֵּית־יהוה וּלְכָל־כְּלֵי עֲבוֹדַת בֵּית־יהוה:
יד לַזָּהָב בַּמִּשְׁקָל לַזָּהָב לְכָל־כְּלֵי עֲבוֹדָה וַעֲבוֹדָה לְכֹל כְּלֵי
טו הַכֶּסֶף בְּמִשְׁקָל לְכָל־כְּלֵי עֲבוֹדָה וַעֲבוֹדָה: וּמִשְׁקָל
לִמְנֹרוֹת הַזָּהָב וְנֵרֹתֵיהֶם זָהָב בְּמִשְׁקַל־מְנוֹרָה וּמְנוֹרָה
וְנֵרֹתֶיהָ וְלִמְנֹרוֹת הַכֶּסֶף בְּמִשְׁקָל לִמְנוֹרָה וְנֵרֹתֶיהָ
טז כַּעֲבוֹדַת מְנוֹרָה וּמְנוֹרָה: וְאֶת־הַזָּהָב מִשְׁקָל לְשֻׁלְחֲנוֹת
הַמַּעֲרֶכֶת לְשֻׁלְחָן וְשֻׁלְחָן וָכֶסֶף לְשֻׁלְחֲנוֹת הַכָּסֶף:

the meaning in the only other place in Scripture in which we find the combination עמו ... רוּחַ — see Numbers 14:24.

Perhaps the commentators' indication lies in the use of the definite article בָּרוּחַ, the spirit rather than בְרוּחַ, a spirit. A definite, known spirit is meant — the spirit of prophecy.

לְאֹצְרוֹת בֵּית הָאֱלֹהִים וּלְאֹצְרוֹת הַקֳּדָשִׁים — For the treasuries of the House of God and the treasuries of all that was consecrated. The first contained the monies earmarked for the upkeep of the building, the second those that were to be used for the purchase of sacrifices (Metzudos).

13. וּלְמַחְלְקוֹת הַכֹּהֲנִים וְהַלְוִיִּם — And for the divisions of the Kohanim and the Levites. This verse continues from the previous one. In addition to the Temple plans, David gave Solomon the detailed dispositions which he had made concerning the twenty-four mishmaros for the Kohanim and the Levites (see chs. 23-26). Ralbag points out that since v. 19 indicates that all the items mentioned in our passage came to David by the hand of HASHEM, the implication is that the Kohanite and Levite divisions were also Divinely inspired.

וּלְכָל־מְלֶאכֶת עֲבוֹדַת בֵּית־ה׳ — And concerning all the activities involved in the service of the House of HASHEM. What form the Divine service was to take, how the shir [song] was to be performed, and the positions to be assumed by the various participants in the service (Malbim).

Ralbag, however, thinks that the vav in וּלְכָל is redundant and the phrase should be read without it. [For other examples of such redundant vavs see above 27:4 and

ArtScroll Genesis 36:24.] In that case our phrase is read together with the previous one — and the divisions ... 'for' all the activities. Thus, the entire phrase is the exact equivalent of the one in v. 21.

וּלְכָל־כְּלֵי עֲבוֹדַת בֵּית־ה׳ — And for all the utensils for the service of the House of HASHEM. David conveyed to Solomon the form of the various utensils to be used in the Temple service[1] (Metzudos). [In this view it would seem that the word וְתַבְנִית in v. 12 is to be brought down to our phrase.] Mefaresh, though, thinks that the issue here was not the form of the utensils but their weight and the number required.

14-18. The exact meaning of these four verses cannot be determined from the text. Coming as they do in the middle of the section which tells that David handed Solomon the plans for the Temple, it would be logical to take these verses as teaching that David also told Solomon the details concerning the manufacture of the utensils — that is, their number, size, weight, and other pertinent information.

However, Metzudos seems to have understood these verses not as describing the instructions which David gave Solomon concerning the manufacture of the utensils but as referring to the gold and silver David gave Solomon to make them. The wording of these verses seem to bear this out.

14. לַזָּהָב — For gold. For those utensils which were to be made from gold (Metzudos).

בַּמִּשְׁקָל לַזָּהָב — By the weight of gold. The

1. See Ramban to Exodus 25:9 for a discussion of whether the utensils in Solomon's Temple had to have the same form as those used in Moses' Tabernacle.

treasuries of the House of God and the treasuries of all that was consecrated. ¹³ And for the divisions of the Kohanim and the Levites, and concerning all the activities involved in the service of the House of HASHEM, and for all the utensils for the service of the House of HASHEM. ¹⁴ For gold, by the weight of gold, for utensils of each type of service; for all the silver utensils by weight, for all the utensils for each type of service. ¹⁵ And the weight [of gold] for the golden candelabra and their golden lamps, according to the weight of each candelabrum and its lamps; and for the silver candelabra by weight for each candelabrum and its lamps, in accordance with the use of each candelabrum. ¹⁶ And the weight of gold for the tables of the ordering, for each table, as well as silver for the silver tables. ¹⁷ And the forks, bowls, and stands, pure gold; and for the golden

units of weight which were used were those appropriate to gold *(Metzudos).*

לְכֹל כְּלֵי הַכָּסֶף — *For all the silver utensils.* Neither in *Kings* nor in *II Chronicles* is there any record of Solomon making any silver vessels for the Temple. *Malbim* suggests that Solomon made none from silver because his immense wealth was such that *silver ... counted for nothing at all in Solomon's days (I Kings* 10:21). David could not have known just how wealthy Solomon would be and anticipated that there would also be silver utensils.[1]

15. וּמִשְׁקָל לִמְנֹרֹות הַזָּהָב — *And the weight [of gold] for the golden candelabra.* Solomon made ten golden candelabra in addition to the one which Betzalel had made for the Tabernacle. [See *II Chronicles* 4:7 and *Menachos* 98b, 99a] *(Radak).*

וְנֵרֹתֵיהֶם זָהָב — *And their golden lamps.* נֵר is used for the receptacle in which the oil and wick are placed *(Metzudos).*

בְּמִשְׁקַל־מְנֹורָה וּמְנֹורָה — *According to the weight of each candelabrum.* All the golden candelabra were to weigh exactly one כִּכָּר, *talent,* of gold, as laid down in connection with Moses' candelabrum in *Exodus* 25:39. By contrast, the end of our verse uses *in accordance with the use of each candelabrum,* in connection with the silver candelabra, because for these no specific weight is ever assigned by the Torah and their size would be determined by use

(Malbim).

וְלִמְנֹרֹות הַכֶּסֶף ... — *And for the silver candelabra ...* We do not find Solomon making any silver candelabra. *Radak* and *Metzudos* suggest that these candelabra were not to be used in the Temple service but were used to light the halls in which the Kohanim ate and slept.

Malbim suggests the same solution as he offered above. David anticipated that some of the candelabra would have been made of silver. In fact, Solomon became so wealthy that this became unnecessary.

16. לְשֻׁלְחֲנֹות הַמַּעֲרֶכֶת — *For the tables of the ordering* [of the *Panim*-bread]. The Torah *(Exodus* 25:23-30) commands that a table be kept in the Sanctuary for the purpose of holding the לֶחֶם הַפָּנִים, *Panim-bread.* In addition to the table which had stood in the Tabernacle, Solomon made ten additional tables (see *II Chronicles* 4:8 and *Menachos* 98b and 99a).

וְכֶסֶף לְשֻׁלְחֲנֹות הַכָּסֶף — *As well as silver for the silver tables.* Again, we have no record of any silver tables made by Solomon. However, as we saw above, it is possible that not everything that was used in the Temple service is listed in the Scriptural record.

The *Mefaresh* writes that silver tables were used for skinning the sacrificial animals in the Temple courtyard. However, this does not accord with the Mishnah in

1. See *Menachos* 28b that even vessels like the Menorah (candelabrum), for which the Torah specifies gold, could be made from lesser metals if gold was too expensive.

In addition, it is possible that there were minor utensils which were used in the sacrificial service but which were not mentioned in the text. Thus, the Mishnah in *Yoma* 43b talks of a silver shovel which was used to take care of the altar for the purpose of offering up the incense.

יז וְהַמִּזְלָגוֹת וְהַמִּזְרָקוֹת וְהַקְּשָׂוֹת זָהָב טָהוֹר וְלִכְפוֹרֵי הַזָּהָב
בְּמִשְׁקָל לִכְפוֹר וּכְפוֹר וְלִכְפוֹרֵי הַכֶּסֶף בְּמִשְׁקָל לִכְפוֹר
יח וּכְפוֹר: וּלְמִזְבַּח הַקְּטֹרֶת זָהָב מְזֻקָּק בַּמִּשְׁקָל וּלְתַבְנִית
הַמֶּרְכָּבָה הַכְּרוּבִים זָהָב לְפֹרְשִׂים וְסֹכְכִים עַל־אֲרוֹן

Shekalim 6:5 which records that those tables were made out of marble.[1] *Malbim* offers the same solution as he did in the previous verses, that David anticipated the need for silver tables but that they did not prove necessary. Alternatively, he suggests that reference might be to a silver table which stood inside the אוּלָם, *Hall*, on which the *Panim*-bread was laid before it was ordered on the golden table in the Sanctuary (see mishnah there). However, there is some question about whether this table was made of silver or of marble — see *Shekalim* 17b, *Menachos* 99a,b and *Tosafos* there, and *Rambam, Beis HaBechirah* 3:16.

According to all opinions, there was a silver table standing to the west of the ramp leading up to the altar upon which the utensils to be used during the sacrificial service were laid out (see *Shekalim* 17b and *Rambam, Beis HaBechirah* 2:15).

17. ... וְהַמִּזְלָגוֹת — *And the forks* ... Four utensils are listed in our verse. Of these, the word קְשָׂוֹת, *stands*, appears in *Exodus* 25:29 where it is used in the description of the table of the *Panim*-bread that was to stand in the Sanctuary. For this reason, *Ibn Ezra* (there) assumes that our verse is a continuation of the previous one and that all four of the utensils mentioned here were to be used in connection with the table. He points out that only the קְשָׂוֹת find a parallel in *Exodus* and thinks that the other three utensils replace the others which are mentioned there in the following manner:

Chronicles	Exodus
מִזְרָקוֹת	קְעָרֹתָיו
כְּפוֹרִים	כַּפֹּתָיו
קְשָׂוֹת	קְשׂוֹתָיו
מִזְלָגוֹת	מְנַקִּיֹּתָיו

He expresses surprise at the substitutions and surmises that these are new utensils envisioned by David for Solomon's Temple.

Ramban (there) thinks that our verse does not refer back to the verse immediately preceding it, but to v. 13, which talks of all the utensils to be used in the Temple. Thus, there is no reason to associate any of the utensils, with the exception of the קְשָׂוֹת, *stands*, with the table. They are vessels used in other parts of the sacrificial service. Our translation follows this approach.

וְהַמִּזְרָקוֹת — *Bowls.* The word derives from זרק, *to throw.* Thus, these are bowls used in the sprinkling of the sacrificial blood upon the altar (*Metzudos*).

וְהַקְּשָׂוֹת — *Stands.* On either end of the table of the *Panim*-bread there were stands which supported the ventilation tubes on which the *Panim*-bread lay. These stands are the קְשׂוֹתָיו mentioned in *Exodus* [מְנַקִּיֹּתָיו mentioned there are the ventilation tubes] (*Metzudos*). *Rashi* (there) considers the possibility that the two words may have the opposite meaning and in that case our קְשָׂוֹת should be rendered *ventilation tubes.*

It is not easy to understand why of all the parts of the table just the *stands* should be singled out for mention. In the context of our verse, *Ibn Ezra's* rendition of קְשׂוֹתָיו as *cups* or *receptacles* seems to fit in much more smoothly. This translation seems based on *Aruch* under קַסְיָא, which in turn is based on *R' Hai Gaon* to *Machshirin* [see *Aruch HaShalem*, there, and *Karnei Ohr* (Mechokekei Yehudah) to *Ibn Ezra*, there]. Given this translation, the word fits smoothly between מִזְרָקוֹת and כְּפוֹרִים.

וְלִכְפוֹרֵי הַזָּהָב — *And for the golden wiping bowls.* These are also utensils used in connection with the sacrificial blood (*Metzudos*). The name derives from כפר, *to cleanse,* because the *Kohen* would wipe the slaughtering knife on the edge of this utensil in order to clean off the blood which was on it (*Rashi* to *Genesis* 32:21; *Radak* and *Metzudos* here).

18. וּלְמִזְבַּח הַקְּטֹרֶת — *And ... for the Altar of Incense.* The golden altar which stood

1. There is, of course, the possibility that in the First Temple, in which silver abounded, they were made of silver but that in the straightened circumstances of the second Temple, marble was substituted. However, it appears from *Shekalim* 6:5 that marble was used by design, because the cold stone would inhibit the putrification of the flesh that was placed upon it.

wiping bowls, by weight for each wiping bowl, and for the silver wiping bowl, by weight for each wiping bowl. [18] *And refined gold by weight for the Altar of Incense; and for the pattern of the Merkavah, the Cheruvim made out of gold spread out, so that they*

inside the Sanctuary was used mainly for the daily offering of incense *(Exodus 30:1-10)*, in contrast to the altar which stood in the Temple courtyard on which most sacrifices were brought.

Rashi to *I Kings* 6:20 expresses surprise that it was necessary for Solomon to make a new incense altar. *R' Yitzchak Isaac HaLevi (Tekufos HaMikrah* ch. 17) suggests that many of the golden utensils may well have been plundered from the Tabernacle during the period of the Judges, when Israel was frequently under the control of foreigners and particularly when Shiloh was sacked by the Philistines. He speculates that the golden incense altar made by Moses was among the items stolen.

In *II Chronicles* 4:1 we learn that Solomon also made a מִזְבַּח נְחֹשֶׁת, *a copper altar* (see also 7:7 there), whose dimensions were evidently different from the one that Moses had made. We note that this altar is not mentioned among the utensils for which David gave Solomon the plans. Nevertheless, from *Chullin* 83b it is clear that the Sages considered the outer altar to be included in the general directions contained in our v. 19 and that the dimensions of all the utensils were determined by Divine fiat. We may perhaps surmise that, since the outer altar was not a moveable object but was, on the contrary, built into the ground (see commentators to *II Kings* 16:14), it is perhaps included in the *courtyards of the House of HASHEM* mentioned in v. 12. This may well explain the absence of the altar from the list of the utensils here, but it does not explain why none of the copper vessels are mentioned. *I Kings* ch. 7 makes a point of stressing that Solomon manufactured sacred objects out of copper, and we would have expected directions from David concerning these vessels. The comentators offer no explanation.

וּלְתַבְנִית הַמֶּרְכָּבָה הַכְּרוּבִים ... — *And for the pattern of the Merkavah, the Cheruvim ...* In *I Kings* 6:23ff and *II Chronicles* 3:10ff we learn of two human figures — *Cheruvim* or cherubs which Solomon made in the Holy of Holies. These *Cheruvim* were meant to symbolize the *Merkavah*, the 'chariot' vision of Yechezkel which is

described in the first chapter of *Ezekiel*. This is the meaning of *Merkavah* in our verse. The *Cheruvim* were *patterned* after the *Merkavah* in the sense that they had a human face, just as one of the faces in the *Merkavah* vision of Ezekiel was human *(Metzudos)*.

הַכְּרוּבִים זָהָב לְפֹרְשִׂים — *The Cheruvim made out of gold spread out.* The spacing of the verses follows the *trop* (cantillation). The wings of the *Cheruvim* were to spread out over the top of the Ark of the Covenant. See *Exodus* 25:20 *(Radak)*.

If this section describes the actual materials which David handed over to Solomon (see pref. remarks 14-18), the meaning may be that sufficient gold was set aside for the wings of the *Cheruvim* to spread out and cover the Ark (R' Y. Danziger).

19. This verse teaches that David's plans for the Temple were grounded in Divine revelation. The Talmud derives from here a prohibition against interfering with the basic structural design of the Temple precincts and the sacred utensils.

Scripture never makes entirely clear what the source of the Divine inspiration was. To some extent this would depend on an accurate rendering of our verse. In the comm. to v. 2, the midrash was quoted as saying that a מְגִילַת בְּנְיַן בֵּית הַמִּקְדָּשׁ, *scroll containing the building plans for the Temple*, was handed to Moses at Sinai and passed on to David by the prophets. *Yerushalmi (Megillah* 1:1) has Samuel handing the scroll over to David.

Rashi to *Succah* 51b writes that our verse means that God informed David of details of the plans for the building through Gad the seer and Nathan the prophet. This may well have taken place by means of the Scroll.

Mefaresh, apparently based on a source that has been lost to us, has Samuel deriving the required dimensions by means of Divinely inspired study of Torah texts.[1]

Radak to v. 12 is uncertain whether the prophecies concerning the Temple structure were given to Samuel or to David

---

1. He adduces an example from the dimensions of the Temple Mount, which is given in *Middos* 2:1 as 500 x 500 cubits. This is said to be derived from a homiletical interpretation of *Exodus* 27:18. *Rosh* to *Middos* cites the same interpretation, and *Gra* (there) writes that the source is in *Yerushalmi*. But

יט בְּרִית־יהוה: הַכֹּל בִּכְתָב מִיַּד יהוה עָלַי הִשְׂכִּיל כֹּל
מַלְאֲכוֹת הַתַּבְנִית: כ וַיֹּאמֶר דָּוִיד לִשְׁלֹמֹה
בְנוֹ חֲזַק וֶאֱמָץ וַעֲשֵׂה אַל־תִּירָא וְאַל־תֵּחָת כִּי יהוה
אֱלֹהִים אֱלֹהַי עִמָּךְ לֹא יַרְפְּךָ וְלֹא יַעַזְבֶךָּ עַד־לִכְלוֹת
כא כָּל־מְלֶאכֶת עֲבוֹדַת בֵּית־יהוה: וְהִנֵּה מַחְלְקוֹת הַכֹּהֲנִים
וְהַלְוִיִּם לְכָל־עֲבוֹדַת בֵּית הָאֱלֹהִים וְעִמְּךָ בְכָל־מְלָאכָה
לְכָל־נָדִיב בַּחָכְמָה לְכָל־עֲבוֹדָה וְהַשָּׂרִים וְכָל־הָעָם לְכָל־

---

directly. *Metzudos,* there, implies that David was the prophet.

Malbim to our verse is of the opinion that there were two levels of revelation. Samuel received prophecies concerning the plans and taught them to David. David, in turn, required Divine inspiration (רוּחַ הַקֹּדֶשׁ) to apprehend the hidden meanings

and implications of these plans.

הַכֹּל בִּכְתָב מִיַּד ה' עָלַי הִשְׂכִּיל כֹּל מַלְאֲכוֹת הַתַּבְנִית — *It is all in writing, as it was elucidated to me from the hand of HASHEM — all the work of the plan.* The wording here is obscure and there are a number of ways to phrase the verse:

Targum		
הִשְׂכִּיל כֹּל מַלְאֲכוֹת הַתַּבְנִית	מִיַּד ה' עָלַי	הַכֹּל בִּכְתָב
Radak		
כֹּל מַלְאֲכוֹת הַתַּבְנִית	עָלַי הִשְׂכִּיל	הַכֹּל בִּכְתָב מִיַּד ה'
Malbim		
[עָלַי הִשְׂכִּיל] כֹּל מַלְאֲכוֹת הַתַּבְנִית	מִיַּד ה' עָלַי הִשְׂכִּיל	הַכֹּל בִּכְתָב

The phrase הַכֹּל בִּכְתָב can be interpreted in two ways. It could describe how David was given the plans in writing (*Rashi* to *Zevachim* 62a and *Succah* 51b) or it could mean that David gave the plans (*Radak*) or the weights and various measures (*Mefaresh*) to Solomon in writing.

Radak joins הַכֹּל בִּכְתָב to מִיַּד ה' and renders: See, I am giving all the plans over to you in writing as they were received from the hand of God. For God explained it all to me (by means of prophecy). [In *Shorashim* under שכל, *Radak* explains that הִשְׂכִּיל has the connotation *to explain* or *make clear.*] The translation has followed this explanation.

The word עָלַי, in the first person, implies that David is talking. Since from v. 11 onwards the entire account has been in the third person, we must assume that there is an implied, *And David said ...* at some point. *Metzudos* has it at the beginning of this verse. David is saying to Solomon: Look! I am giving you in writing all that has been given to me by God ... *Malbim* has the first phrase הַכֹּל בִּכְתָב in the third

person, following onto v. 11: *And David gave to his son Solomon ... everything in writing.* Then David turns to Solomon and says: *Of all this I was informed by God.*

According to *Malbim* the phrase מִיַּד ה' עָלַי הִשְׂכִּיל is to be taken together, as indicated by the *trop* (cantillation). However, in his view the words עָלַי הִשְׂכִּיל do double duty. They refer both to David's receiving Samuel's prophecy concerning the Temple plans and to his own inspired understanding of those instructions. This inspiration came to him through the Divine spirit. According to this, הִשְׂכִּיל refers to the deep, fundamental understanding which was required and which was granted him by God.

Targum takes הִשְׂכִּיל as *to look upon* (לְאִסְתַּכָּלָא). It fits well into the context although the more usual meaning would be *to teach* or *make clear.* Nevertheless, there is precedent for *Targum's* translation in *Targum Onkelos* to *Genesis* 3:6 where לְהַשְׂכִּיל is also translated לְאִסְתַּכָּלָא בֵּיהּ. According to *Targum,* the verse should be translated: *It was all in writing; it came to*

---

see *Talmudic Encyclopedia* under הַר הַבַּיִת note 22 which points out that no such *Yerushalmi* is known to us.

28

19-21

covered the Ark of the Covenant of HASHEM. ¹⁹ 'It is all in writing, as it was elucidated to me from the hand of HASHEM — all the work of the plan.' ²⁰ David said to Solomon his son, 'Be strong and persevere and do, do not fear and do not falter; for HASHEM, God, my God, is with you. He will neither forsake you nor abandon you, until all the work of the construction of the House of HASHEM is finished. ²¹ See! There are the divisions of Kohanim and Levites for all types of service for the House of God; and with you for all the work are those whose spirit moves them with skill for all the tasks; and the

---

me by the hand of HASHEM to look upon all the work of the plan.

20‑21. In this final exhortation to Solomon, David assures him that God will help him to complete the arduous task of building the Temple, and that all the assistance which he will require will be available to him.

20. חֲזַק וֶאֱמַץ וַעֲשֵׂה — *Be strong and persevere and do.* For חֲזַק וֶאֱמַץ see comm. to 22:12. *Mefaresh* writes that David is exhorting Solomon to be strong and persevere so that he will deserve to retain the eternal kingship which had been promised to him.

However, the cantillation combines חֲזַק וֶאֱמַץ, *be strong and persevere,* with עֲשֵׂה, *and do.* This, in turn, is to be read with the final phrase in the verse — עַד ... וַעֲשֵׂה ... לִכְלוֹת, *and do ... until [it] is finished ...* (*Malbim*). In this context it seems more likely that the exhortation to be strong and persevere refers to the building of the Temple. In spite of the long time it will take to complete the building, he is not to lose heart but to see the work through to the end.

אַל־תִּירָא וְאַל־תֵּחָת — *Do not fear and do not falter.* See comm. to 22:12 for this phrase.

Metzudos adds: Do not fear that you will not be up to the task of completing the whole building.

מְלֶאכֶת עֲבוֹדַת בֵּית־ה׳ — *The work of the construction* [lit. *labor*] *of the House of HASHEM.* The term עֲבוֹדָה here does not refer to the Temple service but to the construction of the Temple.

21. In this verse David assures Solomon that everything he may possibly require will be available to him. If he is worried that once the Temple is built it will not function efficiently, he is reassured that the

divisions of *Kohanim* and Levites are there. If he is worried that there will be a dearth of skilled labor, he is promised that able artisans will be with him. And if, finally, he is not sure of sufficient supplies to do the necessary work, David tells him that both the officials and the people will provide all that is needed (*Malbim*).

וְעִמְּךָ בְכָל־מְלָאכָה לְכָל־נָדִיב בַּחָכְמָה לְכָל־עֲבוֹדָה — *And with you for all the work are those whose spirit moves them with skill for all the tasks.* The translation follows *Radak.* He seems to read לְכָל without the first ל, as though it were written כָל. [*Ibn Janach, Sefer HaRikmah* 6, adduces many examples for such a redundant ל, among them עַד לִכְלוֹת of the previous verse.]

He writes that לְכָל־נָדִיב בַּחָכְמָה לְכָל־עֲבוֹדָה is comparable to, כָּל אֲשֶׁר יִדְּבֶנּוּ לִבּוֹ לְקָרְבָה אֶל הַמְּלָאכָה לַעֲשׂוֹת אוֹתָהּ. Now, there is no such verse in the Torah. We have כָּל־ אִישׁ אֲשֶׁר יִדְּבֶנּוּ לִבּוֹ at *Exodus* 25:2 in connection with the donations for the Tabernacle, and we have כֹל אֲשֶׁר נָשָׂאוֹ לִבּוֹ לְקָרְבָה אֶל־הַמְּלָאכָה לַעֲשׂוֹת אֹתָהּ at *Exodus* 36:2. It seems likely that *Radak* had this second verse in mind and that instead of יִדְּבֶנּוּ we should read נָשָׂאוֹ.

If so, *Radak* would seem to be drawing a parallel between [בַּחָכְמָה] נְדִיבוּת and נְשִׂיאוּת לֵב.

Now at *Exodus* 35:21 we have the two expressions together: כָּל־אִישׁ אֲשֶׁר־נְשָׂאוֹ לִבּוֹ וְכֹל אֲשֶׁר נָדְבָה רוּחוֹ אֹתוֹ ... and *Ramban,* there, makes a point of defining them differently from one another. נְדִיבוּת describes an act of generous giving; נְשִׂיאוּת לֵב, a state of pride and confidence in one's abilities. [See also above, 25:19.] *Ibn Ezra* (*Exodus,* there) explains: a proud heart (לֵב רָם).

It is possible that *Radak* feels that they are closer in meaning to one another.

The combination of נָדִיב with בַּחָכְמָה in

א וַיֹּאמֶר דָּוִיד הַמֶּלֶךְ לְכָל־הַקָּהָל אֶת־דְּבָרָיו: א דִּבְרֵיךְ:

שְׁלֹמֹה בְנִי אֶחָד בָּחַר־בּוֹ אֱלֹהִים נַעַר וָרָךְ וְהַמְּלָאכָה

ב גְדוֹלָה כִּי לֹא לְאָדָם הַבִּירָה כִּי לַיהוָה אֱלֹהִים: וּכְכָל־

כֹּחִי הֲכִינוֹתִי לְבֵית־אֱלֹהַי הַזָּהָב ׀ לַזָּהָב וְהַכֶּסֶף לַכֶּסֶף

וְהַנְּחֹשֶׁת לַנְּחֹשֶׁת הַבַּרְזֶל לַבַּרְזֶל וְהָעֵצִים לָעֵצִים אַבְנֵי־

שֹׁהַם וּמִלּוּאִים אַבְנֵי־פוּךְ וְרִקְמָה וְכֹל אֶבֶן יְקָרָה וְאַבְנֵי־

ג שַׁיִשׁ לָרֹב: וְעוֹד בִּרְצוֹתִי בְּבֵית אֱלֹהַי יֶשׁ־לִי סְגֻלָּה זָהָב

וָכֶסֶף נָתַתִּי לְבֵית־אֱלֹהַי לְמַעְלָה מִכָּל־הֲכִינוֹתִי לְבֵית

ד הַקֹּדֶשׁ: שְׁלֹשֶׁת אֲלָפִים כִּכְּרֵי זָהָב מִזְּהַב אוֹפִיר וְשִׁבְעַת

---

our verse recalls *Exodus* 35:26: אֲשֶׁר נָשָׂא לִבָּן אֹתָנָה בְּחָכְמָה which might argue for *Radak's* equating of the two expressions.

Finally, the word חָכְמָה seems to mean not only general wisdom but also the skill required by the artisan — see *Exodus* 31:6.

Our rendering *whose spirit moves them,*

accommodates both the idea of voluntarism implied in נדב and the inspired self-confidence implied in נשא לב.

לְכָל־דְּבָרֶיךְ — *For your every command.* They stand ready to execute your every command *(Commentators).*

XXIX

◆§ David's Final Charge to the People

After charging Solomon, David now turns to the people, exhorting them to help the young king in his great task. The people respond by donating great treasures toward the project.

1. שְׁלֹמֹה בְנִי אֶחָד — *Solomon my son is only one.* Even a hundred people would find the task of building this huge edifice staggering. How much more, then, my son Solomon who is only one person and, moreover, is still young and tender *(Mefaresh).*

בָּחַר־בּוֹ אֱלֹהִים — *[And] God has chosen him.* God has chosen him to rule over Israel — itself a task that can consume all his time. How then will he be able to undertake the task of building *(Metzudos)?*

נַעַר וָרָךְ — *Young and tender.* He is young in years and has been brought up in a sheltered environment which has not prepared him for the taxing tasks which lie ahead of him *(Metzudos).*

In the tradition of the Sages, Solomon

was just twelve years old when he became king[1] *(Radak).*

כִּי לֹא לְאָדָם — *For ... is not for man.* If the house were for a human occupant it would be possible to build a smaller house. But a dwelling place for HASHEM, God, must have the bold design which makes the task so intimidating *(Metzudos).*

הַבִּירָה — *The Palace.* That is, the Temple *(Metzudos).* The use of the word בִּירָה for Temple does not recur in Scripture except at v. 19 below. In Talmudic literature it occurs frequently with this meaning (e.g., *Yoma* 9b).

This Talmudic usage seems to accord with *Resh Lakish* who, based on our verse, holds that בִּירָה is used for the entire Temple complex. By contrast, R' Yochanan thinks that it refers only

---

1. *Radak* supplies the data on which this tradition is based. Solomon was born at the time of the story of Amnon and Tamar. Absalom assassinated Amnon two years later and then fled to Geshur for three years. He returned to Jerusalem and spent two years readying himself for his rebellion against David. His rebellion was followed by a famine which lasted three years. The census which David then initiated lasted nine months, which brings us to David's final year during which he made his preparations for the building of the Temple. We thus have a total of twelve years [2+3+2+3+1 (9 months) +1 = 12].

29

1-4

Then King David said to the whole congregation: 'Solomon my son is only one [and] God has chosen him although he is young and tender;· and the work is great, for the Palace is not for man but for HASHEM, God. ² With all my might I have prepared for the House of my God the gold for the [things of] gold, the silver for the [things of] silver, the copper for the [things of] copper, the iron for the [things of] iron, the wood for the [things of] wood, the shoham and setting stones, puch stones, and tapestries, together with all manner of precious stones and great quantities of marble stones. ³ Moreover, because of my desire for the House of my God, I have treasures of gold and silver; I have given [these] to the House of my God over and above that which I have previously prepared for the sacred House. ⁴ Three thousand talents of gold, of the gold of Ophir, and seven thousand talents of refined silver to overlay the walls of

to a citadel which stood on the Temple Mount. See *Yerushalmi, Pesachim* 7:8 and *Zevachim* 104b. See also *Aruch HaShalem* under בִּירָה.

2. ... וּכְכָל־כֹּחִי הֲכִינוֹתִי — *With all my might I have prepared.* I have done my best. Everything that I was able to do I did *(Malbim)*.

הַזָּהָב לַזָּהָב ... — *The gold for the [things of] gold.* The gold which I have amassed is to be used for those utensils which are to be made from gold *(Metzudos)*.

אַבְנֵי ... וּמִלּוּאִים — *Setting stones* [lit. *filling stones*]. The precious stones were set into sockets, thus filling the holes *(Metzudos)*.

אַבְנֵי־פוּךְ — *Puch stones.* These are precious stones the color of פוּךְ, a substance used to color the eyes *(Metzudos,* and see *Metzudos* to *Isaiah* 54:11). *Ibn Ezra* to *Isaiah* (there) writes that *puch* is a precious stone colored black.

Since the precise identity of both this stone and the *shoham* stone is unclear, the translation has retained the Hebrew names rather than offer speculative translations.

וְרִקְמָה — *And tapestries.* These are curtains woven from strands of colored thread *(Metzudos)*. *Radak* translates *colored garments.*

Ralbag, presumably because the word occurs in a list of precious stones, believes that רִקְמָה is also a stone. It is of a type which tapestry makers used to use as sequins in the fabrics which they made and which are therefore called *tapestry stones.*

וְאַבְנֵי־שַׁיִשׁ — *And ... of marble stones.* These

were for pillars, the tables (see *Shekalim* 6:4 and comm. to 28:16) and the floor *(Mefaresh)*.

3. ... וְעוֹד בִּרְצוֹתִי בְּבֵית אֱלֹהַי — *Moreover, because of my desire for the House of my God ...* Because I am so eager that the Temple be built, I have gathered and donated even more treasures for it, as detailed below *(Mefaresh; Metzudos)*.

סְגֻלָּה זָהָב וָכָסֶף — *Treasures of gold and silver.* סְגֻלָּה is a storage place in which a person keeps his most precious possessions (see *Rashi* to *Exodus* 19:5).

נָתַתִּי לְבֵית־אֱלֹהַי לְמַעְלָה מִכָּל־הֲכִינוֹתִי — *I have given [these] to the House of my God over and above that which I have previously prepared.* The translation follows *Metzudos,* who reads לְמַעְלָה together with the following phrase, despite the *trop* which has it with the previous phrase.

Malbim explains the progression from the previous verse to ours as follows: With all my might I have prepared all the essentials for the building (v. 2). But, because I wish to honor my God's House more than with the minimum requirement, I am donating my own wealth so that it can be used for non-essentials, that is to coat the walls in gold, for which the material which I have prepared would not suffice.

4. מִזְּהַב אוֹפִיר — *Of the gold of Ophir.* The gold of Ophir was highly prized, as can be seen from the account in *I Kings* 9:28, where Solomon sent ships to Ophir for gold.

ה אֲלָפִים כִּכַּר־בֶּסֶף מְזֻקָּק לָטוּחַ קִירוֹת הַבָּתִּים: לַזָּהָב
לַזָּהָב וְלַכֶּסֶף לַכֶּסֶף וּלְכָל־מְלָאכָה בְּיַד חָרָשִׁים וּמִי
ו מִתְנַדֵּב לְמַלֹּאות יָדוֹ הַיּוֹם לַיהוה: וַיִּתְנַדְּבוּ שָׂרֵי הָאָבוֹת
וְשָׂרֵי | שִׁבְטֵי יִשְׂרָאֵל וְשָׂרֵי הָאֲלָפִים וְהַמֵּאוֹת וּלְשָׂרֵי
ז מְלֶאכֶת הַמֶּלֶךְ: וַיִּתְּנוּ לַעֲבוֹדַת בֵּית־הָאֱלֹהִים זָהָב כִּכָּרִים
חֲמֵשֶׁת־אֲלָפִים וַאֲדַרְכֹנִים רִבּוֹ וְכֶסֶף כִּכָּרִים עֲשֶׂרֶת
אֲלָפִים וּנְחֹשֶׁת רִבּוֹ וּשְׁמוֹנַת אֲלָפִים כִּכָּרִים וּבַרְזֶל מֵאָה־
ח אֶלֶף כִּכָּרִים: וְהַנִּמְצָא אִתּוֹ אֲבָנִים נָתְנוּ לְאוֹצַר בֵּית־
ט יהוה עַל יַד־יְחִיאֵל הַגֵּרְשֻׁנִּי: וַיִּשְׂמְחוּ הָעָם עַל־הִתְנַדְּבָם
כִּי בְּלֵב שָׁלֵם הִתְנַדְּבוּ לַיהוה וְגַם דָּוִיד הַמֶּלֶךְ שָׂמַח
י שִׂמְחָה גְדוֹלָה: וַיְבָרֶךְ דָּוִיד אֶת־יהוה לְעֵינֵי כָּל־
הַקָּהָל וַיֹּאמֶר דָּוִיד בָּרוּךְ אַתָּה יהוה אֱלֹהֵי יִשְׂרָאֵל אָבִינוּ

לָטוּחַ קִירוֹת הַבָּתִּים ... כֶּסֶף ... — *Silver ... to overlay the walls of the chambers.* The chambers are evidently the Holy of Holies and the Sanctuary (*Rashi, I Kings 6:21*). However, the *Kings* passage makes clear that the Temple walls were coated with gold, not silver. For this reason *Radak* and *Metzudos* suggest that *to overlay the walls of the chambers* refers only to the three thousand talents of gold, not to the seven thousand talents of silver.

Alternatively, it may perhaps be that just as in the previous chapters (v. 15) David had anticipated that silver would be required — because he did not realize just how wealthy Solomon would be — so, here too, David may have planned for some of the coating to be done in silver, but in the event this proved unnecessary when enough gold was available.

5. לַזָּהָב לַזָּהָב — *Gold for the [things of] gold.* The phrase is a continuation of v. 3: *I have given ... the gold [that is required] for [that which is to be made out of] gold.*

The use of לַזָּהָב in place of the more usual אֶת הַזָּהָב [that is, the substitution of ל for אֶת] an Aramaism which occurs frequently in *Chronicles.* Two examples which come from this chapter are ... וַיְבָרְכוּ ל in v. 20 and ... וַיַּמְלִיכוּ ל in v. 22. In pure Hebrew both these verbs normally appear with אֶת. [An example among many of

this development with the root ברך: תְּבָרְכוּ כֹה אֶת־בְּנֵי יִשְׂרָאֵל (*Numbers 6:23*) as compared to כֹּהֲנִים מְבָרְכִים לְיִשְׂרָאֵל in *Chullin* 48a.]

וּמִי מִתְנַדֵּב — *Now who will donate.* The materials for the building are at hand; the artisans are skillful and willing to work. But the house of God requires the heart of the people. Would the people show their love for God by giving of their wealth for the building (*Malbim*)?

לְמַלֹּאות יָדוֹ הַיּוֹם לה׳ — *So that he may consecrate himself to HASHEM on this day.* The idiom לְמַלֹּאת אֶת הַיָּד, lit. *to fill the hand,* is used in Scripture to describe a consecration (חֲנוּךְ) towards a given purpose. See, for example, *Exodus 29:9.* The idiom conveys a sense of completing something that had been missing; bringing something to perfection (*Sforno to Exodus 28:41*). Thus, in our context it would mean that by donating towards the fund for the building, the people were consecrating themselves towards further efforts in that direction. Whatever they would give on this occasion would only be a beginning (*Metzudos*).

6. The list of officials in this verse covers all those mentioned in 28:1 but not in the same order and not by the same names:

CHAPTER 28	CHAPTER 29
(a) שָׂרֵי הַשְּׁבָטִים, *leaders of the tribes*	(a) שָׂרֵי הָאָבוֹת, *leaders of the families*
(b) שָׂרֵי הַמַּחְלְקוֹת, *leaders of the divisions*	(b) שָׂרֵי שִׁבְטֵי יִשְׂרָאֵל, *leaders of the tribes of Israel*
(c) שָׂרֵי הָאֲלָפִים, *officers of the thousands*	(c) שָׂרֵי הָאֲלָפִים, *officers of the thousands*

29

5-10

the chambers. ⁵ Gold for the [things of] gold and silver for the [things of] silver, for all the work of the artisans; now who will donate so that he may consecrate himself to HASHEM on this day.' ⁶ So the leaders of the families, the leaders of the tribes of Israel, the officers of the thousands and the hundreds and the officials in charge of the king's work donated. ⁷ And they gave for the construction of the House of God five thousand talents of gold and ten thousand adarkonim, ten thousand talents of silver, eighteen thousand talents of copper and one hundred thousand talents of iron. ⁸ And whoever had stones donated them to the treasury of the House of HASHEM through Yechiel the Gershonite. ⁹ The people rejoiced over their having donated, for they donated to HASHEM wholeheartedly; and King David also rejoiced with great joy. ¹⁰ Then David praised HASHEM in the presence of the entire congregation, and David said, 'Blessed are You HASHEM, God of Israel our forefather, from the most distant past to the remotest future. ¹¹ Yours, O HASHEM, is the

CHAPTER 28	CHAPTER 29
(d) שָׂרֵי הַמֵּאוֹת, officers of the hundreds	(d) שָׂרֵי הַמֵּאוֹת, officers of the hundreds
(e) שָׂרֵי כָל רְכֻשׁ וּמִקְנֶה, officials ... of all property and livestock	(e) שָׂרֵי מְלֶאכֶת הַמֶּלֶךְ, officials ... of the king's work

שָׂרֵי הָאָבוֹת — The leaders of the families. This is the title given to the officials who headed the monthly relays at 27:1ff. In ch. 28 they are called שָׂרֵי הַמַּחְלְקוֹת, leaders of the divisions (Mefaresh).

וְשָׂרֵי שִׁבְטֵי יִשְׂרָאֵל — The leaders of the tribes of Israel. These are given at 27:16ff.

וּלְשָׂרֵי מְלֶאכֶת הַמֶּלֶךְ — And the officials in charge of the king's work. These are the officials listed at 27:26ff (Metzudos). In ch. 28 they are called the officials in charge of all the king's property and his livestock.

The ל in וּלְשָׂרֵי seems to be redundant. Sefer HaRikmah 6 notes the Scriptural idiosyncrasy of occasionally adding an unneeded ל. Its use in a list similar to our verse would be Leviticus 11:46 where the ל in וּלְכָל־נֶפֶשׁ הַשֹּׁרֶצֶת is also redundant.

7. וַאֲדַרְכֹנִים — And ... adarkonim. An ancient coin (Metzudos).

8. אֲבָנִים — Stones. Targum renders pearls.

יְחִיאֵל — Yechiel. See 26:21.

9. כִּי בְלֶב שָׁלֵם הִתְנַדְּבוּ לַה׳ — For they donated to HASHEM wholeheartedly. They had neither been forced nor shamed into giving. They had no reservations about their generous donations (Mefaresh).

וְגַם דָּוִיד הַמֶּלֶךְ שָׂמַח שִׂמְחָה גְדוֹלָה — And King

David also rejoiced with great joy. The word וְגַם hints at the fact that David's joy was greater than the others' — because he had initiated the matter (Mefaresh).

◄§ In Praise of Hashem

10-19. In this passage, David sings a song of praise to God. Superhuman efforts had been made and stupendous sums had been amassed so that the dream of a Temple might become a reality in Solomon's time. But for none of this does any praise accrue to David or the people. If they found the energy to perform their great deeds, if they possessed the gold and silver which made their generous donations possible, it was all a gift from God. They were returning to God but a fraction of the bounty which He had showered upon them.

10. וַיְבָרֶךְ דָּוִיד אֶת־ה׳ — Then David praised HASHEM. ברך has been rendered here as praise rather than bless in accordance with Ibn Janach and Radak in their respective dictionaries. They demonstrate conclusively that when used in connection with God, the word means praise.

אֱלֹהֵי יִשְׂרָאֵל אָבִינוּ — God of Israel our forefather. The translation is in accordance with Bereishis Rabbah 70:2, and as accepted by the commentators, that אָבִינוּ refers to the patriarch Israel [Jacob] and is

[355]   I Chronicles

יא מֵעוֹלָם וְעַד־־־־עוֹלָם: לְךָ יְהוָה הַגְּדֻלָּה וְהַגְּבוּרָה וְהַתִּפְאֶרֶת וְהַנֵּצַח וְהַהוֹד כִּי־כֹל בַּשָּׁמַיִם וּבָאָרֶץ לְךָ

not an appositional noun to God of Israel. (Thus: Praised are You ... HASHEM [Who is] God of Israel [who was] our forefather.)

In this interpretation Jacob, and not the other patriarchs, is mentioned because it was he who first consecrated his property to God (*Genesis* 28:20), and David and the people were now walking in his footsteps (*Midrash*). Or, as *Radak* explains, because he was the first one concerned with the building of a House for God (v. 22 there). *Malbim* adds that he was also the first to describe the site as the 'House of God' (v. 17).

מֵעוֹלָם וְעַד־עוֹלָם — *From the most distant past to the remotest future.* The translation follows *Hirsch's* treatment of this phrase (*Siddur*). The word עוֹלָם is used throughout Scripture to denote *eternity*, both looking backwards (*Isaiah* 46:9) and looking into the future (*Deuteronomy* 32:40).

Targum, followed by *Metzudos*, renders: *From this world to the next world.*[1]

Ralbag points out that this formula was used in all blessings which were made in the course of the Temple worship (see *Berachos* 54a and 63a).

11. This verse may be understood at a number of different levels (see *Siddur Bais Yaakov*). It has found its way into the siddur as part of the liturgy recited when the Torah is taken out of the ark to be read. In response to the reader's call: 'Exalt God with me and let us praise His Name together,' the congregation responds by reciting our verse. Of all the sections of

Scripture which could have been chosen, it seems that just our verse is considered the most apt with which to exalt God and to praise Him; perhaps it is the most comprehensive.

Another approach is that the verse is part of the jubilant thanksgiving which filled David's heart at the moment at which he saw his efforts to lay the groundwork for the building of the Temple crowned with success. Short of the actual building of the edifice, David had accomplished as much as a human being could accomplish towards creating a focus for the Divine Presence on earth. As David looks back, he passes before his mind's eye the many personal attributes upon which he had to call in order to bring his efforts to fruition. As he considers each one, he realizes that each one of them is a gift from God. For each of them he must sing God's praises. It is thus possible to interpret each word in a narrow sense — entirely within the context of the moment within which this paean was first uttered.

On yet another level, the masters of the *Kabbalah* find in it a listing of the *sefirah*-emanations, those mystic manifestations through which man can apprehend God (see ArtScroll *Zemiroth* p. 226). It is in this context that the verse appears in the *Hoshana* service on Succos. [See ArtScroll *Hoshanos* on Hoshana 1 st. 3 and on p. 45.] However, this approach does not fall within the scope of this commentary.

We may sum up that we have here two different perspectives, the comprehensive one and the particular one. Most of the classical commentators to *Chronicles* tend towards the second, or particular, perspective, although it seems clear that they

---

1. It seems likely that the source for *Targum's* translation is the Mishnah in *Berachos* 54a. There we learn that originally it was the custom that all blessings made during worship in the Temple had the wording: בָּרוּךְ אַתָּה ה' אֱלֹהֵי יִשְׂרָאֵל עַד הָעוֹלָם and then concluded with the appropriate ending [such as בָּרוּךְ חוֹנֵן הַדָּעַת — see *Rashi* there. This phrase was misinterpreted by the heretics to indicate that there was no life after death; i.e., that there was only one עוֹלָם, *world*, not two. Because of this Ezra and his colleagues instituted a new reading. Henceforth one would say מִן הָעוֹלָם וְעַד הָעוֹלָם, *from this world to the next world.* [There are other readings in the Mishnah according to which the original custom was to say מִן הָעוֹלָם and Ezra added עַד הָעוֹלָם. This does affect the present discussion.]

However, what was meant by the original version בָּרוּךְ אַתָּה ה' אֱלֹהֵי יִשְׂרָאֵל עַד הָעוֹלָם? If עוֹלָם means *world* in this context, what could possibly have been meant with the phrase: *up to the world?* It seems clear that the original meaning was *forever* [as for example in *Psalms* 28:9]. The heretics distorted the meaning and claimed that it meant *world* and that the phrase meant that God should be praised 'up to [the end of] the world' but not beyond — because there was no life beyond this world. The new reading, which did not change the basic meaning implying eternity, would not be able to be distorted because even if the heretics would claim the meaning *world*, there would still be mention of two worlds.

If this is correct then the basic meaning of the phrase would remain as it has been translated.

greatness, the might, the glory, the triumph, and the splendor, for Yours is all that is in the heavens and upon the earth. Yours, O

would not deny the possibility of a more comprehensive understanding. The Talmud inclines towards the first, or comprehensive, perspective, although there too we find that the Sages distill the general terms — *greatness, might* and so on — into concrete events in which these particular attributes were manifest. We shall offer three levels of interpretation deriving from these two perspectives. First the particular application to the Temple preparations will be given, then the more general meaning grounded in the comprehensive approach, and then some of the concrete historical occurrences in which the Sages saw these general qualities manifested.

לְךָ ה' ... — *Yours, O HASHEM* ... According to the second, or particular, perspective in which David sees all his personal attributes coming to him from God, this לְךָ must be understood as מִמְּךָ, *from You (Siddur Bais Yaakov).* According to the other perspective the term has its more usual meaning: Yours, O God, are all these qualities.

הַגְּדֻלָה — *The greatness.* The greatness with which I find myself endowed *(Metzudos).*

Mefaresh goes back to 17:19 where David speaks of the גְּדוּלָה, *greatness,* which God had granted him. He interprets that phrase as referring to the promise that Solomon would build the Temple. [But see there, in context, where it seems to refer to the perpetuation of the Davidic line.] Alternatively, the *Mefaresh* points to 22:5 where David describes the Temple to be built as לְהַגְדִּיל לְמַעְלָה, *to make exceedingly great.* Both these interpretations assume the second perspective. David is ascribing his ability to make the Temple preparations to God.

Ralbag [first perspective] writes: *Yours, O HASHEM, is the greatness:* in that You are immeasurably exalted over everything that exists.

Berachos 58a offers two acts in which God's greatness was manifest. It refers to the act of creation or to the splitting of the Red Sea.

וְהַגְּבוּרָה — *The might.* David had to fight many battles in order to amass the wealth which he had set aside for the Temple (see ch. 18). Here he thanks God for giving him the might to fight those battles *(Metzudos).*

Ralbag writes: ... *and the might* to do whatever You desire. By contrast, all creatures are subject to limitations for they cannot change their nature.

Berachos 58a sees the expression referring either to the *Exodus* from Egypt or to the death of the firstborn.

וְהַתִּפְאֶרֶת — *The glory.* Isaiah 60:13 describes the beautifying of the Temple as לְפָאֵר מְקוֹם מִקְדָשִׁי, *to glorify the place of My Sanctuary,* and above at 22:5 David talks of the Temple as being לְשֵׁם וּלְתִפְאֶרֶת, *famous and glorious.* Thus, with this expression David is thanking God for enabling him to collect the treasures for the building of the Temple *(Mefaresh).*

Ralbag writes: Only *You have glory.* For if a man were to prevail over another or even over many who are much stronger than he, still neither glory (תִּפְאֶרֶת), nor victory (נֶצַח), nor splendor (הוֹד) would accrue to him but only to You — for it is You Who are the source of his strength.

Berachos 58a sees תִּפְאֶרֶת, *glory,* as referring either to the time when the sun and the moon stood still for Joshua or to the giving of the Torah at Sinai.

וְהַנֵצַח — *The triumph.* This refers to David's victories (נֶצַח from נצח, *to triumph)* over the nations which enabled him to consecrate the spoils towards the Temple *(Mefaresh* and *Metzudos).*

Berachos 58a has it refer to the eventual victory over Rome [that is, the resolution to the present exile]. Another possibility offered there is that it refers to Jerusalem — Israel's fortress, surrounded as it is by mountains, and thus a help in gaining victory over their enemies *(Maharsha).*

וְהַהוֹד — *And the splendor.* The splendor that is mine comes to me from You *(Metzudos).* The expression הוֹד מַלְכוּת, *royal splendor,* in v. 25 leads us to suppose that reference is to David's kingship, which He ascribes to God.

Berachos 58a has it refer either to the war at the river Arnon *(Numbers 21:14)* or to the holy Temple.

כִּי־כֹל בַּשָׁמַיִם וּבָאָרֶץ — *For [Yours] is all that is in the heavens and upon the earth.* The translation has inserted the word *Yours* in this phrase in accordance with *Mefaresh* and *Metzudos,* who have it refer back to

יב יהוה֩ הַמַּמְלָכָ֨ה וְהַמִּתְנַשֵּׂ֤א לְכֹ֣ל ׀ לְרֹ֔אשׁ וְהָעֹ֖שֶׁר
וְהַכָּבוֹד֮ מִלְּפָנֶ֒יךָ֒ וְאַתָּה֙ מוֹשֵׁ֣ל בַּכֹּ֔ל וּבְיָֽדְךָ֖ כֹּ֣חַ וּגְבוּרָ֑ה
יג וּבְיָ֣דְךָ֔ לְגַדֵּ֥ל וּלְחַזֵּ֖ק לַכֹּֽל: וְעַתָּ֣ה אֱלֹהֵ֔ינוּ מוֹדִ֥ים אֲנַ֖חְנוּ
יד לָ֑ךְ וּמְהַלְלִ֖ים לְשֵׁ֥ם תִּפְאַרְתֶּֽךָ: וְכִ֨י מִ֤י אֲנִי֙ וּמִ֣י עַמִּ֔י
כִּֽי־נַעְצֹ֣ר כֹּ֔חַ לְהִתְנַדֵּ֖ב כָּזֹ֑את כִּֽי־מִמְּךָ֣ הַכֹּ֔ל וּמִיָּֽדְךָ֖
טו נָתַ֥נּוּ לָֽךְ: כִּֽי־גֵרִ֨ים אֲנַ֧חְנוּ לְפָנֶ֛יךָ וְתוֹשָׁבִ֖ים כְּכָל־אֲבֹתֵ֑ינוּ
טז כַּצֵּ֧ל ׀ יָמֵ֣ינוּ עַל־הָאָ֗רֶץ וְאֵ֥ין מִקְוֶֽה: יהו֣ה אֱלֹהֵ֔ינוּ כֹּ֣ל
הֶהָמ֤וֹן הַזֶּה֙ אֲשֶׁ֣ר הֲכִינֹ֔נוּ לִבְנֽוֹת־לְךָ֥ בַ֖יִת לְשֵׁ֣ם קָדְשֶׁ֑ךָ
°הוֹא ק׳ יז מִיָּֽדְךָ֥ °הִ֖יא וּלְךָ֥ הַכֹּֽל: וְיָדַ֣עְתִּי אֱלֹהַ֔י כִּ֥י אַתָּה֙ בֹּחֵ֣ן

the לְךָ, *Yours*, at the beginning of the sentence. Greatness, might, glory, triumph and splendor are all Yours because Yours is everything in the world.

This must be the meaning of the phrase if we follow the *trop* which makes a stop after our phrase. *Radak* and *Ralbag*, though, read this phrase together with the next — Yours, O HASHEM, *is the kingship over everything in heaven and on earth.*

Berachos 58a has this phrase referring to the wars against Sisera (see *Judges* ch. 4).

לְךָ ה' הַמַּמְלָכָה — *Yours, O HASHEM, is the kingdom.* It is You Who gives kings the power to rule *(Metzudos).*

Berachos 58a has this refer to the wars against Amalek.

וְהַמִּתְנַשֵּׂא לְכֹל לְרֹאשׁ — *And [You] are the One Who is exalted over every leader.* רֹאשׁ, which usually means *head*, is used here as *chief*. God is greater than any leader could be *(Radak* and *Metzudos).*

Berachos 58a has a different interpretation. It is You Who cause the elevation of everyone who is appointed chief over something. No one becomes a leader without Divine Providence influencing the choice. 'Even the superintendent of the wells is appointed by heaven!'

In another interpretation, *Berachos* has the phrase hinting at the wars of Gog and Maggog (see *Ezekiel* chs. 38 and 29).

12. וְהָעֹשֶׁר וְהַכָּבוֹד מִלְּפָנֶיךָ — *Wealth and honor come from You.* You are the source of all the wealth and honor which any man can acquire *(Metzudos).*

Mefaresh has the statement apply specifically to the gold and silver which David had gathered in preparation for building the Temple. It all came from God.

וְאַתָּה מוֹשֵׁל בַּכֹּל — *For You rule over all.* The

prefix וַ, *vav*, is to be understood here as *because.* Because You rule over everything, it follows that all wealth and honor must derive from You *(Mefaresh).*

... וּבְיָדְךָ כֹּחַ וּגְבוּרָה — *In Your hand is power and might. Ralbag* reads this together with the next phrase. Because strength and might are in Your hands, You are able to make great and strengthen anyone.

13. מוֹדִים אֲנַחְנוּ לָךְ — *We thank You.* We thank You for the great wealth which You have given us *(Metzudos).*

מוֹדִים has been translated as *thank* in accordance with *Metzudos.* In fact, though, the root ידה often means *to praise.* Therefore, מוֹדִים here could well have a parallel meaning to מְהַלְלִים in the next phrase, as it does in expressions such as לְהוֹדוֹת לְהַלֵּל which occur in the *Siddur.*

לְשֵׁם תִּפְאַרְתֶּךָ — *Your majestic Name.* This expression occurs only once more in Scripture. *Isaiah* 63:14 talks of a שֵׁם תִּפְאֶרֶת. There *Radak* explains: A name which causes God's majesty to be known and appreciated.

While the combination שֵׁם תִּפְאֶרֶת occurs only in these two places, we do find the two concepts linked together in one context. Thus, for example, we have phrases like לִתְהִלָּה וּלְשֵׁם וּלְתִפְאֶרֶת in *Deuteronomy* 26:19. In all these and similar cases the word שֵׁם has the connotation of *fame* rather than simply *name.*

14. וְכִי מִי אֲנִי ... — *For who am I ...* The question is rhetorical. Could anyone possibly suppose that I or my people could have collected these vast treasures on our own *(Metzudos)?*

כִּי־נַעְצֹר כֹּחַ — *That we can muster the strength.* The idiom עָצַר כֹּחַ is found several times in *Chronicles* and twice in *Daniel.* The root עצר usually means *to gather* or

HASHEM, is the kingdom and [You] are the One Who is exalted over every leader. ¹² Wealth and honor come from You, for You rule over all; in Your hand is power and might, and it is in Your hand to make anyone great and strong. ¹³ So now, our God, we thank You and praise Your majestic Name. ¹⁴ For who am I and who are my people that we can muster the strength to donate like this; for surely it is all from You and we have given You only that which has come from Your hand. ¹⁵ For we are but strangers before You and sojourners, as were all our fathers. Our days on earth are like a shadow and there is no hope. ¹⁶ O HASHEM, our God, all this vast store which we have prepared to build a house for You for Your Holy Name, it is from Your hand and all belongs to You. ¹⁷ And I know, my God,

---

hold in, thus to gather up the energy and retain it in sufficient capacity to make a spurt of strength possible.

כִּי־מִמְּךָ הַכֹּל — *For surely it is all from You.* Surely then we must conclude that it all comes from You.

וּמִיָּדְךָ נָתַנּוּ לָךְ — *And we have given You only that which has come from Your hand.* No praise accrues to us for what we are donating to the Temple; we are giving nothing which we did not first receive from You.

The Mishnah in *Avos* 3:7, based on our verse, teaches: Give to Him from His own — for you and yours are His.

Vayikra Rabbah 27:2 comments on the verse in *Job* 41:3, *Who has preceded Me that I should pay?* Who praised Me before I gave him a soul; who fulfilled the command to circumcise before I gave him a son; who built a fence [to prevent anyone from falling] before I gave him a roof; who affixed a *mezuzah* before I gave him a house; who built a *succah* before I gave him a place; who used a *lulav* before I gave him the money [with which to buy it]; who put *tzitzis* on his garment before I gave it to him; who left the corner of his field for the poor before I gave him the field; who gave the *Kohen terumah* before I gave him his silo; who gave *challah* before I gave him the dough; who brought a sacrifice before I gave him the animal?

15. כִּי־גֵרִים אֲנַחְנוּ לְפָנֶיךָ — *For we are but strangers before You.* Relative to the infinity of Your existence, we are as strangers in the land. How then could we possibly have amassed such wealth without Your help *(Metzudos)?*

וְתוֹשָׁבִים כְּכָל־אֲבֹתֵינוּ — *And sojourners, as were all our fathers.* And even if we view ourselves as more permanent residents (תּוֹשָׁב), our permanence is certainly not greater than that of our fathers who have

already died. Indeed, then, we are really only strangers *(Metzudos).*

כַּצֵּל יָמֵינוּ עַל־הָאָרֶץ — *Our days on earth are like a shadow.* Just as the shadow never remains long in one place, but changes location constantly with the movement of the sun *(Metzudos),* so too are our days on earth — transient and impermanent *(Radak).*

וְאֵין מִקְוֶה — *And there is no hope.* There is no possibility for anyone to extend his life beyond the period fixed for him by God *(Radak).*

16. כָּל הֶהָמוֹן הַזֶּה — *All this vast store.* All this wealth of silver and gold and other materials which have been prepared *(Radak).*

מִיָּדְךָ הִיא וּלְךָ הַכֹּל — *It is from Your hand and all belongs to You.* The thought expressed here seems identical with that in v. 14. But what is the purpose of the repetition?

A careful study of the two passages (see chart on next page) yields a definite difference in nuance between (A) and (B). This can be clearly detected in 6 where in (A) the giver is still in evidence — the verb נָתַנּוּ, *we have given,* is used — and the verse simply makes the point that what he gives came to him from God. There is a recognition of God's role in granting the wealth, but after God has given it, it is the recipient's and it is he who *gives* it. By contrast (B)6 does not mention the act of giving at all. The wealth not only comes from God but is still God's.

This difference is also reflected in 3 where (A) uses לְהִתְנַדֵּב, *to donate,* while (B) has הֲכִינוֹנוּ, *to prepare.* The implication is clear. In (A) the recipient of God's bounty

לֵבָב וּמֵישָׁרִים תִּרְצֶה אֲנִי בְּיֹשֶׁר לְבָבִי הִתְנַדַּבְתִּי כָל־
אֵלֶּה וְעַתָּה עַמְּךָ הַנִּמְצְאוּ־פֹה רָאִיתִי בְשִׂמְחָה לְהִתְנַדֶּב־
לָךְ: יהוֹה אֱלֹהֵי אַבְרָהָם יִצְחָק וְיִשְׂרָאֵל אֲבֹתֵינוּ שָׁמְרָה־
יח זֹּאת לְעוֹלָם לְיֵצֶר מַחְשְׁבוֹת לְבַב עַמֶּךָ וְהָכֵן לְבָבָם

(A) V. 14	(B) Vs. 15 and 16
(1) כִּי מִי אֲנִי וּמִי עַמִּי, *For who am I and who are my people*	(1) כִּי־גֵרִים אֲנַחְנוּ לְפָנֶיךָ ... כַּצֵּל יָמֵינוּ עַל־הָאָרֶץ וְאֵין מִקְוֶה, *For we are but strangers before You ... Our days on earth are like a shadow and there is no hope*
(2) כִּי־נַעְצֹר כֹּחַ, *that we can muster the strength*	(2)
(3) לְהִתְנַדֵּב, *to donate*	(3) כֹּל הֶהָמוֹן הַזֶּה, *All this vast store*
(4) כָּזֹאת, *like this*	(4) אֲשֶׁר הֲכִינֹנוּ לִבְנוֹת־לְךָ בַיִת לְשֵׁם קָדְשֶׁךָ, *which we have prepared to build a house for You for Your Holy Name,*
(5) כִּי־מִמְּךָ הַכֹּל, *for surely it is all from You*	(5) מִיָּדְךָ הִיא, *it is from Your hand*
(6) וּמִיָּדְךָ נָתַנּוּ לָךְ, *and we have given You only that which has come from Your hand.*	(6) וּלְךָ הַכֹּל, *and all belongs to You.*

is the active giver. In (B) he only sets aside that which is already God's.

The same qualitative nuance is obtained by the vivid descriptive and subjective sense of wonderment suggested by the phrase כָּל הֶהָמוֹן הַזֶּה, *all this vast store*, at (B)3, which contrasts sharply with the neutral objective כָּזֹאת, *like this*, at (A)4.

The different perspectives reflected in the (B) passage would seem to derive from a deeper view of man's transience vis-á-vis God's immutability. (A) begins with an exclamation of wonder — *Who am I and who are my people?* But this expresses only a sense of disproportion. We are few and weak, the amounts of gold and silver are enormous. How could we possibly have done all this!

(B), however, begins with a much more general and more profound reflection on the entire human state. The progression is as follows: At (A)6 David states the proposition that *We have given You only that which has come from Your hand*, that our most valiant efforts are no more than returning to God what He had given us.

This thought leads David to thinking of the futility of any human pretensions and of the transience of the human state. In (B), he articulates this in three escalating descriptions: We are as strangers; we are like a shadow; we are without hope. The last of the three, in its terse finality, marks the low point of man's impotence when measured against God's omnipotence.[1]

Under the impression of this final realization, David rethinks his earlier assumption. Where before he had recognized God's role but had not allowed the human factor to be ignored, he now sees that human factor receding entirely into insignificance. Overwhelmed by the unbelievable vastness of the treasure (3), he realizes that in reality it is even now all God's (6) and that the human role is limited to no more than a preparation of the material (4).

17. כִּי אַתָּה בֹּחֵן לֵבָב — *That You examine the heart.* You are well aware of the thoughts which motivate a person (*Metzudos*).

1. These reflections of David take on added significance if they were uttered immediately before his death. See comm. to v. 21.

*that You examine the heart and You desire integrity — I have
donated all this in the integrity of my heart; and now, Your people
who are present here, I have seen that they joyfully donate to You.*
*18 HASHEM, God of Abraham, Isaac and Israel, our forefathers,
preserve this forever, so that it may be the formation of the thoughts
of Your people's heart; and direct their heart towards You. 19 And*

Because of the use of the word לֵבָב
instead of לֵב (two letters *beis* instead of
one), *Mefaresh* sees a reference to two
'hearts' — a good one which inclines a
person to do what is right, and a bad one
which tries to entice him into error (see
Rashi to *Deuteronomy* 6:5). God knows
which of the two hearts is motivating the
person.

וּמִישָׁרִים תִּרְצֶה — *And You desire integrity.*
The word derives from יָשָׁר, *straight*. It has
a number of different connotations.
Targum renders, *decent, good actions* (see
Targum to *Deuteronomy* 6:18).

אֲנִי בְּיֹשֶׁר לְבָבִי הִתְנַדַּבְתִּי — *I have donated ...
in the integrity of my heart.* Here *Targum*
renders *truth.* Thus, my donation was
given from true and straight motives. I had
no personal interest in my giving.

וְעַתָּה עַמְּךָ — *And now, Your people.* For
myself I can say that my motives were
pure. I cannot really know what went on in
the minds of others; but they are *Your
people* so You surely know their hearts.
From the joy of their giving I feel that their
motives must have been correct *(Commentators).*

הַנִּמְצְאוּ־פֹה — *Who are present here.* 28:1
had listed all the various categories of
people whom David had gathered. But
there were many wealthy men who lived
outside Jerusalem and were not present and
thus could not donate their part. If all had
been here the treasure would have been far
greater *(Radak).*

18. ה' אֱלֹהֵי אַבְרָהָם יִצְחָק וְיִשְׂרָאֵל — *HASHEM,
God of Abraham, Isaac and Israel.* In
contrast to v. 10, David involves here the
memory of all the three patriarchs. Perhaps
because, as he contemplates the people and
the exemplary way in which they have
joined with him in the great task at hand,
he sees them as true children of each of
their exalted forebearers.

שָׁמְרָה־זֹּאת לְעוֹלָם — *Preserve this forever.*
Help the people to preserve the state of
integrity which they demonstrated today,
forever *(Radak).* *Mefaresh* translates שָׁמְרָה
as *remember.* David prays that God always
remember the generosity of the people.
[We find שמר used as *to remember* in
Genesis 37:11.]

Metzudos takes it in the sense *to store
up.* May You store up the merit of today's
actions for always.

לְיֵצֶר מַחְשְׁבוֹת לְבַב עַמֶּךָ — *So that it may be
the formation of the thoughts of Your
people's heart.* According to *Radak*, the
prefix ל means *in order that.* David asks
God to preserve the people's state of
generosity so that it may continue to be
their constant state of mind. According to
Mefaresh, the phrase appears to be in
apposition to זֹאת. David had asked that
God remember *this* — i.e., the thoughts of
generosity which had risen up in the
people's hearts or minds.[1]

According to *Metzudos*, David prays
that God store up the merit which accrued
from the product of their mind when they
generously decided to donate their wealth.

יֵצֶר derives from יצר, *to form.* It is used
frequently together with לֵב, *heart.* See
ArtScroll *Genesis*, vol. I, p. 189 to *Genesis*
6:5.

As in v. 17, *Mefaresh* notes the use of
לֵבָב here. The entire heart, its good and bad
components, had in this case joined in the
meritorious act of giving.

וְהָכֵן לְבָבָם אֵלֶיךָ — *And direct their heart
towards You.* *Targum* renders וְאַתְקֵן. The
root תקן is used by the *Targumim* for words
like תְּכֵן, *to establish*, and הֵטִיב, *to do well.*
Thus there is a connotation of a firm
commitment to a good and proper path.
This idiom occurs frequently in Scripture;
cf. *I Samuel* 7:3.

Mefaresh again attaches significance to
the use of לֵבָב. Let their [potentially]

---

1. See *Sefer HaRikmah* 6 under *lamed* for such a use for the prefix ל, *lamed.* He adduces *Exodus*
14:28 where לְכֹל חֵיל פַּרְעֹה is understood to be in apposition to אֶת־הָרֶכֶב וְאֶת־הַפָּרָשִׁים.

יט אֵלֶיךָ: וְלִשְׁלֹמֹה בְנִי תֵּן לֵבָב שָׁלֵם לִשְׁמוֹר מִצְוֺתֶיךָ
עֵדְוֺתֶיךָ וְחֻקֶּיךָ וְלַעֲשׂוֹת הַכֹּל וְלִבְנוֹת הַבִּירָה אֲשֶׁר־
כ הֲכִינוֹתִי: וַיֹּאמֶר דָּוִיד לְכָל־הַקָּהָל בָּרְכוּ־נָא
אֶת־יהוה אֱלֹהֵיכֶם וַיְבָרְכוּ כָל־הַקָּהָל לַיהוה אֱלֹהֵי
כא אֲבֹתֵיהֶם וַיִּקְּדוּ וַיִּשְׁתַּחֲווּ לַיהוה וְלַמֶּלֶךְ: וַיִּזְבְּחוּ לַיהוה ׀
זְבָחִים וַיַּעֲלוּ עֹלוֹת לַיהוה לְמָחֳרַת הַיּוֹם הַהוּא פָּרִים
אֶלֶף אֵילִים אֶלֶף כְּבָשִׂים אֶלֶף וְנִסְכֵּיהֶם וּזְבָחִים לָרֹב לְכָל־
כב יִשְׂרָאֵל: וַיֹּאכְלוּ וַיִּשְׁתּוּ לִפְנֵי יהוה בַּיּוֹם הַהוּא בְּשִׂמְחָה
גְדוֹלָה וַיַּמְלִיכוּ שֵׁנִית לִשְׁלֹמֹה בֶן־דָּוִיד וַיִּמְשְׁחוּ לַיהוה

---

divided heart become one in Your service.
See comm. to 28:9.

19. עֵדְוֺתֶיךָ — *Your testimonies.* These are
the commandments which testify to certain
events, e.g., the Sabbath [creation], Passover [exodus from Egypt], Succos [God's
care for Israel during the forty years in the
wilderness] (*Ramban* to *Deuteronomy*
6:20).

וְלַעֲשׂוֹת הַכֹּל — *To do everything.* To fulfill
all the precepts of the Torah (*Metzudos*).

אֲשֶׁר הֲכִינוֹתִי — *for which I have prepared.*
By stocking up all the materials which
would be required for the building
(*Metzudos*).

If, as the Sages have the tradition, David
dug the foundations of the Temple (see
comm. and fn. to 28:2), reference might be
to that act of preparation (*Daas Soferim*).

In the prefatory remarks and Section Two to
ch. 17 the idea was put forth that David's
turbulent years can be viewed as the prepara-
tory stage to the tranquillity of Solomon's reign. Both
in national and personal terms, David's task was
to achieve the harmony which was the essence of
Solomon's being and which enabled him to be
chosen as the builder of the Temple. The victory
which David wrested from his enemies without
and within himself found vindication in the
peace which he bequeathed to his son. All this
may well be hinted at in the words, ... *for which
I have prepared.*

◆§ The Coronation of Solomon

20. בָּרְכוּ־נָא ... — *Praise now* ... See comm.
to v. 10.

אֶת ה׳ אֱלֹהֵיכֶם ... לַה׳ אֱלֹהֵי אֲבֹתֵיהֶם — *HASHEM
your God ... HASHEM the God of their
fathers.* David exhorted the people to
praise *their* God; he thought that they
themselves deserved the merit of their

generous donations. The people, however,
praised the God of their fathers. They did
not claim the merit for themselves, but for
their ancestors (*Malbim*).

וַיִּקְּדוּ וַיִּשְׁתַּחֲווּ — *And they bowed low and
prostrated themselves.* Prostration
(הִשְׁתַּחֲוָיָה) is more than bowing (קִידָה). The
Sages have explained that *bowing
low* refers to bowing of the head; *prostration* is
spreading out hands and feet on the ground
[פְּשׁוּט יָדַיִם וְרַגְלַיִם] (*Berachos* 34b).

21. עֹלוֹת ... זְבָחִים — *Sacrifices ... burnt-
offerings.* זְבָחִים refers to שְׁלָמִים, *peace
offerings* which are eaten in part by the
Kohanim and those bringing the offerings;
עֹלוֹת are *burnt-offerings* which, except for
the hide, are burned completely on the
altar.

וַיִּזְבְּחוּ ... וַיַּעֲלוּ ... לְמָחֳרַת הַיּוֹם הַהוּא — *And
they slaughtered ... and offered ... on the
next day.* Immediately after David ended
his exhortation, the people went out to buy
animals for sacrifices. There was no time
left during that day to bring them, so they
waited to the next day (*Mefaresh*).

פָּרִים ... וּזְבָחִים לָרֹב לְכָל־יִשְׂרָאֵל — *Bulls ... and
a multitude of sacrifices for all Israel.* The
structure of the verse is chiastic. The earlier
part mentioned *sacrifices* first and then
burnt-offerings. Our section first details
the number of *burnt-offerings* and then
goes back to the *sacrifices* (*Mefaresh* and
Malbim).

Yerushalmi Beitzah 4:2 has another
explanation of why the sacrifices were only
brought on the next day. Apparently the
Sages had a tradition that David died on
the very day that the convocation took
place, which happened to coincide with the
Yom Tov of Shavuos. The burnt-offerings

give to Solomon, my son, a whole heart, that he may keep Your commandments, Your testimonies, and Your laws; to do everything and build the Palace for which I have prepared.' ²⁰ And David said to all the congregation, 'Praise now HASHEM your God.' And all the congregation praised HASHEM the God of their fathers and they bowed low and prostrated themselves. ²¹ And they slaughtered sacrifices and offered up burnt-offerings to HASHEM on the next day, a thousand bulls, a thousand rams, a thousand sheep and their libations; and a multitude of sacrifices for all Israel. ²² And they ate and drank before HASHEM on that day with great joy; and they crowned Solomon the son of David a second time, and anointed [him] as prince to HASHEM, and Tzadok as Kohen. ²³ And Solomon

would anyway not have been offered on that day because they may not be brought on a Yom Tov (see *Beitzah* 19a). Even the שְׁלָמִים, *peace offerings*, which, according to the ruling of Beis Hillel, could be offered on Yom Tov, were left to the next day. This was in accordance with the halachah which states that when a king dies the entire nation has the status of אוֹנֵן, *a mourner on the day a relative dies*, and that they could consequently not offer any sacrifices on that day.

This tradition of *Yerushalmi*, however, is not compatible with *Shabbos* 31b, which has the tradition that David died on the Sabbath. If that were so, then it would have been impossible to offer the sacrifices quite apart from David's death because voluntary sacrifices are prohibited on the Sabbath. Similarly, the question of bringing sacrifices on Yom Tov would have been moot *(Mishneh LaMelech, Hilchos Evel* 3:10).

The story of David's death as it is told in *Shabbos* implies that he did not die on the day of the convocation. The Talmud (there) describes David sitting alone studying the Torah and then going out into the garden to investigate the source of a noise which he had heard. He died out in the garden and Solomon had to send a message to the Sages of the times to obtain a ruling on how to handle the body on the Sabbath. None of this seems compatible with the day of the convocation when Solomon was crowned king (v. 22) and when David would not have been alone in the setting described in the Talmud. It is evident that in that tradition David must have died some time after the events described in our chapter. See further in

comm. below.

22. וַיֹּאכְלוּ וַיִּשְׁתּוּ ... בְּשִׂמְחָה גְדוֹלָה — *And they ate and drank ... with great joy.* Certainly this description seems to argue in favor of the tradition that David did not die on the day of the convocation. It is difficult to imagine such a joyous celebration on the day after David's death.

If, indeed, David had died the previous day, we must ascribe the joy to the fact of the uncontested succession and the consequent preservation of peace in the land *(Daas Soferim).*

לְפְנֵי ה' — *Before HASHEM.* This term usually describes the courtyard of the Temple or of the Tabernacle. It is possible that all these sacrifices were brought in Giveon where the people may have gone to celebrate Shavuos. However, a similar expression also appears in *Exodus* 18:12, where it is said that at Jethro's visit, they brought sacrifices and ate them *before God.* From *Rashi* there, it seems that the expression simply describes an exalted and inspired state of mind, '... as one who basks in the glow of the Divine Presence.' *Sforno* there explains that eating the sacrifices before the altar on which they were brought can also be described as *before God.* Thus, all this may have taken place in Jerusalem *(Daas Soferim).* [During the years when the Tabernacle was at Giveon, private altars were permitted in other parts of the Land. See *Zevachim* 112b.] See comm. to 11:3.

וַיַּמְלִיכוּ שֵׁנִית לִשְׁלֹמֹה בֶן־דָּוִיד — *And they crowned Solomon the son of David a second time.* Solomon had already been crowned once at the time of Adoniyahu's pretension *(I Kings* 1:39), but that had

כג לְנָגִיד וּלְצָדוֹק לְכֹהֵן: וַיֵּשֶׁב שְׁלֹמֹה עַל־כִּסֵּא יהוה l
לְמֶלֶךְ תַּחַת־דָּוִיד אָבִיו וַיַּצְלַח וַיִּשְׁמְעוּ אֵלָיו כָּל־יִשְׂרָאֵל:

כד וְכָל־הַשָּׂרִים וְהַגִּבֹּרִים וְגַם כָּל־בְּנֵי הַמֶּלֶךְ דָּוִיד נָתְנוּ יָד
כה תַּחַת שְׁלֹמֹה הַמֶּלֶךְ: וַיְגַדֵּל יהוה אֶת־שְׁלֹמֹה לְמַעְלָה
לְעֵינֵי כָּל־יִשְׂרָאֵל וַיִּתֵּן עָלָיו הוֹד מַלְכוּת אֲשֶׁר לֹא־הָיָה
כו עַל־כָּל־מֶלֶךְ לְפָנָיו עַל־יִשְׂרָאֵל: וְדָוִיד

כז בֶּן־יִשַׁי מָלַךְ עַל־כָּל־יִשְׂרָאֵל: וְהַיָּמִים אֲשֶׁר מָלַךְ
עַל־יִשְׂרָאֵל אַרְבָּעִים שָׁנָה בְּחֶבְרוֹן מָלַךְ שֶׁבַע שָׁנִים
כח וּבִירוּשָׁלַם מָלַךְ שְׁלֹשִׁים וְשָׁלוֹשׁ: וַיָּמָת בְּשֵׂיבָה טוֹבָה
כט שְׂבַע יָמִים עֹשֶׁר וְכָבוֹד וַיִּמְלֹךְ שְׁלֹמֹה בְנוֹ תַּחְתָּיו: וְדִבְרֵי
דָּוִיד הַמֶּלֶךְ הָרִאשֹׁנִים וְהָאַחֲרֹנִים הִנָּם כְּתוּבִים עַל־דִּבְרֵי

been in the presence of only the people of Jerusalem. This time he was crowned in the presence of representatives of all Israel (Radak). See comm. to 23:1.

לְנָגִיד — *As prince.* See comm. to 11:2.
Mefaresh thinks that the word derives from the Aramaic root נגר, *to pull along.* The prince is called a נָגִיד because he leads the people and they follow him.

וּלְצָדוֹק לְכֹהֵן — *And Tzadok as Kohen.* At the same time that they anointed Solomon king, they also anointed Tzadok to be *Kohen Gadol* [High Priest] (*Radak* and *Metzudos*).
Seder Olam Rabbah 14 teaches that Eviathar had been removed and replaced by Tzadok as *Kohen Gadol* much earlier, during Absalom's rebellion. Thus the anointment mentioned in this verse was necessary to confirm him in this position because of the great influence which the deposed Eviathar still wielded in the affairs of the Tabernacle. Because Eviathar continued to undermine Tzadok's position, Solomon eventually found it best to banish him from Jerusalem, as taught at *I Kings* 2:35 (*Mikra U'Massores*).

23. וַיֵּשֶׁב שְׁלֹמֹה עַל־כִּסֵּא ה' — *And Solomon occupied the throne of HASHEM.* This may describe events which occurred after David's death — perhaps the very next day, if David died on the day of the convocation (see comm. vs. 21 and 22). Or, it is possible that Solomon assumed the kingship while David was still alive, since in his feeble old age David could not provide the strong leadership required in the wake of Adoniyah's rebellion — see *I Kings* 1:51:53

and 2:1.

עַל־כִּסֵּא ה' — [*On*] *the throne of HASHEM.* On the throne from which he administered HASHEM's laws (*Metzudos*).
The Sages (*Sanhedrin* 20b and *Shir HaShirim Rabbah* 1:10) render *Divine Throne,* and see this phrase as defining Solomon's kingship in more than simple human terms. See Overview/p. xlif.

וַיִּשְׁמְעוּ אֵלָיו כָּל־יִשְׂרָאֵל — *And all Israel obeyed him.* Saul had not immediately commanded the allegiance of all Israel (see *I Samuel* 10:27), and even David had originally ruled only over his own tribe at Hebron. Solomon, however, was immediately accepted by everyone (*Mefaresh*).

24. וְגַם כָּל־בְּנֵי הַמֶּלֶךְ דָּוִיד — *And also all the sons of King David.* Daas Soferim notes that almost all the sons of David were older than Solomon (3:1-9). Nevertheless, with the exception of Adoniyahu (see *I Kings* 2:13ff), they all willingly accepted his kingship.

נָתְנוּ יָד תַּחַת שְׁלֹמֹה הַמֶּלֶךְ — *Declared fealty* [lit. *gave a hand*] *to King Solomon.* Mefaresh explains that this is an idiomatic expression implying a declaration of loyalty. R' Shmuel ben Chofni, Gaon (*Genesis* 49:24) thinks that it is an expression connoting obedience.
Radak (*Shorashim,* s.v. יד) compares the expression ... נָתְנוּ יָד תַּחַת to *Genesis* 24:2, שִׂים־נָא יָדְךָ תַּחַת יְרֵכִי, *Place now your hand under my thigh.* He writes that it was the custom in those days for one who wanted to place himself under another's control to

occupied the throne of HASHEM as king in place of his father David, and he was successful; and all Israel obeyed him. ²⁴ And all the leaders and the mighty men, and also all the sons of King David, declared fealty to King Solomon. ²⁵ And HASHEM greatly exalted Solomon in the eyes of all Israel; and He bestowed upon him royal splendor such as had not been upon any king before him in Israel. ²⁶ Now David the son of Jesse reigned over all Israel. ²⁷ The time he reigned over Israel was forty years: in Hebron he reigned for seven years and in Jerusalem he reigned for thirty-three years. ²⁸ He died in a good old age, full of days, wealth and honor; and his son Solomon ruled after him. ²⁹ The history of King David from

place his hand underneath the person whose mastership he accepted, so that the symbolic support offered would be a sign of homage (see *Ibn Ezra* there).

Targum understands it in the sense of *support*. He renders: They placed their hands under King Solomon to help him and to strengthen his rule over the whole kingdom.

25. הוֹד מַלְכוּת — *Royal splendor.* Everyone who saw him knew instinctively that he had those qualities needed to be a great king (*Mefaresh* and *Metzudos*), or, instinctively feared and respected him (*Radak*).

אֲשֶׁר לֹא־הָיָה עַל־כָּל־מֶלֶךְ לְפָנָיו עַל־יִשְׂרָאֵל — *As had not been upon any king before him in Israel.* If the term king is taken in its narrowest sense, the expression *upon any king* seems inappropriate, since Solomon was preceded by only two kings, Saul and David [or by three if we count Ish Bosheth (*II Samuel* 2:10)]. In a broader sense *king* may refer to other leaders of Israel who had the halachic status of *king*, such as Judah himself (see *Bereishis Rabbah* 84:14); Moses (see commentators to *Genesis* 36:31 and to *Deuteronomy* 33:5); and Joshua (see references in ArtScroll *Joshua* p. 98, fn. to 1:7).

Perhaps the term may even incorporate other leaders. We find *Shemos Rabbah* 15:26 speaking of the kingship in Israel lasting for thirty generations, beginning the count from Abraham through all the generations leading up to David.

But, can it be said that the splendor of Solomon's kingship as it was defined above exceeded even that of Moses or Abraham, or even of his father David?

We may be able to understand what is meant in the light of the midrash in *Shemos Rabbah* which we quoted above. In the thirty generations of Israel's kingship Solomon is the fifteenth. As the midrash teaches there, the kingship is

compared to the moon which, after increasing constantly for the first fifteen days of its cycle, peaks on the fifteenth day when it is full and then declines. So, too, Solomon's reign is compared to the full moon. Surely, a part of what is meant is that Solomon's reign was unique in the annals of Jewish history in that every single condition for the fulfillment of the entire Torah was filled. The land was theirs; the Temple stood in their midst; prophecy was rife among the people; the *Kohen Gadol* had access to Divine guidance through the *Urim VeTumim*; the entire nation lived together in the land, making the fulfillment of the *Yovel* (Jubilee) celebration possible.

If such ideal conditions could be meant by הוֹד מַלְכוּת, *the splendor of kingship*, then indeed it can be said that no other man in history had ever attained such splendor.

26. וְדָוִיד ... מָלַךְ עַל־כָּל־יִשְׂרָאֵל — *Now David ... reigned over all Israel.* Although Solomon had now been crowned, David continued ruling until his own death — see v. 28 (*Malbim*).

If David died on the day of the convocation (see comm. to v. 21), then this verse must be seen as a kind of flashback. As David's life is brought to a close, *Chronicles* gives one final and concise review of his reign.

27. בְּחֶבְרוֹן מָלַךְ שֶׁבַע שָׁנִים — *In Hebron he reigned for seven years.* See comm. to 3:4.

28. שֶׁבַע יָמִים עֹשֶׁר וְכָבוֹד — *Full* [lit. *satisfied*] *of days, wealth and honor. Metzudos* points out that שָׂבַע, *satisfied* or *full of*, goes not only on days but also on wealth and honor.

29. וְדִבְרֵי דָוִיד הַמֶּלֶךְ הָרִאשׁנִים וְהָאַחֲרֹנִים — *The history of King David from beginning to end* [lit. *the earlier and the later*]. Translation follows *Mefaresh. Malbim* thinks that רִאשֹׁנִים, *earlier*, refers to the history of David before he became king

שְׁמוּאֵל הָרֹאֶה וְעַל־־דִּבְרֵי נָתָן הַנָּבִיא וְעַל־־דִּבְרֵי גָד
ל הַחֹזֶה: עִם כָּל־מַלְכוּתוֹ וּגְבוּרָתוֹ וְהָעִתִּים אֲשֶׁר עָבְרוּ
עָלָיו וְעַל־יִשְׂרָאֵל וְעַל כָּל־מַמְלְכוֹת הָאֲרָצוֹת:

עַל־דִּבְרֵי שְׁמוּאֵל הָרֹאֶה וְעַל־דִּבְרֵי נָתָן הַנָּבִיא
וְעַל־דִּבְרֵי גָד הַחֹזֶה — *In the records of Samuel
the seer, in the records of Nathan the
prophet, and in the records of Gad the seer.*
Samuel recorded the history which
transpired during his lifetime. The events
which happened after his death were
written in the respective books of Nathan
and Gad *(Malbim)* which have been lost to
us *(Metzudos).*

Daas Soferim notes that according to
Bava Basra 15a the parts of the book of

and that these were written by Samuel (see
below). The אַחֲרֹנִים, *later ones,* is the
history of his kingship which took place
after Samuel's death.

[The phrase דִּבְרֵי … הָרִאשֹׁנִים וְהָאַחֲרֹנִים
never appears in *Kings* but is used in
Chronicles in connection with most of the
kings. (Exceptions are Aviyah, Yoash,
Yotham, Chizkiah, Menasheh and
Yehoiachim.) This indicates a formula for
which, perhaps, no individual explanation
is necessary.]

beginning to end is recorded in the records of Samuel the seer, in the records of Nathan the prophet, and in the records of Gad the seer; [30] *as are all the affairs of his reign and his might, and the times which passed over him and Israel and over all the kingdoms of the lands.*

Samuel which deal with the events which took place after Samuel's death were completed by Nathan and Gad. Thus it is possible that our phrase simply describes the book of Samuel, which was written by the three men mentioned here.

30. וְהָעִתִּים אֲשֶׁר עָבְרוּ עָלָיו — *And the times which passed over him.* The times of sorrow. As David says in *Psalms 31:16,* בְּיָדְךָ עִתֹּתָי הַצִּילֵנִי מִיַּד־אוֹיְבַי וּמֵרֹדְפָי, *My times are in Your hands. Save me from the hands* of my enemies and those that pursue me. [The implication is that עִתֹּתָי in the plural carries a connotation of *sad* times. Compare *Psalms 9:10* and *60:1*] *(Mefaresh).*

Malbim, though, writes that both good and bad times are meant.

וְעַל כָּל־מַמְלְכוֹת הָאֲרָצוֹת — *And over all the kingdoms of the lands.* Those of the other nations with whom Israel came into contact *(Mefaresh).*

תם ונשלם שבח לאל בורא עולם

Section Two
Analyses and Expositions

Chapter One

Ezra wrote the genealogy of *Chronicles* up to his own [family tree] *(Bava Basra 15a)*.

Ezra's purpose in listing those parts of the genealogy that are already given in the Torah cannot have been to preserve an accurate record. From the time of Moses there had been regular public readings of the Torah, and Ezra himself had ordained an extra reading for *Shabbos* afternoon and increased the portion to be read on Mondays and Thursdays *(Bava Kamma 82a and Rambam, Tefillah 12:1)*. Moreover, ever since the Torah had been given at Sinai it had been diligently studied, and its details known to all the people (Halevi, *Tekufas HaMikra*). Even in the difficult times preceding the destruction of the Temple, Torah learning was in no way diminished *(Ran to Nedarim 81a)*. Surely, therefore, all the details of man's ancestry were well known.

Rather, we must conclude that Ezra began his account from Adam because only so could he put his narrative into the correct perspective. *Chronicles* is to be an account of man's journey towards the ultimate goal (קֵץ) that God had set for him. That story must begin from Adam-Man, in whom God's plans had been vested.

Adam

אָדָם — *Adam.* Adam is comprehensive man (אָדָם כּוֹלֵל הַכֹּל) *(Gra).* There was no facet of creation, from the most mundane to the most sublime, that Adam did not encompass. The entire universe lay at his feet. It had been created with him alone in mind *(Sanhedrin 37a)*. His physical and spiritual parts were finely balanced, perfectly tuned, to create a harmonious whole; he was ideally suited for the sublime task that God had set for him *(Derech HaShem)*.

Adam, created by God and therefore with none of the shortcomings which result from imperfect parents, was physically and spiritually the ideal man. He could be described as a Godly being [בֶּן אֱלֹהִים, see *Ramban, Genesis 6:4 (Kol Yehudah)*], and he was destined to bear children who would live at the same exalted level *(Kuzari)*.

Thus, when God called man (and woman — *Genesis 5:2*) אָדָם, *Adam*, He clearly defined humanity's place in the Divine scheme. God created man יָשָׁר, *upright* and unblemished *(Koheles/Eccl. 7:29)*, ready to realize the infinite potential of which he was possessed. This ability defined his essence and informed his whole being. There was no aspect of his existence which needed to be defined (and therefore named) beyond that one, basic, all-encompassing, essential nature.

And the very nature of his task was conveyed to him in his name, Adam — אָדָם, from אֲדָמָה, *the earth. Maharal (Tiferes 3)* explains that he was not called אָדָם, *Adam*, because he had been created from the earth. All the animals were made from the earth *(Genesis 1:24)* and such a name would not have conveyed any unique meaning. Rather, by calling him אָדָם, God taught him the true nature of his being. Nothing is as valueless as a clod of earth, but again, there is nothing which does not ultimately derive from the earth. The earth is that which, while valueless in itself, nevertheless carries an infinite potential for growth and development. And that is the nature of Man. He is the only one of God's creations concerning whom the Torah does not testify that *God saw that what He had made was good*, because it was Man's duty not to remain as he had been created but to achieve greatness out of the infinite resources with which he had been endowed *(Sefer Halkkarim)*. The seemingly insignificant אֲדָמָה [*adamah*], *earth*, has within itself the life-supporting system for the entire globe. Each אָדָם, *Adam*, too, has within himself an entire, individual and unique universe *(Sanhedrin* 37a).

For each individual is indeed an entire world in himself: 'For this reason was man created singly [that is, not in crowds as was the rest of creation; God created millions of fish to fill the seas and so on with all creatures except for Adam, who was created as the only person], to teach that if one destroys a single Jewish soul the Torah considers him as having destroyed an entire world, and one who sustains a single Jewish soul the Torah considers him as having sustained an entire world' (Mishnah, *Sanhedrin* 31a).

Thus, the book of *Chronicles* begins with Adam — Man par excellence — and — after his decline — moves, by way of Israel's story, towards the creation of just such another *Adam* — the כְּנֶסֶת יִשְׂרָאֵל, the Community of Israel.

Chronicles is Ezra's account of Jewish and, therefore, world history. It describes man's path towards the קֵץ, that *end* or *purpose* for which God had created the world.

It is not presumptuous to equate Jewish history with world history. *Ramban* renders the phrase *(Genesis* 5:1): זֶה סֵפֶר תּוֹלְדֹת אָדָם, *this book* (the Torah) *is the chronicle of man*. If Israel is the successor to the Adam of creation then its story holds center stage in the history of man. All other events must be seen as subordinate to Israel's development.

The קֵץ, *end,* is the time when man will once more become that which Adam might have been. (See *Ramban, Deuteronomy* 30:6.) By putting Adam and Seth and Enosh into the first verse of the Book, Ezra places the historical process into its correct perspective. Only by understanding God's purpose in creating Adam, by grasping Seth's role in replacing the slain Abel, and by coming to grips with the decline presaged by Enosh's name can the true significance of Israel's *Chronicles* be comprehended.

Adam's Sons

After Adam's sin and spiritual decline it was to become the task of history to recapture this perfection. No single human would ever be able to rise to those heights again, but there would be a community — Israel, God's chosen — who in their totality would become the 'Adam' of God's intention *(Yevamos* 62a; see ArtScroll *Ezekiel* Overview IV). The seed of greatness which lay in Adam, the man, was to be passed from generation to generation, guarded and nurtured, until it would find its realization in Abraham and his descendants. In each generation there would be one, the 'perfection and heart' (סְגוּלָה וָלֵב) of his times — to whom his cohorts would relate as a shell relates to the fruit which it protects — who would be the conduit through which the strain of Godliness would be passed on. These are the people listed in the family trees of *Genesis*. Each of them was the spiritual giant of his times; even those among them who were wicked had the potential for greatness within themselves. They were the carriers of God's plan for humanity *(Kuzari* 1:95).

Adam had three sons whom the Torah specifically mentions — Abel, Cain, and

Seth. *Maharal (Gur Aryeh* to *Genesis* 9:23) discusses the essential nature of these three sons.

These three men were the ones from whom the whole human race was to develop. Abel had the nature of the body (גּוּף) whose being tends to lethargy and plasticity. Cain had the nature of the life-force (נֶפֶשׁ) shared by all living beings, an initiating forcefulness easily swayed towards self-serving desires. The body (Abel) standing by itself — unsublimated by spiritualizing force — is הֶבֶל [*Abel*], *insubstantial,* and unable to stand up against the self-serving all-consuming onslaught of the life-force which animates Cain; he is soon killed by Cain.

Cain's progeny thus sinks into an abyss of filth and depravity *(Pirkei d'Rabbi Eliezer* 22) from which there can be no salvation. They would be annihilated by the flood. If Adam's seed is to be perpetuated — if God's purpose in creation is not to be frustrated — Adam must bear another child.

So God gives Adam another son, Seth, who is to assume the true (spiritual) essence of man, and will therefore have it in him to bring the plastic and lethargic body of Abel into Divine service. As the Torah puts it, this third son is to be: *Instead of Abel whom Cain had killed (Genesis* 4:25). The implication is that Seth is not just another son. He is to replace Abel.[1]

The lethargic, plastic body, unable to stand up against the consuming passion of the life-force, will henceforth have that nature subsumed under Seth's spiritual drive and thereby come into its own. [The Sages *(Midrash Shochar Tov)* interpret the phrase: וְעָלֵהוּ לֹא יִבּוֹל, *its leaves shall never wither (Psalms* 1:3), as referring to Abel, and the next phrase: וְכֹל אֲשֶׁר יַעֲשֶׂה יַצְלִיחַ, *and everything he does will succeed,* as referring to Seth. The fusion of body and spirituality must lead to ultimate success.]

Thus the name שֵׁת takes on the meaning which the Sages *(Bamidbar Rabbah* 14:24) ascribed to it: שֶׁמִּמֶּנּוּ הֻשְׁתַּת הָעוֹלָם, *in him the world received its foundation* (שָׁתָה is a foundation — *Psalms* 11:3). Man is to be a fusion of the sublime human spirit and the willing, plastic body. Together they can stand up against the passions of the unsublimated life-force.

Gra (comm. to *Koheles)* has a different perception of the respective roles of Cain, Abel and Seth. In his view Cain is the grossly physical force (נֶפֶשׁ) which tends towards a crassly sensual approach to life. Abel is the spirit (רוּחַ) which, if not yet sanctified and sublimated by the imprint of divinity, nevertheless shies away from the sensual, the purely physical. The imperfections of the spirit, however, express themselves in a tendency towards conceit and pride. The spiritual striving is self-oriented.

In this system, too, the gross physical force overpowers the unsublimated spirit — and Abel falls before Cain.

In *Gra's* view the (more) spiritual strivings of Abel which, while disdaining the grossly physical, nevertheless found their fulfillment in self-aggrandizement and pride, had to be sublimated. Henceforth, the focus of those strivings would be God (in Seth) rather than self (as in Abel). Once more, Abel's faculty lives on in Seth.

---

1. Indeed, the verb שית which the Torah uses: כִּי שָׁת לִי אֱלֹהִים זֶרַע אַחֵר, occasionally carries the denotation: *to exchange.* This is rare in Scriptural usage (cf. *Jeremiah* 2:18), but its frequent use in post-biblical Hebrew (cf. *Mechilta* 5, ראשון אחרון ואחרון ראשן, בא הכתוב להשית ראשון) indicates that this root can readily have such a meaning.

From Adam to Noah

But history is not the story of man's unbroken march towards ever-greater heights. It is all too often also the tragic story of man's failure to achieve what might have and, indeed, should have been his lofty destiny.

Seth had been born in Adam's 'likeness and image' *(Genesis 5:3)*. Adam, formed by God Himself, had been able to pass on his own perfection to his child — even, as the Sages point out *(Midrash Shocher Tov 9:17)*, to the extent that Seth was born already circumcised.

Not so Enosh. No mention of 'likeness and image' is made at his birth *(Gra)*. Mankind has moved one step further from its glorious beginnings.

As אָדָם, אֱנוֹשׁ also means *man*. Just as the first man had been called simply 'Man,' because that concept found its fullest expression in him (see above), so also אֱנוֹשׁ is called Man because he was the progenitor of mankind at a lower level.

The decline in man's state is reflected in the name. אָדָם describes man at the pinnacle of his greatness [*Mechilta d'Rabbi Shimon bar Yochai, Tazria:* 'Man is called by several names ... the greatest among them is אָדָם] — not because it describes an attainment but because it looks at his infinite potential for growth. אֱנוֹשׁ [from אנש, *to be weak* or *sick (Radak, Sefer HaShorashim)*], on the other hand, is generally used to describe man at his lowest ebb (cf. *Isaiah 51:12, Psalms 9:20-21*).

Chapter four of *Genesis*, which records Cain's descendants, concludes with two verses describing Adam's fathering of Seth, and Seth's fathering of Enosh. Chapter five then begins *This is the account of the descendants of Adam*, by repeating the birth of Seth and Enosh. It is thus clear that the last two verses of chapter four form a separate section, the purpose of which is not clear.

The Sages *(Bereishis Rabbah 23:9)* ask this question: [Why does the passage tell of] Adam, Seth and Enosh [and then remains] silent? [The answer is that] up to that time [man was created] in [His] likeness and [His] image, but from then on the generations declined and were created as brutes [קֵינְטוֹרִין, from the Greek *Kentairos — centaurs; brutish, insensitive people* who — in mythology — were pictured as half-man half-beast; commentators to the Midrash variously explain the term as denoting one from whom the Divine image has parted]. The Midrash goes on to say that in Enosh's time people began to have faces like apes — וְנַעֲשׂוּ פְּנֵיהֶן כְּקְפוֹת.

Obviously the generation of Enosh was a watershed in the affairs of man, and history may be divided into pre-Enosh and post-Enosh periods.

It was in Enosh's time that pure monotheism was first compromised *(Rambam, Avodah Zarah 1:1;* see ArtScroll *Bereishis* vol. I, pp. 164-165) and, as the Sages teach, sin not only atrophies man's spiritual state but also induces physical decline. 'Since [in Enosh's time] idol worship began, weakness and helplessness became the lot of mankind' *(Ramban, Genesis 6:4)*.

Indeed as man began sinning in Enosh's generation, a deterioration set in throughout the physical world: 'Four things changed in the days of Enosh: The mountains became barren rock, the dead were given over to worms; men's faces became ape-like, and they became prey to demons' *(Bereishis Rabbah 23:8)*.[1]

---

1. Man had indeed been granted ascendancy over the physical world. Thus: ... *and rule over the fish of the sea, the birds of the sky and every living thing that moves on the earth (Genesis 1:28)*. But as

These, then, are the three first generations of man: Adam, God's own handiwork, created in Divine 'likeness and image'; Seth, born of mortal man but still retaining 'likeness and image'; and Enosh, progenitor of a weaker race whose history is now the struggle to regain their original greatness *(Gra)*.

As Adam, man at his most exalted, had borne a Cain, so Enosh, progenitor of a lower level of man, bore a Kenan. [According to a tradition preserved in *Seder Olam* the connection between the two men went beyond an assonance of names. Cain's descendant, Lemech, married two daughters of Kenan, thereby joining the two families.] The erosion of ideal man which had begun in Enosh's time continued in the next generation.

'Why was his name Kenan? Because he bequeathed evil to his generation' (see comm. to v. 2).

In the next generation, however, the pendulum swung back. The sins of Enosh and Kenan stimulated a reaction and Mahalalel found his way back to God. 'Why was his name Mahalalel? Because he repented and began praising God' (see comm.).

But this upward trend did not last long. Mahalalel had a son Yered. 'Why was he called Yered? Because in his time his generation descended to the lowest depths' [יֶרֶד from ירד, *to descend*] *(Torah Shleimah* 50).

Antediluvian man could not maintain his upward progress. Whatever peaks he conquered seemed only to serve as a higher platform from which to fall with ever greater force. Yet the vision of what might have been, which was even at this late date not yet beyond reach, remained within him. This propelled him to yet another, and this time positive, reversal of course with the birth of the righteous Chanoch [Enoch].

Chanoch means to inaugurate (see comm.). He inaugurated a new and even unique attempt on the part of man to regain his spiritual bearings. *And Chanoch walked with God (Genesis* 5:22). This unusual approbation is made for the first time for Chanoch and it does not occur again until Noah. And in Chanoch's case it is even repeated (v. 24). The Midrash and commentaries give numerous explanations of this unique phrase, but in whatever sense it is understood it speaks of an unusual devotion to God. The Talmud comments: 'Is it possible, then, to walk before God? It means to serve Him and emulate His ways' *(Sotah* 14a).

But the world had sunk lower than Chanoch had imagined and the pervasive evil threatened to swamp even the righteous Chanoch. *And Chanoch walked with God; then he was no more, for God had taken him* (v. 24). *Rashi* explains this to mean that God cut short his life (Chanoch died at the comparatively young age of 365) because He foresaw that Chanoch would eventually succumb

---

Rashi notes here, this ascendancy is conditional. The word used for rule — רדו — derives from רדה, *to be master of* or *to control*. But it is also related to ירד, *to descend* or *lower*. Thus, 'If you merit it you shall rule but if you do not merit it you shall be lower than all the rest of creation.'

The Sages surely do not mean that every wicked deed is automatically followed by a deterioration in man's relationship to his surroundings. Scripture and the Talmudic and Midrashic literature are full of the problematics of the wicked who prosper. Nevertheless, there is an assumption that, as we would expect of a world which was created to serve man in his service to God, a decline in humanity's spiritual status would bring about a decline in the cooperation which humanity can expect from the physical world. This would be an extension of God's curse upon Adam when, as a result of his sin, he was told that the ground would be accursed because of him and that it would sprout thorns and thistles where previously his food came to him with ease. See further, *Pirkei d'Rabbi Eliezer* 14, *Ramban* to Genesis 6:4 and *Ramchal, Derech Hashem* 1:3:8.

to the enormous evil pressures of his generation. To avert this, he took him *while he [still] walked with God* (see ArtScroll comm. to that verse).

Even in his short life, however, Chanoch managed to impress the ways of righteousness on his son Methuselah (see comm.). But again, the righteousness of the few could not sway the masses from their headlong rush towards spiritual and physical extinction.

We have seen that there were individual righteous people during the first thousand years of history. But the period as a whole is one during which all the generations angered God to the point where He decided to wipe them all out by means of the Flood.

It is no coincidence that these earliest generations of man failed in their calling. They were giants of the spirit, but in the two millennia before Abraham, their lives lagged behind their perceptions. The Torah which could have sanctified their daily lives had not yet been given and their physical being, unhallowed by adherence to God's commands, stood in direct competition with their spiritual strivings. In such a direct confrontation the physical must eventually overpower the spiritual, much as a tree whose branches are more abundant than its roots must topple *(Maharal, Derech Chaim, Avos 5:2)*. These years [the first two millennia] are *years of futility (Avodah Zarah* 9a). In them God's purpose in creation could never be realized.[1]

The world would have to wait for the second two thousand years, those described by the Sages *(Avodah Zarah* 9a) as *years of Torah,* for the generation of people who would be able to strike such strong roots that even the wildest storms would never be able to tear them up. Their physical existence would have to be hallowed by adherence to the Torah's commands to stand as an ally rather than as an opponent to the strivings of their souls.

Noah

Noah was a man of the שְׁנוֹת תֹּהוּ, the *years of futility.* Only the last six years of his life overlapped into the שְׁנוֹת תּוֹרָה, the two thousand *years of Torah* which were ushered in with Abraham's fifty-third year *(Rashi, Avodah Zarah* 9a). Nevertheless, even in *his generations (Genesis* 6:9) he achieved תְּמִימוּת, *perfection.*

Perfection implies harmony. Every part of his being was pressed into the service of God; nothing rebelled. Noah had complete mastery over himself, but it was a mastery of control, not of sublimation. In the 'years of futility' the body is never sanctified; it is at the very most reigned in.

And this defines Noah's place in history. Prior to his advent, absolute chaos had reigned in the world. 'When God had created Adam he gave him control over everything. The cow was obedient to the ploughman and the earth allowed a true furrow to be ploughed. When man began to sin nature rebelled against him. Neither cow nor the earth would listen to the ploughman' *(Bereishis Rabbah* 25:2). By the time Noah was born, they did not reap that which they had sown.

---

1. *Chovos HaLevovos (Shaar Avodas HaElokim* ch. 2) adduces three causes for the ascendency of man's physical longings over his spiritual strivings: (1) The craving for fulfillment of physical needs is instinctive from birth. Awareness of the spiritual comes only with maturity. (2) Man lives in a physical world where his physical needs are reinforced by every aspect of his physical surroundings. His soul is a stranger in this world. (3) Man's physical cravings are instinctive and therefore function constantly without his active volition, but he must make a conscious decision to engage in pursuit of the spiritual.

'They sowed wheat and harvested thorns and thistles' *(Tanchuma Bereishis).*

Adam had been granted dominion over the whole earth *(Genesis* 1:28). But man himself was a creature of the earth *(Genesis* 2:7); by what right was he to subdue it? Surely it is the נִשְׁמַת חַיִּים, the *soul of life,* that part of him which is ready to receive God's image, which, as it controls those parts of man which are themselves from the earth, entitles him to rule over all of physical existence.

In the ten generations between Adam and Noah that dominion had been dissipated. Far from being a creature of the Divine, man had degenerated into a creature of the flesh (see *Ramban* to *Genesis* 6:3). There was no more moral basis for his rulership and so the earth rebelled against it.

But Noah was a righteous man, a צַדִּיק, one who was an administrator of justice, apportioning his emotions, time, wisdom and resources according to the wishes of their ultimate Owner (Overview, *Noah and Abraham,* ArtScroll *Bereishis,* p. 199).

Noah's body, it was true, remained of the earth (see *Genesis* 9:20) but he exercised control over it, and, by virtue of that control, was able once more to subdue the earth. Man was once more made master of the physical world *(Genesis* 9:2-5). But, as a mastery of control rather than of sublimation, it could not last. The 'years of futility' took their toll and the world was once more plunged into darkness, pending the coming of Abraham.

The Sons of Noah

The world had just been destroyed to cleanse it of its evil and degeneracy. But destruction of evil does not lead automatically to purity; it merely provides a clean canvas upon which a new work may be begun. This was the task which fell to Noah and especially his three sons on their emergence from the ark. A new world lay before them to be conquered and molded; a great opportunity opened to them to recast the world and the history of man in the image of the Divine plan. In this, they were akin to Adam emerging from the Garden of Eden who, although greatly fallen from his previous state, had the ability and opportunity to strike out on the road that would eventually return him to that garden. No evil influences as yet existed to lead either Adam or the sons of Noah astray, no external pressures were there to hamper their progress. Good and evil existed, but only within the breasts of a handful of individuals. Their relative influence on future events was immense and theirs alone to determine the goals towards which society would strive. The general course to be followed towards achieving those goals would, to a large extent, be charted by these progenitors of the new humanity. The world, both physical and spiritual, was theirs to rule.

However, when God offers man another chance it is for the purpose of rectifying his previous errors. For this reason, when history repeats itself, the tale is as encumbered as previously with challenges and pitfalls.

Maharal (Gur Aryeh to *Genesis* 9:23) who, as quoted above, defines the essential nature of each of Adam's three sons, notes their counterparts in the three sons of Noah. Just as Abel's nature was that of the body, tending towards lethargy and plasticity, so too was the nature of his Noahide counterpart, Japheth. Just as Cain was moved primarily by his basic life-force, whose direction is easily swayed towards self-serving desires, so too was his post-diluvian alter ego, Ham. And just as Seth assumed the true spiritual essence of man and had within him the ability to mold the plastic body into a vehicle for Divine service, so too did his latter-day analogue, Shem.

Adam's son שֵׁת, *Seth*, had been so called because מִמֶּנּוּ הוּשְׁתַת הָעוֹלָם, *in him the world received its foundation*, to indicate his role in the perpetuation of mankind. In the same fashion, Shem, who played a similar role among Noah's sons, in that the full destiny of man was to be realized through him, was given a name to symbolize that role. שֵׁם means *name*, and a name, says *Maharal*, is given in accordance with the main and essential nature of a thing. Shem, as Adam had been before him (see above), represents 'man' as God would have wanted him to be. Shem was righteous, born circumcised, God's name was upon him, Abraham was to be descended from him, he was High Priest and the Temple was destined to be built in his portion ... *(Bereishis Rabbah* 26:3). [See comm.]

The name *Ham* also describes the essential nature of its bearer. Ham epitomizes the life-force (נֶפֶשׁ) which tends towards the craving of physical fulfillment. This is suggested by the name חָם, related to חוֹם, *heat*, and descriptive of the חוֹם טִבְעִי, *natural heat* (desire), in a person's heart.

Maharal suggests that the name of the third son, יֶפֶת [*Japheth*], is related to יוֹפִי, *beauty*. He explains that beauty is a property of the body (גוּף), rather than of the intellect (שֵׂכֶל) or the life-force (נֶפֶשׁ), and therefore fits to Japheth, who represents the body among Noah's three sons.

Since Japheth plays a major role in Jewish, as well as world history, this concept needs further elaboration. (See ArtScroll *Bereishis* p. 216, *Shem and Japheth*, for a discussion of *Hirsch's* view of this seminal subject. Our analysis will focus on *Maharal's* interpretation.)

In *Maharal's* view the dominant feature of the body is lethargy (עַצְלוּת). It is therefore plastic and pliant, readily influenced, shaped and mastered by the more active, driving forces in man. If the spiritual force of man predominates, the body can become handmaiden of the soul and be sublimated to a degree that even the body becomes wholly suffused with the spirit. [Cf. *Ramban, Leviticus* 18:5 concerning Elijah and Chanoch whose bodies became immortal together with their souls.] Where the passionate life-force is stronger, the body becomes the chattel of the desires and is dragged into dissipation and depravity.

This vacillation is the hallmark of Japheth's path through history.

There were instances when he chose the road to greatness. Faced with his father's drunken stupor *(Genesis* 9:20-29), he allowed himself to be borne along by Shem's initiative *(Rashi* there, v. 23) and defended Noah's honor. In the same vein, the Persian Cyrus listened to the call of Israel's prophets and lent support and encouragement to the building of the Second Temple (see *Rashi* there, v. 27).

At other times he threw in his lot with the forces of evil. Haman would have held no terror for the Jews if Ahasuerus, the Persian descendant of Japheth, had not been a willing puppet in his hands.

History can be viewed as the struggle between the holy and the depraved for control of Japheth — the neutral gifts of culture and beauty which God gave man. God's wish was that: 'The beauty of Japheth should dwell in the tents of Shem' *(Megillah* 9b, based on *Genesis* 9:27), but Ham and the dark, searing passions for which he stands do not give up the struggle easily.

The final test of history will show Japheth's ultimate failure. When Gog will wage the last — and decisive — battle against holiness just before the Messianic redemption, his forces (Magog) will be drawn mainly from Japheth's descendants. (See *Yechezkel* chs. 38 and 39 and ArtScroll ed., footnote to 38:1.) Beauty and culture will have fallen into Ham's clutches and will only be redeemed for the service of the Divine in the time of the Messiah.

Accordingly, Noah's blessing to Japheth can be understood as יַפְתְּ אֱלֹהִים לְיֶפֶת וְיִשְׁכֹּן בְּאָהֳלֵי שֵׁם, *May God extend Japheth that he may dwell in the tents of Shem (Genesis* 9:27). Noah knew the vacillating nature of his son. His blessing was that God should help him to plant himself firmly in Shem's tents. Japheth had experienced the beauty of submitting himself to Shem's initiative for holiness. There could be no more fitting blessing for Japheth than that his act should once and for all establish his descendants in that camp. It was to be the tragedy of Japheth and of the world as a whole that this would prove not always to be the case.

The Development of the Nations

The descendants of Noah's three sons comprise the seventy nations of which Talmudic tradition speaks.

Although Abraham, and therefore the Jewish people, is descended from Shem through Arpachshad (vs. 24-27), Israel is not considered part of the seventy nations. *Berachos* 16b teaches that: Only three [Abraham, Isaac and Jacob] are considered 'fathers.' As human beings in common with the rest of mankind, Israel traces its ancestry to Adam *(Malachi* 2:10). As God's chosen people it knows no lineage beyond Abraham. *Behold a people who dwell alone, and among the nations they are not reckoned (Numbers* 23:9). It makes its way through history alone — unique by nature, isolated by destiny.

The relationship of Israel to the seventy nations is one of the great themes of aggadic literature. It leaves no facet of Judaism untouched, and its ramifications are abundant. It is obvious that an understanding of *Chronicles,* Ezra's account of Jewish history, must also include an accurate perception of Israel's role in history, defined in terms of its relationship to the other nations.

The definitive explication of the nature of this relationship is contained in Rabbi Moshe Chaim Luzzatto's *Derech HaShem:*

When God created man, He decided in His wisdom that the generations descending from Adam would all occupy certain predetermined levels in the scheme of history. Some generations would be primary, and others would be secondary, like the roots and branches of a tree. Later generations would grow from the earlier ones and share their characteristics, like branches from a tree. The number of trees and branches was carefully determined from the very beginning.

The early generations of the human race were to be the 'roots' of mankind; there would be gifted people in those generations who would father entire nations, each of which would carry their forebears' nature and characteristics. Subsequent generations would only have the nature of branches — they would be individuals but not founders of nations.

Had these 'root' people been born of Adam in the elevated state in which he was before he sinned, then the entire family of man would have shared in his exalted state passed to them through the 'root' people who were their ancestors.

As it was, Adam sinned and lost his exalted status and all his children, including the 'root' people, were born at a much degraded level, far removed from the ideal envisioned by God.

It would be the task of mankind — particularly the 'root' people — to try and regain Adam's exalted state. Thereby they would father nations who would make their way through history at the level which God would have originally wished. God's wisdom determined that there would be a time limit within which this return to the primary state could be accomplished. The 'root' people who had not succeeded within that time would be forever unable to do so and would consequently only be able to father nations whose entire existence would be lived at man's depraved level. The time limit which was set carried mankind until the דּוֹר הַפְלָגָה, the Generation of the Separation.

When the time limit was reached, not a single person besides Abraham had managed to recapture Adam's original state. Consequently, all the 'root' people — seventy in all — fathered nations who represented man at his degraded level.

By contrast, Abraham had chosen greatness. He was to father a people who would — in their totality — be the 'Adam' of God's intention: Not always righteous, not always living up to the potential that lay within them, but never losing the inner spark which defines man at his most exalted.

And thus Israel, unique among the families of man, became the bearer of God's presence on earth. They are 'Adam', the expression of God's purpose in creation. The rest of mankind would henceforth be judged according to the degree to which they would allow themselves to be instructed and uplifted and thus drawn towards the 'Adam' destiny which they had lost.

Abraham, Isaac, Jacob

R' Berachyah said in the name of R' Chanina [the Torah's cursory examination of the development of the 70 nations in contrast to the detailed recounting of the life of Abraham] is reminiscent of the parable of a king who, while traveling from place to place, had a precious pearl fall from his crown. Immediately, he halted his entire entourage and had them make heaps of all the sand in the area. He then brought sieves and they all began sifting the sand. Each pile, after being sifted, was cast aside, until the king finally recovered his pearl and all rejoiced. So, too, did Hashem say: 'What need had I to sift through the genealogy of Arpachshad through Terach — only to find [Abraham].' This is what is meant by the verse (Nehemiah 9:8): And You 'found' his heart to be faithful to You (Bereishis Rabbah 39:13, repeated at the end of Ruth Rabbah).

As the Mefaresh comments (1:1), God impatiently sifts through the genealogy of the nations until he finds Abraham, the pearl He had lost at Adam's decline.

The genealogies — and, indeed, the whole historical account of the lives of the patriarchs in Genesis — is a description of a process of refinement (בֵּרוּר) designed to produce that person who would once more recapture Adam's perfection. In each generation the best is chosen, and from his children once more the best, until an Abraham could be born. He again was picked from among his brothers, as Isaac was from among Abraham's sons, and as Jacob was while Esau was rejected (Kuzari).

But having recovered his pearl, the King does not merely replace it in its setting. Rather, He crafts for it its own unique place in His crown. Thus, Chronicles does not merely list Abram, but adds Abram, that is Abraham (v. 27). In Genesis 11:26 Terach's son is called Abram. In a later, Divinely ordained change of name *(Genesis* 17:5), he became known as Abraham. Since, as we have seen in the commentary, *Chronicles* assumes a knowledge of *Genesis*, it is inconceivable that Ezra would have found it necessary to point out such an elementary piece of information. The Sages, therefore, read deeper meanings into this verse.

According to *Berachos* 13a this verse hints at a progression. At first he was [only] father to Aram [אַבְרָם is taken as two words — אַב רָם, father of אֲרָ(ם)] but then he became father to the whole world. *For I have made you the father of a multitude of nations* (אַב הֲמוֹן גּוֹיִם).

This, according to *Rambam (Bikkurim* 4:3), implies that he is 'father to whomever from among the nations chooses to enter the protective wings of God,' that is, to become a proselyte by accepting Judaism. Abraham, according to *Succah* 49a, was 'the first of the proselytes,' and all subsequent proselytes are to be considered his children.

God changed Abram's name to Abraham in order to indicate that henceforth it would be possible for gentiles to throw in their lot with the Jewish people by becoming proselytes. This moment was a watershed in the historical process which is to lead mankind back to God.

Maharal (Zevachim 116a) points to the fact that the Torah recognizes only one kind of conversion, that of a non-Jew becoming a Jew. There is no way in which a non-Jew of one nation can convert and join another non-Jewish nation. If, for example, a Moabite would want to become an Edomite, he would not be able to do so; the different rules pertaining to marriage with an Edomite and Moabite would remain as before.

Maharal offers the following explanation. Each nation has its own genius — that which defines its essence. That essence is unique to that particular nation and cannot be assumed by another. Only the Torah is universal and only Israel's essence is defined by the Torah. No individual exists who cannot join Israel because there is no one who cannot find place within the universality of Torah.

Above, we saw that the first two thousand years of history were described by the Sages as שְׁנוֹת תֹּהוּ, *years of futility (Avodah Zarah* 9a). With Abraham, the second two millennia, which are described as שְׁנוֹת תּוֹרָה, *years of Torah*, began. From now on the chaos of the earlier years would yield to the harmony of a Torah-ordered society. All this is implied in the evolution of Abram into Abraham.

In this context, the Sages explain our verse as follows. The genealogy from Shem was listed because of Abram. But this Abram would have had no significance if he had not been that Abram whom God eventually renamed Abraham to symbolize that he, among all the generations, was the one whom God had 'found.'

But although a 'father' to a multitude of nations, his family was only Israel. *For through Isaac will offspring be considered yours (Genesis* 21:12). It is only through Isaac — not Ishmael — that Abraham would achieve true posterity, for only the righteous Isaac would follow in his father's footsteps. It is only Isaac, therefore, who is the recipient of both Abraham's genes and spiritual essence, and only he who may therefore rightfully be considered his true offspring. What greater tragedy for a great man than to battle all his life for an ideal only to father a clan which bears his name but desecrates his life's work. Or to leave behind children who will parody his face while depriving the world of his true legacy.

True, Abraham can be a father even to a multitude of nations, but he must first assure the proper development of his true family.

For this reason, Abraham was confronted with the agonizing decision of sending away his own natural children, Ishmael and the sons of his concubine, Keturah, in order that his true family, Isaac, might flourish. Abraham's actions towards the sons of Keturah must not be viewed in the narrow context of his immediate family circle but rather as part of the process of nurturing the Jewish people to spearhead man's odyssey towards Messianic redemption.

The true significance of the genealogies of *Genesis* is that they recount the process of refinement which, by isolating in each generation the לֵב וּסְגוּלָה, *heart and perfection* of that generation, would ultimately produce Jacob through whose twelve sons the tribes of Israel would be established.

Only one in each generation was a worthy carrier of the seed of greatness that had been passed down from Adam; his cohorts were no more than shells among whom that one would be nurtured.

Jacob and Esau

It is noteworthy that whereas vs. 4 and 28 ignored chronology and listed Noah's and Abraham's sons according to their importance rather than their ages, v. 34 lists Esau before Jacob.

The explanation of this may lie in the difference between the relationship of Ishmael to Isaac on the one hand and that of Esau to Jacob on the other.

According to *Ramban*, the first part of our verse, Abraham fathered Isaac (not Ishmael), refers to the bearer of Abraham's true legacy. From the point of view of Abraham's spiritual heritage, Ishmael did not exist. Such was not the case with Esau. *Genesis* 21:12 taught that כִּי בְיִצְחָק יִקָּרֵא לְךָ זָרַע, *through Isaac will offspring be considered yours.* This unambiguously excluded Ishmael from consideration. But, although *Nedarim* 31a excludes Esau from the same verse: בְּיִצְחָק וְלֹא כָּל יִצְחָק, *in part of Isaac* [i.e., a portion of his offspring] *but not all of Isaac's* [offspring will be considered descendants of Abraham], this exclusion is not unambiguous. We know only that not all of Isaac's children will be chosen; it could be either Esau or Jacob. The choice of Jacob occurred only when Isaac finally passed Abraham's blessings on to him (Genesis 28:4).[1]

For this reason, in the genealogy which deals with the father-son relationship at birth, the chronologically older Esau is mentioned first. At birth there was no way of knowing that it would not be he who would carry on the line from Abraham.[2]

This may offer insight into the undying hatred which Esau harbors for Jacob. According to *Rambam (Teshuvah* 2:10), this eternal enmity seems to be the very hallmark by which Esau's essence is defined. *Sifri* (to *Numbers* 9:10) goes so far as to say that it is an immutable law (הֲלָכָה) that Esau hates Jacob. This consistent and undeviating enmity is unique to Esau.

It could well be that it derives from Esau's unique potential for greatness. He

---

1. The above is based on *Rabbi Chaim Soloveitchik's* explanation of the relevant passages in *Genesis*. For a detailed discussion see ArtScroll *Genesis*, p. 1019. See also *Derashos HaRan* 2.

2. Accordingly the contrast between the first and second part of our verse is analogous to Joshua 24:3-4. Joshua, tracing Jewish history from Abraham, says: '... and I gave him [Abraham] Isaac. And I gave Isaac, Jacob and Esau ...' Thus Abraham was only 'given' Isaac, but Isaac was 'given' both Jacob and Esau *(Rabbi Chaim Soloveitchik).*]

was Isaac's son, Jacob's twin, equally endowed with the seed from which true spirituality could have grown. He could have nurtured that seed and found it within himself to be the carrier of Abraham's line. His children could have stood at Sinai; his descendant could have been the Messiah who will ultimately lead mankind to its pinnacle of achievement. He lost all this because he chose to lose it. No one had ever come so close and no one had, through his own folly, lost so much. It is that which so easily might have been which rankles in Esau's bosom. In Jacob, his twin, he sees his own better self — now forever beyond his grasp. In himself he sees a bitter caricature of Jacob — outwardly similar but, where it counts, separated by an unbridgeable abyss.

We can picture the bitterness with which Esau packed up his household and: ... *went to a land because of his brother Jacob (Genesis* 36:6). The Land of Israel, beloved by God, focus of man's striving for sanctity, could not be his. He left for 'a land,' an unspecified place, not because it was the golden opportunity of a new land that was beckoning but because of the need to leave the land of his fathers. And he left it not to a stranger, which would have been bitter enough but bearable, but to his brother Jacob, embodiment of all that he could have been, the constant, intolerable reminder of his own rejection.

Here we have the agony of the wasted chance, the failed opportunity, from which the bitterest, most unrelieved hatred can be born (see *Derashos HaRan* 2).[1]

The presence of Edom's inviolable borders right next to Israel has profound historical and moral implications.

Devarim Rabbah (1:16) states: Once, David wanted to wage war against Edom (and take some of its territory). God said to him, 'I know that you are eager and powerful enough to do this, but I need them to control My world.' Others say, He said, 'I must preserve them for the future.'

In this passage, the Sages reveal the secret of Esau-Edom's function in history. Providence had assured that Jacob, not Esau, was to receive Isaac's main blessing. But that same Divine Providence had made certain that Esau, too, would receive the blessing of earthly riches and military power. [*Ramban, Genesis* 27:4 explains that it was by Divine Providence that Rebecca never revealed to Isaac that God had told her that of her twins, Jacob would be the greater one. Had she done so Isaac would certainly have planned to bless only Jacob and God's plan to have Esau receive the blessing of the sword would have been frustrated. *Rabbi Avraham ben HaRambam* notes the fact that Esau came back from the hunt at exactly the right moment. Had he come earlier Jacob would not have been blessed; had he come later, after the Divine spirit had already left Isaac, no blessing would have been given him. It was by Divine Providence that his hunting was successful at precisely the right moment.]

Jacob is indeed God's beloved. But if it is to be assured that throughout the long centuries Jacob will never lose his bearings and will always retain the awareness of his holy destiny, then he needs the stern discipline of Esau's sword. Esau's presence and military prowess is an indispensable part of God's plan for Jacob. [See further *Yalkut* to *Psalms* 10:14 and 17:13.]

The second answer carries even more profound implications.

---

1. The interplay between Jacob's and Esau's descendants throughout history is one of the great themes of aggadic literature and goes beyond the scope of this essay. It is dealt with in detail in ArtScroll *Bereishis* p. 1018, An Overview: *The Birthright — Esau's vs. Jacob's.*

Why does God wish to preserve Edom for the future? *Matnos Kehunah* explains that the purpose is so that Edom's final destruction can be at the hands of the Messiah (based on *Numbers* 24:17-18).

In Messianic times, the evil introduced into the affairs of man by Adam's sin will finally be eradicated. God will take away our hearts of stone and replace them with hearts of flesh *(Ezekiel* 36:26), and God will punish the Mountain of Esau so that His kingship may be established *(Obadiah* 1:21).

These two functions of Messianic times are not really different from one another. We perceive an evil drive within ourselves (יֵצֶר הָרַע) and another form of evil which takes the guise of the nations who make war against God and Israel. Essentially these two forces are one. The Sages teach that Samael, guardian angel of Esau, was riding on the snake when it came to persuade Eve to rebel against God's command *(Pirkei d'Rabbi Eliezer* 13).

Esau's entry into history coincided with the exact moment in which man decided to become a sinner. It will be finally annihilated only at that moment when man returns to the pristine purity in which he was created.

If Edom is to be destroyed, it is God Himself Who will direct his destruction at the hands of His Messiah. The ultimate removal of evil from the world is His prerogative alone.

Edom's presence on Israel's boundaries, and the prohibition against conquering their land, symbolizes the existence of an implacable force of evil in human affairs. With such a tangible manifestation of evil on its border, Israel would be constantly and acutely aware of the יֵצֶר הָרַע, *evil inclination*, within itself. Such an awareness would carry profound implications for Israel's perception of itself and its historical destiny.

There is another aspect to this relationship which can help us understand why Ezra includes the passage about the Edomite kings (vs. 43-54) in *Chronicles*. When Rebecca in her travail went to inquire of God *(Genesis* 25:23), she was told that she was to bear twins and that, 'Two nations are in your womb; two regimes from your insides shall be separated; the might shall pass from one regime to the other.' This last prophecy is interpreted by the Sages *(Megillah* 6a) to mean that the two of them will never be mighty simultaneously — when one of them rises the other falls. [For a full discussion of the nature of the interplay between the fates of these two nations, see ArtScroll *Bereishis* p. 1023ff.]

A nation reaches the full bloom of its flowering in the person of its king. Through him it expresses its aspirations; in him its character and genius are projected. For this reason, there can be no king in Israel and Edom at the same time. During the reign of Saul, Israel's first king, there was already no functioning king in Edom. If Edom was able to have eight kings, these must have functioned, ... *before a king reigned over the children of Israel* (v. 43 and *Genesis* 36:31).

If Israel is not to waver on the path towards its destiny it must be aware of the dynamics which animate its historical experiences.

Chapter Two

◄§ Zerach, Zimri

[ו] וּבְנֵי זֶרַח זִמְרִי וְאֵיתָן וְהֵימָן וְכַלְכֹּל וָדָרַע כֻּלָּם חֲמִשָּׁה.

[6] *And the sons of Zerach — Zimri, Ethan, Heman, Calcol and Dara, five in all.*

A. [His name] is given as Zimri [in *Chronicles*] and Achan [in *Joshua*]. [Why?] Rav and Shmuel both answered. One said: His real name was Achan [as in *Joshua*]. Why then was he called Zimri? Because he acted like Zimri [the Shimeonite prince who sinned with the Midianite women, and was then killed by Pinechas; see *Numbers* 25:1-15]. The other said: His real name was Zimri [as in *Chronicles*]. Why then was he called Achan? Because he *rolled back* [from עכן, *to undulate*, as a snake does] Israel's sins upon them [i.e., caused their sins to be remembered] (*Sanhedrin* 44b).

B. Rabbi Yehoshua ben Levi said: Zimri is Achan. [He is called Zimri] because he acted like Zimri. Rabbi Shmuel bar Nachman said: Heman is Achan. [He is called Heman] because [Achan said]: Truly I have sinned (*Joshua* 7:20) [אָמְנָה from אמן, *to be faithful*, the same root from which הֵימָן derives] (*Yerushalmi, Sanhedrin* 6:3).

C. Zimri is Achan ... Ethan is Abraham ... Heman is Moses ... Rabbi Shmuel bar Nachman said it is Achan ... Calcol is Joseph ... Dara is the generation which traveled through the wilderness. [A play on the word וָדָרַע (or דַּרְדַּע, as it is written in *Kings* 5:11). It is read as: דּוֹר דֵּעָה, the generation of enlightenment (*Vayikrah Rabbah* 9:1).]

D. Why does it say: כֻּלָּם חֲמִשָּׁה — *Five in all?* [To teach] that all of them [including Achan] have a portion in the World to Come (*all three sources quoted above*).

All the sources agree that Achan is mentioned here among the sons of Zerach. He is to be identified either with Zimri or with Heman. This, in spite of the fact that it is clear from *Joshua* 7:1 that Achan was a great-grandson of Zerach [not a son], and v. 7 here expressly states that his father was Carmi, whom we identified (see comm.) as a son of Zimri/Zavdi.[1]

It is obviously the purpose of the Sages to underline homiletically Achan's descent from Zerach. In actual fact he was Zerach's great-grandson; essentially, however, he was his 'son' (see *Joshua* 7:24), for Achan's nature was inherited from his ancestor Zerach.

As told in *Genesis*, when Zerach and his twin Peretz were born, the younger twin, Zerach, stretched out his hand first but then withdrew it, allowing Peretz to be born first. The word 'hand' is repeated four times in that narrative, to hint at the four bans which Achan (Zerach's descendant) would transgress (*Bereishis Rabbah* quoted by *Rashi, Genesis* 38:30). *Maharal* in *Gur Aryeh* points out that the story of Zerach's birth would not have contained allusions to Achan if the connection were not an essential one. Zerach's nature, as expressed at his birth, was later reflected in the actions of his great-grandson, Achan.

---

1. See *Rashi* to *Sanhedrin* (there), and *Maharsha, Chamre VeChaye,* and *Margalios HaYom.* Since from Source C we see that the Sages included Abraham, Moses and Joseph in this list of בְּנֵי זֶרַח, *the sons of Zerach,* it is obvious that this passage is an example of the דְּרָשׁ, *homiletical interpretation,* of *Chronicles* which functions entirely independently from the plain meaning of the verse.

Gur Aryeh explains as follows: Judah, the father of Peretz and Zerach, was endowed with the qualities of kingship. Both his children by Tamar inherited those traits. Now the Torah grants a king a right of eminent domain, allowing him to encroach on other people's property in the exercise of his kingship [מֶלֶךְ פּוֹרֵץ לַעֲשׂוֹת לוֹ דֶרֶךְ, *a king may 'break through' in order to lay a road for himself (Yevamos 76b)*]. However, there are moral boundaries which inhibit this royal prerogative. There is, so to speak, a legitimate 'breaking through' but, in excess, this right can be abused. One who abuses it shows himself unfit for royalty.

Herein lay the difference between the twins. Peretz, as his name implies [פֶּרֶץ from פרץ, *to break through*], forced his way to birth, but was within his rights. He became the progenitor of the royal house of David. Zerach went beyond seemly boundaries by pushing out his hand ahead of the brother who was to be born first. His was a kingly nature which tended toward the abuse of the royal prerogative. This nature would express itself in his descendant Achan, who would also be unable to contain himself within legitimate boundaries.

Though there was a fatal flaw in Zerach's royal reach which disqualified him from the kingship of Israel, there was another kind of royalty in Israel for which, far from being disqualified by his unfettered ambition, he was uniquely suited. Israel's rabbis, its teachers, are considered kings (*Gittin* 62a). They set out to conquer territories which, by logic, should be far beyond them. For Torah belongs to God and must be won if it is to become man's own (*Avodah Zarah* 18b). Even after the most intense efforts they can only 'find' it, never 'acquire' it (*Megillah* 6b).

Thus, those same qualities which denied him his father's kingship made him heir to Judah's other function, that of the Torah scholar and teacher. For this too was the function of Judah. The Sages teach that when Jacob sent Judah to prepare the way for the descent into Egypt (*Genesis* 46:28), it was so that he would establish a house of learning from which the law of the Torah would be taught (*Bereishis Rabbah* quoted by *Rashi*). It is in this sense that *Vayikra Rabbah* lists Abraham, Joseph, Moses and the generation of the wilderness among the sons of Zerach, to indicate that Zerach is considered the prototype of wisdom in Israel and all its wise men can be said to be 'descended' from him.

The verse in *I Kings* 5:11 quoted in the commentary now takes on special significance: *And he [Solomon] was wiser than all men: than Ethan the Ezrachite, Heman, Calcol and Darda, the sons of Machol.* Solomon's wisdom exceeded that of the four sons of Zerach. Although Solomon was descended from Peretz who had been heir to Judah's kingship, while it was Zerach who had been given wisdom, still Solomon was wiser than the descendants of Zerach, because his wisdom had come to him as a special gift from God.

R' Shmuel bar Nachman identifies Achan with Heman (source B). [R' Shmuel bar Nachman may well agree that Zimri is Achan. He just adds that Heman, too, is Achan. As can be seen from *Megillah* 13a, it is possible for two different names in the same context to refer homiletically to the same person.] Thus, R' Shmuel bar Nachman teaches that Achan's descent from Zerach is not only significant because of his sin, but also because of his repentance. His ability to admit his guilt (הֵימָן=אָמֵן=אֲמָנָה) transcended his individuality. Here, too, his strength of character was inherited.

Vayikra Rabbah 9:1 teaches that Achan taught penitents the way to true repentance (שֶׁהֶרְאָה לַשָּׁבִים אֶת הַדֶּרֶךְ). In this he acted in the tradition of his family.

Judah had stimulated his brother Reuven to penitence by his own admission of guilt in the matter of Tamar (*Sotah* 7b and *Rashi* there). David would one day commit an act entirely unworthy of his exalted level of sanctity (with Bathsheva), so that if an individual would ever sin he could look to the great David as an example of the possibility of penitence (*Avodah Zarah* 4b). David, moreover, was called the one who 'established the yoke of penitence' (*Moed Katan* 16b).

It was in this tradition that Achan left his mark. God had commanded Joshua to discover the violator of the ban by casting lots (*Joshua* 7:14). When the lot fell on Achan, Joshua adjured him to confess: *My son, give, I pray you, give honor to HASHEM, God of Israel, and confess to Him ... And Achan answered Joshua and said, 'In truth, I have sinned against HASHEM, God of Israel. Thus and thus have I done'* (v. 19,20). Knowing that his fate was sealed, that his repentance would not lift the death sentence decreed upon him (see v. 15), he yet found the courage to publicly confess so that the people realize the justice of the Divine sentence. In this he showed that the true goal of repentance is not to gain relief from Divine wrath but to submit to God's judgments, to accept the rightness of His ways, and to thereby glorify His Name.

The ability to bow before greater wisdom, to accept moral judgment, is a mark of true royalty (see *Maharal* to *Bava Kamma* 16a). No man in Israel stands so straight as does the royal line of Judah. And therefore no man can bow so low before God.

Achan, it is true, committed a great sin. But on realizing the enormity of what he had done he summoned the dignity of his royal lineage to enable him to admit his guilt. If Achan is Zimri the son of Zerach, he is also Heman the son of Zerach.

◆§The Royal Line of Judah

[י־יב] וְרָם הוֹלִיד אֶת־עַמִּינָדָב וְעַמִּינָדָב הוֹלִיד אֶת־נַחְשׁוֹן נְשִׂיא יְהוּדָה: וְנַחְשׁוֹן הוֹלִיד אֶת־שַׂלְמָא וְשַׂלְמָא הוֹלִיד אֶת־בֹּעַז: וּבֹעַז הוֹלִיד אֶת־עוֹבֵד וְעוֹבֵד הוֹלִיד אֶת־יִשָׁי.

[10-12] *And Ram fathered Amminadav, and Amminadav fathered Nachshon, prince of Judah. And Nachshon fathered Salma, and Salma fathered Boaz. And Boaz fathered Oved, and Oved fathered Jesse.*

The line of Jewish kingship descended from Judah through Peretz, down to his son Chetzron, and through his son Ram. Several members of this distinguished line were famous in their own right while others are known primarily for having been links in the royal line. One, in fact, had this expressed in his name — Salma, whose name is explained by the Sages to mean *a rung on the ladder of the princes* (see comm.). But even those who achieved personal fame such as Nachshon and Boaz were seen by the Sages as having been outstanding for their contributions to the development of the royal house of David.

'By which merit did [the tribe of] Judah deserve kingship? When the tribes stood by the [Reed] Sea [they argued]. This one said: I will go in first and this one said: I will go in first. ... While they were debating among each other Nachshon ben Amminadav and his tribe leaped into the waves. For this reason, they deserved to become kings ... God said to them: Let he who hallowed My

Name by the sea come and rule over Israel' *(Mechilta, Beshalach* 5).

A careful reading of Jacob's blessing of his son Judah *(Genesis* 49:8ff) leaves no doubt that his descendants were already then destined to become kings (see *Rashi* there). Reuben, who by virtue of his birthright should have received the gift of royalty *(Genesis* 49:3, see *Rashi),* had lost it because of his impetuous temperament *(Rashi* to vs. 3 and 4 there) and, as *I Chronicles* 5:1 and 2 makes clear, it passed from him to Judah.

Surely, then, the *Mechilta* cannot be understood in a literal sense. It was not as a *result* of Nachshon's action that God decided to give the gift of royalty to Judah. Rather, the meaning must be that Nachshon, in leaping into the sea, displayed those innate traits of the family of Judah which made just this family fit to produce Israel's kings.

The ability to break down barriers and spread beyond the confines of ordinariness is a quality essential to the exercise of royal prerogative (see above). The father of royalty was Peretz, whose very name implies this faculty. With his leap into the hostile waters, Nachshon proved himself a true son of the royal house of Peretz.

Israel needed a path through the waters and 'all of Israel are of royal blood' *(Shabbos* 67a). A king is entitled to break a path through private property in order to create a road for himself *(Yevamos* 76b). With this assurance, Nachshon jumped into the water. Supremely confident in Israel's innate royalty, he showed himself and his tribe to be the worthy bearers of its most overt expression.

This tradition was furthered and deepened by Nachshon's grandson, Boaz. 'Ivtzan *(Judges* 12:8-10) is [identical with] Boaz. ... All [his sixty children] died during his lifetime. [This teaches us the truth of] the proverb that says: Rather than bear sixty children [who will not outlive you], bear one child whose value will exceed that of the sixty' *(Bava Basra* 91a).

Maharal to this passage in *Bava Basra* writes: 'Know that it was no coincidence that his sons and his first wife died and that he married Ruth and bore Oved. For Boaz had two names, Ivtzan and Boaz — each expressing the two aspects of his being. One [aspect] married the Moabite Ruth and the other his Jewish wife. From Ruth the royal house of David, in whose merit the world exists, was born and developed, while from his Jewish wife a futile seed was born with no real existence. For it was not Boaz' destiny to bear any but the royal house of David. It was for this reason that he was called Boaz [a contraction of the two words בו עז, *in him is strength*], for in him lay kingship [which is called עז, *strength*, in *I Samuel* 2:10].

Kingship expresses itself in עז, *an aggressive expansive force*, which attempts to spread the orbit of its influence beyond its natural boundaries (see *Maharal, Nesivos Olam, Nesiv HaBushah* 1). Boaz was richly endowed with this faculty (בו עז). It had been preordained that it would be his destiny to expand Judaism's orbit to include the Moabite Ruth who, until his re-establishing of the halachah that the prohibition against marrying Moabites was limited to the males, had in practical terms been excluded. He would need a full range of aggressive vehemence to establish this principle.

He had lived a long life before Ruth came back from Moab. [According to *Ruth Rabbah* 6:2, he was eighty years old when he married Ruth.] He had already fathered many children. But none of this was relevant to his true essence. His early experiences had been as Ivtzan, not as Boaz. The noble kernel of royalty within him had not been involved.[1]

It was in Ruth that the 'Boaz' within him was revealed. It was through her that he found the fulfillment of his destiny.

For yet another facet of Boaz' personality, see page 414.

⋖§ Calev, Miriam and David

וְכָלֵב בֶּן־חֶצְרוֹן הוֹלִיד אֶת־עֲזוּבָה אִשָּׁה וְאֶת־יְרִיעוֹת וְאֵלֶּה בָנֶיהָ יֵשֶׁר וְשׁוֹבָב [יח-יט]
וְאַרְדּוֹן: וַתָּמָת עֲזוּבָה וַיִּקַּח־לוֹ כָלֵב אֶת־אֶפְרָת וַתֵּלֶד לוֹ אֶת־חוּר.

[18-19] *And Calev the son of Chetzron fathered by Azuvah, a wife, and by Yerioth; and these were her sons — Yesher, Shovav and Ardon. And Azuvah died and Calev took for himself Ephrath, and she bore him Chur.*

A. Azuvah is identical with [Moses' sister] Miriam. Why then is she called Azuvah [from עזב, *to forsake*]? Because all [potential suitors] ignored [forsook] her. [Because she was an invalid, as her other name Yerioth indicates,] and was sickly, as indicated by her being called Chelah (4:5) [from חלה, *to be sick*] *(Sotah 12a, Rashi).*

B. *And Calev fathered Azuvah.* Did he not marry her? Rabbi Yochanan answered: [It is to teach us that] anyone who marries a woman for pure motives is considered as though he had fathered her *(Sotah ibid.).*

C. [Why was she called] Yerioth? Because her face was like a sheet [without any color; her sickness made her look pallid *(Rashi).* יְרִיעוֹת from יְרִיעָה, *curtain* (usually white)].

D. *And these were her sons — Yesher, Shovav and Ardon.* [All this refers to Calev:] Do not read בָנֶיהָ, *sons*, but בּוֹנֶיהָ, *her builder.* [Calev built her up by marrying her.]

[Calev is called] Yesher [from ישר, *to be straight*] because he preserved his straightness [by not deviating from the truth together with the other spies *(Rashi)*].

[He is called] Shovav [from שׁוֹבֵב, *backturning, rebellious*] because he forced his inclination to rebel [against his fellow spies *(Rashi)*].

[And he is called] Ardon [from רדה, *to rule* or *control*] because he controlled his inclination [which was urging him to follow the other spies *(Rashi)*] *(Sotah ibid.).*

E. *Now Ashchur Avi Tekoa had two wives — Chelah and Naarah* (4:5). [This verse also refers to Calev:] Ashchur is Calev. He was called Ashchur [from שָׁחוֹר, *black*] because he blackened his face by fasting [praying that he would not be caught up in the plot of the spies *(Rashi)*].

[He was called] Avi (from אָב, *father)* because he became a father to her [to Miriam, providing her with food and medicines for her illness, as a father would do *(Rashi)*].

[And he was called] Tekoa [from תקע, *to fasten*] because he fastened his heart to God [in his efforts not to be dragged into the plans of the spies *(Rashi)*] *(Sotah there).*

---

1. In the absence of any aggadic source concerning the interpretation of the name אִבְצָן, *Ivtzan,* the following suggestion is offered. Since homorganic letters are interchangeable, the *beis* of his name may well be in place of a *phey,* the *tzaddik* in place of a *samech.* The name would thus be אִפְסָן from אֶפֶס, *nothingness* or *futility.*

F. *Now Ashchur Avi Tekoa had two wives.* [This means that] Miriam was like two women. [One aspect was called] Chelah [from חלה, *to be sick*] because at first she was sick. [And one aspect was called] Naarah [from נַעֲרָה, *a young girl*] because in the end [she became] a young girl. [She was cured of her sickness and regained the appearance of a young girl *(Rashi)*] *(Sotah,* there).

G. *And the sons of Chelah — Tzereth, Tzohar, and Ethnan* (4:7). [These are not the names of Chelah/Miriam's children but descriptions of her after she had been built up, strengthened and cured *(Rashi)*.]

[She was called] Tzereth [from צָרָה, *sorrow*] because she caused trouble to all other wives. [Her new-found beauty made all women less beautiful by comparison *(Rashi)*.]

[She was called] Tzohar [from צהר, *to shine*] because her face was as beautiful as the glow of the afternoon [צָהֳרַיִם].

[She was called] Ethnan [related to נתן, *to give*] because whoever saw her would send a gift to his wife. [Because the sight of her would awaken desire in other men *(Rashi)*.]

H. [Moses' sister] Miriam married Calev *(Sifri Behaaloscha* 78).

I. David was descended from Miriam *(Sotah* 11b).

In the sources quoted here Calev appears under six different names (Yesher, Shovav, Ardon, Ashchur, Avi and Tekoa), and these are not the only names in the genealogical lists which the Sages assign to him. (See further at 4:8 and 18.) In v. 9 his name appears in the plural form, Cheluvai, which may, in fact, indicate that *Chronicles* looks at him as a complex, multifaceted personality.

Miriam, too, has many different names (Azuvah, Yerioth, Chelah, Naarah and Ephrath) and again, these are not the only ones assigned to her by the Sages (see further at 4:8).

The many names which the Sages interpret as referring to Calev and Miriam indicate the importance which the Sages attached to their marriage. It seems plausible that this importance derives from the fact that David, and therefore the Messiah, are descended from them. If this is so, it follows that the many facets of their characters, as revealed by their various names, contribute in some material way to the Messianic ideal.

In the case of Calev these names center on two aspects of his life. The majority (Yesher, Shovav, Ardon, Ashchur and Tekoa) deal with his refusal to join the spies in their perfidy. One (Avi) describes the attention which he lavished upon his sick wife.

In the case of Miriam, three (Azuvah, Yerioth and Chelah) describe the sickly state in which she was when Calev married her. One (Naarah) describes her rejuvenation while the one (Ephrath) which she earned through her heroism in Egypt (see comm.) is the name which conveys to us that David was descended from her.

The Messianic idea is often expressed in Scripture as a *sprouting* (צְמִיחָה) of salvation [cf. *Jeremiah* 23:5; 33:15; *Zechariah* 3:8; *Psalms* 132:17]. Sprouting is a process in which the decay and disintegration of the seed promotes growth and generates new life. In much the same way the darkness of the preceding generations will, ultimately, produce the Messianic light. This is the most fundamental of all the forces which animate the historical process as taught by the Torah.

Adam's sin introduced a dimension of evil into the world that made it impossible for God to reveal Himself to man in the unstinting abundance of His goodness with the immediacy which He had intended. Man's perception of Him had become distorted. God's absolute oneness seemed to be called into question in a world in which apparently evil could coexist with good.

The purpose of the historical process is to demonstrate the illusory nature of that evil. God's oneness is not in the slightest compromised by the horrors and the suffering which has become part of man's travail. There are not, as ancient heresies would have us believe, שְׁתֵּי רְשׁוּיוֹת, *two independent forces* — the one from whom all good emanates and the other, source of absolute evil — locked in unending conflict. All comes from God and all derives from His infinite mercies. God wills only man's absolute good, but man will not be able to apprehend that good until he has recognized the catastrophe which lies in any alternative to the will of God. Indeed, history is replete with the blighted hopes and frustrated aspirations of entire people and civilizations whose dreams had led them away from the path of God. Their lives which had once been so full of strength and glory have become no more than a salutary lesson to posterity of the utter futility of a Godless existence.

History will have run its course when man will have realized that in truth, *there is none beside Him (Deuteronomy 4:35).*

The full grandeur of the light of truth will be the more beautiful to man at the time of redemption because of the long ages through which he experienced the heartbreak of futility in his pursuit of the mirages of falsehood. (See *R' Moshe Chaim Luzzatto* in *Daas Tevunos* who elaborates upon this theme.)

In the monthly ritual of בִּרְכַּת הַלְּבָנָה, *the blessing over the moon,* the proclamation: דָּוִד מֶלֶךְ יִשְׂרָאֵל חַי וְקַיָּם, *David King of Israel lives and endures,* plays a central role. The source for this proclamation is *Rosh Hashanah 25a,* where we find David's royal line compared to the moon (see *Rashi* there). There are many different dimensions to this comparison (cf. *Rabbeinu Bachya* to *Exodus* 12:2), among them the promise of renewal and rejuvenation implied in the constantly waning and waxing moon cycle (see *Ramban, Genesis* 38:29). Israel knows that it is to be 'renewed' one day even as the moon is constantly renewed *(Sanhedrin* 42a and text of the *Bircas HaLevanah).* That destiny of renewal is vested in the royal line of David from whom the Messiah will come; and every month when Israel sees the first sliver of light as the new moon begins to make its appearance it knows that David, King of Israel, lives and endures within its collective consciousness.

But David is more than the symbol of renewal. It is also he who taught Israel not to be overwhelmed by the seemingly endless darkness of its travail. In his *Psalms* he always points to the timeless essence which lies within every concrete occurrence. He is constantly aware of the thread of eternity which lies just beneath the surface of the here and now.

'In David's life, ideas — and above all the idea of the omnipresence of God — acquired a singular actuality. The awareness of the Divine occupied his existence to such a degree that it completely overshadowed all other aspects of being. Where others perceived a world made and moved by concrete facts and forces and where — if recognized at all — the forces of the spirit led a shadowy existence in the background of reality, David saw a different world. To him it was a world of the spirit, of the all-pervading and all-sustaining reality of the Divine, animating and ennobling the mechanism of the universe. This invisible reality was his true reality; the world of the idea, his world. All his thoughts and feelings, his words and actions, his wishes and impulses, were directed by the influences of that unseen reality.

'To David every event spelled its eternal meaning; nature and history could not conceal their immutable core of truth. Without hesitation, without perceptible effort, every concrete event was, in his soul, traced to its timeless essence. The treacherous inhabitants of Ziph appear as evil incarnate, Doeg the Edomite as the cruelty of man to man personified. When the Philistines caught him in Gath, or Saul's persecutions drove him to hide in caves; whatever event, grievous or joyous, occurred in his life, was in his meditations recast in the mold of eternity. Hence the immediacy and the directness with which the *Psalms* appeal to man. They speak of what moves man's heart at all times and places, of ever-recurring human problems divorced of the incidentals of place and time. The *Psalms* are forever present, forever alive. Through them David speaks to every Jew in every age' (Introduction to H. Biberfeld's *David, King of Israel*).

These, then, are two aspects of David's function within Israel. He represents the force of rejuvenation which lies within it and is at the same time our guide in perceiving the potential which lies within the seemingly unrelenting darkness of the present.

Perhaps these two gifts, that of renewal and the faculty to see beneath the surface and to apprehend the true nature of the historical process, came to David from Calev and Miriam.

The name Ephrath, which teaches that David was descended from Miriam (comm. v. 18), is mentioned specifically at that point in Miriam's life when Calev took her after Azuvah's death which, as the Sages teach, was at the moment of her return to youth. Surely it is no coincidence that her ancestry of David is stressed just at that particular moment. A return to youth is akin to a new creation [see *Maharal, Gevuros Hashem* 16, in his explanation of the return to youth which the Sages teach concerning Miriam's mother Yocheved]. From the death-like torpor of her *tzara'as* Miriam was 'recreated.' She was not just cured, she was reborn. And thus will the Davidic Messiah descended from her bring about a rebirth of Israel, breathing a new life into the dry bones of a seemingly moribund Israel (see *Ezekiel* ch. 37).

But Miriam's rebirth did not take place in a vacuum. It happened in the context of her marriage to Calev. This marriage was no ordinary one. It was undertaken as a result of such pure motives that it was as though Calev had fathered Miriam. They were truly 'one' as a father is one with his daughter, and within the perfection of that union Miriam, as part of Calev, was able to develop to her full potential (see *Maharal, Ohr Chadash* to *Esther* 2:7).

Calev had truly 'built' Miriam, but this building had been possible for him because of the same insight which enabled him to withstand the pressures of his fellow spies. Where they had seen a 'land consuming its inhabitants' (*Numbers* 13:32), he had apprehended its inner goodness (*Numbers* 14:7). Where the young men of Israel had seen a sickly invalid and had forsaken Miriam, Calev, with a deeper insight, set about patiently to build her back to health and reveal her inner beauty. If Miriam's life portends the Messianic renewal, it is Calev who is the source of David's ability to see the seed of light within the darkness.

Chapter Three

◄§ Zerubavel

[יז] וּבְנֵי יְכָנְיָה אַסִר שְׁאַלְתִּיאֵל בְּנוֹ.

[17] *The sons of Yechoniah — Assir, his son Shealtiel.*

The commentary has noted two peculiarities concerning Zerubavel: that although his real father was Pedaiah he is always described as a son of Shealtiel; and the importance which is attached to the fact that he was conceived in Babylon.

As quoted in the commentary, *Vayikra Rabbah* interprets the name Shealtiel that God 'asked' [שָׁאַל, *to ask*] that the oath which He had made [that Yechoniah die childless] be nullified. *Sanhedrin* 37b adds another interpretation. The name is related to שתל, *to plant*, and connotes: 'He whom God planted.' His conception was truly miraculous in that the dungeon was too narrow to allow for normal conjugal relations between Yechoniah and his wife. She conceived him in a position in which, under normal circumstances, conception would have been impossible.

The complete name זְרֻבָּבֶל בֶּן שְׁאַלְתִּיאֵל, then, is heavy with associations with that miraculous event. This child was conceived in Babylon of a father whose own conception was miraculous in the sense that there should have been no physical possibility that he be conceived and that, moreover, it resulted from God's decision that the oath which He had made be nullified.

All this must be understood against the background of the Sages' tradition (comm. v. 16) that this Zerubavel was to be the link through which the Davidic line was to be perpetuated and was therefore to be ancestor of the Messiah.

That the Messianic line was perpetuated by means of a miracle, in defiance of natural laws which maintained that Shealtiel could never be born, is reminiscent of how Israel came into being. Isaac, too, had been born miraculously, for the Sages teach that both Abraham and Sarah were physically incapable of having children.

Israel lives in defiance of every rule of history because its genesis owes nothing to natural law. It remains eternal in the teeth of time-bound and crumbling national entities because it came into being by Divine fiat, unfettered by the temporal limitations of a nature-bound world.

And what is true of the people is true of the idea which animates and defines their trek through history. Israel lives because of its firm, unshakable knowledge of its Messianic future. And if the one man in the whole world upon whom the realization of that future rests is incarcerated in a Babylonian dungeon without any possibility of fathering a child — because God Himself had decreed that he should be barren and because the physical circumstances make a mockery of any spark of hope that might have existed that perhaps a way could be found — then God will 'retract' nature and will forgo its claims, and a child will be born.

But it is not only the fact of the conception in the king's dungeon which is significant. It is the fact that the dungeon is in Babylon that sets Shealtiel's birth and Zerubavel's destiny into their true perspective.

Moses, too, was born in Egypt, and, what is more, had been reared by the very Pharaoh whose nemesis he was destined to become. The Messiah himself 'sits at the gates of Rome,' the mighty kingdom which he is destined to replace

(*Sanhedrin* 98a). Or, as *Shemos Rabbah* (1:26) teaches, he is even now being readied for his mission in the lands of Gog, king of Magog, whose mighty forces he will one day smash.

The lesson which the Sages seek to teach by revealing these truths seems clear. There is no irrevocable degeneration in the world. As a seemingly absolute degeneration approaches, then that degeneration carries the seed of regeneration within itself. If we could conceive of a world unrelated to God's providence, then an Egypt could sink, dragging the world along with it, into an abyss from which there is no rising. As it is, it nurtures a Moses within its bosom. Gog and Magog are part of a world order which brings humanity to a state in which it teeters on the brink of destruction — but it harbors the Messiah within its borders.

The same is true of Babylon. It is the first of the four mighty kingdoms which, from their advent, were destined to span world history. These kingdoms would comprise world empires and would be devoted to the propagation of all that is evil and degenerate. They would be animated by only one purpose — to drive out the Divine from the affairs of man.

And so, it is eminently fitting that just Babylon should be the cradle of the Messianic future. As Egypt nurtured Moses and as Magog will produce the ultimate Messiah, so Babylon, the first of the four major kingdoms to foster mankind's rebellion against God, generated the seed from which the Messiah would grow.

Chapter Four

◄§ The Symbolism of Wine

[א־ח] בְּנֵי יְהוּדָה פֶּרֶץ חֶצְרוֹן וְכַרְמִי ... וְקוֹץ הוֹלִיד אֶת־עָנוּב ...

[1-8] *The sons of Judah — Peretz, Chetzron, Carmi ... and Kotz fathered Anuv ...*

The commentary has noted the association of Calev with names relating to the vine, e.g., כַּרְמִי, *Carmi (my vineyard)*, and עָנוּב, *Anav (grapes)*. It would seem that the apparent affinity between Calev and the idea of wine is highly significant to *Chronicles'* presentation of Calev. Moreover, the name Carmi which recalls this affinity is particularly apt in our passage whose thrust is towards underlining the significance of his great-grandson, Betzalel, as the builder and chief artisan of the Tabernacle in the wilderness (see v. 2).

Above (p. 290), two aspects of David's function within Israel were identified. He represented the force of rejuvenation and renewal which underlies the Messianic idea, and also taught the people how to intuit that potential within the seemingly unrelenting darkness of the present. It was shown there how both these faculties had their source in the characters and union of Calev and Miriam, who, in the tradition of the Sages, were ancestors of David.

In ch. 58 of *Pachad Yitzchak* to *Pesach*, R' Yitzchak Hutner discusses one aspect of the significance of wine in aggadic symbolism. In contrast to most other things which spoil with the passage of time, wine improves with age. It is only with the passing of years that its true goodness can be savored.

Now, time poses the great challenge to the concept of a finite world begun by God's free, untrammelled will and ending should God withdraw His favor.

Determined by the inexorable, undeviating motion of the celestial bodies around the sun, with no apparent beginning and no discernible end, time functions without revealing the hand of God Who ordained it. God hid Himself behind a facade of natural law when He made this world, and it is the phenomenon of time, more than any other, which serves to obscure His providence.

It is not only the finiteness of the world that is hidden by time. God 'renews daily the act of creation' (Siddur, morning prayers). The passage of time is no more than an illusion which hides God's constant, active and indispensable involvement in physical existence. In reality, each second is a new gift of God, a new granting of life, self-contained and independent of the second which preceded it.

But all this is true only at the essential level of existence. The facade of nature is truly an opaque veil which effectively hides these truths from our observation. In our daily experience time moves linearly and infinitely and all of nature is subject to its ravages.

Except wine! Wine is that unique part of nature which allows us a glimpse of the truth. By defying the debilitating weakening of age, by becoming stronger and more robust as the years go by, wine helps the discerning mind to intuit the illusory nature of time and to detect the creating hand of God which is the true and constant source of life.

And so Çalev, whose task in life — together with Miriam — was to teach of renewal and rejuvenation, and whose keenly perceptive eye allowed him to perceive youth and beauty where all others saw only an aging, sickly woman, is truly a man of 'wine,' a *Carmi*, vintner, able to apprehend the true dynamics of creation.

It is fitting that this aspect of Calev's nature should be stressed in the particular passage which leads to an appreciation of his great-grandson Betzalel. As will be seen below, the Tabernacle which Betzalel built was symbolic of the inner world which lies hidden from the physical eye but which animates and gives meaning to the world as we know it by relating to it as the soul relates to the body. In this context the *'vineyard'* nature of Calev is particularly significant.

◂§ Betzalel

[ב] וּרְאָיָה בֶן־שׁוֹבָל הֹלִיד אֶת־יַחַת וְיַחַת הֹלִיד אֶת־אֲחוּמַי וְאֶת־לָהַד ...

[2] *And Reaiah the son of Shoval fathered Yachath, and Yachath fathered Achumai and Lahad ....*

The commentary has quoted the Sages' statement that all the names here refer to Betzalel. Although certainly not the simple meaning of the verse, such a homiletic reading may well be supported by some curious textual points. Two textual irregularities may underlie the teaching of the Sages:

(1) Why in 2:50 which, as noted in comm. 1-4, is really the beginning of our section, is Calev given as the son of Chur, rather than as his father? [See comm. there for the opinion of the *Mefaresh*.]

(2) The strange formulation of verse 1, which lists Chur by name but gives Calev as Carmi and Uri as Shoval [see comm. there].

Both these irregularities can be explained if the subject of our verse is Betzalel and that it deals with the names of endearment [see comm.] with which God made known the essence of that great man's contribution to history.

As learned from *Maharal* (see comm. to 4:22), *Chronicles* is the book in which we expect individuals to be lifted out of the narrow confines of specific events and to be seen from the perspective of their historical significance.

Within such a context, Betzalel seems unique among the personalities with whom Scripture deals. From the very moment of his introduction, he is presented not as a person of the moment but as one belonging to history. *See! I have called by name Betzalel the son of Uri the son of Chur (Exodus 31:1). 'See!* this "Book of Adam" in which are inscribed all generations which are destined to exist from creation until the resurrection of the dead. Each generation with its kings, each one with its leaders and its prophets. Every person have I destined for his purpose in life from that moment. Betzalel, too, was predestined from that moment' *(Shemos Rabbah 40:3).* [See further in *Ramban* to *Exodus* 31:1: 'God said to Moses that he should consider this miracle [which is Betzalel] ... whom He had created for His honor, for He is the creator of history [קוֹרֵא הַדּוֹרוֹת מֵרֹאשׁ].' As God said [to Jeremiah (*Jeremiah* 1:5)]: *Before I formed you in the womb I set you aside and before you were born have I hallowed you* ...

While everyone has been eternally destined for his role in life, it is only in the case of Betzalel that this is stated openly, as though it is only within the larger perspective of history that his personality can be comprehended.

'R' Yehudah taught in the name of Rav: Betzalel knew how to combine the letters through which heaven and earth were created' *(Berachos 55a).* He saw with his keen and complex mind the structure and pattern of the universe, he understood the forces and interactions of the cosmos, and he knew the symbols and formulae expressing the powers of creation. Thus he was able to fashion the Sanctuary, to recreate on a small, symbolic scale the Temple of creation. He built the microcosm to receive and house the glory of the living God — *Whose glory fills the world (David, King of Israel,* H. Biberfeld, p. 74).

It need not concern us here why a creation in microcosm was necessary at this point. [For an example of how the matter is understood in Chassidic thought, see *Sefas Emes* to *Exodus* p. 224ff.] But if it was needed, then surely the soul of the man who would be entrusted with that 'creation' must be an all-encompassing one; one who can master the cosmos and not be mastered by it.

This idea seems to be expressed in the Midrash *(Shemos Rabbah 40:3).* Moses had originally thought that he himself was to build the Tabernacle. When God explained that he, as king, would not be able to do the work himself he was puzzled. Who, then, would be able to do it? To this God answered as quoted above. Betzalel had been predestined from the moment of creation for this momentous task.

Perhaps we can understand Moses' perplexity as follows: Moses himself had a soul which was all encompassing. 'There was a woman in Egypt who bore six hundred thousand in her womb ... this was Yocheved who bore Moses, whom the Torah considers as the equivalent of the whole of Israel' *(Mechilta, Beshalach;* see *Maharal, Gevuros HaShem* 19). Had he been called upon to build, i.e., create, the Tabernacle he would have been able to do so. But if not he, who then? Was there another soul in Israel which was great enough to be lifted, as it were, above the stars, and have the cosmos at its feet? To this the answer was that indeed there existed such a one. Betzalel, destined from creation for this moment, had indeed been granted a soul which would be equal to the task.

When the Torah tells of Moses' birth the account begins with the words, *Now*

a man from the house of Levi went and took a daughter of Levi (Exodus 2:1).
Maharal (Gevuros HaShem 16) asks why the names of Amram and Yocheved,
Moses' parents, are not clearly stated. *Maharal* answers that if their names had
been given, it would have appeared that Amram and Yocheved — as individuals
— were significant in Moses' birth. But since Moses was destined to be the
redeemer from the moment of creation and his being was already determined, it
was only necessary to bring him into the world [in contrast to ordinary children
whose nature and being depends on their parents]. If Amram and Yocheved had
not been worthy of doing so, then some other parent would have served. Thus,
they are not identified by their given names.

Sometimes, then, a soul is too great to be defined in terms of individual
parents. If Calev's and Uri's names had been given, then Betzalel would have
appeared as just another link in the chain of the Calevite family. Just as Amram
and Yocheved as individuals disappeared behind the anonymity of 'a man and a
daughter of Levi,' so Betzalel's father and great-grandfather were turned into
concepts rather than flesh and blood people to be presented in a truer
perspective.

But what of Chur?

Chur had earned the right to be mentioned as an individual. By an act of
extreme heroism he had established himself as the one from whom Betzalel was
to be descended. When the people wanted to build the golden calf, Chur tried to
prevent them and was martyred for his efforts. So God rewarded him and said:
'By your life, your descendants will be given a great name in the world, as it is
written: *See! I have called by name Betzalel ...*' And that is why Betzalel's name
is given in the Torah as *son of Uri, son of Chur (Shemos Rabbah* 48:3).

Perhaps we can now understand why 2:50 gives Calev as Chur's son whereas,
in truth, it was Chur who was Calev's son. Perhaps in the context of tracing
Betzalel's ancestry the physical sequence is less important than the essential
truth. It is true that in a physical sense Calev fathered Chur, but essentially it was
Chur who was Calev's 'father' — the cause for his existence. In the context of
Betzalel, Chur was more important than Calev and Calev existed only so that he
might bear Chur.

⋙ Yabetz and the Rechavites

[פרק ב:נה] וּמִשְׁפְּחוֹת סוֹפְרִים יֹשְׁבֵי יַעְבֵּץ תִּרְעָתִים שִׁמְעָתִים שׂוּכָתִים הֵמָּה הַקִּינִים
הַבָּאִים מֵחַמַּת אֲבִי בֵית־רֵכָב.

[2:55] *And the families of scribes, dwellers in Yabetz — the
Tirathites, the Shimathites and the Suchathites; they are the Kenites
who are descended from Chammath, father of Beth Rechav.*

[ט־י] וַיְהִי יַעְבֵּץ נִכְבָּד מֵאֶחָיו וְאִמּוֹ קָרְאָה שְׁמוֹ יַעְבֵּץ לֵאמֹר כִּי יָלַדְתִּי בְּעֹצֶב. וַיִּקְרָא
יַעְבֵּץ לֵאלֹהֵי יִשְׂרָאֵל לֵאמֹר אִם־בָּרֵךְ תְּבָרְכֵנִי וְהִרְבִּיתָ אֶת־גְּבוּלִי וְהָיְתָה יָדְךָ עִמִּי
וְעָשִׂיתָ מֵּרָעָה לְבִלְתִּי עָצְבִּי וַיָּבֵא אֱלֹהִים אֵת־אֲשֶׁר שָׁאָל.

[9,10] *Now Yabetz was the most honored of his brothers, and his
mother called him Yabetz saying, 'For I have borne in pain.' And
Yabetz called to the God of Israel saying, 'If You will surely bless me,
and enlarge my boundaries, and Your hand will be with me, and You
will avert evil that I not be saddened.' And God granted what he had
asked.*

A. Rabbi Simai taught: There were three people consulted in [Pharaoh's] plan [to enslave Israel]: Balaam, Job and Yithro [Jethro]. Balaam who suggested [the plan] was [eventually] killed; Job who kept silent [neither encouraging nor opposing it] was punished with suffering; Yithro who [opposed the plan and] fled had the merit that his descendants sat [as judges] in the לְשְׁכַּת הַגָּזִית, *Hall of Hewn Stone* [the Temple chamber in which the Great Sanhedrin sat]. As it is written: *And the families of scribes* [i.e., judges], *dwellers in Yabetz ... they are the Kenites ...* And [to prove that these Kenites are descended from Yithro] it is written *(Judges* 1:16): *And the sons of Keni, father-in-law of Moses ... (Sotah* 11a).

Sanhedrin 104a has the identical passage except that it substitutes the merit of having invited Moses into his home *(Exodus* 2:20) for the merit of his having opposed Pharaoh's plan.

B. [Moses father-in-law was called] Chovav because he loved the Torah (חוֹבָב from חבב, *to love).* No proselyte ever loved the Torah as much as Yithro did. And even as he loved the Torah so did his children. [*Sifri* continues with a description of Jeremiah's experiences with the Rechavites cited in the comm.] [Now, as a reward] God appointed them scribes as it is written: *And the families of scribes* ... תִּרְעָתִים [from the Aramaic תַּרְעָא, *gate],* for they sat [as judges] at the gates of Jerusalem; שִׁמְעָתִים [from שמע, *to hear],* for they listened to their father's commands; שׂוּכָתִים, *Suchathites* [from סכך, *to cast shade],* for they lived in huts.

[What is the meaning of] יֹשְׁבֵי יַעְבֵּץ, *dwellers in Yabetz?* [It teaches that] they left Jericho and traveled to Yabetz to learn Torah from him. As it is written (4:10): *And Yabetz prayed to the God of Israel ... and God brought about that for which he had asked* (4:11) [see there]. They lacked a teacher and he lacked students. So they who sought a teacher went to him who sought students, as it is written *(Judges* 1:16): *And the sons of Keni, father-in-law of Moses, went up from the city of the date trees ... (Sifri Behaaloscha).*

C. We have learned: Othniel [ben Kenaz, the first Judge in Israel after Joshua (see *Joshua* 15-17, *Judges* 1:3)] is [identical with] Yabetz ... [Why was he called] Othniel? Because God answered him. [There is a phonetic relationship between עָתְנִיאֵל and עָנָה אתוֹ א-ל, *God answered him.*] [Why was he called Yabetz? [Because] he counseled [יַעְבֵּץ from יעץ, *to counsel*] and spread Torah in Israel.

Now how do we know that God answered him? For it is written (4:10): *And Yabetz called to the God of Israel saying: If You will surely bless me, and enlarge my boundaries, and Your hand will be with me, and You will avert evil that I not be saddened ... And God granted what he had asked.* [We now interpret.] *If You will surely bless me* — with Torah [that is, that I will know much Torah]; *and enlarge my boundaries* — with students; *and Your hand will be with me* — that I will not forget my learning; *and You will avert evil* — that I will meet friends who complement my nature [a play on the word מֵרָעָה, as though it derived from רֵעַ, *friend]; that I not* — that my evil inclination will not prevent me from learning Torah; *be saddened* — If You do all this for me — good; if not I will go to my grave in sorrow. [This is the teaching of R' Nosson.] R' Yehudah HaNassi explained: *If You will surely bless me* — by allowing me to be fruitful; *and enlarge my boundaries* — with sons and daughters; *and Your hand will be with me* — in my business affairs; *and You will avert evil* — that neither my head, ears nor eyes will trouble me; *that I not* — that my evil inclination will not prevent me from learning Torah; *be saddened* — if You do that for me — good. If not, I will go to my grave in sorrow (Temurah, 16a).

The migration of the Rechavites from the lush and fertile surroundings of Jericho to the arid Judean desert is a drama of epic proportions.[1] Its implications go far beyond the inspiring story of a family, thirsting for knowledge, giving up wealth and comfort for the rigors of desert dwelling in order to be near a man whose craving to share his knowledge equaled their own longing for wisdom. In a sense their lonely trek to the desert presaged the mighty flow of nations who, in Isaiah's majestic vision (Isaiah 2:3), will one day leave everything in order to go up to God's House to learn His ways, knowing that Torah emanates from Zion and God's word from Jerusalem.

There can be no doubt that the Rechavite saga must be interpreted in Messianic terms. No other explanation is possible for the prominent place which it occupies in the visions of the 'end of days' with which Balaam ended his ill-fated attempt to curse Israel (Numbers 24:14ff, particularly vs. 11 and 22). Immediately after Balaam had seen the ultimate destruction of Amalek, he turned his prophetic gaze towards the Kenites. Amazed at the firmness with which these descendants of his former colleague, Yithro, are ensconced among the Jewish people, honored judges in the nation's highest court [based on our passage (2:55) — see Rashi to Numbers 24:21], he assures them that their place there is indeed permanent and that even if, in the course of history, they should suffer through an exile, they will return to share in Israel's future.

Indeed, as Mechilta to Yisro points out, the promise which God made to the Rechavites (Jeremiah 35:19) — Therefore thus says HASHEM of hosts, the God of Israel: There will never cease to be a man from [the family of] Yonadav ben Rechav for all days — was made unconditionally. These children of proselytes were to be an inseparable part of the Jewish people.

From where did the Rechavites draw their inspiration for their desert trek? What is Yithro's place in Jewish history? Who was this Yabetz to whom they felt themselves so strongly drawn?

Balaam prophesied concerning the Kenites immediately after his vision of the ultimate destruction of Amalek. Surely this juxtaposition is no coincidence.

Earlier in the Torah the two are also brought together. The description of how Yithro joined Israel in the desert (Exodus ch. 18) comes immediately after the account of Amalek's defeat at Joshua's hands at Rephidim (there 17:8).

The Sages (Shemos Rabbah 27:8) note this and explain it on the basis of Proverbs 19:25 which teaches: You smite the scoffer [who does not take the lesson] but the simple-minded person [takes heed of the lesson and] becomes wise. Thus, Amalek did not draw the lessons of its defeat, continued to defy God, and was therefore doomed to ultimate destruction. Yithro, on the other hand, saw Amalek's downfall, drew the correct conclusions, and leaving behind

---

1. The following is from Sifri Zuta, Behaaloscha 29:10.

'Now what kindness did Israel bestow on Yithro? [see Numbers 10:32]. When [Israel] entered the Land they set aside the fertile area surrounding Jericho and declared that whichever tribe would have the Temple built in its territory would be compensated for the land it was giving up with this tract of land. This [piece of land] they gave to Yithro [and his family], who ate its produce for 440 years (i.e., until the Temple was built).

Others say that they only remained near Jericho during the lifetime of Joshua because he was available to teach them Torah. After his death they declared: Our whole intention in forsaking all we had was in order to learn Torah and now [should we spend our time] plowing and reaping? When will we learn Torah? So they were told about one man who taught Torah in a barren place where no grain would grow. Immediately upon hearing this they went ...'

wealth and comfort, threw in his lot with the desert wanderings of Israel. In the same manner, his descendants would one day leave the luxuries of their Jericho inheritance to join Yabetz in the wilderness of Judah.

Thus, Amalek and Yithro represent two poles within the gentile world. Amalek is unbending and inflexible; he has never learned to bow down. He is the archetypal לץ, scoffer, to whom nothing is ever holy, nothing worthy of respect. Even if his bitter hatred of God and Israel would allow him to apprehend the Messianic light, it could never serve him as a beacon by which to correct the terrible errors of his blighted life. In his mind he is the repository of the only truth. He will not and cannot search for another because he is convinced that there can be nothing to find. Bitter and alone in the face of a universal recognition of Israel's God which will permeate the Messianic era, but in which he cannot share, he is doomed to oblivion.

Not so Yithro. He is a driven man; driven by an intuitive certainty that there is a truth external to himself which he must find. He spent a lifetime probing and analyzing every conceivable belief. He found them all wanting, and confronted with the truth, he was intellectually prepared to recognize it (see *Shemos Rabbah* 1:32). But more; he was a man of action. Once his mind had been engaged he followed where it led with uncompromising energy and unflagging vigor. No consideration of the practical difficulties which lay in his path could hold him back. In absolute contrast to Amalek, he is the prototype for all the nations who will be able to share in the Messianic future. When the light of truth finally bursts over the world, they will find it within themselves to reject their misguided past and stream to Jerusalem in their myriads to sit at Israel's-feet and learn of God and His Torah.

The passion of the ancestor was passed on to the children. After Joshua's death they knew that they would once more have to make a trek into the desert if they were to be able to quench their thirst for understanding. And so these ideal students set out into the Judean wilderness to find the perfect teacher — Yabetz. Who was this Yabetz? From *Temurah* 16a we know that Yabetz was another name for Othniel ben Kenaz, Israel's first Judge after Joshua. The Talmud (there) teaches that in the period immediately following the death of Moses, the mourning was so great that sections of the Torah were forgotten. It was Othniel, who, with uncompromising tenacity of purpose, studied hard and rediscovered the lost parts of the Torah.

This story can help us to understand Othniel's place in history.

Rabbi David Cohen (in *Ohel David*, Part II) suggests the following explanation for our passage (4:9), which teaches that Yabetz was given his name by his mother: ... *for I have borne in pain.*[1]

When the mantle of leadership passed from Joshua to Othniel, a great qualitative change came about in Israel's relationship to the Torah. The Sages teach that had the first Tablets not been broken at Sinai, no one would ever have forgotten any Torah *(Eruvin 54a)*. At the point when these first Tablets were given, Israel had reached the very heights of human potential and they had regained the lofty status of Adam before he sinned *(Michtav MeEliyahu* vol. II, p. 27ff). Thus, a perfect union of man and the Torah would have come about which could never have been sundered. It was not to be. Israel sinned by making

---

1. יעבץ derives from עבץ which is an inverted form of עצב, *to be sad*. See *Ibn Ezra* in *Safah Berurah* for a discussion of this unusual etymology.

the golden calf, the tablets were broken, and henceforth Torah would have to be acquired through difficult, unrelenting struggle. The Torah would be as difficult to attain as precious gold and as easy to lose as fragile glass (*Chagigah* 15a).

But Joshua had not been present when the golden calf had been made. Alone with his master Moses, he had had no part in that tragic error. The Torah of Joshua was untainted by that sin and he achieved a total fusion with Torah. No word of Torah ever escaped his memory [except once, on occasion as punishment for a specific act; see *Temurah* there]. He knew nothing of the struggle needed to wrest truth from the darkness of ignorance. He taught a Torah clear in all its details, never clouded by doubt or uncertainty. His was a Torah of Adam before the sin.

The sin of Adam introduced pain to the process of childbirth and, in a larger sense, the pain of creativity into human experience. בְּעֶצֶב תֵּלְדִי בָנִים, *in pain will you bear children* (Genesis 3:16), Eve was told after her sin had been revealed; and in pain did Othniel's mother bear him: כִּי יָלַדְתִּי בְּעֹצֶב, *for I have borne [him] in pain*, and called him Yabetz. He was the first bearer of the Torah as it was to be for man after Israel's sin. He was the first to taste the anguish of ignorance and the resulting craving for knowledge which was henceforth to be the hallmark of the Torah scholar. His lot it was to teach that harsh struggle which must precede attainment.

This thirst for Torah knowledge was not coincidental to his existence. Rather, it formed the very essence of his being. Only this can explain the surprising formulation of his prayer, 'If You do all this for me — good, if not I will go to my grave in sorrow.' Only one who knows his very life to be at stake can couch his prayers in such uncompromising, almost demanding, terms. Not for him the uncertain approach of the supplicant. He knows that if God wishes him to live, He must grant him that which is the *sine qua non* of his life. Othniel knew himself for what his essential being demanded that he become — the supreme Torah teacher of the post-desert generation. He needed Torah, needed students, needed an understanding group of friends, needed, above all, to know that he would be granted the energy to follow the path of his destiny. And therefore — all this he was able to demand of God.

It is noteworthy that the prayer of Yabetz should be given so much more prominence than his activities as teacher and Torah scholar. These latter are hinted at but never explicated; his prayer is quoted at length.

In light of the fact, however, that with Yabetz a new, much less-elevated, era began in Israel's relationship to the Torah, it is entirely fitting that prayer should occupy such a central role in Ezra's assessment of Yabetz's historical significance.

King David taught (*Psalms* 130:1) that prayer is to be מִמַּעֲמַקִּים, *from the depths* (see *Berachos* 10b). The more acutely man is aware of his distance from God the more he must feel compelled to seek Him out in prayer. And so, at a watershed of history, when a sudden distancing between man and God occurs, man must feel the urge to bridge by prayer the chasm which has been created.

So it was in the age of Enosh, Adam's grandson. Enosh's generation also marked a turning point in history. Henceforth man was to live at a weaker, lower level of existence [אֱנוֹש from אָנַש, *to be weak or sickly*] (see p. 373). And it was just in his generation that man began to pray, as *Genesis* 4:26 teaches: אָז הוּחַל

לִקְרֹא בְּשֵׁם ה', *then [man] began to pray* [lit. *to call God's name*].[1]

And so it was once more in the case of Yabetz. The change from the Torah of the first Tablets to that of the second Tablets was a cataclysmic one. Light had changed into darkness, exhilarating clarity into a groping uncertainty (see *Tanchuma, Noach* 3). An overpowering yearning was born in man and was expressed in its most sublime form by Othniel-Yabetz, the spiritual giant of his generation. That yearning expressed itself first and foremost in prayer.

As a true leader of his generation Othniel-Yabetz's craving for Torah fulfillment was not limited to himself. It was necessary for him that his people too should regain as much as possible of the light of Torah which had been lost to them. Thus was born the need to 'widen his boundaries with students' and thus Yabetz became the teacher par excellence, with untold spiritual riches to share and an overwhelming desire to share them.

R' Yehudah HaNassi sees Yabetz's prayer as referring to a request for material blessings (see source C). In both versions we are struck by the forcefulness of what is clearly more a demand than a supplication. Yabetz seems to be staking out a right rather than soliciting a favor. Although this is a strange way of addressing God, its justification lies in the object of Yabetz's request. He, who knew himself destined to be the Torah teacher par excellence of the post-desert generation, knew that the tools which he needed for his Torah studies were the prerequisites of his existence. If God wished him to be, then God must grant him the wherewithal for this life — students who would learn from him; friends who could understand and encourage him; and energy to pursue his goal of excellence in Torah studies. All these he needed if he was to achieve his destiny and he could confidently face God and ask for them.

But what of a large family? What of business success and good health? Are these matters which one can demand of God? Are they not rather the gifts of love which God showers upon those who find favor in His eyes? Would not the modest entreaty of the supplicant be more appropriate for these than the firm demand of the claimant?

The explanation may lie in his final request: *That I not* — that my evil inclination will not prevent me from learning Torah. All the other things for which he asked were subsidiary to that final request. If the object of his life remains the propagation of God's Torah, then even the physical amenities of life are his by right.

Yabetz lacked students; the Rechavites lacked a teacher, and Providence brought them together.

---

1. Our translation of this phrase follows *Ibn Ezra*. The Sages, quoted by *Rashi* and other commentators, translate the phrase in a way which implies that in Enosh's generation idol worship began (see ArtScroll *Genesis*, there, for details). However, since the idiom, *to call in God's name*, is always used in Scripture to denote prayer (cf. *Exodus* 33:19 and 34:5), it seems that *Ibn Ezra's* interpretation is in accord with the פְּשַׁט, *the simple meaning*, while the Sages mean their interpretation at the level of דְרַשׁ, *homiletical interpretation*. The two approaches are entirely in consonance with one another. Man began to serve idols because he felt himself distant from God and thought himself in need of an intermediary to intercede for him (see *Rambam, Avodah Zarah* ch. 1). The same feeling of alienation which caused some to turn to idols stimulated others to seek out God in prayer. Both reactions resulted from the same cause.

[יח] וְאִשְׁתּוֹ הַיְהֻדִיָּה יָלְדָה אֶת־יֶרֶד אֲבִי גְדוֹר וְאֶת־חֶבֶר אֲבִי שׂוֹכוֹ וְאֶת־יְקוּתִיאֵל אֲבִי
זָנוֹחַ וְאֵלֶּה בְּנֵי בִתְיָה בַת־פַּרְעֹה אֲשֶׁר לָקַח מָרֶד.

[4:18] *And his Jewish wife bore Yered father of Gedor, and Chever
father of Socho, and Yekuthiel father of Zanoach, and these are the sons
of Bithiah the daughter of Pharaoh whom Mered had married.*

The commentary has noted the difficulties in translating this verse. In the
opinion of the Sages, only one wife is meant here — Bithiah the daughter of
Pharaoh — and all the names of the sons refer to Moses.

The following meanings are assigned to the names: [*Megillah* 13a and *Vayikra
Rabbah* 1:3 assign different meanings; both are given here.][1]

Yered [from ירד, *to descend*]: In whose days manna 'came down' to Israel
(*Megillah*). Or, who 'brought down' the Torah [or the *Shechinah*] from heaven
(*Vayikra Rabbah*).

Avi Gedor [from גדר, *to fence in*]: He 'filled in' the breaches in Israel
(*Megillah*). [The Talmud does not at this stage interpret the word *Avi*. Later it
assigns it a separate meaning. By contrast the Midrash interprets both words
together.] Or, there were many who 'protected' Israel; he was the chief [אֲבִי,
father] of them (*Vayikra Rabbah*).

Chever [from חבר, *to join*]: He 'joined' Israel to their Father in heaven
(*Megillah* and *Vayikra Rabbah*).

Avi Socho [from סכך, *to protect* or סכה, *to see*]: He was a 'protecting canopy'
for Israel (*Megillah*). Or, he was the chief [אֲבִי] of all of Israel's 'seers' and
prophets (*Vayikra Rabbah*).

Yekuthiel [from קוה, *to hope*]: In his time Israel's 'hopes' centered upon God
(*Megillah* and *Vayikra Rabbah*).

Avi Zanoach [from זנח, *to forsake*]: He caused Israel's sins 'to be forgotten'
(*Megillah*). Or, he was the chief [אֲבִי] of all those who caused Israel 'to forsake'
idol worship (*Vayikra Rabbah*).

The three words אֲבִי, which according to *Megillah* have not yet been explained,
are given as: 'father' in Torah; 'father' in wisdom; and 'father' in prophecy.[2]

The verse then goes on to say that all these are [considered to be] the children

---

1. It should be noted that, although we have combined the interpretations of *Vayikra Rabbah* and
Megillah, the Midrash's understanding of the verse differs substantially from that of the Talmud in
as much as the אִשְׁתּוֹ הַיְהֻדִיָּה, in the view of the Midrash, is Yocheved rather than Bithiah. She is called
a 'Jewish' wife because: '... she brought Jews (יְהוּדִים) into the world' (presumably, when as a midwife
in Egypt she refused to obey Pharaoh's orders to kill the children as they were born).

2. *Gra*, in what appears to be a combination of the two versions, explains that the six names
interpreted here refer to the three major benefits which came to Israel through Moses and the three
situations in which Moses averted a major catastrophe. The major benefits were:
   (1) Bringing the Torah to Israel (Yered).
   (2) Building the Tabernacle, thereby establishing a close relationship between God and Israel
(Chever).
   (3) Sustaining Israel in the desert by bringing down the manna, thereby focusing Israel's hopes
upon God (Yekuthiel).
   The major catastrophes he averted were:
   (1) Moses 'filled in' the breach (see *Exodus* 32:25) created by the sin of the golden calf and saved
Israel from punishment with his prayers (Gedor).
   (2) He acted as a 'canopy' (Socho) in front of the fire which began destroying them when Israel
grumbled about its long trek into the wilderness (*Numbers* 11:1-3).
   (3) He averted the destruction of Israel for the sin of trusting the false reports of the spies
(*Numbers* 13:11ff). Moses' intercession caused their sin to be forgotten (Zanoach).

of Bithiah whom Mered married. Mered is taken to be another name for Calev. It is an apt name in this context, for it is fitting that Calev, who rebelled against the prevailing attitude of the spies [מֶרֶד from מרד, *to rebel*], should marry Bithiah who had rebelled against the prevailing idol worship of her father's kingdom.

Vayikra Rabbah adds that the name בִּתְיָה, *Bithiah*, itself is to be interpreted. It can be seen as a contraction of two words: בַּת יָה, *daughter of God*. She had taken Moses as a son although he was not really her son. In return, God would consider her a daughter although she had not been born in Israel.

This verse, then, adds entirely new perspectives to the vague figure of Pharaoh's daughter who appears in *Exodus*. Not only did she eventually marry the princely Calev, but all of Moses' great accomplishments in leading Israel are laid at her door. How can this be? Can all of Moses' accomplishments really be ascribed to the education given him by this Egyptian woman?

There are two additional comments of the Sages to this verse which are very thought provoking and which point to a clearer understanding of this matter.

Yalkut states: *And she brought him to Pharaoh's daughter and he became a son to her, and she called his name Moses* [מֹשֶׁה from משה, *to draw out*], *for from the water have I drawn him out (Exodus 2:10)*. But his father called him Chever [from חבר, *to join*], for because of him he was rejoined to his wife whom he had divorced. But his mother called him Yekuthiel [from קוה, *to hope*], because [even after she had put him into the river] she hoped to have him returned to her so that she could nurse him — and he was. But his sister called him Yered [from ירד, *to descend*], because it was for his sake that she had gone down to the river. But his brother called him Avi Zanoach [from זנח, *to forsake*], as if to say: My father forsook my mother but took her once more because of this one. But Kehath, his grandfather, and his nurse called him Avi Socho [from סכה, *to protect*], as though to say: For three months he was protected as by a roof from the descendants of Ham [the Egyptians] *(Yalkut, Shemos 166)*.

And she called his name Moses. From here we can learn how great is the merit of those who deal kindly with people. Although Moses had many names, the Torah invariably uses the name Moses which was given him by Bithiah, daughter of Pharaoh. Also God never called him by any other name *(Shemos Rabbah 1:26)*.

If we postulate that all the various aggadic and midrashic explanations of these names do not conflict but rather complement one another, the following picture emerges. The names which were subsequently to describe the main elements of Moses' inspired leadership [as analyzed according to *Gra* in the footnote above] were initially given from a much narrower perspective. Thus, for example, the name Chever was always meant to describe a joining. But whereas it eventually came to be the name which projected Moses as the one who erected the Tabernacle and thereby joined Israel to their Father in heaven, Amram, who had originally given the name, had no such inkling. He saw his child only as the cause for his rejoining his wife after he had once divorced her.

This is the case with all the names of Moses to which we are introduced in our verse. Each had been given by an individual who was projecting his individual perception. Moses, however, led his life in such a way that these narrower implications were eventually discarded in favor of the full breadth of meaning assigned to them by the Talmud and Midrash.

Not so the name מֹשֶׁה, *Moses*, given by Pharaoh's daughter to the foundling whom Providence had assigned to her care. She called him מֹשֶׁה [from מֹשֶׁה, *to draw out*] because *from the water have I drawn him out*. But, as *Midrash Lekach Tov* points out (see also *Sforno* there), this seems grammatically incorrect. One who is drawn out should be called מָשׁוּי (in the passive) not מֹשֶׁה (in the active), lit. *one who draws out*. But, the Midrash answers, Bithiah realized that the fact that she had found this child in the water was not just an accident. She recognized that it pointed to his destiny. It was not for nothing that she had drawn him from the water; surely this implied a great future for him. He would one day become a person who himself would, on a much grander scale, save others as he himself had been saved.

Thus, alone among all the people who had given the child a name, Bithiah allowed her own narrower perspective to recede behind the larger implications. This was the kindness for which *Shemos Rabbah* 1:26 praises her. Small wonder, then, that God chose just the name which she had given to be the one by which Moses was to be known for all eternity.

And this is the reason why all of Moses' later accomplishments are laid at her door. It was from Bithiah that he learned the selflessness which is the hallmark of great leadership. Bithiah, in contrast to all the others around Moses, had been able to focus entirely on the child and deny herself the satisfaction of giving him a name in which her own, not insignificant, role might be perpetuated. It is from the upbringing of such a 'mother' that true greatness can grow.

◆§ The Descendants of Shelah

[כא-כג] בְּנֵי שֵׁלָה בֶן־יְהוּדָה עֵר אֲבִי לֵכָה וְלַעְדָּה אֲבִי מָרֵשָׁה ... וְיוֹקִים וְאַנְשֵׁי כֹזֵבָא ... הֵמָּה הַיּוֹצְרִים וְיֹשְׁבֵי נְטָעִים וּגְדֵרָה ...

[21-23] *The sons of Shelah the son of Judah — Er the father of Lechah, Ladah father of Mareshah ... And Yokim and the people of Cozeva ... They were the potters, dwellers in Netaim and Gederah ...*

The wealth of aggadic material about these verses in so many different midrashim makes it obvious that these interpretations were widely accepted.

There are minor variations between the various midrashim, but the common trend is to identify the people mentioned in these verses with various non-Jewish people who became proselytes and were subsequently rewarded for following their determination to come closer to God. The Sages use these experiences to derive a lesson of how richly a Jewish person who sacrifices much in order to attain a greater spiritual standing will be rewarded.

The proselytes hinted at in these verses are, as noted in the commentary, Rachav, the Giveonites and Ruth. Needless to say these proselytes have no place in the פְּשָׁט, *the simple meaning* of the verse, which deals with the descendants of Judah's son, Shelah. Indeed, most of the midrashim preface their identifications with the statement which has been discussed in Overview I, that the Book of *Chronicles* is meant, in the first place, to serve as a basis for homiletical interpretation.

In accordance with the system which we have used throughout the commentary, we must examine why the stories of these proselytes are subsumed under Shelah. In what sense can these proselytes be seen, homiletically speaking, as descendants of Shelah?

As a possible solution, we offer the following analysis of the pertinent teachings of the Sages:

(A) The following passage explains the form which the Torah uses to report Shelah's birth *(Genesis* 38:5). In contrast to the account of the birth of his two older brothers (Er and Onan), where the text says simply, *She conceived [again] and bore a son,* at Shelah's birth the text reads: *And [she conceived] yet again* (וַתֹּסֶף עוֹד) *and she bore a son.* Concerning the expression וַתֹּסֶף, *yet again,* *Yalkut* remarks:

When God makes an 'addition' (תוֹסַפְתּוֹ שֶׁל הַקָּבָּ"ה), then that addition is made more generously than the original. [The *Midrash* then adduces a number of examples where when something was added over and above an original gift the addition always is made with great abundance. Among the examples cited is the following:] Er was the original son, but Shelah, since he was an addition [based on the וַתֹּסֶף, *yet again,* of the text], fathered ten heads of courts, as it is written ... [Our verse in *Chronicles* is cited. The descendants of Shelah which are listed are assumed to be the heads of various courts] *(Yalkut, Melachim* 243).

(B) When Israel lives according to God's will then God searches throughout the world to find some righteous person and to bring him into Israel's fold. Examples are Yithro (Jethro) and Rachav *(Yerushalmi, Berachos* 2:8).

(C) [He was called] Shelah [from שלשל, *to draw along*] because the world was descended from him *(Bereishis Rabbah* 85:4).[1]

In analyzing these passages several ideas emerge:

1. The institution of *gerus* (conversion) — the fact that a non-Jew can become a proselyte or *ger* and thereby fully join the community of Israel — is not just one among the many institutions which, together, constitute Jewish peoplehood. It is, rather, its most basic component, the one which defines as no other the unique nature of that community.

The Torah recognizes no *gerus* other than that of a non-Jew joining the community of Israel. For example, if a Moabite would want to convert into the Midianite community [a switch which could affect his halachic status if he ever decided to become Jewish; a proselyte from Moab is never allowed to marry a native Jewish woman *(Deuteronomy* 22:4) but a *ger* from Midian would be allowed], this conversion would not be recognized by the Torah.

Maharal explains as follows: Each nation has been endowed by God with a unique genius. It is that which animates its being, it is that which defines its existence. This genius, unique as it is to one particular people, cannot be shared by another. *Gerus* (conversion) from one gentile nation to another is thus impossible. But the soul of Israel is the Torah, that universal truth which excludes no one and which, on the contrary, can encompass the whole of humanity within itself. A non-Jew who joins the community of Israel is partaking of something for which he was always destined *(Chidushei Aggadah, Zevachim* 113a).

Just how essential the institution of *gerus* is to the very nature of the Jew can be seen from the fact that the very name of Israel's father, Abraham, was specifically given in order to contain this truth within itself: *You shall no longer be called by your name Abram, but your name shall be Abraham; for I have made you the father of a multitude of nations (Genesis* 17:5) [see *Rambam,*

1.[The text in *Bereishis Rabbah* is corrupt and we have quoted it as *Radal* emends it. Other commentators offer different emendations, and *Matnos Kehunah* points out that the whole passage seems to have been missing in some texts of the *Midrash.*]

Bikkurim 4:3]. This universality was the blessing which God bestowed upon Abraham at the very beginning of his mission: וְנִבְרְכוּ בְךָ כֹּל מִשְׁפְּחֹת הָאֲדָמָה, *and all the families of the earth shall bless themselves by you,* is also to be taken as: *And all the families of the earth shall be grafted upon you,* i.e., that all the families of the earth will wish to intermingle with you for you will not be considered a foreigner in their midst (see ArtScroll, *Genesis* 12:3).

2. Thus we see that Abraham was to be a source of blessing [ברך] for the whole world by affording all humanity the opportunity of 'grafting' [ונברך] themselves upon Israel and, through the institution of *gerus,* becoming one with them. This is possible only because Israel's essential being is, through the Torah, permeated by an all-embracing Godliness within which every human being can find his own destiny.

The symbol, among Abraham's descendants, of this all-pervasive Godliness, was to be Judah. His name is identical with God's Name, with only the addition of the letter *daleth* to hint at the fact that he was the fourth son. In Judah was presaged the Messianic era in which the righteous people are destined to be called by God's own Name *(Bava Basra* 78b). R' Tzadok HaKohen *(Tzidkas HaTzadik* 184) explains, we understood this to mean that their perception of themselves [implied in an individual name] as independently functioning beings will change into a realization that they are no more than manifestations of God's will on earth. All this is implicit in the name יְהוּדָה, *Judah,* and it is for this reason that the *ger* who separates himself from idol worship in order to become part of the community of Israel is called a 'Yehudah'-person. [See comm. to v. 18 and cf. *Esther* 4:17.]

It is significant that the 'Yehudah' description is not limited to a non-Jew who embraces Judaism. The source for the 'Yehudah' description is, after all, *Daniel* 3:12 where Chananiah, Mishael and Azariah are called *Yehudim* because of their refusal to bow down to Nebuchadnezzar's statue. The fact that it is a term shared by both the *ger* and the Jewish rejector of idolatry points to the universality of the concept. Jew and non-Jew can meet at the point of absolute self-abnegation before God.

3. After Joseph had been sold into slavery Judah 'went down' from his brothers and 'turned away' towards an Adullamite man whose name was Chirah *(Genesis* 38:1). There, he saw the daughter of a Canaanite man[1] and married her. She bore him three sons. The elder two, Er and Onan, sinned and died childless. The third, Shelah, was blessed with the families of dignitaries enumerated here (Source A).

Judah had reached the nadir of his existence. His brothers had deposed him from his role of kingship among them and blamed him for the tragedy of Joseph's slavery. They felt that if Judah had exercised his leadership he could have persuaded them to release Joseph. Judah had failed and Joseph had been lost.

In his rejection Judah turned away. He forgot his destiny as progenitor of the Messiah *(Aggudos Bereishis),* desecrated his essential sanctity *(Bereishis*

---

1. See ArtScroll comm. to *Genesis* ch. 38 concerning the disagreement among the commentators as to the nationality of Judah's first wife. Many, based on *Pesachim* 50, explain that she was not of Canaanite descent and that the words אִישׁ כְּנַעֲנִי which describe her father are to be translated: *prominent merchant.* Many others, based on Midrashic sources, believe that Judah's first wife was indeed a Canaanite woman — an opinion which seems borne out by the simple meaning of *I Chronicles* 2:3. Our discussion is based on this second opinion.

Rabbah), and forged a union with a woman of Canaan — that nation which God had cursed and from which it was unthinkable that a Jewish king, much less the Messianic king, should descend.

But Judah could not escape his destiny as progenitor of the royal house of Israel. He took Tamar, daughter of the great and holy Shem, as a wife for his son, Er. Divine Providence then brought about a confluence of events which eventually led Judah himself to this noble woman. Peretz and Zerach were born and the foundations of the monarchy were laid.

But the union of Judah and Tamar was built on the ruins of his former marriage. God said: 'Let the Canaanite woman die … let her sons die … so that Judah may marry Tamar' *(Aggados Bereishis).*

What of Shelah? Here was a child born of that ill-fated union, burdened by a Canaanite heritage in his blood. What could be his future within the community of Israel?

4. Shelah was a special gift from God. As Source A teaches, the words וַתֹּסֶף עוֹד, *And [she conceived] yet again,* indicate that without God's special bounty the union between Judah and his Canaanite wife would only have produced the older two sons. And, while the initial gift which God grants is measured to the exact need and merit of the recipient, an extra gift taps the limitless resources of God's loving kindness. A great outpouring of goodness attended Shelah's birth which would one day be expressed by the ten noble families whom he would father.

But, as we saw in the commentary to these verses, the Sages interpret that these families hint at the various proselytes who were to join Israel through the ages: Rachav, the Giveonites and the Moabite Ruth.

Surely the intent of the Sages is no other than to teach that Shelah himself was the very first to find a cure for his Canaanite antecedents in the all-permeating Godliness of his father's being.

If Abraham is the father of all proselytes *(Rambam, Bikkurim* 4:3) that is in the sense that he was the one with whom God established His covenant and formed the Jewish people. But his antecedents were noble. He was descended from Shem, priest to Almighty God and heir to all that was great and holy in the human race. Shelah, on the other hand, was burdened by a Canaanite legacy. Despicable and accursed, Canaan seemed forever excluded from the possibility of sublimation. But Shelah, losing himself in the 'Yehudah' nature of his father, accomplished just that. Eradicating everything that was negative in his nature, he became the prototype of such proselytes who would be able to surmount their seeming disabilities and find their place in the universal all-embracing Godliness implied in Judah's name. If, as we learned above, it is Judah to whom all future proselytes will learn to cleave [through his Messianic descendant], then it is through his son Shelah that that destiny began to be fulfilled.

Thus, the blessing which attended Shelah's birth (Source A) continues to reap harvests through the ages. When God searches throughout the world to find righteous non-Jews who can be led to Judah (Source B), these people are following Shelah's path — are in fact the spiritual descendants of Shelah, the 'families' which he established in Israel.

And thus, Shelah becomes the one from whom the world is to be descended (Source C). Eventually the whole world will be drawn towards the God Who manifests Himself upon this world through the 'Yehudah' people, whose being and essence is defined only by His Presence. That is the purpose of creation, and as God's plan becomes fulfilled and the nations flow towards Zion, it will be as though they are drawn along [שְׁלָה from שלשל, *to draw along*] by example which, millennia before, Shelah had created for all posterity to follow.

Chapter Five

⊷§ The Hagrite Wars

[י] וּבִימֵי שָׁאוּל עָשׂוּ מִלְחָמָה עִם־הַהַגְרִאים וַיִּפְּלוּ בְּיָדָם ...
[10] *Now in the days of Saul they waged war against the Hagrites, and they fell into their hands* ...

[יט־כ] וַיַּעֲשׂוּ מִלְחָמָה עִם־הַהַגְרִיאִים וִיטוּר וְנָפִישׁ וְנוֹדָב. וַיֵּעָזְרוּ עֲלֵיהֶם וַיִּנָּתְנוּ בְיָדָם הַהַגְרִיאִים וְכֹל שֶׁעִמָּהֶם כִּי לֵאלֹהִים זָעֲקוּ בַּמִּלְחָמָה וְנַעְתּוֹר לָהֶם כִּי־בָטְחוּ בוֹ.
[19-20] *And they made war on the Hagrites, Yetur, Naphish and Nodav. And they were helped against them, and the Hagrites and all that were with them were given into their hands; for they cried out to God in the war, and He answered them because they trusted in Him.*

While Israel was conquering and dividing the land, the tribes Reuven and Gad were with them, having left their small children behind *(Numbers ch. 32, Joshua 1:12-18, 22:1ff).* [They returned home after the seven years of war and the seven years of dividing the land.] One who had left his son aged ten found him now at twenty-four ... [While they were gone] three evil tribes attacked [their families] — Yetur, Naphish and Kedmah. This is what is meant by the verse (here): *Now in the days of Saul* — this [refers to] Joshua. Why is he called Saul? Because his kingship was a 'borrowed' one [שָׁאוּל from שאל, *to borrow*].

[The meaning of the next few lines in the midrash is unclear. According to *Yepheh Toar* based on *Os Emmes* the correct reading yields a description of the warring factions.] Both the attacking Arabs and the Jewish fighters wore their hair long. As a result, the returning armies of Reuven and Gad did not, at first, realize that their own children were involved in the fighting. So God inspired the children so that they called out: 'Answer us, O God of Abraham, Isaac and Jacob,' as it is written, *And they were helped against them, and the Hagrites and all that were with them were given into their hands ... (Bereishis Rabbah 98:15).*

The story of how the Reuvenites and Gadites were given their portion of the land on the east side of the Jordan is given in *Numbers ch. 32.* The Midrash, based on our verse, yields additional information concerning this episode. We learn that although the two tribes willingly accepted Moses' strictures and agreed to join their brothers in the conquest of the land, their carefully laid plan for the protection of their families went awry. The fortified cities in which they hoped to keep their children safe did not, in fact, protect them from attack. They were exposed to the dangers of war and were only saved because God miraculously intervened and enabled their returning parents to help them.

If we are to understand this midrash we must first seek the answer to two questions: (1) What forced the Sages to give the verse this midrashic interpretation? (2) What is the meaning of the idea that Joshua's kingship was a 'borrowed' one? And why is that important just in the present context?

Maharzav to *Bereishis Rabbah* there points out that verse 18, which seems to be the introduction to the war described in verse 19 [which, as we have seen in the comm., is the same war as the one mentioned in our verse], gives the combined armies of Reuven and Gad as 44,760 soldiers. But I Chronicles gives the number of soldiers who attended David's coronation from the eastern bank of the Jordan as 120,000. If in Saul's reign these tribes could only have mustered 44,760, it is inconceivable that by the time of David's coronation their armies could have increased so much. For this reason, the Sages felt that שָׁאוּל could not refer to King Saul, and they consequently interpreted it as referring to Joshua for the reason explained below. In the time between Joshua and David it would be perfectly natural for a great increase in the population to occur.

Whether or not Joshua had the status of a King or only that of a judge is a matter concerning which there is no unanimity among the authorities (see e.g., *Rambam, Sanhedrin* 18:6; *Ramban* to *Deut.* 33:17; *Derashos HaRan* 11). But even if he had the status of king, it was vested only in his person; there was no assumption that his royalty would be passed on to his descendants. Commentators to the midrash believe that this is the meaning of the term, a borrowed kingship — one that ends with the death of the person of the king without being passed on to his family.

While this definition may explain the term, it does not explain why it should be applied to Joshua in just this particular war.

Maharzav (there) offers a different explanation. Joshua's kingship was limited to the execution of the war against the Canaanites and the distribution of the land. It is the narrowness of his mandate which defines his reign as a 'borrowed' kingship. Accordingly, he explains the Sages' interpretation of this verse as follows: Since Joshua was not a real king, the Reuvenites and Gadites felt free to wage a war without first consulting him, which they could not have done had he really been king. This would explain why Joshua is called שָׁאוּל, *borrowed*, just here. However, there is really no textual evidence that this war was waged without Joshua's approval.

We suggest a different meaning for the midrash. We are dealing with a case of paranomasia, a play on words. Joshua is called שָׁאוּל, *Saul*, because his kingship is to be defined under the rubric 'Saul.' Because the name שָׁאוּל is related to the idea שׁאל, *to borrow*, the Sages expressed this thought by saying that his kingship was 'borrowed' from Saul.

The connection between Joshua's kingship and that of Saul may be explained as follows:

A function of Saul's kingship was the eradication of Amalek. *Pesikta Rabbasi* 12 teaches that when Joshua fought Amalek immediately after the exodus (*Exodus* 17:8ff), he wanted to eradicate them completely. God forbade him to do so. He was permitted only to weaken them, but not to destroy them — that was to be left to Saul.

Now, when the Torah commands that Amalek be destroyed the condition is made that this should be done only after *God has given you rest from all your enemies round about* (Deuteronomy 25:19). Thus, the eradication of the seven Canaanite nations had to precede Saul's destruction of Amalek. That duty fell to Joshua — it was the essence of his kingship. But since the eradication of the Canaanite nations is only a prelude to the ultimate removal of Amalek, Joshua's kingship can be seen as a prelude to Saul's kingship. The purpose of Joshua's kingship is, in effect, to lay the groundwork for Saul's. His kingship is thus 'borrowed from Saul.'

The story of Reuven's and Gad's request that they be given their portion on the eastern side of the Jordan is discussed in depth by *R' Dessler* in *Michtav MeEliyahu* vol. 2. He demonstrates how the request itself was in no way objectionable. The fertility of the land coupled with the vast flocks possessed by these two tribes could indeed have been taken as a Divine sign that God wanted them to inhabit the eastern shore of the Jordan. At issue was only the question of whether or not they would bear their part in the battles with the Canaanites in Israel proper. Moses suspected that they would not be willing to do so. After Moses' impassioned speech demonstrating how destructive to the common good such an attitude would be, the two tribes willingly shouldered the burden of war — and went heroically beyond that which had been asked of them. Moses requested only that they remain on the western side for as long as it would take to conquer the land. Voluntarily, they doubled their obligation and elected to stay the extra seven years it took to divide the land.

From the narrative in the Torah it would seem that throughout, the bearing of the two tribes was beyond reproach.

Nevertheless, the Sages criticize the Reuvenites and the Gadites for their action. *Proverbs* 20:21 reads: *If an inheritance is initially approached in haste, its end will not be blessed.* The Sages teach that this refers to the Reuvenites and Gadites. Because they approached their inheritance with undue haste, they were the first of the ten tribes to be taken into the Assyrian exile (vs. 25,25).

What was the haste for which the two tribes were taken to task?

On many different occasions the Torah warned that if the Jews were to be able to flourish in Israel as they were meant to flourish, they would first have to eradicate all vestiges of idol worship from the land. The Canaanite nations, who were the very embodiment of idol worship *(Rambam, Sefer HaMitzvos)*, had to be destroyed. Once the land was cleansed of all negative and destructive influences the Jews would be able to live the life of holiness for which the land was so eminently suited. This was to be the crowning glory of their historical development. Once such a life would become a reality a very different attitude would become possible vis-a-vis the gentile nations. Far from meriting destruction, they would be irresistibly drawn to the sanctity of Jewish life in Zion. All the prophecies envisaging the flowing of all mankind towards God and His people would become a reality.

Many centuries of sorrow could have been avoided if the people would have adhered to the Torah's program. But, as a careful study of *Joshua* and *Judges* will yield, the tendency was to jump to the second stage and to shy away from the eradication of evil which the Torah had defined as an indispensable pre-condition to the more positive approach. *Pesikta d'Rav Kahana* goes so far as to blame Joshua himself for just such a misdemeanor. Tradition has it that Joshua married Rachav, the Canaanite woman who had saved his spies. [That is, the second, positive approach, which centuries later Solomon was to inaugurate by marrying many women born into gentile nations.] God said to Israel: 'I told you to destroy the Hittites and Emorites ... but you did not do so, but Joshua married Rachav ...'

We may conjecture then that this too was the unseemly haste for which the Reuvenites and Gadites were blamed. Though their intentions were above reproach, and as noted there were even indications of the Divine will for the

Transjordan to be settled, yet the time for settlement had not yet come. As long as the purity of the core of the Holy Land had not yet been consolidated by the complete eradication of idol worship, it was premature to consider any expansion of the land.

This rashness had an immediate impact. Their children, whom they had thought safe in the fortified cities built for them, fell prey — first to the customs (the long hair) and then to the armies of the neighboring Arab nations.

The passage stresses that this took place in the days of Joshua-Saul, during the time mandated for the eradication of evil from the land. The Reuvenite and Gadite tribes, in ignoring this reality and hastening to a second stage of development for which the time was not yet ripe, suffered for that impetuousness.

Chapter Seven

⊷§ The Sons of Ephraim

‏[כ-כא] וּבְנֵי אֶפְרַיִם ... וַהֲרָגוּם אַנְשֵׁי־גַת ... כִּי יָרְדוּ ...

[20-21] *And the sons of Ephraim ... But the men of Gath ... killed them as they came down ...*

In the commentary we have seen the tradition of the Sages that these verses refer to the Ephraimites who anticipated the redemption. This episode is remarkable for the paucity of material available. The story itself is repeated, with minor variations, in many midrashic sources but the classical commentators do not seem to address it directly.

To better understand this almost unknown chapter of Jewish history, we must first ascertain how the Sages viewed Ephraim's place among the tribes of Israel. In *Vayikra Rabbah* 2:3 we learn that prior to his death Jacob told Ephraim that he was to be רֹאשׁ הַשְּׁבָטִים, *foremost among the tribes*, and רֹאשׁ הַיְשִׁיבָה, *head of the Yeshivah*. Moreover, he told him that the best and most exalted people of Israel [examples are, Samuel; Jesse, father of David, and Elimelech and his sons] would be called by his name. [All these people are described as אֶפְרָתִי, *Ephrathi*, which seems to have the literal meaning, *an officer, a man of importance* (see *Aruch HaShalem* under אֶפְרָתִי), but which the Midrash interprets as, *one who is worthy to bear the name Ephraim.*] Ephraim, then, is seen as a central figure among the twelve tribes.

It would seem that Ephraim's centrality derives from the fact that he was the more important of the two sons of Joseph who, in turn, was that son among the twelve in whom Jacob himself was most clearly alive. This thought is expressed by *Bereishis Rabbah* 84:6 which takes note of the unexpected formulation in the verse, אֵלֶּה תֹּלְדוֹת יַעֲקֹב יוֹסֵף, *These are the generations of Jacob — Joseph ...* (*Genesis* 37:2). This formulation implies to the Midrash that the תֹּלְדוֹת, *the details of Jacob's life* (see *Genesis* 2:4), were all reflected in Joseph. Indeed, the Midrash lists numerous examples of occurrences in Joseph's life which paralleled Jacob's experiences.

Thus, Joseph can be said to have been the 'Jacob' of his generation. And as the primary spiritual heir of Joseph, Ephraim can be said to have been the 'Jacob' of his generation.

This assessment underlies *Maharal's* explanation of why it was just Ephraim among all the tribes who anticipated the redemption. In his *Chidushei Aggadah, Sanhedrin* 92b, he states: '... For Jacob revealed the [secret of] the time of the redemption (מָסַר הַקֵּץ) to Joseph, and Joseph [in turn] revealed it to Ephraim who was the main one of his children.[1] Jacob wished to reveal the [secret] time of the redemption for there was none among the Patriarchs as involved with [the idea] of redemption as Jacob (see *Netzach Yisrael* 44); and after him, Joseph, as it is written: *And these are the generations of Jacob — Joseph.* And the main one among Joseph's descendants was Ephraim. For this reason the children of Ephraim were more involved in the redemption (קְרוֹבִים אֶל הַקֵּץ) than any of the other tribes.'

The following picture emerges. As the Sages teach, Israel's suffering in Egypt began only after Jacob's death. Even then it did not really intensify until the last of the twelve sons had died. As *Maharal (Gevuros Hashem* chs. 9 and 12) understands this, the explanation is that Jacob himself existed at such an exalted level of holiness that it was impossible for the Egyptians to subjugate him in any way. Even his twelve sons were sufficiently removed from the possibility of Egyptian dominance that the real servitude could begin only after their deaths.

Jacob, then, could not be subjugated in any way by Egypt. The idea of redemption was vested in him. He passed it on to Joseph, his spiritual successor in the next generation, who in turn passed it on to Ephraim, the 'Jacob' among Jacob's grandsons.

Thus, Ephraim also could not be restrained by Egypt, and his descendants were powerful enough to escape from Egypt by the might of the sword. This, although according to the tradition of the Sages Egypt's boundaries were so well guarded that no slave had ever before escaped.

This is perhaps what the Sages meant when they say that the Ephraimites chafed particularly under the yoke of bondage because they were of royal blood. In the comm. we interpreted this to mean that they were destined to rule over the Northern Kingdom because that is how *Radal* in his comm. to *Pirkei d'Rabbi Eliezer* explains it. In light of the above, however, another explanation is possible. *Maharal (Gevuros HaShem* 11) explains why Divine Providence decreed that Joseph was made ruler over Egypt. It was fitting that Joseph — the absolute master of his physical passions as he had demonstrated when he spurned the blandishments of Potiphar's wife — should rule over the Egyptians who, as the Sages explain in numerous places, were the most crassly physical of all the nations.

It will be recalled that Joseph found it in himself to withstand the advances of Potiphar's wife because at the moment of greatest stress a picture of his father Jacob rose up in his mind *(Sotah* 36b). This can mean nothing else but that Joseph recognized the 'Jacob' within himself. That sanctity which had lifted his father beyond any physical temptations found an echo within his own soul and enabled him to become absolute master over himself.

Thus it was that Joseph ruled as the 'Jacob' of his generation and it is in that context that Ephraim is described as being 'of royal blood'. His father had been king over Egypt because of his spiritual ascendancy over them. How, then, could the son, possessed of that same sanctity, be held by Egyptian shackles?

---

1. I have not been able to find the source for *Maharal's* assertion that Jacob passed the secret of the קֵץ, *the time of the redemption,* to Joseph and that he, in turn, passed it on to Ephraim. But see *Baal HaTurim* to *Genesis* 50:25.

This must be the meaning of the Sages when they teach us that the Ephraimites trusted their own strength. In the study of *Chronicles* we learn repeatedly that in the thought-world of Scripture, military valor and prowess go hand in hand with spiritual grandeur [see p. 417ff]. The Ephraimites were great warriors because they were direct heirs to the heritage of sanctity which from Jacob onwards defined the essence of the Jewish people.

As quoted in the commentary, *Shemos Rabbah* (20:10) explains that when God finally took Israel out of Egypt, He took them the long way around instead of leading them straight through Philistia so that they not come across the bones of the Ephraimites who had fallen in their battle with the men of Gath.

The Midrash illustrates this with a parable. A king had taken a wife and set out to bring her to his capital. He placed her in a chariot and embarked on the journey. Just before entering the city she died and was buried by the king by the wayside. Some time later, the king married her sister but rather than have her pass her sister's grave he made sure to bring her to his capital by a different route.

Tiferes Tzion notes that the first wife was *placed in a chariot*. It seems that even the Ephraimites were granted Divine protection as they left Egypt. They were indeed 'men of redemption' whom Egypt could not hold and who merited God's protection when they left the land of bondage. They came to grief only when they sought to enter the Promised Land. This they were prevented from doing since the time that God had ordained for that had not yet arrived.

How, then, did the Ephraimites sin? God had told Abraham that Israel was to be in Egyptian exile for four hundred years. In the tradition of the Sages those four hundred years were to be counted from the birth of Isaac which was to take place thirty years after God's revelation to Abraham. The Ephraimites rebelled against that tradition, ignored the oath that Joseph had imposed upon the brothers not to anticipate the redemption, and decided that the count should begin from the moment of the revelation — that is, thirty years before the right date *(Sanhedrin* 92b). This rebellion against the oral tradition carried by the elders of their generation could not go unpunished, and they were killed before they were able to enter the Land of Israel.

They sinned in their practical application of the halachah and were punished, but the inner compulsion which made them unable to tolerate Egyptian servitude touched upon the very essence of Jewish being. *Exodus* 13:17 reads: וְלֹא נָחָם אֱלֹהִים דֶּרֶךְ אֶרֶץ פְּלִשְׁתִּים, *God did not lead them by way of Philistia.* But the Sages read נָחָם as deriving from נחם, *to comfort*, and interpret וְלֹא נָחָם אֱלֹהִים, *God could find no comfort* (so to speak), and read it as referring to the holocaust that devoured the Ephraimites. 'It is comparable to a king who was marrying off a son when one of his other sons died. He said "I cannot be happy because of the son who died but I cannot mourn because of my son who is marrying." What did he do? He waved one hand in joy and the other one in sorrow' *(Midrash Avkir* brought in *Torah Sheleimah, Exodus* 13:17).

And when God will finally, in the end of days, avenge the horrors which Israel had to suffer during its exile (see *Isaiah* ch. 62), His clothes will be drenched in blood. As *Shemos Rabbah* 2:10 teaches, that blood will be the blood of the Ephraimites who were slain so early in Israel's history. God will say: 'I can find no comfort until I have avenged the death of the Ephraimites.'

Thus, as the Sages teach it, we have a two-sided picture of the Ephraimites. In their motivation they touched the very essence of Israel's sanctity, but came to grief when their actions clashed with the halachah.

Can we possibly explain why the incident, concerning which the Torah was silent, is hinted at in the book of *Chronicles*?

We may surmise as follows. Ephraim was not just one of the twelve tribes, but, as we saw from *Vayikra Rabbah*, the 'head of the tribes.' Countless times throughout Scripture, all of Israel is called Ephraim and that too was part of Jacob's blessing to Joseph (see *Torah Sheleimah* to *Genesis* 48:16).

From *Rambam, Melachim* 11:1 it appears that not only is the belief in the Messiah and the ultimate redemption an integral part of the Jewish experience, but so too is the longing and expectation of those times. '... And all who do not believe in him [the coming of the Messiah] or who do not long for his coming ... deny ... the very Torah which Moses gave us ...'

The story of the Ephraimites' aborted attempt has no place in *Exodus* which is, after all, the story of Israel's actual redemption from Egypt. But *Chronicles*, which places the Jewish experience in the context of world history, taking it from creation up to the intimation of a final redemption (see Overviews) must make room for this episode which helps to define the essence of Israel as the people who carry the consciousness of קץ, *redemption*, in the very fiber of their being.

Chapter Eight

◄§ Boaz and Benjamin

[ח־ט] וְשַׁחֲרַיִם הוֹלִיד בִּשְׂדֵה מוֹאָב מִן־שִׁלְחוֹ אֹתָם חוּשִׁים וְאֶת־בַּעֲרָא נָשָׁיו. וַיּוֹלֶד מִן־חֹדֶשׁ ...

[8-9] *And Shacharaim fathered [children] in the field of Moab from Shilcho Otham [and] Chushim and from Baara, his wives. And he fathered from his wife Chodesh ...*

Yerushalmi Yevamos 8:3 interprets this verse as referring to Boaz. 'Shacharaim is Boaz, who was unburdened [שַׁחֲרַיִם from חרר, *to be free*] by sin. *Fathered in the field of Moab* means that he married Ruth the Moabite. *From Shilcho Otham*, he was descended from the tribe of Judah concerning whom it is written, *And he sent* [שָׁלַח from שלח, *to send*] *Judah ahead of him ... to Goshen* (*Genesis* 46:28). *Chushim, Baara his wives* ... means that he hastened [חוּשִׁים from חוש, *to hasten*] like a leopard and clarified [בַּעֲרָא related to באר, *to explain*] the halachah. And he fathered from his wife Chodesh ... for through her the law that only male Moabites are forbidden, not female Moabites, was renewed [חֹדֶשׁ from חדש, *new*].

Now Boaz is descended from Judah. If in the view of the Sages his story is nevertheless subsumed under Benjamin, this can only mean that in some sense his fight for the establishment of the principle that a Moabite woman is permitted is grounded in a Benjaminite tradition. What is there about Benjamin which could be the source from which Boaz drew his essence or his inspiration?

There is a clear implication that there was much resistance to the establishment of the principle that converted Moabite women are permitted to marry into the Jewish congregation. Indeed, Ploni Almoni refused to marry Ruth because he could not bring himself to accept this teaching (see ArtScroll *Ruth*, pp. 125-126). Indeed, many years later there was still much uncertainty about this law and

Yevamos 77a reports how Amasa girded himself with a sword and declared: 'Whoever refuses to accept this law will be pierced by the sword. This is what was taught in Samuel's court: Ammonite men are forbidden — not Ammonite women; Moabite men are forbidden — not Moabite women.'

Why were men prepared to fight for the establishment of this principle with the vehemence of a Boaz and an Amasa?

When God first appeared to Abraham and apprised him of his destiny *(Genesis* 12:1ff), He promised him that he would be the source of universal blessing: וְנִבְרְכוּ בְךָ כֹּל מִשְׁפְּחֹת הָאֲדָמָה, *through you all the families of the earth will be blessed* (v. 3). The Sages *(Yevamos* 63a) teach that the root ברך which means *to bless* can also be translated *to graft.* According to this translation, they interpret God's promise to Abraham as: I have two excellent boughs which I wish to graft upon you — Ruth the Moabite and Naamah the Ammonite.

Now it is clear that the meaning of the Sages is that the 'grafting' and the 'blessing' are to be one and the same. The universal blessing that was to emanate from Abraham and which was to encompass the whole world was manifested first and foremost by the grafting of the two boughs onto the tree of Abraham. That Ruth and Naamah found shelter among the Jewish people was the first step in the procession of nations who will one day flow towards the 'Mountain of God's House' in order to bask in the Torah which will emanate from Zion and Jerusalem *(Isaiah* 2:2-3). As if to stress the universality of Israel's spiritual treasures, the very Temple — focus of all that is holy in Israel — was described *(II Samuel* 23:20, see *Rashi, Berachos* 18a) as the Temple of the Moabite, i.e., of David who had been descended from the Moabite Ruth. Small wonder, then, that Boaz and Amasa were willing to fight for the establishment of this truth. Israel's whole destiny as a light to the nations depended upon it.

This zeal can be seen as being grounded in a Benjaminite tradition. It is Benjamin's role to play host to the שְׁכִינָה, *the Divine Presence,* in Israel. 'The *Shechinah* dwelt in Israel in three different places: In Shilo; in Nov and Giveon; and in [Solomon's] Temple. In all three places it rested specifically in Benjamin's portion' *(Zevachim* 118b).

Zevachim 53b explains how Benjamin merited that just he should be host to the Divine Presence. As the Sages describe the disposition of the Temple complex, it stood completely in Benjamin's portion. However, there was one strip of land within Benjamin's portion which belonged to Judah; part of the Altar was built in that strip. Benjamin felt a great craving to absorb that strip of Judah into his own inheritance. In the merit of that craving he was chosen to have the *Shechinah* be in his portion.

Maharal (there) explains that this craving for an added portion of holiness was an essential part of Benjamin's nature. Jacob had called him a 'tearing wolf' *(Genesis* 49:27); and as a wolf stalks his prey with the intention of swallowing it up, so Benjamin could never be satiated by sanctity. His whole being was animated by a desire to increase the boundaries of holiness.

This same urge animated those people in Israel who fought so fiercely for the establishment of the principle that the Moabite women be permitted. They understood that it was Israel's destiny to expand the orbit of its sanctity (see below). In that sense Boaz's zeal in making that expansion possible drew its inspiration from Benjamin. 'And Boaz hastened like a leopard to establish the principle that a Moabite woman was permitted' *(Yerushalmi).*

◆§ Elijah the Prophet

[כז] וִירַעַשְׁיָה וְאֵלִיָּה וְזִכְרִי בְּנֵי יְרֹחָם.

[27] *And Yaareshiah, Eliyah, and Zichri, the sons of Yerocham.*

From whom was Elijah the Prophet descended? R' Eliezer said: From Benjamin, as it is written (our verse). R' Nehorai said: From Gad, as it is written ... What explanation does R' Nehorai have for our verse, from which R' Eliezer supports his contention? [The verse is the basis for a homiletical interpretation:] At a time when God causes an upheaval in His world [מַרְעִישׁ עוֹלָמוֹ from רַעַשׁ, *an upheaval;* this is hinted at in the name יִרַעַשְׁיָה, which could be a contraction of two words, יַרְעִישׁ יָ"ה, *God causes an upheaval*], Elijah reminds [God] of the merit of his fathers [זְכְרִי from זכר, *to remember,* in the *hiphil,* causative — *to remind*], and God has mercy upon His world [בְּנֵי יְרֹחָם from רחם, *to have mercy*] *(Bereishis Rabbah 71:9).*

Once, our Rabbis were sitting in the study-hall and discussing the question of Elijah's descent. Some said that he was descended from Rachel and some said that he was descended from Leah. While they were still in the midst of their discussion Elijah appeared to them and said to them, 'My masters! Why do you spend efforts on this matter? Most surely I am descended from Rachel.' [In many parallel sources our verse is then quoted] *(Eliyahu Zuta 15).*

R' Nehorai believes that Elijah was descended from Gad. He could easily have eliminated R' Eliezer's proof from our verse by saying that the Elijah of our verse is not identical with the Prophet Elijah. Instead, he chose to interpret the verse in such a way that at least at the level of דְּרַשׁ, *homiletical interpretation,* there is a reference to Elijah.

Why would the genealogy of Benjamin contain a reference to Elijah who was, in his opinion, descended from Gad? This is another example of the many instances in which a homiletical interpretation is offered by the Sages by which people are introduced into a given genealogical list without having any relationship with that particular family.

The midrash states: בְּשָׁעָה שֶׁהוּא מַרְעִישׁ עוֹלָמוֹ אֵלִיָּהוּ מַזְכִּיר זְכוּת אָבוֹת — *When God causes an upheaval in this world, Elijah reminds [Him] of the merit of the fathers* (see *Yalkut Shimoni*). I.e., when Israel is in danger of destruction Elijah intercedes for them with God.

An example of Elijah's intercession on behalf of Israel can be found in *Esther Rabbah* in connection with the story of Purim. When God decided that Israel deserved to be destroyed because they participated in Ahasuerus' banquet, there was great consternation in the heavenly court. The angels beseeched God to reconsider. What would be their purpose in a world without Israel? Sun and moon withheld their light; they could serve no purpose if Israel were destroyed. At that point Elijah went to the grave of the Patriarchs to awaken them to the danger and to beg them to pray for their children.

God had a purpose in creating His world. That purpose is inextricably bound up with Israel's existence. It was for their sake that the universe came into being (see *Rashi* to *Genesis* 1:1). If Israel were to be destroyed, world order, without any purpose to animate it, would collapse.

There is only one explanation for Israel's centrality. They are the conduit through which the שְׁכִינָה, *Divine Presence,* rests among mankind (cf. *Exodus* 29:46 and *Ramban* there, and *Ramban* to *Deuteronomy* 32:26). A world in which the *Shechinah* can find no welcome is a world in which God can take no interest (see *Ramban, Exodus* 13:16), and which is therefore doomed.

It is Elijah's duty to forestall such a tragedy. When a withdrawal of the *Shechinah* is threatened (מַרְעִישׁ עוֹלָמוֹ) he hastens to remind God of the merit of the Patriarchs. God's love for Israel is rekindled and the danger is averted.

The focus of Divine Presence in Israel — and therefore in the world — is the tribe of Benjamin. It is he, who because of his unbounded craving for the divine (see above), became host to the *Shechinah* [אוּשְׁפִּיזֵיכְנָא לַשְׁכִינָה] (*Megillah* 26a) and, in every Sanctuary which Israel ever had, the *Shechinah* rested specifically in Benjamin's portion (*Zevachim* 118b). As such, the withdrawal of the *Shechinah* from the world is particularly Benjamin's concern. The very craving for sanctity which makes him the ideal host for the Divine Presence makes him more sensitive than any other to the impossibility of a world deprived of the presence of God in its midst.

In that sense Elijah's function, as described in our Midrash, can be said to be rooted in the Benjaminite aspect of the Jewish experience. One who at all costs seeks to preserve the potential for sanctity in the world is a 'Benjaminite' and, at the homiletical level, belongs in the Benjaminite listing even if he was not actually descended from that tribe.

Chapter Eleven

◆§ The Giborim of David

[י-יא] וְאֵלֶּה רָאשֵׁי הַגִּבֹּרִים ... וְאֵלֶּה מִסְפַּר הַגִּבֹּרִים ...
[10-11] *These are the chief mighty men of David ... this is the tally of David's mighty men ...*

The commentary has noted the discrepancies between the list of *giborim* and their respective exploits presented in *Chronicles* and the one in *Samuel,* and many separate solutions. In the light of a number of extant midrashim, however, it would seem that a more general solution is possible and that indeed it may well be that the Sages viewed the issue in just such general terms. Such an approach would obviate the need to address each separate difficulty on an individual basis.

In the first place it seems legitimate to wonder what could have been *Chronicles'* purpose in offering this list. Apart from the fact that the greater part of the people mentioned are already known from *Samuel,* there is the additional problem of what possible significance these names could have had to anyone in Ezra's time, so many centuries after the events described here. If, when *Samuel* was written, the heroes of David's court were still part of the common folklore, this seems unlikely to have still been true in Ezra's time.

Even more problematic is the jarring note which a list of the martial exploits of military heroes introduces into our perception of King David. Our tradition knows nothing of a warrior-king in whose court military prowess would be valued and honored. David the king and David the psalmist are one and the same person. The true nature of David is most eloquently described by *H. Biberfeld* in his *David, King of Israel:*

'... Nature, the profusion of phenomena filling the world, made the chords of David's soul sing. One unending melody reverberates from it — God. This universal theme resounds from all directions of the cosmos. Space is filled with it, for *the heavens declare the glory of God* and *the earth is the Lord's.* Time proclaims it, for, *Day unto day uttereth speech and night unto night showeth knowledge.*

Never once in the *Psalms* does the appearance hide the essence within. This is not poetry in the customary sense; it does not revel in a purely esthetic admiration of the all. A searching and probing mind, a penetrating vision, seeks the spirit within, the life-giving power sustaining nature. A heart full of the awareness of the Divine explores with energy and eager expectation the endless variety of phenomena, to arrive always at the one root-cause of all. Whatever is, is but through Him. This continuous interplay of quest and response, the recurring discovery of the Divine behind all aspects of life is the topic of *Psalms.* It is also the true life story of David, our king.

The roots of the events so tersely described in the narrative books reach deep down. Reading those books is like admiring the calm expanse of the sea. But reading the Psalms is like immersing one's face and gazing down into bottomless depths beholding an unknown world of fantastic vitality, of bizarre shapes and fabulous hues.'

Within the framework of this picture of David, the incongruity of a slayer of three hundred souls at one time (v. 11) being the head of David's followers, based on that act of carnage, is glaring.

There is only one possible conclusion that can be drawn. The might of these *giborim* must have expressed itself in something else besides their prowess on the battlefield. Or, phrased differently, we can say, their might on the battlefield must have been only the outer manifestation of a quite different sort of valor.

The study hall is also a battlefield of sorts. The determination and tenacity which must be invested to make the Torah yield its secrets are no less demanding than the heroism that is required of a soldier in the heat of battle. The thrust and parry of Torah debate requires an intellect no less sharp than the warrior's sword.

And so, the Sages, with the deep and sure feeling with which they approached not only the language of the Torah but also the thought-world within which this Torah has its seat in life, knew that when Scripture speaks of warriors and swordsmen it is not concerned with military exploits but with the wars and battles of the mind and soul.

When the sons of Korach called out, *Gird your sword upon your thigh, O mighty one — your majesty and your splendor (Psalms* 45:4), the Sages *(Shabbos* 63a) knew that by this the Torah scholar is being exhorted to be constantly equipped with the vast amount of Torah knowledge required to render a halachic decision, even as a warrior must carry his weapons at his side *(Rashi* there). And this case is by no means unique. Again and again the Sages regarded references to warriors and swords or weapons which occur in Scripture as referring to Torah study. [For a sampling of instances, see ArtScroll *Tehillim,* fn. to 45:4.] Even the *sixty mighty men who surrounded Solomon's bed, holding swords, practiced in war to guard against the fears of the night (Song of Songs* 3:8), are really 'gripping the sword of tradition, skilled in the battle of Torah' (see *Chagigah* 14a).[1]

---

1. It should not be supposed that when the Sages interpret passages in Scripture in this way that they are disregarding the פְּשַׁט, *the simple meaning.* Rather, they are defining פְּשַׁט as being influenced not only by linguistic, grammatical and lexicographical considerations, but as being determined by the

Thus, among David's *giborim* distinctions between warrior and scholar become blurred. Perhaps it is wrong to view the soldier's sword strictly as metaphor for the scholar's intellect. The two, in fact, become fused within the personality of the *gibor*. The hero's sword flashes in battle powered by the same yearning for closeness to God which animates the scholar's quest for truth in the study hall. And when immersed in Torah study, David's heroes grapple with the complexities of their subject with the same fierceness which drives them into the very thick of the fray on the battlefield.

Let us analyze the nature which the Sages ascribe to Benaiah ben Yehoiada (v. 22), in the light of what we have learned. We do this against the background of the *Gra's* remarks that the important *giborim* numbered thirty-six. [Two groups of three and then another thirty from Elchanan (C7 and S7) through Uriah the Hittite (C37 and S36) who is the last one listed in *Samuel*.] These thirty-six *giborim* were the thirty-six *tzaddikim*, righteous men, upon whom, according to tradition *(Succah* 45b and *Sanhedrin* 97b), the existence of the world depends. It was their purity of soul which led them to victory in battle.

We center on the *Samuel* account where, as noted in the commentary to v. 22, the *k'siv* is בֶּן אִישׁ חַי, *a living man*, while the *k'ri* is בֶּן אִישׁ חַיִל, literally *a valiant warrior*. The *Mefaresh* there understands this to mean that Benaiah's valor on the field of battle was animated by the vibrancy of his essential nature.

Furthermore, *Berachos* 18b derives from this passage the lesson that the righteous, even in death, are considered alive. Death is a function of the physical aspect of man's nature. His soul, however, knows only eternal life. Whether the man, as a totality, undergoes death or not depends upon the balance he has achieved between the two parts of his being. If he leads a physical existence, then his very soul becomes subordinate to his body and becomes degraded into a grossness which is subject to death [רְשָׁעִים בְּחַיֵּיהֶם נִקְרָאִים מֵתִים, *the wicked, even during their lifetime, are considered to be dead*]. If, however, he is a man of the spirit, his 'being' becomes totally identified with his soul. The body becomes no more than an outer shell which, at a given moment, falls away, leaving the essence of the person untouched. Such a man knows no death.

No wonder, then, that Benaiah was victorious in battle. The foes whom he faced may have been numerous and strong, but numbers and physical might are

context within which the particular phrase occurs. In the context of David's psalms, it simply makes no sense to assume that a real warrior is being praised for martial skills. The simple meaning therefore demands that the phrase be taken metaphorically. [This point is discussed at length by *R' Reuven Margalith*, *HaMikrah VeHaMesorah*, ch. 16. He cites three instances: *Kesubos* 111b; *Chullin* 6a; and *Arachin* 8b, in which such metaphorical interpretations are given in answer to the question: פְּשָׁטֵיהּ דִּקְרָא בְּמַאי, *What is the simple meaning of the verse?*]

In this light, a passage in Tractate *Shabbos* is of great interest. The discussion there centers on the question of whether a weapon is to be considered a burden, and therefore not to be worn on the Sabbath, or whether it is considered a normal part of male attire, in the manner of an ornament, and therefore permitted. R' Eliezer attempts to prove that a weapon is considered an ornament from verse 45:4 in *Psalms*. Since the sword there is described as *majesty and splendor*, it is clear that it is to be considered an ornament. The Sages maintain that nothing can be proved from that verse; it is not dealing with a real sword but with the knowledge required of a Torah scholar. To this R' Eliezer retorts that even so, אֵין מִקְרָא יוֹצֵא מִידֵי פְּשׁוּטוֹ, *the plain meaning of the verse cannot be ignored.* The words, 'even so,' which R' Eliezer uses, make it clear that he does not disagree with the basic premise. It is as obvious to him as it is to the Sages that the subject of the verse is the Torah scholar, not the warrior. That, as shown above, is undoubtedly the plain meaning of the verse. Rather, his argument is that even when a phrase is used metaphorically, the metaphor must be consistent within itself. If a real sword were not an ornament it would be illogical to use it as a metaphor for Torah scholarship. [See *Ramban* in his glosses to *Rambam's Sefer HaMitzvos*, *Shoresh* 2 and *R' Reuven Margalith* in the article quoted above.]

merely functions of physical existence. By definition this is limited to its given boundaries. The spirit, however, knows no such limitations; it is stronger than the mightiest, more encompassing than the most numerous. Benaiah was a man of true life. He knew no death because he was no man of the body. And this tenacious hold on חַי, *life*, translated itself into חַיִל, *valor*, on the field of battle. In this manner, all the thirty-six *tzaddikim* whose righteousness supported the world were the warriors who carried David's armies to victory.

Hence we come to the difference between the wars waged by Israel's kings and the so-called 'holy wars' which have left so much horror and suffering in their wake and darkened so many of history's pages. No motive, however exalted, can sublimate an act of violence perpetrated by a gross and lowly nature. Take an army made up from among the debauched and bloodthirsty knighthood of the middle ages and you have the crusaders whose holy wars vie in sheer senseless cruelty and murder-lust with any that was ever waged without the deceiving myths of a spurious sanctity being drawn over it. But take the *talmid chacham* from his study hall and the *chassid* from his house of prayer and, against their entire nature and instinct which knows only peace and purity, place swords in their hands because in a given situation God wills it, then indeed the battles which they will fight may be described as the wars of *Hashem*.

David was himself called עֲדִינוֹ הָעֶצְנִי [see *Moed Katan* 16b based on *II Samuel* 23:8 which parallels our v. 11], because when he sat down to learn Torah he made himself pliant like a worm [עֲדִינוֹ from עדן, *to be smooth* or *pliant*], crouching modestly on the ground and refusing to sit on cushions; but when he went out to war he would be as stiff and unyielding as wood [הָעֶצְנִי from עֵץ, *wood*]. Both aspects of David form his name, both are products of the same essence. David's life was lived before God; the battlefield and study house only provided different arenas. Both, each in its own way, witnessed the same battle.

For David's wars were no ordinary ones. ... *For my Lord wages the battles of* HASHEM *and never have your actions been brought about by any evil intent* [*I Samuel* 25:28 — Avigail's paean to David's greatness; see also *Rambam, Hilchos Melachim* 7:14]. Not once in David's long life of war and fighting did he ever wield a sword for self-aggrandizement. Always he had God before his eyes, always he saw himself as only a tool in His hands. And when David was told that he was not to build the Temple because he had shed much blood (*I Chronicles* 22:8), his fears that this might reflect badly upon him were assuaged by Nathan who said, 'Do not fear, David! The people whom you have killed are like so many sacrifices [brought on the altar] before me' (*Yalkut* vol. 2, 145).

Thus, a completely new perception of David's *giborim* emerges. If we see the Sages interpreting their seemingly martial exploits as referring to heroism in their Torah studies then, far from contravening the simple meaning of the text, it is absolutely within the framework of the Scriptural perspective that they do so.[1]

---

1. It is noteworthy that *R' Shmuel ben Chofni, Gaon*, takes the identity between the people's judges and their army generals for granted and bases it on etymological considerations.

Deuteronomy 1:9ff describes how Moses, feeling unable to bear the burden of leadership alone, asked the people to suggest suitable men who could help in judging and administering the nation. He asked for people who were wise, understanding and acceptable to all. When the men had been nominated and Moses had convinced himself of their suitability, he declared that he would make them, '... *leaders* (רָאשִׁים) *over you, officers over a thousand, officers over a hundred, officers over fifty and officers over ten.*'

R' Shmuel ben Chofni, based on our passage where the word ראש is constantly used as a military term (see e.g., v. 20), explains that the men chosen by Moses were appointed over the army. The

The comm. to vs. 17-18 has quoted just such an interpretration, and the lesson learned from it is of vast significance to an understanding of the relationship between Israel and the Torah. This teaching of the Sages derives from a seeming contradiction between the account in *Samuel* and the one here.

In light of this, both the reason why *Chronicles* lists the *giborim* and the explanation of the discrepancies can perhaps be understood.

In the comm. to the genealogical lists in chs. 1-9, the teaching of the Sages, לֹא נִתַּן דִּבְרֵי הַיָּמִים אֶלָּא לִדְרֹשׁ, that in *Chronicles* the homiletical interpretation (דְּרַשׁ) supersedes the simple meaning (פְּשַׁט), has often been quoted. It has been suggested that this may well be because in many instances there simply is no פְּשַׁט readily intelligible to us. Furthermore, many of the problems in those lists have been traced to the sources from which Ezra drew the genealogical material. In particular, the opinion of the *Mefaresh* at 7:13 and 8:29 has been noted that the genealogical tables do, in fact, contain contradictory material culled from conflicting sources. It is conceivable that the same multiplicity of sources existed for David's *giborim* and that, as lies in the nature of such lists, there were discrepancies between them. But it is just in these discrepancies that the possibility for the rich aggadic interpretations of the Sages is rooted. Had Ezra not recorded the *giborim* and their exploits from the source available to him, and had we been left therefore with only the account in *Samuel*, the lessons which the Sages derived from these discrepancies would not have become evident to us.

Radak to *Samuel* questions the entire approach. Why, he reasons, convert an exploit which, from the whole context, is a demonstration of the *giborim's* heroism, into a quest for halachic guidance? He adduces a number of proofs to the view that the passage is to be taken literally and concludes: '... there is no justification for understanding the passage in any but its simple meaning.'

We have attempted to show that the Sages' approach is not only justified but absolutely necessary if the listing of the *giborim* and their exploits is not to do violence to the entire spirit of Scripture.

For reasons which we cannot know, the Sages' solution to the problems of only vs. 17-18 have been preserved for us. With the loss of the *Sefer HaYuchasin*, the midrash on *Chronicles*, which caused 'the strength of the Sages to be weakened and the light of their eyes to be dimmed' *(Pesachim* 62b, and see *Rashi* there: 'For the explanations of the Torah were now hidden from them'), the explanations of the other discrepancies are not available to us. But we can be sure that just as that incident was explained fully and satisfactorily by the Sages, so also all the other problems were solved. If this perception of these lists is correct, there is really no need to attempt a reconciliation between the lists here and those in *Samuel*.

Chapter Twelve

◄§ The Uniqueness of David

[א־ב] וְאֵלֶּה הַבָּאִים אֶל־דָּוִיד לְצִיקְלָג ... מֵאֲחֵי שָׁאוּל מִבִּנְיָמִן

[1-2] *These are the ones who joined David at Tziklag ... they were*

---

officers over one thousand, one hundred, etc. are described as commanders of units containing these numbers of soldiers (based for example on *I Samuel* 17:18). Although their primary appointments were as judges and administrators, the same qualities which made them suitable for those positions qualified them for their army roles.

from among Saul's brothers, from Benjamin.

It is certainly puzzling why people, and particularly *from among Saul's brothers from Benjamin* (v. 2), would flock to the banner of a man who must, at that time, have come to the nadir of his existence — cut off, as he felt himself to be, from any source of spiritual sustenance, and, at least to outward appearances, no more than a mercenary to a foreign king.

And yet — it was not so. H. Biberfeld in his masterly study, *David King of Israel,* points to the almost lyric accolade which the pagan king Achish gave David as he tried to defend him against the charges of disloyalty which the Philistine officers brought against him: *'... Surely as the Lord lives you have been upright, and your going and comings in the army with me is good in my eyes, for I have not found evil in you from the day you came to me until this day.'* As David protests that he feels wrongly accused, Achish goes on: *'... For you are as good in my eyes as an angel of God.'*

No person in Scripture is ever described as an angel of God except David. Subsequently, in quite different circumstances, two other people, the wise woman of Tekoa *(II Samuel* 14:17) and Saul's son, Mephibosheth *(II Samuel* 19:28), use the same expression. Three such disparate personalities would not have described David by the same — and unique — term if there was not something about David that compellingly suggested this encomium. To quote Biberfeld:

'Thus we see David mirrored in the testimony of his contemporaries. He does not appear to them like other human beings — driven by human passions and doubts. He is free of the compulsion to scheme and plot, free of uncertainty, revenge. His aims and directions — and this too they recognize — are determined by God. He is the source of the true freedom bestowed upon His messengers (מַלְאָךְ), and it is as such that David appears to those around him.

'David himself was well aware of this. The innumerable expressions in the psalms of that absolute suffusion of his person with the will of God so testify. They are neither, as one might be inclined to believe, hyperbolic lyricisms born in moments of transport and ecstasy nor the fervent longings of a soul striving for ever-closer nearness to God. They are statements of an exalted truth. God's words did indeed speak through him. His limbs and organs *were* forever animated by the will of the Most High, his heart was "hollow" in him, a mere receptacle waiting to receive the call of his Master.'

Thus, even in his most depressing exile, did David appear to even the unschooled eye of the pagan king. Small wonder, then, that the great men of Israel were instinctively drawn towards the overwhelming presence of this uniquely awe-inspiring personality.

There is a particular poignancy in the picture of Benjaminites — brothers of Saul — flocking to David's standard at Tziklag.

Immediately before David made his decision to flee the Land of Israel, there had been a dramatic confrontation between him and Saul *(I Samuel* ch. 26). While Saul was fast asleep in his camp, surrounded by an army specially drafted to search out David, David and Avshai had crept silently up to the slumbering Saul. Avshai had wanted to kill Saul but David, recoiling from the idea of attacking God's anointed king, refused him permission. Instead, he took Saul's spear and canteen and left the camp. From a distant hill he called to Saul's general, Avner, to taunt him with his unforgivable laxness in guarding the king.

Saul, hearing David's voice, felt his old love welling up within him and addressed him as 'my son, David.' Then, in an impassioned speech, David took him to task for pursuing him so unjustly and declared his complete innocence, demonstrating to him by exhibiting the spear and canteen how easily he might have killed him.

Chastised, Saul responded with the sentence which was to be the last he would ever speak to David: 'Blessed be you, my son David. You will most certainly do [that is, become king —Targum], and most certainly succeed.'

We might have anticipated that this conversation bring about a rapprochement, but apparently the chasm was too wide. The episode ends with a brief, one might almost say resigned, remark: And David went on his way and Saul returned to his place. Inexorably, now, history would take its course. Immediately after this, David went to Tziklag (see I Samuel chs. 26 and 27).

Thus, at the very end, Saul articulated that which in the depth of his soul he had known all along. And Samuel took the horn of oil and anointed him [David] in the midst of his brothers. And the spirit of HASHEM came upon David from that day forward ... But the spirit of HASHEM departed from Saul and an evil spirit from before HASHEM troubled him (I Samuel 16:13,14). When he proved himself unworthy, the exalted spirituality which had descended upon Saul when he had first shouldered the challenge of his great calling (I Samuel 10:9) left him to find its place in the soul of David.

In the pathos of his last confrontation with David, Saul finally saw the truth with absolute clarity. From now on there was nothing left to him but abject degradation. Mercifully, Saul died the death of one beloved and sweet [in God's sight] (II Samuel 1:23) on Mount Gilboa.

The Benjaminites who found their way to David in Tziklag were thus fulfilling Saul's own tragic prediction. Nothing but the shell was left of Saul's rule. Even while he was a fugitive dependent upon the whims of an idolatrous tribal chieftain, David was the true king of Israel.

⊸§ The Gadites

[ח] וּמִן־הַגָּדִי נִבְדְּלוּ אֶל־דָּוִיד ... וּפְנֵי אַרְיֵה פְּנֵיהֶם וְכִצְבָאִים עַל־הֶהָרִים לְמַהֵר.

[8] From the Gadites there defected to David ... their faces like the face of a lion, and as fleet as roedeer upon the mountains.

As noted in the comm. to this verse, the detachment of Gadite warriors was the first tribal unit to throw in their lot with David. Midrash Lekach Tov sees a hint of this coming of the Gadites in Jacob's blessing to Gad. The many different opinions concerning the precise meaning of this extremely difficult verse in Genesis 49:19 are given in detail in ArtScroll Bereishis pp. 2168-70, and need not be repeated here. The midrash assumes that the first part of the verse, גָּד גְּדוּד יְגוּדֶנּוּ, Gad will recruit a regiment, means that a phalanx of soldiers will one day be mustered out of Gad's ranks — and that this refers to the Gadites who led the battle formation into the promised land in Joshua's time. The second half, וְהוּא יָגֻד עָקֵב, means that he [i.e., another company of soldiers] will [one day] follow in their footsteps,[1] and that this refers to the Gadite warriors who joined David as

1. We have used follow in their footsteps, on the assumption that the midrash takes עָקֵב as heel and in the sense of a path trodden by the heel as many commentators take it there. It is also possible that the midrash takes עָקֵב, heel, as a later time (as a heel follows or terminates the body). See below that this is the meaning that another midrash adduces.

described in our passage.

Since, as we see in our chapter, there were also other tribal units which joined David, it seems likely that the particular importance attached to Gad's coming must be associated with the fact that he was the very first. It was he who, so to speak, broke the ice and initiated the general shift from Saul to David.

The almost lyric description which our verse gives of the Gadites — *faces like the face of a lion, and as fleet as roedeer upon the mountains* — underscores the importance which *Chronicles* attaches to their coming. The choice of words seems designed to elevate a seemingly unremarkable event to the realm of the extraordinary. [In this vein, see also *Gra's* unusual explanation of verse 16.]

The key to this may be the interpretation of Jacob's blessing found in *Bereishis Rabbah* (99:12), which explains the phrase וְהוּא יָגֵד עָקֵב as referring to the ultimate redemption. In the tradition of the Sages (see comm. to 8:27), Elijah the prophet was descended from Gad, and Jacob was hinting at Elijah's involvement in the coming of the Messiah [עָקֵב, *heel*, in the sense of *the end (of days)*]. As Gad was the first to enter the Holy Land at the head of Joshua's army, so too will be the herald of the Messianic era.

On the assumption that this midrash does not stand in disagreement with the *Midrash Lekach Tov* quoted above, in which וְהוּא יָגֵד עָקֵב is interpreted as referring to the time that the Gadites joined David, then this event is presented in a perspective which places it midway between two seminal points in Jewish history: Gad is the first to enter the land, the first to recognize David as king, and the first to recognize the Messianic age.

All three of these events have this in common: Only one who can detect the spark of light within the darkness, the sheen of a diamond covered with dross, could act as Gad did. The land of Canaan was a cesspool of iniquity — Gad saw its potential sanctity and rushed towards it. David was languishing in Philistine exile — Gad saw the future king.

When Gad's greatest son — Elijah — will one day herald the Messianic redemption it will be no more than the continuation of his tribe's glorious heritage. For the herald of the Messiah must also be able to apprehend the spark of redemption which lies hidden in the darkness of exile.

Chapter Fourteen

☙ Ascendancy over Tyre

In the introduction to this chapter the discrepancy between the sequence of events as given here in *Chronicles* and the one given in *Samuel* has been noted. *Abarbanel* shows in *Samuel* that the true sequence of events seems to be the one given in *Samuel*, namely that the abortive transfer of the Ark *followed* Churam's presentation of gifts to David, David's additional marriages and the two Philistine attacks. According to him, *Chronicles* is not following a chronological order. *Abarbanel*, however, does not offer any explanation for the order adopted by *Chronicles*.

If *Abarbanel's* assumption is accepted, then it is clear that the one event which seems out of place in *Chronicles* is the abortive transfer of the Ark (number 2 on the list presented in comm.). It is interjected earlier in the sequence than it actually took place.

As has been noted a number of times, *Chronicles* addresses itself more to the essence than to the form of history (see Overview). It therefore seems likely that the transfer of the Ark was inserted out of its proper historical setting because it has something to teach us about that which follows.

The following is offered as a possible solution:

Churam's gesture of sending craftsmen and material to build David's palace marked a seminal point in David's rule. Verse 1, which tells us of the event, is followed by v. 2 which states that: *Thus David realized that Hashem had firmly established him as king over Israel, that his kingdom had been raised high for the sake of His people Israel*. To this verse *Gra* makes the short remark: [He realized that his kingdom was firmly established] since Tyre, which is descended from Edom, subjugated itself before him. To appreciate *Gra's* remark fully, some background is necessary.

When Rebecca was pregnant with the twins, Jacob and Esau, and suffering terrible pains, she went to inquire of God what the future held in store for her. She was told וּלְאֹם מִלְאֹם יֶאֱמָץ, [*And*] *the might shall pass from one regime to the other*. To this *Rashi* remarks: The two of them will never be mighty simultaneously; when one [i.e., one's regime] falls the other will rise.

Thus, history is to be a constant balancing of power between these two brothers. When Israel keeps the Torah and lives in accordance with God's wishes, they will gain the ascendancy. When she transgresses God's will, Esau will throw off her yoke and rise to the top. (See *Genesis* 40:27 and ArtScroll comm. p. 1156.)[1]

Tyre is considered part of Edom *(Bereishis Rabbah* 61:7) and, according to *Megillah* 6a, rejoiced particularly when Jerusalem was destroyed because only now would she be able to come into her own.

This is the meaning of *Gra's* remark. When Churam tacitly granted David's ascendancy by sending him gifts after his coronation, this attested to the fact that Israel had attained the spiritual perfection which was a precondition for its position in world affairs.

Perhaps the insertion of the story of the Ark before the account of Churam's gesture was meant as an affirmation of the fact that Israel had, indeed, attained that high, spiritual level. As discussed at 13:7, *Gra's* interpretation of David's error in placing the Ark upon a carriage was that David had not thought his people worthy to be the direct bearers of the Divine Presence upon the Ark. God's wrath at this error can serve as an unambiguous refutation of this thought. The centuries under the Judges, when idol worship had been practiced in Israel, had not erased Israel's inner core of sanctity. Under Saul and now under David, Israel was once more the nation in which God finds His pride and the justification for the creation of the world. A people able to carry the Ark upon its shoulder is a people in front of whom a Churam might well prostrate himself.

[ח] וַיִּשְׁמְעוּ פְלִשְׁתִּים כִּי־נִמְשַׁח דָּוִיד לְמֶלֶךְ עַל־כָּל־יִשְׂרָאֵל וַיַּעֲלוּ כָל־פְּלִשְׁתִּים לְבַקֵּשׁ אֶת־דָּוִיד וַיִּשְׁמַע דָּוִיד וַיֵּצֵא לִפְנֵיהֶם.

[8] *And the Philistines heard that David had been anointed king over all Israel, so all the Philistines went up to seek out David; and David heard and went out against them.*

1. For an analysis of the dynamics of Scriptural history as the tension inherent in the poles Jacob-Israel: Esau-Edom, see *Derashos HaRan, Derush* 2.

Radak states that it was on the occasion of David's first battle with the Philistines after becoming king that he composed the second psalm. *Radak* brings no source for his assertion and the author has not been able to find one.

If there is a midrashic source, this would be highly significant because this psalm is interpreted by the Sages as referring to the war of Gog and Magog, that final cataclysmic battle when the nations of the world will attempt to pit themselves against the Messiah — God's anointed — in a last futile effort to prevent the ultimate redemption. [For a detailed analysis of the war of Gog and Magog, see ArtScroll *Ezekiel* chs. 38 and 39.] The psalm makes clear that the fight against the Messiah is in reality a fight against God himself [עַל ה' וְעַל מְשִׁיחוֹ, *against HASHEM and against His anointed one*], the focus of Whose presence on earth is Israel.

If the psalm also deals with the Philistine war to which David was exposed immediately upon becoming king, then this would lift these wars out of their immediate dimensions and stamp them with the mark of eternity. With David's ascension to the throne, the Messianic idea becomes a reality in the affairs of man. In a fury of hatred against the vast implications which this idea has for those whose very existence is a denial of the Divine Presence on earth, the Philistines hurl themselves against David — and against his God. In so doing they presage the Gogian wars — the one waged against the seed, the other against the flower of the Messianic idea. [See *Maharal* in *Chiddushei Aggadah* to *Sanhedrin* 95b who defines the war which the four kings waged against Abraham in precisely those terms. That war, at the beginning of Israel's existence, was the harbinger of the final battle which will be waged when history will have run its course.]

This interpretation of these Philistine wars would explain why *Chronicles* included them in its history. In the short view, they seem like individual events which have no place in the broad sweep of *Chronicles'* historical survey. In fact, they are highly significant steps in Israel's march towards redemption, which is the essential subject of *Chronicles*.

Chapter Fifteen

⋞§ A Place for the Ark

[א] וַיַּעַשׂ־לוֹ בָתִּים בְּעִיר דָּוִיד וַיָּכֶן מָקוֹם לַאֲרוֹן הָאֱלֹהִים וַיֵּט־לוֹ אֹהֶל.

[1] *And he built for himself houses in the City of David; and he prepared a place for the Ark of God and pitched a covering for it.*

It seems likely that when David diverted the Ark to the house of Oved Edom, he did not mean this as a permanent arrangement. There is no doubt that the Ark, symbol of the Divine Presence in Israel, belonged in the City of David. Rather, a temporary irresolution was created by the sudden tragic death of Uzza.

This, according to *Malbim*, is the meaning of 13:12 which reads: 'And David feared God *on that day.*' In one terrible moment, the joyous expansive love of God which had animated David when he first initiated the transfer of the Ark, was transmuted into an inhibiting fear born out of an all-pervading awareness of the smallness of man and the awesome weight of responsibility he shoulders when he chooses to stand in the presence of the Divine. Saddened by Uzza's death, in which he knew himself to be partially to blame, and crushed by the fear of his own failings, he could not bring the Ark to Jerusalem. But surely he must have expected that the time would come when, buoyed by a love of God which could be overshadowed but never extinguished, he would feel ready once more to escort the Ark to its rightful place.

But at which point was David ready for the move? In this, *Samuel* and *Chronicles* say seemingly different things. *Samuel* has: *And it was told to King David, saying: God has blessed the house of Oved Edom and all that is his in the merit of the Ark of God. So David went and brought up the Ark of God from the house of Oved Edom to the City of David in joy.*

By contrast our verse says nothing of all this and seems to attribute David's decision to the cryptic building of houses. What are these houses and in what way do they bear on David's decision to bring the Ark to Jerusalem?

To understand the phrase we should first take a closer look at the simpler phrase in *Samuel*. Why did the information that Oved Edom's house had been blessed convince David that it was time to bring up the Ark?

As the Sages explain it *(Bamidbar Rabbah* 4:20), it brought on a deep sense of shame in David for having feared the presence of the Ark: 'Why was Oved Edom given the strange name Edom [which recalls Israel's archenemy, Esau, and would seem an unsuitable name]? Because he reddened David's face with embarrassment [אָדֹם, from אָדוֹם, *red*].' What had this man done, after all, to deserve such abundant blessings? He had lit a light in front of the Ark, swept and kept clean the place where it rested. Could not he, David, do the same?

As the Sages teach us, shame is the foundation upon which true repentance is built. The shattering awareness of inadequacy which the feeling of shame engenders can loosen the hard soil of lethargy which is brought on by sin and ready it for a new flowering of the self. David came to himself and knew the direction which he must take.

What of the phrase in *Chronicles*? There is much that is problematic in this phrase. In the first place there is no logical cohesion between the first and second parts of the sentence. The building of houses seems irrelevant to the preparation of a place for the Ark. Again, 11:8 already tells of the rebuilding of the City of David, and the implication of that passage is that it describes a complete project. This would surely have taken care of any houses that David needed.[1]

Another point worthy of note is the expression וַיַּעַשׂ לוֹ בָתִּים which literally means *he made* for himself houses, rather than the expected וַיִּבֶן, *he built*.

This last point is so striking that we are inclined to see the phrase as idiomatic. The phrase in this form occurs only once more in Scripture, and that is at *Exodus* 1:21 where it describes the reward which the midwives received for defying Pharaoh's edict. When God saw that they feared Him, וַיַּעַשׂ לָהֶם בָּתִּים, literally, *He made houses for them.* But what does it imply? The Sages (see *Rashi* there) interpret: houses of *Kohanim,* Levites and royalty; meaning that the midwives were rewarded by having Aaron, the father of the *Kohanim,* and David, the

---

1. This problem could be solved if this verse were interpreted to mean not that he now built houses and prepared a place for the Ark but that he had previously done so. The verse would then, in fact, be referring back to the passage in ch. 11. An advantage of this interpretation would be that the preparation of a place for the Ark would already have taken place before the first, abortive, attempt at a transfer. Translated to mean that he only now built the houses and prepared the place leaves open the question of what would have happened to the Ark had the earlier attempt been successful.

father of royalty in Israel, among their descendants.

But that is surely not the simple meaning of the phrase. Rather, we must view the phrase as an idiom (see *HaKesav VeHaKabbalah* there) and see if we can identify at least the rough meaning of it. Now, we do have a very similar — and clearly idiomatic — usage in Scripture which can help us. When Abigail foresees David's glorious future as Israel's king, she says (*I Samuel* 25:28): ... *may HASHEM make a lasting house for my master* (יַעֲשֶׂה ... בַּיִת נֶאֱמָן). Again, the prophet Nathan reminds David (*II Samuel* 7:11) of God's promise to him that, כִּי בַיִת יַעֲשֶׂה לְּךָ, *For* [HASHEM] *will establish a house for you.* And Solomon also speaks (*I Kings* 2:24) of HASHEM, *Who had made a house for me* (עָשָׂה לִי בָּיִת). Clearly, in all these cases we are not dealing with an actual house but with a figurative one; that is, with the kingship granted to David and Solomon. Thus, we can equate *making a house* with establishing an honored, permanent position in Israel (see *Gur Aryeh* to *Exodus* 1:21). In the case of the midwives that is the promise that God made to them and, as the Sages taught, this became fulfilled when they counted Aaron and David among their descendants.

In our context we would not be far off the mark, then, in rendering: *And David established himself* [into the situation which granted him permanence and honor in Israel]. The plunge into despair occasioned by Uzza's death was seen to have been an aberration and now the real David came through once more.

In short, then, it is really precisely the same thought as the one expressed in *Samuel* — the moment when he was ready to forget the fears of the past and bring back the Ark to the location in which it really belonged.

◆§ Dancing Before the Ark

[כז] וְדָוִיד מְכֻרְבָּל בִּמְעִיל בּוּץ ... וְעַל־דָּוִיד אֵפוֹד בָּד.

[27] *And David was hooded in a linen robe ... and David wore a linen ephod.*

The commentary has pointed out that, at least according to *Metzudos'* explanation, *Chronicles* makes mention of an additional garment worn by David for this occasion — the מְעִיל בּוּץ, *linen robe*, which the parallel verse in *II Samuel* 6:14 does not mention. Why?

A careful analysis of the two passages shows that the thrust of the account is quite different in *Chronicles* than in *Samuel.* Whereas in *Samuel* David's uninhibited dancing is central to the account, it is not even mentioned in *Chronicles*, except obliquely in v. 29 as an explanation of Michal's attitude towards David.

Given this difference in emphasis a possible solution to our problem is suggested. If we take v. 14 in *Samuel*, we are struck by an apparent lack of cohesion between the first and second parts of the verse. We read: *And David danced with all his might before HASHEM; and David was girded with an ephod of linen.* What does the one have to do with the other? Perhaps the answer can be found in the Midrash. As the Sages tell it (*Bamidbar Rabbah* 4:20), Michal taunted David with the perceived wildness of his dance: 'Come,' she said, 'see the difference between you and my father's family. They were modest and holy. It was said concerning them that no man ever saw their heel or their toes [i.e., their clothes were long enough to cover their whole body] ... Now they were so modest and [in contrast] you lay back your clothes like some clown'. Thus, it was the fact that in dancing David allowed his clothes to be flapped around revealing parts of his body which disgusted Michal. As the Midrash has David answer her, it was specifically to this point that he addressed himself. 'I am like an infant in front of its mother' (based on *Psalms* 131:2). 'Just as a child can reveal himself before his mother without shame, so I stand before God, not allowing myself to be embarrassed, in order to do Him honor.'

It seems likely that this is how the Sages understood v. 14 in *Samuel*. *David danced with all his might before HASHEM — and was girded with an ephod of linen.* It is the ephod which flapped open in the wildness of David's dance, and for this reason mention of the ephod was central to the narrative from the perspective of *Samuel*. The מְעִיל, *robe*, has no place in that account.

Now the abandon of David's dance is highly significant in the life story of David, the man. It indicated his love for God and his willingness to debase himself in His service, and it is justifiably central to the account in *Samuel*. But this is not the perspective from which *Chronicles* approaches the incident. As has been noted a number of times, *Samuel* and *Kings* treat their subjects from their standing as individuals, while *Chronicles* has the long-range view of history in mind. In that context, it is the contrast between David and the house of Saul which is important rather than David's own spiritual attainments. This is evidenced by the fact which we noted above, that David's dancing is not mentioned at all except in the context of Michal's disapproval. The object of the story from the point of view of *Chronicles* is that David, in bringing the Ark to Jerusalem, acted as a king of Israel should have acted and that Michal, scion of Saul's house, was not able to comprehend the significance of what was happening. In this context, it was important to underline that David's clothing for the occasion was entirely suited to his high perception of the service of God. If he was less than modest in the ecstasy of the dance, in the sober moments prior to the beginning of the celebration he was certainly dressed becomingly.

On the contrary, as the Midrash words it [based on our verse and not on the אֵפוֹד בָּד of *Samuel*]: 'David could have walked in front of the Ark dressed in his royal garments. Instead, he wore suitable clothes (בְּגָדִים נָאִים) to honor the Ark.' The commentators explain that he specifically wore the same clothes as the Levites were wearing so that he was dressed as one who seeks communication with God rather than as a king. To counteract the statement in *Samuel* that he was *girded with an ephod* of linen which, as we saw above, resulted in the perceived immodesty of his dance, *Chronicles* finds it important to stress that in addition to this ephod [end of verse] he also wore a hooded robe.

Chronicles	Samuel
1. ... וְדָוִיד מְכֻרְבָּל בִּמְעִיל בּוּץ, *And David was hooded in a linen robe* ...	1. וְדָוִד מְכַרְכֵּר בְּכָל עֹז לִפְנֵי ה', *And David danced with all his might before HASHEM*
2. וְעַל־דָּוִיד אֵפוֹד בָּד, *and David wore a linen ephod*	2. וְדָוִד חָגוּר אֵפוֹד בָּד, *and David was girded with an ephod of linen*

Phrases 2 are exactly the same, and *Chronicles*, in its phrase 1, counteracts whatever negative impression might have been left by phrase 1 in *Samuel*. Thus, as we have seen in so many other instances, the parts of the two verses in *Samuel* and *Chronicles* exactly cover one another.

Chapter Sixteen

◄§ Chapter Analysis

8-36. According to *Seder Olam* 14, the songs of praise contained in this section were divided into two parts. The section consisting of vs. 8-22 was sung in the morning, while the section consisting of vs. 23-36 was sung in the evening. *Seder Olam* brings no source for this assertion, so we must assume that it is relying on oral tradition.

Sedar Olam continues that these psalms were recited mornings and evenings throughout the forty-three years that elapsed from the time David brought the Ark to Jerusalem until the completion of Solomon's Temple. At that time the Ark was once more reunited with the altar and the Temple service, which had up to that time been in Giveon, became the sole service.

As was noted at 6:16-17, it is not quite clear from *Seder Olam's* words whether these psalms continued to be recited in Solomon's Temple. On the one hand, the mention of forty-three years seems to imply that the recitation of these psalms was later discontinued. On the other hand, the fact that according to most rites these psalms have become incorporated into the daily *Shacharis* service seems to indicate that they were indeed a permanent feature of the service. *Tur* in *Orach Chaim* 51 seems to assume a permanent ordinance.[1]

Seder Olam's tradition that this song of praise was recited in two parts may be based on the fact that the two sections seem to derive from two separate psalms. It would seem that the first section corresponds to *Psalms* 105:1-15 while the greater part of the second section corresponds to *Psalms* 96:1-13. The final three verses are vs. 1 and 47-48 of *Psalms* 106. However, although the resemblance to these *Psalms* is striking — most of the verses being exact repetitions of those found in *Psalms* — it is quite possible that the sections used here take on a slightly different meaning in their new form. By choosing only certain parts of larger *Psalms*, and by dedicating them to the daily service before the Ark, David subtly altered their focus. This may account for the differences which exist between the two texts.

We must now examine the contents of this song of jubilation, paying particular attention to its unusual structure. In this analysis, the whole psalm will be treated as one cohesive unit in spite of the fact that it apparently derives from three different psalms and that *Sedar Olam* splits it into two parts for the purpose of the service before the Ark.[2] This assumption seems justified firstly

---

1. Sephardic and Ashkenazic customs differ in the placing of the הודו psalm in the *Shacharis* prayer. The Sephardic ritual has it together with the recitation of the daily sacrifice (פָּרָשַׁת הַתָּמִיד) because of its association with the morning and evening sacrifice. In the Ashkenazic rite it comes after בָּרוּךְ שֶׁאָמַר because it, too, together with the other psalms which are recited, can be described as, *The songs of your servant David*, to which בָּרוּךְ שֶׁאָמַר serves as an introduction.

It is possible that the Ashkenazic ritual is not concerned with having the הודו recited together with the daily sacrifice because, as discussed at 6:16-17, the site of the daily communal sacrifice during the forty-three years in which the Ark rested in David's tent was not Jerusalem but Giveon. Thus, the initial ordinance for the recitation of these psalms was in no way connected to the sacrificial service. It was a new form of *shir* which David originated as a fitting service for the Ark while it rested alone in Jerusalem. Even if Solomon then continued with the recitation after the sacrificial service was transferred to Jerusalem, the connection to the daily sacrifice remained coincidental rather than integral.

2. There is, of course, the possibility that the psalm in the form in which it appears in *Chronicles* came first and that the other psalms were abstracted from it.

on textual grounds. The text presents the psalm as one and does not allude even by implication to the fact that it derives from various different psalms, nor to the fact that it was not all recited at one time. Secondly, in spite of the fact that David drew the verses of this psalm from various other psalms, the profound changes which he made in the text when he made it part of the daily ritual give the work the stamp of a new and independent creation. Thus, in its new form, there is no reason to see it as anything but a cohesive whole. However, it remains true that this new work falls naturally into two parts, and thus no violence was done to its integrity when it was decided to split it into two parts for ritual purposes.

We turn first to the first part, which comprises vs. 8-22 and which, in all but a few phrases, is identical with *Psalm* 105:1-15. However, *Psalm* 105 comprises forty-five verses, but only one-third of that psalm, vs. 1-15, is used in the song before the Ark. It seems likely then that the thrust of the passage and its emphasis are quite different when it stands by itself than when it is only a fraction of a much larger piece. This assumption yields the following conclusion: *Psalm* 105 is a paean of thanksgiving to God for the way He fulfilled all the promises which He had made to Abraham (see v. 42 there: ... *For He remembered His holy promise, to Abraham, His servant*). Now if we take vs. 1-5 as a general introduction exhorting Israel to thank God for what is to follow, then vs. 6-45 comprise a list of those fulfilled promises. They cover a wide range of topics, including Joseph's rulership over Egypt, a partial list of the plagues, the clouds of glory with which God surrounded Israel in the wilderness, and the manna and meat with which He sustained them. Within such a litany of praise the point made in vs. 6-15, that God promised the land to Abraham's descendants and subsequently made them the object of His special providence and protection, provides just one more example of God's faithfulness to His promise.

If, however, we lift vs. 1-15 out of the larger psalm, then, standing alone, its emphasis is an entirely different point. Verses 1-5 become an exhortation to praise God; but for what? For the unique status of Israel among the nations. This aspect of the section, which is submerged by the general theme of God's faithfulness in the larger psalm, is now the *only* point made and becomes the focus of the whole song. Based on this analysis, the changes which David made in the two key phrases become self-explanatory.

Chronicles v. 13, 15	Psalms 105:6,8
13. זֶרַע יִשְׂרָאֵל עַבְדּוֹ, *O seed of Israel, His servant;*	6. זֶרַע אַבְרָהָם עַבְדּוֹ, *O seed of Abraham, His servant,*
בְּנֵי יַעֲקֹב בְּחִירָיו, *the children of Jacob, His chosen ones*	בְּנֵי יַעֲקֹב בְּחִירָיו, *the children of Jacob, His chosen ones.*
15. זִכְרוּ לְעוֹלָם בְּרִיתוֹ, *Remember forever His covenant,*	8. זָכַר לְעוֹלָם בְּרִיתוֹ, *He remembered His covenant forever —*
דָּבָר צִוָּה לְאֶלֶף דּוֹר, *the word He ordained for a thousand generations.*	דָּבָר צִוָּה לְאֶלֶף דּוֹר, *the word He commanded for a thousand generations.*

The Abraham of *Psalms* becomes Israel in *Chronicles*; the זָכַר, *He remembers* (God's faithfulness affirmed), becomes זִכְרוּ, *Remember!* (an exhortation to Israel).

The changes are entirely natural. God's promises were made to Abraham and God's faith was kept with him (זָכַר). That is the context of the whole psalm and any other wording would have been inconsistent with the intent of the whole work. In the form which the psalm takes in connection with the service of the Ark, however, it becomes a song of praise for Israel's having been picked out from among the nations. Israel as a chosen people is the *seed of Israel*. The nationhood of Israel began with Jacob's sons. The burden of the song is that Israel is always to remember that it is unique among the nations of the world (זִכְרוּ).

It is entirely natural that the theme of Israel's uniqueness should be celebrated daily in front of the Ark. As has been noted several times, the Ark was the focus of God's presence on earth. There is no more eloquent statement of Israel's particularization than that God chooses to dwell among them — in Jerusalem, His and their holy city.

But if Israel has been picked out that does not mean that the nations of the world are to be excluded. Solomon made that same point in his inaugural prayer for the Temple (see I *Kings* 8:41ff), and it is to this too that David addresses himself in the second part of the psalm.

For a clearer understanding of the second part of our psalm, vs. 23-33 must be analyzed. These correspond essentially to *Psalm* 96:1-13. In this section the changes which David made upon using these verses for the song before the Ark are quite complicated. Yet, they seem entirely consistent with the intent of the psalm in its new form. To highlight the essential points the changes are numbered A-C.

A

Note, first of all, that our v. 23 is a telescoped version of vs. 1 and 2 of *Psalm* 96.

Chronicles v. 23	Psalms 96:1 and 2
	1(a) שִׁירוּ לַה' שִׁיר חָדָשׁ, *Sing to* HASHEM *a new song,*
23(a) שִׁירוּ לַה' כָּל־הָאָרֶץ, *Sing to* HASHEM, *all the earth,*	(b) שִׁירוּ לַה' כָּל־הָאָרֶץ, *sing to* HASHEM, *all the earth*
	2(a) שִׁירוּ לַה' בָּרְכוּ שְׁמוֹ, *Sing to* HASHEM, *bless His Name,*
(b) בַּשְּׂרוּ מִיּוֹם־אֶל־יוֹם יְשׁוּעָתוֹ, *announce His salvation daily.*	(b) בַּשְּׂרוּ מִיּוֹם־לְיוֹם יְשׁוּעָתוֹ, *announce His salvation daily.*

The first halves of vs. 1 and 2 are omitted in *Chronicles* and vs. 23 here is made up of the second halves of the two verses.

B

In v. 27, which corresponds to v. 6 in *Psalms*, there occurs a change of expression.

Chronicles v. 27	Psalms v. 6
27(a) הוֹד וְהָדָר לְפָנָיו, *Glory and majesty are before Him,*	6(a) הוֹד־וְהָדָר לְפָנָיו, *Glory and majesty are before Him,*
(b) עֹז וְחֶדְוָה בִּמְקֹמוֹ, *might and delight are in His place.*	(b) עֹז וְתִפְאֶרֶת בְּמִקְדָּשׁוֹ, *might and splendor in His Sanctuary.*

C

A subsequent change is more complicated.

Chronicles vs. 29-33	Psalms vs. 9-13
29(b) הִשְׁתַּחֲווּ לַה' בְּהַדְרַת־קֹדֶשׁ, *Prostrate yourselves before* HASHEM *in majestic holiness.*	9(a) הִשְׁתַּחֲווּ לַה' בְּהַדְרַת קֹדֶשׁ, *Prostrate yourselves before* HASHEM *in majestic holiness,*
30(a) חִילוּ מִלְּפָנָיו כָּל־הָאָרֶץ, *Tremble before Him, all the earth,*	(b) חִילוּ מִפָּנָיו כָּל הָאָרֶץ, *tremble before Him, all the earth.*
	10(a) אִמְרוּ בַגּוֹיִם ה' מָלָךְ, *Declare among the peoples, '*HASHEM *reigns!'*
(b) אַף־תִּכּוֹן תֵּבֵל בַּל־תִּמּוֹט, *indeed, the world is fixed so that it cannot falter.*	(b) אַף תִּכּוֹן תֵּבֵל בַּל תִּמּוֹט, *Indeed, the world is fixed so that it cannot falter,*
	(c) יָדִין עַמִּים בְּמֵישָׁרִים, *He judges the nations with equity.*
31(a) יִשְׂמְחוּ הַשָּׁמַיִם וְתָגֵל הָאָרֶץ, *Let the heavens rejoice and the earth be glad,*	11(a) יִשְׂמְחוּ הַשָּׁמַיִם וְתָגֵל הָאָרֶץ, *Let the heavens rejoice and the earth be glad,*
(b) וְיֹאמְרוּ בַגּוֹיִם ה' מָלָךְ, *let them declare among the peoples, '*HASHEM *reigns.'*	
32(a) יִרְעַם הַיָּם וּמְלֹאוֹ, *Let the sea and its fullness roar,*	(b) יִרְעַם הַיָּם וּמְלֹאוֹ, *let the sea and its fullness roar.*
(b) יַעֲלֹץ הַשָּׂדֶה וְכָל־אֲשֶׁר־בּוֹ, *let the field and everything in it exult.*	12(a) יַעֲלֹז שָׂדַי וְכָל אֲשֶׁר בּוֹ, *Let the field and everything in it exult,*
33(a) אָז יְרַנְּנוּ עֲצֵי הַיָּעַר, *Then the trees of the forest will sing joyously*	(b) אָז יְרַנְּנוּ כָּל עֲצֵי יָעַר, *then all the trees of the forest will sing joyously*
(b) מִלְּפְנֵי ה' כִּי־בָא לִשְׁפּוֹט אֶת־הָאָרֶץ, *before* HASHEM, *for He comes to judge the earth.*	13(a) לִפְנֵי ה' כִּי בָא כִּי בָא לִשְׁפֹּט הָאָרֶץ, *Before* HASHEM, *for He comes, for He comes to judge the earth.*
	(b) יִשְׁפֹּט תֵּבֵל בְּצֶדֶק וְעַמִּים בֶּאֱמוּנָתוֹ, *He will judge the world with righteousness, and nations with His faithful truth.*

Note two major changes in this last section: Firstly, *Psalm's* reference to God's judgment of the nations (10c and 13b) are entirely omitted in the *Chronicles* version. A more striking change is structural. A glance at the *Psalms* verses shows an entirely logical sequence. Vs. 9 and 10 describe how the nations will relate to God, while vs. 11 and 12 describe the joy which nature will evince. In this development the nation's proclamation that God is king (10a) is listed quite properly in the earlier section. *Chronicles* upsets this logical structure by placing this proclamation (31b) in the section dealing with nature's adoration, which would not seem to be its logical place. Moreover, in order to do this the phrase אַף תִּכּוֹן תֵּבֵל בַּל תִּמּוֹט, *indeed, the world is fixed so that it cannot falter* (30b), is left dangling since the conjunction אַף, *indeed*, has no phrase preceding it. [Note that in the passage from *Psalms* this phrase (10b) is part of the proclamation made by the nations.]

In the form which this psalm takes in *Psalms*, it is a song for the future — a call to the whole earth to sing God's praises during the Messianic era. This is evident from the heading, שִׁירוּ לַה' שִׁיר חָדָשׁ, *Sing to HASHEM a new song* (section A, 1a), with the masculine שִׁיר חָדָשׁ rather than the feminine שִׁירָה חֲדָשָׁה. Now the Sages teach that up to the Messianic era all songs of jubilation are to be expressed in the feminine form, for just as a woman is relieved from her birth pangs by the birth of her child only to be subjected to them again when she conceives once more, so all of God's salvations will only be temporary ones. Only the ultimate, triumphant song of the Messianic era will be called שִׁיר חָדָשׁ (see *Shemos Rabbah* 23:11).

It therefore follows from the fact that David eliminated this phrase from section A when he incorporated this psalm as the second half of the psalm to be sung in front of the Ark, that he wanted to change this connotation and bring the song into the present. In doing so he made the initial phrase of the psalm שִׁירוּ לַה' כָּל הָאָרֶץ, *Sing to HASHEM all the earth*, which immediately gives the song universal connotations. The whole earth, including the gentile nations, are to sing to God. This universality is augmented by phrase 2b, בַּשְּׂרוּ מִיּוֹם לְיוֹם יְשׁוּעָתוֹ, *announce His salvation daily*, but phrase 2a (which in *Psalms* balances phrase 1a) adds nothing to it and is therefore omitted. Thus in its new form, v. 23 is a call for universal praise of God, and the psalm continues on the same theme through vs. 24-26.

This change from a song of the future to one of the present readily explains the changes in section B. Once the Messiah has come and the Temple is rebuilt, it will be possible to speak of the *splendor in His Sanctuary (Psalms* 6b). In David's time, the Temple did not yet exist, and there was only the tent in which the Ark rested. The nations could know that there is *delight in His place (Chronicles* 27b), but, for the moment, not more than that.

The changes in section C are also readily understandable. The Messianic era is one in which the nations of the world will recognize God's majesty and formally proclaim this kingship. As part of his vision of an ideal society which is to flourish then, the Psalmist calls out to them *(Psalms* 10a), *Declare among the peoples, 'HASHEM reigns.'* They will gladly subject themselves to God's justice which is both equitable (10c) and true (13b).

As conditions were in David's time, however, this all still lay in the future. There could be no talk of the nations happily subjecting themselves to God's judgment nor of a formal proclamation that God is King. The most that could be said in the context of a song which seeks to elicit a hymn of jubilation from all the nations of the world was that it could be hoped (וְיֹאמְרוּ, *let them declare*, instead of the imperative אִמְרוּ, *declare)* that intuitively, in harmony with the song of praise which all of nature sings, the nations, too, will realize — although not yet express — God's kingship.

We have now uncovered the underlying ideas of this song. As the Ark, and through it the Divine Presence, came to rest in Israel, David ordained that the implicit particularization of Israel be celebrated, but that at the same time the point be made that the manifestation of the Divine Presence on earth was significant for all nations.

The three final verses, which are, respectively, the first and last two verses of *Psalm* 106, are not easily accommodated in this system.

Chronicles

34. הוֹדוּ לַה' כִּי טוֹב כִּי לְעוֹלָם חַסְדּוֹ, *Give thanks to* HASHEM, *for He is good, for His kindness endures forever.*

35. וְאִמְרוּ הוֹשִׁיעֵנוּ אֱלֹהֵי יִשְׁעֵנוּ, *And say, 'Save us, O God of our salvation,* וְקַבְּצֵנוּ וְהַצִּילֵנוּ מִן־הַגּוֹיִם, *gather us and deliver us from among the peoples,* לְהֹדוֹת לְשֵׁם קָדְשֶׁךָ לְהִשְׁתַּבֵּחַ בִּתְהִלָּתֶךָ, *to give thanks to Your Holy Name, to glory in your praise.'*

36. בָּרוּךְ ה' אֱלֹהֵי יִשְׂרָאֵל מִן־הָעוֹלָם וְעַד־הָעֹלָם, *Blessed is* HASHEM, *God of Israel, from the most distant past to the remotest future.* וַיֹּאמְרוּ כָל־הָעָם, *Then all the people said:* אָמֵן וְהַלֵּל לַה', *'Amen, and praise to* HASHEM.'

While v. 34 could well be seen as a concluding, generalized sentence of praise to God, v. 35 seems entirely out of place. If *Psalm* 106 predicts and describes with the prophetic eye of the Psalmist some of the exiles to which Israel would be subject and concludes with a prayer for the gathering-in of the exiles, then that is entirely apt and presents no problems. But what place does this prayer have as part of a daily ritual in front of the Ark?

Malbim goes so far as to suggest that, in fact, the whole *Psalm* 106 was recited but that only the first and last verses are explicated in the text. Alternatively, he thinks that perhaps just the first and last sentences were said but that the purpose was to hint at the contents of the whole psalm. [*Mefaresh* seems to say something similar but his language at this point is difficult to understand.]

Perhaps when we consider the very last phrase in the song: *Blessed be* HASHEM, *God of Israel, from the most distant past to the remotest future* (v. 36), the following solution beomes possible. After vs. 23-33, which sing of the universal adoration of God, the Psalmist returns once more to the opening theme. It is true that all the nations of the world can and should sing to God; but still — Israel is special. When all else is said and done, God is still HASHEM, *God of Israel.* Thus, v. 34 is an echo of the first verse of the psalm (v. 8) in which Israel is called upon to sing the praises of God. Verse 35 picks up the theme of the following verses which expressed Israel's being uniquely chosen in that God protected them throughout their travels among the nations, recognizing them as His anointed and His prophets (v. 22). The logical outgrowth of this is that even if the Ark, the presence of which was now being celebrated, would ever be exiled from its place and Israel would be scattered among the nations, they would know that that exile can not be a permanent one. They can never cease to be God's anointed ones just as God will never be any but HASHEM, *God of Israel* (v. 36).

The commentators have not attempted a similar structural examination and have satisfied themselves with explaining the individual verses. In general, they have interpreted in such a way that many of the references in the psalm can be understood as applying to the Ark and the various miracles which occurred while it was captive in Philistia and while it was being returned. According to these commentators, no other reason for the choice of this particular psalm to be recited in front of the Ark needs to be sought. There are, however, commentators, of whom *Metzudos* is representative, who read no references to the Ark in the psalm but who nonetheless do not offer any explanation of why these particular sections of psalms were picked for the daily ritual. Perhaps the explanation may lie along the lines which have been suggested here. Perhaps they feel that no further explanation is needed for the ordination that a song of jubilation be sung in front of the Ark. The presence of the Ark — and therefore also of the *Shechinah* — in Jerusalem was surely in itself reason enough for the praises to God contained in these sections.[1]

There is one other possibility which could explain the choice of these particular passages. *Avodah Zarah* 24b teaches that the cows which were pulling the wagon upon which the Philistines had placed the Ark in order to return it to Israel were 'singing' praises to God as they pulled it along.[2]

Now, various opinions are recorded in *Avodah Zarah* as to which song the cows were singing. None identify our psalm. However, there is one opinion there, that of R' Yochanan, that they sang the passage from *Isaiah* 12:4 which begins with the same words as our psalm — *Give thanks to God, proclaim His name.* R' Solomon ben Shimshon of Worms in his commentary to the *siddur* suggests that this may have been the reason this particular psalm was chosen to be recited before the Ark on its return.

Chapter Seventeen

◄§ Analysis of the differences between Chronicles and Samuel in this chapter

As pointed out throughout this chapter, there are many significant differences in the way this chapter is presented here and in *II Samuel* chapter 7.

These contrasts are particularly striking in the introductory verses to the passage.

---

1. In the commentary we have also quoted from *Rashi's* and *Ibn Ezra's* commentaries to *Psalms*. If our assumption is correct, that David — by condensing the various sections and making the changes which he did — was creating a new work entirely, then methodologically there may be some inconsistency in this. It can be argued that what *Rashi* or *Ibn Ezra* said in their commentary to *Psalms* would not have been said had they written a commentary on *Chronicles*. Nevertheless, to the extent that these comments concern the meaning of individual phrases it seems reasonable to include them.

2. *Maharal* to *Avodah Zarah* explains that the Sages did not mean that the cows actually sang these songs. No such miracle is indicated in the text. Rather, the strong, undeviating path which the cows took as they carried the Ark — and this in spite of the fact that as nursing mothers they might have been expected to stubbornly refuse to be separated from their young (see *I Samuel* 6:10) — showed God's providence by implication as eloquently as if it would have been expressed in actual song.

Chronicles	Samuel
1(a) וַיְהִי כַּאֲשֶׁר יָשַׁב דָּוִיד בְּבֵיתוֹ, *It was when David lived in his house*	1(a) וַיְהִי כִּי־יָשַׁב הַמֶּלֶךְ בְּבֵיתוֹ, *It was when the king lived in his house,*
	(b) וַה' הֵנִיחַ־לוֹ מִסָּבִיב מִכָּל־אֹיְבָיו, *and HASHEM had given him rest from all his enemies round about,*
(b) ... וַיֹּאמֶר דָּוִיד אֶל־נָתָן הַנָּבִיא, *that David said to Nathan, the prophet*	2(a) ... וַיֹּאמֶר הַמֶּלֶךְ אֶל־נָתָן הַנָּבִיא, *that the king said to Nathan, the prophet ...*

One is immediately struck by the fact that where *Samuel* speaks of *the king*, *Chronicles* has *David*, and that phrase 1(b) from *Samuel* — *And Hashem had given him rest from all his enemies round about* — is missing entirely from *Chronicles*.

The omission of this phrase seems of particular significance since it can be argued that it is the key phrase of the entire narrative. *Deuteronomy 12:10* teaches that the obligation to build a Temple begins only after all of Israel's enemies have been defeated — *When God shall have given you rest from all your enemies round about and you dwell in tranquillity*. David would not have suggested that the time to build the Temple had arrived if he had not perceived that requirement as having been fulfilled. Indeed, as *Malbim* interprets the passage in *Samuel*, it is the refutation of this assumption which is the subject of Nathan's prophecy. It would be many years before Israel would be truly at peace — the quiet he now experienced was not destined to last — and the military campaigns described in the next chapter still lay in the future.

The legal principle — that the eradication of Israel's enemies must precede the building of the Temple — is formulated in *Sanhedrin* 20b, where two sources are adduced, one of which is this phrase in *Samuel*. [*Rambam (Melachim* 1:2), in fact, cites the phrase in *Samuel* as the only source for this halachah.]

Chronicles, which omits the phrase, is thus left without the rationale upon which the entire episode is based.

Again, when considering God's answer to David through Nathan, we are also struck by the difference in wording between *Samuel* and *Chronicles*. Where *Samuel* has God's denial couched in a rhetorical question, *Chronicles* has an absolute prohibition.

Chronicles	Samuel
4. לֹא אַתָּה תִּבְנֶה־לִּי הַבַּיִת לָשָׁבֶת, *You shall not build for Me the house to dwell in.*	5. ...,הַאַתָּה תִּבְנֶה־לִּי בַיִת לְשִׁבְתִּי, *Will you build a house for My dwelling?*

Neither *Samuel* nor the parallel account in *Chronicles* offers a reason for God's denial of David's aspirations. However, in chapter 22 of *Chronicles*, David himself gives the reason for the rejection. There it tells how, towards the end of his reign, David began to make serious preparations for the building of the Temple. In charging his son Solomon with the responsibility for executing his plans, David says (vs. 7,8): *It had been my intention to build a house for HASHEM, my God. But the word of HASHEM came to me saying: You have shed blood abundantly and waged many wars. You shall not build a house for My Name, for you have shed much blood upon the earth before Me.* Now Scripture nowhere records this prophecy to David [*God came to me saying ...*] and there is a presumption, therefore, that it was given as part of Nathan's message here. But, if so, why is it not clearly stated in the text?

Let us first consider an aggadic tradition *(Shabbos* 30a) which sheds much light on the entire matter. According to that tradition, it would seem that David's aspiration to bring the Ark to its permanent resting place was, after all, not frustrated. Although not accomplished in his lifetime, it was, nevertheless, achieved only through his merit.

After God had forgiven David for the sin which he had committed in the matter of Bathsheva, David asked that God give him a sign that the transgression had indeed been eradicated. God answered him that He would indeed give such a sign, but that it would not be given in David's own lifetime but rather in that of his son, Solomon.

When Solomon finally erected the Temple, he attempted to bring the Ark in and place it in the Holy of Holies. But as the Ark approached, the Temple gates refused to open. Solomon uttered many prayers, but all in vain; the gates remained closed and the Ark could not be brought in. Finally, Solomon asked that God remember the righteousness of his father David. Immediately the gates swung open, and the Ark was brought in. This was the ultimate vindication of David and proof that his sin had indeed been forgiven.

Surely it is no coincidence that David's vindication came in connection with the entry of the Ark into the Temple. It can only mean that the hope which had been denied him during his own lifetime was finally granted after his death. It was David who, through Solomon, brought the Ark into the Holy of Holies.

Since David's ability to bring the Ark into the Temple became a signal that his transgression in the matter of Bathsheva had been forgiven, there is an implication that the original denial had resulted from that sin. How can this agree with our passage, which ascribes no reason at all, and with the passage in ch. 22 which ascribes it to the fact that David had shed much blood?

R' Tzadok HaKohen, in his *Tzidkas HaTzaddik,* discusses the places which David and Solomon, respectively, filled in the establishment of the Davidic royal line, and he thereby provides the key to the problems which our passage poses.

David's reign was constantly plagued by wars with a variety of Israel's neighbors, while Solomon's reign was blessed by sustained peace. In *R' Tzadok's* thought, the wars which beset Israel are no more than the outward manifestation of the spiritual turbulence within the heart of Israel's king — a heart described as 'the heart of all the community of Israel' *(Rambam, Melachim* 3:6). Israel's peace reflects the perfect tranquillity born of harmony and fulfillment in the breast of the perfect man. When no evil finds welcome in Israel's soul, no human enemy can find the strength to lift a sword against Israel's people.

David lived the life of a warrior. But much greater than the mighty efforts which he expended on the field of battle were the ones he spent on conquering his own inner conflicts. With the ebb and flow of the conflicts within his soul, the neighboring armies waged their military campaigns — never ultimately succeeding; just as the base drives hidden in David's pure spirit never succeeded in overpowering him.

David lived a life of utmost purity and fought himself relentlessly for every second of that life. He never knew the sweetness of peace and repose until the very end of his life when at last final victory was his. It fell to Solomon to savor the fruits of his father's valiant efforts. His very name, שְׁלֹמֹה [from שָׁלוֹם, peace], reflects the inner harmony which was his and which expressed itself in the peaceful relations which Israel enjoyed with its neighbors during his reign (see 22:18).

The reigns of David and Solomon were thus one long continuum, the parts of which relate to one another as do labor and rest, effort and fruition. David finally wrested peace and harmony from the rigors of battle, and Solomon's reign was the expression of that victory.

God denied David the right to build the Temple. Israel would first have to attain a state of spiritual perfection which would not be subject to the inner struggles of the king. David had shed much blood before God — his troubled life had demonstrated how difficult was his hold on sanctity and how constant were his battles to maintain his standing. The building of the Temple had to wait until the inner and outer enemies had finally been vanquished; it would be left to Solomon, the man of peace, to be the hands which would execute his father's dreams.

We are now in a position to understand the aggadic tradition cited above (Shabbos 30a). The implication that David's inability to establish a permanent home for the Ark was somehow connected with his shortcoming in the matter of Bathsheva is not contradicted by the failure of the Scriptural sources to make mention of this connection. Once we realize that the wars which plagued David's reign were but the tangible expressions of the inner turmoil of his soul, the solution is evident. David's inner conflicts revolved around the very drives and inclinations which led him astray in these tragic occurrences (see Psalms 51). It was they who allowed him no rest and drove him to ever greater heights of heroism in both his personal battle and in the wars waged against Israel's enemies. When peace was finally attained in Solomon's reign — born of David's mighty victories — this showed that these drives had also finally been laid to rest. And it was only with the realization of this true victory — the public vindication of David — that the Temple doors swung open to receive the Ark, making it the permanent House of God.

This analysis reveals that the issue of whether or not David was to build the Temple involved two aspects of David's being. There was David, the king, upon whom the duty fell, as part of his royal obligations, to initiate the building — if the conditions laid down by the Torah had indeed been fulfilled. But there was also David, the man; whether or not David would be able to undertake his royal prerogative would depend upon his own spiritual readiness.

It seems possible that the explanation of the differences between the two passages lies in the distinctness of these two aspects of the problem. Samuel addresses the question from the perspective of the king in his role as ruler of the people. Chronicles, however, records the inner tensions of David, the man. For this reason, Samuel uses the expression the king (1a), while Chronicles talks of David.

Within this context, *Chronicles'* omission of the phrase *(Samuel* 1b), *and HASHEM had given him rest from all his enemies round about,* is understandable. In *Samuel,* which deals with the external situation, viewing it from the standpoint of the monarchy, the phrase is apt. There existed an objective political and military situation which seemed to comply with the conditions laid down by the Torah for the building of the Temple. As was his duty under those circumstances, David turned to Nathan for guidance in this matter. But *Chronicles* is concerned with the inner state and motivations of David, the man. From the point of view of personal motivation, David's desire to build the Temple derived not from an objective evaluation of an external situation but from a deep-felt conviction of the essential wrongness of a state in which he, the king, lived in a permanent and luxurious palace while God's presence was consigned to a temporary shelter (see comm.).

And just as David's query of Nathan took place at two levels — as the formal request of the king and as the inner conviction of the man — so God's answer was given at two levels. The words which Nathan actually spoke are recorded in *Samuel.*[1] They are in the form of a rhetorical question because Nathan himself was not to know of the inner turmoil of David's soul. In his prophetic vision, he was told to put the question to David: Do you really believe that you ought to be the one to build the Temple? Are you ready for it?

David, however, was also attuned to the unspoken part of that reply. What was couched in the form of a question on Nathan's lips was to David a clear and unyielding response. That message is told in *Chronicles* — *You are not to build the house.* When the question was posed to him, David understood with complete clarity that indeed he was not the one destined for this great task. To him the message was clear. His warrior-status was to disqualify him.

Later, he was to tell his son Solomon that God had appeared to him and told him that he was not to build the Temple because of the great amount of blood that he had shed. It was never necessary for the prophet to verbalize this message because the question which Nathan had put to him had made the whole matter abundantly clear. David, in his inner being, knew that there could only be one answer to Nathan's question. God had indeed revealed the truth to him.

In the course of this chapter several other differences in the wording of God's answer to David's request are apparent. These, too, can be explained on the basis of the difference in approach between the two passages. What Nathan *said* addressed the question of the royal house of David, its future and its involvement in the kingly prerogatives of building a Temple. What David *comprehended* was the promised vindication of his life in Solomon's career. These two different elements are therefore further reflected in the differences in the prayer of thanks which David offered at the end of the incident.[2]

Entirely consistent with the above is the subtle shift of emphasis found in the second part of verse 1.

---

1. See footnote in Section Two to 21:3.

2. This perception of the relationship between David and Solomon in this matter can help us to solve another of the puzzles in the difference of approach between *Samuel* and *Chronicles.*
   The book of *Samuel* ends with David's discovery of the appropriate site for the Temple on the threshing floor of Aravna the Yevusite. The book of *Kings* then takes up the story of the end of David's reign. Nowhere in these books is there the slightest hint of the vast preparation which David

Chronicles	Samuel
1(a) ... אָנֹכִי יוֹשֵׁב בְּבֵית הָאֲרָזִים	1(a) ... אָנֹכִי יוֹשֵׁב בְּבֵית אֲרָזִים
(b) וַאֲרוֹן בְּרִית־ה' תַּחַת יְרִיעוֹת	(b) וַאֲרוֹן הָאֱלֹהִים יֹשֵׁב בְּתוֹךְ הַיְרִיעָה

It can be seen that *Samuel* places no definite article before אֲרָזִים, but has it in front of יְרִיעָה, while in *Chronicles* the opposite is true. Thus if we compare the translation to one another we have:

Chronicles

1. ... I am living in 'the' house of cedars while the Ark is 'under curtains'.

Samuel

1. ... I am living in 'a' house of cedars while the Ark reposes in 'the' tent [lit. curtain].

The connotations are entirely different. *The house of cedars* identifies the palace (see comm.) but does not stress the permanence of its structure, while *under curtains* does not identify the particular structure in which the Ark was housed but rather its impermanence. By contrast *a house of cedars* stresses the permanence of David's house while *the tent* identifies the particular structure in which the Ark was presently housed.

In *Samuel* the problem is clear. Once peace has been established it is the obligation of the king to initiate the building of the Temple. David, thinking that this condition has been realized, feels that there is no more excuse to leave the Ark in the tent. This is not so because of the flimsiness of the curtains but because the Torah commands that when certain conditions are fulfilled, the Ark is to be housed in a Temple. The urgency of the matter is brought home to him by the knowledge of how established the monarchy has become — even a new and permanent palace has been built. There is perhaps also a note of guilt in this, a suspicion that he may have been lax in his duty because he was too busy attending to his own comfort.

The thoughts of David, the man, ran in a different direction. As seen above, his desire to build the Temple derived not from an objective evaluation of the external situation but from a deep-felt conviction of the essential wrongness of a state in which he, the king, lived in a permanent and luxurious palace while God's presence was consigned to a temporary shelter.

This is how the commentators explain the phrase and it may indeed mean no more than this. However, the use of the definite article seems to indicate a

---

made for the building of the Temple, either in terms of the material which he gathered or in terms of the Kohanic and Levitic *mishmaros* which he organized, as described in *I Chronicles* from ch. 22 onwards. In effect, *Chronicles* makes a major issue of the role which David played as the one who laid the groundwork for Solomon's Temple, while the books of *Samuel* and *Kings* ignore this aspect of David's activities completely.

In the light of the above, the matter becomes clear. *Chronicles*, which deals with the essential rather than the overt aspects of the pivotal events described in our chapter, has portrayed David as the one who made Solomon's reign possible. His hard-won victories in battle produced the peace and harmony which were the hallmark of Solomon's time. By the same token, the physical preparations which David made for the Temple were the outer form and manifestation of the role which he played at the essential, hidden level — the subject of *Chronicles*. Thus, the detailed description of these preparations grows naturally out of the teachings of our chapter — and is completely absent from the books of *Samuel* and *Kings*.

different thrust. Something other than the permanence of his palace disturbed him. He was troubled by the historical implications which lay in the story of how his house had come to be built.

The cedar from which the palace had been built had come to him from Churam, king of Tyre (14:1). In sending them, this Edomite king had subjugated himself to an ascendant Israel, thereby tipping the scales of history and proclaiming Israel to have attained the spiritual standing expected of it (see Section Two to ch. 14). Each time that David sat in his house and contemplated the cedar with which it had been built, he realized the enormity of the implications. He, as Israel's king, had led them to the fulfillment of the Patriarch Jacob's vision — the older of Rebecca's twins was indeed serving the younger. But David knew that he as king was nothing but the outer expression of God's presence in Israel. What irony when the symbol displaces this essence! What sense did it make for Edom to bow before David if God, the fount of David's inspiration, was less firmly established than he?

But David erred. Far from implying a second-class status for God's presence among His people, the very impermanence of the cover over the Ark served to bring home how little God cared for the externals of a relationship whose bonds were strong enough to withstand the vicissitudes of circumstances.

This truth is brought home in the *Chronicles* account but is not relevant to *Samuel*. The two books therefore diverge in their presentation of the descriptions of the situation since the Exodus up to the present time.

Chronicles	Samuel
5. וָאֶהְיֶה מֵאֹהֶל אֶל־אֹהֶל וּמִמִּשְׁכָּן	6. וָאֶהְיֶה מִתְהַלֵּךְ בְּאֹהֶל וּבְמִשְׁכָּן

Samuel translates as: *And I traveled in tent and tabernacle; Chronicles* [literally] as: *I existed* [in a state of flux, moving] *from tent to tent and from tabernacle* [to an unspecified place].

Samuel, which had begun with the legal question of whether or not it was time to build the Temple, continues with an assessment of the present situation. God tells David that for many centuries the Ark and thus God's presence had found its place in temporary quarters: There is no urgency to build a Temple.

In *Chronicles* the answer addresses itself to David's concern as explicated there. David had been troubled by the implication of impermanence inherent in the flimsy tent at Jerusalem. To this God answers that this very transience can in a way demonstrate His love for Israel: The flimsy externals serve to underline the strength of the essential bond. The impermanence of the structure makes movement possible. He can follow His children in all their wanderings as He had done in the wilderness. There, the people had moved from one location to another, never knowing where the next resting place would be, and God went with them. The text says worlds by omitting the implied לְמִשְׁכָּן, *to tabernacle*. It underlines the seeming arbitrariness of the travel schedule. The 'where' is totally insignificant. It is His presence among His children that matters.

In the next verse God then states that in spite of the fact that throughout these years there was never a permanent Temple to house His presence, He never once requested that one should be built.

A very similar pattern can be found in verse 9 here. Where *Samuel* (v. 10) has וְלֹא־יֹסִיפוּ בְנֵי־עַוְלָה לְעַנּוֹתוֹ — *Nor shall men of evil continue to afflict him*, *Chronicles* substitutes לְבַלֹּתוֹ, *to wear him away*. Again the two expressions reflect the difference in perspective we observed above. In *Samuel* the matter is treated from the point of view of the royal prerogative. Foreigners will have no power to afflict David's people. *Chronicles* is less concerned with the fact of the afflictions than with the effect which this affliction has on the spiritual level of the people. As seen above, Israel's enemies can be viewed as the outward manifestation of the forces of evil within them. When they are at the mercy of their enemies they are in a situation in which brute physical forces hold sway over them, and something of the core of inner sanctity becomes corroded. God promises that in the future this will not happen any more.

From all that we have seen from the previous verses we would expect that the thrust of Nathan's message (vs. 7-14) would be different in *Chronicles* than it is in *Samuel*. We would expect that David's inner ear would detect nuances which would remain hidden to one who heard only the actual words spoken by Nathan. And indeed there are a number of seemingly small, but nevertheless highly significant, changes which point to an entirely different perspective.

On the assumption that there is a likelihood that the tenor of the whole message would be oriented towards the final sentence (v. 14), we begin by contrasting this sentence as it appears in the two narratives.

Chronicles	Samuel
14(a) וְהַעֲמַדְתִּיהוּ בְּבֵיתִי וּבְמַלְכוּתִי עַד־הָעוֹלָם, *And I will install him in My house and in My kingdom forever,*	16(a) וְנֶאְמַן בֵּיתְךָ וּמַמְלַכְתְּךָ עַד־עוֹלָם לְפָנֶיךָ, *Your house and your kingship shall be secured forever before you,*
(b) וְכִסְאוֹ יִהְיֶה נָכוֹן עַד־עוֹלָם, *and his throne shall be established forever.*	(b) כִּסְאֲךָ יִהְיֶה נָכוֹן עַד־עוֹלָם, *your throne shall be established forever.*

The contrast is apparent in both (a) and (b). Where in (a) *Samuel* talks of *David's house* and *David's kingship*, *Chronicles* has *My house* and *My kingdom*, referring to God. In (b) *Samuel* talks of David's throne while *Chronicles* talks of Solomon's throne.

The key to the understanding of this contrast is in an earlier verse in which the difference in wording points clearly to two quite different perceptions.

Chronicles	Samuel
10(a) וּלְמִיָּמִים אֲשֶׁר צִוִּיתִי שֹׁפְטִים עַל־עַמִּי יִשְׂרָאֵל, *And as from the days that I appointed Judges over My people Israel*	11(a) וּלְמִן־הַיּוֹם אֲשֶׁר צִוִּיתִי שֹׁפְטִים עַל־עַמִּי יִשְׂרָאֵל, *And as from the day that I appointed Judges over My people Israel*
(b) וְהִכְנַעְתִּי אֶת־כָּל־אוֹיְבֶיךָ, *I will subdue all your enemies*	(b) וַהֲנִיחֹתִי לְךָ מִכָּל־אֹיְבֶיךָ, *and I will give you peace from all your enemies*
(c) וָאַגִּד לָךְ, *and I have told you,*	(c) וְהִגִּיד לְךָ ה׳, *and HASHEM has told you*
(d) וּבַיִת יִבְנֶה־לְּךָ ה׳, *that HASHEM will build a house for you.*	(d) כִּי־בַיִת יַעֲשֶׂה־לְּךָ ה׳, *that HASHEM will build a house for you.*

The changes which seem important are in (b) and (c). In the opening remarks to this analysis we noted how significant was *Chronicles'* omission of the key phrase in verse 1 of *Samuel*, ... וַה' הֵנִיחַ־לוֹ מִסָּבִיב, *and HASHEM had given him rest from all his enemies round about.* In our verse we see that both *Samuel* and *Chronicles* remain entirely consistent with this earlier difference. Where a word is needed to describe the state of peace that lay in the future, *Samuel* uses וַהֲנִיחֹתִי, and this makes *Chronicles'* substitution of וְהִכְנַעְתִּי doubly noticeable.

Chronicles' treatment of (c) requires particular attention. Although it is possible that the sense of the verse is: *I have told you that HASHEM will build a house for you* — the equivalent of the verse in *Samuel* [as we have translated it; see commentary], the use of the *vav* [וּבַיִת] to mean *that* is certainly irregular. If we take it in its usual sense — *and* — then the message mentioned in *I told you* is left unstated with the verse continuing with a new promise — *and HASHEM will build a house for you.* Thus, where *Samuel* states what it was that God said to David — that He would make a house for him, *Chronicles* only hints at a message: *I told you* — something; *and* [in addition] *God will build a house for you.* What is this message which David evidently 'heard' but which Nathan never articulated?

In *Samuel* the issue revolved around David's kingly duties. His premise had been that the conditions which the Torah had laid down for the building of the Temple — that God should have given Israel rest from its enemies — had been fulfilled. To this God replies that the granting of peace is not yet complete. But He promises that a time will come when וַהֲנִיחֹתִי לְךָ, *I will give you* [true] *peace from your enemies.*

In *Chronicles*, the inner turmoil of David's soul, of which Israel's enemies are but the outer manifestation, had been the issue — not the formal requirement of 'being at peace.' God's promise to him is couched, therefore, in words appropriate to that concern. The time will come when וְהִכְנַעְתִּי אֶת־כָּל־אוֹיְבֶיךָ, *I will* [completely] *subdue all your enemies.* As David finally conquers those inner drives which aim to divert him from his holy destiny, so too all strength will be sapped from the forces of evil which personify those drives. This will not be a mere peace but a vanquishing of evil.

And so David was allowed to hear that which Nathan could not utter openly. Just as Nathan had been permitted only to ask the question: *Are you the one to build the house?* and it was left to David to comprehend the categorical denial which was implied in those words (see above), so now too, Nathan is prophetically told only the facts of the promise that David's royal house is to be firmly established, but the implications are not explicated. It is enough that David understands.

Against this background, the changes in the final verse become abundantly clear. In *Samuel* the point of God's promise to David is that his dynasty will be established as the royal house of Israel. In contrast to the Judges who ruled Israel in the preceding centuries, and in contrast to Saul whose progeny had never really ruled over all Israel, David's line is to be firmly established and kingship in Israel would forever be identified with him. In such a context it is only logical that reference should be to David's house, kingship and throne. He is the founder of the dynasty and it will always be associated with his name.

In contrast to this formal announcement of the establishment of the Davidic dynasty, David's inner ear picks up a different message. His concern is for his son Solomon. Will he attain that inner state of harmony which has eluded David during his whole life and thus become the final vindication of David's terrible struggles? This God reveals to David alone. Solomon's house and kingship will be God's house and kingship. Solomon's entire existence will be lived in the presence of God. Solomon's throne will be firmly established, in contrast to his father's whose hold upon it had never been certain and who had remained king only by dint of his many struggles.

The different focuses of the two accounts are echoed even in the subtlest nuances of this chapter. Where our verse has וְהָיָה כִּי־מָלְאוּ יָמֶיךָ לָלֶכֶת עִם־אֲבֹתֶיךָ, *And it shall be when your time will have come to go the way of your fathers,* Samuel has כִּי יִמְלְאוּ יָמֶיךָ וְשָׁכַבְתָּ אֶת־אֲבֹתֶיךָ, *When your time will have come, and you will lie with your fathers. Samuel,* which deals with the royal obligation to build a Temple, makes clear to David that the condition of sustained peace has not yet been achieved. Therefore this task is not David's responsibility. It will fall to another king, a son, who, after David has completed his life's work, will succeed him. Thus, the verse states simply that when David's life will be completed he will *lie with his fathers. Chronicles,* however, deals with the spiritual state necessary for the construction of the Temple. It is David's conquest of the weakness of his soul and the evil forces within him that makes possible the erection of a Temple. In a sense, then, although his royal duties will, at his death, have been fulfilled, his spiritual life is not yet complete until this House of God has been raised. For this reason, *Chronicles* substitutes לָלֶכֶת, *to go,* for וְשָׁכַבְתָּ, *and you will lie.* The connotation is that even after his death, David's life will continue to find fulfillment through Solomon's accomplishments. The phrase is reminiscent of *I Kings* 2:2 where David charges Solomon before his death with the words: *I am [about] to go in the way of all the land. Be strong and be a man.* Commentators note the use of הָלַךְ, *go,* to describe death. They explain that David meant to convey the idea to Solomon that if he would become strong and be a man then David too would continue 'going' and advancing even in death. The next phrase follows accordingly. *Samuel* has אֲשֶׁר יֵצֵא מִמֵּעֶיךָ, *who will come forth from your insides.* The wording in *Samuel* is impersonal; the issue is the perpetuation of the Davidic dynasty. David's inner ear, as portrayed in *Chronicles,* projects a tangible human being, אֲשֶׁר יִהְיֶה מִבָּנֶיךָ, *who shall be from among your sons* — a son, in whom he will find fulfillment.

[The differences between verse 13 here and *Samuel* verses 14 and 15 have been explained in the commentary. Verse 14 has already been explained above.]

Since the thrust of God's message to David is different here than in *Samuel,* the prayer of thanksgiving which David offers also differs slightly, and in a manner consistent with the previous differences. Just as David not only heard Nathan's actual words but also perceived their true significance, so did David, in his outpouring of gratitude to God, respond on two levels. On the one hand, he responded verbally to the actual message of Nathan, as described in *Samuel;* on the other hand, this response carried within it yet another level of meaning, which addressed the perceived message of Nathan's communication. This, by a subtle shift in wording, is revealed to us in *Chronicles.*

Verse 17 is a prime example of this. As explained in the commentary, *Radak* shows that the meaning of the corresponding verses is essentially the same. Yet the differences between them are substantial enough to point to a shift in focus.

Chronicles	Samuel
17. וּרְאִיתַנִי כְּתוֹר הָאָדָם הַמַּעֲלָה, *and You have seen me as a man of noble nature*	19. ... וְזֹאת תּוֹרַת הָאָדָם, *and this as befits a noble man*

In *Samuel* the phrase is a rhetorical exclamation. The kindness which God has shown him goes far beyond what he deserves. It befits a man of a stature greater than that which David has attained.

In *Chronicles* there is simply a statement of fact: God has looked upon him as a man of high attainments and there is no implication that this is unjustified.

It is as though David's conscience or inner awareness provides an answer to the questions which David's words imply. David's words said that the treatment he had received would be more suited to a greater man. David's soul hears the implication: If so, then I must be more worthy than I had thought myself. God's kindness revealed a depth of soul to David which he had never suspected within himself. In such a context the change from the feminine תּוֹרָה to the masculine תּוֹר is entirely appropriate. In David's rhetorical exclamation the weakness [as signified by the feminine form] of his own capabilities is uppermost in his mind. The conclusions which he draws make him aware of the strength [masculine form] within him.

In the context of *Chronicles*, this is entirely apt. When David hears that his own life of struggle will finally find vindication in Solomon's reign, he is full of gratitude to God for having shown him unambiguously to be a man of exalted attainments. The battles which he has fought within himself have come not from weakness but from strength; victory will, in the end, be his.

The next two verses, again by means of a subtle change in wording, continue to give the passage in *Chronicles* a different thrust than in *Samuel*.

Chronicles	Samuel
18(a) מַה־יּוֹסִיף עוֹד דָּוִיד אֵלֶיךָ, *What more can David proceed [to ask] of You*	20(a) וּמַה־יּוֹסִיף דָּוִד עוֹד, *And what more can David proceed*
(b) לְכָבוֹד אֶת־עַבְדֶּךָ, *to honor Your servant*	(b) לְדַבֵּר אֵלֶיךָ, *to say to You*
(c) וְאַתָּה אֶת־עַבְדְּךָ יָדָעְתָּ, *when You know Your servant?*	(c) וְאַתָּה יָדַעְתָּ אֶת־עַבְדְּךָ ..., *when You know Your servant ...*
19(a) ה', בַּעֲבוּר עַבְדְּךָ וּכְלִבְּךָ, *HASHEM, for Your servant's sake, and in accordance with Your heart,*	21(a) בַּעֲבוּר דְּבָרְךָ וּכְלִבְּךָ, *For the sake of Your word, and in accordance with Your heart,*
(b) עָשִׂיתָ אֵת כָּל־הַגְּדוּלָה הַזֹּאת, *You have done this great thing,*	(b) עָשִׂיתָ אֵת כָּל־הַגְּדוּלָה הַזֹּאת, *You have done this great thing*
(c) לְהוֹדִיעַ אֶת־כָּל־הַגְּדֻלּוֹת, *to make known all the greatness.*	(c) לְהוֹדִיעַ אֶת־עַבְדֶּךָ, *to inform Your servant*

The key to understanding the different thrusts of the two passages is the (a) section of the second verse. Our analysis of this chapter has shown *Chronicles* as depicting the message which David's inner ear picked up from Nathan's words. Where Nathan spoke of kingship in Israel, David heard a vindication of himself as a person. And this follows through here, too. Where *Samuel* sees God's promises (דְּבָרְךָ, *Your word)* to David as the fulfillment of His plan for a proper monarchy, *Chronicles* has David regarding it as a personal commitment to himself (עַבְדְּךָ, *Your servant).*

With the two passages defined in these terms, the rest of the changes fall into line. Phrases (a) and (b) in the first verse from *Samuel* are really one thought. David says that after God has given him the kingship there is nothing more for him to ask. *Chronicles*, which has another thought to add, puts the word אֵלֶיךָ, *of You,* [which *Samuel* has in (b)] into the (a) phrase, which now contains the entire content of (a) and (b) in *Samuel.* In the (b) phrase it introduces a new dimension. He is speechless in the face of God's bounty because of the personal honor and therefore vindication with which it has provided him. In promising him the kingship, God has honored him as a person.

It remains for us to note the change in the (c) phrase of the second verse. In *Samuel,* David thanks God for having informed him of the intention to have the kingship vested in his family. In *Chronicles*, David's gratitude is inspired by the inner greatness which he found within himself which God, so to speak, revealed to him by appointing him king.

In verses 20 and 21, a related pattern of changes emerges.

Chronicles	Samuel
20(a)	22(a) עַל־כֵּן גָּדַלְתָּ ה׳ אֱלֹהִים, *Therefore, You are great,* HASHEM *God,*
(b) ה׳, אֵין כָּמוֹךָ וְאֵין אֱלֹהִים זוּלָתֶךָ, HASHEM, *there is none like You and there is no God besides You,*	(b) כִּי־אֵין כָּמוֹךָ וְאֵין אֱלֹהִים זוּלָתֶךָ, *for there is none like You and there is no God besides You*
(c) בְּכֹל אֲשֶׁר־שָׁמַעְנוּ בְּאָזְנֵינוּ, *in all that we have heard with our ears.*	(c) בְּכֹל אֲשֶׁר־שָׁמַעְנוּ בְּאָזְנֵינוּ, *in all that we have heard with our ears.*

The difference in tone is set by phrase (a) of the first verse, which has no parallel in *Chronicles.* The conjunction עַל כֵּן, *therefore,* creates a bridge to what went before in *Samuel,* where in *Chronicles* a new thought is expressed.

Samuel had previously viewed the establishment of the Davidic line as a fulfillment of God's promise for a lasting monarchy (v. 21 — בַּעֲבוּר דְּבָרְךָ). All this is part of God's plan to bring about a state in which all of mankind will recognize His greatness. The establishment of the Davidic line is one step in this plan and, as a result of it (עַל כֵּן), God's Name will indeed become great.

In contrast, *Chronicles* has viewed the establishment of the Davidic line from David's personal perspective [as explained above in v. 19 — בַּעֲבוּר עַבְדְּךָ], and his personal vindication is not cause for God's aggrandizement. Verse 20 must therefore be seen as introducing an unrelated thought.

This thought can readily be understood in context. Israel's king stands, as it were, between God and His people. As David's exalted destiny becomes clear to him, his thoughts turn automatically to God Whom he must now represent on earth, and then (v. 21) to the people whom he must now lead on their great spiritual march.

Chronicles	Samuel
21(a) וּמִי כְעַמְּךָ יִשְׂרָאֵל גּוֹי אֶחָד בָּאָרֶץ, *And who is like Your people, Israel, a unique nation in the land,*	23(a) וּמִי כְעַמְּךָ כְּיִשְׂרָאֵל גּוֹי אֶחָד בָּאָרֶץ, *And who is like Your people, like Israel, a unique nation in the land*
(b) אֲשֶׁר הָלַךְ הָאֱלֹהִים לִפְדּוֹת לוֹ עָם, *whom God went to redeem for Himself as a nation,*	(b) אֲשֶׁר הָלְכוּ־אֱלֹהִים לִפְדּוֹת־לוֹ לְעָם, *whom God went to redeem for Himself as a nation,*
(c) לָשׂוּם לְךָ שֵׁם גְּדֻלוֹת וְנֹרָאוֹת, *to provide a name for Yourself for greatness and awesomeness,*	(c) וְלָשׂוּם לוֹ שֵׁם, *and to make a name for Himself,*
(d)	(d) וְלַעֲשׂוֹת לָכֶם הַגְּדוּלָה וְנֹרָאוֹת לְאַרְצֶךָ, *and to perform this greatness for you and awesome deeds for Your land,*
(e) לְגָרֵשׁ מִפְּנֵי עַמְּךָ אֲשֶׁר־פָּדִיתָ מִמִּצְרַיִם, *to drive out ... from before Your people whom You redeemed from Egypt*	(e) מִפְּנֵי עַמְּךָ אֲשֶׁר פָּדִיתָ לְךָ מִמִּצְרַיִם, *[driving out] ... from before Your people whom You redeemed for Yourself from Egypt*
(f) גּוֹיִם, *nations.*	(f) גּוֹיִם וֵאלֹהָיו, *nations and their gods.*

Against this background, the changes in the next verse can be readily understood. A glance at phrases (c), (d), (e) and (f) will show that in spite of a superficial similarity there is, in fact, a major difference between them.

The conjunction *vav, and,* in (d) of *Samuel* makes (c) and (d) into two distinct ideas. Besides redeeming a nation for Himself (b), God had two other purposes: to make a name for Himself (c); and to do great things for Israel and awesome things to the [inhabitants of the] land (d).

The idea of *making a name for Himself* (c) must be understood as part of God's plan of history. He had taken Israel out of Egypt in order that there be a focus on earth for the perception of the Divine Presence (see *Exodus* 29:46 and *Ramban* there). This was the purpose of the Tabernacle in the wilderness and that would be the purpose of Solomon's Temple when it would be built. This is the meaning of phrase (c) in *Samuel*. In this context the word שֵׁם is not to be understood as *name = fame* but as *presence* (see comm. to 13:6).

By consolidating phrases (c) and (d) into one phrase (c), *Chronicles* eliminates this thought entirely. God made Himself *a name for greatness and awesomeness,* i.e., fame, by driving out the nations from before the nation which He had redeemed from Egypt. In David's personal perspective, God's purpose to create a universally recognizable 'presence' for Himself is not part of the immediate thought.

Following this, verse 23 has יֵאָמֵן עַד עוֹלָם, *Let* [the promise] *become true for ever. Samuel* has הָקֵם עַד עוֹלָם, *establish it forever*. The difference is readily understandable. *Samuel* talks about the kingship; David prays that it should be permanently established. *Chronicles* deals with the personal suitability of the Davidic kings for their high office. David prays that the trust which God has put in him by promising eternal kingship should be shown to be justified.

This brings us to the final section — verse 27.

Chronicles	Samuel
27(a) וְעַתָּה הוֹאַלְתָּ לְבָרֵךְ אֶת־בֵּית עַבְדְּךָ, *Now, You have desired to bless the house of Your servant*	29(a) וְעַתָּה הוֹאֵל וּבָרֵךְ אֶת־בֵּית עַבְדְּךָ, *Now let it please You to bless the house of Your servant*
(b) לִהְיוֹת לְעוֹלָם לְפָנֶיךָ, *that it remain before You forever*	(b) לִהְיוֹת לְעוֹלָם לְפָנֶיךָ, *that it remain before You forever*
(c) כִּי־אַתָּה ה' בֵּרַכְתָּ, *and because You, HASHEM, have blessed it,*	(c) דִּבַּרְתָּ ... כִּי־אַתָּה, *for You ... have spoken*
(d) וּמְבֹרָךְ לְעוֹלָם, *it is blessed forever.*	(d) וּמִבִּרְכָתְךָ יְבֹרַךְ בֵּית־עַבְדְּךָ לְעוֹלָם, *and from Your blessing, the house of Your servant will be blessed forever.*

The explanation of the differences could well be as follows: It is clear that the verse deals with David's family *(the house of Your servant)* as opposed to the formal kingship. In *Samuel* this is a perspective which has not been dealt with up to this point. After David had devoted his whole prayer to the kingship in Israel, he ends on a personal note asking God's blessing *(Now let it please You to bless)* upon his household, כִּי־אַתָּה ... דִּבַּרְתָּ, *for You ... have spoken* [that is, promised this thing]. This particular promise of God had not been involved before, so David underlines that the promise was made.

In contrast, this subject had been the thrust of the entire prayer in *Chronicles*. To repeat it once more would have been redundant. Instead, it is made in the form of a statement *(You have desired to bless)*. God's promise is so certain of fulfillment that, even though its actual realization still lies in the future, it can be spoken of as an accomplished fact. God has blessed — and it can therefore be said with absolute certainty that David's house will be blessed forever more.

Chapter Eighteen

◆§ The Edomite War

[יב] וְאַבְשַׁי בֶּן־צְרוּיָה הִכָּה אֶת־אֱדוֹם בְּגֵיא הַמֶּלַח שְׁמוֹנָה עָשָׂר אָלֶף.
[12] *And Avshai the son of Tzeruiah smote Edom in the Valley of Salt — eighteen thousand men.*

The commentary has given *Radak's* resolution of the seeming contradictions between the verse here and in *Samuel*. Although *Radak's* explanation eliminates the problems of the apparent discrepancies, it does not address the problem of why a war that engaged both nations is presented in *Samuel* as a war against Aram, while in *Chronicles* as a war against Edom. What underlies the two different perspectives?

To gain an understanding we must first analyze the significance of the governors which David established in Edom (v 13). We can do this best by quoting *Derashos HaRan* 2 in his discussion of the constant balance between the fortunes of Israel and Edom; how from the time of Jacob's blessings, the two never rose or fell together but how one would be ascendant and the other subservient. He notes that *Genesis* 36:31 lists the kings of Edom as having reigned, *before a king ruled in Israel.* In his view this can only mean that Edom could not have had ruling kings once the monarchy had been established in Israel. He writes:

'For if the monarchy had flourished in Israel there could have been no king in Edom. As, indeed, we see that their monarchy disintegrated as soon as a king rose in Israel — for David established governors [in Edom] and did not permit them to keep a king. This situation continued through the reign of Yehoshaphat, as it is written *(I Kings* 22:48), *In his days there was no king in Edom — a governor was* [*in the place of a*] *king.* This continued until the days of Yoram, concerning whom it is written that as a result of his sins and his cleaving to the ways of Ahab, *in his days Edom rebelled from under the hands of Judah and appointed a king over themselves (II Kings* 8:20)

'They had kings until the days of the exile ... for Israel was not sufficiently righteous to eliminate the monarchy from Edom ... but in the days of the Second Temple, Edom was again subjugated by Israel ...

'From all this we see that as long as God allowed us to flourish, He subjugated Edom under us; but as we were driven out of our city, Edom became ever more powerful. As our Sages have taught us, we are today in an Edomian exile. For although Rome ... took us captive ... their emperors were of Edomite descent and there were many Edomites among the populace ...'

From *Ran* we see that the establishment of governors in Edom was a watershed of David's reign. The process begun with Churam's ambassadors (14:1 and see Section Two there) was consolidated by this act, and an era began which foreshadowed the Messianic era, which Ovadiah the prophet defines as the time at which *saviors will ascend Mount Zion to judge the mountain of Esau — at which time kingship will be God's.*

Israel's main opponent from a military and political standpoint was Aram. In terms of the geo-political realities of the time, Edom was no match for the mighty Aramean empire. If, in the course of a campaign against Hadadezer, the Jewish armies met an Edomite army, that was of no particular significance and did not need to be mentioned. To *Samuel*, which, as we have seen throughout these past chapters, deals with the history of its time, the war was an Aramean — not an Edomite — one. It is only *Chronicles*, with its longer view of history, which views the campaign at its essential level. In the context of eternity the Aramean empire means very little; the spiritual ascendancy of Israel implied in a decisive victory over Edom means everything. From the perspective of *Chronicles*, therefore, it is an Edomite war.

This may also help to explain why *Samuel* speaks of the campaign as David's war while *Chronicles* ascribes it to Avshai. While the victory over Edom carried the seeds of eternity within itself, it was not a war which could be ascribed to David. According to *Yerushalmi, Rosh Hashanah* ch. 1, the six months which Yoav spent on that campaign were not counted towards David's reign. This, because God had commanded that Edom not be attacked by Israel and this war was waged in defiance of that command.[1] Thus, it stands to reason that from the point of view of the campaign against Edom it should not be called David's war.

Chapter Nineteen

⋅§ David and Ammon

As pointed out in the commentary, though our chapters 18-20 parallel chapters 8, 10 and 11 of *II Samuel*, they noticeably omit chapter 9 of *Samuel*, which describes David's kindness in seeking out Jonathan's son, Miphibosheth, and establishing him as a member of the royal household. This omission significantly effects the perspective with which *Chronicles* views the Ammonite wars.

The treatment of these wars may well be influenced by another major difference between the two books. At 20:1 we learn of Yoav's attack against the land of Ammon, and the verse concludes: '... *While David stayed in Jerusalem. And Yoav smote Rabbah* [the capital of Ammon] *and laid it waste. David took the crown of their king* ...

Between the phrase, '... *While David stayed in Jerusalem'* [which in *Samuel* is at 11:1] and the statement that Yoav smote Rabbah and that David took the crown [which in *Samuel* is at 12:27 ff.], *Samuel* has the whole story of David and Bathsheva, with all the details of Uriah's death, the birth of the infant who died and Solomon's birth. None of this appears in *Chronicles*. This omission may also significantly affect the perspective with which *Chronicles* views these wars.

Verse 1 begins *And it was after that*. The chapter in *Samuel* starts with the same phrase but the meaning there would seem to be quite different. As noted above, this chapter in *Samuel* follows from the story of David's kindness to Miphibosheth, the sole surviving son of Jonathan. The phrase *after that*, therefore, apparently refers to that incident. In our context, however, this phrase can only refer to the wars described in the previous chapters, since the Miphibosheth story is not mentioned in *Chronicles*. It may well be that the difference in this introductory phrase set the tone for the whole account.

We can best ascertain the thrust of the account in *Samuel* by setting a phrase from the previous chapter dealing with Miphibosheth side by side with a key phrase in the account of David's approach to the Ammonite king.

---

1. *Ramban* (end of *Sefer HaMitzvos*) explains that although there was a justification for this attack, since Edom had previously dealt treacherously against Israel, there was no justification for the extreme severity with which Yoav executed the war. According to *I Kings* 11:16, Yoav wiped out every single male he found. In view of the Torah's prohibition, he should not have gone so far in this punitive action.

II Samuel 10:2	II Samuel 9:1
(a) וַיֹּאמֶר דָּוִד, And David said,	(a) וַיֹּאמֶר דָּוִד הֲכִי יֶשׁ־עוֹד אֲשֶׁר נוֹתַר לְבֵית שָׁאוּל, And David said, 'Is there yet one left from the house of Saul
(b) אֶעֱשֶׂה־חֶסֶד עִם־חָנוּן בֶּן־נָחָשׁ, 'I will show kindness to Chanun the son of Nachash,	(b) וְאֶעֱשֶׂה עִמּוֹ חֶסֶד, that I may show him kindness
(c) כַּאֲשֶׁר עָשָׂה אָבִיו עִמָּדִי חֶסֶד, As his father showed kindness to me.'	(c) בַּעֲבוּר יְהוֹנָתָן, for Jonathan's sake?'

The similarity between the (b) and (c) sections of the two sentences is self-evident. David, by dint of many hard-fought wars, had considered his position and felt that he had no more to fear from any external enemies. It was now time to exercise magnanimity with former enemies who could be assumed to be amenable to gestures of friendship. He made his peace with the house of Saul and then attempted a show of goodwill to Ammon.

As it turned out, this latter attempt was a terrible mistake. His intentions were misread and this resulted in much bloodshed and suffering.

Why did a well-intentioned gesture turn into such a major catastrophe? The Sages provide the answer:

'Although I have written in My Torah: *When you approach a city to make war against it, invite it to make peace*, to these [Ammon and Moab] do not do so: *Do not seek their peace or their benefit!*'

It can be shown that whoever deals mercifully with them will eventually be embarrassed and be involved in suffering. Who is [an example of] this? David — *And David said, 'I will show kindness to Chanun, the son of Nachash.'*

'God said to him, 'You intend to transgress My commands, for I have written, *Do not seek out their peace and their benefit* — and you wish to deal kindly with them! *Do not be excessively righteous! (Ecclesiastes 7:16).* No one has the right to ignore the words of the Torah — and this one sends messengers to comfort the Ammonites and to do kindness to them.

'Eventually he became embarrassed ... and became involved in wars ... Who caused all this? David, who ignored God's command and attempted to show kindness to them' *(Bamidbar Rabbah 21:5).*

What, then, was David's motivation? Surely he would not have willingly transgressed the Torah's covenant that we are not to seek out the peace and benefit of Ammon and Moab.

The commentary has suggested two possible reasons: either that the prohibition does not apply to the repayment of a kindness or that the prohibition applies only to seeking the peace of a city about to be attacked, not to personal relationships between individuals.

According to this last explanation, although David was not guilty of any violation of the letter of the law, he was guilty of violating its spirit. Although the Torah does not actually prohibit friendly overtures between individuals, it is clear from the language of the verse that the Torah frowns on such gestures too. Why then did David do so?

David's reasoning may well have been as follows: The fact itself, that the Torah satisfied itself with indicating its displeasure at any kindly initiative without formally forbidding it, indicates that in a practical sense the Torah wished to leave the application of this principle to the individual's discretion. It is as though the Torah had told us: It is most undesirable to make advances to these two nations and it is highly unlikely that a situation should arise in which it would be the right thing to do. Nevertheless, if in the discretion of one of you it seems to be indicated — I do not forbid it.

David thought that in his situation the friendly approach seemed indicated. To understand his reasoning we have the comparison of the two verses from *Samuel* which we made above. Having made his peace with Saul's house he felt that he could be at peace with other enemies also.

To take this analysis one step further, we should now compare the verse in *Samuel* with its parallel verse in *Chronicles*.

Chronicles	Samuel
2(a) אֶעֱשֶׂה־חֶסֶד עִם־חָנוּן בֶּן־נָחָשׁ, *I will show kindness to Chanun the son of Nachash*	2(a) אֶעֱשֶׂה־חֶסֶד עִם־חָנוּן בֶּן־נָחָשׁ, *I will show kindness to Chanun the son of Nachash*
(b) כִּי־עָשָׂה אָבִיו עִמִּי חֶסֶד, *for his father showed kindness to me*	(b) כַּאֲשֶׁר עָשָׂה אָבִיו עִמָּדִי חֶסֶד, *as his father showed kindness to me*

The difference in wording in the (b) section is noteworthy. כַּאֲשֶׁר, *as*, carries a quite different connotation than כִּי, *for*. The latter implies a strict repayment. He did me a certain favor (see comm. to v. 2 for the specifics); I shall therefore repay him.

כַּאֲשֶׁר, *as*, implies a much more general approach. I shall model my behavior towards him on the mode of behavior that he displayed towards me. In this reasoning the individual favor which Nachash may have done to David is taken as a symbol of an attitude. It is as though David had said: It is time to reassess our attitude towards Ammon; they have deserved our goodwill by changing their attitudes towards us. The Torah would surely not want us to maintain our enmity towards an Ammon which has elected to become our friend.

Thus David displayed a readiness to see the best in Ammon — a readiness which the Sages castigated as an overreadiness. Do not be overly righteous, God calls to David. Do not be so ready to forgive and forget the cruel streak in them which the Torah dreaded so seriously. A gesture of goodwill towards Ammon is something quite different than one to Miphibosheth.

Thus, the perspective of *Samuel*. From its very inception the approach to Ammon has been inappropriate. David miscalculated and his error ended in tragedy. But that tragedy was not exhausted in the shame and bloodshed which resulted from it. It was during the subsequent Ammonite war that the catastrophic incident with Bathsheva occurred. Perhaps *Samuel*, by its treatment of David's approach to the Ammonite, seeks to create the background against which that sad story is to be understood. David was in a state of confusion because of his error in the matter of the Ammonites, and this made his terrible mistake in the matter of Bathsheva possible.

Chronicles' approach to the whole matter is quite different. It does not deal with David's gesture of goodwill to Miphibosheth and it does not report the whole incident of Bathsheva. The Ammonite wars appear as just another of the series of wars which David waged, and a source of spoils for funding the building of the Temple. David's miscalculation in this matter was not relevant to *Chronicles* and it reports the incident without any overture of sin. David was simply repaying a favor which the Ammonites had done to him.

This may explain a subtle difference in wording in the opening verses. A comparison with the parallel verse in *Samuel* yields the following:

Chronicles	Samuel
1(a) וַיָּמָת נָחָשׁ מֶלֶךְ בְּנֵי־עַמּוֹן, *Nachash the king of Ammon died*	1(a) וַיָּמָת מֶלֶךְ בְּנֵי עַמּוֹן, *The king of Ammon died*
(b) וַיִּמְלֹךְ בְּנוֹ תַּחְתָּיו, *and his son became king in his place.*	(b) וַיִּמְלֹךְ חָנוּן בְּנוֹ תַּחְתָּיו, *and his son, Chanun, became king in his place.*

Samuel does not give the name of the dead Ammonite king (a) but does identify the son (b). In *Chronicles* the treatment is the exact opposite. Nachash's name is given and Chanun's is not.

In *Samuel's* perspective the particular favor which Nachash had done to David as an individual is not the issue. David was initiating a rapprochement with the Ammonite rulers. The Ammonite king had died and he wanted to pay his respects to the present Ammonite king — Chanun.

From *Chronicles'* perspective, it is only the favor which Nachash, the man, had done which is significant. David's wish to do kindness was directed to *his son*, not in his capacity as the Ammonite king, but as the son of Nachash.

Based on the above, we may now be able to explain why verse 4 of *Chronicles* omits any mention of the fact that only half the beards of David's messengers were cut off (see comm.). The concept of halves appears in Scripture in connection with the forging of a covenant. Abraham divides the animals into two (see *Genesis* 15:10 and *Rashi* there). At the forging of the covenant at Sinai the blood of the sacrifice is to be divided into two halves; the one half is to be sprinkled upon the people as a symbol of the covenant, while the other is poured onto the altar (*Exodus* 24:6-8). The sharing of the sacrificial blood between the altar and the people symbolizes their unity in this covenant.

Perhaps this was the idea which Chanun was trying to express. In the perspective of *Samuel*, which views David's initiative from the point of view of a gesture from nation to nation — that is, as a covenantal one — Chanun, with utter disdain, was saying: Of the two halves, the one representing our people is adorned and respectably clothed; the one representing you, the Jews, is naked and disgraced.

Such symbolism plays no role in *Chronicles'* perspective which sees no overtones of a covenantal relationship but only a private advance made from David to Chanun. Here the stress is on the nakedness: the naked faced denuded of its beard; the naked buttock denied the covering of the clothes. Perhaps this was also meant to symbolize the spying of which Chanun accused David. When

Joseph accused his brothers of coming to spy upon Egypt he used the phrase: *You have come to see the nakedness of the land (Genesis 42:12).* Thus, the symbolism which Chanun chose reflected exactly the duplicity of which he suspected David.

Chapter Twenty

⇥§ The Crown of Ammon

[ב] וַיִּקַּח דָּוִיד אֶת־עֲטֶרֶת־מַלְכָּם מֵעַל רֹאשׁוֹ ...

[2] *And David took the crown of their king from upon his head ...*

According to *Rashi* to *Sanhedrin* 21b, a gold bar traversed the crown on the inside and it would only fit onto a head the contour of which could accommodate such a bar, that is, a head indented at a given place so that the bar could fit into the hollow.

It seems strange that legitimacy for the Davidic throne should be determined by whether a crown captured from Ammon would fit or not. That there is a deeper significance to this crown is further indicated from the fact that *Chronicles* repeats the story of its capture. We have seen that *Chronicles'* interest in the wars of David is limited to the extent to which the spoils of these wars were set aside for the building of the Temple. Thus, the second part of our verse, which tells of the many spoils which David took out of the city, is a legitimate part of that story. But this crown was patently not used for the Temple treasury. Why then does *Chronicles* include it in its account?

A thorough treatment of this subject would take us beyond the scope of a commentary to *Chronicles*. For our purposes it is sufficient to note that the Sages (see *Zohar* 1:110b) explained that in God's inscrutable Providence, Israel's kingship was to grow out from the descendants of Abraham's nephew, Lot. David himself, in whose *person* the kingship was vested, was a descendant of Lot's son Moab through his ancestor Ruth. The *legitimization* of that kingship was to come through Lot's other son, Ammon. Thus, Moab produced the person of the king, and Ammon his legitimization. [The interested reader can pursue this analysis in *Shelah, Torah Sheba'al Peh* to *Lech Lecha* and in Rabbi Yehudah Bachrach's *Imah shel Malchuth*.]

The insight gained from the above may help us to understand the inclusion of the word וַיִּמְצָא, *and he found it,* in our passage which does not occur in *Samuel* and seems unnecessary here. In Section Two to 2:11 the resistance to David's kingship was traced to his descent from Moab. Fierce determination was required to establish the fact that only male Moabites were forbidden to intermarry with Israel and that David, who was descended through the female, Ruth, was entirely legitimate. *Yevamos* 77a tells of David's delight at finding Scriptural justification for his legitimacy.

Genesis (19:15) describes the two daughters of Lot who were to become mothers of Moab and Ammon, as שְׁתֵּי בְנֹתֶיךָ הַנִּמְצָאֹת, *your two daughters who are to be found here,* while in *Psalms* 89:21 we read, מָצָאתִי דָּוִד עַבְדִּי בְּשֶׁמֶן קָדְשִׁי מְשַׁחְתִּיו, *I found David, My Servant; with My holy oil I anointed him.* The use of the root מצא, *to find,* in both places connects the two passages. 'David was found! Where was he found? In Sodom' *(Bereishis Rabbah* 14:4). Thus we see that in the legitimization of the Davidic kingship, the word מצא, *to find*, plays a major role. A possible reason for this is that if indeed the Davidic kingship was vested in Lot and his descendants, it was hidden deeply under a layer of negative qualities with which Lot is portrayed in the Torah — see *Shelah* quoted above. The essence of nobility within him had to be 'found.' It is perhaps for this reason that *Chronicles* inserted the root מצא into our narrative.

◄§ The Destruction of Ammon

[ג] וְאֶת־הָעָם אֲשֶׁר־בָּהּ הוֹצִיא וַיָּשַׂר בַּמְּגֵרָה וּבַחֲרִיצֵי הַבַּרְזֶל וּבְמַגְרוֹת וְכֵן יַעֲשֶׂה דָוִיד לְכֹל עָרֵי בְנֵי־עַמּוֹן וַיָּשָׁב דָוִיד וְכָל־הָעָם יְרוּשָׁלָם.

[3] *And he brought out the people who were in it and cut them with saws and with iron files and with axes. So did David treat all the Ammonite cities. Then David and all the people returned to Jerusalem.*

The idea of a Jewish king, in particular David, submitting his enemies to torture [for this seems to be what he did — see *Rashi* and *Metzudos* to *Samuel*] seems shocking to us. In general, as we would expect, Israel's attitude towards its fallen enemies was one of consideration and mercy. Thus, during the Edomite wars (chap. 18 above) we are taught *(II Samuel* 8:13) that: *David made a name for himself. Rashi* quotes the Sages who explain that David made sure that all the enemy dead were buried. This spread Israel's fame as benign conquerors. This recognition of the innate dignity of the human body certainly prevailed in all Israel's wars and would surely have been translated into a forbearance towards the living Ammonite captives as well.

It is necessary, however, to consider the background against which the Ammonite wars took place. Chanun had not only spurned David's friendly advances but had shamefully humiliated David's messengers by shaving off half their beards and tearing away their clothes to expose their buttocks. To understand the full implications of Chanun's action, we must remember that David's task was to create an Israel free from the burdens of foreign dominion which could therefore turn its full attention to its exalted task of acting as conduit for the Divine on earth. Chanun's derisive scorn endangered that mission. If David's messengers of goodwill could be stripped naked and sent upon their way, then this shattered David's image as man at his highest and finest — an example which all mankind would wish to emulate. Which nation would recognize Israel's uniqueness if it could be treated thus?

David had learned a salutary lesson in the safeguarding of royal dignity from the fate of his predecessor, Saul. *Yoma* 22b teaches that Saul forfeited his right to the kingship when he showed himself to be unworthy of it by not defending its honor. When people would make fun of him and declare him impotent as a warrior and king, his innate modesty would keep him silent. But the Sages teach that: 'Any wise man who does not defend his [and therefore the Torah's] honor as fiercely as a snake, does not merit the name *Talmid Chacham.'* Saul should have realized that his silence compromised the very institution of the monarchy. How much more then was David obliged to assert the prerogatives of his office when so much more was at stake. The insult was not a personal one from some disaffected subjects but one which was hurled at David by a monarch whose actions would reverberate throughout the world. It would not only be David's internal influence which would suffer but his ability to establish the safety and peace of Israel. This was all the more true in light of David's role as the model and forerunner of the Messiah who will rule at the end of days (see *Rambam, Melachim* 11:1).

David knew, then, that Israel's kingship, indeed even the very fate of its universal beneficence, lay in his hands. He would have to show unambiguously that Israel's king could not be trifled with.

But what language would Ammon and the neighboring nations understand? An inkling of the methods of subjugation employed by the heathen kings of that era can be gleaned from the boast of Adoni Bezek, king of Bezek, that seventy kings whose thumbs and toes he had cut off used to scramble for crumbs under his table (*Judges* 1:7). The Ammonites were hardened brutes whose obscene idolatry, Molech, involved the burning alive of infants to their idol. Surely David knew the people with whom his duty forced him to communicate and knew the minimum which was required to make them understand. A savage people cannot be educated civilly; they must be taught by the lessons they understand.

The comm. to 18:2 speculated that *Chronicles'* omission of any mention of the harsh treatment to which David subjected his Moabite captives was because this treatment, although justified, in no way furthered the preparations which David was making for the building of the Temple, God's House of Mercy, the subject with which *Chronicles* is concerned. Why then is his treatment of the Ammonites mentioned? Perhaps the reason is that, in contrast to the crime which Moab had committed — the wanton murder of David's parents and family which is not explicated in Scripture but is known to us only through the tradition of the Sages — the Ammonites' treatment of David's messengers is indeed spelled out. If the punishment which David meted out to them would not have been mentioned, the narrative would have been incomplete.

This would explain an omission from the account in *Chronicles*. Besides the punishment mentioned here, *II Samuel* describes yet another one: הֶעֱבִיר אֹתָם בַּמַּלְבֵּן, *he passed them through* [burned them] *the kiln where bricks are burned.* Now *Radak* notes that מַלְבֵּן, *kiln*, is written מַלְכֵּן [a כ, *caf*, instead of a ב, *beis*], to allude to the Ammonite idol, Molech, and to indicate that the 'kiln' was not really a place where they manufactured bricks but the place were child-sacrifice took place and infants were burned to Molech. It seems likely that this particular punishment was not given because of Chanun's despicable action in the matter of the messengers, but was administered to punish them for the murder of their own children. This, therefore, is not a matter of concern to *Chronicles* any more than the harsh treatment of Moab which was also not mentioned.

There are some commentators, however, who do not interpret this verse as dealing with torture at all. As they explain it, the verse means that David exacted forced labor from them and made them work with the instruments mentioned here [וַיָּשַׂר is rendered: *He caused them to saw* ...] (see *Wolf* to *Samuel*).

◄§ David / Elchanan ben Yair

[ה] וַתְּהִי־עוֹד מִלְחָמָה אֶת־פְּלִשְׁתִּים וַיַּךְ אֶלְחָנָן בֶּן־יָעִיר אֶת־לַחְמִי אֲחִי גָּלְיָת הַגִּתִּי וְעֵץ חֲנִיתוֹ כִּמְנוֹר אֹרְגִים.

[5] *And there was another war with the Philistines, and Elchanan the son of Yair killed Lachmi the brother of Goliath the Gittite; the shaft of his spear was like a weaver's beam.*

The commentary to v. 5 has noted that the Sages interpret the passage in *Samuel* as referring to David's conquest of Goliath. If this is so, why is David not identified by his real name? Why should an incident which is so central to the Davidic saga be recorded in so indirect a way?

In comm. 4-8 we notice that where *Chronicles* records only three skirmishes, *Samuel* has a fourth — with Yishvi Benov — in which David would have lost his life if not for Avshai's intervention.

In the name Yishvi Benov the Sages *(Sanhedrin* 95a) see a reference to the priestly city of Nov which Saul destroyed after David had sought and found refuge there (for details see *I Samuel* ch. 22). It may well be that David's near calamity with the Philistine was no coincidence, but a punishment for that terrible catastrophe. David had caused, albeit indirectly, the destruction of Nov, and for this he would fall prey to the sword of Yishvi Benov.

That David was nevertheless saved by Avshai's intervention may be understood as follows: David, the man, should indeed have been killed. His rescue came about not because of his personal merit but because the Davidic line had to be spared. It was David, the king, not David, the man, to whom ultimate victory came.

We noted in the commentary that the encounter with Goliath did not really happen at the same time as the other three encounters. Nevertheless, they are dealt with as one so that all the occasions on which David the descendant of Ruth clashed with the descendants of Orpah be told together. It seems likely that the reason for this is not only the physical fact that they came from the same mother, but rather that within the Davidic saga they all played a similar role. In all of them, such victories as David would have would be to David the king, not David the man. As an individual David would have succumbed to Orpah's descendants. If he was victorious it was because of the eternity that lay within him.

This readily explains the interpretation which the Sages gave to these verses. They may well have been, as *Malbim* interprets them (see comm.), the storytellers' version of the events described in *Chronicles*. However, they were made part of Scripture, and were included in the book of *Samuel* as a cloaked reference to David's victory over Goliath. In the Scriptural annals this victory would not be ascribed to David the man, his name would not be used. Rather, he would be described in terms which would point to his essence rather than to his person. David became Elchanan, one who learned God's grace. His family — the source from whom his essence was drawn — was to be identified only with the establishment of the Tabernacles (see comm.), that most essential of the functions of Israel's king.

Chapter Twenty-One

ᴥ§ The Census and Its Aftermath

The differences in the account of David's census between *Chronicles* and *Samuel* are numerous and need to be seen in the context of the different perspectives of the two books to the entire incident.

The story of the census which David initiated, together with its tragic aftermath, is the final chapter in *Samuel* and brings the account of David's reign to an end. The details surrounding his death are perceived as a prelude to Solomon's assumption of the kingship, and are told in *Kings*. By contrast, our chapter, which tells essentially the same story, is followed by detailed descriptions of the preparations and dispositions which David made for the Temple which Solomon would build (chs. 22-29). Some forty-four percent of the *Chronicles* account of David's reign [there are 291 verses in chs. 11-21 and 230 in chs. 22-29] is devoted to matters upon which the earlier books do not even touch.

This difference in approach between the two books need not concern us here. It is part of the pattern which has been carefully traced and analyzed in the Overviews that *Chronicles'* treatment of the life of David follows its interest in the Messianic or eternally 'living' David, and is therefore quite different from that of *Samuel* which presents the story of the historical David. Here we need deal only with the influence which these differences in approach have on the story of the census — and these are considerable.

Samuel tells the story of the census, the plague and of the sacrifice on Aravnah's (Ornan) threshing floor, but makes no mention at all of the fact that the incident led to the discovery of the Temple site. In *Chronicles* this is given prominent play and, indeed, it can be seen as the goal and thrust of the entire *Chronicles'* narrative, inasmuch as it leads into the final eight chapters which deal with David's preparations for the building. Thus, *Samuel* treats the census and its attendant plague as significant events in their own right in the life and reign of the historical David, while *Chronicles*, having no need merely to retell the story, instead treats it as the prelude to the discovery of the Temple site and David's preparations for its construction.

The two accounts tell different aspects of a complex story: In *Samuel* we learn of sin and ignoble motives followed by swift and terrible retribution. All this is true, but it is not the whole story. The burning fevers of the plague could and did serve as harsh punishment for inexcusable shortcomings, but they could also generate the purifying heat needed to reveal the luster and brightness of unalloyed matter. It was in this capacity that the plague served as prelude to the building of the Temple, as we shall see.

To understand this, it is necessary to consider that David may have been moved to count the people by more than one motive. At the conscious level, he may have seen the census as a legitimate step in preparing for the building of the Temple and this, while misguided, was not ignoble. In response to this error, the plague would teach him the true nature of his people and thereby ready him and them to become bearers of the Divine Presence. Subconsciously, however, there were also baser motives at work; an inappropriate satisfaction at the size of the nation over which he ruled *(Ramban)*; or an undue concern with military prowess *(Ralbag* and *Malbim;* see comm.). These were sinful, and because he succumbed to them, David became the unwitting cause of the overwhelming tragedy which was to mar the final years of his reign.

These are two complementary stories; *Chronicles* tells the one, *Samuel* the other.

Chronicles	Samuel
(a) וַיַּעֲמֹד שָׂטָן עַל־יִשְׂרָאֵל, *An adversary rose up against Israel*	(a) וַיֹּסֶף אַף־ה' לַחֲרוֹת בְּיִשְׂרָאֵל, *The wrath of HASHEM was once more kindled agaist Israel*
(b) וַיָּסֶת אֶת־דָּוִיד, *and provoked David*	(b) וַיָּסֶת אֶת־דָּוִד בָּהֶם לֵאמֹר, *and instigated David agaist them, saying:*
(c) לִמְנוֹת אֶת־יִשְׂרָאֵל, *to count Israel.*	(c) לֵךְ מְנֵה אֶת־יִשְׂרָאֵל וְאֶת־יְהוּדָה, *'Go count Israel and Judah'.*

Where *Samuel* has God's wrath inciting David *against Israel* by having him count the people, *Chronicles* states only that an *adversary* (his own evil inclination — see comm.) *provoked David* into counting them.

Exodus 30:12 teaches that improper counting of Israel may cause a plague to come upon them. If God wishes to punish Israel — as *Samuel* states — then this end can be brought about if David succumbs to the subconscious blandishments of his evil inclination to count them for the wrong motives. Surely, God would not make David the instrument of His anger unless he acted in a base and ignoble way. To this end, David is instigated to sin. Needless to say, his wrongdoing was not forced upon him. Had he stood firm, the plague would not have come — or, at least, would not have come through him. In the event, he sinned, and tragedy followed. This is the story of *Samuel*.

But at a conscious level David may well have told himself that there were good and legitimate reasons to count the people at this time. David may have seen the census as one more of the many steps which he was taking in preparation for the building of the Temple. He may have drawn an analogy from the building of the Tabernacle in the wilderness where Moses was commanded to count the Israelites by having each of them donate half a silver shekel. These were to be tallied for the census but were also used to fashion the sockets which supported the walls of the Tabernacle. [See *Exodus* 30:11 ff.]

The idea of counting the people by means of the donation of a given amount for communal use is explained by *Hirsch: '...* Not by mere existence, by living for himself, has his נֶפֶשׁ, his personality, value and meaning; not by his just being there is he an integral part of the nation. His mere existence does not even give him the right to be there; only by giving, doing something, is he to be counted; only by giving, doing, does he gain the right for the continuance of his existence ...'

This lesson taught in connection with the building of the Tabernacle leads to the following principle: The community of Israel consists of individuals, each a being of infinite value, whose identity is expressed in its most exalted form when he does his part in bringing the Divine Presence to rest among man. It is only in this context that he is to be counted.

David may well have been moved by this precedent. He too would count the people so that each would be able to contribute his part to the building of the Temple.

In this David miscalculated. As *Ramban* explains *(Numbers* 1:3), David erred in counting even those who were below twenty. The idea itself was reasonable, inasmuch as David had no way of knowing when the actual building would take place, and he may have wished to place at Solomon's disposal a list of those who would be over twenty then. But the whole of Israel may never be counted — for reasons explained in the commentary to v. 1. Nevertheless, it was not a pernicious error; not the result of being *incited against* Israel but rather a form of test to which he was exposed to see whether he understood fully the sacred nature of his people. This nature lifted them unequivocally out of the realm in which numbers are significant.

David's error resulted in tragedy. It may well be that, in this sense, it is to be regarded as being in line with at least two other catastrophes which marred other occasions which had been fraught with joyful anticipation of an encounter with the Divine. These, too, ended in sorrow when the full weight of responsibility which such close proximity to the sacred fire of Godliness imposes was not fully appreciated. The day of the inauguration of the Tabernacle turned into one of mourning when the righteous Nadav and Avihu paid the price for permitting their religious ecstasy to seduce them into coming closer than they should have *(Leviticus* 10:1ff, and commentators there). The potentially joyous occasion of bringing the Holy Ark to Jerusalem was shattered by the death of Uzza (ch. 13), whose intentions were good but whose actions fell short of what the presence of the Ark demanded.

So too did David's craving to be meaningfully involved in the preparations for the Temple betray him into a tragic miscalculation.

The prohibition against counting the people makes unambiguously clear that Israel's significance does not lie in its numerical strength but in the elemental striving for holiness which is its essential nature. This knowledge needed to be fixed in the awareness of the people, and if it could only be established by the suffering which came as a result of the plague which struck them when David forgot that truth, then this too is a 'sanctification through those that are honored by Me' (see *Rashi* to *Leviticus* 10:3 in the matter of Nadav and Avihu) and justified David being put to the test.

The moment that the plague had run its course was the moment at which Israel's unique status as an uncounted people became forever seared into their consciousness. And it was at that precise moment that God made the Temple site known to them. They were now ready to begin the first step towards building the Sanctuary through which they would attain their exalted destiny.

We are dealing, then, with two disparate but complementary aspects of David's actions. Consciously, his was an enlightened and legitimate idea which, if it was in error, was at least not pernicious *(Chronicles)*. This did not result from an *incitement against Israel* but rather it came about because David was being tested (וַיָּסֶת, *provoked)*. Both in the event of his passing the test or even through the tragedy of the many deaths that would ensue from his failure, a more earnest awareness of the implication of having God in their midst might be planted in Israel's mind. Subconsciously, though, David's motives were not pure and both he and Israel suffered the terrible punishment of God's anger *(Samuel)*.

These are the approaches of *Samuel* and *Chronicles* respectively. As noted above, *Samuel* has no interest in David as precursor to Solomon — only in his reign taken on its own terms. For this reason it does not deal with that aspect of the story which sees the event as a step towards the building of the Temple. Its concern is God's anger against Israel — the incitement of David against them and the grievous sin which he committed of his own free will — as a result of this incitement. *Chronicles* has no reason to repeat the story which has already been told and instead, in line with its consistent interest in the David who spans eternity, tells the story from that aspect which provided the first step in the building of the Temple. Based on this, we now proceed to analyze the rest of the differences in this chapter.

Verse 3 records Yoav's demurral to David. Yoav's speech is markedly different in the two accounts:

Chronicles	Samuel
(a) יוֹסֵף ה׳ עַל־עַמּוֹ, *May HASHEM add upon His people*	(a) וְיוֹסֵף ה׳ אֱלֹהֶיךָ אֶל־הָעָם, *and may HASHEM your God add to the people*
(b) כָּהֵם מֵאָה פְעָמִים, *a hundred times as many as they are now;*	(b) כָּהֵם וְכָהֵם מֵאָה פְעָמִים, *a hundred times as many as they are now*
(c) הֲלֹא אֲדֹנִי הַמֶּלֶךְ כֻּלָּם לַאדֹנִי לַעֲבָדִים, *are they not, my lord king, all servants to my lord?*	(c) וְעֵינֵי אֲדֹנִי־הַמֶּלֶךְ רֹאוֹת, *and may the eyes of my lord the king see it*
(d) לָמָּה יְבַקֵּשׁ זֹאת אֲדֹנִי, *Why does my lord seek this thing?*	(d) וַאדֹנִי הַמֶּלֶךְ לָמָּה חָפֵץ בַּדָּבָר הַזֶּה, *but why does my lord king desire this thing?*
(e) לָמָּה יִהְיֶה לְאַשְׁמָה לְיִשְׂרָאֵל, *Why should it be the occasion of guilt upon Israel?*	

Phrases (c) and (e) from *Chronicles* are not paralleled in *Samuel*. The different tones of Yoav's admonition reflect accurately the two perspectives described above.

In *Samuel* Yoav speaks of הָעָם, *the people* [in contrast to עַמּוֹ, *His people*]. Israel is treated as simply an object. Yoav's tone seems to say: This people in whose numbers you wish to take delight — their present size is really meaningless. God wishes them to be infinitely more numerous than they are now [the repeated כָּהֵם וְכָהֵם, lit. *as many and as many (b)*], and this should occur in your own lifetime so that you may have even more pleasure from it than now (c).

He is showing David that the subconscious idea which is really motivating him is giving him a distorted perspective of his people. They are indeed many — should even become many more — but that is not the view which David should take of them. David's understanding is *in itself* wrong (d) — not because it will bring about a plague but because this is no way for a Jewish king to look upon his people.

By contrast, in *Chronicles*, where David's conscious thinking was, in itself, proper, Yoav's admonition has an entirely different tone. There is no question of the people being treated as an object. They are עַמּוֹ, *His people,* whom David was trying to ready for their supreme destiny of becoming bearers of the Divine Presence. Yoav blesses them that they may increase many fold (b), but omits the sarcastic doubling of the word כָּהֵם, *as many,* since it was not their numbers which had attracted David's attention. In (c) he argues that the census was unnecessary because Israel, as the king's servants, would in any case be available for the building of the Temple when the time came. The counting was inappropriate (d) not because such a census could have no justification ever, but because in the present circumstances it could bring about a plague upon Israel.[1]

(v. 4) As has been noted in the commentary, *Chronicles* omits many of the details of the census given in *Samuel,* such as the names of the places which Yoav visited. It is obvious that the details of the story do not concern *Chronicles. Chronicles* presents the narrative only as an introduction to the identification of the Temple site. Because of this, the places which Yoav visited are less important here. In the narrative in *Samuel* they have a legitimate place because, as *Yalkut* points out there, Yoav picked those places specifically because he knew that the people there would be actively opposed to the census and he hoped that they would physically prevent him from carrying it out.

The commentary (vs. 5-6) has also noted the discrepancy in the tallies and given the various explanations for it. As *Malbim* explains, *Samuel's* number does not include the tribes of Levi and Benjamin. If our understanding of the different perspectives which *Samuel* and *Chronicles* take of the census is correct, then this may explain why *Samuel* gave the lesser and *Chronicles* the greater number. The purpose of the census as it is projected in *Samuel* was sinful. Israel should *not* be counted for the reasons which are assumed there to have motivated David. Yoav attempted to thwart the full impact of David's unfortunate decision and managed to mitigate the full negative impact by leaving out two tribes from the census. The narrator in *Samuel* follows his lead and gives only that incomplete number which the actual census yielded.

By contrast, David's rationale as seen by *Chronicles* was not sinful. A census in preparation for building the Temple, which would enable each one in Israel to be actively involved in bringing the Divine Presence to rest among them had a precedent in Moses' census in the wilderness. David's error was in the form, not in the concept. Within this context there was no need to hide the true number of Israel, and therefore the total, including Benjamin and Levi, was given.

1. The idea of the two perspectives which we have delineated can serve well to explain a difference of thrust or emphasis between the two narratives or the fact that a given incident is either ignored or given minor play in the one while being central to the other. But what of speeches which are recorded in both narratives — each from the appropriate perspective? Surely only one set of words was used. How can the two books report them differently? For example, Yoav's speech here, in which the different approaches of the two accounts seem to be borne out, leaves us with the problem: which words did Yoav really use?

This problem is by no means unique to our chapter, and such a system can be observed in countless other places. [For one example among many, see the disparate accounts of David's prayer on the occasion of God's refusal to allow him to build the Temple — ch. 17.]

The explanation must surely be that neither of the two books quotes verbatim. The actual words used on any given occasion are not revealed to us. Rather, they are paraphrased in such a way as to reveal the truth of the particular perspective of a given narrative. Thus it is eminently possible that Yoav used language which could have conveyed one message to David's subconscious, where he felt guilty about the impure motives which he had not allowed to rise to the surface of his mind, and another to his awareness, at which level a different nuance of Yoav's words would have been significant.

(v. 7-8) In describing God's displeasure and David's recognition of error, the account in *Chronicles* differs sharply with that in *Samuel*.

Chronicles	Samuel
7(a) וַיֵּרַע בְּעֵינֵי הָאֱלֹהִים עַל־הַדָּבָר הַזֶּה, *And this matter was bad in the eyes of God,*	10(a) וַיַּךְ לֵב־דָּוִד אֹתוֹ, *And David's heart pained him*
(b) וַיַּךְ אֶת־יִשְׂרָאֵל, *so He smote Israel.*	(b) אַחֲרֵי־כֵן סָפַר אֶת־הָעָם, *after he had counted the people;*
8(c) וַיֹּאמֶר דָּוִיד אֶל־הָאֱלֹהִים ..., *And David said to God ...*	(c) וַיֹּאמֶר דָּוִד אֶל־ה' ..., *and David said to* HASHEM . . .

Chronicles knows nothing of David's pangs of conscience (a), while *Samuel* does not explicitly report God's displeasure nor the fact that He smote Israel, as is recorded in *Chronicles*.

It seems perhaps that David's conscience pangs are relevant only to *Samuel's* narrative. Only the motives which *Samuel's* narrative assumes were, in themselves, unworthy. David regretted what he had done not because of any act of God but because, on reflection, he realized that the motives which had, albeit unconsciously, goaded him into his terrible error were unworthy. He immediately turned to God to beg His forgiveness.

The motive with which *Chronicles* deals — David's conscious thinking which persuaded him to undertake the census in order to emulate Moses' census prior to erecting the Tabernacle — was entirely appropriate and did not cause David any regrets. Consequently, the (a) phrase from *Samuel* has no place in *Chronicles*. Actually, *Chronicles* could have moved immediately from v. 6 to the prayer in v. 8. But then the narrative would have had no inner logic: Why did David pray for forgiveness? To answer this question v. 7 is inserted in order to provide the understanding that even at the level with which *Chronicles* deals, David had erred and God was, in fact, displeased with him.

For this reason we have the (c) phrase in *Chronicles* which, in *Metzudos'* view, (see comm.) looks into the future. It underlines the seriousness of God's anger — a plague would result from it — and explains why David was moved to his prayer for forgiveness once he perceived his fault.

(v. 10) This verse tells of the choice of punishments David was given. It is entirely fitting that he should have been offered this choice and that much should depend on whether he would choose the correct one of the three alternatives.

The plague which *Exodus* threatens for a census that goes against the will of the Torah would be the result of the motives which are assumed in *Samuel*. These are precisely of the kind which perceive Israel as the object of David's pleasure — the very antithesis of God's will for them — and which bring the plague in their wake.

However, this is not so in the case of the motive which animated David in the *Chronicles* account. If David erred in that consideration and deserved to be punished, it was not in the concept of the census which, as we saw above, was legitimate, but in the form which it took. The punishment for that error in judgment would not necessarily have been the plague which is forecast in *Exodus*.

We have assumed that in his conscious mind David thought of the census only in legitimate terms. He resisted Yoav's urgings only because he honestly believed himself to be in the right. He was conscious only of the legitimate motive with which *Chronicles* deals. The less worthy ideas which are the subject of the account in *Samuel* played their role in a less overt way.

The choice was given to David in order to test whether he would admit these baser motives to himself. Would he realize that indeed it was the plague which he should choose? The fact that he chose correctly is a measure of the true feelings of penitence which animated him.

There is a noticeable difference between the way the last two of the three alternatives are presented in *Samuel* and verse 12 here:

Chronicles	Samuel
(a) ... וְאִם־שְׁלֹשָׁה חֳדָשִׁים נִסְפֶּה מִפְּנֵי־צָרֶיךָ, *... or three months to be swept away before your oppressors,*	(a) ..., וְאִם־שְׁלֹשָׁה חֳדָשִׁים נֻסְךָ לִפְנֵי־צָרֶיךָ *...or three months in which you flee before your oppressors*
(b) וְחֶרֶב אוֹיְבֶיךָ לְמַשֶּׂגֶת, *with the sword of your enemies overtaking you;*	(b) וְהוּא רֹדְפֶךָ, *while he pursues you;*
(c) וְאִם־שְׁלֹשֶׁת יָמִים, *or three days*	(c) וְאִם־הֱיוֹת שְׁלֹשֶׁת יָמִים, *or whether there be three days*
(d) חֶרֶב ה' וְדֶבֶר בָּאָרֶץ, *with the sword of HASHEM, a plague in the land,*	(d) דֶּבֶר בְּאַרְצֶךָ ..., *a plague in your land ...*
(e) וּמַלְאַךְ ה' מַשְׁחִית בְּכָל־גְּבוּל יִשְׂרָאֵל ... *and the angel of HASHEM destroying throughout the borders of Israel ...*	

In (a) and (b) *Samuel* uses נֻסְךָ, *you flee,* and רֹדְפֶךָ, *he pursues you,* while *Chronicles* has נִסְפֶּה, *to be swept away,* and מַשֶּׂגֶת, *overtaking you.* There is a qualitative difference between fleeing and being pursued, and being swept away by one who overtakes you.

Again (d) in *Samuel* simply mentions the plague, while (d) in *Chronicles* describes it as God's sword, and (e), which is entirely missing in *Samuel,* describes God's angel destroying throughout Israel's boundaries — a stronger expression than *in your land* in (d) of *Samuel.*

Why in both instances is the picture drawn in *Chronicles* so much grimmer than that in *Samuel?*

The solution may lie in two other differences between the two accounts which seem small in themselves but assume significance in the context of the whole. In v. 10 *Chronicles* has נֹטֶה, *offer,* the basic meaning of which is *to incline,* while *Samuel* has נוֹטֵל, which is closer in meaning to *impose* or *place upon.* Again, v. 11 in *Chronicles* has the phrase קַבֶּל לָךְ, *accept upon yourself,* which implies that David's role is not limited to making a decision among the three alternatives but that he is to be actively involved in accepting God's judgment upon himself. This whole phrase is missing from the account in *Samuel.*

Thus, in *Samuel* the punishments are *imposed* and David is not called upon to *accept* them upon himself, only to choose between them; but in *Chronicles* they are *inclined* [offered] to him and he is exhorted to *accept* them upon himself.

Our perception of the difference in approach between the two accounts can explain the discrepancy. For the motives with which *Samuel* deals, David was indeed deserving of punishment. It was imposed on him and he had no part in accepting it upon himself. *Chronicles*, however, deals with David's being tested, to see if he understood the nature of his people and their mission. In this context it makes sense for the prophet to ask David to accept God's judgment upon himself and for the punishments to be only offered, not imposed upon him.

Against this background we can perhaps understand why the punishments in *Chronicles* seem so much more severe than those in *Samuel*. In the *Samuel* perspective David was totally passive: What would happen, would happen. God's justice is reigned in by His mercy and the full fury of retribution is never released. But, from the point of view of one who actively and willingly subjects himself to the terrors of plague or military defeat — these catastrophes must loom terrible, indeed, when he contemplates his decision.

This entire thesis is brought into sharp focus by God's final charge to David. Where our verse 12 has וְעַתָּה רְאֵה, *now see!*, *Samuel* has דַּע וּרְאֵה, *know and see!* The connotation is: Realize your guilt in this matter. This would be apt in *Samuel*, where David's baser, subconscious motives are dealt with. Realize that subconsciously your motives are not the pure ones you think they are.

(v. 15) In the description of the plague's end there is a significant difference between our verse and the one in *Samuel.*

Chronicles	Samuel
(a) וַיִּשְׁלַח הָאֱלֹהִים מַלְאָךְ לִירוּשָׁלַם לְהַשְׁחִיתָהּ, *And God sent an angel to Jerusalem to destroy it,*	(a) וַיִּשְׁלַח יָדוֹ הַמַּלְאָךְ יְרוּשָׁלַם לְשַׁחֲתָהּ, *And the angel stretched out his hand towards Jerusalem to destroy it,*
(b) וּכְהַשְׁחִית רָאָה ה', *but as he destroyed, HASHEM saw*	(b)
(c) וַיִּנָּחֶם עַל־הָרָעָה, *and reconsidered the evil;*	(c) וַיִּנָּחֶם ה' אֶל־הָרָעָה, *but HASHEM reconsidered the evil;*
(d) וַיֹּאמֶר לַמַּלְאָךְ ..., *and He said to the angel ...*	(d) וַיֹּאמֶר לַמַּלְאָךְ ..., *and He said to the angel ...*

The significant differences are that whereas in *Samuel* it seems to be the angel who stretches out his hand against Jerusalem independently, in *Chronicles* it is God who sends him there.

Again, the (b) phrase in *Chronicles*, which is evidently inserted to explain why God decided to spare the city (see below), is missing entirely in *Samuel.*

Structurally this latter discrepancy is easily explained. In *Samuel* the angel (whom God must have entrusted with executing the plague against Israel) goes to Jerusalem as part of his general mission. When God sees this, He 'reconsiders' the original mandate which He gave the angel. However, in *Chronicles* it is God Who sends the angel against Jerusalem specifically. There would be no logical reason to 'reconsider' that mandate if God had not 'seen' something to, as it were, change His mind.

What did God see [*Chronicles* (b)] which caused a change of heart and persuaded Him to spare the city? The Sages have a number of explanations which have been quoted in the commentary, but for the purpose of this analysis we will follow *Pirkei d'R' Eliezer*. God saw David's sincere repentance which is described in v. 16. For a clearer understanding, that passage too must be examined against its parallel in *Samuel*.

Chronicles	Samuel
(a)	(a) וַיֹּאמֶר דָּוִד אֶל־ה', *And David said to* HASHEM
(b) וַיִּשָּׂא דָוִיד אֶת־עֵינָיו וַיַּרְא אֶת־מַלְאַךְ ה' עֹמֵד בֵּין הָאָרֶץ וּבֵין הַשָּׁמַיִם וְחַרְבּוֹ שְׁלוּפָה בְּיָדוֹ נְטוּיָה עַל־יְרוּשָׁלִַם, *David lifted up his eyes and saw the angel of* HASHEM *standing between earth and heaven, with his sword drawn in his hand, stretched out over Jerusalem;*	(b) בִּרְאֹתוֹ אֶת־הַמַּלְאָךְ הַמַּכֶּה בָעָם *when he saw the angel who was striking the people,*
(c) וַיִּפֹּל דָּוִיד וְהַזְּקֵנִים מְכֻסִּים בַּשַּׂקִּים עַל־פְּנֵיהֶם, *and David and the elders, covered in sackcloth, fell upon their faces.*	(c)
(d) ... וַיֹּאמֶר דָּוִיד אֶל־הָאֱלֹהִים, *And David said to God ...*	(d) וַיֹּאמֶר ..., *and he said ...*

Two entirely different pictures emerge. In *Samuel* David sees the terrible slaughter. Under the impression of this catastrophe, he turns to God willing to shoulder the whole blame and to absorb the punishment upon himself and his family rather than have any more of Israel's people fall.

In *Chronicles* it is not the death of the people that shocks David into action, but the heavenly sword stretched out against Jerusalem. When he sees the terrible danger to which his city is exposed, he and his elders fall to the ground in an act of penitence (c) (which is missing entirely from the *Samuel* narrative), and he prays that he and his family might be struck instead of the people.

In an analysis of the two passages we have shown that in *Samuel* the focal point is the plague itself, while in *Chronicles* the entire thrust of the narrative is to act as an introduction to the location of the Temple site. For this reason, in the *Samuel* perspective there is no particular significance to Jerusalem. The death of so many Jews is tragic wherever it occurs. The angel of death came to Jerusalem in the course of executing his mandate and intended to spread the plague there as he had done in other places. David lived in Jerusalem and, while he had surely known of the deaths which were occurring elsewhere, it was the sight of the tragedy which brought its full enormity home to him. There was no need for a new act of repentance — he had already acknowledged his guilt in v. 10 (see our v. 8). And so David simply turned to God in prayer, begging Him to halt the carnage.

In *Chronicles'* perspective there is another story playing out. The purpose of the entire incident is only accomplished when the angel turns to Jerusalem, because the plague is to be the means by which David is to learn the location of the Temple site. In that sense God *sent* the angel to Jerusalem to destroy it. Jerusalem was to be the site of the ultimate test of whether or not Israel could be bearers of the Divine Presence by means of the Temple in their midst. If Israel's perception of itself was not up to the task — then there could be no Temple in it, and Jerusalem would be destroyed because it could serve no useful purpose.

David *raised his eyes* and saw the heavenly sword suspended over Jerusalem. He realized that there was more involved than the actual sin which he had committed when he initiated the census. For that sin he had already repented, as told in v. 8. Now he saw that the very essence of Israel's being hung in the balance, and his previous repentance would not suffice now. Indeed, it was not he alone who had to come to a different realization of the nature of Israel. The elders of the people had to join him in his prostration.

With his prostration, God's purpose was fulfilled and, as told in the next verses, the site of the Temple was now revealed to David.

(v. 18) It is interesting that *Samuel* has Gad the seer telling David to build the altar but does not mention that Gad had been ordered by the angel to do so, as does our v. 18. This can be readily understood when we consider that in *Samuel* the angel only appears as an agent of God's wrath and, in that capacity, would not be involved in the bringing of the sacrifice. In *Chronicles* where, in line with *Aggados Bereishis* (see comm. to v. 15), we recognize identification of the angel as one of mercy, it is entirely in character that it should be he who urges David to build the altar.

(v. 20) This verse here, *and he saw the angel*, has no parallel in *Samuel*. And where in our v. 21 we have וַיַּבֵּט אָרְנָן, *and Ornan looked*, *Samuel* has וַיַּשְׁקֵף, *and he looked out*. *Rashi* there writes that this expression hints at the fact that Ornan had been hiding because of the angel as told in our verse.

It seems that in *Samuel* no issue is made of the fact that Ornan saw the angel because the angel had not figured prominently in the narrative. When v. 17 there says, *When David saw the angel striking the people, he spoke to HASHEM ...*, it is not the sight of the angel but of the slaughter which turned David to God (see above). In *Chronicles*, on the other hand, the vision of the angel was central, and therefore our verse points out that not only David but also the *Yevusite* and his sons saw this heavenly sight.

Our analysis of this chapter has shown the different perspective which *Chronicles* brings to bear on this entire tragic episode. Far from being contradictory to the *Samuel's* account, it offers us by its various changes a depth of perception of this event which would have otherwise remained beyond our view. It is by this method that *Chronicles* adds immeasurably to our comprehension of historical events while seemingly only repeating what has already been told in the earlier books.

⊷§ Appendices

Appendix I
The Authorship of Chronicles

In the first nine chapters we occasionally made reference to Ezra as the author of the book while in subsequent chapters this identification was not made. This, because a careful analysis of the sources leaves the authorship of the bulk of the book unclear.

It is imperative to examine precisely what is and what is not said in the Talmudic discussion since in at least one instance — that of the family of Yechoniah in ch. 3 — the listings seem to go far beyond Ezra's lifetime, as will be shown at the end of this article.

The relevant passage reads as follows:

עֶזְרָא כָּתַב סִפְרוֹ וְיַחַס שֶׁל דִּבְרֵי הַיָּמִים עַד לוֹ ... וּמָאן אַסְקֵיהּ? נְחֶמְיָה בֶּן חֲכַלְיָה.
Ezra wrote his book [the book of Ezra] and the genealogy of Chronicles up to him ... And who finished it? Nehemiah the son of Chachaliah.

This translation can serve as a working basis for our analysis of the passage, but parts of it are not necessarily accurate. This excerpt is part of a larger passage which discusses the authorship of all the books of Scripture, and the following observations may be made concerning the terms which are used here:

(1) The term 'So and so wrote his book' does not necessarily mean that he wrote the whole book, even when there is no qualifying statement such as '... up to this or that point.' This can be demonstrated from the phrase, 'Ezra wrote his book.' In the passage under discussion, the books of *Ezra* and *Nehemiah* are considered to be one book. [Their division into two books came together with the division of *Samuel*, *Kings* and *Chronicles* into two books. None of those divisions are known to the Talmud.] Now it is clear that the second part of the book of *Ezra* [the part which we know as *Nehemiah*] was not written by Ezra but by Nehemiah (see *Rashi, Nehemiah* 1:1). Nevertheless, the Talmud makes the unqualified statement: 'Ezra wrote his book.'[1]

(2) The term אַסְקֵיהּ should not be translated *finished* but *carried forward*. It is quite clearly used in the Talmud even when it does not describe the actual conclusion of a book. The word derives from the root נסק, the basic meaning of which is *to light a fire*. The association of ideas is that as someone who lights a fire causes the flames to rise, so a given situation can be said to 'rise' towards its ultimate conclusion. The actual conclusion is not implicit except in a word like

---

1. *Maharshal* (there) addresses this question and suggests that the question וּמָאן אַסְקֵיהּ, *And who finished it?* refers to the earlier statement, 'Ezra wrote his book' and not to the Book of *Chronicles* at all. However, *Maharshal* himself admits that the early commentators do not agree with his interpretation. However, *Yad Ramah's* reading of the passage actually has: '... and who completed the book of *Ezra?'*

מַסְקְנָא, conclusion, which is simply the end result of the process of the 'carrying forward towards a conclusion.'

This can be demonstrated from the following passage:

> יְהוֹשֻׁעַ כָּתַב סִפְרוֹ. וְהָכְתִיב וַיָּמָת יְהוֹשֻׁעַ בִּן־נוּן עֶבֶד ה'? דְּאַסְקֵיהּ אֶלְעָזָר. וְהָכְתִיב
> וְאֶלְעָזָר בֶּן־אַהֲרֹן מֵת? דְּאַסְקֵיהּ פִּינְחָס.
>
> *Joshua wrote his book. But is it not written, 'And Joshua the son of Nun, the servant of God died?' [Joshua could not have written about his own death.] Eleazar [son of Aharon] completed it. But is it not written, 'And Eleazar the son of Aharon died?' Pinechas [son of Eleazar] completed it.*

Now, the original answer, דְּאַסְקֵיהּ אֶלְעָזָר, cannot have meant that Eleazar finished the book. The Talmud must have known that the last sentence in the book which reports Eleazar's death cannot have been written by him. It is clear that the phrase was used to describe exactly what Eleazar had done — he carried the book forward towards its conclusion, but he did not actually complete it.

(3) The expression יַחַס שֶׁל דִּבְרֵי הַיָּמִים, *the genealogy of Chronicles*, seems to indicate that the discussion centers on the genealogical tables contained in the first nine chapters of the book. There would seem to be no reason why the whole book should be described as 'the genealogy of *Chronicles.'*

That this is so can be demonstrated as follows. *Dikdukei Soferim* brings one reading which omits the words עַד לוֹ entirely. The reading is simply: וְיַחַס שֶׁל דִּבְרֵי הַיָּמִים.[1] According to this reading it is obvious that not the whole book but only the genealogical tables are ascribed to Ezra.

Inasmuch as this is an extremely fundamental assertion concerning the authorship of the book it is important to adduce whatever evidence seems to confirm or contradict it.

Firstly, it must be stated that *Ramban* in *Sefer HaGeulah* seems to disagree. He asserts that the final two verses of *Chronicles* are identical with the first two verses in the book of *Ezra*, in order to show that the two books were written by the same person. The implication is clear that the whole of *Chronicles* was written by Ezra.

However, *Yad Ramah's* reading of the passage in *Bava Basra* is a clear confirmation of the thesis.

> עֶזְרָא כָּתַב סִפְרוֹ וְיַחַס בְּדִבְרֵי הַיָּמִים עַד לוֹ ... וּמַאן אַסְקֵיהּ לְסֵפֶר עֶזְרָא ...
>
> *Ezra wrote his book [Ezra] and the genealogy contained in Chronicles up to* לוֹ *... Who completed [the book of Ezra]? ...*

The phrase 'the genealogy *contained in Chronicles'* makes it perfectly clear that not the whole book is under discussion, but only the genealogical lists. Moreover, it is of extreme interest that *Yad Ramah* interprets the question, 'Who completed it?,' as referring to the book of *Ezra* [the second half of which was

---

1. This presents an attractive alternative reading. The words עַד לוֹ are extremely difficult. If they are to be read עַד לוֹ, *up to his [own genealogy]*, as most commentators do, then the word לוֹ is grammatically incorrect. It should be, עַד שֶׁלוֹ or עַד עַצְמוֹ שֶׁל עַד. For this reason *Maharshal* suggests an entirely different reading — עֵד לוֹ, *in testimony for himself*, meaning, as testimony for his own impeccable family tree. [See *Tosafos* there for an entirely different interpretation of the phrase, and see Appendix II for details.]

If, however, it is a later interpolation then the original statement was simply that Ezra wrote the genealogy. Subsequently, someone was bothered by the problem that the genealogy seems to go beyond Ezra's time, and so emended [incorrectly] the words עַד לוֹ to qualify the Talmud's statement.

written by Nehemiah] rather than to *Chronicles*. According to this interpretation, the authorship of the historical part of *Chronicles* is left open. Perhaps because of the lack of a reliable tradition no attempt is made to identify an author.

This interpretation may have found its justification in a responsum of the *Geonim*. In a fragment reprinted in *Ginsberg's Geonica* (V. 2, N.Y. 1909) we read: 'Know then that the book of *Chronicles* was divided in its authorship into two parts. Ezra traced genealogies in it up to וְלוֹ אַחִים (*II Chronicles* 21:2) ... and as for the rest, the Men of the Great Assembly (אַנְשֵׁי כְנֶסֶת הַגְּדוֹלָה) wrote it.' The assertion of the *Gaon* that the book was completed by the Men of the Great Assembly would contradict the passage in *Bava Basra* unless we interpret it as does *Yad Ramah*.

It must also be noted that the *Geonim* interpret עַד לוֹ in *Bava Basra* differently than we have assumed till now. Rather than translating: 'Up to his own genealogy,' as *Rashi* had done, they read it as though it were written עַד [וְלוֹ] and hold it to refer to a verse in *II Chronicles* 21:2. Ezra wrote up to that verse. The rest was completed by the Men of the Great Assembly.

If so, their choice of words would seem to contradict our thesis. 'Ezra traced the genealogies' (יִיחֵס בְּדִבְרֵי הַיָּמִים) seems to apply to all parts of the book, even the historical parts. Thus, our assertion that the phrase יַחַס שֶׁל דִּבְרֵי הַיָּמִים in *Bava Basra* refers only to the genealogical tables seems contradicted.

R' David Cohen, however, pointed out to me that this is not necessarily so. There is after all no reason why the term יַחַס should be used for the historical portions of the book. Rather it seems likely that it refers to the genealogical tables and to those passages in the latter parts of the book which concern themselves with genealogy. It is quite possible that although Ezra did not write the historical parts of the book he nevertheless interlaced genealogical data into the appropriate passages if these were written earlier, or that a later author told the story which he had to tell around the structure of genealogical material which had been provided by Ezra. [See further in Appendix II.]

If this thesis is indeed correct, then the Talmud's question מָאן אַסְקֵיהּ, *Who carried it forward?* must refer to the book from ch. 9 onwards. Who wrote the historical section of the book?

Thus, according to the Talmud's answer, we have Nehemiah writing the historical parts of the book [I: ch. 10 and onwards] with no real indication whether the complete genealogical table contained in the first nine chapters come from Ezra's pen or whether there may be later additions there. This, since noted above, the expression 'Ezra wrote ...' does not have to mean that he completed them.

The issue needs to be solved in connection with the descendants of Yechoniah (3:17ff). As a study of the commentary shows, either fifteen (*Gra*) or nine (*Malbim*) generations are given. Since, as the commentary to 3:17 demonstrates, Yechoniah had no children at all until after he was taken to Babylon, this clearly takes us not only beyond Ezra's lifetime, but also beyond Nehemiah's.[1]

The conclusion is inescapable that hands other than those of Ezra and Nehemiah completed the genealogical lists and, as we have seen, the Talmudic

---

1. According to dates given in *Anvil of Sinai*, Yechoniah was imprisoned in 3327 and Nehemiah came to Jerusalem in 3426. *Malbim* claims that these ninety-nine years could accommodate his nine generations if we postulate that each had his first child at age thirteen or fourteen. Clearly this is no solution for *Gra's* fifteen generations.

tradition can well accommodate such an assumption. However, we should also bear in mind the possibility that Ezra indeed wrote the entire book and that the later genealogy came to him in prophetic vision. This is in fact suggested by an anonymous tenth-century commentator ascribed to the school of R' *Saadiah Gaon.*

In connection with this last discussion, note should be taken of an account concerning the descendants of Yechoniah found in *Seder Olam Zuta* which has been accepted and quoted by major Jewish historians. [See the listings of *Abraham ibn David's Sefer HaKabbalah,* and of *R' Moshe Isserles'* rendering of *Yesod Olam* quoted in *Sefer Yuchasin.*]

According to this account the exilarchate passed from Yechoniah to his son Zerubavel (3, 390); his son Meshullam; his son Chananiah; his son Berachiah; his son Chasdaiah; Yeshaiah; his son Ovadiah; his son Shemaiah; Shechaniah; his son Chizkiah (3994); his son Akuv. We have quoted here the dates of Zerubavel and Chizkiah only to demonstrate the time lapse of six centuries that separates them. The description 'his son' is left out by Yeshaiah and Shechaniah (but *Seder HaKabbalah* and *Yesod Olam* have it by these two also). Thus Chananiah is listed as a son of Meshullam; Berachiah is listed as a son of Chananiah; Chasdaiah is listed as a son of Berachiah although in the account in *Chronicles* the later three are all brothers of Meshullam. Ovadiah is given as a son of Yeshaiah whereas in *Chronicles* he is either his great-grandson *(Gra)* or his brother *(Malbim).*]

This listing spans some six centuries and brings the exilarchate up to almost two hundred years beyond the destruction of the Second Temple. This is obviously incompatible with the fact that these names are listed in *Chronicles.* This may not, however, be a problem since *Seder Olam Zuta* makes no claim that his list derives from *Chronicles,* and it is conceivable that we are dealing with a completely different family line — this one, descended through Zerubavel's son Meshullam for whom *Chronicles* offers no record at all — and that the names, which may have been common in the family, just happen to coincide with those listed in *Chronicles.* This would obviate the problem of *Seder Olam Zuta's* listing several people as sons who in *Chronicles* are listed as brothers, and would also explain why in *Seder Olam Zuta's* list Shemaiah precedes Shechaniah although in *Chronicles* he is given as his son.[1]

However, this solution is not attractive for a number of reasons:

(1) It would be remarkable if nine generations from Meshullam spanned many centuries while the same number of generations from his brother Chananiah passed sufficiently quickly to have still been listed by Nehemiah.[2]

(2) Even if we accept the possibility that the identical names in an almost

---

1. This last discrepancy has been 'corrected' in the lists of *Sefer HaKabbalah* and *Yesod Olam,* both of whom list Shechaniah before Shemaiah.

2. This problem could perhaps be solved if the term 'his son' in *Seder Olam Zuta* could be interpreted as descendant rather than as an actual son. This seems indicated by the fact that some of the reigns listed in *Seder Olam Zuta* seem unreasonably long. For example, Chananiah is appointed in the twelfth year of the Greek period and his 'son' Berachiah in the 140th year of the same period. If it could be postulated that Berachiah was a grandson or great-grandson of Chananiah and that after Chananiah's death the Exilarchate remained unoccupied for a given period until it was once again taken up by a descendant of the previous office-holder, then this could be readily understood. However, from a textual viewpoint this solution seems unlikely since the formula is mostly: 'So and so died and his son, so and so, was appointed,' which implies that the death of the earlier and the ascension of the later occurred at the same time.

identical order remained in the family over a period of close to six hundred years, it is still an unreasonable coincidence that no other names should have occurred within such a long period of time.

R' *David Cohen* has suggested that some of the problems may find their solution in the following thesis.

The names which *Seder Olam Zuta* records for these early exilarchs may not be given names at all. Rather they may be official names, assumed as part of their ascension to office. The practice of assuming the name of the original office-holder to go with a position of power, which is common among royal lines, seems to have been widespread in the era of the Second Temple. For example, we can deduce from *Shekalim* (ch. 5; see *Tiferes Yisrael* there and *Tosafos* to *Menachos* 64b) that a number of functionaries in the Temple were known by the names of the first person to have held their office rather than by their given names.

It may well be that in the early centuries of the exilarchate, it was the custom to choose such official names from among those listed as Yechoniah's descendants in *Chronicles*. The fact that the custom was subsequently discontinued need not disprove this thesis.

As noted in the commentary to 3:24, special esoteric significance seems to have attached to Yechoniah's family line. The inner nature and implication of these names may have been recognized and understood in those early years and, as each of these great men assumed the mantle of leadership [invested with his power by the Sages of his generation, as *Seder Olam Zuta* repeatedly stresses], he would choose that name which he felt to be appropriate to his unique personality and function within Jewish history. As the centuries passed, and with the loss of the book of *Genealogies*, the true understanding of the names of *Chronicles* was forgotten (see Overview) and the custom was discontinued.

Appendix II
The Genealogical Tables

In Appendix I we noted the possibility that when *Bava Basra* 15a ascribes the authorship of *Chronicles* to Ezra and states that it was completed by Nehemiah, a differentiation between the genealogical tables and the historical narrative may have been intended. Ezra is the author of the genealogical sections (יחס של דה"י) while Nehemiah wrote the historical parts.

Given this division we may legitimately ask, in what way do these two sections belong together to form one book? There seems little inner connection between the family records of the various tribes and the story of the Davidic royal house which is picked up at ch. 10.

A careful reading of the *Ramban* in his *Sefer HaGeulah* may yield an explanation.

The key may lie in an understanding of ch. 9 which comes between the genealogical lists which end with Benjamin in ch. 8 and the account of Saul's death in ch. 10 which begins the narrative part of the book.

A detailed analysis of ch. 9 is to be found in the comm. there. For our purpose here, it is sufficient to say that it gives an accounting of how Jerusalem and various cities of Judah and Benjamin were settled by the exiles returning from Babylon.

Such an accounting, serving, as it were, as a culmination of the eight chapters of genealogical data, lends credence to *Ramban's* opinion (there) that Ezra set up the genealogical lists in order to establish the descent of the families who returned with him to Jerusalem. If that is the case, it would surely be logical to cap the tables with an account of how the settlement was accomplished.

We note further that, in contrast to *Kings* which ends with the destruction and the trek into exile, *Chronicles* in the last two verses (II:36:22-23) points to the return at Cyrus' instigation. These same two verses which bring the *Book of Chronicles* to its close are also the opening two verses of *Ezra*, from which *Ramban* deduces that the two books really form one entity.

That being so it seems likely that *Ramban* perceives the *Book of Chronicles* as a kind of introduction to the *Book of Ezra*. It sets the stage for the history of the return to Zion by tracing the descent of the returnees and describing their settlement in the land. The narrative section would then be a retracing of the historical developments which led to the exile and from which the history, which Ezra was about to describe in the book which bears his name, derived.

This analysis of the book points to an understanding of how the genealogical lists do indeed belong together with the narrative parts of *Chronicles*.[1] Indeed,

---

1. In Appendix I we discussed the statement of the Talmud that 'Ezra wrote the genealogy of Chronicles.' We surmised there that perhaps the meaning of this is that only the first nine chapters

we may even consider a possibility whereby the genealogical lists and the last two verses of the Book form one entity and the entire narrative section is, in a sense, an interpolation.

We can best reach a fuller understanding of this basic question if we first address ourselves to two others: (1) What was Ezra's purpose in compiling these lists; and (2) how did he go about fulfilling his appointed task?

In *Bava Basra* 18a we learn that R' Yehudah taught in the name of Rav that: Ezra traced his own descent before he went up from Babylon to the Land of Israel. There is no indication in the Talmud to tell us in what connection Rav had made this statement. Certain it is that he did not make it in order to explain the presence of the genealogical lists in *Chronicles*, since the Talmud offers these lists as a proof for his statement rather than as its source.

A careful examination of the עד ... לא formula which Rav used (לֹא עָלָה עֶזְרָא מִבָּבֶל עַד שֶׁיִּחֵס עַצְמוֹ) yields that it is invariably used when a passage in Scripture needs an explanation (see e.g., *Gittin* 88a; *Sanhedrin* 106b and 108a and many more). We therefore conclude that Rav's statement was meant as an explanation of *Ezra* 7:1-5 where, when Ezra is first introduced, his family tree is traced all the way to Aaron the *Kohen Gadol*, a total of seventeen generations. Rav explains that this was done only because of Ezra's insistence that his own family tree should be in order before he went up to Israel.

However, Rav offers no explanation for Ezra's concern. Why was it so important to him that his line of descent should be firmly established?

Ezra's concern for established and pure family lives extended beyond his own ancestry and indeed became a hallmark of his leadership of Israel. *Kiddushin* 69b teaches that Ezra would not go up from Babylon to Israel until he had made Babylon 'like the purest flour' [i.e., he determined all the people of questionable descent and insisted that they accompany him to Israel, thus making sure that the community remaining in Babylon should be of established and impeccable lineage]. This is offered as an explanation of the mishnah in the fourth chapter of *Kiddushin* which records that among those who accompanied Ezra to Israel there were ten categories of family groupings of which only three (*Kohanim*, Levites and Israelites) were of unquestioned lineage, whereas the other seven categories were all of questionable or defective lineage.

Rashi (there) explains Ezra's concern: Ezra's whole purpose was to cleanse Babylon [from people of questionable lineage]. He realized that such people had become integrated into the community and knew that all the great people of Babylon were about to go with him to Israel, and there would be no one left to concern himself with the people's genealogies. Therefore he separated the people with questionable ancestry and took them with him to Israel. In this way everyone knew who these people were and could be expected to exercise care when marrying. He did not fear that in succeeding generations these people would once more become integrated into the community, since the High Court which had its seat in the Temple building had the task of checking genealogies and would be aware of any problems.

are ascribed to Ezra and that the rest was completed by Nehemiah or by the Men of the Great Assembly. We noted there that *Ramban*, who proves that *Chronicles* and *Ezra* were written by the same person from the fact that the same two verses that end the one begin the other, seems to ascribe the whole book to Ezra. According to our thesis here this may not be the case. It could well be that Ezra wrote the genealogical tables through ch. 9 and then ended the book with the two verses which were to tie this book to Ezra. The narrative of the events which led up to this may have been inserted by Nehemiah or by the Men of the Great Assembly.

Ezra's concern for family purity in Babylon was well rewarded, because centuries later the Talmud (*Kesubos* 111a) ruled that: 'All lands are a mixture relative to the land of Israel, and [even] the land of Israel is a mixture relative to Babylon.' In practical terms this ruling meant that if a Babylonian Jew wanted to marry someone from Israel, he would have to check out that person's lineage while the partner who came from Israel would not need to check the descent of the Babylonian. It was assumed to be impeccable.

Seemingly then, the establishment of clear genealogical lines was so important to Ezra as just one among the many needs of the hour which he, as his people's great leader, recognized, and which he therefore felt called upon to fill.

There is, however, another possibility. *Kiddushin* 70b teaches that: 'The Divine Presence will rest only upon genealogically pure families (מִשְׁפָּחוֹת מְיֻחָסוֹת) in Israel.' Ezra, as the leader of Israel at a time when they were about to reestablish themselves in their own land and once more live their lives around the Temple which again stood in their midst, had the duty to ready them to be worthy hosts for the *Shechinah* (Divine Presence), which was once more to dwell among them.[1] In this readying, an examination of their genealogical status was of primary importance.

All that we have discussed up to this point may underlie *Ramban's* short statement in the *Sefer HaGeulah* that: 'Ezra the Scribe wrote this Book [*Chronicles*] ... in order to make known the genealogy of the tribes who returned with him to Jerusalem.'

We have found a plausible explanation for the compilation of these lists; we should now submit the lists themselves to closer scrutiny.

There are two features of the lists which are immediately striking. First, there is the seeming inconsistency with which the various tribes are dealt. In some cases — e.g., Judah — the lists are extremely detailed, while in others — e.g., Naphtali — the treatment is entirely cursory, and again, Zevulun and perhaps Dan (see comm. to 7:12) are missing completely from the lists. Secondly, there is the style in which the lists are written. Many passages are so obscure that, as attested by the attempts of the commentators, it is for all practical purposes impossible to read meaning into the text as it stands; and, while there are many parts of which the meaning is clear and unambiguous, even those sections are replete with syntaxical and lexicographical irregularities, a seeming lack of organization in presenting the material, and in general, a measure of obscurity which makes these lists unique within Scripture.

We shall discern each of these features separately and then attempt to draw the conclusions to which they may point.

In the view of all standard commentators, the Book itself addresses the first problem. Verse 9:1 reads: *Now all of Israel had its lineage traced and it is written in the Book of the Kings of Israel. But Judah was exiled to Babylon because of its sins.* We quote *Radak* as being representative of most other comments: Even though our Book has mentioned a part of [Israel's] genealogy, it has not mentioned all of it. But it is all recorded in the Book of the Kings of Israel. This

1. Although *Yoma* 21b teaches that there was no *Shechinah* in the Second Temple, our thesis is not contradicted. The Second Temple did indeed fall far short of an ideal Temple. However, this need not have been so. The midrash (see *Rashi* to *Ezekiel* 43:11) teaches that had Israel chosen to heed the call to greatness, the Temple which they built upon their return from Babylon could indeed have been the ultimate one. They sinned and it therefore did not achieve its potential. Certainly Ezra, in his preparations for the return, would have been allowed, and perhaps obliged, to anticipate the optimum circumstances and to assume that the *Shechinah* would indeed come to rest on their handiwork.

Book is not extant [because it probably accompanied the ten tribes into their exile (*Metzudos* and *Ramvan* in *Sefer HaGeulah*)] and is just like the *Sefer HaYashar* (*Joshua* 10:13) and the *Sefer Milchamos Hashem* (*Numbers* 21:14). [*Radak* means that we are not to be surprised the Scripture makes reference to a non-canonical book. He brings two other examples where this is done.]

Metzudos explains the latter part of the verse to mean that in contrast to the ten tribes who were exiled to faraway places, and whose records are therefore lost to us, Judah went to Babylon and Ezra, who was also from Babylon, therefore had access to their records.

A picture emerges of Ezra, by making use of such lists and records as were available to him, attempting to establish the genealogy of as much of Israel as was possible to him under the circumstances. [See further comm. to וְהַדְּבָרִים עֲתִיקִים in 4:22 and particularly *Gra's* opinion cited there.] See also comm. to 7:12 where we find that Ezra even went so far as to include an unconnected fragment of a genealogical list and, at least according to the *Mefaresh*, was himself in doubt concerning the correct placing of that fragment.

An even clearer picture of the methodology which Ezra used can be gleaned from the *Mefaresh* to 7:13 and to 8:29.

In the earlier passage the *Mefaresh* addresses the problem of Naphtali's genealogy; only names which are already recorded in the Torah are mentioned. He comments: The reason why the genealogy is not taken further is for the reason explained at the end of *Megillas Yerushalmi*. Ezra found three books, each containing genealogical lists. If he found something he recorded it; what he did not find he could not record. He found nothing more concerning Naphtali's descendants. Now this is the reason why throughout these genealogical lists there are sudden breaks from one family to another because he [Ezra] moved from one book to the next and then joined them all together.[1]

---

1. A cursory reading of the *Mefaresh's* comment here and at 8:29 (see quote in comm.) yields that there is, in fact, a Talmudic source for his assertion that there were three books which Ezra consulted and that the use of these varying sources accounts for the apparently disorganized presentation of the material.

This assumption is not entirely correct. The printed versions of the *Mefaresh's* comments quote a *Megillas Yerushalmi*. We know of no book of that name. From the more detailed quote contained at 8:29 it is obvious that reference is to the *Yerushalmi* in *Taanis* 4:2, and indeed early prints of the *Mefaresh's* commentary speak of the *Yerushalmi* rather than a *Megillas Yerushalmi*. Now if that is indeed his source, then his reading differed radically from the generally accepted version. The *Mefaresh* evidently read: 'Ezra (עזרא) found three books,' whereas our reading is: 'Three books were found in the Courtyard (עזרה) [of the Temple]' (see *Baer Rathner's*, *Ahavas Zion V'Yrushalayim* there). Furthermore according to our reading the significance of these books their variant readings of certain words in Scripture and we find no reference to any genealogical data.

[The passage in the *Yerushalmi* reads as follows: שלשה ספרים מצאו בעזרה ספר מעוני וספר זעטוטי וספר היא, *They found three books in the Temple courtyard: The Meoni book, the Zaatuti book and the Hi book*. The *Yerushalmi* them goes on to explain that these books were Torah scrolls which had divergent readings in their texts. The various names — Meoni, Zaatuti and Hi — refer to the words or passages in which these divergent readings occurred.

In view of the fact that the whole section of the *Yerushalmi* in which this passage occurs deals with genealogical data, it has been suggested that the original wording of this passage was limited to the statement that three books by these names were found in the Temple Courtyard or, if the reading of the *Mefaresh* (עזרא) instead of (עזרה) is accepted, were found by Ezra. These books may well have been genealogical lists and the various names refer to the families whose records were preserved in them or, perhaps the places in which they were found. [*Avos d'Rabbi Nosson*, according to some readings, contains the information that the *Sefer Meonim* was found in Beth Maon.] The explanation which assumes them to have been Torah scrolls may have been a later addition by someone who did not understand the original statement correctly, and the *Mefaresh* may have had a text of the *Yerushalmi* which contained only the original statement.

Be that as it may, the *Mefaresh's* source is not to be found in the extant versions of the *Yerushalmi*.

He is even more explicit in a later passage. The passage, beginning at 8:29, is repeated almost verbatim at 9:35. It is to this problem that he addresses himself. [But note that other commentators offer different explanations — see there.] We quote: 'This passage is written twice in this book as also ... [quoting other examples of the same phenomenon]. It is this which is explained at the end of *Megillas Yerushalmi* that Ezra found three scrolls ... and they established the correct reading by following the majority. [I.e., if two of three scrolls had the same version of a given word or passage, that version became authoritative.] He also found many genealogical tables and there also the majority rule applied. If, however, he found pairs [i.e., two versions which were essentially similar with only minor differences between them], as e.g., our passage, he had to incorporate both of them [in the Book of *Chronicles*] in order to accommodate the minor differences between them ...'

Thus we see that, although there may be disagreement among the commentators concerning the degree to which Ezra's methodology influenced the structure of the Book, the general consensus seems to be that the thoroughness with which the respective tribes were dealt with was indeed influenced by the availability of sources from which to draw.

We now turn to the second part of our inquiry — the extreme obscurity of style in these lists. We shall offer a list of instances where the plain text yields no meaning at all and where, in order to elicit meaning, assumptions are made by the various commentators which cannot be said to be implicit in the text. It must be stressed that such instances are not unique to the genealogical lists in *Chronicles*. Examples occur, here and there, in other parts of Scripture. But it is beyond dispute that whereas in the rest of Scripture such instances are a tiny exception to a generally clear text, in *Chronicles* they seem to be the norm. The list is by no means complete and is offered only as a sampling of unusual styling of these passages. Some of the examples will be seen as less problematic than others and these are given only inasmuch as they contribute to the general picture.

(1) 2:30: וַיָּמָת סֶלֶד לֹא בָנִים is meaningless unless we read לֹא בָנִים as though it were written בְּלֹא בָנִים.

(2) 2:42: The commentators note that it is frequent usage in these lists to interrupt a given list and then [without apparent logic] to take it up again at a later point.

(3) 2:42: מֵישָׁע בְּכֹרוֹ הוּא אֲבִי־זִיף וּבְנֵי מָרֵשָׁה אֲבִי חֶבְרוֹן. It is clear that Mesha the first-born is described as father of Ziph. But what does the phrase וּבְנֵי מָרֵשָׁה אֲבִי חֶבְרוֹן mean? Both *Radak* and *Gra* explain that the word זִיף or אֲבִי־זִיף must be interpolated after וּבְנֵי. The meaning is that מָרֵשָׁה father of Hebron was a son of [אֲבִי] זִיף.

(4) 2:47: וּבְנֵי יָהְדָּי רֶגֶם. No יָהְדָּי was mentioned up to this point. *Radak* and *Metzudos* suggest that יָהְדָּי is another name for one of the people mentioned in the previous verse. According to *Gra* the word וּבְנֵי does double duty and must be read with the end of the previous verse and also with the verse in which it appears. The previous verse ended with the phrase וְחָרָן הֹלִיד אֶת־גָּזֵז. We must now interpret as though the following phrase reads: וּבְנֵי גָּזֵז יָהְדָּי] וּבְנֵי יָהְדָּי רֶגֶם]. [See comm. to 8:31.]

(5) 2:50: The phrase בְּנֵי כָלֵב בֶּן־חוּר which means: The sons of Calev the son of Chur must, according to the *Mefaresh*, be read as though it were written: וּבְנֵי כָלֵב בְּנוֹ חוּר, *And the sons of Calev whose son was Chur.*

(6) 3:21: וּבֶן־חֲנַנְיָה פְּלַטְיָה וִישַׁעְיָה בְּנֵי רְפָיָה בְּנֵי אַרְנָן בְּנֵי עֹבַדְיָה בְּנֵי שְׁכַנְיָה. The second half of the sentence beginning with the words בְּנֵי רְפָיָה conveys no meaning. We are not told who רְפָיָה, אַרְנָן, etc. are nor who their sons were. *Gra* assumes two changes in order to make sense of the words. (1) בְּנֵי (plural) must be understood as בֶּן (singular); and (2) it is to be read together with the name which goes before rather than with the name which follows it. Thus: [וּבֶן יְשַׁעְיָה] רְפָיָה [וּבֶן רְפָיָה] אַרְנָן [וּבֶן אַרְנָן] עֹבַדְיָה [וּבֶן עֹבַדְיָה] שְׁכַנְיָה. See comm. for *Malbim's* view.

(7) 3:22: וּבְנֵי שְׁכַנְיָה שְׁמַעְיָה וּבְנֵי שְׁמַעְיָה חַטּוּשׁ ... שִׁשָּׁה. The number of sons is given as six although only five are counted. *Gra's* solution is to read as though it were written: וּבְנֵי שְׁכַנְיָה שְׁמַעְיָה וּבְנֵי [שְׁמַעְיָה] שְׁמַעְיָה חַטּוּשׁ ... שִׁשָּׁה — another son called שְׁמַעְיָה is added.

(8) 4:1: בְּנֵי יְהוּדָה פֶּרֶץ חֶצְרוֹן וְכַרְמִי וְחוּר וְשׁוֹבָל. The listing seems without any logic since 2:7 lists כַּרְמִי among the descendants of זֶרַח rather than פֶּרֶץ. See comm. for the solutions which are offered. None are conveyed by the simple meaning of the verse.

As noted, examples such as these abound in the lists. How are we to explain this strange style?

In the first place there is the possibility that we are dealing with a technical style peculiar to genealogical lists in general. The sources from which Ezra drew are for the most part not extant, and it may well be that they were written in just such a style and, that for the scribes whose task it was to write and preserve these records, it was perfectly intelligible. An analogy might be the directions contained in *Kings* and *Ezekiel* for the architectural design of the First and Third Temples respectively. Quite apart from the difficulty of committing a description of such complex buildings to writing, there is a definite, complicated styling in the presentation which puts these passages into a category of their own. Again, we cannot exclude the possibility that we are dealing with a technical language which presents difficulties only to the layman.

Another possibility would be that, as *Malbim* notes in various places (see comm. 1:7), Ezra may have used existing genealogical lists for his source but copied only those parts which were relevant to his needs. If the lists in *Chronicles* are indeed incomplete quotes from more detailed sources, this could account for some of the obscurity.

There seems to be a real possibility that the rule formulated by the Sages, 'The Book of *Chronicles* was given for homiletical interpretation (דְּרַשׁ) [rather than for its simple meaning]' (see first Overview) resulted from the problems which we have isolated here. The text of the lists is so obscure as to make it impossible to communicate much meaning at the level of פְּשַׁט. Therefore, the Sages chose to view them as a vehicle for דְּרַשׁ. As noted numerous times in the commentary, whatever fragments of their commentary have been preserved give explanations of the verses totally at variance with whatever 'simple meaning' would otherwise have been adduced.

Appendix III
The Targum on Chronicles

In the commentary we have made extensive use of the *Targum Rav Yoseph* which is printed in some, but not all, editions of the *Mikraos Gedolos Tanach*. Some remarks concerning this *Targum* are in order.

Many of the early commentators were unaware of this *Targum's* existence. Thus, *Sefer Yuchasin* (under *Rabban Gamliel*) writes: 'I have seen *Targum* on *Kesuvim* except for [the Books of] *Daniel, Ezra* and *Chronicles.'* R' Eliyahu Bachur in *Meturgeman* (under *Kur*) writes expressly that there is no *Targum* to *Chronicles*. *Radak*, who in his commentaries throughout *Tanach* constantly quotes the *Targum* of whichever Book he is explaining, never once mentions the *Targum* of *Chronicles* in his commentary. Indeed, he backs up his various interpretations here with quotations from *Targumim* to other Books when he could equally well have made his point by quoting the *Targum* of *Chronicles*. The implication is quite clear, that *Radak* was not aware of the existence of this *Targum*.[1]

Chida in *Maareches Sefarim* has a short notation as follows: '*Targum* on *Chronicles*: I saw it printed some twenty years ago and it was written there that it was found in Cambridge, England. [N.B. An edition of the *Targum* was published in 1715 by D. Wilkins on the basis of Cambridge manuscript from 1347.] At that time I covered almost all of it and gathered a number of novellae from it. Later, I made efforts to locate it but it could not be found.'

Strangely, *Maharatz Chayos*, who subjects the *Targumim* to *Kesuvim* to extremely close scrutiny in his *Imrei Binah*, makes no mention at all of a *Targum* to *Chronicles*.

Because of the comparatively late discovery of the *Targum* we are left without any indication of either its authorship or the reliability of its aggadic traditions.

It seems that the title, *Targum Rav Yoseph*, is erroneous. *Tosafos* to *Shabbos* 115a point out that those who say that the *Targum* to *Kesuvim* was authored by Rav Yoseph are in error, and that on the contrary, the *Targum* of *Kesuvim* was already extant from the time of the *Tannaim*.[2]

---

1. For some examples of instances in which *Radak* gives interpretations which he could have proven from *Targum*, but failed to do so, see: 2:17: יתר הישמעאלי; 3:3: יתרעם לעגלה אשתו; 4:15: ‎ובני כלב בן; 8:33: ‎ונר הוליד את-קיש; 21:15: ‎ובהשחית ראה. For instances where *Radak* adduces proof for his interpretations from *Targumim* to other books but where the *Targum* to *Chronicles* would have served see his comm. to 11:22 and 20:5.

2. The error of ascribing the *Targum* to Rav Yoseph seems to have arisen from the frequency of the expression: ‎כדמתרגם ר' יוסף, *as R' Yoseph translated,* throughout the Talmud. However, *Tosafos* (*Bava Kamma* 3b) point out that this need only mean that R' Yoseph was particularly well versed in the *Targum*. There is no indication that he was its author.

It is possible that the publishers of the early *Tanachs*, who gave the *Targum* the title *Targum Rav Yoseph*, made the same mistake as that which caused the *Targum Yonasan* on the Torah to be ascribed to Yonasan ben Uzziel. It has been convincingly demonstrated that this *Targum* was not written by Yonasan ben Uzziel at all (see *Chida, Maareches Sefarim* under *Targum* Yonasan) and it is

However, *Tosafos'* opinion is not universally accepted. *Rashi* to *Megillah* 21b states categorically that 'there is no *Targum* to *Kesuvim.'* Commentators have difficulty with this *Rashi* since throughout his commentary to the Talmud, *Rashi* often quotes our *Targum* to *Kesuvim. Maharatz Chayos (Iggeres Bikores* p. 515) suggests that *Rashi's* opinion is that this *Targum* is of late origin — possibly even post-Talmudic — and that the meaning of *Rashi* to *Megillah* is not that there is no *Targum* to *Kesuvim*, but that the *Gemara* could not have known of it.

This general difference of opinions concerning the age of the *Targum* to *Kesuvim* presumably applies to the *Targum* to *Chronicles* as well.

What of the aggadic content of this *Targum?*

It can be shown that there is a close similarity between our *Targum* and the *Targum* *'Yonasan'* to the Torah [see, e.g., the identification of the nations at the beginning of ch. 1 and the verbatim quote in 1:50 from *Targum Yonasan* to *Genesis* 36:39]. Concerning the aggadic content of that *Targum* we have two relevant passages from very early *Rishonim.*

Rav Hai Gaon deals with *Targum Yonasan* in a number of responsa. He writes: 'We do not know who authored the *Targum Eretz Yisrael*, moreover we have not seen it and have only heard small excerpts from it. But if there is a tradition that it was read in public from the days of the early Sages, then it is to be considered as important as our own *Targum*, for were it not so it would not have been recited in the presence of these great people.' In a subsequent responsum he writes: 'The homiletics contained in it are pleasing' *(Harkavi Zikaron LaRishonim VeGaon L'Acharonim* pp. 124-125). This indicates *Rav Hai Gaon's* approbation of the aggadic material in *Targum 'Yonasan'* to the Torah and therefore, perhaps by inference, for that in our *Targum.* However, in another responsum, addressed to an inquirer who asked him why the *Targum* to *Kesuvim* had been 'hidden,' he replied: '... Furthermore, who wrote the *Targum* [on *Kesuvim*] which you possess? Yonasan ben Uzziel did not make a *Targum* on *Kesuvim* at all. Surely the *Targum* which you have is one made by laymen (תַּרְגּוּם שֶׁל הֶדְיוֹטוֹת) ...' *(Otzar HaGeonim, Megillah).*

On the other hand, we have the statement of *R' Yehudah ben Barzillai* (12th century, in *Sefer Halttim, Hilchos Birkas VeOneg Shabbos* 175): 'The *Targum Eretz Yisrael* contains aggadic sayings added by those who led in prayer (חַזָּנִין שֶׁלָּהֶם) against their [i.e., the Sages] will, saying that it is permitted to say them in the synagogue since they are interpretations of the Bible text.'

The implication is that at least some of the aggadic material in *Targum Yonasan* to the Torah, and by implication in our *Targum* to *Chronicles*, is not part of the original text but was added later. This would of course affect the degree of reliability of a given aggadic statement for which no confirmation exists in Talmudic or midrashic sources.[1]

assumed that the printers misread the heading תר״י which was originally attached to this *Targum.* Its real meaning is תַּרְגּוּם יְרוּשַׁלְמִי, *Jerusalem Targum.* [See *Maharatz Chayos, Imrei Binah* p. 911.] In much the same way these same letters תר״י could have been misread as תַּרְגּוּם רַב יוֹסֵף.

1. *R' Yechiel Yaakov Weinberg* in an article entitled, *The History of the Targumim — A Description of the Genesis and Development of the Aramaic Targumim (Jubilee Volume for Rabbi Dr. Abraham Weiss*, New York 1964) makes the same point. He demonstrates that the earliest *Targumim* were literal translations. These were read in the synagogue as an accompaniment to the Torah text.

In response to the needs of the people, the *Metargemim* (public readers of the *Targum)* would embellish these simple translations with aggadic material, sometimes to explain obscure passages in the Torah, sometimes to instruct their listeners in important aspects of Torah knowledge which are not explicated in the text, and sometimes in order to answer questions which may have troubled their

Of these there are quite many. The aggadic material in our *Targum* can be divided into three categories: (1) Where *Targum* cites an interpretation mentioned in either Talmud or midrash, e.g., the identification of Ephrath with Miriam (2:19). (2) Where he cites an interpretation which is found in the Talmud or midrash but not in the form in which he brings it, e.g., *Targum* to 2:18. The Talmud mentions that some women had the skill to be able to spin the thread directly from the backs of the goats but nowhere do we find this to be the interpretation of the name Yerioth. (3) Occasionally he brings an interpretation which is not found in other sources, e.g., the identification of the 'family of scribes' at 2:55 with Rechaviah, the grandson of Moses.

Within these limitations the *Targum* to *Chronicles* is nevertheless an invaluable source for the interpretation of the text. Particularly in the genealogical tables, where aggadic insights play such a primary role, we draw on it as an important aid in understanding the difficult text.

---

congregants for whom the synagogue was the place to turn for the resolution of their problems.

In the course of time the simple translation of the *Targumim* became involved with midrashic material and it was no longer clear which were the original translations and which the late additions. A new and more simple *Targum* became necessary, and it fell to the lot of *Onkelos* to work out this new *Targum* based on what he had learned from his teachers Rabbi Eliezer and Rabbi Yehoshua (*Megillah* 3a). This is what the Talmud means when it says that Onkelos' *Targum* became necessary because the original one had been forgotten. There is no reason why a *Targum* which was in constant use in the synagogue should have been forgotten. More likely, the original text had become submerged by the later additions.

Rabbi Weinberg thinks that in the course of such a development it is very possible that material may have crept into the *Targum* which was not acceptable to the Sages. Since, in contrast to halachic questions which were dealt with by the Sanhedrin, there was no central authority to pass on aggadic teachings, each *Metargem* had the freedom to teach his listeners according to his own wisdom and inclinations. Thus, a critical attitude towards some aspects of *aggadah* developed among the Sages, of which we find traces in the two Talmudim.

As an extreme example, Rabbi Weinberg cites *Yerushalmi Maassros* 3:10 which reports that R' Zeira used to describe aggadic texts as 'books of sorcery' (סִפְרֵי קוֹסְמִים). It is unlikely that R' Zeira objected to the aggadic approach in general (see *Yerushalmi Sanhedrin* 2:3 where he himself voices approbation of aggadic teachings) but rather, he objects to specific sayings which had entered the corpus of aggadic literature by the means which we have described.

Appendix IV (to 3:15)
The House of Yoshiahu

◆§ The Identity of Tzidkiahu

We identify Tzidkiahu as the son of Yoshiahu, and brother of Yehoachaz and Yehoiakim in accordance with *Horios* 11b and *Kerisos* 5b. Although the Sages (ibid.) offer solutions to some of the problems posed by this identification, certain difficulties remain unanswered. Many commentators suggest identifications which, to a greater or lesser degree, differ from the Talmudic tradition. [See *Radak* to *II Kings* 23:30 for *Ibn Ezra's* and his own ideas, and *Abarbanel* to *II Kings* 24.]

We shall attempt to trace the thinking of the Sages, and to remove the seeming difficulties.

That King Tzidkiahu was a son of Yoshiahu and not of Yehoiachin (whom he succeeded, and who in fact did have a son, named Tzidkiahu — see v. 16) is based on *II Kings* 24:17, where Tzidkiahu is called a דוד, uncle, of Yehoiachim. It is thus established that he was Yoshiahu's son.[1]

We thus have the following sequence for the last four kings of Judah:

1. Yehoachaz, son of Yoshiahu (*II Kings* 23:30).
2. Yehoiakim, son of Yoshiahu (23:34).
3. Yehoiachin, son of Yehoiakim and grandson of Yoshiahu (24:6).
4. Tzidkiahu, uncle of Yehoiachin and son of Yoshiahu (24:17).

◆§ The Unknown Shallum

A problem arises out of Jeremiah's prophecy (*Jeremiah* 22) in which he addresses three kings. The first is *Shallum the son of Yoshiahu ... who rules in the place of Yoshiahu, his father* (v. 11). The second is Yehoiakim (v. 18), and the third is Chenaiahu (an obvious variant of Yehoiachin) (v. 24). Who is this Shallum of whom no mention is made in the book of *Kings?* The Sages (*Horios* loc. cit.) seem to address themselves to this problem in their interpretation to v. 15 here in *Chronicles*. This verse reads: *And the sons of Yoshiahu: the first-born, Yochanan; the second, Yehoiakim; the third, Tzidkiahu; the fourth, Shallum:*

Rabbi Yochanan taught: Yochanan is identical to Yehoachaz. He is called הַבְּכוֹר, *the first-born*, because he was the first to rule, although he was in fact younger than Yehoiakim [as evidenced by *II Kings* 23:31 and 36]. Tzidkiahu and Shallum are one and the same person. He is described as both the third and the fourth son because although he was the third of Yoshiahu's sons, he was the fourth king after his father (since Yehoiachin the grandson of Yoshiahu preceded him as king) ... Tzidkiahu is called Shallum either because he was

---

1. However, *Abarbanel* ad loc. suggests that the correct translation may be *a friend* (as דוד is always translated in *Shir Hashirim*); i.e., Nebuchadnezzar appointed his (Nebuchadnezzar's) friend Tzidkiahu king.

'perfect in his deeds' [שָׁלֵם=שָׁלוֹם, *perfect*] or, because 'the Davidic monarchy ceased in his days ' [שָׁלַם, *ceased*] (*Horios* 11b, *Kerisos* 5b).

It would thus appear that the Shallum of *Jeremiah* 22 is in fact Tzidkiahu.

On the surface this seems to be the Talmudic tradition. However it leaves several problems.

1. It is at variance with the simple meaning of the verse here in *Chronicles*.

2. The verse in *Jeremiah* 22:11: *Shallum, the son of Yoshiahu ... who rules in the place of Yoshiahu, his father,* implies that Shallum succeeded Yoshiahu immediately after the latter's death. Surely this would equate Shallum with Yehoachaz, not with Tzidkiahu.[1]

3. In *II Chronicles* 36:10, Tzidkiahu seems to be described as a brother of Yehoiachin rather than an uncle. (But see *Mefaresh* and *Metzudos* ad loc.)

◆§ Two Identities

We suggest that the Shallum of *Jeremiah* is, in fact, Yehoachaz (but see *Rashi* and *Metzudos David* ad loc.), and that Rabbi Yochanan's identification of Shallum with Tzidkiahu refers only to the Shallum mentioned in *Chronicles*.

According to *Vayikra Rabbah* 1:3, *Chronicles* occupies a unique place in Scripture. Whereas in the rest of Scripture, דְּרָשָׁה, *the aggadic exegesis,* may never displace פְּשָׁט, *the simple meaning* (אֵין מִקְרָא יוֹצֵא מִידֵי פְּשׁוּטוֹ), *Chronicles* has no simple meaning in the usual sense of the word. The exegesis is always pre-eminent. [See Overview and *Rabbi Zvi Hirsch Chayes* in *Mevo HaTalmud* ch. 22 for an analysis and elaboration of this concept.] Because of this rule, we need not be surprised to find an interpretation which cannot be justified according to normal interpretational usage.

The sequence in which the *four* sons of Yoshiahu are listed in *Chronicles* (with Shallum given last) could follow either chronological order, or the order in which they reigned. Neither of these criteria would permit the identification of Shallum with Yehoachaz. He was the first to reign, and he was older than Tzidkiahu. For this reason, Rabbi Yochanan preferred to identify Yehoachaz with the Yochanan of *Chronicles*, and to assume that the sequence was determined by the order in which they reigned.

This, however, would leave Shallum unidentified. He could not be a son who never became king, because *Jeremiah* refers to Yehoachaz by the name Shallum (see above), and Yoshiahu would not have had two sons with the same name. Because of this difficulty (and licensed by the special character of *Chronicles*), Rabbi Yochanan explains that the Shallum mentioned there is not a fourth son at all, but that the name is added in order to lend an added dimension to the personality of Tzidkiahu, to indicate either his perfect righteousness or the tragic end of the Davidic dynasty which occurred in his days.

◆§ Why the Double Identity?

Moreover, it is not impossible that Tzidkiahu is pictured as two people in order to underline the essential duality of his character. Scripture describes him as a רָשָׁע, *a wicked person* (see especially *Ezekiel* 21:30), while the Sages teach that he was an entirely righteous man (see Overview to ArtScroll *Yechezkel*). We must deal with both aspects in order to understand all that we are taught about

---

1. If Shallum can be identified with Yehoachaz, then the sequence in the chapter would be eminently logical. The kings would be addressed in chronological sequence of their reigns: first Yehoachaz, then Yehoiakim, then Yehoiachin. But if Shallum is Tzidkiahu then he is mentioned out of order.

this king, and for this reason he is projected as two people.

Perhaps he is presented as two people for another reason. According to *II Kings* 24:17, it was Nebuchadnezzar who changed his name to Tzidkiahu. According to the Sages the purpose was to drive home the seriousness of the oath of loyalty which Nebuchadnezzar had exacted from him (see preface to ch. 17 of ArtScroll *Yechezkel*). Thus the name Tzidkiahu projects the Babylonian view of the king, while Shallum teaches his significance from the Jewish standpoint.

◆§ The Tradition of the Sages

Finally, *II Chronicles* 36:10, where Tzidkiahu is called Yehoiachin's 'brother,' bears out the Sages' tradition. While we have found several times in our Book the word אָח used in the wider sense of *relative* (specifically for nephews; *Genesis* 14:16, 29:12; and *Leviticus* 10:4), it is never used to describe a son. If Tzidkiahu the king was Yehoiachin's son (based on v. 16 here in *Chronicles)* he would not have been called his *brother*. However, for an uncle the term is appropriate.

For the reader's convenience, we cite the Scriptural passages relevant to the above discussion.

II Kings 23:30-36

וַיַּרְכִּבֻהוּ עֲבָדָיו מֵת מִמְּגִדּוֹ וַיְבִאֻהוּ יְרוּשָׁלַם וַיִּקְבְּרֻהוּ בִּקְבֻרָתוֹ וַיִּקַּח עַם־הָאָרֶץ אֶת־יְהוֹאָחָז בֶּן־יֹאשִׁיָּהוּ וַיִּמְשְׁחוּ אֹתוֹ וַיַּמְלִיכוּ אֹתוֹ תַּחַת אָבִיו. בֶּן־עֶשְׂרִים וְשָׁלֹשׁ שָׁנָה יְהוֹאָחָז בְּמָלְכוֹ וּשְׁלֹשָׁה חֳדָשִׁים מָלַךְ בִּירוּשָׁלָם וְשֵׁם אִמּוֹ חֲמוּטַל בַּת־יִרְמְיָהוּ מִלִּבְנָה. וַיַּעַשׂ הָרַע בְּעֵינֵי יהוה כְּכֹל אֲשֶׁר־עָשׂוּ אֲבֹתָיו. וַיַּאַסְרֵהוּ פַרְעֹה נְכֹה בְרִבְלָה בְּאֶרֶץ חֲמָת בִּמְלֹךְ בִּירוּשָׁלָם וַיִּתֶּן־עֹנֶשׁ עַל־הָאָרֶץ מֵאָה כִכַּר־כֶּסֶף וְכִכַּר זָהָב. וַיַּמְלֵךְ פַּרְעֹה נְכֹה אֶת־אֶלְיָקִים בֶּן־יֹאשִׁיָּהוּ תַּחַת יֹאשִׁיָּהוּ אָבִיו וַיַּסֵּב אֶת־שְׁמוֹ יְהוֹיָקִים וְאֶת־יְהוֹאָחָז לָקָח וַיָּבֹא מִצְרַיִם וַיָּמָת שָׁם. וְהַכֶּסֶף וְהַזָּהָב נָתַן יְהוֹיָקִים לְפַרְעֹה אַךְ הֶעֱרִיךְ אֶת־הָאָרֶץ לָתֵת אֶת־הַכֶּסֶף עַל־פִּי פַרְעֹה אִישׁ כְּעֶרְכּוֹ נָגַשׂ אֶת־הַכֶּסֶף וְאֶת־הַזָּהָב אֶת־עַם הָאָרֶץ לָתֵת לְפַרְעֹה נְכֹה. בֶּן־עֶשְׂרִים וְחָמֵשׁ שָׁנָה יְהוֹיָקִים בְּמָלְכוֹ וְאַחַת עֶשְׂרֵה שָׁנָה מָלַךְ בִּירוּשָׁלָם וְשֵׁם אִמּוֹ זְבוּדָה בַת־פְּדָיָה מִן־רוּמָה.

Ibid. 24:6

וַיִּשְׁכַּב יְהוֹיָקִים עִם־אֲבֹתָיו וַיִּמְלֹךְ יְהוֹיָכִין בְּנוֹ תַּחְתָּיו.

Ibid. 24:17

וַיַּמְלֵךְ מֶלֶךְ־בָּבֶל אֶת־מַתַּנְיָה דֹדוֹ תַּחְתָּיו וַיַּסֵּב אֶת־שְׁמוֹ צִדְקִיָּהוּ.

Jeremiah 22:11

כִּי כֹה אָמַר־ה' אֶל־שַׁלֻּם בֶּן־יֹאשִׁיָּהוּ מֶלֶךְ יְהוּדָה הַמֹּלֵךְ תַּחַת יֹאשִׁיָּהוּ אָבִיו אֲשֶׁר יָצָא מִן־הַמָּקוֹם הַזֶּה לֹא־יָשׁוּב שָׁם עוֹד.

Ibid. 22:18

לָכֵן כֹּה־אָמַר ה' אֶל־יְהוֹיָקִים בֶּן־יֹאשִׁיָּהוּ מֶלֶךְ יְהוּדָה לֹא־יִסְפְּדוּ לוֹ הוֹי אָחִי וְהוֹי אָחוֹת לֹא־יִסְפְּדוּ לוֹ הוֹי אָדוֹן וְהוֹי הֹדֹה.

Ibid. 22:24

חַי־אָנִי נְאֻם־יהוה כִּי אִם־יִהְיֶה כָּנְיָהוּ בֶן־יְהוֹיָקִים מֶלֶךְ יְהוּדָה חוֹתָם עַל־יַד יְמִינִי כִּי מִשָּׁם אֶתְּקֶנְךָ.

I Chronicles 3:15-16

וּבְנֵי יֹאשִׁיָּהוּ הַבְּכוֹר יוֹחָנָן הַשֵּׁנִי יְהוֹיָקִים הַשְּׁלִשִׁי צִדְקִיָּהוּ הָרְבִיעִי שַׁלּוּם. וּבְנֵי יְהוֹיָקִים יְכָנְיָה בְנוֹ צִדְקִיָּה בְנוֹ.

II Chronicles 36:9-10

בֶּן־שְׁמוֹנֶה שָׁנִים יְהוֹיָכִין בְּמָלְכוֹ וּשְׁלֹשָׁה חֳדָשִׁים וַעֲשֶׂרֶת יָמִים מָלַךְ בִּירוּשָׁלָם וַיַּעַשׂ הָרַע בְּעֵינֵי ה'. וְלִתְשׁוּבַת הַשָּׁנָה שָׁלַח הַמֶּלֶךְ נְבוּכַדְנֶאצַּר וַיְבִאֵהוּ בָבֶלָה עִם־כְּלֵי חֶמְדַּת בֵּית־יהוה וַיַּמְלֵךְ אֶת־צִדְקִיָּהוּ אָחִיו עַל־יְהוּדָה וִירוּשָׁלָם.

Appendix V
The Levitical Functions

Chapters 23-26 describe the dispositions made by David for the organization of the Levites and *Kohanim* for their respective tasks, as a part of the general groundwork which he laid in preparation for the Temple which Solomon would build. The extreme complexity of these chapters requires that we subject them to a more rigorous analysis than is possible in the commentary to the individual passages.

We shall examine two aspects of the Levitical service: the range of tasks which were assigned to them, and the nature of the *mishmaros* into which they were divided.

We begin by quoting some relevent passages from *Rambam* in *Klei HaMikdash*:

"... It is a positive command that the Levites should be available and ready to serve in the Sanctuary ... Their service is that they should guard the Sanctuary and that some should be gatekeepers to open the gates of the Sanctuary and to close its doors; and that some should be choristers to sing and the daily sacrifice ... Samuel the seer and King David divided the Levites into twenty-four *mishmaros*, one *mishmar* to serve each week ..." (3:1-9).

"The *Kohanim* were separated from the rest of the Levites for the task of offering the sacrifices ... Moses organized the *Kohanim* into eight *mishmaros*, four from Eleazar and four from Ithamar, and so it was till the days of the prophet Samuel. Samuel and David divided them into twenty-four *mishmaros* ..." (4:1-3)

We have, then, two basic premises. Both Levites and *Kohanim* were divided into twenty-four *mishmaros* by Samuel and David. The Levite duties involved the guarding of the Sanctuary, the servicing of the portals, and the musical accompaniment of the sacrificial service. The *Kohanim* were to perform the actual service of offering the sacrifices.

The *Kohanim* present no particular difficulties. Their duties are explicated in the Torah, and their division into twenty-four *mishmaros*, assigned proportionately to Eleazar and Ithamar, is made clear in 24:1-9.

We now turn to an analysis of the Levite's contribution to the Divine service: the range of their duties and the nature of their *mishmaros*.

The Levite duties: The relevant passages are, 23:4-5, 28-32 and 26:20-32.

The first section lists four categories of service:

1. לְנַצֵּחַ עַל מְלֶאכֶת בֵּית ה׳, *to oversee the administration of the House of Hashem.*

2. שֹׁטְרִים וְשֹׁפְטִים, *sherrifs and judges*
3. שֹׁעֲרִים, *gatekeepers*
4. מְהַלְלִים לַה' בַּכֵּלִים, *to praise Hashem with instruments*

The third and fourth categories seem clear enough. The Levites are servicers of the portals and musicians, as known to us from *Rambam* quoted above. But what, precisely, are the first two categories? The first may well be subsumed under the fourth. In comm. to 23:4 we find *Metzudos* and *Gra* defining it as a musical function — choral music as opposed to the instrumental music referred to in #4.

The second may not be, strictly speaking, a Levitical function at all. *Ralbag* defines it as judicial activities. The Levites were the most learned segment of the people, and therefore, although this was not a halachic requirement, they tended to be heavily represented on the nation's courts. In a formal sense, then, we are not dealing with a Levitical function.

If we maintain this interpretation we have the Levites limited to the two well-known categories — מְשׁוֹרְרִים and שׁוֹעֲרִים, musicians and gatekeepers.

But many commentators understand לְנַצֵחַ as *to oversee* and thus #1 becomes, *... to oversee the work of the House of HASHEM*. Indeed, a careful reading of 26:20-28 together with 23:28-29, and then, 26:29-32 yields a picture of many administrative duties centered both inside the Temple and over the far-flung reaches of the nation. [Note that 26:29 has שׁוֹטְרִים וְשׁוֹפְטִים — our category #2 — in an apparently non-judicial context. See comm. ad loc.] These are an aspect of Levite activity not reflected in *Rambam*.

There is, however, a source in *Sifrei* for such Levitical activities. In *Numbers* 18:2 we read that Aaron the *Kohen* was told that the Levites were ... *to be associated with you and minister to you*. To this *Sifrei* remarks: Appoint them as administrators and officials [פְּקִידִים וַאֲמַרְכְּלִין]. Thus we find an entirely new sphere of activity for the Levites and this is reflected in the passages in *Chronicles*, although we do not find it codified in *Rambam*.

The Levite Mishmaros: It will be the purpose of this section to demonstrate that although the Levites had *mishmaros* just as the *Kohanim* did, the make-up of these groupings was quite different. While the Kohanic *mishmaros* were family based, the Levite *mishmaros* were grouped together on the basis of the various skills which were required. Family did not enter into consideration.

This assertion is offered as a thesis based on textual and other evidence from *Chronicles*, as it will now be presented. With the exception of *Gra* and *Malbim*, who stand in disagreement with this thesis, the commentators do not address this issue.

The *Gra* and *Malbim* interpret 23:7-23 in a way which assumes that the families listed there are the twenty-four [family-based] Levite *mishmaros*. We propose that the fact that no other commentators join them in this interpretation tends to show that they disagree with it. Accordingly, *Chronicles* contains no listing of the twenty-four Levite *mishmaros*, and that therefore no [family-based] listing is possible. Internal evidence tends to support this view.

The passage in 23:7-23 must be examined in conjunction with 24:20-31 and 26:20-32. To simplify the analysis, we shall number the various points.

(1) It is true that the names listed in the section in ch. 23 come tantalizingly close to twenty-four. But it is also true that the simple meaning does not seem to yield precisely that number. It would appear that really only twenty-two qualify.

This, because Yeush and Beriah are combined into one at v. 11 and Eleazar at v. 22 died without sons (see comm.). In order to find the full complement of twenty-four, the *Gra* is forced to count Eleazar, although he has no sons, and to interpret v. 11 as referring to Ezra's rather than David's time (see comm.). *Malbim*, who does not wish to make either of these two assumptions, is forced to make up the number twenty-four by augmenting the listing in ch. 23 with two names which do not appear there but in ch. 24.

We may thus conclude that the simple reading of the passage does not yield the number twenty-four.

(2) The very clarity with which ch. 24 lists the twenty-four *mishmaros* of the *Kohanim*, and ch. 25 describes the correspondence between the small groups of musicians with the Kohanic *mishmaros*, makes it unlikely that in ch. 23 twenty-four Levite *mishmaros* are listed. Had this been the case there seems to be no discernible reason why the same clear system could not have been used. The style of the listing is reminiscent of the genealogical lists in the first eight chapters of the book and is entirely dissimilar from the style of chs. 24 and 25.

(3) Whether ch. 23 is a listing of the *mishmaros* or a genealogical list similar to the ones in the earlier part of the book will influence the correct rendering of the word בְּנֵי, *sons*, in this context. The lists seem to take the Levite families of Gershon, Kehath and Merari down two or three generations, and clearly these people could not have been contemporary with David. [Compare the lists of the choristers in ch. 6.]

(4) A careful comparison with the listings in 24:20-31, and particularly an examination of the precise meaning of 24:20, argues for the probability that we are dealing with a genealogical listing rather than the twenty-four *mishmaros*.

Let us first inquire into the relationship of these two listings.

It is obvious that the two passages are related and that the passage in ch. 24 is an extension of the one in ch. 23 in that it adds generations in most cases.

We begin our analysis by noting that of the three Levite families — Gershon, Kehath and Merari — Gershon is missing entirely from ch. 24.

For Kehath the relationship follows:

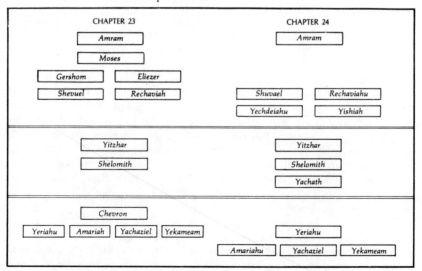

N.B. We have an irregularity in that Yeriah is not introduced as coming from Chevron and the three who are given as brothers in ch. 23 are listed as sons in ch. 24 (see 24:23 in contrast to 23:19).

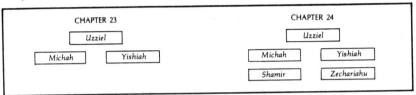

Thus, for Kehath, in each case the listing is identical except that a generation is added — for Chevron, through listing brothers as sons.

For Merari we have as follows:

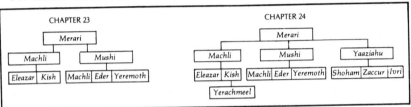

Thus for Merari also an extra generation is added, for Kish and a son of Merari not even mentioned in the Torah is added with children of his own.

The impression is that which we encountered countless times in the genealogical lists in the earlier part of the book — that more than one source of the genealogical lists of the Levites was available to *Chronicles* and that the one went a little further than the other, although that too had gaps [Gershon is missing completely and Yeriah is not introduced as a Chevronite].

This would readily explain the heading (24:20), *As for the remaining Levites* ... that is, for the additional Levites of which there were records but which were not listed in the source quoted in ch. 23.

(5) In point 3 we argued that by treating ch. 23 as a genealogical listing rather than as a list of the *mishmaros* we can be consistent in rendering בֶּן as *son* and do not have to assume that occasionally it means *descendant*.

We must now analyze how this relates to the duties assigned to various Levites in 26:20-32.

That list, too, makes the impression of being fragmentary in much the same way that we found occasionally in the earlier genealogical lists. Firstly, although the Gershonites who are listed there are prominently identified as such, as are the descendants of Amram, Yitzhar, Chevron and Uzziel (see below) [but note that these later are not identified as Kehathites — another notable irregularity], no descendants at all are given for Merari. Secondly, although v. 27 clearly introduces the following listings as coming from all four of Kehath's sons, in the end nothing is said of any descendant of Uzziel. Both these rather blatant omissions give the section the hallmark of being a fragment of an earlier record, parts of which had been lost.

The listings in ch. 26 plainly are based on the earlier ones from chs. 23 and 24 and should therefore throw some light on the meaning of those.

The Gershonite listing (21-22) limits itself to Ladan — Shimei's descendants are not given (see 23:7-11) — but does assign an office to Zetham and Yoel who are given as Ladan's grandsons (see comm. there). If, as the commentators assume, the Ladan of ch. 23 is another name for Gershon's son, Livni, then it is manifestly impossible that his grandsons functioned in David's days. This could argue for the merits of rendering בֶּן in ch. 23 as *descendant*. However, it should be noted that no indication is given in which era they were appointed over *the treasure houses of the House of HASHEM* (v. 22), and this may well have been in earlier years [unless we assume that בֵּית ה' indicates Temple rather than Sanctuary]. See comm. there for another possibility.

The same assumption would have to be made for Shevuel, Moses' grandson (v. 24), whose appointment over the *treasure houses* may well have been in earlier times.

[The logic for giving the names of appointees from earlier generations could be as follows: We have noted before that from *Shekalim* ch. 5 (*Tiferes Yisrael*, there) and *Tosafos, Menachos* 64b we see that positions in the Temple were generally named after the original office holder. It is therefore quite possible that the guardianship of the various repositories mentioned here retained the names of Zetham, Yoel and Shevuel centuries after these people had died. See, for example *II Chronicles* 25:24 where the Temple treasurers are said to be in the charge of Oved Edom during the reign of Amatziah at a time when surely the original office-holder was not alive anymore.

The Shelomith mentioned in v. 25ff as being in charge of the treasures deposited by David and his contemporaries would be the tenth generation from Levi (see comm. there) and could conceivably have lived during David's time since David himself was the eleventh generation from Judah (*Ruth* 4:18ff).

The Chenaniah mentioned as a descendant of Yitzhar (v. 29) and the Chashaviahu mentioned as a descendant of Chevron (v. 30) do not occur in the earlier lists and may well have lived many generations later.

For the other Chevronite mentioned in v. 31, see comm. there.

Our analysis has yielded that there is no clear evidence from the listings in ch. 26 as to the nature of the lists in chs. 23 and 24.

(6) Chapter 26 lists the gatekeepers and the twenty-four locations to which they were assigned. A careful reading of vs. 1, 10 and 19 yields that these gatekeepers were drawn exclusively from the Korahites (descended from the Kehathite, Yitzhar) and the Merarites. If ch. 23 is listing the Levite *mishmaros*, then these were manifestly drawn from all the three of the Levite families. Gershon, Kehath and Merari. But how is this possible if the gatekeepers, who surely had to be part of *every mishmar*, were drawn from only two families?

(7) If ch. 23 is a list of the twenty-four *mishmaros*, then it transpires that these were divided as follows: Ten from Gershon; nine from Kehath; and five from Merari. (See comm. to ch. 23. We have here followed *Gra* for simplicity's sake.) But ch. 25 lists the subgroupings of musicians. According to v. 8 there, these twenty-four subgroupings rotated by a system that corresponded to the Kohanic *mishmaros*. But those subgroupings were divided as follows: The Gershonite, Asaph, — four; the Merarite, Yeduthun — six; and the Kehathite; Heman — fourteen.

These subgroupings, then, do not correspond to the listings in ch. 23. If the subgroupings corresponded to the Kohanite *mishmaros*, and the Levite *mishmaros* corresponded to the Kohanite *mishmaros*, then the listings in ch. 23 cannot be the Levite *mishmaros*.

We conclude that a strong case can be made that the list in ch. 23 is not a listing of the twenty-four *mishmaros* of the Levites but a genealogical record which is later augmented by that given at the end of ch. 24.

Certainly, as the tradition has it, there were twenty-four Levite *mishmaros*, and that is the probable meaning of 23:6. However, for reasons to be explained below, no listing is given of these *mishmaros* in the same way that the Kohanic *mishmaros* were given in ch. 24.

We suspect that the Levite *mishmaros* were fundamentally and essentially different from the Kohanic *mishmaros*. These later ones were determined by family — see *Rambam* quoted above — and see also 24:4. The Levite *mishmaros* may not have been divided by family at all but may have been put together as the exigencies of the service required. That is, that they would be staffed by choristers, musicians, gatekeepers and all the other functionaries which were required. In a sense these Levite *mishmaros* would not have an independent status at all but would quite literally be subsidiary to the *Kohanim* and be organized in a way which would make their service the most efficient as determined by the requirements.

This would explain the structure of ch. 23. David counted the Levites (v. 3), determined the number required for each particular service (vs. 4-5), and from this available pool formed the required number of *mishmaros*.